THE
NEW BOOK
OF
KNOWLEDGE

Grolier Incorporated, Danbury, Connecticut

VOLUME 2

B

ISBN 0–7172–0524–X (set)

The publishers wish to thank the following for permission to use copyrighted material:
Abington Press for excerpts from *The Bible Story for Boys and Girls, Old Testament*, and *The Bible Story for Boys and Girls, New Testament*, by Walter Russell Bowie, copyrights 1952 and 1951 by Pierce & Smith.

Trademark
THE BOOK OF KNOWLEDGE
registered in U.S. Patent Office

B, the second letter of the English alphabet, was also the second letter of the Phoenician, Hebrew, and Greek alphabets. The Phoenicians and Hebrews called it *beth*. The Greeks called it *beta*.

Many scholars believe that the Phoenician letters were pictures of objects. *Beth,* they say, was probably a simple picture of a house. It looked like this: ꓸ.

The Greeks borrowed this basic form for their *beta,* but they made a double-looped version. Since the Greeks wrote from left to right instead of from right to left like the Phoenicians, the *beta* was also reversed. By the 5th century B.C. it looked like this: Β.

In adapting the Greek alphabet, the Romans kept the form of the *beta* but changed its name to *be*—the name it still has today in most European alphabets.

The B is most frequently pronounced as in *baseball* or *bishop,* although in some English words, such as *comb* or *debt,* the letter is silent.

The English B stands for many things. It has even been used in punishment. In Europe during the Middle Ages, and in the United States at the time of the Puritans, anyone who spoke against God was called a blasphemer. Sometimes a B was branded on the foreheads of the guilty ones as a sign of their sinfulness.

In chemistry B stands for the element boron. In a list of things, it labels the second item. On a report card it means above-average work. In music B is the name of a note as well as an abbreviation for bass, the lowest part in a musical composition.

B occurs in abbreviations. The college degree bachelor of arts is shortened to B.A. When used in dates, B.C. means "before Christ," as in "48 B.C." The British Broadcasting Corporation is called the B.B.C. Some B abbreviations employ the small b. "Born," for instance, is indicated before dates by a small b, as in "Queen Elizabeth I, b. 1533."

Reviewed by MARIO PEI
Author, *The Story of Language*

See also ALPHABET.

SOME WAYS TO REPRESENT B:

The **manuscript** or printed forms of the letter (left) are highly readable. The **cursive** letters (right) are formed from slanted flowing strokes joining one letter to the next.

The **Manual Alphabet** (left) enables a deaf person to communicate by forming letters with the fingers of one hand. **Braille** (right) is a system by which a blind person can use fingertips to "read" raised dots that stand for letters.

The **International Code of Signals** is a special group of flags used to send and receive messages at sea. Each letter is represented by a different flag.

International Morse Code is used to send messages by radio signals. Each letter is expressed as a combination of dots (•) and dashes (––).

Newborn babies can do very little by themselves, but by the age of a few months, they are alert and interested in what they see—and they learn to smile.

BABY

A baby cat is called a kitten, and a baby dog is called a puppy. A human baby is often referred to as an infant. All of these babies are mammals.

Mammals are animals whose young, or offspring, are born alive after a period of development inside the mother. (Only two primitive types lay eggs.) After birth the offspring depend on their mother's milk for survival. Mammals may be very large, like the elephant, or very small, like the mouse.

▶BEFORE THE BABY IS BORN

By the time the human mammal, or baby, enters the world, it has spent 9 months in a complicated process of growth and development. This process begins when the **ovum,** or egg, of the mother unites with the **sperm,** or seed, of the father. The fertilized egg begins to grow inside the mother's **uterus,** or womb. In about 3 weeks various organs begin to form. The tiny fertilized egg is then known as an **embryo.** The embryo continues to develop. Later it is called a **fetus.** When the fetus is 3 months old, it is about 3 inches long (8 centimeters) long. By 4 months, it is about twice this length.

When the fetus is 4 or 5 months old, the fetal heartbeat may be heard through a stethoscope placed on the mother's abdomen. At about the same time, the mother may become aware of little movements within her body. These movements bring her great joy, for she knows she has begun to "feel life."

The fetus is developing and moving around in the bag, or sac, of fluid that surrounds and protects it. Inside the sac, the fetus is attached at the belly (abdomen) to the placenta by a cord containing blood vessels. The placenta is a pancake-shaped organ through which the mother's blood flows to give nourishment to the fetus until it is ready to be born.

After 9 months in the uterus of the mother, the fetus is ready to come into the world. More than 90 percent of all babies are born after 9 months, known as full term.

If the fetus is born too soon, or prematurely, it may be difficult for it to survive. Medical advances have made it possible for more than half of all babies born after 20 weeks in the uterus to survive. However, the risk of long-term defects increases as the fetus spends less time in the uterus before birth. The biggest problem faced by premature babies is breathing, because their lungs are immature, and they lack a crucial substance (surfactin) that helps them absorb oxygen into their lungs. That is why they are placed in incubators (special beds in which the environment can be controlled) that provide extra oxygen.

For many months, the baby's parents wonder what their infant will be like. Will it be a boy or girl? What color hair and eyes will it have? Will it inherit any diseases? These and other matters are determined long before the baby's birth. The father's sperm and mother's egg contain the ingredients (called chromosomes) that carry all the characteristics the baby will inherit from its parents. The sex of the baby is determined by chromosomes in the father's sperm. These chromosomes are present in the amniotic fluid that surrounds the fetus before it is born. An analysis of this fluid can identify certain medical disorders, and the sex of the baby, before birth.

▶ AFTER THE BABY IS BORN

At last the baby is born. If it is an average baby, it weighs about 7 or 8 pounds (3 or 3.5 kilograms), and it is about 20 inches (about 51 centimeters) long. Male babies are slightly larger than female babies.

The healthy baby's first action after birth is to utter a sharp cry. With a good loud cry the baby's lungs expand and adapt to the outside world. The lungs enable the baby to breathe the air that now surrounds it. The cry also indicates that the baby is off to a good start.

Most human mothers give birth to a single baby. In about 1 out of every 80 births twins are born. Some twins are **identical.** This means that they have developed from a single fertilized egg. Other twins are **fraternal,** which means that two eggs may have been fertilized at the same time. Identical twins are usually very much alike. Fraternal twins may be quite different from one another. Triplets are born about once in 6,400 births, quadruplets about once in 500,000. Quintuplets, five babies born at one time, are very rare indeed.

Healthy infants have a strong tendency to suck. For the first months of life, sucking enables babies to obtain the nourishment necessary for their growth.

During the months of pregnancy, the mother's breasts have been getting ready to make milk. If the mother chooses not to feed the baby with her own milk, the use of a "formula" is recommended. The formula is usually made of cow's milk mixed with a form of sugar and water. Sometimes vitamins are added. It is put into a bottle that has a nipple made to resemble the nipple of the mother's breast. When the baby's mouth is put to the nipple of the breast, or to the bottle, the strong sucking reflex makes it possible for the infant to suck and swallow this first important food.

Growth and Development

Although babies vary a great deal, there is a general timetable for their growth and development, especially during the first year.

The newborn period in a baby's life is the first month after birth. This is a period of great change not only for the baby, but also for the rest of the family who have awaited the arrival for 9 months.

Newborn babies can do some things by themselves. They can breathe, cry, sleep, and move their arms and legs. They can suck and swallow food, and their bodies can take care of eliminating waste products. But since human babies have little control over these simple actions, they are completely dependent on others for their care.

Very young babies sleep most of the time, about 16 hours per day. When they are awake they are usually eating or crying. Their hearing is good, especially for human voices, and they will react to loud noises. Newborns have trouble focusing but see best at a distance of about 7 to 9 inches (18 to 23 centimeters). They also are the most alert when they are held upright; in that position they can absorb the most information (smells, lights, sounds). When babies are about 2 weeks old, their eyes will follow light and fix on an object. At about the age of 2 months, babies can see colors and, to the delight of their parents, begin to smile.

Babies must be carefully guarded against illness. People with colds or other infections should not handle the baby or get close to it, especially if the baby is premature or delicate. If the baby is bottle-fed, the formula must be prepared carefully. The bottle and nipple should be sterile (free of germs).

Small babies, especially premature infants, have a very limited capacity to control their temperature. They are poorly insulated because they do not have much fat. So it is important to keep babies warm.

After the first few months the baby should be examined by a pediatrician (a doctor who specializes in treating babies and older children), who will discuss the baby's progress with the parents or other caretaker. The pediatrician may suggest the addition of vitamins

The development of babies is the object of extensive research. Doctors and psychologists are attempting to find out what infants know at birth and how they organize and use that knowledge during their early years.

talking back to the baby. Babies start to babble consistently, with some indication of meaning, around 6 to 9 months of age. They start to vocalize in response to others much earlier.

They learn the words of their own language by listening and copying. The process of using and understanding language depends on individual development.

Most babies have a few teeth by the time they are a year old. When babies are born, they have no teeth. But even at birth a baby's teeth are under the gums in the form of tooth buds. As the baby grows, the teeth begin to show through the gums.

▶ ARE YOU A SIBLING?

Brothers and sisters in a family are called **siblings.** Siblings have an important role to play when a new baby arrives, just as parents do.

Parents sometimes worry that older siblings might be jealous of a new baby. Older children often feel that some of their parents' love and attention will have to be shared. Usually, however, siblings also welcome the arrival of a baby. They are proud of the newcomer and quickly discover the excitement of watching an infant grow.

Children who have the opportunity to live with a baby in the family gain valuable experience. If they are old enough, their parents will let them help take care of the new baby. They will learn to help feed the baby, change the diapers, and take the younger child for a walk in the carriage. All of this experience will help siblings to become good baby-sitters when they are old enough. It will also help them become good parents when they are adults.

In a family where love, tenderness, and respect for each member are important, babies and older siblings will thrive. Although no one really remembers what it was like to be a baby, what happened to all of us in our early years will probably have a great effect on us as we grow up.

JEAN PAKTER, M.D., M.P.H.
Director, Bureau of Maternity Services
and Family Planning
New York City Department of Health
Reviewed and updated by MICHAEL E. LAMB,
PH.D.
Professor of Psychology,
Psychiatry, and Pediatrics
University of Utah

and some foods, such as cereal, fruits, and vegetables, to the baby's diet. The pediatrician will also give the baby "shots," or oral vaccines that will protect the baby from certain diseases, such as measles, whooping cough, and polio.

Two- or three-month-old babies can hold their heads up. But babies cannot sit up alone until they are about 6 or 7 months old. By about 9 months, most learn to stand while holding on to something. By this time, babies are quite good at crawling around and exploring their world. The baby usually can take a few steps at about the time of its first birthday.

When do babies learn to talk? Well, if you listen carefully, you will notice that they begin to make sounds when they are still very young. We call these sounds "baby talk." Unfortunately, we do not understand baby talk very well, but we enjoy listening to it and

BABYLONIA

Babylonia was a region in what is now southern Iraq where a talented people built a great civilization almost 4,000 years ago. Among their accomplishments, the Babylonians developed the exact sciences, especially mathematics and astronomy. Because the Babylonians sought to use their science to predict the future, their astronomy gave way to astrology, a belief that the motion of the heavenly bodies affects the course of human events. Thus, while the Babylonians laid a foundation for modern science, it remained for the later Greeks to separate science from superstition.

The Babylonians were a Semitic people whose language was related to Hebrew and Arabic. They were influenced by a people who lived earlier in the region, the Sumerians. Like the Sumerians, they used a style of writing called cuneiform ("wedge-shaped") and developed a culture built around large cities.

The Tower of Babel. The most distinctive type of Babylonian building was the ziggurat, a towerlike temple, built in stages and topped by a religious shrine. Though the ziggurat was first developed by the Sumerians, the Babylonians carried on the tradition. The most famous ziggurat is the Tower of Babel mentioned in the Bible. The god of the Babylonians was Marduk, whose cult spread with the growth of the Babylonian Empire.

The capital of Babylonia was the city of Babylon, situated near the Euphrates River where it approaches the Tigris River, not far from present-day Baghdad, the capital of Iraq.

The Code of Hammurabi. Babylon became important after 1800 B.C. under a succession of kings known as the First Dynasty of Babylon. The most famous monarch in that line was Hammurabi (Hammurapi), who ruled from about 1792 to 1750 B.C. By the use of shrewd diplomacy and strong armies, he defeated his rivals, the kings of other city-states, and carved out the most powerful empire of his day. Hammurabi also established a code of laws that regulated society strictly, with justice but little mercy. For example, a builder was to be executed if the house he built collapsed and killed the homeowner. And an incompetent surgeon who cost a patient his or her eye or life was to have his operating hand cut off. Though harsh, Hammurabi's laws protected his subjects from injustice.

Hammurabi's Code, one of the world's oldest sets of laws, was inscribed about 4,000 years ago on this tablet. The seated figure is that of Hammurabi, king of Babylon.

Nebuchadnezzar II. The next great king of Babylon arose a thousand years later. Nebuchadnezzar II, who reigned from 605 to 562 B.C., made Babylon the greatest city on earth. He beautified his capital with structures such as the Hanging Gardens, famed as one of the Seven Wonders of the Ancient World. Nebuchadnezzar conquered many nations, including the Jews, whose Temple in Jerusalem he destroyed in 586 B.C.

The long rule of Babylon ended with its capture by the Persians under Cyrus the Great in 539 B.C. At least one great monument of the Babylonians survives, however. The development of modern Iraq is due in large measure to its restoration of the ancient irrigation canal system built by the Babylonians, which made the region between the Tigris and Euphrates rivers the most fertile in the world.

CYRUS H. GORDON
New York University
Author, *Hammurapi's Code*

A brilliant composer and organist, Bach wrote much of his music for the church. His work influenced such great musicians as Mozart, Haydn, and Beethoven.

BACH, JOHANN SEBASTIAN (1685–1750)

Johann Sebastian Bach was born on March 21, 1685, in Eisenach, Germany. He was the greatest member of a renowned musical family of more than 50 musicians who lived in central Germany between 1500 and the 1800's.

At the age of 10, Bach was left an orphan and went to live with his older brother, a church organist at Ohrdruf. When he was 15, Bach went to Lüneburg, where a scholarship allowed him to attend school. There he sang in the choir and learned much of the best music of the time. He also studied with the great organist George Böhm.

In 1703, Bach became church organist at Arnstadt and immediately began to compose for the organ, the harpsichord, and voices. He went to Mühlhausen in 1707, and while he was an organist in that city he married his cousin, Maria Barbara Bach. The following year they moved to Weimar, where Bach remained in the service of the Duke of Weimar for ten years.

Most of Bach's music at Weimar was composed for the organ and church choirs. When Bach wanted to change jobs again, the Duke put him in jail to try to make him stay. But Bach was determined to leave and journeyed to Cöthen, where he entered the service of Prince Leopold of Anhalt. During his six years at Cöthen, Bach composed many of his best-known instrumental works, such as the *Brandenburg* concertos, the English and the French suites for harpsichord, and much chamber music.

Bach's wife died in 1720. The following year he married Anna Magdalena Wilcken. Bach became the father of 20 children, and several of his talented sons became well-known composers.

Bach changed jobs for the last time in 1723 and became director of music at St. Thomas' Church and School in Leipzig. Though he was not happy with the post, he remained there for 27 years, until his death. Most of Bach's greatest religious works were composed during these years, including the *Magnificat,* the *St. John* Passion, the *St. Matthew* Passion, the B-minor Mass, and many cantatas. In Leipzig, Bach also completed *The Well-Tempered Clavier,* a collection of 48 preludes and fugues in all the keys. Like most of Bach's music, it was not published until long after his death. Bach was well known as an organist, but during his lifetime he never became a celebrated composer like his famous contemporary, George Frederick Handel.

In 1747, Bach journeyed to Potsdam to visit his son Karl Philipp Emanuel, who was a musician at the court of King Frederick II of Prussia. The King admired Bach and wanted to hear him play. To the King's delight Bach improvised on a melody that the King had given him. When Bach returned to Leipzig, he repaid the royal friendship by composing the *Musical Offering* based on the King's theme and dedicating it to the King.

Bach then turned to his last great work, *The Art of Fugue,* which remained unfinished at his death. It is the fruit of Bach's lifelong study of a musical technique called counterpoint. As Bach grew older his eyesight became increasingly poor, until toward the end of his life, he was totally blind. He died in Leipzig on July 28, 1750. It was not until almost 100 years later that the world recognized Bach as one of its greatest composers.

Reviewed by KARL GEIRINGER
Author, *The Bach Family*

BACKGAMMON

Backgammon is a game of luck and skill played with dice and checkers on a special board. The game was probably introduced into Europe by the Crusaders. In the eastern Mediterranean area, it has been played with such enthusiasm that for many years the better players of this region were the best in the world. But excellent players have developed elsewhere as the game's popularity has spread.

▶ EQUIPMENT

Each player has a set of 15 checkers. The checkers can be of any two different colors, but usually one set is dark and the other is light in color. Each player also has two dice and a cup in which to shake them.

The backgammon board is a rectangle. It is divided into two halves by a vertical line called the *bar*. One half of the board is called the *inner,* or home, *table.* The other half is called the *outer table.*

Twelve triangles, called *points,* stick out from each of the two long sides of the board. Six points are on each side of the inner table, and six points are on each side of the outer table. The players, usually identified as Black and White according to the color of their checkers, sit on opposite sides of the board.

▶ OBJECT OF THE GAME

At the start of the game, the checkers are arranged as shown in Diagram 1. Each player tries to move all his checkers to his own inner table by advancing according to the numbers rolled on the dice. The white checkers move clockwise and the black move counterclockwise. Each player is moving his checkers from the opponent's inner table around the board by way of the two outer tables and then to the inner table on his own side of the board. After all checkers are in a player's own inner table, the player *bears off* (removes the checkers from the board). The first player to bear off all of his checkers is the winner.

▶ NOTATION

Each point on the backgammon board has a number as shown on the outer rim of the board in the diagrams below. The numbers are used by writers of books and columns on backgammon to describe the moves that the players have made. These numbers do not appear on a real backgammon board, but a beginning player might find it helpful to lightly pencil them onto the board. This would enable the player to follow a written game or instructions move by move.

The points on both sides of the board are numbered from 1 through 12, going from the inner table to the outer. The initials B and W, referring to Black and White, indicate which side of the board the point is on. When a move is described, it indicates the point moved from, followed by the point moved to. For example, assume that White throws a 6 and a 1 as an opening move and chooses to move

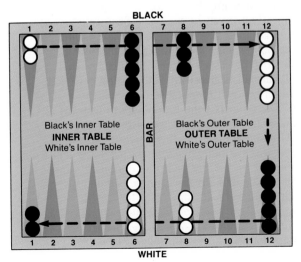

Diagram 1. A board set up for play. White will move in direction of arrows, black the opposite direction.

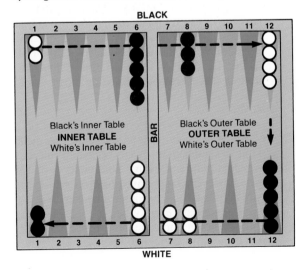

Diagram 2. White rolled a 6 and a 1 and has made an opening move. The notation is White: B12—W7, W8—W7.

the checkers as indicated in Diagram 2. White has moved one checker from Black's 12 point to White's 7 point and another from White's 8 point to White's 7 point. The move would be notated as follows: White: B12–W7, W8–W7.

▶ START OF THE GAME

To begin a game, each player rolls one die. The player who throws the highest number plays first by using the numbers on both his and his opponent's dice. After this, the players take turns rolling their dice onto the board from their cups and moving their checkers.

▶ THE PLAY OF THE GAME

The numbers on the two dice, taken separately, show the number of points over which the player's checkers may be moved. When one checker has been moved the number of points indicated by one die, the number on the other die may be used to move the same checker further—or it may be used to move a different checker. For example, if a player throws a 5 and a 6, the player could choose to move one checker 5 points and a different checker 6 points, or he could opt to move one checker 11 points. No other combinations are possible—in other words, the total of 11 cannot be divided into moves of 7 and 4 or 8 and 3. The split can only be made according to the numbers on the individual dice.

If a player should happen to roll doubles (both dice the same), the player may move twice as many points as the total shown on the dice. For example, a roll of 3–3 counts as four 3's rather than the two 3's shown. The player can move a total of 12 points rather than 6. This move can be made in units of 3 using as many as four checkers. A possible opening move for White throwing double 3's might be: White: B1–B7 (2). The (2) shows that two separate checkers made the same move.

▶ MOVES

If a player has two or more checkers on a point, he has *made* that point. White has made point W7 in Diagram 2. His opponent can pass over that point but cannot land on it. A player can, however, land on a point on which the opponent has only a single checker. Such a point is called a *blot*. When a checker of the opposite color lands on a blot, the checker that was originally there has been *hit* and is re-

moved from the board and placed *on the bar*. A player who has a checker on the bar may re-enter the game by throwing a number that will place the hit checker on any open point on the opponent's inner table. All checkers on the bar must be entered before the player can move any of his other checkers.

Whenever possible, a player *must* move his checkers using both (or all four, in the case of doubles) numbers thrown. There will be cases, however, where the opponent's points prevent a player from moving any of his checkers. In this case, the play passes to the opponent. If only one number of a roll is usable, it must be the higher one.

▶ BEARING OFF

When a player has advanced all 15 of his checkers to his own inner table, he may begin to bear off.

A checker is borne off a point that matches the number rolled on one die. For example, on a 4–2 roll, a checker may be removed from the 4 point and another from the 2 point. When a number on one die is higher than the highest point on which a player has checkers, the player takes the checker off the highest occupied point. That is, if the player throws a 5, and the 5 point is empty but there is a checker on the 4 point, the player bears off the checker from the 4 point. It is not permitted to bear off a checker from a point higher than the number on the die.

If all the player's checkers are in his inner table, it is not required that they be borne off with each roll of the dice. Instead, they could be moved further into the inner table.

If a player's checker is hit during the bearing off, it is put on the bar. The checker must re-enter the game and move all the way around the board again to its inner table before bearing off can start again. In other words, a player can bear off *only* if all of his checkers are in his own inner table.

The winner is the first player to bear off all his or her checkers. If the loser has not borne off a single checker, this player is *gammoned* and loses a double game. If the loser has a checker on the bar or in the opponent's inner table, she or he is *backgammoned* and loses a triple game.

CHARLES H. GOREN
Author, *Goren's Modern Backgammon Complete*

BACKPACKING. See HIKING AND BACKPACKING.

BACON, FRANCIS (1561–1626)

Francis Bacon, an English statesman, philosopher, and essayist, was born in London on January 22, 1561. He showed great brilliance as a child and at the age of 12 entered Cambridge University. After two years at Cambridge, he began the study of law.

Bacon completed his law studies, and in 1584 was elected to Parliament. Ambitious as well as intelligent, he rose to political prominence under King James I. He was knighted and appointed attorney general. In 1618 he was made Baron Verulam and named lord chancellor, the highest legal post in England. He was created Viscount St. Albans in 1621.

Bacon was one of the King's closest advisers. But in 1621 he was charged with accepting gifts from persons whose cases were waiting to be tried in the courts. Since giving and receiving gifts was a common practice at the time, it was obvious that Bacon's political enemies were using the charge in order to rid the kingdom of his influence. He was convicted and imprisoned in the Tower of London. After a few days he was released, but his political career was over.

Bacon had begun to write his famous essays and other works during his busy years as a man of public affairs. Now he devoted the remainder of his life to philosophical and scientific writing. He had planned a long work that would reform philosophical and scientific study. "I have taken all knowledge as my province," he stated. But he was able to finish only two parts of the great work. Among his completed writings are *The Advancement of Learning*, *History of Henry VII*, and the collected *Essays*. Bacon made the essay a popular literary form in England.

Bacon's scientific curiosity led to his death. One winter day, it occurred to him that food could be preserved by cold. To demonstrate this, he bought a chicken and stuffed it with snow. While working in the snowy weather, he caught cold. The illness grew worse, and he died on April 9, 1626.

Reviewed by ELIZABETH S. WRIGLEY
Director, The Francis Bacon Library

BACON, ROGER (1214?–1292?)

Roger Bacon, an English scientist and philosopher, helped lay the foundations of modern scientific thinking. He recognized the need for research and accurate methods of scientific study at a time when many people still relied on myths and superstitions to explain events in the world around them.

Little is known for certain about Bacon's life. He was born sometime between 1214 and 1220, the son of a well-to-do family in Ilchester, England. He may have entered Oxford University as early as the age of 13. In the 1240's he taught at the University of Paris.

Europe during Bacon's lifetime was having a revival of learning, based on the discovery of great written works from ancient Greece and Rome. Most scholars simply accepted and taught this knowledge from the ancient world. But Bacon did something different. He learned from living people and from the world around him, as well as from ancient wisdom.

Bacon also conducted his own experiments. He spent years studying how the eye works. He sprayed water into the air to study the nature of rainbows. He tested superstitions by performing experiments with the actual materials.

About 1250, Bacon returned to England, entered the Franciscan order of monks, and began to teach science at Oxford. But his experiments made his superiors angry. In 1257 they sent Bacon back to Paris. He was told to write and teach only what they approved.

Nevertheless, Bacon secretly obtained a commission from Pope Clement IV to write a report on the importance of science. One part of it, the *Opus majus* ("Greater Work"), was an outline of scientific knowledge. The importance of this report lies in Bacon's emphasis on the need to observe, test, and measure.

In 1278, Bacon's religious superiors imprisoned him in Paris for his unusual ideas. He was freed in 1290, but he had become a weak old man. He returned to England and is thought to have died in Oxford in 1292. Today Bacon's ideas—unusual for their time—are considered an important part of modern science.

JOHN S. BOWMAN
Author and science editor

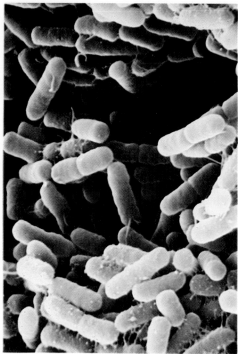

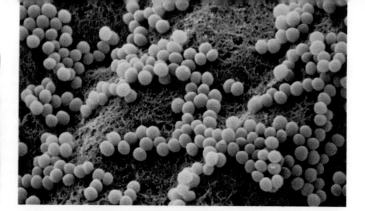

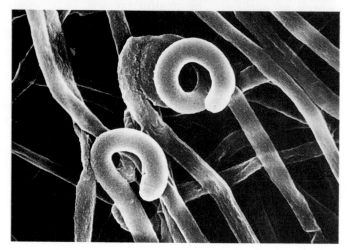

Rods, balls, and spirals are the three shapes that bacteria take. Their proper terms are bacillus (*above*), coccus (*top right*), and spirillum (*bottom right*). Each is magnified more than 1,000 times.

BACTERIA

Bacteria are probably the most common form of life on earth. They are also among the simplest and smallest living things. They are micro-organisms, which mean they can be seen only under a microscope.

Some bacteria cause disease, but most do not. There are at least 2,000 species, or kinds, of bacteria. Most of them are harmless and some are actually helpful to other forms of life, including people.

Size

A bacterium consists of only one cell. ("Bacterium" is the singular of "bacteria.") The largest bacterium is about 200 times bigger than the smallest. A single drop of sour milk may contain 100,000,000 bacteria. A thousand of even the largest bacteria can sit side by side on the tip of a pencil.

Shape

Bacteria have three basic shapes, which take their names from Latin words. A rod-shaped one is called a bacillus, meaning "little rod." The ball-shaped kind is the coccus, meaning "berry." And the one shaped like a corkscrew is the spirillum, meaning "spiral."

Habitat

Bacteria are everywhere. Some live in the mouths, noses, and intestines of animals and of people. Others live on fallen leaves or animal wastes, and still others in water, milk, dust, and soil. Some bacteria use hydrogen gas, ammonia, and iron compounds as their food. A few bacteria feed on gases and acids that are poisonous to us.

Most bacteria are killed by heat, yet a few kinds are able to live in hot springs. Freezing does not usually kill bacteria, but it slows their growth. Some kinds of bacteria resist drying, strong chemicals, or extreme temperatures by changing into tough-walled spores. The bacteria may last a very long time in this resting form. Under favorable conditions, the spore walls burst, and the bacteria become active again.

Are bacteria plants or animals?

Simple organisms like bacteria have some features of both plants and animals. Scientists have never entirely agreed on how to classify bacteria. Bacteria lack chlorophyll, the green coloring matter that most plants need to make their own food. In their use of outside sources of food, bacteria seem like animals. But in their sizes, shapes, and general living habits most bacteria resemble lower plants such as fungi and algae. Many scientists classify bacteria and other micro-organisms that have characteristics of both plants and animals as protists, or "first things."

Reproduction

Most bacteria reproduce by fission—that is, the cell of a bacterium divides in two. Depending on the kind of bacterium, division may take place every 15 to 40 minutes. In theory this means that bacteria could multiply by the millions or billions within a few hours. But in actual practice there is not enough food or moisture in any one place to support such numbers. Competition for food and exposure to harmful conditions keep the bacteria population down.

Oxygen Use

Like all living things bacteria need oxygen to burn up food materials for energy. (Bacteria eat anywhere from 2 to 1,000 times their own weight in an hour.)

Most bacteria take oxygen from the air, but some get oxygen by breaking down chemical compounds in their food. For example, bacteria that ferment milk (cause it to turn sour) get oxygen from milk sugar. Some kinds actually cannot live in the presence of oxygen. These bacteria are called strict **anaerobes,** meaning "without air."

Harmful Bacteria

Certain bacteria cause disease in people and animals. Some of the common human diseases caused by bacteria are cholera, diphtheria, pneumonia, tetanus, and tuberculosis. Other bacteria produce disease in plants. Black rot in cabbage and fire blight in pears are caused by bacteria.

Food is spoiled by still other bacteria, such as those that cause meat to rot. Some bacteria damage food in unseen ways. For example, botulism, a dangerous disease, is caused by a poison-producing anaerobe in improperly canned foods. Another bacterium, Salmonella, found in contaminated meat and eggs, causes a severe digestive disease.

Helpful Bacteria

Most bacteria are useful. Some are even necessary to life. Others have been put to work for a specific purpose.

Bacteria in the Cycle of Life. Bacteria cause the decay of dead plants and animals, both on land and in water. Without such bacteria the earth would soon be covered with material from dead organisms.

As they take in food, bacteria break down plant and animal tissue into simple chemical substances. The substances are then restored to the soil, water, and air in forms that can be used for nourishment and growth by living plants and animals.

Bacteria also play an important part in the digestive processes of people and animals. There are a great many bacteria in the human intestine. As the bacteria eat, they break down foods. At the same time they make certain vitamins, which the body then uses. The bacteria inside the stomachs of grass-eating animals can break down cellulose, the stiff wall of green plant cells. By enabling cows to digest grasses, bacteria play a part in the production of milk.

Colonies of bacteria thrive on a special growth substance called agar. These bacteria, grown on agar containing sheep's blood, cause strep throat in humans.

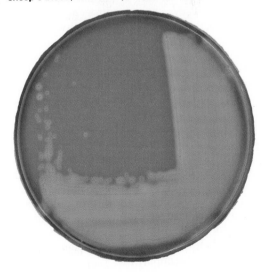

Cheddar cheese obtains its distinctive flavor and aroma from the harmless bacteria that are allowed to grow in it during the curing process.

Scientists have developed a way to produce methane from the manure (solid wastes) of cattle. Methane is a flammable gas and a valuable fuel. It is used for heating homes and factories and for other energy needs. When methane gas is produced, protein and minerals in the manure are removed and can be used for cattle feed.

Bacteria in the Community. Another use for bacteria is in sewage disposal plants. Waste water carries impurities into the sewage tanks. The tanks are really "gardens" where large colonies of bacteria grow. While feeding on the sewage, the bacteria break down the impurities into a gas and into solids. The solid material sinks to the bottom of the tanks, and the water is drained off. After further treatment the water may be safely released.

New Uses for Bacteria

Scientists have discovered ways to change bacteria so that they produce valuable medical, agricultural, and industrial products. This involves changing certain characteristics, or traits, that are inherited.

Units of heredity, called **genes,** pass traits from generation to generation. Genes are made up of long, twisted chains of a chemical called deoxyribonucleic acid (DNA). To change particular traits of an organism, scientists make changes in its genes, using **genetic engineering.** This method is also called **recombinant DNA** and **gene splicing.**

For example, gene splicing is used to change bacteria so that they produce human insulin. This substance is extremely important in regulating the body's use of sugar and other nutrients. The insulin made by bacteria is used to help diabetics—people whose bodies produce little or no insulin.

To change the genes of bacteria, scientists remove a small section of DNA. They replace it with a section of DNA taken from human cells. This human DNA controls the making of insulin. The bacteria follow the "instructions" of the transferred human DNA and produce human insulin. When a changed bacterium divides, each of the newly formed bacteria is able to make human insulin.

SARAH R. RIEDMAN
Author, science books for children.

See also DISEASES; FERMENTATION; FOOD SPOILAGE AND CONTAMINATION; GENETIC ENGINEERING; MICROBIOLOGY.

Bacteria in Agriculture. All living tissue—plant as well as animal—needs nitrogen, the gas that makes up almost 80 percent of the air. Some bacteria, called nitrogen-fixing bacteria, are the only organisms that can take nitrogen from the air. These bacteria live in the soil. They change nitrogen into substances that plants can use. They live in partnership with plants such as peas, beans, and alfalfa.

Bacteria are also responsible for the fermentation process by which such products as cheese, buttermilk, yogurt, and vinegar are made.

Bacteria in Industry. The process of fermentation is used to make substances needed for paints, plastics, cosmetics, candy, and certain drugs. Other industrial uses of bacteria include curing tobacco leaves, tanning hides, eating away the outer covering of coffee and cocoa seeds, and separating certain kinds of fibers for the textile industry. Mineral-eating bacteria help to refine metal and petroleum by eating away the impurities.

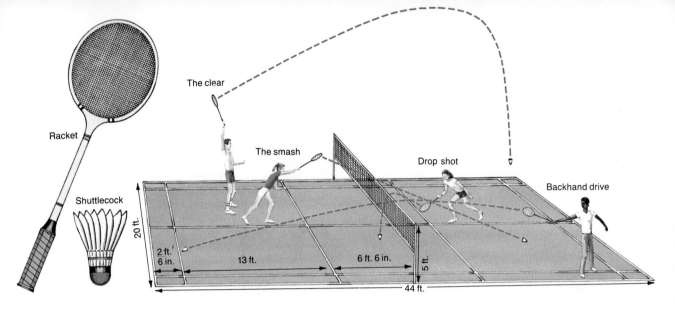

Racket

The clear

The smash

Drop shot

Backhand drive

Shuttlecock

20 ft.

2 ft. 6 in.

13 ft.

6 ft. 6 in.

5 ft.

44 ft.

BADMINTON

Badminton is a fast game played with rackets and a shuttlecock on a wood, dirt, or grass court. The court is somewhat like a tennis court, but smaller. The shuttlecock, often called simply the shuttle, or "bird," is hit back and forth over a net 5 feet (1.5 meters) high. It must be returned before it strikes the court. The game can be played by two persons (singles) or four persons (doubles). It can be played both indoors and outdoors. Official tournaments are played indoors.

Badminton developed from Battledore and Shuttlecock, an ancient game that was popular with children. There are several explanations of how the modern game began; one is that about the year 1870, English army officers brought a version of it to England from India, where it was called Poona. The new game took its name from the Duke of Beaufort's estate, Badminton, where the game was probably played indoors for the first time. Badminton became popular in England, and in the 1890's the Badminton Association was formed. In 1934 the International Badminton Federation was organized. The two international badminton championships are the Thomas Cup competition for men and the Uber Cup for women.

▶ PLAYING BADMINTON

The game starts with the player in the right service court serving to an opponent in the diagonally opposite right service court. Allowed only one serve at the start of each point, the server continues serving to alternate courts until the rally is lost. If a rally is lost, a point is not lost, only the serve. This is called side out. An opponent then takes a hand at serving.

Any of the following is called a fault, and results in side out if committed by the serving side or loss of a point if committed by a receiver:

Server
(1) Serving outside the service court.
(2) Contact with the serve anyplace above the waist.

Server or receiver
(1) Hitting the shuttle out of bounds, or twice in succession on the same side of the net, or under or through the net, or before it crosses the net.
(2) Carrying the shuttle with the racket.
(3) Touching the net or its supports during play.
(4) Serving or receiving the serve with the feet on the line, or with both feet not in contact with the floor until the shuttle is hit.

A shuttle falling on a boundary line is good.

▶ SCORING

Points can be scored only while serving. A game is won by the first player or side to score 15 points, except in women's singles, in which game is 11 points. If a tie score of 13 all is reached (9 all in women's singles), the side that reached the tie score first may, if it chooses, set the game at 5 (or 3 in women's singles). This means that game will not be reached until either side has scored 5 (or 3) more points. Similarly, if the score becomes tied at 14 all (or 10 all in women's singles), game may be set at 3 (or 2) more points.

The side that wins a game serves first in the next game. The opposing sides change ends of the court after each game.

THE BASIC STROKES

Overhead shots are played from above the head; underhand shots are those played from below waist level. Any stroke hit on the right-hand side of the body is a forehand; on the left-hand side of the body, a backhand. The descriptions and instructions in this article are for right-handed players. If you are left-handed, substitute "left" for "right" and "right" for "left."

The serve is the most important stroke because it puts the shuttle in play at the start of each point.

The smash, or kill shot, is the principal point-winning stroke in badminton. It is hit downward from an overhead position with as much speed as possible.

The clear is a shot that sends the shuttle high to the opponent's back boundary line.

The drop shot causes the shuttle to drop close to the net in the opponent's court. It may be hit either overhead or underhand.

The drive sends the shuttle skimming low over the net in a line parallel to the floor.

Several auxiliary shots are often useful in badminton. The hairpin and crosscourt net shots can be used to return a drop shot with a drop shot. They can be hit from one side of the court to the other (crosscourt), or directly back over the net (hairpin).

The round-the-head shot is an overhead backhand played as a forehand. It is protection against a weak backhand. The half smash is used to angle the shuttle downward sharply.

GRIPS AND FOOTWORK

There are different grips for holding the racket to make the various shots.

For the forehand and serve grip, hold the throat of the racket with your left hand. Keep the face of the racket perpendicular to the floor. Then place your right hand on the handle, as if shaking hands with it. Your fingers should be slightly spread.

For backhand shots the hand is turned slightly to the left, the thumb placed flat along the back of the handle, not around it.

Keep your wrist firm and yet flexible, not stiff and tense. The wrist must be cocked back at the beginning of the backswing. As the arm comes forward the wrist snaps or whips the racket head to meet the shuttle.

Good footwork enables you to move quickly in any direction and to have your feet properly placed while stroking. The weight must be on the balls of the feet, and the knees should be mobile. For forehand strokes the left foot is advanced toward the net and the left side faces the net. On the backhand the right foot is advanced and the right side faces the net. These same principles apply to overhead forehands and backhands.

TACTICS AND STRATEGY

The object of the game is to win the required number of points by forcing opponents to make errors. If opponents do not make outright errors they can be forced to make weak returns that can be put away—that is, placed beyond their reach.

Basic strategy in singles involves forcing your opponent to "set up" the shuttle high in the forecourt, where it can be put away with a smash. Use the clear and drop shots to run an opponent to the corners of the court. If an opponent is in the backcourt, try to drop shot. Use a clear shot against an opponent in the forecourt. Drive the shuttle to give an opponent less time.

Generally the singles serve is hit high and deep to the back boundary line. In doubles it should skim over the net and drop near the short service line. The value of a good low serve in doubles cannot be overestimated.

In doubles, attack by hitting the shuttle downward whenever possible. The shuttle is placed strategically to force the opponents to hit upward, or defensive, shots. In mixed doubles the woman usually plays the shots in the front half of the court. The man stands behind her and plays the shots coming to the backcourt.

WHAT MAKES A CHAMPION?

The outstanding characteristic of a champion at badminton is the ability to react in split-second time with eyes, mind, feet, and hands. Becoming a champion takes physical and mental effort at all times. Constant practice, physical fitness, reading instructional books, and observing expert players help make a winner. Habits of concentration, confidence, and self-determination are necessary. The great players of the game almost always have been good sports. This is apparent in their conduct on and off the court.

MARGARET VARNER
Former World Badminton Champion

BAGHDAD

Baghdad is the capital and largest city of Iraq and ranks among the largest cities of the Middle East. It is situated on the banks of the Tigris River and lies about 25 miles (40 kilometers) from the Euphrates. The two rivers form what is often called "the cradle of civilization," a fertile region whose history dates back over 4,000 years.

The Modern City. Baghdad spreads out on both sides of the Tigris River, which is spanned by twelve bridges. The hub of the city is Tahir Square, from which fan out Baghdad's main thoroughfares, including Rashid and Sadun streets. The city's wide boulevards, high-rise buildings, and colleges and universities give much of Baghdad a modern appearance. Its population is about 4 million.

Baghdad is the country's manufacturing center. Its chief industries include petroleum refining and the production of petrochemicals, textiles, processed foods, engineering equipment, and leather goods. The city is also noted for its handicrafts of gold, silver, and copper.

History. Baghdad is part of a region that saw the rise and fall of many of the world's earliest civilizations, including those of Sumer, Akkad, and Babylonia. Assyrian, Greek, Roman, Arab, Persian, and Turkish empires succeeded them. Baghdad itself was the creation of the Caliph al-Mansur, of the Abbasid dynasty of Muslim rulers, who in the 700's A.D. ordered 100,000 workers to build the city for him. For 500 years Baghdad was one of the great cities of the world, attracting merchants and goods from India, Persia (Iran), Egypt, and the Mediterranean region. Under the Caliph Harun al-Rashid (ruled 786–809) of *The Arabian Nights* fame, the city saw the flowering of Arab culture. Grand palaces, imposing mosques (Muslim houses of worship), colleges, places of entertainment, well-paved streets, and public baths reflected the city's wealth, splendor, and sophistication. The city attracted scholars and artists from all over the Islamic world.

Baghdad was almost destroyed by invading Mongols in 1258. For centuries thereafter it was largely a provincial town, first under the Persian and then the Ottoman Turkish empires. The development of the modern city dates from the 1900's. Baghdad came

The Gold Mosque is a modern reminder of Baghdad's long history as a center of the Muslim world. The 1,200-year-old city was once the seat of a great Islamic empire.

under British rule in 1920, and the following year it was made the capital of the newly established kingdom of Iraq. The discovery of large quantities of oil in Iraq provided money for the further modernization of the city. When the monarchy was overthrown in 1958, Baghdad became the capital of the present Republic of Iraq.

Baghdad's economy was strained by Iraq's long war with Iran (1980–88). The city also suffered severely from U.S. and allied bombings during the 1991 Persian Gulf war, which followed Iraq's invasion of Kuwait.

BALKRISHNA G. GOKHALE
Director, Asian Studies Program
Wake Forest University

BAGPIPE. See FOLK MUSIC INSTRUMENTS.

BAHAMAS

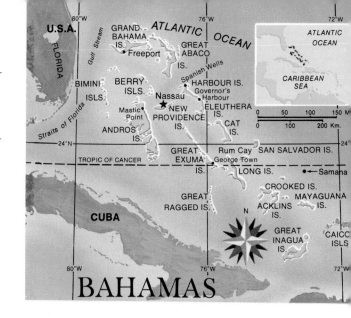

BAHAMAS

The Bahamas is a nation made up of many small islands in the Atlantic Ocean. They form an archipelago (a chain of islands) lying between the Florida coast of the United States and the Caribbean islands of Cuba and Hispaniola.

Christopher Columbus is believed to have first stepped ashore on one of the islands of the Bahamas during his voyage to the Americas in 1492. San Salvador (Watling Island) is long thought to have been the island. Recently, however, some scholars have suggested that Columbus may have first landed on another site in the Bahamas, Samana Cay.

▶THE PEOPLE

Most of the people of the Bahamas are blacks whose ancestors were brought to the islands as slaves. Over half of the people live on New Providence Island, mostly in the area of Nassau, the capital city. Nassau's fine hotels, quaint streets and houses, and a variety of shops selling goods from all over the world

Eleuthera has some of the loveliest beaches in the Bahamas.

at low prices attract many tourists. The only other city of any size is Freeport on Grand Bahama, the second most populous island.

The country has an extensive primary and secondary school system, which contributes to its high literacy rate. School is free and compulsory for all children between the ages of 5 and 14. Students seeking higher education generally attend the College of the Bahamas on New Providence or the University of the West Indies in Jamaica or study in the United States, Canada, or Britain.

▶THE LAND

There are about 700 islands and 2,000 tiny sand cays (keys) and exposed bits of coral reef in the Bahamas. The islands extend in an arc for some 1,200 kilometers (750 miles) to the northern edge of the Caribbean Sea. They are formed largely of coral and are mostly low-lying. The highest elevation is almost 120 meters (400 feet). Only a relatively small number of the islands are permanently inhabited.

The climate of the Bahamas is semitropical. Temperatures vary little with the seasons and are moderate in both winter and summer. Rainfall averages about 1,270 millimeters (50 inches) a year, which is enough for most types of farming. On the smaller islands there is less rainfall, and often there are shortages of fresh drinking water. The islands are subject to hurricanes in the fall. The heavy rains and strong winds that accompany these violent storms occasionally cause severe damage.

THE ECONOMY

The mainstay of the economy is the tourist industry. Well over 1,000,000 visitors a year are attracted by the climate, beautiful beaches, and clear water. Nassau and Freeport are the most popular tourist spots. But the waters near the Bimini Islands off the coast of Florida are famous for big game fishing. In the spring anglers gather there for annual fishing tournaments.

Nassau is also a center of finance because the tax laws of the Bahamas have encouraged the growth of international banking there. Nassau's importance to the Bahamas is so great that the islands other than New Providence are called Out Islands and their people are called Out Islanders.

Petroleum refining has become an important source of income for the Bahamas. Petroleum and petroleum products now rank as one of the country's leading exports. The islands are also a transfer point for petroleum being shipped to the United States.

Manufacturing and agriculture play a relatively small role in the economy. There is light manufacturing on Grand Bahama Island, where a deepwater port has been dredged at Freeport. Alcoholic beverages, tobacco, textiles, chemicals, paper, rubber goods, and plastics are produced.

Only about 1 percent of the land is cultivated, and this is used mostly for growing crops for domestic use. Eleuthera Island, one of the first islands to be settled, is an important farming area. Vegetables, pineapples, and dairy and poultry products are shipped from Eleuthera to Nassau. At Rock Sound, a prosperous farming community on Eleuthera, beef cattle are raised and shipped to New Providence.

Although the waters of the islands teem with fish, only crayfish (spiny lobster) are caught commercially. The country has little in the way of mineral resources except for salt, which is produced on the southernmost island, Great Inagua. There seawater is channeled into shallow basins. When the sun evaporates the water, the salt is left behind. Straw handicrafts provide additional income for the islanders. New ways to expand the economy and provide more jobs are constantly being sought. An influx of Haitian refugees has added to unemployment problems.

FACTS AND FIGURES

THE COMMONWEALTH OF THE BAHAMAS is the official name of the country.

CAPITAL: Nassau.

LOCATION: Archipelago in the Atlantic Ocean off the coast of Florida. **Latitude**—20° 50' N to 27° 25' N. **Longitude**—72° 37' W to 80° 32' W.

AREA: 13,935 km² (5,380 sq mi).

POPULATION: 230,000 (estimate).

LANGUAGE: English.

GOVERNMENT: Constitutional monarchy. **Head of state**—British monarch, represented by governor-general. **Head of government**—prime minister. **International co-operation**—United Nations, Commonwealth of Nations, Organization of American States (OAS).

NATIONAL ANTHEM: "March On, Bahamaland."

ECONOMY: Agricultural products—vegetables, pineapples, dairy and poultry products. **Industries and products**—tourism, textiles, cloth, paper, rubber goods, plastics, petroleum refining, chemical products. **Chief exports**—petroleum and petroleum products, cement, alcoholic beverages, pulpwood, crayfish, salt. **Chief imports**—food, drink, tobacco, raw materials. **Monetary unit**—Bahamian dollar.

HISTORY AND GOVERNMENT

The Spanish explored the islands in the 1500's but made no serious efforts to colonize them. The few Indians who lived there were shipped to the West Indies to work in mines and on plantations. In the 17th century the British gained control of the Bahamas and began to settle some of the larger islands. During the United States Civil War, Nassau was a meeting place for blockade runners from the Confederate states and ships from England. There cotton from the South was traded for English goods.

The Bahamas became self-governing in 1964, although Britain still handled foreign affairs, defense, and internal security. When complete independence came in 1973, the Bahamian Government took over the management of these affairs.

The government of the Bahamas is headed by a prime minister, while a governor-general represents the British monarch, who is head of state. Parliament has two houses—the elected House of Assembly and the Senate, to which members are appointed.

JOHN F. LOUNSBURY
Arizona State University

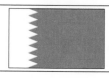

BAHRAIN

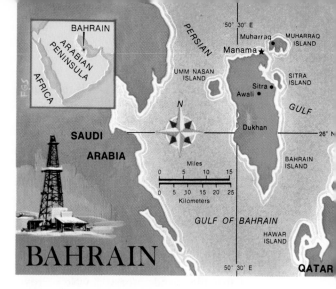

Bahrain is a country made up of a group of islands lying in the Persian Gulf off the coast of Saudi Arabia. It is the smallest in area of all the states of the Arabian Peninsula. Indeed, it ranks among the smallest of the world's nations. In spite of its size, however, Bahrain has for centuries been one of the more flourishing states of the region. Its location made it important as a port and a center of trade for the countries bordering the gulf. It was famed for its pearls and for the skill of its boatbuilders. The discovery of oil brought further prosperity to Bahrain, although its reserves of oil are not nearly so large as those of some of its neighbors. Over the years Bahrain has used its income from oil to establish an extensive social welfare program for its citizens and to continue its economic development toward the day when its oil will be completely gone.

▶ THE PEOPLE

Bahrain is by far the most densely populated country of the Arabian Peninsula. Most of the people are Arabs, some of whom have immigrated to Bahrain from neighboring countries. There are sizable numbers of Pakistanis, Iranians, and Indians, some of whom work as merchants in the cities. It is estimated that about 30 percent of the people are non-Bahraini. Many came to Bahrain because of the relatively high standard of living and to work in the oil industry. The foreign communities include Europeans (mainly British) and Americans. The Arabs are Muslims, about equally divided between the Sunni and Shi'a sects, the two main branches of Islam.

About half the population is concentrated in the two leading cities of Manama and Muharraq. Manama is the largest city, the capital, and chief port. It is connected with Muharraq, which is on another island, by a 2.5-kilometer (1½-mile) causeway. The two cities present interesting contrasts. Manama, a commercial city, has been modernized, while Muharraq, with its old houses and narrow streets, retains a traditional look. The port of Muharraq is the center of Bahrain's boatbuilding industry. The boats are dhows, rather small vessels with triangular sails once common throughout the Arab world.

Traditional ways of life in the Arab states of the Persian Gulf began to change when oil was discovered. Bahrain was the first of the gulf states in which oil was found, and the effects of modernization are most evident here. The country has a growing middle class and a skilled work force. This is largely a result of Bahrain's emphasis on education. Schooling is free and compulsory for all children between the ages of 6 and 16. Schools of higher education include Gulf Polytechnic and the University College of Arts, Science, and Education. These are being combined to form a National University of Bahrain. A Gulf University also is being built.

Revenue from oil provides Bahrainis with a number of social welfare programs. These include free medical and hospital care and low-cost housing.

▶ THE LAND

Bahrain is made up of about 33 islands, islets, and sandbars, most of them uninhabited. The largest island is Bahrain, from which the country takes its name. Other important islands include Muharraq, Sitra, Umm Nasan (Umm Na'san) and Hawar, which lies near Qatar. The land is mainly flat desert, with the only fertile area in the north. The highest elevation, 137 meters (450 feet), is at Jabal Dukhan on Bahrain

Island. Most of Bahrain Island is barren. However, a narrow strip of land in the north, watered by springs and wells, can be cultivated. The main crops grown here are dates, vegetables, and alfalfa, used to feed livestock. The waters of the Persian Gulf have abundant fish and are one of the world's richest sources of natural pearls.

Bahrain's climate is extremely hot and humid in summer. Winters are relatively cool. Rainfall is slight, averaging less than 100 millimeters (4 inches) a year.

▶ THE ECONOMY

Most of Bahrain's income is derived from oil. Bahrain had the first oil refinery in the Middle East and refines not only its own crude oil but also oil from nearby Saudi Arabia. Before oil was discovered in 1932, Bahrain depended on commerce and trade, agriculture, fishing, pearling, and boat building. The development in Japan of cultured, or artificially induced, pearls led to the decline of Bahrain's industry. Shrimp abound in the gulf. Harvesting and freezing them for export is an important part of the fishing industry.

Oil experts predict that Bahrain's deposits of oil, never very large to begin with, will be exhausted before the end of the 20th century. To help diversify the economy, the government has encouraged foreign investment.

Bahrain is becoming a major transportation and commercial center for the Persian Gulf.

FACTS AND FIGURES

STATE OF BAHRAIN is the official name of the country.

CAPITAL: Manama.

LOCATION: Persian Gulf near Saudi Arabia.

AREA: 622 km² (240 sq mi).

POPULATION: 350,000 (estimate).

LANGUAGE: Arabic.

RELIGION: Islam.

GOVERNMENT: Emirate. **Head of state**—emir. **Head of government**—prime minister. **International cooperation**—United Nations, Arab League.

ECONOMY: Agricultural products—dates, vegetables, alfalfa. **Industries and products**—oil, fish, aluminum, boatbuilding. **Chief exports**—oil and oil products, shrimp, aluminum. **Chief imports**—machinery and transportation equipment, manufactured goods, food, chemicals. **Monetary unit**—dinar.

A new aluminum smelting plant and other industrial plants have been constructed. Port and storage facilities and ship repair yards are being enlarged at Mina Sulman, southeast of Manama. The Bahrain airport handles the largest planes. Engineering and international banking are developing rapidly.

▶ HISTORY AND GOVERNMENT

Bahrain's history goes back to very ancient times. In the northern part of Bahrain Island are many thousands of burial mounds, some extremely large, which indicate that people lived here perhaps as long ago as 3000 B.C. The Sumerians, who belonged to one of the world's oldest civilizations, had contacts with ancient Bahrain, which even then was known as an important port. Later the Greeks and Romans visited the islands.

Bahrain was colonized by the Portuguese in the 16th century and then fell under the rule of the Persians. In the 18th century the al-Khalifa family, who came from the Arabian mainland, became the ruling sheikhs of Bahrain and for a time exercised control over neighboring Qatar. Their descendants rule as emirs, or princes, in Bahrain today.

Early in the 19th century Bahrain came under British influence. A series of treaties was negotiated with Britain similar to the treaties with Britain signed by other gulf states. In return for British protection, Bahrain agreed, among other things, not to engage in slavery or piracy. Bahrain remained a British protectorate until 1971, when it gained complete independence.

Bahrain is ruled by an emir, who is the head of state and governs through an appointed prime minister and Cabinet. A legislature, the National Assembly, was provided for under the country's constitution, but it was dissolved by the emir in 1975.

In 1986, Bahrain completed a 25-kilometer (15½-mile)-long causeway, linking Bahrain Island with Saudi Arabia. The causeway is expected to have important economic benefits for Bahrain, including lower prices for its basic imports and increased tourism.

Reviewed by MAJID KHADDURI
Director, Center for Middle East Studies
Johns Hopkins University

BAKING. See BREAD AND BAKING.

Balboa was the first European to sight the Pacific Ocean. Stepping into its waters, he claimed the great ocean and all the land it touched for Spain in 1513.

BALBOA, VASCO NÚÑEZ DE (1475–1519)

Vasco Núñez de Balboa, a Spanish explorer and adventurer, was the first European to see the Pacific Ocean.

Balboa was born at Jerez de los Caballeros, Spain, in 1475. Little is known about his early life until about 1500, when he joined an expedition to seek his fortune in America. Finding no gold, he settled as a farmer on the island of Hispaniola (now Haiti and the Dominican Republic). Balboa soon found himself deeply in debt. To escape his creditors, he hid in a large barrel and was carried on board a ship bound for the settlement of San Sebastián, in Colombia.

When the ship was safely at sea, Balboa came out of hiding. The commander of the expedition, Martín Fernández de Enciso, was furious at the stowaway and threatened to abandon him on a desert island. However, Enciso allowed him to remain after Balboa convinced the crew that he would be valuable to them as a soldier.

This proved to be true, for when the expedition reached San Sebastián, they found it in ruins. Balboa took charge and led the survivors to Panama. There they started a new colony, which he called Darien.

But soon a quarrel broke out between Balboa and Enciso over who should be in command. Enciso was overthrown and sent back to Spain, and Balboa became governor of the new colony.

Balboa then set out to explore the surrounding country, hoping to find gold. His generosity won him the friendship of the Indians, who ordinarily distrusted and fought the Spaniards. The Indians had little use for gold. But seeing that Balboa prized it so highly, they told him of a marvelous land to the south where people ate from golden plates and drank from golden cups. They also said that just beyond the mountains lay a great sea. Balboa did not know that only a narrow strip of land (the Isthmus of Panama) lay between the Atlantic and Pacific oceans. He thought that this sea might be the route to Cathay (China), which Columbus had sought in vain.

Meanwhile, Enciso had returned to Spain and angrily complained about Balboa to King Ferdinand. Anxious to regain the King's favor, Balboa set out to discover the great sea the Indians had described. With 190 Spaniards and 1,000 Indians he cut his way across the jungle-covered mountains of Panama. On September 25, 1513, Balboa left his companions and climbed the last mountain peak by himself. From its summit he saw the gleaming Pacific Ocean stretching as far as the eye could see. He named it the South Sea and claimed it and all the land it touched for the King of Spain.

Balboa then planned to explore Peru—the land of gold. Before he could carry out his plans, a new governor, Pedrarias Dávila, arrived from Spain. Pedrarias, jealous of Balboa, had him arrested on a false charge of treason. And in 1519, not far from the colony he had founded and the ocean he had discovered, Balboa was executed.

Reviewed by KENNETH S. COOPER
Author, *World Ways*

BALDWIN, JAMES (1924–87)

James Baldwin was a black American novelist, playwright, and essayist. He was a leading literary voice in the civil rights movement of the 1950's and 1960's.

Baldwin was born in New York City on August 2, 1924, the oldest of nine children. His father, a Baptist preacher, was a violent man who died when James was a teenager. A gifted student, James read widely and displayed a talent for writing. By his early twenties, he was writing essays and reviews for *The Nation* and other respected periodicals.

Baldwin's first novel, *Go Tell it on the Mountain* (1953), is perhaps his best. The partly autobiographical work tells of a black teenager and his struggles with a tyrannical stepfather at home and with racial injustice in the outside world. Baldwin continued to explore racial conflict in his later works, including the novels *Another Country* (1962), *Tell Me How Long the Train's Been Gone* (1968), and *Just Above My Head* (1979), and the play *Blues for Mister Charlie* (1964).

Noted writer James Baldwin explored the experiences of black Americans.

Baldwin's essays, which reached a wide audience, were highly acclaimed for their insights into black experience in a white-dominated society. His most important essay collections were *Notes of a Native Son* (1955), *Nobody Knows My Name* (1961), and *The Fire Next Time* (1963). *The Evidence of Things Not Seen* (1985) is an essay on the murders of 28 black children in Atlanta in 1980 and 1981.

After 1948, Baldwin lived mainly in France, returning to the United States to teach and lecture. He died in St. Paul de Vence on December 1, 1987.

Reviewed by PETER CONN
Author, *Literature in America:
An Illustrated History*

BALFOUR, ARTHUR JAMES (1848–1930)

Arthur James Balfour is considered one of the most brilliant and intellectual of all the British prime ministers. A member of Parliament (MP) for 48 years, he served as Conservative prime minister from 1902–05.

Born on July 25, 1848, at Whittingehame in the Scottish border country, Balfour was 6 when his father died. He was greatly influenced by his mother, whose brother, the Marquess of Salisbury, would later serve four terms as prime minister.

At Cambridge University it was thought that Balfour would become a philosopher. In 1874, however, he chose to enter politics. At first he seemed to be little more than a lightweight, witty conversationalist, whose career advanced in his uncle's shadow. But he rapidly won a reputation for firmness and fairness. As government leader in the House of Commons (1891–92 and 1895–1902), Balfour became so skillful in debate, he was the natural choice to succeed Salisbury as Conservative prime minister in July 1902.

Balfour's government achieved little, however, apart from the school reforms brought about by the Education Act of 1902. Furthermore, disputes with Joseph Chamberlain over tariff reform caused the Conservatives to lose the 1906 general election to the Liberals. Despite criticism, Balfour continued to lead his party in opposition until 1911.

The Balfour Declaration

During World War I, Balfour returned to government office as foreign secretary (1916–19). His most famous achievement was to issue the Balfour Declaration (1917), a statement pledging British support for the establishment of a Jewish homeland in Palestine following the war (providing the non-Jewish communities already living there would be safeguarded). Balfour also helped draw up the Treaty of Versailles (1919) and other postwar settlements. Later, as Earl Balfour, he served in Stanley Baldwin's cabinet (1925–29).

ALAN PALMER
Author, *The Penguin Dictionary of
Modern History*

BALKANS

The Balkans are a region of southeastern Europe of great strategic and historical importance. Physically, the region consists of a peninsula jutting southward into the Mediterranean Sea. The peninsula is bounded on the west and southeast by the Adriatic, Ionian, and Aegean seas (arms of the Mediterranean) and on the east by the Black Sea. Politically, the Balkans are usually considered to include the present-day countries of Albania, Bulgaria, Greece, Romania, and Yugoslavia. But Yugoslavia is in the process of breaking up, four of the six republics making up the country having declared their independence.

The Land. The word *balkan* is of Turkish origin and means "wooded mountain range." The name is apt, for rugged mountains are the dominant feature of the Balkan landscape. There are several great mountain chains. The Carpathians in Romania extend, as the Balkan Mountains, into Bulgaria. The Dinaric Alps run parallel to the Adriatic coast in Yugoslavia and Albania and continue, as the Pindus Mountains, into Greece. The Rhodope range forms the boundary between Bulgaria and Greece.

The mountains isolated the different peoples of the region and tended to create a number of small states, which were often in conflict with one another. At the same time, certain valleys and rivers, particularly the Danube, the region's chief river, provided access for foreign invaders. The mountainous terrain also limited the amount of land that could be used for farming, although the valleys can be fertile.

The climate ranges from the continental, with long, cold winters and relatively short summers, to the Mediterranean, with mild winters and long, hot summers.

The People. The Balkan Peninsula is home to varied peoples. The majority are Slavs, the descendants of South Slavic peoples who arrived in the region in the A.D. 500's and 600's. Greeks, Romanians, Albanians, and Magyars (Hungarians) are the main non-Slavic groups, and there are Turkish, German, Macedonian, and other minorities.

The six major languages of the region are Serbo-Croatian, Slovenian (both spoken chiefly in Yugoslavia), Albanian, Bulgarian, Greek, and Romanian. Serbo-Croatian, Slovenian, and Bulgarian are Slavic languages.

THE BALKANS

Romanian is a Romance language, derived from Latin. It is a legacy of the time when Romania was a Roman colony.

Most Balkan peoples traditionally have belonged to the Roman Catholic or Eastern Orthodox churches. There is a considerable Muslim population as well, a reminder that the region was long ruled by the Ottoman Turks.

Early History. The first great civilization in the region was that of ancient Greece, followed, in the 300's B.C., by the short-lived empire of Alexander the Great. The Balkans became part of the Roman Empire in the A.D. 100's and 200's. With the division of the Roman world in 395, the region came under the rule of the Eastern Roman, or Byzantine, Empire, centered in Constantinople (modern Istanbul).

The arrival of the Slavs and the decline of Byzantine power permitted the development of distinct Balkan nationalities, the forerunners of today's Balkan states. There were, at different periods, large Bulgarian and Serb empires. Between the late 1300's and the mid-1500's, the region was conquered by the Ottoman Turks. As Ottoman power itself began to wane in the late 1600's, parts of the Balkans fell to an expanding Austria.

The Struggle for Independence. The struggle for Balkan independence began in earnest in the early 1800's, with the rise of Serbia and the liberation of Greece from Turkish rule. Over the next century, Montenegro, Bulgaria, and Romania won independence. In 1912 an alliance of Serbia, Bulgaria, Greece, and Montenegro defeated Turkey in the First Balkan War. As a result, Albania gained its independence and Turkey was forced to give up almost all of its remaining European lands. Disputes over territorial claims, however, led to the Second Balkan War in 1913, in which Bulgaria was defeated by its former allies, joined by Turkey.

The Modern Balkans. Meanwhile, the great European powers, particularly Britain, France, Austria-Hungary, and Russia, had also become entangled in Balkan affairs. World War I (1914–18) arose out of a Balkan issue—the ambition of Serbia to take Bosnia and Herzegovina from Austria-Hungary. The war brought about the destruction of the Austro-Hungarian empire. Out of its ashes a new nation, Yugoslavia, was formed from Serbia, Bosnia and Herzogovina, Montenegro, and other states, and the present-day Balkan states came into being. The war also led to the final collapse of the old Ottoman Empire.

The Balkans fell under Nazi German domination between 1941 and 1945, during World War II. After the war, a Communist political system was imposed on the Balkan countries, except for Greece. Communism crumbled in the late 1980's and early 1990's as reformers sought to establish more democratic governments in the region. In Yugoslavia, however, the changeover led to the revival of ancient rivalries and animosities, and eventually to civil war, especially between the two most numerous peoples, the Croats and Serbs. In 1992 a United Nations peacekeeping force was sent to Yugoslavia in an effort to maintain a fragile truce between the warring factions.

ARTHUR CAMPBELL TURNER
University of California, Riverside

BALL

All over the world, people play ball and have done so since prehistoric times. Some early people wove reeds into rounded shapes. Others used leather stuffed with feathers for ball playing. Later, Greeks and Romans used an air-filled leather ball called a *follis* in games of catch. They also inflated balls of larger sizes, with which they played a kind of football and other kicking games.

Balls have been made from many materials, depending upon what was available in the country. Native Americans used balls made of deer hide, while across the world from them, Japanese children played with balls of tightly wadded tissue paper wrapped with string. It is said that Columbus found the Indians of Central America playing with solid, black balls made of vegetable gum and took some of these bouncy rubber balls back to Europe with him.

We learn from the history of people and their folklore that many of our modern ball games started as religious and magical ceremonies. The Egyptians seem to have been among the first people to have ceremonial ball games. Each spring two large groups of people, each representing one of their gods, acted out a contest that used a round, wooden ball and crooked sticks. The object was to drive the ball through the opposing goal. The side that knocked the ball past the defenders won.

Today a ball and crooked stick are used in playing such games as polo, field hockey, and lacrosse. Each team tries to score while keeping the other side from scoring goals.

At first, ball games were played mainly to develop skill in tossing and catching. Over time, many different sticks, bats, and rackets were added to strike or otherwise control the motion of the ball, and many special games were invented. Today there are over thirty major sports in which a ball is the key object used in the game. These balls range from the oval football to the tiny table-tennis ball.

The ball has played a part in many other customs unrelated to sports. The phrase "to blackball," meaning to reject for membership in a club or organization, goes back to the Greeks' use of white and black pebbles in voting. They used an urn or vase to represent the candidate. The voter tossed a white pebble into the urn if he was in favor of the candidate, a black one if he was voting against him. The ballot, used in voting, is named after the Italian *ballotta*, meaning "little ball."

The ball belongs to everyone, so it is difficult to find out who invented it or from what country it first started to roll to the four corners of the world.

JACQUE HETRICK
Spalding

BALLADS

The ballad is a type of folk song that tells a story using simple words and a simple melody. The words are often in the form of a dialogue between two people.

The ballad developed in Europe during the Middle Ages. The name comes from the Latin word *ballare* ("to dance"). Originally ballads were dancing songs, but by the 1200's they had become solo songs. Today they may or may not be danced or performed with an instrumental accompaniment, but they always emphasize the story and are sung in a way that stresses the words over the melody. Ballad melodies are, nevertheless, beautiful and varied. They range from those based on Gregorian chants in Western Europe to Slavic types in Eastern Europe.

Scholars once believed that the ballad dated back to primitive times and was composed by groups of people. Since then, experts have decided that it has far more recent and sophisticated beginnings. Ballads were composed by individuals with some artistic background and training. As the songs were passed from singer to singer and from generation to generation, they were varied, shaped, and recreated to reflect the concerns, beliefs, and tastes of the time.

The ballads sung in America can be divided into three groups: traditional British ballads, later products of British city presses, and native American narrative songs.

Traditional ballads were first created in Great Britain six or seven centuries ago. Passed on by word of mouth, they usually rhyme and are divided into stanzas. The best ones are strikingly beautiful and moving. The traditional ballads are sometimes called Child ballads, named after Professor Francis James Child, who collected 305 of them in his classic five-volume book, *The English and Scottish Popular Ballads* (1882–98). "Lord Randal," "Sir Patrick Spens," "Barbara Allen," and "The Twa Corbies" are some well-known Child ballads.

Ballads from the British presses of the 1600's to the 1800's are known as broadside ballads. Many were printed on large sheets of paper called broadsides and were sold for a penny. Others were printed in small books called chapbooks. These songs usually recounted tales of mistaken identity, disguised lovers, or cruel crimes. Often the broadsides were based on traditional ballads. They were performed and sold by professional singers on city streets and at country fairs.

Using these British songs as models, Americans composed ballads about outlaws like Jesse James and Billy the Kid, folk heroes like John Henry, and tragic young women like Young Charlotte and Naomi Wise. Sometimes these songs are American versions of British stories.

Of course, English-speaking countries are not the only ones with highly developed ballad traditions. Scandinavia has a large stock of ballads, many of which are variants of well-known British and American songs. In Yugoslavia the ballad is an important form of literature, preserving many national themes and patriotic legends. The ballads of Bulgaria and the Ukraine are also outstanding.

French and Italian ballads often stress emotion and melody instead of story. Ballads are less common in Germany and the Low Countries; Germany, however, has many ballad-like pieces based on political and religious themes.

Spain's ballads, called *romances*, are frequently semihistorical, focusing more on personality then on factual details. Many of them consist of groups of songs on a single theme.

Russian *byliny* are narrative songs, like British ballads. They usually deal with the exploits of fabulous heroes. *Byliny* do not rhyme and are not divided into stanzas.

Traditional ballads continue to survive from ages past. The old songs are reshaped and new songs are created from the older models. These songs spread to more distant areas, where they continue to undergo change. Thus the ballads that people sing are a good indication of their present concerns, beliefs, and musical tastes.

TRISTRAM P. COFFIN
American Folklore Society
Revised by MELVIN BERGER
Author, *The Story of Folk Music*

See also FOLK MUSIC.

Rudolf Nureyev and Margot Fonteyn in *Romeo and Juliet*, based on the play by Shakespeare.

BALLET

A ballet is theatrical entertainment combining dance with other art forms, usually stage design and music. It may tell a story or merely depict an idea or mood. Ballet is a French word that comes from the Italian *ballo,* "a dance."

The exercises, or techniques, of ballet are designed to display the human body in the most elegant and harmonious way possible. Ballet technique is strict, and the training is strenuous. But the result on stage is natural and beautiful.

Ballet is nearly 500 years old. Yet it is very young compared with dance itself, which began with primitive people. Ballet began in Italy about the time of Columbus' voyages to America. It was quite different then from what it is today. At that time ballet was a court entertainment for the amusement of the nobility at lavish balls and banquets. Dancing, music, pantomime (acting without words), poetry, and drama were combined. The first ballet dancers were the royalty and nobles of the court, since there were no professional dancers. The steps were modeled on the elegant but rather simple social dances of the day.

Ballet as we know it is the product of many countries. The French organized the technique and gave it liveliness. The Russians added strength and passion. The English gave it delicacy and tenderness. The Americans gave it speed and variety.

▶ BALLET IN FRANCE

Queen Catherine de Médicis of France was familiar with the elaborate dance productions of Italy, her native land. In 1581, she ordered a grand entertainment—a ballet—to celebrate a royal wedding. The result was most spectacular. Thousands of people witnessed its lavish blending of dance, dramatic scenes, music, and complex scenery. Hundreds of dancers, singers, and actors took part, portraying the goddess Circe and all of her friends and enemies. Huge machines and stage effects were moved about the room so that the audience, seated on three sides, could see them.

All this was the work of an Italian musician best known by his French name, Balthasar de Beaujoyeulx. He was probably the first choreographer, or maker of dances, as we know the word today. He called his work *Le Ballet Comique de la Reine* ("The Queen's Comic Ballet"). Ever since then, performances of this kind have been called ballets.

Catherine's grandson, Louis XIV, loved to dance. He received lessons daily. At the age of 13, he danced in the *Ballet de Cassandre.*

1st position   2nd position   3rd position

The ballets in King Louis' time were formal and quite solemn. Usually they dealt with mythology or history. For a while only members of the court danced in them, but the King soon tired of their lack of skill. He had already brought together professional writers like Molière, Philippe Quinault, and Isaac de Benserade; the composer Jean-Baptiste Lully; and the choreographer Pierre Beauchamp. To improve the dancing, King Louis organized the Royal Academy of Dance in 1661. This academy was the beginning of the Paris Opera Ballet and today's Paris Opera Ballet School.

By 1681, France had its first prima ballerina, the leading female dancer in a ballet company. She was Mademoiselle Lafontaine. Pictures of the time show her to be lovely and very dignified in her long, stiff gown, her high-heeled slippers, and her plumed headdress. She danced that year in *Le Triomphe de l'Amour* (''The Triumph of Love''), with choreography by Beauchamp and music by Lully. Mademoiselle Lafontaine was the first of a series of professional ballet dancers. Each of these experts brought something new to the art of ballet.

In a children's ballet class, a teacher helps a young student position his body correctly. The long wooden railing, called a barre, helps dancers keep their balance while practicing.

4th position   5th position

Several names stand out in the history of ballet in the 1700's. Marie Camargo boldly shortened the ballet costume to mid-calf. She also removed the heels from her slippers. Thus she could move more quickly and perform small, intricate steps like the *entrechat-quatre,* a double crossing of the feet in midair. Gaetan Vestris was the first male dancer to show in his *jetés* (leaps) and *tours en l'air* (turns in the air) that men could develop a ballet style very different from that of women. Danish and Russian dancers later stressed this difference even more.

But no matter how versatile they are, dancers depend on the imagination of choreographers. The great choreographer Jean Georges Noverre looked at the productions around him and saw that ballet was deteriorating into a mere display of technique. He believed that ballet should express strong emotions. After his reforms, ballet became more like drama. Noverre's ballets are not danced today. But his book, *Letters on Dancing and Ballets,* is still widely read by choreographers.

Marie Taglioni (1804—84)

All of us have at some time wished to fly. The female dancers of the early 1800's felt that way, too. As imaginary creatures like ondines (water sprites) or sylphides (tree sprites), they were actually attached to wires so that they could soar above the stage. More often they gave the illusion of lightness by rising to the very tips of their toes. Pictures of Marie Taglioni, one of the foremost dancers of the time, show her this way.

In 1832, Taglioni's father, Filippo Taglioni, created a ballet especially for her. Called *La Sylphide,* it was about a mysterious forest creature so playful and so touching that she lured a young Scot, James, away from his fiancée on his wedding day. Poets and composers of this period, known as the romantic age, loved sadness. In *La Sylphide,* as in most romantic ballets, the end was tragic. The sylphide died, leaving James alone in the forest to mourn her.

Carlotta Grisi (1819—99)

While Taglioni was touring in Russia, an Italian dancer, Carlotta Grisi, arrived at the Paris Opera. Jules Perrot, a celebrated dancer, fell in love with her, as did the poet Théophile Gautier. Gautier wrote a ballet story for her. It was *Giselle* (1841), the tragedy of a gentle peasant girl who loved to dance. Jean Coralli was the choreographer, but *Giselle's* variations (special solos) were made by Perrot.

A scene from *La Sylphide,* a romantic 19th-century ballet, is performed by members of the American Ballet Theatre.

A scene from *The Nutcracker,* **which is often danced during the Christmas season.**

Giselle is even more tragic than *La Sylphide* because Giselle is a real girl and not a sprite. She is wooed by the handsome Albrecht. She falls deeply in love with him, not knowing that he is a count in disguise and can never marry her. To make matters worse, he is already engaged to the Countess Bathilde. When Giselle learns of the betrayal, she goes insane and dies. Later, she rises from her tomb to dance with the remorseful Albrecht and to protect him from being destroyed by the Wilis, spirits of young girls who died before marriage.

▶ **RUSSIAN BALLET**

If you were to ask a friend to name two favorite ballets, the answers might be *Swan Lake* and *The Sleeping Beauty* or *Scheherazade* and *Petrouchka*. These—and many more—came from Marius Petipa and Michel Fokine, two Russian choreographers whose ballets are now performed all over the world.

Marius Petipa (1819–1910)

Petipa, born in France, won fame as a choreographer in St. Petersburg. In 1862 he devised a three-act spectacle called *The Pha-*

raoh's Daughter. Like his later ballets, it took all evening to perform and had a complicated plot. This gave plenty of opportunity for a stilted kind of mime that described what was going on but told the audience very little about the person doing the mime. There were also interludes of beautiful pure dance, usually solos, called variations. They had little or nothing to do with the story. But they were beautifully made and were perfectly suited to the music.

For his most celebrated ballets, Petipa was fortunate to have the composer Peter Ilyich Tchaikovsky. His music was so inspired and so perfectly made that it could stand on its own when played separately from the ballets. The grandest collaborations of Petipa and Tchaikovsky were *The Sleeping Beauty* (1890) and *Swan Lake* (1895). In *Swan Lake,* Petipa shared the choreography with his assistant, Lev Ivanov. This ballet returned to a theme very popular during the romantic period—that of a young prince falling in love with a bewitched creature. And like the romantic ballets, *Swan Lake* ends in death. Two of its variations, the *White Swan Pas de Deux* and the *Black Swan Pas de Deux,* are very often danced separately from the ballet. (A pas de deux is a dance for two people.)

Petipa planned the action of *The Nutcracker* (1892) and gave complete musical instructions to Tchaikovsky. But the choreographer fell ill, and Ivanov actually staged the ballet. It has become a favorite for the Christmas season, and children often have starring roles.

When Petipa planned a new ballet, he did not care whether the costumes and sets were suited to the period and place of the story. They were done according to a formula. This bothered Michel Fokine, who was a student at the Imperial School of Ballet when Petipa was director of its company.

Michel Fokine (1880–1942)

Many of the students at the Imperial School of Ballet were satisfied merely to learn technique and dance in Petipa's ballets. But Fokine had a lively, curious mind. He studied history and painting and spent hours in museums.

One day Fokine wrote a letter to the director of the school and said that he would like to make a new kind of ballet. The mime and the variations would not be separate. They would be part of the action. The style of movement and the style of the costumes and sets would be suited to the period of the ballet. And the stories of the ballets would be simple and believable.

Fokine was not allowed to go ahead, so he began to work on his own. His smallest dance, a five-minute solo called *The Dying Swan* (1905), became his best known. It was made for his classmate Anna Pavlova to dance at a charity ball. To this day it is associated with her.

Then, to show that he knew his craft and that he knew the styles of different periods, Fokine created a ballet in the romantic style, *Les Sylphides.* He borrowed the atmosphere but not the story of *La Sylphide.* The music was a series of piano pieces by Frédéric Chopin. The delicacy of this ballet and the ease with which the movement flows along with the music have made it Fokine's best-known and most performed ballet.

Fokine was staging ballets outside of the Imperial Ballet in Russia. But his first important opportunities came when Sergei Diaghilev formed his Ballets Russes in Paris.

Sergei Diaghilev (1872–1929)

In St. Petersburg, the home of the Imperial Ballet, a group of young authors, painters, and composers often met in the evenings to talk about their work. They started a magazine called *The World of Art,* with Sergei Diaghilev as its editor.

Diaghilev could not write or paint or compose. But he had exquisite taste, and he knew how to bring the right people together to make interesting things happen. He arranged an exhibit of Russian painting in Paris in 1906, and he produced the opera *Boris Godunov* in Paris in 1908. In 1909 he put together his own ballet company. He turned to Fokine as his chief choreographer, and he gave Fokine four of the world's greatest dancers as the principals for his ballets. They were Anna Pavlova, Tamara Karsavina, Vaslav Nijinsky, and Adolph Bolm.

Given this freedom, Fokine's imagination began to soar. In quick succession he turned out the wild *Polovtsian Dances* from the opera *Prince Igor;* the playful *Carnaval;* the lush *Scheherazade,* with its brilliant leaping dance for Nijinsky as the Golden Slave; the myste-

Anna Pavlova in a 1910 production of *The Dying Swan,* the role she made famous.

Marina Kondratieva and Maris Lieta in the Bolshoi Ballet's production of *Spring Water.*

rious Russian fairy tale *Firebird;* and *Petrouchka,* a touching story of puppets brought to life. The last two ballets introduced a new ballet composer, Igor Stravinsky.

Diaghilev was restless. One choreographer was not enough for him. He was constantly searching for new talents in the different arts, and he combined them imaginatively. For example, the choreographer Léonide Massine worked with the painter Pablo Picasso and the composer Manuel de Falla for *The Three-Cornered Hat.* The choreographer George Balanchine worked with the painter Georges Rouault and the composer Sergei Prokofiev for *The Prodigal Son.* Nijinsky, as choreographer, came together with the painter Nicholas Roerich and the composer Igor Stravinsky for *The Rite of Spring.*

Other ballets that were made famous by the Ballets Russes include Massine's *La Boutique Fantastique* and Balanchine's *Rossignol,* in which 12-year-old Alicia Markova danced the nightingale.

Diaghilev's company was disbanded after his death, but the ballets he produced are still presented. Russian dancers have continued to play an important part in ballet. Some, such as Vladimir Vasiliev, Yekaterina Maximova, Galina Ulanova, and Maya Plisetskaya, danced with the Bolshoi Ballet, Russia's leading company. Others, such as Rudolf Nureyev, Natalia Makarova, Aleksandr Godunov, and Mikhail Baryshnikov, left to live and work in other countries.

▶ BALLET IN ENGLAND

When the Diaghilev company was disbanded, several of its dancers settled in London, where the company had often toured. Two of them, the Irish-born Dame Ninette de Valois and the Polish-born Dame Marie Rambert, became the pillars of British ballet.

Like Diaghilev, Marie Rambert liked to take chances on young and unknown artists. Thus she gave a first start to two of England's finest 20th-century choreographers, Sir Frederick

Ashton and Antony Tudor. Their first ballets appeared in Rambert's tiny Mercury Theatre.

Ninette de Valois was an organizer. She wanted a national ballet company and would settle for nothing less. In 1933 she became head of the Vic-Wells Ballet. Alicia Markova was its ballerina. The company grew in size and support to become the Sadler's Wells Ballet. For this company, De Valois gambled on an unknown 16-year-old dancer, who made her debut as the Swan Queen in *Swan Lake*. She was Margot Fonteyn, who later became one of the world's best-loved dancers. Finally, in 1957, De Valois saw her dream come true. As Dame Ninette, she was artistic director of Britain's Royal Ballet.

In the meantime, she had engaged Frederick Ashton as choreographer for the company. His ballets—whether witty, as in *A Wedding Bouquet*, or serious, as in *Ondine*—showed a refined, poetic style and respect for the classical tradition. They provided Fonteyn with some of her finest roles. Ashton's style is shown at its best in two works produced after his retirement as the company's artistic director in 1970. They were *Enigma Variations*, created to music by Edward Elgar, and *A Month in the Country*. In these ballets, every detail of movement was not only precisely made but seemed perfectly suited to the person performing it.

▶ **DANISH BALLET**

In the 1950's, the Royal Danish Ballet began to travel outside Denmark. It had a tremendous impact. The Danes gave special attention to the acting parts of ballets. In the hands of artists such as Niels Bjorn Larssen and Gerda Karstens, standard roles came alive in a new way.

The Danes had an interesting tradition from the 1800's. It came from the teaching and choreography of August Bournonville, which the Danes had lovingly preserved. The Bournonville style stressed the differences between men and women dancers. It featured strong movements and brilliant leaps for the men and intricate *terre-à-terre* (close to the ground) steps for the women. Because he traveled much during his career, Bournonville created ballets in a variety of styles. Many are performed today, among them *Napoli, Far from Denmark, Flower Festival at Genzano,* and *La Ventana.*

La Fille Mal Gardée (The Unchaperoned Girl) is a comic ballet with a happy ending.

George Balanchine's ballet *Jewels* is in three parts: *Emeralds*, *Rubies*, and *Diamonds*.

Some present-day Danish dancers combine the Bournonville style with the stronger Russian style. They have made their mark on companies in other parts of the world where they have gone to live and work. Among them are Toni Lander, Erik Bruhn, Peter Martins, Helgi Tomasson, and Peter Schaufuss.

▶ BALLET IN CANADA

The Royal Winnipeg Ballet is Canada's oldest company. It began as the Winnipeg Ballet Club in 1938 and became a fully professional company in 1949. Today it is famous for performing the works of 20th century choreographers such as Gweneth Lloyd, Arnold Spohr, Brian MacDonald, and Michel Conte.

The National Ballet of Canada, based in Toronto, was established in 1951. The company is noted for its performances of original works by Grant Strate and David Adams. Les Grands Ballets Canadiens began in Montreal in 1952 as a television troupe. The company performs classics and original works.

▶ BALLET IN THE UNITED STATES

In the 1800's, the United States produced such fine ballet dancers as George Washington

Smith, Mary Ann Lee, and Augusta Maywood. But it was not until the 1900's that ballet began to find a wide and enthusiastic public. It all began with the tours of Anna Pavlova between 1910 and 1930. Pavlova was tireless. She went to every community that would have her. She did not encourage daring choreography. The members of her company were often modestly trained young dancers acquired along the way. But to many people of the United States, Pavlova was ballet.

Two years after Pavlova's death in 1931, the Ballet Russe de Monte Carlo arrived in the United States. Some of its dancers were from Diaghilev's company. Others were new. Audiences fell in love with stars such as Alexandra Danilova, Natalie Krassovska, Mia Slavenska, Irina Baronova, Tatiana Riabouchinska, Tamara Toumanova, and Igor Youskevitch.

At first the Ballet Russe depended on Russian choreographers such as Léonide Massine, David Lichine, and Michel Fokine. Gradually it turned to Americans such as Agnes de Mille, whose *Rodeo* (1942) gave an image of cowboys and ranchers that audiences still enjoy when it is performed today.

Dancers and choreographers of the United States soon began to found their own companies. Lincoln Kirstein, a wealthy young Harvard graduate with a strong writing talent, lured former Diaghilev choreographer George Balanchine to New York. The promises were a company of his own with a school behind it to train the dancers. It took time. Their modest company first performed in 1933. The company grew and in 1948 became the New York City Ballet.

The repertory of the New York City Ballet is extremely varied. Yet it is dominated by Balanchine and by the United States choreographer Jerome Robbins, who has blended jazz and modern dance with more traditional elements in ballets such as *Fancy Free*. Outstanding artists such as Maria Tallchief, Melissa Hayden, Suzanne Farrell, Jacques D'Amboise, Edward Villella, and Mikhail Baryshnikov have danced with the company.

In 1940 another major company, Ballet Theatre (later called the American Ballet Theatre), was created. It has developed the careers of many choreographers, among them Agnes de Mille, Jerome Robbins, and Eliot Feld. While developing new talents, it has kept the classics alive. Antony Tudor, the British choreographer who began his career with Marie

Two great stars of ballet, Mikhail Baryshnikov and Natalia Makarova, in *The Sleeping Beauty*.

Rambert in London, was associated with the company from its earliest days.

In the United States, the American Ballet Theatre and the New York City Ballet are the equivalent of the great national companies of Europe and the former Soviet Union. But smaller companies contribute to dance in the United States. Among them are the Dance Theater of Harlem, a classically oriented company of black dancers, and the Joffrey Ballet. The Joffrey Ballet has presented the works of its resident choreographer, Gerald Arpino. It has also staged 20th-century classics such as Kurt Jooss's *Green Table* and modern works such as José Limón's *The Moor's Pavane*.

While these companies have made New York City a world center of dance, the entire country has come alive with companies such as the Boston Ballet, the Pennsylvania Ballet, the Houston Ballet, and the Minnesota Dance Theatre. These and many more hold the key to the future of ballet in the United States.

DORIS HERING
Critic-at-large, *Dance Magazine*

See also DANCE.

BALLOONS, RESEARCH. See BALLOONS AND BALLOONING.

Karen Brown and Keith Saunders of the Dance Theater of Harlem, in *Allegro Brillante* by George Balanchine.

BALLOONS AND BALLOONING

Have you ever wondered what it would be like to float on the wind, drifting silently above your town? You could find out—if you were a balloonist. Every flight would be an adventure because in ballooning, you must travel where the wind takes you.

Balloons are aerostats, or lighter-than-air craft. A modern balloon is a bag made of a light material such as nylon or plastic. Air is blown into the bag and is then heated by a burner. Or the bag may be filled with a gas such as helium or hydrogen. The gas or hot air causes the balloon to rise. The pilot and passengers ride in a basket or gondola suspended underneath the balloon.

Not all balloons carry passengers. Scientists launch balloons carrying instruments to study the upper atmosphere and to gather information about the weather. And balloon satellites orbit the earth. Today balloons have two main uses—as tools in research and as a means of recreation in the sport of ballooning.

▶ HISTORY

Early in the 18th century Bartholomeu de Gusmão, a Portuguese priest, developed a small hot-air balloon. But the first big balloon was built by two French brothers, Joseph Michel and Jacques Étienne Montgolfier, in 1783. They made a huge bag of paper and cloth, which they held over a fire. When they released the smoke-filled balloon, it soared into the sky.

Encouraged by their success, the Montgolfier brothers built a balloon with a basket underneath to carry passengers. In the basket they put a rooster, a duck, and a young sheep. The balloon was filled with hot air from a fire and was released. The basket, with its animal passengers, floated upward. High above the earth the warm air inside the balloon cooled off, and the balloon slowly floated to earth. Live passengers had been carried into the air and returned safely for the first time in history.

This feat inspired two men to become the first human beings to fly above the earth. They were Jean François Pilâtre de Rozier, a French physician, and François Laurent, the Marquis d'Arlandes. A huge blue and gold hot-air balloon carried them aloft over Paris on November 21, 1783.

Colorful balloons rise into the air at the beginning of a race in Iowa. Ballooning is best in open country, far from tall buildings, traffic, and high-tension wires.

Fire was always a danger at these early balloon launchings. One spark could send a balloon up in flames. But in the same year that the hot-air balloon was developed, Jacques A. C. Charles, a French scientist, invented the gas balloon. Charles built a sphere of rubberized silk and filled it with hydrogen, a gas that is lighter than air without being heated. The balloon soared into the air and landed in a field near Paris, where it was destroyed by frightened farm workers.

With the help of others, Charles later developed a balloon that could carry passengers. To rise higher, the balloonist released sand from bags tied to the side of the basket. To come down, the balloonist pulled a rope that opened a valve located at the top of the balloon. The open valve allowed hydrogen to escape, so that the balloon would slowly deflate and return to earth.

The Age of Ballooning

The popularity of the safer gas balloons soon surpassed that of the hot-air type, and a ballooning craze swept Europe. Balloonists of this period were daring souls whose exploits were memorable.

In 1785, Jean Pierre Blanchard, a French balloonist, and John Jeffries, an American, crossed the English Channel in a gas balloon. Blanchard later made the first free flight in the United States, in Philadelphia, on January 9, 1793. President George Washington was among those who watched his ascension. On this occasion, Blanchard carried the first airmail letter and made scientific observations of the effects of altitude on the human body. For example, he discovered that his heart beat more rapidly at high altitudes. And he brought bottles filled with air back to earth. When the air was studied, it was found to contain less oxygen than air near the ground.

Blanchard's wife, Madeline-Sophie, was famous for spectacular ascensions at night. In 1819 she was killed when fireworks she had carried aloft ignited her balloon.

Ballooning was furthered by several inventions. In 1797 a French balloonist, André Garnerin, astonished spectators by leaping from a balloon and floating safely to the earth. In secret, he had invented the first practical parachute. In 1839, John Wise, an American, invented the rip line. By pulling this line, a

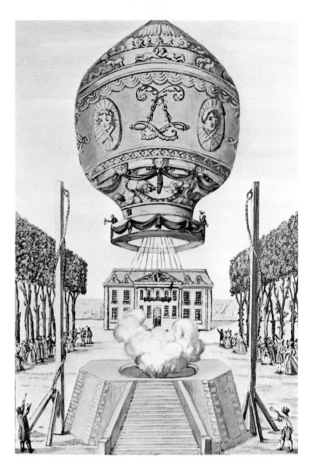

Above: The balloon that carried two French balloonists on the first piloted flight in 1783. Below: Preparing for the first successful piloted balloon flight in the United States—in Philadelphia, 1793.

balloonist near the ground could open a large panel in the balloon and deflate it quickly in an emergency.

The jet streams—long currents of air moving at high altitudes—had not been discovered in Wise's time. But he was convinced that a balloon could cross the Atlantic Ocean by traveling on rivers of wind.

Balloons in War

Balloons became important in military operations during the U.S. Civil War (1861–65) and the Franco-Prussian War (1870–71). Balloonists were sent up in tethered balloons—balloons anchored to the ground by long lines—to observe the enemy troops and even to report descriptions of battles from an aerial position. From their high positions, they could direct cannon fire more accurately. Balloons were also used to carry messages.

During World War I, balloons were again used for observation. In both world wars, barrage balloons were anchored by long cables along Britain's coast to block enemy aircraft. During World War II, Japan sent balloons carrying bombs across the Pacific Ocean toward the northwestern coast of North America. But few of the balloons completed the trip, and most of those that did landed in remote areas.

Reaching for Height and Distance

Balloonists have ventured to the limits of their endurance to learn about the upper atmosphere and to discover how high and how far balloons can travel.

In 1862, James Glaisher, an English scientist, and Henry Coxwell, his balloon pilot, rose to a height of more than 9,000 meters (30,000 feet) without oxygen. But early high-altitude research could be dangerous. At high altitudes, the air contains so little oxygen that a person can suffocate. In 1875, three French balloonists floated up in a balloon called the *Zenith,* carrying bottles of oxygen with them. But they lost consciousness at about 7,500 meters (25,000 feet), before they could use their equipment. When the *Zenith* returned to the earth, only one was alive.

In 1927, an American military balloonist, Captain Hawthorne Gray, also died during a high-altitude ascension. He lost consciousness at about 13,400 meters (44,000 feet),

although he was wearing an oxygen mask. Notes made by Gray gave valuable information about the atmosphere at high altitudes.

Auguste Piccard, a Swiss scientist and inventor, developed a way to explore the upper atmosphere safely in a balloon. He invented an airtight aluminum gondola that was round, like a ball. Inside it he put oxygen and pressure tanks. In 1931 he ascended to more than 15,500 meters (51,000 feet) and became the first person to look without a telescope into the black depths of outer space. Piccard made many other ascents into the upper atmosphere, as did his brother, Jean Piccard. They brought back information about cosmic rays and high-altitude electricity. Since then, balloons have risen higher and higher. In 1961, Malcolm Ross and Victor A. Prather, Jr., of the U.S. Navy, reached a height of over 34,500 meters (113,500 feet).

Balloonists have attempted to set records in distance as well. But the dream of crossing the Atlantic was not realized until 1978. Three U.S. balloonists—Ben Abruzzo, Maxie Anderson, and Larry Newman—made the crossing. Their helium balloon, *Double Eagle II,* traveled from Maine to France. In 1980, Anderson and his son Kris attempted a flight across North America. Their craft, *Kitty Hawk,* set an overland distance record, floating about 5,000 kilometers (3,100 miles) from California to Quebec. In 1981, four balloonists crossed the Pacific. Ben Abruzzo, Larry Newman, Ron Clark, and Rocky Aoki flew the *Double Eagle V* from Japan to California, a distance of about 9,500 kilometers (6,000 miles).

What makes a balloon rise?

A big balloon soars up into the sky because it is filled with a gas that is lighter than air.

Air itself is made up of gases, the chief ones being oxygen and nitrogen. Certain other gases are lighter than air. One of these is helium, and that is why a balloon filled with helium rises.

Hot air will also make a balloon rise because hot air is lighter than cold air. It is lighter because as air is heated, its gas particles spread out and become less dense.

You can demonstrate with this simple experiment that air expands as it is warmed. Snap the open end of a small balloon over the top of an empty soda bottle. The balloon hangs limp. Now set the bottle in a pan of hot water. The hot water heats the bottle and warms the cold air inside it. Gradually the warm air in the bottle pushes its way into the balloon. The balloon slowly fills with air and begins to inflate.

▶BALLOONS IN SCIENTIFIC RESEARCH

Balloons are of value in scientific research because they can go very high and stay up a relatively long time. Rockets can go higher, but they stay up only briefly and so cannot collect as much information as balloons can.

Three types of gas balloons are most commonly used in scientific research today—extensible balloons, zero-pressure balloons, and superpressure balloons. They are made of various kinds of plastic. Tethered hot-air balloons are sometimes used as observation platforms—to study the skies, for example, or to locate archeological sites.

Extensible balloons are small. As a balloon of this type rises, the gas inside it expands because the pressure of the surrounding air is less at high altitudes. When the balloon reaches a certain height, the pressure inside it causes it to burst. A parachute opens and carries the instruments back to the earth.

Zero-pressure balloons are among the largest balloons. They can carry heavy loads to high altitudes. They are only partly filled with gas when they are launched. But as they rise, the gas expands to fill the balloon. Excess gas escapes through a vent. Zero-pressure balloons usually stay aloft for several days.

Superpressure balloons can remain aloft for months. Like zero-pressure balloons, they are launched partly filled with gas. But then they are sealed, so that the expanding gas will not escape. The excess pressure that builds up as the balloon rises keeps it aloft at a constant altitude.

The instruments sent up in these balloons include devices that measure the temperature, pressure, humidity, and chemical composition of the air. The information they provide is used in studying the atmosphere and the weather. Communications equipment is also sent aloft in balloons.

Radiation—in the form of visible light, X rays, gamma rays, cosmic rays, or infrared or ultraviolet radiation—gives us information about space. But the earth's atmosphere blocks much of the radiation from space. From the edge of the atmosphere, instruments in a balloon can gather more information about the sun, the planets, and distant stars—their temperatures, speed and direction of motion, chemical composition, and so on—than can be gathered on the earth. The instruments in-

Research balloons help scientists gather information not easily obtained on earth. This balloon, shown during launching, carries an infrared telescope.

clude telescopes, spectroscopes, photometers, and cosmic ray counters.

During the 1950's, balloons paved the way for people to enter outer space. Balloons as tall as 50-story buildings rose to gather information about cosmic rays and other radiations from outer space. Monkeys were sent aloft in balloons as a test of what happens to the body at high altitudes. Guided missiles were carried aloft by balloons and then fired from the edge of space out into space. Since then, several balloon satellites have been launched into orbit by rocket. New equipment is often tested in balloons before being sent up in rockets or space probes.

In 1978, *Double Eagle II* carried three United States balloonists on the first flight across the Atlantic Ocean.

▶ THE SPORT OF BALLOONING

Ballooning has become popular as a sport that offers competition and the enjoyment of floating freely above the earth. Many rallies and events are held each year. In one of the best-known events, balloonists from all over the world travel over the Alps from Switzerland to Italy.

Competition takes various forms. There are long-distance races, in which the winner is the balloonist who travels farthest. There are cross-country and spot-landing contests, in which the pilot must take off and land within a specified time. In the cross-country event, the balloonist who travels farthest is the winner. In spot-landing contests, balloonists attempt to land at a designated point. In a hare-and-hounds chase, a single "hare" balloon flies off, followed minutes later by the other balloons, or "hounds." The hound balloon that lands closest to the hare is the winner.

Both gas and hot-air balloons are used in competition. Modern hot-air balloons that carry propane burners to heat the air have become increasingly popular since the early 1960's. Several hot-air balloons that rely on the heat of the sun have also been developed.

Sport balloons vary in size. The smallest are flown by a pilot dangling in a harness beneath the balloon. The average sport balloon can carry three people.

To inflate a typical hot-air balloon, the ground crew assembles the gondola, lays the balloon (a huge nylon bag) flat on the ground, and attaches the gondola to it. A fan is directed into the mouth of the balloon until the balloon is almost half filled with cold air. Then a propane burner is lighted, and the flame is directed into the mouth of the balloon to heat the cold air. As the air in the balloon is heated, the balloon begins to drift upward. The ground crew lets the balloon rise slowly until it has reached the necessary height. The gondola is held on the ground until the pilot has finished a preflight inspection and is ready for takeoff.

The propane burners are carried at the mouth of the balloon, above the gondola. They enable the pilot to regulate the air temperature. In this way the pilot can control the altitude of the balloon—but nothing else. Balloons travel where the wind takes them. The pilot can do nothing except change the altitude of the balloon to take advantage of air currents blowing in different directions.

In the United States, both the balloon and the pilot must be licensed by the Federal Aviation Agency. You may obtain a student balloon license when you are 14 years old. A student balloonist may fly alone but may not carry passengers. When you are 16 years old, you may become a private balloon pilot. To earn the license, you must have ten hours of instruction in balloons, including one ascent to 915 meters (3,000 feet) and a solo flight. You must also pass a flight test and an examination on weather conditions and on federal aviation rules.

BALLOON FEDERATION OF AMERICA

BALLOT. See ELECTIONS.

BALTIC SEA. See OCEANS AND SEAS OF THE WORLD.

BALTIMORE

Baltimore is the largest city in Maryland and one of the major ports of the United States. It lies on the banks of the Patapsco River near Chesapeake Bay, 40 miles (about 65 kilometers) northeast of Washington, D.C. Baltimore is a center of industry, culture, education, and transportation. To visitors, it has the flavor of both an old southern city and a modern industrial community.

Through the years, manufacturing industries grew along with shipping and other port activities. Today the chief industries turn out steel and other metal products, chemicals, electronic equipment, and processed foods. Nearly 740,000 people live in the city proper. Baltimore's greater metropolitan area contains more than half the population of the state.

Baltimore was chartered in 1729 and was named after the Lords Baltimore who founded the Maryland colony. The Continental Congress met in Baltimore during the Revolutionary War. The Cumberland Road brought prosperity to the city in the early 1800's. But when the Erie Canal opened in 1825, Baltimore was threatened with a loss of trade. The city met this threat by building the first railroad in the United States—the Baltimore and Ohio.

Many monuments and landmarks reflect the city's long and colorful history. The oldest U.S. warship still afloat, the wooden frigate *Constellation*, is anchored not far from where it was launched in 1797. During the War of 1812, Fort McHenry in the Baltimore harbor was heavily bombarded by the British fleet. This event inspired Francis Scott Key to write "The Star-Spangled Banner" (1814). Baltimore also contains such landmarks as the nation's first Roman Catholic cathedral and the home and burial place of writer Edgar Allan Poe.

Since the 1950's the city has been a leader in urban renewal. Rows of handsome red brick houses have been restored, and a civic center and modern office and apartment complexes have been built in the heart of the city. One of the most ambitious projects has been the redevelopment of the Inner Harbor. A popular attraction of the Inner Harbor is the National Aquarium in Baltimore where visitors can view many kinds of exotic plant and animal life.

Among the city's many universities is Johns Hopkins University, which has a world-famous school of medicine. Residents and visitors enjoy the city's symphony orchestra and opera company and the outstanding art collections at the Walters Art Gallery and the Baltimore Museum of Art. Sports fans cheer baseball's Orioles at Oriole Park and watch horses run in the Preakness each spring at Pimlico Racetrack.

GEORGE BEISHLAG
Towson State University

See also MARYLAND.

Shops, restaurants, and commercial buildings line Baltimore's Inner Harbor, where the warship *Constellation* is anchored. At the far right is the National Aquarium in Baltimore.

BALZAC, HONORÉ DE (1799–1850)

The French writer Honoré de Balzac is known around the world for the novels and shorter works of fiction that he collected under the general title *La Comédie humaine (The Human Comedy)*. His ambition in this great work was to describe all of French society.

Balzac was born on May 20, 1799, in Tours, where his father was a civil servant. At the age of 8, he was sent to boarding school. He was an undisciplined child, and he was often sent to detention, or "kept in." He looked on this punishment as a blessing in disguise because it gave him all the time he wanted for reading. When his family moved to Paris in 1814, he went to school there.

For a while Balzac studied law, but he had no taste for legal work. He wanted to write plays, but his first play, *Cromwell* (1819), was a failure. He turned to writing sensational novels under various pen names. Realizing that he would never make his fortune this way, he went into business as a publisher and later as a printer. But he earned only debts.

In 1829, Balzac started the novels that made him famous. Some were fantastic, like *The Wild Ass's Skin* (1831). This novel tells how a young man acquires a magic piece of leather that grants his every wish but shrinks a little every time he uses it. He knows he will die when the leather has shrunk to nothing. Others were realistic, like *Eugénie Grandet* (1833), the story of a miser who loves his gold more than his daughter.

Balzac lived extravagantly, and he was always in debt. His many women friends inspired the sensitive portraits of women in his novels. Just before his death, he married a Polish countess, Eveline Hanska.

Balzac worked as intensely as he lived. By writing as much as 16 hours a day, he published over 80 titles between 1829 and 1847. This great labor brought on a serious illness before he was able to complete *The Human Comedy*. But when he died in Paris on August 18, 1850, he left a vivid record of his time.

F. W. J. HEMMINGS
Author, *Balzac: An Interpretation of La Comédie humaine*

BAMBOO. See GRASSES.

BANANA

The banana is a tropical fruit. People used it as a food even before history began to be written. The armies of Alexander the Great found bananas growing in India in 327 B.C. No doubt they grew there long before that time. Because of an old story that the sages of India rested in the shade of the plant and ate its fruit, the banana is often called the "fruit of the wise men."

Plant scientists believe that roots of banana plants were carried to the east coast of Africa by a people who moved there in ancient times. From there the banana plant was carried across the African continent to the Guinea Coast by early Arab traders.

When Portuguese explorers discovered the Guinea Coast of Africa in 1482, they found bananas growing there. These explorers took roots of the plant, and its African name, banana, to the Portuguese colonies in the Canary Islands. The next step in the journey of the banana plant was across the Atlantic Ocean to the New World. In 1516, only a few years after Columbus' famous voyages of discovery, a Spanish missionary brought this useful plant to the Caribbean island of Hispaniola. Other missionaries followed his example and planted bananas on the other islands of the Caribbean and on the tropical mainland. Thus, the banana plant had to go more than halfway around the world to reach Central America, where so many of the world's bananas are grown today.

It was not until the latter part of the 19th century that bananas were brought into the United States in quantities for sale in stores. Before that time, very few Americans other than those who had traveled in tropical countries had ever seen or tasted a banana. Even after banana schooners began entering New Orleans, Boston, and other ports, only people who lived in or near the port cities were able to eat bananas. The banana is perishable. Unlike some other fruits, it cannot be stored. Within a period of ten to twenty days, bananas must be harvested, shipped several thousand kilometers, ripened, and sent to the stores where they are sold. Today's modern transportation —fast, refrigerated ships, trains, and trucks— makes it possible for families in Chicago, in the United States, or Calgary, in Canada, to eat bananas every day of the year.

▶THE BANANA PLANT AND ITS GROWTH

The banana plant is often called a tree. But it is not a real tree because there is no wood in the stem that rises above the ground. The stem is made up of leaves growing very close together, one inside the other. The leaves that spread out at the top of the stem usually are from 2.5 to 3.5 meters (8 to 12 feet) long and more than 0.5 meters (about 2 feet) wide. These leaves spread out and rise in the air, making the banana plant look like a palm tree. When the plant is old enough to bear fruit, it is from 4.5 to 9 meters (15 to 30 feet) tall.

Bananas grow in bunches. Each bunch consists of 9 to 16 clusters of fruit, called "hands," and each hand contains from 12 to 20 separate bananas, called "fingers." A bunch of bananas usually weighs from 25 to 45 kilograms (55 to 100 pounds).

The size of the plant and the size of the bunch of fruit depend on the climate and the kind of soil in which the plant grows. Bananas grow best where the soil is deep and rich and the climate is warm and moist. They cannot be grown satisfactorily in any place where temperatures fall below 13°C (55°F). For good fruit, the temperature should not go below 21°C (70°F) for any length of time.

Bananas grow in all the moist, tropical areas of the world. Most of the bananas sold in North America and Europe are grown in Central America, northern South America, tropical Africa, and the Caribbean islands. Bananas are grown in Taiwan and the Philippines for sale in Japan. In other tropical areas, bananas are grown mainly for local use.

To grow new banana plants, pieces of rootstock (bits cut from the base of growing plants) are planted in holes about 3 meters (10 feet) apart. Each piece of rootstock must have one or more sprouts, or "eyes," like the eyes of a potato. Green shoots appear above the ground three or four weeks later. Only the strongest shoot is allowed to become a plant. This plant forms its own rootstock, from which other plants continue to grow. Careful pruning

Bananas grow well in tropical Costa Rica. This bunch will be cut while still green and sent to far-off markets.

ensures that one strong, fruit-producing plant follows another.

Banana plants need care and attention to produce fruit of good quality. They must be provided with water by irrigation if the normal rainfall does not supply at least 250 centimeters (100 inches) per year. The leaves must be sprayed to prevent damage by insects and diseases. The area around the plants must be kept free of weeds and grass. The plants must be fertilized with nitrogen and potash. On a large plantation, many workers are required to care for the plants and harvest the fruit.

About eight to ten months after planting, a flower appears on the banana plant. This flower is at the end of a long stalk, which grows from the base up through the center of the stem and turns downward when it emerges from the top. Small bananas form on this flower stalk as it grows downward. Bananas really grow upside down. As the small bananas form on the stalk, they point downward, but as they grow they turn and point upward. In three months they are plump and ready to harvest. Bananas are harvested while they are still green. Even when they are to be eaten where they are grown, they are not allowed to ripen on the plant. A banana that turns yellow on the plant loses its flavor. Also, the peel bursts open and insects get into the fruit. The finest flavor develops only when the fruit is cut while green and ripened afterward. The bananas sold in stores in the United States, Canada, and Europe are shipped there under refrigeration while still green. They are then ripened in special rooms where cool tempera-tures of 16 to 21°C (60 to 70°F) and moist air combine to allow the best-tasting fruit to be developed.

Each banana plant bears only one bunch of fruit. When the bunch is harvested, the plant is cut down. But as the plant has been growing to maturity and producing fruit, another plant has been growing beside it from the same rootstock. Soon this plant's fruit will be ready to harvest. This cycle of production will continue for years, if the plants are not destroyed by diseases, high winds, or floods.

NORWOOD C. THORNTON
Formerly, United Fruit Company

BANDS AND BAND MUSIC

Everyone loves a band. No football game, parade, circus, or Fourth of July celebration would be quite complete without a rousing march. Not only does everyone love to hear a band, but almost everyone loves to play in one. In the United States alone there are millions of people who play in bands now or who have played in school, college, or town bands.

The word **band** is a broad term that describes a group of musicians performing on wind and percussion instruments. One thinks immediately of a brightly uniformed marching band, perhaps part of an army or navy unit or the band of a college or high school.

Aside from marching bands and bands that entertain at fairs, public ceremonies, and informal social gatherings, there are other bands that exist only to perform music in a concert, just as an orchestra does. Such bands are known as concert or symphonic bands, or wind ensembles. What all bands have in common is that they are composed of wind and percussion instruments in various combinations. Bands usually have at least 50 players.

Since bands often perform out-of-doors, they require instruments whose sounds carry easily. Trumpets, trombones, tubas, horns, drums—all are instruments capable of making plenty of noise with little effort on the part of the player. The large family of woodwinds, including clarinets, oboes, bassoons, and flutes (and their relatives, bass clarinets, English horns, saxophones, and piccolos), also has this advantage.

A second requirement is that the instruments be easy to carry. It is impossible to march while playing a cello or a double bass; even the violin is not easy to play while one is walking. But one can easily play brass and woodwind instruments while marching. And of course the band has always required instruments that create the proper military excitement. For this the brass and percussion instruments are perfect.

There is a special type of band called a brass band. As its name implies, it uses only brass instruments and no woodwinds. Many excellent Salvation Army bands are of this type. They usually have 24 players and produce a good, well-blended sound despite their limits of tone quality and range.

A fife and drum band from Newport, Rhode Island.

EARLY HISTORY

Bands of some sort have existed almost from biblical times. Armies have always marched to the beat of drums, and soldiers have always taken their signals from the sounds of a trumpet or bugle of some sort. Little groups of wind-instrument players have sounded the hours of the day. (In 16th-century Germany the players assembled on the tower of the town's tallest building for this.) Bands have added to the beauty and impressiveness of church services and accompanied all kinds of outdoor public ceremonies.

Until the middle of the 18th century, however, there were practically no regularly organized bands. The combination of instruments used for any occasion was determined by whatever instruments were available in the town and whatever players were free at the moment and could be assembled for the occasion. New instruments were being invented (the clarinet, for instance, appeared around 1700) and old ones improved. Great excitement was created in Europe when, around 1750, a whole family of new percussion instruments was introduced by traveling bands from Turkey. Composers were soon busy writing "Turkish music," with parts for tambourines, cymbals, triangles, bass drums, and other clanging and beating instruments.

In 1763 King Frederick the Great of Prussia was the first to regulate the kinds and number of instruments used in his bands. He ordered that all of his military bands have at least two oboes, two clarinets, two horns, and two bassoons. To this basic group other instruments, including flute, trumpet, and drum, were gradually added. By the end of the 18th century, the bands were playing regularly not only for military parades but also for special court functions and popular outdoor concerts.

BEGINNINGS OF THE MODERN BAND

The modern band was born in the year 1789 as a result of the French Revolution. In that year Bernard Sarrette (1765–1858) founded the Band of the National Guard in Paris. This group of 45 players was immediately in demand for the popular demonstrations and numerous public ceremonies of the new government. By 1790 this band had 70 players and led to the formation of many military and town bands throughout Europe.

Many of the leading composers of the time served as bandmasters and wrote pieces for their bands. François Joseph Gossec (1734–1829) served for a time as bandmaster of the National Guard Band, with Charles Simon Catel (1773–1830) as his assistant. Their symphonies and overtures are still played by bands today. Others who composed for band included Luigi Cherubini (1760–1842), Ferdinando Paër (1771–1839), Etienne Mehul (1763–1817), and even the great composer Ludwig van Beethoven (1770–1827). The French band tradition reached its highest point in the great *Funeral and Triumphal Symphony* of Hector Berlioz (1803–69). It was written for a band of 208 players for the dedication of the Bastille Column in 1840.

WILHELM WIEPRECHT (1802–72)

Wilhelm Wieprecht was chiefly responsible for organizing the band as we know it today. A forward-looking musician, he experimented with mechanical improvements for the instruments. It was through his example that the use of horns and trumpets with valves, or keys, became universally accepted. It was then possible to play these instruments in more difficult kinds of music, and a greater variety of sound in band music resulted. This and the work of Adolphe Sax (inventor of the saxophone) and Theobald Boehm (who developed the modern flute) contributed to the development of the modern band and its music.

Wieprecht was responsible for the first of the massed-band festivals and band contests, forerunners of today's school and college band festivals. In 1838 he organized a grand festival in which over 1,000 players plus 200 extra side drummers performed. The occasion was the visit of the Russian Emperor Nicholas to the King of Prussia. What a royal welcome it must have been!

By the middle of the 19th century, bands in Europe had become an important part of every country's musical as well as military life. Among the most famous bands in England were the band of the Royal Horse Guards and the band of the Grenadier Guards led by Sir Daniel Godfrey (1831–1903). Godfrey was probably the best-known bandmaster of his time. His many arrangements for band are still performed in England and America. .

BANDS IN THE UNITED STATES

The development of bands and band music in the United States is one of the most colorful stories in American history. The earliest American bands were based on British models, and even before the American Revolution there is record of a band led by Josiah Flagg, of Boston. He was one of the first organizers of concerts in the American colonies. It is an interesting fact that Flagg's *Collection of the Best Psalm Tunes* was engraved by Paul Revere.

Although there is little historical record of bands in America before 1800, we know there was a wealth of band music composed in Revolutionary times and shortly thereafter. People, then, must have enjoyed band concerts and employed small bands for military purposes and public celebrations. Every American schoolchild knows the famous painting *The Spirit of '76*.

Marches were composed to celebrate patriotic occasions. The *Federal March* of Alexander Reinagle, performed in 1788, was written for the Fourth of July procession in Philadelphia celebrating the ratification of the United States Constitution. There were also many marches written in honor of the country's leading citizens and military heroes, such as *General Washington's Grand March* and *Jefferson's March*. During this period almost every town had its local band, attached to the town's militia.

PATRICK SARSFIELD GILMORE (1829–92)

Patrick S. Gilmore, born in County Galway, Ireland, in 1829, arrived in the United States at the age of 19. He was a man of enormous energy and vivid imagination and a born showman. In 1859 he took over the Boston Brigade Band, clad the players in bright new uniforms, rehearsed them over and over, and began an enormous schedule of performances. His band played for concerts, parades, and public ceremonies of all kinds. Also, as was the custom then, he provided dance music for balls and other events.

During the Civil War Gilmore conceived the idea of a huge band festival. With the help of the Army, he organized a Grand National Band consisting of 500 Army bandsmen plus a number of additional drum and bugle players. They were accompanied by a chorus of 5,000 schoolchildren. As a crowning touch Gilmore added 36 cannons, firing them by pushing hidden electric buttons. The great event took place in New Orleans on March 4, 1864.

Spectacular as this event was, it was only a hint of greater things to come. Returning to Boston after the war, Gilmore began to work on his next celebration, the National Peace Jubilee, given in 1869. This time he used an orchestra of 500, a band of 1,000, a chorus of 10,000, two batteries of cannons, and 100 firemen with hammers and anvils. The Jubilee lasted 5 days.

But Gilmore had even grander ideas. For 10 days, in 1872, he presented a World Peace Jubilee. His performers included an orchestra of 1,000, a band of 2,000, a chorus of 20,000, cannons, anvils, organ, and bells.

In 1873 Gilmore moved to New York, where he became leader of the 22nd Regiment Band. This became known as Gilmore's Band. He made several tours with the band in the United States, Canada, and Europe. He died in 1892.

JOHN PHILIP SOUSA (1854–1932)

John Philip Sousa was perhaps the greatest bandsman who ever lived. Trained as a violinist, he was only 24 years old when he was asked to take over the United States Marine Band. During Sousa's 12 years as director of the Marine Band, it achieved a national reputation for brilliance of performance that it retains to this day.

In 1892 Sousa left the Marine Band and formed a band of his own. He then toured extensively throughout the United States, Canada, and Europe. Sousa's band was probably the greatest band in the history of America. Its members included the leading virtuoso players of the day. His band had something that no band before him had and that every band since his has depended upon: Sousa's own marches. Brilliant in sound, rousing in spirit, and absolutely perfect for a band, they still form the backbone of band music everywhere. In fact, when most people think of band music, it is the sound of a Sousa march that they usually have in mind. Sousa wrote about 140 marches, including the famous *Stars and Stripes Forever, The Washington Post,* and *El Capitan.*

The United States Marine Band at Washington, D.C.

EDWIN FRANKO GOLDMAN (1878–1956)

In the 20th century the nature of the band changed. The great touring bands of Sousa's time disappeared. Movies, television, and radio took the place of the old-time touring band that gave concerts wherever it went.

There is, however, no lack of popularity for the concert band, the kind that does not go on tours. The leading band of this type in the United States is the Goldman Band, founded in 1911 by Edwin Franko Goldman. Trained as a trumpet player, Goldman was for 10 years a member of the Metropolitan Opera Orchestra, in New York City. While he was playing there, he conceived the idea of forming a permanent concert band. By 1918 he was giving a regular series of outdoor summer band concerts; his players were among the leading musicians of the day. The summer concerts he started have become a tradition in the musical life of New York. They are now given under the direction of his son, Richard Franko Goldman.

Edwin Franko Goldman was the first bandmaster to encourage leading composers of the day to compose original works for band. It is through his efforts that today we are able to hear a large variety of music composed especially for bands.

RICHARD FRANKO GOLDMAN

See also PERCUSSION INSTRUMENTS; WIND INSTRUMENTS.

The Band of the Canadian Guards at Ottawa, Ontario.

Visitors enjoy strolling or relaxing by the shores of scenic Lake Louise (*above*). They may also watch the deer and other animals that are protected within the park.

BANFF NATIONAL PARK

Banff National Park in Alberta is the oldest and one of the largest of Canada's national parks. Engineers were surveying a route for the Canadian Pacific Railway in the 1880's when they discovered hot springs on the eastern slopes of the Rocky Mountains, at the spot where the town of Banff now stands. When the discovery of these springs amid the beautiful, snow-capped peaks became known, the Canadian Government decided to preserve the mountain scenery and wildlife of the area as a public park. In 1885 an area around Banff was set aside as Rocky Mountains National Park. Later it was renamed Banff National Park. The area has been expanded until now it covers more than 6,500 square kilometers (2,500 square miles).

Through the deep valleys of Banff National Park, between such famous mountains as Eisenhower, Rundle, and Temple, glacier-fed streams flow into crystal-clear lakes. The main river is the Bow, which runs southward through most of the park. The most famous lake is Louise, renowned for its magnificent natural setting. The towns of Banff and Lake Louise are two world-famous resorts located in this park. People come long distances to enjoy such sports as skiing and tobogganing in winter and hiking, golf, and mountain climbing in summer. Banff's popular swimming pools use water from the hot springs at the foot of Sulphur Mountain. Wild animals are protected from hunters so that tourists may see moose, elk, mountain goats, and bears close by the highways.

Lake Louise is on the main Canadian Pacific Railway line at the east end of Kicking Horse Pass. Banff is also on the Canadian Pacific Railway and on the Trans-Canada Highway as well.

The Banff School of Fine Arts, now a part of the University of Calgary, was established at Banff in 1933 as a summer school to teach subjects connected with the theater. Since then it has grown tremendously. It offers courses in drama, ballet, opera, creative writing, and fine arts. Every summer students come from many countries to attend this unusual school.

JOHN S. MOIR
University of Toronto

BANGKOK (KRUNG THEP)

Bangkok is the capital, largest city, and cultural center of Thailand and one of the leading cities of Southeast Asia. It lies in a bend of the broad Chao Phraya River, not far from the Gulf of Siam (Gulf of Thailand). Bangkok is famous for its beautiful Buddhist temples. Today, the glittering spires of more than 300 temples rise on the skyline beside modern skyscrapers.

In 1982, Bangkok celebrated the 200th anniversary of the Thai royal family, the Chakri dynasty. The first Chakri king, Rama I, moved the capital from Thonburi (now part of Bangkok) across the river to the tiny village known as Bangkok. The Thais call their capital Krung Thep—sometimes translated as ''city of angels''—a shortened form of the name Rama I gave his new capital.

People once moved about Bangkok mainly by boat—and many still do. As the city spread outward from the riverbanks, canals were built to provide transportation links to the river. Streets on land were often only narrow lanes for walking and for use by bicycles and carts. People went to market, visited neighbors, and transported goods by water. Shops and houses crowded the banks of the canals.

After World War II, the number of cars and trucks increased, and new streets were needed. Many of the canals were filled in and paved. Road building has changed the face of Bangkok more than any other kind of construction.

Bangkok is a city with no single center. Instead, it has many centers that developed as the city grew. In the oldest part of the city is the Grand Palace. It is almost a small city itself, with many buildings inside a high wall. They include the famous Temple of the Emerald Buddha, which houses a statue of Buddha that is the most sacred of all objects for the Buddhists of Thailand. The lovely emerald-green statue is actually carved from a piece of jasper. Across the river is another landmark, the Temple of the Dawn.

Near the Grand Palace are many large government buildings, theaters, museums, and Silpakorn and Thammasat universities. To the north is the palace where the present king lives. To the south is the old Chinese part of the city, where Thai merchants and artisans of Chinese ancestry own small stores and shops. In the newer parts of the city, modern shopping centers have been built. Tall office and apartment buildings and hotels rise many stories above much older shops and houses.

Bangkok is Thailand's center of industry and banking, its busiest port, and a hub of international air and railroad transportation. Factories in the city and in new industrial areas in the suburbs turn out a wide variety of goods. These include processed foods, metal and electrical goods, pharmaceuticals, textiles, and jewelry.

The population of Bangkok's metropolitan area, which includes Thonburi, is approximately 5,400,000. Like other big cities, Bangkok faces traffic jams, pollution, and other problems, such as lack of jobs and housing. Parts of the low-lying city are subject to floods, especially during times of heavy rain. But Bangkok is still a showcase of Thai culture and an exciting place to live in or visit.

JAMES BASCHE
Author, *Thailand: Land of the Free*

The Bangkok skyline, with its gilded temples and modern skyscrapers, reflects the mixture of past and present.

BANGLADESH

Bangladesh is a nation in South Asia almost entirely surrounded by the territory of its giant neighbor, India. Though small in area, Bangladesh is one of the most heavily populated, and one of the poorest, countries in the world. Formerly known as East Pakistan, Bangladesh declared its independence from Pakistan following a civil war in 1971.

▶THE PEOPLE

Bangladesh means "Bengal Nation," and the vast majority of the people are Bengalis who are related to the Bengalis of neighboring India. The largest minority groups are the Biharis, who emigrated from India, and the tribal people of the Chittagong Hills. Most of the people are Muslims. There are a sizable number of Hindus and some Buddhists and Christians. The hill tribes practice traditional religions. Bengali (or Bangla) is the official language, but English is also widely spoken.

FACTS
and figures

PEOPLE'S REPUBLIC OF BANGLADESH is the official name of the country.

LOCATION: South Asia.

AREA: 55,598 sq mi (143,998 km²).

POPULATION: 115,600,000 (estimate).

CAPITAL AND LARGEST CITY: Dhaka.

MAJOR LANGUAGES: Bengali, or Bangla (official); English.

MAJOR RELIGION: Muslim.

GOVERNMENT: Republic. **Head of state**—president. **Head of government**—prime minister. **Legislature**—Jatiya Sangsad (National Assembly).

CHIEF PRODUCTS: Agricultural —jute, rice, tea, sugarcane, fruits, oilseeds, wheat. **Manufactured**—jute products, cotton textiles, refined sugar, leather goods, fertilizer, paper. **Mineral**—natural gas.

MONETARY UNIT: Taka (1 taka = 100 poisha).

Bengalis place great value on education, and almost every village has one or more local schools. The government provides free primary school education for five years. Bangladesh has a number of colleges and universities. The oldest and largest is the University of Dhaka, founded in 1921, which is located in Dhaka, the capital.

The basic unit of life in Bangladesh is the village. It is usually located along the course of a river or canal with rice fields nearby. Communication between villages is chiefly by boat. There are thousands of boats, of all sizes and shapes, and they travel up and down the rivers carrying people and goods.

The everyday diet in Bangladesh consists of rice and fish with some vegetables. The typical house is built of reeds, bamboo, and mats and is plastered with clay or mud. Men usually wear the lungi, a length of colored cotton cloth worn wrapped around the waist and stretching to the ankles. At work the lungi is tucked up to the knees. Women often wear saris—long, colorful garments draped around the body from the shoulder to the ankles. Traditionally, Muslim women cover their faces, especially around strangers.

▶THE LAND

Bangladesh is a land largely of low plains crisscrossed by rivers. The most important rivers are the Ganges and the Brahmaputra and their tributaries. In the south the rivers, by depositing sediment, have created areas of very rich soil.

The only elevated areas are in the southeast, in the Chittagong Hills. This hill country, the home of the tribal people, is covered with dense tropical forest.

Bangladesh is a tropical country. The average temperatures range from over 60°F (16°C) to over 90°F (32°C). It is also a land of torrential monsoon rains, which fall from June to September. In addition, violent winds called cyclones (or typhoons) regularly bring heavy flooding to the region, causing many deaths and widespread devastation. Since Bangladesh's independence alone, cyclones have killed hundreds of thousands of people and left many millions more homeless.

▶THE ECONOMY

Bangladesh is an agricultural country. The main food crop is rice. Jute is the major

Most of Bangladesh's people are Bengalis.

BANGLADESH

commercial crop. Bangladesh is one of the world's leading producers and suppliers of jute, a plant fiber used to make burlap, sacking, and twine. Exports of jute are the country's chief source of income. Tea, grown in the hill region, is the second most important cash crop. Other crops include sugarcane, wheat, mangoes, coconuts, pineapples, and oilseeds, from which cooking oil is derived.

The manufacture of jute products is Bangladesh's chief industry. Other manufactured goods include cotton textiles, refined sugar, leather goods, fertilizer, and paper and paper products.

Aside from natural gas, Bangladesh has few useful mineral resources. It has deposits of coal, but they are difficult to mine.

The average farm is small, and the farming methods usually do not enable farmers to produce large crops. Bangladesh is one of the most densely populated areas in the world, and the population is rising very rapidly. Unless agriculture is modernized and effective means of population control are adopted, the country will face problems in attempting to feed its people adequately.

The many rivers and canals are both a blessing and a problem. They provide the chief means of transportation of people and goods. But to be used efficiently, they require effective methods of flood-control and mechanization. The great hydroelectric potential of the country can be utilized for industrial growth only if the rivers are harnessed. This

A farmer watering his rice fields. Rice is the staple food in Bangladesh.

Left: Riverboats are a common form of transportation.
Above: A typical small Bangladesh village.

would enable Bangladesh to provide power for industrialization. But such projects require vast amounts of money, which the country cannot easily supply.

▶CITIES

There are fewer than a dozen major urban centers in Bangladesh. The most important of these is Dhaka, the capital and largest city. Formerly the capital of East Pakistan, the city has many historic buildings and is an educational and cultural center. It is also the nation's chief industrial area. Chittagong, on the Karnafuli River east of the Bay of Bengal, has a good natural harbor and is the nation's chief port. It is also a major industrial and rail center.

▶HISTORY AND GOVERNMENT

Bangladesh is a young nation, but the history of the region goes back to ancient times. In the beginning, Bangladesh was part of the larger Bengal region of eastern India. It was ruled by successive groups of invaders—the Turks, the Moguls, and the British. In 1947, India gained its independence from Britain. East Bengal (now Bangladesh) became part of Pakistan. This new nation was created because the Muslim League demanded an independent and separate nation for the parts of the former British Indian Empire where the Muslims were a majority.

Pakistan was born with built-in flaws. It was made up of two parts, East Pakistan and West Pakistan, which were separated by about

Bicycles and pedicabs crowd the busy city of Dhaka, the capital of Bangladesh.

1,000 miles (1,600 kilometers). India lay between them. The two parts of Pakistan were quite different in their peoples and cultures. Groups from West Pakistan soon took control of the new nation. East Pakistan turned out to be a good place for commercial investments. But the Bengalis charged that most of the profits were drained off to West Pakistan. The West Pakistani leaders were accused of neglecting the interests of the eastern region and treating it as a colony. The East Pakistanis also complained that they were not receiving their fair share of political power. They believed they were entitled to a greater voice because they made up more than 55 percent of the nation's total population.

Other issues led to frustration and discontent among the Bengalis of Pakistan. The government at first refused to accept Bengali as one of the national languages. Popularly elected local governments in the East were dismissed on charges of wanting to secede from Pakistan. Bengali leaders were imprisoned as traitors. There were frequent riots, and a long period of military rule (from 1958 to 1971) created dangerous tensions in the East.

The Birth of Bangladesh

The climax came in the elections of 1970. The Awami League, led by Sheikh Mujibur Rahman (Mujib), won most of the seats in the East Pakistani provincial legislature and a majority in the national legislature. The victory would have given Sheikh Mujib a decisive role in Pakistani politics. This situation was unacceptable to General Yahya Khan, the leader of the national government, and Zulfikar Ali Bhutto, the leader of the Pakistan People's Party, the majority party in West Pakistan. They objected especially to the Awami League's Six Point Program, which included self-government for the eastern region. West Pakistani leaders believed this would lead to the breaking up of Pakistan.

The two parts of Pakistan tried to form a plan for restoring civilian rule and drafting a new constitution. Their failure to do so set off riots in the East. The West Pakistani army brutally suppressed the riots. It is charged that millions of people lost their lives and hundreds of villages were destroyed. Some 10,000,000 Bengalis, mostly Hindus, fled to India. This placed a great economic burden on India. As a result, India became involved in what was essentially a civil war between the two parts of Pakistan.

Incidents mounted until, in December, 1971, India and Pakistan went to war in both the eastern and western regions. The war was swift. In less than two weeks, the Indian Army, with the aid of the Bengali guerrillas, had compelled the Pakistani forces to surrender. The Bangladesh provisional government had been formed earlier in India. Its members arrived in Dhaka and took control.

Sheikh Mujibur Rahman, who had been arrested and imprisoned in West Pakistan, was released. On January 10, 1972, he arrived in Bangladesh and became prime minister of the new nation. He later became its president.

Recent History

Bangladesh faced enormous problems. Millions of people had become refugees. The economy had been disrupted, and the country was torn by political quarrels. In 1975 the government was overthrown by army officers, and President Mujib was killed.

Bangladesh was governed under martial (military) law by General Ziaur Rahman (known as Zia). In 1978, Zia was elected president. Martial law was lifted in 1979, and elections were held for the legislature. In 1981, Zia was killed during an attempted coup.

In 1982, General Hussain Mohammed Ershad seized power and reimposed martial law. After many postponements, new elections for the presidency and legislature were held in 1986. Ershad was elected president and later lifted martial law. His opponents, charging widespread fraud, refused to take part in the elections. Elections held in 1988 also were boycotted by the opposition. Widespread protests forced Ershad to resign in late 1990. In new elections in 1991, the Bangladesh Nationalist Party won the largest number of seats in the legislature. The party leader, Khaleda Zia, widow of the former president, was named prime minister.

BALKRISHNA G. GOKHALE
Director, Asian Studies Program
Wake Forest University

See also INDIA; PAKISTAN.

BANJO. See FOLK MUSIC INSTRUMENTS.

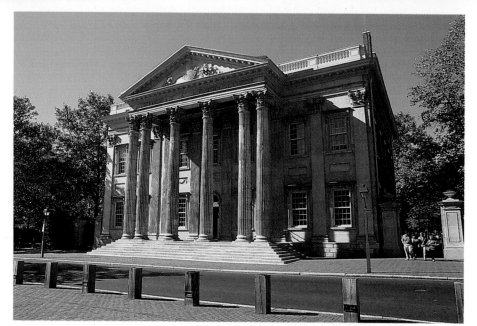

The Bank of the United States, which received its charter in 1791, was the country's first federal bank. In 1797 it moved into this building, which is considered to be the oldest U.S. bank building. The bank stayed in business only until 1811 when its charter expired, but the building still stands on South Third Street in Philadelphia.

BANKS AND BANKING

What can you do when you have money that you do not want to spend, or carry around, or keep at home? You could deposit the money at a bank in a checking or savings account. On the other hand, if you didn't have enough money to meet your needs, you could ask a bank to lend you money. By providing these two functions—holding money and lending money—banks play a very important role in the United States economy. They make the money in bank accounts available to people who need to borrow money.

When you deposit money in a bank as savings, you also earn interest. The interest is a fee paid to you for the use of your money. Suppose, for example, that you deposit $100 in a bank offering an interest rate of 5 percent on savings. At the end of one year the amount of money in your account would be $100 plus the additional interest.

Money deposited in a bank as savings is loaned to borrowers at a higher interest rate than is paid to savers. For example, a bank that pays 5 percent interest on savings may charge 10 percent interest on the money when it is loaned to borrowers. The interest the bank receives is income for the bank. It is used to pay interest to depositors, as well as to pay for the salaries of bank employees, and for equipment, supplies, and other costs of operating the bank.

Banks are owned by stockholders who have invested money in the bank. Part of a bank's total assets are the funds invested by these stockholders. But most of a bank's assets come from money that people have deposited and from interest paid on loans.

▶HISTORY OF BANKING

Banking activities are almost as old as the earliest civilizations. The earliest bankers were moneychangers or moneylenders. These people had strongboxes in which to keep money, and people left money with them for safekeeping or borrowed money from them in exchange for a fee. As early as A.D. 534 the ancient Romans had laws and regulations concerning moneylending and banking activities.

Today most banks have safe-deposit boxes in their vaults, which customers may rent and use to store important papers and other valuable items.

Modern banking is generally thought to have begun in Italy during the late 1500's. In fact, the word "bank" comes from the Italian word *banco*, which means bench. The term became associated with banking because many early Italian bankers conducted their business from benches in the street.

In England during the 1600's it became common practice for people to give their gold and silver to local goldsmiths for safekeeping. These goldsmiths, who made jewelry and other items, had strong vaults in which they kept precious metals. It was only natural that people who did not have safe places for their valuables would want to keep their gold and silver in these vaults. The goldsmiths issued paper receipts, or notes, to the people who left precious metals with them. Eventually, people began to use these paper notes as money; the goldsmiths became bankers.

As trade flourished in Europe in the 1600's and 1700's banking became so important that commercial banks were set up. These commercial banks were privately owned, and their chief business was to help merchants finance trading activities. They accepted deposits of money, made loans, collected bills, and acted as places of exchange in which money from one country could be converted into the money of another country.

Banking in the United States

The first banks established in the United States were state banks. In 1781, the Bank of North America, the first bank to receive a charter, or license to operate, was organized in Philadelphia. Other states soon issued charters to banks of their own. The first national bank, the Bank of the United States, was established in 1791 and had branches in several cities.

During the late 1700's and early 1800's many state banks in the United States followed unsound banking practices. They issued far too many loans in the form of paper bank notes (paper money). The Bank of the United States had the authority to control the amount of paper money issued by the state banks, but in 1811 its charter expired and the Bank of the United States no longer had any control.

Increasing numbers of people became concerned about the value of their paper notes and asked state banks to exchange the notes for gold and silver coin (called **specie**). Many banks, however, did not have enough precious metals to back the notes and they stopped exchanging gold and silver for paper notes. As a result, the notes quickly lost their value. This dangerous financial situation led to the failure of many banks. When the banks failed, depositors lost their life savings.

The National Bank Act of 1863, which was amended in 1864, created a national banking system in the United States. Under the provisions of this system, the state banks were driven out of the business of issuing paper notes. The national banks were allowed to continue issuing bank notes until 1935. Federal laws then gave the power to issue paper notes solely to a centralized banking system called the Federal Reserve.

Bank tellers help customers with many different transactions, including making deposits to and withdrawals from their accounts and taking care of bills such as loan payments.

▶ THE AMERICAN BANKING SYSTEM

The banking system in the United States today is made up of many banks operating at different levels. All these banks, however, must operate under the jurisdiction and rules of the Federal Reserve System, the centerpiece of American banking.

The Federal Reserve System

The Federal Reserve System was established by Congress in 1913 in an effort to correct some serious problems that existed in American banking. Prior to the establishment of the Federal Reserve System, the United States experienced several severe financial panics during which many businesses failed and many banks were forced to close. The national banking system at the time was unable to deal with these crises. It was decided that major reforms were needed, and the Federal Reserve System was the result.

The Federal Reserve System—or the Fed, as it is commonly called—is made up of three levels of organization. The top level consists of the Board of Governors, the Federal Open-Market Committee, and the Federal Advisory Council. The Board of Governors is the most important of these three groups. It is the central policy-making body of the Federal Reserve System. It consists of seven members appointed by the president and confirmed by the Senate. Each member is appointed for a 14-year term and is ineligible for reappointment. The Board of Governors remains relatively independent of politics. Board decisions do not have to be approved by the president or Congress, and board members do not have to fear losing their jobs when a new president is elected.

The second level of the Federal Reserve System consists of the Federal Reserve Banks. The United States is divided into twelve districts, and there is a separate Federal Reserve Bank for each district. The twelve Federal Reserve Banks are located in Boston, New York, Philadelphia, Cleveland, Richmond, Atlanta, Chicago, St. Louis, Minneapolis, Kansas City, Dallas, and San Francisco. The activities of these Federal Reserve Banks are coordinated by the Board of Governors. The Federal Reserve Banks do not deal directly with the public. They are "bankers' banks" that deal only with other financial institutions and the government.

The third level of the Federal Reserve System consists of other financial institutions, including commercial banks, savings and loan associations, credit unions, and savings banks. These financial institutions utilize the services of the Federal Reserve System and are subject to reserve requirements established by the Fed. They perform the regular day-to-day business of banking in the nation.

The Federal Reserve System performs many important functions, the most important of which is controlling the nation's money supply. It also plays a major role in clearing checks. The Fed supervises member banks and serves as a depository for the money that banks are required to keep as reserves. The Fed is also responsible for supplying the nation's paper money in the form of Federal Reserve Notes.

Types of Banks

There are several different types of financial institutions in the United States that are commonly thought of as banks.

Commercial Banks. Commercial banks make up the largest banking group in the United States. At one time, commercial banks could easily be distinguished from other financial institutions by the fact that only they could

---

The Savings and Loan Crisis of the 1980's

Before the 1980's, savings and loan institutions were allowed to make loans only to individuals to buy houses. This changed in 1982 with the enactment of a deregulation act that changed the way the savings and loan industry operated. The deregulation of the industry led to one of the worst financial disasters since the Great Depression and was one of the worst scandals in American history.

As a result of deregulation, an estimated $250 billion of depositors' money was lost through poor management practices or, in some cases, fraud. Questionable construction projects — shopping centers in the desert, suburban developments with almost nobody to live in them, and unneeded high-rise office buildings — were financed by the savings and loan industry. A massive building binge occurred, and buildings of all types were built, often on pure speculation; that is, on the chance that buyers would be found.

When developers could not sell these properties, they defaulted on (could not repay) their loans. Since the savings and loan institutions could not sell these properties either, many went bankrupt. The government took over these bankrupt institutions and the unneeded real estate became the property of the American taxpayers. Most of the property will probably be sold eventually at a fraction of its cost, and taxpayers will have to absorb an estimated loss of at least $250 billion.

Savings and loan associations, which have always offered loans to their customers for building or buying houses or for buying real estate, now provide many other types of loans and services, including checking accounts.

offer checking accounts. However, changes in the banking laws now allow other financial institutions to offer checking accounts as well.

Commercial banks can be established and operated only after being granted a charter by either the federal government or a state government. Commercial banks chartered by the federal government are called national banks. Those chartered by one of the states are called state banks. The primary functions of commercial banks are to receive deposits, make loans, and provide checking and other services to customers. Commercial banks primarily make short-term commercial loans to businesses and personal loans to individuals.

Savings and Loan Associations. Savings and loan associations are owned and operated by individuals who, as shareholders, elect a board of directors to manage the organization. Historically, savings and loan associations primarily made long-term loans—twenty years or longer—to individuals for the purpose of building homes or buying existing homes and other real estate. Today, however, savings and loan associations make many other types of loans as well. They also make checking account services available to depositors.

Savings Banks. Savings banks specialize in individual savings accounts. These banks may be owned by stockholders, although most function as **cooperatives**, or **mutuals**, and are owned by their depositors. Mutual savings banks originated in the United States in the early 1800's when commercial banks were not interested in handling the small savings deposits of wage earners. By pooling their savings in a mutual savings bank, wage earners with individual savings could find profitable investment opportunities for their money.

Credit Unions. Credit unions are cooperative nonprofit associations owned and operated by their members. They are often organized by the employees of large companies or the members of labor unions for the benefit of their membership. The primary purpose of credit unions is to offer high-interest savings accounts and low-interest loans to members.

Investment Banks. Investment banks specialize in distributing the **securities**, or stocks and bonds, of corporations to the public. Investment banks purchase newly issued stocks and bonds from companies and then resell these securities to individual investors in smaller quantities. Investment banks buy securities from a company at a particular price with the intention of reselling them at a higher price. The difference between the purchase price and the sale price is the investment bank's profit. Investment banks provide companies with the money they need without the companies having to wait for the general public to buy stock.

The World Bank. While some of the nation's major banks do business with foreign countries, there are a few specialized banks that deal exclusively in international finance. One of these, the International Bank for Reconstruction and Development (IBRD), more commonly known as the World Bank, officially began operating in 1944. The original purpose of the World Bank was to help finance the reconstruction of areas of the world damaged during World War II. Since that time, the World Bank has also assisted in the economic growth of underdeveloped countries by providing them with long-term loans. In 1956, the World Bank established the International

Bank customers often find themselves in long lines during their lunch hours or just before bank closings on Fridays. This is when many people deposit or cash paychecks, or make withdrawals for weekend trips.

period of time. Savings accounts are a type of time deposit. Most people who put money in a savings account plan to leave it there until it is needed—perhaps to buy a house, to pay for a child's education, or to use during retirement. Banks pay interest on the money deposited in a savings account, so the amount of money left in an account will gradually increase.

A person who deposits money in a savings account often receives a savings passbook. This passbook shows the amount of money in the deposit. When money is deposited or withdrawn from the account, the balance in the passbook will be updated. Periodically, the bank will add the interest that has been earned on the account to the balance.

People who have large amounts of money to deposit as savings often put the money in a special account called a **certificate of deposit (CD)**. An advantage of certificates of deposit is that they usually pay higher interest rates than passbook savings accounts. However, certificates of deposit are only payable at a definite date in the future, called the maturity date. This maturity date might range from 30 days to several years. If a person withdraws money from a certificate of deposit before the maturity date, he or she will have to pay a penalty in the form of lost interest.

Demand Deposits. Demand deposits are checking accounts, which allow individuals to deposit, withdraw, and transfer their money whenever they want. Checking accounts pro-

Finance Corporation (IFC), the purpose of which is to stimulate private investments in developing countries. While the World Bank lends money only for public, or publicly sponsored, projects, the IFC helps to finance private enterprise.

Banking Services

Banks provide many services to the public and the government. But most of the regular business of a bank involves accepting deposits from savers and making money available to borrowers in the form of loans.

Time Deposits. In time deposits, money usually stays in an account for an extended

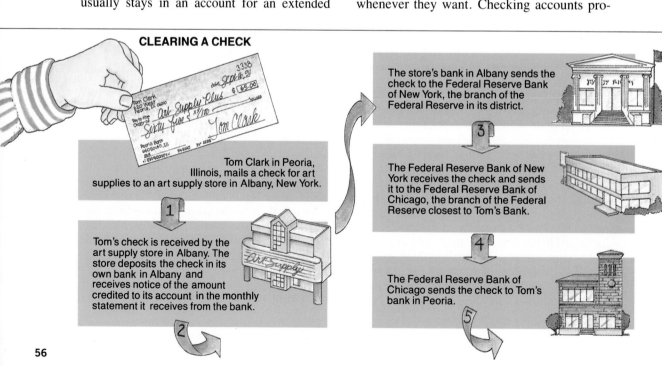

CLEARING A CHECK

Tom Clark in Peoria, Illinois, mails a check for art supplies to an art supply store in Albany, New York.

1

Tom's check is received by the art supply store in Albany. The store deposits the check in its own bank in Albany and receives notice of the amount credited to its account in the monthly statement it receives from the bank.

2

The store's bank in Albany sends the check to the Federal Reserve Bank of New York, the branch of the Federal Reserve in its district.

3

The Federal Reserve Bank of New York receives the check and sends it to the Federal Reserve Bank of Chicago, the branch of the Federal Reserve closest to Tom's Bank.

4

The Federal Reserve Bank of Chicago sends the check to Tom's bank in Peoria.

5

vide a convenient way for people to have access to their money without having to carry it around as cash. A person can write checks against a checking account at any time. These checks can be made payable to oneself to withdraw money, or they can be made payable to someone else to transfer money to that person. Banks sometimes pay interest on checking accounts, usually with the provision that a minimum amount of money be kept in the account at all times.

Each month banks send detailed statements to customers with checking accounts. These statements show how much money was deposited during the month, the number of checks written and the amount of each, and the current balance of the account. Enclosed with the statement will be the checks that were written, cashed, and returned to the bank during the month. These checks, for which money has been withdrawn from the checking account, are called cancelled checks. They can serve as receipts for any bills paid by check.

Loans. Banks make many types of loans to individuals or businesses. One major type of loan is a home mortgage loan, which is provided to people who want to buy or build a home. Home mortgage loans usually require repayment over a loan term, perhaps as long as twenty to thirty years. After the buyer pays a down payment on the home, the bank finances the balance of the cost. The buyer then pays off this amount, plus interest, in periodic (usually monthly) installments. On a large

Many banks post the rates they offer for making loans to customers for different items. Customers may compare the rates of different banks to find which one offers the best rate for their needs.

loan repaid over many years, the buyer will pay a large amount of interest as a part of each payment.

Banks make many short-term loans to both individuals and businesses. For example, a person might borrow $1,000 from a bank for a period of six months. The person signs a note promising to repay the money borrowed in addition to interest charged by the bank for the use of its money. Usually, the person must also offer something of value, such as an automobile, as security, or collateral. If the person fails to repay the loan, the bank can take possession of this collateral.

The rate of interest that banks charge depends on the type and length of the loan. The **prime rate** is the rate of interest that large city banks charge their best customers (large businesses that have excellent credit ratings). The rate of interest paid by the average borrower is usually higher than the prime rate.

Other Services. Banks also provide many other services to their customers. Most banks have safe-deposit boxes in their vaults, which they rent to customers for safekeeping of valuable possessions. Banks also provide financial advice to their customers, sell traveler's checks, and issue credit cards.

Financial experts in a bank's trust department provide a variety of services. They manage real estate and collect rents, invest money in stocks and bonds, sell securities, give advice on drawing up wills, and manage company pension and health-insurance plans. Money left to charities is often handled by the

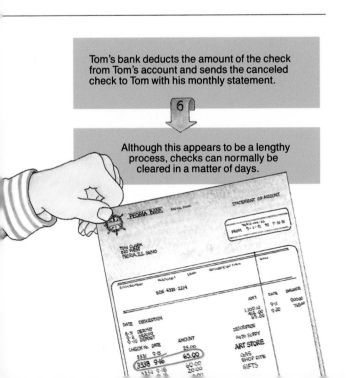

Tom's bank deducts the amount of the check from Tom's account and sends the canceled check to Tom with his monthly statement.

6

Although this appears to be a lengthy process, checks can normally be cleared in a matter of days.

trust departments of banks as well. Of course, the bank charges a fee for all of these services.

Many banks also offer bank credit cards to their customers. These credit cards enable people to buy items on credit by charging the items on their cards. The banks pay the merchants for the purchases and then bill the credit card holders, who make payments to their banks. The banks charge interest only on the amounts of the monthly bills that are not paid on time. Bank cards can also be used by customers to get cash advances from banks.

Many banks today have automatic teller machines (ATM's) that let customers have access to their accounts 24 hours a day. The bank customer inserts a special card into the machine and then enters a secret identification number. Once this is done, the customer has access to his or her bank account and can deposit, withdraw, and transfer money without the assistance of a bank employee.

Another service offered by many banks is electronic funds transfer (EFT). An electronic funds transfer system moves money into or out of a customer's account electronically. For example, some employees have their salaries electronically credited to their accounts, eliminating the need to cash or deposit paychecks. Electronic funds transfer speeds service to customers and also eliminates much of the paperwork involved in various banking services.

Safety of Bank Deposits

During the Great Depression of the 1930's many people lost their life savings when banks failed. In order to prevent that from happening again, government insurance funds were created. These insurance funds guaranteed that depositors would be paid the full amount of their deposits if a bank failed.

Prior to 1989, accounts in savings and loan associations were insured by the federal Savings and Loan Insurance Corporation (FSLIC), and accounts in commercial banks were insured by the Federal Deposit Insurance Corporation (FDIC). In the late 1980's, however, the failure of many savings and loan associations caused the bankruptcy of the FSLIC insurance fund. As a result, beginning in 1989, the FDIC became responsible for insuring accounts in both commercial banks and savings and loan associations.

To handle all these accounts, two separate insurance funds were established within the FDIC—the Banking Insurance Fund (BIF) and the Savings Association Insurance Fund (SAIF). The BIF insures deposits in commercial banks up to $100,000 per deposit. The

Above: By using automatic teller machines (ATM's), customers have quick and easy access to their accounts day or night. *Right:* Banks provide statements to their customers every month that show opening and closing balances, cancelled checks, and transactions such as deposits, withdrawals, and service charges.

SAIF insures deposits in savings and loan associations up to a total of $100,000. If a bank or savings and loan association has financial troubles and is unable to repay depositors, repayment will be made out of the insurance funds. Credit union deposits are also insured up to $100,000 by insurance funds.

▶BANKING IN CANADA

Attempts to establish a Canadian bank go back to the late 1700's. But it was not until 1817 that the first bank in Canada was successfully launched. Early banks in Canada were established as private partnerships, by provincial law, or by royal charters obtained in England. However, by 1867 the federal government had assumed sole responsibility for the country's banking system.

Canada's central bank, the Bank of Canada, is the centerpiece of Canadian banking. It was founded in 1934 and nationalized in 1938. In addition, there are five large banks chartered under Canadian law, each of which has a nationwide network of branch banks.

The Bank of Canada is directed by law to regulate credit and currency in such a way as to promote the best interests of the Canadian economy. It carries out banking policies by changing rates of interest on loans, altering the amount of reserves that must be held by chartered banks to back up deposits, buying and selling securities, and responding to changes in foreign exchange rates. Canadian banks provide basically the same services as American banks. There are some differences, however, in policy and in the services provided.

▶CAREERS IN BANKING

Most of the people working in banks are either bank officers or clerical workers. Bank officers, depending on their rank, usually have some authority to make business decisions involving the bank. Bank officers might include positions such as president, vice president, treasurer, and comptroller. Some, such as loan and trust officers, head specific departments.

Clerical workers in banks include secretaries, bank tellers, bookkeepers, and various other employees who do clerical work. These positions generally outnumber bank officers by a ratio of about six to one.

ALLEN SMITH
Professor of Economics
Eastern Illinois University

See also ECONOMICS; INFLATION AND DEFLATION; MONEY; CREDIT CARDS.

BANTING, SIR FREDERICK GRANT (1891–1941)

Frederick Grant Banting, a Canadian doctor and scientist, was born on November 14, 1891, in Alliston, Ontario. He is remembered for his contribution to the control of diabetes, a serious disease in which the pancreas, a large gland near the stomach, produces too little insulin. Insulin is a chemical needed by the body to use and store sugar. Scientists knew that insulin from a healthy animal could help human patients, but no one—until Frederick Banting—knew how to obtain it.

Banting earned a medical degree at the University of Toronto and served with the Canadian Army Medical Corps in World War I (1914–18). He was awarded the Military Cross for his courage.

After the war Banting returned to his medical practice and to teaching in London, Ontario. While preparing a lecture on the pancreas, he suddenly realized how he might obtain insulin. Working in the laboratory of Professor John J. R. Macleod at the University of Toronto, Banting set to work in May 1921. He was assisted by Charles H. Best, a young graduate student.

Within several weeks Banting and Best obtained the first insulin from the pancreas of a dog. By January 1922, after many tests, they gave insulin to a diabetic, who showed immediate improvement. When insulin was given to other patients, they, too, improved. Another researcher, James B. Collip, perfected the method of preparing insulin.

In 1923, Banting and Macleod were awarded the Nobel prize, which they shared with Best and Collip. The University of Toronto set up a new medical research institute named after Banting, and he was knighted in 1934. Banting was killed in an airplane crash in Newfoundland on February 21, 1941.

JOHN S. BOWMAN
Author and Science Editor

BARBADOS

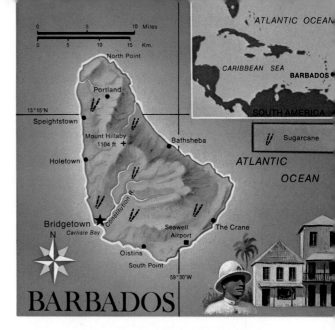

Barbados is an island nation in the West Indies. Although it has been independent of Britain since 1966, there are many reminders of over 300 years of British rule. People play cricket, a British game, and take afternoon tea. Drivers use the left-hand side of the road, as they do in Britain. And the hills are dotted with tiny cottages that remind one of Britain.

▶ THE PEOPLE AND THE ECONOMY

Most of the people are black, descendants of slaves brought from Africa centuries ago. The rest are mainly of British origin. English is the official language, but is spoken in a distinctive, lilting way. The people are known as Barbadians, though they often call themselves Bajans.

Barbados has a high standard of living compared to other developing countries; still, overpopulation is a major problem. The island's economy was once dominated by sugar and related industries, such as the production of rum and molasses. But Barbados' fine beaches and pleasant climate have made tourism the chief source of the country's income.

▶ THE LAND

Barbados lies in the Atlantic Ocean but is considered the easternmost of islands in the Caribbean Sea. From its highest point—Mount Hillaby, 1,104 feet (336 meters)—the island slopes gently to the sea. The Atlantic coast is rugged, with a high surf. The Caribbean coast has smooth, wide beaches and calm, blue waters. Bridgetown, the capital, is located on the Caribbean side of the island. The climate is warm, but the trade winds have a cooling effect on the temperature. Rainfall is abundant, especially in the north.

▶ HISTORY AND GOVERNMENT

Barbados was uninhabited when the Portuguese Pedro a Campos landed there in the early 1500's. He named the island Barbados, meaning "bearded," probably for the beard-like vines or moss that hung from the trees.

The British established the first permanent settlement in 1627. Slaves were imported to work on the tobacco, cotton, and sugarcane plantations, until slavery was abolished in the 1800's. Barbados gained self-government in 1961 and full independence in 1966.

Barbados recognizes the British monarch, represented by a governor-general, as the head of state. Real political authority, however, rests with the Barbadian Parliament. It is made up of the House of Assembly, elected by popular vote, and the Senate, whose members are appointed by the governor-general. The prime minister is chosen from the majority party in the House of Assembly.

BRANFORD M. TAITT
Former Consul General of Barbados

BARKLEY, ALBEN. See VICE PRESIDENCY OF THE UNITED STATES.

FACTS AND FIGURES

BARBADOS is the official name of the country.

THE PEOPLE are known as Barbadians.

LOCATION: West Indies.

AREA: 166 sq mi (430 km²).

POPULATION: 250,000 (estimate).

CAPITAL AND LARGEST CITY: Bridgetown.

MAJOR LANGUAGE: English (official).

MAJOR RELIGION: Christian (Protestant).

GOVERNMENT: Constitutional monarchy. **Head of state**— British monarch, represented by a governor-general. **Head of government**—prime minister. **Legislature**— Parliament (consisting of a House of Assembly and a Senate).

CHIEF PRODUCTS: Agricultural—sugarcane, sweet potatoes, corn, cassava, beans. **Manufactured**—sugar, rum, molasses, cotton clothing, pharmaceuticals.

MONETARY UNIT: Barbados dollar (1 dollar = 100 cents).

NATIONAL ANTHEM: "In plenty and in time of need."

BAROMETER

The air around you is heavy. It has weight. There is about 1 ton of air over every square foot (about 10 metric tons over every square meter) of the earth's surface. The name for the air's weight pressing down on the surface of the earth is **air pressure.** A barometer is an instrument that measures this air pressure.

You may have seen a barometer hanging on a wall. Inside it there is a small box, or chamber, with thin metal walls. Most of the air has been drawn out of this chamber. The thin walls move in or out slightly when there is an increase or decrease in the air pressure outside. A pointer on the front of the barometer is connected by a lever to the chamber walls and shows these small changes. The pointer moves in front of a dial that is marked off in units of air pressure. The units are usually inches or centimeters.

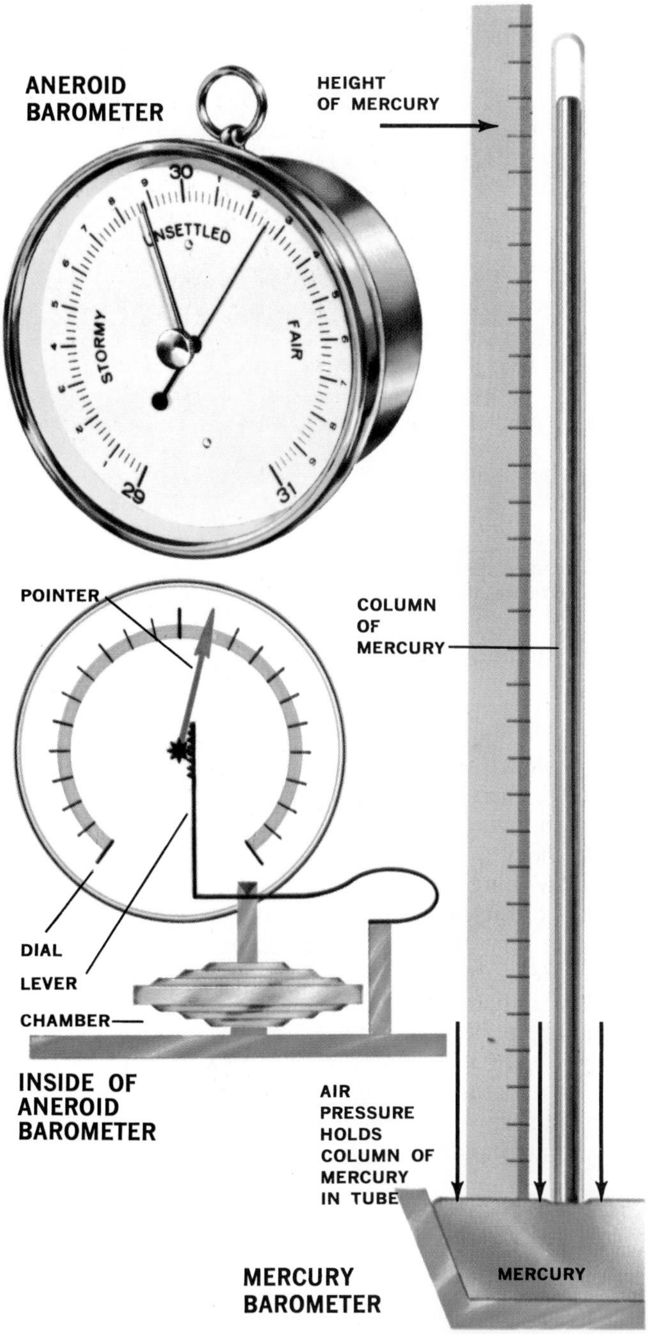

Air pressure is important in weather forecasting. A change in air pressure usually means a change in weather. A drop in pressure often means that bad weather is coming. A rise in pressure usually means that clear weather is on the way. Ships and airplanes carry barometers. Weather forecasters also use barometers.

Air pressure also changes when you move from sea level to higher altitudes. When you climb a mountain, you find that the air grows thinner. It weighs less, and so it presses down less strongly. Airplane pilots often use barometers called **altimeters** to tell them how high they are above the ground.

The barometers you have read about so far are called aneroid barometers. Aneroid means "without liquid." There are other barometers that do use liquids. The very first barometer was of this type. An Italian scientist named Evangelista Torricelli (1608–47) designed it in 1643. He took a long glass tube that was closed at one end and filled it with mercury. He turned this tube upside down in a pan that contained more mercury. The mercury in the tube started running out, of course. Soon the mercury stopped running out. The weight of the mercury in the tube was balanced by the pressure of air on the mercury outside.

Mercury barometers are still used today. Scientists read a mercury barometer by seeing how high the column of mercury in the tube is. When air pressure increases, the mercury column goes up. When the pressure decreases, the column goes down.

Mercury barometers are very accurate. But they are clumsy to move around, and they have to be kept upright so that the liquid stays level. That is why ordinary barometers in homes or on ships and airplanes are aneroid barometers. Mercury barometers are used mainly in scientific laboratories.

Reviewed by SERGE A. KORFF
New York University

See also WEATHER.

ANEROID BAROMETER

HEIGHT OF MERCURY

POINTER

COLUMN OF MERCURY

DIAL

LEVER

CHAMBER

INSIDE OF ANEROID BAROMETER

AIR PRESSURE HOLDS COLUMN OF MERCURY IN TUBE

MERCURY BAROMETER

MERCURY

Church of Santa Maria della Salute, in Venice, Italy, by Baldassare Longhena (1604-82).

BAROQUE ART AND ARCHITECTURE

Baroque is the name given to the art of the 17th century. But the baroque style, like all other styles in the history of art, began gradually. It started in the latter part of the 16th century and continued to be used well into the 18th century.

The 17th century was a period of great change. Some Europeans were exploring and settling new lands. Others were exploring the whole universe, from the distant heavens to the tiniest drop of water, by using the newly invented telescope and microscope. Whether they stayed at home or whether they traveled, the people of the 17th century looked at their own world with lively, inquiring eyes and minds. Their artists depicted what they saw in such a way that we are led to look and feel with them.

Describing their art as "baroque" is curious. The word itself has a strange sound, and this is the very reason why the term was first used. A large, irregularly shaped pearl is called a baroque pearl. It differs from the smooth, perfectly round pearls that we usually see. In the 18th century, architects who thought that all buildings should have smooth, simple shapes disliked the more complicated, elaborate buildings of the 17th century. They therefore angrily called them absurd, fantastic, and baroque. While the word has continued to be used ever since, this first meaning has now largely been forgotten. Today we simply use the term to describe the special qualities of 17th-century art.

The painters of the 17th century, for example, wanted to draw the viewer into the picture. Instead of using horizontal and vertical lines, they tended to use curves and diagonal lines that pull the viewer into the action on the canvas. The paintings are full of movement and dramatic lights and colors. Often baroque painters tried to give the illusion of unending space.

The architecture of this period also gives a feeling of excitement, motion, and drama.

Vision of Saint Theresa (1645–52), by Giovanni Lorenzo Bernini. Church of Santa Maria della Vittoria, Rome.

The façades, or fronts, of buildings were ornamented and the interiors richly decorated. Curving shapes were frequently used —the dome was the most typical architectural form. Another common feature of baroque buildings was great sweeping staircases.

Architects became interested in the surroundings of their buildings. They placed elaborate gardens around palaces. They set off important buildings in the cities by open squares decorated with fountains or colonnades. Roads leading from the squares give a dramatic view of stairways, sculpture, or other buildings far in the distance.

▶BAROQUE ART IN ITALY

Rome was the birthplace of baroque art, and from that artistic center the style spread all over Europe and to the European colonies in North and South America. One of the pioneers of baroque art was Michelangelo Merisi (1571–1610), always known as Caravaggio. In Caravaggio's painting *The Conversion of Saint Paul,* we see nothing but two men and a large work horse, yet we are made to feel that this is a scene of very special importance. Caravaggio gives us this feeling by placing the scene as if we were a part of it. He has used a very strong, almost blinding light and has left out any details that might be distracting.

Caravaggio thought of the people of the New Testament as if they were people living in his own time, and painted them to look real. This may appear to us a reasonable way to paint, but it seemed startling and new in his day. Some people objected violently to this new style, but many of the younger artists, both in his day and the years that followed, were so struck by what he did that they painted in his way. They too made figures look like real human beings, moving near us as though they were in the same space as ourselves. These figures are painted as though there were no separation between ourselves and the work of art. The followers of Caravaggio also used light to make their figures seem like solid objects with empty space between them. Light was used for dramatic effects. By illuminating certain figures, Caravaggio indicated the important ones, making the picture clear and memorable.

Malle Bobbe (date unknown), by Frans Hals. Metropolitan Museum of Art, New York City.

The Conversion of Saint Paul (1601?), by Caravaggio. Church of Santa Maria del Popolo, Rome.

Caravaggio painted at the beginning of the 17th century, and his work seems much more simple than later baroque art. In many ways Caravaggio laid the foundations for the complex works of sculpture and architecture—as well as painting—that followed.

One area in which later Italian baroque artists excelled was ceiling decoration. An outstanding example is the painted ceiling of the church of Sant'Ignazio in Rome, painted by Andrea Pozzo (1642–1709). Looking up at the ceiling, we get even more of a sense of distant spaces and the vast expanse of heaven than we could by looking through the telescopes used at that time. Columns and arches appear to tower far above our heads, but these columns, which seem to reach far into the sky, are not real but painted ones.

The four continents Asia, Africa, Europe, and America are shown as human beings. These large figures dominate what seems to be hundreds of figures swirling and rising higher and higher into the painted sky. In the distance is the small figure of Saint Ignatius being received into heaven. Everything leads to this one crucial point, so that the scene is clear even though it includes many forms and many rich and gay colors: icy pinks, light greens and blues, silver, plum, chocolate-brown, and gold.

Bernini

Giovanni Lorenzo Bernini (1598–1680) was one of the most brilliant and energetic of all the 17th-century artists. A painter, sculptor, and architect, Bernini is said to have

Landscape with the Flight into Egypt (1647) by Claude Lorrain. Royal Gallery, Dresden.

Head of a Young Girl (1665?) by Jan Vermeer. Royal Picture Gallery, The Hague.

Peasant Dance (1636–40) by Peter Paul Rubens. Prado Museum, Madrid.

written music, composed operas, and even designed stage sets. All of Bernini's many interests can be seen in his work as a sculptor and architect.

The *Vision of Saint Theresa* shows an angel appearing to the saint. The sculpture is presented as a scene on the high altar of a chapel. This chapel is built to resemble a theater so that if we enter it we are part of the audience. A stage is suggested by a great, gilt-bronze frame that curves forward in our direction. A beam of light shines down on the two carved figures, whose gestures lead us into the action on stage. But we are not all of the audience. Carved on the walls of the chapel are figures seated in theater boxes. They too are aware of the miracle being enacted before their eyes and ours.

As an architect Bernini makes us actually become the actors on a stage he builds for us. One of the largest and most splendid churches in the world, St. Peter's in Rome, gives us a sense of acting in an important occasion. Bernini was responsible for much of what we see and feel in this church. Many of the colored marbles, paintings, gilt-bronze ornaments, and sculpture were made by him or his assistants and followers.

Bernini also designed the large square in front of St. Peter's. Two fountains with sparkling jets of water are placed as accents in the wide, open space before the entrance. As an approach to the church, he built a great curving colonnade on either side of the square. The colonnade was made low in height and simple in shape to set off the façade of the church, which seems to rise as steeply as a mountain.

▶ FRENCH ARTISTS IN ITALY

Nicolas Poussin (1594–1665), a Frenchman, was one of the greatest of the many foreign artists who traveled to Rome in the 17th century. Many artists were attracted to Italy and especially to Rome. Some made rather short journeys; others, like Poussin, stayed the rest of their lives. These foreign artists helped to spread all over Europe a feeling for the new kinds of art produced by such men as Caravaggio and Bernini.

Poussin is typical of a large and important group of artists. These men looked very carefully both at the new art of their time and also at the works of earlier men, as far back as the ancient Romans. Poussin loved Rome and the Roman countryside, the river valleys, and the nearby mountains. He studied and sketched the ruins of ancient buildings and drew copies of ancient statues. He thought of the gods and goddesses of Greece, the heroes of Roman legends, the figures of the Bible as having lived in just this kind of setting. He painted them as they might have been, wearing Roman costumes and living in Roman buildings in the city or country.

Bernini once spoke of Poussin as a great storyteller who always worked with his mind. Poussin read and thought about the real meaning of stories and then worked steadily to find the very best way of telling his story as a painter. He felt that tragic or sad stories should be painted in a sober, severe way. Gay and happy subjects he painted in a more cheerful, lively manner, with glowing lights and colors and flowers sprinkled about as graceful ornaments.

Whatever the subject he chose, Poussin always organized his paintings very carefully, building them as firmly as a carpenter. In the *Holy Family on the Steps,* each figure is very clearly formed and is part of a group that is as stable and solid as a pyramid. The pyramid is balanced by the flat, horizontal steps and by the high, vertical columns above. The whole painting seems exactly right, so perfectly balanced that no single part could be changed even a fraction of an inch without destroying the effect of the whole work.

However, Poussin was a man of the 17th century who shared many ideas with the artists of his own day. Like other baroque painters he often used strong lights and deep shadows. His colors are deep, rich, and glowing. Poussin's paintings show a feeling for space and atmosphere—looking at his paintings we feel a part of them. In the *Holy Family on the Steps,* he has placed a group of objects so near our eyes that we can almost reach out and touch them. A strong light shines from somewhere on our left—it seems to fall on ourselves as well as on the painted scene before us. In short, we feel as close a connection with this work as we do with Caravaggio's *Saint Paul;* Poussin has simply used other means for the same end.

Another French artist, who spent most of

his working life in Rome, was Claude Lorrain (1600–82), called Claude. His interest was entirely in landscapes or scenes with rivers or seaports and harbors.

Claude, an orphan, went to Rome to work as a pastry cook, but he became an apprentice landscape painter instead. His love of nature and his eye for composition gave his paintings an agreeable sweetness. His *Landscape with the Flight into Egypt* is pleasant to look at. The peaceful countryside has a little river winding its way back into the distance, and trees and bushes placed at just the right points lead our eyes back toward the horizon, where land and sky meet. A longer look at such paintings shows us the quiet seriousness beneath their surface sweetness.

▶ SPANISH ART

Diego Velázquez (1599–1660), court painter to King Philip IV of Spain, is best known for his many royal portraits, but he treated every subject with equal interest and respect. His pictures of beggars or soldiers, dwarfs or tiny children have just as much dignity as those of the King himself. In every case Velázquez painted with a great concern for the actual way we see. He was interested in changes in light and shade and the effects of these changes on color and form.

Velázquez used his paintbrush very freely. Thin, broad strokes or long, tapering ribbons of paint are laid easily on the canvas. Almost magically these strokes fuse together. When we look at one of Velázquez' portraits, such as the one of Pope Innocent X, we feel that we are in the same room with the person at the very moment he was painted. The result of Velázquez' sensitivity to what he saw and his way of painting is that we believe what he shows us. We feel that we know as much as can be known of his people from the way they look at a given moment.

Two other famous Spanish painters of the 17th century were José Ribera (1591–1652) and Francisco de Zurbarán (1598–1664). These artists painted religious pictures with strong dramatic lighting and realistic details that are similar to Caravaggio's.

▶ NORTHERN BAROQUE ART

The northern counterpart of Bernini in Italy was Peter Paul Rubens (1577–1640) in Flanders. He was equally brilliant. Rubens produced a vast number of works by training many younger artists who learned from him by working with and assisting him.

All Rubens' drawings, oil sketches, and paintings reveal his great sense of pleasure and enjoyment of everything he saw. In his *Peasant Dance* we can almost feel the ground shake as the great circle of dancing people wheels forward and away from us in the golden light spreading all over the land.

One of Rubens' most gifted younger artists was Anthony Van Dyck. Like Velázquez he is best known for his portraits of royalty. Van Dyck painted King Charles I of England and his court with such grace, elegance, and distinction that they are always remembered as he saw and recorded them.

▶ DUTCH ART

The cackling laugh we seem to hear in the vigorous painting of an old fishwife, *Malle Bobbe,* by Frans Hals (1580–1666) is a far cry from the quiet, gentle, rather sad figures by Van Dyck. Frans Hals and all the Dutch took pride in their independence. The people of the tiny Dutch Republic had fought long and bravely for their freedom and had earned all the good things of life they knew in this period. One of the things they valued most was painting. And hundreds of artists provided many different kinds of paintings for them. Some painters specialized in landscapes, some in seascapes. Some painted flowers or fruits and flowers; others, animals. Some painters recorded buildings, while still others presented scenes from everyday life.

No matter what the subject matter is, almost every Dutch painting is really a portrait —a record of the people, places, or objects that were part of Dutch life.

In Frans Hals's portraits we feel the same interest and closeness to the subject as in Caravaggio's paintings or Bernini's sculpture. But all the noise, fun, and gaiety of Hals's portraits are absent in the paintings of Jan Vermeer (1632–75). Vermeer's paintings are as quiet and orderly as those of Nicolas Poussin. Vermeer's subjects are very different from Poussin's large historical paintings but they have the same feeling of seriousness. In the *Head of a Young Girl,* the sphere of the girl's pearl earring echoes the perfect shape

An early self-portrait by Rembrandt van Rijn, painted about 1629. Royal Picture Gallery, The Hague.

A later Rembrandt self-portrait (1658). The Frick Collection, New York.

of her whole head and her dark eyes. Vermeer repeats the same shape in different kinds of objects to show the basic order of all things.

Vermeer studied with great care the effect of light on different textures—on crusty bread or creamy milk. He shows the number of colors reflected on a bare plaster wall and the brightness of colors even in shadows. But Vermeer never let these careful observations clutter his paintings. Everything in his paintings is controlled to make a thoughtfully arranged scene. The perfection of Vermeer's paintings makes the few examples of them that remain with us today both rare and precious.

Rembrandt

Fortunately, hundreds of drawings, prints, and paintings exist to show the astonishing genius of Rembrandt van Rijn (1606–69).

Rembrandt seems to have been interested in everything in his world—from pigs and elephants to a side of beef, from quiet, sunny landscapes to stormy scenes on rainy days. He drew, painted, or prepared prints of these subjects and countless others, but his constant interest was always in human beings. Rembrandt studied and recorded human beings of all sorts and kinds, of all ages and types, in every kind of situation: a tiny child tottering unsteadily in its first steps or an old, worn, blind man. Some of these records are merely swift pen sketches; others are formal paintings of single persons or groups of people.

Rembrandt made studies of his own appearance from the time he was a gay and lively young artist until he was a very tired and ill old man. In these self-portraits Rembrandt never made himself look handsome or brave. He was always honest and used these many studies to train his hand in recording what he saw and to increase his understanding of himself and other people.

Rembrandt was deeply religious. The scenes and figures of the Bible were profoundly important to him. Most of his countrymen in Holland were Protestants who felt that religious figures and scenes should not be represented in art. But Rembrandt interpreted what he read and believed in the Bible in his own way, as an artist.

His way of presenting religious scenes changed as he grew older and wiser. Some of his paintings done as a young man are like a splendid theatrical performance, with the figures in colorful, rich clothes. In 1631 Rembrandt painted a picture of Christ appearing before his disciples after the Crucifixion. The disciples are shocked and frightened. Their gestures are dramatic—Rembrandt painted them as though they were actors recreating the scene under powerful spotlights. But in his later works Rembrandt told stories in simpler and more human terms. He painted the same scene again in 1648. This time, however, the disciples sit quietly, and the face of Christ reflects his great suffering.

▶ FRANCE

The French King Louis XIV was determined to make his country the strongest in all Europe. From the very beginning of his long reign, Louis XIV thought of the arts as an important part of his campaign. He encouraged painting, sculpture, and architecture to provide an appropriate setting for himself as the new monarch.

In the late 17th century, France became the new center of artistic interest. French art became known, admired, and copied all over Europe. Louis XIV appointed a very able man, Charles Le Brun (1619–90), his superintendent of the arts. Le Brun acted for the King in supervising everything from a new factory for tapestries to the training of young artists in the Academy of Fine Arts in Paris and the French Academy in Rome.

The Chateau of Versailles is evidence of Le Brun's energetic activity for the King. An army of workmen and the talents of dozens of artists were organized to create this new palace. What was once a small hunting lodge was enormously enlarged and transformed into a city-palace. Dozens and dozens of rooms and hundreds of acres of gardens are all connected with one another in a design that is as clear and orderly as it is huge and ambitious. Gardens with terraces, pools, and fountains seem to stretch for miles in the distance. The paths of the gardens and the three highways that lead to the palace are all directed toward the royal apartments.

▶ LATER BAROQUE ART

In the 17th and 18th centuries, the Portuguese and the Spaniards brought the baroque style to their colonies in South America. The cathedrals built during this time combined the native artistic tradition with the baroque. The abundance of the carved and gilded ornaments that decorate these churches was especially influenced by the old native crafts.

In Europe itself the baroque style did not die with the closing years of the 17th century. It was carried forward and flourished especially in Germany and Austria, and then became the basis for the new style that developed in the course of the early 18th century. This style was called rococo, a lighter, more fragile, and decorative form of art than the baroque art of the 17th century.

ELEANOR D. BARTON
Chairman, Department of Art
Sweet Briar College

See also ARCHITECTURE: DECORATIVE ARTS; PAINTING; SCULPTURE.

BAROQUE MUSIC

"Baroque" is a term used to describe the music of the period extending roughly from 1600 to 1750. The word originally was used to describe the architecture of the 17th century, which was heavy and elaborate in style and full of decoration and ornamental details. Musical compositions during this period were often huge and elaborate, and often required a great number of singers and players to perform them. The melodies were complicated and had highly ornamented passages. The way in which voices and instruments were combined often resulted in complex musical patterns. The characteristics of this music seemed to resemble those of baroque architecture. Musical scholars decided, therefore, that the word baroque could also be used to identify the music of that time.

The baroque era includes all the music from the time of Claudio Monteverdi in the late 16th century to Johann Sebastian Bach and George Frederick Handel in the 18th. Many of the most important musical forms were developed during this period. These forms include the sonata, symphony, concerto, suite, opera, oratorio, and many others.

The composers of baroque music struggled to express intense human emotions such as rage, passionate love, fear, exaltation, awe, wonder, joy, and despair. As a result, music became much more dramatic than it had ever been before. Furthermore, secular music came to be regarded as equally important as—if not more than—religious music. While most of the best music of earlier times was composed for the church, a great quantity of baroque music was composed for other purposes.

▶ THE NEW MUSIC

The new music of the baroque era started in Florence, Italy, near the end of the 16th century. There a group of amateur poets, musicians, and painters met to discuss art, music, and the drama. This little group, known as the Florentine Camerata, wanted to revive ancient classical Greek drama. They knew that Greek drama had been accompanied by music, but they were not sure what kind of music it was or how it was used in the drama. In imitation of the Greeks, they decided to write plays based on classical subjects and to set the plays to music. Polyphony, the musical style of that day, was poorly suited for this purpose. Polyphony is a Greek word meaning the sounding together of many different sounds. In polyphonic music several melodies in combination are sung together at the same time. In polyphonic music it was difficult to hear the words clearly. Can you imagine a musical play in which all the singers sing their parts to different melodies at the same time? Of course the words would not be clearly understood and no one would be able to follow the story.

A new kind of music, then, was needed and it was soon invented. It was called **recitative.** It consisted of a single melodic line for a solo voice with a simple instrumental accompaniment. Through the recitative, words could be clearly expressed and the story could be easily followed.

The composers of the Florentine Camerata began writing this new kind of music for classical dramas. But instead of reproducing the drama of ancient Greece as they had hoped, they produced something entirely new—the opera.

▶ VOCAL MUSIC

The world's first opera was *Dafne.* It was the work of two members of the Florentine Camerata. The poet Ottavio Rinuccini wrote the play. Jacopo Peri (1561–1633) composed the music. *Dafne* was first performed in 1597. Unfortunately it has been lost, but Peri's second opera, *Euridice* (1600), still exists. The success of both *Dafne* and *Euridice* removed any doubt that opera was to become an important form of music.

Opera now needed the imagination of a musical genius. Such a genius soon appeared in Claudio Monteverdi (1567–1643). Monteverdi was the most daring composer of his time. Only a decade after the first performance of Peri's *Dafne,* Monteverdi composed an opera that is still performed. That opera is *Orfeo,* which was first performed in Mantua, Italy, on February 22, 1607. Monteverdi was the first to write ensemble numbers such as duets and trios, and to give an important role to the orchestra. With orchestral interludes Monteverdi created the mood of a whole scene. He made expressive use of colorful orchestral effects. He enlarged the orchestra and developed new techniques of performance. For this reason many people consider Monteverdi the father of the symphony orchestra.

Monteverdi's music possessed a human element not found in Peri's operas. He expressed human emotions through his music so well that audiences were said to burst into tears sometimes at a performance of one of his operas. Monteverdi showed the same power of expression in his wonderful madrigals, for which he is equally famous.

The opera developed rapidly. In Naples Alessandro Scarlatti (1660–1725) established many of the traditions of Italian opera that later composers followed. In France Jean Baptiste Lully (1632–87) laid the foundations of French opera. Lully emphasized the drama in his operas and gave the orchestra a more important part. He also established the ballet in French opera. In England Henry Purcell (1659–95) composed *Dido and Aeneas* (1689), which has remained the most important English opera.

While baroque musicians created opera, they also enriched church music. They developed large new forms such as the oratorio and the Passion. These required choruses, recitatives, solo and ensemble numbers, and orchestral interludes and accompaniment. Both the oratorio and the Passion were dramatizations of Bible stories. They were meant to be performed usually without scenery or costumes.

The Oratorio

The oratorio got its name from the place where some of the earliest oratorios were first performed. The place was the oratory of St. Philip Neri's Church in Rome. Here in the late 16th century, composers began to write music for dramatized stories from the Bible. The early oratorios were very simple in design. The first composer to write a fully developed oratorio was Giacomo Carissimi (1605–74).

A favorite solo instrument of the baroque age was the harpsichord. It also played an important part in the performance of chamber music and orchestral works.

Carissimi's oratorio *Jephtha* (about 1660) established some of the traditions that later oratorio composers followed. Carissimi was one of the first to leave out scenery and costumes (oratorios given at St. Philip Neri's Church had been staged). He was also one of the first to use the narrator, who kept the story moving. Finally, he was one of the first to write dramatic and expressive choruses. For these reasons Carissimi's *Jephtha* is considered the first modern oratorio.

The Passion

The Passion was a musical setting of Christ's Passion according to the Gospels. It had been used occasionally by the Renaissance composers but it underwent great change in the baroque era. The Passion of the Renaissance was a composition for an unaccompanied chorus. The baroque Passion, however, added solo voices and orchestra. A new kind of episode was also introduced—the chorale. The church congregation was supposed to join in the singing of the chorales. Heinrich Schütz (1585–1672) was the first important composer of Passions. Schütz studied in Italy, and was strongly influenced by the Italian composers, especially Monteverdi. Besides Passions and many other works, he wrote music for all the psalms in the Bible.

The Cantata

The cantata was another important musical form that developed in the baroque era. It began as a secular form of music. Carissimi realized that many churches did not have enough musicians to perform large works like the oratorio. He therefore introduced the cantata into the church. The cantata was a small composition that required only a few musicians to perform. They were composed for one or two solo voices accompanied by a small instrumental group. These pieces usually began with an introduction for instruments alone. Contrasting sections consisting of recitatives and arias followed. Church cantatas were based on biblical texts.

The cantata became very popular in 17th- and 18th-century church music. Its form was perfected by Dietrich Buxtehude (1637–1707). Many of Buxtehude's cantatas use chorale melodies of the Lutheran Church. Next to Heinrich Schütz, Buxtehude is Germany's finest composer of church music before Bach. The most famous Italian composer of cantatas was Alessandro Scarlatti, who is better known for his operas. Scarlatti wrote 600 or more cantatas in addition to over 100 operas and about 150 oratorios.

The Aria

Arias were usually in A-B-A form; that is, the first part was repeated after the end of the contrasting second, or middle, part. These are called *da capo* arias, a form that became very common in baroque opera, cantata, and other vocal music. *Da capo* means to repeat from the beginning of a piece. In the *da capo* aria singers often had an opportunity to show off their skill in singing high notes and difficult florid passages called coloraturas.

▶ INSTRUMENTAL MUSIC

In the baroque era instrumental and vocal music became equally important for the first time. Probably nothing else in this period has had more far-reaching effects than the development of instrumental music. As in vocal music, all the baroque instrumental forms began in Italy. Baroque composers developed music with only one melody and a supporting accompaniment. This style of music allowed composers to give more attention to inventing new and interesting harmonies.

The Figured Bass

The importance of harmony in the baroque era is shown in a new kind of harmonic notation called the figured bass. It was so widely used that the baroque era in music is sometimes called the figured-bass period. It was used in both instrumental and vocal music. Figured bass is a kind of musical shorthand. The composer indicated the harmony by writing figures (numbers and letters) under the bass part below the staff. Only the melody and bass needed to be written out in the musical score. The keyboard player, who played the bass part with the left hand, filled in the harmony according to the figures. As the system of notation became more complicated so did the harmony. In baroque music, therefore, we can see the beginnings and early development of modern harmony.

Renaissance composers like Giovanni Gabrieli (1557–1612) and Jan Pieters Sweelinck

Often several kinds of instruments were used in the performance of baroque church music.

(1562–1621) wrote many pieces for the organ. But they wrote them in the polyphonic vocal style, as though the organ were a combination of human voices rather than an instrument. Beginning with Girolamo Frescobaldi (1583–1643), however, composers of organ music began to develop a distinctly instrumental style of writing. They emphasized the tonal qualities for which the organ was best suited. In doing this Frescobaldi perfected some of the chief forms of organ music. These included the organ toccata, fugue, and partita.

Frescobaldi's most important successor was Buxtehude. With Buxtehude, organ music reached a stage of development that remained unsurpassed until Johann Sebastian Bach. Music for instruments other than the organ also had to develop a non-vocal style before it became independent from vocal music.

Instrumental music developed rapidly because brilliant new stringed instruments were being made by the famous violin-making families of Cremona, Italy. First the Amati family and later the Guarnieri and Stradivari families made wonderful new violins, violas, and cellos. These instruments have never been surpassed for their beautiful tone and perfect craftsmanship. The most renowned of all violin makers is Antonio Stradivari (1644–1737). One of his violins is worth several thousands of dollars today.

The Sonata and the Concerto

Early in the baroque era a new musical idea emerged for which a new term was invented —sonata. A sonata was a composition that could be performed only on an instrument, just as the cantata was a piece of music that was meant only to be sung. Once composers started making this distinction, they began to develop a strictly instrumental style completely different from vocal music.

The first master to do so was Arcangelo Corelli (1653–1713). Corelli was the foremost violin virtuoso of his time and the first important composer of violin music. He produced two epoch-making works. One of these consisted of 12 sonatas for violin and keyboard accompaniment. In these sonatas a new style of violin performance was demonstrated fully for the first time. His second great contribution was a set of 12 *concerti grossi* (grand concertos) for a combination of instruments. Corelli's violin sonatas and concertos were the ancestors of the later solo sonata and the classical concerto.

The practice of contrasting the tone color of instruments with each other, singly or in groups, was a baroque invention. For the first time on a large scale the special tone quality of individual instruments was fully used. This formed the basis upon which modern orchestral writing was built. Baroque composers wrote many concertos for violin, flute, cello, and keyboard. Later in the period, concertos for other instruments such as the horn and the oboe also became popular.

The sonata and the concerto developed rapidly. The leading composers were Antonio Vivaldi (1675?–1741), Giuseppe Tartini (1692–1770), and Domenico Scarlatti (1685–1757), the son of Alessandro. Scarlatti was the first important composer in Italy to write sonatas for a keyboard instrument. He also created a brilliant new style of keyboard writing and perfected a new technique of performing on the harpsichord.

The Dance Suite

Outside of Italy, too, great advances were being made in instrumental music. Composers were creating a treasury of smaller pieces for keyboard instruments. These pieces were often based on dances. Composers began to arrange them in groups called suites. The dance suite consisted of several dance movements contrasting in mood, tempo, and rhythm. The basic arrangement consisted of four dances: an allemande in moderate tempo; a courante, or running dance; a slow and stately saraband; and a quick and lively gigue, or jig. Composers often added dances between the saraband and gigue, such as the minuet, gavotte, bourrée, or passepied. Outstanding composers of dance suites and other beautiful keyboard pieces were Johann Froberger (1617–67) in Germany, Henry Purcell in England, and François Couperin (1668–1733) and Jean Philippe Rameau (1683–1764) in France.

▶ HANDEL AND BACH

Baroque music reached a climax with two of the greatest composers who have ever lived: George Frederick Handel (1685–1759) and Johann Sebastian Bach (1685–1750). With these giant creators, baroque music came to its final fulfillment. With Handel, opera in the old Italian tradition reached its highest development. Henceforth opera would develop in completely new directions. With Handel, too, the oratorio—and with Bach the Passion—reached a stage of perfection upon which it was not possible to improve.

Few composers before Bach and Handel wrote instrumental music with such expressiveness, emotion, and beauty. Both these masters composed sonatas, concertos, suites, and solo instrumental music that fully achieved all the possibilities of the baroque style. They also pointed the way for the future. Bach and Handel not only represent the end of the baroque era, they anticipate the beginnings of the classical period that followed.

DAVID EWEN
Music Historian

BARRIE, SIR JAMES MATTHEW (1860–1937)

James Matthew Barrie, the creator of Peter Pan, was born in the Scottish town of Kirriemuir on May 9, 1860, the son of a local weaver. When James was six, his older brother David was drowned in a skating accident. Their mother was heartbroken, but consoled herself with the idea that in dying so young, David would remain a boy forever. It was this idea that Barrie later turned into his most famous play, *Peter Pan*.

Barrie knew from an early age that he wanted to be a writer. He was graduated from Edinburgh University in 1882, and in 1885 he moved to London and began writing novels. The most famous was *The Little Minister* (1891). But Barrie is best known as a writer for the stage. His first successful play, *Walker, London* (1892), was followed by *The Admirable Crichton* (1902), *What Every Woman Knows* (1908), and *Dear Brutus* (1917).

Barrie married the actress Mary Ansell in 1894, but they had no children of their own. One day in the summer of 1898, while walking his dog in Kensington Gardens, Barrie met three young brothers, George, Jack, and Peter. Their parents, Arthur and Sylvia Llewelyn Davies, and the Barries soon became friends. The story of Peter Pan had been in Barrie's mind since childhood, and now he started writing it as a play to entertain the Davies boys. But instead of making Peter a tragic boy who *could* not grow up, Barrie changed him into the carefree boy who *would* not grow up. *Peter Pan* was first performed in London on December 27, 1904, and it has been revived at Christmastime ever since.

Barrie was created a baronet in 1913. In 1929 he donated the entire copyright in *Peter Pan* to a London children's hospital. He died on June 19, 1937.

ANDREW BIRKIN
Author, *J. M. Barrie and the Lost Boys*

See also PETER PAN.

BARRYMORE FAMILY

Ethel Barrymore said of herself and her brothers Lionel and John: "We became actors not because we wanted to go on the stage, but because it was the thing we could do best."

The Barrymores said that their family went back to the strolling players of Shakespeare's day. They made the name Barrymore a synonym for actor, although they appeared together only twice—in a childhood production of *Camille* in an old barn, and 45 years later in the 1932 film *Rasputin and the Empress*.

Ethel Barrymore (1879–1959) became a star at the age of 21 in *Captain Jinks of the Horse Marines*. She appeared in a series of drawing-room comedies before graduating to plays by Barrie, Ibsen, and Shakespeare. She crowned her stage career in 1940 as the spirited schoolteacher in Emlyn Williams' *The Corn is Green*. During her later years in films, she won an Academy Award for *None But the Lonely Heart*.

Lionel Barrymore (1878–1954) preferred painting to acting. He disliked romantic roles, and with his first hit as an Italian organ grinder in *The Mummy and the Humming Bird* in 1902, he established himself as a skillful character actor. In 1918 he made a great hit as Milt Shanks in *The Copperhead*, followed by *The Jest* in 1919 (with his brother), *Macbeth* (1921), and *The Claw* (1921). After that he devoted most of his time to motion pictures. When a broken hip and rheumatism confined him to a wheelchair, he won an even greater following as Dr. Gillespie in the Dr. Kildare film series.

Stunning portrayals of Richard III and Hamlet established John Barrymore (1882–1942) as one of the greatest actors of the English-speaking stage. But in the 1920's, he fled to Hollywood—where the pay was better and the work less demanding. He starred in a variety of films, including *Grand Hotel* (1932) and *Twentieth Century* (1934). His charm, his classic profile, and his 'headline romances added a new chapter to the Barrymore legend—a legend that lives on in younger generations of Barrymores.

JAMES KOTSILIBAS-DAVIS
Author, *The Barrymores: The Royal Family in Hollywood*

BARTÓK, BÉLA (1881–1945)

Béla Bartók, the great 20th-century composer, was born in Nagyszentmiklós, Hungary (now in Rumania), on March 25, 1881. At age 5 he was given his first piano lessons by his mother. Four years later he began to compose.

In 1899, Bartók was admitted to the Academy of Music in Budapest as an advanced student in piano and composition. During 1903, his last year at the academy, he won much praise for his brilliant piano recitals. His symphonic poem *Kossuth,* written in the same year, brought him international recognition.

As a young man, Bartók was greatly influenced by the spirit of Hungarian nationalism. In 1905 he began making field trips to the Hungarian countryside to learn about the folk music of his land. There he discovered that the villagers had often taken the music of neighboring areas of Eastern Europe and mixed it with their own. He began to use the melodies and rhythms of these mixed styles in his compositions, combining them with a new approach to harmony for which he would become famous. Later he collected folk songs from other countries and wrote books on the special features of folk music. His work encouraged other composers to make use of folk music in their own compositions.

In 1907, Bartók was appointed professor of piano at the Academy of Music. Shortly afterward he began to compose the first of his six string quartets, which were completed between 1909 and 1939. They are thought to be among the finest string quartets ever written.

During the 1920's, after studying old Italian keyboard music, Bartók achieved a completely original style of composing. He combined the sounds and rhythms of folk music with the techniques of composers such as Frescobaldi, Beethoven, and Debussy, as in the First Piano Concerto. He also began his *Mikrokosmos,* pieces for piano students.

Political unrest in Hungary caused Bartók to settle in the United States in 1940. For a time he was associated with Columbia University, where he was able to continue his study of folk music. Bartók was also a successful pianist until ill health forced him to stop performing in public. But he made recordings and continued to compose. His popular Concerto for Orchestra was written in 1943. Bartók died in New York City on September 26, 1945.

BENJAMIN SUCHOFF
Author, *Guide to the Mikrokosmos of Béla Bartók*

BARTON, CLARA (1821–1912)

Clara Barton devoted most of her life to helping people. Her greatest accomplishment was the founding of the American Red Cross.

Clarissa Harlowe Barton was born on Christmas Day, 1821, on a farm near Oxford, Massachusetts. The youngest of five children, she received her early education from her brothers and sisters. At the age of 15, Clara became a teacher.

After 18 years of teaching, Clara Barton moved to Washington, D.C., where she worked in the Patent Office. When the Civil War broke out, reports on the suffering of wounded soldiers troubled her. She urged people to contribute medicines and bandages. She often took these supplies to the battlefield herself, caring for the wounded during action.

When the war was over, Clara Barton headed a group that searched for missing soldiers. She also gave lectures on her war experiences. After four years of this work, she became ill and went to Switzerland to recuperate. There she first learned of the international Red Cross, an organization for the relief of suffering caused by war. When the Franco-Prussian War began in 1870, she remained in Europe to work with the Red Cross.

In 1873, Clara Barton returned to the United States. Although she was not well, she devoted all her energy to establishing an American branch of the Red Cross. In 1881 she succeeded and became its first president, serving for over 20 years. As a result of her efforts, the work of the Red Cross was enlarged to aid victims of peacetime disasters such as earthquakes and floods. In 1904, at the age of 83, Clara Barton retired. She died eight years later, on April 12, 1912, at Glen Echo, Maryland.

Reviewed by ALLEN F. DAVIS
Temple University

See also RED CROSS.

BASEBALL

Baseball is called the American "national pastime." Every spring and summer, millions of fans watch professional major-league games in ballparks or on television. There are also professional minor leagues, which serve as a training ground for the "majors," as well as thousands of college, high school, Little League, and other amateur teams. In addition to organized competition for every age group, the game is played on an informal basis in parks, school yards, and sandlots. Hardly a child in the United States has grown up without playing baseball, and hardly an adult is not familiar with at least some of the rules, terms, and stars of "the great American game."

Baseball began in the United States during the mid-1800's. Through the years, baseball has developed a rich and colorful history. The popularity of the game today owes much to its

Articles on BABE RUTH and JACKIE ROBINSON may be found in Volume R of *The New Book of Knowledge*. Biographies of the following baseball players and managers may be found by looking them up in the Index: Hank Aaron, Grover Cleveland Alexander, Johnny Bench, Yogi Berra, Roy Campanella, Rod Carew, Steve Carlton, Roberto Clemente, Ty Cobb, Dizzy Dean, Joe DiMaggio, Bob Feller, Jimmy Foxx, Lou Gehrig, Bob Gibson, Hank Greenberg, Lefty Grove, Rogers Hornsby, Carl Owen Hubbell, Miller James Huggins, Reggie Jackson, Walter Perry Johnson, Sandy Koufax, Mickey Mantle, Roger Maris, Christy Mathewson, Willie Howard Mays, Joseph Vincent McCarthy, Stan Musial, Mel Ott, Satchel Paige, Gaylord Perry, Frank Robinson, Pete Rose, Nolan Ryan, Tom Seaver, Warren Spahn, Tris Speaker, Casey Stengel, Bill Terry, Honus Wagner, Ted Williams, Carl Michael Yastrzemski, and Cy Young.

tradition and folklore. Many fans spend hours recalling dramatic moments and great achievements of the past, reciting statistics, and comparing old-time and present-day stars. Some fans root for the same team for their whole lives, watching games or reading about them in the newspaper every day.

Baseball is so much a part of American life that its terms have been adopted into the everyday speech of the people. "Pinch-hit," "going to bat," and scores of other baseball terms are used even by people who are not well acquainted with the game.

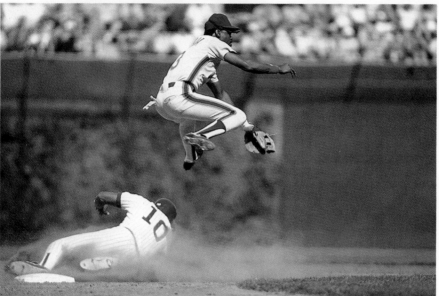

As baseball became the national pastime of the United States, it also spread to other countries. Today the sport is popular in Latin America, Canada, Japan, and elsewhere.

Colorful, exciting, and rich in tradition, baseball is often called the American "national pastime." During the spring and summer, millions of fans flock to major league stadiums to root for their favorite teams. Before the game starts, some youngsters are lucky enough to get the autograph of a star player. When the action begins, attention focuses on the batter (*top right*), the pitcher (*bottom right*), and the fielders (*bottom left*).

▶ HOW BASEBALL IS PLAYED

The basic rules of baseball have undergone little change in more than 100 years. Two teams, consisting of nine or ten players each, play the game on a large field. During the course of the game, the two teams alternate between **batting** (offensive play) and **fielding** (defensive play). The equipment needed to play baseball includes a bat, a ball, and padded gloves worn by players in the field. The object of the game is to score more **runs** than the opposing team. Generally, a run is scored when a batter hits the ball with the bat and runs safely around four bases, starting from home plate. The fielders try to catch the batted ball and halt the runner's progress.

Field and Equipment

A baseball field has two main sections—the **infield** and the **outfield.** The infield is often called the diamond because it contains four bases—called **home plate, first base, second base,** and **third base**—arranged in the shape of a diamond. The outfield extends to a fence or grandstand that encloses the playing area.

The infield and outfield are contained within two straight lines extending diagonally from home plate—one past first base, the other past third base. These two lines are called foul lines. The area between them is **fair territory;** the area outside them is **foul territory.**

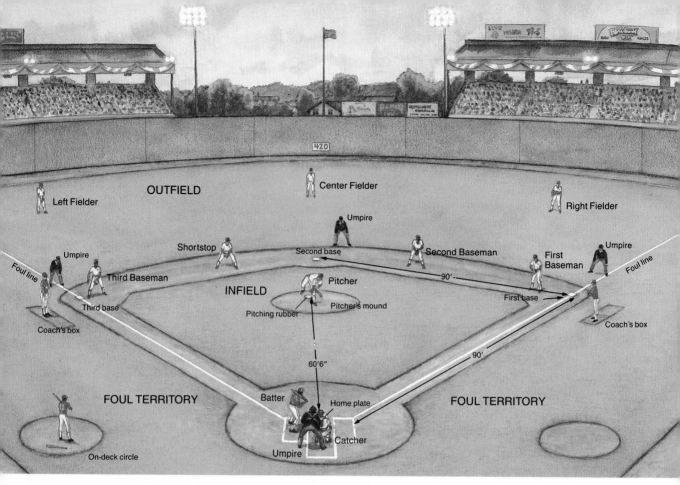

OUTFIELD

Left Fielder

Center Fielder

Right Fielder

Umpire

Shortstop

Second base

Second Baseman

Umpire

Foul line

Umpire

Third Baseman

INFIELD

Pitcher

First Baseman

Foul line

90'

First base

Third base

Pitching rubber

Pitcher's mound

Coach's box

Coach's box

60'6"

90'

FOUL TERRITORY

Batter

Home plate

FOUL TERRITORY

On-deck circle

Umpire

Catcher

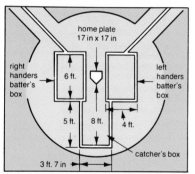

home plate
17 in x 17 in

right
handers
batter's
box

6 ft.

left
handers
batter's
box

5 ft.

8 ft.

4 ft.

catcher's box

3 ft. 7 in

Defensive players occupy nine positions on the field: pitcher, catcher, first base, second base, shortstop, third base, left field, center field, and right field. The batter (offensive team) stands in the "batter's box" (*left*) at home plate and tries to hit the ball beyond the reach of the fielders. Base runners try to advance to home plate, thereby scoring a "run."

cowhide, is stitched on with thick red thread. The ball weighs between 5 and 5¼ ounces (142 and 149 grams) and is 9 to 9¼ inches (23 to 24 centimeters) in circumference.

Until recently, all **bats** had to be made of wood (usually ash but sometimes hackberry or hickory). Today aluminum bats are permitted at every level of competition up to the minor and major leagues, where wood is still required. A bat must be no more than 2¾ inches (7 centimeters) in diameter at the thickest part and no more than 42 inches (107 centimeters) long.

The nine defensive players all wear padded leather **gloves,** or mitts, when they go out in the field. The gloves allow them to catch the ball without hurting their hands. Different fielders use different kinds of gloves.

Baseball uniforms usually include a cap, jersey, knicker-style pants, socks, and shoes. The shoes have metal spikes or rubber cleats on the soles to give the player a solid footing. Batters are required to wear a hard plastic helmet to prevent injury if the ball hits them in the head.

In a standard baseball diamond, each base is 90 feet (27.4 meters) apart. The size of the outfield varies from field to field. In major league stadiums, the outfield fence or grandstand is generally between 300 and 450 feet (91 and 137 meters) from home plate. Except for dirt areas around each base, most of the infield and all of the outfield is grass. (Some major league stadiums use artificial grass.)

An official **baseball** has a cork center, surrounded by layers of rubber and tightly wound yarn. The outer cover, made of bleached white

BASIC BASEBALL EQUIPMENT

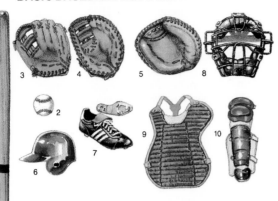

The basic equipment used in baseball includes a wooden or metal bat (1), a ball (2), and leather gloves for fielding. Most fielders use a standard five-fingered glove (3); a first baseman's mitt (4) has a larger "pocket"; a catcher's mitt (5) is round and heavily padded. Other gear includes a batting helmet (6); spiked or cleated shoes (7); and a mask (8), chest protector (9), and leg guards (10) for the catcher.

Players and Positions

Each of the nine players in the field occupies a specific position and performs a specific defensive role. Together they try to keep the team at bat from getting on base and scoring runs.

The main defensive player is the **pitcher.** From a dirt mound in the middle of the diamond, the pitcher throws the ball to the batter. In an effort to keep the batter from hitting it, the pitcher may use a variety of overarm or sidearm pitches—fastballs, curveballs, knuckleballs, and others. The pitcher also fields batted balls (catches and throws them to a teammate), keeps a watchful eye on base runners so they will not advance, and covers first base or home plate when necessary. The pitcher has the most responsibility for seeing that the team at bat does not score. If the pitcher loses control of the game and lets too many opposing players get on base and score

Throwing different kinds of pitches at different speeds, the pitcher tries to keep the batter from hitting the ball. With one foot on the "rubber," the pitcher winds up, takes a long stride toward home plate, and hurls the ball with full force. The motion should be smooth and easy, with a strong follow-through. It is important to end up in a balanced position, ready to field a batted ball.

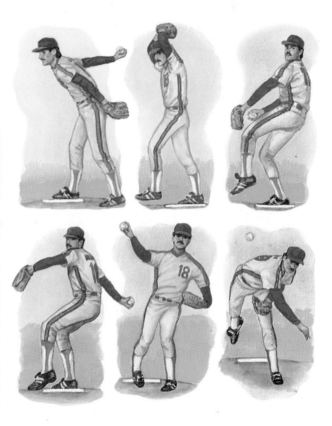

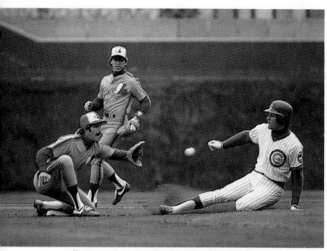

Teamwork in the field is an essential ingredient of winning baseball. *Above:* With the infielder in perfect position, a throw arrives at third base just ahead of the sliding runner. *Below:* An outfielder catches a fly ball as his teammate tries to avoid a collision.

ners who try to score, and to field batted balls that fall near home plate. The catcher must play in close harmony with the pitcher. The catcher studies opposing batters and gives signals to the pitcher indicating what type of pitches to throw. The catcher wears a metal face mask, a padded chest protector, and plastic shin guards to prevent injury from balls tipped by the bat. The catcher's mitt is very thickly padded because pitches are thrown very fast.

Four other members of the defensive team are called infielders. These players try to catch any balls hit by the batter within the infield. The **first baseman** guards first base and the area around it. The **second baseman** plays on the side of second base toward first, while the **shortstop** plays on the other side of second base; together they defend the middle of the infield. The **third baseman** covers third base and the area around it.

Finally, three players called outfielders try to catch any balls hit over or past the infielders. These players are the **left fielder** (on the third-base side), the **center fielder,** and the **right fielder.**

For the offensive team, players take their turns at bat in an order listed before the game starts. This batting order, or **lineup,** normally consists of nine players who also have positions in the field. But because pitchers are not usually good hitters, the American League in 1973 decided to allow another player—the "designated hitter"—to bat instead of the pitcher. This created a ten-player team. The designated hitter does not play a fielding position.

If substitute batters, called **"pinch hitters,"** come into the game, they normally bat in the same places in the lineup as the players they replace. But if two or more substitutes (other than pinch hitters) enter at the same time, they can be inserted in any vacant spots in the lineup.

The person in charge of the players and strategies for each team is the **manager,** often a former player. The manager sets the team's lineup, makes substitutions, and directs many plays on the field. The manager also has several coaches, who help train members of the team in skills and strategies. During a game, coaches stand just outside first base and third base, where they make hand signals to base runners and batters.

runs, the starting pitcher may be replaced by a relief pitcher.

The next most important defensive player is the **catcher,** who crouches in a boxed area behind home plate. The catcher's job is to catch all the pitcher's throws that are not hit by the batter, to guard home plate against run-

Every batter has his or her own way of standing at the plate, gripping the bat, and swinging. All good batters assume a balanced position and concentrate fully on the pitch. In the split second it takes the ball to reach home plate, the batter must decide whether or not to swing. If the batter decides to swing, the bat begins to level out as the ball approaches. When contact is made, the batter's head should be down, eyes still focused on the ball. A quick snap of the wrists and a full follow-through add power and distance to the hit. Once contact has been made and the swing is completed, the hitter drops the bat and runs toward first base.

Conduct of Play and Basic Rules

The visiting team takes the first turn at bat. It remains at bat until the home team, fielding, has gotten three **outs** (put out three visiting players). The home team then bats until three of its players have been put out. When each team has had a turn at bat and a turn in the field, one **inning** is over.

A complete baseball game normally consists of nine innings. However, if the home team is ahead after 8½ innings or takes the lead in the last half (or "bottom") of the ninth inning, then the home team is automatically the winner, and the game is over. Also, if play is stopped because of rain or any other reason after five innings (4½ innings if the home team is ahead), the game is considered complete; if play is stopped before five innings of play, the game is continued at a later date. Finally, if the score is tied at the end of nine innings, the game goes on until the tie is broken and both teams have had an equal number of times at bat.

The focus of action in any baseball game is the confrontation between pitcher and batter. The batter stands in a boxed area on either side of home plate, depending on whether he or she bats right-handed or left-handed. The

The strike zone is the area directly over home plate between the top of the shoulders and the top of the uniform pants to the top of the knees. If the batter does not swing at a pitch in this zone, the umpire calls a "strike." If the pitch is outside the strike zone, the umpire calls a "ball."

pitcher throws the ball toward the batter, and the batter tries to hit it. The pitcher aims the ball at an area called the **strike zone.** To be in the strike zone, the ball must pass over home plate within an area extending from the midpoint between the top of the batter's shoulders and the top of the uniform pants to the top of the knees. If the pitch passes through the strike zone and the batter does not swing, a **strike** is called on the batter. A strike is also called if the batter swings at the ball and misses, or if the batter hits the ball into foul territory. The batter is out when three strikes have been made. (A foul ball is not counted as the third strike unless it is a foul bunt or a foul tip caught by the catcher before it touches the ground.)

There are other ways in which a batter can be put out. If the batter hits a ball in the air (fair or foul) that is caught before it touches the ground, the batter is said to have "flied out." If the batter hits a fair ground ball that is caught by a fielder and then thrown or carried to first base before the batter gets there, the batter is said to have "grounded out."

There are also a number of ways in which a batter can get on base. If a batted ball lands in fair territory and the batter reaches first base before the fielder gets the ball there, the batter has made a **single.** If the batter can reach second base safely on the same hit, it is a **double.** If the batter can reach third base, it is a **triple.** A fair ball hit over the fence or into the stands is a **home run.** The batter can also make a home run by hitting a fair ball onto the playing field and running around all the bases before the fielders get the ball back to home plate. This exciting (and rare) play is an "inside-the-park" home run. Any single, double, triple, or home run is called a **hit.**

A batter sometimes can proceed to first base without getting a hit. Each pitch to the batter that passes outside the strike zone is called a **ball.** After four balls, the batter is credited with a **walk** and advances freely to first base. The batter also is awarded first base if hit by a pitched ball; if interfered with by the catcher; or if the catcher drops the ball on a third strike and fails to throw it to first base before the batter arrives there.

In addition to pitching, fielding, and batting, **base running** is an important part of the game of baseball. Once a batter gets on base, the object is to advance to each of the next bases and finally to score a run by reaching home plate. Base runners may advance to the next base any time they think they can do so safely. Usually they wait until the batter hits the ball and then decide whether or not to try to advance. On a fly ball, however, they must wait (**"tag up"**) at the last base they held until the ball is caught; after tagging up, they may run to the next base. If a runner advances to the next base without the aid of a batted ball or a fielder's error, the runner is said to **"steal"** a base.

But base runners must always be alert because the fielding team can put them out in several ways. Base runners are out if they are tagged with the ball by a fielder when they are off base or if they go outside the base lines to avoid being tagged. Base runners also can be "forced out." For example, if the runner is on first base and the batter hits a ground ball, the runner must advance to second base so that

A "play at the plate" is one of the most thrilling in baseball. As a base runner slides into home, the catcher receives a throw from another fielder and tries to tag the runner before his foot touches the plate. The two players collide in a cloud of dust, and the umpire signals "safe" (*as left*) or "out."

BASEBALL TERMS*

Assist: A play by one fielder that makes it possible for another to make a put-out.

Balk: An illegal motion by the pitcher, entitling base runners to advance one base each.

Bases loaded: When there is a runner at each base.

Battery: A team's pitcher and catcher.

Batting average: Number of hits divided by times at bat (as: 18/60 = .300). If a batter reaches base safely on an error or fielder's choice, the batter does not get credit for a hit. If the batter hits a sacrifice or gets a base on balls or is hit by a pitched ball, the batter is not charged with a time at bat.

Bullpen: A special area where relief pitchers warm up.

Bunt: A batted ball tapped with the bat rather than hit with force.

Doubleheader: Two games played consecutively on a single day.

Double play (DP): A play in which the batter and a runner, or two runners, are put out.

Dugout: The seating area, often below the level of the playing field, reserved for players, managers, and coaches.

Earned run: Any run scored except one that results from a fielding misplay.

Earned run average (ERA): Number of earned runs charged against a pitcher divided by total innings pitched times 9 (as: $10/50 \times 9 = 1.80$).

Error: Any play on which a fielder misses a reasonable opportunity to put out a batter or runner, or a misplay that allows a runner to advance.

Fielder's choice: An attempt by the fielder of a fair ground ball to put out a runner instead of the batter who hit the ball.

Fielding average: Total put-outs and assists divided by total chances (put-outs, assists, and errors)

(as: $\frac{66 + 33}{66 + 33 + 1} = \frac{99}{100} = .990$).

Force play: A play in which a runner is put out when forced to advance to the next base to make room for the next runner.

Full count: When there are three balls and two strikes on the batter.

Grand slam: A home run with the bases loaded.

Infield fly: A fair fly ball hit above the infield when there are runners on first and second or on all three bases and there is not more than one out. The umpire declares "infield fly," and the batter is automatically out.

Line drive: A ball hit in the air but on a straight line, usually not far off the ground.

No-hitter: A game in which the pitcher does not give up a single hit.

Passed ball: A failure of the catcher to hold a pitched ball (other than a wild pitch), permitting a runner to advance; not scored as an error.

Percentage (team or pitcher): Number of games won divided by total games won and lost

(as: $\frac{15}{15 + 9} = \frac{15}{24} = .625$).

Pickoff: A throw by a pitcher or catcher to another fielder, catching a runner off base.

Rookie: A player in his first year in the major leagues, or a young player trying out for a big-league team.

Runs batted in (RBI): A run that scores and is credited to a batter as a result of the batter's safe hit, sacrifice, or infield out; or the batter's reaching first base on a fielder's choice; or the batter's getting a base on balls or being hit by a pitched ball with the bases full, forcing in a run.

Sacrifice: A successful attempt by the batter (before two are out) to advance a runner or runners by means of a bunt or a long fly out.

Shutout: A game in which a team fails to score.

Spring training: The period before the start of the regular season when major league teams train and play exhibition games to prepare for the season. Many teams hold their spring training camps in Florida or Arizona.

Squeeze play: An attempt to bring home a runner from third base by means of a bunt.

Stolen base: The act of a runner in advancing one base without the aid of the batter or any misplay by the defending team.

Switch-hitter: A player who can bat right-handed or left-handed.

Wild pitch: A pitch too high, low, or wide for the catcher to handle, allowing a base runner to advance.

* Common terms not defined in text.

first base will be left open for the batter. If the ground ball is caught and thrown to a fielder at second base before the runner arrives, the runner is forced out.

On the same play, if the fielder at second base then throws the ball to a fielder at first base and the ball arrives there before the batter, then the batter is out as well. This is called a **"double play,"** because two outs were made on one batted ball. A double play also can occur if a fielder catches a fly ball and throws the ball to a base before the runner gets back to it. Sometimes the fielding team can even get three outs on one batted ball—a rare "triple play."

A Game of Inches

Baseball is often called a "game of inches." For example, a speedy ground ball may pass within an inch or two of a infielder's reach, making the difference between a hit or an out. Sometimes even a fraction of an inch can determine whether a pitch is a ball or a strike, whether a batted ball is fair or foul, or whether a base runner is safe or out. Even one close play can decide the outcome of a whole game.

The job of making these decisions and enforcing the rules of the game falls on a group of **umpires** stationed around the field. Major league games usually have four umpires—one each at home plate, first base, second base, and third base. The home plate umpire decides whether pitches are balls or strikes and whether runners attempting to reach home plate are safe or out. The other umpires rule on plays at or near their designated bases.

While even the most basic rules of baseball may seem complicated to those unfamiliar with the game, a good player must know every detail, understand many strategies, and react quickly to every situation. Almost every play is different, presenting batters, fielders, and base runners with a variety of choices and opportunities. To play well requires speed, power, pinpoint accuracy, split-second timing, and a special instinct for the game.

▶ **LEAGUES AND COMPETITION**

Millions of Americans play baseball on a formal, organized basis. They participate on teams that compete regularly against a group of other teams, usually about six to ten in number, that together make up a league. Following a preset schedule, all the teams in a league play each other at least once—usually twice or more—during the course of a season. The team that has won the most games at the end of the season becomes the champion. Sometimes the top several teams in a league compete in a special post-season tournament to determine the champion.

In the United States today, there are baseball leagues for nearly every age group. The best adult players are paid money to play on a team. They are called professionals. The top professionals play in the major leagues. But most people who play baseball are not paid any money for it. They are called amateurs, and they play the game for the enjoyment and competition. Amateur baseball programs range from Little League for youngsters to high school, college, and adult leagues.

Major Leagues

There are a total of 28 teams in major league baseball today—26 based in U.S. cities and two based in Canadian cities. These 28 teams are divided into two leagues: 14 in the **American League**, and 14 in the **National League**. Each of the two leagues is made up of an Eastern Division and a Western Division. The two divisions in each league have an equal number of teams, seven each in the American and National leagues.

A major league season starts in April and lasts until October. Every team plays a total of 162 games during the **regular season**. Games are played only between teams in the same league. A majority of games are played between teams from the same division, although there is some interdivision competition. Each team plays half of its games at home and half of them away. There are day and night games, and occasionally teams will play two games in one day. This is called a **doubleheader**.

At the end of the regular season, the top teams in each division play a best-of-seven-game series for the league title, or pennant. The two pennant winners then meet in the **World Series**, sometimes called the "Fall Classic." The winner of this best-of-seven series is recognized as the world champion. The World Series is one of the major sporting events anywhere. Many millions of people in the United States and other countries watch the games on television or listen to them on the radio.

Another highlight of the major league season is the **all-star game.** This is a special game, played midway through the regular season, between the best players in the American League and the best players in the National League (as voted by the fans). The game has no effect on the standings, but fans enjoy it because they see the top stars compete against each other.

MAJOR LEAGUE TEAMS

American League

Eastern Division	Western Division
Baltimore Orioles	California Angels
Boston Red Sox	Chicago White Sox
Cleveland Indians	Kansas City Royals
Detroit Tigers	Minnesota Twins
Milwaukee Brewers	Oakland Athletics
New York Yankees	Seattle Mariners
Toronto Blue Jays	Texas Rangers

National League

Eastern Division	Western Division
Chicago Cubs	Atlanta Braves
Miami Marlins	Cincinnati Reds
Montreal Expos	Denver Rockies
New York Mets	Houston Astros
Philadelphia Phillies	Los Angeles Dodgers
Pittsburgh Pirates	San Diego Padres
St. Louis Cardinals	San Francisco Giants

Minor Leagues

Major league teams get many of their players from the minor leagues. Each major league club provides financial support to minor league teams. These "farm" teams give training and experience to promising players. When a minor league player performs well, the "parent" team will bring the player up to the major leagues.

There are a number of minor leagues in the United States and Canada. They are generally classified into three groups, according to level of play—Class A, Class AA, and Class AAA. In addition, there are winter leagues and leagues for rookies (first-year players)—some in Mexico and other Latin American countries.

Amateur Competition

Organized baseball for amateurs begins with Little League, for youngsters age 8 to 12. The rules of Little League baseball are very similar to those followed in the major leagues. The biggest difference is the size of the diamond. In Little League the bases are 60 feet (18.3 meters) apart, as opposed to the standard 90 feet (27.4 meters), and the pitcher's mound is closer to home plate. Also, Little League games last seven innings instead of nine. A separate article on LITTLE LEAGUE BASEBALL can be found in Volume L.

For teenagers, American Legion and Babe Ruth leagues offer an opportunity to continue competitive play. In addition, most high schools and colleges have baseball teams that belong to established leagues.

Finally, local groups everywhere—park and recreation boards, Boys' Clubs, companies, and others—organize programs for boys and girls, pre-Little Leaguers and rusty adults, and just about anyone else who wants to play.

▶ AN INTERNATIONAL GAME

Although baseball is regarded as the American national pastime, the game is enormously popular in many other countries. Organized competition for youngsters is extensive in Canada and Mexico. Minor leagues in both countries have been feeding players to U.S. professional teams for many years. In 1969 the Montreal Expos became the first major league team based outside the United States. Another Canadian team, the Toronto Blue Jays, was added in 1977. In 1992 the Blue Jays became the first Canadian team and the first team outside the United States to win the U.S. World Series.

Baseball is also widely played, and enthusiastically followed, throughout Latin America. Competition at all levels is held year-round in Puerto Rico, the Dominican Republic, Cuba, Venezuela, the Virgin Islands, Panama, Nicaragua, and other lands. During the winter months, many Latin and U.S. professionals take part in highly competitive league play. Latin countries also have developed a number of major league stars, including Roberto

---

SOME IMPORTANT MAJOR LEAGUE RECORDS ESTABLISHED SINCE 1900

Highest lifetime batting average: .367, Ty Cobb, Tigers, 1905–26, Athletics, 1927–28.

Highest season batting average: .424, Rogers Hornsby, Cardinals, 1924.

Most hits, lifetime: 4,256, Pete Rose, Reds, 1963–78, Phillies, 1979–83, Expos, 1984, Reds, 1984–86.

Most hits, season: 257, George Sisler, Browns, 1920.

Longest consecutive-game hitting streak: 56 games, Joe DiMaggio, Yankees, 1941.

Most runs batted in, lifetime: 2,297, Hank Aaron, Braves, 1954–74, 1977, Brewers, 1975–76.

Most runs batted in, season: 190, Hack Wilson, Cubs, 1930.

Most home runs, lifetime: 755, Hank Aaron. Other leaders: Babe Ruth, 714; Willie Mays, 660; Frank Robinson, 586; Harmon Killebrew, 573; Reggie Jackson, 563; Mike Schmidt, 548; Mickey Mantle, 536.

Most home runs, season: 61, Roger Maris, Yankees, 1961 (162-game season schedule); 60, Babe Ruth, Yankees, 1927 (154-game schedule). Other leaders: Babe Ruth, 59; Hank Greenberg, 58; Jimmy Foxx, 58; Hack Wilson, 56.

Most stolen bases, lifetime: 1,042 (end of 1992 season), Rickey Henderson.

Most stolen bases, season: 130, Rickey Henderson, Athletics, 1982.

Most consecutive games played: 2,130, Lou Gehrig, Yankees, 1925–39.

Most games won by a pitcher, lifetime: 511, Cy Young, 1890–1911. Other leaders: Walter Johnson, 416; Grover Cleveland Alexander, 373; Christy Mathewson, 373; Warren Spahn, 363.

Most games won by a pitcher, season: 41, Jack Chesbro, Yankees, 1904.

Longest winning streak by a pitcher: 24 games, Carl Hubbell, Giants, 1936–37.

Most strikeouts, lifetime: 5,668 (end of 1992 season), Nolan Ryan.

Most strikeouts, season: 383, Nolan Ryan, Angels, 1973.

PENNANT AND WORLD SERIES WINNERS—YEAR-BY-YEAR RECORD

The winning team is indicated by an asterisk (*).

Year	American League	National League	Games Won–Lost		Year	American League	National League	Games Won–Lost	
1903	*Boston	Pittsburgh	5	3	1948	*Cleveland	Boston	4	2
1905	Philadelphia	*New York	4	1	1949	*New York	Brooklyn	4	1
1906	*Chicago	Chicago	4	2	1950	*New York	Philadelphia	4	0
1907	Detroit	*Chicago	4	0	1951	*New York	New York	4	2
1908	Detroit	*Chicago	4	1	1952	*New York	Brooklyn	4	3
1909	Detroit	*Pittsburgh	4	3	1953	*New York	Brooklyn	4	2
1910	*Philadelphia	Chicago	4	1	1954	Cleveland	*New York	4	0
1911	*Philadelphia	New York	4	2	1955	New York	*Brooklyn	4	3
1912	*Boston	New York	4	3	1956	*New York	Brooklyn	4	3
1913	*Philadelphia	New York	4	1	1957	New York	*Milwaukee	4	3
1914	Philadelphia	*Boston	4	0	1958	*New York	Milwaukee	4	3
1915	*Boston	Philadelphia	4	1	1959	Chicago	*Los Angeles	4	2
1916	*Boston	Brooklyn	4	1	1960	New York	*Pittsburgh	4	3
1917	*Chicago	New York	4	2	1961	*New York	Cincinnati	4	1
1918	*Boston	Chicago	4	2	1962	*New York	San Francisco	4	3
1919	Chicago	*Cincinnati	5	3	1963	New York	*Los Angeles	4	0
1920	*Cleveland	Brooklyn	5	2	1964	New York	*St. Louis	4	3
1921	New York	*New York	5	3	1965	Minnesota	*Los Angeles	4	3
1922	New York	*New York	4	0	1966	*Baltimore	Los Angeles	4	0
1923	*New York	New York	4	2	1967	Boston	*St. Louis	4	3
1924	*Washington	New York	4	3	1968	*Detroit	St. Louis	4	3
1925	Washington	*Pittsburgh	4	3	1969	Baltimore	*New York	4	1
1926	New York	*St. Louis	4	3	1970	*Baltimore	Cincinnati	4	1
1927	*New York	Pittsburgh	4	0	1971	Baltimore	*Pittsburgh	4	3
1928	*New York	St. Louis	4	0	1972	*Oakland	Cincinnati	4	3
1929	*Philadelphia	Chicago	4	1	1973	*Oakland	New York	4	3
1930	*Philadelphia	St. Louis	4	2	1974	*Oakland	Los Angeles	4	1
1931	Philadelphia	*St. Louis	4	3	1975	Boston	*Cincinnati	4	3
1932	*New York	Chicago	4	0	1976	New York	*Cincinnati	4	0
1933	Washington	*New York	4	1	1977	*New York	Los Angeles	4	2
1934	Detroit	*St. Louis	4	3	1978	*New York	Los Angeles	4	2
1935	*Detroit	Chicago	4	2	1979	Baltimore	*Pittsburgh	4	3
1936	*New York	New York	4	2	1980	Kansas City	*Philadelphia	4	2
1937	*New York	New York	4	1	1981	New York	*Los Angeles	4	2
1938	*New York	Chicago	4	0	1982	Milwaukee	*St. Louis	4	3
1939	*New York	Cincinnati	4	0	1983	*Baltimore	Philadelphia	4	1
1940	Detroit	*Cincinnati	4	3	1984	*Detroit	San Diego	4	1
1941	*New York	Brooklyn	4	1	1985	*Kansas City	St. Louis	4	3
1942	New York	*St. Louis	4	1	1986	Boston	*New York	4	3
1943	*New York	St. Louis	4	1	1987	*Minnesota	St. Louis	4	3
1944	St. Louis	*St. Louis	4	2	1988	Oakland	*Los Angeles	4	1
1945	*Detroit	Chicago	4	3	1989	*Oakland	San Francisco	4	0
1946	Boston	*St. Louis	4	3	1990	Oakland	*Cincinnati	4	0
1947	*New York	Brooklyn	4	3	1991	*Minnesota	Atlanta	4	3
					1992	*Toronto	Atlanta	4	2

Clemente, Juan Marichal, Tony Oliva, Orlando Cepeda, and a host of others.

Another country in which baseball has become extremely popular is Japan. The game was introduced there by an American teacher named Horace Wilson in 1873. Japan today has two professional leagues, the Pacific and Central, each with six teams. After a 130-game regular season, the top teams in each league compete in the Japanese version of the World Series. Games throughout the season attract huge audiences, both at the stadiums and on television. The level of play is very high, and Japanese baseball has produced many of its own stars. The most famous was Sadaharu Oh of the Yomiuri Giants, who hit an amazing 868 career home runs. Over the years, a number of American stars also have played professionally in Japan.

Elsewhere in Asia, the game has caught on in such countries as Taiwan and South Korea —especially with youngsters. Since the 1960's, teams from the Far East have won the most Little League World Series championships.

Because of its worldwide popularity, baseball in 1984 became a "demonstration" sport in the summer Olympics and will become an official medal sport in 1992. Since that time there has been a surge of interest in many more countries—from Italy, England, and the Netherlands to Australia, Tunisia, and even the Soviet Union. Who knows? Maybe some day there will be a true *World* Series.

▶HISTORY OF BASEBALL

Games with a stick and ball were played as early as 5,000 years ago, as part of the religious rites of ancient Egypt. In the Middle Ages, the Christian church in France popularized a game in which a ball was swatted with sticks by two teams of worshipers. This custom spread throughout Europe, giving rise in England to a children's game called rounders.

Rounders was surprisingly similar to modern baseball. A batter hit a thrown ball and ran around one or more bases (in the form of rocks, sticks, milk stools, or wooden posts). But in rounders, fielders threw the ball at base runners. If the runner was off base and struck by the thrown ball, the runner was out.

In the United States, children in the 1800's called the game "town ball." When there were not enough players for two full teams, they played "one old cat," "two old cat," or "three old cat," depending on the number of bases used.

Origins and Early Growth

According to a popular legend, baseball was invented in 1839 by a young West Point cadet named Abner Doubleday at Cooperstown, New York. But most baseball historians now dispute that story, emphasizing the evolution of the sport from such earlier bat-and-ball games as rounders and town ball.

The person generally given credit for the biggest role in the evolution of modern baseball is Alexander J. Cartwright. In 1845, Cartwright drew up some rules that are very much like those followed today. Cartwright's rules set four bases at 90 feet apart. They also established the foul lines, the strikeout, three-out innings, and nine-player teams. But the ball had to be pitched underhand, runs were called "aces," and 21 or more aces made a game.

Baseball today is played much as it was in the late 1800's (*above*), when the first professional leagues were organized. One major difference is the vast stadiums, some with plastic domes and artificial grass. Houston's Astrodome (*right*) was the first indoor ballpark.

BASEBALL'S NATIONAL HALL OF FAME AND MUSEUM

When a player is elected to the National Baseball Hall of Fame in Cooperstown, New York, his career highlights and portrait are immortalized on a bronze plaque. The first five plaques were installed in 1936 at the building's dedication. They honored, from left, Ty Cobb, Walter Johnson, Christy Mathewson, Babe Ruth, and Honus Wagner.

The National Baseball Hall of Fame and Museum, located in Cooperstown, New York, was dedicated on June 12, 1939, to the pioneers and great players of the game. Members of the Hall of Fame are elected by the Baseball Writers' Association of America and by a special Committee on Veterans. Only the very best players in baseball history are honored in the Hall of Fame. To be elected is considered the greatest honor a player can receive. In addition to bronze plaques for each member, the Cooperstown museum displays a vast collection of baseball-related objects.

The Hall of Fame was established in Cooperstown because it was long regarded as the "home of baseball." According to legend (now rejected by most baseball historians), the game was invented on a Cooperstown field by Abner Doubleday. In 1935 a farmer living in a village near Cooperstown discovered an ancient trunk in his attic. The trunk, which had gone unopened for generations, contained the belongings of a schoolboy of a century before. Among the articles in the trunk was a battered homemade ball that had been used in a game. Unlike any baseball seen today, it was small, out of shape, and stuffed with cloth. Possibly used by many Cooperstown youngsters, the ball became known as the Abner Doubleday baseball. The antique baseball was bought the same year by Stephen C. Clark. He decided to exhibit the ball, and any other old obtainable baseball objects he could find, in a room in the Village Club.

Clark's exhibit interested the top officials of major league baseball. Ford C. Frick, the president of the National League, suggested that a National Baseball Hall of Fame and Museum be built. Plans were immediately approved to erect a building that would house a museum and a hall of fame where the great players would be honored. Contributions and valuable baseball objects from the past poured in from everywhere.

According to the rules, candidates for the Hall of Fame are chosen "on the basis of playing ability, integrity, sportsmanship, character, and their contribution to the team on which they played and to baseball in general."

Modern players are chosen by an annual secret ballot of the Baseball Writers' Association. To be eligible, a player must have played at least ten years in the major leagues, during a period that began 20 years before and ended five years before the election. The first five modern players elected to the Hall of Fame were Ty Cobb, Honus Wagner, Walter Johnson, Christy Mathewson, and Babe Ruth. The five-year rule was set aside in 1939 for Lou Gehrig, who was gravely ill, and in 1973 for Roberto Clemente, who was in a fatal air crash while transporting supplies to earthquake victims in Nicaragua. Clemente was the first Latin American player to be elected to the Hall of Fame.

The Committee on Veterans (appointed by the board of directors of the Hall of Fame) votes on players who have not played in at least 25 years. They also select outstanding managers, coaches, umpires, and executives who have been retired from the game for at least five years.

Because black players were excluded from the major leagues before 1947, many early stars failed to qualify for the Hall of Fame. To honor outstanding players from the Negro Leagues before 1947, the Hall of Fame changed its admission requirements in 1971 so these players could be admitted. A special committee was set up to select Negro League players. The great pitcher Satchel Paige was the first to be named.

Since the first election in 1936, more than 200 players, managers, executives, and other people who have made major contributions to the sport of baseball have been honored in the Hall of Fame.

The early years of major league baseball produced some of the game's most legendary stars. *Left to right:* Outfielder Ty Cobb played 24 seasons (1905–28), compiling a career batting average of .367, the highest ever. Cy Young pitched for 22 years (1890–1911), winning a total of 511 games—still a major league record. No player had a greater impact on baseball than George Herman "Babe" Ruth. His 714 home runs in 22 seasons (1914–35) revolutionized the game and raised it to a new level of popularity.

Cartwright also helped organize the first regular baseball team, the New York Knickerbockers. On June 19, 1846, the Knickerbockers lost the first recorded game to the rival New York Nine, 23–1, in four innings, at Hoboken, New Jersey. After that, amateur baseball spread to other eastern cities. Baseball attracted wide interest during the Civil War (1861–65), when groups of soldiers took up the new game.

The Rise of Professional Baseball

By the 1860's, the teams were paying some of their players a share of the money paid by fans to watch baseball games. But the first professional team to pay all its players a regular salary was the Cincinnati Red Stockings of 1869.

Modern professional baseball got its true start in 1876, when the eight-team National League was founded. A rival American Association was formed in 1881 but disbanded after ten years. The present American League had its first season in 1901, also with eight teams. The rivalry between the National League and the American League greatly increased popular interest in baseball. In 1903 the championship teams of the two leagues met in the first World Series, won by the Boston Red Sox.

The Modern Era

It was during the first decades of the 20th century that baseball truly became the "great American game." Stadiums were built with grandstands for thousands of spectators. Soon games were broadcast on radio, later on television. The best players became celebrities. Record-setting performances, dramatic World Series games, memorable plays, and colorful personalities became part of a history and folklore that continue to grow.

The period from 1900 to 1919 is sometimes called the "dead ball" era in baseball history. The balls used during that time were not very lively and were used in games until they were battered out of shape. Very few home runs were hit, and games usually ended with low scores.

The early years of major league baseball produced some of the greatest players in the history of the game. Pitcher Cy Young, who retired in 1911 after 22 seasons, won a total of 511 games—still the major league record. (Today the top pitcher in each league is honored by being named winner of the annual Cy Young Memorial Award.) Outfielder Ty Cobb of the Detroit Tigers had a career batting average of .367, the highest ever; his total of 4,191 hits stood as the record for nearly 75 years. Other famous players from this era

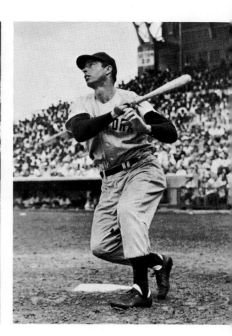

included pitchers Walter Johnson, Christy Mathewson, and Grover Cleveland Alexander; shortstop Honus Wagner; outfielder Tris Speaker; and second baseman Nap Lajoie.

The leading teams during this period were the Chicago Cubs and New York Giants in the National League, and the Philadelphia Athletics and Boston Red Sox in the American League. The Cubs, featuring the fabled double-play combination of "Tinker to Evers to Chance," played in four World Series in five years, winning in 1907 and 1908. The Athletics, managed by the legendary Connie Mack, appeared in four of five World Series from 1910 through 1914, winning three.

Baseball's darkest moment came in 1919, when the Cincinnati Reds defeated the heavily favored Chicago White Sox in the World Series. It was later discovered that eight White Sox players had accepted bribes from gamblers to lose the series. In what became known as the "Black Sox Scandal," the eight players were banned from baseball for life.

The next two decades, from 1920 to 1939, have been called the "golden era" of major league baseball. In 1920 the New York Yankees purchased from the Boston Red Sox a hard-hitting former pitcher named Babe Ruth. Many still regard "The Babe" as the greatest baseball player ever. In 1920, Ruth hit an amazing 54 home runs, exceeding his own

single-season record of 29 (set the year before). In 1921 he hit 59 home runs, and in 1927 he hit 60—a record that was to last 34 years. The era of the dead ball was over. Fans flocked to the stadium to see The Babe play.

In addition to the great feats of Babe Ruth, several off-the-field developments boosted the image and popularity of professional baseball. In 1921, Judge Kenesaw Mountain Landis was named the major league's first commissioner. Landis' chief contribution was to restore honesty and integrity to the game in the aftermath of the Black Sox Scandal. Meanwhile, many radio stations began broadcasting play-by-play accounts of games, bringing baseball to vast new audiences. Like so much else in American life, baseball thrived during the Roaring Twenties.

In the following decade more milestones were reached in the growth and development of major league baseball. The first all-star game was played in 1933 at Comiskey Park in Chicago. The first night game was played in 1935 in Cincinnati. The Hall of Fame was dedicated in 1939. And the first television broadcast of a game was made in 1939 from Ebbets Field in Brooklyn.

Besides Babe Ruth, other stars were attracting fans to major league ballparks. Ruth's teammate on the Yankees, slugging first baseman Lou Gehrig, played in 2,130 consecutive

Far left to right: New York Yankee first baseman Lou Gehrig played in a record 2,130 consecutive games. Jackie Robinson of the Brooklyn Dodgers became the major leagues' first black player in 1947. Joe DiMaggio set one of baseball's most cherished records in 1941 by hitting safely in 56 consecutive games. Willie Mays is considered one of the top all-around players in history; in 22 seasons (1951–73), he hit 660 home runs. Mickey Mantle hit 536 homers in 18 seasons (1951–68) with the Yankees.

games—a record that may never be broken. Rogers Hornsby of the St. Louis Cardinals batted .424 in 1924, the highest ever. Other greats of the 1920's and 1930's included pitchers Lefty Grove, Dizzy Dean, and Carl Hubbell; outfielders Mel Ott, Paul Waner, and Al Simmons; and first basemen Jimmy Foxx and George Sisler.

Led by Ruth, Gehrig, and others, the Yankees began one of the greatest success stories in professional sports history. From 1921 through 1939, the "Bronx Bombers" won a total of eleven American League pennants and eight World Series. Another strong team of this era was the New York Giants, who won seven pennants and three World Series.

Over the next three decades, major league baseball continued to grow and change. An important breakthrough came in 1947, when 28-year-old Jackie Robinson signed a contract with the Brooklyn Dodgers and became the first black player in the major leagues. From

Strikeout specialists Sandy Koufax (*left*) and Tom Seaver (*right*) were among the greatest pitchers of modern times. In twelve years (1955–66) with the Dodgers, Koufax won the National League Cy Young Award (top pitcher) three times and hurled four no-hitters. Seaver compiled a 311–205 record over 20 years (1967–86) and also won three Cy Young Awards.

the very beginning of professional baseball, black players had been barred from competing in the major leagues. For many years they competed in their own "Negro Leagues," which produced some of the game's best players—such as Satchel Paige, Josh Gibson, and "Cool Papa" Bell. Robinson's breaking of the "color line" in 1947 opened the door to the major leagues for new generations of black players.

Another important change after World War II was the movement of existing franchises (teams) and the addition of new ones. Among the several teams that changed cities during the 1950's were the Brooklyn Dodgers, who moved to Los Angeles, and the New York Giants, who went to San Francisco. In 1961 the American League expanded to ten teams, as the Senators were installed in Washington, D.C. In 1962 the National League added the New York Mets and Houston Colt .45s (now Astros). By 1969 each league had grown to twelve teams. And in 1977, with the addition of the Seattle Mariners and Toronto Blue Jays, the American League expanded to a total of 14 franchises.

Meanwhile, new stars were born, new records were set, and new memories were made. In 1941, Joe DiMaggio hit safely in a record 56 consecutive games, a feat that has not yet been equaled. In 1951, Bobby Thomson clinched the pennant for the Giants with a dramatic ninth-inning home run in a special,

three-game playoff against the Dodgers. In 1956, Don Larsen pitched the only perfect game (no batters reaching first base) in World Series history. In 1961, Roger Maris broke Babe Ruth's great record by hitting 61 home runs in the regular season (expanded from 154 to 162 games).

The Yankees continued to produce great players and win championships. With Ruth and Gehrig giving way to Joe DiMaggio, Yogi Berra, Mickey Mantle, Roger Maris, Whitey Ford, and others, the Yankees won an amazing 18 pennants and twelve World Series from 1941 through 1964. But not all of the standout players were Yankees.

The 25 years after World War II gave fans the treat of watching a galaxy of stars. Among the many top hitters of the era were Hank Greenberg, Ralph Kiner, Duke Snider, Ted Williams, Stan Musial, Hank Aaron, Willie Mays, Ernie Banks, Eddie Mathews, Roberto Clemente, and Frank Robinson. Great pitchers included Bob Feller, Robin Roberts, Bob Lemon, Warren Spahn, Early Wynn, Sandy Koufax, Don Drysdale, Juan Marichal, and Bob Gibson.

The late 1960's signaled another new era in baseball history. The leagues expanded, new ballparks were opened, attendance climbed from year to year, television coverage increased steadily, and baseball became big business. In 1965 the first of many indoor stadiums with artificial turf—the Houston As-

Each new generation of players brings new stars, some of whom will break long-held records. *From left to right:* In 1974, Hank Aaron broke Babe Ruth's record of 714 career home runs; Aaron retired in 1976 with 755 home runs and 2,297 runs batted in, also the most ever. Reggie Jackson, nicknamed "Mr. October" for his playoff and World Series heroics, hit 563 homers in a colorful 21-year career. In 1985, Cincinnati's Pete Rose broke Ty Cobb's record of 4,191 career hits.

In the United States —as well as many other countries—the basic skills and a love of the game of baseball are passed on from parents to children.

trodome—was opened. With the expansion of the two leagues in 1969, the present post-season play-off format (League Championship Series) was introduced. In 1973 the American League adopted the designated-hitter rule. In 1993 two new teams, the Denver Rockies and the Miami Marlins, were added to the National League, giving each league 14 teams.

The mid-1960's also marked the end of the old Yankee dynasty. Since then, only a few teams have been able to repeat as world champions: the Oakland Athletics won the World Series in 1972, 1973, and 1974; the Cincinnati Reds in 1975 and 1976; and the Yankees in 1977 and 1978. A powerful Oakland team won three pennants in 1988, 1989, and 1990, but just one world championship, in 1989.

Some of the game's most cherished records have fallen. In 1974, Hank Aaron hit his 715th home run, surpassing Babe Ruth's all-time mark. (Aaron ended his career with 755 home runs.) Pete Rose overtook and passed Ty Cobb's record of 4,191 lifetime base hits. Several pitchers have exceeded Walter Johnson's career total of 3,508 strikeouts, with the record now held by Nolan Ryan, the undisputed strikeout king of baseball.

An important change came in 1976. For the first time, players with at least six years of experience in the major leagues could become **free agents**. Formerly, players were required to stay with the same club until traded, sold, or released. Now they were free to offer their services to any team. With franchise owners bidding against each other to get good players, many veteran stars signed multimillion-dollar contracts and moved to new teams.

With all that has changed in baseball since Alexander Cartwright first set down the rules in 1845, the game today is still played very much the way it used to be. The biggest change is the long and colorful tradition that has built up over time. Each spring marks a new beginning but also brings to mind the great eras of the past. Stories are passed down from generation to generation. Parents take their children in the backyard to teach them how to bat and throw. Baseball is "the great American game."

Reviewed by PETER V. UEBERROTH
Former Commissioner of Baseball

See also LITTLE LEAGUE BASEBALL; ROBINSON, JACK ROOSEVELT (JACKIE); RUTH, GEORGE HERMAN (BABE).

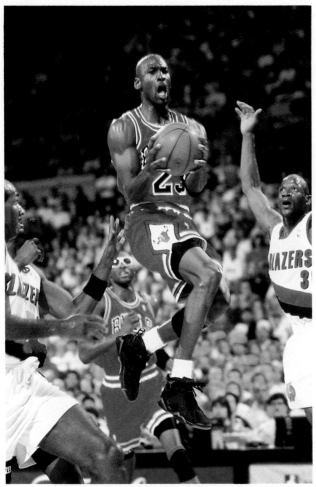

Michael Jordan floats toward the basket and another score. His spectacular play led the Chicago Bulls to championships in the National Basketball League.

BASKETBALL

Basketball is the most popular indoor sport in the world. It is also one of the few sports whose year of birth and originator can be traced accurately. The game was invented in 1891 by Dr. James A. Naismith. Although basketball grew and developed in the United States, the game today is played and watched in more than 150 countries.

Two teams, of five players each, play the game on a court. At each end of the basketball court is a round metal rim, or hoop, placed 10 feet (3 meters) above the floor. The rim is attached to a backboard made of wood or fiberglass. Hanging from the rim is a white cord net. The rim and net together are called the basket, or goal. The object of the game is to score points by shooting a large ball through the basket—and to prevent the other team from doing so. The winning team is the team that has scored the most points during the course of the game.

Basketball is a fast-paced, exciting game. Much of its appeal lies in its unique blend of teamwork and individual athletic skills. Speed, strength, stamina, quick reflexes, leaping ability, and shooting accuracy are just some of the important skills for a basketball player to possess. Taller players generally have an advantage over shorter players because taller players can reach closer to the basket. Shorter players, however, can be valuable for their quickness, ball-handling ability, and other contributions. For any player, the most important asset is the ability and willingness to play in close harmony with the other players on the team. Above all, basketball is a team sport, not an individual sport. At any level of competition—from playground to professional—the most successful teams are the teams that work together as a unit.

When Dr. Naismith invented the game of basketball, he was a physical education instructor at the International Training School of the Young Men's Christian Association (YMCA) in Springfield, Massachusetts. It was winter, and his students needed a fast-action game that could be played indoors. He decided on a game in which the players would have to throw a ball into baskets. So he attached a couple of old wooden peach baskets to the ends of the gym balcony and established some basic rules.

Although the rules laid down by Dr. Naismith are still basic to the game, basketball has come a long way since it was first played in the Springfield YMCA. Every four years, amateur players from all over the world compete in an Olympic basketball tournament. In the United States, millions of fans attend games in sports arenas and gyms. Many millions more watch on television. The top male

You can find biographies of the following basketball players and coaches by looking them up in the Index: Kareem Abdul-Jabbar; Elgin Baylor; Larry Bird; Wilt Chamberlain; Bob Cousy; Julius Erving; Joseph Lapchick; George Mikan; Bob Pettit; Oscar Robertson; Adolph F. Rupp; Bill Russell; and Jerry West.

players compete as professionals. Colleges and high schools sponsor teams for both male and female players. Recreational centers and youth organizations run leagues for younger players.

Part of basketball's popularity stems from the fact that it can be played in many ways. Although organized competition calls for five-player teams, the game can be played for practice or recreation with any number down to "one-on-one." It can even be played alone. In addition, basketball does not cost much money to play, as little equipment is required —only a ball and a hoop.

THE COURT AND EQUIPMENT

A full-size, regulation basketball court is 94 feet (28.7 meters) long and 50 feet (15.2 meters) wide. However, a smaller court is generally used for competition up through the high school level. Indoor courts have a hardwood surface, while outdoor courts are made of asphalt or some other weather-resistant material. The boundaries of a basketball court are marked by two pairs of parallel lines called the side lines and end lines (or baselines). The court is divided in half by a midcourt line parallel to the end lines. Other lines on the court mark off special areas, such as the free-throw lanes, free-throw circle, and center circle.

The basket at each end of the court is attached to a backboard suspended above the floor. The backboard is set midway between the side lines and parallel to the end line. The backboard is usually rectangular in shape, but a fan-shaped backboard also can be used. Painted on the backboard, directly above the rim, is a large rectangle. This helps a player aim when trying to bounce the ball off the backboard and into the basket.

The metal rim should be exactly 10 feet (3 meters) above the floor. It is 18 inches (45.7 centimeters) in diameter, nearly wide enough to fit two basketballs at the same time. The net hanging from the rim is open at the bottom so the ball can fall through.

A regulation basketball is 30 inches (76.2 centimeters) in circumference and weighs from 20 to 22 ounces (567 to 624 grams). (The ball used in the women's game is slightly smaller.) The surface of the ball is made of leather or rubber, usually orange or brown in color. It has a pebble grain for easy gripping. The ball is inflated with air so that it bounces easily.

The only other equipment really needed to play basketball are a pair of athletic socks and sneakers with rubber soles. In formal competition, the two teams also wear uniforms. Each team wears a different color uniform. The standard basketball uniform includes shorts and a sleeveless jersey or T-shirt. On the back of each jersey is a number to identify the player.

Basketball Court

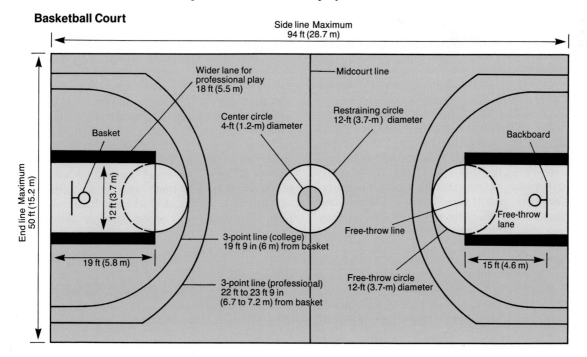

Side line Maximum
94 ft (28.7 m)

End line Maximum
50 ft (15.2 m)

Wider lane for professional play
18 ft (5.5 m)

Midcourt line

Center circle
4-ft (1.2-m) diameter

Restraining circle
12-ft (3.7-m) diameter

Basket

Backboard

12 ft (3.7 m)

3-point line (college)
19 ft 9 in (6 m) from basket

Free-throw line

Free-throw lane

19 ft (5.8 m)

15 ft (4.6 m)

3-point line (professional)
22 ft to 23 ft 9 in
(6.7 to 7.2 m) from basket

Free-throw circle
12-ft (3.7-m) diameter

Left: Two of basketball's greatest centers, Wilt Chamberlain (with headband) and Kareem Abdul-Jabbar, maneuver into position for a rebound. They are the only players to have scored more than 30,000 points in their professional careers. Behind them is another all-time great, guard Jerry West. Right: Guard Bob Cousy (number 14), known for his adept ball handling, dribbles past a defender. Far right: Two centers vie for a "jump ball," tossed up between them by an official, at the start of a college game.

▶ HOW THE GAME IS PLAYED

Each team defends the basket at its own end of the court (backcourt) and tries to shoot the ball into the basket at the other end (frontcourt). The team in possession of the ball, and trying to score, is said to be on **offense.** The team without the ball, and trying to prevent the other team from scoring, is said to be on **defense.** Players can advance the ball up and down the court only by passing (throwing) it or dribbling (bouncing) it.

The Team

The five players on the court for each team normally are a **center,** two **forwards,** and two **guards.** The center is usually the tallest player and takes a position close to the basket. A good center can dominate a game by scoring baskets, rebounding (grabbing missed shots), and blocking the opponents' attempts at the basket. The two forwards are stationed to the sides of the center, along the end lines or farther out on the wings. They are strong players who try to maneuver for close shots at the basket; they should also be good rebounders. The two guards are usually smaller and quicker than the center and forwards. They also play farther away from the basket. The main responsibilities of the guards are to guide the offense and set up the plays. The guards should be good dribblers, passers, and outside shooters.

Although the center, forwards, and guards have somewhat different roles, their positions are not fixed or stationary. They can move anywhere on the court and perform any role in the offense or defense. In fact, a team can change the positions at any time. For example, it might use three forwards and two guards, or two centers and three guards.

In addition to the five players on the court, a basketball team has several substitute players. The substitutes are brought into the game to give the other players a rest or to take advantage of their own special abilities. For example, a substitute who is especially good at defense may be brought into the game to guard the other team's best shooter. Or the team's best shooter may be brought into the game when scoring is especially needed.

The person who runs a basketball team is called the **coach.** He or she organizes the team and instructs the players in important skills. The coach holds regular practice sessions to drill the team and to prepare for each game. In addition, the coach designs special plays and strategies to use against the opposing team. During the game the coach determines which players to use, tells them what to do, selects substitutes, and decides when to call timeouts. The coach of a professional or college team normally has at least one assistant coach to help with all these responsibilities.

Officials

The conduct of play is controlled by two officials on the court. (Sometimes three are used.) They ensure that the game is played

according to the rules. The officials carry whistles. When a player has committed a foul or violation, an official will blow the whistle to stop play and assess the appropriate penalty. The head official has the final decision in any dispute. Otherwise, the officials have the same duties. The officials are assisted by a scorekeeper and a timekeeper. They sit at a table alongside the court.

Time

The team that scores more points in the specified amount of time wins the game. A high school basketball game is played in four 8-minute quarters, while younger teams play 6-minute quarters. College games are divided into 20-minute halves, professional games into 12-minute quarters. There is a rest period at halftime. (In the second half of the game, the teams "trade" ends of the floor, and each now shoots for the basket that it had defended during the first half.) In case of a tie score at the end of the last period, overtime periods are played—3 minutes in high school games, 5 minutes in college and professional games.

During the course of a game, the clock is stopped when the buzzer sounds to end a quarter or half or when an official blows the whistle for any reason. For example, an official will blow the whistle when the ball goes out of bounds, or to signal that a foul or violation has been committed, or when a team calls a time-out. Each team is allowed only a limited number of time-outs during the game.

The Action

The game begins with a "jump ball" at the center of the court. Two opposing players, usually the centers, face each other at the midcourt line. Their teammates get in position around the center circle. The referee tosses the ball in the air between the two facing players. Each one jumps up and tries to tap the ball to a teammate.

As soon as one team gains possession of the ball, it goes on the offense and advances toward the other team's basket. A shot for the basket may be made from anywhere on the court. It is best, however, to move the ball as close to the basket as possible before shooting.

Players may pass the ball back and forth or from side to side in order to confuse the defensive players. If this happens, one member of the offensive team can get under the basket for

Left: Earvin ("Magic") Johnson keeps his head up while dribbling to watch for a teammate to whom he can pass. Middle: John Havlicek shoots a free throw, taking a one-hand set shot. Right: All-time great center Bill Russell (number 6) grabs a rebound.

a clear, easy shot. Passes do not have to stay in the air—the bounce pass is commonly used. But the ball must stay on the playing court. Should it go out-of-bounds, the official decides which player touched it last. The ball is then awarded to the opposing team.

The only other legal way a player can move the ball is by bouncing it along the floor with one hand. This is called **dribbling.** Once a player stops dribbling and holds the ball with both hands, it must be either passed or shot for a basket. If the player dribbles again, before another player touches the ball, or walks or runs while holding the ball **(traveling),** the ball is turned over to the other team.

When a basket is scored, the opposing team gains possession of the ball and passes it inbounds from behind the end line. That team goes on offense and tries for a basket at the other end of the court. The team that just scored now becomes the defensive team. Defensive players try to guard their opponents closely. They attempt to steal the ball, intercept a pass, block a shot, or force the offensive team to take only a difficult shot.

A very important part of the game of basketball is **rebounding.** Every missed shot re-

sults in a rebound (unless the missed shot goes out-of-bounds). Whichever team can catch the rebound keeps possession of the ball and goes on the offense. Tall players generally get the most rebounds because they are positioned close to the basket and they can reach very high. But smaller players can also grab rebounds if they get in a good position and legally block their opponents.

Rules and Scoring

Players may not interfere with the progress of an opponent by holding, pushing, slapping, or tripping. Such violations are called **personal fouls.** If a player commits five personal fouls (six in professional competition), that player is disqualified from the game and replaced by a substitute. Another kind of foul is called the **technical foul.** A technical foul is assessed for unsportsmanlike conduct or such other violations as delaying the game, calling too many time-outs, or having too many players on the court.

In basketball, points are scored on either a **field goal** or a **free throw** (also called a "foul shot"). A field goal is a basket made from the court during normal play. A field goal counts

2 points. In professional basketball, 3 points are counted for a field goal shot from beyond a line marked in an arc ranging from 22 feet to 23 feet 9 inches (6.7 to 7.2 meters) from the basket. In men's college basketball, 3 points are counted for a field goal shot from beyond a line 19 feet 9 inches (6.0 meters) from the basket.

A free throw is awarded to a player after certain fouls. The player who is fouled takes a free (unguarded) shot from the free-throw line, which is 15 feet (4.6 meters) from the basket. The other players line up along the free-throw lane to await a rebound. A successful free throw counts 1 point. Two free throws are allowed for a personal foul against a player in the act of attempting a field goal. (If the field goal is made, it counts 2 points, and the fouled player gets one free throw.) In some situations, a **one-and-one** free throw is allowed. That is, if the first free throw is made, the shooter is awarded a second free throw. (The one-and-one free throw is not used in professional basketball.) Free throws are also awarded to a team if the opposing team commits a technical foul.

Several rules in basketball concern time limitations. From out-of-bounds, a player has 5 seconds to pass the ball inbounds to a teammate. If a team gains possession of the ball in the backcourt, that team has 10 seconds to advance the ball across the midcourt line. Once the ball is across the midcourt line, it may not be passed or dribbled back behind the midcourt line. In high school and college games, no guarded player may hold the ball for more than 5 seconds without dribbling or passing. In any game, no offensive player may stay inside the free-throw lane for more than 3 seconds. In professional basketball, the offensive team has 24 seconds, from the moment of gaining possession of the ball, to attempt a field goal; in a men's college game, the limit is 45 seconds; in a women's college game, the limit is 30 seconds. (There is usually no such restriction in high school basketball.) If any violation of these time limits is committed, the official stops play and gives the ball to the opposing team.

A defensive player may block a shot that is on its way up. But the defensive player may not block a shot that is on its way down; knock the ball off the rim or away from the area above the basket; pin the ball against the backboard; or block a shot that has already hit the backboard. Any of these illegal blocks, called **goaltending,** results in the shooting team being awarded a field goal.

In trying to score a basket, the offensive team works together to free one player for a good shot. The guards, forwards, and center move around constantly to get free of the defense. They pass the ball among them and dribble when necessary, trying to create an opening for someone to shoot. Breaking through the defense is sometimes very difficult, requiring skillful passing, clever fakes, and acrobatic shooting.

There are two basic styles of offensive play. One is called the **set-pattern** offense. This is a deliberate, pre-arranged series of movements and passes. Each player begins from an assigned spot on the court and follows a specified route through or around the area in front of the basket. Such a pattern can be very complicated. Sometimes the pattern has to be altered or rerun several times, with many passes, before any player gets free for a shot. In a set-pattern offense, **picks** and **screens** are very effective in getting someone free. In a pick or screen, an offensive player takes a firm, stationary position to block the path of one or more defensive players. Another offensive player can then get away for a clear shot. Set-pattern offenses are designed to include many picks and screens.

The other basic style of offense is called the **fast break,** or **running game.** In a fast break, the offensive team tries to score as quickly as possible after gaining possession of the ball. A fast break begins with a rebound at the defensive basket. Then the offense moves the ball downcourt as fast as it can, trying to beat the defensive players to the basket.

▶ASPECTS OF DEFENSE

Good defense is as important as good offense to the success of a basketball team. When the other team has the ball, all five players must work hard on defense to keep the opponents from scoring.

There are two basic types of basketball defense. One is **man-to-man,** in which each defensive player is assigned a certain offensive player to guard. Sometimes a defender will have to help a teammate guard a particular

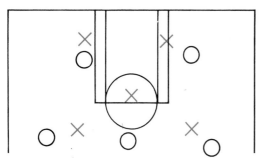

A 2-1-2 zone defense: Two defensive players (X's) are between the free-throw line and midcourt, one is near the free-throw line, and two are near the basket. Placement of the zone may shift depending on the locations of the offensive players (0's).

offensive player. This is called "double teaming." The other basic defensive system is called **zone defense.** In this type, each defensive player is assigned a certain area of the court to protect. The player guards any opponent who enters that area. In a zone defense, the players can be arranged in several different ways. The various arrangements have such names as "2-1-2," "1-3-1," "2-3," and "3-2." For example, in a "2-1-2" zone defense, two defensive players are positioned between the free-throw line and midcourt, one is positioned near the free-throw line, and two are positioned close to the basket.

Zone defenses are used extensively in high school and college basketball, though teams also play man-to-man defense. Teams often will switch their defense during a game, perhaps changing from one zone to another or from a zone to a man-to-man. These changes may confuse their opponents. In professional basketball, zone defenses are illegal, and only man-to-man defense is allowed.

▶ **HINTS ON PLAYING BASKETBALL**

For the individual player, success in basketball depends on the ability to perform certain basic skills. Coaches call these the **fundamentals** of the game. Young players should concentrate on learning the fundamentals. Even experienced players should practice them often. The most important areas are footwork, dribbling, passing, shooting, and defense.

Basketball "superstars": Oscar Robertson (number 1), one of the game's greatest all-around players, flips a pass between a defender's outstretched arms; Jerry West (number 44), a deadly accurate shooter, takes a lay-up shot despite the presence of opponents Dave De-Busschere and Willis Reed; and Julius Erving (number 6) slams one of his famous dunk shots into the basket.

Footwork. Good footwork is important in every aspect of the game. Balance, speed, quick changes of direction, and the ability to stop and go suddenly give any player a big advantage. To be in a position to move fast, stand with one foot slightly forward. Your knees should be bent slightly, your shoulders a bit forward. Hold your arms out a little, with the fingers spread. When you start to run, use your rear foot as a spring. Take short steps. To move to the side or rear, pivot on the back foot. Use the front foot to guide you in whatever direction you want to go.

Dribbling. Dribbling must be done with one hand. Any player should be able to dribble with the right hand or the left hand. Always keep your head up while dribbling so you can be alert for a teammate to whom you can pass.

When you are unguarded and dribbling the ball down court, use the high, or normal, type of dribble. Lean forward a little and bend your knees slightly. The hand that controls the ball should have the fingers spread wide. Your other hand should be at your side for balance. The ball should be bounced about waist high.

If a defender is near, use a low dribble and protect the ball with your body. The stance is the same as for the high dribble except that you bend your knees more. When you are crouching, keep the ball closer to the floor, bouncing it easily as you move around.

Passing. The fastest way to get the ball down court is by passing it. Passing is the key

ingredient in offensive play. There are several different kinds of passes. Always use the simplest pass you can to complete the play.

The **chest pass** is the most widely used for short, quick throws. Hold the ball chest high with both hands, fingers forward, thumbs behind the ball. As you get ready to pass, bring the ball back toward your chest, turning it so that your thumbs are now under the ball. Then step out with your forward foot while pushing your arms straight ahead. With your wrists snap the ball to the receiver.

The **bounce pass** is effective when your defender keeps his or her hands in the air. With your knees bent, hold the ball waist high with both hands. When your receiver is clear, bend your back knee almost to a kneeling position. Straighten your arms and flip the ball downward on a single bounce toward your receiver.

To throw high to a teammate, you can use the **two-hand overhead pass.** Hold the ball as you would for a chest pass, but with your fingers a little more behind the ball. Keep your feet just apart, and bend your knees slightly. Lift your hands above and a little in front of your head. Take a step forward and bend your wrists back. Then push the ball forward with a quick snap of the wrists.

For getting the ball to a teammate on the run, the best choice might be a **shovel pass.** This is a two-handed underhand pass. It should be short and soft, with no spin on the ball.

To make a long pass, especially on a fast break, you may use the **football pass.** It is made with one hand, the ball cocked behind your head. As you begin to throw, step forward with the opposite leg—just as if you were throwing a football. (Interestingly, this pass is also called the baseball pass, because a baseball is thrown the same way.)

It is also important to learn how to fake. Look high, pass low. Look low, pass high. Fake a pass one way and then pass another. When you have mastered the basic passing techniques, you can try more difficult passes. Just make sure the ball gets to your teammate.

Shooting. No basketball skill is more important than shooting for the basket. In trying to make a basket, a player can choose any of several different kinds of shots. Always choose the easiest shot for the situation. Whatever the shot, maintain good balance, concentrate on the rim, and do not rush. To become a good shooter, practice, practice, and practice some more.

The easiest shot in basketball is the **lay-up.** Dribbling the ball, stride hard toward the basket and jump off one foot. In the air, lay the ball gently off the backboard and into the hoop. When you take a lay-up, push off the floor with the foot opposite your shooting hand. Practice taking lay-ups with either hand, from either side of the basket.

The **dunk** is the most spectacular shot in basketball. The player leaps high in the air,

bringing the ball well above the rim. Then the player simply slams it down through the hoop. Usually, only very tall players can reach high enough to perform a dunk. But shorter players who are extremely good leapers can often perform dunks too.

Another shot for tall players is the **hook shot.** Use the hook only when you are near the basket. After getting the ball, turn so that you are sideways to the basket. With the hand farther from the basket, raise the ball in a circular motion above your head. At the highest point, release the ball with a quick snap of the wrist.

Shots taken farther away from the basket are called "outside" shots. There are two basic ways of shooting from the outside. One is the **set shot.** The two-hand set is best for younger players. Keep your feet slightly apart, knees bent. Hold the ball on each side, with the seams running horizontally. Keep your fingers spread and thumbs back. As you raise the ball near your chin, bend your knees a bit more. Bring your wrists back so that the ball is cupped in your hands. Then straighten your knees and arms, pushing the ball toward the basket with a snap of the wrists. For a one-hand set shot, put the weight of the ball on one hand and use the other hand to guide the ball as you raise it toward the basket.

For more experienced players, the **jump shot** is the most commonly used outside shot.

It is taken like a one-hand set shot, except that the player jumps before shooting. Bend your knees and jump slightly off the floor with both feet. At the peak of your jump, release the ball toward the basket with the same wrist-snapping action.

Always try to take an outside shot the exact same way. Maintain good balance and rhythm. Feel comfortable. It is very important to concentrate on the basket. Snap your wrists, putting backward spin on the ball. Follow through on the release, as if guiding the ball after it has left your hands.

Defense. Guarding an opponent well requires as much concentration as shooting does. Always know where the ball is. Always know where your opponent is. Also know your opponent's abilities and playing habits. Can this player make long shots? Can this player dribble well with either hand? Also be alert for a teammate who needs defensive help. Most of all, work hard and hustle.

When on defense, always keep your knees bent. In guarding, spread your feet with one slightly in front. If your left foot is forward, hold your left arm head-high with fingers spread. Hold out your right arm to the side, between knee and hip. When your opponent has the ball, stand in front and move your arms constantly. Your object is to block any pass and keep a shot from being taken. The

Left: Kareem Abdul-Jabbar releases a hook shot over Artis Gilmore. Hook shots taken by tall players are nearly impossible to block. **Right:** Larry Bird shoots a jump shot with perfect form. He concentrates on the rim, maintains his balance, and follows through.

hand on the side is for blocking a pass. The raised hand is for blocking a shot or high pass. If your opponent tries to get away from you by dribbling to the side, move in the same direction with a shuffle, or side step.

When your opponent is in scoring territory, guard as closely as possible. But be careful not to foul. When your opponent is out in the middle of the court or beyond, you can stay a few feet away. If your opponent is awaiting a pass near the basket, stand a bit behind in a straddle position and keep one hand in front to knock away the ball.

In guarding an opponent, try never to leave your feet. Work hard with your legs, not your hands. If your opponent shoots, put both arms straight in the air. Try not to jump—if you do, you will probably foul your opponent. If you must jump, make sure to jump straight up, not toward your opponent.

▶EARLY HISTORY

When Dr. Naismith invented basketball in 1891, the game was played with peach baskets and a soccer ball. Every time a goal was made, someone had to climb a ladder to retrieve the ball. Over the next several years, changes were made to improve the game. In 1893, hoops with net bags began to be used. In 1894, backboards and a slightly larger ball were introduced. The standard metal rim and bottomless netting first appeared in the early 1900's. The modern seamed ball was developed by the 1930's.

When the game was first played, nine people formed a team. Later it was changed to permit nine, seven, or five to play. Standard rectangular courts were established in 1903. As the game spread and formal competition was organized, other regulations gradually were introduced. By the mid-1930's, most of the modern rules had been set.

▶MODERN COMPETITION

Basketball today is still played most widely in the United States. There is organized league competition for boys and girls, men and women, amateurs and professionals. And the popularity of the game continues to grow, both in America and throughout the world.

High School. Most high schools in the United States today, whether public or private, sponsor basketball teams for both boys and girls. A school's top team is called the varsity.

For freshmen and sophomores, many high schools also field a junior varsity squad. Schools within the same general area are organized into a league, with a full schedule of games among all the teams. In some states, high schools are divided into groups based on the number of students enrolled. After the regular season, a statewide tournament is held to determine the champion in each group. Large cities such as New York and Chicago also hold championship tournaments.

In the United States, the National Federation of State High School Associations is the governing body of organized basketball for players of high school age and under. The federation is made up of 50 state high school athletic associations. It determines the rules for high school and junior high competition.

College. The game of basketball began to catch on in American colleges and universities within only a few years after its invention. By the beginning of the 20th century, the game was being played by more than 50 U.S. colleges. By the 1930's, some intercollegiate games were attracting thousands of fans. Still, it was not until after World War II that college ball became extremely popular. Competition improved and rivalries developed. Some colleges began building big arenas and giving scholarships to good players. Then television brought the excitement into everybody's living room. Since the 1970's, women's college basketball has boomed along with men's.

The National Collegiate Athletic Association (NCAA) governs major college basketball competition. The largest schools compete in Division I; those with smaller enrollments compete in Division II and Division III. Certain other small colleges belong to the National Association of Intercollegiate Athletics (NAIA).

Most colleges also belong to conferences of eight to twelve teams each. The schools in each conference are located in the same part of the country. Each team plays the other teams in the conference at least twice each year. Then there might be a tournament to determine the conference champion. Some of the best-known basketball conferences are the Big Ten, Atlantic Coast Conference, Big East, Big Eight, Southeastern Conference, and Pacific 10. During the regular season, a team also plays several schools from outside its own conference.

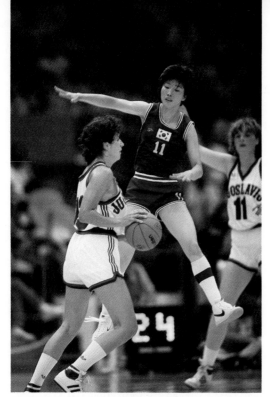

Reflecting a surge in popularity, women's basketball became an Olympic sport in 1976. South Korea and Yugoslavia compete in the 1984 games.

International. Organized basketball competition continues to grow and spread throughout the world. Outside the United States, most formal competition is either amateur or semi-professional. The rules used in international basketball are established by the International Amateur Basketball Federation (FIBA). The game is played basically as it is in the United States, though with certain minor differences. The free-throw lane, for example, is larger and shaped differently from the one used in American basketball.

Olympic basketball tournaments are held for both men and women. The first official basketball competition in the Olympic Games was held in 1936, for men only. The U.S. men's teams have won every Olympic tournament except that of 1972, when the Soviet Union won, and that of 1980, when Yugoslavia won. The first women's Olympic tournament was held in 1976. The USSR won in 1976 and 1980; the U.S. women took the gold medal in 1984.

Professional. The first professional basketball teams also date from the early days of the game. The most famous early pro team was the Buffalo Germans. They were created in 1895 and lasted 30 years. During one stretch, the Germans won 111 straight games.

The greatest professional team of the 1920's was the Original Celtics of New York City. The Celtics were the first basketball team to sign players to exclusive contracts. Some of the most famous Celtic players were Nat Holman, Henry "Dutch" Dehnert, and Joe Lapchick. In the 1930's the Renaissance Big Five, or Rens, a team of black players, dominated the game. One of its famous players was center Charles "Tarzan" Cooper.

Probably the best-known professional team of all time is the Harlem Globetrotters. They are not part of any league. This team of black players was formed in 1927 by Abe Saperstein. Their combination of skill and clowning continues to entertain spectators all over the world. Among the most famous Globetrotters have been Reece "Goose" Tatum, Marques Haynes, and Meadowlark Lemon. In 1985 the Globetrotters added the first woman to their roster, Lynette Woodard.

The National Basketball League, the first league to have a bearing on today's professional game, was formed in 1937. It was composed of professional and industrial teams

The highlight of the college basketball season is the NCAA championship, a tournament held after the regular season and conference championships. In men's Division I play, 64 teams are selected for the NCAA tournament; in women's play, 32 teams compete. Tournaments are also held in Divisions II and III, for both men and women.

The men's NCAA tournament has been held every year since 1939. The most successful team has been the University of California at Los Angeles (UCLA). Coached by the legendary John Wooden, UCLA won ten NCAA titles in the 1960's and 1970's. Other teams that have won several NCAA championships include the University of Kentucky and Indiana University. The first women's NCAA tournament was held in 1982.

There have been many excellent college players over the years. The top men go on to play professionally. Because there is no professional league for women, college usually marks the end of their competitive careers. Some of the great women collegiate players have included Ann Meyers, Nancy Lieberman, Carol Blazejowski, Pam McGee, Lynette Woodard, and Cheryl Miller.

Some Common Basketball Terms

Assist — A pass to a teammate that leads directly to a field goal.

Backboard — The surface of wood or fiberglass to which the basket is attached.

Backcourt — The half of the court away from the basket under attack.

Basket — (1) The iron rim (or hoop) and the attached net through which goals are scored; (2) a field goal.

Blocking — A foul by a defensive player who blocks the legal path of an offensive player.

Charging — A foul by an offensive player who runs into a defensive player having legal position.

Dribbling — Continuous bouncing of the ball with one hand, the only legal way a player may move with the ball.

Fast break — A style of offense in which a team attempts to race to the offensive basket before the defense can get set.

Field goal — A basket made from the court during normal play. A field goal is worth 2 or 3 points, depending on the part of the court from which it is attempted.

Free throw — A free (unguarded) shot from the free-throw line, awarded to players after certain fouls by the opposing team.

Free-throw lane — The area on the floor bounded by the free-throw line, the end line under the basket, and connecting lines forming a 12-foot lane (high school and college) or 16-foot lane (professional). The free-throw lane is also called the "foul lane."

Free-throw line — A line, 15 feet from the basket, behind which the shooter must stand in attempting a free throw. The free-throw line is also called the "foul line."

Frontcourt — The half of the court in which the basket is under attack.

Goaltending — An illegal block of an attempted field goal.

Held ball — Possession of the ball by opposing players at the same time. In professional basketball, a jump ball determines which team will get possession of the ball; in college basketball, possession is determined on an alternating basis.

Jump ball — A means of putting the ball into play in which an official tosses it upward between two opposing players. Each player jumps and tries to tap the ball to a teammate.

Man-to-man defense — A style of team defense in which each player is assigned one specific opponent to guard anywhere on the court.

Offensive foul — A personal foul committed by a member of the offensive team, usually not involving a free throw as part of the penalty. Also called "player control foul."

Palming — An illegal means of carrying the ball while dribbling.

Personal foul — Any of a variety of body-contact fouls. A player who has committed five personal fouls (six in professional basketball) is disqualified from the game.

Pick — A legal method of providing shooting room for a teammate by taking a stationary position that "picks off" or blocks a defensive player.

Pivot — A position taken by a player with his or her back to the basket, at the head of or alongside the free-throw lane, from which the player can spin or shoot or pass the ball to teammates moving toward the basket.

Post — A synonym for pivot. "High post" means farther from the basket, "low post" means closer to the basket.

Press — A style of defense in which defensive players closely guard the offensive players. (A "full-court press" is applied all over the court; a "half-court press" is applied only after the ball is brought across the midcourt line.)

Rebound — The recovery of a missed field goal attempt.

Shot clock — A timer that indicates how much time remains for the offensive team to attempt a field goal. In professional basketball, for example, a team has 24 seconds to attempt a field goal after gaining possession of the ball.

Steal — The capture of the ball from the hands of a player by the defender; also, an intercepted pass.

Technical foul — foul imposed for misbehavior or some technical rule infraction. The penalty is a free throw (sometimes two free throws). In high school and college games, the team shooting the free throw also receives possession of the ball.

Ten-second rule — The rule that a team must bring the ball across the midcourt line within 10 seconds after gaining possession in the backcourt.

Three-point shot — A field goal made from behind a line marked in an arc a certain distance from the basket; such field goals are credited with 3 points.

Three-second rule — The rule that offensive players may not take set positions within the free-throw lane for more than 3 seconds.

Traveling — Running or walking with the ball without dribbling it. Also called "steps" or "walking."

Turnover — Loss of possession of the ball without attempting a field goal.

Violation — Any infraction of the rules that is not classified as a foul. The penalty is loss of possession of the ball.

Zone defense — A style of team defense in which each player is assigned to guard a designated floor area rather than a specific opponent.

Some signals used frequently by officials

| Jump ball | Personal foul | Points scored (1, 2, or 3 fingers) | Traveling | Illegal dribble | Offensive foul |

NATIONAL BASKETBALL ASSOCIATION

EASTERN CONFERENCE

Atlantic Division	Central Division
Boston Celtics	Atlanta Hawks
Miami Heat	Chicago Bulls
New Jersey Nets	Cleveland Cavaliers
New York Knickerbockers	Detroit Pistons
Philadelphia 76ers	Indiana Pacers
Washington Bullets	Milwaukee Bucks
	Orlando Magic

WESTERN CONFERENCE

Midwest Division	Pacific Division
Charlotte Hornets	Golden State Warriors
Dallas Mavericks	Los Angeles Clippers
Denver Nuggets	Los Angeles Lakers
Houston Rockets	Phoenix Suns
Minnesota Timberwolves	Portland Trail Blazers
San Antonio Spurs	Sacramento Kings
Utah Jazz	Seattle SuperSonics

The American Basketball Association (ABA) began in 1967 as a league for those cities without NBA teams. It was dissolved in 1976, and some of its teams and best players were absorbed into the NBA.

The first women's professional league, the Women's Professional Basketball League (WBL), was organized in 1978. However, women's pro basketball did not prove to be as popular as men's, and the WBL ceased operating in 1981.

The NBA players are tall, fast, and highly skilled and are considered by many to be the best all-around athletes. The best players are paid very large salaries, and their fans pack vast arenas to watch them compete. Many games are broadcast on television and radio.

The NBA has 27 teams, representing major cities from around the country. The league is divided into two conferences. The Eastern Conference consists of the Atlantic Division and Central Division; the Western Conference has the Midwest Division and the Pacific Division. Each team plays a regular-season schedule of 82 games. Many of those games are against teams in the same division, but all the teams play each other a few times every year. At the end of the regular season, the top 16 teams compete in a series of playoffs to determine the NBA champion.

The most successful team in NBA history has been the Boston Celtics. Since the 1950's the Celtics have won 16 league championships. From 1959 to 1966 they took the crown eight years in a row. Since the 1970's the Los Angeles Lakers have also been a dominant team, earning the NBA title four times.

Over the years the NBA has had many great players. Some of the outstanding centers have been George Mikan, Bill Russell, Wilt Chamberlain, and Kareem Abdul-Jabbar. Stellar forwards have included Bob Pettit, Elgin Baylor, Julius Erving, and Larry Bird. Among the great guards have been Bob Cousy, Jerry West, Oscar Robertson, John Havlicek (who also played forward), Earvin "Magic" Johnson, and Michael Jordan.

The Basketball Hall of Fame is located in Springfield, Massachusetts, the birthplace of the sport.

Reviewed by DAVE DEBUSSCHERE
Member, Basketball Hall of Fame

BASTILLE. See FRENCH REVOLUTION.
BASUTOLAND. See LESOTHO.

from small midwestern cities. Another pro league, the Basketball Association of America, was established in 1946.

In 1949, owners of Eastern hockey arenas wanted to sell seats when hockey was not being played. With these large playing areas available, the National Basketball League merged with the Basketball Association of America to form the modern National Basketball Association (NBA).

NATIONAL BASKETBALL ASSOCIATION CHAMPIONS

1951	Rochester Royals	1972	Los Angeles Lakers
1952	Minneapolis Lakers	1973	New York
1953	Minneapolis Lakers		Knickerbockers
1954	Minneapolis Lakers	1974	Boston Celtics
1955	Syracuse Nationals	1975	Golden State Warriors
1956	Philadelphia Warriors	1976	Boston Celtics
1957	Boston Celtics	1977	Portland Trail Blazers
1958	St. Louis Hawks	1978	Washington Bullets
1959	Boston Celtics	1979	Seattle SuperSonics
1960	Boston Celtics	1980	Los Angeles Lakers
1961	Boston Celtics	1981	Boston Celtics
1962	Boston Celtics	1982	Los Angeles Lakers
1963	Boston Celtics	1983	Philadelphia 76ers
1964	Boston Celtics	1984	Boston Celtics
1965	Boston Celtics	1985	Los Angeles Lakers
1966	Boston Celtics	1986	Boston Celtics
1967	Philadelphia 76ers	1987	Los Angeles Lakers
1968	Boston Celtics	1988	Los Angeles Lakers
1969	Boston Celtics	1989	Detroit Pistons
1970	New York	1990	Detroit Pistons
	Knickerbockers	1991	Chicago Bulls
1971	Milwaukee Bucks	1992	Chicago Bulls

Bats are the only mammals that fly. They are also among the most social of mammals. Some species have been known to live in colonies of more than a million members.

BATS

In the animal kingdom bats are classed as mammals. Like all mammals, bats nurse their young on milk. Like most mammals, they have hair and bear living young. But in one way bats are different from all other mammals: Bats can fly.

There are mammals known as flying squirrels and flying lemurs, but they do not truly fly. Rather they glide from tree to tree. Bats are the only mammals that move through the air with wings.

A bat's wing is not like a bird's wing. The bird's wing is formed chiefly of feathers. The bat's wing is a double layer of skin stretched over the thin bones of its arm and fingers. A bat's skeleton is the framework for these wings. The arm extends from a shoulder socket, bends at the elbow, and ends with long, slender fingers. The fingers are almost as long as the rest of the body. They support the main part of the wing and are covered with skin.

The wing covers all fingers except a short thumb, which is left free. A sharp claw on the end of the thumb forms a hook at the top of the wing. When its wings are folded, the bat uses its hooks to climb tree trunks, rocky walls, and other rough surfaces.

The skin connecting the webbed fingers is also attached to the bat's clawed feet. This makes the back part of the wings. Most bats have an extra flap of skin connecting their feet. While flying, many can fold this flap into a pocket for catching insects.

Since its leg bones and leg muscles are included in its wings, a bat can fly more easily than it can walk. But the feet are far from useless. Like human hands, a bat's feet can turn inward, which enables them to grasp objects like twigs and branches. Sharp claws hook securely into cracks or around bumps in the wall or ceiling of a cave. These claws are so strong that they support the bat's whole weight, even during sleep.

When resting, a bat can use its claws to cling to a wall or tree trunk—or it may hang upside down, suspended by its feet. Bats hang upside down because it is easier for them than perching upright.

Bats may be less than 1 inch (2.5 centimeters) in length or as long as 15 inches (37.5 centimeters). Their wing spread can be as wide as 5 feet (1.5 meters). Bats have fur that may be white, red, brown, gray, or black.

▶HOW BATS LIVE

There are nearly a thousand different species, or kinds, of bats. They live in almost every part of the world except the polar regions. Each kind of bat has different habits, though the various species also have many things in common.

Bat Colonies

Bats are usually social animals. That is, they live in groups. Often they can be found living in caves. If you see one bat flying into a cave, you can be reasonably sure there are other bats inside. In some caves thousands of bats crowd together on walls or ceilings. Smaller bat colonies numbering only ten or twelve bats may live in a hollow tree.

Caves and hollow trees are not the only places where bats live. Some bats simply roost in trees, hanging like leaves from twigs and branches. Two kinds of tropical bats make tents from palm leaves. Such a bat slits the leaf with its teeth, then hangs inside the folds.

Bats live in the pyramids of Egypt and in the fruit trees of Australia. In North America and Europe people sometimes share a house with bats and never know they are there. A bat can squeeze through narrow cracks and roost between layers of wall and ceiling.

Night Creatures

Most bats are nocturnal. This means that they are active only at night. They sleep in the daytime and come out at night to find food. Only a few kinds of bats venture out in bright sunlight. Bats are probably night creatures for the same reasons that most small mammals are. A small animal is in less danger at night. In the daytime it is in constant danger of being eaten by larger animals that sleep at night. Also, at night bats can catch insects with less competition from birds.

The Search for Food

Most bats live on insects alone. Some eat only fruit. Some eat both insects and fruit. A few kinds of bats eat other things—meat, fish, and even flower nectar.

In Canada and the United States the most familiar bats are insect eaters, though there are nectar-feeding bats in Arizona and California. Probably the best-known fruit bats are the huge flying foxes. In Australia these giant bats have become a serious nuisance to fruit growers. They swarm over the orchards, devouring fruit at night and roosting in the trees by day.

In India one kind of bat has been seen eating mice, birds, and lizards. When captured, the large spear-nosed bats of tropical America will eat almost anything. They have been fed bananas, horsemeat, liver, and hamburger. They will even eat smaller bats.

The bats with the most unusual diets are found in the tropics. *Noctilio* bats of South and Middle America eat fishes. They skim over a pond or lake, dragging their sharp claws

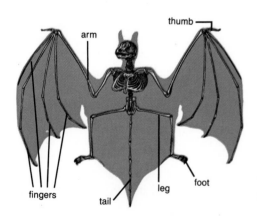

The bat's anatomy is specially adapted for flying. The hands and arms form the wings. The highly developed arm bones hold out flaps of skin from the bat's back and belly. A double layer of thin, flexible skin covers the elongated bones of the fingers.

thumb
arm
fingers
tail
leg
foot

Bats eat a wide variety of food, some species consuming up to half their weight each night. At left, a bat uses its long tongue to obtain nectar. At right, a mother and baby bat at rest. Bats roost by hanging upside down with their wings folded over their bodies.

through the water to catch small fishes swimming near the surface. Another group of jungle bats, the tiny hummingbird bats, eat chiefly the pollen and nectar of flowers.

Probably the most famous tropical bats are the vampires, found only in South and Middle America. The vampire bat has inspired legends, superstitions, and horror tales—all of them false. A vampire bat does bite other animals and drinks their blood. But a vampire bat may bite a sleeping horse, cow, or goat—or even a person—without being noticed. Its sharp teeth make a shallow cut. Then the bat simply laps up a small amount of blood and flies away. The chief danger to the victim is not loss of blood but rather infection. Vampire bats—as well as several other species—are known carriers of rabies.

Migration and Hibernation

Bats cannot survive in extremely cold weather. So some fly to warmer climates for the winter. When spring comes, these bats return to a favorite roost. They may fly as far as 800 miles (1,287 kilometers) during a migration.

Instead of migrating, other bats hibernate deep in caves, where the temperature changes very little from season to season. For many weeks hibernating bats hang head downward, sometimes packed together in thick clusters. They each have an extra layer of body fat that provides the fuel they need to keep alive until spring.

Birth of Young

Bats mate in the fall, before hibernating or flying away for the winter. When the weather begins to warm up, female bats gather in the roosts that will become nurseries. In late spring or early summer the baby bats are born. Most mother bats have just one baby at a time. (Some have up to four, but this is as rare as twins in human families.)

When a baby bat is born, the mother forms a living cradle by hanging belly-up from the ceiling or a branch. She may hang by the hooks at the top of her wings as well as by her feet. The newborn bat rests in this cradle. The baby bat is able to hang on to its mother's fur, using its own sharp teeth and claws.

Young bats grow so rapidly that a 10-day-old bat can be too heavy for its mother to carry. Within a month after birth, the baby bat has grown to its full size. A bat born in June is flying on nightly hunting trips by August. It may live as long as 10 to 14 years, a remarkably long lifetime for a small mammal.

▶ANCESTORS

Ancestors of today's bats were flying about the earth at least 50,000,000 years ago. Since that time some bats have changed very little. One 40,000,000-year-old bat fossil found in Europe looks very much like the skeleton of a modern bat.

Some scientists think that the first bats may have evolved from a tree-climbing mammal that could leap and glide after insects. Over millions of years the limbs of some gliding animals may have developed into wings. These winged animals would have been the first bats. Scientists are still looking for fossils that would prove this theory.

▶HOW DO BATS FIND THEIR WAY IN THE DARK?

For centuries people who studied bats wondered how they found their way in the dark. Many people thought that bats had unusually keen eyesight and could see by light too faint for human eyes to detect. Scientists now know that a bat's ability to navigate depends not on its eyes but on its ears and vocal organs.

The first steps toward understanding how bats navigate were taken in the 1780's. An Italian zoologist named Lazzaro Spallanzani suspected that bats could not see in the dark. To find out, he blinded some bats and released them into a room crisscrossed with silk threads. The bats flew through the maze without touching the threads. Then he tried plugging their ears with wax. The animals blundered about, flapping their wings helplessly and becoming entangled in the threads.

Spallanzani's work was almost forgotten until 1920. That year, at Cambridge University in England, Professor H. Hartridge suggested that bats sent out signals that were beyond the range of human hearing. (Such sounds are called **ultrasonic.**) He thought bats might use the echoes of these signals to navigate in the dark. But Hartridge could not prove his theory. He had no way of listening to ultrasonic sounds.

In 1941 two scientists in the United States proved that Spallanzani and Hartridge had been on the right track. Donald R. Griffin and Robert Galambos of Harvard University placed bats in front of a new electronic instrument that could detect ultrasonic sounds. The men could hear no sounds, but patterns on a screen showed that the bats were uttering high-pitched cries.

Griffin and Galambos strung a room with a network of wire and repeated some of Spallanzani's experiments. They added their own modern equipment—microphones and recording devices. Patterns on the electronic screen showed that the bats were constantly squeaking as they flew successfully through the maze of wires.

A bat sends out signals—high-pitched squeaks that bounce off anything in its path. A sound that is bounced back, or reflected, is called an echo. The bat uses echoes to locate things in the dark. So scientists call this system **echolocation.** It is often compared to man-made radar and sonar systems, which also use reflected signals to locate objects. But radar and sonar are newcomers. Bats have been using echolocation for millions of years.

BARBARA LAND
Columbia Graduate School of Journalism
Reviewed by KARL F. KOOPMAN
The American Museum of Natural History

See also ECHO; RADAR, SONAR, LORAN, AND SHORAN; SOUND AND ULTRASONICS.

A bat locates and judges distance to its prey by bouncing ultrasonic signals off it. The same technique, called echolocation, helps a bat navigate in the dark.

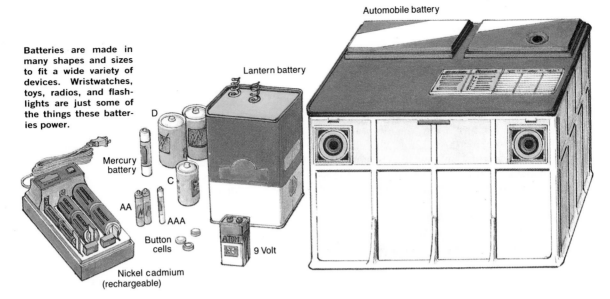

Batteries are made in many shapes and sizes to fit a wide variety of devices. Wristwatches, toys, radios, and flashlights are just some of the things these batteries power.

Automobile battery

Lantern battery

D

Mercury battery

C

AA

AAA

Button cells

9 Volt

Nickel cadmium (rechargeable)

BATTERIES

When you enjoy music from a portable radio or find your way in the dark with a flashlight, you are using the most common portable power source known—the battery.

Batteries are very much a part of our lives. Without them many toys would not work, automobiles would not start, and digital wristwatches would not tell time. Even satellites in orbit would stop relaying their signals to earth.

▶ WHAT IS A BATTERY?

A battery is a device that produces electrical energy, usually by means of a chemical reaction. This chemical reaction takes place in the part of the battery known as the **cell.** Cells are the battery's building blocks. Each battery contains one or more cells. The common transistor radio battery, for example, is made up of six cells. The common "D" battery is just a single cell.

Batteries can be either **primary** or **secondary** devices. Primary batteries are those that can be used only as long as the supply of chemicals inside them lasts. (The process of producing electricity uses up the chemicals.) When a primary battery stops producing power, it is thrown away.

Secondary batteries, on the other hand, can be recharged. When these batteries are exhausted, an electrical current can be applied to the battery to reverse the chemical reaction that took place inside the cells. The result is a battery with a new supply of energy; it can be used until it runs down again.

▶ HOW PRIMARY BATTERIES WORK

The most common primary battery is the "D" battery, also known as the flashlight battery or the dry cell. The dry cell is not really dry. It contains a central carbon rod surrounded by a damp chemical paste. These are enclosed in a container made of zinc. When the battery is being used, the carbon and zinc react with each other to produce electricity.

To start the chemical reaction, the battery must be in an electrical circuit. Only when there is a demand for power will the battery produce electricity. When the "on" switch is moved—on a flashlight, for example—a complete path, or electrical circuit, is formed that includes the battery, switch, connecting wires, and bulb. Electricity can now flow through the circuit, and the flashlight bulb lights.

Often more than one battery is needed to provide sufficient power to run a device. Several batteries can be used together if they are lined up in a certain way. In a **series connection,** the positive end of one battery must be in contact with the negative end of another battery. This type of arrangement multiplies the force that pushes the electricity (like a pump pushing water) through the device being powered.

Sometimes cells can be wired in a **parallel connection,** that is, positive end to positive end and negative end to negative end. When this is done, the "push" available is the same as from a single battery, but the amount of electricity is multiplied. This type of connection is used where heavy loads, such as electrical motors, must be powered.

Types of Primary Batteries

The flashlight battery is just one of many kinds of primary batteries. Another common type of dry cell, also based on a carbon-zinc chemical reaction, is the 9-volt battery, also known as the transistor radio battery. This device is made up of six flat, 1.5-volt cells stacked one upon the other in a package that will easily fit the small spaces in pocket-size transistor radios and calculators. (These devices do not all use 9-volt batteries. Some take "A" or "AA" cells.) The battery's connecting posts, called **terminals,** are made into clips, and both are located on the top of the package. This helps avoid the problem of putting the battery into a device upside down.

Another type of primary battery is the alkaline battery, which is becoming more and more popular because of its longer life. Its operation is similar to that of the carbon-zinc dry cell—the only difference is the chemicals used. The basic package is almost identical.

Other types of primary batteries are the mercury battery, the silver-oxide battery used in electronic wristwatches, and the new, very long-life lithium battery. These batteries are named for the chemicals that they contain.

Because all primary batteries in time will run down and have to be replaced, they are most widely used in products or applications where low cost is important or where recharging is not practical, such as in a wristwatch.

▶ HOW SECONDARY BATTERIES WORK

Secondary batteries are often referred to as "wet cells" since many do contain liquids (unlike the dry or damp chemicals in primary batteries). Secondary batteries are also often called storage batteries because when they are being recharged, they can be thought of as storing energy.

The most common secondary battery is the lead-acid automobile battery. This device is made up of six cells, each of which contains metal plates made of lead and lead dioxide. The plates are immersed in a weak solution of sulfuric acid and water. On the outside of the battery, positive and negative terminals are used to make the electrical connection to the metal plates and acid solution inside.

The automobile battery is turned on by the ignition switch in the car. This action forms a completed electrical circuit. As the battery is being used, or discharged, the lead plates chemically change into different compounds of lead. This process can provide electricity as long as enough lead is present on the plates.

When the battery runs low, however, it can be recharged by forcing electricity to flow into it in the reverse direction. This is the process called charging. It is carried out in a car by a device called an alternator, which is a small electrical generator run by the automobile engine. During charging, the chemical compounds change back into the original lead and lead dioxide. The life of such a battery is measured in years, because it can be charged thousands of times as it runs down.

Types of Secondary Batteries

Other types of secondary batteries are the nickel cadmium and silver cadmium batteries, which are named for the chemicals they contain. Like the lead-acid automobile battery

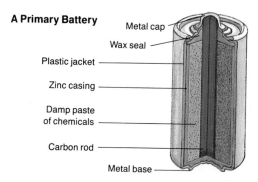

A Primary Battery

Metal cap
Wax seal
Plastic jacket
Zinc casing
Damp paste of chemicals
Carbon rod
Metal base

The carbon-zinc dry cell, or flashlight battery, is the most common type of primary battery. A chemical reaction between the carbon, zinc, and damp chemical paste causes an electrical current to be produced.

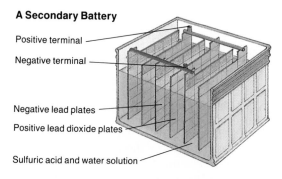

A Secondary Battery

Positive terminal
Negative terminal
Negative lead plates
Positive lead dioxide plates
Sulfuric acid and water solution

The lead-acid automobile battery, a type of secondary battery, contains lead and lead-oxide plates set in a solution of sulfuric acid and water. This kind of battery can be charged and used over and over again.

they can be charged many times. This is done with a charging device that plugs into an electrical outlet. These batteries can be used in the same applications as primary batteries. They also are used to power rechargeable flashlights, portable two-way radios, and a variety of other battery-operated household appliances that are supplied with their own chargers.

In general, secondary batteries are used where large amounts of power are needed or where charging is practical to carry out. Though they initially cost more than primary batteries, secondary batteries can be very economical because they are not discarded and replaced every time they run down.

▶ HOW POWERFUL ARE BATTERIES?

The amount of power that a battery can deliver is directly related to the amount and type of chemicals it contains. This power is measured in both amperes and volts. An ampere is the amount of electricity the battery can produce in 1 second. Volts are a measure of the "push" the battery can give to electricity flowing through a wire.

The amount of chemicals in a battery also influences the battery's size, so a large battery is more powerful than a small one. Small "AAA" penlight batteries (1.5 volts and $\frac{1}{8}$ ampere) will run a penlight for an hour or so. An automobile battery (12 volts and 50 amperes) will provide enough power to start a car or run an electric golf cart.

The life of a battery also depends on the amount of power it must deliver to the device it is running. An automobile battery can start a car and keep it running for a short while, but it will very quickly run down if the car's alternator (turned by the engine) does not begin to charge it. On the other hand, tiny button-size batteries will operate a digital wristwatch for a year or more. This is because the power requirements of a wristwatch are very small.

▶ NEW TYPES OF BATTERIES

All of the batteries described ultimately will run down and have to be replaced. Even rechargeable units will reach a point where they will not respond to charging. As a result, scientists are constantly trying to develop the ideal battery that will last for years (when not in use) and will deliver maximum power for long periods of time when needed. Two candidates are the solar cell and the fuel cell.

Solar Cells

Solar cells are unique because no chemical reaction occurs to use up material. Electricity is produced when light, particularly sunlight, strikes the surface of the cell. This surface is a thin wafer of specially treated, pure silicon.

The power produced by such cells is directly related to the amount of light present. With enough light, a 3-inch (8-centimeter) solar cell will produce about one third the amount of electrical energy of a "AAA" penlight battery. It will do so, however, as long as light falls on the cell—even for years.

Individual solar cells are almost always connected together to form solar batteries. They are used in applications where it is impractical or even impossible to replace worn-out batteries. The power source for most satellites circling the earth consists of large solar batteries made up of hundreds of individual cells. Solar batteries may one day be used as inexpensive power sources for our homes.

Fuel Cells

Another candidate for the ideal battery is the fuel cell. This device produces electricity from the interaction of two gases—typically hydrogen and oxygen. This battery works by passing hydrogen and oxygen gas over a heated substance in a specially constructed chamber. A complex chemical process combines the two gases and produces electricity as a result.

An interesting by-product of the operation of the fuel cell is pure water. Because the gases are obtained inexpensively and the by-product is useful, fuel cells may become a major source of power for our cities.

Nuclear Batteries

A third type of battery that exhibits extremely long life is the nuclear battery. It produces electricity as the result of the decay of radioactive material. A nuclear battery has a lifetime that is measured in hundreds or even thousands of years. The problem with this device is the danger of radioactive contamination. For this reason its widespread use probably will not occur in the near future.

IRWIN MATH
Author, *Wires and Watts:
Understanding and Using Electricity*

See also ELECTRICITY.

BAUHAUS. See GERMANY, ART AND ARCHITECTURE OF.

A large bear is a powerful animal. If it is cornered or attacked, it can be very dangerous.

BEARS

A shaggy giant wades into a stream. Ducking its head, it lunges forward. Then it comes up, a big salmon flopping between its jaws. The huge beast clambers ashore to eat its meal in comfort. This expert catcher of fish is the Kodiak bear, one of the great Alaskan brown bears. It is the world's largest land-dwelling flesh eater, often measuring nearly 3 meters (about 9 feet) in length.

Alaskan brown bears feed almost entirely on fish when salmon are running upstream to spawn. At other times the bears make a meal of whatever is available. They may dig for roots and bulbs and eat grass, berries, fruits, eggs, and insects. Or they may burrow after squirrels and other small mammals.

▶ "BEASTS THAT WALK LIKE PEOPLE"

Although they eat many different kinds of food (and much of it vegetable), bears make up one family of the Carnivora, or meat-eating mammals. Raccoons and pandas are their close relatives, but bears also share a common ancestry with dogs. All bears have bulky bodies and stubby tails. Their legs are thick and powerful. When they walk, their heels touch the ground, just as ours do. The prints of their hind feet are remarkably like those of a huge, flat-footed human being. In fact, the American Indians called grizzly bears "the beasts that walk like people." Bears ordinarily move at a lumbering walk, but they can run at nearly 50 kilometers (about 30 miles) an hour when necessary. Some are skilled tree climbers. Bears live from 15 to 30 years in the wild and even longer in captivity.

In the wild, most bears are found in parts of Asia, Europe, and North America. There are no bears in Africa, Antarctica, or Australia, and only one species lives south of the equator. This is the South American spectacled bear. The main types that inhabit North America are big brown bears, grizzly bears, and American black bears. Polar bears live in the Arctic region.

▶ THE BLACK BEAR APPEARS IN SEVERAL COLORS

The American black bear, which weighs up to 225 kilograms (500 pounds), is the smallest of the North American bears. It is a wide-ranging species, found from Alaska and northern Canada to central Mexico. In spite of its name, the black bear appears in a variety of colors. In the eastern part of their range, most of these bears grow shiny black fur. To the west, many of them have brown or cinnamon-colored coats. Brown cubs are often born in the same litter with black ones. A race with grayish blue fur—the glacier, or blue, bear—lives in southern Alaska. The creamy white Kermode's bear appears on islands off British Columbia.

Like bears everywhere, the American black fills up on many different kinds of food during the summer and fall. By the time cold weather comes, the bear is very fat and ready for a long winter's nap. It curls up in a den under a ledge or under the roots of a tree and goes to sleep. Eating nothing and living off its fat, the bear usually stays in this snug retreat until spring. Once in a while it may wake up briefly and grumble. On mild days it may even leave its den for a short walk.

The bear's winter sleep is not true hibernation. The animal's temperature remains almost normal, and it breathes regularly four or five times a minute. In true hibernation a mammal's body temperature may drop close to freezing, while its heartbeat and breathing are very slow and faint. To all appearances, the animal seems to be dead. Woodchucks and many ground squirrels hibernate in this way, but bears do not.

Cubs are born in late January or early February while the mother is in her den.

Most bears appear even larger than they are because they have loose skin and dense, shaggy fur. Bears have an excellent sense of smell, but their eyesight and hearing are usually poor. Their ears are small and are set close to their heads.

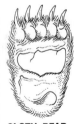

Bears have five toes on each foot and a strong, curved claw on each toe for digging and climbing. The claws are not retractile (cannot be drawn in, as a cat's claws can), but they can pick up very small objects. The feet of tree-climbing bears have soles with a rough surface. Polar bears have thick fur on the soles of their feet to help them grip on ice.

SLOTH BEAR

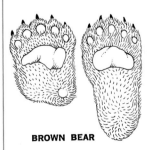

BROWN BEAR

POLAR BEAR

Above, polar bears in northern Canada. They roam ice packs and coasts of the Arctic Ocean. Right, Alaska grizzly. Notice its shoulder hump. These bears have almost disappeared south of Canada.

Left, black bears climbing a tree. They are the smallest North American bears. Below, Alaskan brown bear with salmon. When full-grown, these bears are the world's largest land-dwelling flesh-eaters.

Usually she has two cubs, but sometimes three or four are born. Their eyes are closed, and they are almost naked. Each one is less than 25 centimeters (10 inches) long and weighs under 0.5 kilograms (1 pound). They remain in the den with the mother until late March or early April. By then they are covered with thick coats of wooly hair. They come out and wander through the spring woods with her. The mother keeps a constant watch over the cubs. She teaches them how to hunt for food. If danger threatens, she sends them up a tree. If they disobey, she cuffs

them soundly. The cubs usually stay with the mother until they are 1½ years old.

▶ THE GRIZZLY, A VANISHING MONARCH

The grizzly bear weighs up to 450 kilograms (1,000 pounds). It is much larger than its cousin the black bear. The black bear has a straight profile, but the grizzly's face has a concave (curved-in) appearance. The grizzly also has a shoulder hump and very long, straight claws. In color it ranges from a yellowish shade to almost black. Some individuals have light-tipped hair, giving them the grizzled appearance for which these bears are named. Such bears are also called silvertips.

This mighty bear once ranged from Alaska to Mexico. Now grizzlies have almost disappeared south of the Canadian border. Only small numbers still roam wilderness areas of Idaho, Montana, and Wyoming. The most likely place to see a grizzly bear is in a national park in the American West.

Grizzlies are closely related to Alaskan brown bears. Some experts consider that the two are different races of the same species. Kodiak bears, which are larger than grizzlies, weigh up to 780 kilograms (1,700 pounds).

▶ THE GREAT WHITE BEAR

The polar bear roams the ice packs and coasts of the Arctic Ocean, all the way around the earth. This great white bear may weigh as much as 450 kilograms (1,000 pounds). It is a powerful swimmer and is sometimes found far at sea, traveling from one iceberg to another. The polar bear has keen eyes and an extra-sharp sense of smell. It is an expert hunter. It stalks seals, walrus pups, and other prey. Often it hides its black nose with its paws so that it will not be seen against the ice and snow.

The only polar bear that stays in a den during the Arctic winter is a female that is expecting cubs. Before winter comes, she travels inland and digs a den in deep snow. There she sleeps through the months-long night. And there her cubs, each about 25 centimeters (10 inches) long, are born. Like black bear cubs, they may stay with their mother until they are 1½ years old. Today, the hunting of polar bears for sport or for commercial purposes is limited by international agreement.

▶ BEARS IN OTHER PLACES

The spectacled bear lives in the Andes mountains of South America. Many variations of brown bears inhabit mountains in Europe and Asia. Asia also has such interesting species as the Himalayan black bear, which has a kind of mane; the insect-eating sloth bear of India and Sri Lanka; and the small, short-haired Malayan sun bear. All three have white or yellowish crescents on their chests.

ROBERT M. MCCLUNG
Author, science books for children

The South American spectacled bear was named for the markings of light fur around its eyes.

The Himalayan bear is a hunter of livestock. It is black in color, with a light crescent marking.

The Beatles in 1966. *Clockwise from left:* John Lennon, Paul McCartney, George Harrison, and Ringo Starr.

BEATLES, THE

During most of the 1960's, the Western world seemed to move to the beat of four young rock musicians from Liverpool, England. They called themselves the Beatles.

John Lennon (1940–80), a guitarist and singer, was the original leader of the group. He explained the name Beatles in this way: "When you said it, it was crawly things [beetles]; when you read it, it was beat music." The other members were Paul McCartney (1942–) and George Harrison (1943–), also guitarists and singers, and the drummer and singer Ringo Starr (1940–), whose real name was Richard Starkey.

Before the Beatles, many people thought rock was American music that was not to be taken seriously. The Beatles proved them wrong.

Each Beatle brought different strengths to the group. John had a strong personality and a sharp wit. Paul was a showman, who charmed audiences with his melodic voice. George was known as a gifted and serious musician. Ringo was adored for his "goofy," down-to-earth personality.

Brian Epstein, a young record dealer, became their manager. He was a major force in their success. With great difficulty, he found a record company willing to sign the Beatles. Their first single recording, "Love Me Do" (1962), quickly became popular. Their second record, "Please Please Me" (1963), was a big hit. Teenagers—in a frenzy known as "Beatlemania"—struggled to get close to their new heroes.

The Beatles appeared in New York for the first time in 1964. Their engaging personalities and energetic sound turned Britain's most popular rock group into an overnight success in the United States. Within weeks, the top five best-selling records there were all by the Beatles.

Before long, adults found it hard to ignore the Beatles' talents. John Lennon's first book, *In His Own Write,* and the group's first movie, *A Hard Day's Night,* won enthusiastic reviews. Beatles tunes like "Yesterday" were recorded by hundreds of other artists in many musical styles. In 1965, Queen Elizabeth II honored the Beatles by making them members of the Order of the British Empire.

As time went on, the words of their songs, written mainly by Lennon and McCartney, became more poetic. The subjects ranged from the haunting loneliness of "Eleanor Rigby" to the fantasy of "Yellow Submarine" (the theme song for the full-length cartoon of the same name). Their music changed, too. The Beatles began experimenting with electronic effects and instruments from around the world. And they invited jazz and classical musicians to perform on their recordings.

The Beatles made their last stage appearance in 1966. They produced their masterpiece, the album *Sergeant Pepper's Lonely Hearts Club Band,* in 1967, the year of their manager's death. Later that year, the four wrote and directed a film, *Magical Mystery Tour,* in which they toured the English countryside in search of wonder, magic, and fun.

The Beatles made several more recordings as a group, including the hit songs "Hey Jude," "Get Back," "Come Together," "Something," and "Let It Be." But the members had also begun to pursue separate interests, and in 1970 the group disbanded. All four continued to enjoy some success as solo artists during the 1970's. Many fans hoped for a reunion. But in 1980, John Lennon was assassinated in New York City. The "magical mystery tour" was truly over.

NICHOLAS SCHAFFNER
Author, *The Boys from Liverpool*

See also ROCK MUSIC.

BEAUMONT, WILLIAM (1785–1853)

William Beaumont was a frontier surgeon who discovered how the human stomach works. He made his discoveries in a remarkable way: by acquiring a patient with a hole in his stomach. His work ranks as a landmark in medicine. Yet compared with modern doctors, Beaumont had almost no training.

Born on November 21, 1785, in Lebanon, Connecticut, he was one of nine children. His father was a veteran of the Revolutionary War. Young William received some schooling, but no one knows how much. In 1806 he moved to upstate New York, where he taught school. Here he began to read many books about medicine. Four years later he became an apprentice to a doctor and did everything from sweeping floors to assisting in surgery. That was his first medical training. In 1812 he entered the army as a surgeon's assistant.

When the War of 1812 ended, Beaumont practiced medicine in Vermont for a few years. Then he re-enlisted in the Army and was assigned to Fort Mackinac, an outpost in northern Michigan. Before going west in 1821, he married. In time he and his wife had three children.

Beaumont was post surgeon at the fort. One day in 1822 he was called to treat a wounded French-Canadian Indian named Alexis St. Martin. St. Martin, who was 18, had been accidentally shot. The bullet had both exposed his stomach and made a hole in it the size of a man's finger.

Beaumont placed him in the post hospital. There, for almost a year, Beaumont treated the wound and kept St. Martin alive. Later Beaumont took St. Martin into his own home and fed and clothed him.

By 1825 St. Martin was well enough to chop wood, but he still had a hole in his stomach. A small flap had grown over the hole, but it could be easily pushed aside. This meant Beaumont could study a human stomach at work and see how it digested food —if St. Martin would let him. Beaumont made an offer. If St. Martin would serve as a human laboratory, Beaumont would give him food, drink, and lodging.

St. Martin agreed, and Beaumont began 10 years of experiments that were to make

William Beaumont, as he appeared around 1821.

him famous. He tied bits of food to string and held them in the opening. In this way, he discovered that the stomach produces gastric juice, which dissolves food. He collected the juice in bottles and noted that it continued to dissolve food there. He saw how the movements of the stomach muscles helped to shred the food. Beaumont also found that some meats were digested more easily than others and that small pieces were digested more easily than large ones. His studies still stand as the greatest single contribution to understanding digestion.

The Army assigned Beaumont to various posts and he always took St. Martin with him. But St. Martin often tired of being a human laboratory. He twice left and returned to Canada.

Beaumont received some help from other scientists and some support from the U. S. Government. But for the most part he carried on the work on his own. He paid St. Martin's expenses even after St. Martin married and had children. When Beaumont finished writing his classic book about his work, he had to pay for publishing it.

In 1834 St. Martin left for the third time, and Beaumont could not persuade him to return. Still, the important discoveries had been made. Beaumont retired from the Army in 1840 and settled in St. Louis as a private doctor. He died on April 25, 1853.

JOHN S. BOWMAN
Author and Science Editor

The beaver is a talented lumberjack that uses giant chisel-like front teeth and well-developed chewing muscles to fell trees.

BEAVERS

Beavers inhabit ponds and streams in wooded areas from Alaska to northern Mexico. Their bodies are ideally constructed for their varied activities on land and in the water. A beaver's large hind feet are webbed for swimming. Its broad, flat tail is scaly and naked, except for a few bristles. The tail serves as a prop when the beaver stands up to gnaw on trees; it becomes an alarm signal when slapped against the water; it also is a rudder and an oar to aid in swimming.

Although they are air breathers, beavers are thoroughly at home in the water. They can remain submerged for 15 minutes at a time. When a beaver dives, flaplike valves in its ears and nostrils close, shutting out the water. Except for its tail, the beaver is clothed in a shiny coat of soft, thick underfur; this is overlaid with longer, coarser guard hairs. Glands on either side of the tail supply oil, which keeps the coat waterproofed and glistening. The two inner claws of the beaver's hind feet are grooved; they make efficient combs for grooming the coat and spreading the oil through it.

▶CHAMPION HEWERS OF WOOD

Beavers live in family groups, or colonies. The family usually consists of the parents and their young of the past two years. Together they cut trees, build and repair their dams and lodges, and store branches for the winter food supply. This work makes them the most remarkable engineers among the Rodentia, the order of gnawing mammals to which they belong. And among mammals, only human beings are better engineers than beavers.

For felling trees, a beaver uses its four front teeth—the orange-colored, chisel-edged gnawing teeth (incisors). With these sharp tools it takes only a few minutes to cut down a small willow tree. Occasionally beavers fell trees as big as 2 feet (0.6 meter) in diameter. Favorite beaver trees are softwoods like aspen, poplar, and willow. But the beaver also cuts birch, sugar maple, wild cherry, alder, hemlock, and pine.

Building dam

After selecting a tree to cut, the beaver gouges out first one chip and then another a few inches below. Next it tears out the middle chip of wood. Working in this way, the beaver girdles the tree, then cuts deeper and deeper until the tree falls. The beaver cannot control the direction in which the tree will fall. As it begins to totter the beaver dashes for safety.

When all is quiet, the work begins again. But first the beaver may make a meal of tender green bark, buds, and twigs. Holding a section of wood in its front paws, the beaver nibbles away like a person eating corn on the cob. Stomach full, it starts cutting the tree into convenient lengths for moving to the pond.

▶ BUILDING DAMS AND LODGES

In deep streams with high banks, beavers sometimes make underground dens in the bank instead of building lodges. Digging the entrance underwater, they tunnel upward beyond the water level. There they hollow out a living chamber in the bank. In such a den the beaver family is safe from most enemies. Even in shallow streams beavers often build bank dens when they first settle in an area. Then they start to dam the stream.

The dam blocks the flow of water and creates a pond where the beavers will live. The dam keeps the pond level constant during spring rains and summer droughts. It is deep enough not to freeze solid in winter.

To build a dam, the beavers drag branches to the place they have selected in the stream. The branches are laid side by side, parallel to the current. Their ends are often thrust into the bottom mud to anchor them. Mud and debris are piled on top. Layer upon layer, the dam is built up. To prevent leaks, the beavers plaster the upstream face with mud, leaves, and stones scooped up from the stream bottom.

Beaver dams vary considerably in size. They can be from 3 feet (1 meter) in length to more than 100 feet (31 meters). Exceptionally large dams may be as much as 10 feet (3 meters) in height.

In the pond that forms behind their dam the beavers usually build an island lodge. Pulling boughs and branches into the water, they build up a broad foundation of sticks and wood—sometimes more than 30 feet (9 meters) across. Making the huge pile slope inward, they construct mounds that may stand up to 8 feet (2.4 meters) above the pond's surface. When the outer structure is complete, the beavers plaster the chinks and holes with mud and debris. A section of the roof is left unchinked, as an air hole. Underwater entrances lead to

Beavers are industrious builders. They use wood, mud, and rocks to construct lodges and dams. Inside the lodge, beaver parents shelter their young. A beaver colony builds a dam to make sure the entrances to the lodge are safely hidden under the water's surface. Beavers also forge canals to make transporting supplies easier.

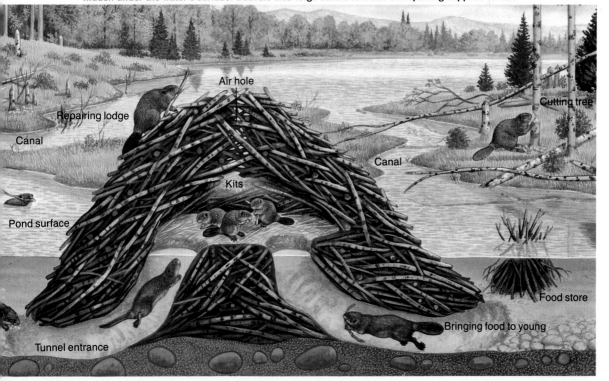

Woody plants are important to the colony's way of life. Gnawing on a tender shoot (*left*) helps satisfy the beaver's nutritional needs. A beaver uses a tree branch (*above*) to make underwater repairs to the lodge.

the main living space. This chamber may be as big as 8 feet (2.4 meters) across and 5 feet (1.5 meters) high.

As time goes by, the beavers have to travel farther and farther from the pond to find suitable trees. Dragging branches and logs, they wear smooth paths, or "tote roads," through the woods. To make the going even easier, they dig canals from the pond to connect with the tote roads. Whenever the job of bringing wood in from increasing distances becomes too difficult, the beavers leave the area. Then in a new location, they start all over again.

▶ FAMILY LIFE OF THE COLONY

From early spring until late fall, all the members of the beaver colony are busy. They repair their dams after the spring floods. They build or enlarge their lodge. They stock food for winter eating. By the time ice and snow arrive, the beavers have a huge quantity of branches stored in the bottom of the pond, close to the lodge. These are thrust into the pond bottom, where they stay fresh.

When the surface of the pond freezes over, the beavers retire to their lodge. Whenever they are hungry, they simply swim out under the ice, cut a fresh branch from the food supply, and carry it into the lodge. Stripped of its tender bark, the branch is finally thrown out.

It may be used the next spring for repairing the dam or lodge.

As spring approaches, the expectant mother beaver prepares a soft nest of wood and bark shavings on the floor of the lodge. Here her young, usually three or four in number, are born during April or May, nearly four months after mating. When the female is expecting, the father beaver moves out for the time being. The year-old youngsters may move out with him. The 2-year-olds leave home for good at this time; they search for mates with whom they will live for the rest of their lives.

The baby beavers, called kits, weigh about 1 pound (0.5 kilogram) at birth. They are born with their eyes open, and they can move about. They grow rapidly and may reach 25 pounds (11 kilograms) in a year's time.

▶ THE BEAVER AND CONSERVATION

In a few areas beavers may become nuisances when their dams flood roads, croplands, or timber areas. But the beaver's good points far offset such problems. Beaver ponds act as fire guards in the forests. They provide homes and breeding places for fish, water birds, and other wildlife. Beaver dams help to control floods and conserve water. They keep soil from washing away. Rich silt backs up behind the dams year after year. When the beavers finally move on, the ponds gradually fill in. They become part of wide, gentle valleys covered with fertile soil.

ROBERT M. MCCLUNG
Author, science books for children

BECKET, SAINT THOMAS À
(1118?–1170)

Thomas à Becket was archbishop of Canterbury during the reign of Henry II of England. As archbishop, he clashed with the king over the rights of the church against the rights of the crown. The conflict led to Thomas' death. It has become one of the most famous episodes in English history and literature.

Thomas was born in London, probably on December 21, 1118. His father, a merchant, came from Normandy, in France. Thomas was educated in London and Paris. While in his 20's, he entered the service of Theobald, archbishop of Canterbury. In 1154, he was appointed archdeacon of Canterbury. That same year, 21-year-old Henry of Anjou came to the English throne as King Henry II. He made Thomas his chancellor, or chief official. Thomas served the king faithfully, and a warm friendship grew up between them. After Theobald died in 1161, Henry offered Thomas the office of archbishop. Thomas accepted reluctantly. He feared that the policies of the strong-willed king would conflict with his own views of his duty as head of the church.

In 1164, the king had a document prepared known as the Constitutions of Clarendon. Its purpose was to restore some of the power of the crown, which had been weakened during the period before Henry became king. Among other things, it provided that members of the clergy who were convicted of crimes by church courts were to be punished by civil courts. Previously, the church had both tried and punished its own members. Thomas refused to sign the document. This infuriated the king, who had expected his friend's support.

Thomas fled to France, where he continued to speak out on the rights of the church. In 1170, Thomas and the king were partly reconciled, and Thomas returned to England. But his refusal to lift the ban against two excommunicated bishops angered the king again. On December 29, 1170, four of Henry's knights murdered Thomas in the cathedral of Canterbury. Henry denied that he had ordered Thomas' death. But he did penance at Thomas' tomb in the cathedral, which at once became a shrine for pilgrims. In 1173, Thomas was made a saint.

Reviewed by ROBERT LACEY
Author, *Majesty*

BECQUEREL, ANTOINE HENRI
(1852–1908)

Antoine Henri Becquerel is known as the man who discovered radioactivity—a discovery that influenced the development of atomic weapons, nuclear energy, and radioactive medical treatments.

Becquerel was born on December 15, 1852, in Paris, France. Both his father, Alexandre Edmond Becquerel, and his grandfather, Antoine Cesár Becquerel, one of the founders of electrochemistry, were physicists.

Becquerel worked as an engineer as well as a professor of physics. His discovery of radiation occurred in February 1896. A few months before, Wilhelm Roentgen had discovered X rays—invisible penetrating forms of radiation. Becquerel wanted to find out whether or not phosphorescent materials—materials that glow in the dark after being stimulated by sunlight—would also give off X rays. What he discovered was that certain substances, such as uranium, would give off X rays even when they had not been stimulated by light.

Soon scientists discovered that other elements give off energy in this way. These are the radioactive elements, whose atoms are decaying. Particles from the atoms break away and release the energy that held the atoms together. When harnessed, this produces the enormous energy needed to produce nuclear power.

In 1901, while experimenting with radium, Becquerel developed what looked like a reddish-brown sunburn on his skin. He reasoned that the burn was caused by the radium—that the rays emitted were able to penetrate and cause changes to living things. His discovery led to the controlled use of radioactivity in the treatment of some diseases. For his discoveries he was awarded, along with Marie and Pierre Curie, the Nobel prize in physics in 1903.

Becquerel died on August 25, 1908, in Le Croisic, France.

RACHEL KRANZ
Editor, Biographies
The Young Adult Reader's Adviser

See also CHEMISTRY, HISTORY OF; URANIUM.

BEECHER, HENRY WARD (1813–1887)

Henry Ward Beecher was the most famous American preacher of his time. He was born on June 24, 1813, in Litchfield, Connecticut. His father, Lyman Beecher, was a distinguished Presbyterian minister, and four of Henry's brothers also became clergymen. Among his sisters, Catharine Beecher was a notable educator, and Harriet Beecher Stowe won fame for her novel *Uncle Tom's Cabin.*

Beecher graduated from Amherst College, in Massachusetts, in 1834. He was not a disciplined student, but he loved literature and read widely. He was athletic, fun-loving and friendly, and a fine storyteller. After Amherst, he studied at Lane Theological Seminary, in Cincinnati, Ohio. In 1837, he married Eunice White Bullard and began his ministry. Soon he became pastor of a church in Indianapolis, Indiana. He developed his skill as a preacher and in 1847 moved to Brooklyn, New York, as minister of Plymouth Church of the Pilgrims (Congregational). He remained there until his death, on March 8, 1887.

Beecher's sermons were informal, impulsive, witty, emotional, and dramatic. They mirrored his warm personality and attracted between 2,000 and 3,000 people each week. He had a fine voice and a poetic command of language. His physical appearance helped make him a striking figure in the pulpit. He had a strong build and a lionlike head with hair that reached his coat collar. Beecher aimed for the hearts of his listeners and stressed God's love for sinners. He was tolerant of other views. For example, he defended the theory of evolution when most of the clergy attacked it. And he spoke out on the social and political issues of the day, opposing slavery and championing the right of women to vote.

ARI HOOGENBOOM
City University of New York,
Brooklyn College

BEER AND BREWING

Beer is an alcoholic beverage that has been drunk for thousands of years. The making, or brewing, of beer appears to have begun very early in many parts of the world. A beerlike beverage was made in Mesopotamia as early as 6000 B.C. Beer was also brewed in ancient Egypt, Greece, and Rome.

During the Middle Ages most beer was brewed by monks, and almost every monastery had a brew house. Eventually others took over this task and brewing grew into an industry with organizations, or guilds, of brewers. Beer in the Middle Ages was a thick, heavy beverage with a much higher alcohol content than today's beer. This thick, nourishing beer, almost as much a food as a drink, was an important item in people's daily diet.

In medieval England, beer, or ale, was often the chief drink at festivals and celebrations. It was such an important part of these revels that the word "ale" was sometimes used to mean a festival. Lamb-ales were celebrations held at lamb-shearing time. College-ales were parties at which students drank the ale they had brewed. The word "bridal" comes from "bride-ale," which was a wedding feast.

The knowledge of brewing beer was brought to the New World by the early colonists. At first, beer was made in small home breweries. However, as the colonies grew, brewing was established as an industry. One of the first breweries was built in 1683 at Pennsbury, Pennsylvania. Within a hundred years, the brewing industry had become an important part of the nation's economic life.

▶ HOW BEER IS MADE

The brewing of beer starts with grain, primarily barley, although corn or rice is sometimes used as well. The grain is mixed with water and is kept warm until it begins to germinate, or sprout. After a week, the grain is roasted and the germination stops. This partly sprouted grain is known as **malt**.

The malt is mixed with water and boiled to form a sweet liquid called **wort**. The dried seed cones of a plant called the hop vine are added to the wort and the mixture is boiled again. These seed cones, called **hops**, have a slightly bitter taste and give beer its characteristic tangy flavor. All solid matter is then filtered out of the mixture and **yeast** is added. Yeast contains microscopic organisms that

Hop Back

Wort Cooler

The copper brew kettle at left is located at the Boston Beer Company brewery. Here an employee carefully monitors the simmering of malt and water, which forms the liquid called wort.

feed on sugars and starches. As these organisms feed on the sugars of the wort they release alcohol as a waste product. The change from sugar to alcohol is called **fermentation**, the most important step in the brewing process. Fermentation also produces carbon dioxide gas, which gives beer its bubbles.

After fermentation, the beer is pumped into closed storage tanks where it ages. Then it is filtered again before it is put into barrels, bottles, or cans. From start to finish, the brewing process may take several months.

There are several common types of beer. **Lager beer** originated in Germany. Its name comes from the German word for "storage" (*lager*) because the beer is stored or aged before it is packaged. Lager is usually pale yellow in color, and it has an alcoholic content of about 3 or 4 percent. Special kinds of lager beer include **bock beer**, a darker and heavier type of lager, and **Pilsner**. **Light beer** is a type of lager with reduced carbohydrate contents and fewer calories. **Dry beer** is a lager that is specially brewed to be less sweet than other lagers. **Ale** has a paler color and sharper taste

than lager beer and has an alcoholic content of about 4 or 5 percent. **Porter** is a dark brown beer with a slightly sweet taste. **Stout** is one of the darkest, heaviest, and strongest beers. Its alcoholic content is about 5 to 6.5 percent.

In many parts of the world, people prefer to drink beer chilled. In some places, however, beer is served either at room temperature or slightly warmed. Differences in climate and culture may have something to do with this.

Despite their skill at brewing, old-time brewers could never be certain that each batch would be the same. Today, however, brewing is a highly scientific process—all ingredients are carefully tested and each step is closely controlled. As a result, today's beer is as uniform in quality as any other manufactured product. The amount of beer produced has also changed over the years. In the past, beer was usually brewed for personal use or in small quantities by professionals. Today, most beer is mass-produced in large quantities, although in some places home-brewing or small breweries have become quite popular.

UNITED STATES BREWERS ASSOCIATION

A honeybee (*left*) laden with pollen, which it has stored in special "pollen baskets" on its hind legs, burrows within dandelion petals to suck up the flower's sweet nectar. A beekeeper (*above*) collects the honey produced in a hive from the gathered nectar.

BEES

In a field of blooming flowers, bees are a familiar sight buzzing about seeking the rich stores of nectar and pollen held within the flower blossoms. Bees gather the nectar and pollen for food. They turn the nectar into delicious, sweet honey, which people eat. They also produce beeswax, which is used to make candles, crayons, and cosmetics. Many plants would not grow without their help. As bees fly about searching for food, they fertilize plants by spreading pollen from one plant to another. This allows the plants to reproduce.

There are about 20,000 different kinds, or species, of bees. They are found on every continent except Antarctica. There are two general groups of bees: **solitary bees**, which live alone, and **social bees**, which live together in large groups called **colonies**. A colony of bees can contain hundreds, sometimes thousands, of members.

▶ THE BODY OF A BEE

Like all insects, the bee has three body parts: head, thorax, and abdomen. Its body looks fuzzy because it is covered with many fine hairs. Even its antennae, or feelers, are covered with tiny hairs. In addition to a pair of antennae on its head, the bee has five eyes and has chewing and sucking mouthparts. The bee uses its eyes—one pair of large compound eyes and three small eyes—to distinguish colors and different flower shapes. The antennae, or feelers, have sense organs that provide the bee with the senses of touch and smell. Along with the **mandibles** (jaws) that it uses to cut

and chew, the bee has a long tubelike tongue that it uses for sucking.

The thorax of the bee is composed of three segments. The bee has two pairs of wings on its thorax—a large front set and a smaller hind set. The wings, which move up and down and forward and backward, allow the bee to fly forward, backwards, and sideways, and even hover in midair. A pair of legs is attached to each of the thorax segments.

The abdomen of the bee has two very important features. One is a special sac called the **honey stomach**. In it, the bee carries the nectar it collects. The other is its sting. The sting is attached to the abdomen and is found only on female bees. Some species of bees have better developed stings than others. Within one species, there is also a difference between the sting of the female worker bee and that of the queen bee. The worker bee has a straight sting with hooks. The queen bee has a smooth, curved sting. The worker bee defends its life and home with its sting, while the queen bee only uses its sting to kill other queens.

▶SOCIAL BEES

The honeybee is the most social bee of all. An average honeybee colony has about 30,000 bees, but there may be up to 80,000. The bees live together in their home, called a **hive**, dividing the labor of the colony. Within the hive, the bees produce wax, which they use to build **honeycombs**. A honeycomb is made up of a mass of six-sided compartments, or **cells**.

The colony contains three different kinds of bees: the queen, the drones, and the worker bees. The **queen bee** is a large female who lays all the eggs in the colony. Although the queen lays eggs from January to November, the majority of eggs are laid between the first warm days of spring and the end of the summer.

At the height of the season, the queen may lay as many as 1,000 to 2,000 eggs a day. Since she lives about five years, she may lay up to 1 million eggs in her lifetime. The queen is the mother of the entire colony, and the whole hive is one big family of bees.

The **drones** are the males of the colony. They take no part in the work of the hive. They have only one function—to fertilize the eggs of a queen. A typical colony has several hundred drones.

The **worker bees** are all females. They are smaller in size than the queen. They are able to lay eggs, however, they usually do not lay eggs when the colony has a queen. Worker bees do all the labor in the hive necessary for

The External Body Structures of a Honeybee

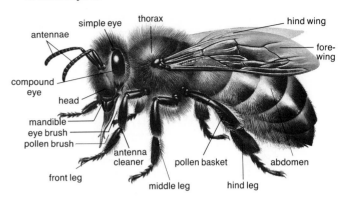

the maintenance and growth of the colony. Tens of thousands of worker bees live in a typical hive.

Inside the Hive. The beehive is a smoothly run, organized society. Each bee has a job to do. If you watch the entrance of a beehive, you will see the busy traffic of bees coming and going. One after another, bees fly out of the hive. Other bees, heavily loaded with the food needed to supply the colony, land and enter the hive.

Workers called **foragers** fly out to flowers and collect pollen and nectar. Pollen, necessary for the formation of seeds in plants, is a source of protein, vitamins, and minerals for bees. When the bees who collect pollen groom themselves, they put the pollen grains that cling to the fine hairs of their bodies into special "pollen baskets." These baskets are flattened areas on their hind legs surrounded by long hairs. Nectar is a sweet, sugary liquid. It is 40 to 80 percent water. The bee sucks it into its mouth with its flexible tongue and stores it in its honey stomach.

When a bee returns to the hive, it spits up its load of nectar through its mouth. The nectar is handed over to other worker bees that place it in empty cells. Special chemicals called **enzymes** are added to the stored nectar. As the nectar dries out, it changes into honey and is a great source of energy for the bees. The nectar gathered by one bee during its entire lifetime is enough to produce about 1.5 ounces (45 grams) of honey.

Duties of a Worker Bee. Some worker bees build the honeycomb. Some clean out empty cells and prepare them for the eggs that the

Within the bee colony, there are three different kinds of bees: (a) the female worker bee, (b) the male bee, called a drone, and (c) the queen bee.

From An Egg to An Adult Bee

The queen bee (1) deposits one egg in the cell, and a wormlike larva (2) hatches from the egg. The larva grows as it is fed royal jelly or bee-bread. When the larva finishes spinning its cocoon, workers seal the cell with wax (3); the larva starts to pupate, its wormlike body changing into the form of an adult bee. With its growth complete, the young adult bee breaks through the wax cap and (4) emerges from its cell.

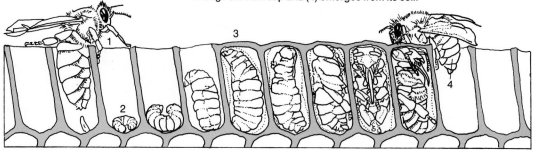

queen will deposit there. Some feed and nurse the growing young. Guard bees stand at the entrance to the hive and protect the hive against enemies, such as wasps, wax moths, and bees from other colonies. Fanning bees ventilate the hive. Still other worker bees take care of the nectar and pollen.

The task of a worker bee depends on its age. For the first three days of its life, the worker cleans a section of the hive called the **brood nest**, which is the part of the hive where the eggs are laid and the young bees are raised.

During the time the worker bee is preparing the brood nest for new eggs, special glands in its head are developing. Once the glands fully develop, they will secrete a creamy substance called **royal jelly**. Then the worker becomes a **nurse bee**, tending the developing larvae (wormlike grubs that hatch from the eggs) and feeding them royal jelly. After several days, the worker stops producing royal jelly and be-

gins to produce wax from glands in its abdomen. At about 12 days, the same bee is a builder of wax cells.

At about 16 days, some workers stop building and start standing guard at the entrance to the hive. There they defend the hive against intruders. Other workers this age receive the nectar and pollen brought by foragers. From the age of 3 weeks until the end of its life, the worker bee shifts to its last and longest job—the collecting of nectar and pollen.

Every bee gathers its own information about the needs of the hive. In any one day it spends part of its time patrolling the hive, inspecting cells and larvae, interacting with other workers, and looking over the building areas and the stores of food. From such inspection tours, new forms of activity start—nursing, building, or cleaning, as each need arises.

In summer when there is a lot of work in the hive, a worker bee may live to only 5 or 6

This page, left: The queen bee checks the brood nest for empty cells in which to lay her eggs. *Right:* Wormlike larvae hatch from the eggs the queen has deposited in the cells. *Opposite page, left:* After the larvae have spun cocoons, the worker bees crawl over the cells in the brood nest, sealing the cells with wax. *Right:* Breaking through the wax cap of its cell, a full-grown bee emerges.

weeks. During the fall and winter there is less work, so a worker may live several months.

The Mating Flight of the Queen. Each time the hive has a new queen, there is a mating flight. A new queen is needed when the old queen dies, leaves to establish a new hive, or becomes feeble. Special cells in the brood nest house developing queen bees. The first queen to emerge destroys those developing in other cells. If two queens emerge at the same time, they fight until one is killed. An old queen may fight the new queen or leave the hive. Only one queen will emerge from the battles.

When the new queen is about a week old, she leaves the hive for her mating flight. During the flight, she will mate with one or more drones. When they mate, the drone transfers sperm (male sex cells) into the queen's body. The queen stores the sperm until she is ready to lay eggs.

The drones die after mating and the queen returns to the hive. A few days later, the queen starts to move over the honeycombs, looking for empty cells in which to lay her eggs.

From Egg to Adult Bee. If the queen exposes her eggs to the sperm she is storing just before they are laid, the eggs will be fertilized. If she does not, the eggs will be unfertilized. All the unfertilized eggs become males (drones). All the fertilized eggs become females (either egg-laying queens or workers).

The eggs develop into larvae after three days. All the larvae receive the same food, royal jelly, for the first three days. Then some of the larvae receive a mixture of honey and pollen called **beebread**. The larvae that are fed beebread will become worker bees. Some lar-

WONDER QUESTION

Are there really "killer" bees?

The so-called "killer" bees are just very good at protecting themselves when bothered. They are the descendants of bees brought from Africa to South America as part of an effort to develop a stronger breed of honeybee. But before a breed could be developed, 26 queen bees escaped from the research hives.

The sting of the Africanized "killer" bee is no different from that of any other honeybee. However, the Africanized bees are quicker to attack and more of them will join in an attack. For the bees to actually kill anything, a mass stinging involving hundreds of bees would have to take place.

vae are selected to be fed only royal jelly. These larvae will develop into queen bees.

The nurse bees carefully tend the larvae, visiting each larva with food nearly 1,300 times a day. At 6 days, the larva starts to spin a cocoon, a shell of silk, inside its wax cell. When the cocoon is completed, the cell is sealed with wax by the worker bees. The larva changes into a pupa within the cocoon. During the pupa stage, the wormlike body of the larva changes into the form of an adult bee. A full-size queen bee emerges from the cell after 16 days. A full-size worker bee makes its way out of its wax cell in 21 days.

Unfertilized eggs go through the same

stages as fertilized eggs. They change into larvae and then become pupae. Full-size drones emerge from the cells in 24 days.

With a queen laying 1,500 eggs a day, a new bee emerges almost every minute to take its place in bee society.

How Bees Communicate. Some foragers, acting as "scouts," return from a food hunt and tell other bees from their hive about the food source they have found. The scouts pass on their information by performing a "dance." There are two basic dances that are used to tell the direction and distance from the hive to a source of nectar and pollen: a **round dance** and a **waggle** dance. If the returning scouts do a **round dance**, it means that food is near the hive. The scouts use the **waggle dance** to describe the exact distance to the food and the direction of the food in relation to the sun. The faster the dances, the closer the food.

In the darkness of the hive, the other worker bees surround the dancing scouts. Using the sense organs on their antennae, the worker bees pick up the flowers' nectar scent clinging to the dancers. The worker bees become excited and start to follow the dancers.

After following the dance, the workers leave the hive and—without the dancing bees to lead them—fly directly to the area of the food source. Once there, the workers search the area for the flowers with the particular scent that clung to the dancing scouts.

The bees form groups just large enough to collect the available food. When the source of the food is plentiful and rich, the worker bees recruited by the scouts also dance on returning

While scouts search for a new location for the colony, the queen and her group of workers cluster in a swarm around a fence post.

to the hive. When the amount of food is reduced, the incoming bees simply deliver the nectar and pollen and do not dance. In this way many bees appear at a good source of food and as the supply wanes, fewer and fewer bees visit those flowers.

Bees also communicate information by the secretions in their bodies. Bees that attend the queen constantly lick a substance from her body and share it with other members of the colony. If the hive loses its queen, the other bees of the colony become aware of her absence in a few hours. They look for her, and if she cannot be found, they immediately set about replacing her with a new queen.

Swarming. When a hive gets overcrowded, the queen lays fewer and fewer eggs. The worker bees build a new type of cell in the

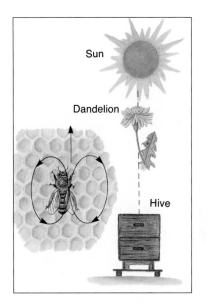

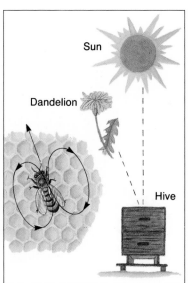

During the waggle dance (which has a figure-eight pattern), the scout tells others about the food source. Here the scout shows the relationship of the food source, dandelion, to the sun by starting the dance facing toward the sun (*left*) or away from the sun (*right*).

hive. These are much bigger than the other wax cells and are shaped somewhat like peanuts. Inside these special cells, the queen deposits the eggs from which a new queen will emerge. After the larvae develop from the eggs, the cells are covered with wax.

Soon after the cells are covered with wax, the old queen gathers many of the workers and leaves the hive to start a new colony. The departing queen and her group of workers is called a **swarm**. Their journey from the hive to find a new home is called a **swarming**. Left behind in the hive are workers that will tend the new queen and developing larvae.

Many scouts search for a new location for the colony. While the scouts search, the swarm gathers around a tree branch or other support. The scouts report back to the swarm using their "dance" language to describe the various locations they have found. The scouts then check out each site. Once one is chosen, the entire swarm travels to the new site.

Bumblebees are another familiar kind of social bee. Their colonies are not as large or complex as those of honeybees, and they do not produce as much honey. Also, the duties of the bumblebee queen are quite different from those of the honeybee queen.

Each spring the bumblebee queen must start a new colony because all of her workers die each year when winter comes. At first, the queen performs the work for the entire hive. She gathers pollen and nectar, builds wax cells, and feeds the young. Not until the larvae become adult workers does the queen have any help with her duties.

The hive thrives for a short time. In the fall, cold weather kills all but the new queens that hatched, and then mated, late in the season. The new queens hibernate and start new hives when the warm weather returns.

▶SOLITARY BEES

Many of the solitary bees have curious habits. **Carpenter bees** bite tunnels through solid wood. In the tunnels they make a series of cells, one on top of the other and separated by walls of tiny wood chips. **Mason bees** cement pieces of stone together, forming groups of cells that are attached to cliffs or stone walls. **Leaf-cutter bees** use their jaws like scissors and snip out pieces of leaves or flowers. They use this plant material to line their nests and make partitions between the cells. **Burrowing bees** tunnel into the ground.

Most solitary bees live alone. The female solitary bee puts pollen and nectar in the cells of the nest. She lays an egg on each lump of food, seals the cells, and flies away. She usually dies at the end of the summer. When the eggs hatch, the developing young feed on the food left for them. They are completely on their own, having no contact with the mother. When they are adults, male and female mate.

MILLICENT E. SELSAM
Author, science books for children
Reviewed by GENE E. ROBINSON
Department of Entomology
University of Illinois

See also FLOWERS AND SEEDS; HONEY; INSECTS.

Nests of Solitary Bees

Mason bee

American carpenter bee

Leaf-cutter bee

BEETHOVEN, LUDWIG VAN (1770–1827)

The great composer Ludwig van Beethoven was born in Bonn, Germany, on December 16 or 17, 1770, and was baptized on December 17. His father, Johann, and his grandfather Ludwig van Beethoven were both musicians.

Beethoven revealed his own musical talents when he was very young. His father, an irresponsible drunkard, hoped the boy would be a profitable child prodigy like Mozart. Beethoven was often dragged out of bed in the middle of the night and forced to practice the piano. At the age of 7 he was playing in public. When Beethoven was 13, the elector of Cologne made him assistant organist at his chapel in Bonn.

In 1787 Beethoven traveled to Vienna and met his idol, Mozart. When Beethoven improvised on a melody that Mozart had given him, the great master was astounded.

But Beethoven could not stay in Vienna. His mother fell ill, and he rushed back to Bonn. The death of his mother left Beethoven and his brothers at the mercy of their drunken father. At the age of 18 Beethoven assumed full responsibility for the family.

In 1792 Beethoven returned to Vienna, where he spent the rest of his life. He became a pupil of Haydn. But he was dissatisfied with Haydn's method of teaching, which he considered not thorough enough. To avoid offending the famous master, he took lessons in secret from another composer, Johann Schenk.

Beethoven presented a strange appearance to the people of Vienna. He was a short, stocky man, untidily dressed, with dark, piercing eyes and a wild shock of black hair. Knowing himself to be a genius, he lived by his own rules. The German poet Goethe called him an "utterly untamed personality."

Nevertheless, he quickly became famous. Several princes became his patrons, and for a few years he was happy. Then, about 1800, tragedy struck. He discovered that he was slowly becoming deaf. This was the great crisis of his life.

After this, Beethoven's music became more profound. He developed a completely original style of composing. It reflected his violent emotions, his sufferings and joys. At this time Beethoven composed the most popular of all symphonies, his fifth. Other famous works of

Beethoven with the score of his great *Missa solemnis*.

this period are the *Eroica* and *Pastoral* symphonies, the *Appassionata* Sonata, the *Emperor* Concerto, his only opera, *Fidelio*, and the *Rasumovsky* string quartets.

In 1815 Beethoven became the guardian of his nephew Karl. Beethoven adored the boy, who gave his uncle nothing but trouble. Beethoven's hearing problems steadily increased; by 1820 he was almost totally deaf and had to carry on all conversation in writing.

Despite his deafness Beethoven now composed his greatest works. These include the last five piano sonatas, the *Missa solemnis*, the Ninth Symphony, with its choral finale, and the last five string quartets, which many people consider the finest of all his works.

In 1826 Beethoven became seriously ill. It is said that as he lay unconscious on his deathbed, on March 26, 1827, there was a loud clap of thunder. In response Beethoven sat straight up, shook his fist at the heavens, and fell back dead.

Beethoven is perhaps the most popular and revered of composers. He was a man of profound vision and his music has deeply moved its listeners for generations.

Reviewed by KARL GEIRINGER
University of California—Santa Barbara

Beetles vary greatly, not only in appearance but also in lifestyle. While the dung beetle (*left*) busily forms a dung ball to use as a nest for its eggs, the locust borer beetle (*above*) lays its eggs on plentiful goldenrod.

BEETLES

Wherever you look, on the ground, in the air, or in lakes and ponds, they can be found. They go busily about their daily tasks—whether it is nibbling on plant leaves, chewing wood from rotting logs, or cleaning the bones of dead animals. They are beetles, the most common of all the insects. In North America alone, there are more than 30,000 different kinds, or species, of beetles. Throughout the world, about 300,000 species of beetles can be found; and every year, new species are being discovered.

Beetles make up the insect order, or group, called Coleoptera. It is the largest order of the animal kingdom. The name Coleoptera, which means "sheath wing" in Greek, refers to the beetle's pair of hard, inflexible outer wings. The wings, called **elytra**, lock together down the beetle's back to provide a protective shell for the beetle.

Sometimes called the armored tank of the insect world, the beetle owes much of its ability to survive to the leathery elytra. With this tough outer shell, the beetle can live under stones and in other sheltered areas that insects with soft bodies cannot use, because they would be crushed. The beetle's shell also makes it resistant to dryness. This allows the beetle to live in places that are drier than the habitats of many other insects.

▶ THE CHARACTERISTICS OF BEETLES

There is a great variety in the appearance of beetles. Some beetles are dark brown so that they blend in with the soil. Other beetles have bright colors or complex patterns on their elytra. Still others are iridescent, changing color in the sunlight. Although beetles vary greatly in size, shape, and color, they all share the same body plan. Like that of other insects, the beetle's body is divided into three main parts: the head, the thorax, and the abdomen.

Body Parts. The **head**, at the front of the body, holds the main sense organs (eyes and antennae), chewing mouthparts, and a primitive brain. Projecting from the head, the beetle's two antennae are covered with tiny hairs. The hairs are special sense organs that help the beetle detect sounds and odors. A pair of compound eyes, one on each side of the head, gives the beetle a well-developed sense of sight.

The chewing mouthparts of most beetles are designed to crush or break food into small pieces before the food actually enters the

The External Body Structures of a Beetle

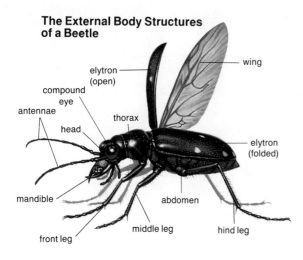

- wing
- elytron (open)
- compound eye
- antennae
- head
- thorax
- elytron (folded)
- mandible
- abdomen
- front leg
- middle leg
- hind leg

mouth. Plant-eating beetles have mouthparts that allow them to slice leaves, cut stems, bore under bark, or crush seeds. Beetles that eat other insects or animals have mouthparts that allow them to pierce, stab, or crush their prey. Some of these beetles can cause painful bites to an inexperienced insect collector.

The **thorax** forms the middle part of the body and holds the beetle's three pairs of legs as well as the elytra and a pair of hind wings. Different kinds of beetles have different kinds of legs. Many predatory beetles have long, slender legs that enable them to pursue their prey swiftly. Beetles that dig through the soil have legs that are flattened with toothed edges,

allowing the beetles to sweep large amounts of soil behind them.

The **abdomen** houses the organs that help the beetle digest food, get rid of waste, and produce offspring. The beetle does not have special organs, like our lungs, to help it breathe. Instead, holes called **spiracles** pierce the abdomen. Air enters the beetle's body through the spiracles and passes through tubes into open spaces in the abdomen and the rest of the body.

Locomotion. If the beetle needs to fly, it unlocks the elytra and the hind wings unfold. Only the hind wings are used for flight. When the beetle is not flying, the elytra cover and protect the thin, delicate hind wings.

Some beetles spend most of their life in water. An aquatic beetle has flattened legs that are used for paddles as it pushes through the water. A built-in air tank helps the beetle swim and dive underwater. The space between the elytra and the soft body underneath fills up with air. While the beetle is under water, it breathes using the stored air.

Behavior. Most beetles, unlike many types of bees, ants, wasps, and termites, are solitary insects. They live alone rather than in large nests or hives. Different types of beetles have

Two behaviors that are important to a beetle's survival are its ability to defend itself and its ability to reproduce. The bombardier beetle (*below*) effectively repels its enemies with a hot pulsing jet of chemicals. The mating blister beetle (*right*) provides for its offspring by laying its eggs near a larval food source.

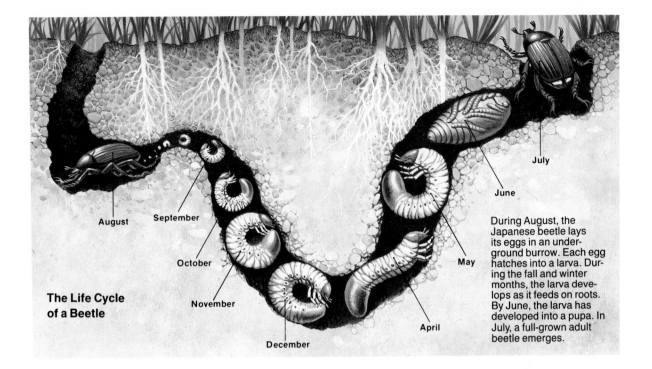

The Life Cycle of a Beetle

August · September · October · November · December · April · May · June · July

During August, the Japanese beetle lays its eggs in an underground burrow. Each egg hatches into a larva. During the fall and winter months, the larva develops as it feeds on roots. By June, the larva has developed into a pupa. In July, a full-grown adult beetle emerges.

different types of behavior that allow them to adapt to their environment, feed, defend themselves from predators, and breed.

People have been interested in some of the more unusual beetles for hundreds, even thousands, of years. In ancient Egypt, people were fascinated by the scarab, or dung beetle. This insect makes a ball of dung to lay its eggs in. Often the ball is as large or larger than the scarab itself. Some beetles make dung balls as big as softballs.

The Egyptians considered the ball of dung and the life of the scarab to be symbols for the world and the cycles of nature. So important was the scarab that it was used as a seal on many important Egyptian documents.

Another beetle with unusual behavior is the tortoise beetle. As it grows, it is protected by a collection of its own waste and shed skins. Stuck to its body, this material helps camouflage, or hide, the young beetle from predators. It also serves as a defense, because the foul odor of the pile of wastes discourages other insects and animals from coming close for an attack. Nicknamed the trash peddler, the young tortoise beetle develops into a brilliant, shiny metallic adult.

The bombardier beetle has an even more dramatic defense against predators. When an attacking animal approaches, the bombardier beetle raises its rear end into the air and shoots out a hot spray of burning liquid at the attacker. The spray is released with an explosion that is quite loud. The combination of the surprising sound and harmful spray wards off most animals that would prey upon this beetle.

▶ **THE LIFE CYCLE OF THE BEETLE**

Beetles, like many other insects, have a life cycle during which they pass through several different stages before becoming an adult. This process of growth and change is called **metamorphosis**.

The Egg. Most beetles begin the first stage of life as an egg. Beetle eggs are generally oval in shape with a tough but flexible outer shell. Inside the egg, the growing beetle feeds on the large yolk. The first stage ends when the developing beetle cuts its way through the shell, hatching into a beetle larva.

The Larva. The larval stage is the only one in which the beetle grows in size. Because beetles lay eggs on or in a food source, a newly emerged larva does not have to hunt for food. The larva, also called a grub, spends most of its time eating. When the larva grows too large for the hard shell (called an exoskeleton) that covers its body, the shell splits. The soft grub that emerges will quickly grow a new, larger exoskeleton. The new covering

Some Common Beetle Families

Firefly
Family: Lampyridae
Common name:
lightning bug or firefly
  The name *Lampyridae* means "shining fire" in Latin. In some species, the eggs, larvae, pupae (plural of pupa), and adult fireflies all emit a glowing light.

Two-spotted Ladybug
Family: Coccinellidae
Common name: ladybird beetle or ladybug
  The name *ladybug* originated in the Middle Ages. Named the beetle of Our Lady, this insect was dedicated to the Virgin Mary.

Colorado Potato Beetle
Family: Chrysomelidae
Common name: leaf beetle
  There are more than 25,000 species of leaf beetles in the world. Both the larvae (plural of larva) and the adult leaf beetles feed on leaves. This makes many leaf beetles serious crop pests.

Dung Beetle
Family: Scarabaeidae
Common name: scarab
  The scarab beetles are one of the largest families of beetles, with almost 1,300 North American species and 20,000 species in the world.

Striped Blister Beetle
Family: Meloidae
Common name: blister beetle
  When a predator attacks a blister beetle, the beetle discharges a drop of blood containing an oily chemical. This chemical causes severe blistering of the skin.

Fiery Searcher Ground Beetle
Family: Carabidae
Common name: ground beetle
  Almost all ground beetles are nocturnal, so they hide during the day and search for food at night. They are very aggressive predators, even climbing trees to get their prey.

Boll Weevil
Family: Curculionidae
Common name: snout beetle or weevil
  With 40,000 species of snout beetles, this is the largest family of beetles in the world. These beetles get their name because they have a long snout, with their mouthparts attached at the farthest end.

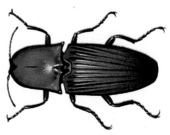

Click Beetle
Family: Elateridae
Common name: click beetle or snapping beetle
  When attacked, the click beetle falls backward and plays dead. To right itself, the beetle bends at the thorax and hooks a long spine into an abdominal groove. It unhooks the spine with a click, throwing itself in the air and flipping end over end.

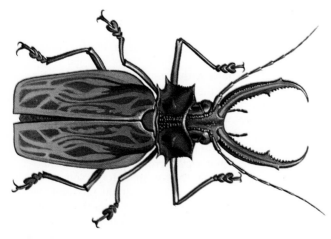

Tiger Beetle
Family: Cicindelidae
Common name: tiger beetle
  Tiger beetle larvae wait for prey at the entrance of their vertical burrows. They attach themselves to the burrow wall with a hooklike spine on the abdomen that prevents them from being pulled out of the burrow when capturing large prey.

Giant Longhorn Beetle
Family: Cerambycidae
Common name: long-horned or wood-boring beetle
  Larvae of this family are wood borers. They are easy to capture because they can be picked out of the wood with hooked sticks. Partly for this reason, the larvae are used as food in many parts of the world.

will also be shed as the larva continues to eat and grow. This process of growing and shedding the outer layer is called **molting**. A larva may molt three to seven times before it enters the next stage.

The Pupa. As it enters the pupal stage, the beetle buries itself underground or in a tree trunk or a plant so that it will not be attacked by predators. It usually forms a hard casing around itself for protection. Then it stops all movement for several days or weeks. On the outside it looks as if nothing is happening. But inside its case, the insect is transforming itself. The pupa forms legs, wings, and elytra. Its digestive system changes, and its reproductive system develops. When its development is complete, an adult beetle emerges and crawls or flies away.

The Adult. Although long-lived compared with most other insects, adult beetles live for less than a month. During this time they must mate, and the females must find a suitable place to lay their eggs. These ends accomplished, the adult beetle dies.

▶**BEETLES AND THEIR ENVIRONMENT**

Many plant-eating beetles are considered serious pests because they feed on farm crops, trees, bushes, and other plants. One of the most destructive of these beetles is the boll weevil. Until 1843 the boll weevil lived only in Mexico, where it fed on a wild relative of the cotton plant. By 1892 the boll weevil had reached the southern tip of Texas, where there were vast fields of domesticated cotton. The boll weevil was able to spread quickly through the acres and acres of cropland, spreading northward into the southern United States at a rate of about 60 miles per year. Nothing the farmers could do prevented the expansion of this beetle's range.

One reason the boll weevil was able to spread so quickly is that a female boll weevil can lay as many as 300 eggs in her lifetime. The entire life cycle of the boll weevil takes only two or three weeks. Therefore, several generations of boll weevils can hatch in one summer, quickly increasing the population. Today, cotton farmers use a variety of methods to control the spread of the boll weevil, from insecticides and fertilizers to the introduction of sterile boll weevils that prevent the beetle from breeding successfully. But the boll weevil is a very adaptable insect. No method has

As a larva and an adult, the plant-eating Mexican bean beetle (*top*) is considered a pest. Carrion beetles (*above*) provide a beneficial service by feeding on animal wastes and dead animals.

enabled farmers to get rid of the boll weevil completely.

Other beetles are considered important in controlling insect pests on farm crops and in gardens. Ladybugs, or ladybird beetles, attack and eat aphids, scale insects, mites, and other pests. They have been used commercially since 1888 to control these insects in greenhouses and orchards. Many gardeners use ladybugs today to try to get rid of unwanted insects without using pesticides.

GAIL M. TERZI
Forest Biologist
Contributor, *Insect Biochemistry* journal

See also INSECTS; PLANT PESTS; VECTORS.

BELARUS

Belarus, once known as Belorussia (also spelled Byelorussia), is a new nation of Eastern Europe. Formerly a part of the Soviet Union, it won its independence as a result of the breakup of the Soviet Union in 1991. Belarus is surrounded by five other nations—Poland on the west; Lithuania and Latvia on the northwest; Russia on the north and east; and Ukraine on the south. This location, at the crossroads of Eastern Europe, has played an important role in Belarus' history.

The People. The Belarusians trace their origins to Eastern Slavic tribes that settled in the region between the A.D. 500's and 600's. The name *Belarus* means "White Russia," but the origins of the name are lost in time. The Belarusian language belongs to the Eastern slavic language group, which also includes Russian and Ukrainian. Both Belarusian and Russian are official state languages.

Native Belarusians make up about 80 percent of the population. Russians are the largest minority, with about 13 percent. Poles and Ukrainians are the other major ethnic groups. Most of the people adhere to the Eastern (or Greek) Orthodox faith. There are smaller numbers of Roman Catholics and members of the Greek Catholic, or Uniate, Church, which recognizes the supremacy of the pope but observes the Orthodox rite. There is also a significant Jewish community.

At one time, the majority of Belarusians were engaged in agriculture and lived in small rural farming communities. Intensive development of the country's resources led to greater economic diversity. It also brought about great changes in where the people lived. The population today is concentrated mainly in the industrial central and northern parts of the country, especially around the cities of Minsk, the capital and largest city, Gomel, and Mogilyov.

The Land. Most of Belarus consists of flat or rolling plain. A small area of uplands near the city of Minsk reaches a height of about 1,135 feet (436 meters). The Pripet Marshes occupy most of the southern part of the country. A region of rivers, lakes, bogs, and woodlands, it is inhabited by a wide variety of wild animal life. Large parts of the marshes have been drained to create new farm land.

FACTS and figures

REPUBLIC OF BELARUS is the official name of the country.

LOCATION: Eastern Europe.

AREA: 80,154 sq mi (207,600 km²).

POPULATION: 10,300,000 (estimate).

CAPITAL AND LARGEST CITY: Minsk.

MAJOR LANGUAGES: Belarusian, Russian (both official).

MAJOR RELIGIOUS GROUPS: Eastern Orthodox, Greek Catholic (Uniate), Jewish.

GOVERNMENT: Republic. **Head of state and government**—president. **Legislature**—Supreme Council.

CHIEF PRODUCTS: Agricultural—wheat, rye, and other grains, potatoes, sugar beets, and other vegetables, fodder, flax, hemp. **Manufactured**—processed agricultural products, textiles, machine tools heavy farm equipment, fertilizers. **Mineral**—oil, coal, potash.

Galloping horses enjoy a moment of freedom on a horse farm in western Belarus. The grassy plains that make up most of Belarus' land are especially suited to the raising of livestock, an important part of the country's agriculture.

About one third of Belarus is covered with forests, one of its most important natural resources. Its mineral deposits include oil, coal, and potash. Peat, obtained from the southern bogs, is used as fuel.

The climate is moderately continental, with hot summers and cool winters.

The Economy. Before the collapse of the Soviet Union, Belarus had a Communist economic system, centrally planned and controlled by the state. Economic reforms now taking place are based on a market, or free-enterprise, system.

About two thirds of the country's income comes from manufacturing, but agriculture is also important to the economy. Major crops include wheat, rye, and other grains; potatoes, sugar beets, and other vegetables; fodder, or feed for livestock; flax (from which linen is made); and hemp (used to make rope). The raising of cattle and other livestock is an important part of Belarusian agriculture. The chief manufactures include processed agricultural products, textiles, machine tools, heavy farm equipment, fertilizers, and other goods.

Early History: Polish Rule. By the A.D. 800's, Belarus was ruled by various princes who were linked to the ancient state of Kievan Rus (whose center was located in what is now Ukraine). The Kievan state was eventually destroyed by invading Mongols, and in the 1300's Belarus fell to Lithuania. For more than 400 years, Belarus was dominated first by Lithuania and then by Poland, which united with Lithuania in the 1500's. During this period the Belarusians, separated from the Eastern Slavs of Russia and Ukraine, developed their own language and culture, and emerged as a distinct people.

From Russian to Soviet Rule. When Poland was partitioned (divided) among its neighbors in the late 1700's, Belarus became a part of the Russian Empire. The Russian imperial government discouraged Belarusian cultural activities and prohibited the use of the Belarusian language in schools. This policy, however, did not succeed in destroying the idea that Belarus was a distinct nation with a history and tradition worth preserving.

During the social and political confusion caused by World War I and the Russian revolutions of 1917, Belarusian leaders issued a declaration of independence. But the infant state was crushed by political and military events and the attempt to establish independence failed. Under the Treaty of Riga (1921), Belarus was partitioned between newly independent Poland and Soviet Russia, the state that succeeded the Russian Empire. When the Union of Soviet Socialist Republics (or Soviet Union) was founded in 1922, Belarus—then called Belorussia—was one of its founding republics. In 1939, on the eve of World War II, the part of Belarus ceded to Poland in 1921 was taken over by the Soviet Union.

Independence. During all the years that followed, however, Belarusian national self-awareness remained alive. On July 27, 1990, as the Soviet Union began to break apart, the Belorussian parliament approved a declaration of sovereignty. The name Republic of Belarus was adopted in August 1991. In December 1991, with the complete collapse of the Soviet Union, Belarus and ten other former Soviet republics formed the Commonwealth of Independent States, with its administrative headquarters in Minsk.

The government, which is in the process of change, is that of a parliamentary republic. The Supreme Council, the legislative body, elects the president. Under proposed constitutional changes, the president would be elected directly by the people.

PETER CZAP, JR.
Amherst College

BELGIAN ART. See DUTCH AND FLEMISH ART.

BELGIUM

Belgium is a small nation located in north-western Europe. Although not much larger than the state of Maryland in the United States, Belgium has always been more important than its small size suggests. This is due partly to its strategic location. Situated at a crossroads of Europe, Belgium points toward Britain, which lies just across a narrow strip of the North Sea, and shares borders with the Netherlands, Germany, Luxembourg, and France. Because of its location, Belgium historically has been caught up in the struggles and quarrels of more powerful countries.

Belgium is a fairly young nation, having won its independence in 1830. But the region that is now Belgium has a long history. During the Middle Ages, it was one of the most prosperous parts of Europe, famous for both its woolen textiles and lace and for its great culture. Today, Belgium is a highly industrialized country, sometimes known as the Workshop of Europe. It is the second most densely populated European nation, after the Netherlands, and has one of the continent's highest standards of living. In addition, it plays an important role in the affairs of modern Europe.

▶THE PEOPLE

The Belgian people are divided into two large groups—the Flemings and the Walloons. The Flemings, who make up a little more than half of the population, live in the northern part of Belgium, mainly in a region called Flanders. The Flemings are descended from ancient Germanic peoples and speak Dutch.

The Walloons are French-speaking. Most Walloons live in the south, in that part of Belgium called Wallonia. The Walloons are descended from an ancient Celtic people, the Belgae, and from the Romans who conquered the Belgae in the 1st century B.C. The Belgae gave their name to the country.

Language. When Belgium first became independent in 1830, French was the official language in government and schools. Toward the end of the 19th century the Flemish people protested against the exclusive use of French, and eventually the Dutch language won legal equality. Today, Belgium is divided into distinct linguistic (language) regions. In Flanders, Dutch is the official language. French is the official language of Wallonia. Brussels, the capital, is officially bilingual; that is, both French and Dutch are used. Some German also is spoken in the eastern part of Belgium, near the border with Germany. Through the years disputes over the status and use of French and Dutch have caused considerable friction among Belgians.

Religion. Although Belgians are divided by language, they are united in their religion. Most of the people are Roman Catholics. Religious freedom, however, is guaranteed by the constitution. Although the government may not interfere in religious matters,

---

FACTS AND FIGURES

KINGDOM OF BELGIUM is the official name of the country. It is called Royaume de Belgique in French and Koninkrijk België in Dutch.

THE PEOPLE are known as Belgians.

LOCATION: Northwestern Europe.

AREA: 11,781 sq mi (30,513 km²).

POPULATION: 10,000,000 (estimate).

CAPITAL AND LARGEST CITY: Brussels.

MAJOR LANGUAGES: Dutch, French, German.

MAJOR RELIGION: Roman Catholic.

GOVERNMENT: Constitutional Monarchy. **Head of state**—king. **Head of government**—prime minister. **Legislature**—parliament, consisting of a Senate and a Chamber of Representatives.

CHIEF PRODUCTS: Agricultural—wheat, oats, barley, potatoes, sugar beets, rye, flax, fruits, flower bulbs, tobacco, livestock. **Manufactured**—iron and steel, textiles, machinery, railroad equipment, armaments, processed metals, processed food, lace, cut diamonds, glassware, chemicals, cement, tobacco products. **Mineral**—coal, phosphates.

MONETARY UNIT: Belgian franc. (1 franc = 100 centimes).

NATIONAL ANTHEM: *La Brabançonne* ("The Song of Brabant").

it does pay part of the salaries of recognized ministers of all faiths.

Education. All Belgian children between the ages of 6 and 14 must go to school. There are public and private primary and secondary schools. Most private schools in Belgium are run by religious groups. Private as well as public schools may receive financial support from the government. Higher education is provided by several excellent universities. The university at Louvain, just east of Brussels, was founded in the 1420's. It was divided into separate Dutch- and French-speaking universities in 1970.

Way of Life

The Belgians live much the way people of other modern industrial nations do. Because Belgium has a high standard of living, many homes have modern appliances such as television sets, refrigerators, and washing machines. More and more Belgians are able to afford an automobile, and traffic problems are serious in the winding streets of the old towns. But superhighways have been built to span the countryside and ease traffic congestion.

Belgians enjoy their modern way of life,

BELGIUM

Coal
Industry
Wheat, Oats

but many old buildings remain to beautify the towns and villages. Although Belgians put great emphasis on the new, they think of these old landmarks as valuable relics of their past. Belgians are proud of the fact that more than 90 per cent of Belgian homes have electricity. They are also proud that housing is generally far above average—even for prosperous northwestern Europe.

One of the canals in the city of Bruges.

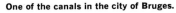

Belgian girls learn the art of lacemaking in school.

In the begonia festival held every August, displays are made entirely of flowers.

Steelworkers ride motor bicycles to foundries in Athus, an area of heavy industry.

Flax, the source of linen, drying near Courtrai.

Food. The Belgians are expert cooks and enjoy good food and pleasant dining. Every region of Belgium has its own specialties, but certain dishes are popular all over the country. A typical Belgian meal might begin with a kind of chicken soup called *waterzooï de poulet*. The main course might be *carbonnade à la flamande,* which is a beef stew made with beer. For dessert there might be sweet tarts or tiny, paper-thin, jelly-filled pancakes called *crêpes.*

Recreation. Movies, theaters, radio, and television are very popular in Belgium. Spectator sports such as soccer attract large audiences. Bicycling, bowling, and basketball are favorite sports, and ice skating on the frozen waterways is special winter fun for children in Belgium. Visitors from all over the world flock to the many richly filled art galleries.

The Arts. Belgium has been the home of many famous composers, writers, and painters. Among the 15th- and 16th-century musicians who won great fame were Guillaume Dufay, Josquin des Prez, and Roland de Lassus. The best-known modern Belgian composer, César Franck, lived in the 19th century.

Belgium's artists have been world famous for many centuries. Many famous Flemish artists lived between the 15th and 18th centuries. They include Jan van Eyck, Hieronymus Bosch, Pieter Brueghel the Elder and his son Jan, Peter Paul Rubens, Sir Anthony Van Dyck, and David Teniers the Younger. In modern times two Belgians, Paul Delvaux and René Magritte, have won fame for their surrealistic paintings.

Belgians have also made important contributions to world literature. Three of the outstanding Belgian authors who wrote in Dutch are the novelist Hendrik Conscience and the poets Guido Gezelle and Karel van de Woestijne. Among the most noted Belgians who wrote in French are the poet Emile Verhaeren; Charles de Coster, who wrote about the legendary prankster named Till Eulenspiegel; and Maurice Maeterlinck, who won the Nobel prize for literature in 1911. Georges Simenon, the popular modern mystery story writer, was born in Liège.

▶ THE LAND

Belgium is shaped almost like a triangle. There is also a tiny 18-square-kilometer (7-square-mile) fragment of Belgium, called Baarle-Hertog, that is entirely surrounded by the territory of the Netherlands. The Netherlands borders Belgium on the north and northeast. Germany and Luxembourg are on the east. France is on the south and west. Belgium's northwestern boundary is formed by the North Sea.

Belgium can be divided into three equal sections. They are the lowlands in the north and west, a low plateau in the center, and the uplands in the south and southeast.

The lowland north is generally level, and in some sections it is practically flat. Parts of the northwestern lowlands were reclaimed from the sea and marshes during the Middle Ages. Picturesque windmills, which once pumped away excess water from the earth, used to dot the lowlands. Now engine-driven pumps do the work of the old windmills. The Kempen (Campine) is the name given to the sandy, gravelly, and in places marshy northeastern lowlands. The short, straight Belgian coastline has many wide beaches that are popular resorts in summer. Much of the coast is bordered by sand dunes, and dikes have been built to protect the coast against sea flooding.

The southern two thirds of Belgium is more elevated. Central Belgium is on a low and rolling plain. Belgium's highest point is the Botrange, in the rugged Ardennes Plateau in the east.

Major Rivers. From northwest to southeast the principal Belgian rivers are the Lys, Scheldt, Sambre, Meuse, and Ourthe. Most Belgian rivers are tributaries of the Scheldt or Meuse. Northern and central Belgium are crisscrossed by many waterways. Some of the waterways are artificial ones used for drainage and navigation.

Climate. Belgium's climate is of the type known as marine west coast, which is typical of northwestern Europe. This kind of climate has changeable and cloudy weather with frequent rains and moderate temperatures. Winters are generally mild except in the interior uplands. Summers are usually cool rather than warm. Daytime temperatures are rarely higher than 27°C (80°F).

About 750 millimeters (30 inches) of precipitation—mostly in the form of rain—fall on northern Belgium in an average year. The uplands receive even more precipitation.

Natural Resources. Belgium has become a great industrial nation even though it is quite poor in natural resources. Only coal and phosphates (which are used in fertilizers) are found in large quantities. Coal, which has been taken from pits in Belgium since Roman times, is found in the Sambre and Meuse river valleys. Newer fields are being worked in the eastern Kempen. Earth, sand, and clay, used in the manufacture of glass, brick, and cement, are also found.

Belgium's agricultural resources are important. About 50 percent of the land is cultivated. Some of this is land that has been reclaimed from the sea and marshes. Centuries of skillful farming have also made the soil fertile in many other sections that once had no value.

▶ THE ECONOMY

Industry. Belgium is able to keep its high standard of living because it is a highly industrialized nation. About half of all Belgian workers are engaged in mining and industry. Many Belgian cities have industrial specialties. The capital, Brussels, is the general center of manufacture and commerce. Textiles and lace come from the cities of Ghent, Tournai, and Courtrai. Liège produces firearms. Mechlin is a furniture-making center. Woolens are made in Verviers. Charleroi, Mons, and Namur are the center of iron and steel processing.

Belgian industries depend to a large extent on imported raw materials. For example, Belgian steel is made from iron ores imported from France and Luxembourg. Belgium produces over 11,000,000 metric tons (over 12,000,000 tons) of steel a year, making it one of the world's important steel-producing countries. Other leading industries include the manufacture of railroad equipment and armaments and the processing of such metals as zinc, copper, and lead. The manufacture of woolens and other textiles has been important in Belgium since the Middle Ages. Today hundreds of thousands of metric tons of cloth goods are made in Belgian mills. "Made in Belgium" also is found stamped on such products as glassware, foods, tobacco goods, timber, and paper products.

The products of Belgium's industries are sold all over the world. Foreign trade is very important to the Belgian economy, which has widespread commercial interests, particularly in Europe. Belgium is a member of the European Communities and also has trading connections with the United States.

Agriculture. Although industry is dominant, many Belgians earn their living from farming. The average Belgian farm is small, covering only about 6.5 hectares (16 acres). But the farms are intensively cultivated. Many farmers combine farming with some other occupation such as factory work.

The major crops produced by Belgian farmers are wheat, oats, barley, potatoes, sugar beets, and rye. Flax, used for linen making, and tobacco are also grown. Truck gardening of vegetables and fruits is a leading occupation in Flanders. Bulbs for flowers are also grown in Flanders.

Belgium's climate is good for grass growth, and as a result the country has a flourishing livestock industry. Livestock feed crops are widely grown and occupy about one half of the cultivated acreage. Dairy cattle, beef cattle, and hogs are the most important livestock. Belgian horses were once widely used as draft animals. Today they have largely been replaced by farm machines in Belgium, as elsewhere.

Transportation and Communication. Belgium's farms and industries are served by an excellent transportation system. Roads reach every corner of the country. Belgium has one of the world's densest networks of railroad facilities, and an extensive system of navigable rivers and canals.

Belgium has a small merchant navy and an airline, Sabena, which is partly owned by the government. Antwerp, Belgium's most important port, on the Scheldt, competes with Rotterdam in the Netherlands and Hamburg in Germany as northwestern Europe's leading port.

▶ **GOVERNMENT**

Belgium is a hereditary, constitutional monarchy. The king is the head of the state and commander of the army. The king must approve all laws passed by Parliament. When a king dies, he is succeeded by his son. Daughters may not succeed to the throne. If a king has no sons, he may nominate his successor. But his choice must be approved by Parliament.

Although the Belgian king seems to have great powers, the actual government is headed by a prime minister, who is helped by other ministers. The Belgian Parliament is divided into two houses—the Senate and the Chamber of Representatives. The minimum voting age is 18. All qualified voters are required by law to vote.

▶ **HISTORY**

Julius Caesar wrote, "Of all the tribes of Gaul, the Belgae are the bravest." These words of the man who conquered the Belgic tribes in the 1st century B.C. have been echoed by others who tried to conquer Belgium during its long history. But the Belgians sought independence during centuries of foreign rule and finally won it in 1830.

Roman rule over Gallia Belgica lasted about 500 years. During the early Middle Ages, Belgium's history was very complicated and closely interwoven with that of its neighbors. By the end of the Middle Ages, however, northern Belgium, under the rule of the counts of Flanders, had grown strong and prosperous. Commerce, manufacture, and the arts grew. Towns slowly grew up, and guilds and other trade organizations were established. A powerful, wealthy, and well-educated middle class developed. Even so, Belgium was often involved in the military adventures of her larger neighbors.

After being tied to the Austrian Empire for over two centuries, Belgium passed to Spanish control in 1519. Then, in 1598, Belgium began a brief period of independence. This ended in 1621, when the Spanish once again took over the area they called the Spanish Netherlands. In 1713 Belgium was again made a part of the Austrian kingdom, but in 1797 France annexed the country. After the final defeat of the French emperor, Napoleon, at Waterloo, near Brussels, in 1815, Belgium and the Netherlands were set up as a united kingdom. The Belgians were unhappy about this union and on October 4, 1830, declared their independence.

The first king of the newly independent nation was a German prince, Leopold of Saxe-Coburg-Gotha. During the rule of Leopold, Belgium became one of the pioneer leaders of the industrial revolution in Europe.

The late 19th century was a period of active European colonization, but Belgium did not participate directly. However, King Leopold II, acting more or less as a private individual, claimed a huge expanse of land in Africa's Congo River basin. In 1908 the Belgian Congo colony was placed under the direct control of the Belgian Parliament.

In 1909 Albert I became king. The early years of his reign were prosperous and happy ones for Belgium. But at the outbreak of World War I in 1914, German armies invaded and quickly occupied most of Belgium. Some of the bloodiest battles of the war were fought in Belgium at Ypres, Antwerp, Namur, and Mons.

At the end of the war, the Belgians began restoring their war-torn country. Acting with their usual vigor, they quickly re-equipped and modernized their industries. Then in May, 1940, shortly after the beginning of World War II, Belgium again became a European battleground. Belgian soldiers, aided by British and French allies, were unable to resist a German invasion. After 18 days of combat, Belgium came under German occupation for the second time in a generation.

Allied armies succeeded in driving the Germans out of Belgium in September, 1944, but in December of that year German armies re-entered the country. The savage Battle of the Bulge was fought in the Ardennes region during the winter of 1944–45. It was a desperate counteroffensive, which was doomed to fail. At last in February, 1945, Belgium regained its freedom.

The Belgians once again set about re-

The City Hall on the Grand' Place in Brussels is a baroque building completed in the 17th century.

building their country. Prosperity and high employment marked the postwar years. But there were also serious problems. The conflict between the Flemings and the Walloons became more bitter. King Leopold III abdicated because many Belgians disapproved of his wartime behavior, and in 1951 his son, Baudouin, became king.

Early in the 1960's, Belgium granted independence to the Belgian Congo (now the nation of Zaïre) and to the Trusteeship Territory of Rwanda-Urundi (now the nations of Rwanda and Burundi). At home, Parliament tried to settle the language dispute. Limited self-rule was granted to Dutch-speaking Flanders and French-speaking Wallonia in 1980. Brussels remained officially bilingual.

The headquarters of many international organizations, including the European Communities and the North Atlantic Treaty Organization (NATO), are in Brussels.

KENNETH THOMPSON
University of California—Davis

Reviewed by J.-A. GORIS
Former Commissioner of Information
Belgium Information Service

BELIZE

Belize is a small nation located on the eastern, or Caribbean, coast of Central America. Formerly a British colony known as British Honduras, it gained its independence in 1981. Belize is unusual in being officially an English-speaking country in a region where Spanish is the common language.

▶ **THE PEOPLE**

Belize is the home of many different peoples. The Creoles form the largest ethnic group. They are chiefly descended from black Africans, who were originally brought to the region as slaves. Mestizos, or people of mixed Indian and European ancestry, make up the next largest group. There are smaller numbers of Maya and Carib Indians, East Indians, Europeans, Syrians, and Chinese.

While English is the official language, Spanish is also widely spoken. The Indians speak their own languages. Many Creoles speak an English dialect that contains numerous African words and is often difficult for other English-speaking people to understand.

Over half the people are Roman Catholics. The remainder are Protestants.

Most of the people live along the Caribbean coast. About one third of the population lives in Belize City, the largest city, chief port, and former capital.

▶ **THE LAND AND THE ECONOMY**

Belize has a long, swampy, and irregular coastline, fringed by small islands known as cays. The low coastal plain rises gradually toward the interior. In the south are the Maya Mountains and the Cockscomb Mountains. Victoria Peak, in the Cockscombs, rises to 1,122 meters (3,681 feet).

The hot and humid climate is cooled along the coast by northeast trade winds. In the south more than 4,300 millimeters (170 inches) of rain may fall each year. Belize lies within the Caribbean hurricane belt, and storms have caused great damage in the past. Belize City was nearly destroyed twice by hurricanes. For this reason a new capital, Belmopan, was built inland about 80 kilometers (50 miles) from Belize City. Belmopan has been the official capital since 1972.

Belize has many rivers, but most are shallow, and none is very long. The most important is the Belize River. A considerable part of the land is still covered with dense tropical forests. For much of Belize's history, lumber-

Belizeans gather to watch British troops on parade in Belize City. Some British forces still remain in Belize because of neighboring Guatemala's claims to its territory.

ing was its most important economic activity. African slaves were brought to the territory to fell the valuable hardwood trees. Sugar is now the leading export. Other important products include citrus fruits, fish and lobsters caught in the waters of the Caribbean Sea, and bananas.

▶ **HISTORY AND GOVERNMENT**

Belize was once a part of the vast Maya Indian Empire. The first known European settlers were British sailors who had been shipwrecked off the coast in 1638. Other British settlers followed. For many years, Spain, which ruled the surrounding region, disputed Britain's possession of the territory. When Guatemala won independence from Spain in 1821, it assumed the Spanish territorial claims.

British Honduras became a British crown colony in 1862. It was granted internal self-government in 1964, and in 1973 its name was changed to Belize, which came from an older name for the territory. Belize's movement toward independence was complicated by Guatemala's continued claims to the territory and by threats of a Guatemalan invasion. Even after Belize won its independence in 1981, the territorial dispute was still not resolved; and British troops remain in the country.

The government of Belize is based on the British model. The British monarch, represented by a governor-general, is the head of state. Real political power, however, lies with the National Assembly, which is composed of an elected House of Representatives and an appointed Senate. The leader of the majority party in the House of Representatives becomes prime minister, or head of government.

Belize is a member of the Caribbean Community and Common Market (CARICOM).

Reviewed by SIR PETER STALLARD
Former Governor, Belize

Most of Belize's rivers are shallow and not very long. But they provide transportation for small craft, such as dugout canoes, carrying village produce to market.

FACTS AND FIGURES

BELIZE is the official name of the country.

THE PEOPLE are known as Belizeans.

LOCATION: Central America.

AREA: 8,867 sq mi (22,965 km²).

POPULATION: 170,000 (estimate).

CAPITAL: Belmopan.

LARGEST CITY: Belize City.

MAJOR LANGUAGES: English (official), Spanish.

MAJOR RELIGION: Christian (Roman Catholic, Protestant).

GOVERNMENT: Constitutional monarchy. **Head of state**— British monarch, represented by a governor-general. **Head of government**—prime minister. **Legislature**— National Assembly (composed of a House of Representatives and a Senate).

CHIEF PRODUCTS: Agricultural—sugarcane, citrus fruits, bananas, rice, corn, beans. **Manufactured**—refined sugar, processed citrus fruits, lumber, clothing.

MONETARY UNIT: Belize dollar (1 dollar = 100 cents).

NATIONAL ANTHEM: "Land of the Gods."

Although Bell invented the telephone and made important contributions in many fields of science, he described his occupation as "teacher of the deaf."

BELL, ALEXANDER GRAHAM
(1847–1922)

The date was March 10, 1876. The place was a small laboratory in a Boston boardinghouse. A young man was working with an electrical instrument that was wired to one in another room. Suddenly the instrument spoke: "Mr. Watson, come here. I want you." Watson rushed into the other room, where his employer, Mr. Bell, had spilled some acid. Both men forgot the acid in their excitement over Watson's report: Bell's words, spoken near one instrument, had issued clearly from the other. These words had become the first spoken telephone message.

Alexander Graham Bell was born on March 3, 1847, in Edinburgh, Scotland. He was born into a family with an interest in speech and hearing. Both his grandfather and his father were teachers of correct speech. His father had developed "visible speech," a method of helping the deaf and hearing impaired to learn how to speak. From his mother, who was a portrait painter and an accomplished musician, he inherited a talent for music.

Bell's schooling was far from regular. In his early years he was taught at home along with his two brothers. At the age of 13 he spent a year in London with his grandfather. In his grandfather's library he read all he could about sound and speech—about the vibrations set up by the voice. He later recalled this year as the turning point of his life. By the age of 16 Graham, as he was called by his family and close friends, was teaching music and speech at a boys' school. Within a few years he was teaching his father's visible speech to deaf and hearing impaired children.

While studying how the human voice works, Bell came upon the writings of Hermann von Helmholtz. Helmholtz was a German scientist who had used electric vibrations to make vowel sounds. Interested, Bell at once began to study electricity so that he could repeat Helmholtz's experiments.

Bell's family had moved to London, and he joined them there in 1868. But by 1870 both of Bell's brothers had died of tuberculosis, and his own life was in danger. Seeking a more healthful climate, the Bells left Britain and moved to Brantford, Ontario.

With his health improved, Bell went to Boston, Massachusetts, in 1871. There he again took up his life's work of teaching the deaf and hearing impaired. Bell also continued his experiments. By now his work with electricity had led him to think about inventing a harmonic telegraph. This was a system that could carry several messages over one wire at the same time.

Bell needed money to carry on his experiments. It was given to him by two wealthy men, Gardiner Hubbard and Thomas Sanders. Hubbard had a deaf daughter, and Sanders a deaf son, both of whom were receiving instruction from Bell. It was arranged that the two fathers would share in any profits from Bell's work. Bell was now able to hire a skilled assistant, Thomas A. Watson.

It was during the summer of 1874 that Bell's thinking first went beyond his plan for a harmonic telegraph. What if an electric current could be made to vary, just as the air varies with sound waves? Then any sound— including human speech—could be carried by electricity. This was the idea of the telephone.

The next year was a busy one for Bell. Now that he had the idea of a telephone, he wanted to develop it. On June 2, 1875, Bell and Watson were experimenting with their telegraph, which made use of thin steel reeds. One of the reeds was stuck, and Watson plucked it with his finger. In another room Bell heard a reed in his instrument vibrate as if he himself had plucked it. The electric current had reproduced in this second reed the vibrations of the first.

If the current had done this, then surely it should also reproduce vibrations caused by the human voice. Bell now knew that the telephone was a practical idea. It was only a matter of time before he could perfect an instrument that would send words clearly. Success came on March 10, 1876, with the famous words, "Mr. Watson, come here. I want you."

By the end of 1877 the Bell Telephone Company had been formed, and many phones were in use. Bell himself did not take part in the telephone business that developed. Rather, he leased the right to build a company around his invention.

In the meantime Bell had married Mabel Hubbard, the deaf girl whom he had taught.

They had two daughters. In 1882 Bell became a citizen of the United States. He divided his time between Washington, D.C., and his summer home, Beinn Bhreagh, on Cape Breton Island, Nova Scotia.

Bell had invented the telephone before he was 30. In the remaining 45 years of his life he applied his talents to many questions. He experimented with sending sound by light waves. He was interested in heredity and carried on breeding experiments with sheep. As early as the 1890's, Bell was experimenting with the problems of airplane flight. Throughout his life Bell continued working for the deaf and hearing impaired. His work in all these fields won him many honors. Bell died on August 2, 1922. He was so greatly admired that during the funeral the telephones of North America were silent in his honor.

JOHN S. BOWMAN
Author and Science Editor

See also ELECTRICITY; TELEPHONE.

BELLINI FAMILY

During the 1400's, Jacopo Bellini, a Venetian painter, owned one of the busiest workshops in Italy. He painted portraits for rich people and altars for the Church and taught young artists who came to study under him. Among his students were his sons, Gentile and Giovanni. Gentile was the elder.

Jacopo was born about 1400, and his sons were born about 1429 and 1430. The three artists worked in the shop for years, experimenting with a new medium, oil paint. The brothers continued to paint after Jacopo died (about 1470). In 1474, they began a series of historical paintings for the palace of the chief magistrate of Venice.

The sultan of Turkey asked the rulers of Venice to lend him one of their best painters. Gentile was chosen and was sent to Constantinople in 1479. Giovanni remained in Venice, working at the palace, teaching, and painting. He was the first of the great Venetian painters to capture a sense of open space and light. Today, he is regarded as the greatest of the Bellinis. When Gentile returned to Venice in 1480, the brothers worked together again.

Gentile died in 1507, and Giovanni in 1516. In 1577, a fire burned through the pal-

Madonna of the Trees (1487), by Giovanni Bellini.

ace. It destroyed countless Bellini canvases—among the first masterpieces of oil painting.

Reviewed by ADRIANE RUSKIN BATTERBERRY
Author, *The Pantheon Story of Art for Young People*

BELLOW, SAUL (1915–)

Saul Bellow is one of the foremost American writers of the period after World War II. His finely crafted novels of modern life won him the Nobel prize for literature in 1976.

Bellow was born on July 10, 1915, in Lachine, Quebec, Canada. His parents, who were Jewish, had gone there two years before from Russia, where his father had been a businessman. Saul was the youngest of four children. Until he was 9, the family lived in Montreal, where he grew up learning four languages—French, English, Yiddish, and Hebrew. In 1924 the family moved to Chicago, and he afterward thought of that city as his hometown.

Bellow attended Chicago schools. He graduated with honors from Northwestern University and started graduate studies at the University of Wisconsin. But he left in his first year, determined to become a writer.

Bellow taught at colleges and universities and also worked as an encyclopedia editor. His first two novels, *Dangling Man* (1944) and *The Victim* (1947), are rather grim stories. His next novel, *The Adventures of Augie March* (1953), shows the humor for which he has become known. It was his first big success, and it won a National Book Award. *Henderson the Rain King*, about an American in Africa, followed in 1959.

In 1962, Bellow became a professor at the University of Chicago. Two later novels, *Herzog* (1964) and *Mr. Sammler's Planet* (1970), won National Book Awards. *Humboldt's Gift* (1975) won the Pulitzer prize for fiction in 1976. Bellow has also written nonfiction and plays. *Him With His Foot in His Mouth and Other Stories* (1984) is a collection of his short stories.

Reviewed by JEROME H. STERN
Florida State University

BELLS AND CARILLONS

A bell is a hollow cup-shaped vessel that rings when struck. A bell may be struck on the outside by a hammer or mallet or by means of a clapper suspended inside the bell.

Most modern bells are made of metal—usually bronze, an alloy of copper and tin. In bell casting, two molds of baked clay are made. One forms the bell's interior, and the other forms the curved outside surface. Molten bronze is poured between the two molds. When the metal is cool and hard, the molds are removed. Bells are tuned by filing metal strips from their inside surfaces.

For centuries bells have been rung to mark the passing hours. But they have also been used for many other purposes: to sound an alarm, to announce a birth or a death, to call a congregation to worship, even to ward off evil spirits. The Egyptians wore bells on their ankles as a protection against lightning. In old England, folk dancers jingled bells to awaken the spirit of spring from a long winter's sleep.

In ancient Rome, bells announced public assemblies and church services. In the Middle Ages, bells woke the city at dawn, signaling morning prayers. Through the day, bells marked the hours, the half hours, and the quarters. They pealed for weddings and tolled for funerals and were heard at Easter and Christmas.

A modern-day bell tower in Atlanta, Georgia, holds a set of carillon bells. This carillon can be programmed by computer to play a sequence of tunes.

The First Bell Music. The earliest attempts to make music with bells occurred in the Middle Ages, with the *cymbala*, or bell chime. This was a small set of bells hung from a rack.

The clock bell originated in the monastery. The bells rang from a tower, regulating not only life in the abbey but in the surrounding town as well. So necessary were the bells to a town that they became civic property.

Since the first clock bells could not ring by themselves, someone was hired to strike them at the proper times. The human bell ringer was soon replaced by clock machinery. It was then possible to ring many bells, and it became customary to ring a short tune as a warning that the hour bell was about to strike. This is known as a clock chime tune.

From Bells to Carillons. A carillon is a set of bells with a range of between two and four octaves. Usually a carillon has at least 23 bells. The first carillons were made in the 1500's in Flanders (a region in present-day Belgium and northern France). At first the bells were rung automatically; later a keyboard, operated by a **carillonneur**, was added.

The carillon keyboard consists of levers and pedals. The levers resemble small broomstick handles. The carillonneur sits at a bench and strikes the levers with clenched hands while playing the foot pedals.

The oldest carillon in the world is in the Rijksmuseum in Amsterdam. It has 24 bells cast in 1554. A famous carillon is at Saint Rombold's Cathedral in Mechelen, Belgium. It has 49 bells. The first carillon in North America was installed at Notre Dame University in South Bend, Indiana, in 1856. The largest carillon in the world is at the Riverside Church in New York City. It contains six octaves of bells, of which the **bourdon**, or bass bell, weighs more than 18 tons.

Electronic carillons imitate the sound of bells through the use of electronic equipment; they are very different from true carillons.

JAMES R. LAWSON
Carillonneur, Riverside Church (New York City)

BEN-GURION, DAVID (1886–1973)

David Ben-Gurion became the first prime minister of Israel after the country became independent in 1948. He served as prime minister and minister of defense from 1949 to 1953 and from 1955 to 1963.

Ben-Gurion was born David Gryn on October 16, 1886, in Plonsk, Poland. His father, Avigdor Gryn, was a Zionist who inspired young David with the hope that some day a homeland for the Jewish people could be established in Palestine.

In 1906 David decided that the time had come for him to go to Palestine, then a part of the Turkish Empire. The new land was strange to someone who had always lived in Poland, but he soon found work as a farm laborer. In 1910 David became editor of the Palestine Labor Party's magazine. He signed one of his articles "Ben-Gurion," Hebrew for "son of the young lion." From then on he was known as David Ben-Gurion.

When World War I broke out in 1914, Ben-Gurion was arrested by the Turks and expelled from Palestine. First he fled to Egypt and later to the United States. In America he encouraged young people to emigrate to Palestine.

One of these Americans was a nurse named Paula Munweis, who eventually became Ben-Gurion's wife. In 1917 Ben-Gurion helped organize the Jewish Legion to fight with the British Army against the Turks. In 1918 he returned to Palestine.

For the next 20 years Ben-Gurion devoted himself to Zionism and politics. He helped organize Histadrut (the General Federation of Jewish Labor). In 1935 he became chairman of the Jewish Agency for Palestine, an organization that assisted Jewish immigrants who wanted to settle in Palestine.

Israel declared its independence on May 14, 1948. Under Ben-Gurion's leadership the new nation became a modern democracy as well as a home for Jews seeking refuge. Ben-Gurion died in 1973, a national hero.

Reviewed by HOWARD M. SACHAR
George Washington University

BENIN

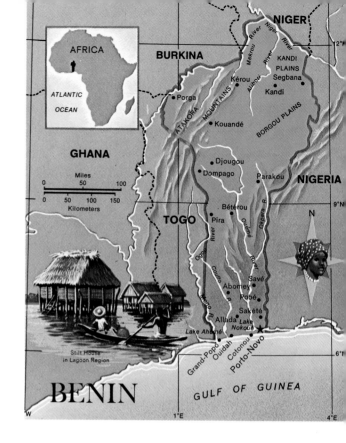

Stilt House in Lagoon Region

BENIN

Benin, which was formerly called Dahomey, is a small nation on the west coast of Africa. It traces its history back to the powerful kingdom of Dahomey in the 1600's. Later the region came under the control of France, which governed it until 1960. Unlike the old kingdom of Dahomey, Benin today is one of the poorest countries in Africa.

▶THE PEOPLE

Most of the people in Benin live in the southern part of the country, which has the richest soil. The northern region is more sparsely populated. Of the many different ethnic groups in Benin, the most numerous are the Fon, the Adja, the Bariba, and the Yoruba. The majority of the people follow traditional African religions, but there are considerable numbers of Christians and Muslims. French is the official language, but Fon and other African languages are widely spoken.

FACTS and figures

REPUBLIC OF BENIN (République du Bénin) is the official name of the country.

LOCATION: West coast of Africa.

AREA: 43,484 sq mi (112,622 km²).

POPULATION: 4,500,000 (estimate).

CAPITAL: Porto-Novo (official).

LARGEST CITY: Cotonou (center of government administration).

MAJOR LANGUAGES: French (official), Fon, other African languages.

MAJOR RELIGIONS: Traditional African religions, Christian, Muslim.

GOVERNMENT: Republic. **Head of state and government**—president. **Legislature**—National Assembly.

CHIEF PRODUCTS: Agricultural—palm kernels, coconuts, peanuts, cotton, shea nuts, cassava, corn, beans, millet, sweet potatoes, rice. **Manufactured**—palm oil, palm kernel oil, copra, processed fish, cotton textiles.

MONETARY UNIT: African Financial Community (CFA) franc (1 CFA franc = 100 centimes).

Most of the people are farmers who produce food chiefly for their own use. The main food crops are cassava, maize (corn), beans, millet, sweet potatoes, and rice. Cassava is used in making bread and tapioca (*gari*). The farmers also keep cattle, sheep, and goats. Fish are an important source of food and one of the country's exports.

Improvement in education is essential to the country's development. Most schools are in the south, but the government is trying to provide education for the scattered population in the north. Most of the schools of higher education are located in Porto-Novo, the official capital, and Cotonou, the largest city and center of government administration.

▶THE LAND

Benin occupies a long, narrow strip of land that includes both lowlands and highlands. It has a short coastline on the Gulf of Guinea, a part of the Atlantic Ocean.

The country has four geographical regions. In the south is a flat coastal area along the Gulf of Guinea. Next is a region of lagoons and lakes. Farther north the land rises to a broad plateau that reaches as high as 1,500 feet (460 meters). In the far north the land is divided between the Atakora Mountains and the broad plains of Borgou and Kandi. The major rivers are the Ouémé (the country's longest), the Mono, and the Couffo. Ships can travel up the Ouémé for about half its length in the rainy season.

The northern and southern parts of the country have different climates. The south is hot and humid; the north is drier, with less rainfall.

▶ THE ECONOMY

Benin is a poor and underdeveloped country. Its economy is largely agricultural. The major industries are those that process the chief export crops—palm oil, palm kernels, and nuts. Palm products supply most of the country's exports. Palm oil is used in making soap and margarine. Copra (dried coconut meat), shea butter (the fat of shea tree nuts), cotton, peanuts, and castor oil are among the other important agricultural exports.

▶ HISTORY AND GOVERNMENT

The three great kingdoms of Ardra, Jakin, and Dahomey flourished in the early 1600's. During the 1700's, the strong kings of Dahomey gained control of Ardra and Jakin in the south.

In 1738 the Yoruba from Nigeria seized Abomey, the capital of the kingdom of Dahomey, and forced the Dahomean rulers to pay tribute for nearly 100 years. In the late 1800's, the great Dahomean king Gezo reorganized the Dahomean Army, which in-

cluded a famous band of female warriors. He succeeded in shaking off the yoke of the Yoruba.

During this time, the French were extending their influence along the Gulf of Guinea. Gezo signed the first trade agreement with the French in 1851, but the kings who came after him did not respect the agreement. In 1894, France forcibly deposed the last of the Dahomean kings, Béhanzin, and annexed the territory to French West Africa.

France gradually began to give Dahomey and other French African territories more control over their own affairs. Dahomey elected its own legislature in 1952. In 1960 it proclaimed its independence.

After gaining independence, Dahomey suffered years of political instability. Military coups in the 1960's and early 1970's led to frequent changes of government. In 1972, Major (now General) Mathieu Kérékou came to power and established a revolutionary Marxist-Leninist (Communist-style) government. In 1975 he changed the name of the country from Dahomey to Benin.

Kérékou governed as president and head of Benin's sole political party, the People's Revolutionary Party, until 1990, when anti-government demonstrations forced him to resign. In 1991, in the first free elections in more than twenty years, Nicephore Soglo, who had served as prime minister, was elected to the presidency, defeating Kérékou.

L. GRAY COWAN
Columbia University

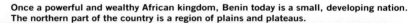
Once a powerful and wealthy African kingdom, Benin today is a small, developing nation. The northern part of the country is a region of plains and plateaus.

BEOWULF

Beowulf is the longest and greatest of the poems that have come down to us in Old English. It is a hero's story made into a poem, so that all the pleasures of poetry are added to the lively events of a hero's life. *Beowulf* had to be exciting and easy to understand, because when it was composed, literature was not read quietly out of books but was recited after feasts in the halls of kings and nobles. The *scop* or *gleeman*—early words for "poet" —spoke *Beowulf* and other poems aloud, probably striking a small harp to mark the rhythm. Such poems often inspired warriors before battle or celebrated a victory.

Though *Beowulf* was composed by a *scop* who called England his native land, the scene of the story is not England. Beowulf was a Geat, which means that he came from the south of Sweden. Hrothgar, the king he came to help, was a Dane, and most of the story happens in Denmark. Though the poem could not have been written down before A.D. 700, the events in it probably happened in the 500's. Like writers of historical novels today, the *scop* went back in time and far away in space to find his story.

The only copy of *Beowulf* that we have was written down about A.D. 1000 in the West Saxon dialect. This manuscript looks to us now as if it were in some strange language. These are the opening lines:

> Hwaet! we Gar-Dena   in geardagum,
> þeodcyninga   þrym gefrunon,
> hu þa aeþelingas   ellen fremedon!
> Oft Scyld Scefing   sceaþena þreatum
> monegum maegþum   meodosetla ofteah,
> egsode eorlas,   syððan aerest wearð
> feasceaft funden;

The unfamiliar þ and ð are only ways of showing the sounds we write as *th*. Some words in *Beowulf* are still in our language.

Many things about the poem must have stirred the listening warriors. Old English is very powerful, with harsh consonant sounds like K, D, G, KH, and GH. The Old English *scops* used alliteration, the repetition of one consonant sound, instead of rhyme. "Great was the *grief* of the *gold*-friend of Scyldings" shows how the *scop* tied his line together with the sound of G.

The rhythm is as strong as the beat of marching feet. Each line has two parts and is divided by a pause. Each of the two parts has two strong beats. So there are four strong beats in each line, two on one side of the pause and two on the other:

> *Great* was the *grief*//of the *gold*-friend
> of *Scyld*ings . . .

If we say the line aloud, accenting the words in italics and pausing at the double line, we will feel the rhythm that could make warriors wish to grasp their spears and march.

Old English poems are rich in images— words that make pictures. That is because the *scops* used *kennings*, colorful ways of saying ordinary things. The *scop* who composed *Beowulf* calls the sea a whale-path; a traveler an earth-stepper; a battle, spear-play. Since his England was misty, craggy, and gloomy, with many empty wildernesses, his images are often mysterious and frightening.

The Story

The main story of *Beowulf* runs as follows: Hrothgar, King of the Danes, built a great house called Heorot. Here his warriors gathered to drink mead and listen to the *scop* sing his songs. Their revelry enraged an evil monster named Grendel, who lived in the marshes. He began attacking the mead-hall at night, killing the men while they were sleeping. Finally Hrothgar was forced to abandon Heorot.

Beowulf, a young hero, heard in Geatland of Hrothgar's grief and determined to help. He crossed the icy sea with 14 companions-at-arms, told Hrothgar his good intentions, and got permission to try his might. After

At night the monster Grendel attacks the Danish warriors in their mead hall.

the Danes had feasted the visiting Geats in Heorot, Hrothgar and his warriors went elsewhere, and Beowulf and his companions stayed in the hall. Grendel came, opened the iron-bolted door at a touch, fell upon one of Beowulf's sleeping friends, and killed him. But before Grendel could carry the body off to the marsh, Beowulf caught the beast's hairy arm and dragged on it until he wrenched it out of its socket. Grendel fled, leaving his arm and a trail of blood behind. The next morning Geats and Danes followed the trail to a pool that was boiling with the blood of the dead monster. They returned happy. That night the Geats again lodged elsewhere, and the Danes went back to sleep—safely, they thought—in Heorot. But Grendel's mother, a monster-hag, came to the hall seeking vengeance and killed a Danish warrior. Again Beowulf followed the trail of Grendel's blood to the pool in the wasteland and leaped in. Under the water, inside a vaulted room, he found and killed the monster-hag. He also found the dead body of Grendel and cut off the head and carried it back to the king.

Beowulf contains other stories telling how the hero became king of the Geats and killed a dragon, but the best part of the poem is his visit to Hrothgar.

Beowulf is a strange mixture. It refers to pagan rites and Christian beliefs. It tells about real things, such as lordly feasts and sea journeys, and imaginary things, such as monsters and dragons. It contains at least one event that we know happened in history, and many events that could happen only in fairy tales. Although it is not so great an epic as Homer's *Iliad*, it is a noble and exciting poem that shows us much about the earliest heroes—their courage, generosity, and faithfulness and their love of glory and danger. Like a rich barbaric bracelet found by excavators, no one knows who made it or exactly when it was made. It is rough and dark, but strongly beautiful. It speaks to us of old times, old customs, and men and women who would be quite forgotten if the *scop* had not told of them in the king's hall.

GLADYS SCHMITT
Author, *The Heroic Deeds of Beowulf*

BERING, VITUS (1680?–1741)

In the early 1700's, many people still believed that a bridge of land connected Asia and North America. Vitus Bering, a Dane in the service of the czar of Russia, discovered that this land bridge did not exist. His explorations helped map what was at that time a little-known part of the world and led to the discovery of Alaska.

Bering was born at Horsens, Denmark, in 1680 or 1681, and entered the Russian Navy when he was 23. In 1724, Czar Peter the Great appointed him to lead an expedition to the Kamchatka Peninsula on the northeast coast of Siberia. Here, Bering was to build a ship in which to seek the reputed bridge between the continents.

The long journey across Siberia was filled with great hardships. After more than three years, the expedition finally reached a little village on Kamchatka. Bering had a ship built and in 1728 set sail across an uncharted sea, now called the Bering Sea. He discovered an island, which he named St. Lawrence Island. Then he sailed north through the strait (now called Bering Strait) that separates Asia and North America. The discovery of this strait proved that the two continents were not linked.

Bering returned to Russia in 1730 to report his findings and to plan a new expedition. In 1741 he sailed from Kamchatka again with two ships—his, the *St. Peter*, and the *St. Paul*, which was commanded by Aleksei Chirikov. The ships soon drifted apart, and on July 15–16 both Chirikov and Bering sighted the southern coast of Alaska from different points. The *St. Peter* stopped briefly at Kayak Island. But before exploring further, Bering, who was ill, decided to return to Kamchatka for the winter. On the return voyage the *St. Peter* was buffeted by violent storms and wrecked on an uninhabited island off the coast of Kamchatka. Here, on December 8, 1741, Bering died and was buried. The island now bears his name.

Reviewed by HELEN DELPAR
Editor, *The Discoverers: An Encyclopedia of Explorers and Exploration*

BERLIN

The city of Berlin has long been a center of German political, economic, cultural, and intellectual life. Twice during the course of history it has served as the capital of a unified Germany.

Berlin first became the national capital in 1871, when the various German states were united into a single country. However, in the years that followed the defeat of the Nazi German regime in World War II (1939–45), Berlin—like Germany itself—was divided into two parts. East Berlin became the capital of East Germany (the German Democratic Republic), while West Berlin became one of the federal states of West Germany (the Federal Republic of Germany). During these years, the small university town of Bonn served as the capital of West Germany.

With the reunification of East and West Germany in 1990, however, the division of the city was ended, and Berlin once again became the official capital.

A sunny day draws Berliners to an outdoor café. In the background, the ruins of the old Kaiser Wilhelm Memorial Church stand as a stark reminder of the destruction of World War II.

Location, Area, and Population. Berlin is situated in northeastern Germany, on the Spree and Havel rivers. Its location has made it a traditional crossroads of trade between eastern and western and northern and southern Europe. Lying on the great sandy plain of the North German lowlands, the city has an average elevation of only about 112 feet (34 meters) above sea level.

Berlin makes up an urban area of about 441 square miles (1,142 square kilometers). With a population of nearly 3.5 million, it is the largest city in Germany and one of the ten largest cities in Europe. Yet the city's numerous parks, forests, lakes and other waterways give some of its districts a rustic, or country-like, setting.

Places of Interest. In the center of the former West Berlin the ruined tower of the Kaiser Wilhelm Memorial Church stands as a stark reminder of the destruction of World War II. Next to it is the new, modernistic church building, completed in 1961. The two structures are situated at the eastern end of the Kurfürstendamm, an elegant avenue of fashionable shops, restaurants, and theaters.

The reconstructed Reichstag, the old parliament building, is a landmark of historical importance. The original building was burned in 1933, soon after the Nazis took power. The present German parliament (or legislature) meets there on festive public occasions. Nearby is a Soviet war memorial, the Tiergarten, and the new Congress Hall. The Tiergarten, a park near the center of the city with a zoo and aquarium, is especially popular with Berliners. Other new buildings include the Berlin Philharmonic concert hall, the opera house, and several museums.

For years the wall that divided the city attracted millions of visitors. It was torn down in 1990, and all that remains of this relic of the Cold War is a swath of open space.

The Brandenburg Gate, one of Berlin's best-known monuments, is situated in the historic center of the city, in what was formerly East Berlin. A triumphal arch some 85 feet (26 meters) high, it faces the Tiergarten and stands at the western end of a tree-lined boulevard, Unter den Linden ("Under the Linden Trees"). This thoroughfare was once the site of military parades and the funeral processions of German rulers. Most of the government buildings, palaces, and foreign embassies that at one time lined the avenue were destroyed during World War II, but those that could be saved were restored.

At the eastern end of Unter den Linden is a giant square, which the East Germans named Marx-Engels-Platz, after the two major figures in the founding of Communism. It is also the site of the former royal palace. The huge Palace of the Republic, which once housed the East German parliament, stands nearby. Numerous museums are located on the appropriately named Museum Island.

Cultural Life. Berlin has been a cultural center of Germany for much of its modern history. During the Weimer period (1919–33), it was the entertainment capital of the world. Its numerous cabarets, theaters, and motion pictures enjoyed an international reputation, lost during the Nazi era that followed.

Top: East German border guards looked on calmly in 1989 as West Germans celebrated the coming reunification of the long-divided city. A reunited Berlin was soon followed by the reunification of Germany itself. *Right:* A poster for the German silent film classic *Metropolis* dates from 1926, when Berlin was famed as the popular entertainment capital of the world. *Far right:* This war memorial was dedicated to the thousands of Soviet troops killed in the 1945 battle for Berlin.

The city's division into eastern and western sectors from 1949 to 1990 meant that each developed its own distinct cultural life. Attempts were made, however, to preserve a common heritage. The great pre-war museum collections, for example, were divided between East and West Berlin's museums.

Berlin has recaptured some of its past glory through its Philharmonic Orchestra concerts, opera houses, theater groups, a yearly cultural festival, and jazz and rock performances. The Free University and Humboldt University play an important role in the city's intellectual life. Its many museums include the world-famous Pergamon Museum, noted for its collection of classical art.

The Economy. Before World War II, Berlin was a center of commerce and banking as well as an important industrial city. By the 1950's, West Berlin had recovered from the war's destruction and was in the midst of an economic boom. At the same time, East Berlin was integrated into the Communist economic system of East Germany. The standard of living was considerably higher in the West than in the East.

The major industries in the Greater Berlin area involve the production of electrical and electronic equipment, machinery and motor vehicles, engineering products, processed foods, chemicals, and clothing. The city also has the largest number of scientific and technological research institutions in the country.

Since the reunification of Germany in 1990, the federal government has provided substantial economic assistance to the former eastern sector.

The City's Origins. The city of Berlin developed out of two small trading settlements, Kölln and Berlin, which are first mentioned in documents of the 1200's. The two settlements merged in the 1300's. In 1486, Berlin became the seat of the electors (or rulers) of what was then the small state of Brandenburg. The Thirty Years' War (1618–48) laid waste to the city, but it was rebuilt by the Great Elector Frederick William.

Capital. In 1701, Berlin became the capital of the kingdom of Prussia, which had grown out of the original core of Brandenburg. In spite of military occupation by foreign armies during the wars of the 1700's and 1800's, Berlin, along with Prussia, grew steadily in importance. When the German states united around Prussia to form the German Empire in 1871, Berlin became its capital.

During World War II, much of Berlin was destroyed by bombing and in the

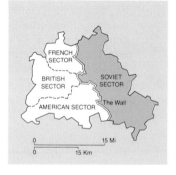

Above: Berlin was divided among the four victorious Allied powers in 1945, at the end of World War II. In 1949 the U.S., British, and French sectors were joined to form West Berlin. The Soviet sector became East Berlin. The city remained divided until 1989–90. *Left:* When the Soviet Union blockaded West Berlin in 1948–49, cutting off all land access to that part of the city, its people were supplied through a massive airlift by U.S. and British planes.

As onlookers cheer, a young Berliner adds his own blows to the crumbling wall that for nearly thirty years had physically divided the city. Erected in 1961, the Berlin Wall was designed to stop the flood of Germans escaping from Communist East Germany to West Germany, which had become a drain on the East German economy. The wall was also a symbol of the division of Germany itself, which lasted until 1990, when both Germany and Berlin were again united.

heavy ground fighting that took place in the closing weeks of the war in Europe. On May 2, 1945, Soviet armies captured the city. By agreement, U.S., British, French, and Soviet forces each occupied a sector of Berlin (see map). Germany as a whole was divided along the same lines. The United States, Britain, and France occupied the western part of the country (which later became West Germany). The Soviet Union controlled the eastern part (later to become East Germany). Berlin itself lay deep within the Soviet area of occupation of Germany. An inter-Allied governing authority administered the city jointly.

Blockade and Airlift. In 1948, Berlin became a focal point of the Cold War, the period of hostility that developed between the Soviet Union and the nations of the West after the war. The Soviets informally withdrew from the governing authority and tried to force the Western powers to end controls over their three sectors. When this failed, the Soviets cut off all land and water communications between western Germany and the three western sectors of Berlin in an effort to gain control over the entire city.

In response, the Western Allies launched a massive airlift of food and other supplies to the isolated western sectors. The blockade lasted eleven months, until May 1949, when the Soviets, not having gained their objective, lifted it.

The City Divided. In 1949 separate East and West Germanys were established. The U.S., British, and French sectors of Berlin were joined to form West Berlin; the Soviet sector became East Berlin. But the four Allied powers still had final control over the city.

In 1953 a revolt by workers in East Berlin against the East German government was crushed by Soviet tanks. Increasing numbers of East Berliners fled to West Berlin in subsequent years, until 1961, when the East German authorities erected a fortified wall, physically separating the two parts of the city.

Reunification. The easing of political tensions and a new agreement between the Western Allies and the Soviet Union in 1971 eased travel restrictions for Germans. Nevertheless, the Berlin Wall remained a symbol of a divided city and nation for nearly twenty more years. In November 1989, however, following widespread protests by its own people, the East German government opened the guarded crossing points of the wall.

As East Berliners poured into West Berlin in celebration, the dismantling of the wall and of a divided Germany was already underway. On October 3, 1990, the two Germanys were united, the special privileges of the four powers ended, and a separate West and East Berlin ceased to exist.

GERARD BRAUNTHAL
University of Massachusetts, Amherst

BERLIN, IRVING (1888–1989)

The American songwriter Irving Berlin helped define the modern American popular song. During his long career he wrote some 1,500 songs. Many—"Always," "Blue Skies," "Puttin' on the Ritz," and countless others—have become classics, recorded again and again by new generations of singers.

Berlin was born Israel Baline in Tyumen, Russia, on May 11, 1888, the youngest of eight children. He moved with his family to New York City at the age of 5. He had barely begun school when his father died, and he sold newspapers and sang in the streets to help support his family. He learned to play piano by ear and began to compose melodies by trial and error. He became Irving Berlin when his first song was mistakenly credited to "I. Berlin," and he decided to change his first name as well.

In 1909, Berlin got a job writing lyrics for a music publisher; he became world famous two years later for writing "Alexander's Ragtime Band," which sold more than one million copies of sheet music. Berlin formed his own music company in 1919. During the 1920's the composer developed his unerring touch for

U.S. songwriter Irving Berlin entertained generations of Americans with his popular tunes.

ballads. In 1935 he wrote *Top Hat*, the first of many film scores. In 1939 he composed "God Bless America," which became one of the country's best-loved patriotic songs.

Among Berlin's greatest successes was the song "White Christmas," which won an Academy Award in 1942 and became a modern Christmas carol. He also wrote hit Broadway musicals, notably *Annie Get Your Gun* (1946), with its rousing showstopper, "There's No Business Like Show Business."

Berlin's last major work was the Broadway show *Mr. President* (1962). He died in New York City on September 22, 1989, at 101 years of age.

Reviewed by CHARLES MORITZ
Editor, *Current Biography*

BERLIOZ, HECTOR (1803–1869)

Louis-Hector Berlioz, an innovative French composer, was born near Grenoble, France, on December 11, 1803. Because of pressure from his father, a physician, Hector went to Paris in 1821 to enroll in medical school. While there he attended many opera performances. He also studied music at the Paris Conservatory.

In 1824 the young student abandoned medical studies but continued to compose music. When his parents refused to support him, Hector taught music lessons and wrote articles. He completed his most individual work, *Symphonie fantastique*, in 1830. That year he also won a prestigious music prize that required him to live in Italy.

After his return to Paris in 1832, Berlioz met the Irish actress Harriet Smithson, whom he married the following year. Because his unusual compositions failed to win any recognition in France, Berlioz was forced to earn a living as a music librarian and by writing essays and music criticism.

Finally, Berlioz did begin to win fame outside France. In 1843 he made a triumphant tour of Germany, conducting his own compositions. He had equally successful tours to Austria, Hungary, Russia, and England.

In Paris, though, his genius continued to go unrecognized. His great opera, *The Trojans at Carthage*, was only a partial success at its first performance in 1863. Discouraged, Berlioz stopped composing and writing. He died in Paris on March 8, 1869.

Since then his reputation has steadily grown. Berlioz is now regarded as one of the world's foremost composers, one of the first great orchestral conductors, and a very skilled writer on musical topics.

Reviewed by MARGERY MORGAN LOWENS
Peabody Conservatory of Music
The Johns Hopkins University

Bermuda is made up of many small islands situated in the western Atlantic Ocean. Their mild, sunny climate and natural beauty make the islands popular with vacationers, most of whom come from the United States.

BERMUDA

Bermuda, or the Bermudas, is a group of about 300 coral islands situated in the western Atlantic Ocean, about 670 miles (1,075 kilometers) southeast of Cape Hatteras, North Carolina. Most of the islands are small and only about 20 are inhabited. Also called Somers Islands, Bermuda is a British crown colony. The islands' natural beauty and their mild, sunny climate have made tourism the most important economic activity. Most vacationers come from the nearby United States.

The People. Bermuda has a population of about 58,000. About two thirds of the people are of black African or mixed ancestry, descendants of slaves brought to the islands in the 1700's. White Bermudians are largely of British ancestry. English is the official language. Most of the people are Christians, with the Anglican Church the largest Protestant denomination. The capital is Hamilton.

Part of the islands' charm is the unhurried tempo of life. Until 1946 automobiles were not permitted, horse-drawn carriages and bicycles being used instead. Even today the size and number of automobiles are limited.

The Land. Shaped roughly like a fishhook, Bermuda has a land area of about 21 square miles (54 square kilometers). The largest island, Bermuda (or Main Island), the site of Hamilton, is about 14 miles (23 kilometers) long. It is connected by causeways and bridges with other important islands. There are no natural lakes or streams, and Bermudians are dependent on collected rainwater for drinking.

The Gulf Stream gives Bermuda an unusually mild climate for a region so far north of the equator, allowing palm trees and other tropical vegetation to flourish. The average yearly temperature is about 70°F (21°C). Ocean breezes keep the summers from being oppressively hot.

Economy. Tourism, the mainstay of the economy, accounts for about half of Bermuda's income and provides about 65 percent of all employment. Some crops are grown for local use, and cut flowers, particularly Easter lilies, are cultivated for export. There is some light industry, chiefly ship repairing, boat building, and the manufacture of pharmaceu-

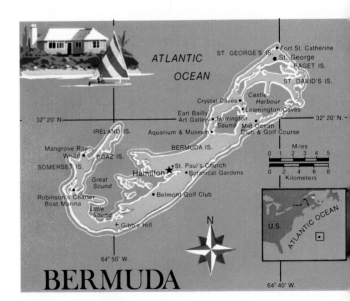

BERMUDA

ticals (medical drugs). Ship registry, finance, and insurance have become important sectors of the economy. Bermuda must import much of its food, fuel, and other necessities.

History and Government. The islands take their names from two ships' commanders—the Spaniard Juan de Bermúdez, who first sighted the islands in the 1500's; and Sir George Somers, whose ship, carrying English colonists to Virginia, was shipwrecked there in 1609. The first permanent English settlement of the then-uninhabited islands was made in 1612, at St. George. In 1815 the capital was transferred to Hamilton. The tourist industry developed in the 1900's. In 1941, during World War II, the British granted the United States a 99-year lease for naval and air bases on the islands. Several hundred U.S. military personnel are stationed on the islands.

Bermuda's constitution, which was amended in 1979, gives the colony considerable self-government. The British monarch is represented by an appointed governor, who is responsible for the islands' foreign affairs, de-

WONDER QUESTION

What is the Bermuda Triangle?

It is a triangular area of the Atlantic Ocean, with Bermuda, southern Florida, and Puerto Rico making up its approximate corners. It is also known, more ominously, as the Devil's Triangle, because of the numerous ships and airplanes that reportedly have vanished in the region, usually without trace. Some authors have sought to explain the disappearances as due to mysterious weather conditions in the area of the triangle. But this has not been borne out by any evidence.

fense, and police. The legislature consists of an appointed Senate and an elected House of Assembly. The leader of the majority party in the assembly serves as prime minister.

Reviewed by THOMAS G. MATHEWS
Secretary General, Association of Caribbean
Universities and Research Institutes

BERNINI, GIOVANNI LORENZO (1598–1680)

During the 1600's, the city of Rome was filled with elegant statues, chapels, fountains, and palaces. Many of them were designed by Giovanni Lorenzo Bernini, the Italian sculptor, painter, and architect who ruled the artistic life of Rome for more than fifty years.

The strong and graceful lines in the statue of King Louis XIV of France show both Bernini's technical skill and his ability to produce dramatic effects.

Bernini was born on December 7, 1598, in Naples. His father, a sculptor, received a commission from the pope and moved his family to Rome about 1605. Except for a short trip to Paris in 1665, Bernini spent his entire life in Rome. In 1639 he married Caterina Tezio; they had eleven children.

At 20, Bernini received his first important commission: a series of statues for the villa of Cardinal Borghese. Among them is the famous *David*, whose tense figure, portrayed with great feeling, shows the taste of the baroque period. Another of his great works is a study for a statue of King Louis XIV of France on horseback.

Bernini died on November 28, 1680. He had been a painter, scenic designer, and decorator. But he was most famous for his sculpture and architecture. The square in front of St. Peter's Basilica, with its stately rows of columns and 162 statues, is one of his most powerful achievements.

Reviewed by HOWARD HIBBARD
Columbia University

BERRIES. See GRAPES AND BERRIES.

BESSEMER, SIR HENRY (1813–1898)

The industrial city of Bessemer, Alabama, is named in honor of Sir Henry Bessemer, the English inventor who made the steel industry possible. In 1855 and 1856 he patented a method of purifying iron so that it could be made into steel cheaply and easily. This method, called the Bessemer process, and a machine called the Bessemer converter are still used in steel manufacturing.

Henry Bessemer was born January 19, 1813, in the village of Charlton in southern England. His father, also an inventor, had a factory there for casting type. Young Henry spent his spare time in his father's workshop, learning to make use of his natural mechanical ability.

When he was 17 years old, Bessemer went to London, where he cast metal into artistic figures that were exhibited by the Royal Academy. Then he turned to embossing designs on cards and cloth. In 1833 he invented a method of canceling tax stamps so that they could not illegally be used again.

During his busy life Bessemer worked out and patented 114 inventions. One of the most profitable was a method of making gold paint. The money from this invention enabled him to experiment and develop his steelmaking process, his most important invention.

The Bessemer process practically created the modern steel industry. Before the invention of this process, steel could be made only in small batches. As a result, it was very expensive. Bessemer's discovery made possible large-scale production of steel. It has been ranked with printing, the magnetic compass, and the steam engine as an invention that changed the world.

In 1879, Bessemer was knighted in reward for his tax-stamp canceling process. He died in London on March 15, 1898.

Reviewed by DAVID C. COOKE
Author, *Inventions That Made History*
See also IRON AND STEEL.

BETHUNE, MARY MC LEOD (1875–1955)

Mary McLeod Bethune rose from poverty to become a famous educator, a leader of black women, and an adviser to presidents. She was born on July 10, 1875, near the small town of Mayesville, South Carolina. Her parents, Patsy and Sam McLeod, were recently freed slaves who made their living as farmers.

Even after the Civil War ended, there were not many schools for black children in the South. Mary was 11 years old before a mission school was opened in Mayesville. She completed her education at the Moody Bible Institute in Chicago. When she was turned down for a post as a missionary in Africa, she went home to the South to teach. After her marriage to Albertus Bethune, a teacher, she moved to Florida. In 1904, she opened a school for black girls in Daytona Beach.

The Daytona Normal and Industrial Institute for Negro Girls was only a shack, but its goals were high. The school's motto, "Enter to learn, depart to serve," described the aim of its founder, which was to educate black girls to become teachers.

The early years of the school were difficult. Few of the students were able to pay tuition. Mary Bethune raised money by selling food to winter visitors in Daytona Beach. Before long, the institute received donations that made it possible to add a high school, a small hospital, and then a college. The institute was merged with a boys' school in 1923 and became Bethune-Cookman College in 1925.

In 1935, Mary Bethune founded the National Council of Negro Women. She helped President Franklin D. Roosevelt start the National Youth Administration, which provided employment for young people. She was a member of the President's unofficial "Black Cabinet," which advised him on ways to improve conditions for black people. During World War II, she served as a special assistant to the secretary of war to help end discrimination in the armed services.

The last years of Mary Bethune's life brought her many honors and awards. She died in Daytona Beach on May 18, 1955.

DANIEL S. DAVIS
Author, *Struggle for Freedom:
The History of Black Americans*

BHUTAN

The tiny kingdom of Bhutan lies high in the Himalaya mountains of south central Asia. For most of its history, it was a forgotten and seldom-visited part of the world. Even today Bhutan remains largely undeveloped and remote from modern 20th-century life.

▶ THE PEOPLE

The majority people of Bhutan are the Bhotes (or Bhotias), who are related to the people of neighboring Tibet. They speak Dzongkha, a Tibetan dialect, and practice a form of Buddhism known as Lamaism, or Tibetan Buddhism. A few Bhutanese still follow the old religion of Bon—the worship of things in nature—that was common before the arrival of Buddhism. The Nepalese, who live in the south, are immigrants from the nearby country of Nepal. They practice the Hindu religion and speak Nepali.

Most Bhutanese are farmers or animal herders; others are skilled artisans. Settlements often cluster around a *dzong* (a fortresslike monastery). The people are extremely isolated, and travel is difficult in all parts of the country. There are no railroads and only a few good roads.

There are few towns; the largest is Thimbu, the capital. Most of the people live in widely scattered villages. A typical village house consists of a two-story building made of stone or mud-brick. The family lives on the upper floor, while farm animals occupy the lower floor. The yak, a long-haired ox, is the main beast of burden.

In the past, fewer than one person in a hundred in Bhutan could read and write. To correct this, the government has built elementary schools and is planning more. Most of the teachers come from India, which is helping to develop Bhutan. Most children of well-to-do Bhutanese attend school in India.

▶ THE LAND

In Bhutan the snowy Himalaya peaks and mountain highlands tower only a short distance away from dense jungles and valleys lush with rice fields. There are three distinct land regions—the High Himalayan region in the north, the Inner Himalayan region in central Bhutan, and the Duars plain in the south.

The High Himalayan region borders China. Many peaks in this part of Bhutan belong to

Towering mountains, lush valleys, and dense jungles make up the varied landscape of Bhutan. Most of its people live in the high, fertile valleys of central Bhutan.

154

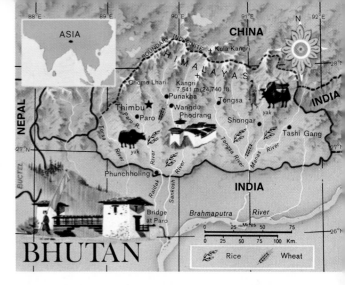

BHUTAN

the Great Himalayan range. They tower as high as 7,300 meters (24,000 feet). Even the lowest part of the region is more than half that height above sea level. Except for a few scattered Buddhist monasteries, the Great Himalayas are uninhabited.

Most Bhutanese live in the valleys of the Inner Himalayan region. These valleys are as high as 2,400 meters (8,000 feet) above sea level. Rainfall is moderate, and the valleys are broad, fertile, and healthful. Paro, the former capital, and Thimbu, the new and still-developing capital, are both found here.

South of the Inner Himalayan region is a narrow strip of the Duars plain. The plain must be crossed to reach the narrow valleys that lead through the jungle-covered Himalayan foothills into the valleys of central Bhutan. The southern part of the Duars plain is covered with tall grass and bamboo. The north is rugged and heavily forested. There are many wild animals. Few people live on the Duars plain because of the heavy rainfall, dense vegetation, and malaria-ridden swamps.

The climate of Bhutan is as varied as the land. The high elevation gives the northern interior bitterly cold winters. But the lowlands of southern Bhutan have a humid, tropical climate throughout the year.

▶THE ECONOMY

Bhutan's economy is based on farming. Most farms are in the fertile valleys of the Inner Himalayas. The land is cultivated in a series of terraces, each terrace bordered by a stone embankment. Rice and wheat are grown in the valleys and on the lower slopes. Rice is the country's leading export. Vast forests make timber an important resource.

Yaks, sheep, and goats are raised in all parts of Bhutan. The Yak, besides being used as a beast of burden, provides meat, milk, and hides. Yak hair is used to make blankets. A creamy, yogurtlike cheese is prepared from yak milk.

▶HISTORY AND GOVERNMENT

Little is known about Bhutan's early history. According to old Tibetan manuscripts preserved in Buddhist monasteries, about 300 years ago a Tibetan lama, or priest, named Sheptoon La-Pha became the first man to proclaim himself king of Bhutan. During the 18th and 19th centuries, the *penlops* (regional governors) acquired great power, and the king became a figurehead. In 1907 the most powerful of the *penlops*, Ugyen Wangchuk, became king. His descendants have continued as rulers of Bhutan. The present king, Jigme Singye Wangchuk, came to the throne in 1972.

Bhutan has no constitution, but it does have a legislative body, the Tsongdu, or National Assembly. Most of its members are elected indirectly by the people through village leaders; others are chosen by the king and the lamas. The king has a council of ministers, who serve as a kind of cabinet.

Bhutan is guided in its foreign affairs by India. A member of the United Nations, it is developing diplomatic relations with other countries.

P. P. KARAN
University of Kentucky

FACTS AND FIGURES

KINGDOM OF BHUTAN is the official name of the country. The Bhutanese call their country Druk-Yul, which means "Land of the Dragon."

THE PEOPLE are known as Bhutanese.

LOCATION: South central Asia.

AREA: 46,620 km² (18,000 sq mi).

POPULATION: 1,400,000 (estimate).

CAPITAL AND LARGEST CITY: Thimbu.

MAJOR LANGUAGES: Dzongkha (official), Nepali.

MAJOR RELIGIONS: Buddhist, Hindu.

GOVERNMENT: Monarchy. **Head of state and government**—king. **Legislature**—Tsongdu (National Assembly).

CHIEF PRODUCTS: Agricultural—rice, wheat, and other grains; fruit; livestock. **Manufactured**—handicrafts, processed food, timber, textiles. **Mineral**—coal, graphite, limestone, marble, lead, zinc, talc, copper.

MONETARY UNIT: Ngultrum (1 ngultrum = 100 chetrum).

NATIONAL ANTHEM: *Gyelpo Tenjur* ("Royal Anthem").

BIBLE

The Bible, a collection of diverse books written in ancient times, is one of the world's most famous pieces of literature. The English word "Bible" comes from the Greek word *biblia,* meaning "books," and aptly describes this library of religious writings. The books form the sacred scripture of Jews, Christians, and, to some extent, Muslims. The Bible has had more influence on art, drama, language, and other literature than any other single collection of books. It has been translated into more languages and published in more editions than any other single collection, and it has remained a best seller up to modern times.

The Bible may be divided into three major sections: the Old Testament, the New Testament, and the Apocrypha. "Testament" comes from the Latin word *testamentum,* meaning "will," "covenant," or "agreement," and described for ancient Israelites and early Christians the type of relationship that they had with their God.

The Old Testament, composed of 39 books, makes up the sacred literature of Judaism. In addition, Christianity also accepts the 27 books of the New Testament. The remaining 14 books, called the Apocrypha, are sometimes referred to as the Inter-Testament, since they fall chronologically between the Old

Testament and the New Testament. Acceptance of this part of the Bible has varied from time to time among Christian groups.

Transmission and Translation

How did these collections come down to us from ancient times? This handing down of Biblical materials is properly called transmission. Since the Old Testament is the earliest part of the Bible, its transmission must be considered first. Ancient Hebrews, whose literature this was, began to tell of their God and his relation to them long before they began to write. As a result, the material that finally became the Bible began in oral form. Around the campfires, at the village gates, and in religious services, this sacred history had its beginning. After a while some of the material was put into written form, and other material was written and added. The collections grew and were reworked through the centuries as men felt they had new insights from God or about God. Eventually "books" were put together and became fixed in written form. These were finally accepted as authoritative for religious use. The list of such accepted books is called canon (from a word meaning "rule"). The making of such a list is called canonization and took place at various times for various books or collections of books. Since the apocryphal books were never accepted by Judaism, they did not form part of the official canon in the Hebrew Bible.

Transmission of the New Testament was considerably different. The reason is that by the time Christianity began, the civilized world was using written language as a means of communication. As a result, the stories about the life and ministry of Jesus, the missionary work of the Apostles, letters to churches, and similar material soon spread all over the Roman Empire in written form. In the course of time, individual collections of these materials were made, books were formed, and eventually the whole collection known as the New Testament came into being and was accepted as canonical by the early Christian Church. There is also a New Testament Apocrypha, but it has never been widely used by Christians because of the high esteem in which the canonical books were held.

Hebrew, except for some Aramaic in Ezra and Daniel, was the language in which the

Old Testament was written. The New Testament books were recorded in Greek ("everyday," or *koinē,* Greek). How did the Bible get into English, then, along with so many other languages? This, of course, came about through translations, called versions, from the original Hebrew and Greek. Thus there are as many versions of the Bible as there are translations of it. Some of these have become very famous. They were either very early, in a language that had a wide use, or became the Bible for a particular group.

Earliest translations were obviously of the Old Testament. Probably the most important of these was the Greek translation called the Septuagint. The name of this translation, meaning "seventy," was derived from the tradition that it had been done by 70 scholars (actually 72—6 from each tribe of Israel) at the request of one of the Ptolemies of Egypt in the 3rd century B.C. About a century earlier the Samaritans, who also followed Jewish law, had made a translation of the first five books of the Hebrew Bible (the Pentateuch). In the early Christian period, another important translation, called the *Peshitta,* was made from the Hebrew Bible by Syriac-speaking Christians. Jewish scholars likewise made translations for popular use (more properly a paraphrase with commentary) called the *Targumim,* in Aramaic.

Early Christians had adopted the Greek version of the Old Testament because it could be understood by most of them. After a while, however, a need was felt to have both the Old Testament and the New Testament in the language that was becoming more widely used—Latin. One very early Latin translation was made (using the Greek Old Testament for that part of the Bible), called the Old Latin, or Itala. The most famous early Christian translation, however, was that made by Saint Jerome in the early 4th century A.D. Since this was in the common ("vulgar") language of the day, the version is still called the Vulgate. Jerome used both the Hebrew and Greek versions for his translation. The Church accepted Jerome's translation, and it became the official version of the Bible, although the older Latin translation of certain books continued in use. The most famous edition of this version is the Sixtine edition, done at the order of Pope Sixtus V in 1590.

Christian missionaries had also gone to all parts of the ancient world and carried the Bible with them. In many places the Hebrew, Greek, and Latin versions were translated into the language of the people among whom they worked. As a result, translations appeared in Arabic, Gothic, Coptic, Ethiopic, Armenian, and a myriad of other languages.

All these translations were written by hand. When the printing press was invented about 1450, the production of individual translations of the Bible, as well as editions in the original languages, was tremendously advanced. In the 16th century the Christian Church was divided into Roman Catholic and Protestant branches by the Church dispute called the Reformation. From that time both Catholics and Protestants began to make their own translations independently.

Many printed editions of the Bible appeared. Of them, the German translation (1522–32) of Martin Luther set the pattern for many others. Just about the same time, an English printed edition was issued by William Tyndale but was quickly suppressed by the authorities in England. About 1535, however, Myles Coverdale published an English translation, probably in Zurich. This time the Church was less opposed to a "popular" version, and Coverdale's Bible became widely read. A whole series of English Bibles then began to appear, with the names of translators (Matthew's Bible, Taverner's Bible) or of the cities of publication (the Geneva Bible) or even with descriptive titles (the Great Bible, because of its size) to identify them. Finally an approved Bible called the Bishops' Bible (a revision of the Geneva Bible) was published in England in 1568.

In France a group of English-speaking Roman Catholics also felt the need for a translation of the official Latin version of the Bible. As a result, an English translation of the Vulgate was completed between 1582 and 1610 and is still known as the Rheims-Douai Version, in honor of the two cities in which it was done.

King James I called a conference at Hampton Court in 1604 in an effort to reconcile the religious parties of England. Out of this conference came the King James Version of the Bible, published in 1611. This is perhaps the best-known English Bible and has continued in use up to the present time. It was supposed to be only a revision of the Bishops' Bible, but other editions and newly discovered manuscripts in the original languages were also used.

As English changed and more new copies of ancient Biblical manuscripts (texts) were found, revisions of the King James Version were made from time to time. The English Revised Edition was completed in 1881; the American Revised Edition (or American Standard Version) appeared in 1901; and the Revised Standard Version was published between 1946 and 1952. At the same time a great number of independent translations were made of all, or part, of the Bible. These include many translations into modern speech as well as many versions for special use.

OLD TESTAMENT

In Hebrew the Old Testament is divided into three parts: the Law, the Prophets, and the Writings. These divisions are not followed exactly in the English Bible but make the contents of the Old Testament easier to summarize. Traditionally attributed to Moses, the first five books of the Old Testament make up the Law, or Pentateuch. In Hebrew they are named after the first word of each book, but in English the names are derived from the Greek Bible: Genesis, Exodus, Leviticus, Numbers, and Deuteronomy. These books trace the relationship of man to God, in a series of agreements, beginning with creation, through the division of people into nations, to the days of Abraham. Then the record of the special relation of the Hebrews to God is told, from the time of Abraham's call by God into the land of Canaan.

Abraham and his descendants, the patriarchs, traveled through Canaan until the family of Joseph finally entered Egypt. There they were ultimately enslaved, made their escape under Moses (the Exodus), and fled to the Sinai Peninsula, between the Mediterranean Sea and the Red Sea. At Mount Sinai the people, now properly called Israelites, received the Law from God and prepared to enter the Promised Land. Because of arguments among some of the people, they were all forced to wander for 40 years in the desert wilderness. At the end of that time the Israelites were permitted to enter Palestine under the leadership of Joshua.

This group of five books contains a great variety of literary styles and types. Some of the stories illustrate great religious truths: the creation, the fall of man, the flood, the Tower of Babel, the Passover and Exodus, the giving of the tablets of the Law, and other short narratives. Certain of the books contain great poetry: the Song of Lamech, the Blessings of the Patriarchs, the Song of Moses, and the Blessing of Moses. Others tell about specific people: Noah and his scoffing neighbors, Abraham's faith, Lot's inquisitive wife, the cunning of Jacob, and the frustration of Balaam when all his curses against Israel became blessings. The land, the nations, and the local customs are also described: the wilderness experience, the fire and smoke at Mount Sinai, the varied inhabitants of Canaan, the building of the Ark of the Covenant, the casting of metals and weaving of cloth, the marriage of Rebecca and Isaac, and other details of everyday living. In addition, long lists of ancestors and descendants, codes of law, rules for festivals and sacred ceremonies, are also presented. Yet with all this diversity, the entire Pentateuch is held together by the religious faith that the God of Israel cared for his people, from the first man to the birth of the Israelite nation, and that He had made a covenant, or agreement, with that people. Obedience to the covenant brought Israel to the promised land, but disobedience to its terms brought disaster.

Next in the Hebrew Bible is the group of books called the Prophets because it contains those books that the Jews considered to be the work of men speaking for God. The word "prophet" comes from the Greek word *prophetes,* "one who speaks forth." This division of the Bible is composed of the Former Prophets—Joshua, Judges, I and II Samuel, I and II Kings; and the Latter Prophets—Isaiah, Jeremiah, Ezekiel, and the Book of the Twelve. This last "book" contains the books of Hosea, Joel, Amos, Obadiah, Jonah, Micah, Nahum, Habakkuk, Zephaniah, Haggai, Zechariah, and Malachi. Some books that are generally found among the prophetical books in the English Bible are not included in the Hebrew Bible under that title but are placed among the Writings. Certain of the prophetic books also have slightly different names in the Hebrew and Greek Bibles and in the versions used by Roman Catholics and Protestants.

The Former Prophets are books that consider the history of Israel from the conquest of Canaan under Joshua down to the release from prison of Jehoiachin, Israel's last king, by the Babylonian king, Evilmerodach, in about 561 B.C. Here, then, is the great story of the wars fought, the settlement of the land, the rise of the monarchy under Saul, the history of King David, Solomon's reign and the building of the first Temple, the split of the united monarchy into the kingdoms of Israel in the north and Judah in the south, the fall of Jerusalem, and the Babylonian exile.

This part of the Bible is probably the most interesting to read as literature because it is a connective history and contains stirring tales of battles, stories of great people, the life of David, and tales of court intrigues and plots. It also tells of the sad downfall of the two kingdoms of Judah and Israel. Also, since Hebrew literature was in its classical period at this time, one can find some of the best examples of both poetry and prose.

The Latter Prophets are less easy to summarize, since each has its own specific message. Isaiah, Jeremiah, and Ezekiel make up the Major, or Greater, books because they are the longer ones in this section of the Bible. Historically these prophets span the period from King Uzziah in the 8th century B.C., to the time of the exile during the 6th century B.C. Isaiah is concerned with the religious and political problems of Judah in his day as relations with Assyria became more and more difficult for the people. A great promise of new hope for Israel has been added to Isaiah's words (Deutero-Isaiah) as a fitting climax to his book. Isaiah's "call" to prophecy (Chapter 6) is one of the most impressive accounts in ancient Hebrew literature.

Jeremiah lived at the end of the monarchial period, during the trying days of the destruction of the city of Jerusalem. He, too, speaks against the religious and social decay of his own day, but gives to the people going into exile the promise of a new covenant. God, says Jeremiah, has now made a covenant with Israel that shall not be kept on tablets of stone, but shall be in the heart of every man, no matter where he goes. This was a message of great hope to a people saddened by the loss of their great city and forced to live in a strange land.

Ezekiel might be called the planner of Judaism because he gave to the Israelites in exile a plan whereby they could keep their faith alive in times of strife and struggle. With the writings of Ezekiel, the religion of Israel became known as Judaism and was closely linked with the Law and the Temple. The God of Israel became known as the Holy One in Israel, and Jews tried to honor this holiness by strict observance of the proper religious ritual and duties.

Not less important, however, are the Minor, or Lesser, Prophets. Their books are just "smaller in size," the meaning of the Latin word *minor* used to describe them. In the Hebrew Bible the Book of the Twelve just fills one scroll of writing material, so these prophetical books have been put together for that reason. Here, again, each prophet has his own particular message, and each is a separate book in itself. Amos is really the oldest of the prophetic writers and is the first literary, or written, prophet. Amos, Hosea, and Micah all preach against the social, political, and religious abuses of their individual periods, and each one declares that God will punish His people for their evil. Nahum, Zephaniah, and Habakkuk give their attention to specific foes of Israel—the Assyrians, the Scythians, and the Neo-Babylonians—and use those threats to the nation to stress the need for the people to trust and obey God. A little later, in the 6th century B.C., the prophet Obadiah uses the example of the fall of Edom, one of Israel's neighbors, to illustrate the action of God in the world and to stress hope for the future of his own people. Jonah, with the famous story of the great fish, urges the Jews, now restored to their homeland, to reform themselves. In the same way, the prophets Haggai, Zechariah, and Malachi speak to the new generation. In Haggai religious duty is centered upon the rebuilding of the Temple, and in Zechariah there is hope offered of a better age to come. In Joel, the last book among the prophets in terms of date, hope is again given to the people during a new time of national disaster.

Thus, the prophetical books of the Old Testament furnish a great array of religious ideas, individual styles and approaches, and relate to many historical situations. From these books have come many of the religious beliefs of Judaism and Christianity as well as many influences upon other literature through the ages. In English, for example, there are many expressions in common use today that have their origin in the Old Testament: "the fat of the land," "a man after his own heart," "the skin of my teeth," "one among a thousand," "angels' food," "eat, drink, and be merry," "see eye to eye," "holier than thou," "no new thing under the sun," "to every thing there is a season."

The final division of the Old Testament in the Hebrew Bible might be called Miscellaneous. In the section known as the Writings are those books that the Jewish leaders considered to be of religious worth but not of the same type as those of the other two divisions. Therefore, in this category are found Psalms, a collection of hymns or religious poems said to be composed by David; Proverbs, which gives helpful advice on everyday living; Job,

in which the whole meaning of human suffering is considered; The Song of Solomon, a love song, once seen to have religious application; Ruth, a story of deep personal devotion as well as a protest against racial bigotry; Lamentations, a series of sorrowful reflections concerning the exile and the sad plight of the people; Ecclesiastes, a book of "wisdom," or religious philosophy; Esther, which explains the festival of Purim; Daniel, a book of stories of heroes, which urges religious faithfulness in a time of oppression; I and II Chronicles, Ezra, and Nehemiah, which summarize Israel's history up to the exile and then give an account of the events that followed.

Here, again, the individual books of this part of the Bible are all different and each one has its own special characteristics. Likewise, each of these books has had its own influence upon religious thought and upon the literature of the world. Psalms, for example, has furnished the basis for many hymns still sung in places of worship; Job has provided much material for modern literature; Ruth and Esther have given the world two great heroines; while Daniel and his friends have found their place in folk songs, art, and in such popular quotations as "the handwriting on the wall" or "into the lions' den."

PHILIP C. HAMMOND
Princeton Theological Seminary

APOCRYPHA

The Apocrypha were written between the 3rd and 1st centuries B.C. Although they have come down to us in Greek, Latin, and other translations, including the English of the King James Bible that was published in 1611, fragments of the Apocrypha in the original Hebrew and Aramaic have been found among the Dead Sea Scrolls from the caves around Qumran, in northwest Jordan.

For Catholics most of the Apocryphal books are sacred. For Protestants and Jews the Apocrypha are respected as instructive writings, but not as divinely inspired.

Judaism between the 3rd century B.C. and the 1st century A.D. was split into many sects. The rabbis felt it necessary to put an end to the developments that were dividing the peo-

ple. They chose a simple way out. By excluding all books written after the fall of the Persian Empire in the 4th century B.C., the rabbis removed the authority of all the later writings that were splitting the community. This is why the Old Testament does not include any books that were thought to come from the period after Alexander's conquest in the 4th century B.C.

The Apocrypha begin with the First Book of Esdras. This book has to do with the return of the Jews from their Babylonian exile to Palestine in the days of the Old Testament leaders Ezra and Nehemiah. The most famous passage from this book is the tale of the Three Guardsmen (3:1—5:6), showing that truth is the most powerful force in the world.

The Second Book of Esdras justifies God's ways through divinely inspired visions.

The Book of Tobit is a story about virtue and love. It has enough magic to make the tale doubly interesting. The dog appears as man's pet and companion in Tobit for the first time in Jewish literature.

The Book of Judith is about the trials of the Hebrew people. The heroine Judith saves her people by cutting off the head of the enemy general, Holofernes.

There are six additions to the Book of Esther. These additions, examples of how reverent the Apocryphal books are, add religious tone to the Old Testament Book of Esther, which never even mentions the name of God.

The most important literary books in the Apocrypha are known as Wisdom Literature. This type of writing has as its aim the improvement of men through virtuous and sensible living so that they may be respected in society and successful in their careers. The first of these Apocryphal books is The Wisdom of

An 11th-century Psalter (Book of Psalms) in Greek.

An illuminated page, in Latin, from the Gutenberg Bible. Johann Gutenberg invented printing from movable type.

This page from a Hebrew Bible begins the history of the Israelites in Egypt.

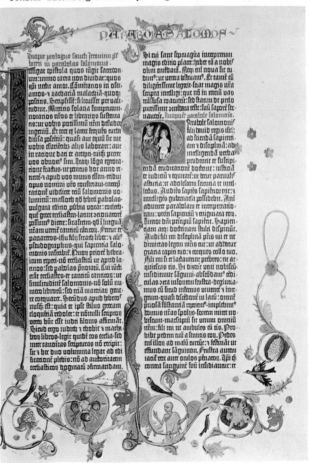

Jonah

Paintings of famous prophets are a part of Michelangelo's work in the Sistine Chapel, St. Peter's, Rome.

Jeremiah

Zechariah

Isaiah

Ezekiel

Solomon, which praises "Lady Wisdom," not a woman of flesh and blood, but wisdom treated as a divine person. The author of The Wisdom of Solomon is not only interested in teaching wise principles. He wants, in addition, to save the people from uncivilized heathenism.

The other book of Wisdom Literature is in many ways the finest composition in the Apocrypha. It is called Ecclesiasticus or The Wisdom of Jesus, Son of Sirach ("Jesus" is simply the Greek form of the old Hebrew name "Joshua"). Ecclesiasticus is a practical as well as a reverent teacher. While he advises us to turn to God with piety and prayer to save us from misfortune and illness, he reminds us that physicians and medicines have been created by God for our benefit (38: 1–15). He praises the practice of justice and reminds us that good character brings rich rewards. Life is short but a good name endures forever. Ecclesiasticus ends his book by telling us, "Work your work betimes, and in his time he will give you your reward."

The Book of Baruch is supposed to come from the pen of Baruch, the secretary of the Prophet Jeremiah. Among the books of the Apocrypha, this one comes closest to Old Testament prophecy. It ends with an appendix, The Letter of Jeremiah, in which the prophet tells the Jewish exiles in Babylonia to avoid worshiping idols.

There are three additions to the Old Testament Book of Daniel. (1) The story of Susanna tells how Daniel saved Susanna from the false accusations of two evil elders. (2) The story of the Three Children tells about Shadrach, Meshach, and Abednego, who according to the Book of Daniel were thrown into the fiery furnace. It is typical of Apocryphal literature to fill gaps in the "authoritative books." Since the Book of Daniel does not tell us what happened to the three men after they were thrown into the fiery furnace, a later author took advantage of the opportunity to write this story. (3) The story of Baal and the Dragon tells how Daniel proved to the king of Babylon that idols are false and God is true.

The Prayer of Manasseh is supposed to be the prayer recited, according to the Biblical II Chronicles 33:18, by the repentant King Manasseh of Judah. This composition is of high religious and literary quality.

The Apocrypha end with First and Second Maccabees. First Maccabees, covering the years 167–134 B.C., is a reliable historic account of the Jewish war against Antiochus Epiphanes and the developments that followed. Antiochus, whose empire included Palestine, tried to force the Jews to conform to Greek culture at the expense of their ancestral religion. The Jews rebelled under the leadership of the Maccabean brothers. Their victory is still celebrated by the Jews during the feast of Hanukkah.

Second Maccabees is more emotional than First Maccabees and is concerned with its special kind of Jewish viewpoint. Second Maccabees covers the period 175–160 B.C. It is not a continuation of First Maccabees but another account covering some of the same years.

CYRUS H. GORDON
Brandeis University

NEW TESTAMENT

The New Testament is that part of the Bible that is the heritage of Christians. It states a new relation between man and the God of Israel, in the person of Jesus of Nazareth. He is seen by the writers of the New Testament as the long-awaited Messiah of Israel and of the whole world, and is known by the Greek word for "Messiah," or "Saviour," which is "Christ."

The New Testament was written mainly in the days of the Roman Empire and covers the historical period from the last part of the reign of King Herod (37–4 B.C.) to just after the destruction of Jerusalem in A.D. 70. Often this period is referred to in Christian writings as "the fullness of time," because of the religious significance of the coming of Jesus. But it was a "full time" historically as well. Roman government had brought peace to most of the civilized world; Greek language had made international communication easy; and the weakening of the hold of old pagan gods on

For a Bible published in 1866 Paul Gustave Doré did
this illustration of the miracle of the loaves and fishes.

the people had provided an atmosphere that
welcomed a new faith.

Followers of Jesus, called the Apostles,
began to spread the story of the risen Lord to
all the world. The Apostles themselves went
from town to town, preaching and teaching.
From that activity the New Testament was
born. First came collections of Jesus' own
words; then the stories about his life and
work, as well as letters to various individuals
or groups explaining Christianity. Since writing had now become more common, these
materials were written down very quickly or
even appeared in written form originally (for
example, the letters). As a result, the New
Testament evolved into written form, then
into collections of written books, and finally
into the collection of canonical books, much
more rapidly than the Old Testament did.
Very soon these writings were considered to
be equal in importance, in the religious sense,
to the Old Testament, which Christians
shared with their Jewish neighbors. Thus the
New Testament was also regarded as holy, or
sacred, literature for Christians.

When we examine the New Testament, we
again see a collection of diverse books under

one cover. Again divisions can be made in
the material, just as the earliest Christians
made them. In the New Testament the two
main divisions consist of Gospels and Epistles, plus a single book called Revelation.

The Gospels are books that tell the story of
Jesus—what he did, what he said, how he
acted in relation to people. These books are
four in number and bear the names of their
writers, Matthew, Mark, Luke, and John. The
early Church considered these to be the four
best books of the many written about Jesus.
Thus, they attributed them to Apostles or to
close associates of the Apostles. They are
called Gospels because that word means "good
news"—the good news of Jesus' message and
life for the world.

The Gospel of Mark stresses the human
side of Jesus and explains many of the Jewish
customs and words for Gentile readers. It is
therefore referred to as the "human" Gospel
or the "Roman" Gospel (to explain that it
was written for non-Jewish readers). It begins
the story of Jesus with his baptism in the river
Jordan and ends with his appearances to the
Apostles after his Crucifixion.

The Gospel of Matthew, on the other hand,
is sometimes called the "Jewish" Gospel because of the arrangement of its material. In
this book Jesus' teachings are carefully set
down into categories for easy reference, just
as the Jewish teachers in that period classified
their teachings. There are really five such
divisions in Matthew: Jesus' ancestry and
birth, which introduces his baptism and temptation, leading up to his first "sermon"; stories
of healing, with instructions to the disciples;
Jesus' relation to John the Baptist and to
other religious leaders, with a series of parables, or teaching stories; more healing stories,
the feeding of the multitude, and the story of
the Transfiguration; the Judaean ministry of
Jesus, the triumphal entry into Jerusalem,
parables, other teachings, and a conclusion
that tells of his death and resurrection.

The Gospel of Luke is really a letter and
should be read with Luke's other book, The
Acts of the Apostles. Both books form what is
called an apologia, or defense, of Christianity
to the non-Christian world. Luke begins his
Gospel with the birth of Jesus and a brief
narrative of his boyhood, his ancestry, and his
work. Since Luke tells so many stories about

Jesus' ministry to the common people, this Gospel is often spoken of as the "social" Gospel. In the Book of Acts the "history" of Jesus' message is continued, as it was carried out into the Gentile world by the Apostles and other missionaries. Again Luke is concerned with the effect of this message on people and their lives. The book therefore tells about the early Christian Church as it developed and grew from Jerusalem and other early centers of the ancient world.

The Gospel of John is quite a different book. It is not so much a story about Jesus as it is an interpretation of who and what he was. The language is more philosophical and is therefore harder to read. In early Christian art John was depicted as an eagle because his writings soared to such great height. John likes to contrast light and darkness, for example, in speaking about Jesus' relation to the world, and he likes to use many similes and metaphors. He begins his Gospel "In the beginning . . ." and shows how God entered the world because of his love for man. This view of Jesus is called the Incarnation (that is, God becoming man and living among men), and John stresses the reality and meaning of it for the world.

These four Gospels were written down to preserve the sayings and works of Jesus for future generations. They were all written relatively soon after his death, probably all before A.D. 100. At the same time that the Gospels were being put into writing, so were the Epistles, or Letters, which form the second main division of the New Testament. As people began to join the Christian sect questions were asked, problems came up, communications were sent, and disputes arose. Thus, letters began to be written by important Church leaders such as Paul, James, John, and others. They were carefully preserved by those who received them, often recopied, and were gradually collected. Since they dealt with important matters, they were finally joined with the Gospels and became part of the official literature of Christianity.

Traditionally the Epistles are classified into Pauline Epistles, attributed to the Apostle Paul, and General, or Catholic (in the sense of worldwide), Epistles, which were not addressed to any one particular church. To these are added the Epistle to the Hebrews, whose author is unknown, and the Book of Revelation.

The Pauline Epistles include the letters to individual churches: Romans, Galatians, I and II Thessalonians, I and II Corinthians, Philippians, Colossians, and Ephesians; along with letters to two young Church leaders named Timothy and Titus. Most of these letters are concerned with specific problems Paul wished to discuss with particular churches or groups, as well as answers to questions that they had asked him. One additional letter, however, known as Philemon, concerns a runaway slave.

In the letter to the Romans, Paul presented a system of Christian belief as he saw it, in order to instruct the people. To the Galatians, Paul wrote about the independence of Christians from some aspects of the Jewish law and gave warnings about falling away from the teachings that he, himself, had given them. Moral and theological problems arose in Thessalonika and Corinth, and Paul's letters to those people consider those issues, as well as matters of Church discipline and his own authority to deal with them. The letters to the Philippians, Colossians, and Ephesians stress the need for loyalty to Jesus' teachings and for loyalty within the Church itself. By this time

The German artist Albrecht Dürer created this engraving called *The Holy Family*.

some teachers had arisen in the Church who wished to modify or change the teachings of the original disciples of Jesus. As a result, Paul was often called upon to decide issues of faith and warn the people against false ideas. The letters to Timothy and Titus reflect somewhat the same problems. They are called pastoral letters, since Paul was giving advice to young men in charge of churches in regard to meeting theological problems, to conducting themselves, and to settling problems within their churches. The letter of Philemon stands by itself in the Pauline collection because it did not result from any question asked Paul, but from his own interest in a runaway slave, Onesimus, whom he had met. Paul sent Onesimus back to his master, Philemon, with a message stressing Christian brotherhood and freedom in Christ.

The anonymous letter to the Hebrews is unusual not only because it is unsigned, but the name of its author never seems to have been known in the early Church. Like the Gospel of John it is a more philosophical letter. Its purpose was to urge faithfulness to Christianity in a time of great persecution. It accomplishes its purpose by using much of the Old Testament to trace the history of faith down to the writer's own time, with Jesus seen as the fulfillment of the ancient promises of God.

Seven letters, the General Epistles, are known by their writers' names but were not addressed to any particular groups. These letters also arose from specific problems or from theological disputes in the Church, just as did the letters of Paul. The letter of James thus stresses good works along with faith, in order to keep Christians active as well as faithful. The two letters of Peter try to answer questions about suffering (I Peter) and to stress morality as an important Christian virtue (II Peter). John's first two letters meet problems arising out of false teachings by insisting on the "reality" of Jesus as human, as well as asserting his divine aspect. These letters thus mirror a controversy in the early Church concerning the nature of Jesus. Such controversies are termed Christological because they were about interpretations of Christ. The third letter of John is administrative and considers matters of Church government and authority. Jude returns to the matter of false teachings and again insists on the Christian interpretation of the life and ministry of Jesus. Many of the General Epistles relate to matters of interpretation, both of theological and administrative affairs. The early Church was growing rapidly, and many new converts had no background in the Old Testament viewpoints from which much of the thinking of Christianity had come. In addition, groups began to arise within the Church who wished to modify or change the words of Jesus, or to offer new interpretations. As these issues arose they had to be settled, reconciled, or denied by the leaders of the early Church.

The book called The Revelation of John is an apocalypse. That is a particular type of writing, full of hidden symbols and word pictures and often oriented toward some indefinite "end of time" sometime in the future. The symbols used by the writer of Revelation were such that they were familiar to Christians but hidden from non-Christians. When this book was written, Christians were undergoing persecution. The author therefore urged them to remain faithful, for Christianity would finally triumph over evil through Jesus, the Christ. The word pictures also helped to make the author's ideas alive—people could "see" what the author was trying to say in words. Since the Rome authorities could not understand the symbols and word pictures in the book, Christians could read it publicly and not be in danger of arrest. This book is very rich in beautiful allusions and has had a great effect on other Christian literature through the ages.

The Bible is a book of variety: the Old Testament gives us the record of ancient promise, while the the New Testament discusses its fulfillment for Christians in the person and message of Jesus. The period between the two is spanned in both history and ideas by the Apocrypha.

PHILIP C. HAMMOND
Princeton Theological Seminary

Entire article reviewed by JAMES I. McCORD
President, Princeton Theological Seminary

A. L. SACHAR
President, Brandeis University

MSGR. JOHN J. VOIGHT
Secretary of Education, Archdiocese of New York

See also BIBLE, PEOPLE IN THE; BIBLE STORIES.

The following is a brief description of some of the important people in the Bible.

Aaron was the older brother of Moses and the first Jewish high priest.

Absalom, one of the sons of King David, led a rebellion against his father and was slain by Joab, David's military general.

Adam and Eve were the first man and woman. God created Adam out of dust and Eve from one of Adam's ribs. They were expelled from the Garden of Eden for eating fruit from the tree of knowledge.

Barabbas was a criminal awaiting execution at the same time as Jesus. When the people of Judea were asked to choose who to free, they chose Barabbas.

Bathsheba, the wife of a Hittite army officer, fell in love with King David and married him after the death of her husband. One of their four sons, Solomon, succeeded his father as king.

Belshazzar was a king of Babylonia. During a feast, mysterious handwriting appeared on a wall and was thought to be a sign that Babylonia would fall. That night Belshazzar was killed and Babylonia was conquered.

Caiaphas was the high priest who presided at Jesus' trial before the Sanhedrin, Jerusalem's ruling council.

Cain and Abel were the sons of Adam and Eve. Cain killed his brother and was condemned by God to a life of wandering.

Daniel, an early Hebrew prophet, interpreted the handwriting on the wall at Belshazzar's feast.

Deborah was a prophetess and the only woman judge of the early Israelites.

Delilah was a Philistine who was loved by Samson. After discovering that the secret of Samson's strength was his hair, she cut it off and betrayed him.

Eli was a Hebrew judge and high priest. His two sons lost the sacred Ark of the Covenant in a battle with the Philistines.

Elizabeth was the mother of John the Baptist and a cousin of the Virgin Mary.

Enoch was the name of two biblical figures. One was the eldest son of Cain. The other was the father of Methuselah.

Esau, the son of Isaac and Rebekah, was the older twin brother of Jacob. He traded his birthright as eldest son to Jacob for a bowl of stew.

Esther, a Jewish woman who married the king of Persia, helped prevent the Persians from killing the Jews. This is celebrated in the Feast of Purim.

Gideon was a Hebrew judge who raised an army and saved Israel from the Midianites. Under his leadership, the tribes of Israel were united.

Hagar was one of Abraham's wives. She bore him a son, Ishmael. At the insistence of Abraham's first wife, Sarah, Hagar and Ishmael were cast out into the desert.

Hezekiah was a king of early Judah who instituted religious reforms, restored religious spirit, and abolished idolatry.

Ishmael, the son of Abraham and Hagar, was exiled into the wilderness with his mother. The Arab peoples are said to be descended from him.

Jacob, the younger twin son of Isaac and Rebekah, inherited the covenant given by God. He passed this covenant to his sons, who founded the 12 tribes of Israel.

Jephthah was a judge of Israel. Called to lead his people in battle, he vowed, if victorious, to sacrifice the first of his household to greet him on his return. He sacrificed his little daughter, his only child, in fulfillment of this vow.

Joel, an early Hebrew prophet, predicted a plague of locusts and events associated with the coming of the Messiah.

Jonathan was the eldest son of King Saul. A heroic military leader, he was a loyal friend of the future king, David. Jonathan was killed along with his father in the wars against the Philistines.

Judas Iscariot, one of Jesus' disciples, betrayed Jesus for 30 pieces of silver. He led soldiers to Gethsemane and identified Jesus with a kiss.

Lazarus was the brother of Mary and Martha. After he died, he was resurrected by Jesus.

Leah was the first wife of Jacob, who was supposed to marry Leah's sister Rachel. Their father tricked Jacob and substituted Leah for Rachel on the wedding night.

Martha, the sister of Mary and Lazarus, was gently reprimanded by Jesus for complaining that Mary listened to him instead of helping prepare their meal.

Mary Magdalene was a Galilean woman from whom Jesus cast out demons. She became a devoted follower of Jesus and was present at the Crucifixion.

Methuselah, the grandfather of Noah, was said to have lived 969 years.

Miriam, the sister of Moses and Aaron, was a prophetess. God rebuked her for being jealous of her brother Moses and she was stricken with leprosy.

Naomi and her family left their home in Bethlehem because of famine. After her husband and two sons died, she returned home with her daughter-in-law Ruth. She arranged Ruth's marriage to Boaz.

Nathan, a Hebrew prophet, served as advisor to King David and King Solomon.

Nicodemus was a member of the Jewish ruling council, the Sanhedrin. He became a secret disciple of Jesus and after the Crucifixion took expensive spices to cover the body of Jesus for burial.

Nimrod, the great-grandson of Noah, was a famous hunter and a mighty king of ancient Babylon.

Noah built a great ship, the Ark, and filled it with two of every kind of animal. When the great Flood came, Noah and his family were safe on the Ark. When they finally reached dry land they gave humanity and the animal kingdom a fresh start.

Pontius Pilate was the Roman governor of Judea who condemned Jesus to death.

Rachel was the best-loved wife of Jacob and the sister of Leah. Rachel bore Jacob two sons, Joseph and Benjamin.

Rebekah was the wife of Isaac. She bore him twin sons, Esau and Jacob. She helped Jacob, her favorite son, receive Isaac's blessing, which rightfully belonged to Esau.

Rehoboam, the son of King Solomon, caused Solomon's united kingdom to be divided into Israel and Judah. He then ruled Judah for some 17 years.

Ruth was the faithful daughter-in-law of Naomi. Her loyalty was rewarded by marriage to Boaz. Their first son was the grandfather of King David.

Salome, the daughter of Herod Philip and Herodias, danced for Herod Antipas, ruler of Galilee and Perea. As a reward, she demanded the head of John the Baptist.

Samson, a judge of Israel, had great strength, the source of which was his hair. When Delilah cut his hair, the Philistines captured him, blinded him, and chained him to their temple. As Samson's hair grew, his strength returned and he destroyed the temple, killing himself and many Philistines.

Samuel was Israel's last judge, a role that incorporated military, political, judicial, and spiritual leadership.

Sarah was the wife of Abraham and the mother of Isaac. After giving birth to Isaac, Sarah became jealous of Hagar, Abraham's other wife, and urged Abraham to banish Hagar and her son Ishmael into the desert.

Saul was the first king of Israel. Defeated and wounded in battle with the Philistines, Saul committed suicide rather than be captured.

Seth was the third son of Adam and Eve. According to the New Testament, Seth was an ancestor of Jesus Christ.

See also ABRAHAM; BIBLE; BIBLE STORIES; DAVID; ELIJAH; EZRA; ISAAC; ISAIAH; JESUS CHRIST; JEREMIAH; JOHN THE BAPTIST; JOSEPH; JOSHUA; MARY; MOSES; PETER; SOLOMON.

BIBLE STORIES

The Bible is great literature. Many writers have retold its stories for boys and girls. The following selections from the Old and New Testaments were adapted by Walter Russell Bowie.

▶ NOAH'S ARK

From the years far back, before the Bible was written, there had been handed down the tale that one time the earth had grown so wicked that there seemed nothing for God to do but to wash it clean and to start again.

God had to find someone fit to make the new start, and the one he found was Noah. God told Noah that there was going to be such a flood as had never been seen before. The waters would be so wide and deep that they would cover all the earth. God said that Noah must build a boat that would be big enough to take in all his family and also two of every sort of bird and animal he could find in the whole world. The boat was to be like a floating house, and it should be called the ark. It needed to be big, considering all that was going to be in it!

So Noah began to build the ark. It was a hard job to build such a tremendous boat, and it must have been all the harder when the neighbors stood around and laughed. "Who ever heard of building a boat in a dry meadow?" they asked. There the sun was shining down, and there was not enough water to float a stick, much less a thing like this huge ark. Noah must be crazy! But Noah kept on working.

Then one day it began to rain. Noah and his family went into the ark and took with them a male and female of every kind of living thing that came walking and running and creeping and flying from the face of the earth. As the water came up higher, the ark was lifted up and floated above the meadows.

When it started to rain, Noah, his family, and a male and female of every kind of animal went into the ark.

Goliath, armed with a sword, a spear, and a shield, came toward David. David drew back his arm and whirled his sling with deadly aim.

It kept on raining, and it rained harder. Day after day the water poured out of the sky as if the earth had been turned upside down and the ocean put on top. Forty days and forty nights it rained.

All the other people and creatures had climbed up to the tops of the hills to try to be out of the reach of the flood. But at last every spot of earth was covered, and nothing was left alive except Noah and his family and what they had with them in the ark.

At last the rain stopped and the sun came out, but for a hundred and fifty days the ark floated on the waters, above the empty earth. Then, little by little, the flood began to go down. One day Noah felt the bottom of the ark jolt on something, and there it was, scraping the top of the highest mountain that had been in all that part of the earth—Mount Ararat. No other land could be seen around it, but Noah knew that before long the rest of the earth would begin to be uncovered.

Noah went into the part of the ark where the birds were. He took a dove and opened a window and let the dove fly away. But presently the bird came fluttering back in the window again, because it had not found a single dry spot anywhere to rest.

A week longer Noah waited. Then he sent the dove out again. This time when the dove came back it carried in its bill a green olive leaf. Noah knew by this that somewhere the earth and the trees were rising above the water. Once more he sent the dove out. This time the dove did not come back at all, and Noah knew that it had found a place to build its nest.

Then at last the ark itself settled down on solid ground. Noah opened the doors, and he and his family and all the beasts and birds and everything else came flying and running and scrambling out, glad to be back on the earth again.

Noah thanked God, and when he looked up he saw a rainbow in the sky. The rainbow was God's sign—the sign of his promise that "while the earth remaineth, seedtime and harvest and cold and heat and summer and winter and day and night shall not cease."

▶ DAVID AND GOLIATH

About that time the Philistines collected an army again and marched up into a valley in the land of Israel. They had with them a man who was as huge as a giant. His name was Goliath. On his head he wore a helmet of brass, and he had armor on his body and on his legs. His spear was as thick as a wooden beam, and his armor-bearer went before him with his great shield.

Every day Goliath came out into the valley between the camp of the Philistines and the camp of Israel and dared any man to come and fight him. But nobody dared, not even Saul. So Goliath shouted and strutted and shook his spear. "I defy the armies of Israel," he cried. "Give me a man that we may fight together!"

Now the three elder sons of Jesse, the brothers of David, were in Saul's army. David had gone back to Bethlehem for a while to take care of his father's sheep. One day, while the armies of Israel and of the Philistines were watching each other, Jesse decided to send his soldier sons some food—parched corn and bread and cheese. He told David to carry the food to the camp and give it to his brothers, and to find out how they were.

Early the next morning David left the sheep in charge of another shepherd, and started off. When he reached the camp of Israel there was a great stir in both armies, and a noise of shouting as of a battle about to begin.

David ran ahead until he found his three brothers. As he stood there talking with them, out came Goliath. He was shouting, as he always did, "What are you here for? I am a Philistine, and you are servants of Saul. Choose a man on your side, and let him come out and fight me. If he can kill me, we will be your slaves; but if I kill him, you shall be slaves to us. I defy you!"

The men around David drew back. None of them had any idea of going out to fight Goliath. They said to David, "You see that man? Whoever kills him will be rich. And Saul will give him his daughter to marry, and will make his family great in Israel."

As David looked at Goliath, he was filled with anger and contempt. "Who is this Philistine," he said, "that he should defy the armies of the living God?"

Eliab, his oldest brother, heard David say that, and was annoyed. "Why did you come down here?" he demanded. "And who have you left to keep those few sheep in the wilderness? I know your pride, and I know that you have come down here just to watch us fight."

David asked Eliab what he had done to make him speak like that. There was reason for his being there, and he would show it, too. He was not going to be frightened by Goliath, or by anyone else.

Presently the army began to talk of this young man, David, who had turned up in the camp, and word about him came to Saul. Saul sent for him. Here was the same lad who had been his armor-bearer and had played for him on the harp!

"Nobody need be troubled about Goliath," David said to Saul. "I will fight with this Philistine."

"You cannot fight with this Philistine," said Saul. "You are only a boy, and this man has been a fighter ever since he grew up."

But David had a different idea. "I have kept my father's sheep," he said, "and once there came a lion, and another time a bear, and took a lamb out of the flock. I went out after those beasts and killed them, and saved the lambs. Both the lion and the bear I killed, and this heathen Philistine shall be like them, since he has defied the armies of the living God. The Lord God who saved me from the paw of the lion and from the paw of the bear will save me from this Philistine."

Saul looked at David and thought for a moment. Then he said, "Go, and the Lord be with you." He put his own armor on David, helmet and breastplate and all, and he gave David his own sword. But David said he could not do anything in that heavy armor. He had never worn armor before, and he did not know how to handle a sword. He took them off, and gave them back to the king. Then David went down to a brook that ran through the valley. There he chose five smooth stones. He put these into the shepherd's bag which he wore at his waist. In one hand was his shepherd's staff, and in the other, his sling. With these David went out to meet the giant Philistine.

On came Goliath, with the man who carried his shield walking in front. When Goliath caught sight of David, he laughed. "Am I a dog," he shouted, "that you come to me with a stick?" And he cursed David by all his gods. "Come on," he said, "and I will give your flesh to the birds and beasts!"

But David answered: "You come to me with a sword, and with a spear, and with a shield; but I come to you in the name of the Lord of Hosts, the God of the armies of Israel, whom you have defied. This day the God of Israel will deliver you into my hands. I will kill you, and take your head from your body. The carcasses of the army of the Philistines I will give this day to the birds and the beasts, that all the earth may know that there is a God in Israel. Yes, all these people shall know that the Lord does not save with the sword and spear. The battle is the Lord's, and he will give you today into our hands."

The Philistine came on with heavy steps. David ran toward him. Putting his hand into his bag, David took out a stone and fitted it into his sling. His arm drew back and whirled with deadly aim. Out from the sling the smooth stone shot, and whistled through the air. It caught Goliath between the eyes and sank into his forehead. Goliath, the giant, pitched forward on his face.

As he fell, David ran and stood over him. He drew Goliath's own sword out of its sheath and cut off his head.

When the Philistines saw that, they fled in panic. The Israelites, shouting, poured after them along the valley and down across the country as far as the gates of Ekron. Then the army of Saul came back and took everything that was in the tents of the Philistines. But all David wanted was the armor of Goliath.

The sailors threw Jonah overboard. He had hardly touched the water when a whale came up and swallowed him.

▶ JONAH

Jonah was commanded by God to go and preach to the great and wicked city of Nineveh. This was the very city from which armies had often come to make war against the people of Israel.

Jonah did not want to go to Nineveh. Instead, he went down to the city of Joppa on the sea. There he found a ship that was going in the opposite direction from Nineveh. He paid his fare, went on board, and sailed away.

The ship had not gone far before a tremendous storm arose. The sailors were frightened and they began to pray. They threw overboard much of the cargo to lighten the ship and give it a better chance to keep afloat when the great waves broke over it. In spite of all the commotion, Jonah was asleep down below the decks. The captain went down and awoke him, and asked him to pray to God that they all might be saved.

But the sailors thought that this storm had come because there was an especially wicked person on the ship. They drew lots to see who it might be. The lot fell upon Jonah. Then the sailors asked him who he was, and what he had done, and why he was on the ship.

Jonah admitted that he was running away from God and from what God had told him to do.

The sailors tried to bring the ship to land. When they could not do this, they took Jonah and threw him overboard.

Hardly had Jonah touched the water, when up came a huge fish, like a whale, and swallowed him. Inside the fish, Jonah had plenty of time to think about God and to change his mind.

After three days, the fish came close to shore and cast up Jonah, unhurt, on the dry land. Now again Jonah heard the voice of God speaking in his heart. Once more it told him to go to Nineveh and preach there. This time he went. He preached that Nineveh and all its people would be destroyed unless they repented of their wickedness.

To Jonah's surprise, the people of Nineveh listened and repented. They fasted and put on sackcloth in sorrow for their sins. Even the king took off his royal robes, dressed himself in sackcloth, and sat down in ashes as a sign of being ashamed for the city's sins. And he gave a command that all the people should pray to God, and that everyone should turn away from whatever wickedness he had been doing.

But instead of being glad that his preaching had had such a great and wonderful result, Jonah was annoyed. He did not like Nineveh. He had not wanted to go there in the first place, and he did not want any good to come to Nineveh because of him. He began to complain to God. He said he had known that God was merciful and slow to anger and full of love and kindness, but he had not wanted God or anyone else to feel that way toward Nineveh. So far as he was concerned, he would rather die than see Nineveh blessed by God. So Jonah went outside the city. He made himself a little shelter and sat there alone and pouted, waiting to see what would happen.

It was very hot in the sun where Jonah sat. When God made a gourd vine to grow and cover Jonah's thin shelter with its cool green leaves, Jonah was pleased. But the next morning worms began to eat the gourd vine, and it withered.

When the sun rose there came a sultry east wind. The sun beat down so hot on Jonah's head that he fainted, and again he wished that he were dead.

At last God spoke to Jonah in a way to bring him to his senses. "You are angry because your gourd vine is withered," he said.

Jonah blurted out, "Yes, I am angry. I do well to be angry."

Then said the voice of God: "You did not make this gourd vine in the first place, and you did not make it grow. It was a thing that came up overnight and lasted only a day. And you are angry because it is gone. Yet here is Nineveh, the great city with more than a hundred thousand people in it and all the cattle upon which they depend, and you want to have it all destroyed."

So the Book of Jonah ends, and at least some men among the people of Israel began to appreciate its meaning: that God has pity upon all peoples, and that men must have pity too.

▶ DANIEL IN THE LIONS' DEN

Belshazzar was slain, and Darius, the king of Media, took his throne.

At first Daniel was honored by the new king even more than he had been honored before. Darius appointed a hundred and twenty princes as governors in the kingdom. Three of these he put in authority over all the others, and among these three Daniel stood first, so that he was next to the king.

That made the princes jealous. They did not want Daniel to be greater than they were. So they began to whisper among themselves, and to try to plan a way to get rid of Daniel. They knew that they could not find Daniel doing wrong. Everything that he did for the king was done well. But suppose they could persuade the king, without his thinking much about it, to make some law that Daniel would think was wrong. They knew that Daniel would not obey such a law. Then, if the king had solemnly declared that anyone who disobeyed it should be punished, they would have Daniel in a trap.

So the princes went to the king. They said to him that it was a dangerous thing to have people of other religions in his kingdom. Why could not everyone think as the king thought and believe what he believed? They suggested that the king give an order that for the next thirty days no one in the kingdom should pray to any god, or act as though even in heaven there could be anyone more important than the king.

The king, without stopping to understand just what might happen, gave the order and signed it with his royal seal. Then the princes who had persuaded him to do that persuaded him also to say that a law, signed and sealed in that fashion, would always be the law, and never could be changed.

Now they were ready to have their revenge on Daniel. When the law had been proclaimed, they watched to see what he would do. Daniel did just what they thought he would do. Law or no law, he went into his house at his regular times to pray. With the windows wide open, he knelt down, with his face turned toward Jerusalem, the Holy City, and prayed to God, just as he had always done.

The men who were trying to trap Daniel went off to tell the king. Had not the king made a law that for thirty days no one in his kingdom

Daniel was thrown into a den of lions, but the lions did not hurt him.

should pray to any god or make any petition to anyone except the king himself? And had it not been declared that any person who dared to disobey that law should be thrown into a den of lions? Well, there was one man who had paid no attention; one man who had gone right on praying as though what the king ordered did not matter.

"Who has done this?" the king wanted to know. And the princes told him it was Daniel.

Now the king was exceedingly sorry and distressed. All day long he thought and tried to find some way by which he could save Daniel. But he had made the law. Besides that, he had been persuaded into declaring that it should be one of the laws of the Medes and Persians that never could be changed. There was nothing left for him to do but to give the order that Daniel should be brought and thrown into a den of lions.

And so Daniel was put into the den where the lions were. The gate was fastened, and sealed with the king's own seal, so that no friend of Daniel could come and let him out.

The king grew more and more distressed. That night in his palace he would not eat, and he would not let any musicians play. When he lay down on his bed he could not sleep. Early the next morning he got up and went to the mouth of the den. In a miserable voice, hardly hoping for anything, he called, "Daniel, servant of the living God, has your God been able to save you from the lions?"

To his amazement and joy, he heard the voice of Daniel from the den, saying, "God has sent his angel and shut the lions' mouths so that they have not hurt me."

The king was filled with great joy. He ordered that Daniel should be taken out of the lions' den immediately. And there he was, safe and sound, not even scratched.

When the king thought of the men who had planned to have Daniel thrown into the den of lions, he ordered that they and everybody connected with them should be thrown in there themselves.

▶ THE BOY JESUS

When Jesus was twelve years old, he went with Joseph and Mary to Jerusalem to celebrate the Feast of the Passover. This was the greatest festival of the Jewish year. It had begun far back in the time of Moses, when the people of Israel were slaves in the land of Egypt. They had worked there making bricks for the temples and for the great monuments which Pharaoh, king of Egypt, commanded to be built. The story of all that happened then is written in the Old Testa-ment Book of Exodus. The Feast of the Passover was the glad reminder of the way in which Moses helped the people of Israel to escape from Egypt and led them across the Red Sea to Palestine, the Promised Land. Everyone was happy when this festival came. It made men proud to remember God's help long ago, and it filled them with belief that God was with them still.

Jewish families always wanted to celebrate the Passover in Jerusalem, where the Temple was. Thousands and thousands of people, beyond anybody's counting, went up to the Holy City at Passover time. All of them were happy at the thought that they were going to see Jerusalem, the Holy City. They sang the beautiful old songs called the "pilgrim songs," which had first been written hundreds of years before.

One of them began:

"I was glad when they said unto me,
Let us go into the house of the Lord.
Our feet shall stand within thy gates,
    O Jerusalem."

And another song began:

"As the mountains are round about Jerusalem,
So the Lord is round about his people from
    henceforth even for ever."

Hardly anything could have been so exciting to Jesus as this first journey to Jerusalem. Joseph's family and their friends walked together in the midst of the growing crowds. The neighbors went too, and people from other towns along the way joined them. They stopped now and then by the roadside to eat the food they had brought with them. It was much more than one day's journey from Nazareth to Jerusalem. So at night they made a place to sleep on the ground and lay down under the open skies and the stars.

The Passover was in the spring, when the fruit trees were blossoming and the fields were bright with flowers. The road from Nazareth to Jerusalem led across the wide Plain of Esdraelon. Jesus knew the stories of the heroes who had walked on that same ground. Gideon had been there with his three hundred men; and David, and Jonathan, and Saul. Many armies had marched across it. Here and there in the earth one might come upon a broken sword blade or a piece of rusty iron from a chariot that had lain there for hundreds of years, left from some battle with the Philistines or the Egyptians or the terrible armies of the Assyrians.

After the pilgrims to Jerusalem had crossed the Plain of Esdraelon, they did not keep straight on. Instead, they crossed the Jordan River and

The young Jesus talked with the oldest and wisest teachers in the Temple court.

went through the country on the east side of the river. Jesus knew that this was because the people of Israel despised the Samaritans, who lived in the country just beyond the Plain of Esdraelon, and did not want to go into the Samaritans' land.

Along the valley of the Jordan River the roads ran south as far as the fords opposite the old city of Jericho. Here the travelers went back across the river. Then they began to climb up through the steep hills that led toward Jerusalem. Up and up they went, until at last they came to where they could see the Holy City. The first sight of it made them stand still in happy wonder.

Outside the walls of Jerusalem, and also within the walls, were green gardens that belonged to rich men's houses. On the highest hill was the splendid palace which Herod the king had built. A great tower of it rose against the sky. But the most glorious thing was the Temple. It was even more magnificent than the Temple of Solomon which had stood on the same ground long before. The walls and columns were of colored marble, and great gates opened from each court to the court beyond. At the end of the farthest court there stood the holiest part of the Temple, so beautiful that hardly any other building in the world could be compared to it. Its marble walls were richly carved, and its roof was of shining gold.

Now that Joseph and Mary and Jesus had reached Jerusalem, they made ready for the Passover. Each family ate the Passover supper by itself. As the evening grew dark, a lamp was lighted, and the old, old prayers were said. Then the family ate a roasted lamb, and bread that had no yeast in it. They ate with their belts

tightened and their sandals tied, because they were remembering the night when Moses had told the Hebrew people to be ready to leave Egypt the instant he should give the word. The people of Israel were no longer in Egypt, but again they were not free. Rome ruled over them. Roman soldiers were there in the castle on the hill, next to the Temple. Many men who kept the Passover were hating the Roman rule and wishing to get rid of it.

Jesus may have been thinking that what they needed more was to get rid of their hatred and bitterness. Certainly he was thinking much about God and asking himself how he could know surely what God wanted for his people.

When the days of the Passover were finished, the people from Nazareth started for home. Again there was the great throng of friends and neighbors journeying along together. Joseph and Mary thought that Jesus was walking with some of the other groups. But when evening came and they stopped to camp for the night, they could not find Jesus anywhere. Then they were frightened. They went straight back to Jerusalem, looking for him. At last they came to the Temple. In one of the Temple courts some of the wisest teachers—teachers who knew most about the sacred books and the law of God—used to sit and let people ask them questions. There, in the midst of them, Mary and Joseph found Jesus. They were glad, and yet a little annoyed. Why had Jesus stayed there and let them be so worried?

"Son," said Mary, "why did you treat us so?"

Jesus was surprised. He thought they should have understood where he would be. "Did you not know," he answered, "that I must be in my Father's house?"

Bicycling is enjoying a dramatic rise in popularity. Cyclists of all ages are taking to the roads for recreation, fitness, transportation, and sport.

BICYCLING

Bicycling is fun because it gives you the freedom of the road—freedom to travel almost anywhere under your own power. People have traveled around the world by bicycle. Cyclists have ridden to the heart of China, up mountains in Africa, and across the Australian desert. But it is not necessary to do anything quite so exotic to have fun on a bicycle. You can explore your neighborhood, your town, and your state by bicycle, discovering places and things you might never see from a car.

More than 85,000,000 Americans ride bicycles. Almost half of them are under the age of 16. They ride for many reasons. For children, a bicycle provides personal transportation—to school, to the store, and to friends' homes. Many adults consider the bicycle a means to better fitness. Bicycling strengthens the heart and lungs without putting severe strain on the body.

The chance to explore new places at a leisurely pace is another reason for bicycling. Bicycle tours are popular in Europe, and many countries have special bicycle paths and trails. In the United States, cycling groups such as those organized by the American Youth Hostels, Bikecentennial, and the League of American Wheelmen offer supervised outings for people of all ages. Bicycling is also a competitive sport, with races of various kinds.

▶ **TYPES OF BICYCLES**

The most familiar bicycles are probably the lightweight models designed for touring. They usually weigh about 25 pounds (11 kilograms) and have ten or more speeds, or gears, to make pedaling easier on hills and in other situations. They have narrow tires and hand brakes, operated by levers on the handlebars. Racing bikes are similar but lighter, weighing about 20 pounds (9 kilograms).

The turned-down handlebars on some racing and touring bikes shift the body forward, into an efficient pedaling position. Similar but heavier and sturdier bicycles, with one to five speeds and level handlebars, are popular for short trips. The high-riser, with raised handlebars and a banana-shaped seat, is a popular children's bicycle. The BMX (bicycle motocross) bicycle, which looks similar to a high-riser, is favored by many young riders because it has a strong frame and fat tires and can take a lot of heavy use. These bicycles have coaster brakes, which are operated by pedaling backward.

All-terrain bicycles (ATB's), also known as mountain bikes, are similar to BMX bicycles. ATB's are strongly built, with wide, knobby tires and up to 18 speeds. They were designed to be ridden on dirt trails, but many are now used on city streets. Other bicycles include folding bicycles, which can fit in the trunk of a car, and tandem bicycles, which carry two

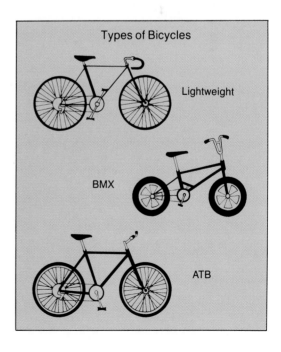

Types of Bicycles

Lightweight

BMX

ATB

people, one behind the other—each with a separate set of pedals. Still another type of bicycle is the recumbent, on which the rider sits in a reclining position and reaches forward in order to pedal.

Bicycles are available in different sizes, based on the diameter of the wheels and on the frame size, or distance from the top of the seat tube to the pedals. Adults are usually comfortable with 26- or 27-inch wheels, while 16 and 20 inches are typical sizes for a child's bicycle. (In countries that use the metric system, the corresponding sizes are 70 and 40 or 50 centimeters.) To choose the correct frame size, straddle the bicycle. For touring models, there should be about 1 inch (3 centimeters) or so between your body and the horizontal bar that runs from the seat to the handlebars. For ATB's, there should be about 3 to 4 inches (8 to 10 centimeters). The seats of most bicycles can be adjusted to make the fit precise.

▶ **BICYCLE RACING**

The four main types of bicycle racing are road, track, off-road, and BMX racing. Road races are run over streets and highways, which are sometimes closed to other traffic. The racers use lightweight ten- to 15-speed bicycles with hand brakes. Track races are run on closed, banked tracks called velodromes. Cy-

Left: Track races take place on oval tracks called velodromes. The distance around the track ranges from about 1/10 of a mile to 1/3 of a mile (0.2 to 0.5 kilometer). *Below left:* Road racers ride over streets and highways on lightweight bikes. The course may be as short as 6.2 miles (10 kilometers) or as long as the Tour de France, which covers about 2,500 miles (4,000 kilometers). *Below:* BMX (bicycle motocross) is an off-road sport run on a bumpy, curvy dirt track, usually less than 1/4 mile (400 meters) long.

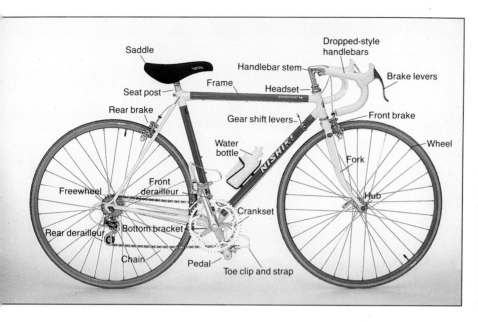

Saddle
Dropped-style handlebars
Handlebar stem
Frame
Seat post
Headset
Brake levers
Rear brake
Front brake
Gear shift levers
Water bottle
Wheel
Fork
Front derailleur
Freewheel
Hub
Crankset
Rear derailleur
Bottom bracket
Chain
Pedal
Toe clip and strap

A well-maintained bicycle is a safe bicycle. **Every time you ride** — Check tire pressure; make sure brakes work; test lights, horn or bell; give a quick visual check for anything obviously wrong. **Every week** — Pump up tires and check pressure with gauge; check tires for cuts, bulges, or glass. **Every two weeks** — Clean and lubricate chain. **Every month** — Lubricate moving parts of derailleurs and brakes and check for worn brake pads; check adjustment of brakes and derailleurs and all bearings (headset, hubs, bottom bracket and pedals); check wheels for wobbling. **Every year** — Clean and lubricate both wheel hubs, bottom bracket, headset and pedal bearings; tighten all nuts and bolts.

clists compete on single-speed bicycles with no brakes. Off-road races, ridden on ATB's, are one of the newest cycling events. BMX racing, popular with young riders, is done on short dirt tracks with jumps, bumps, and curves.

Probably the best-known bicycle race in the world is the Tour de France. This yearly race lasts up to 25 days and covers about 2,500 miles (4,000 kilometers) or more. In 1986, Greg LeMond became the first U.S. cyclist to win the race. His victory did much to make bicycle racing more popular in the United States, as did the success of U.S. cyclists who won nine medals at the 1984 Olympics. By the late 1980's, some 250,000 Americans were riding bicycles in competition.

On a worldwide basis, road and track racing is governed by the Union Cycliste Internationale, based in Switzerland. Road and track racing in the United States is under the authority of the U.S. Cycling Federation (USCF), which has some 500 affiliated (member) clubs. Based in Colorado Springs, Colorado, the USCF issues racing licenses, sponsors training programs, and oversees the U.S. Olympic cycling program. Riders as young as 9 may race in USCF-approved events.

Off-road races are usually authorized by the National Off-Road Bicycle Association. BMX events are overseen by the National Bicycle League or the American Bicycle Association.

▶ **THE HISTORY OF BICYCLES**

Sketches of a bicycle were made by the great 15th-century Italian artist and inventor Leonardo da Vinci. But the first working vehicle was designed by Baron Karl von Drais, of Germany, in 1818. It had no pedals—he pushed himself along with his feet. Similar machines were soon developed and came to be called **velocipedes,** from Latin words for speed and walking. In 1839, Kirkpatrick Macmillan, a Scottish blacksmith, added foot cranks connected by rods to the rear wheel of a velocipede. Later, Ernest Michaux, of France, put rotating pedals on the front wheel.

The first U.S. bicycles were produced after 1876 by Colonel Albert Pope of Massachusetts. They were **ordinaries,** a type of bicycle with a high front wheel and a tiny rear wheel. They cost more than $300 (over $1,500 in today's dollars). In the 1890's the **safety** bicycle replaced the ordinary. It had wheels of equal size and was driven by a chain. Basic bicycle design has changed little since then, but great improvements and refinements have been made.

Bicycling reached its peak in the United States in the late 1890's, when cyclists supported the Good Roads Movement for better highways to ride on. But as more cars took to the roads, bicycling declined. It became popular again in the 1970's, as a result of a gasoline shortage and increased interest in fitness.

Rules of the Road for Bicyclists

Follow lane markings. Do not turn left from the right lane. Do not go straight in a lane marked "Right turn only."

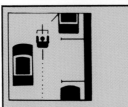

Ride in a straight line whenever possible and ride with traffic. Keep to the right, but stay about a car-door width away from parked cars.

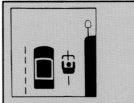

Obey traffic signs and signals. Bicycles must behave like other vehicles if they are to be taken seriously by motorists.

Use hand signals. Hand signals tell motorists what you intend to do. Signal as a matter of law, of courtesy, and of self-protection.

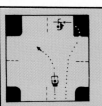

Choose the best way to turn left. There are two ways to make a left turn: (1) Like a car. Look, signal, move into the left lane, and turn left. (2) Like a pedestrian. Ride straight to the far-side crosswalk. Walk your bicycle across.

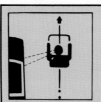

Scan the road behind. Learn to look back over your shoulder without losing your balance or swerving left. Some riders use rearview mirrors. Always look back before changing lanes or changing positions within your lane, and only move when no other vehicle is in your way.

Ride a well-equipped bicycle. Always use a strong headlight and taillight at night and when visibility is poor. Be sure your bicycle is adjusted to fit you properly. For safety and efficiency, outfit it with bells, rearview mirrors, fenders (for rainy rides), and racks, baskets, or bicycle bags.

Go slow on sidewalks and bicycle paths. Pedestrians have the right-of-way. By law you must give pedestrians audible warning when you pass. Do not cross driveways or intersections without slowing to a walker's pace and looking very carefully for traffic (especially traffic turning right on a green light).

▶ BICYCLING SKILLS

The traffic laws of every state say that people who ride bicycles have the same rights and duties as people who drive cars. In other words, a bicycle is a vehicle, and a bicyclist is a vehicle operator. Thus every bicyclist must know and follow the rules of the road.

Some important rules and tips for safe cycling appear in the boxes above. In addition, cycling is safer if you take these steps:

• Ride on routes with few cars, slow traffic, and easy intersections and on streets that have room for cyclists and motorists.

• Wear bright clothing that makes you stand out during the day. At night, wear white or reflective clothing (and make sure your bicycle is outfitted with a headlight, taillight, and reflectors). But remember that riding at night is dangerous, and avoid it.

• Wear a hardshell bicycle helmet with a sticker of approval from the American National Standards Institute (ANSI) or the Snell Memorial Foundation. It will shelter your head from the weather and make you more visible to motorists, and it may save your life. The USCF and other racing organizations require riders to wear helmets in their events.

• Ride a safe bicycle. A well-maintained bike is dependable and easy to ride. You can have a bicycle shop overhaul your bicycle once a year. Once a week or so, check to be sure that all nuts and bolts are tight, that the brakes stop the bicycle quickly, that the chain is lubricated, and that the pedals and handgrips (or handlebar tapes) are tight. Check the tires for cuts and wear, and be sure they are inflated to the pressure shown on the sidewalls. See that the wheels spin freely, without binding or wobbling, and that there are no broken spokes.

Cycling is more fun, as well as safer, when you practice good cycling skills, wear a helmet, and ride a well-maintained bicycle.

JIM FREMONT
Education Director
Bicycle Federation of America

How to rack balls for eight ball

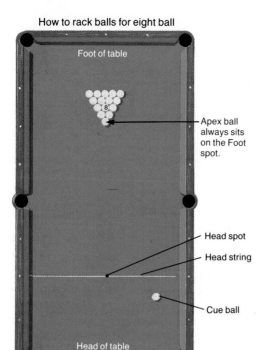

Foot of table

Apex ball always sits on the Foot spot.

Head spot

Head string

Cue ball

Head of table

How to rack balls for rotation

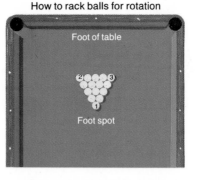

Foot of table

Foot spot

How to rack balls for nine ball

Foot of table

Foot spot

Cue

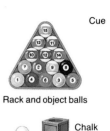

Rack and object balls

Chalk

Cue ball

The various forms of the game of billiards are played on a rectangular cloth-covered table. Equipment includes a leather-tipped stick known as a cue, a white cue ball, and colored balls called object balls. The balls are racked (arranged) in different positions for different forms of the game.

BILLIARDS

Billiards is the general term for a number of different games played on cloth-covered rectangular tables on which balls are struck by sticks, called **cues**. The playing surface is always twice as long as it is wide and is lined by raised rubber cushions. On each turn, the leather tip of the cue is used to strike a white ball, called the **cue ball**, and drive it into what are called **object balls**. Points are scored in some versions by making the cue ball hit two or three object balls, sometimes striking the cushions in between hits; in other versions the goal is to drive object balls into openings, or **pockets**, in the cushions.

▶FORMS OF THE GAME

The style of play most popular in the United States is called **pool**, or sometimes **pocket billiards** to separate it from the carom, or pocketless, games. Pool is played on a table 4½ feet (1.4 meters) wide by 9 feet (2.7 meters) long, or smaller. The most often played games are **eight ball**, **nine ball**, **rotation**, and **straight pool**. In England, Canada, Australia, and India, the favorite game is **snooker**. It is similar to pool but is played on a much larger table (usually 6 by 12 feet, or 1.8 by 3.7 meters) with smaller balls and smaller pockets.

▶RULES OF GAMES

Only the highlights of major games are given here. In every game described, players shoot until they miss, they win the game, or they commit a foul. Examples of fouls are jumping a ball off the table or hitting the cue ball twice on a single stroke.

Eight Ball. The balls are **racked** (arranged with the aid of a triangular frame that is then removed) as shown in the diagram with the 8 ball in the center. One player is chosen to **break** the balls by driving the cue ball into the rack from a position behind the **head string**. When a ball goes into one of the pockets, the shooter is restricted for the rest of the game to the balls in the same group, either those numbered higher than eight (the stripes) or those numbered lower than eight (the solids), while the opponent must aim at only those balls in the other group. Each player tries to **pocket** all the balls in his or her group, which means driving them into any of the pockets with the cue ball. Once that is done, the player can shoot at the 8 ball, the pocketing of which wins the game. Pocketing the 8 ball out of order loses the game.

Nine Ball. In the last 20 years, nine ball has replaced straight pool (see below) as the game of choice for tournaments and matches for expert players. The balls, numbered one through

The cue stance should be relaxed and comfortable. The feet should form a line at about a 45-degree angle to the line of aim. The head should be directly over the cue, sighting as if through a gun sight. Keep the left arm straight and the feet in a comfortable position.

The bridge (position of the hand) must be solid to give firm guidance to the cue.

Another form of the bridge involves placing the fingers firmly on the table and using the thumb to guide the cue.

nine, are racked in a diamond shape as shown, with the 9 ball in the center and the 1 ball at the front. Whoever pockets the 9 ball wins. When breaking the balls, the cue ball must hit the 1 ball first. Players must always hit the lowest-numbered ball on the table first; if they do and any ball goes into a pocket, they shoot again. If a ball other than the lowest ball is contacted by the cue ball before other balls and a ball is pocketed, the pocketed ball is returned to the table on the foot spot and the next player shoots. If the 9 ball goes in on a legal shot, the game is over, even if other balls remain on the table.

Rotation. All 15 balls are racked in a triangle with the 1 ball in front and the 2 ball and 3 ball at the other corners. The 1 ball must be hit first on the break. On each shot, the cue ball must hit the lowest-numbered ball first; if it does and any ball goes in, the player shoots again. All balls pocketed during a player's turn at the table are totaled and credited to the player. Each ball is worth its number; for example, the 10 ball counts ten points. Since the numbers from one to 15 add up to 120 points, whoever scores 61 points or more wins.

Straight Pool. This game is considered the best test of skill by many top players. On each shot, the player must indicate which ball is intended for which pocket, a form of play termed "call shot." The numbers on the balls have no significance. Each legally pocketed ball counts one point, and a game consists of an agreed-on number of points. When only one ball remains on the table, the other 14 are racked in a triangle with the front ball missing. If the player can pocket the remaining ball and break the rack at the same time, that player can continue shooting.

Straight Billiards. Straight billiards is more popular than any other cue game in Europe, North Africa, Latin America, and Asia. A pocketless table and only three balls are used, a cue ball for each player and a red ball (sometimes two red balls). To start, the red ball is placed on the foot spot, one cue ball on the head spot, and the other cue ball 6 inches (15.2 centimeters) to one side of the head spot. A point is scored if the shooter can make the cue ball hit the other two balls, and the game is over when an agreed-on number of points is reached. By keeping the balls close together and near a cushion, experts can make hundreds, even thousands, of points in a row.

Three Cushion. In this difficult but beautiful game, points are scored by making the cue ball hit the other two balls; however, before it hits the second ball, it must contact three or more cushions. Many of the greatest players in the world prefer this game over all others. National championships are held in many countries, including the United States, and a world championship is held every year.

▶ **TIPS FOR SUCCESS**

To become a good player, much practice is necessary and a great amount of thought and skill is required. The best way to learn is to take lessons from an accomplished player or to watch pool or billiards tournaments. You can also improve your game by reading books or magazines and by watching videotapes. These teaching tools are readily available in libraries, bookstores, and billiard supply stores.

ROBERT BYRNE
Author, *Byrne's Standard Book of Pool and Billiards*

BILL OF RIGHTS

The Bill of Rights—the first ten amendments to the Constitution of the United States—ranks alongside the Constitution and the Declaration of Independence as one of the nation's most treasured documents. Since its adoption in 1791, the Bill of Rights has served as the cornerstone of basic American freedoms. Its laws specify the fundamental rights and most cherished liberties of the American people and protect them from the whims of popular majority opinions and abusive government officials.

The Bill of Rights became part of the Constitution of the United States on December 15, 1791. On the 150th anniversary of this event in 1941, President Franklin Roosevelt proclaimed December 15 as Bill of Rights Day. He wanted to make Americans aware of their rights and to remind them of their duties as citizens of the United States. On this day in 1991, Americans recognized the 200th anniversary of these important amendments that have proved so essential to the American political tradition.

The Bill of Rights, on display at the National Archives in Washington, D.C., summarizes the basic rights and freedoms of American citizens.

▶ WHY THE BILL OF RIGHTS WAS ADDED TO THE CONSTITUTION

At the Constitutional Convention of 1787, delegates rejected a motion made by George Mason, author of the Virginia Declaration of Rights (1776), to preface the Constitution of the United States with a bill of rights. The failure to mention basic rights soon became a major issue in the subsequent debates over whether or not the proposed Constitution would be ratified, or approved.

When the Constitutional Convention ended, delegates went back to their respective states to hold their own ratifying conventions. Each state would decide for itself whether or not to approve the new framework for the American government.

The debate over the need for a bill of rights was sparked by a proposal made by a dissenting minority in the Pennsylvania ratifying convention. Some delegates believed that guarantees of certain basic rights and liberties were missing from the proposed Constitution. They called for a number of amendments that would secure a wide range of liberties, such as the free exercise of religion, freedom of speech and press, and protection against unreasonable searches and seizures. Majorities in the ratifying conventions of New Hampshire, Massachusetts, New York, Maryland, Virginia, North Carolina and South Carolina also called for numerous amendments to the proposed Constitution. Although the substance of these recommended amendments differed from state to state, most contained provisions that would limit the powers of the new federal (national) government and protect the people from inconsistent and oppressive rule.

"....a bill of rights is what the people are entitled to against every government on earth, general or particular, and what no just government should refuse, or rest on inferences."

From a letter Thomas Jefferson wrote to James Madison, December 20, 1787.

The Anti-Federalists (those who were opposed to ratifying the Constitution) argued that the broad powers of the new federal government would threaten the powers of the individual states and the liberties of the people. However, the Federalists (those who supported ratification) argued that a bill of rights was unnecessary. Alexander Hamilton, for example, maintained that because the proposed federal government would possess only specifically assigned and limited powers, it could not endanger the fundamental liberties of the people. "Why," he asked, "declare that things shall not be done which there is no power to do? Why, for instance, should it be said that the liberty of the press shall not be restrained, when no power is given by which restrictions may be imposed?"

Nevertheless, the Federalists had to pledge their support for the addition of a bill of rights to the Constitution once the new government began operations. Otherwise they would risk endangering the Constitution's ratification in certain key states and face the possibility of another constitutional convention.

▶ DRAFTING THE BILL OF RIGHTS

James Madison, the "Father of the Constitution," may also be considered the "Father of the Bill of Rights." In his campaign for a seat in the House of Representatives under the new Constitution, he promised his voters that he would energetically push for the adoption of a bill of rights. True to his word, he took the lead in the First Congress in pressing for the desired amendments.

On June 8, 1789, drawing from proposals made by the various state ratifying conventions, Madison proposed to the Congress nine amendments to the Constitution, containing nineteen specific provisions (many of which are now contained in the Bill of Rights). Madison and members of a House committee then went through the complex process of drafting a bill that would secure the necessary two-thirds approval of both houses of Congress. The House and the Senate modified some of Madison's proposals, eliminated others entirely, and added some new ones as well.

As it finally emerged from Congress, the proposed Bill of Rights consisted of twelve amendments and was offered to the states for ratification. The first two proposed amendments were never ratified by the states. (One was related to the size of the House of Representatives and the other to laws regarding the compensation, or payment, for senators and representatives.) On December 15, 1791, Virginia ratified the remaining ten amendments, and the Bill of Rights officially became part of the Constitution.

▶ WHAT THE BILL OF RIGHTS SAYS

The first eight amendments of the Bill of Rights set forth specific guarantees and liberties. The Ninth Amendment acknowledges that the American people have rights that are not even specified in the Constitution or the Bill of Rights. (The Federalists argued for this particular amendment, stating that it would be impossible to list all of the rights and liberties that should be protected.)

The Tenth Amendment emphasizes the national character of the United States constitutional system. It declares that the states or people retain those "powers not delegated to the United States by the Constitution."

Most people, however, believe that their most important rights are those guaranteed by the First Amendment. Commonly called "First Amendment freedoms," these are the fundamental freedoms of religion, speech, and press, as well as the right of the people to assemble and to petition a government.

Other vital provisions contained in the first eight amendments also deal with the rights of individuals. They are designed to protect people against inconsistent or abusive government, particularly in criminal proceedings.

For example, the Fourth Amendment protects individuals from unreasonable searches and seizures (either of themselves or of their property and possessions) by law enforcement officials.

The Fifth Amendment prohibits double jeopardy, which means that someone cannot be tried twice for the same crime. The Fifth Amendment also states that people cannot be compelled to testify against themselves (self-incrimination), and it guarantees "due process," which means people accused of a crime must be properly notified of the charges and given a fair hearing.

The Sixth Amendment establishes the right of an accused person to a public trial by jury. The accused also has the right to have a lawyer, to confront hostile witnesses, and to obtain witnesses in his or her defense.

Finally, the Eighth Amendment prohibits the infliction of "cruel and unusual punishments" (either mental or physical) on those convicted of a crime.

The remaining amendments (the Second, Third, and Seventh) do not cover individual rights in criminal proceedings but address other specific concerns. The Second Amendment is the most noteworthy and controversial of these remaining amendments. After noting the need for a "well regulated militia" (a body of citizen soldiers called to serve during times of emergency or war), this amendment declares that the people's right ". . . to keep and bear Arms, shall not be infringed."

The Third Amendment prevents the government from making citizens shelter soldiers in their homes. This amendment was drafted in response to abuses by British forces during the Revolutionary War.

The Seventh Amendment was included to meet the demands of many Anti-Federalists who wanted to insure trial by jury in civil suits.

▶ **THE ORIGINS OF THE BILL OF RIGHTS**

The Virginia Bill of Rights (proclaimed in 1776, only days before the Declaration of Independence) was the first of ten such declarations by the states during the Revolutionary War period (1775–83). All of these declarations contained provisions that eventually found their way into the national Bill of Rights. Major portions of the First, Fourth,

The Bill of Rights

The First Ten Amendments to the Constitution of the United States
(Ratified December 15, 1791)

Amendment 1

Congress shall make no law respecting an establishment of religion, or prohibiting the free exercise thereof; or abridging the freedom of speech, or of the press; or the right of the people peaceably to assemble, and to petition the government for a redress of grievances.

Amendment 2

A well regulated Militia, being necessary to the security of a free State, the right of the people to keep and bear Arms, shall not be infringed.

Amendment 3

No Soldier shall, in time of peace be quartered in any house, without the consent of the Owner, nor in time of war, but in a manner to be prescribed by law.

Amendment 4

The right of the people to be secure in their persons, houses, papers, and effects, against unreasonable searches and seizures, shall not be violated, and no Warrants shall issue, but upon probable cause, supported by Oath or affirmation, and particularly describing the place to be searched, and the persons or things to be seized.

Amendment 5

No person shall be held to answer for a capital, or otherwise infamous crime, unless on a presentment or indictment of a Grand Jury, except in cases arising in the land or naval forces, or in the Militia, when in actual service in time of War or public danger; nor shall any person be subject for the same offense to be twice put in jeopardy of life or limb; nor shall be compelled in any criminal case to be a witness against himself, nor be deprived of life, liberty, or property, without due process of law; nor shall private property be taken for public use, without just compensation.

Amendment 6

In all criminal prosecutions, the accused shall enjoy the right to a speedy and public trial, by an impartial jury of the State and district wherein the crime shall have been committed, which district shall have been previously ascertained by law, and to be informed of the nature and cause of the accusation; to be confronted with the witnesses against him; to have compulsory process for obtaining witnesses in his favor, and to have the Assistance of Counsel for his defence.

Amendment 7

In Suits at common law, where the value in controversy shall exceed twenty dollars, the right of trial by jury shall be preserved, and no fact tried by a jury shall be otherwise re-examined in any Court of the United States, than according to the rules of the common law.

Amendment 8

Excessive bail shall not be required, nor excessive fines imposed, nor cruel and unusual punishments inflicted.

Amendment 9

The enumeration in the Constitution, of certain rights, shall not be construed to deny or disparage others retained by the people.

Amendment 10

The powers not delegated to the United States by the Constitution, nor prohibited by it to the States, are reserved to the States respectively, or to the people.

Fifth, Sixth, and Eighth amendments, for example, can be traced directly to the Virginia Bill of Rights.

The origins of many of the other rights and liberties contained in the Bill of Rights can be found in the English tradition, dating as far back as Magna Carta (1215), a document that marked the first step toward constitutional law in England. For example, the clause in the Fifth Amendment, which declares that individuals cannot be deprived of their "life, liberty, or property, without due process of law" is rooted in Chapter 39 of Magna Carta.

England's Petition of Right (1628) and Bill of Rights (1689) further expanded individual liberties and placed increased limitations on the ruler's powers and authority. English liberties and rights, such as trial by jury, protection against self-incrimination and unreasonable search and seizure, were, in fact, included in the charters establishing the American colonies. They were considered to be the "rights of Englishmen."

▶ENFORCING THE BILL OF RIGHTS

The courts, both state and national, are responsible for enforcing the Bill of Rights, when instances of abuse are brought to their attention through proper legal channels. The Supreme Court of the United States, however, has the final word in determining whether or not the principles contained in the Bill of Rights have been violated.

Making such a determination is seldom an easy matter. The Court, for example, must answer such questions as, What constitutes "unreasonable" search and seizure? What limits can be placed on the free exercise of religion for reasons of public morality, safety, or health? Under what circumstances may speech be legally curtailed to prevent violence or property damage?

Originally, the Bill of Rights applied only to the laws and activities of the national government. It was not until after the Civil War that the Bill of Rights' provisions were applied to the states. The 14th Amendment (1868) was the first to declare that no state "shall . . . deprive any person of life, liberty, or property without due process of law."

Today, for all intents and purposes, the fundamental rights and liberties guaranteed by the Bill of Rights apply with equal force to both the national and the state governments.

▶STATE BILLS OF RIGHTS

All of the fifty state constitutions contain a bill of rights. The Illinois Bill of Rights borrows from the Declaration of Independence in stating, "All men are by nature free and independent and have certain inherent and unalienable rights among which are life, liberty, and the pursuit of happiness."

Some states' declaration of rights are even far more extensive and detailed than the national Bill of Rights. The California Declaration of Rights, for example, says, "A person may not be disqualified from entering or pursuing a business, profession, vocation, or employment because of sex, race, creed, color, or national or ethnic origin."

▶THE CANADIAN BILL OF RIGHTS

The Canadian Charter of Rights and Freedoms, officially proclaimed on April 17, 1982, applies to both the national and provincial governments. Certain sections of the charter deal with distinctly Canadian concerns, such as declaring the French and English languages to have equal status in the official proceedings of the national government. Other sections deal with rights not specifically mentioned in the American Bill of Rights. For example, a clause concerning mobility rights gives citizens the right to enter and leave Canada, as well as any of the provinces.

The charter details major rights and liberties under the headings of **Fundamental Freedoms** and **Legal Rights**. The fundamental freedoms correspond to those found in the First Amendment in the American Bill of Rights, but they are more extensive. In addition to freedom for the press and media, peaceful assembly, and freedom of speech and religion, they include freedom of association, conscience, thought, belief, and opinion.

The legal rights of the Charter are similar to those found in the Fourth, Fifth, Sixth, and Eighth amendments in the American Bill of Rights. These include, among others, protection against self-incrimination, double jeopardy, unreasonable search and seizure, and cruel and unusual punishment.

GEORGE CAREY
Author, *The Federalist: Design for a Constitutional Republic*

See also UNITED STATES, CONSTITUTION OF THE; UNITED STATES, GOVERNMENT OF THE; UNITED STATES, HISTORY OF THE; FEDERALIST, THE.

BIOCHEMISTRY

Biochemistry forms the meeting ground of two great sciences: biology and chemistry.

There is a Greek word, *bios,* which means "life." For that reason **biology** is the name given to the study of living things—animals, plants, and microscopic forms of life. Biology takes in the description of living things. It takes in their ways of living and growing and reproducing.

Chemistry is the name given to the study of the composition of various substances. It includes the manner in which the composition changes or can be changed. Chemists are interested in all substances: those in rocks, in sea water, and even in distant stars.

Now suppose you combine biology and chemistry. You have the study of the substances that make up living things, their composition and the changes they undergo. This is **biochemistry**.

▶ THE ORIGINS OF BIOCHEMISTRY

Biochemistry is a fairly new science, but many of its processes are as old as life. The means by which green plants make their food is a biochemical process. So is digestion in human beings and in other animals. Long before people knew anything about science, they stumbled upon biochemical processes. Cooking is one. Some substances in food are changed when the food is cooked. The food is made tastier and easier to digest. Primitive people also found that if fruit juice was allowed to remain in a warm, dark place, certain changes took place in it. The juice fermented and changed to wine.

Such discoveries were accidental. People did not understand what happened during cooking or fermentation. They understood only that by certain methods they could change various substances. Then in the late 1700's modern chemistry was developed.

How Chemistry Led to Biochemistry

The early chemists were concerned with what we call inorganic chemistry, or the chemistry of nonliving things. For example, they were interested in minerals. Yet they could not ignore living things altogether. Certain substances existed both in living organisms and in the nonliving world. For instance, all creatures are made up mostly of water; this is the same water that we find all about us.

However, chemists also knew that many substances of living organisms are not at all like those of the nonliving world. One important difference has to do with what happens when they are heated.

When inorganic substances are heated, no basic change takes place in them. Iron that is melted is still iron. Water that is boiled is still water. If a copper bowl is broken up and melted down, a second bowl can be made of the material.

With organic substances the basic form is easily changed by heat. They char, smoke, or burn. And then they are no longer what they were to begin with. There is no way that a cooked or burned egg can be made back into a raw egg.

Because organic substances are easily changed, the chemists who studied them had to work more carefully and slowly than the chemists who studied rocks and minerals. Even so, between 1750 and 1850 chemists learned much about the nature of these substances. Organic chemistry, or the chemistry of living things, became the first approach to biochemistry.

Among the early discoveries were the three main kinds of organic substances that make up all living matter. Chemists called them carbohydrates, fats, and proteins. Examples of carbohydrates are starch and sugar; wood is mostly cellulose, which is another kind of carbohydrate. Butter and olive oil are examples of fats. Gelatin and egg white are examples of protein.

The human body uses carbohydrates and fats for energy. It uses protein to form new tissue.

Both fats and carbohydrates are made up of three elements. They are carbon, hydrogen, and oxygen. In the body these combine with oxygen from the air to supply energy. Before long, chemists discovered that proteins were far more complicated than either fats or carbohydrates. Protein contains not only carbon, hydrogen, and oxygen, but also nitrogen. The body uses nitrogen in building new tissue.

In spite of these discoveries, scientists still thought that organic matter had no connec-

Friedrich Wöhler (1800–82) proved that it was possible to make an organic substance from inorganic chemicals.

tion with inorganic chemicals. They believed it was impossible to change inorganic substances into organic substances.

Then in 1828 a German chemist named Friedrich Wöhler accidentally proved that false. While heating some inorganic chemicals he happened to make an organic substance, urea. Up to that time scientists believed that only a living body could make an organic substance.

Wöhler's discovery was the first real breakthrough into biochemistry. Scientists then realized there could be no clear dividing line between chemical processes and life processes. Chemists and biologists found that their work was overlapping more and more.

▶ WHAT BIOCHEMISTS STUDY

Biochemists today explore a great range of subjects. These fall into several main areas.

Pharmacology

One of the oldest branches of biochemistry is called **pharmacology.** It is the study of how chemicals affect living tissue. Everyone who orders drugs or a prescription from the pharmacist comes in touch with this branch of biochemistry.

The fact that certain plants could be used to cure various diseases had long been known. In the 1800's scientists began to learn about the chemical basis of these cures. They also learned to make new substances that resembled natural chemicals in many ways but were not found in living tissues. Some of these substances that they made had powerful effects on living tissue.

Among the great discoveries of the 1800's were the antiseptics, chemicals that could kill germs. Scientists also discovered chemicals that could deaden pain. These are the anesthetics.

Chemotherapy

Chemotherapy, a special branch of pharmacology, is the treatment of diseases with chemicals. In the 20th century laboratories made new chemicals that could destroy germs without hurting human beings. Other chemicals, called antibiotics, were obtained from microbes. They were even more deadly to germs. By the 1970's chemotherapy had brought many ancient diseases under control. Other diseases, such as cancer, were under constant attack by researchers.

Dietetics

Toward the end of the 1800's the science of **dietetics** became very important. This is the study of how the body makes use of foods. Biochemists began by using animals in experiments. They fed special diets to rats or guinea pigs and studied the effects on the animals.

By 1900 biochemists realized that it was not enough just to eat food. People had to have the proper foods. Certain substances were important to health and to life, even though these substances were present in the body only in tiny quantities. Many of these substances could not be made by the body, so they had to be present in the diet. Some of these substances were inorganic. Others were organic. They were given the name "vitamins."

If vitamins are missing from the diet, a person can develop a deficiency disease such as anemia or scurvy. The most common form of anemia is caused by a lack of iron in the blood. Scurvy was once common among sailors on long ocean voyages. It was caused by a lack of vitamin C.

To fight such deficiency diseases, biochemists have learned what foods are necessary to good health. They have also learned how to make vitamins in the laboratory.

Endocrinology

Shortly after 1900 the biochemists discovered that certain organs in the body produce substances that keep the body in proper working order. These chemical substances are called hormones. The study of hormones is called **endocrinology.**

If the body's organs do not produce the proper amount of hormones, serious disorders can result. The most common disease of this sort is diabetes; it is caused by a lack of the hormone called insulin. Biochemists have learned how to take hormones such as insulin from the glands of animals. People with diabetes can use insulin that has been obtained from cattle. Diabetics can now lead almost normal lives if they use insulin carefully. And biochemists are learning how to make other hormones in the laboratory.

The Body's Chemistry

Since 1900 biochemists have concentrated more and more on the chemical changes that go on in people. The changes that can occur are so many and so complicated that it takes long, hard work for the biochemist to untangle all the threads.

The most complicated organic substances are the proteins. They are made of long

Modern techniques have made possible important advances in biochemistry. Left, radioactive phosphorus in the leaf shows how different parts of the leaf take up different amounts of phosphorus as food. Below, biochemist studies an experimental antibiotic. He is comparing its effect on a bacteria culture with the effect of a known antibiotic on a culture of the same kind of bacteria.

Below: cells of a green leaf as seen through an electron microscope, showing chloroplasts.

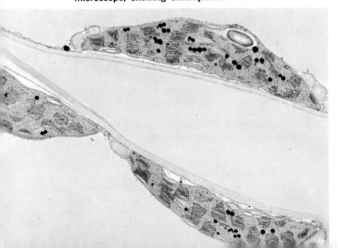

chains of organic chemicals called amino acids. Although there are only about two dozen different kinds of amino acids, the body can put them together in millions of different ways. Each different protein has its own special purpose in the human body.

For example, there are special kinds of proteins called enzymes. Each of the millions of changes that take place in the body depends on one particular kind of enzyme. If this particular enzyme is missing from the body, then the body cannot change one substance into another. There are special enzymes, for example, that make it possible for food to be digested. Biochemists have also discovered that enzymes are responsible for the fermentation of bread dough and fruit juice.

▶ **FUTURE DEVELOPMENTS**

The most exciting future developments in biochemistry lie in two directions.

Photosynthesis

For many years scientists wanted to work out the exact changes that go on in green plants when they combine the carbon dioxide of the air with water and form starch. The green plant uses the energy of sunlight to bring about this change, and the process is called **photosynthesis.**

It is photosynthesis that creates the world's food supply. And when plants form starch, oxygen is given off to the air. It is photosynthesis, therefore, that keeps the air breathable and prevents us from ever using up the world's oxygen supply.

Until 1945 practically nothing was known about photosynthesis. Now the details are being revealed at a fast rate. If biochemists can learn enough about photosynthesis, they may be able to bring about the same chemical reactions. Then they may be able to learn ways of making food out of air, water, and sunlight so that we will depend less on rainfall and good harvests.

Genetics

The other exciting development involves the study of the way in which the pattern of chemical change in a body is inherited. Children inherit far more than outward appearance from their parents. Many of the internal substances and processes that make us what we are—the diseases we may have or how long we live—are determined by our inherited chemical patterns. The study of these patterns is called **genetics**.

This science takes its name from the genes, tiny elements in certain body cells that determine heredity. Biochemists have discovered that the genes are made up of special proteins called nucleic acids. Each nucleic acid brings about the formation of a particular enzyme by what is called the "genetic code." In the 1950's and 1960's biochemists began to work out the genetic code.

Once the code is fully understood, scientists may be able to correct many human conditions that cannot now be helped. It may become possible to assure health and long life from the beginning.

Biochemistry as a New Science

Many of the important advances in biochemistry have been made possible only by modern tools and techniques for investigation. More has been learned since 1945 about chemical changes in the body than in all history before that time. As biochemists learn more and more about the workings of the body they come closer to understanding such disorders as hardening of the arteries and high blood pressure. Some biochemists are working hard to learn how cancer attacks the body. Others are studying the virus —the smallest form of living matter. Viruses are responsible for many serious illnesses like polio and diphtheria, as well as for the common cold.

In reading about biochemistry you may have noticed that almost everything biochemists discover is put to use by doctors to help them fight disease. Today, in fact, medicine can hardly be separated from biochemistry. And in biochemistry itself it is hard to say where chemistry stops and biology begins. But it is important to realize that the name "biochemistry" represents far more than a convenient label for certain scientific activities. It indicates a completely new view of the nature of life.

ISAAC ASIMOV
Boston University School of Medicine

See also BIOLOGY; BODY CHEMISTRY; CHEMISTRY, HISTORY OF; GENETICS; PHOTOSYNTHESIS.

BIOGRAPHY, AUTOBIOGRAPHY, AND BIOGRAPHICAL NOVEL

Biography is both a craft and an art. As a craftsman the biographer begins with research, gathering all the available information about a person's life. There are first the surface facts about a chosen subject. Then the biographer looks beneath the surface for evidence of inner truths—what the man or woman thought, felt, desired, suffered.

The biographer as an artist sets down the meaning of a person's life. With his research at hand, the writer chooses the facts he will use. Sometimes it is the bulk of detail; sometimes it is the essence, or pith. With this task of selection comes the task of writing the story in a clear, convincing way. The artist must so construct his book that every portion of the person's life fits into an understandable, moving whole. The writing must have style; the structure must have architectural form. That is the meaning of art.

▶ BIOGRAPHY OLD AND NEW

Modern biography, as an independent and popular literary form, is fairly new. Writing about individual lives, however, is an old practice. The Bible is full of stories about the prophets and saints. The earliest Greek biographical writing was done by Xenophon, who wrote about Socrates in the 4th century B.C. Plutarch's *Parallel Lives* (about A.D. 100) is still famous. The best-known Latin biographer is Suetonius, author of *Lives of the Caesars* in A.D. 120. Tacitus set down an account of the life of his father-in-law, Agricola, in A.D. 97–98. The purposes of these early Greek and Roman biographers were mixed. Some tried to tell the history of a dynasty or of a war. Others attempted to justify a moral or philosophical system. As a result the human story was sometimes lost.

Modern biographers' aims are varied. Some wish to tell an exciting, dramatic, and often inspirational human story. Others study the life of a person so that we can profit by another's experience and better understand ourselves and the world about us. Still others wish to make the past more alive. Instead of writing about the impersonal forces of history, the biographer tells of the impact of an individual on the life of his times. There is Lytton Strachey's *Eminent Victorians,* which describes an interesting age in England. Douglas S. Freeman's *George Washington* portrays the beginning of the American nation. Hendrik Willem van Loon's *R.v.R.,* a biography of Rembrandt, serves as an introduction to art. René Jules Dubos' *Louis Pasteur* gives us a picture of the scientist at work.

Biography may be written out of love or hate but never out of indifference. It may take years to write. It may require thousands of hours of study in libraries, law courts, halls of records, city halls, museums, family archives. Frequently many miles must be traveled to visit the places where the subject lived and worked, to interview men still alive who can add to the body of knowledge. This concentrated effort can be achieved only by people who love deeply—such as the biographers of Jefferson or Michelangelo or Edison—or by those who hate deeply, such as the biographers of Torquemada or Hitler or Mussolini.

Often the search is frustrating. For a conscientious biographer the easily available material won't be half enough. A researcher is a detective. He hunts down clues, pursues scraps of evidence, never gives up looking for material he senses must exist. In his hero's life there are always blank spaces that must be filled in if the biography is to be complete and true. To a good biographer everything is findable. When he comes up empty-handed, he must return to the quest with fresh ideas and renewed courage. For it is not enough to know everything a man did. It is also important to know why he did what he did—his reasoning, his fears, his failures before he achieved something important.

Once all his material is collected, the biographer faces a new challenge. The reader must feel that he is in the hands of a thorough and honest workman. Therefore, the biographer has to be objective. He has to tell the complete truth, based on his findings. He must not conceal his hero's faults, omit his shortcomings, bury his failures. He must not allow his own prejudices to take over. What is known as his "principle of selection," that is, his choice of materials to use, must be strictly ethical. Otherwise the reader will sense that something is wrong. He will feel that he is being deceived.

But when he reads an honest, well-balanced biography, such as Benjamin Thomas' *Abraham Lincoln* or Muriel Rukeyser's *Willard Gibbs* or Carl Van Doren's *Benjamin Franklin,* he will know that the strands of each story are accurately woven.

Biography is one of the most enjoyable forms of reading and learning. While reading biographies, one can sit at home yet roam the realms of time and space with *Genghis Khan* (Harold Lamb), *Napoleon* (Emil Ludwig), *Aristotle* (W. D. Ross), and *Madame Curie* (Eve Curie). A good biographer will become as one with the person he is writing about. This union enables the reader, in turn, to live another's life in his imagination.

▶ AUTOBIOGRAPHY

Autobiography is a very different medium. "Auto" comes from the Greek for "self," "one's own." An autobiography is the story of a person's life written by himself. Sometimes an autobiography is ghostwritten, that is, written by someone else, frequently with journalistic experience. Sometimes the real writer is completely unknown. Sometimes there is an "as told to . . ." approach.

Autobiography is a difficult art form, yet it looks easy. Perhaps that is what tempts so many thousands to try it.

A man sometimes writes his own story because he has experienced some kind of self-discovery. The discovery may be about his relationship to life, to his fellow man, or to God. Others write about their struggles against great odds and their eventual success. The autobiographies of Alfred E. Smith and Helen Keller show a refusal to be held down or defeated. Some autobiographies, like those of Booker T. Washington and Jane Addams, glow with an individual's dedication to a life of serving mankind. Greatness of character, which seems to spring from selflessness and courage, often reveals itself in an autobiography. The best of these life stories raise the stature of the human race. They inspire the reader and deepen his understanding.

Not all autobiographies are written for noble purposes. Many are written for selfish reasons—to get money, attention, sympathy, or revenge. Yet all too often the writer of autobiography conveys the exact opposite of the impression he had hoped to impart.

Every kind of American has written an autobiography. As a group, clergymen are more interested in writing about themselves than any other single category. Authors and politicians follow close behind. Industrialists, scientists, and engineers tend to remain silent. In between come the educators, the reformers, the military and the professional men. It has become fashionable for actors and athletes to have their stories ghostwritten.

▶ THE BIOGRAPHICAL NOVEL

In recent years a third biographical form has become increasingly popular and important. It is called the biographical novel. This is biography presented in the form of a novel, with dialogue, suspense, and plot structure. The biographical novelist can use his creative imagination to develop these aspects of the novel. But he must do so only within the framework of truth. The novelist will have found the truth in documents—diaries, letters, journals, notes, recorded deeds.

The biographical novel is thus the fruit of a marriage between the research of biography and the fictional devices of the novelist. Books like *I, Claudius* (Robert Graves) and *The Romance of Leonardo da Vinci* (Dimitri Sergeevich Merezhkovski) are fine examples of the biographical novel. It offers a more emotional approach to life, with more personal interpretation by the author. Facts can be forgotten, but rarely an emotional experience. The biographical novelist tries to catch up his readers in the emotions of his hero. Emotions felt while reading a biographical novel can be almost as unforgettable as the emotions one experiences in real life.

Not every life will fit into the form of the biographical novel. Dramatic elements must be present, along with an overall pattern into which the parts can be fitted. Many lives, important in their achievement, do not lend themselves to the nature of the novel. Other lives seem to have been lived as though the subject were constantly aware that he was creating a dramatic structure.

Biography, autobiography, and the biographical novel are personal books. They tell the story of men's lives, in order to help us understand mankind.

IRVING STONE
Author, *Lust for Life, The Agony and the Ecstasy*

BIOLOGICAL CLOCK

As the sun rises on a warm, sunny day, the trumpet-shaped flowers of the morning glory unfold. It is in the afternoon, as the morning glories close, that the buds of moss roses uncurl. When darkness comes, moss roses curl shut. Only then do evening primrose flowers open, pale and ghostly in the night. In the morning, before daylight, they close again.

The opening and closing of the flowers is one of the natural cycles, called **biological rhythms**, that occur in living things. The biological rhythms of the morning glories, moss roses, and evening primroses occur within a single day. Such rhythms are called *circadian rhythms*, from the Latin words *circa* and *diem*, meaning "about a day." But not all biological rhythms are based on a day. Some, such as the beating of the heart, occur every few seconds. Other rhythms are repeated each month and still others are repeated each year.

Scientists use the term **biological clock** to describe the internal timing mechanism that controls biological rhythms. Where is this biological clock and what is it? In animals, the brain is thought to play a role; however, plants, fungi, and microscopic organisms lack brains and still exhibit biological rhythms. There is increasing evidence that chemicals produced by living things trigger the cycles. These chemicals, in turn, are controlled by factors outside the living organism including the light-dark cycle of a day and the changing seasons of a year. Yet, even if an organism is shut off from all clues in the environment, it will still display biological rhythms.

▶ BIOLOGICAL CLOCKS IN NATURE

The biological rhythms of seashore organisms are often linked to the rise and fall of the ocean's tides. Clams, mussels, and barnacles feed by filtering food from the water. When the tide is in, their shells open and they feed. As the tides go out, the shells close and the animals are protected from the drying air.

The migration of animals is an event that is triggered by a signal from an animal's biological clock. One of the most dramatic examples of a migration is the journey some birds make in spring and autumn. These migrations are associated with changes in day length. As days grow longer, birds leave their winter feeding grounds in the south. By the time they reach their northern destination, the plants they depend on for food are flourishing there. When the birds reach their summer feeding grounds, another biological rhythm is triggered: They are ready to mate and raise young. As autumn approaches, days shorten, temperatures drop, and plants begin to die. Birds' biological clocks signal the return to the south where there is food and warmth.

Like flowers, birds, and other animals, humans have biological clocks that control their biological rhythms. Humans have daily, weekly, monthly, and seasonal biological rhythms. Body temperature, blood pressure,

The jimsonweed, which blooms at night, is a desert flower with a biological rhythm opposite that of most flowers. *Right:* Throughout the hours of daylight, the flower of the jimsonweed remains tightly closed. *Far right:* After the sun has set, the funnel-shaped flower slowly opens.

sleeping and waking, and the levels of many chemicals in the body have a 24-hour rhythm. Many illnesses appear to have a yearly rhythm. Colds, flu, and pneumonia are most common in autumn and winter. Outbreaks of childhood diseases such as measles most often occur in spring and summer.

▶CHANGES IN BIOLOGICAL CLOCKS

More is known about circadian rhythms in humans than about any other kind of biological rhythm. When people travel by plane across several time zones, their internal clocks are no longer in tune with where they are. This is called jet lag. The effects of jet lag are worse when people travel to a place with a later time (that is, west to east) than it is when they travel to a place with an earlier time (east to west). People with jet lag feel cranky and tired. Their hand-eye coordination is not as good as usual and they may be forgetful. It takes several days for the body's biological clock to reset to the new time zone.

People who work night shifts also experience problems with their biological clocks. They are generally not as productive or alert as people who work during the day, and they have more accidents on the job. They also have more health and sleep problems than

At a signal from their biological clocks, monarch butterflies gather in huge swarms to make a yearly migration that covers thousands of miles.

people who work day shifts. Scientists studying this problem found a possible solution by conducting a test study. At night, people worked under very bright lights. When they went home to sleep, they slept in totally darkened bedrooms. After three days, the workers' biological clocks had been reset. Now their temperature cycles were the same as day workers: highest when they were at work, and lowest when they were sleeping.

▶ADVANCES AND DISCOVERIES

Exciting breakthroughs are being made with new medical treatments. Certain medical problems are associated with different times of the day. Heart attacks, strokes, and sudden death happen most often during the waking hours before noon. Asthma and ulcer attacks occur most often between midnight and 8 A.M. This information can be used in treatment. Heart medication taken right after waking may help protect a person with heart disease. Medication for asthma and ulcers is available in time-release tablets. When these tablets are taken at night, an individual is helped most during the high-risk time.

Biological clocks control the biological rhythms that make the world a familiar place. As scientists learn more about these rhythms, especially those in humans, new solutions can be found to make travel more comfortable, working conditions safer, and medical treatment more effective.

KARIN L. RHINES
Co-author, *Discover Science*

See also HIBERNATION; HOMING AND MIGRATION.

Workers who switch between day and night shifts, such as these firefighters, experience problems with their biological clocks similar to the effects of jet lag.

The science of biology is the study of all living things.

BIOLOGY

Since the beginning of human history, people have taken an interest in what they saw, particularly in everything that moves or grows and can be called alive. **Biology** is the name given to this study of living things. Much of the study has been, and still is, simply a process of looking at what can be seen and thinking about it. This activity may be broadened by carefully dissecting (taking apart) living things so that more internal (inside) structure can be seen. The study may also be broadened by use of a lens or a microscope. And since all living things are active in some ways, the action may be interfered with; that is, the action may be experimented with, just as one can experiment with any piece of working machinery to discover what stops it or changes the manner in which it works.

▶ GREAT BIOLOGISTS OF THE ANCIENT WORLD

All we know of ancient efforts to study the nature of living things comes from the records made by the early biologists. Unfortunately, only some of those records survived to later times. What is now known is mainly the work of Aristotle, who lived in Greece about 2,300 years ago. Aristotle observed the world of nature, thought about it, taught about it, and left records. And he was undoubtedly one of the best naturalists of all time. He described in a remarkably accurate manner the animal life that was familiar to him and attracted his attention—particularly the habits of fishes, the breeding habits of octopuses, the behavior of bees, and the nature of whales, dolphins, and porpoises. All are still being studied by biologists today. Aristotle also attempted to analyze the nature of reproduction, heredity, and sex, with which biologists are still deeply concerned. Aristotle, in fact, represents the climax of the great intellectual adventure of the ancient Greeks. For nearly 2,000 years afterward no one really tried to improve on his ideas concerning the nature of life.

We have a record of only one other important biologist of ancient times. This is Galen, a Greek who spent most of his active life in Rome during the 2nd century A.D. Aristotle was an observer, who saw things as they were and thought about their nature. Galen was outstanding for his skill and inventiveness in making experiments. He paid much attention to the flow of blood in the

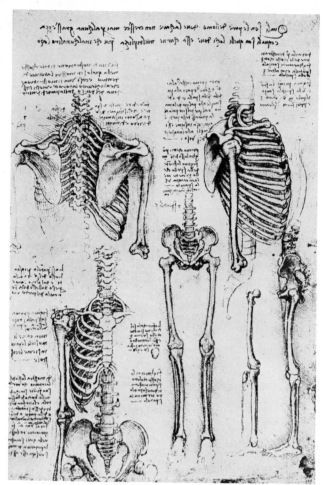

These drawings of the human skeleton were made by Leonardo da Vinci, who lived from 1452 to 1519.

were greatly interested in the exact portrayal of animal and plant forms, as well as the structure of the human body. These artists needed also to be scientists because they were intensely curious about the real nature of what they were attempting to portray on canvas or in stone. For the first time in ages men began to look at plants and animals as they really were, rather than studying old drawings and descriptions.

At the same time the discovery of the New World and of the Far East took place. Explorers brought home accounts of an exciting variety of strange forms of life.

All of this happened at the same time as the invention of printing and of reproducing drawings by means of wood engravings. So it became an easy step for other students of nature to produce the first biological textbooks of this new period of biology. In Germany the first books of this sort dealt with plants. In Italy, at the University of Padua, great advances in the study of the human body were made by Vesalius and Fabricius. And somewhat later another great advance was made by William Harvey, an Englishman who had been a student under Fabricius at a time when Galileo was also present at Padua. In 1628 Harvey published his demonstration that blood circulates through the body, a fact previously unknown.

Harvey and the Founding of Physiology

Proof that the blood must circulate through the body depended in part on observations. It also depended on measurement, of a kind proposed by Galileo. The procedure is familiar to us but was new at the time. Harvey first showed that blood can leave the ventricle (chamber) of the heart only in one direction because of the valves in the heart. He then measured the capacity of this chamber. Since the normal heart beats 72 times a minute, it was possible to calculate the amount of blood that passes through it. (If the capacity of the chamber is 2 ounces, then in 1 hour the heart pumps $60 \times 72 \times 2$ ounces, a total of 8,640 ounces, or 540 pounds, of blood into the blood vessels.) This amount is about three times the weight of the body. Where did it all come from? Where did it go? The answer was that the same blood must be going round and round. This knowledge that

body. He was also much concerned with the effect of injuries to the spinal nerve cord with regard to paralysis and death. Galen stands for the second period of biology.

After Galen biology ceased to be an active science. It made no progress throughout the Dark Ages and most of the Middle Ages. It came to life again only as part of the general reawakening of scientific interest during the Renaissance.

▶ BIOLOGY DURING THE RENAISSANCE

The Renaissance, which means "rebirth," was the great surge of intellectual activity that came into full force during the 1500's. It showed itself in art, science, and exploration. Biological science has its roots in all three of these activities.

This was a time of great painters and sculptors, such as Botticelli, Leonardo da Vinci, Dürer, and Michelangelo. All of them

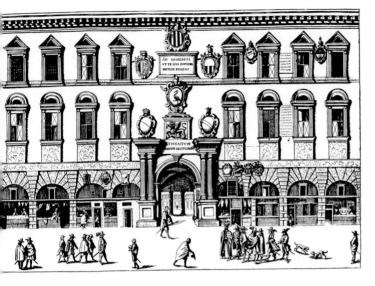

Above, the University of Padua in Italy. Many discoveries were made here. For 1,300 years, since the days of Galen, medical scholars had merely read about the body. Around the 1500's they began to study how it actually worked. One of these new scholars was Andreas Vesalius, a professor at Padua. His book on the workings of the human body led him to be called the father of modern anatomy. The book's Latin title was *De humani corporis fabrica*. One of its woodcuts is shown at the right.

CIRCULATION OF BLOOD

Also trained at Padua was the Englishman William Harvey (*below*). He discovered that blood travels in a complete path through the body, as shown in the diagram at left. Blood goes from the arteries to the capillaries in the body tissues, where gases are exchanged. Then the blood goes into the veins and so back to the heart. Until the 17th century, men believed blood ebbed and flowed out of the heart, like a tide.

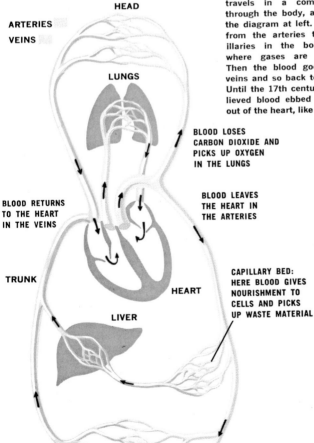

HEAD

ARTERIES

VEINS

LUNGS

BLOOD LOSES CARBON DIOXIDE AND PICKS UP OXYGEN IN THE LUNGS

BLOOD RETURNS TO THE HEART IN THE VEINS

BLOOD LEAVES THE HEART IN THE ARTERIES

TRUNK

HEART

LIVER

CAPILLARY BED: HERE BLOOD GIVES NOURISHMENT TO CELLS AND PICKS UP WASTE MATERIAL

LEGS

Leeuwenhoek, Dutch lens maker, holds one of his tiny early microscopes. They showed an unknown world.

of physiology since Harvey's time has been the answering of questions such as these. Gradually a clearer picture of the animal body as a working mechanical model has been obtained.

Advances with the Microscope

Although he was not concerned with biology, Galileo worked out and described the construction of the compound microscope; in it a system of two or more lenses was employed. It gave biologists a means of seeing what had previously been invisible.

During the second half of the 1600's the great pioneers in the use of the microscope were at work. The most important of these men were Robert Hooke in England, Anton van Leeuwenhoek and Jan Swammerdam in Holland, and Marcello Malpighi in Italy. All contributed to the growth of the new biology, each in his own way. Malpighi, for instance, saw and described the circulation of the blood in the fine capillary vessels in the lung of a frog. Swammerdam's magnificent book called the *Bible of Nature* is probably the finest collection of microscopic observations ever published and is still used. Leeuwenhoek drew attention to the complexity and beauty of microscopic structure in plant and animal tissues. Hooke showed that plant material is made up of small units enclosed by cell walls. Thus began **microscopy**, which is the name given to the use of microscopes generally; **histology**, which is the study of tissues; and **cytology**, which is the study of cells. However, little headway was made in those fields for another 150 years. Then, in the early 1800's, important improvements in microscopes made more rapid advances possible. Meanwhile, biology had been divided into **botany** (the study of

blood circulates has formed the foundation of the science of **physiology** (how living organisms work). It raised many questions: What does the blood carry on its rounds, and why? How and where does it pick up its loads? How, where, and why does it give them up? And what does it bring back? The main task

A model of one of Leeuwenhoek's microscopes. The scale shows size. Object was placed on the needle point, and viewed through a lens set in the center hole of the flat stage at left.

Inches 1 2 3

plants) and **zoology** (the study of animals). And it had made progress in various ways.

▶**BIOLOGY AFTER THE RENAISSANCE**

The 1600's and 1700's were periods of worldwide exploration. And so the need arose for cataloging and describing in an orderly way the great variety of animals and plants that were being collected. This was early undertaken by John Ray, an English naturalist; he paved the way for the great work of Carolus Linnaeus of Sweden.

Linnaeus and Classification

Linnaeus' scheme for classifying and describing living things was adopted by naturalists in all countries. He described the parts of an animal or a plant in a regular and sensible way, according to definite rules; he also drew up a scheme in which all kinds of plants and animals had their place. Thus, plants were divided into classes, and classes into orders, according to the number and arrangement of the parts in the flower. Animals were grouped as the classes of Mammals, Birds, Reptiles, Fish, Insects, and Vermes, the last name meaning "worms." Linnaeus also developed the system of giving every living thing two Latin names, first of the genus and second of the species, as in *Homo sapiens* for man.

However, Linnaeus chiefly observed, described, and classified the external (outside) characteristics of plants and animals. It was the French anatomist Georges Cuvier who showed the importance of the structure and relations of the inner parts of the animal body.

Cuvier and the Correlation of Parts

Cuvier was actually more concerned with structure than function—that is, with **morphology** rather than physiology. But his great contribution was his principle of the correlation of parts. This principle states that if we know the structure of a certain organ or part of an animal, we can reconstruct the whole. For example, if we have a feather or a certain kind of bone, we can be sure that it belonged only to a bird. If we find a certain kind of tooth, we can safely say that it belonged to a mammal and to no other kind of animal. This principle has been very useful in the study of fossils, or **paleontology**. Here we often have small parts of an animal. Yet

Cuvier in his laboratory. On his left is a microscope of the early 1800's. In the background is a fossil elephant's skeleton. Cuvier excelled in rebuilding extinct animals from a few bones.

from these fragments it is usually possible to work out the structure of the whole.

This process of comparing and contrasting the structures of living things is known as **taxonomy**. It occupied many biologists during the first half of the 1800's. Other biological advances took place during the same time. And this period saw the slow coming together of various separate approaches into what we now regard as modern biology. These approaches were principally: the development of the general theory of evolution; the devel-

RED-FOOTED BOOBY

FUR SEAL

GALÁPAGOS PENGUIN

GALÁPAGOS TORTOISE

PELICAN

FLAMINGO

LAND IGUANA

By studying the animals of the lonely Galápagos Islands, "a little world in itself," Charles Darwin got important ideas for his world-shaking book *The Origin of Species.*

opment of the cell theory; and a deepening understanding of the living organism as a functioning mechanism.

▶ THE THEORY OF EVOLUTION

Animals and plants have slowly changed, one way or another, throughout the ages. That is, they have undergone **evolution**, and simpler kinds have given rise to more complex kinds. That idea grew slowly. It was based in part on this realization: Living things can be arranged in some order from simple to complex. Aristotle long ago drew up his "ladder of nature," with simple forms of life at the bottom and man at the top. The vast information acquired during the early 1800's about animal and plant structures unmistakably pointed to an orderly and evolutionary pattern of relationships.

The Forerunners: Lamarck and Lyell

The Chevalier de Lamarck, a French zoologist, was among the first to propose such an idea. He suggested that animals had not always been as they are today. Rather, the various kinds had undergone progressive change; the cause had been changing external circumstances. During the same period the Scottish geologist Charles Lyell added im-

portant evidence. Lyell was an expert on rocks and fossils. He showed that each layer of rocks contained its own distinctive fossil remains of animals and plants. And the nature of the fossils showed a gradual change within succeeding layers. The idea of evolution and the evidence of progressive change were therefore being discussed by scientists in 1830. This was just before young Charles Darwin set out on his famous voyage aboard the *Beagle.* That 5-year voyage led to Darwin's theory of evolution.

Darwin's Theory of Evolution

Darwin himself later wrote that three things above all influenced him in favor of the idea of evolution. These were:

(1) The discovery of fossil remains of giant armored animals clearly related to the small living South American armadillos.

(2) The way in which species of animals gave way to close relatives as Darwin went south.

(3) His experience in the Galápagos Islands. These are young, volcanic islands in the equatorial Pacific Ocean. They are far removed from continental land. On them live peculiar kinds of giant tortoises and lizards, and various birds, including some flightless

sea birds. The significant fact was this: The tortoises and certain birds were common to all the islands but were in small ways different on each particular island. It became clear that since the group of islands had first acquired its animals and plants, those on each separate island had undergone change.

So the principle of evolution was firmly established in Darwin's mind. He spent the 20 years after his voyage building up an immense quantity of evidence in support of the theory. He published it in 1859 in his book *The Origin of Species*.

Darwin finally showed that:

(1) The offspring of every kind of living thing vary among themselves.

(2) Every kind breeds to excess, and the numbers are continually cut down through the struggle for survival.

(3) The result is a process of natural selection of some varieties rather than others. This causes a race or species to adapt to its external conditions.

The general theory of evolution stated that all living things are related to one another and that the animal and plant kingdoms have each had an immensely long and changing past. The theory rapidly became one of the most influential ideas in the history of human thought.

The general theory of evolution was the outcome of a broad, far-reaching study of living things. Other biological advances came about in very different ways. One of these depended on improvements in the microscope. And it led to the development and acceptance of the **cell theory**.

▶ THE CELL THEORY

The microscopists of the 1600's had studied infusions—liquids made by boiling hay or dead leaves in water. When the infusions were allowed to stand awhile, a large variety of microscopic organisms could be seen swimming about in them; these organisms were called infusorians.

In the 1800's, through the use of better microscopes, microscopists slowly came to an important conclusion: Almost all organisms that can be seen without a microscope are aggregates (collections) of cells, while the infusorian organisms consist of single cells. Biologists gradually recognized that organisms consist of one cell or of many cells. In living things the cell is the unit of construction.

Also, during the first part of the 1800's, it was seen that each cell has a central nucleus; this was regarded as the controller of the cell. It was seen that living matter is a sticky, slimy substance with very definite optical, chemical, and physical qualities; this substance was given the name protoplasm. And it was recognized by Theodor Schwann that all eggs are cells, whatever their size may be.

Schwann, a German, concluded that an entire animal or plant is composed either of cells or of cells and substances thrown off by cells; that cells have a life that is to some extent their own; and that this individual life of all the cells is under the control of the organism as a whole. Those are three of the widest general conclusions reached in biology. We must add to them the conclusion of Rudolf Virchow, a German: Every cell originates from a cell. Together these constitute the cell theory.

▶ DEEPER UNDERSTANDING OF LIVING FORMS

One other major development in biological science took place during the first half of the 1800's. It lay in applying chemistry to investigations into the nature of living processes.

Liebig's Work

Baron Justus von Liebig in Germany classified foods in relation to their use in the animal body—that is, as fats, carbohydrates, and proteins. He taught that plants obtain carbon dioxide and ammonia in the atmosphere and from ammonia and nitrates absorbed through their root systems. He taught that these substances are eventually returned to the atmosphere and soil through the process of decay. He claimed that carbon dioxide,

Plant cells (much enlarged) contain chloroplasts (dark spots) that make starch out of carbon dioxide and water.

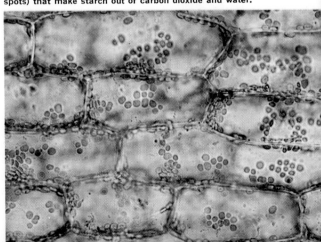

ammonia, and water contained all the necessary elements for the production of vegetable matter. And, he said, these substances were used over and over again through death and decay. Liebig adopted the term "chlorophyll," which is Greek for "green leaf," and used the term as a name for the green pigment of plants. Somewhat later Julius von Sachs, another student of plant nutrition, showed that chlorophyll is not spread all through the plant cell; it is confined within small bodies called chloroplasts. He also showed that sunlight is needed for chloroplasts to absorb carbon dioxide.

Pasteur's Work

In the middle 1800's Louis Pasteur in Paris discovered the cause of fermentation and decay. The changes were caused by the activity of microscopic organisms. He then turned to the question of the origin of these organisms. By 1859 Pasteur was engaged in a scientific argument concerning the origin of such living things. In a beautifully simple experiment he put some fermentable fluid in a flask; he heated the neck of the flask and drew it out into a long, narrow S with an open

Louis Pasteur sealed boiled fluid in a flask to show that life does not start up by itself.

end. Next, he boiled the fluid repeatedly to kill anything alive. Finally, he left it to stand for several months. Nothing happened. Pasteur broke the neck of the flask, thus exposing the fluid to the fall of atmospheric dust. Within a few hours fermentation started, and organisms were discovered swimming about in the liquid; they arose from spores (seed-like cells) drifting about in the atmosphere. The old belief that such life sprang into being without a cause could be held no longer.

▶ THE START OF MODERN BIOLOGY

The modern period of biology begins about 1860. It begins with the launching, almost at the same time, of Darwin's theory of organic evolution and Pasteur's theory of **biogenesis** (that is, living matter always arises through already existing living matter). In that same period, in an Austrian monastery garden, the Abbé Mendel was performing his famous breeding experiments concerning hereditary features of pea and bean plants. However, his experiments did not become generally known until 1900; so, in effect, they belong to a later period.

Within 20 years following 1860 the whole outlook of biology underwent a complete change. The causes were:

(1) The discovery that plants and animals reproduce in basically the same way—by means of sex cells.

(2) The discovery that living substance, or protoplasm, is similar in both plants and animals.

(3) The discovery that processes of nutrition and respiration (breathing) are practically the same in all living things.

(4) The recognition that plants use the chlorophyll apparatus to make their food and so, indirectly, the food of animals.

(5) The realization that the cell is the unit of life in all organisms.

(6) The evolutionary view of life.

(7) The realization that all living organisms come from living organisms; life, therefore, has been continuous throughout the ages.

During this later part of the 1800's biologists gave great attention to the evolutionary relationships of animals and plants, both living and extinct. They studied the development of eggs and embryos, and whole life histories in the hope that more light would be thrown on evolutionary history. And they turned to the working of the animal body. The studies of the French physiologist Claude Bernard were outstanding here.

Bernard discovered, for instance, that the liver builds up substances obtained from the blood, stores them, and breaks down substances for distribution to the body. Bernard also introduced an extremely important idea: The various forms of body activity are closely related and respond to the body's general needs. He emphasized the importance of what is called "the internal environment of the body." It consists of (1) neighboring cells and their products, (2) substances contributed by the blood, (3) substances thrown off by the cells and removed by the blood, and (4) the messages, or impulses, brought by nerves. Modern physiological research is mainly the continuing investigation of those four areas.

▶ BIOLOGY TODAY

During the 1900's, biology has developed along several major lines. In physiology, great advances have been made in our understanding of the nervous system (the brain and the nerves). The physiology of the nervous system is known as **neurophysiology**. Studies in this field show that nerves function by means of an electrochemical system. Messages, or nerve impulses, moving along nerve fibers are electrical currents. At the junction, or **synapse**, of two nerve fibers, chemicals control whether or not the impulse will move from one nerve to another. These chemicals are called **neurotransmitters**.

This electrochemical system produces a very complex network of nerve impulses moving constantly through the body. The nervous system is now known to be in direct or indirect control of all that goes on in the body. The beating of the heart, the moving of a limb, and the learning of algebra are examples of the many activities controlled by the brain. Many mental states, such as happiness or sadness, can sometimes be controlled by the brain. And these mental states may sometimes act through the brain to affect the body.

Much of the new knowledge about the functioning of the nervous system has been made possible because of new techniques and in-

Research technician adjusts an electron microscope.

struments. Tiny needlelike probes inserted into nerve tissue help to track nerve impulses. A new chemical technique, called **fluorescence histochemistry**, has enabled scientists to identify and measure tiny amounts of some neurotransmitter chemicals in the brain. This growing knowledge of neurotransmitters may point the way to new treatments for certain diseases, particularly mental disease.

Knowledge of microscopic cell structure has grown continually as microscopes have improved or changed. Some of the most important advances in **cytology** (the study of cells) were made toward the end of the 1800's. They were made through improvements in various techniques of staining and in the use of the microscope. As a result, the fine detail of the mechanism of cell division was observed. It was observed both in the cell as a whole and in the nucleus with its chromosomes. Division of the nucleus was seen to be so exact that each resulting nucleus was the image of the parent nucleus.

Improvements in ordinary (light) microscopes provided better and better views of bacteria. Then in 1939 a new kind of microscope, which provided the first view of viruses, was developed. This was the electron microscope. The powerful electron microscope can magnify an object 200,000 times. It reveals

Linus Pauling, Nobel prizewinner in chemistry, has studied the structure of giant molecules (model at left).

parts of the cell not visible with the best magnification of the light microscope. In the 1960's and 1970's, the scanning electron microscope (SEM) and the scanning transmission electron microscope (STEM) provided three-dimensional views of microscopic objects.

Studies of the cell were extended to the reproductive cells of both sexes. The chromosomes of the cell nucleus were recognized as the bearers of the hereditary agents, called **genes**. The science of heredity is called **genetics**.

During the first half of the 1900's, geneticists carried out extensive breeding experiments with plants and with a kind of fruit fly called *Drosophila*. At the same time they investigated the nucleus of the sex cells of these organisms. Further progress in this field has come from the study of bacteria and viruses. These studies have given scientists a good understanding of heredity.

Scientists now know that bacteria reproduce by a process much like that of plants and animals. But viruses can reproduce only when they are inside bacterial cells or the cells of plant or animal tissues. Scientists know also that viruses are able to transfer hereditary qualities from one cell to another. Work with viruses and bacteria has become the center of the newest genetic research.

While the geneticists were studying the functioning of the cell, chemists were using new instruments to unravel the structure of the huge chemical molecules in the cell. This new science is called **molecular biology**.

The major discovery in molecular biology was that chromosomes are made of very long molecules of a chemical called DNA (deoxyribonucleic acid). Parts of each DNA molecule are the genes. Chemists soon discovered that by using certain chemicals, they could split genes away from the DNA. A single gene —a fragment of DNA from one form of life— could then be recombined with the DNA of another form of life. The result would be a new kind of DNA, known as **recombinant DNA**. Such re-arrangement of genes is called **genetic engineering**.

When it is put into a form of life such as a bacterium, recombinant DNA would give that life a new gene. The bacterium would then be a new bacterium. And it would multiply into many more of this new bacterium. In effect, recombinant DNA gives scientists the ability to redesign life. This ability frightens many people. One reason is that new bacteria might prove to be disease organisms. But recombinant DNA also holds the promise for many benefits. Already scientists have used it to produce a bacterium that makes a hormone vital for treating a disease of the pituitary gland.

In the 1960's, 1970's, and 1980's, we have learned a great deal more about the many species of life around us. Special techniques, such as radio tracking of animals, and instruments, such as computers, have helped provide much of the information we now have. From Aristotle's notes about fish life to radio tracking of a sea gull, biology has come full circle—back to the study of living creatures.

N. J. BERRILL
Author, *Biology in Action*

See also BIOCHEMISTRY; CELLS; DARWIN, CHARLES ROBERT; EVOLUTION; FERMENTATION; FOSSILS; GENETICS; HARVEY, WILLIAM; MEDICINE, HISTORY OF; MICROBIOLOGY; PASTEUR, LOUIS; PHOTOSYNTHESIS; TAXONOMY.

Left: Vividly colored glowing corals are animals that live on the Great Barrier Reef off the eastern coast of Australia. *Above:* Some species, or kinds, of fireflies have light-emitting glands in their abdomens that are used to flash mating signals.

BIOLUMINESCENCE

Light from fireflies and other living things is called **bioluminescence**. There are many bioluminescent things in nature—plants, animals, and bacteria.

The glowing plants include only a few kinds, such as certain toadstools and molds. But animals that light up are more numerous; they range from tiny one-celled sea creatures to sponges, clams, worms, and insects. The most numerous glowing forms of life are found in the salt water of oceans. The most familiar forms are found on land—fireflies, glowworms, and fox fire fungus.

Bioluminescence is called "cold" light to distinguish it from incandescence, or heat-giving light. (For example, electric light bulbs, oil lamps, and candles give off "hot" light.) Living plants and animals could not produce incandescent light without being burned up. Their light is caused by chemicals combining in such a way that little or no measurable heat is given off.

The substance that gives off the light in living things is called luciferin. This "glowing" chemical was named in 1887 by one of the earliest scientists to study living light, Raphaël Dubois, of France. Dubois named this chemical substance "luciferin," meaning "light bearer." Through his experiments using the glowing fluid taken from a clam, Dubois found that the light was caused by a team of chemicals working together. Luciferin would not light up except in the presence of a second chemical, which Dubois called "luciferase."

Scientists have since learned that living light is produced when luciferin and oxygen combine in the presence of luciferase. Other substances are also needed to produce light in some living things, such as adenosine triphosphate (ATP) in fireflies. It is the additional substances that give the light a range of color from yellow to blue, green, and red.

In some cases, the function of the light seems obvious. Marine fireworms use glowing light as mating signals. During the mating season, the female fireworms come up from deep waters to the surface of the sea and glow. Seeing the light, the males join the females. A mating dance follows and then both sexes release their reproductive cells into the water.

Bulblike organs, called photophores, on the bodies of many deep-sea fish attract mates or prey and illuminate the search for them in the darkness of the ocean depths. Some luminescent fish zigzag through the water with lights flashing to confuse predators and escape being eaten. In other cases, such as the many blind light-emitting deep-sea species, the light seems to have no function.

Much remains to be learned about the chemistry of bioluminescence. Perhaps some day enough will be known to produce this cold light for everyday use instead of the energy-wasting electric light we use now.

W. D. McElroy
Author, *Light: Physical and Biological Action*

Large herds of zebras and wildebeests roam across the vast grasslands, or savannas, of Africa, grazing on the abundant plant life that includes a variety of grasses.

BIOMES

The hot, humid rain forest, the dry desert, and the icy tundra all have something in common: Each one is a biome. A biome is a community of specific types of plants and animals that covers a large area of the earth's surface. Each biome is made up of many **habitats**—the places where a particular plant or animal normally lives and grows. The type of biome in a region is generally determined by the kind of climate in that region. Deserts cover dry regions. Rain forests cover hot, humid regions. Tundras cover cold and icy, dry regions.

On every continent except Antarctica, most of the different kinds of biomes can be found. Each place has unique species of plants and animals, yet the plants and animals of a particular biome, all around the world, tend to be similar. For example, spine-covered cacti are common plants in the deserts of the American Southwest. In African deserts, plants called euphorbs grow in abundance. Euphorbs have fleshy, leafless stems and prickly spines, very much like the American cacti. Euphorbs and cacti have developed similar adaptations that allow them to live in the hot, dry desert biome. Similarities among plant species in biomes around the world allow scientists to identify the different kinds of biomes. Scientists also study a biome's **ecology**; that is, the interactions of living things with the environment and with each other.

▶KINDS OF BIOMES

The major land biomes include the following: grasslands; deserts; chaparral; deciduous forests; coniferous forests; tundra; and tropical rain forests. Aquatic biomes also exist in rivers, lakes, ponds, and in the oceans. However, this article concentrates on the land biomes.

Grasslands

Known as prairies in North America, savannas in central Africa, steppes in central Asia, and pampas in South America, grasslands are among the earth's richest biomes. The world's main agricultural crops, including corn, wheat, oats, and barley, were all bred from grasses—the main plants in the grassland environment.

Grasslands are found in climates slightly drier than the climates that support deciduous forests. Average rainfall in the grasslands varies from 10 to 40 inches (254 to 1,016 millimeters) annually. Fires, which can destroy deciduous forests, cause grasslands to thrive. Burned grasses enrich the soil and allow new plants to grow. Some grassland wildflowers cannot sprout unless their seeds are exposed to a fire's searing heat. Fires also keep certain plants from growing that would change the grassland environment, such as deciduous trees.

Grasslands that receive the most rain produce tall, dense grasses, as in America's tall-grass prairies. Grasses there can reach heights of 12 feet (3.7 meters). Early settlers riding through the grasslands had to stand up in the stirrups of their saddles to spot their cows grazing in these tall grasses. Grasslands that receive the least precipitation have short grasses. Short-grass prairies are dotted with clumps of grasses that grow less than 2 feet (0.6 meters) tall. Grasslands also include wildflowers, which add vibrant color to the green backdrop. An occasional shrub or tree dots the landscape, springing up in places where there is adequate moisture.

The dominant grassland animals are grazers. In Africa, millions of gazelles, zebras, and wildebeests migrate across the savannas, each grazing on a different part of the grass plant. Predators, including lions, tigers, and hyenas, stalk the old and sick grazing animals. Vultures feed on the decaying carcasses while insects strip the bones clean. In their natural state, grasslands support the largest herds of animals in the world.

Deserts

Regions that receive less than 10 inches (254 millimeters) of rain each year are generally classified as deserts. Desert rains are infrequent. Sometimes it will only rain once or twice a year. When it does rain, a great quantity of rain may fall so rapidly that a quick, heavy flood (called a flash flood) occurs. Deserts also tend to have extreme variations in temperatures. Days are very hot, but temperatures plummet at night, sometimes dipping down below freezing. Desert plants and animals have to be quite hardy to adapt to these difficult conditions.

Succulents, plants that store water in their leaves or stems, are among the major plants of the deserts. Cacti and euphorbs are two different types of succulents. Shrubs with small leathery or waxy leaves also thrive in some desert environments. These plants may shed their leaves and remain dormant through the desert's harshest seasons. Some desert plants live short lives, sprouting, flowering, setting seed, and dying in the few days during and after a heavy rain. The seeds of these plants lie dormant in the sand for months or years until adequate rain once again falls.

Desert animals must also find ways to adapt to the extreme dryness and heat. Many rest in their underground burrows during the day and only come out at night. Others, such as certain iguanas and other types of lizards, are active during the day. They spend most of their time out of the sun, venturing from the shade of one plant only to scurry to the shade of another. Some animals can survive with very little water. The kangaroo rat is one animal that does not need water to drink. It gets its water from the seeds and leaves it eats.

Chaparral

Scattered along certain coastal areas is the chaparral biome. The Mediterranean coast, the coast of southern California, the coast of central Chile, the southern tip of Africa, and the southern coast of Australia all are covered by chaparral. Like the desert, the chaparral gets little rainfall. Some regions average as little as 10 inches (254 millimeters) of rain a year, all of which falls during the winter months. However, warm, moist air from the oceans helps balance the chaparral environment and prevents conditions from being as severe as those in the desert.

The main plants of the chaparral are tough evergreen shrubs with small leathery leaves. Animals adapted to a dry climate, including lizards, rodents, rabbits, hawks, and owls, inhabit the chaparral. Deer and songbirds migrate to the chaparral during the wet winters, when food is more plentiful.

The scattered evergreen shrubs of the chaparral, which are the plants found most often in this dry coastal biome, help prevent soil erosion.

During the hot, rainless summers, brush-fires often rage across the chaparral. However, chaparral plants are well adapted to what would be a disaster in other places. Many species produce fire-resistant seeds. Others send shoots from the base of charred stumps. It takes as little as ten years for a burned area of chaparral to recover completely.

Deciduous Forests

Spanning eastern North America, central Europe, eastern China, and the southeast coast of Australia, deciduous forests grace the land. Such forests are made up of trees that grow and shed their leaves in a distinct seasonal pattern. In spring the trees bud, in summer they grow, in autumn they lose their leaves, and in winter they stand dormant. Ample rain falls throughout the year, averaging about 40 inches (1,016 millimeters) annually. In this constantly changing environment, many different types of plants and animals flourish.

Deciduous forests, such as the maple-beech forests of North America, tend to have rich soil that supports numerous types of plants. Shrubs grow in the shade of the leafy maple and birch trees. Ferns, flowers, and mosses carpet the floor of the deciduous forest. Mushrooms and other fungi grow on rotting leaves and logs.

Animal life, too, is quite abundant in these woods. Earthworms and insects tunnel through the dark, moist soil. Songbirds flit among the tree branches and on the ground. Amphibians, such as newts and salamanders, scurry through the thick cover of fallen leaves. Deer browse and rodents burrow. Predators, such as foxes, weasels, and bobcats, stalk their prey. Such activity, especially during the summer months, makes deciduous forests inviting places in which to study wildlife.

In the winter, when the trees have shed their leaves and the woods stand under a blanket of snow, life in the forest slows down. Many living things adapt to the cold by becoming dormant. Some mammals hibernate, burrowing in dens for a long

Snowy owl

Pronghorn antelope

Black bear

American elk

Raccoon

Rufus hummingbird

Bell's vireo

Mountain Biomes

Every mountain creates its own set of biomes. As the climate changes with the altitude, so does the biome. One mountain may have as many as five different biomes.

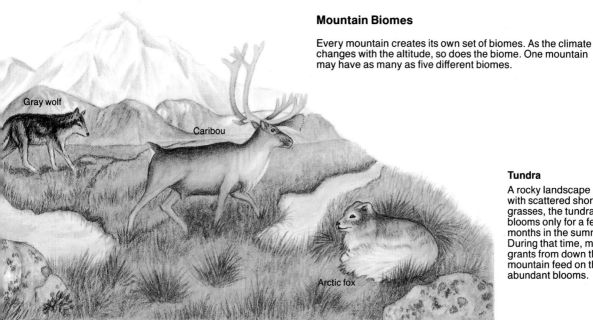

Tundra

A rocky landscape with scattered short grasses, the tundra blooms only for a few months in the summer. During that time, migrants from down the mountain feed on the abundant blooms.

Grasslands

The coniferous forest meets the grassland at the tree line. In summer, many animals migrate above the tree line. In winter, however, the harsh weather drives most animals down from the grasslands to the forests below.

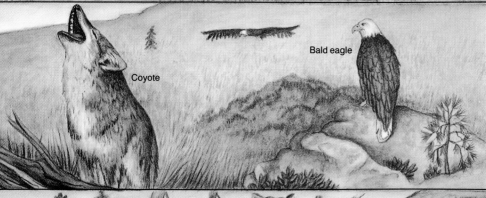

Coniferous Forests

The colder, drier coniferous forest lies upslope from the deciduous forest. Many animals shelter in the coniferous forest during the winter months. They move up to the grasslands during the summer.

Deciduous Forests

The deciduous forest carpets the foothills of the mountain. The forest provides ample food for many types of animals, including hummingbirds, vireos, deer, raccoons, and squirrels.

period of inactivity. Others, including three quarters of the birds, migrate, spending the winter in warmer climates. A few, including sparrows, raccoons, and rabbits, stay through the winter, searching out food as best they can.

Coniferous Forests

Coniferous forests are forests that are largely made up of cone-bearing trees. There are two distinct types of coniferous forest biomes: the temperate coniferous forest and the northern coniferous, or boreal, forest.

The temperate coniferous forest is found in moist, coastal environments, including the northern Pacific coast of North America and the eastern coast of Australia. These forests contain the largest trees in the world—the giant sequoia trees of California, which are also called redwoods, and the towering eucalyptus trees of Australia. The boreal forests are much more extensive than the temperate coniferous forests. They stretch across the northern reaches of North America, Europe, and Asia. In these regions, winters are long and cold. The short, cool summers allow only a brief growing season.

Pine, spruce, hemlock, and fir trees are the most common trees in the boreal forests. All have needle-like leaves that help prevent water loss in the cold, dry winter air. The soil in

During the summer months, a wide variety of animals—elk, moose, birds, rabbits, and insects—populate the coniferous forest, feeding on tree leaves and grasses.

coniferous forests tends to be acidic, and few types of plants can grow in it. Blueberry shrubs and heather plants, however, thrive in the acidic soil.

Many different types of animals live in the boreal forests, especially in the warmer summer months. Moose, elk, and deer browse on tree leaves. Migratory birds eat the plentiful insects, which hatch in the late spring and summer. Porcupines gnaw on pine bark. Snowshoe hares, whose coats change so that they blend in with both summer's fallen leaves and winter's blanket of snow, dart from under cover. Wolverines and bears stalk their prey.

Tundra

North of the boreal forest lies the tundra. Under this treeless region is a layer of frozen ground more than 1,000 feet (305 meters) thick, called permafrost. The soil on top of the permafrost thaws for only eight weeks during the short Arctic summer. The small flowering plants and dwarf trees of the tundra have to grow, bloom, and set seed quickly to survive. The outburst of growth in the tundra during the summer creates a colorful carpet of low-lying flowers that dazzles the eye. Adding to the colorful display are the numerous types of lichens, which are really a combination of algae and fungi living and growing together, that cover the rocky landscape.

Not many animals spend the long winter months in the tundra. Some small rodents, such as lemmings, have adapted to the harsh winter environment. Arctic foxes, wolves, and polar bears also stay feeding on whatever they can find during the quiet winter months.

When summer comes, the tundra once again teems with life. Herds of caribou and also reindeer graze on the tundra's quick-growing grasses. Flocks of migrating birds make the tundra their destination. Many birds feed on the numerous insects that hatch in the ponds and puddles of the tundra's soggy ground. As summer fades away, the caribou and many other mammals travel to the forests and the birds fly south. The tundra again becomes a snowy, silent world.

Tropical Rain Forests

Tropical rain forests are damp, humid places where lush, leafy plants abound. In most tropical rain forests, annual rainfall averages between 80 and 200 inches (2,032 and

MAJOR BIOMES OF THE WORLD

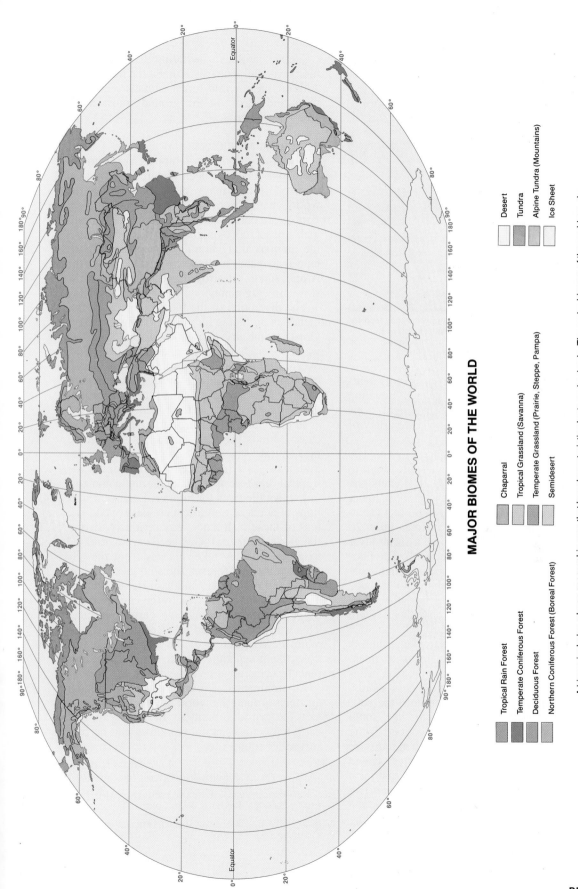

Tropical Rain Forest

Temperate Coniferous Forest

Deciduous Forest

Northern Coniferous Forest (Boreal Forest)

Chaparral

Tropical Grassland (Savanna)

Temperate Grassland (Prairie, Steppe, Pampa)

Semidesert

Desert

Tundra

Alpine Tundra (Mountains)

Ice Sheet

A biome includes a large geographic area that has characteristic plants and animals. The major biomes of the world are shown on the map above. Each biome has a certain type of climate and soil to which plants and animals of the region have adapted.

The continued destruction of the rain forest may lead to such dramatic climate changes that life in all of the other biomes around the world will be threatened.

5,080 millimeters). The rain falls evenly year-round. Temperatures hardly vary, hovering just below 80°F (27°C) day and night. This steady environment has the greatest variety of plant and animal species of all the biomes.

The leafy branches of tall trees, 75 to 100 feet (23 to 30 meters) in height, spread out to form a canopy that shades and shelters the tropical rain forest. Beneath the canopy, lower trees form leafy umbrellas 40 to 60 feet (12 to 18 meters) tall. A few smaller trees grow 20 to 30 feet (6 to 9 meters) above a shrub layer that is at most 10 feet (3 meters) tall. The floor of the rain forest receives so little light that only plants able to grow in almost total shade can live there. Thick jungle growth occurs only along river edges or other places where light easily penetrates to the ground.

The most lively part of the tropical rain forest is the canopy and upper layers of trees. Colorful flowers use the higher tree branches as platforms to reach the sun. These plants, called epiphytes, send no roots into the soil. They get their nutrients from the small amounts of dirt and dust that collect in the forks of tree branches. They gather moisture from the misty air. Some epiphytes, called bromeliads, have overlapping leaves that form a cup at their base. The bromeliad cup can hold several quarts of water to nourish the plant. These miniature ponds are the breeding grounds for snails, insects, and tiny frogs.

Larger animals, including lizards, birds, monkeys, and leopards, inhabit the rain forest. Although a few rain forest animals search for roots and seeds on the ground, most dwell solely in the trees.

▶ THE CHANGING BIOMES

These descriptions of biomes apply to regions that have not been disturbed by human activity. But in many places throughout the world, nature's biomes have been altered. Forests are cut down for farms. Domestic animals are set loose on grasslands, crowding out the animals that naturally live there. Desert land is irrigated to grow crops. Oil rigs in the Arctic tundra destroy large patches of the slow-growing plants.

The disruption of the biomes can cause tremendous problems for people living in the regions. In the dry grasslands of the Sahel, in western Africa, domestic goats and sheep have overgrazed the land. The thin layer of topsoil has blown away and the Sahel is becoming a desert. This process, called desertification, threatens other parts of the world.

In other places, disturbing the biomes may cause serious problems in the future. People in Central America, South America, and Southeast Asia have been burning down the tropical rain forests to make farmland and cutting down the trees for lumber. Each year millions of acres of rain forest are destroyed. The loss of these lush lands may seriously disrupt the global climate. Plants need carbon dioxide to grow and they take this gas from the air. Without the rain forests, the amount of carbon dioxide in the air will increase tremendously. This gas holds heat close to the earth, warming the atmosphere and the earth's surface. This warming is called the **greenhouse effect**. With the destruction of the tropical rain forests, the greenhouse effect could cause our planet to heat up at an unhealthy rate.

Environmental groups and government agencies around the world are working to protect the world's biomes. In this way, the earth's precious natural resources can be preserved for future life.

ELIZABETH KAPLAN
Author, *Biology Bulletin Monthly*

See also DESERTS; ECOLOGY; FORESTS AND FORESTRY; GRASSES; PRAIRIES; RAIN FOREST; TUNDRA.

BIOSPHERE. See LIFE (Living Things and Their Environments).

Each day, no matter what kind of environment you are in, you will see some kind of bird. It may be a pair of courting swans (*left*), a proud sparrow hawk with its prey (*below left*), or some helpful oxpeckers plucking parasites off a black rhinoceros (*below*).

BIRDS

Throughout the ages, birds have been a source of wonder to all who have observed their soaring flight or listened to their sweet song. As a group, birds are unique—they are the only animals covered with feathers. This evolutionary development separates birds from all other animals.

Birds can travel faster than any other animal —the fastest bird can fly more than 100 miles (161 kilometers) per hour! Although all birds have feathers and wings, not every bird can fly. Some birds walk, run, or swim instead of flying.

Birds are **vertebrates** (animals with a backbone), as are fish, amphibians, reptiles, and mammals. Like many vertebrates, birds lay eggs from which their young hatch. They are warm-blooded animals; that is, their body temperature always remains about the same no matter what the temperature of their surroundings. They differ from other vertebrates in that they are toothless and have a hard beak, or bill, that they use to get and eat food.

The more than 9,000 kinds, or species, of birds belong to the class of animals called Aves. Because of their superb flying skills, birds have been able to reach virtually every area of the world: forests, mountains, oceans, and deserts. Birds have adapted to a great variety of habitats, living in places too harsh for people or any other animal. The large snowy owl is able to survive in the Arctic, where temperatures dip below −50°F (−46°C) during the long winter. Its thick feather coat even covers its bill and feet. Birds are able to live in the middle of the world's oceans. The albatross family lives most of its life on the wing, soaring over the open ocean searching for food. It only comes to shore to build a nest and to breed.

▶BIRDS AND PEOPLE

Birds as Food. Humans have hunted birds since prehistoric times. Along with hunting birds, early humans also gathered bird eggs and nestlings (babies).

People eventually learned to tame and raise birds, and over time this has led to the domes-

Probably the greatest use of feathers was by native Hawaiians. Helmets, staffs, and huge feather cloaks (*above left*) were made for royal chiefs from the feathers of native honeycreepers. Since ancient times, people have engaged in the sport of hunting with trained birds of prey, such as the eagle (*above right*). Macaws (*left*) and other brightly colored tropical birds are among the most prized bird pets.

tication of several species: ducks, chickens, turkeys, and pigeons. Domestic ducks, a form of the mallard, appeared in Egypt around 1500 B.C. and spread quickly to Europe. Greylag geese were also domesticated at about the same time. Even earlier, people in Southeast Asia had tamed the red junglefowl, a bird recognized today as a chicken. Native Americans in Mexico and Central America successfully domesticated the wild turkey. Pigeons were domesticated in Europe and were used as food and to carry messages since Roman times. Birds, both wild and domestic, continue to be an important source of food today.

Products from Birds. The people of many societies used, and some still use, the feathers and skins of wild birds. Eagle feathers were exchanged much like money in some native North American tribes. The feather cloak of the Hawaiian king Kamehameha I took at least a hundred years to make and used about

450,000 feathers from more than 80,000 birds! It is not surprising that the king collected taxes from his subjects in honeycreeper feathers. The Inuit people of the Arctic use waterfowl feathers for pillows and clothing. The skins, especially eider skins, are used to make warm and waterproof blankets. On the other side of the world, the aborigines of Australia still wear feathers of cockatoos and emus as decoration.

Birds in Religion, Art, and Literature. Birds are powerful symbols used to represent everything from peace (the dove carrying an olive branch) to wisdom (the wise owl) to politics (the bald eagle that is the national symbol of the United States).

From the earliest times, birds have played almost as great a role in people's religion and art as in their diet. The religious paintings of early humans on the walls of Lascaux Cave near Montignac, France, include birds among the animals depicted. Ancient Egyptians used birds in their art. Painting and sculptures of birds adorn buildings and tombs of royalty.

Birds are also found in early literature. The Bible mentions almost forty species of birds—most often doves—in ways that show a knowledge of their habits and an appreciation of their grace and beauty. The religion of the Egyptians has many gods, including real and imaginary birds. They believed in the legendary phoenix, a bird that serves as a symbol of immortality. The ibis was so sacred that they were often mummified and buried with royalty in their family tombs.

Birds as Pets. Birds are also popular pets. Except for dogs and cats, more people have pet birds than any other animal. People share their homes with an amazing variety of birds, including finches, waxbills, and parrots.

The great horned owl fans its feathers in a defensive threat display. Along with their use as a defense measure, feathers keep birds warm and help them fly.

▶ WHAT MAKES A BIRD A BIRD?

All animals share certain characteristics, such as having the ability to move about and needing food to live. Some animals even share the same methods for performing these tasks and securing those substances that are necessary for life. However, birds are unique. There is no other animal with the same combination of features.

Feathers

Other animals have wings and can fly, but no other creature is covered with feathers. Feathers, which are formed in special skin cells from a protein called keratin, perform many different jobs. Body, or contour, feathers smooth and streamline the bird's body so it can move easily through the air or water. Contour feathers also protect the bird's skin from wind and, sometimes, from water. Beneath the contour feathers are tiny down feathers. Down acts as an insulator to help the bird maintain its body temperature even in temperatures below zero. In addition to contour and down feathers are filoplume feathers, which provide information on the position of movable feathers, and bristles that form eyelashes, which provide sensory information in much the same manner as a cat's whiskers.

Molting. Molting is a process that involves shedding thousands of feathers, and then growing new ones. Most birds molt twice each year: before the spring migration and after nesting. Replacing all of a bird's feathers is a

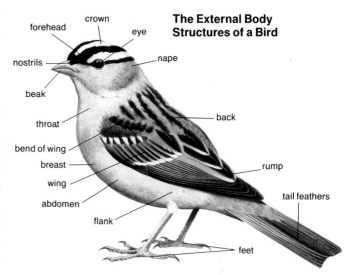

The External Body Structures of a Bird

crown
forehead
eye
nostrils
nape
beak
throat
back
bend of wing
breast
wing
abdomen
rump
flank
tail feathers
feet

How a Feather Grows

Inside a tube called a feather sheath, the feather starts to grow. Soon a rolled up tuft of feather emerges. As the feather grows, the feather unrolls and becomes flat. Finally, the protective sheath falls away from the fully grown feather.

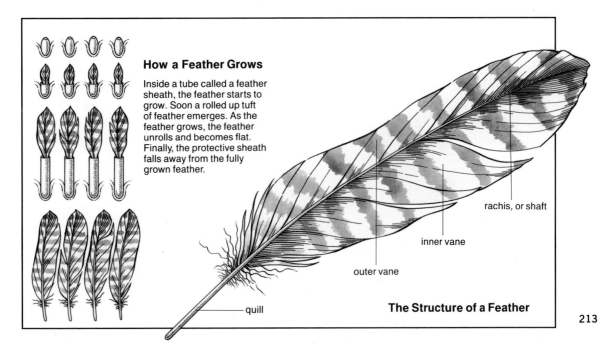

rachis, or shaft

inner vane

outer vane

quill

The Structure of a Feather

213

major undertaking—it takes a lot of energy to molt. Feathers are so important to birds that many birds do not nest a second time; instead, they save their energy for the molting process.

The spring molt replaces flight feathers that will be needed to make the long journey north to the breeding grounds. The males of many species molt their drab winter plumage and replace it with spectacular breeding colors—bold reds, yellows, oranges, and blues—that will help attract a mate.

After nesting, most species molt for the second time. The bright colors needed to attract a mate and defend a territory are now dangerous. Standing out makes it difficult to hide from and escape from predators. Ducks and geese even lose their ability to fly because they molt all of their flight feathers at once. During this period of flightlessness, and before they grow a new camouflage plumage, they hide in remote marshes.

Flight

The dominant forces that affect a bird's flight are lift and propulsion. The shape of a bird's wings helps create lift: Air moves more quickly over the curved top of the wing than it does under the flattened bottom of the wing. This difference in speed creates lower air pressure over the wing than under the wing. Because air moves from a high-pressure area to a low-pressure area, the higher pressure bottom air moves toward the lower pressure top air, lifting the wing upward. A bird can increase

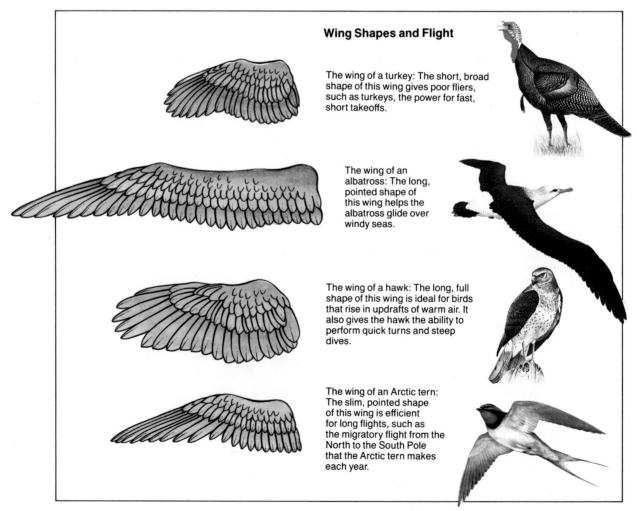

Wing Shapes and Flight

The wing of a turkey: The short, broad shape of this wing gives poor fliers, such as turkeys, the power for fast, short takeoffs.

The wing of an albatross: The long, pointed shape of this wing helps the albatross glide over windy seas.

The wing of a hawk: The long, full shape of this wing is ideal for birds that rise in updrafts of warm air. It also gives the hawk the ability to perform quick turns and steep dives.

The wing of an Arctic tern: The slim, pointed shape of this wing is efficient for long flights, such as the migratory flight from the North to the South Pole that the Arctic tern makes each year.

During the flight of the mallard duck, the bird is thrust forward by the flapping wing strokes.

or decrease the lifting force to travel up or down by tilting the forward edge of its wing upward or downward.

Propulsion, which is a forward-moving force, is created by long wing feathers that close together and overlap so air cannot pass through. In much the same manner as a boat paddle pushes against water, the closed structure of the wing pushes down against air, propelling the bird forward. On the return stroke, the wing feathers separate and allow air to pass between them.

Wing feathers are not the only feathers that aid flight. The long, strong tail feathers are used much as the tail fin of an airplane to steer while the bird is flying. The tail feathers also act as a brake when landing.

There are three basic types of flight: flapping, gliding, and soaring. Most birds use flapping flight, that is, after they take off, they continue to fly by flapping their wings. When gliding, birds keep their wings extended and coast downward. During soaring flight, birds use the energy of rising columns of warm air, called thermals, to move without having to flap their wings. With wings extended, a soaring bird circles lazily as the thermal current lifts it higher and higher. Other air movements, such as prevailing winds, are also used by birds to soar.

Walking and Running

When most people think of how birds get from place to place, they think of flight. However, there also are birds that walk, run, hop, or swim. Some birds, such as the ostrich, emu, and rhea, have evolved into flightless, swift-running birds. Typically, birds that nest and feed on the ground walk and run by moving one foot forward at a time. Most birds that nest in trees hop on both feet when they are on the ground. Some birds run and hop.

The snow goose (*above left*) uses its feathered wings for flight. Rapidly beating wings power this pair of grebes (*above*) across the water's surface during a courtship dance. The male peacock (*left*) fans its lush plumage to attract females.

A bird's legs and feet match their habits and environment. Legs serve as good shock absorbers and can launch the bird from the ground during takeoff. There is a great variety in the length of their legs. The swift-running birds have very long legs. Other birds, such as water-loving penguins, have very short legs that make walking on land difficult. Most birds have four toes—three pointing forward and one pointing backward. Some climbing birds, such as woodpeckers, have two toes pointing backward that help them to cling to tree trunks. The osprey has an outer toe that can point either forward or backward. In swifts, all the toes face forward.

Toes for grasping perches, climbing, capturing prey, and carrying and manipulating food are tipped with sharply curved and pointed nails. Strong toes for running and scratching have thick blunt nails. Toes for swimming and paddling are sometimes webbed or they may have fleshy lobes attached to them. South American jacanas appear to walk on water. Their extremely long toes spread out the bird's weight so that the bird can be supported by the underwater weeds growing near the water's surface.

hunting

perching

golden eagle

black-capped chickadee

walking

climbing

eastern meadowlark

pileated woodpecker

swimming, three webbed toes

running

common goldeneye

ostrich

The long-legged ostrich (*left*) can reach speeds of 40 miles (64 kilometers) per hour. The blue-footed booby performs a tapping dance during courtship (*below*). On its stilt-like legs, the flamingo (*below right*) wades into deep waters to feed.

Food and Feeding

Birds use their bills, flexible necks, feet, and ability to fly in order to find, secure, and eat their food. They feed on a wide variety of food—from fruit and seeds to dead animals.

A bird's bill is made up of upper and lower halves, called mandibles. The mandibles are the visible part of the bill and are made of layers of keratin, the same protein found in feathers. In most birds, the bill is black.

Bills come in a variety of shapes and sizes. Birds of prey have powerful, hooked bills to tear apart their victims. Wading birds, such as the heron, have long, sharp, daggerlike bills that they use to spear fish and frogs. Shorebirds have long, slender bills to probe mud for food. Seed-eaters have strong wedge-shaped bills to crack open the hard shells of seeds. The sawlike edges on the bill of a fish-eater, such as the merganser, is ideal for grasping and holding slippery prey.

Along with food, birds need water. Some birds, such as fruit- and insect-eaters, may get the water they need from the food they eat. Others find a water source and scoop water up in their bills. Still others have devised special ways to get water. The sand grouse lives in some of the driest deserts on earth. They travel long distances to a water source, soak the special feathers on their bellies, and carry water back to the nest. The young grouse suck on the feathers to get the water.

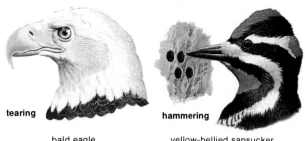

tearing

bald eagle

hammering

yellow-bellied sapsucker

spearing

black-crowned night heron

cracking

common redpoll

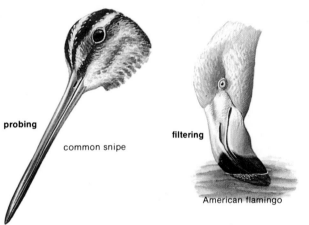

probing

common snipe

filtering

American flamingo

Many birds, such as the blue jay (*left*), feed on seeds and nuts; others, such as the western gull (*below left*), eat small water animals and insects; still others, such as the bald eagle (*below*), prey on larger animals—fish, frogs, and even other birds.

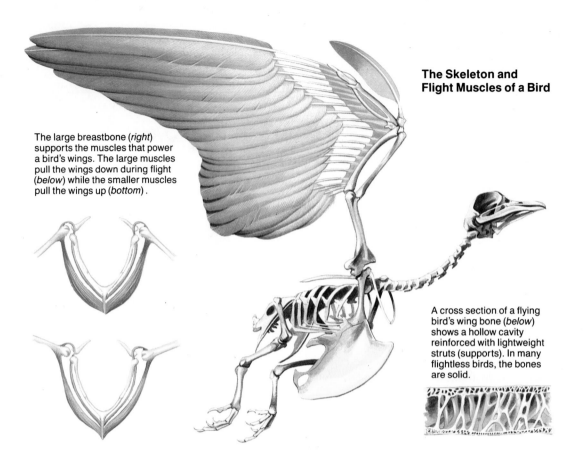

The Skeleton and Flight Muscles of a Bird

The large breastbone (*right*) supports the muscles that power a bird's wings. The large muscles pull the wings down during flight (*below*) while the smaller muscles pull the wings up (*bottom*).

A cross section of a flying bird's wing bone (*below*) shows a hollow cavity reinforced with lightweight struts (supports). In many flightless birds, the bones are solid.

▶ **THE BODY SYSTEMS OF BIRDS**

There are many physical features that are shared by birds and mammals. For instance, both groups of animals have backbones, are warm-blooded, and have four limbs. However, the body systems of birds are adapted to flight.

Bones and Muscles

Over time, the skeleton of the bird has developed into an airy, lightweight, yet strong, frame. Since the earliest birds, many body parts, such as teeth, have disappeared—lightening the frame. Other parts, such as the vertebrae of the back, have become fused (joined) —giving the frame more strength.

While a bird's many neck vertebrae are shaped so that the neck is extremely flexible, most of the rest of the skeleton has become stiffened. Birds have a large breastbone, or sternum, that protects the internal organs and provides strong support for the attached muscles that power flight. The heaviest, strongest bone is the coracoid. Together with the ribs, it holds the sternum and the rigid backbone apart when the flight muscles contract.

The largest muscles in a bird are the pectoral (breast) muscles. These muscles may account for as much as one fifth of a bird's entire weight. They are attached to the long bone of the wing. When they contract during flight, the wings are pulled down. Smaller muscles, called the supracoracoideus, contract during flight and the wings are pulled up.

Digestive System

Since birds have no teeth, the digestive system must grind up food so that the energy stored in it can be used. A hollow digestive tube extends from the mouth through the entire length of the body to an external opening called the cloaca. The tube is divided into the throat (pharynx), esophagus, stomach, small intestine, and large intestine.

Food passes from the mouth through the pharynx into the esophagus. Some birds, such as pigeons, doves, and hawks, have a portion of their esophagus enlarged to form a storage pouch called a crop. The crop allows birds to feed quickly and digest its meal later in safety.

Nearly all birds have a stomach made up of two parts. The first part of the stomach, called the proventriculus, secretes strong digestive juices, which in some birds are strong enough to digest bones! The second part of the stomach, called the gizzard, has strong muscular walls that act like teeth to grind and pulverize foods. In addition to the muscular walls, birds often swallow small pebbles and grit that get trapped in the gizzard and aid in the grinding process.

From the stomach, food passes into the small intestine where the nutritious end products of digestion are absorbed into the bloodstream. The remaining indigestible matter travels into the large intestine where it is stored until it is eliminated from the body through the cloaca.

Metabolic System

A bird's metabolic system guides all the chemical changes that provide energy for vital processes and activities such as new cell growth and maintenance of body temperature. Birds, which have a higher body temperature, a faster heart rate, and a greater need for oxygen than mammals, must eat a great deal of food to get the necessary energy to fuel the body functions. Small birds have a relatively higher metabolic rate, and therefore higher energy needs, than large birds. An ostrich can go several days without food, however, a small hummingbird needs so much energy that it must feed almost constantly during the day.

Birds are endothermal, or warm-blooded. That means they have an internal furnace, fueled by food, that generates heat and allows them to keep their bodies at a constant temperature, even though the temperature of their en-

The tiny hummingbird (*above*) requires between fifty and sixty meals a day to sustain its high metabolic rate. With wings beating at a rate of between fifty and eighty times a second, the hummingbird can hover (*right*) without rest for four hours at a time.

vironment changes. Birds are also able to regulate their body temperature by conserving or losing heat through a variety of ways—feathers help retain heat, while panting helps get rid of heat.

Circulatory System

A bird's circulatory system consists of a four-chambered heart and blood vessels. With each beat, or stroke, of the heart, a large volume of blood is carried throughout the bird's body by vessels called arteries. Blood is then returned to the heart by vessels called veins. Birds are nature's best athletes. With their powerful hearts, they can keep up extraordinary levels of physical exertion for long periods. A ruby-throated hummingbird's heart is about 3 percent of its total body weight, but it is strong enough to supply fuel and oxygen to the flight muscles for a nonstop flight across the Gulf of Mexico.

The high metabolism of birds requires rapid circulation of the blood because waste products build up quickly in the cells and must be removed before they reach a toxic level. Typically, small birds have a higher metabolism than large birds and therefore have a faster heart rate.

The Internal Body Structures of a Bird

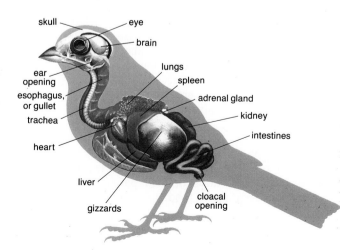

skull
eye
brain
lungs
spleen
ear opening
esophagus, or gullet
adrenal gland
trachea
kidney
heart
intestines
liver
cloacal opening
gizzards

How Birds See

The owl, whose eyes are on the front of its head, has a wide overlapping field of vision in front and good depth perception.

The falcon, whose eyes are on the sides of its head, has a narrow overlapping field of vision in front.

The woodcock, whose eyes are far back on the sides of its head, has a narrow overlapping field of vision both in front and behind.

Respiratory System

The high metabolism and athletic life-style of birds require a great deal of oxygen. Four organs work together to bring oxygen from the atmosphere to the cells: nostrils, trachea, lungs, and air sacs. With each breath, air moves through the nostrils, down the trachea and into the lungs and air sacs. From the lungs, oxygen passes into the bloodstream and then to the body cells. The air that passes into the air sacs cools the internal organs and helps maintain body temperature. Nearly all of the air in the lungs is replaced with each breath. At rest, birds breathe slowly. When flying, birds require ten to twenty times more oxygen than at rest. To supply the extra oxygen, birds increase their breathing rates.

Nervous System

The nervous system of a bird is similar to that of other vertebrates and consists of the brain, sense organs, and nerves. Nerves carry messages from sense organs, such as the eyes, to the brain. Nerves also carry messages from the brain to the muscles.

As a group, birds have the best vision of all animals. Their large eyes, which sometimes weigh more than their brain, provide keen sight and excellent color perception. Birds that are most active at night, or nocturnal, also have well-developed sight. The range of vision that a bird has depends on whether the eyes are located on the sides of the head or on the front of the head.

Hearing is also well developed in birds, with some night birds having especially acute hearing. Only a few birds, such as the kiwi, have a highly developed sense of smell. The kiwi is nearly blind and relies on its sense of smell to find food.

Reproductive System

A bird's reproductive system is composed of the sex organs and a series of tubes, or ducts, which act as passages for the sex cells produced within the organs. The male sex organs, called the testes, produce sperm; the female sex organs, called the ovaries, produce eggs.

When birds mate, sperm from the testes pass from the male to the female. The sperm fertilize the eggs, which have formed in the ovaries. After an egg is fertilized, it begins to travel down a narrow tube called the oviduct toward the external opening, or cloaca. On the way down the oviduct, it first receives a coating of the protein called albumen (the egg white). Further down the oviduct, the albumen is surrounded by a shell composed of calcium. As the egg nears the end of the oviduct and before it is laid, it also may receive various colored pigments.

▶THE BEHAVIOR PATTERNS OF BIRDS

Birds have many behaviors that help them to survive. Some of these are learned behaviors, but many others are not learned. Behaviors that animals are born with are called instinctive behaviors. Some instinctive behaviors help birds recognize enemies. Great kiskadees display an instinctive behavior related to coral snakes, which eat young birds. Even though they have never seen a snake, hand-raised great kiskadees are frightened by sticks that have been painted to look like coral snakes. Newly hatched herring gulls know by instinct to peck at the red spot on the bill of their parents in order to be fed. Pecking becomes more accurate as the baby gulls learn to anticipate the position of their parents' bills when they return with food.

Bird-watching

Birds are fascinating creatures. You do not have to be an ornithologist to enjoy watching birds. Many amateurs have contributed to the understanding of birds by recording their observations and reporting interesting or significant sightings to their local bird club. Information provided by amateur bird-watchers can then be used to compile information about population changes within a specific area or to document the introduction of a new species into an area.

Some people simply watch birds at a backyard feeder; others hike the forests, fields, and marshes to get a close look at birds. Whichever way you decide to bird-watch, recording what you observe is fun as well as helpful. Information that will help you recall a bird sighting includes the date, time of day, location, weather conditions, and persons with you (if any). Some observations to keep track of are the species, number of birds, and behaviors of the birds you see. Quick sketches of plumage or flight patterns can also be made. Along with a notebook and pencils, supplies such as field guides, binoculars, camera, and tape recorder (for recording bird calls) are all useful.

Birds also learn very well. Young birds learn to recognize predators by observing the behavior of other birds. Many species of birds make loud, scolding calls when they discover predators such as owls, cats, or snakes. Flocks of birds attack and usually drive away the

Birds have different bathing behaviors that keep their feathers free of parasites and dirt. A swan (*above left*) thrashes its wings in water, while the helmeted guinea fowl (*above right*) digs a small pit in the ground and shuffles its feathers in the dirt.

Not all species of birds have the same activity cycle. Great gray owls (*left*) rest during the day and hunt during the night. Egrets (*below*) follow the typical cycle —they feed during the day and rest during the night.

predator—a behavior called mobbing. Inexperienced birds quickly learn to associate danger with mobbing. Some birds learn how to build better nests as they get older and more experienced.

Living in a Community

Flocks. Birds that stay all winter in northern regions have little time to do anything but find food, water, and shelter. Some species form large social groups called flocks. Among these species, some form flocks in the winter, some remain in flocks year-round, and others never form flocks at all. Living in a flock has two big advantages: It is easier for the many eyes of the group to find food and to spot predators. A bird in a flock is much less likely to be killed by a hawk than a lone bird singled out for attack. Usually all the birds in a flock do the same thing at the same time—they sleep together, feed together, and sometimes even breed together.

Dominance. Often winter birds living in small flocks establish a system of dominance, which is sometimes called a **pecking order**. Pecking order is organized so that each bird pecks another bird lower in standing within the group and submits to pecking by birds of higher rank.

In flocks with dominance systems, the highest ranking bird gets first choice of food, water, even mates, while others wait their turn. Dominance helps all the birds in the flock to survive by reducing competition. Being lowest bird in the pecking order is better than fighting over every scrap of food with all the members of the flock.

Defense. Birds use a variety of methods to protect themselves and their offspring against

For most birds, defending territory is the focus of the males' day. Threat displays by the sage grouse (*right*) warn intruders that they had better leave the territory. Occasionally, fighting erupts. Brown pelicans (*below right*) use their beaks to peck and grab at the enemy.

enemies. Some birds that are colored or patterned so that they blend with their surroundings can often remain undetected if they stay still. This type of **protective coloration**, or natural camouflage, not only helps a bird avoid enemies, but it also helps a bird get close to prey without being seen.

Other birds may flee or hide. As a last resort and if it cannot escape or hide from danger, a bird will fight using its beak, legs, or wings, depending on its species. Sometimes, a bird will try to distract an intruder from its nest by making a noisy disturbance or pretending to be hurt and, therefore, easy prey. Once the intruder follows the "wounded" bird away from the nest, the "wounded" bird flies off.

Establishing a Territory

In general, male birds migrate north before females. They need to arrive early to stake claim to a territory. A territory is a fixed area that is defended continuously for a period of time. Most birds defend territories during breeding; some defend territories all year long. Both males and females defend territories, but most often it is the male who works hardest to defend the territory. Birds establish, maintain, and defend breeding territories in order to attract mates, find appropriate nest sites, and find enough food to raise hungry nestlings.

Communicating

Bird song may sound beautiful, but birds do not sing to make music; birds sing to attract mates and to tell other males to stay off their territory.

Birds are capable of an enormous variety of vocalizations. Traditionally they are divided into two groups: calls and song. Calls are

short, simple vocalizations such as calls of distress, feeding, flight, flocking, and warning. Songs are long vocal displays with specific repeatable patterns. Normally only males can sing. However, some females, such as northern cardinal females, sing quite well.

Birds can sing more than just one specific song. Birds generally have between 5 and 14 songs, but some species have many more. Northern mockingbirds and wrens are capable of producing hundreds of songs. Besides helping males to defend their territories and attract mates, songs can warn others about potential dangers; can say "Here I am . . . where are you?"; and can tell other birds the species, age, sex, and experience of the singer.

No two birds sing exactly the same song. Subtle differences in the pitch and timing of songs are used to recognize individuals. Birds are able to identify their mates, young, parents, and neighbors. Penguins returning to nesting colonies that may have tens of thousands of birds are able to locate their mates by picking out their unique call from the deafening chorus of the colony.

During courtship, the male sage grouse (*left*) inflates its neck pouches and lets out booming calls to attract females. The male frigate bird (*right*) seeks the attention of a female by inflating his huge red throat pouch and keeping it inflated, sometimes for many hours, until he has lured a female to his side. During courtship, a pair of great blue herons (*below*) collect twigs and sticks and build their nest together.

▶ THE LIFE CYCLE OF BIRDS

A year in the life of a bird is controlled by a series of rhythms and cycles. Every year birds pass through the phases of breeding, molting, and migrating. What is amazing is that birds do these things with astonishing precision. This is because they have an internal biological clock that controls their daily and annual schedules and regulates when they sleep, feed, migrate, breed, and molt.

Mating

In spring, males arrive at the breeding ground before females. After establishing a territory, they defend it against neighboring males and sing to attract a mate. When the females arrive, they may choose a mate in one of several ways. Northern mockingbirds prefer males with a large number of different songs. Red-winged blackbirds select males with the best territories. Regardless of how the choice is made, a strong tie known as a pair bond is formed between the male and female. Canada geese and bald eagles form pair bonds with their mates that last their entire lives. At the other extreme, ruby-throated hummingbirds form a pair bond for only a few minutes. In most birds, the pair bond lasts the entire summer, as the birds build a nest, incubate eggs, and raise fledglings to adulthood.

Most birds are monogamous, which means they only have one mate at a time. Some birds have more than one mate at a time; they are called polygamous. Promiscuity is a form of mating without bonding. The male and female come together briefly to mate and then part. The female builds the nest and cares for the young alone.

Nesting

All birds lay eggs and care for them in one way or another. The place where birds lay their eggs is called a nest. Nests hold and cushion eggs before they hatch. Some birds, such as murres, do not build any type of nest to hold their eggs. They simply lay them on bare cliff ledges overlooking the sea. Other birds build elaborate structures to hold the eggs. Some nests are used year after year.

Birds must choose the safest possible place to nest if the young and the adults are to survive. The nest must provide protection from predators, who like to eat eggs, nestlings, and even adults sitting on the nest. The nest must also protect the eggs from bad weather.

Types of Nests. Although birds build nests in a variety of places, using many different types of materials, members of the same species generally build similarly styled nests.

The first birds probably built nests that were just a slight depression scratched in the ground or fallen leaves. This type of nest is called a scrape and is still used by many birds today. Shorebirds, terns, nighthawks, and falcons are some of the species that make scrapes. Other birds, like belted kingfishers and petrels, nest in a scrape at the end of long burrows they have dug deep within stream banks or the ground.

When most people picture a bird's nest, they think of a cup-shaped nest. These cup nests are the most common type and can be built almost anywhere. Warblers, American robins, and blackbirds all build cup nests.

Other birds are well equipped to chisel out a home in a dead tree. Woodpeckers, parrots, and hornbills dig nest cavities. Cavity nests are widespread among birds because they provide especially good protection. Male hornbills seal the female into their nest cavity and she does not leave until the chicks have hatched!

Many species build flat platform nests in just about every type of habitat imaginable—from treetops to water environments. Bald eagles build the largest tree nests of any bird. These large platform nests

are used year after year and can be more than 9 feet (3 meters) wide! Great blue herons also make large tree nests and place them close together in what are called colonies. Grebes build floating platforms, anchoring them to plants growing in shallow water. The horned coot of South America even builds its own island! Thousands of small stones are piled up over several years, making a custom-designed nesting island that may weigh as much as a ton.

One of the most unusual nests belongs to the dusky

Nests come in many forms. The northern flicker (*above*) has settled into a cavity it has made in a giant cactus. The nest of the Caribbean flamingo (*left*) is a cone of mud about 1½ feet (.5 meter) high. The eggs are laid in a small depression formed at the top of the cone. Nestlings within their snug cup-shaped nest (*below left*) call for food. The cup-shaped nest is the most common type of nest. At one time the mud nests of the cliff swallow (*below*) were only found at cliff sites; today they can be found under the eaves of buildings and under concrete bridges.

scrub fowl of Australia. Males of this species build gigantic mounds of rotting leaves, sticks, and grass that can sometimes measure 36 feet across (11 meters) and more than 16 feet (5 meters) high! The female lays her eggs in the mound, where they are warmed by the heat generated from the rotting vegetation and by the sun. The male dusky scrub fowl carefully checks the temperature of the mound with his bill and adds or removes layers of vegetation as needed.

Eggs and Egg Laying

Once an egg is fertilized, it develops quickly in the female's oviduct and is surrounded with a protective eggshell. As soon as the egg is fully formed, it is laid before the next one has grown very large. Usually females lay an egg each day, or every few days, until the group of eggs, called a clutch, is complete. Most birds wait until all the eggs are laid, then they sit on the eggs to warm them with their bodies. They will warm the eggs in this manner, in the process called incubation, until the eggs hatch. In this way, all the young birds hatch at about the same time.

Other birds, like owls, start incubating as soon as the first egg is laid. The eggs hatch at different times and the young are much different in size.

Eggs vary tremendously in size and color. The flightless ostrich lays a gigantic egg that can weigh up to 4 pounds (1.8 kilograms). It is so big and the shell is so thick that few animals can break it open. On the other hand, the tiny Cuban bee hummingbird's egg is only ¼ inch (.5 centimeter) long and weighs ¹⁄₁₀₀ ounce (.25 gram). More than 5,000 hummingbird eggs would fit inside an ostrich egg!

Often eggs are perfectly colored to blend in with their background. Ground-nesting birds usually have pastel gray, blue, or green eggs that are speckled with shades of brown or black.

Eggs show countless variations, not only in size and color but in shape. The shape of eggs varies from long and elliptical, or oval, to nearly round. Most eggs are shaped like the familiar chicken egg. Streamlined birds, such as swifts and hummingbirds, lay long, elliptical eggs that help females keep their efficient body shape. Murres, which nest on narrow

Bird Eggs

Blue grouse

Mountain plover

American crow

European starling

Golden-fronted woodpecker

Ostrich

American robin

Northern cardinal

Bobolink

Black-chinned hummingbird

The shape, color, and size of egg that a bird lays varies with each species. Some eggs are round, others are oval; some eggs are glossy white, some are black, still others are speckled with color. The ostrich lays an egg that weighs about 3 pounds (1 kilogram), while the hummingbird lays an egg that is only ¹⁄₁₀₀ ounce (0.35 gram).

When temperatures soar, the heron (*left*) partially extends its wings to provide cooling shade for the eggs in its nest. The trumpeter swan (*right*) turns the eggs to make sure they are warmed evenly. Eggs may be turned from once every few minutes to about once an hour. The cowbird lays its eggs in other birds' nests. Here (*below*), a yellow warbler cares for cowbird nestlings.

cliffs, have eggs shaped like toy tops. These eggs roll in a tight circle, which is important if rolling out of the nest means a fall of several hundred feet. Cavity-nesting birds tend to lay round eggs that pile neatly in the bottom of the nest hole. Shorebirds lay four pointed eggs that fit together like pieces of a pie.

Incubation. A few days before a bird lays its first egg, the bird loses some of the feathers on its belly. The blood vessels in the area also enlarge and form what is known as a brood patch. When a bird incubates its eggs, it settles itself down so that its brood patch is in direct contact with the eggs. In general, brood patches develop only in the birds that incubate. If both sexes incubate, both develop brood patches.

Birds that nest in places where the temperatures are above 100°F (38°C) need to keep their eggs cool. Some birds will stand over the eggs, shading them with partially opened wings. Mourning doves nesting in Arizona have been found to use their brood patches to cool their eggs down to body temperature. The birds pant heavily while incubating, to get rid of the extra heat.

The incubation period of an egg is the time from the start of incubation until hatching of the egg. In general, larger eggs need longer incubation periods. The wandering albatross, one of the largest flying birds, needs 75 to 82 days of incubation. Small finches and warblers need only 11 to 12 days.

Some birds neither build nests nor take care of their young. Instead, they lay their eggs in the nests of other species, and rely on them to incubate the eggs and rear the offspring. This

behavior is called brood parasitism. Some birds, such as cuckoos, are always brood parasites, while others, such as redhead ducks, are irregular brood parasites.

Redhead ducks are irregular brood parasites, which means that sometimes they have their own nests and incubate their own eggs, and sometimes they lay eggs in the nests of different duck species. Honeyguides, found in Asia and Africa, are totally parasitic and have lost all courtship and nesting behaviors. Honeyguides usually lay a single egg in the nest of a closely related species. Newly hatched honeyguides, while still blind and featherless, will eliminate the other nestlings that compete with them for food. They use the sharp hook on the tip of their beaks to bite and kill the other nestlings or, one by one, they push the host's young out of the nest.

Hatching of a Chick

When the offspring inside the egg is fully developed, hatching begins. The chick uses the egg tooth on the tip of its beak to peck an opening in the shell. Pushing through the opening it has made, the chick tumbles out of the shell. Depending on the species, hatching may take as little as five hours or as long as four days.

The brown-headed cowbird, which is widespread throughout North America, is also a brood parasite. Cowbird eggs have been found in the nests of more than 150 species. The abundance of cowbird parasitism has been an important factor in the decline of some birds, such as the endangered Kirtland's warbler.

Hatching. Inside the egg, the growing bird develops a short, pointy structure on the tip of the upper beak called an egg tooth. When the incubation period is complete, the fully developed offspring uses its egg tooth to break out of the shell. Small birds, such as warblers, finches, and sparrows, may complete the hatching process in five hours. Larger birds, especially seabirds, may take as long as four days.

Imprinting. Birds exhibit a very special type of learning called imprinting. Imprinting only occurs during a critical period early in life, and once something is learned by imprinting it cannot be changed or forgotten. For instance, the moving object that a duckling follows in the first 24 hours after hatching is accepted as its "mother." Usually the moving object is the adult female duck; however, it has been shown that a duckling will follow and imprint on humans or even a moving box with a ticking alarm clock inside.

Later in life, birds will select mates and other members of their flock based on what has been imprinted. Baby birds raised by people do not imprint correctly and never select an appropriate mate for nesting. Birds also imprint on the type of nest and its location, which is important information when they need to select a good spot to build their nest.

Because these peregrine falcon chicks are being raised by humans, they will not learn how to perform some of the tasks necessary for their survival in the wild.

Care of the Young

Feeding. A nestling bird is an ugly thing. It is all belly and head with two large bulging eyes. Almost immediately, a nestling can lift its wobbly head and open its mouth. The inside of the mouth is usually brightly colored, providing a food target for the parents. On either side of the nestling's mouth are sensitive nerve endings. When touched, the mouth automatically snaps shut. The combination of the nestling's wide-open mouth and constant begging for food is powerful stimuli for the adults. The instinct to feed young is so strong that they will occasionally feed other birds' young.

Some birds are altricial—that is, they are helpless when they are born. They are born featherless and blind. At first, altricial nestlings cannot maintain their own body temperature. If the parents are gone too long, they grow cold. Fortunately, in a few days, the nestlings grow a coat of downy feathers. They also take in huge quantities of food and grow very rapidly. A common cuckoo, which is only about 0.07 ounces (2 grams) at hatching, weighs about 3.5 ounces (100 grams) after three weeks. By the time it leaves the nest, its weight is almost that of the adult female. Young albatrosses and petrels weigh much more than either parent when they leave the nest. Their tremendous fat reserves are slowly used up after the parents abandon them and return to sea. By the time young albatrosses have reached normal adult weight, they are ready to leave the nest and soar over the ocean in search of food.

Precocial birds spend more time in the egg than altricial birds do, so they are better developed when they hatch. However, they grow more slowly than altricial birds after hatching. The killdeer is typical of most precocial birds. It is born with its eyes open, a thick layer of down, and well-developed legs and bill. Shortly after hatching, it is able to run around and find its own food.

In the Nest

Life in the nest is not easy. Very few of the young live long enough to nest themselves. Eight or nine out of every ten birds die during their first year. For most species, weather and predators are the greatest threats to young

To satisfy the seemingly boundless appetite of nestlings, a parent bird makes many trips to and from the nest—sometimes as many as 900 trips per day.

The 27 Orders of Living Birds

Coliiformes
blue-naped mousebird

Psittaciformes
gray parrot

Apodiformes
ruby-throated hummingbird

Passeriformes
blue jay

Coraciiformes
carmine bee-eater

Gruiformes
crowned crane

Rheiformes
common rhea

Columbiformes
victoria crested pigeon

Tinamiformes
variegated tinamou

Casuariiformes
Australian cassowary

Anseriformes
wood duck

Falconiformes
bald eagle

Apterygiformes
brown kiwi

T. BOYER

Piciformes
keel-billed toucan

Trogoniformes
collared trogon

Cuculiformes
white-eared turaco

Procellariiformes
gray-headed albatross

Caprimulgiformes
common nighthawk

Struthioniformes
ostrich

Strigiformes
snowy owl

Ciconiiformes
black-crowned night heron

Charadriiformes
ruddy turnstone

Pelecaniformes
great frigate bird

Galliformes
Lady Amherst's pheasant

Sphenisciformes
king penguin

Gaviiformes
arctic loon

Podicipediformes
western grebe

birds. Bad weather can reduce insect populations and thus reduce the birds' food supply, or it can interfere with the parents' ability to find food for their young. Mammals, especially raccoons, foxes, and squirrels, can be very destructive. Nestlings can also suffer heavy losses from parasites, such as mites and blow fly larvae. These insects attach themselves to the skin of the nestlings and feed on their blood, weakening them so much that they are unlikely to survive.

Regardless of their regular diet, the adults feed their young foods rich in proteins. Young birds, like children, need large amounts of protein in order to grow. Even hummingbirds, which as adults feed mainly on flower nectar, bring small insects to their young. Some birds have unique ways of feeding their young. Pigeons and doves (a member of the pigeon family) feed their young on pigeon's milk, a

The trumpeter swan is an attentive parent that sometimes carries its young, called cygnets, on its back. More often, however, the swan simply escorts its brood from one place to another.

material high in fat and protein that is formed in their crop (the storage portion of their stomach). Pelicans catch and store fish in their huge mouths and let their young dip into the enormous pouch and help themselves to the food there. Cormorants swallow the heads of their young and the young feed right from the adult's stomach.

The large amount of food brought to a nest full of young results in the production of much waste. If not removed, this material would foul the nest, attract predators and parasites, or cause disease. Many young birds eliminate undigested food and wastes in a small membrane called a fecal sac. The sacs are then eaten by the adults or carried away.

Before long, the nest becomes overcrowded with the rapidly growing nestlings and soon it can no longer hold them. Then it is time for the baby birds to leave the nest; this is called fledging. In some birds, the young make their first flight when they fledge. In others, the fledglings (baby birds) simply move out of the nest to a nearby limb.

The masked booby (*left*) carefully preens its offspring, combing through the feathers to remove dirt and parasites. Spreading its wings to create shade, the egret (*below*) protects its downy offspring from the hot sun. In a few species of birds, such as the emperor penguin (*below right*), the male has much of the responsibility for taking care of the offspring. Here, the emperor penguin chick huddles under the warm belly of its parent.

By fall, the young birds that were born in late spring have learned a great deal. They have practiced flying and can now find their own food, although they still may beg for their parents to feed them. In many cases, they have been on their own for months. Many birds nest more than once in a summer. The young from the first nest fend for themselves while the parents start a second brood. In some birds, the young from the first nest stay with the parents and help raise their siblings.

The Migration Cycle

There are ancient records of the appearance and disappearance of birds. Early naturalists did not know if birds migrated or hibernated. People told stories of swallows that were found frozen in marshes and would fly away when thawed. Now we know that billions of birds make astonishing migrations, traveling to distant places to breed and winter. Each spring, an estimated 5 billion birds migrate from the Central and South America to North America in search of nesting sites. An equal number leave the warmth of Africa and set out for breeding grounds in Europe and Asia. The migration of birds is truly one of the most spectacular feats in the natural world.

Residents and Migrants. Some birds never make a long-distance migration. These birds are called residents. Other birds fly incredible journeys to spend winters in tropical areas. These birds are called migrants.

There are advantages and disadvantages to both resident and migrant life-styles. Residents face long, cold winters and scarce food supplies. If a bird cannot find enough food to burn for energy during the long, cold winter night, it will freeze to death. It is much easier to survive the winter in the warm tropical forests of Central and South America. However, long-distance migrations are dangerous. Many birds are killed during migration by storms and man-made hazards, such as radio and television towers. Many forest areas have been destroyed to provide land for construction and development, so good places to stop and rest during migration are harder and harder for birds to find.

Migration. As fall approaches, the days get shorter and the nights grow cooler. With nesting over, things begin to change. The territories that were defended so vigorously in the beginning of summer no longer matter. Many species have urges to join large flocks of birds —for safety and to prepare for the migration to come.

Whether in a flock or not, birds feed heavily at this time of year to build up the fat reserves they will need to fly back to their wintering grounds. Before long, the alarm goes off on their biological clocks and it is time to migrate south.

Some birds migrate by day, others migrate at night. Hawks ride the thermals created as the sun warms the ground below. Humming-

With winter on the way, snow geese leave their nests in high Arctic regions to form large flocks for the journey southward. They fly during the day and night, coming down at regular intervals to rest and feed.

birds migrate alone and during the day, stopping to feed as needed. However, most small land birds, including flycatchers, thrushes, warblers, and orioles, migrate at night when temperatures are cooler and the tremendous quantities of heat generated by flapping flight muscles are quickly lost to the cool night air. Predation is less likely at night and the daylight hours can be used to find food and refuel for the next night's journey. As the day dawns, large flocks of migrating songbirds descend into patches of woods in what is known as a fallout, to rest and feed.

Many birds, especially duck and geese, follow narrow paths as they migrate north and south. These paths are called flyways. The main migration routes in North America run north to south, much as most of the mountain ranges and major rivers do. In Europe and Asia, birds migrate east to west as they travel from their breeding grounds to wintering ground.

In spring the days grow longer, and once again the changing daylight sets off the bird's biological clock. It is time to molt and begin preparations for the migration north. Longer days do more than just trigger the molting process. The increasing day length also triggers an increase in appetite and an increase in fat storage, which help to prepare the bird for spring migration.

After traveling all the way to the tropics, why do birds not stay and nest there? The costs of migration are great, but the benefits

Under clear skies and with a good tail wind, Canada geese can cover many hundreds of miles in a single nonstop flight.

Each year in their migratory journey between the Arctic and the Antarctic, Arctic terns log up to 25,000 miles (40,225 kilometers) of travel.

of returning north to breed are even greater. The tropics are full of predators that would quickly gobble up young birds. In North America, there are not as many reptile and small mammal predators.

Birds also migrate north to breed because there is an extremely large supply of the insects that are needed to feed growing young. In the long days of the northern summer, birds have time to find plentiful amounts of food for their young. In the Arctic, the mid-summer sun never sets, allowing birds to hunt 24 hours a day.

How Birds Migrate

How do birds know where to go? How do they find their way? Why do some birds travel during the day, while others travel during the night? These are questions that **ornithologists** (scientists who study birds) have tried to answer for at least a century. Birds have an astonishing ability to return to an exact location after wintering in South America or Africa. Homing pigeons can return to their home loft from places hundreds of miles away.

Recently ornithologists have started to learn how birds know where they are and navigate during their great migrations. Near your house, it is unlikely that you would ever get lost. You know the way because you recognize landmarks; birds also use landmarks to find their way. But they also have other ways of navigating when they fly out of their neighborhood. They have several sources of information that tell them which way to go. Migrating birds can use the sun by day and the stars by night. Research shows that they can even use the earth's magnetic field (the same field detected by a compass) and that they sometimes use odor clues, and maybe even low-frequency sounds.

However birds find their way, they are rarely very late. One of the extraordinary things about migration is its precision. Birds that travel across a continent, or farther, arrive at their destination within a few days of the same time each year.

A bird's internal clock is mostly responsible for the start of migration, but weather is also a factor. Many species, such as American robins, time their arrival to match the spring thaw. Birds are sensitive to changes in atmospheric pressure. Strong favorable winds cause birds to migrate in large numbers.

The Birds Around Us

Some birds spend most of their lives in deserts, others can be found along seacoasts, still others are found in woodlands and forests. In the following section, a variety of birds are shown in the kind of habitat, or environment, in which they can typically be found. The habitats include seacoasts, deserts, woodlands and forests, grasslands, polar regions, tropics, and residential areas. Below is an alphabetical listing of the birds presented and the habitats in which they live.

Bird	Habitat	Bird	Habitat
American kestrel	Grasslands	Hairy woodpecker	Woodlands and forests
American oystercatcher	Seacoasts	Herring gull	Seacoasts
American robin	Residential areas	Hoatzin	Tropics
Baltimore oriole	Residential areas	Long-billed curlew	Seacoasts
Blue jay	Residential areas	Mockingbird	Residential areas
Bobwhite	Grasslands	Phainopepla	Deserts
Bohemian waxwing	Woodlands and forests	Purple finch	Woodlands and forests
Burrowing owl	Grasslands	Quetzal	Tropics
Cactus wren	Deserts	Red-tailed hawk	Deserts
Chipping sparrow	Residential areas	Ruffed grouse	Woodlands and forests
Common cormorant	Seacoasts	Sandpiper	Seacoasts
Common pigeon	Residential areas	Scarlet ibis	Tropics
Common tern	Seacoasts	Snowy owl	Polar regions
Eastern meadowlark	Grasslands	Tawny owl	Woodlands and forests
Emperor penguin	Polar regions	Toco toucan	Tropics
Gila woodpecker	Deserts	Wandering albatross	Polar regions
Great hornbill	Tropics	Western kingbird	Grasslands
Great skua	Polar regions	Wilson's storm petrel	Polar regions
Greater roadrunner	Deserts	Yellow warbler	Woodlands and forests

Birds of the Seacoasts

Many birds are found along the coasts of the world's continents. Some are shorebirds; that is, they live most of the time on the shore. The most widely distributed and probably the best-known shorebird is the gull. Gulls are scavengers — they forage along the shore for dead animals and even search through garbage dumps for food. They also hunt the shallow waters for fish or clams and other mollusks. The gull must break the mollusk's shell to get to the soft meat inside. It does this by carrying the mollusk aloft, then dropping it on rocks or other hard surfaces. Other birds found along the coasts are seabirds; they live most of the time at sea, coming ashore only to breed and nest. Terns are seabirds that stay at sea for long lengths of time, sometimes months or even years. Some seabirds spend so much time flying that they have lost the ability to walk on land or to swim. Not all of a seabird's time is spent flying; seabirds also soar and glide.

Herring gull

Common tern

Long-billed curlew

Common cormorant

Sandpipers

American oystercatchers

Birds of the Deserts

Only the hardiest of birds survive in the desert. The days are very hot, and during the night the temperatures plunge, sometimes even dipping below freezing. The desert is also a dry place. Because it is so dry, desert birds must get their water from the foods they eat. Rather than eating dry seeds and other plant products, most desert birds eat insects or small animals, such as lizards, snakes, and tree frogs, that supply the moisture they need. It is difficult to escape the hot desert sun. Few birds build nests on the hot ground; most build nests in the scattered thickets of low trees and shrubs. Cacti and prickly, thorny shrubs are the favorite nesting sites of the cactus wren. The nest is built deep among the protective spines of the cactus. Within the nest, the cactus wren is shaded from the sun. The Gila woodpecker excavates a cavity in the giant saguaro cactus. The bird uses the same hole for several years. When the nest is abandoned, other birds take it over.

Red-tailed hawk

Gila woodpecker

Phainopepla

Cactus wren

Greater roadrunner

Birds of the Woodlands and Forests

Woodlands and forests provide habitats to many different kinds of birds. Some birds are found in dense forests of evergreen trees; others prefer the open areas among the scattered thickets of shrubs and leafy trees of the woodlands. Some birds build their nests high in the treetops, while others make their nests in the lower branches or on the ground. The ruffed grouse builds its nest on the ground in thick woods and dense cover — at the base of a tree or rock, under a log, or in dense brush. The hairy woodpecker, which digs a cavity in a tree or tree stump, is a year-round resident whether it is found in woodlands, wooded swamps, or mountain forests. It is active even on the most frigid winter days. One part-time resident of wooded areas is the yellow warbler. It builds its nest in shrubs or low trees close to streams and lakes. After raising its young, it heads for warm southern climates.

Tawny owl

Bohemian waxwing

Purple finch

Ruffed grouse

Hairy woodpecker

Yellow warbler

Birds of the Grasslands

Whether they are called prairies, savannas, pampas, or steppes, grasslands provide an abundant source of food and water for a variety of birds. The rich food supply supports birds that eat plant matter, such as grasses and seeds, as well as those birds that eat small animals, such as insects and spiders. Some birds, such as bobwhites, seek the dense cover provided by the tall grasses to hide their ground nests. While nesting, the bobwhite jealously guards its territory deep within the grassland. The meadowlark is also a ground nester that forms its nest from surrounding grasses. However, it prefers to be in more open areas. Perched at the edge of a field, the meadowlark can be heard singing its cheerful song. The burrowing owl does not burrow into the ground to make its nest; instead, it searches for the abandoned burrow of other animals, such as the prairie dog.

American kestrel

Western kingbirds

Burrowing owl

Bobwhites

Eastern meadowlark

Birds of the Polar Regions

The polar regions, the Arctic and Antarctic, are the coldest regions of the Northern and Southern hemispheres. Not all polar birds stay in this harsh environment all the time. Some birds leave the polar regions during the freezing winters and return during the spring to breed and rear their young; others leave to spend months at sea. Birds within these regions have developed in special ways that allow them to withstand the severe environment. Some have specialized body features. The emperor penguin is a flightless bird with short flipperlike wings, webbed feet, and a stiff rudderlike tail. Although it does not fly, it is an excellent swimmer. It also has a thick layer of body fat that serves as insulation against the cold. The skua is a seabird that breeds in the polar regions. Part of its special adaptation is its method of feeding: The skua is a predatory bird that pirates the prey captured by gulls and terns.

Wandering albatross

Great skua

Wilson's storm petrel

Emperor penguin

Snowy owl

Birds of the Tropics

The tropics are damp, humid places where lush, leafy plants abound. Day and night, the temperatures hover just below 80°F (27°C). This steady environment has the greatest variety of animal species, including birds, of anywhere on earth. The brilliantly colored male quetzal is one of the most beautiful birds in the world. Humid mountain forests are home to the quetzal. Some tropic birds, such as the hoatzin, are found feeding on the plentiful supply of leaves and fruit in the dense vegetation that lines the rivers and streams of South American rain forests. Other tropic birds live in the thick canopy formed by the leafy branches of tall trees. There they feast on a great variety of insects and other small animals such as frogs and lizards. The rain forests of India and Indochina are home to the great hornbill. The ibis, which is a wading bird that can be found in most of the warmer areas of the world, nests in huge coastal colonies.

Quetzal

Scarlet ibis

Great hornbill

Toco toucan

Hoatzin

Birds of Residential Areas

The variety of habitats in which birds are found includes patches of grass and trees within the noisy city and in the trimmed backyards and gardens of the suburbs. The mockingbird can be heard singing its varied song, composed of other birds' songs, animal calls, and other common sounds. The cooing of pigeons is a familiar sound in cities as well as in less populated areas. Pigeons are quite social and often breed in colonies and gather in flocks during the nonbreeding season. In some places, the robin is a year-round sight; in other places it is only a resident during the warmer months. The blue jay is a big, bold, dashing bird. Its presence does not go unnoticed. It is a noisy bird that is abundant in backyards and wooded areas.

American robin

Blue jay

Chipping sparrow

Baltimore oriole

Common pigeon

Mockingbird

▶THE HISTORY OF BIRDS

Since the days when dinosaurs roamed the land, millions of years ago, birds have inhabited the earth. They have become one of the most widely distributed of all the wild creatures. Many evolutionary changes have occurred on the path that has led those first primitive forms to modern-day birds.

The First Birds

If you have ever closely examined a bird's scaly foot or watched an anhinga sunning itself on a mangrove or a roadrunner dashing across the desert, you may have noticed how much birds look and act like reptiles. There is a good reason for the similarities—birds and modern reptiles evolved from a common ancestor.

What did this ancestral bird look like? When did it live? The answer is found in fossils that are more than 200 million years old. At that time there was a group of primitive reptiles, dinosaurs called thecodonts, that were covered with scales, had long, strong hind legs for running and jumping, and had teeth set in sockets. There were many different types of dinosaurs, and competition for food forced some of these animals to live in trees. The trees provided safety and plenty of food for them, and their descendants became very good at climbing among the branches.

Over long periods of time, these tree-living reptiles began jumping from branch to branch, then gliding from branch to branch, and eventually from tree to tree, using skin folds similar to the wings of modern birds. The scales on the outside edge of the wings and along the edges of the tail became modified—they lengthened, widened, and lightened into feathers. Feathers were a big advantage for gliding over long distances. Eventually muscles developed that were able to flap the wings and allow these animals to make the first true flight. The descendants of the thecodonts, over a million or more years, learned to fly; they became birds.

Modern Birds

As the ability to fly evolved, birds developed the higher metabolism necessary to provide the fuel for the flight muscles; they also developed the trait of warm-bloodedness. Some experts believe that feathers may have developed as an insulating covering to conserve body heat and that feathers became an aid to flying later. Others argue that feathers emerged to help primitive birds fly and later became useful in keeping the body at a constant temperature.

By the end of the Cretaceous period, 65 million years ago, the toothed birds had vanished and a wide variety of bird life had evolved. The ancestors of modern birds, such as penguins, rheas, loons, tropic birds, and even some perching birds, were already flying across the skies and swimming in the seas. Fifty-three million years ago there was a marked change in the life on earth. Gone were the dinosaurs and the early reptiles that had dominated the environment. Birds, warm-blooded and able to fly, spread and multiplied quickly, taking advantage of every available habitat on earth.

The Decline of Birds

In the past 20 million years or so, there have been more bird extinctions than evolutions of new species. Humans have caused the decline of many birds, in direct and indirect ways.

Environmental pollution caused by humans is a constant threat to the welfare of birds. This bird is a helpless victim of an oil spill.

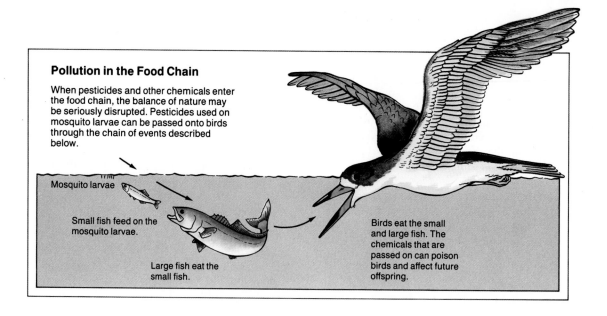

Pollution in the Food Chain

When pesticides and other chemicals enter the food chain, the balance of nature may be seriously disrupted. Pesticides used on mosquito larvae can be passed onto birds through the chain of events described below.

Mosquito larvae

Small fish feed on the mosquito larvae.

Large fish eat the small fish.

Birds eat the small and large fish. The chemicals that are passed on can poison birds and affect future offspring.

At one time, the hunting of birds for food and feathers destroyed a large part of the bird population. Barrel after barrel of salted birds and bale after bale of feathers were shipped to market. In 1878, a single Michigan hunter shipped 3 million passenger pigeons to market. Eleven years later, the passenger pigeon was extinct in that state.

The popularity of bird pets has also contributed to the decline of birds. The international trade in species from Africa, Asia, and South America is one of the major causes of a decline in their numbers—especially hard hit are the world's parrots. Of this beautiful bird family, 78 species are in danger of extinction. Conservationists estimate that for every bird that reaches the pet shop alive, another four perish during the trip to the market.

People have introduced into new lands animals, such as rats, cats, and mongooses, that are bird predators. Cattle, rabbits, pigs, and sheep do not kill birds directly, but they destroy the habitats that birds live in.

The most damage to bird populations has been caused by the human destruction of habitats: Woods and forests have been cut down, marshes drained, and swamps filled to provide more land for development, farming, and grazing.

The Future of Birds

The combination of hunting, destruction of natural habitats, and environmental pollution has proved to be too much for many plants and animals. More than one hundred known birds have become extinct, although many more species must have disappeared before they were even discovered.

Conservationists describing the status of birds categorize them as endangered, threatened, or rare. A species is considered endangered when the population has been so severely reduced that it is unlikely to survive if the cause of the bird's decline is not stopped. Endangered species are in immediate danger of extinction. Threatened species are likely to move into the endangered category in the near future. Rare species have small populations that are not yet in trouble, but could be quickly driven toward extinction.

The need for effective measures on behalf of the world's birds has never been more urgent. Humankind needs birds. We no longer depend on them for food, but we still need them. Birds are part of a healthy, thriving planet. Coal miners used to bring a canary into the mines with them to warn them when the air became too poisonous to breathe. Birds are like the coal miner's canaries for the whole planet. When they can no longer survive, we are in danger. Saving the birds is in our own best interest. By preserving the environment for birds, we take the first steps in saving all life on earth, including our own.

TODD A. CULVER
Education Specialist
Cornell Laboratory of Ornithology

See also ANIMALS; BIRDS AS PETS; ENDANGERED SPECIES; HOMING AND MIGRATION; OSTRICHES AND OTHER FLIGHTLESS BIRDS.

BIRDS AS PETS

Everyone has a different idea of what kind of animal makes a good pet. Some people want an animal that is friendly and will be a good companion; others want an animal that is entertaining—one that can talk, do tricks, or sing; and still others want an animal that is inexpensive to keep. It is possible to have all these things when the pet you have is a bird.

Birds have been popular pets for centuries. Records show that pigeons were tamed in Egypt nearly five thousand years ago. Canaries were luxury pets of wealthy Europeans about five hundred years ago. Alexander Wilson, a pioneer and scholar of American bird life, kept a Louisiana parakeet as a companion. Wilson even took the bird on long horseback journeys exploring the West. The parakeet rode in Wilson's pocket during the day and perched beside his campfire at night.

One of the best features of keeping a pet bird is that most kinds take up little space. They usually live in cages that fit easily in small homes or apartments. Pet birds keep themselves clean and need little daily care. There are also many unusual and interesting varieties to choose from.

▶PARAKEETS

The parakeet is among the most popular of all house pets, feathered or furred. It is called by several names. Budgerigar, or "budgie" for short, is its Australian name, for parakeets originally were native to Australia. In the Far East, these birds are known as shell parakeets.

Parakeets belong to the parrot family. There are certain characteristics that help identify such birds. The feet have two toes in front and two behind. The bill is thick, strong, and hooked. The body is short and compact, with a short neck, large head, and thick tongue. The plumage (feathers) comes in a variety of bright colors. Parakeets are hardy birds and long-lived. These pets also have the wonderful ability to imitate a human voice.

The best place to buy a parakeet (or other cage bird) is at a reliable pet store. There you can learn the age and the sex of the bird you are buying. You can also ask for advice on the correct size and type of cage.

These birds can eat boxed mixtures of small-sized seed like wheat, millet, and canary seed. Many of them have tastes for certain snacks. With some it is apples; others enjoy bits of vegetable greens. Drinking water must always be within reach.

▶PARROTS AND MYNAHS

A parrot or a mynah bird does not have to say anything really funny to be amusing. The way these birds talk is funny enough. They seem to know what they are saying and why they are saying it. Of course this is not true.

WONDER QUESTION

Can people get parrot fever?

Parrot fever, also known as psittacosis, can be passed along to people from infected birds. Although the disease occurs most often in members of the parrot family, it is also found in other birds such as pigeons. In people, the disease is an infection somewhat like pneumonia. It can spread to humans when they handle sick birds or come into contact with infectious articles (bird droppings, perches, cages). The best way to avoid it is to buy pet birds from a reliable dealer, keep their cages clean, and never handle sick birds.

Choosing a Bird

Everyone wants to have a healthy pet. Before selecting a bird, it is important to watch the bird during its normal activities. Look for one that has bright, fully opened eyes and is completely feathered without any bald spots or deformities, such as crooked toenails or overgrown beaks. A bird that looks tamer than the others in its cage may actually be quiet and inactive because it is sick. Other signs that may mean a bird is ill include an unwillingness to eat, runny nose, ruffled feathers, coughing and sneezing, and excessive scratching.

and completely untrained, while others are older and used to talking and living with people. Be prepared to care for a parrot for a long time. Depending on the type of parrot, these birds can live from 25 to 50 years.

The mynah bird is quick to imitate human talk. It is also likely to startle its owner with a piercing squawk or scream. Native to Southeast Asia, mynahs are members of the starling family. There are several kinds of mynahs, some as small as robins, some as large as crows, but all are bright and perky. Again, proper food (mynah birds like a soft mixture) is to be found at pet shops. Once a day they should be given fruit, such as cut up bananas, apples, and grapes.

▶CANARIES

Like parakeets, canaries are mostly seedeaters. They are easily cared for with foods you find at pet shops, with additional snacks of fresh greens and bits of apple or orange. Since its song is one of the canary's best features, the smart canary shopper will look into this before buying a bird.

There are many kinds of canaries, but all of them may be grouped into two main types of singers—the choppers and the rollers. The choppers are the kind of canary most often found in pet shops. They may be sold when only 5 or 6 months old and without training in singing. The chopper sings loudly with high-pitched, short notes. The rollers are usually older and are often given careful training so that their song is at its best. The roller performs with soft, sweet, rolling trills. The male is always the singer.

They merely imitate sounds they have heard. But it makes them seem almost human.

Pet parrots need a great deal of attention. They must be given roomy living quarters and a well-balanced diet. As with other pet birds, proper seed foods for them will be found at pet shops. But parrots have a definite need for more than seeds. Greens, fruits, and nuts are all important for a parrot. On their own, parrots are likely to sample any food that is around—meat, eggs, cheese, or cake—even though it may not be good for them.

The Amazon parrot, with blue markings on its face, and the African gray are two of the most popular parrots. Both can be taught to speak clearly and often to sing and whistle.

If you are shopping for a parrot, you will find a wide range in price. Some are young

With its cheerful yellow color and its soft, sweet trill, the roller canary is one of the most popular of all pet birds. Canaries, which belong to the finch family, are native to the Canary Islands, off the coast of Africa. Over time, breeders have developed different varieties—some are known for their melodious songs, others are known for their distinctive appearance.

Native to Central and South America, the scarlet macaw is a large long-tailed parrot. It is valued as a pet because it is easy to tame and lives a long time.

People who keep pigeons may own dozens of these birds. They are mainly used for racing or to produce the squabs, or young pigeons, that people eat as a luxury food.

Pigeons are kept in many city areas as well as in the country. Pigeon fanciers sometimes keep them in special houses, or lofts, on the roofs of buildings—if city laws permit. From the rooftops the birds can be released for exercise flights. Wherever they are kept, pigeons need air and light and protection from drafts and mice. Seed mix that can be bought from a pet shop is their chief food. If you feed them by hand, they become very tame and friendly. A pair of pigeons may be purchased for a small amount of money, but a single champion racing bird may be expensive.

▶BACKYARD BIRDS

Chickens, ducks, and geese are birds that are usually thought of as farm birds, but any one of them may be tamed and kept as a backyard pet. A chicken is interesting to watch and to hear. It has a varied and unmistakable "language" all its own. Ducks and geese, too, make interesting and unusual pets.

DOROTHY E. SHUTTLESWORTH
Author, *Exploring Nature With Your Child*
Founder, *Junior Natural History Magazine*

BIRTH CONTROL

When a man and a woman have sexual intercourse and do not want the woman to become pregnant, they use birth control, or **contraception**, to try to prevent pregnancy. Knowing how to prevent pregnancy can help them with family planning. Deciding when to have a child and how much time should pass between the birth of one child and the birth of the next is important. It allows parents to have children when they are ready to love and care for them and be responsible for their many needs.

▶METHODS OF BIRTH CONTROL

To understand how birth control works, you must understand some basic facts about how human beings reproduce. About once every 28 days an egg cell, or ovum, is released from one of a woman's ovaries and begins to travel down a narrow Fallopian tube toward the uterus. This is called **ovulation**. If this ovum is not fertilized by a sperm cell from a man, it will quickly die and pass out of the uterus during a normal menstrual period. But if sexual intercourse takes place while the ovum is in the tube, one of millions of sperm cells deposited in the woman's vagina through the man's penis may unite with the ovum. This is called **conception**—fertilization of the ovum. The fertilized egg may then attach itself to the inner lining of the woman's uterus, and a new life will begin to develop—the woman is pregnant. Some nine months later a baby will be born.

There are a number of birth control techniques. This discussion is limited to descriptions of birth control techniques that prevent conception.

Barrier Methods. Barrier methods of birth control prevent pregnancy by blocking sperm from entering the vagina or uterus so conception cannot take place. The **condom** is a tube of thin latex rubber, closed at one end, that is rolled down over the man's penis before intercourse. Latex condoms treated with nonoxynol-9 also protect against the AIDS virus. A

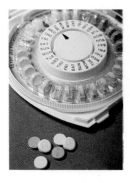

▲ Condom

◀ The Pill

diaphragm is a dome of thin rubber that a woman can insert into her vagina before sex. It covers the opening of the uterus, blocking the entrance of any sperm. Both the condom and the diaphragm are best used with a **spermicide**—a chemical that kills sperm cells. The **vaginal sponge**, which is already treated with spermicide, and the **cervical cap** can be inserted into the vagina; they function much like a diaphragm. Condoms and vaginal sponges can be bought at a pharmacy, or drugstore; diaphragms and cervical caps must be fitted by a doctor. When used properly barrier contraceptives have no bad side effects and they are about 80 to 90 percent effective.

The Pill. Contraceptive pills taken by mouth every day contain tiny amounts of powerful body chemicals known as **hormones**. These hormones prevent the woman's ovaries from producing egg cells so there are none to fertilize as long as the pills are taken. One form of the Pill also makes it hard for any fertilized egg cell to attach itself to the uterus lining and grow.

The Pill must be prescribed by a doctor, who would be able to discuss and monitor any side effects that could occur. The Pill is almost 97 percent effective when used properly. Since ovulation begins again as soon as the woman stops taking the Pill, couples can use it to plan when to have children.

Intrauterine Device (IUD). An intrauterine device is a small coil of metal or plastic that is inserted by a doctor into the woman's uterus. It prevents any fertilized egg cell from attaching itself in the uterus. Younger women who use IUD's sometimes are bothered by cramping or unusual menstrual bleeding. IUD's are more easily used by older women who have already had children. They are over 97 percent effective for preventing pregnancy.

Natural Birth Control. Natural birth control methods attempt to prevent conception without the use of artificial devices. The **Fertility Awareness Method (FAM)**, or rhythm method, depends upon avoiding sexual intercourse on the days before, during, and after ovulation—about 12 days each month—so that no sperm are present to fertilize the egg cell. Unfortunately, because it can be difficult to pinpoint the time of ovulation, the Fertility Awareness Method as well as another natural birth control technique—withdrawing the penis from the vagina just before sperm are ejaculated—are not very reliable.

Other Birth Control Methods. During the 1980's researchers developed **hormonal implants** that prevent ovulation for extended lengths of time by releasing tiny amounts of

▲ Cervical Cap

Intrauterine Device (IUD) ▶

hormones into the woman's body daily. One form is inserted in the uterus, to be replaced yearly. Others are inserted under the skin of the forearm and work even longer. Removing the implant restores fertility. **Sterilization**—surgically cutting and tying off the woman's Fallopian tubes or the man's sperm tubes—is a way to prevent pregnancies permanently. These operations can seldom be reversed once they are performed. Finally, researchers are seeking a reversible pill for men to use to prevent sperm formation as long as the pill is taken. So far, no such "male pill" has been found to work well.

▶ HISTORY OF BIRTH CONTROL

Birth control is a fairly recent idea in human history. Centuries ago large families were important for survival. Many babies died in infancy and childhood, and people had large families to be sure that enough would survive to help gather food and to have children of their own.

In the 1700's and 1800's medical and scientific discoveries enabled many diseases to be controlled and food supplies to be increased. Large families were no longer necessary for survival. People live longer, and the world's population began to grow rapidly.

In 1798 Thomas Malthus (1766–1834), an English economist, predicted that the world's population would quickly outgrow the available food supply. This population increase, he said, would lead to worldwide hunger, wars, and plagues unless people stopped having so many children.

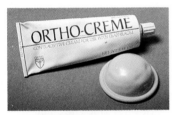
▲ Diaphragm

Spermicidal Cream and Foam ▶

Malthus' prediction proved to be wrong. But as the world population increased rapidly in the early 1900's, the idea of family planning took root. Methods of contraception began to be developed, and a worldwide movement to encourage birth control began.

Margaret Sanger (1879–1966), a trained nurse, became a leader of that movement in the early 1900's. She believed that the poor in America and other countries needed to control the size of their families. Although it was illegal to provide family planning information at that time, Mrs. Sanger published pamphlets and books about it, and eventually helped pass laws that allowed doctors to teach birth control methods. In 1916, she established the first birth control clinic to advise people, and in 1917 she founded the National Birth Control League. This organization and her clinics were combined to form the Planned Parenthood Federation of America in 1942.

▲ Vaginal Sponge

▲ Skin Implants

▶ BIRTH CONTROL TODAY

Widespread use of birth control is becoming more important worldwide every year. The world now has more than 6 billion people, and the number is increasing rapidly, especially in the poor underdeveloped countries. Different countries support birth control in different ways. In Europe and the United States, many birth control methods are readily and legally available. In China, rigid laws control family size. In India, vigorous efforts are being made to make birth control available to millions of people. Family planning is also being taught by satellite television in many remote areas.

Not everyone favors the use of birth control, however. The Roman Catholic Church forbids artificial methods of birth control, believing that sexual love in marriage should never be separated from the possibility of conception. Only **abstinence** (refraining from sexual intercourse) or the rhythm method of family planning are considered acceptable. Some people fear that governments may impose birth control in order to obtain political control over their people. Others charge that teaching birth control encourages people to have sex before marriage—an idea that is not supported by scientific evidence.

Doctors and other knowledgeable people you respect can help you understand the different methods and how they may affect your life and your health.

ALAN E. NOURSE, M.D.
Author, *Birth Control* and
Teen Guide to Birth Control

See also REPRODUCTION (Human Reproduction).

BISMARCK. See NORTH DAKOTA (Cities).

BISMARCK, OTTO VON (1815–1898)

Otto Eduard Leopold von Bismarck-Schön-hausen—the man responsible for the unification of Germany in 1870–71—was born on April 1, 1815, at Schönhausen, in the German state of Prussia (now in East Germany). His father belonged to the Junkers, the Prussian landowning class. His mother came from a middle-class family.

As a boy, Bismarck attended a boarding school in Berlin. Later, he studied law at the universities of Göttingen and Berlin. After graduating in 1835, Bismarck worked in the Prussian civil service and served in the army. He then returned home to help his father manage the family estates. He became religious, partly because he married the devout Johanna von Puttkamer in 1847. That same year, he became a member of the Prussian Diet (parliament), where he represented the conservative traditions of the Junkers.

When France abolished the monarchy in 1848, a wave of change swept across Europe. Germany was still a collection of independent states. Liberals tried to turn the country into a constitutional monarchy headed by the king of Prussia. But the king refused to accept the crown from an elected parliament.

In 1851, Bismarck was Prussia's delegate to the German Diet at Frankfurt-am-Main. There he spoke for Prussia's interests against those of Austria—then the most powerful German state. In 1859 he was named Prussian ambassador to Russia and, later, to France.

In 1862 the new king of Prussia, William I, clashed with his parliament. When the lower house refused to approve money for military reforms, King William appointed Bismarck prime minister and minister of foreign affairs. Bismarck skillfully silenced parliament and gained the power to put his ideas on foreign and domestic policy into effect.

Prussia and Austria defeated Denmark in 1864 in a war over the tiny northern states of Schleswig and Holstein, which had large German populations but were linked to the Danish crown. Prussia then defeated Austria (1866) and gained control of both Schleswig and Holstein. In 1867 Bismarck set up the Prussian-dominated North German Confederation. As chancellor of the confederation, he soon became known as the Iron Chancellor. The nickname came from an 1862 speech in which he had said that "the great questions of the time are decided not by speeches and majority decisions . . . but by iron and blood."

Bismarck had made Prussia the strongest German state. In 1870 he helped provoke the Franco-Prussian War, which united the German states against a common enemy. France was defeated and forced to cede the province of Alsace and most of Lorraine to Germany. The new German Empire was born. It included all the German states except Austria. King William of Prussia became Kaiser (Emperor) William I of Germany.

Bismarck had reached his goal—a united Germany under Prussian leadership. He wanted no more war. He formed alliances that kept a balance of power in Europe and helped nations settle their differences peacefully.

Within Germany, Bismarck played his political rivals off against each other. He never accepted democratic views. But he put through sweeping social reforms to gain liberal support.

William II, who came to the throne in 1888, had his own ideas on running the empire. After much conflict, Bismarck resigned in 1890. His retirement from public life marked the end of an era in European history.

Bismarck died on July 30, 1898. His will included instructions that his tombstone bear the words "A true German servant of Emperor William I." Some historians feel that Bismarck helped pave the way for the Nazi era by not encouraging the growth of democratic institutions in Germany. But he was one of the most skillful and practical politicians the world has ever known.

Reviewed by GERARD BRAUNTHAL
University of Massachusetts, Amherst

BISON. See BUFFALO AND BISON.

As the nation's largest minority group, black Americans represent a powerful political force in the United States. The Reverend Jesse Jackson, a national civil rights leader and two-time candidate for the Democratic presidential nomination, has worked hard to increase voter registration among blacks. By increasing the number of black voters, black concerns can be better represented in government.

BLACK AMERICANS

Black Americans are Americans who are mostly or partly descended from people who once lived in Africa south of the Sahara Desert. More than 30 million blacks live in the United States. They are the nation's largest minority group, making up about 12 percent of the total population.

Black Americans have used several terms to refer to themselves. Until the 1960's, "Negro," which means "black" in Spanish, and "colored" were common terms. Today, "black," "African-American," and "Afro-American" are the terms most commonly used. These terms relect blacks' pride in their color and heritage.

The history of black Americans is rooted deep in their African past. The blacks of ancient Africa were proud peoples, whose rich cultural heritage and civilization thrived under their own rulers. Europeans began to enslave black Africans in the late 1400's and began taking them to the Americas early in the next century. In the United States the history of black people has been largely one of a long and determined struggle to win freedom and equality.

▶THE AFRICAN PAST

The earliest African civilizations developed along the Nile River valley, from Egypt to the north through Ethiopia to the south. At least one black ruler, Ra Nahesi, is known to have occupied the throne of the pharaohs in Egypt. Queen Nefertari—the wife of Ahmose I of Egypt and co-founder (about 1850 B.C.) of the 18th dynasty—was a black woman noted for her beauty and ability. Mutemua, wife of Thutmose IV, was also a black woman. Their son Amenhotep III, who ruled from about 1420 to 1411 B.C., was noted for the great buildings constructed during his reign.

In the 8th century B.C., Ethiopian rulers conquered Egypt. They occupied the throne of the pharaohs for more than 100 years. Greatest of the Ethiopian pharaohs was Taharka, who reigned from 688 to 663 B.C. and called himself emperor of the world.

Early West African Empires

In West Africa south of the Sahara, many tribes were united into empires. The most powerful were Ghana, Mali (or Melle), and Songhai. These empires owed their power to their location on the caravan routes across the Sahara. In their busy markets, wheat, sugar,

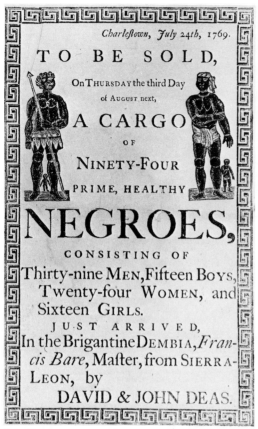

A leaflet from 1769 announces the sale of slaves who have arrived from West Africa. At this time in the American colonies, most blacks were slaves for life.

and salt from the north were exchanged for gold and cattle from the south. Trade with the Arabs of North Africa brought the people of these empires into contact with the written Arabic language and the religious teachings of Islam. Their cities became centers of Muslim learning and culture.

Ghana's beginnings date back to about A.D. 300. Under Tenkamenin, who ruled during the 1000's, Ghana reached the peak of its power. But in the same century, Ghana fell to Muslim conquerors. It was then overwhelmed by the Mandingo people, led by Sundiata, who became king of Mali.

The history of Mali begins in the 600's. Under Mansa Musa I, who ruled from 1312 to 1337, the empire reached its peak. Scholars were brought from all over the Muslim world to establish seats of learning in the cities of Walata, Gao, and Timbuktu. After the death of Musa, Mali's power and glory faded.

The empire of Songhai dates back to the 300's. It rose to prominence in the 1400's under its warrior king Sunni Ali Ber and reached its greatest power under his son Askia Mohammed. In 1590 a military expedition from Morocco invaded Songhai. Once-prosperous towns and cities fell into decay. During the next 100 years, the empire broke up into petty tribal states and decayed.

▶YEARS OF BONDAGE

The first black people to reach the New World were members of Spanish exploratory expeditions in the early 1500's. One of these, Estavanico (Estabanico, or Little Stephen), helped prepare the way for the Spanish conquest of what is now Mexico and the southwestern United States. Blacks accompanied French missionaries to North America during the 1600's. A century later, black people settled in the Mississippi Valley. In the 1770's, Jean Baptiste Pointe du Sable became the first settler in the area of present-day Chicago.

Blacks first traveled to the Western Hemisphere as indentured servants. Later they were taken as slaves. Africans, like people in other parts of the world, had long enslaved one another. Sometimes enslavement was the result of defeat in tribal wars. Sometimes members of a tribe whose crops had failed or whose cattle had died would enslave themselves to more prosperous tribes. Slaving was such a profitable business that North African merchants made long trips across the desert to buy Sudanese slaves for resale in the North. But the Africans' enslavement was relatively mild until they were enslaved by whites, who took them across great oceans to strange lands.

The Slave Trade

When the native Indian peoples in America proved unadaptable to slavery, European colonizers looked elsewhere for cheap labor. They found it in western Africa. There the Portuguese had set up trading posts in the 1400's and were involved in selling slaves to Europe. Control of the profitable slave trade with the New World fell first to the Portuguese, then to the Spanish, Dutch, and English. By the 1800's, about 10,000,000 blacks had survived the horrors of the **middle passage,** as the voyage was called, to work in the fields, plantations, and mines of the Americas.

In 1619, 20 Africans were put ashore at Jamestown, Virginia, as indentured servants. They were treated in much the same way that white indentured servants were treated. The Africans, too, served an indentureship. They worked for their masters for 7, 14, or 21 years. Then they were set free, and each was given a small tract of land. But in the case of the blacks, this practice was gradually stopped. By the late 1600's, most blacks in the American colonies were slaves for life. In Maryland, Virginia, the Carolinas, and Georgia, there were over 640,000 slaves by the end of the 1700's. As agriculture developed, more and more slaves were needed. Tobacco, rice, indigo, cotton, and sugarcane became important crops. The large plantations that grew them depended on slaves.

Attitudes Toward Slavery

On the whole, black slaves in Latin America were treated less harshly than those in the English colonies. The Roman Catholic Church in Latin America played an important part in educating the black slaves and in supporting their desire for freedom. In Latin America there was also greater respect for black people as human beings. Free blacks were accepted more readily in Latin America than in North America.

Almost no one felt easy and comfortable about slavery. Of course the slaves did not like it. They often plotted rebellion or watched for chances to escape, and quite a few did escape.

Their owners, on the other hand, were often troubled by conscience. They knew, too, that the feeling against slavery was growing. This was especially true in France, where there was much talk about people's "natural rights." This idea soon reached England. Slavery was abolished in the British colonies in 1833 and in the French colonies in 1848. The idea of natural rights was also expressed by Thomas Jefferson in the Declaration of Independence.

The right to be free was the idea behind the Revolutionary War in America. Crispus Attucks, a black killed in the Boston Massacre, was among the first Americans to die in that revolution. As many as 5,000 blacks fought in it. They included Peter Salem, who distinguished himself at the battles of Lexington, Concord, and Bunker Hill in 1775. Another black, Salem Poor, also demonstrated bravery at Bunker Hill.

At the time of the Revolutionary War, some blacks in the North were already free. Slaves who ran away to enlist were granted freedom as a result of their wartime service. But many black people had no opportunity to fight. After the war, most of the Northern states did away with slavery. This was not the case in the South.

Slave Life

It was not easy for slaves in America to adjust to the harshness of their lives. All slave owners did not treat slaves badly, but cruelty was so much a part of the system that it was

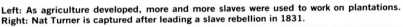

Left: As agriculture developed, more and more slaves were used to work on plantations.
Right: Nat Turner is captured after leading a slave rebellion in 1831.

hard to avoid. Field slaves, including children from the age of 8 or 9 years, worked from dawn to dark. Their food was cornmeal, fat pork, salt fish, and salad greens. They lived under harsh laws. For stealing so much as a pin, slaves could be whipped or branded or have an ear cut off. They could not strike a white person, even in self-defense, without running the risk of being hanged. Some slave owners hired brutal overseers and plantation managers, called slave drivers, who whipped the slaves to get more work out of them. Bolder slaves took revenge for being harshly treated. But most slaves quickly learned that their lives were easier if they did what they were told without complaining.

The slaves found comfort in the Christian religion. They made up religious songs that contrasted their hard life on earth to the happiness they hoped to have in heaven. They sang, for example, "Nobody Knows the Trouble I See" and "Swing Low, Sweet Chariot." These spirituals were among the first songs created in America.

The vast majority of slaves were field-workers. But some were trained as carpenters, millwrights, masons, tailors, and shoemakers. These slave artisans did almost all the skilled work on the plantations and in the cities of the South. When work was slow on the plantations, owners often hired out their skilled slaves to managers of trade and industry in the nearest city. These highly skilled artisans often earned excellent wages, some of which were used to buy their freedom. Sometimes people freed their slaves in their wills or in return for a courageous act.

Almost all personal services were done by slaves. They were the barbers, hairdressers, valets, maids, and nurses of wealthy and educated whites, who generally treated them kindly. Many slaves, among them the seafarer Gustavus Vassa (1745–1801), were taught to read, write, and figure. Some became teachers and preachers to other slaves.

Several slave rebellions occurred in the South in the early 1800's. One of the most ambitious plans was organized in 1822 by Denmark Vesey (1767–1822). He was inspired by the revolts against the French in Haiti led by Toussaint L'Ouverture, Jean Jacques Dessalines, and Henri Christophe. Vesey was betrayed by a house slave and put to death before he could carry out his plan.

The most violent rebellion occurred in Virginia in 1831. Its leader, Nat Turner, believed that he had been called by God to free his people. After more than 100 blacks and about 60 whites had been killed, the rebellion was put down. Turner was captured and executed. New and more severe slave codes (laws) were enforced. Some people blamed educated blacks for encouraging rebellion, and teaching slaves to read and write was made a crime.

SOME INTERESTING PLACES TO VISIT

ALABAMA: Tuskegee—Tuskegee Institute.

DISTRICT OF COLUMBIA: Washington—Frederick Douglass home, 1411 W Street, South East; Howard University.

FLORIDA: Daytona Beach—Bethune-Cookman College.

GEORGIA: Atlanta—Atlanta University.

ILLINOIS: Chicago—Du Sable Marker, Michigan Avenue Bridge; Du Sable plaque and painting, Du Sable High School, 49th and State streets; Underground Railroad marker, 9955 South Beverly Avenue.

MARYLAND: Annapolis—Matthew A. Henson plaque, State Capitol.

MASSACHUSETTS: Boston—Crispus Attucks Monument, Boston Common; Boston Massacre site plaque, State Street; Bunker Hill Monument; monument to Colonel Shaw and 54th Massachusetts Volunteers, a black regiment. **Great Barrington**—James Weldon Johnson cabin.

MICHIGAN: Battle Creek—Grave of Sojourner Truth, Oak Hill Cemetery. **Cassopolis**—Underground Railroad marker, east on route M-60.

MISSOURI: Diamond—George Washington Carver National Monument. **St. Louis**—Old Courthouse, Jefferson National Expansion Memorial (Dred Scott).

NEW HAMPSHIRE: Jaffrey—Grave of Amos Fortune.

NEW YORK: Albany—Original draft of Emancipation Proclamation, New York State Library. **Auburn**—Harriet Tubman home, 108 South Street. **New York City**—Booker T. Washington plaque in Hall of Fame, Bronx Community College; Schomburg Center for Research in Black Culture, New York Public Library.

OHIO: Cleveland—Col. Charles Young Square. **Dayton**—Paul Laurence Dunbar home, 219 North Summit Street **Ripley**—John Rankin House Museum (Underground Railroad station).

PENNSYLVANIA: Philadelphia—Mother Bethel AME Church, 419 South Sixth Street; Negro Soldiers Monument, Lansdowne Drive, West Fairmount Park.

TENNESSEE: Memphis—W. C. Handy Park. **Nashville**—Fisk University; Meharry Medical College.

VIRGINIA: Hampton—Hampton Institute. **Rocky Mount**—Booker T. Washington National Monument.

WEST VIRGINIA: Harpers Ferry—Harpers Ferry National Monument.

WISCONSIN: Milton—Underground Railroad station; Milton House Museum.

Free Black People

No slave codes were passed in the North, where most of the free black people lived. But a black person who got any schooling past the first or second reader was unusual. The mathematician and inventor Benjamin Banneker (1731–1806), one of the best-known blacks of the time, was entirely self-taught. There was no black college graduate until 1826, when John B. Russwurm received a degree from Bowdoin College in Maine. In the following years, a handful of free blacks studied at Harvard College in Massachusetts and at Oberlin College in Ohio. In these colleges they came in contact with faculty members who were **abolitionists** (people who wanted to do away with slavery). Two blacks are known to have gone abroad to study. Alexander Crummell (1819–98) earned a degree at Cambridge University in England. James McCune Smith (1813–65), who studied medicine at the University of Glasgow in Scotland, practiced his profession in New York City.

By 1860 there were nearly 500,000 free blacks in the United States. But few of them enjoyed equality of citizenship rights. Free blacks in the South were hardly free at all. They had to carry passes, or certificates, of freedom. If they were caught without them, they might be sold into slavery. They could not form clubs or discussion groups, and they were not allowed to hold meetings when there were more than five present. Because they were not allowed to own firearms, it was hard for them to protect themselves against criminal whites, who often kidnapped free blacks and sold them "down the river" into slavery.

The controls on the lives of free black people were less severe in the North. But there were enough controls to set them apart from other free Americans. The barriers they faced made many free black people feel that it was a disgrace to have a dark skin. A few blacks took advantage of an offer made by Paul Cuffe, a black shipowner, to transport them to Africa. A similar offer was made by the American Colonization Society, which some prominent white Virginians had organized in 1817. The society set up a colony in Liberia, on the west coast of Africa, especially for former slaves and freeborn American blacks. But the idea of going to Africa did not appeal to many black people. By 1830 only about 1,500 had

Frederick Douglass was minister to Haiti during the Lincoln administration. A writer and lecturer, he fought slavery and was an early supporter of women's rights.

settled there. Many more, who were light enough in color to be mistaken for white, "passed" into the world of whites and thus escaped the handicap of color. But hundreds of thousands had no way of escape, and they developed a way of life inside the barriers that the white world built around them.

The life they made for themselves was modeled generally on the way white people lived. Black people organized their own churches and built their own schools. In New York City, blacks had their own theater, where black actors performed, in the 1820's and 1830's. Black people established societies, clubs, and various "improvement" groups. The first black newspaper, *Freedom's Journal,* edited by John Russwurm, was begun in New York City in 1827.

The Abolitionist Movement

Twenty years later, in Rochester, New York, the black abolitionist Frederick Douglass began publishing a newspaper, *The North Star,* that was to become known around the world. Like many former slaves, Douglass also published the story of his life, which first appeared in 1845. He wrote and spoke out about freedom, justice, and equality—ideals that meant much to people in slavery. One of the most famous antislavery speakers was So-

Both black and white abolitionists in the Underground Railroad helped slaves escape from their masters. The homes of the abolitionists served as "stations" on the Railroad.

journer Truth (1797–1883). Born a slave, she gained her freedom when New York state liberated its slaves in 1827. Declaring "The Spirit calls me, I must go," she set out in 1843 to preach against slavery.

In the South, as well as in the North, a good number of white people, many of them Quakers, were active in the abolitionist movement. Abolitionists' homes served as "stations" on the so-called Underground Railroad, which guided 100,000 slaves to freedom. One of its most famous "conductors" was Harriet Tubman, herself an escaped slave. Two white southerners—James G. Birney, editor of the abolitionist newspaper *The Philanthropist,* and Levi Coffin, "president" of the Underground Railroad—were nearly as famous in the antislavery cause as the white northerners William Lloyd Garrison, editor of *The Liberator,* and Wendell Phillips, the fiery orator from Boston. John Brown, an abolitionist from Kansas, attacked the federal arsenal at Harper's Ferry, West Virginia, in 1859, with the idea of distributing arms to the slaves in the neighboring areas.

There were many white people living in the North who were for slavery. Stephen A. Douglas from Illinois was one of these. In parts of Indiana and Ohio, so many people sympathized with slaveholders that antislavery speakers were afraid of being mobbed.

The proslavery forces won important political and legal victories. In 1820 the Missouri Compromise opened to slavery any new states made out of the Louisiana Purchase that lay south of Missouri's southern boundary. The Compromise of 1850 permitted people in states (except California) made out of territory won from Mexico to decide for themselves (popular sovereignty) whether they wanted slavery or not. The Fugitive Slave Law was passed, requiring people in the free states to help catch escaped slaves. In 1854 the Kansas-Nebraska Act extended popular sovereignty to territories previously closed to slavery by the Missouri Compromise.

The conflict between those who wanted to abolish slavery and those who wanted to keep it grew hotter every year. It was a moral conflict. One side said that slavery was wrong; the other side said that slavery was right. But it was not this argument alone that brought on the U.S. Civil War in 1861.

▶FREEDOM GAINED AND LOST

The causes of the Civil War were political and economic. President Abraham Lincoln himself said that the war was to save the political union of the states. It was not to **emancipate** (free) the slaves. Even the Emancipation Proclamation, issued by the President on January 1, 1863, did not free all the slaves. It freed only those in "states now in rebellion." Indeed, it hardened the slaveholding South's determination to keep the slaves.

Early in the war, black Americans were not allowed to enter military service and fight for their own freedom. But by late 1862, black enlistments were permitted and even encouraged. Black soldiers served in **segregated** (separate) regiments, usually under white officers. Almost 180,000 blacks enlisted in the Union Army, and about 38,000 of them lost their lives.

In 1865 the war ended, and slavery was abolished throughout the country by the Thirteenth Amendment. But the Southern states passed laws, known as black codes, that were intended to keep black people in an inferior position.

When freedom came, the former slaves, who numbered slightly fewer than 4,000,000, did not find life easy. They had been dependent on their masters, and nothing had prepared them for the responsibility of being on their own. President Lincoln understood this and tried to find ways to help. Just a month before he was assassinated, he signed the bill setting up the Freedmen's Bureau. Under the direction of the War Department, this new government agency did some excellent work. It found jobs for former slaves and saw to it that they were paid fair wages. It also looked after their health.

The more than 4,000 schools supported by the Freedmen's Bureau represented the first widespread system of free public education in the South. Schools and colleges were also built with gifts from religious groups and wealthy people in the North. Among the educational institutions started during the years 1865–69 were Shaw University, North Carolina; Fisk University, Tennessee; Talladega College, Alabama; Georgia Baptist (now Morehouse) College, Georgia; Howard University, Washington, D.C.; Hampton Institute, Virginia; and Clark College, Georgia.

The Reconstruction Period

The work of the Freedmen's Bureau and well-meaning northern whites did not solve all the problems. Southern whites disapproved of the Fourteenth Amendment, which upheld the Civil Rights Act of 1866. This act bestowed citizenship on black people and gave them the right to hold office and the right to equal protection of the law. Southern whites were also displeased with the Fifteenth Amendment, which gave black people the right to vote. These whites resented the program called Reconstruction, which was designed to bring the Confederate states back into the Union and to build a new social order in the South.

Reconstruction was meant to protect black people in their new rights. The Civil Rights Act of 1875 guaranteed them equal rights in public places and in serving on juries. Former slaves were elected to local offices, to state legislatures, and to the U.S. Congress. One of these was Robert Smalls, who won fame as a pilot in the Union Navy and was a U.S. representative from South Carolina for twelve years.

Southern whites reacted bitterly. They joined together to stop blacks from exercising their rights. The Ku Klux Klan, the Red Shirts, the Knights of the White Camelia, and other groups of masked whites used methods so harsh—sometimes even murder—that Union soldiers were stationed in parts of the South to protect blacks.

After Reconstruction

Reconstruction lasted about ten years. After 1877, federal troops were withdrawn from the South, and black people were left without protection. In 1883 the U.S. Supreme Court decided five civil rights cases. It ruled that the Civil Rights Act of 1875 did not apply to black people's social rights or to **discrimination** (unfair treatment) by private persons. In 1896, in the case of *Plessy* v. *Ferguson,* the Supreme Court ruled that separate facilities for blacks on railroads must be equal to those of whites. This decision created a precedent. The principle of separate but equal facilities soon was broadened to cover public facilities, education, and many other areas.

Black people's place in the social order dropped almost as low as it had been during slavery. The white people of the South would not allow them to vote. They were barred from any jobs that whites found desirable. Blacks were not permitted to attend schools with whites, and black schools were badly neglected by white school officials. The Jim Crow laws (named for a minstrel show act)

W. E. B. DuBois, a Harvard-educated sociologist, believed that all people of African descent should unite against racial prejudice. He helped found the NAACP.

forced black Americans to live behind a "color line." As time passed, the color line was drawn not only in the South but in the rest of the country as well. It divided blacks from whites as surely as if it had been a brick wall.

But there were white people who crossed the line. Generous people crossed it to bring money and encouragement in support of black people's efforts to improve their situation. These efforts came forcefully to the attention of whites through the work of a former slave, Booker T. Washington. At Hampton Institute, young Washington had been taught that blacks must learn to do useful, practical things. This was the basis of the educational program he set up some years later, when he founded Tuskegee Institute in Alabama. The young men and women at Tuskegee were taught to plow and plant, cook, clean, and sew.

White people of both the North and the South were impressed. It seemed to them that Washington's attitude and his educational program would be good for race relations. The program said nothing about civil rights or political action or social equality. It said nothing about educating blacks to be doctors, lawyers, engineers, or workers in other professions. Many blacks felt that Washington's program would keep blacks inferior economically, politically, and culturally—that it would keep them segregated.

The National Association for the Advancement of Colored People (NAACP) was founded in 1909 by a group of both blacks and whites who believed that black people should have the same rights and privileges that other citizens enjoyed. They opposed Booker T. Washington's program on the grounds that it meant blacks would continue to be looked upon as second-class citizens. W. E. B. DuBois, one of the leaders of the NAACP, said that black people claimed for themselves every single right—political, civil, and social—that belonged to a freeborn U.S. citizen. Until black people got those rights, he declared, they would not cease to protest. *The Guardian,* edited by W. Monroe Trotter (1872–1934), and the *Chicago Defender,* edited by Robert S. Abbott, were among the black newspapers that supported DuBois' stand. In an effort to secure legal rights, the NAACP brought suits in the courts and petitioned Congress and other branches of the federal government. It also made appeals to the conscience of the American people.

Another organization, the National Urban League (NUL), was established in 1910 by whites and blacks. It sought especially to improve the living conditions and employment opportunities for black people in cities.

A number of white people worked with blacks in these and similar organizations. But

Although they did not enjoy many of the benefits of American life, blacks fought in their country's wars. These soldiers served in the Spanish-American War.

the average white person never tried to find out what black people thought and felt or ever read black newspapers, magazines, or books. Fewer still would have guessed how deeply discontented black people were, especially in the South. Black people grew increasingly isolated from white society and came to rely more and more on their own institutions for aid and security. The black church became not only a source of spiritual renewal but also the center of social life and community activity.

But black Americans remained steadfast in their patriotism. During the Spanish-American War (1898), black troops of the Ninth and Tenth cavalries fought alongside the famous First Volunteer Cavalry, or Rough Riders.

IMPORTANT DATES IN BLACK AMERICAN HISTORY

1513 Blacks accompanied Spanish explorers Ponce de León and Balboa to New World.

1538 Estevanico led expedition in the Southwest.

1619 First blacks landed at Jamestown, Virginia.

1663 First serious slave conspiracy in colonial America, by white servants and black slaves, in Gloucester County, Virginia.

1688 First formal protest against slavery in Western Hemisphere, by Quakers of Germantown, Pennsylvania.

1770 Crispus Attucks killed in Boston Massacre.

1777 Vermont became first state to abolish slavery.

1787 Continental Congress excluded slavery from Northwest Territory.

1807 President Thomas Jefferson signed bill abolishing slave trade as of January 1, 1808.

1820 Missouri Compromise.

1822 Slave conspiracy planned by Denmark Vesey.

1831 Nat Turner led slave revolt in Virginia.

1834 American Anti-Slavery Society organized in Philadelphia, Pennsylvania.

1847 Frederick Douglass published first issue of *The North Star.*

1850 Fugitive Slave Act passed by Congress, as part of Compromise of 1850

1854 Kansas-Nebraska Act.

1857 Dred Scott decision by Supreme Court opened federal territory to slavery and denied citizenship to American blacks.

1859 John Brown hanged for attack on federal arsenal at Harpers Ferry, West Virginia.

1861 U.S. Civil War began.

1863 Emancipation Proclamation.

1865 Civil War ended. Freedmen's Bureau established; President Lincoln assassinated; Thirteenth Amendment adopted.

1866 Civil Rights Act passed over President Andrew Johnson's veto.

1867 First Reconstruction acts passed by Congress.

1868 Fourteenth Amendment adopted.

1870 Hiram R. Revels, first black person in Congress, elected senator from Mississippi; Fifteenth Amendment adopted.

1875 Civil Rights Act of 1875 signed.

1877 Last federal troops left South.

1881 Tennessee passed Jim Crow railroad car law, beginning modern segregation movement.

1895 Booker T. Washington delivered "Atlanta Compromise" speech at Atlanta, Georgia.

1896 *Plessy* v. *Ferguson* decision by Supreme Court upheld "separate but equal" doctrine.

1898 Louisiana became first southern state to insert "grandfather" clause in its constitution, excluding blacks from voting by limiting that right to descendants of men who voted before 1867.

1909 NAACP founded; black explorer Matthew A. Henson accompanied Peary to North Pole.

1910 Urban League founded.

1915 Supreme Court declared "grandfather" clause illegal.

1941 President Franklin D. Roosevelt issued Executive Order 8802 prohibiting discrimination in government and defense industries.

1942 CORE founded.

1946 Supreme Court banned segregation in interstate bus travel.

1948 President Truman issued Executive Order 9981 abolishing segregation in armed forces.

1950 Ralph J. Bunche awarded Nobel peace prize.

1951 NAACP began attack on segregation and discrimination in elementary and high schools.

1954 *Brown* v. *Board of Education* decision by Supreme Court overrules *Plessy* v. *Ferguson* decision of 1896; racial segregation in public schools declared unconstitutional.

1955 Interstate Commerce Commission banned segregation in interstate buses and facilities; Martin Luther King, Jr., led bus boycott in Montgomery, Alabama.

1956 Supreme Court ruled segregation on public transportation unconstitutional.

1957 SCLC organized; Civil Rights Act of 1957 passed; federal troops ordered to Little Rock, Arkansas, to prevent interference with school integration.

1960 "Sit-in" demonstrations began at Greensboro, North Carolina; SNCC organized; Civil Rights Act of 1960 signed.

1961 Freedom riders sent into South.

1962 Federal troops ordered to Oxford, Mississippi, to protect James H. Meredith, first black person to register at University of Mississippi; President Kennedy signed executive order banning discrimination in federal housing.

1964 Civil Rights Act of 1964 signed.

1965 Martin Luther King, Jr., awarded Nobel peace prize; federal voting rights bill enacted.

1966 Robert C. Weaver became the first black cabinet member.

1967 Thurgood Marshall became the first black appointed to the U.S. Supreme Court; Carl B. Stokes was elected mayor of Cleveland, Ohio, and Richard G. Hatcher, mayor of Gary, Indiana.

1968 Martin Luther King, Jr., assassinated in Memphis, Tennessee; Civil Rights Act of 1968 signed.

1972 First National Black Political Convention held.

1977 Patricia Roberts Harris became first black woman cabinet member; Andrew Young became first black U.S. ambassador to the United Nations.

1983 Astronaut Guion S. Bluford, Jr., became the first black to travel in space.

1984 Civil rights leader Reverend Jesse Jackson became the first major black candidate for the U.S. presidential nomination. He won Democratic primaries in Washington, D.C., and Louisiana.

1988 Reverend Jesse Jackson campaigned again for the Democratic presidential nomination.

1989 Ronald Brown, chairman of Democratic National Committee, became the first black to lead a major American political party; L. Douglas Wilder, governor of Virginia, became the first black elected chief executive of a state.

▶PROTEST AND PROGRESS

When World War I broke out in Europe, thousands of black people began to leave the South. This alarmed the whites of the South, who saw a source of cheap labor draining away. Southern politicians and public officials tried to stop the migration. But the blacks would not be stopped.

The North seemed to promise a freer, fuller life. There were plenty of jobs in northern cities—an increase in defense production and a decline in immigration had created a labor shortage. Most blacks had never earned the high wages that northern industry paid, and they felt that they had taken a step up. They began to understand the importance of voting and of taking part in civic affairs. Their children could go to decent schools.

But black newcomers soon learned that the North was not a paradise. As more and more blacks moved north, living conditions grew worse. The black population of such cities as Chicago, Detroit, New York, Philadelphia, and Pittsburgh doubled or tripled in the years between 1914 and 1920. Housing was scarce. Often as many as ten people lived in a single room. Sanitary arrangements were poor or did not exist. Black people lived in the poorest sections, but they paid the highest rents of any group in those sections. When they tried to move to better neighborhoods, they found that white people often banded together to keep them out. All through the war years, there were racial riots in the North. In the South more than 270 blacks were lynched (unlawfully killed by mobs) in less than four years.

When the United States entered World War I in 1917 and the military draft began, 400,000 blacks went into service. They joined 20,000 black soldiers who were already in the Army and the National Guard. Segregation was the rule. More than half of the 200,000 black troops who were sent to Europe served in labor battalions. They loaded supplies, kept camps clean, and did other chores. But some black units went into battle. The 369th New York Infantry spent 191 days in the trenches. The 370th Infantry was decorated as a unit with France's Croix de Guerre.

Between the World Wars

When World War I ended, black people met with even greater difficulties than before. Segregation and discrimination were strong. There were 26 race riots in the United States in 1919. In northern cities there was bitter rivalry between whites and blacks for jobs and housing. In the South, lynchings increased. The NAACP managed to get an anti-lynching bill introduced in Congress in 1921. But southern senators kept the bill from coming to a vote. Similar bills met defeat in 1935 and 1940.

Many black Americans of the 1920's were discouraged by the slow progress in civil rights. They were attracted to the Universal Negro Improvement Association (UNIA), organized in 1916 by Marcus Garvey. The UNIA supported a "back to Africa" movement, on the grounds that black Americans could never expect to gain their rights.

One of the social results of the blacks' northern migration and of World War I was an awakening of race consciousness. This was reflected in a cultural movement known as the New Negro Movement (also called the Harlem Renaissance or the Black Renaissance). New York City was its center. The publication in 1925 of the anthology *The New Negro,* edited by Alain Locke, created a new interest in black life. Claude McKay, James Weldon Johnson, Countee Cullen, Langston Hughes, and Arna Bontemps were among the leading writers. In the following years, great fame was won by singers Roland Hayes, Marian Anderson, and Dorothy Maynor; musicians W. C. Handy and William Grant Still; and theatrical performers Paul Robeson, Bill (Bojangles) Robinson, Canada Lee, and Ethel Waters. A few noted black painters included Horace Pippin, Jacob Lawrence, and Henry O. Tanner.

Black scholars and scientists made important contributions. Historian Carter G. Woodson founded the Association for the Study of Negro Life and History. Sociologists E. Franklin Frazier and Charles S. Johnson won international recognition for their work. Percy L. Julian made pioneer discoveries in the uses of soybeans. Daniel H. Williams first successfully operated on the human heart, and Charles R. Drew was a leading authority on the preservation of blood plasma.

Led by track star Jesse Owens, black athletes won honors for the United States in the Olympic Games of 1936. One of the best-known athletes in the world was the black American prizefighter Joe Louis.

Among the prize-winning plays with black themes, written by whites, were *All God's Chillun Got Wings* and *Emperor Jones,* by Eugene O'Neill, and *In Abraham's Bosom,* by Paul Green. DuBose Heyward wrote the opera *Porgy and Bess,* with music and lyrics by George and Ira Gershwin.

Black music—spirituals and jazz—was played everywhere. Harry T. Burleigh, R. Nathaniel Dett, and J. Rosamond Johnson achieved acclaim for their arrangements of spirituals and other musical compositions. W. C. Handy received national recognition for his "St. Louis Blues" and brought about a new American music known as blues. Jazz is another type of music created by black Americans. The first jazz musicians played in New Orleans during the late 1800's and early 1900's. They later moved on to Chicago, making that city a jazz center. Several jazz band leaders such as Louis (Satchmo) Armstrong, Fletcher Henderson, Edward (Duke) Ellington and William (Count) Basie became well known for their respective styles.

In classical music, Roland Hayes, Paul Robeson, and Marian Anderson received international attention for their performances in leading European as well as American cities.

Black people also began to develop economic and political strength. Their purchasing power (the money they could spend for goods and services) leaped from a few million dollars in 1928 to several billion dollars in 1941. The first black in Congress since Reconstruction days, Oscar DePriest, was elected from Illinois in 1928.

President Franklin D. Roosevelt appointed several blacks to government positions. Ralph Bunche held a post in the State Department before he became deputy secretary-general of the United Nations. Roosevelt was opposed to racial discrimination and to the injustices that were thrust upon the poor. His "New Deal" programs helped relieve poverty and hunger, initiated national recovery from the depression and established economic reforms. Black people benefited greatly from the New Deal programs. They were able to get jobs; to obtain loans to purchase homes; to have hospitals, college buildings, and playgrounds built; and to live in low-cost federal government housing. Black actors, writers, and artists also found employment in federal projects.

Louis Armstrong, world-famous jazz trumpet and coronet soloist, was also a band leader, composer, and vocalist.

Joe Louis wearing the heavyweight championship belt in 1937. He held the title longer than any other boxer.

By 1940 there was at least a slight change in racial attitudes in the United States. The worldwide rivalry between democracy and fascism, and the need for democracy to prove itself, had helped. The blacks' efforts had helped, too. But all this was just a step on the long road to full equality in civil rights.

World War II

When World War II broke out, it became clear that victory would call for the unified efforts of all the American people. President Franklin D. Roosevelt took steps to satisfy some of the complaints of black Americans. In 1941 he issued Executive Order 8802. It prohibited discrimination in "employment of workers in defense industries and in government because of race, creed, color, or national origin." When many blacks moved to cities in the North and West to work in defense industries, they often met with violence. The housing problem was serious, and there were frequent racial clashes. The worst riot occurred in Detroit in June, 1943, and took the lives of 25 blacks and 9 whites.

More than 1,000,000 black men and women served in the U.S. armed forces during World War II. They were allowed to join branches of the services that had been closed to them, and they were encouraged to seek promotions. The chief black combat unit, the 93rd Division, fought in many Pacific campaigns. There were squadrons of black pilots. Colonel (later Lieutenant General) Benjamin O. Davis, Jr., won the Distinguished Flying Cross. He was the son of the first black general in the U.S. Army, Benjamin O. Davis, Sr. For shooting down two Japanese planes during the attack on Pearl Harbor, Dorie Miller won the Navy Cross. Four blacks were ship captains in the merchant marine, commanding integrated crews.

But segregation was still the rule in the armed forces. It lowered the spirits of black soldiers. In 1944 the War Department ordered an end to segregation in recreation and transportation in military camps. This order aroused bitter protests in the South, and it was not strictly enforced. The years of change for black people awaited the end of the war.

JAY SAUNDERS REDDING
Author, *Lonesome Road: The Story of the Negro in America*

▶ YEARS OF CHANGE

In August, 1945, World War II ended. The people of the United States, black and white, looked forward to peace and to a better economic future. More and more black people migrated to the cities in search of better job opportunities. Anti-black incidents increased, as did social tensions. Soon racial violence shocked the nation. Mobs in Louisiana, Georgia, South Carolina, and Tennessee set back the newly improved race relations and stirred unrest in the cities.

President Harry S. Truman was called on to stop racial violence and to ensure equality. He responded by establishing the President's Committee on Civil Rights. This committee of black and white leaders was to recommend ways to protect civil rights.

In 1947 the committee produced a report titled "To Secure These Rights." The document recommended the establishment of a permanent commission on civil rights and a fair-employment commission. It also recommended laws against lynching, laws against poll taxes (property taxes imposed as a voting requirement), and civil rights laws with enforcement procedures. The next year, President Truman presented a program to Congress that included the committee's recommendations.

In the meantime, W. E. B. DuBois of the NAACP sent a petition to the United Nations. The petition focused attention on the denial of civil rights to blacks and on the negative effects of slavery, discrimination, and segregation on both blacks and whites. It brought the problems of black people to the attention of the world, and it influenced public opinion.

The President established another committee to study problems of discrimination in colleges and universities. This committee recommended an end to discrimination and

---

SOME NATIONAL BLACK ORGANIZATIONS

Congress of Racial Equality (CORE), founded 1942.

National Association for the Advancement of Colored People (NAACP), founded 1909.

National Black Political Convention, founded 1969.

National Urban League (NUL), founded 1910.

Operation PUSH (People United to Serve Humanity), founded 1971.

Southern Christian Leadership Conference (SCLC), founded 1957.

United Negro College Fund (UNCF), founded 1944.

World Community of Islam in the West (Nation of Islam, Black Muslims), founded 1930.

LITTLE ROCK CENTR

On September 25, 1957, federal troops escorted nine black children into the previously all-white Central High School in Little Rock, Arkansas.

unequal educational opportunity in higher education. A third committee examined progress in integrating the armed forces. Its report, "Freedom to Serve," presented a plan for the complete integration of the armed forces.

Integration spread to civilian housing and education. In 1948 the U.S. Supreme Court outlawed limits on the type of housing open to black people. And a 1954 Supreme Court decision in *Brown* v. *Board of Education of Topeka, Kansas,* affected both blacks and whites. The decision meant that the policy of providing "separate but equal" education for blacks no longer applied. A year later little effort had been made to desegregate the schools, and the court ordered public school authorities to obey the ruling "with all deliberate speed." But discrimination in education remained a problem. In 1957 federal troops were sent to Little Rock, Arkansas, to protect nine black students who were attempting to enroll in Central High School there.

Employment for blacks increased in the years following the war. Black workers were invited to join the Congress of Industrial Organizations (CIO), a labor federation. In 1955 the CIO merged with the American Federation of Labor (AFL). Two black men, A. Philip Randolph and Willard Townsend, became vice-presidents of the new organization.

Blacks also made advances in other fields. Several actors and actresses who had received their start in the 1930's were able to find jobs on Broadway and in Hollywood. Outstanding black dancers, musicians, and artists were recognized for their talents. By the mid-1950's many blacks were contributing to the sciences and receiving recognition for their work. And more attention was given to the history of black Americans. Blacks wrote much of their own history, as little had been included in traditional history books. W. E. B. DuBois was the most influential scholar of the time.

Black writers produced works that presented and interpreted the problems and experiences of blacks. And by the 1960s a new protest movement had brought forth a new set of protest writers. Their works reflected three major themes—liberation, self-determination, and a positive self-image for blacks.

Nonviolent Demonstrations

Despite the improvements of the postwar years, many problems remained for blacks. In the 1960's a new thrust for civil rights began. As the movement gained momentum, new leaders emerged. Stokely Carmichael, H. Rap Brown, and Malcolm X were vocal, and they led large groups of people in the fight for civil rights. The most renowned of the leaders was Martin Luther King, Jr.

King, a minister in Montgomery, Alabama, came to national attention in 1955. He led a boycott of the city's buses after Rosa Parks, a black woman, was arrested for refusing to give up her seat on a bus to a white man. The

The Reverend Martin Luther King, Jr., (*center*) was one of the leaders of the Freedom March on Washington, D.C., in August, 1963. More than 200,000 people participated.

boycott lasted 381 days and inspired blacks in other southern cities. Finally, in November, 1956, the U.S. Supreme Court banned segregation in public transportation.

People soon realized that an organization that could co-ordinate integration activities was necessary. In 1957 the Southern Christian Leadership Conference on Transportation and Nonviolent Integration was founded. It later became known as the Southern Christian Leadership Conference (SCLC). King was its leader.

Young people led the fight for equality. In 1960, four black students from North Carolina Agricultural and Technical College, in Greensboro, sat at a segregated (white) lunch counter in a local store. They sat for an hour without being served. Because they refused to move, the counter was closed early. This practice of sitting in places reserved for whites became known as a sit-in. The sit-in spread rapidly as a form of protest in southern cities.

The SCLC helped to organize the Student Nonviolent Co-ordinating Committee

Patricia Harris, first black woman cabinet member, and Andrew Young, first black U.S. Ambassador to the United Nations.

(SNCC). SNCC members became involved in direct action programs in black communities. They encouraged voter registration, led demonstrations, held classes in nonviolent protest techniques, and distributed food and clothing to the needy. A few well-known members of SNCC were Marion Barry, Julian Bond, John Lewis, and James Forman.

The Congress of Racial Equality (CORE), organized by James Farmer in 1942, also helped the young protest workers. In 1961, CORE organized new protests called freedom rides. Freedom riders forced the integration of interstate buses and waiting rooms. Sometimes they were beaten, or their buses were damaged by angry whites. But the rides proved necessary to guarantee the equal rights that had been granted by the courts.

The work of King and the SCLC gave the organization an international reputation. King took part in many demonstrations and stressed his belief in nonviolence. In 1963 he began to use a form of protest called civil disobedience. He and his followers would allow themselves to be arrested to protest what they felt was an unjust court order.

On August 28 of that year, King led more than 200,000 people in the now-famous March on Washington. The participants listened to his "I have a dream . . ." speech. At the foot of the Lincoln Memorial, they also heard leaders of various civil rights groups call for a "new birth of freedom." The memorial was a significant site, as Abraham Lincoln was known as the Great Emancipator. King received worldwide recognition in 1964, when he was awarded the Nobel peace prize.

Black leaders have approached the fight for equal rights from many directions. From left: James Farmer of CORE; Whitney M. Young, Jr., of the NUL; A. Phillip Randolph, labor leader; and Dr. John Hope Franklin, scholar.

Many nonviolent demonstrations met with resistance from authorities in southern cities. Demonstrators were often injured by police who used nightsticks, electric cattle prods, and streams of water from high-powered fire hoses. Churches and homes used for meetings were sometimes burned to the ground.

But the demonstrations helped bring about change. An executive order issued in 1962 by President John F. Kennedy prohibited discrimination in housing built with federal funds. In 1964 the Twenty-fourth Amendment to the U.S. Constitution prohibited poll taxes. The Civil Rights Act of 1964 did away with segregation and discrimination in housing, employment, voting, and other areas. The Voting Rights Act of 1965 removed other restrictions to voting.

But these laws did not go far enough, and their provisions were often ignored. Many blacks, especially among the young, grew increasingly impatient and militant.

Separatism, Militancy, and Black Power

While King was leading the civil rights movement, a religious group called the Black Muslims began to grow in strength. The Black Muslims had been founded in Detroit in the 1930's by Wali D. Farad (Fard). Later Elijah Poole, who took the name Elijah Muhammad, became the leader of the movement.

The Black Muslims required their followers to separate themselves from whites. During the 1960's one of the most influential Black Muslims was Malcolm X. He became a major leader within the black community. Eventually he began to see that separatism was not the answer to the problems of blacks. But before he could develop this new line of thinking, he was assassinated at a Harlem meeting in 1965.

The next year the Black Panther Party for Unity and Self-Defense was organized in Oakland, California, by Huey P. Newton and Bobby G. Seale. Both young men admired Malcolm X's stress on self-defense and freedom for blacks. They believed blacks had to fight to achieve dignity and freedom.

The Panthers brought attention to unjust rent evictions and instances of police brutality. Soon they were teaching black history classes and informing people who were on welfare of their rights. Branches of the Black Panthers were established in several parts of the United States. But the organization became more militant, and there were many confrontations between Panthers and police. Both blacks and whites began to fear the Panthers.

Macolm X disagreed with the militant separatist philosophy of the Black Muslims and founded his own movement, the Organization of Afro-American Unity.

Shirley Chisholm served seven terms in the U.S. House of Representatives. Harold Washington, elected in 1983, was the first black mayor of Chicago.

The actor James Earl Jones, in costume for his role in *Othello,* and the operatic soprano Leontyne Price are two outstanding performing artists.

In the late 1960's, "black power" became a slogan of the civil rights movement. It meant achievement by blacks, as well as economic and political power. Leaders of the movement focused on voter registration, black ownership of businesses, and control of schools and poverty programs. More important, they stressed self-pride and dignity.

Self-help programs began to emerge in black communities. Black-owned businesses included banks, factories, bus lines, and stores. An SCLC-sponsored program in Chicago, called Operation Breadbasket, received national attention. Its director was the Reverend Jesse Jackson. He organized boycotts against dairy and grocery chain stores that had dealt unfairly with blacks, and he promoted the sale of goods manufactured by blacks.

At the same time, anger and despair at continuing discrimination touched off riots in a number of cities. These "ghetto riots" were largely the result of failure to enforce the Civil Rights Act of 1964. In 1968 the U.S. Senate approved a new civil rights bill. But as the House of Representatives was considering the bill, tragedy struck. On April 4, 1968, Martin Luther King, Jr., was shot and killed in Memphis, Tennessee, by a white man.

Grief and anger were shared by blacks and whites alike as news of the assassination spread. Rioting and looting broke out in over 30 cities. Forty-six people died, and more than 2,500 were injured. Soldiers were called in to stop the rioting.

Although King was dead, several positive things took place. The Civil Rights Act of 1968 was passed by Congress. The Supreme Court declared that discrimination in the sale or rental of property was unconstitutional. And a demonstration designed by King, the Poor People's Campaign, was carried out.

Growing Political Strength

In the 1970's the civil rights movement lost some of its thrust. There was no single national leader. Ralph Abernathy led the SCLC, but his following was not as great as King's. A new organization, People United to Serve Humanity (PUSH), was founded in Chicago by Jesse Jackson. Its purpose was to fight for both economic and civil rights.

Some progress continued to be made in integration. In 1971 the Supreme Court ruled that busing to achieve racial balance in schools was constitutional. In 1976 it held that private schools, except religious schools, could not deny admission to blacks.

Meanwhile, black political strength was growing. Black politicians obtained the votes of blacks and whites, and more blacks held public offices. Black members of the U.S. House of Representatives formed a caucus. They came to national attention in 1971, when they boycotted President Richard M. Nixon's State of the Union address because he had refused to meet with them.

In March, 1972, the first National Black Political Convention was held, in Gary, Indiana. More than 3,300 delegates attended. They were mayors, city council members, state legislators, and others. One result of the convention was a document called "The National Black Political Agenda." This document reflected the major concerns of black Ameri-

SOME LEADING BLACK AMERICANS OF THE 20TH CENTURY

Government, Politics, and the Military:

Thomas Bradley, mayor (Los Angeles, California)
Edward W. Brooke, U.S. senator
Ralph Bunche, United Nations under secretary
Shirley Chisholm, U.S. representative
Ronald Dellums, U.S. representative
David Dinkins, mayor (New York, New York)
Patricia R. Harris, diplomat and cabinet official
Daniel (Chappie) James, four-star U.S. Army general
Barbara Jordan, U.S. representative
Thurgood Marshall, U.S. Supreme Court Justice
Donald F. McHenry, diplomat
Colin Powell, chairman of the Joint Chiefs of Staff
Carl T. Rowan, diplomat and journalist
Harold Washington, mayor (Chicago, Illinois)
Andrew Young, diplomat and mayor (Atlanta, Georgia)
Coleman Young, mayor (Detroit, Michigan)

Scholarship and the Professions:

Kenneth B. Clark, psychologist
John Hope Franklin, historian
John H. Johnson, publisher
Percy Julian, physician
Ernest E. Just, biologist
Rayford Logan, historian
James M. Nabrit, educator and lawyer
Benjamin Quarles, historian
Margaret Bush Wilson, lawyer
Carter G. Woodson, historian

The Arts:

Alvin Ailey, dancer
Marian Anderson, singer
Louis Armstrong, jazz musician
James Baldwin, writer
Imamu Baraka (LeRoi Jones), writer
Count Basie, jazz musician
Kathleen Battle, singer
Harry Belafonte, actor and singer
Chuck Berry, musician
Gwendolyn Brooks, poet
Cab Calloway, jazz musician
Ray Charles, musician
Alice Childress, writer
Eldridge Cleaver, writer
Bill Cosby, actor
Katherine Dunham, dancer
Duke Ellington, jazz musician
Ralph Ellison, writer
Ella Fitzgerald, singer
Dizzy Gillespie, jazz musician
Nikki Giovanni, poet
Lorraine Hansberry, playwright
Langston Hughes, writer
Mahalia Jackson, gospel singer
Michael Jackson, musician
James Earl Jones, actor
Jacob Lawrence, artist
Spike Lee, filmmaker
Wynton Marsalis, musician
Arthur Mitchell, dancer
Thelonius Monk, jazz musician
Toni Morrison, writer
Jessye Norman, singer
Charlie Parker, jazz musician
Sidney Poitier, actor
Leontyne Price, opera singer
Augusta Savage, sculptor
Alice Walker, writer
Ethel Waters, singer
Stevie Wonder, musician
Richard Wright, writer

Sports:

Hank Aaron, baseball
Kareem Abdul-Jabbar, basketball
Muhammad Ali, boxing
Arthur Ashe, tennis
Jimmy Brown, football
Wilt Chamberlain, basketball
Althea Gibson, tennis
Reggie Jackson, baseball
Earvin (Magic) Johnson, basketball
Michael Jordan, basketball
Willie Mays, baseball
Walter Payton, football
Jackie Robinson, baseball
Sugar Ray Robinson, boxing
Wilma Rudolph, track and field
Bill Russell, basketball

Civil Rights:

Ralph D. Abernathy, SCLC
Mary McLeod Bethune, educator
Charles and **Medgar Evers,** NAACP
Wali D. Farad, Black Muslims
Benjamin Hooks, NAACP
Jesse Jackson, Operation PUSH
Vernon Jordan, National Urban League
Coretta Scott King, SCLC
Martin Luther King, Jr., SCLC
Malcolm X, Black Muslims
Floyd B. McKissick, CORE
Elijah Muhammad, Black Muslims
Rosa Parks, activist
Roy Wilkins, NAACP
Whitney Young, National Urban League

Consult the index for biographies on many of these and other prominent black Americans in this encyclopedia.

---

cans. It contained a list of categories that needed improvement and an agenda for blacks in public office.

Black people voted in record numbers in the 1976 presidential election, helping to elect Jimmy Carter. By that time there were black mayors in seven major cities. They faced new problems and changing conditions. Many businesses had moved from the cities to the suburbs. The black population of the cities had increased, but job opportunities had decreased. Crime rose to a new high, and drugs were a major problem. Other areas of concern included transportation, education, pollution, garbage collection, and taxes.

In the 1980's, blacks in high positions spoke out about problems that continued to harm black communities. Unemployment became a major issue. Many felt that the presidency of Ronald Reagan (1981–89) represented a major setback for blacks, as members of the U.S. Commission on Civil Rights questioned Reagan's commitment to civil rights issues. Therefore, in 1984 and 1988, a number of black civil rights and political leaders supported the candidacy of the Reverend Jesse Jackson for the Democratic presidential nomination. Jackson won much popular support and brought black issues into the political spotlight.

In the 1990's, racial unrest came to a head once again when a jury acquitted several Los Angeles policemen accused of brutality in the arrest of a black man, Rodney King. The beating had been recorded on videotape, so the verdict surprised and outraged many people, white as well as black. It led to rioting in Los Angeles, which underscored the despair and anger of those who continue to feel the sting of discrimination.

FLORENCE A. JACKSON
Author, *Blacks in America* series

See also AFRICA; CIVIL RIGHTS; CIVIL WAR, UNITED STATES; COMPROMISE OF 1850; DRED SCOTT DECISION; HYMNS (Spirituals and Other Folk Hymns); KANSAS-NEBRASKA ACT; LINCOLN-DOUGLAS DEBATES; MISSOURI COMPROMISE; RACES, HUMAN; RECONSTRUCTION PERIOD; SEGREGATION; SLAVERY; UNDERGROUND RAILROAD; JACKSON, JESSE; KING, MARTIN LUTHER, JR., and names of other individual black leaders.

BLACKFOOT INDIANS. See INDIANS, AMERICAN.
BLACK HAWK. See ILLINOIS (Famous People).
BLACK HOLES. See STARS.
BLACK SEA. See OCEANS AND SEAS OF THE WORLD.

BLACKWELL, ELIZABETH (1821–1910)

As a young woman, Elizabeth Blackwell earned her living as a teacher. But she was not happy in her work. She longed for independence and became a supporter of women's rights. Searching for a career that would offer her independence and that would also allow her to help people, Blackwell decided to become a doctor.

Born on February 3, 1821, in Bristol, England, Blackwell and her family moved to the United States in 1832. It was in the United States that Blackwell applied to medical school. However, women were not welcome in the medical profession, and Blackwell was repeatedly turned down by the medical schools to which she applied. Finally she was accepted by the Geneva Medical College in Geneva, New York.

Most of her fellow students respected her, but the doctors at a hospital where she went for training treated her less kindly. "When I walked into the wards they walked out," she later wrote of her experience. Still, Blackwell did not give up. She graduated from medical school in 1849, the first woman in the United States to do so. She then went to Europe to continue her studies.

Blackwell returned to the United States in 1851. However, because she was a woman, no hospital would allow her to practice medicine. In 1853, determined to help the sick, she set up her own small clinic in a poor New York City neighborhood. Four years later Blackwell opened the New York Infirmary for Women and Children, a hospital run almost entirely by women. In 1868, Blackwell expanded the hospital to include the Women's Medical College, the first of its kind in America. In 1869, she returned to England, where she helped found the London School of Medicine for Women. She died on May 31, 1910, at the age of 89.

KARYN L. BERTSCHI
Science Writer

BLAKE, WILLIAM (1757–1827)

William Blake, the English poet and artist, was born on November 28, 1757, in London. His father was a shopkeeper, and the family lived simply. William was taught at home by his mother. He read poetry and other literature, including the Bible, theology, mystical writings, and philosophy. Sometimes William would speak of visions he had seen. Once he returned home from a walk and told his parents that he had seen angels in the treetops.

When he was 10, William was able to go to a drawing school. He began to write poems at the age of 12. At 14, he was apprenticed to an engraver so that he could learn a trade.

In 1782, Blake married Catherine Boucher. Blake trained his wife to help him produce hand-colored engravings of his poems and drawings. Blake's drawings enlarge and complete the meaning of his poems.

Blake's chief prose work is *The Marriage of Heaven and Hell* (1790–93), a satire. But he is best loved for his collections of poems called *Songs of Innocence* (1789) and *Songs of Experience* (1794). These works contain his two most famous poems, "The Lamb" and "The Tiger." Blake's engraving of "The Tiger" is reproduced in Volume E, page 278.

Blake's comments on the ugliness, cruelty, and injustice of the world as he saw it play as much a part in his works as do his comments on the beauties and joys of life.

Blake believed that the world of the imagination was more real than the world that people could see or touch. And he was able to bring alive, through words and pictures, the world of his own imagination. As time went on, his art and poetry became increasingly filled with symbols from his visions.

After about 1818, Blake did little writing, but he continued to produce engravings and watercolors. He died peacefully on August 12, 1827. The full appreciation of his genius did not come until long after his death.

EDMUND FULLER
Author, *Man in Modern Fiction*

BLEEDING. See FIRST AID.

BLIGH, WILLIAM (1754–1817)

British naval officer William Bligh commanded the H.M.S. *Bounty*. The scandalous mutiny aboard that ship in 1789 immortalized his name in the annals of maritime history. Bligh was born in the old Devon County seaport of Plymouth, England, on September 9, 1754. At the early age of 22, he became sailing master of the H.M.S. *Resolution* on Captain James Cook's third great Pacific voyage of exploration (1776–80).

In 1787, Bligh was given command of the H.M.S. *Bounty* and ordered to sail to the South Pacific to collect breadfruit plants in Tahiti. The plants were to be transported to the British West Indies and used to feed the slaves on the colonial plantations.

The infamous mutiny on the *Bounty* occurred on April 28, 1789, when Bligh's crew became fed up with his bullying ways. The ship's 2nd lieutenant, Fletcher Christian, took command of the *Bounty* and cast Bligh adrift in a small boat with 19 other loyal crew members. After a stormy and miraculous passage

that covered 3,900 miles (6,240 kilometers) in 43 days, Bligh and his men landed safely on the island of Timor in Southeast Asia. Christian, in the meantime, had sailed eastward with 8 other mutineers and 17 Tahitians and settled on uninhabited Pitcairn Island (where some of their descendants still reside).

The British searched in vain for Christian and his group, but three of the mutineers who had settled in Tahiti were found and hanged for their crime. Bligh was absolved of all blame for the loss of the *Bounty*. His last important appointment was as governor of the British penal colony in Australia (1805–08). He retired as a vice admiral and died in 1817.

SAM McKINNEY
Author, *Bligh: A True Account of Mutiny Aboard His Majesty's Ship Bounty*

BLINDNESS

Some people cannot read the words printed on this page. This is because they are blind. People without eyesight face difficulties in everyday life that can be hard for sighted people to imagine. Try putting toothpaste on a toothbrush with your eyes closed. How would you cook a meal if you could not see? Most of the things we learn by watching others must be taught to people without sight.

Blindness is not simply being without eyesight. There are many degrees of blindness. Some blind people can distinguish light and dark. Others can recognize the direction of a light source.

People who have limited eyesight are said to be visually impaired. Their eyesight may be limited in one or more ways. Some visually impaired people can recognize large objects, such as chairs or tables, but cannot see details on those objects. Some individuals cannot see to the left or right, some have several blind spots in their vision, and some individuals cannot distinguish colors or contrasts.

There are approximately 2.5 million people in the United States alone who are severely visually impaired. Three quarters of these people are 65 years of age or older. This is because many of the causes of eyesight loss are associated with aging.

▶ THE DEGREES OF BLINDNESS

People who study eyesight loss have established guidelines for identifying blindness and visual impairment. The guidelines are based on **visual acuity**, which means the amount of details an individual can see. A person is said to be visually impaired if he or she has a visual acuity of 20/70 or less when wearing corrective lenses (eyeglasses or contact lenses). This means that what a person with normal vision can see at 70 feet away, a visually impaired person can see at only 20 feet away.

A person is considered to be blind if his or her visual acuity is 20/200 or less with corrective lenses. This means that what a person with normal vision can see at 200 feet away, a blind person cannot see at all or at no more than 20 feet away.

These measurements are always determined by the stronger eye. Some people have no eyesight in one eye but some vision in the other eye. They are not considered blind or visually impaired unless the stronger eye meets the above guidelines.

There is one additional measure of blindness that has to do with a person's **visual field**. Visual field refers to how great an area a person can see. It is measured in degrees of an angle. If a person with normal vision looks straight ahead, he or she should be able to see nearly all the objects in a half-circle (180 degrees). Individuals who have a visual field of no greater than 20 degrees are considered to be blind.

▶CAUSES OF BLINDNESS

There are many causes of blindness and visual impairment. Some people are born with this condition. Their blindness or visual impairment is said to be **congenital**, meaning "born with."

Accidents can also cause eyesight loss. Wearing protective eyeglasses or goggles during activities such as using power tools, playing racquetball, or working with chemicals can help prevent such accidents.

Disease is a very common cause of blindness and visual impairment. **Cataracts**, an ailment usually found in elderly people, causes a clouding of the lens in the eye. If you look through a piece of waxed paper, you can experience what some people with cataracts see.

Glaucoma is a disease that causes increased fluid pressure inside the eye. It can cause blindness and also tunnel vision. If you close one eye and look through a paper towel tube with the other eye, you will see what tunnel vision is like. If detected early, glaucoma often can be treated with special eye drops or surgery.

Diabetes causes a swelling and leaking of the blood vessels inside the eye. This can cause blurred vision. If the blood vessels break, the blood interferes with light passing through the eye. This can cause visual impairment or total blindness.

In developing nations, there are additional diseases that cause eyesight loss. **Onchocerciasis**, commonly referred to as "river blindness," is an eye infection caused by a parasite. This disease is common in tropical areas such as Central America and parts of Africa. In some villages, 10 percent of the total population is blind because of this disease.

What to Do When You See a Blind Person

If you see a blind person who seems to need help, offer your assistance. Tell the person who you are and that you are speaking to him or her. If the person says that help is not needed, believe it and simply go on your way.

If the person accepts your help, let him or her take your arm at the elbow. When you lead a blind person, you should always walk slightly in front. If a blind person is using a guide dog, do not pet or distract the animal. The guide dog is a working dog and is not a pet.

Do not be afraid to use words like "see" and "look." Such words do not make blind people uncomfortable. If a person is blind, that does not mean he or she cannot hear. Remember to speak in a normal tone of voice.

When you leave a blind person, tell him or her that you are leaving. Let the person know that you may meet again. "See you soon!"

Using an abacus, the student works on math problems from a braille textbook. Braille is a touch method of reading letters, numbers, and other symbols.

BRAILLE ALPHABET AND NUMERALS									
a	b	c	d	e	f	g	h	i	j
k	l	m	n	o	p	q	r	s	t
u	v	w	x	y	z				
1	2	3	4	5	6	7	8	9	0

Xerophthalmia is the major cause of blindness in young children in many developing countries. It is caused by a severe lack of protein and vitamin A in the diet. This disease is found in overpopulated regions of south and east Asia, Africa, the eastern Mediterranean, and parts of Latin America. In India alone, more than 60,000 children under the age of 6 go totally blind each year due to this disease.

▶ COPING WITH BLINDNESS

Two of the biggest challenges that a blind or visually impaired person must face are moving about independently and communicating with others.

Moving about without sight—or with very limited sight—requires a unique set of skills. Blind people must use their sense of hearing, smell, and touch to learn about their environment. This is called **orientation**. For example, a blind person in the city listens for traffic sounds to know when to cross a street. The person may smell flowers in a park or food from a restaurant to help them know where they are.

To move about safely, blind or visually impaired people can rely on a variety of aids. A long cane, also called a prescription cane, is used when walking to warn of objects, stairs, or street curbs in a person's path. Scientists have developed a laser cane, which can also detect objects at head or chest level. When it senses an obstacle, the cane gives out a warning sound.

Blind teenagers and adults can learn to use a guide dog to move about. Both the dog and the handler attend a special school to learn how to work together. Guide dogs serve the same purposes as the long cane. They help the person move around obstacles or stop before stepping up or down.

Blind and visually impaired people have the same need for information about the world as people with sight. To meet that need, there are many useful aids.

Braille is a touch method of reading. The braille alphabet was developed in France by Louis Braille in the 1800's. The letters of the braille alphabet are based on a system of six raised dots that can be read by the fingertips. There are also special braille symbols for mathematical, musical, computer, and foreign language materials. Braille can be produced by using heavy paper with special braille typewriters.

Large-print books and magazines are useful to people with less severe visual impairments. Audio tapes are frequently used for both leisure and educational reading. Some computers have speech devices that can talk to the user, telling what is happening on the screen.

Two recent developments help blind and visually impaired people gain more immediate access to current information. Talking Newspaper programs allow people to call on the telephone and have the newspaper read aloud to them. Audiodescription Services provides a description of the action, mannerisms, and

What is a Talking Book?

The world of books is open to the blind today through books prepared in braille and through long-playing recordings of books, called talking books. The largest producer of braille textbooks is the American Printing House for the Blind in Louisville, Kentucky.

The Library of Congress of the United States, Division for the Blind and Physically Handicapped, in Washington, D.C., has hundreds of thousands of braille volumes and talking books. Hundreds of new library titles are recorded and brailled each year. Throughout the country there are libraries that act as distributing centers for these books and records. They are mailed postage-free.

Technological advances, such as talking computers and electronic braille machines, have opened up new career opportunities for blind and visually impaired individuals.

other nonverbal communications shown on television programs.

▶ **EDUCATION AND EMPLOYMENT**

The first school for children who were blind was founded in France in 1784 by Valentin Hauy. By 1833 there were three special schools for blind children in the United States. Public school began to educate blind children in the early 1900's. Today, about 90 percent of all the children in the United States who are blind or visually impaired are educated in their neighborhood or community schools. Blind and visually impaired children must learn the special skills needed by people without sight. They also must learn basic concepts in special ways. Because so much of what we learn is through observation, visually impaired children need a great deal of hands-on experience. Concepts such as up and down, streets, rainbows, clouds, and stars are meaningless words unless taught with models or accurate verbal descriptions.

Any career that does not depend on sight is open to a blind or visually impaired person. People without sight can become teachers, farmers, computer programmers, government workers, accountants, or lawyers. Young people can work at jobs such as delivering newspapers, counseling children at summer camp, and serving food at fast food restaurants.

▶ **AGENCIES AND ASSOCIATIONS THAT HELP**

The American Foundation for the Blind helps blind and visually impaired people achieve equal access to opportunities that will help them live independent and satisfying lives. This organization helps pass laws that will help people with limited sight, publishes information about blindness, and provides a directory of consumer groups, agencies, schools, and services that can help. Its headquarters is in New York City.

Three United Nations agencies are concerned with blindness in both industrialized and developing nations. These are the United Nations Education, Scientific and Cultural Organization (UNESCO), the World Health Organization (WHO), and the United Nations Children's Fund (UNICEF).

KATHLEEN MARY HUEBNER
Director, National Consultants Department
American Foundation for the Blind

See also EYE; KELLER, HELEN.

BLOOD

Long before the beginning of recorded history, people realized that blood meant the difference between life and death. When cave dwellers speared an animal and blood gushed from the wound, the beast soon fell dead. A person who lost a lot of blood also died. It is no wonder that blood was often regarded as the mysterious secret of life. People came to believe that good or evil spirits were present in blood itself.

Today blood is no longer a mystery, but as everyone knows, it is vital to certain forms of animal life. For all such animals, blood is the stream of life.

▶ BLOOD'S MAJOR TASKS

The human body contains a vast network of blood vessels. They are the arteries, veins, and capillaries. These vessels, extending throughout the body, carry the stream of blood. The average adult has about 5 liters (just over 5 quarts) in continuous circulation. A child has less. The blood serves the body's needs in the following ways:

The body is made of living cells that need food to grow and to reproduce themselves. Blood supplies food to the cells.

Cells "burn" food, thus producing energy for the body. To burn food, the cells need oxygen from the air. The blood carries oxygen to the cells.

Wastes, such as the gas carbon dioxide, are given off by the burning process. The blood carries these wastes away from the cells.

Cells live surrounded by a watery material called tissue fluid. Blood provides this fluid.

Every part of the body needs water to function. The blood brings water to all parts of the body.

When the body exercises heavily, a great deal of heat is given off by the muscles. Blood distributes heat evenly through the body. Blood also carries excess heat to the skin, where this heat is given off.

Some parts of the body make chemicals needed by cells and body organs. Blood distributes these chemicals.

The body produces cells and chemicals that fight harmful bacteria and viruses. Blood carries these "fighters" to the parts of the body that need them.

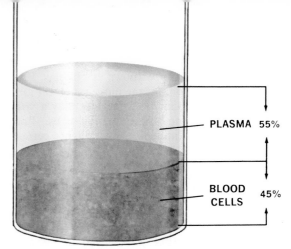

The clear liquid, plasma, makes up about half the blood.

For all these—and other—reasons, blood is called the stream of life.

▶ WHAT IS BLOOD MADE OF?

When you cut yourself, some very small blood vessels—capillaries—break, and a little blood escapes. Soon the blood clots. It forms a thick jelly that plugs the cut. From such experiences we all learn that blood is red, thicker than water, sticky, and salty in taste. Blood contains platelets (one kind of blood cell) and chemicals that make it clot.

If a drop of blood is examined under a microscope, many round cells can be seen. These are the red cells. Seen singly, they appear faint pink or yellow rather than red. Only the thickness of many cells bunched together makes blood look red.

Red cells are only one kind of solid matter that is found in blood. Some of the solids are dissolved in the watery part. Other solids are in suspension. That is, they are distributed through the blood like grains of sand in a glass of water that has been stirred. In laboratories blood can be separated into two major parts: a jellylike mass of cells and a thin, straw-colored liquid.

Blood Plasma

The liquid part of the blood is called plasma. It is thin and clear because it is 90 percent water, but many chemicals are dissolved in it. These chemicals include forms of calcium (which builds bones) and potassium (which is needed by the heart and muscles). Plasma contains a salt, which accounts for the salty taste of blood. Plasma also carries sugar and tiny drops of fat—fuels for the body's cells.

Most of the solids dissolved in plasma are

molecules of the type known as proteins. Proteins perform some of the most important jobs in the human body. Certain ones play a vital part in building and repairing cells. Proteins called antibodies help fight certain disease-causing invaders of the body. Among the proteins are also certain hormones—chemicals that control the work of different parts of the body.

Solids in the Blood

While circulating throughout the body, the blood plasma also carries solids that are not dissolved. The most important of such solids are the corpuscles ("little bodies")—usually called blood cells. Mature blood corpuscles do not grow or reproduce themselves. Unlike most of the body's cells, blood corpuscles do not join together to form tissue. They float singly, in suspension. The blood corpuscles can be separated from plasma. When this is done, the corpuscles form a jellylike mass.

There are three kinds of solid bodies in the blood: red cells, white cells, and platelets. (The drawing shows what the different bodies look like.) Each kind performs one major task. The red cells carry oxygen throughout the body. The white cells attack infection-causing bacteria. And the platelets help to clot the blood.

Blood contains three types of cells: red cells, platelets, and white cells.

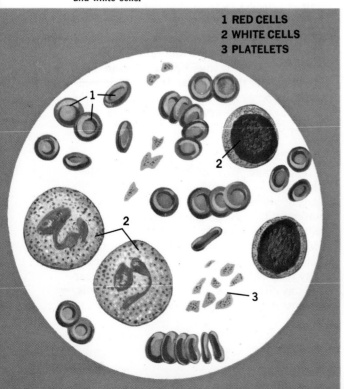

1 RED CELLS
2 WHITE CELLS
3 PLATELETS

Red Blood Cells. Most of the solids in the blood are red cells. Billions and billions of them circulate in the bloodstream. About 1,400 of them placed side by side would stretch one centimeter (about 3,500 to an inch). As they flow through the capillaries, red cells move in single file in these narrow blood vessels.

The red cells contain a protein called hemoglobin. Hemoglobin is a pigment (coloring matter) containing iron. In combination with oxygen, hemoglobin gives blood its red color. More important, hemoglobin also has the ability to combine loosely with oxygen.

This loose combining explains how red cells deliver oxygen to the body cells. Oxygen is part of the air breathed into the lungs. The hemoglobin picks up oxygen as blood passes through the lungs. Then, as the blood flows through capillaries among the body cells, the oxygen escapes through the thin capillary walls.

When the oxygen is released, hemoglobin takes up carbon dioxide from the body cells. This gas is waste formed when cells burn food. Loaded with carbon dioxide, the blood returns to the heart, which pumps it to the lungs. Here an exchange takes place. Carbon dioxide is dropped (to be breathed out) and fresh oxygen is picked up. Then the red cells continue on their way, carrying oxygen to cells throughout the body.

A red cell lives for about 120 days. By then it is worn out and can no longer do its work properly. Passing through the liver, it is caught and destroyed. While most of the red cell is destroyed, the iron from the hemoglobin is stored in the liver. The iron is later used in making new red cells.

New red cells are made in the red marrow of the bones. Bones have a spongy tissue inside the solid outer part. Red marrow fills the spaces in some of the spongy bone parts. New red cells are produced at about the same rate at which the worn-out old ones are destroyed.

White Blood Cells. White blood cells are colorless. They can be seen only when blood examined under a microscope has been treated with a special dye. Unlike the other blood cells, white cells have a nucleus. This is the inner core that enables the body's other cells to divide in two and reproduce themselves. But white cells do not reproduce themselves in the blood-

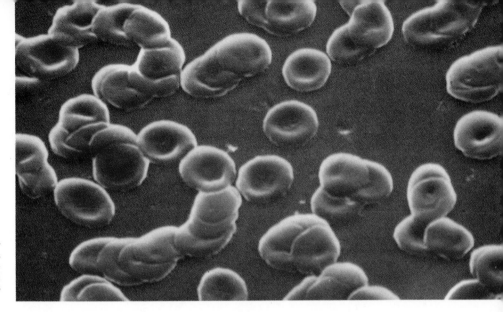

Red blood cells carry oxygen to all parts of the body. They contain a substance, called hemoglobin, that gives blood its red color.

stream. Most of them are formed in the red marrow and in the lymph glands.

Most white cells are phagocytes ("eating cells"). They can move about, even slipping through the walls of capillaries. They are also able to engulf and destroy (by "eating") invading organisms. So they make up one of the body's main defenses against infection.

If infectious bacteria enter the body—through a cut, for example—the white cells rush to the spot where the bacteria are. Great numbers of them gather around the bacteria. If they can engulf the bacteria fast enough, the infection is stopped. The dead tissue, bacteria, and dead and living white cells that collect at the point of infection all make up the matter known as pus.

Normally red cells outnumber white cells by several hundred to one. The number of white cells may increase slightly in response to physical exertion. But in a healthy person the white cells remain fairly constant. Some white cells are killed in the steady battle with harmful bacteria. Others get into the body's digestive and waste-disposal system and are lost to the body. But replacements for lost and destroyed white cells are produced in the bone marrow and in structures called lymph glands.

When harmful organisms infect the body, the total number of white cells may double or triple. One of the ways a doctor can tell whether someone is suffering from some unknown infection is to count the white cells in a tiny sample of blood.

Platelets. These are the third kind of solid in the blood. Their name describes their shape —little plates. These small, colorless bodies are fewer in number than the red cells, but more numerous than the white cells. Platelets are fragments of cells that are produced in the red bone marrow.

The platelets are needed for clotting—the process by which the blood turns into a sticky jelly and stops flowing. Blood clots most easily when exposed to air, rough surfaces, or nonliving matter, such as a bandage.

There are many steps involved in the clotting process. It begins when the platelets come in contact with the rough edges of a cut or other break in the skin. The platelets then release a chemical. This chemical starts a chain of reactions. As a result of these reactions, another chemical called fibrin is formed. Fibrin is a threadlike material. It forms a lacy mesh of fine threads. Blood cells and platelets are trapped in the mesh, like fish in a net. More cells pile up behind and a clot forms. The clot acts like a plug to stop the flow of blood.

▶ BLOOD TYPES

All human blood is made up of basically the same plasma, cells, and dissolved chemicals. But individuals differ in some of the arrangements and proportions of the chemicals in their cells and plasma.

Karl Landsteiner (1868–1943), an Austrian doctor, found in 1901 that the blood of every human being could be classed under one of four main groups, or types. The groups are

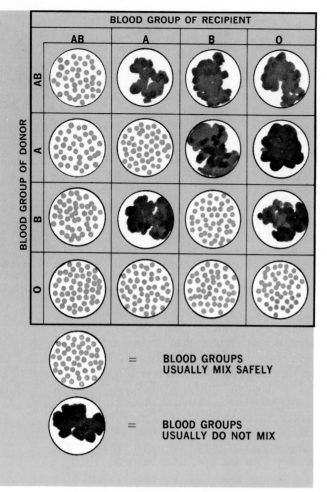

BLOOD GROUP OF RECIPIENT				
	AB	A	B	O

A blood transfusion can be a lifesaving measure if the types of blood are properly matched. The chart above shows which types will clump when mixed.

= BLOOD GROUPS USUALLY MIX SAFELY

= BLOOD GROUPS USUALLY DO NOT MIX

called A, B, O, and AB. They are based on the presence or absence of certain protein molecules in the blood.

When blood from two different groups is mixed, the blood sometimes forms clumps that could clog the body's important blood vessels. This results from a reaction between the protein molecules in the red cells of one group and the plasma of the other. Such chemical reactions make it dangerous for a person to receive a transfusion of whole blood from someone whose blood group is unknown. But if the cells are removed from blood, then the remaining plasma can be given to anyone, no matter what the person's blood group.

In the years since Landsteiner's discovery, scientists have found that the four major groups of blood can be classed chemically into various subgroups.

The presence or absence of certain other protein molecules separates all human blood into two other broad groups—Rh positive and Rh negative. The protein itself is called the Rh factor, after the rhesus monkey, in which the protein was first found.

Couples about to marry are tested for the Rh factor. This is done because of a possible danger that is faced by the baby of an Rh-negative woman and an Rh-positive man. If the baby developing in the womb is Rh-positive, the mother's Rh-negative blood produces substances that destroy many of the baby's blood cells. At one time doctors had to remove and replace all of such a baby's blood at birth to save its life. Today they have a way of learning whether the developing baby is Rh-positive. If it is, the baby is given a life-saving transfusion of concentrated Rh-negative red cells before it is born.

Blood can be exchanged among any human beings whose groups and subgroups are matched. But certain populations may have more of one particular group than another.

Human blood has many different groups and subgroups, but it is basically all the same. Each species of animal, in fact, has its own blood. This blood can be exchanged only among animals of the same species. All cats, for example, have the same kind of blood, just as all dogs have the same kind of blood.

▶ARTIFICIAL BLOOD

Scientists have developed an "artificial blood" that has been used successfully in humans. It is a white fluid, chemically related to the coating used on cookware to prevent sticking. The fluid matches all blood types. It does the job of the blood's hemoglobin, carrying oxygen and dissolving carbon dioxide. But it has no white cells, antibodies, or platelets. It cannot clot. Therefore, it cannot really replace blood. And it stays in the body for only a short time.

The fluid is used in some patients in Europe and Japan. In the United States, it is used only in emergencies for people who refuse to accept blood transfusions.

SARAH R. RIEDMAN
Author, *Your Blood and You*
Reviewed by THOMAS R. FORBES
Yale University School of Medicine

See also CIRCULATORY SYSTEM; CELLS.

BLOOD TRANSFUSION. See TRANSFUSION, BLOOD.

BLUEPRINT

The blueprinting process was discovered by Sir John Frederick Herschel, an English astronomer, in 1842. It was originally called cyanotype and involved coating paper with a special chemical, which resulted in a print of white lines on a Prussian blue background.

The blueprint was used mainly for copying drawings and other clerical work done by architects, engineers, and shipbuilders who needed quick, long-lasting records of designs and figures. It was the simplest, cheapest, and most permanent photographic print and could be easily made by almost anyone.

To make a blueprint, a chemical coating is applied to a piece of paper. When the sensitized paper has dried to a bronze color, it is placed in contact with a drawing, covered with a sheet of glass, and exposed to sunlight for about an hour. After a final cold-water wash, the paper becomes bright blue and the lines of the image are white.

Blueprints were widely used until the 1960's when other techniques were developed. The sepia print and the whiteprint—an image of blue, brown, or black lines on a

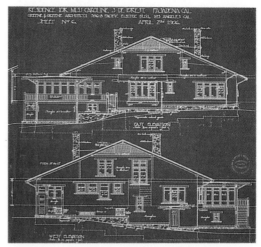

A blueprint like this one serves as a detailed plan for the building of a house. Copies used by everyone in the construction process show both the builder and the owner the exact specifications they have agreed upon.

white background—were faster to make and easier to mark up and read. Architects and engineers continue to use these alternative reproduction methods. No one is sure, however, if they will last as long as blueprints, which survive for many decades without fading.

DONNA ROBERTSON
Director, Barnard College Architecture Program

BLUME, JUDY (1938–)

The American writer Judy Blume is best known for books that deal frankly with issues and problems confronting young people. Her books consistently appear on lists of young readers' favorites.

Blume was born Judy Sussman in Elizabeth, New Jersey, on February 12, 1938. She was an imaginative child who studied dance and earned high honors at school. After graduating from New York University in 1960, she lived in suburban New Jersey with her husband, John Blume, and two children. Looking for a creative outlet, she tried

Judy Blume's fiction deals frankly with issues confronting young people. Her books are sometimes controversial with adults but always popular with her young readers.

writing pop songs and making banners. Finally, she began to write stories, taking a college course in writing for children.

Her first successful book was *Are You There, God? It's Me, Margaret* (1970). It tells of a sixth-grader's preoccupation with religion and with her own developing body. Blume dealt with the issue of parental divorce in *It's Not the End of the World* (1972) and with teenage sex in *Forever* (1975). In all her works she attempted to be completely honest with her readers, saying, "Problems only get worse when there are secrets, because what kids imagine is usually scarier than the truth."

Other books by Judy Blume include *Superfudge* (1980), *Just As Long As We're Together* (1987), *Fudge-A-Mania* (1990); two novels for adults, *Wifey* (1978) and *Smart Women* (1984); and *Letters to Judy* (1986), a collection of letters from her young readers.

Reviewed by CHARLES MORITZ
Editor, *Current Biography*

BLY, NELLIE (1864–1922)

Nellie Bly was once the most daring and celebrated newspaper reporter in the United States. She helped pioneer a sensational eyewitness reporting style that broke new ground for women and journalism. Bly acquired international fame by traveling around the world in record time—72 days, 6 hours, and 11 minutes. Her trip, completed in 1890, sought to outdo the fictitious record of Phileas Fogg, the hero of Jules Verne's popular novel, *Around the World in Eighty Days*.

Nellie Bly was born Elizabeth Cochran on May 5, 1864, in Cochran's Mills, Pennsylvania. She began her journalism career in 1885 as a reporter for the Pittsburgh *Dispatch*. It was there she took the pen name Nellie Bly.

As a novice reporter, Bly took many risks for a woman in her day. She wrote controversial articles on divorce, slum housing, and dangerous factory conditions. Newspapers around the country picked up her articles.

In 1887, Bly moved to New York City and joined Joseph Pulitzer's *World*. For her first assignment, she pretended to be insane to gain admission to the notorious asylum on Blackwell's Island. She wrote a blistering account of her experiences and exposed the asylum's appalling treatment of its patients. Her story sparked a statewide reform effort.

Such stunts became Bly's trademark. She later posed as a prostitute and as a criminal to gain firsthand information on prison life. Her most famous exploit, however, was her 72-

News reporter Nellie Bly became an international celebrity when she completed a record-breaking 72-day trip around the world in 1890. This photograph was taken the day she returned from her journey.

day trip around the world. She recorded her adventures in *Nellie Bly's Book: Around the World in 72 days*, published in 1890.

In 1895, Bly married Robert L. Seaman, a Brooklyn industrialist. After his death in 1904, Bly took over his manufacturing company, where she provided health care and equal wages to men and women. At the age of 50 she resumed her newspaper career but failed to achieve a major comeback. Nellie Bly died of pneumonia on January 27, 1922.

ELIZABETH EHRLICH
Author, *Nellie Bly*

BOARDSAILING

Boardsailing is a modern sport that combines features of two ancient activities, sailing and surfing. It is sometimes called windsurfing because the first sailboard, built in 1968, was named Windsurfer by its inventors, Americans Hoyle Schweitzer and Jim Drake.

Certified schools offer one- or two-day boardsailing courses that help beginners learn correct techniques. With six to eight hours of practice, beginners can learn enough of the basic skills at such schools to enjoy sailing in gentle breezes on smooth water.

Experienced boardsailors have many exciting challenges. There are races from local to international level, including the Olympic Games. Freestyle is a form of gymnastics on the sailboard. Wave jumping combines the speed of surfing and sailing to gain enough momentum to fly off the crest of a large wave and then fly or somersault through the air.

Equipment. A sailboard resembles a surfboard. It may be about 12 feet (3.6 meters) long for sailing and racing or shorter for freestyle and wave jumping. It is equipped with a **mast** attached by a **universal joint**—a device that allows the mast to turn and tilt in all directions. A bar, called the **boom,** curves around both sides of the sail at a height at which the sailor can grip it when standing on the board. The triangular sail usually has an area of from 55 to 65 square feet (5 to 6 square meters). It has a clear plastic window, allowing the sailor a view of the water on either side.

Controlling the Sailboard. When the sailboard is at rest, the mast and the sail lie flat on the water. The sailor stands on the board and pulls them upright with an attached line. The sailor then holds the boom. **Tacking** (turning the board toward the direction from which the wind is blowing) is done by tilting the mast toward the back of the board. **Jibing** (turning away from the wind) is done by tilting the mast forward.

Safety. Boardsailors must follow the general rules found in the article SAILING in Volume S. They must know how to swim and should always wear life jackets. It is important to have a companion nearby to give assistance if required.

Boardsailors must guard against hypothermia—chilling of the body that can cause death. This chilling can be caused by exposing the wet body to wind even when the air and water seem warm. The first symptoms are numbness in the hands and feet and uncontrollable shivering. If this occurs, the sailor must immediately get out of the water, dry off, and get warm. Wet suits are worn by most boardsailors. These suits hold a thin layer of water next to the body, where it is warmed and acts as insulation.

Competition. Boardsailing races are held on triangular, slalom, or long-distance courses. Triangular courses are used in Olympic competition (known as sailboarding), which was instituted for men in 1984 and became a part of women's competition in 1992. Slalom racecourses have six marks set close enough together to test the sailors' ability to tack and jibe. Distance races usually cover 5 to 15 miles (8 to 24 kilometers) and test both skill and endurance.

RHONDA SMITH-SANCHEZ
World Champion

BOAS, FRANZ (1858–1942)

Franz Boas was a pioneer of anthropology, the study of the origin and development of people and their cultures. Before Boas, many believed that some cultures were advanced while others were primitive. Boas did not accept this. He believed that cultures were different from one another because of the differences in their environments. He established that each culture should be judged on the basis of its own environment and history, and not by the standards of others.

Boas also had a great influence on how anthropologists work. He established the importance of field work—the recording of data based on personal observation. He showed that information about language, art, folklore, and mythology was as important to one's evaluation of a culture as the physical details about the people and their surroundings.

Franz Boas was born on July 9, 1858, in Minden, Germany. His parents encouraged his interest in science, and he attended the University of Kiel. His interest in anthropology developed during a scientific expedition to Baffin Island in the Arctic (1883–1884), where he had an opportunity to observe the local Eskimo (Inuit) culture. Many of his ideas were shaped by several trips he made to the northwest coast of North America, over a period of time from 1886 to 1931, to study several Indian cultures, including the Kwakiutl.

In 1887 Boas decided to live permanently in the United States and he became a citizen in 1891. At first he worked for the magazine *Science*. Later, he taught and did research at Clark University in Massachusetts and at Chicago's Field Museum of Natural History. Finally, he settled in New York City to work at the American Museum of Natural History and to study and teach at Columbia University. Boas founded a department at Columbia that produced many of the great anthropologists of the 1900's, including Ruth Benedict, Margaret Mead, and Edward Sapir. He also published many books and several important studies on American Indian folklore and art.

Franz Boas died in New York on December 22, 1942.

RACHEL KRANZ
Editor, Biographies
The Young Adult Reader's Adviser

See also ANTHROPOLOGY.

BOATS AND BOATING

Boating is a fast-growing sport. Every year more young skippers pilot their craft on freshwater lakes and rivers and on the bays and inlets at the ocean's edge. To keep pace with the rapid growth of boating, hundreds of marinas have been built to provide shoreside berths, or places to anchor small craft. *Marina* is a Spanish word meaning "seacoast," and is used in English to describe a modern boat basin with piers and slips for docking boats, launches, and yachts. In a marina large and small boats are repaired, serviced, and stored. Shore electricity, telephones, fresh water, ice, and fuel are available at dockside. Pleasure-boat owners may shop here for supplies and food and drink all within walking distance of their boats. Every type of craft may be seen at a marina. There are sailing dinghies and two-masted schooners, outboard runabouts and big cabin cruisers with facilities to sleep six or more people.

The 14- to 18-foot (4.3- to 5.5-meter) runabouts are the most popular small powerboats. They are wonderful for fishing or for just having fun on the water. The larger ones, fitted with powerful outboard engines, are used for towing water-skiers.

Before beginners learn to run one of these craft or even go for a ride in a dinghy or other small rowboat, they should know the basic rules of safety for themselves and their boat.

▶SAFETY RULES FOR YOUNG SAILORS

(1) Learn to swim. If you cannot swim, wear a life jacket.

(2) Do not go out in a boat alone. Young children should always be accompanied by an adult.

(3) Do not go out in bad weather, or when a storm is forecast, or in a fog. Beginning boaters should stay close to shore.

(4) Never overload your boat.

(5) Sit quietly when boating. Do not scuffle while aboard a boat. Do not change seats when the water is rough or when the boat is in deep water.

(6) Do not try to swim ashore from an overturned boat even if you are a good swimmer. Hold on to the boat and wait for help.

(7) Wear sneakers or rubber-soled shoes to avoid slipping, and wear a hat to protect yourself from the sun.

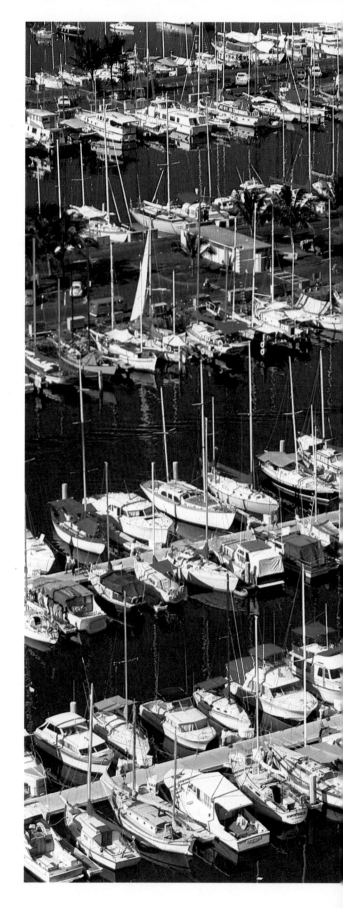

(8) Before diving off a boat into strange water, test for depth, rocks, and weeds. Swim in a safe place.

▶ THE RULES OF BOATING

It is important to know the rules of any sport, but in boating not knowing the rules can mean disaster. The important rules of boating concern whistle signals, the lights for different kinds of boats, and rights of way.

Signal Talk

One blast of a boat's whistle or horn means "I am going right." Two blasts mean "I am going left."

Motorboats are forbidden to respond using a cross signal—that is, answering one whistle with two blasts or two blasts with one. Instead, they are required to answer with the same signal to indicate that the other boat's signal has been understood. Whistle or horn signals, however, are not exchanged between sailboats.

Four or more blasts are the signal for danger. If the skipper disagrees with a signal or does not understand it, the danger signal should be given and the boat stopped. The boat should not proceed until the proper signals have been given, answered, and understood.

Lights Required After Sunset

Class A boats, which are under 16 feet (4.9 meters) long, and Class 1 boats, which are 16 to 26 feet (4.9 to 7.9 meters) long, have a combination red and green light at the front, or **bow** of the boat. The red light indicates the **port**, or left side, and the green light indicates the **starboard**, or right side. Each color should be visible from dead ahead and should show for 10 points around the horizon on each side for a distance of 1 mile (1.6 kilometers). (On a compass, 32 points represent a complete circle.) A white light at the rear, or **stern**, of the boat should show all around the horizon and be visible for about 2 miles (3 kilometers).

Class 2 boats, which are 26 to 40 feet (7.9 to 12.2 meters) long, and Class 3 boats, which measure 40 to 65 feet (12.2 to 19.8 meters), have separate red and green side lights. These boats must also have a white 20-point light at the bow, as well as a white 32-point stern light, which is placed higher than the bow light.

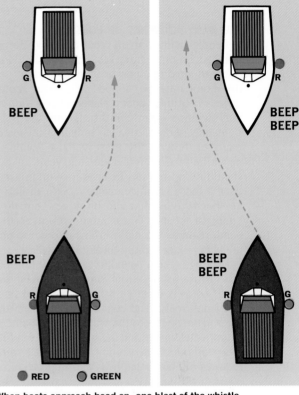

BEEP

BEEP
BEEP

BEEP

BEEP
BEEP

RED   GREEN

When boats approach head on, one blast of the whistle means "going right" (starboard). It is answered by one blast from the approaching boat. Two blasts mean "going left" (port), and are answered by two blasts.

Right of Way

The first rule of the seaway is "Keep to the right." For instance, when two boats are about to meet head on, each skipper should give one blast on the whistle and turn the boat to starboard (right). The boats will then pass port side to port side (left side to left side). This and other passing situations are shown above and on pages 264–265.

Sailboats always have the right of way over powerboats, unless a sailboat is overtaking a powerboat. In any dangerous situation, even though a boat may have the right of way, it is best to turn or back away to avoid collision. Pamphlets on piloting rules are available from the U.S. Coast Guard office in Washington, D.C., or from local coast guard offices. In Canada, boating information is available from the Canadian Department of Transport, Hunter Building, Ottawa, Ontario.

Good boating safety also requires having certain emergency equipment, including a fire extinguisher, a well-stocked first-aid kit, life jackets, and buoyant cushions. A compass is also important for boats that navigate offshore.

▶THE MANY ACTIVITIES OF BOATING

People swim from all types of boats. Before going swimming, however, the boat should be either moored to a pier or lying at anchor, and the motor must be stopped. The boat should have a boarding ladder placed at one side so that swimmers can climb back into the boat. Someone should always remain on board, ready to throw a life preserver if a swimmer needs help. Children under ten years of age should wear life vests and never swim in water over 5 feet (1.5 meters) deep. Skin diving is another activity that can be done from most kinds of boats. Waterskiing, on the other hand, requires a fast powerboat in order to pull the water-skier rapidly through the water.

Fishing is the most popular activity for boaters. Most fishing from runabouts and other small boats is done with light poles and lines and small reels. The boat can be stopped and the bait cast out into the water, or the bait can be pulled along behind the boat as it is moving —a method called trolling. Deep-sea fishing requires big boats and heavy fishing tackle. A

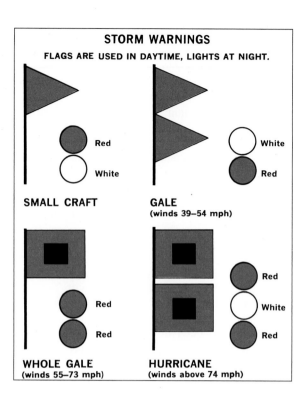

STORM WARNINGS
FLAGS ARE USED IN DAYTIME, LIGHTS AT NIGHT.

Red
White
SMALL CRAFT

White
Red
GALE
(winds 39–54 mph)

Red
Red
WHOLE GALE
(winds 55–73 mph)

Red
White
Red
HURRICANE
(winds above 74 mph)

Left: Sailboats always have the right of way over powerboats. *Center:* Red to red (port to port) means safe to go ahead. *Right:* When you see both red and green lights, blow one blast and pass red to red (port to port).

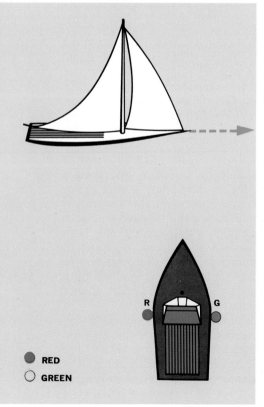

● RED
○ GREEN

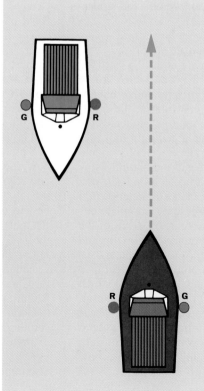

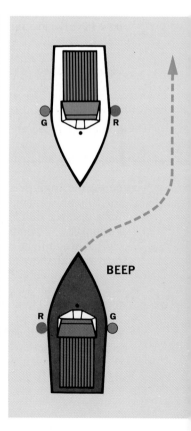

BEEP

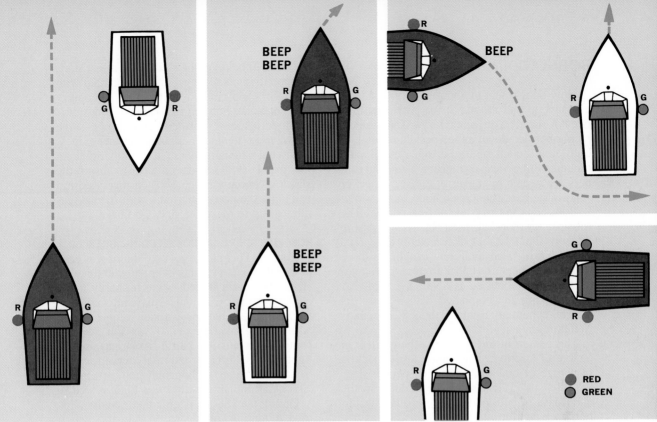

Left: Green to green means safe to proceed. *Center:* Boat astern asks to pass. Lead boat answers and moves to starboard. *Upper right:* Red to starboard gives other boat right of way; signal and go astern. *Lower right:* Green off your port bow gives you right of way.

boat with a "flying bridge," a piloting platform at the top, is used to fish for large game fish, such as marlin or sailfish. When one of these fish is hooked, the skipper must be able to twist and turn the boat quickly to keep the fishing line tight and prevent it from getting under the boat. The person fishing is often strapped into a special chair and may require several hours to land a large fish.

Camping is another activity that almost every boat owner can enjoy. Even a canoe or small runabout can carry the tent, sleeping bags, portable stove, and supply of food that will make a satisfying trip.

▶**POWERBOAT RACING**

A more specialized boating activity is powerboat racing. Most racing requires special boats and motors. Racing boats are classified according to the size of the boat and the type of motor. The largest competition boats are the 25- to 40-foot (7.6- to 12.2-meter) **hydroplanes**. (Hydroplanes are light, flat-bottomed boats.) These boats have powerful engines that enable them to reach speeds of 200 miles

(320 kilometers) an hour. Jet-powered speedboats can reach speeds of almost 300 miles (480 kilometers) an hour.

Racing boats compete in a variety of contests in the United States and throughout the world. The famous Gold Cup race, for example, is held at various cities in the United States. The marathon is a long-distance event often raced on a river. Powerboat races are also held on the open ocean. These races provided a rugged test of boats, their equipment, and their drivers.

Racing requires expert boating skills. However, newcomers to boating can have a great deal of fun using their boats for exploring, for nature studies, for photography, and for simply being on the water. As Kenneth Grahame wrote in *The Wind in the Willows*, "There is nothing half so much worth doing as simply messing about in boats. . . . in or out of 'em, it doesn't matter."

TOM BOTTOMLEY
Author, *Cruising for Fun*

See also DIVING; FISHING; ROWING; SAILING; SKIN DIVING; SWIMMING; WATERSKIING.

BOBSLEDDING

How does it feel to shoot down the side of a mountain and around sharp curves at high rates of speed? You would know if you rode a racing bobsled down an ice-packed bobrun. A bobsled is a plank of steel or other metal alloy mounted on two sets of runners. The front runners are steered by means of either a wheel or ropes. The back runners do not turn.

Bobsleds can carry two or four people. The four-person bobsled used in championship races is about 12 feet (3.5 meters) long. The weight of the sled and crew cannot be more than 1,389 pounds (630 kilograms). A two-person racing bobsled is about 8½ feet (2.5 meters) long and combined with its crew its weight cannot total more than 827 pounds (375 kilograms).

The person in the front of a bobsled is in charge of steering. The person in the back is in charge of braking. On a four-person sled, the other two riders sit in the middle. In the early days of bobsledding, these riders would bob back and forth to make the sled go as fast as possible. This is how bobsledding got its name.

The bodies of today's bobsleds are often made of graphite or other very lightweight material. The body of the bobsled helps protect the riders and the steering mechanism. Streamlined design helps cut down wind resistance, making faster speeds possible. Push handles on each side of the sled are used by the crew to help get the sled off to a fast start. Competitive bobsleds are usually painted with the colors and emblem of the club or country that enters the bobsled in a race.

Modern racing bobsleds incorporate some of the most advanced engineering techniques. Many have runners mounted in rubber that act like the shock absorbers on a car to absorb the shock of bumps. Some bobsled racers design and build their own bobsleds, with special features to try to make the sleds go faster.

▶HOW THE SPORT OF BOBSLEDDING GREW

Long ago people discovered that it was easy to travel and carry loads over snow and ice on sleds. The earliest sleds were probably made of flat boards or animal skins stretched over frames. Later, narrow wooden runners were added. This made the sleds faster and easier to control. Indians of North America used a light, flat-bottomed sled that curved up in front. The name "toboggan" came from the Algonkian Indian word for this kind of sled.

During the 1880's, people in the Swiss Alps tried mounting toboggans on runners, which made them go faster. In fact, they went so fast that they often ran off course, out of control. Members of the Toboggan Club at St. Moritz, a famous winter resort in Switzerland, found that by making these sleds much heavier they could be controlled better. This was the birth of the bobsleigh, or bobsled, as it is called today. A special bobrun was built at St. Moritz, and the first race was held there in 1898.

A United States bobsled crew pushes off for a fast start in an Olympic race.

The first national championship bobsled races were held in Austria in 1908, and bobsledding became a world event in the first Olympic Winter Games, held in France in 1924.

▶ NORTH AMERICA'S FAMOUS BOBRUN

The 1932 Olympic Winter Games were held at Lake Placid, New York. The Van Hoevenberg bobrun was built for these Olympics, and it became one of several bobruns in the world that qualify for international competition. Some others are at St. Moritz, Switzerland; Cortina d'Ampezzo, Italy; and Innsbruck, Austria.

The Van Hoevenberg bobrun is about 1 mile (1.6 kilometers) long. It has 16 curves with sections in between called straightaways. The walls of the curves and straightaways are made of concrete covered with a mixture of ice and snow. Using concrete eliminates the need for building walls of large ice blocks. The base of the bobrun is also made of concrete. Refrigeration under this concrete base keeps the run very cold. When water is sprayed onto the bobrun, it freezes quickly into ice, making the bobrun very fast.

The largest curve at Van Hoevenberg is called Shady; it is one of the most famous curves in the world. The trickiest curve is Zig-Zag. It is actually two curves, one right after the other in opposite directions. If the bobsledders' timing isn't perfect in Zig, they will have trouble going into or out of Zag.

▶ BOBSLED RACING

There is room for only one sled at a time on a bobrun. A bobsled race is therefore a race against time. Each sled is timed with the aid of electronic eyes.

Bobsled racers push their sled from a starting point and leap on it after crossing the starting line. As the sled crosses the starting line, electric eyes cause a clock in the timing booth to start running. Other electric eyes along the bobrun mark the sled's time at intermediate points. At the end of the run a final pair of electric eyes stops the clock in the timing booth. The clock is able to time each run to 1/100 of a second.

Championship races consist of four heats, or runs, for each sled. The sled with the shortest total time for the four heats is the winner. The fastest times on the Van Hoevenberg bobrun are less than 1 minute for a four-person sled and less than 1 minute and 4 seconds for a two-person sled. Bobsleds often reach speeds of about 90 miles (145 kilometers) an hour.

Bobsled racing is governed by the International Bobsleigh and Tobogganing Federation. During races, a jury of three people is in charge of the bobrun and the sleds. If anything should happen to the bobrun during the event, this jury would decide what to do. Bobsled championships are held at the Winter Olympics, as well as at world championship races each year. North American championships are usually held each year also.

▶ BOBSLEDDING FOR FUN

It is not necessary to be a racer to enjoy bobsledding. In winter the Van Hoevenberg bobrun at Lake Placid is open for public pleasure riding. Paying passengers can ride with experienced bobsledders who do the steering and braking. People who want to drive a bobsled must have a license. To obtain one, they must first pass a physical examination. They are then taught by expert drivers. If they pass the driving tests, they are granted licenses.

STANLEY BENHAM
Former World Bobsled Champion

Reviewed by JOHN J. FELL
Bobsled Chairman, XIII Olympic Winter Games

Spectators watch a two-person bobsled climbing high on the sidewall as it takes a curve.

There is a magic to being human. Our bodies let us participate in the world around us in ways unlike any other animal. As humans we have a wide range of wondrous abilities: We can move with grace and precision, learn intricate tasks, feel deep emotion, and survive in an ever-changing environment.

BODY, HUMAN

From the earliest times, people have tried to understand how the human body is made and how it works. Scientists have tried to unlock its secrets to improve health and to help fight disease. Artists have used the human body as a source of inspiration to create art. Athletes and performers have studied the human body to better their performing abilities.

Those who have studied the human body often compare it to a machine. Like a machine, the body needs energy to do its work. A machine such as an automobile engine burns fuel, usually gasoline, to obtain energy. The fuel combines with oxygen from the air, and energy is released. The body's fuel is food. The food is combined with oxygen that is breathed in. Energy is released.

There are many other likenesses between machines and the human body. But it is the differences that make us better than machines.

The body can grow. Machines cannot. Cameras can "see" and computers can "learn" in a way. But machines cannot feel, see, think, and learn as humans do. The body can repair worn-out parts and even produce new humans. Most important, the human body has a very special quality—it is alive.

▶BODY CHEMISTRY

The human body consists of chemical elements—substances that cannot be broken down into simpler substances by ordinary means. The most common chemical elements in the body are carbon, hydrogen, nitrogen, and oxygen; the body also contains many others, such as sodium, calcium, iron, phosphorus, and potassium.

Every element is made up of units called **atoms**. When two or more atoms combine, a microscopic structure called a **molecule** is formed. Some molecules are composed of atoms of only one element. For example, a molecule of oxygen (O_2) consists of two atoms of oxygen. When an atom combines with one or more atoms of different elements, **compounds** are formed. Water (H_2O), for instance, is a compound consisting of molecules that contain two atoms of hydrogen joined with one atom of oxygen.

The compounds of the body must be arranged in a very special way to produce life. The most basic compound in the human body is water. It is necessary for most of the chemical functions. Nucleic acids carry the instructions that pass human traits from one generation to the next.

▶ **THE LIVING CELL**

The cell, which is a collection of compounds, is the basic unit of life in all living things. A cell can take in food, get rid of wastes, and grow. The human body is made up of billions of cells. This tells you something about the size of cells. Most of them are too small to be seen without a microscope. But they are alive. Throughout life, the body continues to grow new cells. These new cells replace those that have worn out.

Most cells have three main parts. A thin skinlike covering, called the **cell membrane**, encloses each cell. Inside the cell is a soft jelly called **cytoplasm**. Within the cytoplasm lies the **nucleus**, which is sometimes called the "control center" because it directs the activities of a cell.

ical reactions that occur. In addition to water, there are four other main compounds in the body: carbohydrates (such as starch), lipids (or fats), proteins, and nucleic acids.

These four compounds are large, complex structures that contain the element carbon. Carbohydrates provide the energy for all of the body's activities. Lipids store extra fuel and serve as building material for the cells of the body. Proteins also perform several duties. Some proteins are used to build cells, others

The cell membrane acts not only as a wrapper but as a sieve: It lets some materials pass into the cell while keeping others out. Food and oxygen carried to the cell must pass through the cell membrane. Wastes given off by the cell when it has burned the food and oxygen pass through the sievelike membrane back into the blood and are carried away.

The cytoplasm makes up most of the cell. Within the cytoplasm are many tiny structures called **organelles**. These are the organs of the

During cell division, two sets of chromosomes are pulled apart toward opposite poles. Completion of the process yields two genetically identical cells.

cell. The **mitochondrion** is one type of organelle. It transforms substances from the food we eat into energy that the cell can use. Cells that are very active such as muscle cells have lots of mitochondria. Another type of organelle is the **lysosome**. It digests and gets rid of unwanted material.

The nucleus is a solid ball in the center of the cell. It contains rodlike structures called **chromosomes**. Each cell has 46 chromosomes —half are inherited from the mother and half from the father. The chromosomes are made up of **genes**. Genes are the basic units of heredity—that is, they carry the characteristics that are inherited from an individual's parents. The fact that a boy has blue eyes like his mother or brown hair like his father is determined by the genes that he has inherited from his parents.

The genes also control what cells do. The genes carry their instructions, or master plans, in a special language called the **genetic code**. The genetic code is formed using a chemical substance called **DNA** (*d*eoxyribo*n*ucleic *a*cid). All living plants and animals use the same genetic code; however, it is the different master plans carried in the genetic code that make every living thing different from all other living things.

Cells not only grow larger, they also reproduce new cells. New cells serve two functions: They help the body grow and they replace injured or dead cells. Cells reproduce by dividing—one cell divides to make two cells. First the nucleus reproduces by dividing into two parts. Then each part becomes a new cell complete with chromosome-containing nucleus, cytoplasm, and cell membrane. When cells divide, each of the two **daughter cells** are exactly like the **parent cell**.

Cells get their nourishment from blood. They convert some of the nourishment to energy. This is called **energy metabolism**. They may also use part of the food for making new cell materials. In some kinds of cells, such as fat cells, food is stored for later use.

▶**THE ORGANIZATION OF THE HUMAN BODY**

The human body has more than a hundred different kinds of cells. Each has a special form that makes it fit with the special job it

The Living Cell

The adult human body contains some 100 trillion cells teeming with activity. Although all the cells do not look alike, they do share the same basic structure and some characteristic parts.

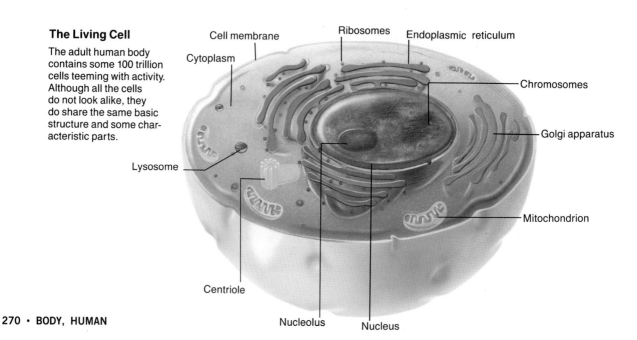

Cell membrane
Cytoplasm
Ribosomes
Endoplasmic reticulum
Chromosomes
Golgi apparatus
Mitochondrion
Lysosome
Centriole
Nucleolus
Nucleus

Cells of the Body

Cells are the building blocks of life. The many different kinds of cells that make up the human body come in all shapes and sizes. Cartilage cells (*right*) form the major supporting tissues of the body. The regularly arranged epithelial cells (*below right*) make up the outer surface of the skin. A cross section of bone (*bottom left*) shows the spidery form of bone cells. Each nerve cell (*below left*) has projections that carry electrical signals to the cell and others that carry electrical signals away from the cell to other parts of the body.

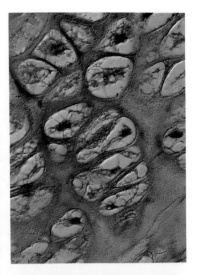

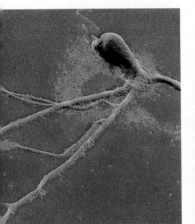

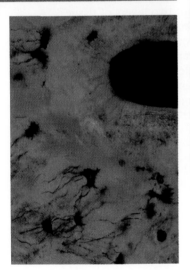

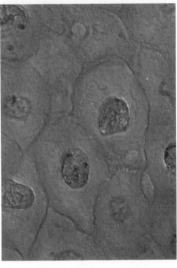

has to do. Cells of one kind are usually joined to make **tissue**. Blood cells are an exception. They are not joined. They travel alone through the blood vessels.

A tissue is a fabric of the same kind of cells. For example, muscles are tissue made up of muscle cells; nervous tissue is made up of nerve cells. There are four main kinds of tissue: **Epithelial tissue**, which covers the surface of the body; **connective tissue**, which helps support and join together parts of the body; **muscle tissue**, which makes body movement possible; and **nervous tissue**, which carries nerve signals throughout the body.

Different kinds of tissue are combined in the body's organs. An **organ** is a body part that does one or more special jobs for the rest of the body. The heart, lungs, stomach, brain, and skin are all organs.

A group of organs working together is called a **system**. For example, the heart, blood, and blood vessels make up the circulatory system. The nose, throat, windpipe, and lungs make up the respiratory (breathing) system. The kidneys, bladder, and connecting tubes make up the urinary system. The systems of the body are like members of a team. Each one has a specific job, but together they make it possible for the body to work, play, grow, and carry out many other functions.

What is the largest organ of your body?

Your skin—the only body organ that is exposed to the outside world—is the largest organ of your body. Skin is a tough, elastic, waterproof protection for the entire body. Even your eyes have a transparent layer of skin, called the conjunctiva, covering them. The skin of an average adult covers an area of about 22 square feet (2.04 square meters) and weighs 8 to 10 pounds (3.6 to 4.5 kilograms).

While the skin is the largest organ of the entire body, the liver—which in an adult weighs about 3 pounds (1.4 kilograms)—is the largest organ inside the body. It is also one of the most active organs. Its tasks include processing nutrients, such as proteins and carbohydrates; metabolizing drugs and hormones; and storing blood, vitamins, and minerals.

▶BODY SYSTEMS AND ORGANS

Body systems help the body remain alive: The skin protects the body; the body obtains oxygen through the respiratory system; the digestive system processes food so it can be used for energy and growth; the heart and blood vessels circulate oxygen and other substances throughout the body; the kidneys eliminate waste materials; and the reproductive system produces offspring. Together the nervous system and endocrine system form a command system that links all of the other body systems.

The Skin

The skin is the largest organ of the body, and it does many jobs. It holds fluids inside the body. It protects the body from air, water, dirt, and germs. By giving off heat, it helps to regulate body temperature. It contains nerves that are sensitive to things such as touch and temperature that provide information about the world around us.

The skin is made up of two layers of tissue. The top protective layer is called the **epidermis**; the inner layer is called the **dermis**. The thickness of the skin varies on different parts of the body. For example, the skin on the soles of the feet is thicker than that on the face.

In addition to forming a protective covering for the body, the epidermis also forms the fin-

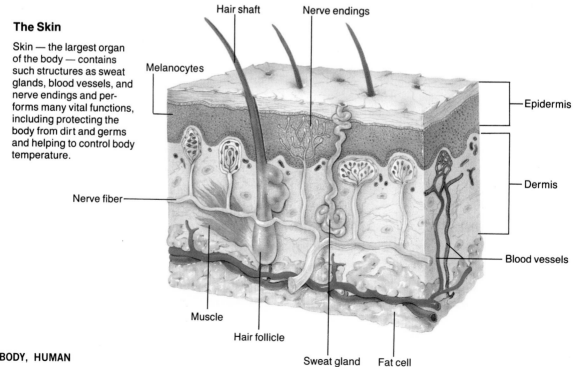

The Skin

Skin — the largest organ of the body — contains such structures as sweat glands, blood vessels, and nerve endings and performs many vital functions, including protecting the body from dirt and germs and helping to control body temperature.

Hair shaft

Nerve endings

Melanocytes

Epidermis

Dermis

Nerve fiber

Blood vessels

Muscle

Hair follicle

Sweat gland   Fat cell

Some people, such as the young boy above, are born with clumps of melanocytes in their skin. These people end up with freckles.

The pigment melanin acts as an umbrella to help protect the skin of these sunbathers (*left*) from ultraviolet rays that could damage cells.

gernails and toenails. Fingernails and toenails are collections of dead cells. That is why it does not hurt when you cut your toenails and fingernails.

The outermost layer of the epidermis is called the **stratum corneum**, and it is made up of a tough protective layer of dead cell material called **keratin**. When you look at a person's skin, all you are actually seeing is dead cells. The stratum corneum is thickest on the soles of the feet and on the palms of the hands. Collections of keratin, called corns, form to protect the foot from ill-fitting shoes.

The epidermis also has special cells called **melanocytes**, some 60,000 in every square inch of skin. Melanocytes produce a dark pigment called **melanin**. Melanin gives skin its color. People with black or brown skin have more melanin in their skin than people with white or yellow skin. Melanin protects the body from the damaging effects caused by the sun. When the skin is exposed to sunlight, the melanocytes produce additional melanin. This is what creates a suntan.

The dermis contains sweat glands, blood vessels, nerves, and cells called **hair follicles**. Each hair follicle contains a hair root. The hair root produces hair cells. These cells die and form the hair that projects from the skin's surface. Hair is present on most parts of the body's surface except for the palms of the hands and soles of the feet.

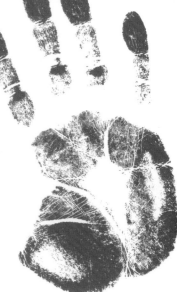

Each person's handprint is a unique pattern of loops, arches, and swirls formed by the ridges and grooves of the skin.

The Skeletal System

The framework that holds the human body erect is the **skeleton**. The skeleton, which is made mostly of bones, has two major jobs. It supports the body—without a skeleton you would be like a jellyfish—and it protects delicate organs, such as the brain and heart.

The skeleton must also be able to move. The parts of the skeleton that let bones move are called **joints**. Bones fit together at joints and are held fast by tough cords or straps, called **ligaments**. Some joints can be moved freely; others cannot be moved at all. When you run, you move your legs at the hip and knee joints. When you throw a ball, you move your arms at the shoulder and elbow joints. The bones in your spine help you stand straight. They do not move as freely as other joints, but they let you bend. Except for the bones in the jaw, the bones in your skull, which protect your brain, do not move at all.

Bone is made up of two types of living tissue. The outer layer of bone is dense hard (or compact) tissue; the inner layer is lightweight spongy tissue. The holes in the spongy tissue are filled with **marrow**. Some of the marrow is yellow and stores fat. Other marrow is red and produces blood cells. Because bone is living, growing tissue, it must be fed. The outside of bone is covered with a thin skin called a periosteum, which holds the tiny blood vessels that carry food to the bone.

The Skeletal System

The human skeleton is a hard, strong, living framework for the body's tissues. It provides the support needed so that we can stand upright and move about freely. It also holds internal organs in place and shelters them from injury.

Cross Section of a Bone

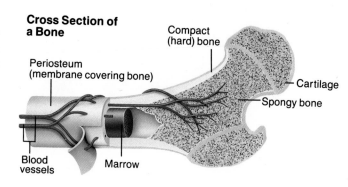

Periosteum (membrane covering bone)

Compact (hard) bone

Cartilage

Spongy bone

Blood vessels

Marrow

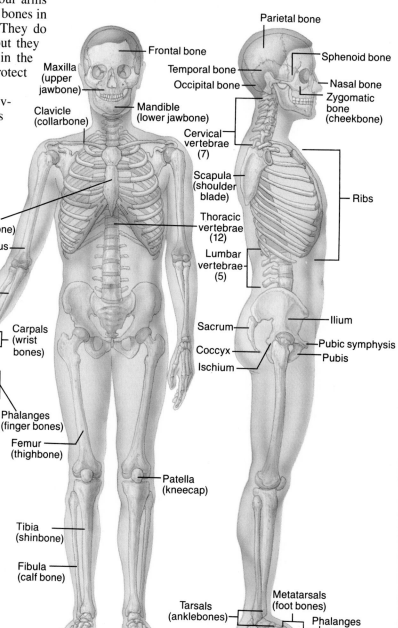

Parietal bone
Frontal bone
Sphenoid bone
Maxilla (upper jawbone)
Temporal bone
Occipital bone
Nasal bone
Zygomatic bone (cheekbone)
Clavicle (collarbone)
Mandible (lower jawbone)
Cervical vertebrae (7)
Scapula (shoulder blade)
Ribs
Sternum (breastbone)
Thoracic vertebrae (12)
Humerus
Lumbar vertebrae (5)
Ulna
Radius
Carpals (wrist bones)
Sacrum
Ilium
Coccyx
Pubic symphysis
Ischium
Pubis
Metacarpals (hand bones)
Phalanges (finger bones)
Femur (thighbone)
Patella (kneecap)
Tibia (shinbone)
Fibula (calf bone)
Metatarsals (foot bones)
Tarsals (anklebones)
Phalanges (toe bones)

The Muscular System

Bones are the framework of the body, but they cannot move by themselves. **Muscles** are the body's movers. For every bone that can move, there are muscles called **skeletal muscles**, that move it. Skeletal muscles are firmly attached to the bones by hard, ropelike tissue called **tendons**.

Muscles have the unique ability to contract, or get shorter. They are able to do this because each muscle cell contains special proteins. It is the proteins that are extended or shortened when the muscle relaxes or contracts. The process of relaxing or contracting is controlled by the central nervous system.

When a skeletal muscle shortens, it pulls on the tendons that are attached to the bone, and the bone moves. Muscles pull, but they cannot push. So they must work in pairs. If you bend your arm, one set of muscles contracts and pulls your forearm up. To straighten your arm, you relax the first set of muscles. A second set pulls in the opposite way, straightening your arm.

The skeletal muscles are under a person's control. They work because you decide to walk, pick up a ball, or take off your sweater. The body also has another body system that works without conscious orders from you. These muscles, called **smooth muscles**, contract automatically. They are found in many parts of the body and are not attached to bones. Smooth muscles do jobs like controlling the pupil of the eye and propelling food through the digestive tract.

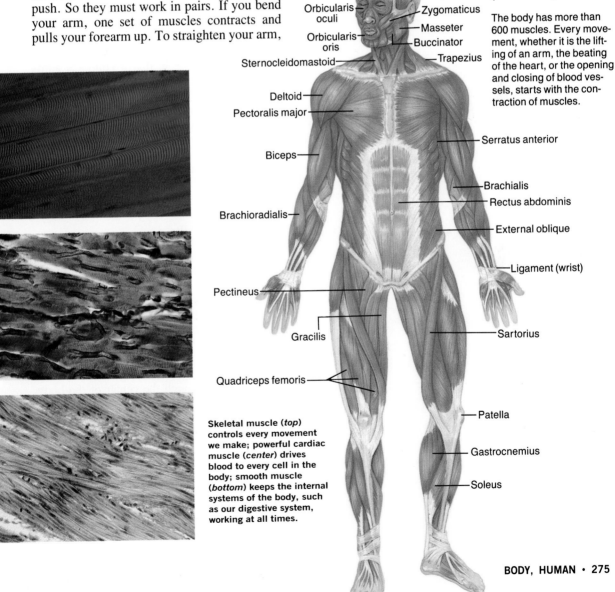

The Muscular System (Front view)

The body has more than 600 muscles. Every movement, whether it is the lifting of an arm, the beating of the heart, or the opening and closing of blood vessels, starts with the contraction of muscles.

Labels (left side): Frontalis, Orbicularis oculi, Orbicularis oris, Sternocleidomastoid, Deltoid, Pectoralis major, Biceps, Brachioradialis, Pectineus, Gracilis, Quadriceps femoris

Labels (right side): Temporalis, Zygomaticus, Masseter, Buccinator, Trapezius, Serratus anterior, Brachialis, Rectus abdominis, External oblique, Ligament (wrist), Sartorius, Patella, Gastrocnemius, Soleus

Skeletal muscle (*top*) controls every movement we make; powerful cardiac muscle (*center*) drives blood to every cell in the body; smooth muscle (*bottom*) keeps the internal systems of the body, such as our digestive system, working at all times.

The Muscular System (Back view)

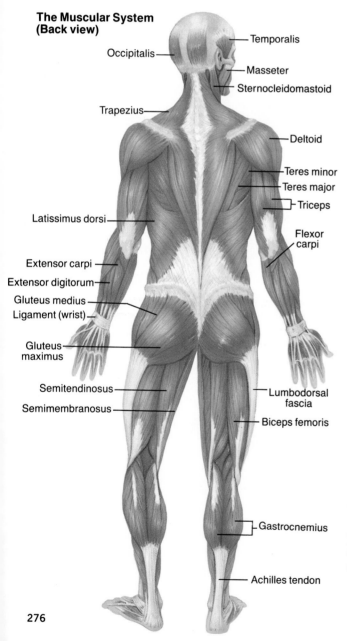

- Temporalis
- Occipitalis
- Masseter
- Sternocleidomastoid
- Trapezius
- Deltoid
- Teres minor
- Teres major
- Triceps
- Latissimus dorsi
- Flexor carpi
- Extensor carpi
- Extensor digitorum
- Gluteus medius
- Ligament (wrist)
- Gluteus maximus
- Semitendinosus
- Semimembranosus
- Lumbodorsal fascia
- Biceps femoris
- Gastrocnemius
- Achilles tendon

The heart is made up of another type of muscle, called **cardiac muscle**. Cardiac muscle is made up of fibers that resemble skeletal muscle. However, cardiac muscle also resembles smooth muscle in that it contracts automatically without conscious control.

The Digestive System

To do work, muscles and other tissue need water and fuel to burn. This fuel comes from the foods we eat and drink. But food cannot be used directly as fuel. Foods must be broken up and changed before they can be used as an energy fuel. This process of converting food to fuel is called **digestion** and takes place in the digestive system.

Digestion begins in the mouth where the teeth are used to break food into small pieces. The saliva that is in the mouth gets the food moist and makes the food easier to swallow. Saliva also contains amylase, an enzyme that starts breaking the starch in food into sugar. Then the moist ball of food is carried to the back of the mouth by the tongue.

Swallowing starts food on its journey through the 25- to 30-foot (8- to 9-meter)-long tube that coils through the center of the body and makes up the digestive system. Muscles force the food into the **esophagus**, the section of the digestive tube that connects with the stomach. Other muscles force the food down the esophagus.

Next, the food enters the pouchlike stomach portion of the tube. Here the food is churned and broken down further. Glands in the stomach add the chemical substances hydrochloric acid and pepsin to the food mixture. Pepsin is an enzyme that breaks down meats and other proteins. The acid sterilizes the food and makes the pepsin work better. A mucous slime, which coats the stomach and protects it from injury by the acid, is also secreted. The stomach works on the food for one to four hours. By then, the food is almost liquid.

From the stomach the food is pushed into the **small intestine**. The small intestine is so called because it is about 1 inch (2.5 centimeters) in diameter. However, it can be very long —about 20 feet (6 meters) in length. The small intestine does the main job of digestion. And it is from the small intestine that food starts its journey to the cells.

In the small intestine, more protective mucus is secreted. Food mixes with juices from the liver and pancreas. The liver makes liver bile, which helps to digest fats; the pancreas secretes enzymes that digest protein, fat, and carbohydrates. The small intestine also makes some digestive enzymes. As the food is digested, it becomes liquid. The starches are broken down into simple sugars. Proteins are split into smaller particles. Fats are changed to fatty acids and glycerol.

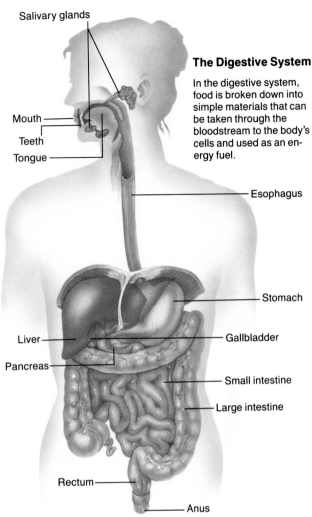

The Digestive System

In the digestive system, food is broken down into simple materials that can be taken through the bloodstream to the body's cells and used as an energy fuel.

Salivary glands

Mouth

Teeth

Tongue

Esophagus

Stomach

Liver

Gallbladder

Pancreas

Small intestine

Large intestine

Rectum

Anus

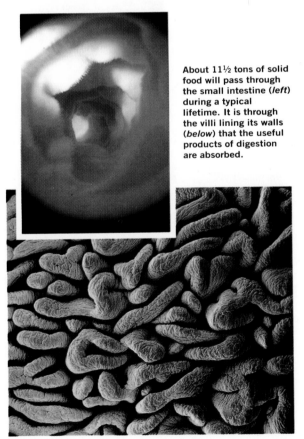

About 11½ tons of solid food will pass through the small intestine (*left*) during a typical lifetime. It is through the villi lining its walls (*below*) that the useful products of digestion are absorbed.

These digested materials pass through the cell membranes of the intestinal cells into the bloodstream. To make sure that none of the small particles are wasted, the small intestine is lined with hundreds of microscopic fingerlike projections called **villi**. These projections reach out and capture the food particles. Because particles can pass through the sides as well as the top of the villi, there is more space for food to be absorbed. Food particles travel from the villi into the bloodstream, then into the cells.

Most of the blood from the intestine passes through the liver before it enters the heart. The liver is like a large chemical factory. It changes many of the food particles. Some of the sugar is changed to a starchy substance called **glycogen** for storage in the body. When body cells need more sugar, the liver changes glycogen back to sugar and releases it into the bloodstream. Other products are used by the liver to manufacture proteins and process fats to be used as fuel. The liver also acts as a storage warehouse. It stores vitamins such as vitamin A and D.

Whatever food is left undigested after its journey through the small intestine moves into the **large intestine**. The large intestine is much wider than the small intestine and also much shorter. It is about 6 feet (2 meters) long. In the large intestine, water and minerals are removed from the undigested material, leaving solid waste material. Most of the body's waste comes from what is left of the food after the body uses what it needs. The solid wastes are then stored in the large intestine until they pass out of the body as bowel movements.

The Respiratory System

Cells have two important needs: They must have oxygen to produce energy, and they must get rid of the waste gas, called carbon dioxide, that forms when energy is produced. The respiratory system provides both of these services for the body's cells.

Oxygen enters the body from the air that is breathed in. Usually the air is taken in through the nose. But at times, when the body needs extra oxygen, air can be also taken in big gulps through the mouth. The moist lining of the nose contains many small hairs that clean the air as it moves through the nose. There are also many blood vessels in the lining of the nose, and the warm blood heats the air.

From the nose, air travels through the **pharynx** (the cavity located behind the nose and mouth), to the **larynx** (or voice box), the **trachea** (or windpipe), and finally, the lungs. Together these structures form the respiratory system.

The larynx contains folds of gristle-like tissue called the **vocal cords**. When air moves through the vocal cords, the cords vibrate and

The life-sustaining exchange of gases, oxygen and carbon dioxide, takes place within the lungs' approximately 300 million tiny air sacs called alveoli.

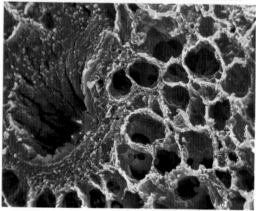

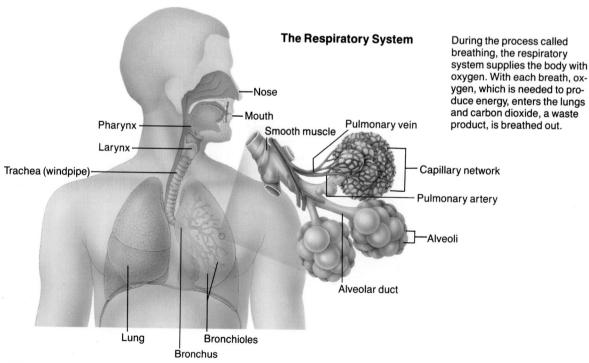

The Respiratory System

During the process called breathing, the respiratory system supplies the body with oxygen. With each breath, oxygen, which is needed to produce energy, enters the lungs and carbon dioxide, a waste product, is breathed out.

Nose
Mouth
Pharynx
Smooth muscle
Larynx
Pulmonary vein
Trachea (windpipe)
Capillary network
Pulmonary artery
Alveoli
Alveolar duct
Lung
Bronchioles
Bronchus

produce sounds, such as talking. Like the strings on a violin, the vocal cords can be tightened or loosened to produce higher- or lower-pitched sounds. The larynx also serves a protective function. When water or other materials enter the throat, the folds close so that the material cannot go into the lungs.

Air moves from the larynx to the trachea. The trachea is a ridged tube that is about 1 inch (2.5 centimeters) in diameter. The ridges, which are made up of firm gristle-like material, keep the trachea from collapsing during the act of breathing. In the upper part of the chest, the trachea divides to form two tubes. Each tube, called a **bronchus**, branches into smaller and smaller bronchial tubes that look like the branches on a tree. Each of the tiniest branches opens into a grapelike cluster of air-filled sacs, called alveoli. The air sacs are covered with a network of capillaries, which are the small blood vessels that connect veins and arteries.

Waste-carrying blood is pumped from the heart into the capillaries of the air sacs. Here a quick exchange takes place. Oxygen moves out of the air sacs into the blood. The waste gas carbon dioxide moves out of the blood into the air sacs and then is breathed out of the body. The oxygen is picked up by the red blood cells and carried back to the heart. From there it is pumped throughout the body.

Aided by the work of muscles, air is moved into and out of the lungs during the process of breathing, or **respiration**. Muscles in the chest wall and a muscle called the **diaphragm**, that separates the chest from the abdomen change the size and shape of the chest. With each breath taken in, the chest muscles contract, lifting the front and sides of the ribs and the breastbone to make a bigger space in the chest. When the diaphragm contracts, it flattens out and makes the space even bigger. As the chest expands, so do the lungs and air rushes in to fill them. With each breath let out, the muscles relax, the space becomes smaller, and air is pushed out of the lungs.

Breathing is automatic. That means you do not have to think about breathing to actually breathe. You continue to breathe even when you are sleeping. People do have some control over their breathing. You can take large or small breaths and you can breathe faster or slower. You can even hold your breath. But you cannot stop breathing altogether.

The Circulatory System

The circulatory system, which includes the heart, blood, and blood vessels (arteries, veins, and capillaries), moves life-giving blood throughout the body. Many thousands of miles of vessels travel through the body, supplying oxygenated blood to the body's tissues and organs.

Blood acts as a transport vehicle, carrying nutrients and oxygen to cells. Blood also picks up unneeded waste materials from the cells, carries important immune cells throughout the body, and picks up and carries heat from the inside of the body out to the skin, where it is released into the air.

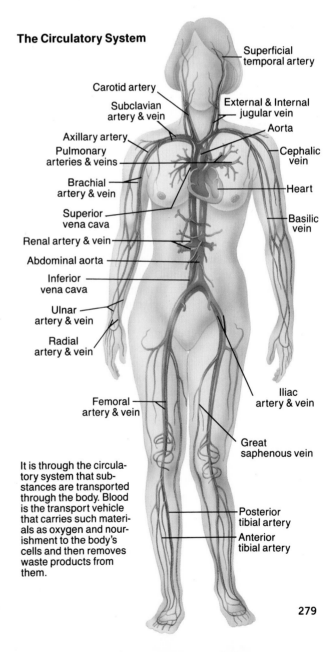

The Circulatory System

Superficial temporal artery
Carotid artery
Subclavian artery & vein
External & Internal jugular vein
Aorta
Axillary artery
Pulmonary arteries & veins
Cephalic vein
Brachial artery & vein
Heart
Superior vena cava
Basilic vein
Renal artery & vein
Abdominal aorta
Inferior vena cava
Ulnar artery & vein
Radial artery & vein
Femoral artery & vein
Iliac artery & vein
Great saphenous vein
Posterior tibial artery
Anterior tibial artery

It is through the circulatory system that substances are transported through the body. Blood is the transport vehicle that carries such materials as oxygen and nourishment to the body's cells and then removes waste products from them.

279

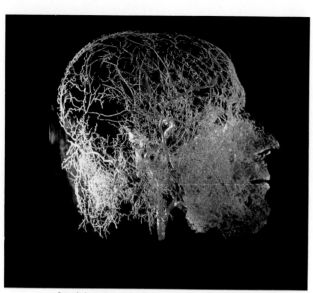

An elaborate and extensive network of blood vessels brings a rich supply of oxygenated blood to the face, head, and brain.

About half of the body's blood is made up of a thin, clear light yellow liquid called **plasma**. It flows through the blood vessels carrying many dissolved materials and solid blood cells. Most of these blood cells are red blood cells. Some 25 trillion red cells move through the bloodstream.

The red blood cells carry out specific jobs. Their main job is to carry oxygen from the lungs to cells in the body. These blood cells have powerful protein molecules called **hemoglobin** that carry the oxygen. Each hemoglobin molecule contains an iron atom that acts as a magnet, snapping up oxygen in the lungs, then clinging tightly to it. When the red cells reach the tissues, the hemoglobin releases the oxygen. Red blood cells also pick up carbon dioxide in the tissues and carry it back to the lungs, where it is removed from the body.

White blood cells are also transported in the blood. These cells kill dangerous bacteria and fight disease. **Platelets** are the third kind of solid material carried in the blood. They are the repair force. More than a trillion strong, platelets start the clotting process when a blood vessel is torn or cut.

The red and white blood cells and the platelets are all made in the bone marrow. Red blood cells live about four months. White blood cells live a much shorter time—some live only a few days. Platelets are not actual cells. They are pieces of larger cells. They live about eight to ten days. The bone marrow replaces blood cells and platelets as they die or are destroyed.

The force needed to push the blood through the many miles of vessels is supplied by a powerful muscular pump: the heart. It lies in the middle of the chest, between the lungs.

The heart is divided into four parts called **chambers**. There are two chambers called **atria** at the top of the heart and two chambers called **ventricles** at the bottom. The atria act as receptacles for blood as it enters the heart and the ventricles act as pumps to force blood out of the heart. The heart pumps the body's 4 to 6 quarts (4 to 6 liters) of blood through many thousands of miles of blood vessels, most of them tiny.

From the heart, blood is pumped into the lungs where carbon dioxide and other wastes are removed, and oxygen from the air breathed in is added to the blood. The oxygen-rich blood returns to the heart to begin its travels to the body's cells.

The Heart

The heart is a hollow muscle that functions as a pump to distribute oxygen-rich blood throughout the body. The round-trip of blood traveling between the heart and a part of the body may take about a minute.

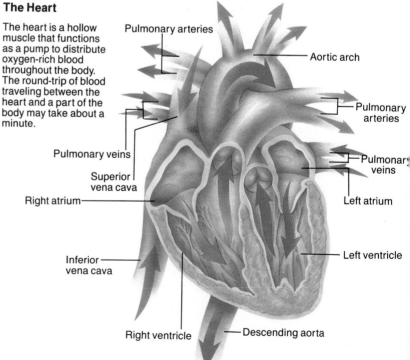

Pulmonary arteries
Aortic arch
Pulmonary arteries
Pulmonary veins
Pulmonary veins
Superior vena cava
Left atrium
Right atrium
Inferior vena cava
Left ventricle
Right ventricle
Descending aorta

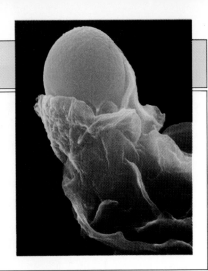

there are more red blood cells in the body than any other kind of cell? Some 25 trillion of the plump, round dimpled cells course through the bloodstream. The sole task of these tiny cells is to bring oxygen to all of the body's tissue and remove carbon dioxide.

Each of the cells travels approximately 173,000 times between the lungs and other tissues before it dies. The red blood cell has a life span of about 120 days. At that time, the aging cell is caught by a macrophage (*pictured at right*) and digested.

When the oxygen-rich blood leaves the heart, it travels in vessels called **arteries**. The **aorta** is the biggest artery in the body. It travels from the heart through the chest into the abdomen. Other large arteries branch from it, and still other arteries branch from them. Blood flows from the smallest arteries into tiny thin-walled tubes called **capillaries**. The oxygen and nutrients from digested food are carried in the blood and pass through the walls of the capillaries to the cells. In much the same manner, the waste materials from the cells pass back into the blood through the walls of the capillaries.

From the capillaries, the waste-carrying blood moves into tiny vessels called **veins**. The tiny veins lead into bigger veins. The bigger veins lead into still bigger veins until the blood finally flows into the large **vena cava**, the vein that enters the heart. From the heart, the waste-carrying blood is pumped into the lungs where the waste gases are removed from the blood and oxygen is added. The oxygen-rich blood returns to the heart and once again begins its travels.

The Urinary System

In order to function properly, the body must be able to get rid of its gaseous, solid, and liquid waste materials. Carbon dioxide, the waste gas, is eliminated through the lungs; solid wastes are eliminated through the large intestine. Some liquid waste evaporates from the skin as sweat; however, most of the liquid waste is removed by the urinary system as **urine**. The two kidneys, the bladder, and the tubes that connect them are the structures of the urinary system.

The Urinary System

Removing liquid waste and regulating fluid balance are the tasks of the urinary system. Each hour, as blood passes through the kidneys, about 2 ounces (57 grams) of urine are produced.

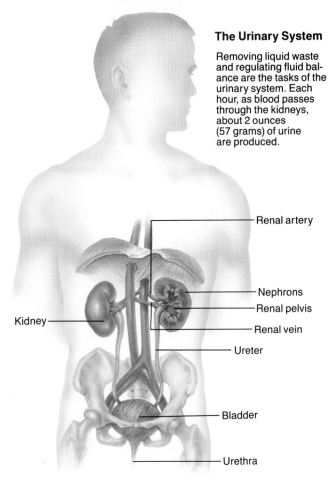

Kidney
Renal artery
Nephrons
Renal pelvis
Renal vein
Ureter
Bladder
Urethra

A **kidney** is bean-shaped and dark red in color. It is about 4 inches (10 centimeters) long. The kidney is like a waste purification system. Within each kidney there are about a million capillary clumps. These capillaries are like sieves. They have small openings that allow water and waste particles, but not blood cells, to leave the blood. The liquid containing waste is collected in small tubes that surround the capillary sieves.

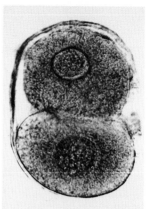

From the tubes, the waste then moves through the kidney and is processed further. Some small particles, such as sugar and salt, are taken back into the body; other waste particles are added to the urine. One familiar substance that is in the waste liquid is water. Water makes up more than 95% of urine. By removing water, the kidneys help keep the balance of water in the blood just right.

After the waste liquid has been processed in the kidney, it moves through the connecting tubes into the bladder. The bladder stores the urine until it is eliminated from the body.

The Reproductive System

The process of reproduction involves the creation of a new human being. It begins when a male's reproductive cell, called a **sperm**, joins with a female's reproductive cell, called an **ovum**. The joining of the sperm and the ovum is called **fertilization**.

Within a fertilized egg are all the instructions that are needed to direct the growth of a new human being. The baby develops as the joined cells divide and form the many organs that make up a new human being. Because the two reproductive cells contain the parents' genes, the baby that is formed will tend to look like both its parents.

The reproductive structures that develop in male babies, both inside and outside, are different from those that develop in female babies. Males and females also produce different chemical messengers, or **hormones**. During puberty and adolescence, these hormones produce noticeable body changes.

In the male, the reproductive structures include the **testes**, two walnut-sized structures

The Reproductive System

The reproductive structures of the male and female, which differ, provide the means to produce a new generation of human beings. The process begins when the male sex cell and the female sex cell unite.

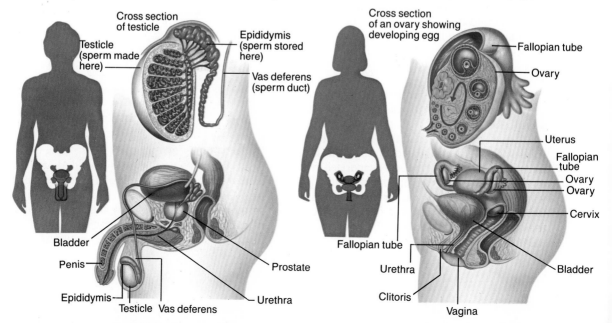

Fertilization takes place when one of the sperm cells thrashing around the egg (*opposite page, far left*) penetrates its gelatinous covering. A new life grows cell by cell as the fertilized egg divides (*opposite page, left*). The fetus floats within a wet, dark world. Now at 4 months (*right*), all its organs have been formed, and the time remaining before birth will be simply a time of growth.

that hang between the legs in a loose skin sac called the **scrotum**. The testes produce and store sperm. The sperm that are produced in the testes are transported through narrow tubes to the **penis**, which is the external reproductive organ of the male. The penis is used for both transporting sperm into the female reproductive system and eliminating urine.

In the female, the internal reproductive structures include the **ovaries** (which produce the ovum) and the **uterus** (which is where babies grow until they are ready to be born). Women have two ovaries. Each ovary is connected to the top of the uterus by a small tube called the **fallopian tube**. At the bottom of the uterus, a canal-like structure called the **vagina** opens to the outside of the body. The external structures of the female are small folds of skin and mucous membranes called **labia**.

Women usually produce only one ovum a month. At the same time that the ovum is developing, changes occur in the uterus. It is preparing a place for the baby to grow. The inside of the uterus gets thicker and forms new blood vessels. If the ovum is not fertilized, the uterus sheds this inside layer. This is called a **menstrual period**. Most women have a menstrual period once a month.

The reproductive process involves an act called **sexual intercourse**. During sexual intercourse, millions of sperm from the penis enter the vagina. The sperm move around and look for the ovum. If an ovum is present, a sperm may join with the ovum and begin the process of creating a new human being.

Communication Systems of the Body

Throughout the body, changes are happening second by second and minute by minute. Even though hundreds of different things are going on at the same time, no part of the body acts alone. For instance, the heart does not just start beating differently. If it did, other systems in the body would act to bring the heart back to the usual rhythm. All of the body systems communicate with each other and work together in the ongoing process called **self-government**. Self-government works whether you are awake or asleep.

When you run, both legs must move at the right time. You breathe more often, your heart beats faster, and your cells use more energy.

Messengers travel from one part of the body to another telling each part what needs to be done and when it needs to be done.

There are two types of messenger systems that work together in the body. One system uses electrical signals; the other system uses chemical signals. Most of the body's electrical messages are sent through the **nervous system**. The many kinds of chemical messages are carried in hormone messengers that travel through the bloodstream and other body fluids. The most common are hormones that are produced by the **endocrine system**.

Although each person is a unique mix of genetic information, individuals within a family tend to share a likeness of features.

The Nervous System

The structures of the nervous system include the brain, spinal cord, **neurons** (or nerve cells), and sense organs (such as the eyes and ears). The brain acts as a central computer for the nervous system, processing many types of orders, sensations, emotional feelings, and thinking behaviors.

Neurons have a cell body that contains a nucleus and wire-like projections called **nerve fibers**. They have input fibers that receive information and a single long output fiber that sends information. Nerve fibers from all over the body go to the brain and fibers from the brain go to all parts of the body.

Within the nervous system, electrical signals are used as messengers. Neurons have been programmed to recognize specific incoming signals. When the correct signal arrives, the nerve cell "fires." Some nerves work like calculators—they add up the incoming signals until they get the correct answer and then they fire.

When a nerve fires, information leaves the nerve through the output fiber. Many of these fibers communicate with other nerves, many of which are in the brain. Some communicate with muscle cells; others communicate with glands, blood vessels, and organs of the digestive tract.

The Nervous System

The complicated tasks of detecting, interpreting, and acting on information from the body's external and internal environments are performed by the nervous system.

Cerebrum — Brain
Cerebellum
Medulla
Spinal cord — Cervical nerves
Thoracic nerves
Radial nerve
Median nerve
Ulnar nerve
Lumbar nerves
Sacral and coccygeal nerves
Femoral nerve
Sciatic nerve

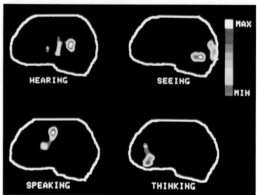

Scans of the brain while an individual is awake show the level of activity in areas of the brain that are dedicated to hearing, seeing, speaking, and thinking.

Different parts of the brain do different things. The **medulla** is the part of the brain that connects with the spinal cord. Its nerve cells carry messages between the spinal cord and other parts of the brain. These nerves are in charge of the muscles and glands that work day and night. Even when you are asleep, nerves in the medulla keep your heart beating and your lungs breathing.

The **cerebellum** controls body movement and balance. Information about many of the habits and skills you have learned is stored there. Once you have learned these behaviors they become automatic. The cerebellum issues orders that enable you to, among other things, walk, ride a bicycle, and play the piano.

The **cerebrum** (or **cerebral cortex**) is where thinking, learning, remembering, deciding, and being aware take place. The sensations of seeing, hearing, smelling, tasting, and touch-

The structures of the nervous system work together to produce conscious and automatic activities. Without the contributions of each part, it would be impossible to engage in such activities as playing the violin (*above*) or jumping hurdles (*right*).

ing are centered there. So are body feelings. The cerebrum enables you to enjoy things, speak intelligently, make up a poem, even design a rocket.

The different parts of the brain work together to accomplish a task. For example, suppose you decide to take a bike ride. The cerebrum, which is the thinking part of your brain, makes this decision. It decides where you will ride, how fast you will pedal. It orders the muscles to work. After that, the cerebellum and other parts of the brain take over. These make the muscles work smoothly and together. The medulla matches the action of the heart and the lungs to the energy needs of the muscles. As you pedal harder, your heart beats faster and you breathe more often.

The Sense Organs. Because we get information about the outside environment through the senses of sight, hearing, smell, taste, and touch, they are often referred to as external senses. Along with the external senses that tell us about the outside world, there are some senses that tell us what is going on inside of our bodies. These senses, called internal senses, let us know such things as when we are hungry or thirsty, whether we are in pain, and if we are sitting up or lying down.

There are **receptors** for every sensation. Receptors are special nerve structures such as those in the eye that let you see. Each receptor processes only one kind of information. That is why you cannot see with your ears or hear with your eyes. The sensory information is sent to the brain through input fibers. The eyes report on a wide range of sensory information, such as the size, shape, color, position, and movement of objects.

The seeing process begins when light coming from an object reaches the eyes. The rays of light go through the **lens** to the **retina**, a sort of screen at the back of the eyeball. From there the message is sent to the brain, and the person sees.

Because the two eyes are a small distance apart, they report slightly different images.

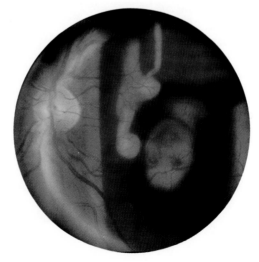

The human eye observes its surroundings as an upside-down image and sends this message along nerve fibers to the brain. The brain interprets this information so that we perceive the world with objects right side up.

The Eye

The eye provides visual information by changing light waves into nerve impulses that are interpreted in the brain.

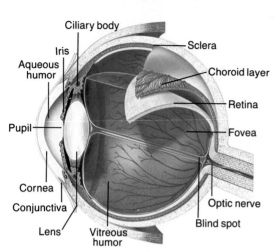

Ciliary body
Iris
Aqueous humor
Pupil
Cornea
Conjunctiva
Lens
Vitreous humor
Sclera
Choroid layer
Retina
Fovea
Optic nerve
Blind spot

The Ear

Sound waves received by the ear are conducted through its structures and converted to nerve impulses before traveling to the brain.

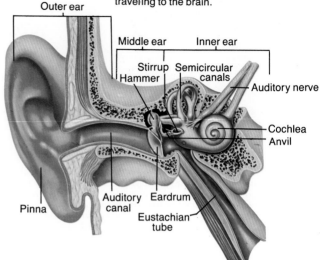

Outer ear
Middle ear
Inner ear
Stirrup
Hammer
Semicircular canals
Auditory nerve
Cochlea
Anvil
Pinna
Auditory canal
Eardrum
Eustachian tube

However, the two images merge, and the important result is that we see things in depth and can therefore judge distances.

Having an ear on each side of our head helps us to judge the direction from which a sound comes. We hear when something sends out vibrations called **sound waves**. The sound waves enter the ear and hit the eardrum, causing a vibration that moves some small bones inside the air-filled cavity of the skull's temporal bone. The bones send a message along the hearing nerves to the brain.

Smelling and tasting work closely together, and much of what most people call tasting is actually smelling. Taste is a chemical sense. As food becomes wet in the mouth and dissolves, a chemical reaction takes place and taste receptors are activated. These receptors, usually called **taste buds**, are contained within the small bumpy structures, or **papillae**, on the tongue. Once activated, taste buds send messages to the brain about whether the flavor of the food is sweet, sour, bitter, or salty. Some tastes seem stronger on certain tongue areas. The tongue also has receptors that report on heat, cold, texture, and pain.

Anything that has an odor is giving off tiny particles of gas, which mix with the air. By breathing, you draw these particles into your nose, where the particles of gas are moistened. Nerve cells sense the wet particles and send a message to the brain. Then you smell whatever the odor is.

Through different kinds of nerve cells in the skin, the brain learns about pain, pressure, heat, cold, and touch. The sense of touch tells whether things are rough or smooth, hard or soft, sharp or rounded. When you feel your way through the dark, you are using your sense of touch. The same sense tells you when and how the skin is being stroked and about something that is pulling on the skin.

The nerve cells of the skin are scattered all over the body, but some parts of the body have especially large collections of them. The fingertips are such parts—you can get much more information by feeling something with your fingertips than with your elbow.

Sometimes the information that is reported by our exter-

The tongue's surface is covered with small budlike projections that house the taste buds.

nal senses seems more obvious and important than information reported by our internal senses. However, the internal senses make us aware of feelings such as hunger, pain, movement, and fatigue. The internal senses help maintain a steady, healthy environment inside the body. They do this by responding to specific chemical and physical changes in internal systems, such as the digestive, respiratory, and nervous systems.

None of the senses work alone. We do not see with just our eyes or hear with just our ears. The senses are reporters. They take in information and send it to the brain. Each kind of information reaches a particular part of the brain, and in a way that scientists do not understand, the brain turns nerve impulses into sounds, tastes, and smells. Not until the messages reach the brain do we actually see, hear, taste, and so on.

Sometimes when one sense does not work, other senses tend to become sharper to make up for the loss. People who are blind tend to develop keen senses of hearing and touch. And people who are deaf tend to develop sharper senses of sight and touch.

The Endocrine System

The endocrine system produces powerful chemical messengers called hormones. Similar to the nervous system, the endocrine system works automatically and we cannot control it. Hormones are most often manufactured by patches of cells called **glands**. Glands that are part of the endocrine system include the thyroid, parathyroid, adrenal, pituitary, and sex glands. However, there are hormone-secreting endocrine tissues in organs such as the brain, kidneys, stomach, and pancreas. Wherever the endocrine secretions are produced, they pass directly into the bloodstream and remain in the body.

Some glands do not produce hormones. Instead, they secrete substances such as saliva or sweat. Such glands are called exocrine glands. Substances such as saliva and sweat perform specific tasks close to where they are released. Their secretions leave the body either from the skin or through the digestive tract.

When sense receptors send conflicting messages to the brain, such as during weightlessness, the mechanism that keeps our internal processes stable is disrupted.

The **thyroid gland** is an example of an endocrine gland that keeps the body working normally. It is a rather large gland in the neck. Its hormone stimulates cells to produce more energy. The thyroid hormone controls the rate at which cells burn food and thus the rate at which they produce energy. It also affects growth and development of the mind. Four tiny glands that function as one make up the

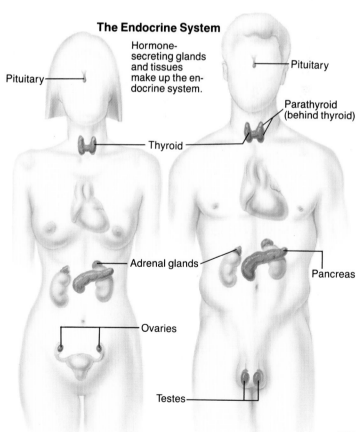

The Endocrine System

Hormone-secreting glands and tissues make up the endocrine system.

Pituitary

Pituitary

Parathyroid (behind thyroid)

Thyroid

Adrenal glands

Pancreas

Ovaries

Testes

Many things contribute to a healthy and well-functioning body and mind, including work, play, and companionship.

parathyroid, which lies close to the thyroid. The parathyroid secretes hormones that control blood calcium and are important in several body processes, such as bone growth and muscle and nerve function.

Another type of endocrine gland is the **adrenal gland**. There are two adrenal glands—one is located on the top of each kidney. Each adrenal gland has two parts, and each part does a different job. Whenever a person is in danger, one part of the gland releases a hormone called **adrenalin** that prepares the body for quick action. Suppose something happens to give you a sudden fright. Your heart begins to pound. Your face turns pale, and the pupils in your eyes open wider. Your muscles tense. You feel "butterflies" in your stomach. This is what adrenalin does to the body.

The other part of the adrenal gland produces hormones too. These hormones help keep your blood sugar up between meals, regulate the salt levels in your blood, and prevent tissue damage due to injury or infection.

The **pituitary gland** is a pea-sized gland at the base of the brain. It is sometimes called the master gland because it makes hormones that control other endocrine glands. For example, one of its hormones controls the action of the adrenal glands. Another makes the thyroid gland work harder.

The pancreas is one of the organs that has endocrine tissue. **Insulin**, which is produced by specialized pancreatic cells, helps to control blood sugar. It carries the message that tells fat cells and muscle cells to take sugar out of the blood.

Hormones and other chemical messengers act through receptors. The chemical messengers fit into the receptors in a lock and key fashion. Each hormone and chemical messenger (the key) has its own specially shaped receptor (the lock). Insulin has a different shape of receptor than the thyroid hormone. Hormones will only communicate with cells that have the right kind of receptor. This is how they manage to travel throughout the body and only communicate with certain types of body cells.

▶**YOUR BODY**

The human body is a complex arrangement of separate parts. Each part performs its own specific task, yet each is dependent on the other to maintain one unique living being: you. Learning about the human body and how it works also helps us examine ourselves and the world around us. When we examine the human body, we find that there are differences that make each person unique and special. However, the basic truth is that we are each of us more alike than we are different.

CAROL MATTSON PORTH
Author, *Pathophysiology: Concepts of Altered Health States*

See also BIOLOGICAL CLOCK; BLOOD; BODY CHEMISTRY; BRAIN; CELLS; DIGESTIVE SYSTEM; EAR; EYE; GLANDS; IMMUNE SYSTEM; LIFE; NERVOUS SYSTEM; SKELETAL SYSTEM.

BODYBUILDING

Bodybuilding is a system of exercises for developing the muscles in order to change the body's appearance. It is also a sport in which contestants are judged for their muscular development.

Bodybuilding grew out of weight lifting. Training with weights produces bigger and stronger muscles because of the body's ability to adapt to stress. Lifting a weight heavier than a muscle is accustomed to lifting causes that muscle to get stronger. Once the muscle adapts to the new level of stress, you must increase the amount of weight you are using in your training in order to force the muscle to continue to adapt. This is called **progressive-resistance training**—you progressively increase the weight, or resistance, to keep pace with the increasing strength of your muscles.

The purpose of weight lifting is to lift as much weight as possible. But the aim of bodybuilding is to use weights, or some other form of resistance to muscular effort, to change the way the body looks. The bodybuilder is not concerned with how much weight he or she can lift but rather with the full contraction of each muscle involved in an exercise. Of course, bodybuilding training does make you stronger. But more important to the bodybuilder is the size, shape, proportion, and definition of the muscle structure. These create the unique physique of a bodybuilder.

▶PRINCIPLES OF BODYBUILDING

There are certain basic principles of bodybuilding training. The first is progressive-resistance training. The bodybuilder also tries to isolate and train each muscle of the body. Using weights or some other form of resistance, the bodybuilder subjects each of the muscles to a series of "sets" that are made up of a specific number of "reps," or repetitions. For example, to build up the biceps, a bodybuilder may do an exercise called "curls," which alternately contract and expand the biceps muscles. Using weights the bodybuilder may do 5 sets of 20 repetitions of curls. Contracting the muscles over and over, with the proper balance of sets and repetitions, is what gives the bodybuilder's muscles the shape and definition that weight lifters lack.

Bodybuilders used to work their whole bodies in each exercise session. Then they

This bodybuilder is doing an exercise called curls to develop her biceps—a muscle in the upper arm. Bodybuilding has become increasingly popular among women.

found that they got better results by training certain body parts one day and others the next. They also learned more about diet and nutrition. They are now able to create maximum muscle mass together with minimum body fat, so that every individual muscle fiber seems to be visible.

Top-level bodybuilding competitors train for many hours each day. As with any athlete, proper rest and nutrition are extremely important. Anything—even emotional factors—can change the way the bodybuilder's physique appears during the day of a contest.

▶THE FIRST BODYBUILDING CONTESTS

The forerunners of modern bodybuilding contests were "physical culture" competitions, which took place in the United States during the 1920's and 1930's. In these contests a variety of athletes, including swimmers, runners, boxers, gymnasts, and weight lifters, were judged on the look of their physiques and on their ability to perform athletic feats. The weight lifters began to dominate these contests because their huge muscles created such an overwhelming impression. Eventually all the competitors in these events were weight lifters, and the modern bodybuilding competition was born.

A competition called the Mr. America contest was held in 1939, but the first of the modern Mr. America bodybuilding events was held in 1940. Competitors were still required to perform some sort of athletic feat, as in the old physical culture contests. But the mass, proportion, and overall development of the contestants' physiques made it clear that they were really bodybuilders and not just weight lifters or physical culturists.

MODERN BODYBUILDING CONTESTS

In modern bodybuilding contests, the judges look at each competitor in order to evaluate the shape and proportions of the body, as well as how much muscle definition the competitor has achieved. The contestants are asked to do a series of poses that reveal the relative quality of the various parts of their physiques. Each also does a posing routine of his or her own choice. This routine is designed to emphasize the especially well-developed parts of the competitor's body.

Presenting the body properly through posing is a difficult art. It involves more than just flexing the muscles. The way a bodybuilder poses can impress or disappoint the judges. In addition, posing for long periods of time requires great endurance. Bodybuilders must practice posing in order to avoid becoming exhausted on stage.

In the late 1970's, the first bodybuilding contests for women were held. Before that time, contests for women were actually physical-culture beauty contests. Today women bodybuilders are held to the same high standards of physical development as men.

BODYBUILDING ORGANIZATIONS

The world governing organization of bodybuilding is the International Federation of Bodybuilders (IFBB), which has more than 120 member nations. The major events sanctioned by the IFBB are the World Amateur Bodybuilding Championships (Mr. Universe), the men's and women's World Professional Championships, the World Mixed-Pairs Championship (in which men and women compete together as teams), and the Mr. Olympia contest, in which the top champions come together each year to see who is the best.

FAMOUS BODYBUILDERS

The first bodybuilder who became well known to the general public was Steve Reeves, an American Mr. Universe winner who played Hercules in a series of "muscle movies" in the 1950's. In the 1970's and 1980's, two other bodybuilders gained celebrity through movies and television: Lou Ferrigno, an American, who played in "The Incredible Hulk" on television, and Austrian-born Arnold Schwarzenegger, who won the Mr. Olympia contest seven times. Both men starred in *Pumping Iron* (1977), a movie about bodybuilding.

BILL DOBBINS
Founding editor, *Flex* magazine

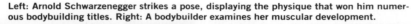

Left: Arnold Schwarzenegger strikes a pose, displaying the physique that won him numerous bodybuilding titles. Right: A bodybuilder examines her muscular development.

BODY CHEMISTRY

The body is a complicated chemical machine. The cell is the engine that runs this machine. If we want to learn how the cell engine works, we must take it apart. We must find out what each part looks like and what job it does.

The body is made up of so many cells that it would be impossible to take each one apart to learn how it works. Fortunately, this is not necessary, because cells resemble one another in many ways. A liver cell, a kidney cell, and a brain cell have much in common even though they do very different jobs in the body. Much of what we learn about one kind of cell applies to others as well. Therefore, from now on we will talk about a typical cell. This is a cell that doesn't really exist but that has the properties of many different kinds of cells.

▶ **WHAT CELLS ARE MADE OF**

The cell is a collection of chemicals called compounds. At first glance these compounds don't seem very unusual. A typical cell is about 65 percent water, 15 percent fatlike material, 15 percent protein, ½ percent carbohydrate, and 4½ percent salt. You could make up a mixture like that for less than a penny's worth of chemicals, but of course you wouldn't have a living cell. These compounds must be arranged in a very special way to produce life.

The most ordinary compound in the cell, water, has several important functions. For one thing, water is a very good solvent, which means it will dissolve many different kinds of chemicals. This is very important because the cell engine runs on chemical reactions. And chemical reactions, in general, take place best when the chemicals are dissolved in some liquid.

Many salts are dissolved in the cell water. Of course, it wouldn't do for all the salts in the body to dissolve in water. If they did, our bones would dissolve and we would collapse like a wet rag. Our bones contain calcium salts, which do not dissolve very much in water.

These simple compounds, water and salts, are found everywhere—in the sea, in the ground, and so on—not just in living cells.

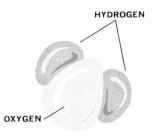

A molecule of water contains two atoms of hydrogen attached to an atom of oxygen. A typical cell is about 65 percent water.

Table salt is one of the simplest compounds known. It contains only two different kinds of atoms, sodium and chlorine. Water is simple, too. It contains two atoms of hydrogen attached to an atom of oxygen.

Not all the compounds in the body are this simple. Some of the most important molecules in the body contain thousands of atoms hooked together in a definite way. The compounds we are most interested in can be divided into four groups. These groups are called: the carbohydrates, the proteins, the lipids, and the nucleic acids.

A compound in a particular group is built on a definite plan. The carbohydrates have a plan, the proteins have another plan, and so on. A chemist can recognize this plan and can tell a carbohydrate from a protein as readily as you can tell an automobile from an airplane.

Within each group there are differences, too, just as there are differences between different makes of automobiles. You must learn a little about these different compounds before we can talk about how the cell works.

▶ **CARBOHYDRATES**

Carbohydrates are made up of carbon, hydrogen, and oxygen atoms. Lots of other compounds contain these same atoms. But carbohydrates can be recognized by the way the atoms are put together. **Sugars** are the simplest carbohydrates. When sugars were first discovered, scientists thought they were just carbon atoms combined with water. So they named the sugars carbo-hydrates, meaning carbon-water. Actually sugars are more complicated than this, and the carbohydrate group includes many compounds other than sugars.

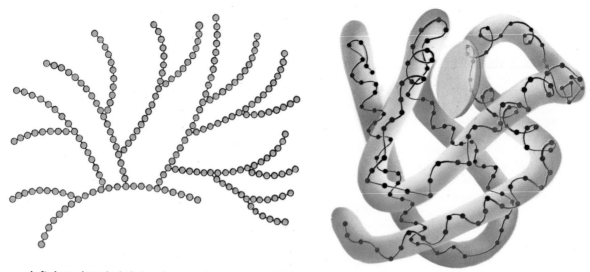

Left: Long, branched chains of glucose form glycogen. Right: Proteins are very important macromolecules. Amino acids (small dots) link together in complex chains and form huge protein molecules.

The word "sugar" makes everyone think of table sugar. But table sugar is actually a particular kind of sugar, which is called **sucrose**. There are many different kinds of sugar. The most important sugar in the body is **glucose**. Glucose is also called **dextrose**. It is one of the body's most important fuels. It is so important that the body stores up a good supply of it in a form called **glycogen**.

Glycogen is not a sugar itself, but is made up of sugar building blocks. Glycogen is produced when glucose molecules are hooked together into chains. The main glucose chain has many shorter chains that branch off it like the branches of a tree.

Starch is another important carbohydrate. Starch comes from plants, and starch molecules are very similar to glycogen. They are made up of glucose chains, too. Starch is the most important carbohydrate in the diet because it furnishes much of the glucose your body needs to function properly.

Compared to the sugars, starch and glycogen are huge molecules. Biochemists (scientists who study the chemistry of living organisms) have a special name for giant molecules like this. It is **macromolecules**. Macromolecules are so important that there cannot be any life without them.

▶**PROTEINS**

Starch and glycogen are not the only macromolecules in the body. Proteins are macromolecules, too. Every cell of every living organism has protein in it. In fact, the word "protein" means "of the first importance" in Greek.

There are many different proteins in the body, and they have many jobs to do. Your skin and hair contain a tough structural protein called **keratin**. Keratin and other structural proteins hold the body together. They are like the frame of your house. Another group, the **functional proteins**, are actively working at all sorts of important jobs. **Hemoglobin**, a blood protein, carries oxygen from the lungs to the cells. A large group of proteins called **enzymes** helps the cell carry out hundreds of chemical reactions.

Proteins are made from simple building blocks, the **amino acids**. Like the sugars, amino acids contain carbon, hydrogen, and oxygen, but they also contain nitrogen. There is a common pattern of carbon, hydrogen, oxygen, and nitrogen atoms in the amino acids that sets them apart from other compounds. However, there are also different arrangements within this basic plan. And so there are many different amino acids. Twenty of them are of particular importance in the body.

The amino acids are hooked together in long chains. One or more of these chains makes up a protein. Sometimes the chains are stretched out like string. Many structural proteins, such as keratin, are like this. In other proteins the chains are coiled and folded into a ball-like structure. Hemoglobin and many other functional proteins have this globular form.

Protein chains are complicated, with 20 different kinds of building blocks. Most proteins contain all 20, but a few do not. Our bodies can produce 12 of the 20 amino acids needed to make cell proteins. The other 8 must come from proteins in our food. A prolonged diet deficient in any of these 8 **essential amino acids** causes serious disease.

The chains in even the simplest protein are more than 30 amino acids long. The chains of many proteins are several hundred units long. The order of amino acids in the chains and the way the chains fold up give the protein the special properties it needs to carry out its particular job in the body.

The sum total of all your body's proteins makes you what you are. They are responsible for both the similarities and the differences between you and your parents. You do not inherit your proteins directly from your parents. But you do inherit the information that tells your cells what kind of proteins to make. This hereditary information is carried by another important group of compounds, the nucleic acids.

▶ NUCLEIC ACIDS

Like proteins, nucleic acids contain carbon, hydrogen, oxygen, and nitrogen. But nucleic acids also contain phosphorus. And like proteins, nucleic acids are made up of long, chainlike molecules within the body's cells. The building blocks of nucleic acid chains are called **nucleotides**.

Nucleotides are divided into two groups, depending on the sugar they contain. One group has the sugar **ribose**; these nucleotides are called **ribonucleotides**. The other group contains the sugar **deoxyribose**; these nucleotides are called **deoxyribonucleotides**. Deoxyribose has one less oxygen atom than ribose.

Ribonucleotides join together and form one type of nucleic acid—**ribonucleic acid**. It is commonly known as **RNA**. The smallest RNA has about 75 nucleotides in a single chain. The largest RNA chains are thousands of nucleotides in length.

Deoxyribonucleotides join together to form the other type of nucleic acid—**deoxyribonu-**

BUILDING NUCLEOTIDES

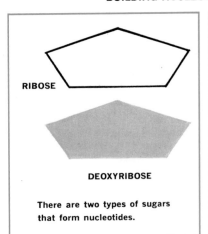

RIBOSE / DEOXYRIBOSE

There are two types of sugars that form nucleotides.

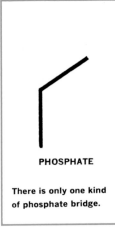

PHOSPHATE

There is only one kind of phosphate bridge.

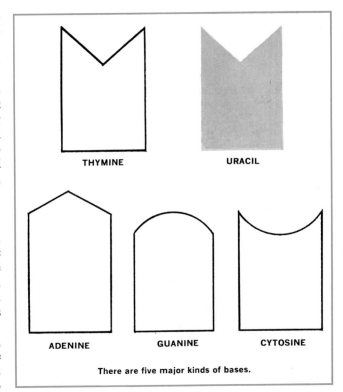

THYMINE   URACIL

ADENINE   GUANINE   CYTOSINE

There are five major kinds of bases.

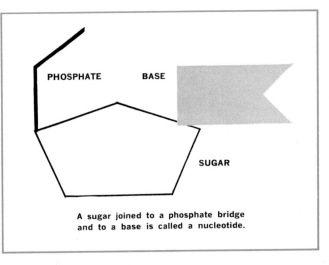

PHOSPHATE   BASE   SUGAR

A sugar joined to a phosphate bridge and to a base is called a nucleotide.

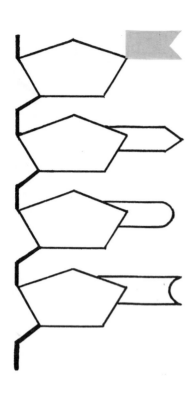

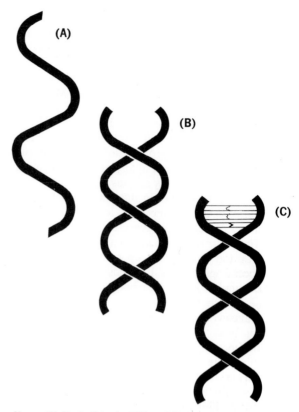

Above: RNA is made of many nucleotides strung together. All the nucleotides in RNA have the sugar ribose. Below: DNA is made of many nucleotides strung together. All the nucleotides in DNA have the sugar deoxyribose.

Above: (A) Nucleotides in DNA and RNA are arranged in a helix. (B) Nucleotides that make up DNA form two helices that wind around each other. (C) The helices are held together by bases that join in pairs. Two bases are always found together, one base on each helix. Below: Model of a DNA molecule.

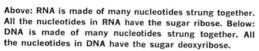

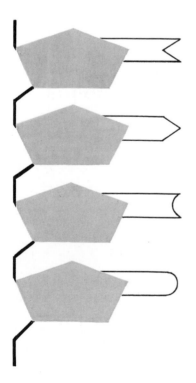

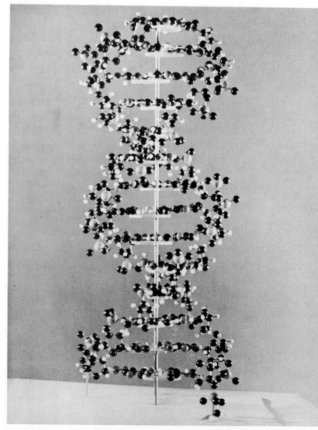

cleic acid, or **DNA**. DNA chains contain many thousands of nucleotides. Usually the DNA molecule has two nucleotide chains exactly the same length. The chains are wound around each other like two strands of rope and form a double helix.

DNA is found only within the nucleus of the cell. DNA carries all the body's hereditary information. All of us inherit DNA from our parents. When the two chains of the DNA helix split apart, each produces a new partner. The result is two DNA molecules exactly like the original one. As this process continues hereditary information is passed on from cell to cell.

Later in this article, you will learn more about the fascinating things nucleic acids do. But there is still one more group of compounds to talk about before we come to how the body machine works.

▶ LIPIDS

All the fatlike or "greasy" compounds in the body belong to the lipid group. The simplest lipids are the fatty acids. There are many different fatty acids in the body. They are building blocks for other lipids. For example, **fats** such as beef fat or lard and **oils** such as olive oil are made when three fatty acids become attached to a molecule of glycerol (glycerin). Fats are an important storehouse of energy in the body.

The **steroids** are also fairly simple lipids. Perhaps you have heard about the steroid **cholesterol**. It serves as the raw material for making many other important steroids such as the **sex hormones**. The body can't function normally without cholesterol. But when the amount gets too high, the cholesterol may deposit in the arteries and lead to the disease atherosclerosis (hardening of the arteries).

Not all lipids are simple. In fact, lipid macromolecules are perhaps the most complex (complicated) molecules in the body. They do not have just one building block, as in glycogen, or a few similar building blocks, as in proteins and nucleic acids. Rather, the **complex lipids** may contain many different kinds of building blocks. Fatty acids are almost always part of these lipids, but the lipids may also contain sugars, amino acids, phosphates, and some special compounds.

These complex lipids make up the various membranes of the cell. The membranes hold important parts of the cell machine together. The cell itself is encased in a lipid membrane —without this membrane there can't be a cell. The cell nucleus also has a lipid membrane. These membranes are so constructed that certain kinds of molecules can pass through them easily. For example, building blocks such as sugars must pass through the cell membrane in order for the cell machinery inside to use them. Waste products such as carbon dioxide must pass out of the cell.

There are other molecules that the cell must keep inside the membrane. The liver cell can't store glucose because glucose molecules pass through the cell membrane. But large glycogen molecules will not go through the cell membrane. So the liver can store glucose as glycogen. When glucose is needed, some glycogen is broken down into glucose.

As you can see, the cell is more than a complicated mixture of chemicals. And these chemicals are not just thrown together like nuts in a bag. They are carefully woven into the complicated chemical structures that make up the different parts of the cell machine.

Now that you know a little about the parts of the machine, we can go on to how they work at the chemical level. The cell machine runs on hundreds of chemical reactions. All these reactions, taken together, are called **metabolism**.

▶ ENZYMES

Many chemical reactions by themselves are quite slow. For example, if the gases hydrogen and oxygen are mixed, nothing happens. When a little finely ground platinum metal is added, the hydrogen and oxygen combine to form water. Sometimes they react so fast in the presence of platinum that the mixture explodes. When the reaction is finished, the metal can be recovered unchanged.

The platinum speeded up the reaction between hydrogen and oxygen without being permanently changed itself. Chemists call compounds that do this **catalysts**.

The body has hundreds of different catalysts. Almost every chemical reaction that occurs in the body has a special catalyst. These body catalysts are called **enzymes**. Enzymes, then, speed up the body's chemistry.

With all catalysts, including enzymes, a

little bit goes a long way. This is because they aren't changed by the reaction they catalyze. So a single molecule of catalyst can work over and over again. However, enzymes have special properties, which are different from those of other catalysts. First of all, enzymes are proteins. (Now you see one reason why proteins are so important.) Second, enzymes have **specificity**. This means that a particular enzyme catalyzes one particular reaction or, at most, one particular group of reactions. It will not work in any other reactions.

Specificity comes in when the enzyme and its **substrate** meet. The substrate is the substance on which the enzyme does its work. The substrate and the enzyme must fit together in the way that a lock and its key fit together. On the surface of the enzyme, the substrate is changed to some other compound. The new compound separates from the enzyme. And so the enzyme is again free to combine with another molecule of the substrate. This can happen again and again.

▶ ENZYME HELPERS

The protein molecules can't always act as catalysts by themselves. Sometimes they need help.

Very often an enzyme has two parts, a protein and a **coenzyme**. A coenzyme is a fairly complicated molecule, but much simpler than a protein. And it is the coenzyme that actually gets the job done. The protein part of the enzyme assures that the job is done on the right substrate.

The body can make coenzymes if it has the right building blocks. The building blocks must be furnished by the diet because the body can't make them. These building blocks are the **vitamins**. For example, vitamin B_2 (riboflavin) is changed into the coenzyme, flavin adenine dinucleotide, or simply FAD. Other vitamins are converted into other coenzymes. Now you can understand why vitamins are important in the diet.

▶ DIGESTION

Enzymes are made inside the cell. Most of them remain in the cell, where they catalyze the complicated cell reactions. A few of them, however, pass out of the cell to do their job. The digestive enzymes are **extracellular** (out-

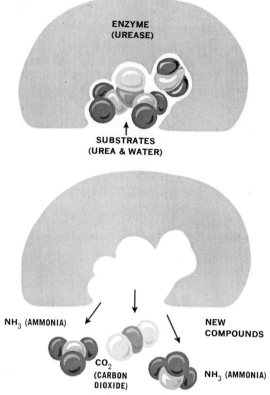

Enzyme and substrates fit together like a lock and key. Chemical reaction alters the substrates while the enzyme remains unchanged. Products of reaction on substrates are separated from the enzyme. The enzyme is now free to act on other molecules of substrates.

side the cell) **enzymes**. Let's see how digestion works at the chemical level.

Suppose you have just had a ham sandwich. This sandwich contains protein and fat in the meat. It contains carbohydrate (starch) in the bread. An enzyme called **ptyalin** or **alpha-amylase** is present in your saliva. This enzyme begins to break down the starch chains. In the stomach the enzyme **pepsin** begins to work on the proteins, splitting the chains into shorter pieces. The finishing touches are carried out in the intestine. There still other enzymes finish the digesting. The protein chains are digested into amino acids. Starch is digested into glucose. Fats are converted to fatty acids and glycerol.

All of these are small molecules. They pass through the intestinal wall and are carried by the circulatory system to the various cells of the body. There they serve as fuel and building blocks for the cell engines. Without the digestive enzymes much of our food would remain as macromolecules. Since these are too big to pass through the intestinal wall, we would starve to death.

Unlike the digestive enzymes, most enzymes act inside the body's cells. There are enzymes that hook the glucose molecules together to form glycogen. There are enzymes that string the amino acids together again. The result is not proteins just like the ones in the meat but new proteins that are needed by the particular cell that is making them. Fatty acids and glycerol are combined again to make fat.

Now you can understand why proteins, carbohydrates, and fats are important in the diet. They are the raw materials. Digestion converts them to important building materials, such as sugars, amino acids, and fatty acids. As we shall see, they are also important fuels for the cell engines.

▶ **MAKING PROTEINS**

It is not too difficult to imagine how cells can make certain vital substances. Enzymes assist in much of the work. Enzymes in the cells can hook glucose units together to form glycogen. Enzymes in the cells can link fatty acids to glycerol to produce fat.

However, making a protein is much more complicated. (The process is called **protein biosynthesis**.) Even the simplest protein contains at least 30 amino acids in a chain. The more complicated proteins contain hundreds of amino acids. Furthermore, the amino acids must be arranged in just the right way if a protein is to carry out its particular job.

The problem of making proteins can best be understood through a comparison. Imagine you are told to make a string of beads representing a chain of amino acids. Each bead (amino acid) is numbered. You are told the string of beads must have a certain length and the numbers must run in a certain order. But you are not told what this length is or what the order of numbers is.

All the parts for solving the problem are set out (Fig. 1). The only information is given by the pattern. In the cell DNA is the pattern. This information is coded in units (nucleotides) of different shapes. There are six units, which means that the string of beads is to be six beads long.

Now the information of the DNA pattern must be decoded to find the order of the amino-acid beads in the chain. Of all the parts, only the shaded blocks (ribonucleotides) fit

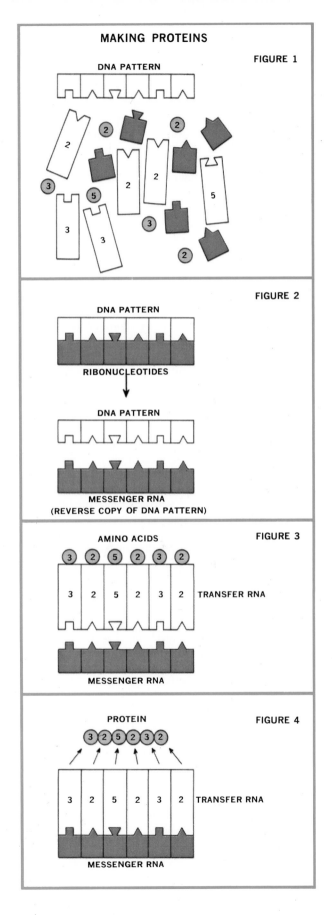

MAKING PROTEINS

FIGURE 1

DNA PATTERN

FIGURE 2

DNA PATTERN

RIBONUCLEOTIDES

DNA PATTERN

MESSENGER RNA
(REVERSE COPY OF DNA PATTERN)

FIGURE 3

AMINO ACIDS

TRANSFER RNA

MESSENGER RNA

FIGURE 4

PROTEIN

TRANSFER RNA

MESSENGER RNA

into the pattern. When the shaded blocks are joined together, the result is a copy of the pattern (Fig. 2). It is not the same as the pattern—everything is reversed. But it contains all the information that was in the pattern. In the cell this reversed copy is called **messenger RNA**.

This reversed copy is like a plaster cast taken of a head or a sculpture. When the proper material is poured into the cast, the original form can be reproduced.

The white blocks represent another kind of RNA, **transfer RNA**. The beads attached to them represent amino acids. There is a different transfer RNA for each different amino acid. When the transfer RNA and its amino acid fit into the messenger RNA copy (Fig. 3), the DNA pattern is reproduced and the order of amino acids is fixed (Fig. 4).

There are 20 kinds of amino acids. Then how does each kind of amino acid hook up with its own kind of transfer RNA and with no other? If a mistake should happen, the order of amino acids in the protein chain would be wrong. Suppose, for example, that a molecule of amino acid 2 becomes attached to a transfer RNA 3. As the protein chain is built, this amino acid will be fitted into a place where an amino acid 3 belongs.

Proteins called **activating enzymes** provide for the correct pairing of transfer RNA and amino acids. A specific activating enzyme links amino acid 2 with transfer RNA 2. Another enzyme does the same for the number 3 pair, and so on.

Arranging the amino acids in the correct order is only part of the problem, however. As you know, it takes work to make something. It requires mechanical work to build a house and electrical work to produce light. It takes chemical work to build proteins and the other compounds the body needs.

▶ **FROM FOOD TO ENERGY**

Work requires energy. The energy to do the body's work comes from the food we eat. Our food is mainly carbohydrate, fat, and protein. It took energy to make these food molecules. And energy is never really lost—it just appears in different forms. So we should be able to get energy back when our body breaks down these molecules.

Let's take a simple example and see how this energy cycle works. The sugar glucose contains 6 carbon atoms, 12 hydrogen atoms, and 6 oxygen atoms. Plants make glucose from carbon dioxide, water, and sunlight. The carbon dioxide provides the carbon atoms and some of the oxygen atoms. The water provides the hydrogen atoms and some of the oxygen atoms. The sunlight provides the energy that hooks these atoms together in a glucose molecule. (As it turns out, when the glucose molecule is finished, there is some oxygen left over. It becomes the oxygen in our air.)

We call this process **photosynthesis**. And we can summarize it as follows:

(plants)
carbon dioxide + water + energy → glucose + oxygen

If we reverse this process we should be able to produce energy:

(animals)
oxygen + glucose → energy + water + carbon dioxide

And that is exactly what people and animals do. Glucose is oxidized, or combined with oxygen, to give energy and waste products (water and carbon dioxide). This energy is used by the cells to make their macromolecules and to carry out their other work assignments, such as moving muscles.

This process of oxidation also occurs when we burn something. That's why a fire needs oxygen to burn. That's why you will often hear that the body "burns" its food to obtain energy. This "burning" is not exactly the same as a campfire, though. There are no tiny flames flickering inside the cell.

Furthermore, we build a fire to produce heat. We use this heat in many ways—to cook our food, to change water into steam that runs a steam engine, and so on. The body has no way to use heat to do work. It needs heat to keep the cells warm. But much of the heat produced by oxidation is a waste product because the body cannot use it directly.

If the body can't use heat to do work, how does it use its energy? The answer lies in a special molecule called **adenosine triphosphate** or **ATP**. ATP is a nucleotide. It is an RNA building block. But it is also able to trap the chemical energy released by oxidation and convert this energy into chemical work. ATP supplies the energy for building macromolecules. It also supplies the energy for muscle contraction, for nerve transmission, and so on.

THE ENERGY DYNAMO

Actually the cell is more like an electrical dynamo than a furnace. In a dynamo water flows over the turbine blades and turns the turbine. The turbine drives an electrical generator, which produces electricity. The electricity is used to produce light, run electric motors, and so on.

In the cell glucose is oxidized by a series of chemical reactions, which are like the turbine wheel. This chemical wheel turns another chemical wheel, which is like the electrical generator. This second wheel produces ATP, instead of electricity. The energy obtained from the ATP is used to do the cell's work.

So far we have talked only about the oxidation of glucose. But the other sugars are oxidized too. Except for the first few steps where preparation for oxidation occurs, all carbohydrates are oxidized by the same reactions. Fatty acids (from fats) and amino acids (from proteins) are oxidized inside the cell by the same energy dynamo.

Each different kind of food can furnish the cells with a definite amount of energy. Suppose you ate the same weight of each foodstuff in a meal. The fat would furnish one half the energy from that meal. The carbohydrate and protein would each furnish one fourth. In other words, fat can furnish about twice as much energy as the same amount of carbohydrate or protein.

As you remember, energy is never lost. What happens if you take in more potential energy in your food than your body can use up? The answer is simple. The body stores the extra food. The body can only store a certain amount of this food as carbohydrate and protein. The rest is stored as fat. It doesn't make any difference what this extra food is. Extra carbohydrate and protein can be converted to fat.

Clearly, if you eat more than your body needs, you will get fat. If you eat less than your body needs, it must draw upon its energy stores. The fat will be broken down to supply energy, and you will lose weight. When the carbohydrate and fat supplies are low, protein will be used to produce energy. If this breakdown of vital proteins continues for very long, a person will die.

CONTROLLING THE CELL ENGINE

When you run a race your muscles work hard. They need a big supply of fuel quickly. Your liver goes to work almost instantly changing glycogen, a carbohydrate that it normally stores, into glucose. The glucose enters the bloodstream, and in seconds it reaches the straining muscles. What controls this process? How does the liver know when to supply glucose for the muscles? Two systems control the work of the body tissues: the **nervous system**, and the **endocrine system**.

The nervous system provides a rapid response to an emergency situation. You know how fast you pull your hand away when you accidentally touch a hot stove. Your nervous system has told your muscles what to do.

The endocrine system acts less quickly, but for a longer time. The eight different glands that make up this system produce special chemicals called **hormones**. These are given off directly into the bloodstream, which carries them throughout the body. Each hormone acts on a particular organ to speed up or slow down its work. For example, the adrenal glands produce epinephrine (adrenaline). This hormone stimulates the liver to change glycogen into glucose. The hormones of the endocrine system act collectively to regulate the body's very complicated chemistry, producing a smoothly running machine.

SUMMARY

As you can see, the body is a complicated chemical machine. Simple chemicals are built into complicated macromolecules. Some macromolecules are woven into various structures that form the cell. Inside the cell hundreds of chemical reactions are going on and these reactions are catalyzed by other macromolecules, the enzymes. The chemical reactions provide the energy to make new cells and to carry out the functions of the body— moving muscles, thinking, and so on. Each cell is an independent unit, but it co-operates with other cells to make the body machine run smoothly and efficiently.

ROBERT WARNER CHAMBERS
New York University School of Medicine
See also BIOCHEMISTRY; CELLS.

BODY SIGNALS

Your body is smart. It knows how to take care of many problems. You do not even have to think about them; your body just acts.

Yawns

No one knows what causes yawns. You yawn when you are tired and when you are bored. Sometimes you yawn just because someone nearby has yawned. Even reading about a yawn can make you yawn. When you exercise, you do not yawn, and you never yawn when you are angry or excited. Probably some yawns are caused by your body's need for extra oxygen. A big yawn brings extra oxygen into your body. However, the need for oxygen does not explain why yawns are contagious.

Snores

People who snore breathe through their mouths when they sleep. Snores occur when soft parts of the mouth and throat wiggle and flop as air goes in and out. Many people snore only when they are lying on their backs.

Blushing

There are more tiny blood vessels, or capillaries, in the skin of your face than anywhere else on your body. When you are embarrassed or angry or overheated, your body sends a message to the blood vessels in your skin to expand, or become larger. When the capillaries expand, more blood flows through them, and your skin looks red. "You're blushing!"

Coughs and Sneezes

Coughs and sneezes are your body's way of reacting to something that is bothering your throat or your nose. When something irritates your throat or when a piece of food goes down your windpipe, you cough to force it out. When you have an itch or irritation in your nose, you sneeze.

Coughs and sneezes are very similar: you take in a big breath, muscles in your chest and abdomen tighten up, your throat closes, and air bursts out. In a cough, the vocal cords close tight, and the exploding sound is the air blasting its way through the vocal cords and out of the mouth. In a sneeze, the air is expelled through your nose as well as your mouth.

Sometimes you keep coughing or sneezing, because the irritation does not go away. That is why you cough and sneeze a lot if you have a cold. During a sneeze, tiny germ particles are forced from the nose at great speeds. This is one of the main ways that colds are spread from one person to another.

Hiccups

You get hiccups when something unusual happens to your diaphragm (the muscle at the bottom of your chest that helps you breathe). When you breathe out, your diaphragm relaxes and bulges up into your chest. That helps push air out of your lungs. When you breathe in, the diaphragm tightens and flattens out. This makes a bigger space in your chest, and air rushes in.

Your diaphragm usually has a regular rhythm of relaxing and tightening. But every so often the diaphragm suddenly jerks itself tight. That sudden jerk is called a spasm.

When your diaphragm is tight, air usually goes into your lungs. But when the diaphragm spasms, a tiny flap at the back of your throat, called the epiglottis, covers up the opening of your windpipe and prevents the air from going down. The "hic" is the sound you make when the air hits the epiglottis. After a "hic" the diaphragm goes back to normal. Then the spasm may happen again.

No one knows what causes the spasms. Sometimes they happen after a scare, or from laughing very hard, or from swallowing food too fast. Hiccups usually just stop after a while, but people have invented many unusual ways to try to cure them.

Burps

Burping is the body's way of getting rid of too much air or gas in the stomach. You swallow air with everything you eat and drink. When you chew food, you mix air with it. When you drink a glass of water, you swallow air. Soda, popcorn, and toast are filled with air. Apples and oranges have gases trapped in them that are set free by the acids in your stomach.

As your stomach digests the food you swallow, the trapped air and gases rise as bubbles and pop, just like the bubbles in soda. As more and more bubbles pop, more and more air presses against the sides of your stomach. Finally the gas pushes up into your esophagus and bursts out your mouth as a burp. The scientific word for burping is eructation.

Stomach Growls

Stomach growls can happen anytime, not only when you are hungry. Usually it is not even your stomach that is growling at all; it is your intestines. When your stomach finishes mashing and grinding your food, it pushes the food into your intestines where muscles then move the food along. It is this squeezing of the liquid food out of your stomach and through the twisted narrow intestines that causes stomach growls.

Gas

Everything you swallow moves into your digestive tract. Your digestive tract is a very long tube that has two openings. One opening is at your mouth; the other is at your anus, through which you expel solid waste and gas. All the air you swallow with your meal goes right to your stomach. The swallowed air that is not burped out goes on from the stomach into your intestines. Other gases are added to this air when millions of bacteria that live in the intestines attack the food.

When air, or gas, comes to the end of the digestive tract, it is held there by a muscle that keeps the exit tightly closed. The muscle is called the anal sphincter. Sometimes a lot of air gets to the anal sphincter and puts so much pressure on it that you cannot hold the muscle tight. The gas just pushes out. Other times you can keep your sphincter tight so the gas will not come out at an embarrassing time. Still other times, you can relax your anal sphincter and push out the gas when you want to.

Goose Bumps

Sometimes you feel chilly or are frightened by something, and you get little bumps all over your body. Those are called goose bumps, or gooseflesh.

If you look closely at the goose bumps, you will see a hair coming out of the middle of each one. Each hair on your body sits in a tiny pocket in your skin (called a follicle) with a little muscle attached to it. Usually those muscles are relaxed and let the hairs lie flat on your skin. But when you are cold or frightened, the muscles tighten. That makes the hairs stand up and the skin bunch up into little bumps.

Scientists think that many years ago, people's bodies were covered with lots of thick hair. When all those bumps formed and the hairs stood up, warm air from the body was trapped by the hairs and kept the body warm. That thick hair is not there any more, but the muscles still are. And they still pull on the tiny pockets, making hairs stand up and causing goose bumps.

SUSAN KOVACS BUXBAUM
Co-author, *Body Noises*

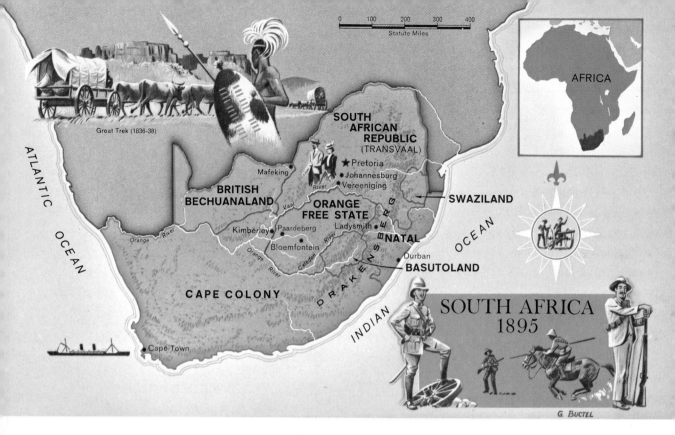

Great Trek (1836-38)

SOUTH AFRICAN REPUBLIC (TRANSVAAL)

★Pretoria
•Johannesburg
•Vereeniging

BRITISH BECHUANALAND

ORANGE FREE STATE

SWAZILAND

Kimberley• •Paardeberg
Bloemfontein

Ladysmith
•NATAL
Durban
BASUTOLAND

CAPE COLONY

ATLANTIC OCEAN

INDIAN OCEAN

DRAKENSBERG

Vaal
Orange River
Orange
Caledon River
River

Cape Town

Mafeking

0 100 200 300 400
Statute Miles

AFRICA

SOUTH AFRICA 1895

G. BUCTEL

BOER WAR

The Boer War, also called the South African War, was fought from 1899 to 1902. It pitted Britain, then the world's leading power, against two small countries in southern Africa.

In the 1600's the Dutch had settled the southern tip of Africa. Britain acquired the territory in the early 1800's. Not wishing to live under British rule, some of the descendants of the original Dutch settlers, called Boers, moved northward. They set up two independent republics, the South African Republic (the Transvaal) and the Orange Free State. The discovery of gold in the Transvaal in 1886 attracted many immigrants, most of them British.

Hostility between the British and the Boers increased as the immigrants began to outnumber the Boers. Fearing the loss of their independence, the Boers passed restrictive measures against the newcomers, refusing them the right to vote. The British Government insisted that the new settlers be granted full political rights. In 1895 a band of British colonists tried to overthrow the government of the Transvaal. These events convinced the Boers that the British meant to take control of their territory. The two republics formed a military alliance and mobilized their forces. The British sent troops to the border areas. When the British refused to withdraw, the Boers declared war in October, 1899.

The Boers were not professional soldiers. But they rode their horses and shot their rifles with great skill. Their mobility and knowledge of the land aided them against the slow-moving British troops. Early in the war the Boers defeated the British in several battles.

The British Government was embarrassed by the defeats and stung by criticism of the war at home and abroad. It sent more troops and new generals to Africa. By 1900 the superior British force succeeded in capturing the capitals of both Boer republics. But the Boers refused to surrender. They waged a guerrilla war for over a year. The British retaliated by burning Boer farms and putting Boer families in concentration camps. Finally, on May 31, 1902, the Boers signed a peace treaty. The two republics became British colonies. In 1910 they became part of the Union (now Republic) of South Africa.

Reviewed by JOHN E. FLINT
Dalhousie University

See also SOUTH AFRICA.

BOGOTÁ

Bogotá is the capital of Colombia and its largest and most important city. It is located in the central part of Colombia, on a wide plateau high in the Andes mountains. It is a city of contrasts, with modern skyscrapers perched next to historic buildings.

The city, which is more than 8,600 feet (2,600 meters) above sea level, is surrounded by mountains on three sides. For centuries, Bogotá was isolated by these high ranges. Formerly it took eight days to reach the city from the Atlantic coast. Now the trip can be made in one hour by airplane.

Bogotá usually bustles with activity. In the downtown sector, the main commercial district, the narrow streets are crowded with people and cars. Children walk or ride donkeys through heavy traffic. Everywhere there are vendors and *campesinos* (farm laborers), who come to the city looking for work. Well-dressed business people and shoppers stroll by or stop at one of the city's many coffeehouses.

The people of Bogotá are of European, Indian, and mixed background. They are known for their conservative manners and gentle dignity. The city's rapid growth to a population of more than 4,000,000 has caused a housing shortage. Many new apartment houses are being built. But the slums have grown enormously, and unemployment has become a problem.

Economic Activity. Bogotá's factories process agricultural and dairy products from nearby farmlands and manufacture furniture, household appliances, construction materials, textiles, and chemicals. The city is a world center for emeralds, which are mined north of Bogotá. The area around Bogotá also produces flowers for export.

Places of Interest. Bogotá has fine restaurants, hotels, and theaters. Concerts and plays are performed in the richly decorated Colon Theater, in the older part of the city. It faces the Palace of San Carlos, where the president of Colombia lives. There are several universities, including the National University of Colombia. Among the art galleries and museums, the National Museum and the Colonial Museum are known for collections of colonial art. The Gold Museum has magnificent gold objects made by Indians before the country was conquered by the Spanish.

Situated high in the Andes mountains, Bogotá, the capital of Colombia, lies more than 8,600 feet (2,600 meters) above sea level.

The city has many old colonial buildings. The cathedral on the Plaza Bolívar, the main square, dates from 1572. Overlooking the city is the church of Monserrate, which can be reached by cable car.

History. Bogotá was founded in 1538 by the Spanish conquistador (conqueror) Gonzalo Jiménez de Quesada. It became the capital of New Granada, which was a center of the Spanish empire in South America. The city was liberated from Spanish rule in 1819, and in 1821 it was named the capital of Gran (Greater) Colombia. This federation, which included the present-day nations of Colombia, Panama, Venezuela, and Ecuador, fell apart by 1830. Bogotá then became the capital of the Republic of New Granada, which was later renamed the Republic of Colombia.

ARLENE GOULD
Former correspondent, *Life en Español*

See also COLOMBIA.

BOHR, NIELS (1885–1962)

Early in the 1900's a young Danish physicist named Niels Bohr began to study the atom. His studies turned out to be both his life's work and extremely important. First he gave science a new view of the atom's structure. Some years later he helped to release the energy of the atom. Still later he worked to control that energy for peaceful uses.

Niels Bohr was born on October 7, 1885, in Copenhagen, Denmark. His father was a scientist and professor at the university there, and Niels was raised in a home where science was naturally of interest. In 1903 he entered the University of Copenhagen. His chief concern was physics, but he was also an outstanding soccer player. By 1907 Niels had won a gold medal from the Royal Danish Academy for his scientific work.

After receiving his doctor's degree in 1911, Bohr wanted to learn more about the atom. He decided to go to England and study with J. J. Thomson and Ernest Rutherford. Both these men were leaders in atomic physics. Bohr first studied under Thomson at Cambridge University; a year later he worked with Rutherford at the University of Manchester. In 1913 Bohr returned to the University of Copenhagen as a lecturer.

It was during this year that Bohr made his first great contribution to atomic physics. By that time many scientists had attempted to explain the atom. Rutherford, for example, had provided one theory. The great German physicist Max Planck had another.

Working from the ideas of Rutherford and of Planck, Bohr set forth a new theory of his own. It dealt with atomic structure and behavior. Bohr's theory became the basis of the branch of modern physics known as quantum mechanics. For his brilliant work Bohr received the Nobel prize for physics in 1922.

Meanwhile Bohr had married a Danish girl, started a family, and continued teaching at the University of Copenhagen. In 1920 he became director of the university's new Institute of Theoretical Physics. He made the institute into one of the world's major research centers. Scientists came from all over the world to study with Bohr. He was sometimes so busy with his work that he forgot about his meals. But he always managed to make time for his wife and five sons.

About 1930 the institute began important studies of the nucleus of the atom. In 1936 Bohr made another major advance in atomic physics: he gave the first correct description of a nuclear reaction. This work later helped the United States develop the atomic bomb.

Bohr arrived in the United States in 1939 to work at the Institute for Advanced Study in Princeton, New Jersey. Some of the world's leading scientists were there, including Albert Einstein. Bohr told them of the work going on in Europe in splitting uranium atoms. His reports spurred United States research in this field.

Bohr returned to Copenhagen a few months after World War II broke out. In 1940 the Germans conquered Denmark. Bohr refused to co-operate with them and closed his institute. In 1943, when he was threatened with arrest, Bohr fled. He went first to Sweden and then to the United States.

Bohr served as adviser at the first atomic bomb laboratory, near Los Alamos, New Mexico. He soon began to worry about the far-reaching effects of the new bomb. After the first atomic bomb test, in 1945, Bohr went to Washington to plead for immediate international control of atomic weapons.

When the war ended in 1945, Bohr returned to work at his institute in Copenhagen. In 1955 he became chairman of the newly founded Danish Atomic Energy Commission. Two years later Bohr received the first Atoms for Peace award—a fitting climax to his life. Bohr died November 18, 1962.

JOHN S. BOWMAN
Author and Science Editor

BOILING POINT. See LIQUIDS.
BOISE. See IDAHO (Cities).

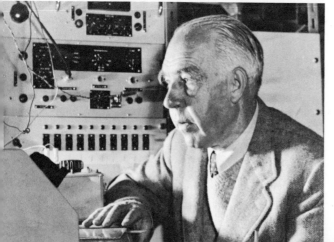

Niels Bohr helped form modern theory of atomic structure. He later served as adviser on the first atomic bomb.

BOLÍVAR, SIMÓN (1783–1830)

For nearly 300 years most of South America was under Spanish rule. Simón Bolívar vowed to free his native land, Venezuela, from Spain. When he died in 1830, he had freed not only Venezuela, but Ecuador, Bolivia, and Colombia as well.

Bolívar was born at Caracas, Venezuela, on July 24, 1783. His ancestors in Spain had belonged to the nobility, and young Bolívar was educated as an aristocrat. When he was 16, Bolívar was sent to Spain to continue his education. For the next seven years he studied and traveled in Europe. The example of the American and French revolutions stirred Bolívar deeply. He swore that he would not rest until he had broken the chains that bound his country to Spain.

In Venezuela a group of patriots, including Bolívar and Francisco Miranda, seized Caracas. On July 5, 1811, they declared Venezuela's independence. But the patriots were crushed by Spanish troops. Miranda died in prison and Bolívar fled from Venezuela.

Years of bloody fighting and heartbreaking defeat followed. Twice again Bolívar was forced to flee into exile. But his stern face and dark, piercing eyes showed a determination to win independence at all costs. In 1819 he boldly marched his patriot army over the snow-covered Andes mountains. It was winter, and in that terrible march many men and all the horses perished. But Bolívar surprised the Spanish Army and defeated it completely at Boyacá, in Colombia. The victory brought independence to Colombia. Two years later, Bolívar liberated Venezuela. And the following year, Ecuador was freed.

Venezuela, Colombia, and Ecuador were united into the republic of Gran Colombia, with Bolívar as its president.

Meanwhile, General José de San Martín, the liberator of Argentina, with Bernardo O'Higgins of Chile, had proclaimed the independence of Peru. Bolívar met with San Martín at Guayaquíl. San Martín generously gave Bolívar command of his army to complete the liberation of Peru. The next year Upper Peru was renamed Bolivia in honor of its liberator.

Bolívar soon had all the powers of a dictator, though his ideals were freedom and jus-

Simón Bolívar led his troops over the Andes mountains in 1819, surprising the Spanish Army. His victories led to the liberation of Colombia, Venezuela, and Ecuador.

tice. He encouraged the creation of constitutional government and urged that more schools and universities be built. There were slaves in South America. Bolívar had freed his, and he insisted that other slave owners do the same.

Bolívar's dream had been to see all the liberated countries united. However, each country wanted its independence. New revolutions broke out and Gran Colombia fell apart. Bolívar's enemies accused him of being a tyrant, and an attempt was made to kill him.

In 1830, weary and ill after years of war and revolution, Bolívar resigned as president of Colombia. On December 17, 1830, he died at the age of 47.

Bolívar's dream of a united South America was a failure. He died a disappointed man, with few friends and many enemies. But to the people of South America he is still *El Libertador*—the liberator.

Reviewed by ERNESTO SÁBATO
Author, *The Graves and the Heroes*

BOLIVIA

Bolivia lies in the heart of South America. Dominated by the great snowcapped peaks of the Andes mountains, it is one of the highest countries in the world. In fact, it is sometimes called the Tibet of South America. The city of La Paz, one of the country's two capitals, is about 3,600 meters (12,000 feet) above sea level. It is the world's highest capital city.

▶THE PEOPLE

Most of the people of Bolivia live in the snowcapped Andes in the western part of the country. Only about one quarter of the people make their home in the east, where the land slopes away into tangled tropical jungles and hot, dry plains.

Bolivia is the most Indian of the South American nations. More than one half of the people are Quechua and Aymará Indians. People of mixed Spanish and Indian descent, or Mestizos, make up one quarter of the population. Only a small fraction of the people call themselves whites. These are mostly descendants of Spanish settlers.

The Indian Way of Life

The Aymará Indians trace their ancestry back more than 1,000 years, to a great Indian civilization that grew up on the banks of Lake Titicaca. Today most Aymará live in the mountain area around Lake Titicaca. They work as farmers, shepherds, and miners.

Bolivia's other major Indian group, the Quechua, are descended from the Inca invaders who came to Bolivia in the 13th century A.D. The Quechua live mostly in the highlands and the deep valleys of the eastern Andes. Like the Aymará, the Quechua have their own language.

The life of the Bolivian Indian is generally harsh and monotonous. Families live in one-room houses of stone or baked mud brick called adobe. Windows are often just slits in the walls. Most Indians are farmers. The gov-

ernment has made many of them owners of their own land; but the life of the Indians is still hard. If they are fortunate, they may have oxen to draw their wooden plows across the fields. After the seed is sown, the children often follow behind to cover the furrows with earth.

The children also tend the herds of llamas and alpacas. These long-necked animals are related to the camel and are found only in the Andes. The Indians use them as pack animals and for their meat and fur.

The foods most commonly eaten are potatoes, corn, and beans. A basic food is *chuño*. It looks like popcorn, but it is really a potato that has been preserved by drying and freezing so that it can be stored for many months.

The life of the Indians who work in Bo-

FACTS AND FIGURES

REPUBLIC OF BOLIVIA (República de Bolivia) is the official name of the country.

THE PEOPLE are known as Bolivians.

LOCATION: West central South America.

AREA: 1,098,581 km² (424,165 sq mi).

POPULATION: 6,000,000 (estimate).

CAPITAL: La Paz (actual), Sucre (legal).

LARGEST CITY: La Paz.

MAJOR LANGUAGES: Spanish, Quechua, Aymará.

MAJOR RELIGION: Roman Catholic.

GOVERNMENT: Republic. **Head of state and government**—president. **Legislature**—Congress (composed of a Senate and a Chamber of Deputies).

CHIEF PRODUCTS: Agricultural—potatoes, corn, beans, wheat, barley, sugarcane, cotton, cacao, coca, coffee, alfalfa, oats, livestock. **Manufactured**—textiles, refined sugar, processed food, lumber. **Mineral**—tin, petroleum, natural gas, zinc, tungsten, silver, antimony, iron ore, copper.

MONETARY UNIT: Bolivian peso (1 peso = 100 centavos).

NATIONAL ANTHEM: *Bolivianos, el hado propicio coronó nuestros votos y anhelo* ("Bolivians, propitious fate has crowned our hopes").

---

livia's mines is a little better than that of the farmers. Miners live in houses built by the mining companies. They can also shop in special stores that sell low-priced goods. But the miners' work is very dangerous, especially in the tin mines that are at altitudes of 3,600 to 5,500 meters (12,000 to 18,000 feet). They are given a daily ration of coca, which is very important to them. Chewing the leaves of this tea-like plant relieves hunger. In 1952 the mines were nationalized, as the first step toward economic and social reforms for the miners.

Feasts and Fairs. The gayest days in the life of Bolivians are holidays and fairs. They delight in the Alacitas Fair, which is held in La Paz each January. The fair is held in honor of the Aymará god of abundance, Ekeko. Ekeko is a cheerful fellow. He looks a little bit like Santa Claus without a beard. Ekeko carries miniatures of all the things people may want or need: tiny sacks of rice and sugar, a miniature sheep or cow, a house, an automobile, a suit of clothes. According to legend, if a person buys one of Ekeko's miniatures, he will get its life-sized equivalent during the coming year.

Spanish missionaries long ago converted the Indians to Catholicism. But many ancient Indian festivals are still mixed with Christian rituals. For example, at carnival time in Oruro dancers perform the Diablada, or Devil Dance. The dance is dedicated to the Virgin of the Mines. The dance is the miners' way of asking the Virgin's protection against the devil, whom they fear meeting deep in the dark mines.

Religion. The majority of Bolivians are Roman Catholic. Catholicism is recognized as the state religion, but members of all religious groups may worship freely.

Language. Spanish is the official language of Bolivia, and most educated people in Bolivia speak it. Bolivia's Indians are taught Spanish in school. At home they may speak the language of their group, be it Aymará or Quechua.

Education. All children between the ages of 6 and 14 are supposed to go to school. But many Bolivian boys and girls are so busy helping their families that it is not always possible for them to attend school. There may not even be a school nearby. Many Indian

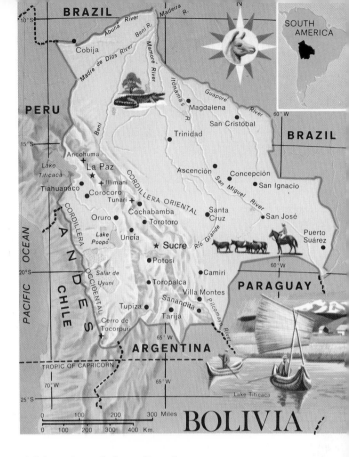

children drop their studies after a year or two. Only a few go on to universities. The government is working to increase the number of people who are able to read and write.

In Bolivia's cities many more children are able to attend school. Some schools are modern, especially the private and parochial schools. Boys and girls usually go to separate schools. In addition, there are universities in leading Bolivian cities such as Oruro, Potosí, Cochabamba, and La Paz. San Francisco Xavier University at Sucre was founded in 1624 and is one of the oldest universities in the Western Hemisphere.

▶**THE LAND**

Bolivia has three major land regions. They are the Andes, the Altiplano, and the lowlands.

The Andes are widest in Bolivia, stretching as much as 640 kilometers (400 miles) across at their widest point. The Bolivian Andes are divided into two main ranges, or cordilleras. The Cordillera Occidental, or Western Range, forms Bolivia's border with Chile. It is the barrier that cuts Bolivia off from the Pacific Ocean. Bolivia's highest mountain, Anco-

Balsas, small boats made of reeds, on Lake Titicaca.

A busy and colorful outdoor market in La Paz.

huma, rises in the Cordillera Oriental, or Eastern Range. Deep valleys called *yungas* have been cut by rushing rivers in the slopes of the Eastern Range. The mild climate of these deep valleys makes them good farming areas.

The Altiplano is the high, bleak, cold, and almost treeless plateau between the mountain ranges. Its average elevation is almost 3 kilometers (over 2 miles) above sea level. Three out of four Bolivians live in this region, many in La Paz and smaller towns.

The lowlands of Bolivia are entirely different from the highland zone, and much larger. The climate throughout this region is hotter. The northern lowlands are heavily forested. Close to the border of Brazil the jungle grows dense and the rivers are a home for giant crocodiles. The southern lowlands are drier than those in the north. Instead of jungles there are great plains where wild cattle roam. Near the Argentine border there are important oil reserves owned by the Bolivian Government.

Lakes and Rivers. Lake Titicaca, at the northern edge of the Altiplano, is the highest navigated body of water in the world. It lies 3,812 meters (12,507 feet) above sea level, on the border with Peru. Small native boats called *balsas* are used for fishing in the lake. Lake Titicaca drains into Lake Poopó, farther south. There is no drainage from Lake Poopó.

The water evaporates, leaving the lake very salty. Great salt flats dot the lonesome landscape south of the lake.

The Beni River and its tributaries drain the northern *yungas*. They flow north to join the Madeira River in Brazil and finally the great Amazon River. The southern *yungas* are drained by the Pilcomayo River and its tributaries. They are part of a river system that flows southeast to join the Paraguay River and the Río de la Plata in Argentina.

Climate. Because of Bolivia's altitude, there are great differences in temperature between day and night. The average annual temperature at La Paz, on the Altiplano, is only 8°C (47°F). At Trinidad, a city in the lowlands of eastern Bolivia, the average temperature is around 21°C (70°F). In Bolivia there is little difference in temperature between summer and winter. Wet and dry seasons are more important. The dry season lasts from May to November. Between December and February there are heavy rains on the Altiplano and drenching tropical storms in the lowlands.

Natural Resources. Bolivia has been described as "a beggar on a throne of gold." The country's mountainous terrain and its turbulent history have kept Bolivia from making full use of its great natural resources.

The little wealth Bolivia has enjoyed has come from the mines on or near the Altiplano. The Cerro Rico ("rich hill") of Potosí is a mountain that is almost a solid mass of tin, silver, tungsten, and other ores. Zinc, antimony, gold, iron, bismuth, sulfur, and asbestos are also mined in Bolivia. And at Corocoro there is one of the world's rare surface deposits of natural copper. Another increasingly important Bolivian resource is oil, which is found mainly in southern Bolivia.

Timber is one of Bolivia's most valuable and least-exploited resources. Timber covers nearly 40 percent of the land. The most valuable trees—mahogany, jacaranda, rosewood, balsa, and cedar—grow on the eastern slopes of the Cordillera Real.

▶ **THE ECONOMY**

Agriculture. The leading Bolivian occupation is agriculture. About one half of Bolivia's farms are on the Altiplano. But the crops have been poor because of the high altitude, the lack of rain, and the primitive methods of cultivation. However, potatoes, barley, a grain called quinoa, broad beans, wheat, and alfalfa are grown. Coca, coffee, cacao, and bananas are grown in the *yungas*. From the fertile valleys around Cochabamba, Tarija, and Sucre come corn, wheat, barley, vegetables, alfalfa, and oats. Only a very small portion of the lowlands east of Santa Cruz de la Sierra are under cultivation. Rice, sugar, cotton, corn, yucca, oil plants, and fruit are grown there. Cattle and hogs are raised in the lowlands.

Industry. Large-scale industries, except for mining, are as yet unknown in Bolivia. The chief source of Bolivia's industrial wealth comes now, as it has for centuries, from mining. Tin is mined in larger amounts than any other mineral, and Bolivia has long been one of the leading exporters of tin in the world. Petroleum and petroleum products are of growing importance to the economy.

Transportation and Communication. Bolivia's future as a united and strong country depends to a large degree on its success in improving its transportation network. At present Bolivia must import a great deal of food and lumber because these products cannot be transported cheaply from the lowlands to the cities of the Altiplano. The hardwood trees of the northern forests die of old age while Bolivia imports lumber because there is no road from the forests. Airplanes sometimes fly beef from the city of Trinidad to La Paz —the only way to get the meat to market.

Most of the communications system in Bolivia is privately owned. There is telephone service in the major cities, but more than half the total number of phones are in the city of

The ancient Indian ruins of Tiahuanaco are among the most important archeological sites in South America.

La Paz, Bolivia's largest city, is one of the highest cities in the world.

La Paz. There are many radio stations and a government-operated television network.

▶MAJOR CITIES

Bolivia's two capitals are Sucre and La Paz. Sucre is the legal capital and the site of the Supreme Court. La Paz is the administrative capital and the seat of government. It is the country's largest city and the center of its commerce and culture. Sucre, founded by the Spanish in 1538, was known by several names. It received its present name, after Bolivia's first president, in 1839. La Paz was founded by the Spanish in 1548 on the site of an Indian village. Other major cities include Santa Cruz, the second largest in population; Cochabamba; Ouro; and Potosí.

▶HISTORY AND GOVERNMENT

Early History and Spanish Rule. The magnificent carved stone Gate of the Sun, ruined temples, and a few ancient roads are all that remains of Tiahuanaco, a great Indian civilization that once flourished on the banks of Lake Titicaca. From about A.D. 600 to 900 the Indians of this region reigned supreme. Then mysteriously their civilization vanished. By the year 1300 the powerful Incas of Peru ruled the region. The Inca Empire in turn was conquered by the Spanish in the 1500's. Spain ruled the area for nearly 300 years, exploiting what were then the rich silver mines at Potosí.

Independence. Harsh Spanish rule had led to a number of uprisings in the 1600's and 1700's, but the most important movement toward Bolivian independence began in 1809. It was inspired by Simón Bolívar's liberation of the northern part of the continent from Spain. It was not until 1824, however, that Antonio José de Sucre, one of Bolívar's lieutenants, completely broke Spanish power in this region. The new nation declared its independence on August 6, 1825. It was named Bolívar in honor of the Liberator. Later the spelling was changed to its present form.

Bolivia's first president was General Sucre. He was followed in office by General Andrés Santa Cruz, who tried but failed to bring about a permanent union between Peru and Bolivia. The next half century of Bolivian history is scarred by a succession of military dictatorships.

The most terrible of these dictators was Mariano Melgarejo, who came to power in 1864. He was illiterate, cruel, dishonest, and tyrannical. During the years of his rule Melgarejo sold and leased national territory to neighboring countries. In later years, wars cost Bolivia much of her original territory.

The first 50 years of the 20th century in Bolivia were marked by some advances in industry and transportation. But since the Bolivian economy depended so much on the world demand for tin, events far from Bolivia shaped the course of Bolivian life. During the depression of the 1930's, when the tin demand was slight, Bolivians suffered. World War II brought a rise in the price of tin and some improvement in the Bolivian economy. But at the end of the war, tin prices dropped, and Bolivia was once again in crisis.

Recent History. A revolution in 1952 brought the National Revolutionary Movement (MNR) to power. Victor Paz Estenssoro, an MNR leader, served as president from 1952 to 1956 and from 1960 to 1964. He nationalized (brought under government control) the country's tin mines, began a program of land reform, and extended the right to vote to all adult Bolivians. Paz Estenssoro was overthrown in a military coup in 1964. General René Barrientos Ortuño, who as vice president had led the coup, was elected president in 1966. His death in an accident in 1969 led to a period of political instability as Bolivia alternated between military and civilian rule. From 1971 to 1978 the presidency was held by General Hugo Banzer Suárez. A civilian, Hernán Siles Zuazo, became president in 1982.

Siles resigned in 1985 because of protests against his policies and new elections were held. The eventual winner was Victor Paz Estenssoro, who thus returned as president after more than 20 years. He was succeeded as president by Jaime Paz Zamora, who took office in 1989.

Bolivia's government is headed by the president, who is elected (together with a vice president) for four years. Presidents cannot serve two consecutive terms of office. The legislature is the Congress. It consists of two houses, the Senate and the Chamber of Deputies, which also are elected for 4-year terms. If no presidential candidate receives a majority of the votes in an election, Congress elects the president.

J. DAVID BOWEN
Author, *Hello, South America*

Bombay's scenic Marine Drive follows the coastline of Back Bay. The spectacular string of lights lining the four-lane highway is known as the Queen's Necklace.

BOMBAY

Bombay, city of story and legend, is the capital of the state of Maharashtra as well as the major port and industrial center of the west coast of India. The main part of the city is built on Bombay Island, which is about 18 kilometers (11 miles) in length and 6 kilometers (4 miles) across at its widest point. Greater Bombay, a metropolitan municipal organization that includes Bombay Island, Trombay Island, and part of Salsette Island, was created in 1957.

More than 8,000,000 people live in Greater Bombay, the second largest metropolitan area in India. Bombay is considered India's most sophisticated and culturally varied city. The majority of the inhabitants are followers of the Hindu religion, but the population includes Muslims, Christians, Jains, Zoroastrians, Jews, and Sikhs. The two major languages are Marathi and Gujarati, although more than 50 different languages are spoken.

The City Today

At the southwestern end of Bombay Island, the coast is indented. It forms a shallow body of water known as Back Bay, which opens into the Arabian Sea. To the west of the bay is a high ridge known as Malabar Hill. The homes of the well-to-do are to be found on the ridge and along the slopes. The Hanging Gardens and Kamala Nehru Park with its giant Mother Hubbard shoe are also in the Malabar Hill area. The summit of the hill offers a superb view of the city. At night thousands of lights form a sparkling outline of Marine Drive, which runs along the northeastern edge of Back Bay. Marine Drive has rows of modern apartments on one side. On its other side are lovely palms and a wide promenade facing the bay.

The port of Bombay is on the eastern edge of the island. Its shore is lined with docks, piers, and warehouses. One of the world's finest natural deepwater harbors, the port covers an area of about 180 square kilometers (70 square miles). Most of India's imported goods enter through this port. Cotton yarn, oilseeds, manganese ore, and manufactured goods are leading exports.

At the entrance to the harbor is the Gateway of India, the most familiar landmark of the city. It is a huge and magnificent stone

arch, which was built in 1911 in honor of King George V and Queen Mary of England. Also in the harbor is Elephanta Island, the site of seven magnificent 8th-century Hindu cave temples.

The major commercial center is west of the waterfront, in a part of the city known as The Fort. Most of the older and larger buildings in this area are of Gothic and other European architecture. In this area are the famed Victoria Terminus and the University of Bombay. Most of Bombay's factories are located in the north, where there are many overcrowded slums.

Among the special attractions of Bombay are the Prince of Wales Museum, the Jehangir Art Gallery, and many religious temples and shrines. Kanheri National Park, on Salsette Island, contains more than 100 ancient Buddhist temple caves. Other places of interest include Victoria Gardens, an aquarium, and a well-stocked zoo.

History

The Bombay area has been inhabited since prehistoric times. The harbor and islands were ceded to Portugal by the kingdom of Gujarat in 1534. In 1662 the British king Charles II married a Portuguese princess, Catherine of Braganza. He received Bombay as part of her dowry, and it soon became the leading center of British power on the west coast of India. But the city did not grow rapidly until it became the world's chief source of cotton during the U.S. Civil War (1861–65).

Today Bombay is more than a great port and textile center. From its busy factories come chemicals, glassware, leather goods, machinery, and other products. Finance, commerce, oil exploration, filmmaking, and publishing are also major activities. Each year the glamour and wealth of what has been called India's most beautiful city attract huge numbers of people seeking a better life. Modern Bombay has become one of the most crowded cities in the world, and many of its people are unable to find housing or jobs.

DAVID FIRMAN
Towson State University
Reviewed by THE CONSULATE
GENERAL OF INDIA

BONDS. See STOCKS AND BONDS.

Victoria Terminus, one of Bombay's main railway stations, was built in the 1860's. It is located in the commercial center of the city, an area known as The Fort.

BOOKKEEPING AND ACCOUNTING

No business could operate very long without knowing how much it was earning and how much it was spending. Bookkeeping and accounting are the methods business firms use to keep track of their earnings and expenses.

Bookkeeping is a formal, organized system of recording financial transactions. (Volumes in which business records are kept are often called books.) It is done according to standardized rules. These rules make it easier to detect errors in the bookkeeping. The bookkeeper's record shows how much was spent in a certain transaction and how much was gained or lost in the transaction. The information is arranged so that it may be easily analyzed, that is, examined to determine the financial condition of the business or person involved.

A bookkeeper often works under the direction of an **accountant.** While the bookkeeper's duties are mainly to keep a record of the company's business transactions, the accountant's work has a broader scope. In addition to supervising the recording of financial information, the accountant analyzes the information. The company relies on this analysis when making business decisions.

▶ THE DOUBLE-ENTRY SYSTEM

The system used in keeping the financial records of a business is the **double-entry** system. Behind this system is the basic idea that every business transaction affects the company's financial position in at least two ways. In the double-entry system every aspect of a transaction is recorded.

Accounts

The records kept by bookkeepers are called accounts. The three main types of accounts used in bookkeeping are assets, liabilities, and capital.

Assets are anything of value owned by the company. Examples of assets are land, buildings, and equipment. Money in the company's bank account also is an asset, as are services that the company has paid for in advance.

Liabilities are debts owed to persons or to other companies. Examples of liabilities are wages owed to employees, money owed to a bank, unpaid bills for supplies, and stocks that have been sold to obtain money to run the business.

Capital, sometimes called **equity,** is the total value of everything that the company owns free of debt. Capital is equal to the company's assets minus its liabilities. For example, if a company's assets are $100,000, and its liabilities total $45,000, its capital would be $55,000.

Each of the company's assets and liabilities, as well as its capital, is given a separate account. Examples of asset accounts are the "cash" account, which is a record of money that a company owns, and the "accounts receivable" account, the record of money owed to the company. One type of liability account is the "accounts payable" account, the record of money owed by the company for such things as purchases of goods, supplies, and equipment.

In a double-entry system, each account has two sides: the left side, called the **debit** side, and the right side, called the **credit** side. One side is used for increases and the other for decreases. In asset accounts, increases are recorded on the debit side of the account, and any decrease in value is shown on the credit side. In liability and capital accounts, increases and decreases are recorded in the opposite way. These accounts are increased on the credit side and decreased on the debit side. Every business transaction affects two or more accounts—any entry made on the credit side of one account must be balanced by an entry on the debit side of another account. Debits must equal credits. Here are two examples of this system:

(1) Suppose the Acme Company decides to pay off a $25,000 bank loan. Payment of the loan decreases the liability account, so Acme's bookkeeper will debit the liability account $25,000. Acme's "cash" account, an asset account, has also been affected by the transaction. It has been decreased by the $25,000 used to pay off the loan. Thus, in order to record the transaction fully, the bookkeeper must also credit the "cash" account $25,000.

(2) Suppose Acme sells a piece of equipment for $2,000. The buyer pays $500 immediately and will pay the other $1,500 later. Acme's bookkeeper credits the "equipment" account $2,000 and then debits the "cash" account $500 and the "accounts receivable" account $1,500.

ACCOUNT: Checking

Date	Item	Debit	Credit	Balance
12/1	Balance			4,500.00
12/8	Cash Sales	1,350.00		5,850.00
12/15	Cash Sales	2,000.00		7,850.00
12/15	Old Farms Dairy		830.00	7,020.00

ACCOUNT: Accounts Payable

Date	Item	Debit	Credit	Balance
12/1	Balance			2,285.00
12/15	Old Farms Dairy	830.00		1,455.00
12/15	Sprinkles 'n' Such		300.00	1,755.00
12/25	Acme Refrigeration Co.		1,500.00	3,255.00

```
                SUE'S ICE CREAM SHOP
                    Balance Sheet
                    Dec. 31, 1989


            ASSETS

Current Assets
  Cash                          10,800.00
  Accounts Receivable            4,500.00
  Materials and Supplies         2,400.00
  Interest Receivable              500.00
                                ---------
        Total Current Assets                18,200.00

Fixed Assets
  Equipment                     20,000.00
  Shop Building                 55,000.00
                                ---------
        Total Fixed Assets                  75,000.00
                                            ---------
Total Assets                                93,200.00
                                            =========



            LIABILITIES AND CAPITAL

Current Liabilities
  Accounts Payable               3,500.00
  Notes Payable                  6,000.00
  Mortgage Interest Payable        600.00
                                ---------
        Total Current Liabilities           10,100.00

Long-Term Liabilities
  Mortgage Payable              38,000.00
                                ---------
        Total Long-Term Liabilities         38,000.00

Capital                                     45,100.00
                                            ---------
        Total Liabilities and Capital       93,200.00
                                            =========
```

Top to Bottom: Each of a company's assets and liabilities, as well as its capital, has a separate account. A checking account is a type of asset account, while accounts payable is a liability account. A balance sheet shows a company's financial state at a given time. Note that assets equal liabilities plus capital.

The use of the double-entry system maintains an up-to-date record of the assets, liabilities, and owner's equity of a business. At any time an examination of the books will show just what the financial situation of a business is. An accountant periodically checks the books to see that the debit and credit entries are equal to one another. If they are not equal, it shows that an error has been made. This is called preparing a **trial balance.**

Journals and Ledgers

Separate entries of all day-to-day transactions are made in a book known as a **journal.** Typically, a journal contains columns for recording the date, the account title, the amount of money debited, and the amount credited. In modern bookkeeping, journal entries often are entered on a computer, which stores the information until it is needed.

At the end of each month, or more frequently, all journal entries are recorded, or **posted,** in a more permanent book of accounts called a **ledger.**

▶FINANCIAL STATEMENTS

Financial statements use the records kept in the accounts to give a picture of the financial activity of the company. Two types of financial statements are most commonly used to report this information: the **balance sheet** and the **income and expense statement.** (Before these statements are prepared, a trial balance is made to be certain that debits equal credits.)

The balance sheet, sometimes called the statement of financial position, is a summary that represents the financial condition of a business at a given time. It shows the company's assets at that moment, as well as its liabilities and capital.

The income and expense statement, sometimes called the profit and loss statement, shows the income and expenses of a business over a specified period of time, usually one year. From this statement the managers of the business can learn whether the company had a profit or a loss for the period covered by the report.

▶ACCOUNTING SPECIALTIES

The three main fields of accounting are public accounting, industrial accounting, and governmental accounting. Each of these fields has special characteristics.

Public accountants offer their services to the public rather than to one organization. Their work often involves advising businesses about investments or taxes. They may also help individuals prepare their income tax returns. Public accountants also perform **audits.** An audit is an examination of a business's financial record and a report on the findings. Audits are made mainly for the benefit of stockholders, creditors, and the public.

Public accountants can become C.P.A.s (Certified Public Accountants) by fulfilling certain requirements of education and experience and passing a written examination. A C.P.A. certificate is the mark of expert competence in the accounting field. This certificate is required in order to certify financial statements.

Industrial accountants are employed by single business firms. They keep the records and make the reports on which the managers of a business rely in planning the operations of the business. The accounting department is, in effect, the nerve center of a company. A gain or loss in business is almost immediately revealed in the figures of the accounting department's records.

Government accountants hold important positions at all levels of federal, state, and local government. Their duties are often similar to those of public and industrial accountants.

In modern business, accounting has such a variety of duties to perform that there are accountants who specialize in certain types of jobs. **Tax accountants** keep tax records and prepare reports that must be sent to government tax agencies. They also advise management about the taxes that the company may have to pay as a result of a business transaction. Many individuals hire tax accountants to prepare their income-tax returns.

Cost accountants deal with the costs involved in all the operations of a business. These may be the cost of a product, a service, a manufacturing process, or the operating expenses of a business. The information provided by the cost accountant helps management to budget the company's money and to plan its future operations.

More and more financial information is assembled using electronic data-processing equipment. Many personal computers can be equipped with accounting programs, so that even small businesses can have computerized record-keeping systems. Today's accountants should have some familiarity with data processing.

▶HISTORY

People have counted and kept records throughout history. In the ancient world, trade between merchants made necessary the creation of some kind of business records. Ancient clay tablets show that a system of positive and negative entries was used, in which the gain or loss of any business transaction was added to or subtracted from the total worth of the business.

The modern system of bookkeeping originated in medieval Italy. Records were kept according to the modern system in the city of Genoa in 1340. Some historians believe that the origins of the system can be traced as far back as the 13th century. Genoa, Lombardy, and Tuscany were all thriving business centers in Italy, and any one of them could have been the birthplace of modern bookkeeping. Gradually merchants in other countries learned of the new bookkeeping system, and it spread throughout Europe.

As the methods of the new bookkeeping system were developed, some people became specialists in this kind of record keeping. They were known as accountants. With the increase of business activity, some accountants began to offer their services to any individuals or organizations that needed accounting work done. This was the origin of public accounting. Public accounting developed mainly in the British Isles, which were a leading center of trade. As early as 1720 an English public accountant was called in by Parliament to investigate a financial scandal.

During the 19th century, corporations became the most important form of business organization. A corporation has many owners. These are the stockholders, people who have bought shares, or stock, in the business in return for a share of the corporation's profits. The stockholders depended on published financial reports to learn how well their corporations were doing and whether the executives they hired to manage them were doing their jobs properly. During this period the basic principles of modern accounting were worked out to ensure that the stockholders got thorough and accurate reports.

Stockholders soon realized that if the reports were to have any value, there had to be a set of common principles for gathering and reporting the information. Without a standard method of reporting financial information, a misleading idea about the condition of a business could be given by reporting some facts and ignoring others.

Many unqualified people claimed to be accountants and attempted to do auditing work. Just as standard accounting methods were needed, it also became necessary to establish standards by which properly qualified accountants could be trained and measured.

Today a college degree in accounting has become essential for a successful accounting career. The possible rewards make it worthwhile to get the education. The accountant's familiarity with nearly all the basic operations of a business provides a good opportunity for promotion to the management of a company. Many business executives began their careers as accountants.

EUGENE L. SWEARINGEN
Bank of Oklahoma, N.A.
Tulsa, Oklahoma

Reviewed by JOHN PETRO
Accounting Teacher

BOOK REPORTS AND REVIEWS

A **book report** is a discussion or an analysis of a book and it is one of the most common school assignments. It can be either written or delivered aloud. Book reports are helpful both to those who prepare them and to those who read or listen to them. When you are assigned a book report, you pay extra attention when reading your book, and you think carefully about what it says. Doing this helps you understand your book better and remember it longer.

Others benefit, too. By listening to or reading each other's reports, students learn about a variety of subjects and discover new books to read.

Readers outside the classroom also benefit from what others have to say about books. Newspapers and magazines regularly publish **book reviews** for readers who want help deciding what new books to read or information about books they might not have an opportunity to read. In a book review, a knowledgeable person offers comments and criticism on a recently published book.

Keep in mind, then, that your book report is a sharing experience. Even if no one but your teacher reads it, prepare it as though you were addressing a wide audience.

▶WRITTEN BOOK REPORTS

Your book report, whether it is written or spoken, should include five major points of information: (1) the author, title, publisher, and date of publication of the book, (2) the type of book it is, (3) what the book is about, (4) the form and style in which the book is written, and (5) your opinion of the book.

Author, Title, Publisher, and Publication Date. The first thing your readers will want to know about your book is its title and the name of its author. Remember, also, whenever you prepare a written record of a book, to include the name of the publisher and the date the book was published. The publisher's name can be found at the bottom of the title page. The date of publication is usually located on the other side of the title page, following the word "Copyright." Put all of this information in a heading—several lines at the top of the first page of your written report.

CHOOSING A BOOK

Your teacher will probably give you guidelines on what kind of book to choose for your book report. He or she may even assign a specific book for you to read. If, however, some decisions about your book are left up to you, the best thing to do is to spend some time at the library. Ask a librarian to help you find the section that has books at your reading level.

Look for a book about a topic that interests you or that you would like to learn more about. If you are interested, you are more likely to pay attention to what you read. This will help you write a better book report. For example, if you like horses, select a book about riding or about a special breed of horses. Or, read a fictional work about horses, such as *Black Beauty.*

If you are assigned a biography, try to find one about a favorite author, artist, or musician. Do you like basketball, baseball, or hockey? Your library probably has biographies of well-known sports figures.

Do not wait until the last minute to choose your book. Be sure to give yourself enough time to finish reading it and write your report.

Type of Book. All books can be classified as either fiction or nonfiction. In a library, all novels and short stories are called fiction, and all other books nonfiction. Within these two divisions, though, books can be put into narrower categories. The book you report on might be a collection of poems, a biography, a history, or a work of science fiction. Add this information to your heading.

What the Book Is About. The longest portion of your report will be devoted to the subject matter of your book. If the book is a work of fiction, you will reveal something of the story in this section. If it is a factual work, you will deal mainly with the information it contains.

In the case of a novel, your report should cover the plot, the characters, and the time and setting. It is not necessary to discuss all of these at equal length. There are many kinds of novels, and you must decide what is most important about the one you have read. For a mystery or adventure tale, in which the plot is usually the outstanding feature, your main job will be to relate the story.

Do not tell too much of it. For most people, reading a novel is a kind of adventure, where the pleasure comes from not knowing what will happen next. Your role in narrating a story is to tell your audience of readers enough about what is going on to make them want to read the book, but not so much as to take away the surprise.

Use the present tense to re-tell a story. Avoid opening phrases such as ''This book is about . . .'' Just tell what it is about. Your summary might be something like this:

The day Henry Jameson turns 12, a lot of strange things begin to happen to him. A package arrives in the mail, and he thinks it is a birthday present. But there is no card or return address, and the box contains only a key on a chain.

The following day, he receives another box, this one containing a map with directions to a place he has never heard of. Every day after that,

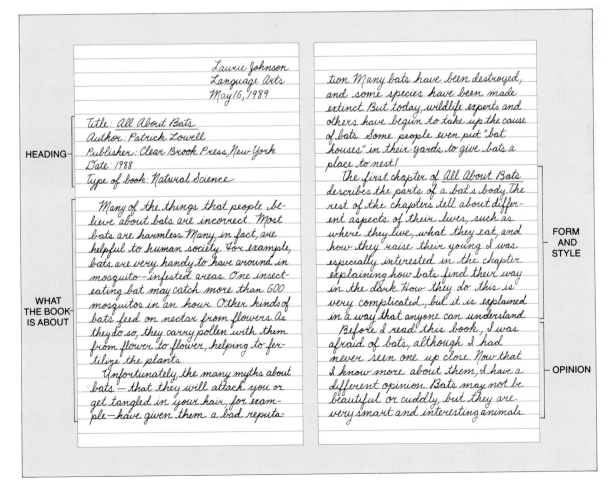

HEADING

Laurie Johnson
Language Arts
May 16, 1989

Title: All About Bats
Author: Patrick Lowell
Publisher: Clear Brook Press, New York
Date: 1988
Type of book: Natural Science

WHAT THE BOOK IS ABOUT

Many of the things that people believe about bats are incorrect. Most bats are harmless. Many, in fact, are helpful to human society. For example, bats are very handy to have around in mosquito-infested areas. One insect-eating bat may catch more than 600 mosquitos in an hour. Other kinds of bats feed on nectar from flowers. As they do so, they carry pollen with them from flower to flower, helping to fertilize the plants.

Unfortunately, the many myths about bats — that they will attack you or get tangled in your hair, for example — have given them a bad reputation. Many bats have been destroyed, and some species have been made extinct. But today, wildlife experts and others have begun to take up the cause of bats. Some people even put "bat houses" in their yards to give bats a place to nest!

The first chapter of All About Bats describes the parts of a bat's body. The rest of the chapters tell about different aspects of their lives, such as where they live, what they eat, and how they raise their young. I was especially interested in the chapter explaining how bats find their way in the dark. How they do this is very complicated, but it is explained in a way that anyone can understand.

FORM AND STYLE

Before I read this book, I was afraid of bats, although I had never seen one up close. Now that I know more about them, I have a different opinion. Bats may not be beautiful or cuddly, but they are very smart and interesting animals.

OPINION

a package arrives with a mysterious object that seems to be connected in some way with what he has received before. He feels as though he is on a treasure hunt, and when, after many weeks, he finally puts all the clues together, he learns something about his ancestors that no one in his family had ever suspected before.

For other novels, you will want to concentrate more on the characters than on the events. To describe a character clearly, imagine that you are telling someone about an old friend. Tell what she looks like and how she behaves. Tell, too, how she feels inside and what she thinks:

Everybody in Maria's family says that she is ''the plain one.'' Her hair is no special color, her eyes are small, her teeth are too big, and her ears stick out. Maria's two sisters, Jane and Laura, are ''the beauties.'' That is what all their aunts call them, adding in a low voice, ''Maria is the plain one.'' After a while, Maria thinks of herself that way, too. She spends most of her time in her room, making up strange fantasies about people she's never met.

In a novel of this type, the plot focuses on changes that cause the character to be different at the end of the book from the way she was at the beginning. Keep this in mind when you tell the story:

When Maria goes to Oklahoma to visit a grandmother she has never known before, she finds herself in a household where what you say is more important than how you look. There are some ''beauties'' in Grandmama's family, and some ''plain ones'' like Maria, but nobody cares about any of that. What matters is how you tell a story, and when Maria relates some of the fantasies she had made up, everybody listens. For the first time in her life, Maria is admired, and pretty soon she begins to admire herself.

Some novels are written to inform readers about a specific culture or historic era. When reporting on this kind of book, concentrate on its setting and time:

Raj Sahni lives in a rural village just west of New Delhi, in present-day India. Life is not easy for Raj. In the summer months, the temperature goes over 100°F in the shade, and in the monsoon season that follows, rain falls for days on end. Very little has changed over the generations in Raj's village. Many people live in mud houses with thatched roofs, and goats and water buffalo wander about on the streets. Raj's father plants corn and wheat in the same fields his father and grandfather farmed before him. Raj, though, wants to do something different when he grows up. He wants to be a doctor in the small hospital down the road from his house.

If, instead of a novel, your book is a collection of short stories, mention a common theme among them, if there is one, and then tell about one or two stories in detail:

All the stories in *After and Beyond* tell of supernatural happenings. The most frightening is ''The Strange Return of Mr. Jensen,'' in which a baker disappears from his shop one day in late 19th century London and is not heard from for nearly ten years. During that time, his family, many of his former customers, and the police try to track him down. When a little girl finally discovers where he is and what he has become, they all wish they had never looked for him in the first place. ''What Became of Jody?'' and ''The Lost Butler'' are also about people who have disappeared and later return in strange and frightening forms.

Follow the same rules when you report on a collection of poems:

Wingsongs is a collection of poems about things that fly, such as airplanes, geese, bees, angels, and pterodactyls. Some of the poems are funny, some are scary, and some are full of unusual images. In ''Washday,'' a flock of geese is compared to a clothesline of wash flapping in the wind. In ''Pterrible Beast,'' the poet makes up crazy words and spellings to describe a pterodactyl.

For a report on a biography, a history, or a science book, you will be relating facts rather than imaginary events. Works of this sort usually contain a great deal of information, and you may have difficulty remembering it all. Keep a notepad at your side as you read, so that you can write down important points and their page numbers as you come across them. Do not attempt to report on all the material in the book. Offer a general statement about the subject, and follow that with a few specific details.

If your book is a biography, begin by explaining why its subject was important and what he or she accomplished. Use the past tense when you report on real events:

Harriet Tubman was often called "Moses" during her lifetime because she led her people out of slavery and into freedom. A runaway slave, she returned to the South over and over to help hundreds of other slaves escape to a new life.

A report on a book of history or science should also open with a general statement, this time offering an introduction to the subject:

The Boston Tea Party of 1773 was an act of rebellion engaged in by Boston citizens who opposed British taxation of tea.

Or, for a science book:

Many of the things that people believe about bats are incorrect. Most bats are harmless. Many, in fact, are helpful to human society.

Use your notes to provide further details about your subject. You might conclude this section of your report on a biography this way:

Harriet Tubman lived to be more than 90 years old, and she devoted most of these years to helping other blacks. Before the Civil War, she worked with the Underground Railroad to rescue slaves. During the war, she helped the Northern army locate enemy camps in the South, and she nursed runaway slaves and black soldiers in hospitals. After slavery was abolished, she set up the John Brown Home in Auburn, New York, where she took care of sick and poor blacks.

Form and Style. Every book has a form and style all its own. The form of a book refers to its structure, or the way it is organized. A novel, for example, might be written in the form of a diary. A biography might be written in the form of an exchange of letters. The style refers to the way the author expresses himself or herself. Styles vary from book to book the way personalities vary from person to person. Some books are written in very formal prose, others in the language you hear around you all the time. You can combine a discussion of the form and the style in a single paragraph:

Each chapter of *The Plain One* is introduced by a letter written by Maria to her grandmother, long after she has returned home from her visit to Oklahoma. The chapter then tells in detail what the letter refers to. The letters are written in simple, everyday language. The chapters often sound like poetry, with long descriptions of cornfields and the Oklahoma sky.

Your Opinion. There are many reasons for liking or disliking a book. The plot of a novel may be exciting, or it may be slow moving. The dialogue may sound authentic, or it may sound false. The facts in a history book may be clear and understandable, or they may be hard to follow. At times, you will like some aspects of a book and dislike others. Whatever your opinion, be specific in stating it. Do not say only that the book was interesting or boring. Tell why:

When I read *The Plain One*, I felt that I myself was Maria. I suffered with her when her family ignored her at home, and I triumphed with her when her storytelling won her so much admiration in Oklahoma. The other characters, though, seemed much less real. They all spoke alike, and they sounded like people on a television show, not like people in the real world.

▶ORAL REPORTS

When you present an oral book report, you should give the same basic information that you would provide in a written report. This time your audience will be listening to, rather than reading, what you have to say. However, you will still have to write out in advance everything you want to tell them. Do not read this written report word for word to your audience. Instead, prepare index cards, each containing a few phrases that will remind you of what your full-length report said. Make one card for each major idea in your report. An index card for the biography of Harriet Tubman might read like this:

Harriet Tubman often called Moses
Led her people to freedom
Runaway slave
Returned to South over and over
Helped hundreds of slaves escape

Glance down at your cards when you need to, but look at your audience as much as you can. Stand up tall and speak in a slow, clear voice. Keep reminding yourself that your audience wants to hear what you have to say. Those who have not read your book will want to hear about something new. Those who have read it will want to compare your understanding of it with their own.

SYLVIA CASSEDY
Author, *In Your Own Words: A Beginner's Guide to Writing*

BOOKS

It is difficult to imagine a civilization without books. Their importance in human history cannot be exaggerated. Valuable ideas and discoveries throughout our history have been recorded in books. Using information from books, scholars and scientists have explored and expanded almost every subject known to us. Without books there would be no modern medicine, no modern science or technology, no television, no space flights to the moon, no teachers, and no schools. In short, without books, life as we know it would not be possible.

Information about fields and crops are etched on this clay tablet, which dates from about 2800 B.C. Clay tablets could be moved from place to place but they were heavy and not very practical.

▶BEFORE BOOKS

The human need to record and pass along stories and information is as old as the human race. For thousands of years, some of our early ancestors preserved their beliefs, legends, and daily activities by painting pictures on walls of caves and other rock surfaces protected from the weather. Unfortunately, in order to "read" these stories, one had to go to the source—a wall could not be carried or placed on a library shelf.

The Need for Books

About 10,000 years ago, people began raising crops in addition to hunting animals and gathering edible plants. As farming expanded and became more complicated, there was a need to count, measure, and record holdings —sheaves of grain, numbers of cattle, bins of rice, and so on. Therefore, people developed simple symbols to help them count and keep track of their animals and crops.

Over time a creative people called the Sumerians, who also built the world's first cities, invented a simple form of writing that was made up of three-cornered marks. This form of writing is called **cuneiform**, which means "wedge-shaped." Using sticks, the Sumerians drew their farm and business records on small slabs, or tablets, of soft, damp clay that were then hardened in the sun. The tablets could be stored and carried, and when they were no longer useful, they were simply thrown away.

The more important Sumerian texts were baked in ovens much like fine pottery and then stored in the world's first libraries. In recent times, thousands of these clay tablets have been discovered; many were found in perfect condition under the dry desert sands.

▶THE FIRST BOOKS

The next advance in the history of books occurred in Egypt, around 3500 B.C. The ancient Egyptians had developed a lovely, but complex, picture writing called **hieroglyphics**, or "sacred writing." In order to reproduce this complicated writing, they invented papyrus sheets. These thin cream-colored sheets were made from the papyrus plant—a tall reed that grew in flooded marshes along the Nile River. To make the sheets, the reeds were split open

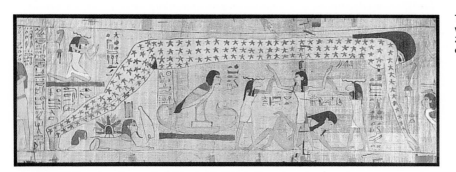

This Egyptian papyrus, which dates from about 2500 B.C., illustrates the creation of the universe.

and cut into strips. Then the strips were flattened and joined together. Brushes and reeds were used to illustrate and write on the long rolled pieces of papyrus, which were called **scrolls**.

Papyrus-making became a major industry in Egypt; blank rolls and scrolls were exported to every corner of the known world, especially to Rome and Athens. Although Egypt was the largest producer, excellent quality papyrus was also grown in other places in the eastern Mediterranean.

Ancient Greece—Books Begin to Travel

The best customers for Egypt's papyrus were the Greeks, particularly the people of Athens, then the world capital of learning. Scribes, people who made copies of scrolls, were busy individuals in Athenian communities, and their work required large amounts of papyrus.

Greek scholars, teachers, actors, and musicians, who often traveled from job to job and from town to town, usually carried with them

many Greek ideas, seized large numbers of Greek books, and moved entire Greek libraries to Rome.

The Romans also wrote their own books on thin wooden boards. Eventually, they decided to join several boards together by punching holes along one side and passing rings through the holes to connect the pages. This kind of wooden book became known as a **codex**, which in Latin *(caudex)* means "tree trunk."

In order to write in an early codex, the pages were first coated with gesso, a liquid mixture of chalk and glue. When the gesso dried to a hard finish, a thin coat of black wax was applied. Then with a pointed instrument called a stylus, the writer scratched the lettering through the wax. The early codices were used mainly as notebooks.

The crude early codices made of wood were soon replaced by ones made of flat papyrus pages that were cut to uniform sizes and bound between two boards. These codices were very popular, largely because they were so easy to use and to carry. When an opened codex was

Wooden boards were spread with gesso and a thin coat of black wax. Using a sharp, pointed tool, it was easy to scratch symbols on the waxed surface. The tablets could be joined together, making a wooden book, or codex. These codices replaced the clay tablets and papyrus scrolls of earlier times.

the latest papyrus scrolls of poetry, geometry, philosophy, music, manners, and morals.

The Greeks greatly advanced writing and the making of books by inventing an alphabet of 24 symbols, called letters. Each letter represented a particular sound in the spoken language. It is far easier to write down a language made up of letters than one based on pictures.

Moving Toward Modern Books

Around 146 B.C., the expanding Roman Empire conquered Greece. The victorious Romans were dazzled by the cultural richness of classical Greece, and they readily adopted

placed on a table, it stayed open, unlike a scroll, which had an annoying tendency to roll back up the moment it was put down. It was also easier to locate sections of a text in a codex. Today, codex is the technical term for any book made up of many pages bound together and not in the form of a roll or scroll.

Parchment Replaces Papyrus

The next step toward the modern book was the use of **parchment**, or processed and stretched animal skin. Parchment was not a new material, but its potential was realized with the invention of the Roman codex.

A "page" from an Indian palm-leaf book. People in India, China, and Nepal sometimes wrote on the backs of palm leaves. When the leaves were fastened together, they could be spread for reading.

Parchment is actually a very smooth thin leather. It is prepared from a sheep's or goat's skin that has been carefully cleaned, bleached white, stretched flat, and then rubbed smooth with pumice, a lightweight volcanic material that works like a fine sandpaper. An especially desirable creamy white parchment called vellum was made from calfskin.

Parchment was more expensive than papyrus, which was made from a plant that grew wild and required much less preparation. But parchment had several advantages over papyrus. It was a tougher material and less likely to tear or decay. Ink could be erased from parchment, unlike papyrus, and parchment could be painted and decorated with bright colors and gold leaf. Parchment also had two usable sides. A single page of parchment could carry twice as many words as a page of papyrus, which had only one usable side.

The codex, with its double-sided parchment pages, was in many ways the first truly modern book—one of Rome's many gifts to the world.

▶ BOOKS OF THE ORIENT

Thousands of miles east of Egypt, Greece, and Rome was the "celestial kingdom" of China. The Chinese developed their language, writing, and books in ways similar to those of their Western counterparts, even though there was very little contact between the two widely separated areas.

The ancient Chinese, like the Sumerians and the Egyptians, began to write with pictures instead of an alphabet. Over the centuries Chinese writing developed into elegant **pictograms** with thousands of separate characters. With some changes, this writing system is still used by the Chinese people today.

The earliest Chinese books were written on the backs of palm leaves and on flattened pieces of wood and bamboo. The Chinese never used the roll or scroll. Instead, their palm-leaf and bamboo books were strips fastened at one end much like a fan and then spread like a fan to be read. The Chinese did not use pens or styluses. They painted their pictograms with brushes and shiny black ink.

The Chinese had no papyrus or parchment, and they desired a better, more practical material than palm leaves or bamboo as a writing surface. They tried using panels of silk cloth for their finest poetry, but silk pages were not durable and were very expensive. Their search for a better material finally ended in A.D. 105 when a Chinese dignitary named Ts'ai Lun invented the world's first sheets of real paper. He concocted a pulp of wood chips, silk and cotton rags, hemp rope, and even old fishing nets, and then molded it into sheets. The Chinese were immediately aware of the great value of paper and they kept the art of papermaking a secret for hundreds of years. Eventually, however, the technique was carried east in the 100's and west in the 200's.

Using their paper, the Chinese at first made books that were written by hand. Later, they developed a printmaking technique, called **woodcut**, which enabled them to illustrate their texts more easily and also allowed them to make multiple impressions of the pages.

The invention of paper changed the format of Chinese books—full-size pages were glued together and accordion-folded. This style of book was the Chinese standard for well over a thousand years, until the introduction of the printing press from Europe.

This illustration of a man collecting bamboo pulp is from a Japanese edition of a Chinese encyclopedia on traditional technology, written about 1637.

MEDIEVAL MANUSCRIPTS

After the fall of Rome in 476, nearly all the making and selling of books stopped as a cultural and political decline, called the Dark Ages, occurred throughout Europe. Later, books began to be made again in small Christian communities called **monasteries**.

Dedicated monks of religious orders began to make exact, handwritten copies, or **manuscripts**, of the most significant Greek and Roman books that had survived. The monks diligently copied the old books—mostly Bibles and other religious and philosophical works—from dawn to dusk, six days a week, year after year. They worked in rooms called **scriptoria** whose windows faced the sun. The presence of such rare manuscripts made the monks very fearful of fire, so the scriptoria were unheated and candles were not allowed.

By the Middle Ages, around the year 1100, monks were making beautiful **illuminated manuscripts**—radiantly colored codices with ornamental borders of animal and plant designs. Nuns sometimes inked in the delicate, perfectly formed letters. But hand-copying, however beautiful, was a very slow process. Even the most diligent monks could not produce enough books to satisfy the growing demand for them.

THE PRINTING PRESS

At the height of the Middle Ages, the first colleges and universities were opening in cities across Europe. Students wanted and needed books. Secular professional copyists, called **stationers**, began to make hurried, unattractive manuscripts for the students, but still there never seemed to be enough books. This situation changed—rapidly and forever—with the invention of the printing press.

The printing press was invented by Johann Gutenberg in the small city of Mainz in Germany around 1450. Gutenberg's press used tiny pieces of metal type to print each letter of the alphabet. The printing press soon replaced the slow work of the manuscript copyist. The printer with his ink-stained hands could create thousands of copies of a book in the time it would take a copyist or stationer to make just one.

The next 50 years were explosive. By 1500 there were printing presses in some 300 European cities. More than 10 million copies of thousands of books had been printed. In order

Illuminated manuscript pages like this one from the *Belleville Breviary* (1343) are as colorful and hauntingly beautiful as the stained-glass cathedral windows of the same period.

to illustrate so many books quickly and easily, Europeans adopted the Chinese woodcut technique. A drawing was carved into a block of wood, and the block was locked into the press with the text. Then the text and illustration were printed as a complete page again and again.

For the first time in history, books were plentiful and popular. Millions of ordinary people developed an intense desire to learn to read now that books were available.

All of the books printed before 1501 are called **incunabula**, the Latin word for "cradle," because this was the infancy of modern bookmaking. By 1500 the printing press itself was so mechanically perfected that it would change very little over the next 400 years.

The form, look, and feel of the books we read today were also worked out and adopted worldwide during the late 1400's. Italian book designers and printers were especially adept at creating typefaces, layouts, and illustrations that were pleasing to look at and to read.

Left: Some unusual types of books include large-print books for the visually impaired, and talking books, shape books, and pop-up books. *Below:* Children's books in braille such as this one are available in many bookstores and libraries.

▶MODERN BOOKS

Most modern books resemble those made 450 years ago—paper pages are bound between a front cover and a back cover. There have been, however, a few variations in the materials and even in the format, used in books over the last 200 years.

In the 1800's the first paperback books were published. Printed on cheap paper with paper covers, they only cost a dime. Just about anyone could read about the exploits of cowboys in the Wild West and other adventurers. Paperback editions of the classics as well as popular fiction and nonfiction were also printed. The paperback book industry is still a big business today.

Since the 1930's when they were first introduced, books on audio tape have become increasingly popular. Well-known actors and sometimes the authors themselves are recorded as they read entire novels or nonfiction books. More recently, children's stories have been recorded to give pre-readers more exposure to language and literature.

Other innovations in children's books have included cloth books with pages that cannot be torn; books with plastic pages that can be taken into the bathtub, and wipe-off books that can be colored with crayons and then wiped clean with a cloth.

Pop-up story books became popular in the late 1800's. These entertaining creations have flat pages that become three dimensional when they are turned. Because they were so expensive to produce, however, publishers stopped

making them. Since the 1980's there has been a renewed interest in this format, and some publishers now produce elaborate pop-ups.

▶BOOKMAKING TECHNOLOGY

The technology involved in making books has changed dramatically with the advent of phototypesetting, computers, and four-color printing processes used in reproducing illustrations and photography. The paper used for the pages of books has also been improved to ensure its durability and longevity.

These advances combined with age-old traditions promise even more interesting and different books in the future.

JACK KNOWLTON
Author, *Books and Libraries*

See also GRAPHIC ARTS; ILLUMINATED MANU-SCRIPTS; ILLUSTRATION AND ILLUSTRATORS; LIBRARIES; PRINTING; WOODCUT PRINTING.

BOOKS: FROM AUTHOR TO READER

Books are one of the miracles of humanity. They make our thoughts, our feelings, our dreams, and our knowledge permanent, and they make them available to everyone.

Millions of books are printed each year in the United States. Have you ever wondered how these books were made? Let us look at the bookmaking process for the type of book you might buy in a bookstore or borrow from your local library. We will begin with the author's manuscript.

▶ FROM AUTHOR TO PUBLISHER

Imagine that you have written a story called *It Rained Every Day*, about a family on vacation. Like most authors today, you have used a word processor to prepare your manuscript. In the past when authors wrote poems, stories, novels, or other material, they prepared handwritten copies of their work. Typewritten copies or printed copies from word processors or computers are much easier to read, and the people who make books prefer them.

You have worked very hard and long on your story and think it is good. Friends and family who have read it agree. They urge you to try to have *It Rained Every Day* made into a book. Fine! But now that the story is finished and you have prepared the manuscript, what do you do?

▶ FINDING A PUBLISHER

When your manuscript is finished, you must find a publisher who is interested in making it into a book. The best way to find a publisher is to go to the library and look at *Literary Market Place (LMP)*. This reference book lists hundreds of different publishers with their addresses, phone numbers, and the names of some of the people who work there. You want to find publishers who publish children's trade books. **Trade books** are fiction and nonfiction works sold in bookstores, and that is where you want your book to end up. Other publishers listed in *LMP* may specialize in textbooks, reference books, or other types of publishing.

February 9, 1992

Ms. Julia Lee, Editor
Children's Book Department
Crabapple Publishing Co.
669 Fifth Avenue
New York, NY 10020

Dear Ms. Lee:

I am enclosing my manuscript, IT RAINED EVERY DAY, which I would like you to consider for publication.

IT RAINED EVERY DAY is about a brother and sister who fight all the time. When they go on vacation with their family, the weather is bad every day. The brother and sister learn that if they keep fighting each other, their vacation will be really ruined. This is the story of how the vacation is saved.

I hope you will enjoy reading the manuscript. I look forward to hearing from you.

Sincerely,

Mary Smith

Mary Smith
8 Lafayette Street
Belmar, NJ 07719
(908) 555-6704

MS/ms
Enc: ms and SASE

Above: Be sure to enclose a one-page letter and a self-addressed, stamped envelope with any manuscript you send to a publisher.

Left: A young author works on her manuscript. Changes in her manuscript are easy to make on a word processor.

Contacting a Publisher

After selecting a number of trade book publishers, the next step is to write a short, one-page letter to the children's book editor at one of them. In this letter you should tell the editor a little about yourself and your book. Send the letter and a copy of your manuscript to the editor in a sturdy envelope. Include a stamped, self-addressed envelope so that the editor can return your manuscript if he or she decides not to publish it.

A book contract is carefully checked before it is sent to an author.

Publishers receive thousands of manuscripts every year, so months may go by before you hear from the editor. The manuscript may be returned with a rejection note, saying that the publisher is not interested. If so, send it to another publisher. Imagine, however, that the editor wants to publish your manuscript as a book. What happens next?

Book Contracts

If the editor is interested in your book, one of the first things he or she probably will do is telephone you and offer you a contract. At this point the editor will want to discuss an advance and a royalty, as well as some of the other terms of a contract.

Advances and Royalties. An **advance** is an amount of money the publisher agrees to give you before your book is published. Usually, the publisher pays half the advance when a contract is signed and the other half when the manuscript is delivered and the editor agrees that it is acceptable. Advances for first novels usually range from $1,500 to $4,000. Well-known authors receive advances many times greater than that.

A **royalty** is a percentage of the price of each copy of your book that is sold. Part of the royalty is used to pay off the money you received as an advance. When the advance has been paid off, an author begins to receive royalty payments twice a year based on the sales of the book.

Contract Clauses. A book contract contains many clauses, or conditions, dealing with such things as territorial and subsidiary rights, warrants, and permissions. It will also include the date on which you, the author, promise to deliver the final manuscript.

Clauses dealing with **territorial rights** specify the countries in which your book can be sold. The contract may state that you agree to sell "world rights," or the rights to sell your book in any country. Or it may agree to sell rights for only certain countries.

Subsidiary rights allow your book to be sold for such things as a paperback edition, a book club edition, a movie or television version, translations into foreign languages, a large print edition, or a serialization in a newspaper or magazine.

Contracts also include **warrants**, or guarantees. One warrant states that you guarantee your work to be original and of your own creation. Another states that the book contains no recipe, formula, or instruction that may be harmful to someone reading your book. Suppose, for example, that you write about a person eating a particular wild plant. If someone reads your book, eats this plant, and becomes ill because the plant is poisonous, this person might sue. The warrant helps protect the publisher from such a lawsuit, and reminds you, the author, of your responsibility to be sure such information is carefully checked and that appropriate warnings are included in your book when they are necessary. The contract will also include a warrant stating that you have not invaded the privacy of another person or written anything that is libelous—that is, that discredits someone's character.

Contracts may also include clauses concerning permissions. **Permissions** are written consents from others saying that you may use materials they have created. Songs, poems, photographs, and excerpts from interviews are all examples of materials that usually require written consent for their use. Contracts normally state that the author must pay any fees required to obtain such permissions.

The Importance of Agents

Dealing with publishers and book contracts can be quite complex. For this reason, it is usually advisable for writers to hire literary agents to represent them in negotiations with editors and publishers. Agents often are able to get better terms in contracts than writers can get negotiating alone. In return for their services, agents will charge commissions of 10 to 15 percent of the income writers earn from their books.

Literary agents are professionals who know the publishing business and the people who work in it. Because of this, the manuscripts of writers with agents are usually given more careful consideration by publishers than ones by writers without agents. Getting an agent is not easy, however. It is almost impossible to find an agent who will take on a young, unknown writer before he or she has been published. Once a writer has been offered a contract, it is much easier to get an agent. Nevertheless, unknown writers can try to find agents by submitting letters of inquiry and samples of their work to them.

▶ THE EDITORIAL AND DESIGN PROCESS

Once a contract has been signed, the publisher begins work on your manuscript of *It Rained Every Day* to make it into a book. The publishing process is quite complex. It involves many stages and a variety of people both inside and outside the publishing company. Since several parts of the process may be going on at the same time, the people involved in making a book work closely together to ensure the book's completion.

The two divisions of a publishing company that are initially involved in creating a book from manuscript are the editorial department and the art department. The publishing professionals working in these departments include the editors, managing editors, copy editors, proofreaders, art directors, designers, and illustrators.

The Editor

Most manuscripts undergo changes after they have been submitted to the publisher. The person responsible for improving a manuscript is the editor. The edi-

tor will read the manuscript and then return it to the author with suggestions for changes, or revisions. These constructive suggestions are not meant as criticisms but are aimed at making the book better. The editor will point out flaws or errors and propose ways the manuscript could be improved. Perhaps he or she will suggest a different ending, or question whether a character's actions make sense. The editor might even suggest that certain parts of the manuscript be rewritten.

Although editing is their primary role, good editors do more than just edit. They must be knowledgeable about new trends, new ideas, and what is being written elsewhere. They must also be on the lookout for new, talented writers and must encourage published writers to continue working. They might also develop ideas for books themselves and try to find writers who can turn those ideas into books.

After a manuscript has been revised and approved, the editor prepares to put it into **production**. The editor estimates the length of the book; sets a date for publication; and determines other specifics, such as the size of each page (the **trim**), the kind of binding, and the

On this page of the copyedited manuscript, note the content changes—"fork" to "spoon" and "plate" to "cereal bowl"—as well as the corrections in grammar and punctuation.

quantity of books to be printed. The editor also prepares a brief description of the book—to be used later for advertising purposes—and a brief biographical note about the author.

The editor's responsibility does not end when a book goes into production. He or she generally reviews the progress of a manuscript during the publishing process to see that everything is proceeding as planned.

An editor often uses a word processor to make changes the author has agreed to in the manuscript.

The Managing Editor

When an editor puts a manuscript into production, the first person to receive it is generally the managing editor. Managing editors are familiar with all aspects of the bookmaking process. Although their duties may vary from publisher to publisher, they are usually in charge of **trafficking** the manuscript. This means making sure that the manuscript is complete, sending it to the appropriate people at the right time, and keeping track of schedules and deadlines. It often takes from nine months to a year for a manuscript to be made into a book and placed in bookstores. The managing editor makes sure that each person involved in the process does his or her job properly and on time.

The Copy Editor

One of the first people to receive a manuscript from the managing editor is the copy editor. Copy editors are responsible for checking a manuscript for accuracy and style—that is, consistency in spelling, grammar, and word usage. The copy editor's most important tools are a collection of specialized reference books that he or she refers to while working.

While working on a manuscript, the copy editor keeps an alphabetical list of proper names and unusual spellings on a piece of paper called a **style sheet**. This style sheet will be used later to double check the accuracy of the manuscript. The copy editor rewrites passages that are not grammatical, corrects misspellings, and punctuates the book according to accepted rules of punctuation. The copy ed-

itor also checks for consistency, making sure that words are spelled the same way throughout the book.

Copy editors are trained to doubt every fact in a manuscript and to check these facts in a variety of source books. For example, if a manuscript says that a character caught a rainbow trout in the ocean, the copy editor will suggest that the author choose another type of fish after checking and learning that rainbow trout are only found in freshwater streams.

In making corrections and changes, copy editors use marks called proofreader's marks. These are special marks used throughout the bookmaking process to ensure that instructions are conveyed accurately.

The Proofreader

One member of the editorial staff—the proofreader—does not become involved in the bookmaking process until much later. The proofreader begins working on a book after the manuscript has been set into type by a typesetter. At that point the proofreader will carefully check typeset copies of the manuscript against the copyedited manuscript to catch any errors and mark them so that they will be corrected. You will read more about typesetting and the job of proofreaders later in the section on composition.

The Art Director

The art director in a publishing house is responsible for overseeing all aspects of a book's design. This includes assigning artists to work on a book, supervising design staff, and often choosing a design for a book's cover. The art director, as well as other artists involved, works with the editorial staff to make sure that the design of a book is appropriate for its content and its intended audience. The art director becomes involved in the publishing process when he or she is given a copy of the manuscript by the editor. At that point, the art director assigns the work to staff members of the art department or to outside artists.

The Book Designer

The design of a book—the physical arrangement of all the materials that make up the book—is the responsibility of the book designer. The primary goal of the book designer is to translate an author's words into a visual design that helps a reader understand the author's ideas.

Determining Book Length. One of the first things the book designer does with the manuscript of *It Rained Every Day* is make a **cast off** or **character count**. A character is any letter, numeral, space, and punctuation mark in the manuscript. A cast off is necessary for calculating how long the finished book will be. An average young person's novel of 160 to 192 pages may contain more than a quarter of a million characters!

Choosing Type. Once the cast off has been done, the designer chooses a typeface and type size that he or she considers most appropriate. The designer also considers the length of each line of type, the space between the words, the space between lines, and the margins around the outside of the type. These elements all help to determine how easy or difficult the book will be to read.

Baskerville

Size 14 pt.   ABCDEfghijklmno

Size 18 pt.   ABCDefghijkl

Size 24 pt.   ABCdefghi

Helvetica

Size 14 pt.   ABCDEfghijklmno

Size 18 pt.   ABCDefghijkl

Size 24 pt.   ABCdefghi

Above: Times Roman and Helvetica are two of the many typefaces used for books. Note the differences in the shapes and sizes of the letters in these examples.

Left: A designer discusses the layout of a book with the art director.

One

Paula Jones grit her teeth. The screen door slammed. Her brother Pete was gone, and she was left at the breakfast table with her parents and her little brother Ted.

She slammed down her spoon. "It isn't fair," she said. "It's Pete's turn to do the dishes. I did them last night."

Her mother stood up. "It's not fair, you're right. I'll do the dishes, but I hope you'll help us with unpacking and setting things up. It's a shame to waste our first day of vacation working, but we have to get organized before we can have fun."

"I'll help." Ted stood up, his cereal bowl in his hand. He reached for his half-full glass of milk, grabbed it tightly, and set it in the bowl. Holding the bowl and the glass of milk with one hand, he began piling silver into the bowl. It wobbled, and the milk sloshed against the side of the glass. A knife fell onto the floor. When Ted lurched for it, the glass tilted, and milk splashed onto the table.

Ted looked miserable, Paula thought. He's always trying to help and makes a mess because he's so little. Paula remembered when she was six.

This two-page layout shows how the text and art will look when the manuscript for *It Rained Every Day* is printed into a book.

The placement of the title, the author's name, and the name of the publisher on the book jacket is important because the book may be placed on a shelf rather than on a table or in a window of a bookstore.

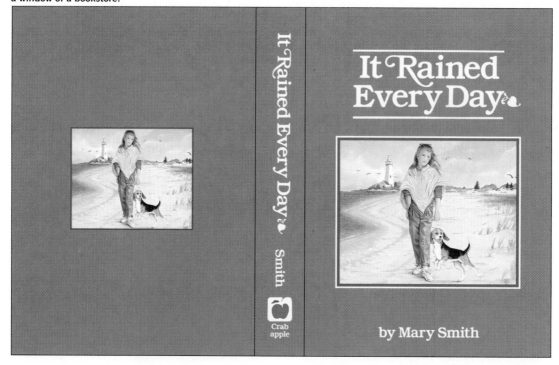

Front Matter and Back Matter. The book designer is not only concerned with the main text, or body, of the book. He or she also designs the material that comes before, and sometimes after, the text. The material at the front of the book, called the **front matter**, normally includes a half-title page, a title page, a copyright page, and often a dedication page. Some books may have additional front-matter pages such as a frontispiece (a page with a map or illustration), a preface, an author's note, a table of contents, or an introduction. Nonfiction books often include **back matter**, such as an appendix, a glossary, a bibliography, and an index.

Layouts. After a design has been created, the designer prepares special sheets, called **layouts**, that show how the book will look. Layouts include detailed plans for every element of the book. Frequently, the designer will ask the **compositor**—the person setting the type—to provide samples that show how these different elements will look after the book is printed. After reviewing the layouts and samples, the designer and editor may decide to make changes in the design.

Preparing for Typesetting and Printing. When the design has been finalized, it is the designer's job to mark the manuscript with coded instructions for setting type. These instructions tell the compositor exactly how to set all the type throughout the book, including the main text, page numbers (folios), headings at the top or bottom of the page, and all front- and back-matter materials.

Before a book is printed, the designer may sometimes be asked to prepare a mechanical. A **mechanical** is a detailed assembly of the book, with every element in place. The mechanical is then photographed and the film is used in the printing process.

The Jacket Designer

While *It Rained Every Day* is being edited and designed, artists are creating its artwork. This could include art for the cover of a paperback book and for the paper dust jacket that protects the cover of a hardcover book.

The cover or dust jacket of a book is very important. It protects the book and serves as an advertisement. The person responsible for designing the cover is the jacket designer. Working with the art director of the publishing house, the jacket designer tries to create an

attractive, eye-catching, and informative cover that is appropriate for the book and conveys all necessary information, including the title and the author's name.

When the jacket designer has created a design, he or she often prepares a **comp**, a mock-up of what the design will actually look like after it is printed. If the editor and art director approve the design, the jacket designer will then prepare a mechanical to be used in the printing process.

The Illustrator

Many books, especially those for young readers, have artwork in the interior of the book as well as on the cover. The artist who creates the original art to be used in the interior of a book is called an illustrator.

While the manuscript of *It Rained Every Day* is being prepared, the editor and art director choose an illustrator to work on the art. Following their guidelines, the illustrator prepares sketches to show what the finished art will look like. These sketches are checked by the editor or an assistant to make sure they are appropriate to the text and that all the details are correct. For example, a section of a story may say that a girl has red hair, wears blue jeans, and is walking with her dog, so the illustration for this portion of the story should show the same things.

If an illustration does not match the text, something will have to be changed. Sometimes the art can be changed. However, since it is often costly and time-consuming to change a piece of art, the editor might ask the author to revise the text as long as it will not hurt the author's storyline or ideas.

▶ THE PRODUCTION PROCESS

After the editorial and art and design departments have completed their work, the actual production of a book begins. This part of the bookmaking process involves several stages, including composition, or typesetting, color separation, printing, and binding. Most of the work at these stages is done outside the publishing house.

Control over the process during these stages is maintained largely by the publishing house's production department and a production manager or supervisor. The role of the production manager or supervisor is a complex and very important one. It is that person's responsibility to select outside groups to work on various production aspects of the book, to act as liaison between these groups and the publishing house, to choose the paper to be used for the book and its cover, to coordinate production schedules, and to maintain control of production budgets.

Composition

During the composition process a compositor, or typesetter, changes a typewritten manuscript into pages of type that can then be printed and made into a book. In the past, typesetting was done manually and involved arranging individual pieces of metal type to create a page. Today, computer technology has made most typesetting much easier, as well as faster and cheaper.

As the typesetting proceeds, the compositor prepares **galley proofs**, which are long sheets of paper showing the typeset material. These galley proofs are sent

to the publisher for approval. A proofreader compares a master set of galley proofs against the original, copy-edited manuscript to find any errors. The author receives a set of galley proofs as well and may request certain changes. These changes are added to the master set, which is then sent back to the compositor for corrections.

The compositor then prepares other stages of typeset material to be checked by the editor and designer. These stages include page proofs, repros, and blues. **Page proofs** are corrected galley proofs that have been broken up into pages. They show how the type on each page of the book will appear. The editor checks page proofs for any additional changes or corrections. **Repros**, or reproduction proofs, show any further changes in typesetting. They are printed on a special coated paper that will be photographed and used in the printing process. Repros are used by the designer to make any mechanicals that might be required. **Blues**, or blueprints, are the last stage in the typesetting process. They are made from photographic film that has been prepared for use in the printing process. Blues show how all the parts of each book page will be assembled, with art, text, and any other

On this galley proof, note the proofreader's correction marks. A "pe" indicates a printer's error; an "aa" indicates an author's or editor's change in the text.

One

Paula Jones grit her teeth. The screen door slammed. Her brother Pete was gone, and she was left at the breakfast table with her parents and her little brother Ted.

She slammed down her spoon. "It isn't fair," she said. "It's Pete's turn to do the dishes. I did them last night."

Her mother stood up. "It's not fair, you're right. I'll do the dishes, but I hope you'll help us with unpacking and setting things up. It's a shame to waste our first day of vacation working, but we have to get organized before we can have fun.

help." Ted stood up, his cereal bowl in his hand. He reached for his half-full glass of milk, grabbed it tightly, and set it in the bowl. Holding the bowl and glass of milk with one hand, he began piling sliver into the bowl. It wobbled, and the milk sloshed against the side of the glass. A knife fell onto the floor. Ted lurched for it, but the glass tilted, and milk splashed onto the table.

Ted looked miserable, Paula thought. He's always trying to help and makes a mess becyause he's so little. Paula remembered when she was six . . .

elements in place as they will appear in the finished book. Corrections can be made at this stage, but they are very expensive.

Color Separation

Printing colored illustrations in a book or on a cover is a much more complicated and expensive process than printing black type. In order to print color, it is necessary to separate a color image into four basic colors first. The colors are red, yellow, blue, and black. The principle behind this is the same as mixing paints. Mixing the three primary colors—red, yellow, and blue—produces all other colors. Black is used to add highlight and depth.

A special machine called an electronic scanner photographs the different hues of each colored illustration or photograph and makes four separate negatives—red, yellow, blue, and black. These negatives are then used to make printing plates that, when combined on a printing machine, will produce a full-color image on the printed pages of the book or cover.

A designer carefully checks the color plates. If the colors are not right, the color separator can change color hues.

A color illustration or photograph is first separated into four basic colors — yellow, blue (cyan), red (magenta), and black. An electronic scanner does the separating.

yellow   blue (cyan)   red (magenta)   black

When the four colors are printed together, they make up more colors. For example, a combination of yellow and blue produces green, and a combination of blue and red produces purple.

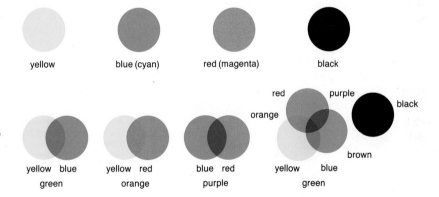

yellow blue   yellow red   blue red   yellow blue
green   orange   purple   green

red   purple
orange
black
brown

This example shows how 32 pages are printed on one sheet of paper. Sixteen pages are printed on each side. Some pages are upside down. They are arranged so that they will fall into the proper sequence when the sheet is folded. This arrangement is called an imposition.

1	16	13	4
8	9	12	5
17	32	29	20
24	25	28	21

3	14	15	2
6	11	10	7
19	30	31	18
22	27	26	23

When the separation has been done, the separator will send a proof to the publisher for approval. If the colors do not seem right, the color separator can make adjustments and change color hues.

Printing

The printing process involves transferring all typed images and art onto large sheets of paper, which can then be folded and bound into a finished book. In the past, printing was done by hand on manually operated printing presses. Today, modern machines do the work.

When the printer receives the film prepared by the compositor, the film is exposed to flexible metal sheets. This process is similar to the way a photograph is developed from a negative. The images on the film are transferred to the metal sheets, which are then treated with chemicals. When these sheets are placed on cylinders in the printing press and passed by ink, the images are transferred to the sheets of paper that become the pages of the finished book.

The pages of a book come off the printing press on large sheets of paper. From 4 to 64 pages may be printed on each side of these sheets, but the usual number is 16 or 32. The pages do not follow each other in order. In-stead, they are arranged so that they will fall into the proper sequence when the sheets are folded. This arrangement is called an **imposition**. When all the pages have been printed, the book is ready for the next stage of the production process.

Binding

Binding is the final stage of the production process. After printing is finished, the printed sheets are sent to a bindery where they are folded, arranged in the correct sequence, and put within the book's cover.

At the bindery, the large printed sheets are put into a folding machine to be folded, gathered, and trimmed by special knives. Each folded section is called a **signature** and is usually made up of groups of 16 or 32 pages. Putting the signatures together in the proper sequence is called **gathering**.

Next, the signatures are sewn together by a large sewing machine. There are three methods of sewing a book. In **saddle sewing**, the book is stitched only through the center from back to front. With this method, books will open flat, but they are not very strong. In **Smyth sewing**, each signature is first individually sewn through its fold. Then the signatures are placed next to each other and sewn together across the back. Smyth-sewn books

Left: Two press operators check the color printing press. *Below:* The signatures—folded groups of 16 or 32 pages—are sewn or glued together before they are bound into a book.

open flat, and they are much stronger than saddle-sewn books. In **side sewing**, stitching runs through all the signatures from the side. Side-sewn books cannot open flat, but they are the strongest type of books.

Some books, such as paperbacks, are not sewn. Instead, a method called **perfect binding** is used. In this method, the folded rear edge of each signature is trimmed and the pages are glued directly to the cover. Perfect binding is not always durable.

After sewing comes smashing and gluing. In **smashing**, a powerful compressor squeezes all the signatures so that the sewing does not cause a bulge along the rear edge of the book. Smashing is usually followed by gluing, in which a mechanical roller and brush force glue between the rear edges of the signatures. This increases the book's strength.

After smashing and gluing, the pages of the book are trimmed and cut again in preparation for attaching the cover. The covers for most books are made of special cloth that can withstand wear and tear and be cleaned easily. This cloth is attached to heavy cardboardlike material called **binder's board**, which acts as a backing to stiffen the cover. After the covers are attached and the book's dust jacket is put on, it is ready to be shipped to the publisher's warehouse.

▶**MARKETING AND SELLING**

After a long complicated process, your book, *It Rained Every Day*, has finally been published. Congratulations! Soon you will receive your first copy, hot off the press.

Long before you see this first copy, however, your publisher will have begun planning how to market and sell your book. It was listed in the publisher's catalog with a photograph of the book jacket and a summary of the story. Advance news about the book was sent to book reviewers and booksellers, and plans were made to exhibit the book, along with other new books, at special conventions and traveling exhibits throughout the country.

When the first copies of *It Rained Every Day* are available, some are sent to book reviewers. Book reviews in newspapers, magazines, or on radio and television are free advertising and can be very important in generating interest in the book. Copies may also be sent to groups, such as library associations, that include booklists in their publications.

Most bookstores have a department where you can find many kinds of books for young readers, including picture books, storybooks, books on special topics such as history, science, or sports, and dictionaries and encyclopedias.

Publishers employ other techniques to market books as well. These may include paid advertisements in magazines and newspapers, posters that are displayed in bookstores or other places where books are sold, special bookmarks, and public appearances by the author (if he or she is well known).

Marketing promotes your book and creates interest in it. Selling the book is what earns money for you and the publisher. Several months before your book was published, it was presented at one of the publisher's sales conferences. At this conference your editor enthusiastically described your book to sales representatives, whose job it is to sell it to bookstores and other booksellers. Once in the hands of booksellers, the long process of publishing *It Rained Every Day* is finally over.

OLGA LITOWINSKY
Executive Editor, Books for Young Readers
Simon & Schuster

See also CHILDREN'S BOOK AWARDS; CHILDREN'S LITERATURE; PRINTING; PROOFREADING; PUBLISHING.

BOONE, DANIEL (1734–1820)

Daniel Boone has become a legend as one of America's greatest pioneers and frontier heroes. He was a dead shot with a rifle and a skillful hunter who could glide through forests as swiftly and silently as an Indian.

Daniel was born on November 2, 1734, at Oley, a frontier settlement in Pennsylvania. By the age of 12, he was hunting game for the dinner table with his first rifle. Indians roamed the nearby woods. Daniel knew that if he were caught by Indians on the warpath against intruders on their land, he would either be tomahawked or taken prisoner. So he learned how to walk through the forest without making a sound.

In 1751 the Boones settled in North Carolina. In 1755, during the French and Indian War, Daniel joined British General Edward Braddock's expedition against the French. The British, who were unused to Indian ways of fighting, were ambushed and slaughtered, but Daniel and a hunter named John Finley (or Findley) escaped into the woods. Finley told Daniel about a mysterious land, west of the Appalachian Mountains, that the Indians called Kentucky. He said its forests were thick with turkeys, bears, and deer, and buffalo thundered across its prairies. These stories inspired Daniel to go to Kentucky.

First Daniel returned to North Carolina to marry 17-year-old Rebecca Bryan, whose family lived near the Boones. For the next ten years they rarely lived very long in one place.

Daniel often was away hunting deerskins and beaver pelts, which he sold to support his growing family.

Finally, in 1769, Daniel set out across the Appalachian Mountains, and for the next two years he explored Kentucky. Then he went back to North Carolina to gather several families who would return with him to establish a settlement. On the journey back to Kentucky, the pioneers were attacked by Indians, and Daniel's son James and several others were killed. The settlers turned back.

In 1775, still determined, Daniel cleared the Wilderness Road, through the Cumberland Gap, into Kentucky and built a fort called Boonesborough on the Kentucky River. Then he returned home to lead another group of pioneers across the mountains to settle there. Daniel's wife and daughter were among the first women settlers in Kentucky.

In 1778, Daniel was captured by Shawnee Indians. Their chief, Blackfish, was so proud to have caught the famous frontiersman, he "adopted" Daniel as his son and named him *Shel-tow-ee*, meaning "Big Turtle." For several months, Daniel lived among the Indians. One day he overheard the Indians plan a raid on Boonesborough, but he was able to negotiate a plan with the Shawnee to surrender his men as prisoners. His quick thinking saved the lives of countless numbers of other settlers. Later, when Daniel discovered the Indians were planning yet another attack on Boonesborough, he made a daring escape and reached the fort in time to warn the settlers.

Daniel later held several public offices, including lieutenant colonel of the militia and representative of the Kentucky state legislature. However, he lost all claim to the land he had been the first white man to explore and settle, because he had not followed the proper procedures to obtain legal title to it.

In 1799, feeling Kentucky had become too crowded with people, he moved westward to Missouri to find, as he put it, "more elbow room." He died in Missouri on September 26, 1820, at the age of 86.

Reviewed by DANIEL ROSELLE
State University College (Fredonia, New York)

BOOTH, JOHN WILKES (1838–1865)

John Wilkes Booth, the infamous assassin of President Abraham Lincoln, came from one of America's most famous theatrical families. His father, Junius, and his brother, Edwin, both were actors of considerable reputation, and John followed in their footsteps.

Born in 1838 near Bel Air, Maryland, on a farm worked by slaves, Booth strongly sympathized with the Confederate cause as a young man during the Civil War. In 1864, as the war turned ever more in favor of the Union, Booth and several other conspirators hatched a plan to kidnap Lincoln and strike a blow against Union morale. They also hoped to exchange the president for Confederate prisoners of war. However, nothing came of their immediate plans. After Confederate General Robert E. Lee's surrender at Appomattox on April 9, 1865, Booth and his followers' kidnapping plot turned toward murder. In addition to Lincoln, their targets included Vice President Andrew Johnson and Secretary of State William H. Seward.

On the evening of April 14, Lincoln, his wife, and two young friends attended the play *Our American Cousin* at Ford's Theatre in Washington, D.C. Booth entered their private box with a small pistol and shot the president in the back of the head at point-blank range. Witnesses reported that Booth then jumped down to the stage, shouting, *"Sic semper tyrannis!"* (Thus always to tyrants), Virginia's state motto. Lincoln never regained consciousness and died the next morning in a rooming house across the street from the theater. As the president drew his last breath, his Secretary of War Edwin Stanton uttered, "Now he belongs to the ages."

In his leap to the stage, Booth had broken his left leg above the ankle, but he managed to escape with one other conspirator. Union soldiers caught up with him several days later and cornered him in a barn near Port Royal, Virginia. Refusing to surrender, Booth was shot to death. His last reported words were, "Tell mother I died for my country."

For the murder of President Lincoln, eight conspirators were quickly brought to trial and sentenced. Four were hanged: George Atzerodt, Davy Herold, Mary Surratt (who owned the boardinghouse in which the conspiracy was said to have taken place), and Lewis Paine

After shooting President Abraham Lincoln on April 14, 1865, John Wilkes Booth leapt to the stage of Ford's Theatre and escaped. Lincoln died the following morning. Booth was later captured and killed.

(who was identified as the man who had attacked and injured Secretary Seward).

The other four were sentenced to life imprisonment, including Dr. Samuel Mudd, who had set Booth's fractured leg after his escape from Ford's Theatre.

Many conspiracy theories regarding Lincoln's assassination cropped up after his death. One story, for example, implicated Secretary of War Stanton as a co-conspirator; others made claims of repeated "sightings" of Booth as late as the 1890's. Such stories take advantage of the fact that, unlike in detective mysteries, many questions regarding historical events can never be answered with certainty.

It is possible that the Confederate government was involved in the assassination plot, but Lincoln's murder was more likely the work of a small group of conspirators living in a society deeply disturbed and divided by war. Many Southerners could not accept defeat and the changes that were to be imposed on them. In Lincoln's last speech, he made reference to extending to blacks the right to vote. For John Wilkes Booth, it appears that this was the final consequence he simply could not endure.

GABOR S. BORITT
Director, Civil War Institute
Gettysburg College

BORAH, WILLIAM EDGAR. See IDAHO (Famous People).

BORGLUM, GUTZON. See IDAHO (Famous People).

BORLAUG, NORMAN. See IOWA (Famous People).

BORNEO

Borneo is the world's third largest island. It is exceeded in size only by Greenland and New Guinea. With an area of about 287,000 square miles (743,000 square kilometers), Borneo is larger than many nations of the world.

Location. Borneo straddles the equator at the western end of the Pacific Ocean. Across the South China Sea is the mainland of Asia, with the Malay Peninsula (part of Malaysia) to the west. Borneo's neighbor to the northeast is the Philippines. The many islands of Indonesia curve in a wide arc from west to east. Farther east is the island of New Guinea.

Political Divisions. Politically, Borneo is divided among three separate nations—Indonesia, Malaysia, and Brunei. Kalimantan, the largest region of Borneo, making up about 75 percent of its territory, is part of Indonesia. It is divided into the provinces of East, West, Central, and South Kalimantan. Sabah· and Sarawak are states of Malaysia, together known as East Malaysia. Brunei is a tiny, oil-rich nation situated on the northwestern coast of the island.

There is a separate article on Brunei in Volume B, as well as individual articles on Indonesia and Malaysia in Volumes I and M.

▶THE LAND

Borneo is a largely mountainous land of dense tropical rain forests and many rivers. Mount Kinabalu, the highest peak, rises 13,455 feet (4,100 meters) above sea level. The Kapuas mountain chain, which runs generally east and west, forms the backbone of the island. The Schwaner Mountains tend to run in a northeast and southwest direction.

Since travel is often difficult in the rugged interior of the island, the rivers provide an important source of transportation. In contrast to the mountainous interior, Borneo's coastal areas are usually flat and swampy.

Climate. Borneo has a tropical climate, with generally high temperatures and humidity and considerable rainfall. The temperature seldom falls below 70°F (21°C), except in the cooler highland areas, and often reaches a high of 96°F (36°C). Depending on elevation and exposure to rain-bearing monsoon winds, Borneo receives from 100 to 200 inches (2,500 to 5,000 millimeters) of rainfall a year.

Plant and Animal Life. Forests cover most of the island. The trees, which may grow to a height of 120 feet (35 meters), are surrounded by giant ferns, creeper vines, and other plants. The forests often are so thickly grown that little sunlight can penetrate their cover. Teak and other valuable hardwoods grow in the interior. Mangrove trees are found in the swampy coastal regions, and sago and coconut palms flourish in other areas.

Borneo is famous for its animal wildlife. Hundreds of species of birds add brilliant color to the forest. Among the numerous kinds of reptiles are several varieties of poisonous snakes; crocodiles live in the rivers. The larger forest animals include two-horned rhinoceroses, honey bears, wild pigs, wild oxen, deer, elephants, monkeys, and gibbons. One of the shiest creatures is the orangutan, a large ape whose name means "man of the forest" in Malay.

▶THE PEOPLE

Borneo has a population of over 9,000,000, more than three quarters of whom live in Kalimantan. The great majority of the people are

Most of Borneo is covered with dense tropical rain forests. Rivers are often the only convenient source of transportation through the rugged interior, where many of the island's Dayak people live.

Dayaks, who are native to the island and belong to a number of different tribes. Malays and Chinese make up the next largest ethnic groups.

Languages and Religion. Major languages spoken in Borneo include Bahasa Indonesia and Bahasa Malaysia (the official languages of Indonesia and Malaysia), various Dayak dialects, English, and Chinese. Many of the Dayaks practice traditional religions, while most of the other people of Borneo are Muslims.

Life in the Interior. The Dayaks of the interior tend to follow older, more traditional ways of life. A traditional Dayak dwelling was the longhouse, which sheltered as many as 50 families and was built on stilts several feet off the ground. Smaller houses connected by walkways are now more common. The people hunt, fish, and plant crops on small plots cleared from the forest.

Coastal Cities. The Dayaks who live in the coastal areas have largely mixed with the other peoples of Borneo and have adopted their customs. The population is most heavily concentrated in the coastal areas, where almost all of Borneo's cities and towns are located. Banjarmasin in Kalimantan is Borneo's largest city, with a population of more than 400,000. Other large cities, also in Kalimantan, are Pontianak, Balikpapan, and Samarinda. Kuching is the capital of Sarawak, and Kota Kinabalu the capital of Sabah. Brunei's capital city is Bandar Seri Begawan.

►ECONOMY

Agriculture and Forestry. The majority of Borneo's people earn their living from agriculture. Rice is the most important food crop; other crops include corn, sweet potatoes, yams, manioc (cassava), and beans. Clearing land for cultivation frequently is carried out by the slash-and-burn method, in which vegetation is first cut and then burned away.

Borneo's chief commercial agricultural product is rubber. Copra (dried coconut), tobacco, and hemp (for making rope) also are produced in large quantities. Timber from its vast forests is one of the island's most valuable natural resources.

Mineral Resources. Petroleum and natural gas are Borneo's most important minerals. Brunei is the single most important petroleum-producing area on the island. Some gold, diamonds, and other minerals also are mined.

BORNEO

Industry. Borneo has limited industry. Most of it involves the drilling for and refining of petroleum and the processing of agricultural products and timber.

►HISTORY

Borneo has a long history. Traders from India arrived in Borneo at least 2,000 years ago. Chinese settled on the island in succeeding centuries. There were also early contacts between Borneo and what are now the Indonesian islands of Java and Sumatra.

Europeans first arrived in the region in the 1500's. The Dutch became the most successful colonizers, gaining control of what is now Kalimantan by the early 1800's. By the mid-1800's the British were dominant in the northwestern quarter of the island, in what is now Sabah, Sarawak, and Brunei.

Recent History. During World War II, Japanese troops occupied most of the coastal areas of Borneo. When Indonesia gained its independence from the Netherlands in 1949, it acquired Dutch-controlled Borneo. Sabah and Sarawak became part of Malaysia in 1963. Brunei remained a British protectorate until 1984, when it won complete independence.

PHILLIP BACON
University of Houston
Author, *Golden Book Picture Atlas of the World*

BOSNIA AND HERZEGOVINA

BOSNIA AND HERZEGOVINA

Bosnia and Herzegovina (sometimes spelled Hercegovina) was formerly one of the six republics making up the nation of Yugoslavia. In 1992, Bosnia and Herzegovina declared its independence from Yugoslavia, becoming the fourth republic to do so.

Bosnia and Herzegovina has an area of about 19,800 square miles (51,280 square kilometers) and a population of slightly more than 4 million. A mostly mountainous land, it is one of the poorer parts of Yugoslavia. But it has a rich and colorful history and is a fascinating patchwork of different cultures and religions.

The People. The people are nearly all South Slavs. (In fact, Yugoslavia means "Land of the South Slavs.") However, they are sharply divided into three major national and religious communities.

About two fifths of the people are Serbs, who belong to the Eastern Orthodox Church. Slightly more than one fifth are Croats, who are Roman Catholics. Most of the rest prefer to describe themselves as Muslims—although they may be either Serbs or Croats in terms of nationality and language. This is a reminder of the long period of rule by the Muslim Ottoman Turks. The official language is Serbo-Croatian. The rugged landscape with its few resources has produced a people of generally hardy and vigorous character.

Sarajevo is the capital of the republic and the largest city. It has a population of about 500,000. Mostar is the second largest city.

The Land. Bosnia and Herzegovina is basically an inland region, with only limited access to the Adriatic Sea. Bosnia, the northern part of the republic, takes its name from the Bosna River. Herzegovina in the south derives its name from the German word for "duke," the title of its onetime rulers.

Roughly half the land is covered by forests, while about one quarter is suitable for farming. Most of the rest is used to pasture livestock. Because of the rugged nature of the terrain, transportation and communication have always been a problem.

Economy. The economy is based mainly on agriculture. Tobacco is the major commercial crop. Wheat and other grains are chief food crops. A variety of fruits are grown, especially plums, from which the national liquor, slivovitz, a plum brandy, is made. The forests provide timber and related products.

History. The migration of Slavic peoples during the Middle Ages gave the region its present racial makeup. An independent Bosnian state of some power emerged in the 1300's, but in the late 1400's, Bosnia and Herzegovina fell to the Ottoman Empire.

After centuries of rule, the Turkish tide began to ebb, and in 1878, the two territories were placed under the administration of Austria-Hungary. Complete annexation by Austria in 1908 fanned the fires of nationalism. In 1914 a Bosnian Serb student, Gavrilo Princip, assassinated the heir to the Austrian throne, Archduke Francis Ferdinand, at Sarajevo, triggering World War I. After the war's end in 1918, Bosnia and Herzegovina became a part of a united Yugoslav kingdom.

The region was under Nazi German occupation from 1941 to 1945, during World War II. In 1946, it became a republic of a newly established Communist Yugoslav state. Yugoslavia began to break apart in 1991, following the collapse of Communist regimes in Eastern Europe. Bosnia and Herzegovina's proclamation of independence, in March 1992, led to the outbreak of bloody fighting between its Serbs, who had opposed independence, and the republic's Muslims and Croats.

ARTHUR CAMPBELL TURNER
University of California, Riverside

BOSTON

Boston is the capital of the Commonwealth of Massachusetts. The city is located in the northeastern United States on a peninsula, where the Charles River flows into a large, well-protected bay of the Atlantic Ocean, forming one of the world's finest natural harbors. Founded in 1630, Boston is at once an old city and a new one. Because many of the major events of the American Revolutionary War took place in or near Boston, it has come to be known as the "Cradle of Liberty."

With a population of about 575,000, Boston is New England's largest city. The city encompasses 46 square miles (119 square kilometers), which is more than 35 times its original colonial size. This growth is due in part to a clever landfill project that was undertaken in the late 1800's to reclaim much of the swampland along the Charles River basin. The project took soil from Boston's hills to create the Back Bay section and the waterfront area. Boston's growth is also due to the annexation of several bordering towns. The modern city of Boston is made up of many neighborhoods, including Downtown Boston, Charlestown, Dorchester, Roxbury, South Boston, East Boston, Back Bay, Beacon Hill, the North End, Brighton-Allston, the Fenway, Jamaica Plain, Roslindale, West Roxbury, Mattapan, and Hyde Park.

Boston's average temperatures range from 31°F (-1°C) in the winter to 71°F (22°C) in the summer. The average yearly precipitation is 43 inches (1,080 millimeters).

Business and Industry

Boston was one of the first industrial cities in the United States. Today it maintains a number of strong industries, including the processing of fresh and frozen fish; electronics assembly; video and film production; the manufacture of medical and dental instruments; printing and bookbinding; and the manufacture of stone, clay, and glass products. An expanding service economy and the success of high technology of defense-weapons manufacturing have contributed to Boston's economic health and high rate of employment.

Major components of Boston's service industry include financial services (banking, insurance, and real estate), health care, education, and tourism.

Transportation

Boston's public transportation system, the oldest in the United States, provides a crisscross of subway lines, trolleys, buses, and trains, which makes it easy for residents of outlying neighborhoods to travel into the center of the city.

Boston is also the major seaport and air terminus for Massachusetts and New England. The port of Boston, with its 25 miles (40 kilometers) of docking space, handles about 26 million tons of cargo annually. Logan Airport, the twelfth busiest in the world, services 20.5 million passengers and 335,000 tons of cargo annually.

Urban Renewal

In the 1960's an extensive project was undertaken to bring new life to the decaying

Modern skyscrapers and historic landmarks grace the Boston skyline. Many high-rise buildings were erected in the 1960's as part of an urban renewal project.

Colorful Quincy Market is a lively place where residents and tourists alike go to shop, dine, and be entertained. Both the market and Faneuil Hall (rear) were successfully restored in the late 1970's.

this day maintains a national reputation for academic excellence. In 1636, across the Charles River in neighboring Cambridge, Harvard University opened its doors.

Today, there are more than 65 colleges and universities serving 250,000 students in the Greater Boston Area. Among these are Harvard University, Radcliffe College, the Massachusetts Institute of Technology (MIT), Boston University, Boston College, Northeastern University, Brandeis University, Emerson College, Tufts University, and the University of Massachusetts.

Libraries. Many world-class libraries are located in Boston. Among them are the Athenaeum, which owns George Washington's book collection; the Boston Public Library, considered one of the finest in the United States; and the library at Harvard, the world's largest university library, with more than 9 million volumes.

Museums. Famous Boston museums include the Museum of Fine Arts, the Children's Museum, the Museum of Science, the Computer Museum, the John F. Kennedy Presidential Library and Museum, and the Isabella Stewart Gardner Museum.

Music and Dance. The Boston Pops Orchestra and the Boston Symphony Orchestra delight audiences at Symphony Hall. The Boston Opera and the Boston Ballet have earned worldwide recognition and perform regularly to full houses.

downtown area. Today, Boston's skyline includes many new skyscrapers and prominent landmarks, such as the Prudential Center, the Government Center, and the John Hancock Mutual Life Insurance Company tower.

Education, Culture, and Recreation

For its size, Boston has an unusually large number of educational, cultural, and recreational facilities. It is a major center for the publication of books, textbooks, and magazines. The city's major newspapers are the *Boston Globe*, the *Boston Herald*, and the *Christian Science Monitor*, which is distributed internationally.

Schools. In 1635, Puritan settlers established the Boston Latin Academy, the first free public school in the United States, which to

---

BOSTON "FIRSTS"

A partial list of many "firsts" that occurred in Boston illustrates the city's importance in American tradition, culture, and technological development.

1639 First post office.
1653 First public library.
1686 First schoolbook printed.
1704 First American newspaper published, the *Boston News-Letter*.
1776 First proclamation of the Declaration of Independence, Old State House, July 18.
1845 First sewing machine.
1846 First anesthesia demonstration.
1857 First American literary magazine published, the *Atlantic Monthly*.
1873 First university to open all departments to women (Boston University).
1874 First words spoken by telephone.
1897 First subway for trolley car operation.
1900 First Davis Cup tennis match.
1903 First modern World Series, won by the Boston Red Sox over the Pittsburgh Pirates.
1929 First computer, developed at MIT.
1944 First automatic digital computer, patented at Harvard.

Parks. Boston Common (the oldest public park in the United States), the Public Garden, the Arnold Arboretum, the Charles River, and Boston Harbor provide beautiful settings within the city for outdoor activities, such as bicycling, jogging, picnicking, and sailing.

Sports. Fenway Park is the home of Boston's professional baseball team, the Boston Red Sox. The city also supports professional teams in basketball (the Boston Celtics), football (the New England Patriots), and ice hockey (the Boston Bruins). Perhaps the one sporting event most identified with the city is the Boston Marathon. Held on Patriot's Day (the third Monday in April), it is the oldest sporting event in the United States and attracts more than 6,000 competitors every year.

▶ **HISTORY**

Ten years after the Pilgrims arrived at Plymouth on the *Mayflower*, English Puritans followed them to New England in search of religious freedom. In 1630, under the leadership of John Winthrop, the first governor of the Massachusetts Bay Colony, the Puritans founded Charlestown and later Boston on the other side of the Charles River.

Although the Indians who inhabited the area called it "Shawmut," the Puritans first re-named it "Trimountaine" for the three hills that dominated the landscape. (To this day, the official symbol of the city includes the "trimount.") The name Boston was later adopted because many of the Puritans had come from a town by that name in England. In 1632, Boston became the capital of the Massachusetts Bay Colony.

For two hundred years after the Puritans arrived, Boston remained populated almost exclusively by their descendants. However, beginning in the 1840's, great waves of European immigrants voyaged to the United States in search of a better life. Many of those who settled in Boston came from Ireland to escape the great famine caused by a four-year blight to their potato crops. Today the Irish form the largest ethnic group in Boston, followed by the Italians. Blacks account for about 22 percent of Boston's population.

Throughout the 1800's, Boston witnessed many religious, literary, philosophical, and social changes. The Christian Science religion was established at The Mother Church, and King's Chapel was the birthplace of American Unitarianism. William Lloyd Garrison made his first antislavery speech in 1829 at the Park Street Church. The Old Corner Bookstore became a favorite meeting place for distin-

Every year millions of people take a walk along the famous "Freedom Trail" to visit Boston's most important historic landmarks, many of which date from colonial days.

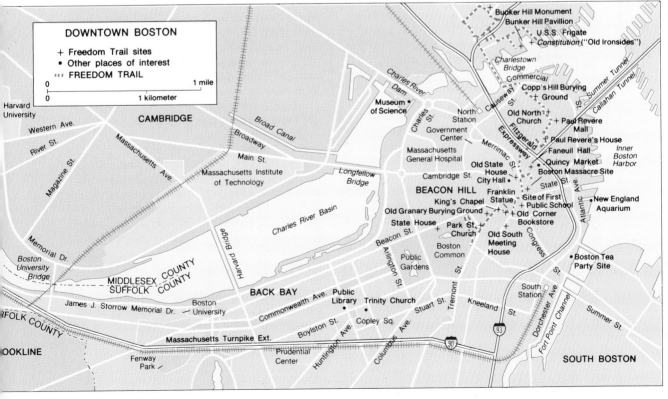

guished writers, such as Henry Wadsworth Longfellow, Ralph Waldo Emerson, and Henry David Thoreau.

Places of Interest

Each year more than 2 million visitors—as well as countless area residents—take a 2-mile (3.2-kilometer) walk along a well-marked path called the "Freedom Trail" to visit the Boston of old. Colonial Boston seems to come alive when one visits the sites of many of the events that led up to the American Revolutionary War (1775–83). Of special interest are the site of the Boston Massacre (1770), where British troops fired at a crowd of American colonists, killing five; the Old South Meetinghouse, where in 1773 the "Sons of Liberty" planned the infamous Boston Tea Party; and Christ ("Old North") Church, where in 1775 Robert Newman hung the "two if by sea" lanterns that sent Paul Revere and William Dawes on their famous midnight rides to warn the Minutemen.

Other sites along the Freedom Trail include Paul Revere's house, the site of Benjamin Franklin's birth, the Old State House, and Faneuil Hall. Since 1742, Faneuil Hall has been used as an all-purpose marketplace (first floor) and meeting hall (second floor). In front of Faneuil Hall is Quincy Market. Today, more than 14 million residents and tourists every year come to visit its 175 shops, restaurants, food markets, and art galleries.

Boston also has a "Black Heritage Trail," a walking tour that explores the history of Boston's black community. The trail begins at the Museum of Afro-American History and includes visits to the African Meeting House (the oldest church established by blacks in the United States) and the Robert Gould Shaw and 54th Regiment Memorial, a monument to one of the black regiments that fought for the North during the Civil War.

Boston's rich historic and cultural heritage makes it an exciting city for its residents as well as its 10 million annual visitors. The unusual variety of attractions makes Boston deserving of another of its popular nicknames—the "Hub of the Universe."

ANNE N. BONNER
Director of Communications and Public Relations
Greater Boston Chamber of Commerce

BOSTON MASSACRE.   See REVOLUTIONARY WAR.
BOSTON TEA PARTY.   See REVOLUTIONARY WAR.

BOTANICAL GARDENS

Botanical gardens are museums that maintain collections of living plants for scientific and educational purposes and for public display. **Botanists** (scientists who study plants) carry out research in the laboratories and test plots of botanical gardens to learn more about how plants grow, how new plants can be developed, and how plants can be useful to people as a source of food and other products.

Sharing knowledge of plants with the public is an important function of botanical gardens. Visitors will find all the plants labeled with their scientific and common names. Botanical gardens may have libraries and information services and may publish books and pamphlets on botanical subjects. School classes might visit local botanical gardens for guided tours or workshops. Sometimes students actually tend small garden plots there to learn about plants.

Most large botanical gardens include greenhouses or conservatories—glass buildings where temperature, humidity, and light can be controlled. These artificial environments can copy natural ones, making it possible to grow plants from many different regions and climates of the world. In one room a tropical rain forest might be created; in another, desert plants can grow in a sunny, dry climate; and yet another room can display the conditions found in a marshy bog.

Some botanical gardens have theme gardens, such as a butterfly garden with flowers that attract those insects. A Japanese garden would have the plants arranged in typical Japanese fashion. A Shakespeare garden would have plants mentioned in Shakespeare's plays or sonnets. Frequently there is an herb garden and often an herbarium—a place where dried plants and parts of plants are preserved and cataloged for study.

One of the most interesting of all botanical gardens is in Uppsala, Sweden, home of Carolus Linnaeus. This great botanist of the

1700's devised a system of classifying and naming plants and animals. He managed the Uppsala Gardens from 1742 to 1777. Today the gardens display plants in beds that Linnaeus himself laid out. A biography of Linnaeus is included in Volume L.

One of the greatest botanical gardens in the world today is the Royal Botanic Gardens at Kew, near London, England. The facility is sometimes known as Kew Gardens. In the 1800's it introduced plants brought back from the voyages of Captain Cook, including coffee, cotton, and cinnamon trees.

One of the best-known botanical gardens in the United States is the New York Botanical Garden in the Bronx, New York, which has more than 13,000 species of plants. The Missouri Botanical Gardens in St. Louis is the oldest in the United States.

Canada has a number of well-known botanical gardens, among them the Montreal Botanical Gardens in Quebec and the Royal Botanical Gardens in Ontario.

LUCY E. JONES
Director of Education
Brooklyn Botanic Gardens

Carefully arranged and labeled gardens offer an opportunity to study as well as to enjoy plants in a natural setting. The Royal Botanical Gardens in Hamilton, Ontario, is known for its late-blooming tulip collection.

BOTANY

Have you ever wondered what is inside a flower? Or what the veins in a leaf are for? If you have, you have asked the same sorts of questions as those asked by a botanist. A botanist is a scientist whose field is botany—the study of plants.

Plants form the basis of all life on earth. Only plants can capture the energy of the sun and use it—in a process called photosynthesis—to make food. Animals cannot do this and so must depend on plants for food. No animal life could exist on earth without plants.

This essential world of plants is a large and varied one. There are about 300,000 different kinds of plants. They range in size from tiny mosses as small as ⅜ inch (1 centimeter) to the giant redwoods, the largest living things on earth. Some plants, such as carrots, are rooted in soil. Others—orchids, for example—grow in air. Some plants reproduce from seeds, others from underground stems.

Botany includes every aspect of plant life. A botanist may study the plant itself—its structure and the function of its various parts. Other botanists may study the development of plants on earth—when they first appeared, how they changed over long periods of time, and how they are related to one another.

Some botanists study plants in relation to their environment. They may, for example, try to determine how soil and water affect the growth and reproduction of plants.

A botanist may specialize in one area of botany, but whatever his or her specialty, the work can benefit people. Thus, botanists may discover plants that yield important new medicines, or they may help to improve crops by developing new and better varieties of plants.

REVIEWED BY NANCY R. MORIN
Missouri Botanical Garden

See also ALGAE; BACTERIA; CACTUS; CELLS; FERNS, MOSSES, AND LICHENS; FLOWERS AND SEEDS; FUNGI; GENETICS; GRASSES; KINGDOMS OF LIVING THINGS; LEAVES; LIFE; PHOTOSYNTHESIS; PLANT PESTS; PLANTS; PLANTS, FOOD; PLANTS, MEDICINAL; PLANTS, ODD AND INTERESTING; PLANTS, POISONOUS; REPRODUCTION; TREES; WEEDS.

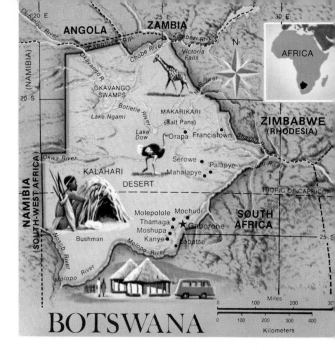

BOTSWANA

Botswana is an arid, landlocked country in southern Africa. Formerly known as Bechuanaland, it was a British dependency before gaining independence in 1966. Much of Botswana's land is desert or grassland suitable only for grazing cattle. Traditionally the country's wealth was measured by counting its cattle, which still outnumber the people.

▶ THE PEOPLE

Most of the people are Tswana, who belong to the large Bantu family. The Tswana are cattle herders and farmers. A number of Bushmen, a distinct people of southern Africa, inhabit the Kalahari Desert, where they live primarily as hunters and food gatherers. Many of the people practice traditional African religions. Others are Christian. The most widely spoken languages are Setswana, a Bantu language, and English, which is the official language. Botswana has few cities. The largest city is Gaborone, the capital. Most of the people live in villages, some of great size.

▶ THE LAND AND THE ECONOMY

Most of Botswana is a vast plateau. In the northwest the Okavango River overflows to create an area of large swamps. Southern Botswana forms part of the great Kalahari Desert.

FACTS AND FIGURES

REPUBLIC OF BOTSWANA is the official name of the country.

THE PEOPLE are known as Batswana.

LOCATION: Southern Africa.

AREA: 600,372 km² (231,804 sq mi).

POPULATION: 1,000,000 (estimate).

CAPITAL AND LARGEST CITY: Gaborone.

MAJOR LANGUAGES: English (official), Setswana.

MAJOR RELIGIONS: Traditional African religions, various independent Christian churches.

GOVERNMENT: Republic. **Head of state and government**—president. **Legislature**—National Assembly.

CHIEF PRODUCTS: Agricultural—cattle, sorghum, millet, corn. **Mineral**—diamonds, copper, nickel.

MONETARY UNIT: Pula (1 pula = 100 thebe).

NATIONAL ANTHEM: *Fatshe La Rona* ("Our Land").

The north and east receive most of the slight rainfall and generally have the only land suitable for cultivation. Most of the population is concentrated in the east.

Botswana's economy is based on cattle raising and mining. Meat and hides, diamonds, copper, and nickel are the chief exports. Farming is limited to a few food crops. Because of unemployment, many of the men spend part of each year working in neighboring South Africa, Zimbabwe, and Zambia.

▶ HISTORY AND GOVERNMENT

Europeans knew little about what is now Botswana before the early 19th century, when British missionaries arrived there. For many years the region was torn by tribal warfare and by clashes between the Tswana and the Boers of South Africa. In 1885 the native chiefs asked Great Britain for protection against the Boers, and the territory—then called Bechuanaland—became a British protectorate. Botswana gained its independence in 1966.

The government consists of a president and a legislature called the National Assembly. There is also an advisory body, the House of Chiefs. Elections are held every five years.

Since independence, Botswana has had continuously elected democratic governments. It has followed a moderate course in African affairs and a policy of non-alignment in its international relations.

HUGH C. BROOKS
St. John's University (New York)

BOTTICELLI, SANDRO (1444?–1510)

The poetic paintings of the Renaissance master known as Botticelli often describe the beginnings of things. With grace and delicacy Botticelli depicted not just love but the birth of the love goddess, not simply faith but the birth of Christ, not only the beauty of nature but the blooming of spring. He turned for subject matter to history and religion, to poetry and legend.

Botticelli's life is somewhat like a legend. Little about it can be proved since much of what we know has come down through the ages by word of mouth. He was born in Florence and died there when he was about 65. His real name was Alessandro Filipepi, but he took the name Botticelli from his older brother, whose nickname was *Botticello,* meaning ''little barrel.'' By 1460 he was probably studying with the well-known artist Fra Filippo Lippi. By the time he was 25, Botticelli had already become teacher to Lippi's son and was considered one of the best painters in Florence.

Among his many admirers was Pope Sixtus IV. In 1481 the Pope invited Botticelli to Rome to help decorate the Sistine Chapel, which had recently been completed. Botticelli's contributions to the chapel include wall paintings illustrating the life of Moses.

The Medici family, rulers of Florence, were the greatest supporters of artists and scholars in all Italy. Botticelli received encouragement from them and may even have lived in the Medici palace. The scholars there were fascinated by the poetry and philosophy of ancient Greece. As his painting the *Primavera* shows us, Botticelli, too, was entranced by the creators of ancient mythology. The spiritual quality of his religious paintings can also be seen in his portrayals of the gods and heroes of ancient Greece.

In his later years Botticelli was influenced by the monk Savonarola, who preached against the vanity and extravagance of the Florentines. Botticelli became very religious and painted only religious subjects.

Botticelli's paintings are famous for their dancing lines, flowing forms, and delicate details, admirably represented in the *Primavera.* His golden-haired Venus, goddess of love, has in her eyes the faraway look of one lost in a daydream, which appears so often in Botticelli's work.

Reviewed by ARIANE RUSKIN BATTERBERRY
Author, *The Pantheon Story of Art for Young People*

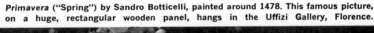

Primavera (''Spring'') by Sandro Botticelli, painted around 1478. This famous picture, on a huge, rectangular wooden panel, hangs in the Uffizi Gallery, Florence.

Bottling is an automated process. Conveyor belts carry bottles to washing, filling, capping, and labeling machines. Machines also pack the bottles in cartons, which are conveyed to shipping areas.

BOTTLES AND BOTTLING

Bottles are made in an endless variety of forms—tall, squat, round, and slender. They range in size from tiny perfume bottles that hold less than an ounce to large industrial bottles that hold many quarts. Some bottles are designed from a practical standpoint. They have very broad bases to keep from being toppled over or long, narrow necks to make pouring easy. Other bottles are shaped in odd and interesting ways for advertising purposes. Many bottles are so beautifully designed that they may be used solely as ornaments.

Glass bottles came into use very slowly over a span of many hundreds of years. The Egyptians learned how to make glass before 3000 B.C. Around 1500 B.C. they began to make bottles by forming molten (melted) glass around a core of sand or clay. When the object had been fashioned and decorated, the core was scraped out. Making bottles in this way was so difficult and expensive that glass bottles were a luxury item for 1,500 years. Then the Romans developed cheaper and quicker methods of production. Using blowpipes, skilled Roman workers blew the molten glass into bubbles. By blowing the bubble inside a mold, they found they could produce bottles of uniform size and shape.

After the fall of the Roman Empire in the 5th century A.D., glass bottles again became a scarce and sought-after luxury in Europe. They were collected and displayed like prize paintings.

Bottles became more of an everyday item in the 18th century, but they were still made by hand by the same methods the Romans used nearly 2,000 years before. Even with the help of molds, an experienced glassblower and a crew of assistants could only turn out about 250 bottles a day.

Some of our most familiar glass containers date from the 19th century. The first baby bottle was patented in 1841. John L. Mason put his famous mason jar on the market in 1858. Dr. Hervey D. Thatcher perfected the milk bottle in the mid-1880's.

Glass manufacturers experimented with various ways to automate the bottle-making process. In 1865 the pressing and blowing machine was invented. In this machine a plunger forces the molten glass against a mold. Then compressed air blows the glass into its final shape.

The first fully successful automatic blowing machine was invented in 1903. The Owens Bottle Machine, invented by Michael Owens, was the first real advance in the manufacture of glass containers since the invention of the blowpipe. Today, modern versions of blowing machines make a variety of products—including jelly glasses, fruit jars, and soft-drink bottles—efficiently and inexpensively.

Bottling

After bottles have been made, they must be filled and prepared for shipment to stores. This task, called bottling, involves a number of steps. These are washing, filling, capping, labeling, and packing. Today almost all the work is done by machines. Conveyor belts move the bottles from one machine to another in an orderly parade, like marching soldiers.

The bottles must first be cleaned. This is especially important with returnable glass containers that are used over and over again. Some soft-drink, milk, and beer bottles are reused as many as 30 times before they are broken or lost.

The clean bottles move along a conveyor belt to a rotary filling machine. Rotary filling machines operate at speeds from 100 containers per minute up to 2,000 containers per minute. A platform lifts each bottle up and presses it tightly against one of many filling valves. The contents pour in. The full bottle is then lowered and moved on to the capping machine.

The capping machine presses a cap onto the mouth of each bottle. These may be cork- or plastic-lined caps or screw caps. A comparatively new type of cap that has taken over a sizable portion of the soft-drink market is a closure made of aluminum and rolled onto the lip of the bottle. Other bottles have corks inserted in the neck.

After capping comes labeling, if required. This is done by a labeling machine that has sets of automatic "fingers." The fingers pick up a label, put glue on it, and press it onto the correct place on the bottle.

After being washed, filled, capped, and labeled, bottles are ready to be packed for shipment to stores. Packing is done by machines that drop the bottles into cases or cartons, seal the boxes, and send them on their way to the shipping platforms.

Recycling

Glass bottles have been replaced for some uses by plastic, metal, and cardboard containers that are not breakable and can be discarded. However, government legislation in many states has discouraged discarding glass, plastic, and metal beverage containers by requiring that deposit fees be paid at the time of purchase. The fees are refundable only if the container is returned.

Bottles and other glassware that are not reusable can be recycled and used to make new glass containers. The used glass is sorted by colors. It is crushed into small pieces and added to a mixture of sand, limestone, and soda ash. This mixture is melted in a furnace and formed into new bottles and other products. By recycling bottles, we conserve the energy resources used in making new bottles. We also limit the costs and other problems of disposing of discarded bottles.

Reviewed by JANET F. FLYNN
Glass Packaging Institute

BOW AND ARROW. See ARCHERY.

BOWIE, JAMES (1796?–1836)

James (Jim) Bowie was a fighter in Texas' struggle for independence from Mexico. Much folklore has been passed down about his adventures. It has been said that he rode alligators, speared wild cattle, and smuggled slaves for profit along the Gulf Coast with the pirate Jean Laffite.

Born about 1796, Bowie grew up in the backwoods of Louisiana. He was said to have invented the bowie knife after he cut his hand on a butcher knife while fighting Indians. He had a crosspiece placed between the handle and the blade to prevent the hand from slipping forward.

In 1828, Bowie settled in San Antonio, Texas, which then belonged to Mexico. About 1832 he joined the Texas independence movement and later became a colonel in the Texas army. In 1836 he and fewer than 200 other Texans were besieged at the Alamo by Mexican General Santa Anna and his large army.

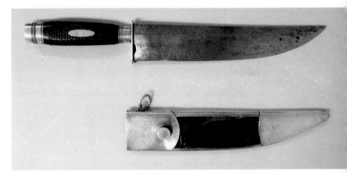

Folklore credits Jim Bowie with the invention of the bowie knife. A metal guard, or crosspiece, separates the blade and handle. Frontiersmen nicknamed this razor-sharp, all-purpose tool the "Arkansas Toothpick."

Although sick with pneumonia, Bowie killed several of the attackers before he was fatally wounded on March 6, 1836. All of the other defenders of the Alamo lost their lives there as well.

Reviewed by DANIEL ROSELLE
State University College (Fredonia, New York)

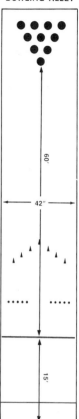

Attractive, modern alleys with electronic pinsetting and scoring equipment have helped bowling become the largest organized competitive sport in the United States. More than 64,000,000 people enjoy the challenge of the game in which they attempt to knock down ten pins by rolling a ball down a 60-foot wooden lane.

BOWLING

The game of bowling has been played for more than 7,000 years. Objects similar to our modern tenpins were discovered in the grave of an Egyptian whose burial has been placed at 5200 B.C.

Just how the sport came to be called bowling is not known. The word "bowl" may have come from the Saxon *bolla* and the Danish *bolle*, meaning "bubble," and through usage, "round."

In its earliest form bowling was a crude recreation and was played with primitive equipment in any space that provided suitable conditions. Today we have automatic pinsetters, automatic scorers, and smooth, well-balanced balls and pins. We bowl in air-conditioned centers amid attractive surroundings. Bowling is very popular with people of all ages.

▶EQUIPMENT FOR THE GAME

The basic idea of bowling is to roll a ball down a wooden lane and knock down the 10 pins set in a triangle. The American Bowling Congress sets the following standards for the equipment used in bowling tenpins.

The length of a bowling lane is 60 feet from the foul line to the head pin. The width of the lane is 42 inches, and the approach must be 15 feet from the rear edge to the foul line. Tenpins are 15 inches in height and must weigh not less than 3 pounds 6 ounces. The distance between pins set for play is 12 inches from center to center. A bowling ball cannot weigh more than 16 pounds. Its circumference must be 27 inches.

The correct clothing for bowling is important. Since the sport involves activity of the entire body, clothing should allow freedom of movement of arms, shoulders, and legs.

Special bowling shoes should be worn on the lanes. One of these shoes has a leather sole and one a rubber sole. The leather sole allows you to make the necessary slide on the last step of your approach. The rubber sole is used as a brake to control the slide. The shoes can be rented for a nominal fee. The use of a bowling ball is included in the price of the game.

FOUR-STEP APPROACH: (A) Face pins, holding ball just above waist. (B) Step 1, right foot, is short. Push ball forward smoothly. (C) Step 2 is a half step, ball passes right leg. (D) Ball is at top of backswing on a full-size Step 3. (E) On Step 4, left foot glides to foul line, ball is released well beyond foul line. (F) Follow through.

A three-finger ball, preferred by most bowlers, is especially recommended for beginners. Grip is very important. If the distance between the holes is too wide or too narrow, it strains or cramps the hand, reducing ball control. Bowling balls come in weights of 6 to 16 pounds. Use a ball weight with the right feel. Never use a ball that is too heavy, for it will tend to make you drop your shoulder and thus put you off balance before you release the ball. Start with a lightweight ball and gradually work up to the heavier weights.

▶THE FOUR-STEP APPROACH

The most popular style of bowling is called the four-step approach. Although five-step and three-step approaches are used, the four-step has proved to be the best for most bowlers.

Champions agree that every bowler eventually develops his or her own style, but for beginners the illustrated way to learn the four-step delivery is strongly recommended.

To determine where you should begin your approach, go to the foul line and place your left foot so that the toes are from 2 to 6 inches on the near side of the line. Then turn around, take one long step, one full step, one half step, and one small step. Again turn around and face the pins. This position indicates approxi-

mately where you should start your four-step delivery. If you are left-handed, start with your right foot on the near side of the line.

▶TIMING

To excel in bowling, as in other sports, you must develop good timing. For example, in baseball a batter will hit the ball far only if his bat connects with the pitched ball at exactly the right moment. If his timing is off, he will miss the ball or merely pop it to the infield.

In bowling, timing is equally important. It consists of the ability to co-ordinate the forward motion of your body with the pendulum swing of your arm. Develop your timing and your bowling scores should improve.

To understand better the value of timing, study some fast-action-sequence photographs of champion bowlers. Be sure to note the smooth, rhythmic flow of their delivery as ball and body work together.

▶CONVERTING SPARES

In each turn you are allowed to roll your ball at the pins twice if necessary. If you knock down all the pins on your first try, it is scored as a strike. If you knock down all 10 pins with two balls, it is scored as a spare. Spares are important in bowling, both to be-

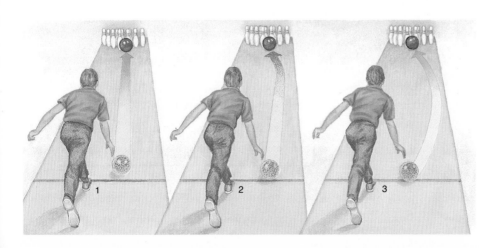

DELIVERING BALLS: (1) Straight: Thumb on top, fingers underneath. (2) Hook: Twist wrist left, remove thumb first, lift and spin with fingers. (3) Curve: Same as hook, less twist of wrist.

ginners and to expert bowlers. They can make the difference between a 190 and a 90 bowling average.

Spares fall into four categories: right-side spares; left-side spares; spares that can be converted with your strike ball; and splits, the most difficult spares. Study the illustrations that show how to convert spares—that is, to knock down all the pins that remain standing after your first bowl. In spare situations where your strike-ball delivery is required, you should take the position you normally apply to your first ball. Splits are very difficult, but with the proper determination and concentration, and confidence in your bowling style, you will find yourself converting more spares than you are missing.

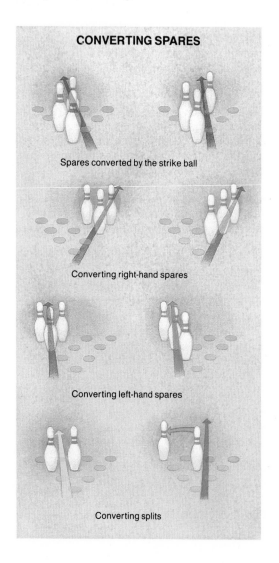

CONVERTING SPARES

Spares converted by the strike ball

Converting right-hand spares

Converting left-hand spares

Converting splits

▶HOW TO SCORE

A game consists of 10 frames. Each bowler rolls two balls per frame unless he strikes, which makes a second ball unnecessary. The symbols used for scoring are **X**, strike; **/**, spare; **—**, possible spare not converted; **O**, split that is difficult to convert; and **Ø**, split that has been converted.

For a strike a player receives 10 pins plus the total number of pins knocked down (called a **pinfall**) by his next two balls. A spare entitles a player to 10 plus a pinfall on the next ball. Now let us score a game you might bowl.

In the first frame you spare.

1	2	3	4	5	6	7	8	9	10
/									

In the second frame you roll your first ball into the pocket for a strike. This gives you 20 in the first (a spare in the first plus a pinfall on the next ball).

1	2	3	4	5	6	7	8	9	10
/	X								
20									

In the third frame you split, but you **bring in** (knock down) one with your second ball for a pinfall of 9. Score in the second is 39 (10 from a strike in the second plus a pinfall of the next two balls, added to the score in the first frame). Add your 9 for a third-frame total of 48.

1	2	3	4	5	6	7	8	9	10
/	X	O							
20	39	48							

In the fourth frame you strike.

1	2	3	4	5	6	7	8	9	10
/	X	O	X						
20	39	48							

In the fifth frame you strike. No score is recorded in either the fourth or fifth frame because for a strike you receive 10 pins plus the pinfalls of the next two balls.

1	2	3	4	5	6	7	8	9	10
/	X	O	X	X					
20	39	48							

In the sixth frame you bring in 8 on your first ball. You then knock down the two standing pins with your second ball for a spare. The score, which is 48 from the third, plus 10 for a strike in the fourth, plus 10 for a strike in the fifth, plus 8 for a pinfall of the first ball in the sixth, totals 76 in the fourth. Score in the fifth frame, which is 10, plus a pinfall from two balls in the sixth, which was 10, makes the total score 76 plus 20, which is 96.

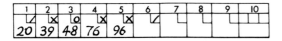

In the seventh frame you bring in 8 on your first ball, then miss two standing pins on your second ball. Score 96, plus 10, plus 8 pins on the first ball, giving you a score of 114 as of the sixth frame. Add 8 for a score of 122 in the seventh frame.

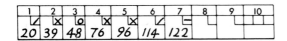

In the eighth frame you spare.

In the ninth frame you bring in 7 on your first ball and then knock down the 3 standing pins for a spare. Score 122, plus 10, plus 7, for a total of 139 in the eighth.

In the tenth frame you throw a strike, adding 10 pins to your spare and giving you a total of 159 points for the ninth frame. Striking in the tenth frame allows you to throw two more balls, of which you make good use and spare. To your 159 from the ninth frame you add 10 for your strike plus 10 for your extra two balls, giving you a final score of 179 for the game.

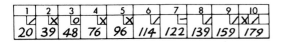

▶BOWLING ORGANIZATIONS AND COMPETITION

Bowling is played in more than 100 countries and in the Olympic Games. More than 10,000 bowling tournaments are conducted in the United States each year. There is competition for bowlers of all ages and all degrees of ability, from beginner to top professional. Prizes range from tiny 2-inch trophies to $250,000.

The Professional Bowlers Association sponsors more than 35 tournaments each year with over $6,000,000 in prizes. At most of these events, young amateur bowlers can compete with the pros in junior Pro-Am competitions. There is also a tournament circuit for a women's bowling association, the Ladies Pro Bowlers Tour (LPBT).

The American Bowling Congress (ABC) is the official organization for adult male bowlers. Standards set by the ABC govern all sanctioned bowling in North America and most of the world. The Women's International Bowling Congress is the counterpart of the ABC for adult women bowlers. The Young American Bowling Alliance regulates youth and collegiate bowling in the United States. All three organizations are headquartered in Greendale, Wisconsin. With more than 5,000 local associations, bowling is the largest organized competitive sport in the United States. There are more than 64,000,000 people who bowl in the country.

▶OTHER BOWLING GAMES

Germans of the Middle Ages played a game in which balls were rolled to knock over wooden clubs, or *kegels*. The players were called *keglers*. From Germany this game spread to other parts of Europe. Varying numbers of pins were used, but the most common game in Germany and Holland was (as it is today) ninepins. The pins were set up to form a diamond.

Early Dutch settlers in New York played ninepins. This is the game that made the sound of thunder Rip Van Winkle heard in the famous story by Washington Irving. By about 1840 ninepin bowling had become such a popular gambling game that some states actually issued laws against playing it. In order to get around the laws against playing ninepins, a tenth pin was added. The ploy was successful because tenpins is the most popular form of bowling in the United States today.

Fivepins is a favorite form of bowling in Canada. The pins, 12⅜ inches tall, are arranged in a V. Balls are 5 inches in diameter and weigh 3½ pounds. A bowler rolls three balls in each of the 10 frames.

Another bowling game, popular in New England and eastern Canada, is candlepins. It is played with long, tapering pins.

Skittles is a game sometimes confused with bowling. It is like ninepins but is played on a smaller scale and with disks instead of balls. The disks are tossed or slid toward the pins.

▶ **DUCKPINS**

Duckpins is a variation of bowling in which smaller pins and smaller balls are used. It is popular in the eastern part of the United States from New England to Baltimore, Maryland.

The game is played on a regulation bowling alley, but the ball used in duckpins is no more than 5 inches in diameter and weighs 3 pounds 12 ounces. It is completely smooth, without grooves for the player's fingers. The 10 bottle-shaped pins are $9^{13}/_{32}$ inches high. Some duckpins have a band of rubber around the middle, but the game using all-wooden pins is considered the real test of skill.

Each player bowls three balls in a frame, rather than two. Even though there are three chances to score in each frame, the total score is usually lower than in regular bowling because the ball is so much smaller and lighter.

In duckpins you hold the ball comfortably and firmly, but not very tightly. You must be able to let it go easily. The ball is rolled straight off the tips of the fingers, without any twisting motion. After the ball has been bowled, the back of your hand should be turned down.

▶ **BOWLS, OR LAWN BOWLING**

The game called bowls is the most popular form of bowling in Britain, Australia, New Zealand, and some other Commonwealth lands. In the United States and Canada, where it is also widely played, it is called lawn bowling, or bowling on the green, to avoid confusion with the tenpin game.

Bowls is usually played on a smooth, level grass court. The object is to roll balls, which are themselves called bowls, as close as possible to the jack, a white ball 2½ inches in diameter. Bowls are made of a composition material or very hard wood and weigh not more than 3½ pounds each. They are about 5 inches in diameter. One side of a bowl bulges less than the other, giving it what is called **bias.** This causes the bowl to lean to one side and curve as it loses rolling speed. A player can roll his bowl so that it will approach the jack in a curve from either side.

In singles or doubles games each player uses four bowls; in triples, three bowls. When full teams of four play, each person rolls two bowls. To start, the first player rolls the jack from a rubber mat at one end of the rink, a division of the green on which the game is played, at least 75 feet toward the other end. In team play two opposing players, called the leads, roll their bowls alternately. Then two other opposing players bowl. Last to bowl are the skips (captains) of the teams, who have been directing the play of their teammates. If a bowl touches the jack, it is marked with chalk to show that it is still alive, even if it goes into the ditch at the end of the rink. Any other bowl going into the ditch is out of play.

When all players have bowled, an end (inning) is over. The team that then has a bowl closest to the jack scores a point for every bowl that it has closer to the jack than the nearest of the opponents' bowls. (Each set of bowls has a special marking so they can be identified.) The players then bowl toward the opposite end of the rink, the side that scored last bowling first. A game consists of 21 points in singles, or in team play a number of ends (usually 21) agreed on at the start.

Similar games were played with balls of stone in very early times. One called "bowles" was popular in England in the 13th century or earlier. The bowls used were generally of wood, and by the 1500's they were made with bias. From England the game spread to Scotland and to the British colonies.

Bowls was played in Jamestown as early as 1611. It was also enjoyed by early New Yorkers in a small area at the lower end of Manhattan that is still called Bowling Green. Lawn bowling has grown in popularity in the United States in the present century. The American Lawn Bowling Association was formed in 1938.

ARTHUR K. SERBO
Brunswick Division, Brunswick Corporation

Reviewed by CHUCK PEZZANO
Author, *PBA Guide to Better Bowling;
Sports Illustrated Bowling*

Dempsey Through the Ropes (1924), by George W. Bellows, depicts 1923 heavyweight championship fight. Jack Dempsey climbed back into the ring to knock out Luis Firpo.

BOXING

Boxing is a sport in which two opponents battle (or fight) each other with their fists. Each boxer tries to score more points than his opponent by the intelligent use of skills in which he has been trained. In amateur boxing, especially, skill is more important than strength.

Boxers wear gloves made of soft leather padded with sponge rubber. Gloves usually weigh from 230 grams (8 ounces) to 280 grams (10 ounces). A boxer's hands are wrapped in soft cotton or linen for protection from the impact of his own blows. Amateur boxers may wear headgear to protect their heads and ears from injuries. All boxers use a rubber mouthpiece that helps prevent injuries to the lips and teeth.

The space in which a boxing match (bout) takes place is called a ring. It is generally 4.9 to 6.1 meters (16 to 20 feet) square, closed in by lengths of muslin-wrapped rope. The ropes are 0.6, 0.9, and 1.2 meters (2, 3, and 4 feet) above the floor of a platform on which the ring is mounted. A canvas floor covering is laid over thick padding. The cornerposts and turnbuckles that hold the ropes are also heavily padded.

The length of a round in most amateur boxing is 2 minutes or less. In professional and some international amateur bouts, a round is 3 minutes long. There is a 1-minute rest period between rounds. During this period the fighters go to corners of the ring opposite one another and are tended by their seconds. Most amateur matches are scheduled for three rounds. Professional championship bouts go as many as 15 rounds. A timekeeper marks the beginning and end of each round by sounding a bell, gong, or buzzer.

The referee is a very important third man in

the ring during a bout. He sees that the rules are obeyed and separates the boxers if they clinch one another. Blows below the beltline, on the kidneys, or on the back of the neck (rabbit punches) are fouls. So too are pushing or butting, or hitting an opponent when he is down (on the floor, getting up, or outside, between, or hanging helpless over the ropes).

If a fighter is knocked down, his opponent must go to a neutral corner—a corner of the ring not occupied by either fighter between rounds. The fighter who is down must get back on his feet within the ring before the referee counts to 10 at 1-second intervals. If he does not do this, his opponent is declared the winner by a knockout (KO). Until 1963, if a round ended before the count reached 10, the man who was down was said to have been "saved by the bell" because he could recover between rounds and continue. In 1963, though, the rules were changed. The count continues despite the bell and the fight can end if the count is completed. The count may not continue after the bell has sounded ending the final round. If a downed boxer gets up before the count of 10, he is usually forced to wait for a count of 8 before action can continue.

The referee is expected to stop a fight any time he feels that a boxer is too badly hurt to continue. A fight ended in this way is called a technical knockout (TKO). A physician must be on hand to determine whether an injured fighter should continue. It is also a TKO if a fighter is knocked down three times in one round. But this rule does not apply to professional championship bouts.

If there is no knockout, usually two judges and the referee decide the bout's winner on a basis of rounds won or points. They note how effectively each man punches his opponent, how well he defends himself, and how aggressive he is. They also allow for knockdowns and for fouls and such minor faults as hitting in a clinch. The decision may be based on the number of rounds won or on total points. In case of a tie, a bout is declared a draw.

▶ BOXING AS AMATEUR AND PROFESSIONAL SPORT

In boxing, as in any physical contact sport, there are bound to be injuries. In 1938 the Society of State Directors of Physical and Health Education adopted an official policy disapproving of boxing as an interscholastic sport. A few years later boxing was dropped from collegiate competition.

Supporters of amateur boxing claim that when it is conducted under proper rules and supervision, it is a safe competitive sport.

Many youth and athletic clubs provide instruction in basic boxing skills. They stress sound body condition, proper training, knowledge of the rules, and principles of fair play. They match only opponents of nearly equal size and experience.

Olympic and other amateur boxing competition around the world is governed by the International Amateur Boxing Federation. In the United States, the Amateur Athletic Union is the chief governing body. The Golden Gloves Association conducts amateur tournaments throughout the country, and the winners compete in national championships.

Professional boxers are those who fight for cash prizes. Their activity is regulated in the United States by the World Boxing Association (WBA) and the World Boxing Council (WBC) and various state and local commissions. Neither the WBA nor the WBC has the power to control boxing. They often disagree on which boxer is champion of his division. Professional boxing in Canada is regulated by the Canadian Professional Boxing Federation and by various provincial and local boards.

▶ BOXING PAST AND RECENT

The people of Sumer in ancient Mesotamia made many carvings in stone. Archeologists have found one of these that shows

---

BOXING WEIGHT LIMITS

	International	A.A.U. World Amateur	Professional
Light Flyweight	48 kg	106 lb	108 lb
Flyweight	51 kg	112 lb	112 lb
Bantamweight	54 kg	119 lb	118 lb
Junior Featherweight	55.5 kg	—	122 lb
Featherweight	57 kg	125 lb	126 lb
Junior Lightweight	59 kg	—	130 lb
Lightweight	60 kg	132 lb	135 lb
Light Welterweight	63.5 kg	139 lb	140 lb
Welterweight	67 kg	147 lb	147 lb
Light Middleweight	71 kg	156 lb	154 lb
Middleweight	75 kg	165 lb	160 lb
Light Heavyweight	81 kg	178 lb	175 lb
Heavyweight	Over 81 kg	Over 178 lb	Over 175 lb

In professional boxing, light welterweight is called junior welterweight, and light middleweight is called junior middleweight.

HEAVYWEIGHT CHAMPIONS *

1882–92	John L. Sullivan	1926–28	Gene Tunney	1951–52	Joe Walcott	1973–74	George Foreman
1892–97	James J. Corbett	1928–30	None	1952–56	Rocky Marciano	1974–78	Muhammad Ali
1897–99	Robert Fitzsimmons	1930–32	Max Schmeling	1956–59	Floyd Patterson	1978	Leon Spinks
1899–1905	James J. Jeffries	1932–33	Jack Sharkey	1959–60	Ingemar Johansson	1978–79	Muhammad Ali
1905–06	Marvin Hart	1933–34	Primo Carnera	1960–62	Floyd Patterson	1979–85	Larry Holmes
1906–08	Tommy Burns	1934–35	Max Baer	1962–64	Sonny Liston	1985–87	Michael Spinks
1908–15	Jack Johnson	1935–37	James J. Braddock	1964–67	Muhammad Ali	1987–90	Mike Tyson
1915–19	Jess Willard	1937–49	Joe Louis	1968–70	Disputed	1990	James (Buster) Douglas
1919–26	Jack Dempsey	1949–51	Ezzard Charles	1970–73	Joe Frazier	1990–	Evander Holyfield

*Various champions have been recognized by the World Boxing Association (WBA), World Boxing Council (WBC), and International Boxing Federation (IBF). Those listed are considered to have the best claims to the title.

two boxers in combat. Greek and Roman athletes fought with their hands wrapped in a kind of leather covering called a cestus. To this the ancient gladiators attached murderous metal studs or spikes. A Roman boxer was called a *pugil,* from which we get "pugilism," another name for boxing.

Revival in England. Little more is known about fistfighting until the 1600's. Then in England the name boxing was given to a contest in which men boxed, or beat, one another with their bare fists. In 1719, James Figg became the first British champion. Figg established a boxing school for young men in London, and interest in the sport spread quickly. Men often fought for prizes, hence the term "prizefighting." Jack Broughton, a champion from 1743 to 1750, drew up the first London Prize Ring Rules.

Boxers of the bareknuckle era stood toe to toe and wrestled, shoved, or struck each other until one man was knocked down. That marked the end of a round. After a brief rest the fight began again. When one man could no longer fight, his opponent was the victor. Many bouts lasted 50 rounds or more.

If a boxer's second, or assistant, in his corner decided to give up the match for his boxer, he could inform the referee by throwing a towel into the ring. From this practice comes the saying that a person who gives up some effort is "throwing in the towel."

In 1865 the Marquis of Queensberry drew up rules that are the basis for those in use today. The rules provided for 3-minute rounds with a 1-minute rest period between rounds. They required fighters to wear "fair-sized" boxing gloves, banned wrestling holds, and set the 10-second count for a knockout. With the adoption of the Queensberry rules, boxing gradually became acceptable in the United

States, where prizefighting had been illegal. Heavyweight bouts were the most popular.

The Modern Era. In 1892, John L. Sullivan, the last of the bareknuckle champions, was defeated by James J. (Gentleman Jim) Corbett in the first heavyweight title bout fought with gloves under the Queensberry rules. Two other great heavyweight champions of the early modern era were James J. Jeffries, who retired undefeated in 1905, and Jack Johnson, who became the first black champion in 1908.

William Harrison (Jack) Dempsey launched the "golden age" of boxing by knocking out Jess Willard in 1919. His bouts began to draw huge crowds. James J. (Gene) Tunney won the title from Dempsey in 1926 before 120,000 onlookers. The next year Dempsey knocked Tunney down in the seventh round; but because Dempsey did not go at once to a neutral corner as he should have, the referee did not start the count for several seconds. Tunney got to his feet at the famous "long count" of 9 and went on to win by a decision.

Joe Louis knocked out James J. Braddock in 1937 to capture the heavyweight crown. Louis went on to a brilliant career with knockout after knockout. He retired in 1949, unbeaten in 26 title bouts. In 1950 Louis tried to regain the championship but lost.

Rocky Marciano retired undefeated as champion in 1956. Floyd Patterson became champion that year but lost to Ingemar Johansson in 1959. Patterson then knocked out Johansson in 1960 to become the first modern heavyweight to regain the title.

Muhammad Ali first captured the heavyweight crown in 1964. In 1967, following his refusal to serve in the armed forces, Ali was stripped of his title. He regained the championship in 1974 by knocking out George Foreman. Leon Spinks won the crown from Ali in

1978. Later that year, Ali defeated Spinks and became the first man to win the heavyweight title three times. During the 1980's the heavyweight division was dominated largely by Larry Holmes and Mike Tyson. In 1990, Tyson lost the title on a surprise KO by James (Buster) Douglas, who then lost it to Evander Holyfield.

There have been notable champions in other weight classes too. Lightweights Joe Gans (1902–08) and Benny Leonard (1917–25) are two of boxing's greats. Henry Armstrong was the first boxer to win three titles, featherweight, lightweight, and welterweight (1937–38). Sugar Ray Robinson held the middleweight title five times (1951–1960) and was welterweight champ (1946–51). Rivals Willie Pep and Sandy Saddler ruled the featherweight class (1946–57). Roberto Durán won lightweight, welterweight, and junior middleweight titles (between 1972 and 1984). Sugar Ray Leonard held welterweight, junior middleweight, middleweight, super middleweight, and light heavyweight championships.

ROCKY MARCIANO
Former World Heavyweight Boxing Champion
Updated by BILL BRADDOCK
The New York Times

BOYLE, ROBERT (1627–1691)

Robert Boyle was a self-taught scientist who during the 1600's carried out experiments that helped to found modern chemistry and modern physics. Boyle was born on January 25, 1627, at Lismore Castle in Ireland. His father was a wealthy, land-owning Englishman who had been made Earl of Cork. Robert was the 7th son and 14th child in a family of 15 children.

An unusually bright child, Robert went to Eton, the famous boys' school, at the age of 8. When he was 11, he went abroad with a tutor. He spent most of the next six years in Switzerland and Italy. During this time Boyle developed an interest in science and began to study the works of Galileo.

When his father died, Robert Boyle inherited a rich estate in England. In 1644 he returned there. He was now in a position to do anything he wanted. Having what he called "an unsatisfied appetite for knowledge," he decided to explore the unknowns of science. Since there were no textbooks and few teachers, Boyle had to proceed on his own. He set up a laboratory and worked alone, but hired assistants when he needed help. One assistant was Robert Hooke, who became an important scientist himself.

Boyle investigated questions in biology, chemistry, and physics. He studied how animals breathe and how blood circulates. He showed how matter burns, boils, and freezes. His investigations ranged from the barometer and crystals to light and sound. The results of these experiments are no longer important. What matters is that Boyle was among the first to use careful scientific methods.

Boyle's work with the air pump is probably best known. The pump was a new device that could both compress air and produce near vacuums. With it Boyle could control the quantity of air in a closed container. His experiments demonstrated the role of air in burning, breathing, and sound. During these experiments Boyle discovered that when pressure on a given quantity of air is increased, the volume of air becomes smaller. This finding became the basis of what is now known as Boyle's law: If the temperature and quantity of a gas remain constant, the volume varies inversely with the pressure.

At this time other people were becoming active in scientific research. By 1645 Boyle had begun to meet with some of these scientists in London. Out of these meetings grew the Royal Society, which is still one of the world's leading organizations for the encouragement of science.

Boyle was a deeply religious man. He learned Greek and Hebrew so that he could read the Bible in the original. He wrote books on religious matters. He spent great sums of money to have the Bible translated, and he supported missionary work abroad.

Boyle never married. He tended to be sickly, but his interest in science was so strong that he worked steadily almost until his death, on December 30, 1691.

JOHN S. BOWMAN
Author and Science Editor

BOYS' CLUBS

Boys' Clubs is one of many organizations that offer a wide range of programs and activities to young people in the United States and Canada. But several key factors make Boys' Clubs specially suited to the needs of boys living in cities today.

Many young people dream of having a place of their own. And that is what a Boys' Club is—an actual building devoted to the needs of boys 7 through 20 years of age. A Boys' Club is equipped for educational, vocational, social, cultural, and recreational activities. And it is open whenever boys need a friendly atmosphere for having fun—every weekday after school and all day on Saturdays.

Every Boys' Club provides full-time professional adult leadership and guidance to all its members. These professionals are at the club every day. They are trained to listen to the boys' problems and offer help and advice.

▶ NATIONAL PROGRAMS

Many programs run by local Boys' Clubs are based on major projects developed by the Boys' Clubs of America national headquarters in New York City. The aim of the National Education and Services Project is to improve health services for children in low-income communities. The project makes medical examinations available to all club members. A follow-up by staff members ensures proper treatment for ailments. There are health education courses for both boys and parents.

Other national projects include programs in prevention of alcohol abuse (Project TEAM —"Teens Explore Alcohol Moderation"), juvenile justice and prevention of delinquency, education for family life (HAK—"Help-A-Kid"), and youth employment ("World of Work"). Several programs involve local Boys' Clubs with the national headquarters on a year-round basis. The Epstein Memorial Foundation raises money to help fund studies for club members who show promise in the fine arts.

The National Association of Keystone Clubs is a citizenship organization within Boys' Clubs. It offers teenage members opportunities in community and club service, fund raising, and the planning of social events. The Boy of the Year program honors outstanding mem-

Boys' Clubs offer a variety of recreational, educational, and social activities, such as guitar lessons.

bers of all Boys' Clubs. The top five finalists meet the president of the United States at the White House.

Individual Boys' Clubs run many day-to-day activities that depend on the interests of members, the location of the club, the size of the staff, and other factors. The activities include arts and crafts, mechanics, music, sports, swimming, cooking, and camping.

▶ ALUMNI

The alumni of the Boys' Clubs of America include sports figures O. J. Simpson and Joe DiMaggio; songwriter Neil Diamond; actors Sylvester Stallone and Telly Savalas; concert pianist Emanuel Ax; comedian Bill Cosby; and U.S. Senator Abraham Ribicoff. Thousands of other former Boys' Club members are now doctors, lawyers, members of the clergy, government officials, civil servants, and businessmen. Many of these leaders have credited their Boys' Club experiences with helping to start them on successful lives.

Today over 1,100 Boys' Clubs in more than 700 communities are serving 1,000,000 boys. Since the founding of the first Boys' Club in 1860, the movement has grown tremendously. The national organization of the Boys' Clubs of America was founded in 1906 and was chartered by Congress in 1956.

The headquarters of the Boys' Clubs of America are located in New York City. The national organization continues to work with local communities across the country, reaching more and more young people as new branches are opened.

EVAN T. MCELROY
Boys' Clubs of America

Camping is one of the many ways in which Boy Scouts work and play to develop mental and physical fitness. Approximately 16,000,-000 Scouts and leaders participate in Boy Scout programs throughout the world.

BOY SCOUTS

Not long ago, a 12-year-old Boy Scout was leaving a tidal pool when he saw two small children bobbing helplessly in the water. The Scout rescued the children from the pool and began mouth-to-mouth resuscitation. One child began to breathe, but the other did not. The Scout instructed people on the beach to continue working on the second child while he called for an ambulance. Both children lived, thanks to the Scout's actions.

This is but one of hundreds of real cases in which Boy Scouts have saved lives by using the skills they learned in Scout training. This worldwide organization teaches young men leadership and good citizenship. It teaches them the skills that enable them to live up to their Scout motto, ''Be prepared.''

Boys get much more from Scouting besides training for emergencies. They find fun and fellowship with other boys and the men who lead them. They find adventure in hiking, camping, boating, and other outdoor sports. They gain useful knowledge and skills and have many chances to take part in the life of their community and nation.

▶THE BOY SCOUTS OF AMERICA

The Boy Scouts of America has more than 5,000,000 members. The organization provides a long-term program for a boy from the time he enters the first grade until his 21st birthday. In the first grade, a boy may become a Tiger Cub; in the second grade a Cub Scout; at age 11 a Boy Scout; and at age 14 a Varsity Scout or Explorer.

Tiger Cubs

Introduced by the Boy Scouts of America in 1982, the Tiger Cub program is for boys in the first grade. They join with an adult partner, usually a parent, and they participate together in a program of activities and fun with the family and as part of a Tiger Cub group. Group leadership is shared among all of the adult partners.

Tiger Cub Promise: ''I promise to love God, my family, and my country, and to learn about the world.''

Tiger Cub Motto: ''Search, discover, share.''

Cub Scouts

Cub Scouting is a program for boys in second through fifth grades.

Many of a Cub Scout's activities and achievements take place in the home with the encouragement of adults in the household. He starts out as a Bobcat. By completing twelve achievements, he earns his Wolf Badge. Then, for earning credits in a variety of activities of his choice, he receives arrow points to wear below his badge. When he completes the second grade (or is 9 years old), he begins to work for the Bear rank. On completion of the third grade (or when he is 10 years old), he may join a Webelos den and earn the Webelos badge and the highest Cub Scout award, the Arrow of Light. Webelos activity badges are awarded for learning special skills. "Webelos" stands for "*We*'ll *Be Lo*yal *S*couts."

A Cub Scout belongs to a den with boys from his neighborhood. The den meets each week under the guidance of its adult den leader, who is helped by a Boy Scout called the den chief. Several dens make up a Cub pack, which has an adult leader called the Cubmaster. The pack meets once a month, often in the form of a group outing.

The Cub Scout uniform is dark blue with yellow trim. A different color neckerchief is worn by the Cub Scout to designate his grade or age. Yellow indicates second grade; blue, third grade; and plaid, fourth- and fifth-grade Webelos Scouts.

Cub Scout Motto: "Do your best."

Cub Scout Promise: "I, [name], promise to do my best to do my duty to God and my country, to help other people, and to obey the Law of the Pack."

Law of the Pack: "The Cub Scout follows Akela. The Cub Scout helps the pack go. The pack helps the Cub Scout grow. The Cub Scout gives goodwill." ("Akela" means "good leader.")

Boy Scouts

A boy may become a Boy Scout at age 11. By understanding the Scout Oath and Law and by passing a few simple tests, he may join and be called a Boy Scout. Skill awards and merit badges lead him on to Tenderfoot, Second Class, and then on to First Class rank. Scouts may earn merit badges in any of more than 100 different fields. Certain merit badges help him achieve the ranks of Star (6 merit badges), Life (11), and Eagle Scout (21), the highest rank in Scouting.

SCOUT UNIFORMS, INSIGNIA, AND BADGES

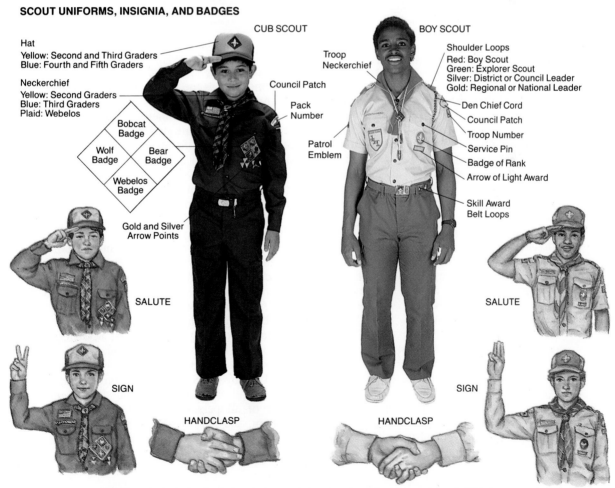

Scouts wear insignia showing their rank, den or patrol, and service and achievement awards. Webelos Scouts may wear blue or khaki and tan uniforms.

A Scout must earn a number of awards, or merit badges, in order to qualify for each new rank. The colorful badges can be earned in many different subject areas.

A small group of Boy Scouts forms a patrol. Several patrols make up a troop. The troop usually meets once a week with its adult leader, the Scoutmaster. Hiking and camping are part of the adventure that Scouts enjoy. They learn how to take care of themselves in the open and how to help others in case of accidents. They also learn to be useful citizens.

Scout Oath or Promise: "On my honor I will do my best to do my duty to God and my country and to obey the Scout Law; to help other people at all times; to keep myself physically strong, mentally awake, and morally straight."

Scout Motto: "Be prepared."

Scout Slogan: "Do a good turn daily."

Scout Law: A Scout is trustworthy, loyal, helpful, friendly, courteous, kind, obedient, cheerful, thrifty, brave, clean, and reverent.

Varsity Scouting

Varsity Scouting is a new Boy Scouts of America program for young men 14 through 17 years of age. It is the "varsity" of Boy Scouting, just as the varsity is the senior team in school sports.

Varsity Scouts are members of a Varsity Scout team. They are under the leadership of an adult Varsity Scout coach. The youth leader of the team is the Varsity Scout team captain. There are youth squad leaders and a youth program manager for each of the five program fields of emphasis.

The fields of interest—advancement, high adventure, personal development, service, and special programs—challenge a young man to use the basic skills learned in Boy Scouting. Participation in Varsity Scout activities and requirements lead to earning the Varsity Scout letter. Advancement toward the Eagle Scout rank is continued in Varsity Scouting.

Varsity Scouting ideals are the Scout Oath or Promise, Law, Motto, and Slogan.

Varsity Scout Pledge: "As a Varsity Scout, I will: Live by the Scout Oath (Promise), Law, Motto, and Slogan; Honor the dignity and worth of all persons; Promote the cause of freedom; and Do my best to be a good team member."

Landscape Architecture · Law · Leatherwork · Lifesaving · Machinery · Mammal Study · Masonry · Metals Engineering · Metalwork · Model Design and Building

Motorboating · Music · Nature · Oceanography · Orienteering · Painting · Personal Fitness · Personal Management · Pets · Photography

Pioneering · Plant Science · Plumbing · Pottery · Public Health · Public Speaking · Pulp and Paper · Rabbit Raising · Radio · Railroading

Reading · Reptile Study · Rifle Shooting · Rowing · Safety · Salesmanship · Scholarship · Sculpture · Shotgun Shooting · Signaling

Skating · Skiing · Small-Boat Sailing · Soil and Water Conservation · Space Exploration · Sports · Stamp Collecting · Surveying · Swimming · Textile

Theater · Traffic Safety · Truck Transportation · Veterinary Science · Waterskiing · Weather · Whitewater · Wilderness Survival · Wood Carving · Woodwork

Exploring

Exploring is a division of the Boy Scouts of America for young men and women from high school age to 21. Young adults—and they need not have been Scouts—may join a general- or special-interest Explorer post or Sea Explorer ship. Exploring offers a choice of activities and a chance for adventure, career experience, education, and recreation. Explorers plan their own programs with the help of an adult adviser or skipper. Young women became full members in 1971.

More than half of all posts are organized around a career interest such as law enforcement, medicine, banking, space exploration, computer programming, or other occupation.

▶THE BOY SCOUT ORGANIZATION

There are about 16,000,000 Scouts and leaders in the world today. They are found in 116 countries. They have different uniforms, badges, and customs, but their aims and ideals are alike. The motto ''Be prepared'' is known in many languages. The headquarters of the Boy Scouts World Bureau is in Geneva, Switzerland.

World jamborees are held every four years. These are huge camps that bring Scouts from many nations together in friendship. The first world jamboree was held in England in 1920. Many countries also hold national jamborees. The Boy Scouts of America held its first jamboree in 1937. Canada held its first in 1949.

United States

The National Council of the Boy Scouts of America is made up of representatives who come from more than 400 local councils across the country. This body elects an Executive Board, which is the governing body of the Boy Scouts of America. The national office is in Irving, Texas. A full-time staff, headed by the Chief Scout Executive, publishes handbooks and magazines for boys and leaders and prepares video and other materials for training leaders. It also controls the manufacture and sale of uniforms and equipment through local Scouting distributors.

The staff of the national organization provides assistance to local councils made up of volunteers who offer to help Scouting in a city, county, or larger area. The council must have, among other things, a camp for its members. A small group of professional Scouting administrators work full time in local councils.

Scouting reaches boys and young men and young women through churches, schools, and other organizations. Each group that receives a charter to operate a troop or other Scouting unit offers a meeting place, good leaders, and other needed support.

Although uniforms and customs in different countries may vary, the aims of Scouting are alike worldwide. Here a group of Canadian Wolf Cubs enjoy a fishing trip.

Today there is an active interest in Scouting in the inner cities. Many city youngsters join Scouting for the outdoor activities it offers, such as camping and water-safety programs.

Scouting for the Handicapped. Today more than 213,000 physically or mentally disabled Scouts are active in various programs throughout the United States. Anyone who has been certified as disabled by a proper medical authority may enroll in Scouting and remain in its program beyond the regulation age limits. This provision allows all members to advance in Scouting as far as they wish.

Canada

The first Scout troop in Canada was formed in 1908. Six years later the Canadian General Council of the Boy Scouts Association was formed by an act of Parliament. In 1961 this name was changed to Boy Scouts of Canada. Today there are more than 300,000 Canadian Scouts and leaders.

The Boy Scouts of Canada principles are:
"Man must, to the best of his ability,
"Love and serve God;
"Respect and act in accordance with the human dignity and rights of individuals;
"Recognize the obligation on himself to develop and maintain his potential."

Canadian Scouts are divided into five age groups: (1) Beavers, age 5 to 7; (2) Wolf Cubs, 8 to 10; (3) Boy Scouts, 11 to 13; (4) Venturers, 14 to 16; and (5) Rovers, young men and women 17 to 26 years old.

▶HISTORY OF SCOUTING

Boy Scouting was started by Robert Stephenson Smyth Baden-Powell, an Englishman born in 1857. As an army officer, Baden-Powell made up many training games and contests, which he later described in a book called *Aids to Scouting*. He became a hero during the Boer War in South Africa and, at 43, became Britain's youngest major general.

On his return to England, he was surprised to find that some leaders of boys had started using his scouting games and contests. He was asked to work out a program of scouting more directly suited to the needs of boys. He began to think of scouting as a game with a goal, so his program was built around the high ideals of the Scout Promise and Law. With Baden-Powell's handbook, *Scouting for Boys* (1908), to guide them, troops of Boy Scouts began to spring up in many other countries.

In 1910, Baden-Powell, Chief Scout of the world, retired from the Army to give all his time to Scouting. He died in Kenya in 1941.

Shortly after the Scouting movement started in Britain, William D. Boyce, a Chicago publisher, became lost one day in a London fog. An English Scout helped him find the address he was looking for, and this led Boyce to become interested in Scouting. On February 8, 1910, he founded the Boy Scouts of America.

Reviewed by BOY SCOUTS OF AMERICA

BRACES, DENTAL. See ORTHODONTICS.

BRAHE, TYCHO (1546–1601)

Tycho Brahe, the great Danish astronomer, was born into an aristocratic family on December 14, 1546. Early in life Tycho decided to become an astronomer. His family disapproved strongly because in those days this was not considered a suitable profession for an aristocrat.

Tycho's early years were spent in the village of Knudstrup, which then belonged to Denmark but is now part of Sweden. In 1559 he entered the University of Copenhagen. While he was there an eclipse took place, as predicted by astronomers. There is a story that this so impressed him that he decided to become an astronomer. At any rate, he did begin to study astronomy and mathematics.

Three years later his family sent him to study law in Leipzig, Germany. Tycho continued to study astronomy in secret. He bought a fist-size globe of the heavens, carried it around with him, and in a month's time had learned all the constellations.

Tycho was not only stubborn but also hot-tempered and arrogant, and he made a number of enemies during his life. In his student years he fought a duel with another young nobleman, who cut off part of his nose. Tycho replaced it with one of gold and silver.

When Tycho returned to Denmark, he set up quarters in an uncle's castle and began his study of the heavens. He used only his eyes, for the telescope had not yet been invented. There, in 1572, he became the first Western astronomer to sight a supernova—an old star that suddenly becomes brilliant because it has exploded. The star was in the constellation of Cassiopeia.

In 1573 Tycho published his observations of the star. That year he also married a peasant girl. Neither of these acts won the approval of his family.

His growing fame as an astronomer drew the attention of King Frederick II of Denmark. To make sure Tycho stayed in Denmark, the King built him an observatory, called Uraniborg, and paid him a salary. Here for 21 years Tycho taught, wrote, studied the heavens, and made astronomical instruments. Night after night he studied the sky, recording the stars and the movements of the planets.

During these years Tycho made many ene-

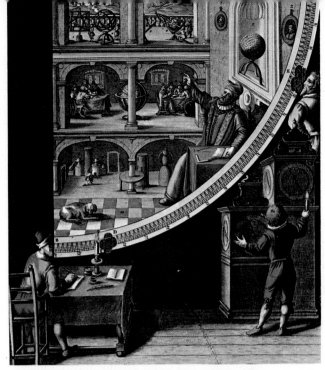

Engraving (1587) shows Tycho in his observatory on the island of Ven, off the southwest coast of Sweden. There was no telescope, since it had not yet been invented.

mies. One result was that when Frederick II died, the new king took away Tycho's observatory and stopped his salary.

Tycho left Denmark. He spent 2 years at universities in Germany. Then, in 1599, the Holy Roman Emperor, Rudolph II, invited Tycho to Prague. There he installed all his instruments from Uraniborg in a castle. In 1600 he hired as his assistant a young German astronomer, Johannes Kepler, who later became famous himself. A year later, on October 24, 1601, Tycho died.

Tycho's great work was completed by Kepler. This was the publication of the Rudolphine tables. The tables summed up Tycho's observations of the positions of the fixed stars and of the motions of the sun, moon, and planets. Working without a telescope and with only the simplest of instruments, Tycho had recorded the positions of 777 fixed stars.

Tycho himself believed that the earth was the center of the universe. The sun, he thought, revolved around the earth, and the other planets around the sun. Yet his careful observations laid the groundwork for men like Kepler, who revealed the true nature of the solar system.

JOHN S. BOWMAN
Author and Science Editor

BRAHMS, JOHANNES (1833–1897)

Johannes Brahms, the son of a poor musician, was born on May 7, 1833, in Hamburg, Germany. With his sister and younger brother, he grew up in the slums of the city. His mother, a major influence in his life, encouraged him in his studies.

At a very early age Brahms showed that he had unusual musical ability. When he was 13, he began to help his family by playing the piano in taverns and restaurants of the city. Two years later, already well known for his skill at the keyboard, he gave a public recital. By the time he was 16, Brahms decided that his chief interest was composing music rather than performing it.

When he was 20, Brahms met Joseph Joachim, the great violinist, and they became lifelong friends. Through Joachim, Brahms met Robert and Clara Schumann, who immediately recognized his talent as a composer.

In 1853 Schumann wrote a famous magazine article entitled "New Paths" in which he hailed Brahms as the coming genius of German music. Aside from being a great composer, Schumann had great influence as a music critic, and his praise of Brahms helped the young composer become better known.

Brahms's native city failed to appreciate his talents, so he went to Vienna in September, 1862, to try his success. Except for conducting engagements, Brahms lived in Vienna for the rest of his life.

The Viennese quickly accepted him for his musical ability, and he soon won an appointment as a choral conductor. After his mother died in 1865, Brahms composed the *German Requiem,* which brought him widespread recognition as a composer. From 1872 to 1875 Brahms was musical director of the famed Viennese Society of the Friends of Music. Brahms, a shy and modest man, lived a simple life in a two-room apartment, content with the companionship of musical friends.

In the later part of his life, Brahms's fame as a composer spread throughout Europe. In 1876 his first symphony, which he had started to work on 22 years before, was finally performed. Three years later Brahms introduced his violin concerto, a tribute to his friend Joachim, who gave the first public performance of the work. The great second piano concerto was finished in 1881, and in 1885 Brahms completed the fourth and last of his symphonies.

For the last 12 years of his life Brahms concentrated on chamber music, compositions for the piano, and songs. His daily life fell into the comfortable routine of the confirmed bachelor. All of Vienna knew and loved him, and his favorite restaurant, The Red Hedgehog, became a center of musical society. The concerto for violin and cello of 1887 was his last orchestral work. Two years later his native city, Hamburg, finally gave Brahms full recognition, and at the age of 56 he received the Honorary Freedom of the City.

In 1894 Brahms was offered the post he had wanted all his life, conductor of the Hamburg Philharmonic Orchestra. But Brahms felt he was too old for the position and declined the offer. He took satisfaction, however, in the many festivals dedicated to his music. When his final illness began in 1896, Brahms faced it calmly, feeling that his life's work had been completed with success. He died on April 3, 1897.

Reviewed by KARL GEIRINGER
Author, *Johannes Brahms*

Johannes Brahms in his home in Vienna.

BRAIN

The brain is the master organ for control and communication within the body. And it is the master organ for communication between the body and its surroundings. It is an important part of the nervous system and is found in all but the most primitive animals.

In a way the brain is unlike any other organ of the body. The brain alone receives, handles, and sends out information.

Flowing into every brain is a never-ending stream of signals carrying sensory (from the senses) information about the world outside the body and about the inside of the body. The brain turns this into another stream of signals, which are commands. This new information is then sent to the muscles and glands by nerves that connect the brain to the rest of the body.

The total complex pattern of activity in muscles and glands of an animal is what we call its **behavior**. Therefore, the brain is responsible for behavior. The different types of behavior that we see in various animals are partly the result of differences in brain structure and organization.

One-celled organisms, such as the amoeba, do not have a nervous system or a brain. (However, they can and do react to stimuli such as light, heat, and food.) Simple, many-celled animals, like sea anemones, have a primitive nervous system. But they have no real brain. That is, they have nerves that connect various parts of the body, but they lack the central grouping of cells that forms a brain.

Larger and more complicated animals have a greater need for an organ to control the activities of the body. In general, therefore, more highly developed animals have more highly developed brains.

No two animals ever have exactly identical brains. But related species may have brains that are much alike. Though there are countless species of insects, their brains share many common features. All fish have similar brains. And because fish, amphibians, reptiles, birds, and humans are distantly related, their brains are basically organized in much the same way.

▶ THE BASIC FEATURES OF A BRAIN

In spite of their great differences, all brains have some features in common.

(1) All brains are composed of nerve cells, or **neurons**.

(2) All brains have at least three major sections: a **sensory section**, which supplies the information on which the brain acts; an **integrating** (putting together) **section**, where the incoming information is processed; and a

All these animals have simple nervous systems, made up of nerves that connect various parts of the body. In addition, the crayfish, earthworm, and planarian have central groups of nerve cells that make up primitive brains.

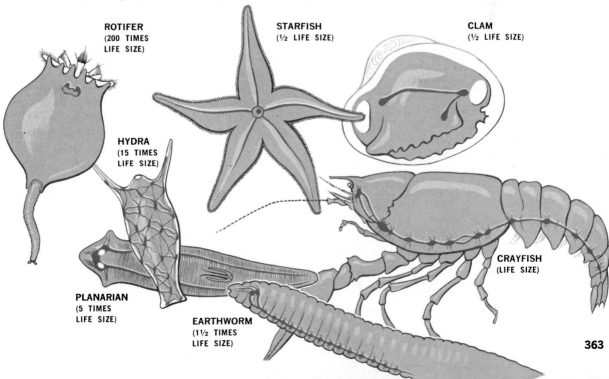

ROTIFER
(200 TIMES
LIFE SIZE)

STARFISH
(½ LIFE SIZE)

CLAM
(½ LIFE SIZE)

HYDRA
(15 TIMES
LIFE SIZE)

PLANARIAN
(5 TIMES
LIFE SIZE)

EARTHWORM
(1½ TIMES
LIFE SIZE)

CRAYFISH
(LIFE SIZE)

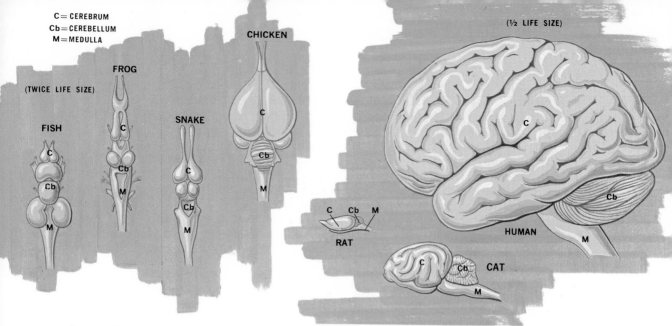

C = CEREBRUM
Cb = CEREBELLUM
M = MEDULLA

(½ LIFE SIZE)

CHICKEN

FROG

(TWICE LIFE SIZE)

FISH

SNAKE

RAT

HUMAN

CAT

In general, the cerebrum, or forebrain, increases in size as it goes up the evolutionary scale, through fish, frog, snake, bird. The cat's cerebrum is bigger than the rat's and more wrinkled. This means that more nerve cells are crowded together at the surface. The human brain is the most complex.

motor section, which generates the final output signals to muscles and glands.

The overall function of the brain, which we see as behavior, is determined by two things: the precise way in which these three divisions are connected and the presence (or absence) of other special brain centers.

To understand the operation of the brain as a whole, you must first know something about the nerve cells themselves and how they are combined into systems.

The Neuron

Primitive brains, such as those found in snails and their relatives, may consist of only a few thousand nerve cells, or **neurons**. In the human brain the number of neurons is probably around 10,000,000,000 (billion).

Although usually too small to be seen without a microscope, each neuron is itself a tiny communication system. A typical neuron is made up of a central part, or **cell body**. The cell body has a nucleus within it, and it may have many threadlike branching parts, like the branches of a tree. These are called **dendrites**, from a word meaning "tree." The dendrites carry signals arriving from other neurons. When certain sets of signals arrive in a nerve cell, the cell becomes active.

The remarkable fact about nerve cells is that when they become active, they produce a tiny, brief, electrical signal. This pulselike electrical signal travels along a main branch leaving the cell; this branch is called the **axon**. On reaching the next cell, the signal does one of two things. Either it causes other cells to relay the signal onward (by causing them to generate their own pulses) or it causes the neurons to stop firing pulses.

The axons and dendrites act very much like wires that carry electrical signals. The particular pattern of pulses streaming along the axon makes up the "message" sent on by the cell. Each cell may fire hundreds of pulses each second, because each one lasts only a small fraction of a second. The pulses travel

Delicate, threadlike dendrites pick up incoming pulses and pass them to the cell body. When a particular set of signals arrives, cell becomes active and pulses are sent out along axon.

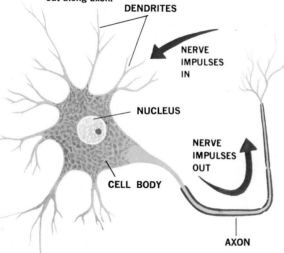

DENDRITES

NERVE IMPULSES IN

NUCLEUS

NERVE IMPULSES OUT

CELL BODY

AXON

Landscape Architecture | Law | Leatherwork | Lifesaving | Machinery | Mammal Study | Masonry | Metals Engineering | Metalwork | Model Design and Building

Motorboating | Music | Nature | Oceanography | Orienteering | Painting | Personal Fitness | Personal Management | Pets | Photography

Pioneering | Plant Science | Plumbing | Pottery | Public Health | Public Speaking | Pulp and Paper | Rabbit Raising | Radio | Railroading

Reading | Reptile Study | Rifle Shooting | Rowing | Safety | Salesmanship | Scholarship | Sculpture | Shotgun Shooting | Signaling

Skating | Skiing | Small-Boat Sailing | Soil and Water Conservation | Space Exploration | Sports | Stamp Collecting | Surveying | Swimming | Textile

Theater | Traffic Safety | Truck Transportation | Veterinary Science | Waterskiing | Weather | Whitewater | Wilderness Survival | Wood Carving | Woodwork

Exploring

Exploring is a division of the Boy Scouts of America for young men and women from high school age to 21. Young adults—and they need not have been Scouts—may join a general- or special-interest Explorer post or Sea Explorer ship. Exploring offers a choice of activities and a chance for adventure, career experience, education, and recreation. Explorers plan their own programs with the help of an adult adviser or skipper. Young women became full members in 1971.

More than half of all posts are organized around a career interest such as law enforcement, medicine, banking, space exploration, computer programming, or other occupation.

▶THE BOY SCOUT ORGANIZATION

There are about 16,000,000 Scouts and leaders in the world today. They are found in 116 countries. They have different uniforms, badges, and customs, but their aims and ideals are alike. The motto "Be prepared" is known in many languages. The headquarters of the Boy Scouts World Bureau is in Geneva, Switzerland.

World jamborees are held every four years. These are huge camps that bring Scouts from many nations together in friendship. The first world jamboree was held in England in 1920. Many countries also hold national jamborees. The Boy Scouts of America held its first jamboree in 1937. Canada held its first in 1949.

United States

The National Council of the Boy Scouts of America is made up of representatives who come from more than 400 local councils across the country. This body elects an Executive Board, which is the governing body of the Boy Scouts of America. The national office is in Irving, Texas. A full-time staff, headed by the Chief Scout Executive, publishes handbooks and magazines for boys and leaders and prepares video and other materials for training leaders. It also controls the manufacture and sale of uniforms and equipment through local Scouting distributors.

The staff of the national organization provides assistance to local councils made up of volunteers who offer to help Scouting in a city, county, or larger area. The council must have, among other things, a camp for its members. A small group of professional Scouting administrators work full time in local councils.

Scouting reaches boys and young men and young women through churches, schools, and other organizations. Each group that receives a charter to operate a troop or other Scouting unit offers a meeting place, good leaders, and other needed support.

Although uniforms and customs in different countries may vary, the aims of Scouting are alike worldwide. Here a group of Canadian Wolf Cubs enjoy a fishing trip.

Today there is an active interest in Scouting in the inner cities. Many city youngsters join Scouting for the outdoor activities it offers, such as camping and water-safety programs.

Scouting for the Handicapped. Today more than 213,000 physically or mentally disabled Scouts are active in various programs throughout the United States. Anyone who has been certified as disabled by a proper medical authority may enroll in Scouting and remain in its program beyond the regulation age limits. This provision allows all members to advance in Scouting as far as they wish.

Canada

The first Scout troop in Canada was formed in 1908. Six years later the Canadian General Council of the Boy Scouts Association was formed by an act of Parliament. In 1961 this name was changed to Boy Scouts of Canada. Today there are more than 300,000 Canadian Scouts and leaders.

The Boy Scouts of Canada principles are:
"Man must, to the best of his ability,
"Love and serve God;
"Respect and act in accordance with the human dignity and rights of individuals;
"Recognize the obligation on himself to develop and maintain his potential."

Canadian Scouts are divided into five age groups: (1) Beavers, age 5 to 7; (2) Wolf Cubs, 8 to 10; (3) Boy Scouts, 11 to 13; (4) Venturers, 14 to 16; and (5) Rovers, young men and women 17 to 26 years old.

▶HISTORY OF SCOUTING

Boy Scouting was started by Robert Stephenson Smyth Baden-Powell, an Englishman born in 1857. As an army officer, Baden-Powell made up many training games and contests, which he later described in a book called *Aids to Scouting*. He became a hero during the Boer War in South Africa and, at 43, became Britain's youngest major general.

On his return to England, he was surprised to find that some leaders of boys had started using his scouting games and contests. He was asked to work out a program of scouting more directly suited to the needs of boys. He began to think of scouting as a game with a goal, so his program was built around the high ideals of the Scout Promise and Law. With Baden-Powell's handbook, *Scouting for Boys* (1908), to guide them, troops of Boy Scouts began to spring up in many other countries.

In 1910, Baden-Powell, Chief Scout of the world, retired from the Army to give all his time to Scouting. He died in Kenya in 1941.

Shortly after the Scouting movement started in Britain, William D. Boyce, a Chicago publisher, became lost one day in a London fog. An English Scout helped him find the address he was looking for, and this led Boyce to become interested in Scouting. On February 8, 1910, he founded the Boy Scouts of America.

Reviewed by BOY SCOUTS OF AMERICA

BRACES, DENTAL. See ORTHODONTICS.

at various speeds along the axon. In the fastest human nerves, the impulses may travel at speeds up to several hundred kilometers an hour. This means that a message can go from brain to toe in much less than a second.

A neuron may send different messages by changing the number or pattern of its pulses. But the individual pulses themselves are always identical.

The axon carries the pulses from one cell to the next. An axon that connects nearby cells may be very short, but some other axons may be very long. For example, a sensory axon joining an elephant's toe to its spinal cord may be several meters long.

The point where an axon passes impulses to another cell is called a **synapse**. An electrical impulse traveling in the axon causes the release of a chemical called a **transmitter agent** at the synapse. This agent stimulates the next cell, thus passing on the impulse. Only a few kinds of transmitter agents are known. Acetylcholine, dopamine, and epinephrine are among them. Certain drugs that mimic the structure of transmitters or interfere with their action can have very serious effects on the working of the nervous system.

Sensory Systems

Sensory systems are those parts of the nervous system that provide the brain with information. In people, sensory systems include sight, smell, and hearing, which provide information about the world outside the body. There are also sensory systems that send signals to the brain about the body's temperature, blood pressure, and other internal conditions. We are not aware of it, but these signals continue day and night.

The first link in a sensory system is usually a **receptor**, a specialized nerve cell sensitive to certain kinds of energy or to certain chemicals. For example, receptors in the retina of the eye are sensitive to light energy but not to heat energy. Certain receptors in the skin are sensitive to heat but not to sound, and so on. The signals sent by all the receptors are interpreted by the brain as visual stimuli, sound stimuli, or other kinds of stimuli.

Each sensory system has its own set of receptors and axon pathways within the brain. Each system is always actively sending information to the brain. For example, from the cells of the retina of the human eye alone, about 1,000,000 axons lead to the brain. These are necessary for sending visual information to the brain. Many of them are always at work, even in the dark. (After all, there must be some signal that the brain can interpret to mean "dark.") These axons are grouped along special pathways in the brain concerned with the processing of visual information. Actually, much information processing is done by the cells in the retina itself. So "busy" is the retina that, for its size, it uses up more energy than any other part of the body.

Integrating Centers

The brain must keep bringing about behavior that is suited to the situation. So there are brain centers into which a large part of the sensory information is fed. These centers decide which sensory signals are the most important. They relate what one sense reports to information from other senses.

When you a ride a bicycle, for example, you do not rely on what sight alone tells you. The actions that your body takes depend on sight, sounds, sense of balance, and many other things. All this information must be integrated (put together). Only then are the final commands sent by your brain to your muscles.

The integrating centers are organized differently in various animals. But their general function is present in every brain.

Motor Centers

Within every brain there is a section called the motor apparatus. This is the set of nerve cells that acts directly on muscles and glands, putting them to work. These cells carry the brain's commands to the rest of the body.

Some of these command signals are followed quickly, taking only a fraction of a second to be completed. The fastest muscles, such as the wing muscles of insects, take less than $\frac{1}{1000}$ of a second to contract. The record for slowness probably belongs to some of the muscles in the sea anemone; these may take five or six minutes to contract after they have been excited by their nerves. The fastest human system is the one that controls eye movements.

There is also a great range in the strength that different muscles can produce. These differences in strength are brought about by slight changes in the command signal from the brain. As a result, we can use our hands for such different tasks as picking up a ripe tomato or hanging from a bar.

DIFFERENCES AMONG BRAINS

All brains share certain features, but they also differ in important ways. Some brains contain a great many more nerve cells than others. The cells of more highly developed brains have more interconnections. In simple nervous systems, a particular neuron may receive signals directly from only a few other cells. But some cells in humans are believed to receive signals directly from thousands of other cells.

Brain size is an important difference. The entire brain of some insects is less than 1 millimeter ($\frac{1}{25}$ inch) across. The brain of the elephant is among the largest. It weighs about 5 kilograms (11 pounds).

Neurons differ in size and in the thickness of their axons. Impulses can be sent faster along thick axons. Thus, thicker axons mean that different parts of the brain can communicate with one another more quickly.

Temperature is another factor. Most nerve activity is faster in warm bodies. This gives warm-blooded animals an advantage over their cooler, more sluggish competitors.

Some animals have brains with sensory systems that other animals do not have. The rattlesnake, for example, has in its face specialized receptors sensitive to heat. With them, it can detect warm-blooded prey, such as mice, several meters away. The receptors enable rattlesnakes to hunt in total darkness.

Bats have specially developed vocal organs for producing very high-pitched sounds—far too high for our own ears to hear. But the bat can detect the echo of its own voice bouncing off distant objects. That is why a bat can fly in the dark without bumping into things and why a bat can pick out tiny insects as prey. This bat system is very much like radar and is of great interest to scientists.

THE HUMAN BRAIN

The human brain is the most complex and highly developed of all brains. It commands the body's hundreds of different muscles, so that we can run, talk, and hold things. The

Does a larger brain mean greater intelligence?

Not necessarily. For instance, humans are the most intelligent members of the animal kingdom. Yet our brains are smaller and they weigh less than the brains of some other animals. A human brain weighs less than 1.5 kilograms (about 3 pounds), while an elephant's brain is more than three times that weight. The clue to intelligence is in the cortex, the surface covering of the brain. Intelligence seems to be related to the amount of folding in the cortex.

brain also commands the thousands of glands that produce vital substances. For example, sweat, tears, and saliva are all under the brain's control.

The brain is located in the head, protected by the skull. It weighs less than 1.5 kilograms (about 3 pounds) in adults. Like most parts of the body, it is mainly water. To the touch, a brain feels very much like a balloon filled with water. Because the brain is delicate in structure, it must have extra protection from bumps and injury. This protection is provided by tough membranes that surround it and by a special fluid that supports it and buoys it up in the skull.

Divisions of the Brain

The largest part of the brain is the **cerebrum**. It has a peculiar surface—twisted, wrinkled, and knotted. This surface is the **cerebral cortex**. Its pink color is due to the presence of very tiny blood vessels. The foldings of the surface are called **convolutions**. They serve to increase the surface area of the cortex. The increase in area means an increase in the total number of cells in the cortex. This is important because, in a way, intelligence is related to the total number of nerve cells in the cortex.

The cerebrum, also called the **forebrain**, consists of two hemispheres. At the base of the hemispheres, and surrounded by them, is a region of the brain called the **diencephalon**, or "between-brain." It connects with the **midbrain**. Overlying the midbrain is the large **cerebellum** (which means "little brain"). The midbrain continues back into the **medulla** and finally into the **spinal cord**. Strictly speaking, the spinal cord is not considered to be part of the brain.

These various parts of the central nervous

system are connected by long bundles of axons. These relay messages back and forth to the collections of nerve cells that are grouped together. Because of their color, these groupings are called **gray matter**. (The bundles of axons, because of their color, are called **white matter**.)

Local Brain Functions

The **spinal cord** is the great link connecting the brain with much of the body. From receptor neurons throughout the body, messages travel up the cord to the brain, carrying information about touch, pain, temperature, and body position. Alongside these **sensory pathways** are the **motor pathways**, coming down from the brain. These relay messages from the cortex, midbrain, and cerebellum, which command activity in muscles and glands.

Higher up, in the **medulla**, are vital centers that automatically control the rate and depth of breathing, heart rate, and blood pressure. Without these centers, life would cease.

In the **midbrain** are important centers for the major sensory systems and important motor centers. (In lower animals, such as fish, amphibia, and reptiles, the cerebrum is not well developed. In these animals the midbrain is the most highly developed part of the brain.) In addition, there are centers here that act to control sleeping, waking, and attention.

The deepest part of the **diencephalon** is the **hypothalamus**. It is involved in such matters as hunger, thirst, regulation of body temperature, and, to an extent, emotional behavior. Hanging down from the hypothalamus is the **pituitary gland**. It acts much like a master control organ for many of the other important glands of the body.

Higher up in the diencephalon is the **thalamus**. It is an important relay center for sensory signals on their way to the cortex and to centers where different sensory signals come together.

From these centers in the thalamus, sensory signals are relayed to the **cerebral cortex**. Many parts of the cortex seem to be concerned with only a single sense. At the back of each hemisphere are areas concerned with vision. At the side of each hemisphere are areas concerned with hearing and touch. Just ahead of these are the main motor centers, which may be concerned with voluntary control of muscles and movement.

Left: A section of the brain, showing some of its inner parts. Right: Position of the brain within the head. The delicate tissue of the brain is protected from injury by the hard bony skull that surrounds it and by the shock-absorbing fluid. The spinal cord is also protected by fluid and by the bones of the spine.

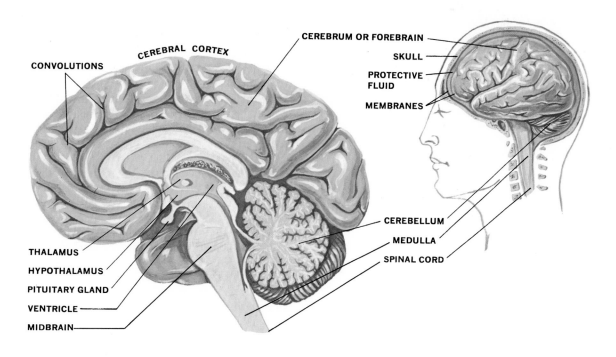

Strangely enough, all these centers in the cortex are chiefly concerned with sensation and movement on the opposite side of the body. That is, a touch on the left arm is relayed to the right cortex; movements of the right hand involve the left cortex.

The leg jerks if you tap one spot on a relaxed knee. This is a body reflex. Signals go from sensory receptors in the muscle to the lower spinal cord, and down to thigh muscles, in a fraction of the time they take to reach the brain. Such a reflex enables the body to protect itself quickly. The brain acts later on the information.

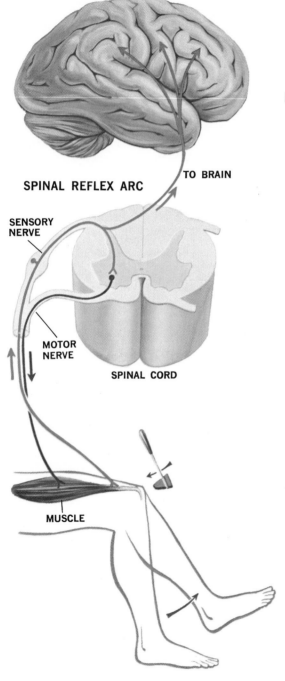

SPINAL REFLEX ARC

TO BRAIN

SENSORY NERVE

MOTOR NERVE

SPINAL CORD

MUSCLE

In humans certain parts of the cortex are necessary for speech, writing, memory, learning, and various kinds of emotional behavior. But the functions of these centers are poorly understood.

It is not yet possible to say which part of the brain "thinks," "sees," "learns," or "wants." We can only say that these activities require many different parts of the brain working together. But at every level of the brain, from the spinal cord to the cortex, there are sensory, motor, and integrating centers. Each has a particular kind of activity. These centers are fairly simple in the spinal cord and unbelievably complicated at the cortex. But scientists are a long way from completely understanding even the spinal cord.

▶ COMPLEX BEHAVIOR

All brains have sensory and motor functions. These are fairly well understood by scientists. However, all brains have other functions that are very complicated and poorly understood.

The Reflex

Most animals, for example, have automatic responses to certain types of stimuli, called **reflex responses**. These are patterns of activity that are produced whenever certain stimuli appear. And they are largely beyond control of the animal.

For instance, when we touch a hot stove, we immediately withdraw our hand. Careful measurement shows that the movement begins before we are aware that the stove is hot. This is because there are **reflex centers** in the spinal cord. They receive sensory warning signals before the signals have reached the conscious parts of our brain. The reflex centers in the cord immediately send signals to the nearby motor centers in the cord. These cause withdrawal of the hand.

The entire mechanism is present in the cord. And it is brought into action whenever a painful event occurs. This obviously helps to protect the body. Precious time would otherwise be lost by the signals' having to travel farther up in the brain and back down again. The reflex in the cord cuts the time to a tenth of what it would otherwise be.

The reflex is present in many functions and at many levels of our nervous system.

There is also a great amount of activity that is under conscious, or voluntary, control.

Instinctive Behavior

Many nervous systems produce very complex patterns of behavior that have not been learned by the animal. This is called instinctive behavior. Many insects and birds, for example, build complicated nests, although they have never seen another animal do so. This must mean that the directions are stored somewhere in the brain at birth. At the right time the proper pattern of activity is "triggered" somewhere in the brain. It may take a long time to build the nest, but each animal of the species will complete the task. (And once they have started, it is hard to stop them.) Instinctive patterns of behavior are very much like phonograph records; once they start, they play through to the end, always the same.

In some animals scientists have discovered which parts of the brain control instinctive behavior. They have learned what stimuli are necessary to start the process. But otherwise very little is known.

Less well-developed brains rely very heavily on reflexes and instinctive behavior. But as the nervous system becomes more advanced the brain is able to become somewhat more independent of the stimuli reaching it. This means also that the animal becomes more independent of its environment.

▶ LEARNING AND MEMORY

Brains can learn different kinds of tasks. Better developed brains can learn more complicated tasks. In the simplest brains learning is very crude. Humans show the greatest learning abilities. Among all animals, only humans can learn verbal (speaking, writing) behavior.

Memory

How and where does the brain store the information that we call memory? That is an easy question to ask, but very difficult to answer. In the human brain, areas of the cortex appear to be involved. When these areas are excited by a weak electrical current, the person "relives" past experiences. Apparently these electrical stimuli force the brain to reproduce experiences that are stored within it

from the past. It is also known that injury to certain areas will result in loss of memory.

But this does not mean that these are the places in the brain where the information is stored. Nor does it tell us anything about the way information is stored. Some scientists think that memory storage is chemical in nature. That is, they think that individual nerve cells have chemically coded information within them. Other scientists believe that memory is a result of some permanent change in the structure of the nerve—in the dendrites, for example.

▶ CONSCIOUSNESS

In humans we have a whole set of functions like consciousness, emotion, verbal expression, and thinking. These functions are the object of much study, and a great deal is known about them. But they are far too complicated to be understood in terms of the activities of nerve cells.

▶ RESEARCH ON BRAINS

Today scientists in many countries are studying the brains of people and other animals. In recent years electronic equipment has been developed that lets scientists observe the tiny electrical signals produced by nerve cells. These signals provide much important information about the operation of the brain. Other instruments permit experimenters to use tiny amounts of electricity to stimulate or prevent activity in certain parts of the brain. These methods have been used to trace pathways through the brain, to discover the connections between cells, and to see how signals are sent from one center to another. These experiments also tell us what functions are served by different areas of the brain.

Nevertheless, we have only begun to uncover the basic processes going on within the brain. As we learn more, many new questions arise. The brain is the most complicated of all organs. And it will be a challenge to scientists as long as people continue to wonder about the workings of the living body.

GEORGE P. MOORE
Department of Physiology
University of Southern California

See also BODY, HUMAN (Body's Senses).

BRAKES. See HYDRAULIC AND PNEUMATIC SYSTEMS; RAILROADS.

Brancusi's *Mademoiselle Pogany* (1931) is a portrait of a young woman sculpted in the smooth, simple shape of an egg. Philadelphia Museum of Art.

BRANCUSI, CONSTANTIN (1876–1957)

Constantin Brancusi was one of the great sculptors of the 20th century. His life was outstanding in its simplicity and devotion to art. For many years he lived alone in his studio in Paris, surrounded by his work.

Brancusi was born in a village in western Rumania on February 19, 1876, the son of land-owning peasants. When he was 11 years old, he left his home to seek his fortune. He worked at odd jobs for five years and then went to Craiova. In 1895 he entered the Craiova School of Arts and Crafts and studied sculpture for the first time. From then on, his education was paid for by scholarships and grants. He graduated from the Bucharest School of Fine Arts in 1902 and in 1905 enrolled in the École des Beaux-Arts (School of Fine Arts) in Paris. His work quickly gained respect.

Brancusi's first sculptures showed the influence of the French sculptor Rodin. Brancusi worked in Rodin's studio in 1906 but left after a short time, stating, "Nothing can grow in the shade of a great tree." His work became personal and inventive. In much of his sculpture, natural shapes are reduced to simpler forms. He sometimes produced several versions of a theme—a smooth, simple egg or a bird with elegant lines—seeking to express its purest form. *Bird in Space*—a work in bronze, dated 1926—was involved in a lawsuit when it was sent to the United States that year for exhibition. Customs officials decided to tax it as a manufactured object rather than admit it free of tax as a work of art. Two years later a court decided in the sculptor's favor.

From 1908, Brancusi's work was almost entirely of wood or stone—carved often in large, simple shapes—and of bronze cast from the carvings and frequently polished to a mirror finish.

Brancusi died on March 16, 1957. His studio in Paris, as he left it, serves as a museum of his work.

Reviewed by MARK ROSENTHAL
Philadelphia Museum of Art

BRANT, JOSEPH (1742–1807)

Joseph Brant was a Mohawk Indian chief and war chief of the Six Nations of the Iroquois. He is known for the help he gave the British during the Revolutionary War.

Joseph, the son of a Mohawk chief, was born in 1742 in what is now the state of Ohio. His Indian name was Thayendanegea, which means "he places two bets." When Joseph was 12, he met Sir William Johnson, the British superintendent of Indian affairs. The next year he accompanied Johnson in a French and Indian War campaign. A few years later, Johnson sent him to school in Connecticut. Joseph became a member of the Anglican Church and began to translate religious works into the Mohawk language.

When the Revolutionary War began, Brant and most of the members of the Six Nations remained loyal to Britain. Brant received the rank of captain in the British Army. He plunged into the conflict and led Indian forces against settlements on the New York frontier. After the war he led members of the Mohawk tribe into Canada, seeking a new home for his people. The British Government granted him a large tract of land in what is now Ontario.

Brant made two trips to England and was presented to King George III. In 1793 he attended a great conference of Indian tribes. He urged the Indian people to live in peace with the settlers. But many of the tribes deserted him and continued to wage war.

Brant died on November 24, 1807. Brantford, Ontario, was named for him.

JOHN S. MOIR
University of Toronto

BRAQUE, GEORGES (1882–1963)

Georges Braque's interest in art began when he was a child in Argenteuil, France, where he was born on May 13, 1882. His father was an interior decorator and an amateur painter. Georges watched and copied his father, and art became the center of his life.

The Braque family moved to the city of Le Havre in 1890, and Georges continued to draw and paint and study. Ten years later he went to Paris, where a great revolution in art was taking place. Braque's first paintings were done in the Impressionist style, but by 1906 he was exhibiting with a new group called *les fauves* ("the wild beasts").

In 1907, Braque met the great young painter Pablo Picasso. They became close friends and for years worked together, experimenting with modern techniques. They helped develop **cubism,** a kind of painting that shows many sides of an object at once. In 1912, Braque invented *papier collé,* or **collage,** a technique of gluing scraps of paper and other objects onto a flat surface, as part of a picture.

During World War I, Braque was seriously wounded while serving in the French Army. After the war he began to work more slowly and thoughtfully. After 1917 he struck out on his own, although he continued to work with cubism, simplifying it as the years passed. He painted many still lifes, often using the table in his studio as a subject.

Braque did not limit himself to painting. He also created stage scenery, book illustrations, and sculpture. In the 1950's he designed a ceiling for the Louvre museum in Paris. Braque died in Paris on August 31, 1963.

Reviewed by PHILIP LINHARES
Director, Mills College Art Gallery

BRASS. See BRONZE AND BRASS.
BRASS INSTRUMENTS. See WIND INSTRUMENTS.

Le Guéridon ("The Pedestal Table") is one of several paintings by Braque using a small, round-topped table as the center of a still life.

BRAZIL

Brazil is one of the world's giant nations. It is the largest and most populous country in South America, with almost half the continent's area and more than half its people. Among the nations of the world, Brazil ranks fifth in area, after the Soviet Union, Canada, China, and the United States.

The name of the country is believed to come from brazilwood, a tree that Portuguese colonists, who first arrived in the region in the 16th century, found in great abundance. Brazilwood yields red and purple dyes, which were highly prized in Europe for coloring cloth. In fact, for a time the only use that Portugal found for its American colony was as a source of brazilwood.

Brazil was ruled by Portugal for over 300 years before gaining its independence peacefully in 1822. Following the reign of two emperors, Brazil became a republic in 1889.

Brazil resembles the United States in several ways. It is a federal republic, made up of a number of states, territories, and the federal district of Brasília, the national capital. It is a land of great variety and contrast. Vast jungles and tropical rain forests, great rivers, and mountains cover much of the interior of Brazil, while rapidly growing modern cities crowd the long coastline of the Atlantic Ocean. Brazil had its gold rush and its pioneers, who helped open up the thinly populated interior of the country. Brazil also became a melting pot, where people of every race and many nationalities made their home. And, like the United States of an earlier age, Brazil is undergoing an economic revolution and becoming an industrial power.

▶THE PEOPLE

Brazil's population is unevenly distributed. Most of its people are concentrated on the eastern edge of the country—along the At-

Brazilians relax on Copacabana Beach in Rio de Janeiro.

BRAZIL

lantic coast between the Amazon River and the border with Uruguay.

More than half of all Brazilians are of European or part-European ancestry, and the majority of these are of Portuguese descent. Since the middle of the 19th century, Europeans of many other nationalities have also settled in Brazil. The descendants of the Europeans live for the most part in the eastern, southeastern, and southern regions of the country.

Sugarcane was Brazil's most important crop during the early days. Portuguese plantation owners at first used Indians to work in the fields. But the Indians resisted. In 1538 the colonists began to bring in large numbers of black Africans to work on the sugar plantations as slaves. Many of these people came from a part of Africa where farming and metalworking were highly developed. First as slaves and later as free people, the black Africans made many important contributions

Carnival, celebrated before Lent, is a three-day festival enjoyed by rich and poor, young and old.

Many different ways of life are found in Brazil. But Brazilians respect tradition, and they have many customs and ideals in common. They speak the same language. Nearly all worship according to the same faith. And they are educated in the same way.

Language

"Buenos días" is the way to say "hello" in every South American country except Brazil. In Brazil, people say *"Bom dia,"* which is Portuguese for "Good morning." Brazil is the only Portuguese-speaking nation in the Western Hemisphere. But because there are many Brazilians, Portuguese has become a major world language. Brazilian Portuguese is much like the language spoken in Portugal except that it is spoken with a different accent. A visitor from Portugal would also have to learn new words that have been added to the language by black Africans and Indians.

Most educated Brazilians also speak Spanish, and many are fluent in English and French. Descendants of European settlers often speak their native language at home. German and Italian are spoken by several million in the southern states. Magazines and newspapers are published in many different languages.

Education

Brazilian law requires all children to attend elementary school for at least three years. Elementary school pupils can be recognized easily by their uniforms. Boys wear khaki shirts and shorts. Girls wear navy-blue skirts and white blouses. They study Brazilian history, arithmetic, science, social studies, and Portuguese. English and French are taught as second languages in the higher grades.

Secondary school consists of four years of junior high school, called *ginásio,* and three years of senior high school, called *colégio.* Most secondary schools are privately run, and only well-to-do Brazilians can afford to send their children to them.

Advanced education is available at technical schools, state colleges, and at national and Catholic universities. Specialized institutes for graduate study in the fields of diplomacy, civil service, government, and medicine—located in Rio de Janeiro—attract students from all over South America.

Brazil has many fine schools and colleges,

to the growth of the country. Today more than one tenth of the people of Brazil are of black African descent. More than one fourth are of mixed black African and European ancestry.

Today very few of Brazil's people are descended from the country's first settlers—the Indians. Most of those of pure Indian descent now live in the Brazilian and Guiana highlands. Brazilians of mixed white and Indian ancestry are found mainly in the interior of the country.

The remainder of Brazil's population includes various other ethnic groups. A number of Japanese, Lebanese, and Syrians make their homes in Brazil.

but there are still not enough for all of the fast-growing and widely scattered population. The number of people who are able to read and write has been increased greatly through a massive government program of school building and teacher training. In addition, adult education courses are being given in some of the larger cities. There are also mobile schools that carry teachers, books, and school supplies to remote villages by truck. However, because many of the people of Brazil are under 18 years of age, more schools are needed every year.

Religion

About 90 percent of all Brazilians are Roman Catholics. This gives Brazil the distinction of having the largest Catholic population of any nation in the world. Freedom of worship is guaranteed by the constitution. Many Protestants, as well as smaller numbers of Buddhists and Jews, make their homes in Brazil. An unusual mixture of African religions and Roman Catholicism is practiced by many Brazilians of black African descent in the big cities and the Northeast.

Family and Social Life

The family is the center of everyday life in Brazil. Most couples marry quite young, often when they are still in their teens. Children are welcomed and loved. Sometimes they are even a bit spoiled. Traditionally the father is the head of the household, but women are assuming increasingly important roles in all aspects of Brazilian society.

Social life in Brazil is often built around family holidays. The birthdays, christenings, and weddings of the immediate family and of vast numbers of aunts, uncles, and cousins are occasions for celebrations and parties.

All Brazilians share in the many Catholic holidays, such as saints' days, when festivals, pageants, and dances are held. The most famous of these holidays is Carnival—the three-day festival that occurs just before Lent. Carnival is celebrated in all Brazilian towns and cities. The best known is the one that is held in Rio de Janeiro. Schools and businesses close, and the whole city is given over to parades, street dances, and masked balls. Strolling musicians play the *samba, marcha,* and *frevo.* Confetti and streamers fill the air. *Cariocas,* as the people of Rio are called, and

tourists join in this huge citywide celebration during which no one sleeps and nearly everyone dances. Even as Lent begins, everyone in Rio—from the wealthiest apartment dweller to the poorest person in the *favelas,* or slums—starts to plan a costume for the great event of the next year.

Sports

Nearly all Brazilians are sports enthusiasts and good athletes. Boating, sailing, and swimming are popular activities, but nothing excites a Brazilian so much as a good *futebol* ("soccer") match. *Futebol* is the national sport, and every school and town has its own team. Professional soccer players are national figures in Brazil, just as baseball players are in the United States. No one is surprised to see soccer fans weep if their team loses or celebrate if it wins.

Maté, a tealike beverage, is the favorite drink of Brazilian cowboys (*gaúchos*) of the southern grasslands. This is an important cattle-raising region of Brazil.

Food and Drink

Cafézinhos—tiny cups of sweet, steaming-hot coffee—are as important a part of daily life in Brazil as *futebol*. Brazilians stop several times a day to sip their *cafézinho* in outdoor restaurants or at home. Even in factories and offices, trays of the small cups are brought to workers for a *cafézinho* break.

The national dish of Brazil is called *feijoada*. It contains black beans, pork sausage, spices, and manioc powder. Manioc is made from mandioca, the root of the nonpoisonous cassava, a tropical plant that is native to Brazil. No one would enjoy eating the root raw, but Indians long ago discovered that when cooked and dried, it could be used in many ways. Brazilians sprinkle it on soups, meat, and stews and use it as flour in bread and puddings. Tapioca is also made from manioc.

Every region of Brazil has its own special foods. *Charque* (dried and salted beef) is traditional in southern Brazil. In the Northeast and along the Amazon River, fish dishes are popular. The cowboys (*gaúchos*) of the southern grasslands eat a form of barbecued beef and drink *maté,* a kind of tea, instead of coffee. Everywhere in Brazil oranges, pineapples, bananas, and other varieties of tropical fruits are inexpensive and far more popular than vegetables.

The Arts

The Portuguese colonists brought a love of music and art from their home country that has become a vital part of Brazilian life. As the colony grew into a nation, many Brazilians won fame in the arts.

Sculpture and Painting. One of the first well-known Brazilian artists was the 18th-century sculptor Antônio Francisco Lisboa, who was known as Aleijadinho—the "Little Cripple." Aleijadinho was a leper. When he could no longer use his hands, he had his tools strapped to his wrists so that he could go on sculpting. His most famous works are the statues of the twelve prophets on the steps of a church in Congonhas, a small town in Minas Gerais.

Brazilian painters have only begun to win worldwide fame in this century. Among the best known are Emiliano di Cavalcanti, Lasar Segall, and Cândido Portinari, whose murals can be seen not only in Brazil but also at the Library of Congress in Washington, D.C., and at United Nations headquarters in New York City.

Architecture. In the field of architecture, too, Brazilians have won international fame. The dramatic capital city of Brasília is the work of Brazil's leading designers—the city planner Lúcio Costa, the architect Oscar Niemeyer, and the landscape architect Roberto Burle Marx.

Music and Dance. Brazilian dances and music, such as the *samba, baião,* and *bossa nova,* are known all over the world. Several Brazilian musicians have won international fame. One is Antônio Carlos Gomes, a 19th-century composer whose opera about a proud Indian is called *Il Guarany.* Heitor Villa-Lobos composed more than 2,000 works based on the folk music of the Brazilian black Africans and pioneers. Guiomar Novaes was a noted pianist.

Authors. Only a few Brazilian writers are known outside their own country. One of them, Joaquim Maria Machado de Assis, is considered one of the greatest South American writers. His portrayals of life in Rio de Janeiro during the early 19th century are found in *Epitaph for a Small Winner, Dom Casmurro,* and *Quincas Borba.* Euclides da Cunha is another of Brazil's better-known writers. His most famous book, *Rebellion in the Backlands,* is an essay on people and the land in the Northeast. One part of the book tells of a military adventure there. Distinguished Brazilian writers of the 20th century include the poets Carlos Drummond de Andrade, Manuel Bandeira, Augusto Frederico Schmidt, and Guimarães Rosa; and the novelists Graciliano Ramos, Erico Veríssimo, Rachel de Queiroz, and Jorge Amado. The sociologist-historian Gilberto Freyre is well known in other countries. His classic works are *The Masters and the Slaves* and *The Mansions and the Shanties.*

The Land

Brazil, like all large countries, has many different kinds of landscape. An easy way to view this variety is by dividing the country into uplands and lowlands. The two main areas of uplands—the Brazilian Highlands and the Guiana Highlands—cover more that one half of Brazil. The three major lowland areas are the Amazon Basin, a small area in southern Brazil drained by the Rio de la Plata system, and the small area of the upper Paraguay river system in the southwest.

Brazilians usually divide their large and varied country into five regions that have a

Mato Grosso ("Great Forest") is a vast but thinly populated state in Central West Brazil. A frontier region, it is still largely undeveloped.

geographic unity and share a common history, economy, and way of life. These regions are the Northeast, the East, the South, the Central West, and the Amazon Basin. Each region contains several states.

The Northeast

In the region known as the Northeast are the states of Maranhão, Piauí, Ceará, Rio Grande do Norte, Paráiba, Pernambuco, Alagoas, Sergipe, and Bahia.

Here on the hot, rainy coastal plain, Portuguese planters of colonial times became

wealthy growing cane sugar on their *fazendas* ("plantations"). The *fazenda* was home to the planter, his family, and the crews of Indian and black African slaves who worked the fields. The port cities of Salvador (formerly Bahia), Brazil's first capital, and Recife flourished. The children of wealthy planters became the leaders of the colony. Their descendants are still among the leaders of the nation today.

The coastal plain soon became crowded, and settlers pushed inland to the *sertão,* or "backland." The *sertão* is a forbidding region of extremes in climate. It has either too much or too little rain. In some years the drought is so severe that people must move away or die of hunger and thirst. In rainy years cotton can be grown, and the land is green with fodder for cattle.

The gauchos on the ranches of the *sertão* must wear leather clothing to protect themselves from the thorny plants that are typical of the region. Many unusual plants grow in the caatinga, a tropical thorn forest of the Northeast. One, the carnauba palm, stays green even during severe droughts because its leaves are coated with a thin film of wax. This wax is used in the manufacture of lipstick, self-polishing floor waxes, and phonograph records.

Other valuable products of the Northeast include sugar, cotton, tobacco, and rice. Brazil lacks sufficient oil to meet the country's needs. But petroleum has been found in Bahia.

Much of the Northeast has been devastated by a severe drought that began in 1978. The drought ruined crops, dried up wells, and sent millions of people streaming into the already overcrowded cities. It wiped out most of the economic gains made by government investment in the region through an organization known as SUDENE (Superintendency for Development of the Northeast).

The East

The eastern region is made up of Rio de Janeiro, Espírito Santo, Minas Gerais, and São Paulo. A combination of favorable climate, rich soils, and abundant natural resources has made these states, with the exception of Espírito Santo, the richest and most important in Brazil.

Thousands of settlers were attracted to this region after the discovery of gold in Minas Gerais ("General Mines") in 1698. During the next 100 years almost half the gold mined in the world came from Brazil. Today gold is mined only in small quantities. But there are tremendous iron reserves at Itabira and a wealth of industrial diamonds, aquamarines, beryls, topazes, and tourmalines elsewhere in the region.

One important result of Brazil's gold rush was that the Northeast lost importance and the East gained its position as the heart of the nation. In 1763 the capital was moved from Bahia to Rio de Janeiro on the central coast. Rio, which had been a sleepy village before the discovery of gold, became the chief port for the shipment of the precious metal abroad. Other businesses grew, too, and soon it was the commercial center of the country. In 1974, oil was discovered offshore near Campos in Rio de Janeiro state.

But the most important city of the eastern region is São Paulo. Founded more than 400 years ago, it was a frontier town until the 19th century, when *terra roxa,* the purplish-red soil of the region, was found perfect for growing coffee trees. Thousands of European immigrants swelled the population of São Paulo, and the number of coffee plantations in the region mushroomed. São Paulo and its port city, Santos, became rich as centers of the coffee industry.

For hundreds of kilometers around São Paulo, the countryside is dotted with huge coffee plantations. The headquarters of these vast *fazendas* are often small towns with movie houses, health centers, churches, and clubs. The people of the *fazenda* are busiest at coffee harvest time when everyone, including the children, goes out to pick the ripe coffee berries from the trees and prepare them for shipment to São Paulo and Santos.

The South

The three southern states are Santa Catarina, Paraná, and Rio Grande do Sul. A pleasant, temperate climate and fertile land attracted large numbers of European settlers to this region in the 19th and 20th centuries. The narrow coastal plain and rolling grasslands of the interior are today the most European parts of Brazil. Some southern towns such as Blumenau and Joinvile look

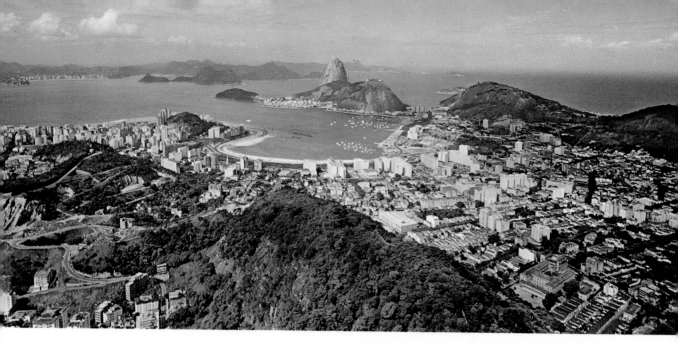

like transplanted German villages. Other cities have populations that are largely of Italian ancestry.

The immigrants brought many of their European skills to the new land. The Italians have made grapes and wines important products of the region. Germans have built breweries and cultivated large farms in the area.

In parts of the South, rolling grasslands like the Pampa of Argentina are used to raise Brazil's largest herds of sheep and high-grade beef cattle. Rio Grande do Sul is the center of the beef industry, and wheat and soybeans are leading products.

Brazil's only source of coal is in the state of Santa Catarina. Low-grade coal mined here is used in the manufacture of steel at Volta Redonda in the East. Santa Catarina and Paraná are important sources of lumber. Paraná is now the largest producer of coffee in Brazil. Cotton, sugar, rice, beans, onions, potatoes, and tobacco are also grown in the region.

The Central West

Brazil's frontier states are Goiás, Mato Grosso ("Great Forest"), and Mato Grosso do Sul on the western plateau. This vast, thinly populated region was first settled by people hunting for gold and diamonds. Only in recent years have travelers been able to go into this region unarmed.

Many people have tried to settle in this region. But huge distances and poor communications have discouraged settlers. In the

Mountains, sea, the modern city, and the jungle beyond it, all meet in a unique way at Rio's Guanabara Bay. Below, the Central Plaza in São Paulo, Brazil's industrial city.

Brasília is Brazil's modern capital city. The twin towers are the congressional office buildings.

southern part of the region there are coffee plantations, but most of the land is used for ranching. Cattle roam the large, unfenced ranches and provide the chief source of income for Brazil's westerners.

The government believes that this vast region may become the heart of the nation. This explains the location of the new capital, Brasília, in Goiás. For hundreds of years Brazilians had spoken of moving their capital to the center of their nation. But it was not until Juscelino Kubitschek de Oliveira became president that the dream turned into a reality. In 1956 the Brazilian Congress decided to build a new capital city. On April 21, 1960, Brasília officially became the capital of Brazil in place of Rio. All Brazilians hope that with the movement of the capital their last frontier has been permanently opened for settlement.

The Amazon Basin

The territories of Rio Branco and Amapá and the states of Acre, Amazonas, Pará, and Rondônia lie in the huge basin formed by the Amazon and its tributaries.

So much rain falls in the Amazon Basin that Brazilians divide the seasons into the "time of the big rains" and the "time of the little rains." The rains and high humidity feed the trees of the world's largest tropical rain forest. The selva, or rain forest, is home to many unusual forms of wildlife, including rare butterflies, giant spiders, huge beetles, boa constrictors, a rat that grows to more than 1 meter in length, and a kind of jaguar called an *onça.* More than 1,000 different species of fish live in the river. One of these is the pirarucu, a giant codfish that often grows to 1.5 meters (5 feet) in length. Another is the piranha, a small flesh-eating fish.

Many of Brazil's Indians still make their home in remote parts of the tropical rain forest. The Indians of Brazil have always lived in scattered groups and have never developed great civilizations like those of the Aztecs or Incas.

Most of the settlers in the Amazon Basin are of mixed Portuguese and Indian descent. They live in family groups or in small clusters of houses built on the riverbanks. In the places where floods occur, the houses are often raised off the ground on stilts.

Because the tropical rains have washed away minerals that make the soil good for agriculture, settlers usually cannot farm one place for more than three years. The few people living in the upper Amazon Basin get much of their food through hunting and gathering. They hunt tapirs, peccaries, monkeys, and parrots for meat. The river provides turtles and many kinds of edible fish.

The Amazon people gather the products of the forest and river such as latex (natural rubber), palm and Brazil nuts, cayman (a type of alligator) skins, and medicinal plants that provide many different kinds of drugs, including cocaine, cumarin, curare, and strychnine. When the people have enough goods to sell, they travel on the river by canoe, boat, or steamer to the nearest trading post. Here they exchange their goods for manufactured products such as knives, needles, and pots.

Brazil's largest gold deposits and a mountain of iron ore have been discovered in Pará. The Amazon Basin also contains large reserves of bauxite (aluminum ore), copper, manganese, and tin. However, some scientists fear that opening the Amazon to large-scale mining, logging, farming, and ranching operations would destroy the fragile balance of the world's largest tropical rain forest.

▶ THE ECONOMY

Throughout Brazil's history, the economy has depended mainly on one product at a time. During the early years of settlement, sugar was the main export. When the soil on the sugar plantations began losing fertility, large deposits of gold were discovered. Throughout the 18th century, Brazil was gripped by "gold fever." As the profits from gold lessened, Brazil turned to agriculture again as the basis of the economy.

Agriculture

Agricultural products are Brazil's chief export. The nation is among the world's leading producers of soybeans, coffee, cacao (the source of cocoa and chocolate), sugar, corn, cassava, oranges, bananas, pineapples, tobacco, and cotton. Cotton is grown in the South for export and in the East to supply Brazil's large textile industry. Beans, rice, and manioc are grown widely for local use. Jute, used for making burlap, sacking, and twine, was introduced by Japanese immigrants. In spite of Brazil's rich agriculture, however, some foods must be imported.

Brazil is now a major cattle-raising nation. It exports large quantities of meat and other animal products. Hogs are also raised extensively, as are horses and other animals.

Industry

Brazil is the leading industrial nation in Latin America. Many foreign companies have built factories in Brazil, although most industrial plants are owned by Brazilians.

Houses along the Amazon are on stilts because of floods.

Food processing and textiles are the industrial giants. Industry centers around São Paulo and Rio de Janeiro but is expanding rapidly in many other cities. Volta Redonda, for example, was once a tiny village. Today it has one of the largest steel works in Latin America. The manufacture of automobiles, commercial vehicles, television sets, chemicals, and consumer goods is also growing rapidly.

The most serious obstacle to industrial growth is the lack of mineral fuels such as coal and petroleum. The building of hydroelectric plants on Brazil's rivers has helped

In Salvador (Bahia), the past and present, the African and Portuguese, meet and mingle.

Pots are sold along the old streets of Belém, capital of Pará (*left*). At right, coffee beans from Pará are spread out to dry in the sun. Brazilians have become world experts in the coffee-growing industry.

provide electricity. The country is also turning to nuclear power as a source of energy. And many vehicles now run on alcohol made from sugarcane and manioc.

Mining and Lumbering

Iron ore is Brazil's leading single export. Manganese, bauxite, chrome, and many other minerals are mined, and new mineral discoveries are constantly being made. Wood is cut for export and is also processed into wood pulp, paper, and other products.

Trade

Brazil sells its products to other countries to pay for imports of fuels and lubricants, machinery, chemicals, foods, and metals and metal products. Imports come mainly from Western Europe, the United States, Venezuela, and Argentina. The chief exports are iron ore, soybeans, coffee, cocoa, textiles, shoes, and sugar. Many exports go to Western Europe and the United States. Brazil supplies many kinds of raw materials and consumer goods to other Latin American countries.

Transportation and Communications

Transportation and communications in Brazil need to be improved because the country is very large. Settlements, towns, and cities are far from one another, and mountains, jungle, and deserts often separate them. The Great Escarpment has made the construction of roads and rails slow. Most highways and railroads are found on the eastern fringe of the country, where most of the people live. The Trans-Amazon Highway is being built to link the Atlantic coast to the border of Peru.

Air travel helps to link all parts of Brazil, and it is expanding rapidly. Brazil's domestic air network has become one of the world's greatest. There are many excellent harbors that are busy centers of world trade.

All major cities are linked by telephone and telegraph. Brazil has hundreds of radio stations, and there is hardly a town or village beyond the reach of television.

▶CITIES

Brazil has many large and bustling cities. Each year, more and more people move from the countryside to the cities in search of jobs and a better way of life.

Rio de Janeiro, in eastern Brazil, is considered one of the world's most beautiful cities. Its fine harbor, steep mountains, and magnificent modern apartment houses strung along the beaches and wide, tree-lined avenues have made Rio one of the most visited and most often photographed cities in the world. There is an article on Rio de Janeiro in Volume R.

Also in the eastern region is São Paulo, the chief industrial city of Latin America and the largest city in Brazil. This bustling, modern city is the center of the nation's textile industry. A separate article on São Paulo can be found in Volume S.

Santos lies southeast of São Paulo and serves as its port. Linking the two cities was a major feat of engineering because of the great difference in elevation. An electric-cable railroad and a highway carved into the Great Escarpment now connect the *fazendas* of the plateau with the port. In Santos the air is perfumed with coffee, and nearly everyone makes a living in some activity related to coffee production.

The flourishing ports of Salvador (Bahia) and Recife are the chief cities of the Northeast. The leading cities of the South are Pôrto Alegre and Curitiba. The leading products of Pôrto Alegre ("Happy Port") are leather, textiles, beer, and wine. Curitiba rivals São Paulo as a center of coffee production. There are only a few large cities on the Amazon. Belém is an important port at the mouth of the river. Manaus, on the central Amazon, was very important during the 19th century, when the Amazonian forest was the world's leading source of natural rubber. The opera house and mosaic sidewalks of Manaus are reminders of the city's prosperous past.

Brasília is the chief city of the Central West as well as the site of the national capital. It is considered an outstanding example of modern large-scale city planning. The city is shaped roughly like a giant airplane. The buildings of its central area are bordered by a V-shaped artificial lake.

▶ GOVERNMENT

Brazil is a federal republic, consisting of 23 states, three territories, and a federal district (the city of Brasília). Brazil's legislative body is the National Congress, which is composed of the Chamber of Deputies and the Federal Senate. Deputies are elected, on the basis of population, for four years. Senators serve 8-year terms, with three senators elected from each state.

The president, who is elected, together with a vice president, for six years, is the head of state and government. From 1969 to 1985, presidents were elected by an electoral college made up of members of the National Congress and delegates from state legislatures. The constitution was amended in 1985 to allow for direct elections of the president. A new constitution was approved in 1988.

Each state has its own elected legislature and governor.

▶ HISTORY

The Portuguese navigator Pedro Alvares Cabral claimed Brazil for Portugal in 1500. However, for some 30 years after Cabral's historic voyage, the Portuguese paid little attention to their new colony, and only a few trading posts grew up along the coast. Portugal's main interest still lay in trade with the Far East. But Portugal's attitude changed after 1530 for two reasons. A new source of wealth was needed, and other European powers were threatening to take Brazil.

Portuguese Settlement

The Portuguese king started the settlement of Brazil by giving favored nobles grants that stretched far inland from the coast. The early settlers had difficulties with the Indians. The settlers also had to face a new and strange tropical environment and unfamiliar soil conditions. The large landowners soon discovered that if they were to run successful settlements, they needed more farm laborers. Black slaves were brought from Africa to work on plantations in the Northeast.

Meanwhile, in the East and the South, a new kind of person appeared. This was the mestizo, of mixed Portuguese and Indian ancestry. Bands of these hardy peoples, called *bandeirantes,* roamed the interior in search of gold and Indians to sell as slaves to the plantation owners of the north. The *bandeirantes* found both gold and slaves—and in doing so helped to explore and settle large regions in the present states of Minas Gerais, Mato Grosso, Goiás, and Mato Grosso do Sul.

By the early 19th century, Brazil's first gold mines had been nearly exhausted, but a large part of the country was permanently settled. Farming was the major occupation. The descendants of the Portuguese settlers now thought of themselves as Brazilians rather than subjects of the King of Portugal.

Just as the first Brazilian movements for independence were developing, the French emperor Napoleon invaded Portugal. In 1808 the Portuguese royal family and more than 1,000 members of the court fled to Brazil. For the next 14 years Rio de Janeiro was the capital of the Portuguese empire. At last, in 1821, the King returned to his native land and left his son, Dom Pedro, to rule Brazil. The next year Dom Pedro, following the advice of José Bonifácio de Andrada, his minister of the interior, declared Brazil independent of Portugal. Peaceful change became the pattern of Brazil's political life.

Independence

Brazil remained an empire from 1822 until 1889. Dom Pedro was emperor for nine years and then turned over the throne to his 5-year-old son, Dom Pedro II, who became emperor in 1840 at the age of 14. Dom Pedro II ruled Brazil for 49 years, during which the nation became larger and richer. Wars with Argentina (1851–52) and with Paraguay (1865–70) were finally settled peacefully. Railroads were built. Rubber from the Amazon jungle doubled foreign trade. Thousands of immigrants swelled Brazil's population between 1874 and 1889.

This peaceful growth ended in 1888, the year the Emperor's daughter Isabella abolished slavery. Many of the large landowners and slaveholders called for an overthrow of the government. But some wanted a republican form of government. The Army itself, which was republican in spirit, favored the change. And in 1889 the old Emperor peacefully left Brazil for the good of the new republic. Ruy Barbosa, leader of the anti-slavery movement, prepared the first constitution of republican Brazil in 1891.

The Republic

During the early years of the republic, when the Army ruled Brazil, there was civil war and political upheaval. But by 1895 order had been restored and Brazil had a civilian government. Brazil became increasingly important in world politics. It fought with the Allies during World War I. But the years between the two world wars were troubled. The over-production of coffee and the fall of world coffee prices during the Depression brought new difficulties to the country. In 1930 the president was overthrown, and Getúlio Vargas became dictator of what he called a "disciplined democracy." Under Vargas' rule living conditions improved and trade grew. During World War II, Brazil was an ally of the United States and sent troops to Italy.

The Second Republic

The Army forced Vargas to resign in 1945. Eurico Dutra was elected as his successor. But in 1950, Vargas ran for office and was elected. At the end of a very serious political crisis, in which he was close to being ousted again, Vargas took his own life. Juscelino Kubitschek de Oliveira then became president.

Kubitschek told the Brazilians that they would "enjoy in 5 years the progress of 50 years." He worked hard to live up to his promise. The government helped to develop hydroelectric plants and some industries. But inflation and falling world coffee prices brought new economic and social problems.

In 1960, Jânio Quadros was elected president, but his attempts to improve conditions were blocked. Quadros resigned within a year, and his vice president, João Goulart, took his place. By 1964, however, Goulart's leftist policies had brought the Brazilian economy to a crisis. Discontent with his government led to a revolution, which brought the military to power. Until 1985, Brazil's presidents all came from the armed forces. In 1985, Tancredo de Almeida Neves, a civilian, was elected president. Neves died before his inauguration, and the vice president, José Sarney, became president.

The 1989 elections were the first since 1960 in which Brazilians voted directly for the president. Fernando Collor de Mello, a conservative, won the presidency after a runoff election. His term was marked by controversy, and in 1992 he was impeached by the Chamber of Deputies on charges of corruption. Collor was replaced by the vice president, Itamar Augusto Canteiro Franco, while he awaited trial by the Senate.

PETER O. WACKER
Rutgers, The State University of New Jersey
Updated by ROLLIE E. POPPINO
University of California, Davis
Author, *Brazil: The Land and People*

See also AMAZON RIVER.

BRAZING. See SOLDERING AND BRAZING.

BREAD AND BAKING

Bread in some form is eaten almost everywhere in the world. It is called "the staff of life" because it can go far in meeting people's need for food—in supporting human life. (A staff is a long stick that is used for support in walking.) And the word "bread" has taken on other special meanings. "Breaking bread" (sharing a meal) is a sign of friendship. "More bread!" (a demand for the basic necessities of life) has been the slogan of many revolutions.

Most North Americans and Europeans tend to think of bread as a food that is moist and crumbly on the inside and crusty on the outside. But breads have many different forms. In Greece, for example, bread is often *pita*, a wheat-flour bread that is simply a thin pocket of crust with a hollow inside. In Mexico, the common bread is a delicate cornmeal pancake known as a *tortilla*.

The breads of the world are of two main kinds—flat and leavened. Flat breads are those such as the Greek *pita* and the Mexican *tortilla*. They also include religious breads—the matzoth eaten by Jews during Passover and the wafers used in Communion in Christian churches.

Leavened breads are lighter than flat breads because they contain a rising, or leavening, agent. They include white or whole wheat bread, rye bread, muffins, and rolls. There are many other bakery products that can be considered forms of bread, such as cakes, cookies, crackers, and pretzels.

In most of its forms, bread is an important source of carbohydrates, which provide energy, and protein, which the body uses in building and repairing its cells. Most breads also contain B vitamins and some minerals.

▶ **BASIC INGREDIENTS**

Most breads and baked goods made in Canada, Europe, and the United States are leavened products. These products always include four basic ingredients—flour, a leavening agent, salt, and liquids and fats.

Flour. Bread contains more flour than any other ingredient. There are many different types of flour. Most are made from grains such as wheat, rye, barley, oats, corn, and rice. White flour is made from wheat that is milled (crushed and sifted) repeatedly until the outer covering has been completely removed.

Different flours produce breads of different flavors. They also produce breads of different textures. This is because the flours contain different amounts of gluten. Gluten is a mixture of proteins found in grain. When it comes in contact with a liquid (such as milk or water) and is pushed about by stirring or some other action, it develops long, elastic strands. The stretchable bands of gluten form an invisible structure that enables a loaf of bread to hold its shape. It is because of the elastic nature of gluten that bread will bounce back if you poke it gently with your fingers.

Leavening Agent. Yeast was the first leavening agent, and it is still the most important. Yeast is a tiny one-celled plant that is present all around us. It is found in the air, on trees, in the soil, and on the skins of fruits. Yeast cells feed on sugars and starches. They change the starch of bread dough into sugar, which they then digest. As they do this, they give off carbon dioxide gas as a waste product. (This chemical change is called fermentation.) Tiny bubbles of carbon dioxide are trapped by the strands of gluten in the dough. The gas blows the gluten into bigger and bigger bubbles and makes the bread rise.

In the early days of baking, the chief source of yeast was the foam that bubbled on the tops of vats in which ale or beer was brewing. This liquid yeast was called barm. (Today, in dry form, it is known as brewer's yeast.) Before modern times, most housekeepers did their own brewing, and ale barm was readily available. But too often it was bitter and unpleasant tasting. To improve the taste, the foamy barm had to be "cleaned" (soaked in several changes of water over a period of days). A steady supply of clean yeast was always kept on hand in a corked jug.

Nowadays, people can easily buy yeast in a food store. Some yeast is compressed into tiny blocks. Other yeast, called active dry yeast, is sold as a powder in small packets.

These little beads of yeast have been stripped of all moisture and remain in a dormant (sleeping) state until they come in contact with liquid.

Breads leavened by yeast are called yeast breads. Those leavened by other agents are often called quick breads because they can be baked immediately, without waiting for fermentation to take place. Baking powder is one leavening agent used in quick breads. Its active ingredients are bicarbonate of soda and an acid such as tartaric acid. When the baking powder is moistened, the bicarbonate of soda reacts with the acid to form new substances. In the process, carbon dioxide is produced and released. The result is a dough that is light and airy.

Baking powder is used chiefly in cookies, crackers, biscuits, and pretzels. It makes these baked goods rise just enough to be light and crumbly. Another leavening agent is a mixture of baking soda and an acid food, such as buttermilk, molasses, or lemon juice. This mixture is often used in making muffins and other quick breads.

Salt. Salt is an important ingredient in most breads and other baked goods. It adds vitality to the flavor. In yeast breads, it helps control the speed at which the yeast works. The rate of yeast growth, in turn, helps determine the texture and crustiness of the loaf.

Liquids and Fats. For plain, ordinary bread, water is the only liquid required. Because of its fat content, milk is sometimes used in addition to, or instead of, water. Milk creates a richer-tasting loaf with a soft crust. For this reason it is often the preferred liquid for making sweet rolls, muffins, cakes, and cookies.

To make a rich dough, butter, margarine, or another fat is added. These ingredients are called shortenings because they often make baked goods "short" (crisp and flaky).

Other Ingredients. There is a great variety of baked goods because many other ingredients can be added to the basic dough. Sugar adds a sweet flavor. It also provides extra nourishment for yeast cells and speeds up their manufacture of gas bubbles. Sugar also helps in the browning of the crust.

Eggs generally are not used in breads, but they are often included in rich cakes. Some cake recipes call for egg whites. The whites are beaten until they are stiff. Then they are carefully folded into the cake batter. Because they contain so many little pockets of air, the whites help to create a very light cake. Angel food cake is made in this way.

Raisins, currants, prunes, dates, and other dried fruits often are included in coffee cakes and holiday cakes. So is the candied peel of citrus fruits such as lemons and oranges. Fresh fruits may be mixed into dough—banana bread is an example. Finely ground nuts are sometimes mixed with flour for an especially moist cake or quick bread with a nutty flavor. Spices such as caraway, dill, cumin, fennel, and aniseed are often used to give breads a crunchy texture or tangy flavor. Sweet spices such as cinnamon, cloves, nutmeg, and allspice are used in cakes.

▶ MAKING YEAST BREAD

Two common ways of making yeast bread are the sponge method and the straight-dough method. In the sponge method, the yeast is first mixed with water and some of the flour. This mixture, called a sponge, is allowed to ferment before the rest of the ingredients are added. In the straight-dough method, all the ingredients are mixed at once.

After the ingredients are mixed together in the proper amounts, several steps remain— kneading the dough, letting it rise, releasing the trapped gas, allowing the bread to rise again, and baking the bread.

For the gluten to develop properly, most breads made at home require about 10 to 20 minutes of kneading. The purpose of kneading is to work the dough into a uniform texture. To knead bread dough, put the dough on a lightly floured board and flatten it with the palm of your hand. Pick up the edge farthest from you and fold it over the edge nearest you. Push the edges together with the heel of your hand. At the same time, push the mass of dough away from you. Then turn the dough a quarter of the way around and repeat the process. This folding, pushing, and turning process is repeated until the dough is smooth and shiny and has lost all of its stickiness.

Next, the dough is allowed to rise until it has doubled in bulk. For this step, the kneaded dough must be placed in a warm, preferably moist place, away from any cold drafts. The temperature should be about 27 to 29°C (81 to 84°F). An ideal spot is an unlighted oven.

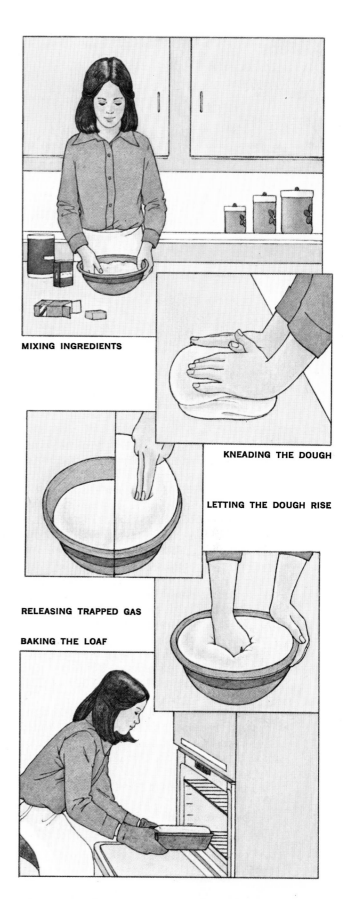

MIXING INGREDIENTS

KNEADING THE DOUGH

LETTING THE DOUGH RISE

RELEASING TRAPPED GAS

BAKING THE LOAF

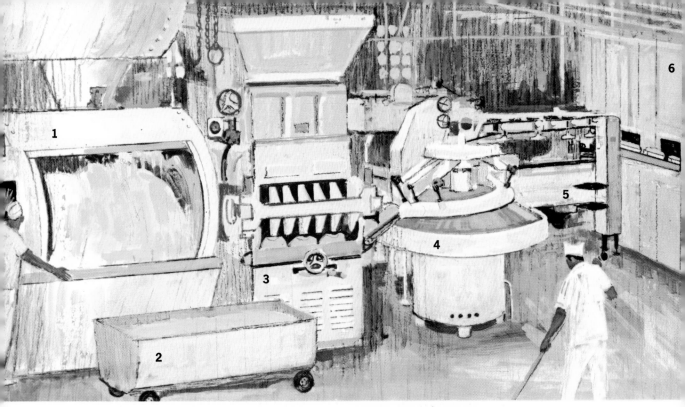

Today bread can be mixed, baked, and wrapped in a completely automatic process. Dough is turned out by the revolving paddles of the mixing machine (1). After fermenting in a trough (2), the dough is transferred to the divider (3), which divides the mass of dough into loaf-sized pieces. The rounder (4) forms the dough into balls. From the rounder the dough passes to a proof box (not shown), where it rises. Conveyor belts carry the

The dough is covered with a sheet of waxed paper or a clean towel. This prevents a dried crust from forming on the outside.

Depending on the recipe and the amount of yeast used, some kneaded doughs take close to 24 hours to double in bulk. Others take as little as 1 hour. To test whether a dough has doubled in bulk, press the tips of two fingers lightly and quickly about 1.5 centimeters (½ inch) deep into the dough. If the dent remains, the dough has doubled.

After the dough has risen, it is necessary to release the gas trapped within it. For hand-kneaded dough, this is done by plunging a fist into the dough to collapse it and then kneading it for a few minutes. Then the bread is allowed to rise again, so that it will have a light and even texture.

Baking is the final stage in the breadmaking process. The dough is placed in a preheated oven. Most wheat bread is baked in pans. Some breads, such as French bread, are formed into loaves and placed directly on baking sheets. It is important that the bread be heated evenly from all sides.

The heat of the oven gives the yeast its last chance to work, and most loaves will rise about 5 centimeters (2 inches) while baking. The yeast is not killed until the inside temperature of the loaf exceeds 54°C (130°F). It takes longest for the center of the loaf to reach that temperature, and the yeast in the center has the longest time to work. As a result, most baked breads have the shape of a gently sloping hill.

▶ MANUFACTURING BREAD

Today, approximately 95 percent of all bread eaten in the United States is produced commercially. In large commercial bakeries, the entire process is carried out by machinery. Machines mix thousands of kilograms of flour into dough every hour and are automatically switched off when the dough is of the proper consistency. Machines also divide the dough into pieces of the desired weight, shape it into loaves, and put it into pans. Conveyor belts move the dough from step to step in the breadmaking process.

The baking itself takes place in a huge oven. The oven may be 23 meters (75 feet) long— big enough to hold almost 3,000 loaves at

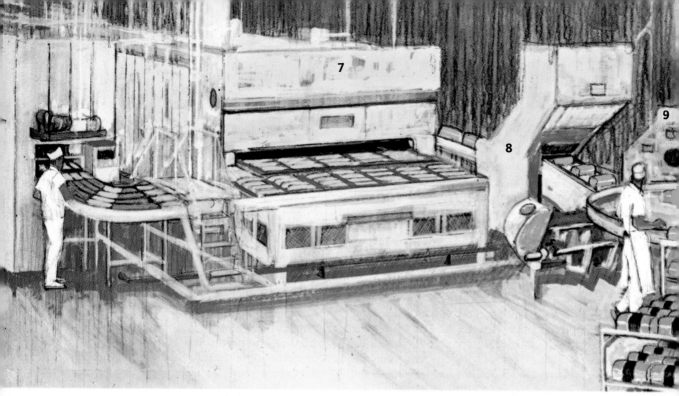

dough from machine to machine. In the molding machine (5), rollers flatten the dough into pancake shape, then form it into loaves. The loaves rise once more in a final proof box (6), then move into a traveling oven (7). When the bread comes out of the oven about ½ hour later, it is fully baked. The loaves are sliced by the steel blades of a slicing machine (8), then wrapped automatically (9).

one time. After they are baked, the loaves are sent on conveyor belts to be cooled, sliced, and wrapped. The slicing and wrapping operations, like the other steps in the breadmaking process, are performed by machines.

Frozen baked goods and brown-and-serve rolls are usually put out by specialty companies. They give people the chance to serve a variety of fresh baked goods without spending hours making them. Brown-and-serve rolls are baked in a few minutes in a hot oven. A frozen cake needs only to be defrosted.

Some cakes and breads are sold in cans. Canned bread was developed to solve a practical problem—armies had to find a way to keep the bread in combat rations from going stale. Canned bread is made by baking the dough in the can rather than in baking pans. The lid is loosely clinched onto the can to permit steam and leavening gas to escape during baking—otherwise, the can would explode. As soon as the can leaves the oven, a machine seals it hermetically (airtight). This keeps out bacteria and molds that cause decay. The can is then cooled rapidly to protect the flavor and color of the bread.

▶ HISTORY OF BREADMAKING

No one knows for sure when people first began to make bread. But many scholars believe that bread was first made more than 10,000 years ago, in the Middle East. Around that time, people made a thick porridge of crushed wheat or barley and water. They shaped the mixture into flat disks. Then they baked it in ashes or on hot stones.

The first leavened bread was probably made by accident. Perhaps a mixture of crushed grain and water was left longer than usual and began to ferment before it was baked. But bread that rises with the aid of wild yeast may turn out quite differently each time because different kinds of yeast may fall on it. The ancient Egyptians learned to control the kind of yeast in their bread. Each time they baked, they set aside some of the leavened dough to mix with the next batch. In this way they could be sure of having the same taste and texture. (The sourdough carried by prospectors in the California and Klondike gold rushes of the 1800's served the same purpose.)

The Greeks were the master bakers of antiquity, with more than 70 different recipes for bread. The Romans turned baking into a large-scale industry and passed many laws governing the quality of bread. Poor people generally ate coarse, dark bread. Fine, white bread was only for the wealthy.

In Europe during the Middle Ages, white bread was also the bread of the rich and privileged. Dark, often sour rye bread was the mainstay of most of the people. This continued to be so until the 18th and 19th centuries, when the Industrial Revolution brought many changes in baking. Large bread factories took the place of neighborhood bakeries. As standards of living rose and wheat became more abundant, people demanded more refined bread. They thought that whiter bread was better in quality. This is not actually true, because the milling that produces white flour removes most of the vitamins and minerals present in wheat. Since 1940, most white bread baked in the United States has been enriched by adding some of the vitamins and minerals lost during milling.

▶ OTHER BAKED GOODS

During the Middle Ages, French travelers, soldiers, and sailors carried a strange, hard bread. The bread had been cooked twice to keep it from spoiling. No one needs to cook bread twice today, but we still eat hard biscuits. The name "biscuits" comes from the early French word for twice cooked. Another form of hard bread—hardtack—was the traditional fare for British sailors.

Cookies, crackers, and pretzels do not look or taste alike, but they are alike in many ways. All are small and crisp, and they keep well. All are made with the same basic ingredients—flour, leavening, shortening, and liquid. Usually the leavening in these products is baking powder.

Crackers appeared in the United States about 1860. Soon every grocery store had a cracker barrel filled with square soda crackers or round butter crackers. Grocery stores were one of the popular centers of social life in small towns during the 1800's and early 1900's. The people who gathered there to exchange news and opinions were called cracker-barrel philosophers.

Part of the fun in eating cookies is their shape. The dough for some cookies is simply dropped by the spoonful onto a baking sheet. These are called drop cookies. For other cookies, the dough is rolled out into a sheet. Then cookie cutters of various shapes cut out pieces of dough, which are placed onto the baking sheet. Still other cookies are made by forcing the dough through a nozzle shaped like the design of the cookie.

Pretzels have a long history. They date back to the early Christians in the Roman Empire. At that time, they were used solely for religious purposes. Fat, milk, and eggs were forbidden during the Lenten season, and people ate dry pretzels instead of bread. They were especially popular on Ash Wednesday. It was only in modern times that pretzels became snacks to nibble on.

In northern Europe and the Scandinavian countries, the pretzel has become the sign of the baker. A large golden pretzel is usually seen hanging outside each bakery.

The Roman honey bread and the later medieval sweet cakes were the forerunners of the iced layer cakes and sponge cakes of today. Pies were made by medieval cooks. But often these were filled with combinations of meat or fish and fruits and eaten as a main course. Gradually pastry cooks began to use pies as sweet desserts. During the 1800's, desserts became elaborate creations. The Viennese and French made such artistic and tasty desserts that people traveled to Vienna and Paris just to try their pastries. Today many home bakers prepare cakes and other baked goods either from packaged dry mixes or from scratch.

The size, shape, and contents of baked goods are forever changing. The basic ingredients—flour, leavening agent, water, and salt—can produce a long crusty loaf of French bread, a soft roll, a crispy pretzel, or a crunchy cracker. Knead in a little oil for pizza dough. Leave out the leavening agent and add some butter, and you have a flaky pie pastry. Stir in a few eggs, some sugar and spice, and you have a pound cake. The possibilities are truly endless.

LORNA J. SASS
Author, *To the King's Taste*

See also FLOUR AND FLOUR MILLING; FOOD AROUND THE WORLD; GRAIN AND GRAIN PRODUCTS; WHEAT.

BRECKINRIDGE, JOHN C. See VICE PRESIDENCY OF THE UNITED STATES.

BREZHNEV, LEONID (1906–1982)

Leonid Ilyich Brezhnev was the leader of the Soviet Union from 1964 until his death. He was the first Soviet leader to be head of state and head of the Communist Party at the same time.

Brezhnev was born in Dneprodzerzhinsk (formerly the village of Kamensk) in the Ukraine, on December 19, 1906. His father was an ironworker. Brezhnev's education exposed him to the two fields in which Communist Party leaders usually have some working knowledge—industry and agriculture. He studied first at a boys' secondary school. Later, at an agricultural school, he learned surveying. He graduated from a technical institute as a metallurgical engineer.

Brezhnev's rise in the Communist Party followed the same pattern as that of Nikita Khrushchev, who was party chief before him. Brezhnev became a member of the Young Communist League in 1923 and joined the party in 1931. He attended party schools and gained experience in agricultural and industrial positions in various parts of the country. He worked in the Ukraine with Khrushchev, who was in charge of reorganizing the party there. He was a political officer in the Red Army during World War II.

After the war Brezhnev held several high-level party positions. From 1953 to 1957, he directed an effort to open the dry regions of Soviet Central Asia to farming. When he returned to Moscow, he was named to the party's ruling Presidium. In 1960 he became chairman of the Presidium of the Supreme Soviet (head of state of the Soviet Union). This position is less powerful than that of general secretary of the Communist Party.

Brezhnev was involved in Khrushchev's dismissal in October, 1964. He had resigned his position as head of the Presidium earlier that year, and he replaced Khrushchev as party general secretary. He later strengthened his leadership. A constitution adopted in 1977 elevated the office of head of state, which he resumed and held with his party job. He died on November 10, 1982, in Moscow.

In his domestic policies, Brezhnev favored the military, and he built up Soviet forces. He also tried to improve production in industry and agriculture. He pushed some projects—such as the Baikal-Amur Mainline railroad, in Siberia—despite difficulties in construction.

Brezhnev showed both a mailed fist and a silk glove in dealing with Eastern Europe. In 1968, reform programs in Czechoslovakia seemed to threaten Soviet control there. He ordered Soviet troops to invade Czechoslovakia and dismiss its liberal leaders. The reason given was that the interests of the Soviet bloc outweighed the right to self-rule of any member country. (This policy became known as the Brezhnev Doctrine.) In contrast, when riots broke out in Poland in 1970 and 1976, Brezhnev ensured that the party leader was removed in the first case and that food prices were lowered in the second. But Soviet pressure encouraged the Polish Government to declare martial law in 1981, after workers had formed independent unions and demanded more political freedom.

Under Brezhnev, the Soviets remained on unfriendly terms with China. They gave aid to pro-Communist forces in other countries. In 1979, Soviet troops entered Afghanistan to support a Communist government.

Brezhnev expressed a policy of détente (easing tension) with the West. The Soviets negotiated on arms control. In 1975, they joined in talks in Helsinki, Finland, that set goals of peace, security, and justice for Europe, the United States, and Canada. But relations with the West were often strained.

ROBERT H. DODGE
Washington and Jefferson College

BRICKS AND MASONRY

Brick is one of the most common and useful building materials. It is also one of the oldest. Bricks are made of fired (baked) clay and can be used to build almost any type of structure.

Early forms of brick were sun-baked and were not as durable as fired bricks. Bricks have been made in many sizes and shapes since they were first used almost 10,000 years ago. At the present time, the standard brick in the United States is a rectangular block measuring about 2¼ inches (5.7 centimeters) thick by 3¾ inches (9.5 centimeters) wide by 8 inches (20 centimeters) long. Bricks are produced in many other sizes, as well as in some special shapes, including curved and sloped brick.

Bricks range in color from nearly white, through tan, red, and red-brown, to dark purple. The color is determined by the type of clay used as well as the amount of iron and other impurities in it. The method of firing is also a factor. Generally, the higher the firing temperature, the darker the brick. Bricks, like pottery, may also be glazed in various colors. Finally, coatings and mechanically applied textures can also change the color and appearance of the brick.

Bricks are extremely durable. Ordinary brick can stand the direct flames of a fire with little damage, and refractory brick (a special brick used for lining fireplaces and furnaces) can stand temperatures as high as 4000°F (2200°C). Because brick is not easily damaged by acids, it resists the chemicals created by air pollution and various industrial processes better than some kinds of stone and painted metal.

The strength of brick also varies a great deal. Brick has high compressive strength; that is, it can withstand forces that press in on it. The average brick can take a load of about 10,000 pounds (4,500 kilograms) a square inch before it is crushed. Several types of brick can stand a load as high as 20,000 pounds (9,000 kilograms) a square inch. However, brick does not have tensile strength—it cannot withstand forces that tend to pull it apart.

▶ FROM CLAY TO BRICK

Bricks are made from clay, which is a common mineral substance. Some types of clay are formed by the disintegration of rocks by weathering. Other types of clay were formed during the Ice Age by the action of glaciers grinding boulders to fine powder. Clay is found over most of the earth's surface, often in lake beds and riverbeds. It is frequently mixed with other substances, such as sand and silt. Clay becomes slippery and plastic (easily molded) when it is wet. When it is dry, it becomes hard and stony.

Workers in Madagascar set bricks out to dry in the sun. Most modern bricks are machine-formed and baked at high temperatures in large ovens.

When clay is heated to about 850°F (450°C), it changes chemically so that it no longer becomes plastic when it is wet. This means that bricks of fired clay will not soften and lose their shape when they become wet, and a wall made of these bricks will not collapse into a sticky heap during a heavy rain. Bricks are baked, or burned, at 1600 to 2200°F (870 to 1200°C). At about 1000°F (540°C) the brick turns from greenish gray to its matured color (for example, red, buff, or white).

Until the 1800's bricks were made by hand. In one common method clay was dug up from the ground and exposed to the air from fall to spring. After the clay was thoroughly dried, the brickmaker spread a small quantity of it on the ground, added a little water, and mixed it into a paste. He pressed the mixture into wooden forms, or molds, which gave the bricks the correct size and shape. Then he removed the sides of the mold and laid the moist brick on the ground to be dried and hardened by the sun. In biblical times chopped straw was usually mixed with the clay to help hold it together.

Because rain might slow up the process or even ruin the soft clay, brickmakers realized that they had to find a better process of drying. As early as 2500 B.C. the technique of baking the brick in ovens, or kilns, was being used in Mesopotamia and India. (Sun-dried bricks, or adobe, are still used in regions where it seldom rains.)

Over the centuries a number of different types of kilns were invented. In older types of kilns only one batch of brick could be made at one time. Most bricks today are made in continuous kilns. Continuous kilns are designed so that they can turn out bricks 24 hours a day, all year long, if necessary. The tunnel kiln, a heated tunnel through which the bricks are pushed or pulled slowly on small railroad cars, is a leading type of continuous kiln.

A mason places a brick in a bed of wet mortar and taps it into place with the handle of his trowel. Mortar holds bricks together and makes the wall watertight.

Some Brick Bonds

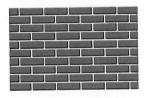

Running bond — stretchers (bricks' long sides) are laid in overlapping courses

Flemish bond — stretchers and headers (bricks' short sides) alternate in each course

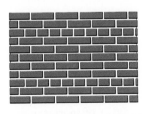

Common, or American, bond — a headers course is placed at every sixth stretcher course

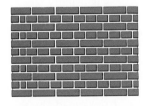

English bond — a course of stretchers and a course of headers alternate up the wall

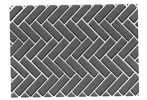

Herringbone bond — often used for paving; bricks may be laid flat or on edge

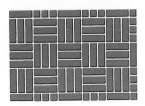

Basketweave bond — used for paving; bricks may be laid flat or on edge

391

Stonemasons carefully select rocks and fit them into this dry stone wall (built without mortar). Strings are used as guides for building the wall straight and level.

Basically the manufacture of bricks has changed little since ancient times, except that machines now perform most of the tasks that were once done laboriously by hand. The clay is now dug by power shovels. After drying, it is ground in power-driven mills and screened to get particles of uniform size.

In the **stiff-mud** process the clay is mixed with water into a stiff paste and then forced out under pressure through nozzles called **dies**. As it comes out, the clay resembles a giant square-cornered strip of toothpaste. The strip is automatically cut into pieces of the proper size by knives or wires. The soft "green" brick is then dried in heated holding areas. Finally the brick is carried on small, flat railroad cars through the kilns for firing.

The **soft-mud** process is older than the stiff-mud process. More water is mixed with the clay than in the stiff-mud process. This produces a softer paste. The soft paste is shaped in individual molds either by machine or by hand. The soft-mud process is usually slower than the stiff-mud process and is used to produce bricks that cannot be formed by other brick-making methods.

In the **dry press** process the ground-up clay is moistened with just enough water to hold it together. Powerful hydraulic presses squeeze the clay into brick shape. Bricks made by this method are as durable as bricks made by the stiff-mud process and usually shrink very little during the drying process. This process is used to make most refractory brick.

▶MASONRY

Masonry is the name for walls, pillars, arches, and other structures made by laying bricks, stone blocks, and other stonelike materials, such as concrete blocks, in a cementing material called **mortar**.

Long ago, primitive people discovered that they could pile naturally occurring stones together to make a rough wall. Later came the idea of trimming the stones so that they would fit together better. This made a firmer and more solid wall. At about the same time, people in regions where stone was scarce discovered how to turn clay into artificial stones—bricks. Bricks were easy to handle and build with because they were the same size and shape and did not need trimming to fit together. An important step in the development of masonry was taken when builders learned that they could use various materials to cement bricks or stone blocks together. In this way they could build rigid walls and more complicated structures, such as arches and vaults.

Brick Masonry

To make a rigid wall of brick, individual bricks are laid together in horizontal layers, or **courses**. The bricks are bound together with mortar.

The mason spreads a layer of mortar with a wide, flat tool called a trowel. The bricks are set on the mortar and pressed down lightly. If a brick is out of line, it is tapped gently into place with the handle of the trowel. Mortar is

Some Stonework Patterns

Examples of ashlar masonry

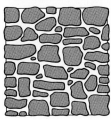  

Examples of rubble masonry

also placed between each brick in a course. When the first course is laid, the mason spreads mortar on top of it and lays the second course on this mortar. This process is repeated until the wall is built.

It is important to make each course level and the wall straight. An uneven wall is not only unsightly but weak. The mason uses a straight level to make sure that the bricks are set level in the mortar. A plumb line (a string with a weight at one end) is used as a vertical guideline. A string stretched tightly from one end of the wall to the other helps the mason line up the bricks horizontally.

The thin horizontal and vertical layers of mortar between the bricks are called the **joints**. The early masons learned that they could build a stronger wall by staggering the joints, or overlapping the bricks so that the vertical joints of one course do not line up with the joints of the course below. The different arrangements or patterns in which the bricks are laid are called **bonds**. A brick laid so that its long end is exposed to view is called a **stretcher**; a brick laid with its short end exposed is called a **header**. Many builders use brick as a facing, or veneer, over the wooden frames of houses and the concrete or steel frames of large buildings.

Stone Masonry

Stones vary widely in size, shape, and composition. The two main types of modern stonework are **ashlar** and **rubble**. Ashlar masonry is constructed of cut and squared stones. They may be set in regular courses, similar to brick, or in random courses where different sizes of stone are used. Rubble masonry is composed of rough, irregularly shaped stones. Rubble stones are usually set in random patterns.

A person who works with stone is called a stonemason. The stonemason's work is more difficult and exacting than the bricklayer's. The stones have rough, jagged edges. To get a smooth surface, the stonemason trims off the projections. This is called dressing the stone and requires experience and skill.

Setting the stones in place in the walls is an art in itself. Because building stones are usually cut in large sizes (to save labor in trimming), they are very heavy. For example, a granite block 6 feet (1.8 meters) long by 3 feet (0.9 meter) wide by 1 foot (0.3 meter) thick weighs about 3,060 pounds (1,377 kilograms) —more than a ton and a half.

Obviously, such stones are too heavy to lay by hand. They must be lifted by powerful derricks and guided into place by the stone setter as they are gently lowered. If the stone is out of line, it cannot simply be tapped into line like a brick. It must be lifted up and lowered into place again.

Stone, like brick, was once a major structural material. It was used where great strength and weight were required, as in dams, bridges, fortresses, foundations, and important buildings. Today steel and concrete have taken the place of stone as a basic construction material. However, stone is still important as sheathing (outside covering) for buildings, as flooring

Built some 4,500 years ago, the Great Pyramid, in Egypt, contains more than 2 million close-fitting stone blocks averaging 2.5 tons (2.3 metric tons) each.

where there is heavy traffic, and for many decorative uses. It is valued for its many colors and textures.

▶HISTORY OF MASONRY

The history of masonry goes back as far as that of civilization. Archaeologists have unearthed bricks that authorities have dated as 9,000 to 10,000 years old. These bricks were discovered at the site of an ancient settlement beneath the biblical city of Jericho. The Old Testament of the Bible contains the earliest written record of brick making.

In Egypt brick making began about 3100 B.C. Although the Egyptians had vast supplies of fine building stone, it took so much labor to quarry the stone, cut it to size, and transport it to the building sites that stone was used only for temples, palaces, and monuments. Ordinary buildings were made of sun-baked brick.

From Egypt brick making spread to other countries around the Mediterranean Sea. The Romans became the master brickmakers of ancient times. Roman bricks were relatively thin and broad, and they were made in a variety of different shapes: rectangular, square, triangular, and semicircular.

One of the biggest problems faced by builders in the ancient world was the lack of a strong mortar to bind their bricks and stones together. Yet in spite of their poor mortar, ancient builders constructed some remarkable brick temples and palaces, with walls 10 to 20 feet (3 to 6 meters) thick. The builders depended mainly on the weight of the walls to hold the bricks in place.

Masonry construction was revolutionized by the Roman discovery of concrete in the 2nd century B.C. With this strong cementing material builders no longer needed to make their walls enormously thick to keep them from toppling over. In fact, the Romans' concrete was so strong that most important Roman buildings were made of concrete with a thin decorative facing of brick or stone.

Perhaps the most famous examples of ancient stone masonry are the pyramids of Egypt, some of which are more than 4,500 years old. These huge stone structures were built as tombs for rulers of ancient Egypt.

Other ancient civilizations besides the Egyptians developed great skill in handling very large blocks of stone. The Myceneans, who lived in central Greece between 2100 and 1300 B.C., built fortifications and tombs of rough stone blocks that weighed several tons apiece. The Greeks became the master stone workers of the ancient world. They were especially skilled at designing and trimming stone blocks.

The Gothic cathedrals of the late Middle Ages are the most complex structures in pure stone ever attempted. The skill of those who built these cathedrals has never again been equaled.

CARL W. CONDIT
Co-editor, *Technology and Culture*
Reviewed by CHARLES N. FARLEY
The Brick Institute of America

See also ARCHITECTURE; BUILDING CONSTRUCTION; CEMENT AND CONCRETE; STONE.

Bridges allow easy passage across rivers and other obstacles. In a city like Pittsburgh, Pennsylvania, bridges are lifelines, allowing people and goods to move into and out of the downtown area.

BRIDGES

Imagine life without bridges. Even the smallest river would be a barrier to travel and trade. To cross a broad river we would have to wade across or wait for a ferry boat. To cross a steep canyon would require trudging down one side and climbing slowly up the other. Before bridges were built, cars and trains lined up at busy crossings, waiting for traffic going in other directions.

There are more than 500,000 bridges in the United States today. Most of them are designed to carry automobile or railroad traffic, but some are intended for pedestrians only. Without bridges we would not have a modern system of highways and railroads. Most bridges are so short that they do not have names, and most travelers do not even notice going over them. There are some bridges, however, that are famous for their length, for their outstanding design, and for their beauty.

▶TYPES OF BRIDGES

A bridge must be strong enough to support its **load**, which includes its own weight as well as that of any traffic it may carry. It must have the stiffness and stability to withstand natural forces such as temperature changes, wind, and earthquakes. A bridge must also stand up to corrosion caused by moisture, polluted air, and road salt.

People have developed a variety of structures that meet these requirements. These structures include beam bridges, truss bridges, arch bridges, cantilever bridges, suspension bridges, cable-stayed bridges, and movable bridges. When deciding which kind of bridge to build, engineers consider how far the bridge must span, how deep in water or earth they must go to find solid support, and how much traffic the bridge must carry. These considerations help them choose the type of bridge and the right materials.

Beam and Truss Bridges. The simplest way to bridge a stream or other obstacle is to lay a beam across the stream so its two ends rest on opposite banks. The first bridges were probably natural bridges formed by fallen trees.

The beam may be made of wood, steel, or concrete reinforced with steel. Beam bridges resting on **abutments** (supports at each end of the bridge) are used to span fairly short distances. Longer beam bridges have additional supports, called **piers** and **trestles**, between the abutments.

Beam bridges are simple and relatively inexpensive to build. They can be found on most highways and expressways, where they are widely used at crossings.

Beam   Truss

Adding a framework called a truss to a beam bridge creates a **truss bridge**. The parts of a truss are connected in a series of triangles. The truss may lie under the bridge **deck** (roadway). Or large truss arrangements may extend above both sides of the bridge deck. Truss bridges are used to span longer distances than beam bridges. Timber trusses helped support wooden covered bridges built in the 1800's.

Arch Bridges. Bridge builders can span greater distances with arch bridges than they can with beam or truss bridges. The roadway can be built above the gracefully curved arch (a **deck-arch bridge**) or be suspended from it (a **through-arch bridge**). Foundations support the load of the arch, which pushes outward and downward on them.

Arch bridges have been constructed of stone, brick, timber, cast iron, steel, plain concrete, and reinforced concrete. The construction of beautiful stone masonry arch bridges reached a peak in the early 1900's, but they are rarely built anymore. Almost all modern arch bridges are constructed of steel, reinforced concrete, or timber.

Most of the great Roman bridges were supported on arches. In the city of Rome alone, six of the eight arch bridges built over the Tiber River almost 2,000 years ago are still standing.

Cantilever Bridges. In its simplest form, a cantilever is a beam that extends or projects beyond its vertical support. A wall bracket is a familiar example of a cantilever. When secured firmly at one end (bolted to the wall), a wall bracket can support a heavy weight. To make a bridge, two cantilevers are ordinarily built projecting toward each other from opposite sides of a waterway. Each cantilever rests on a pier and is anchored to the waterway bank behind the pier. The cantilevers do not meet until they are connected in the center by a truss.

The Forth Rail Bridge in Scotland, opened in 1890, is a cantilever bridge constructed of enormous steel tubes. Some of the tubes are 12 feet (3.7 meters) in diameter. More recently, very strong reinforced concrete has been used to build cantilever bridges.

Suspension Bridges. All of the world's longest and many of the best-known bridges are suspension structures. Suspension bridges are built to span the longest distances—more than 4,600 feet (1,400 meters) between support towers. And with their tall towers and swooping cables, suspension bridges are among the most beautiful bridges.

All suspension bridges have three common parts: towers, anchorages, and cables. The majestic towers are built on firm foundations near either shore. Some stand more than 700 feet (210 meters) above the water.

The anchorages are placed on land at each end of the bridge and are where the main cables are secured. The cables may be anchored in bedrock or huge blocks of reinforced concrete. The anchorages hold the main cables against tremendous forces.

The main cables themselves are made of thousands of strong steel wires bound together. From one anchorage, the cables soar to the top of a tower, then swoop gracefully almost to road level and back up to the top of the next tower. Finally, they swoop down again to the end anchorages.

Once the main cables are in place, smaller support cables are attached to them. These support cables, called **suspenders**, hold up the framework for the roadway.

The first primitive suspension bridges were probably made with vines in a tropical region. Ropes replaced vines as civilization progressed. Bridges were later supported by wrought-iron chains strung over towers. Eventually, cables made of woven strands of iron or steel were developed, making possible the construction of modern suspension bridges.

The first modern suspension bridges were introduced by the German-American engineer

Left: The Sydney Harbour Bridge in Australia supports its roadway by a graceful steel arch. The roadway of an arch bridge can run through the arch or sit completely above it.

Below: The Forth Rail Bridge—a massive cantilever structure in Scotland—crosses the Firth of Forth, an inlet of the North Sea. The spans of a cantilever bridge project toward one another from piers and are connected by shorter truss spans.

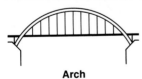

Arch

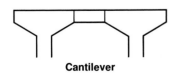

Cantilever

Suspension bridges span the greatest distances. The Golden Gate Bridge reaches across California's San Francisco Bay, stretching 4,200 feet from tower to tower. The roadway is supported by two heavy steel cables that are attached to both shores and hung across both towers.

John A. Roebling. Although Roebling had built earlier suspension bridges, the Brooklyn Bridge in New York City, completed in 1883, was his masterpiece. With its beautifully designed stone towers, the Brooklyn Bridge was one of the first all steel-cable suspension bridges. Its main span of 1,595 feet (486 meters) also made it longer than any bridge previously built.

Roebling never saw the Brooklyn Bridge completed. In 1869, before construction even began, he died following an accident. The work of building the bridge was taken over by his son, Washington A. Roebling. The younger Roebling devoted his life to the bridge's construction for the next 14 years.

Suspension bridge designs, construction techniques, and materials have improved greatly since Roebling's time. Today suspension bridges can be built with main spans nearly three times longer than the main span of the Brooklyn Bridge. The Humber Bridge over the Humber River in England, opened in 1981, holds the record for the world's longest single span—4,626 feet (1,410 meters).

Cable-Stayed Bridges. Dramatic new cable-stayed bridge designs look like suspension bridges. Both types of bridges have towers and cable-suspended roadways. But on a cable-stayed bridge, the cables supporting the roadway run straight from the towers to the bridge deck. The cables may fan out from the tops of the towers or they may be spaced at intervals along the lengths of the towers.

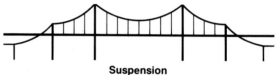

Suspension

But no cables run from one end of the bridge to the other. The result is a bridge that has a sleek, futuristic beauty.

Cable-stayed bridges span up to 2,000 feet (610 meters) and can cost less to build than suspension bridges of the same size.

Movable Bridges. Sometimes it is not possible or convenient to build a bridge high enough for ships to pass underneath. If this is the case, the bridge must be built so that it can be moved out of the way or raised, so that ships can pass under it. Almost all modern movable bridges are driven by electric motors. Among the most common movable bridges are drawbridges and vertical-lift bridges.

A **drawbridge** opens when one or two sec-

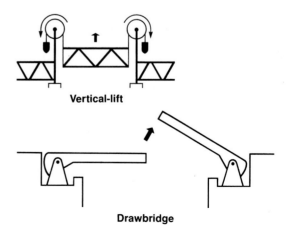

Vertical-lift

Drawbridge

tions swing upward to allow ships to pass through. The **vertical-lift** bridge has a span that can be lifted straight up into the air to allow ships to pass under.

▶BUILDING A LARGE BRIDGE

The construction of a suspension bridge requires the talents and efforts of many people. Many types of information must be collected during the planning phase. Maps of the building site are drawn to show the shape of the land. Other maps showing the underlying soil and rock are prepared, so that proper foundations can be planned. Studies are made to estimate the amount of bridge traffic there will

be. Tides, flood conditions, currents, and other characteristics of the waterway are carefully studied. Information is also gathered on natural hazards such as high winds and earthquakes.

Engineers take all the information collected and produce finished written descriptions and drawings telling what is to be built, the exact location of the bridge, the materials to be used, and how they are to be put together.

Construction starts with the foundations. No matter how strong a bridge is designed to be, it requires good foundations. The piers and abutments must be able to support the load of the bridge and traffic and to resist the forces

Cable-stayed

The Sunshine Skyway Bridge over Florida's Tampa Bay is a cable-stayed bridge. *Above:* During construction, roadway segments are added to both sides of a central tower, supported by cables connected directly to the tower. *Right:* Beam sections and cable-stayed sections have been joined to create a dramatic finished structure.

of wind, water, ice, and earthquakes. Piers must be solidly based on rock or firm ground.

Many bridge foundations have to be sunk into the bottom of a river or bay, where there are layers of mud, sand, and rocks. To support the foundation, the builder may drive long, slender pieces of wood, steel, or concrete called **piles** through these upper layers of loose material to firm soil or rock. This is usually done with a powerful hammering machine called a **pile driver**.

Another method is to dig away the loose mud and silt and build concrete pillars or walls on firm soil or bedrock. For this underwater construction, large watertight compartments called **caissons** are sunk to the bedrock. The water is pumped out of them, and air is pumped in. The higher air pressure inside a caisson acts to keep water out. Then workers enter the caisson, excavate the loose soil, and build the foundations. In the early days of bridge construction, people who worked in caissons returned too quickly to normal air pressure. Such a rapid change in air pressure can cause internal injuries. Many people were seriously injured or died from this condition, which became known as caisson disease, or "the bends."

The bridge towers are constructed on the foundations, and cable anchorages are prepared on each bank of the waterway. Then the placing of the cables can begin.

John A. Roebling designed a way to string cables in place. Individual steel wires fed from each shore are looped back and forth many times over the bridge towers. Once the proper number of strands has been placed, the strands are wrapped tightly together with corrosion-resistant wire. Vertical cables, or suspenders, are attached to giant bands clamped to the newly constructed cables.

After the roadway is completed signs, lighting, guardrails, and other finishing details are installed, and the bridge is ready to use.

SOME NOTABLE BRIDGES OF THE WORLD

Name of bridge	Location	Length of main span feet	Length of main span meters	Year opened
Suspension				
Humber	Humber River, near Hull, England	4,626	1,410	1981
Verrazzano-Narrows	Lower New York Bay, New York, N.Y.	4,260	1,298	1964
Golden Gate	San Francisco Bay, Calif.	4,200	1,280	1937
Mackinac	Straits of Mackinac, Mich.	3,800	1,158	1957
Second Bosporus	Bosporus Strait, Turkey	3,597	1,096	1988
First Bosporus	Bosporus Strait, Turkey	3,524	1,074	1973
George Washington	Hudson River, New York, N.Y.	3,500	1,067	1931
Brooklyn	East River, New York, N.Y.	1,595	486	1883
Cantilever				
Quebec Railway	St. Lawrence River, Quebec, Canada	1,800	549	1917
Forth Rail	Firth of Forth, Queensferry, Scotland	1,710	521	1890
Minato Ohashi	Osaka Bay, Japan	1,673	510	1974
Commodore John Barry	Delaware River, Chester, Penn.-Bridgeport, N.J.	1,644	501	1974
Greater New Orleans	Mississippi River, New Orleans, La.	1,575	480	1958
Howrah	Hooghly River, India	1,500	457	1943
Steel Arch				
New River Gorge	New River, near Fayetteville, W. Va.	1,700	518	1977
Bayonne	Kill Van Kull, Bayonne, N.J.	1,675	510	1931
Sydney Harbour	Sydney, Australia	1,650	503	1932
Fremont	Willamette River, Portland, Ore.	1,255	383	1973
Cable-Stayed				
Alex Fraser	Fraser River, British Columbia, Canada	1,525	465	1986
Second Hooghly	Hooghly River, India	1,500	457	1987
St.-Nazaire	Loire River, France	1,325	404	1975
Dame Point	Jacksonville, Fla.	1,300	396	1988
Sunshine Skyway	Tampa Bay, Fla.	1,200	366	1987
Continuous Truss				
Astoria	Columbia River, Astoria, Ore.	1,232	376	1966
Oshima	Oshima Island, Japan	1,066	325	1976
Croton Reservoir	Croton, N.Y.	1,052	321	1970
Concrete Arch				
Krk	Krk Island, Yugoslavia	1,280	390	1979
Gladesville	Parramatta River, Sydney, Australia	1,000	305	1964

Over the years bridge builders have worked to make their bridges as safe as possible. With proper engineering, construction, and maintenance bridges will be strong and safe. On the other hand, serious engineering flaws, faulty construction, or lack of proper maintenance can lead to bridge failure.

One such catastrophe involved the Tacoma Narrows Bridge over the Puget Sound in 1940. Only four months after it was completed, while exposed to strong winds, the suspension bridge began twisting violently. The roadway was ripped from its suspenders and plunged into the water below. The knowledge engineers gained from that and other bridge disasters led to safer designs.

To remain safe, bridges require constant inspection and maintenance. Scuba divers inspect piers for damage or erosion that may weaken the bridge's foundation. Steel bridges are painted to prevent corrosion from air pollutants and rain.

When a bridge is no longer economical to maintain, it may be demolished and replaced. Some bridges are simply abandoned, and new bridges are built nearby. In rare cases bridges are moved or are maintained as historic sites.

▶ SOME FAMOUS BRIDGES

One of the most famous structures in history is London Bridge, across the Thames River. The original bridge, begun in 1176 and completed in 1209, was a series of stone arches. Until the 1700's it was the only bridge across the Thames in London. The bridge became a center of London life. After the bridge was finished, houses were built on it, and in time it became lined with buildings.

Erosion of the bridge foundations was a continual problem. Some scholars think the song "London Bridge Is Falling Down" originally referred to the bridge's constant need for repairs. The old bridge continued in use, however, until the 1830's, when it was replaced by a new London Bridge, also an arch.

With the passing of time this bridge, too, had to be replaced. In the 1970's, stones from this bridge were shipped to Lake Havasu City, Arizona, where the bridge was reconstructed over an arm of the Colorado River. The present London Bridge, another arch bridge, was begun in 1968 and completed in 1973.

Venice, Italy, has about 400 bridges crossing its many canals. Located in this city is the

WONDER QUESTION

Why were some of the early bridges in America covered?

Covered bridges once dotted the American countryside from the Atlantic coast to the Ohio River. The bridges looked like square tunnels with peaked roofs. Some people claim that the bridges were covered so that horses would not be frightened by the water underneath. Others say that they were built as a shelter for travelers in bad weather. Actually the coverings were designed to protect the wooden framework and flooring of the bridges and keep them from rotting. The pitched roofs, which shed snow, also reduced the amount of heavy snow that collected on the bridges. Wooden bridges became obsolete as traffic loads increased and modern trucks grew in size. Today only a few are still standing. Many people work to preserve the remaining covered bridges.

Bridge of Sighs, built around 1600. It is believed that prisoners sentenced to death could be heard sighing as they crossed the bridge on their way to execution.

The Quebec Railway Bridge over the St. Lawrence River in Canada is the only major bridge to have collapsed twice. When the bridge was nearly finished in 1907, part of it collapsed, killing 75 workers. Work began again on a redesigned and stronger bridge. In 1916 a new span fell while being lifted into place, killing 13 more workers. The bridge was finally completed in 1917.

The Chesapeake Bay Bridge-Tunnel is an unusual combination of trestles, bridges, and tunnels stretching almost 18 miles (29 kilometers) across the entrance to Chesapeake Bay. Most of the roadway is supported by trestles and lies about 25 feet (8 meters) above the water. The trestles join two bridge spans that rise high above the water and two tunnels that dip beneath the channel. Ships can pass under the bridges or over the tunnels.

Other significant bridges, their lengths, and the years in which they were opened are listed in the accompanying table.

Reviewed by NEAL FITZSIMONS
Principal, Engineering Counsel

See also TRANSPORTATION.

BRINKLEY, DAVID. See NORTH CAROLINA (Famous People).

BRITISH COLUMBIA

British Columbia, the most westerly province in Canada, faces the Pacific Ocean. The coast is indented with hundreds of narrow inlets. Some of them extend inland as far as 100 kilometers (60 miles). Vancouver Island and the Queen Charlotte Islands, which are part of British Columbia, lie between the coast and the open sea. The Inside Passage, a natural waterway extending from the state of Washington in the United States to Alaska, separates the islands from the mainland.

▶ **THE LAND**

British Columbia is the most mountainous province in Canada. Row after row of jagged peaks must be crossed to travel from one side of the province to the other. In the northeast corner of the province are the forested, rolling plains of the Peace River district. The Rocky Mountains are the most easterly mountain range. The Rockies are cut by narrow passes such as Crowsnest, Kicking Horse, Yellowhead, and Pine. These passes are used as road and railway routes across the Rockies.

The Coast Mountains form the western rim of British Columbia's mainland. These forest-covered mountains rise steeply from the shores of the coastal inlets and the Inside Passage.

The Interior Plateau, in central British Columbia, is an area of rolling plateaus and valleys from 600 to 900 meters (2,000 to 3,000 feet) high.

The rivers of British Columbia flow directly or indirectly into two oceans—the Pacific and the Arctic. The Columbia River, with its tributaries, and the Fraser, Skeena, Stikine, and other rivers flow into the Pacific. The Peace and Liard rivers in the northeastern part of the province are tributaries of the Mackenzie River, which flows through the Northwest Territories on its way to the Arctic Ocean.

British Columbia owes much of its beauty to its many lakes. Among the best known of the natural lakes are Atlin, Babine, and Kootenay. Williston Lake, the largest lake in the province, was formed by the W. A. C. Bennett Dam on the Peace River.

Climate

British Columbia has a great variety of climates. In winter the climate along the coast is the mildest in Canada. Air masses moving eastward across the Pacific Ocean bring mild winters, cool summers, and much winter precipitation to the coastal area. The average annual rainfall on western Vancouver Island is more than 2,540 millimeters (100 inches), the heaviest in North America.

Summers are hotter and winters are colder in the interior of the province. There is much less precipitation in the interior than there is on the coast.

Natural Resources

Vast forests, powerful rivers, an abundance of well-distributed minerals, fertile valleys, and beautiful scenery are British Columbia's main natural resources.

Forests. The mild, wet coastal climate helps the growth of British Columbia's most abundant natural resource—the vast forests of

---

FACTS AND FIGURES

LOCATION: Western Canada. **Latitude**—49° N to 60° N. **Longitude**—114° W to 139° W.

JOINED CONFEDERATION: July 20, 1871, as 6th province.

POPULATION: 2,889,207 (1986 census). **Rank among provinces**—3rd.

CAPITAL: Victoria, pop. (metropolitan area) 255,547 (1986 census).

LARGEST CITY: Vancouver, pop. (metropolitan area) 1,380,729 (1986 census).

PHYSICAL FEATURES: Area—948,600 km² (366,255 sq mi). **Rank among provinces**—3rd. **Rivers**—Peace, Liard, Fraser, and Columbia. **Lakes**—Atlin, Babine, Kootenay, Okanagan, and Williston. **Highest mountain**—Fairweather, 4,663 m (15,300 ft.)

INDUSTRIES AND PRODUCTS: Lumbering and the manufacture of forest products; mining; farming and the processing of food products; commercial fishing.

GOVERNMENT: Self-governing province. **Titular head of government**—lieutenant governor, appointed by Governor-General of Canada in Council. **Actual head of government**—premier, elected by people of province. **Provincial representation in federal parliament**—6 appointed senators; 28 elected members of House of Commons. **Voting age for provincial elections**—19.

PROVINCIAL MOTTO: *Splendor sine occasu* (Splendor without end).

PROVINCIAL FLOWER: Dogwood.

Vancouver, the largest city in British Columbia, is Canada's major Pacific port.

coniferous trees. These forests cover the eastern lowlands of Vancouver Island and the Queen Charlotte Islands, as well as the lower slopes of the Coast Mountains. Forests also cover most of the Interior Plateau and the valley slopes in southeastern and northern British Columbia. The most valuable tree is the gigantic Douglas fir, which may reach a height of 60 meters (200 feet). Western hemlock, Sitka spruce, and western cedar also are commercially important.

Waterpower. Swift, snow-fed rivers provide an abundance of waterpower. The largest hydroelectric projects are near Kitimat, along the Columbia River and its tributaries, and on the Peace River.

Minerals. Copper, zinc, lead, molybdenum, silver, and tungsten head the list of metallic minerals found in British Columbia. Deposits of mercury, gold, tin, antimony, and other metals also are found. Asbestos is the chief nonmetallic mineral. And there are large quantities of sand and gravel, stone, clay, sulfur, and peat moss. Coal, oil, and natural gas are important mineral fuels.

▶ THE PEOPLE AND THEIR WORK

The population of British Columbia is small for its vast area. Many parts of the province are unpopulated because the land is too rugged for agriculture or forestry. Seventy-five percent of the people live in or near the cities in the southwest. The remainder live in towns or small cities in the southern valleys or along roads or rail lines crossing the interior of the province.

British Columbia is well named because most of the early white settlers were of British origin. This is true of 60 percent of the present-day residents. Many other Europeans moved to the province after 1950.

In the 1880's, Chinese laborers came to British Columbia to help build the western section of the Canadian Pacific Railway. Afterward many of them settled in Vancouver and formed the largest Chinese community in Canada. Many other Asians have become residents of British Columbia since that time.

Another important group is the Indians, who number about 52,000. Most of them live on reserves, which are administered by the federal government in co-operation with local Indian associations.

Industries and Products

The availability of waterpower has played an important part in the growth of industry in British Columbia. Forestry and the manufacture of wood products are the leading industries. The economy of the province also depends on mining and mineral industries, agriculture, fishing, and tourism. An important

Oceangoing freighter takes on cargo of freshly-sawed lumber at Port Alberni sawmill, Vancouver Island.

Many yacht basins are found in the inlets and fiords along the coastline of British Columbia.

share of British Columbia's income is brought in by tourists, who come to enjoy the magnificent scenery.

Forest Industries. More than 65 percent of the softwood lumber produced in Canada comes from British Columbia's forests. Before 1940, most of the large sawmills were on the coast, so that lumber could easily be exported on oceangoing ships. But after 1950, production from forests in the interior increased. New pulp and paper mills were built in the interior after 1960. This development increased British Columbia's pulp and paper production to about 20 percent of Canada's total production.

Mining and Mineral Industries. The gold rush of 1858—up the Fraser River and later into the Cariboo region—brought the first large wave of white settlers into the province. Gold no longer adds much to the income of the province. The most valuable minerals are copper, zinc, lead, asbestos, coal, petroleum, molybdenum, silver, and tungsten. Most of Canada's lead and much of its zinc are produced at Kimberley. These ores are smelted and refined at Trail, on the Columbia River. Copper is shipped to Japan from several mines in southwestern British Columbia. Coal is also mined and then exported to Japan. Oil and gas are produced in the northeastern Peace River area.

In the 1950's the Aluminum Company of

Canada built an aluminum smelter and the town of Kitimat for workers and their families. The site was chosen because the area has an abundance of water to provide hydroelectric power for the industry.

Agriculture. Most of the good farmland is found in the lower Fraser River valley, the valley around Okanagan Lake, the central Interior Plateau, and the Peace River district. The lower Fraser valley is used for dairy farming. There are also truck farms in that area, producing vegetables, berries, and poultry for the nearby cities. Specialty crops of flowers and flower bulbs are grown on Vancouver Island and are exported to eastern Canada. The irrigated Okanagan valley is a major apple-growing area. It also produces peaches, cherries, pears, plums, and the only apricots in Canada. Beef cattle are raised on ranches in the Interior Plateau. The Peace River district produces grain and legume seed crops, as well as cattle.

The processing of foods is an important industry. Dairy products, meat, fish, and fruits and vegetables are the major products.

Fishing. Almost all the Pacific salmon—Canada's most valuable fish—are caught in the river mouths and coastal inlets of British Columbia. The large salmon canneries are south of Vancouver. Prince Rupert is an important port for halibut-fishing fleets.

Transportation and Communication

Transportation in British Columbia has always been a problem because of the mountains, the scattered population, and the high costs of construction. The historic Cariboo Road into British Columbia's gold country, built in the 1860's, had to be cut through the rock wall of the Fraser River's canyon. But by the time the Trans-Canada Highway was completed in 1962, most of the settled regions had paved roads. The Alaska Highway starts at Dawson Creek—the end of the railway in the Peace River district—and extends about 1,000 kilometers (600 miles) through northern British Columbia before entering Yukon Territory.

The Canadian Pacific and the Canadian National transcontinental railways connect British Columbia with the rest of Canada. They are vital to the province's economy. The provincially owned British Columbia Railway

BRITISH COLUMBIA

crosses the province from Vancouver to the Peace River. It carries many of the resources from the interior to the coast.

Passenger boats and cargo vessels stop at the small coastal villages between Vancouver and Prince Rupert. Ferries make regular runs between Victoria, Nanaimo, Vancouver, and ports in Washington state. Many vessels travel from Seattle, Washington, and Vancouver through the Inside Passage to Skagway, Alaska —a voyage of about 1,530 kilometers (950 miles). There are commercial airports in the major cities. Service is provided by a number of airlines.

All major towns and cities have radio stations. Television reaches all parts of the province by use of relay stations. *The Colonist,* one of the first newspapers in British Colum-

Parliament Buildings, Victoria. Flower-filled baskets decorate many street lamps in this lovely capital city.

Towering totem pole dominates Prospect Point in Vancouver's huge Stanley Park. Park contains zoo, aquarium, and theater.

Mount Maxwell Provincial Park in the Gulf Islands of the Inside Passage.

PROSPECT POINT

bia, began publication in Victoria in 1858. Other major newspapers include the *Times* of Victoria; the *Province* and the *Sun,* both of Vancouver; and the *Columbian* of New Westminster.

▶ **EDUCATION**

Education is free and compulsory for children from 6 to 15 years of age. Elementary school extends through the first seven grades; secondary school, from the eighth to the twelfth grade. Children who live in isolated areas may be taught through correspondence courses that are provided by the provincial government.

There are three universities. The largest is the University of British Columbia in Vancouver. The other two are Simon Fraser University in Burnaby, an eastern suburb of Vancouver, and the University of Victoria in the capital city. Numerous community colleges throughout the province provide the first two years of post-secondary education.

Public libraries are maintained in all the larger cities, and mobile libraries serve distant communities. The library of the University of British Columbia in Vancouver and the provincial archives in Victoria are noted for their collections of historical material on British Columbia.

▶ **PLACES OF INTEREST**

Some of British Columbia's magnificent scenery and places of historic interest are preserved in national parks. They provide extensive areas for recreation.

Glacier National Park is located in the Selkirk Mountains of southeastern British Columbia. The Rogers Pass section of the Trans-Canada Highway crosses this park. It can also be reached by railway. Glacier National Park is known for heavy snowfall and many avalanches.

Kootenay National Park, a huge forest preserve, was developed in the Canadian Rockies at the source of the Kootenay River. Deep canyons and waterfalls are among its major attractions.

Mount Revelstoke National Park is a winter sports center in the western Selkirk Mountains. Skiing is its most popular sport during winter months.

Pacific Rim National Park was established in 1971 on the central west coast of Vancouver Island. It includes the longest continuous stretch of sand beach in British Columbia.

Yoho National Park was established in 1886 on the west side of the Continental Divide. It is the site of Takakkaw Falls, which drop about 360 meters (1,200 feet). The park has many lakes and a natural stone bridge. It adjoins Banff National Park in Alberta and is crossed by the Trans-Canada Highway.

Fort Langley National Historic Park is the site of the first government of British Columbia. The fort, which was built as a trading post in 1827, has been restored as a museum.

Other places of interest in British Columbia include museums and more than 175 developed provincial parks. The largest of the provincial parks is Tweedsmuir, in the Coast Mountains. It is mainly a wilderness area.

The Maritime Museum, in Vancouver, has displays emphasizing the importance of the ocean in British Columbia's past and in its present economic life. In a drydock is the RCMP *St. Roch,* the first ship to navigate the Northwest Passage through the Canadian Arctic from west to east. The city archives and museum and a planetarium are nearby.

The Provincial Museum of Natural History and Anthropology, in Victoria, contains fine collections of Indian artifacts. It also has exhibits depicting British Columbia's past. Near the museum is Thunderbird Park, which has a large collection of Indian totem poles.

▶ **CITIES**

More than 80 percent of the people of British Columbia live in cities and towns with populations of more than 1,000. Since about 1900, nearly half of the people have resided in or near Vancouver.

Victoria is the capital of British Columbia. It grew from a Hudson's Bay Company trading post built in 1843 and became the capital of the colony of British Columbia in 1868. Many of the residents do government work, but there are also a few sawmills and small manufacturing plants.

Vancouver is one of Canada's largest cities and its major Pacific seaport. It is the center of British Columbia's industry, finance, and trade, as well as the headquarters of many businesses. Most of the people work in service industries and commerce. An article on Vancouver appears in Volume V.

New Westminster, on the north bank of the Fraser River near its mouth, was founded in

A salmon catch. Most of Canada's Pacific salmon comes from the waters of British Columbia.

1859. It was the capital of British Columbia until 1868. The city has a good freshwater port and several large sawmills. It has a population of about 40,000.

Nanaimo, on eastern Vancouver Island, was an important coal-mining town in the last half of the 19th century. Its major industries today are sawmills and a pulp mill. It is the main wholesale and distribution center for central Vancouver Island. Nanaimo has a population of more than 45,000.

Prince George is a forestry and transportation center for central British Columbia. It has many sawmills and three pulp and paper mills. Simon Fraser established a fur-trading post at Fort George in 1807, near the site of the present city. Prince George has a population of more than 65,000.

Prince Rupert was laid out in 1909 as a planned city at the northern terminal of the railway. It has fish canneries and freezing plants. Its population is about 16,000.

Kamloops is the largest city in the southern interior. It has sawmills, a pulp and paper mill, and an oil refinery. It is also a transportation and distribution center. It has a population of about 65,000.

Kelowna is the largest city in the Okanagan valley. It is the supply and service center for the valley, as well as a recreation center.

Trail is on the Columbia River near British Columbia's southern border. It is the site of a fertilizer plant and a smelter and a refinery that process lead, zinc, and other minerals.

▶**GOVERNMENT**

British Columbia is a self-governing province with a legislative assembly of 57 members. A lieutenant governor, appointed by Canada's governor-general, is the titular head of the province. The actual head of government is the premier of the province, who is the leader of the political party electing the most representatives to the legislature. British Columbia has six appointed senators in the Canadian Parliament and 28 elected members of the House of Commons. The voting age for provincial elections is 19.

▶**FAMOUS PEOPLE**

British Columbia has been the home of many people who have contributed to the economic development of the province and to its political, social, and cultural life.

Simon Fraser (1776–1862) explored much of the territory of British Columbia for the North West Company and established several fur-trading forts, including Fort George and Fort Fraser. In an extremely perilous journey in 1808, he traveled the length of the river that now bears his name. He retired in 1820 and died a poor and lonely man.

Sir James Douglas (1803–77), sometimes called the founder of British Columbia, was born in British Guiana (now Guyana). He was associated with the Hudson's Bay fur-trading company for more than 35 years and was instrumental in establishing Victoria as an important trading center. Sir James was governor of Vancouver Is-

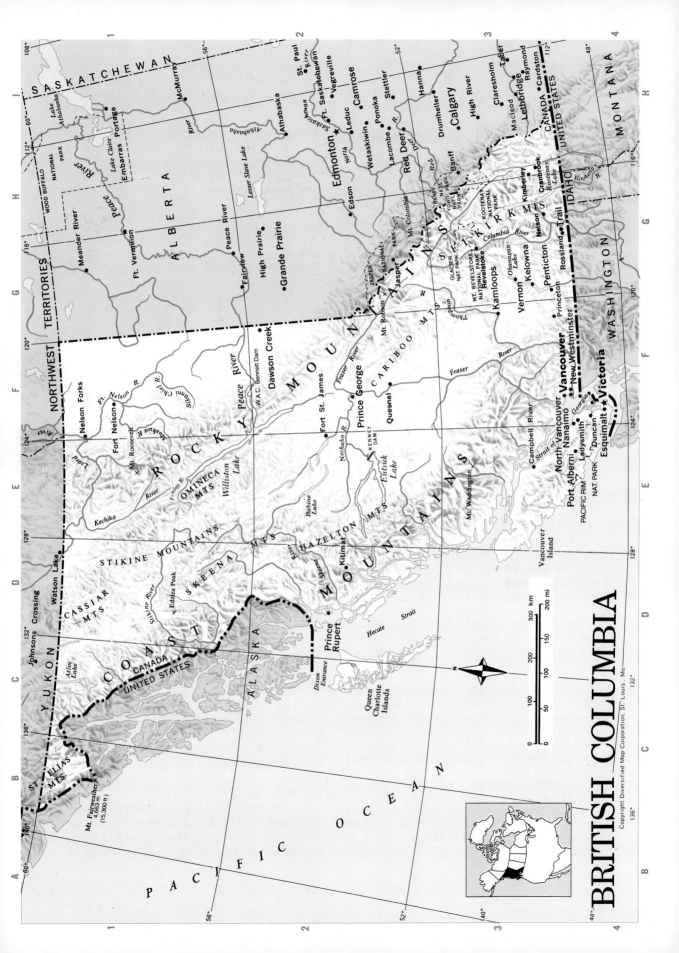

BRITISH COLUMBIA

Copyright Diversified Map Corporation, St. Louis, Mo.

Emerald Lake in Yoho National Park. The park is especially popular with mountain climbers.

land (1851–63) and also of the mainland colony of British Columbia (1858–66). He worked to keep British Columbia and other British colonies on the Pacific coast from becoming part of the United States.

Amor De Cosmos (1825–97) was born William Alexander Smith in Windsor, Nova Scotia. He acquired the name Amor De Cosmos, meaning "lover of the universe," during the California gold rush of 1853. He joined the gold rush in British Columbia in 1858 and in that year founded *The Colonist,* one of the oldest newspapers in western Canada. He was premier of British Columbia from 1872 to 1874.

Peter Vasilievich Verigin (1858–1924) was a Russian-born leader of the Doukhobors, a Russian religious sect that settled in Saskatchewan and British Columbia after 1909. The Doukhobor communities under Verigin's leadership were thriving collective societies for more than ten years. Verigin was killed by an explosion, probably set by a group of followers who became disenchanted with his increasingly dictatorial leadership.

Mary Ellen Spear Smith (1861–1933), born in England, was one of British Columbia's most noted social reformers. Politically active from 1918 to 1928, she was instrumental in the fight for woman suffrage and reforms for women and children. The first woman to sit in British Columbia's legislature, she was also the first woman to hold cabinet rank (as a minister without portfolio), in 1928.

Emily Carr (1871–1945) was a noted painter and writer. Born in Victoria, she was known as Canada's leading woman painter. She took as her subjects the west coast Indians and the forests of British Columbia. Her paintings are on display in Vancouver. Her prose writings include *The Heart of a Peacock* (1953) and *Pause* (1953).

H. R. MacMillan (1885–1976) was a forester in British Columbia. In 1915 he toured the world looking for markets for British Columbia's forest products. He later formed a lumber company, which by the 1960's was the largest in Canada.

Ethel Davis Bryant Wilson (1890–   ) is known for her novels of life in British Columbia. Born in Port Elizabeth, South Africa, she went to Vancouver in 1910. Her novels, noted for their wit and sympathetic character portrayals, include *Swamp Angel* (1934) and *Love and Salt Water* (1956).

William Andrew Cecil Bennett (1900–1979) was premier of British Columbia for 20 years (1952–72), longer than any other political leader in the history of the province. As premier, he promoted the growth of the forest and mineral industries and developed hydroelectric power. As a result, the province experienced an economic boom. Bennett was born in New Brunswick. After moving to British Columbia, he established a hardware business. In 1941 he was elected to the provincial legislature. He became the leader of the Social Credit Party and premier in 1952. His party lost control of the government to the New Democratic Party in 1972. But the Social Credit Party came to power again in 1976, under the leadership of one of Bennett's sons, William R. Bennett.

William Bruce Hutchison (1901–   ), one of Canada's leading journalists, was born in Prescott, Ontario, and grew up in Victoria. He was editor of the Victoria *Times* and the Vancouver *Sun* during the 1950's and 1960's. He wrote several books about Canada, including *The Fraser* (1950).

A biography of fur trader Sir Alexander Mackenzie, who was the first white man to explore the interior of British Columbia, appears in Volume M. A biography of George Vancouver, who explored and mapped the northwest coast of North America and gave his name to Vancouver Island and the city of Vancouver, appears in Volume V.

▶ **HISTORY**

Before the first Europeans reached British Columbia, the land was inhabited by many Indian tribes. They lived by fishing and hunting. Some of them created unusual works of art, such as the totem poles that are treasured in British Columbia today.

In 1774 the Spanish voyager Juan Pérez became the first European known to have reached the coast of British Columbia. Pérez claimed the land for Spain. Four years later Captain James Cook arrived and claimed the land for Britain. For many years Spain and Britain contested the territory, but during these years both countries carried on a lively fur trade with the Indians.

In 1792 Captain George Vancouver explored Puget Sound and surveyed the coastal inlets. A year later Alexander Mackenzie, a trader with the North West Company, completed the first overland journey from eastern Canada to the Pacific coast. Finally Spain was forced to give up its claim and to recognize Britain's right to the territory.

In 1808 Simon Fraser explored the river that now bears his name. By 1811 David Thompson had explored the southeast interior and the Kootenay and Columbia rivers. During these years the only European settlers were fur traders. Trading posts were established along the Columbia River and in the north. In 1843 Victoria on Vancouver Island became the center of the coastal fur trade. Settlers arrived and farming began.

In 1858 the discovery of gold in the Fraser River brought prospectors from eastern Canada and the United States. By 1861 the gold rush to the Cariboo Mountains was in full swing. Ranching and farming began in the interior plateaus and river valleys, and sawmills began harvesting the coastal forests.

Vancouver Island and the mainland settlements were separate crown colonies until 1866, when they were united by the British Government into the single crown colony of British Columbia.

In 1871 British Columbia became Canada's sixth province. In 1885 the Canadian Pacific Railway was completed, and the next year the first transcontinental train arrived at Port Moody. The water around Port Moody was too shallow for an ocean port, so the rail terminal was moved to the little sawmilling town of Granville. Later, Granville was renamed Vancouver.

During the 1890's another mining boom brought settlers to the southeast Kootenay country. Commercial fishing began off the river mouths, and lumber from the tall forests was exported east of the Rockies to build the towns in the prairie provinces. Early in the 20th century, farming began in the irrigated Okanagan valley, and dairy farming expanded across the lower Fraser River valley.

Over the years British Columbia has become ever more closely linked with the economic expansion of all Canada. And the province's wealth of resources is only now coming into full development.

J. LEWIS ROBINSON
University of British Columbia

IMPORTANT DATES

1774 Juan Pérez, Spanish voyager, reached the coast of British Columbia.

1778 Captain James Cook claimed the coastal area for Great Britain.

1792 George Vancouver began explorations along the Pacific coast.

1793 Alexander Mackenzie reached the Pacific coast.

1795 Spain renounced claims to the area.

1805–1808 Simon Fraser explored area of British Columbia; followed Fraser River to the sea.

1843 Fort Victoria established at present site of capital city.

1846 Oregon Treaty set boundary between British Columbia and the United States.

1849 Vancouver Island established as British Crown Colony.

1858 Colony of British Columbia established on the mainland during gold rush to Fraser River.

1866 British Columbia and Vancouver Island united.

1868 Victoria became provincial capital.

1871 British Columbia joined Canadian Confederation as the 6th province.

1885 Canadian Pacific Railway completed to west coast of Canada.

1903 Alaska boundary dispute arbitrated.

1914 First grain elevator was built in Vancouver harbor.

1915 Railway completed across southern British Columbia.

1942 Alaska Highway linked Dawson Creek with Yukon Territories and Alaska.

1957 Natural-gas pipeline completed between Peace River District and Vancouver.

1962 Trans-Canada Highway completed; Rogers Pass section opened.

1965 Columbia River power project, joint venture between the United States and Canada, begun.

1972 The New Democratic Party became the first socialist party to govern British Columbia; it was defeated in the elections of 1975.

1976 Provincial Department of the Environment created.

BRITISH COMMONWEALTH. See COMMONWEALTH OF NATIONS.

BRITISH GUIANA. See GUYANA.

BRITISH HONDURAS. See BELIZE.

BRITISH ISLES. See UNITED KINGDOM.

BROADCASTING. See RADIO (Radio Programs); TELEVISION (Television Programs).

BRONCHITIS. See DISEASES.

Anne, Emily, and Charlotte Brontë, as painted by their brother Branwell about 1835. All three sisters wrote novels about life in 19th-century England.

BRONTË SISTERS

Charlotte, Emily, and Anne Brontë and their brother Branwell lived with their father, the Reverend Patrick Brontë, in a parsonage high above the village of Haworth in Yorkshire, England. Their mother had died when Anne was a year old. There were no other children nearby for the Brontës to play with. They walked on the moors, read books, and wrote stories about imaginary places called Angria, Gondal, and Gaaldine. The stories were more real to them than their own lives.

Charlotte Brontë was born on April 21, 1816. Like her younger sisters, she wrote poetry as well as stories. In 1846 the sisters joined together to publish *Poems by Currer, Ellis and Acton Bell*. To hide their true identities, Charlotte called herself Currer, Emily was Ellis, and Anne was Acton.

The sisters had also been working on novels. Anne's and Emily's were accepted for publication, but Charlotte's novel, *The Professor*, was rejected. Finally one publisher expressed an interest in her work, so she finished *Jane Eyre*, her second novel, and sent it off. She drew on her own life in this novel. Like her main character, Jane Eyre, Charlotte Brontë was once a governess in a large house. The school where Jane Eyre taught was modeled after one that the Brontë sisters attended. *Jane Eyre,* published in 1847, was an immediate success. Her third novel, *Shirley,* was published in 1849, and her last novel, *Villette,* in 1853. *The Professor* was finally published in 1857, after her death.

Emily Brontë was born on July 30, 1818. She wrote only one novel, *Wuthering Heights,* which was published under her pen name, Ellis Bell, in 1847. It was not so popular at the time as *Jane Eyre,* but it is the most imaginative and poetic of all the Brontës' novels. Set on the wild Yorkshire moors, *Wuthering Heights* tells the love story of Catherine Earnshaw and the gypsy Heathcliff.

Anne Brontë was born on January 17, 1820. She worked for many years as a governess, and her first novel, *Agnes Grey* (1847), was about that experience. Her second novel was *The Tenant of Wildfell Hall* (1848).

Fame made little difference in the lives of the sisters, since their identities were still unknown to the public. Their father did not know of their success until much later. Their brother Branwell never knew. A failure at painting and writing, he took to drink and opium and died on September 24, 1848, at the age of 31.

Branwell's death was the first of a series of tragedies for the Brontës. Emily caught cold at her brother's funeral and became very ill. She refused all care and died less than three months later, on December 19, 1848. Her dog, Keeper, followed her coffin to the grave. On May 28, 1849, Anne also died of tuberculosis.

Charlotte lived for six more years, but life seemed empty to her without her sisters and brother. She let her real name be known after a rumor spread that Currer, Ellis, and Acton Bell were all the same person, but she was too shy to enter into society. She did travel to London occasionally. There she met literary celebrities of the day, including the novelists Elizabeth Gaskell, who later wrote a biography of Charlotte, and William Makepeace Thackeray. Charlotte married her father's curate, Arthur Nicholls, less than a year before her death on March 31, 1855.

Reviewed by JULIET MCMASTER
University of Alberta (Canada)

BRONZE AND BRASS

Sometime between 3500 and 3000 B.C., people discovered that mixing copper and tin would yield a new metallic substance, harder and tougher than either copper or tin. This new substance was bronze, and its discovery was an important event in human history.

Before the discovery of bronze, most tools and weapons were made of stone, wood, or bone. Stone could be given a sharp edge, but it was hard to shape, and it broke easily. Bone and wood, being softer than stone, were easier to shape. But they also wore out more quickly.

Copper, which was discovered around 5000 B.C., made better tools and weapons than stone, wood, or bone. It could be cast (melted and poured into a mold) or hammered into many different shapes. When a copper knife broke, it could be melted down and used to make a new knife. But copper was soft, and it bent easily.

Bronze was different. Bronze could be cast into complicated shapes more easily than copper. It would hold a sharp edge much longer. It did not bend in use or grow brittle quickly, as copper did. Durable bronze hoes and spades helped farmers to cultivate their fields better and thus grow more food. Bronze saws and chisels made it possible for carpenters to cut and trim wood accurately.

Bronze brought other changes, too. Armies equipped with bronze weapons easily crushed their more primitive neighbors. From these conquests the first empires were formed.

Archeologists believe that bronze originated somewhere in the mountainous regions of southwestern Asia. Both native copper nuggets and tin ore were found there, often in the beds of mountain streams. Tin was proba- bly discovered shortly before bronze, when an early gold hunter tried to melt the gold out of some gravel containing tin ore. But tin—a soft, pliable white metal—was apparently not used by itself. No tin objects from that time have been found.

Metallurgy (the science of metals) was a mysterious art in those times. Primitive metal-workers experimented with new combinations of metals and ores, just as sorcerers might try new ingredients in their "magical" potions. Copper was already being alloyed with lead and antimony to make it easier to cast. When someone tried adding tin, bronze was the result.

The knowledge of how to make bronze spread gradually from the Near East to other parts of the ancient world. Eventually, people from China to the British Isles were using bronze. The period in history when bronze was the most important material for tools and weapons is called the **Bronze Age.** It lasted from about 3500 B.C. to 1200 B.C., when iron became plentiful and cheap enough for every-day use and took the place of bronze.

▶BRONZE MAKING TODAY

Bronze is made by mixing molten copper with molten tin. The most commonly used bronzes contain up to 10 percent tin.

Traces of other elements are often added to the basic copper-tin mixture to obtain bronzes with special qualities. Phosphorus, for instance, yields a hard, springy bronze that has high resistance to fatigue and corrosion. (Fatigue means that the metal becomes brittle under stresses such as repeated bending or twisting.) Phosphor bronzes are used for products in which these qualities are important, such as bearings, shafts, and diaphragms. Sil-

Brass is made by mixing molten copper and zinc. Here a machine trims the rough edges off long coils of brass. Each coil weighs six metric tons.

icon bronze is used for piston, rings, metal screens, and propeller shafts for ships because it resists corrosion. Aluminum bronze is also used for engine parts and fittings for ocean-going ships.

Bronze may range in color from reddish brown to silvery white, depending on its composition. But the most usual color is golden brown. Bronze is a favorite material for statues and other works of art.

Although "bronze" really means an alloy made chiefly of copper and tin, the name is also used now for some copper alloys that do not contain any tin at all. These tinless bronzes do have some of the characteristics of true bronze, especially its typical golden brown color. Tinless bronze is often used in architectural trim for buildings, as in lobbies and storefronts.

▶ BRASS

Brass, an alloy of copper and zinc, was developed much later than bronze. It appears to have been first used by the peoples of the Middle East around 700 B.C.

Much of our present knowledge of brass comes from the alchemists of the Middle Ages. Their attempts to turn common metals into gold (or at least gold-colored alloys) yielded much information about mixtures of copper, zinc, tin, and lead.

During the 18th and 19th centuries, hundreds of different copper alloys were developed. Most of them were brasses. Today brass is the most widely used copper alloy.

Brass is made in the same way as bronze except that zinc is used instead of tin. Copper and zinc cannot be melted together because copper melts at a much higher temperature than zinc. The zinc would boil away by the time the copper melted. Instead, solid ingots of zinc are added to the molten copper. The two metals may also be melted separately and then mixed.

The resulting alloy ranges in color from deep red through gold to creamy white. The zinc content ranges from 5 to 40 percent. The more zinc, the harder the brass is. Small quantities of other elements—lead, tin, silicon, manganese, or iron—may be added to produce special qualities.

Brasses are divided into two main types, based on the amount of zinc they contain.

Brasses with up to 37 percent zinc are called alpha brasses, and those with more than 37 percent are called beta brasses. Alpha and beta brasses have different crystal structures and therefore different properties.

Alpha brasses are malleable, or easily worked. They are especially suited for cold-working (forming or rolling the metal without softening it by heating). Beta brasses are very malleable when hot, but at normal temperatures they are hard and not easily worked.

Low-zinc, or alpha, brasses are used for such products as water pipes, costume jewelry, cosmetics containers, and artillery shells. High-zinc, or beta, brasses are used for musical instruments, lamps, doorknobs, locks, and hinges.

A small amount of lead makes brass more easily machinable (easier to cut and drill with machine tools). Leaded brass is used in parts that must be accurately shaped, such as watch and clock parts, gears, plumbing materials, and printers' engraving plates.

▶ METHODS OF WORKING

In addition to casting and machining, there are several ways of shaping brass and bronze that also change the properties of these alloys. **Forging** increases the strength of the metal. In forging, the hot metal is pressed with great force between a set of dies. A die is a type of mold that shapes objects by squeezing them.

In **cold-rolling,** the unheated metal is passed back and forth between two heavy rollers, growing longer, wider, and thinner each time. The rolling hardens the metal, but it also creates stresses that make it brittle. **Annealing** (heating the metal and slowly cooling it) relieves the stresses and softens the metal. The cold-working process can then be repeated without danger of cracking the metal.

Seamless tubing and pipe are made by **extrusion.** The heat-softened alloy is squeezed out of a circular die with a plug in its center. As the metal is forced through the die and around the plug, it takes the shape of a hollow tube. While it is still soft, it is drawn, or stretched, to the desired size.

Reviewed by A. H. LARSON
Metals Division, Gould Inc.

See also ALLOYS; COPPER; DIES AND MOLDS; METALS AND METALLURGY.

BROWN, GEORGE (1818–1880)

George Brown was the owner of the most powerful Canadian newspaper of his day, the *Toronto Globe*. He was a leader of the Liberal Party and one of the Fathers of Confederation.

Brown was born in Alloa, Scotland, on November 29, 1818, and went to the United States when he was 18. In 1843 his family moved to Toronto, in Upper Canada. Brown was very close to his father, Peter Brown, and together they founded the *Toronto Banner*. In 1844 they started the *Globe*. The *Globe*'s strong editorials supported the struggle for responsible (cabinet) government and the right of Canadians to rule their own affairs within the British Empire.

In 1851, Brown was elected to Parliament. Canada was then a union of two provinces—Upper Canada and Lower Canada. Brown felt that the country was being controlled by Lower Canadian votes. Yet Upper Canada had the larger population. He demanded representation by population to give Upper Canada the greater number of seats in Parliament. He rebuilt a Liberal Party nicknamed the Clear Grits. In 1858 he became premier, but his government lasted only two days.

Brown's health was poor, so in 1862 he went on a long holiday. While visiting friends in Scotland, he met Anne Nelson. They were married the same year.

Brown was re-elected to Parliament in 1863. He offered to work with his chief foes, John A. MacDonald and George Cartier, to solve Canada's problems. This led eventually to a federal union, or confederation, of all the Canadian provinces. Brown played a major part at the Charlottetown and Quebec conferences, which were held to settle the design of the new union. In 1867 the British North America Act was passed, creating a united Canada.

Brown died in Toronto on May 9, 1880.

J. M. S. CARELESS
University of Toronto

BROWN, JOHN (1800–1859)

John Brown is remembered because of his strong hatred of slavery and for his use of violence in attacking it. He considered himself to be an instrument in the hands of God and believed that only through force and bloodshed would the slaves be freed.

Brown was born in Torrington, Connecticut, on May 9, 1800, but he grew up in Ohio. To support his 20 children, he moved from place to place working as a farmer, sheep raiser, wool merchant, and surveyor. Brown's father had taught him to hate slavery, and over the years his feelings against it grew stronger. In Pennsylvania he used his barn as a hiding place and shelter for runaway slaves.

In order to strike a direct blow at slavery, Brown moved to Kansas in 1855. The Kansas territory was then the center of conflict between slaveholders and those who opposed slavery. On May 24, 1856, Brown headed a party of eight (including four of his sons) that put to death five unarmed proslavery settlers at Pottawatomie Creek.

In December, 1858, Brown led a raid into Missouri. His party seized eleven slaves and conducted them to the Canadian border and freedom. Ten months later he was ready to carry out his long-cherished plan to invade Southern territory in order to free the slaves and organize them into military companies. On October 16, 1859, Brown and twenty-one followers launched an attack on the U.S. arsenal at Harpers Ferry, Virginia (now in West Virginia). A company of U.S. Marines, led by Colonel Robert E. Lee, was sent to crush Brown's band. Ten of Brown's men, among them two of his sons, were killed. Brown and six others were captured.

John Brown was brought to trial for murder and treason. He was convicted and sentenced to hang. As he mounted the scaffold on December 2, 1859, he showed the same dignity and calm that had marked his appearance in the courtroom. To some people, Brown was a lunatic and a murderer who deserved to die. To others he was a martyr. During the Civil War, his memory inspired Union soldiers who sang: "John Brown's body lies a-mouldering in the grave, His soul goes marching on."

BENJAMIN QUARLES
Author, *Allies for Freedom: Blacks and John Brown*

BROWNING, ELIZABETH BARRETT (1806–1861) AND ROBERT (1812–1889)

Two of England's finest poets, Robert Browning and Elizabeth Barrett Browning, are remembered as much for their romance as for their poetry. Elizabeth was born on March 6, 1806, in Durham, England. She was the first of 12 children and her father's favorite. He encouraged her to read and let her be tutored in Greek and Latin along with her brother Edward. When at 13 she composed an epic poem, *The Battle of Marathon,* he had it printed.

Elizabeth was impetuous. One day, when she was 15, she tried to saddle her pony by herself. The pony stumbled, and the saddle fell on top of Elizabeth, injuring her spine. That injury and an infected lung made her a semi-invalid. From then on she spent most of her time indoors, reading and writing.

Robert Browning was born six years after Elizabeth Barrett on May 7, 1812, in Camberwell, near London. Like Elizabeth's father, Robert's had a well-stocked library and encouraged his son to read. Like Elizabeth, Robert began writing verses at an early age. He studied art, music, languages, and literature and published his first poem, *Pauline,* in 1833.

As poetry by both Elizabeth Barrett and Robert Browning began to appear in print, they grew acquainted with each other's work. Then in 1845, Browning found himself mentioned in one of Miss Barrett's poems. He wrote to her, told her how much he admired her poetry, and said he had long wished to meet her. He had, he told her, been as far as her door, but she had not been well enough to receive him. They began corresponding, and on May 20, 1845, Browning called on Miss Barrett in the house on Wimpole Street in London, where the Barretts were living. He visited her frequently afterward, his visits carefully hidden from Mr. Barrett, who had forbidden his children to marry.

Although Elizabeth loved her father, her love for Robert Browning was stronger. On September 12, 1846, the two were secretly married. A week later they left for Italy. Mr. Barrett never forgave his daughter and returned her letters unopened.

The Brownings were extremely happy, and Mrs. Browning's health improved greatly. They both worked on their poetry, although they never discussed or showed their poems to each other until they were finished. They traveled a good deal, yet always returned to Casa Guidi, their home in Florence. It was there that their only child, Robert Wiedemann Barrett Browning, called Penini or Pen, was born on March 9, 1849.

Shortly after the Brownings' third wedding anniversary, Mrs. Browning slid something into her husband's pocket while he stood looking out a window. It was the manuscript of sonnets she had written before they were married. Browning felt they should belong to the whole world and urged his wife to publish them. To hide the identities of the lovers, he suggested she call them *Sonnets from the Portuguese.* No one would know that he sometimes called her his "little Portuguese" after the heroine of her poem "Catarina to Camoens." The sonnets are Mrs. Browning's best-known work.

For 16 years, Elizabeth Barrett and Robert Browning knew a life together of such happiness that it has become legendary. Then on June 30, 1861, Mrs. Browning died at Casa Guidi. A month later, Browning left for England with his son. He could not bring himself to return to Italy until 1878, but from then on he spent most of his time there. He died on December 12, 1889, in the palace his son and daughter-in-law had bought in Venice. His body was taken to England and buried in the Poets' Corner of Westminster Abbey.

Reviewed by REGINALD L. COOK
Middlebury College

This is a sonnet from Elizabeth Barrett Browning's *Sonnets from the Portuguese:*

How do I love thee? Let me count the ways.
I love thee to the depth and breadth and height
My soul can reach, when feeling out of sight
For the ends of Being and ideal Grace.
I love thee to the level of every day's
Most quiet need, by sun and candle-light.
I love thee freely, as men strive for Right;
I love thee purely, as they turn from Praise.
I love thee with the passion put to use
In my old griefs, and with my childhood's faith.
I love thee with a love I seemed to lose
With my lost saints—I love thee with the breath,
Smiles, tears, of all my life!—and, if God choose,
I shall but love thee better after death.

Robert Browning's *Pied Piper of Hamelin* is based on an old legend. The following excerpt tells how the rats followed the piper out of the town of Hamelin.

Into the street the Piper stept,
Smiling first a little smile,
As if he knew what magic slept
In his quiet pipe the while;
Then, like a musical adept,
To blow the pipe his lips he wrinkled,
And green and blue his sharp eyes twinkled
Like a candle-flame where salt is sprinkled;
And ere three shrill notes the pipe uttered,
You heard as if an army muttered;
And the muttering grew to a grumbling;
And the grumbling grew to a mighty rumbling;
And out of the house the rats came tumbling.
Great rats, small rats, lean rats, brawny rats,
Brown rats, black rats, gray rats, tawny rats,
Grave old plodders, gay young friskers,
Fathers, mothers, uncles, cousins,
Cocking tails and pricking whiskers,
Families by tens and dozens,
Brothers, sisters, husbands, wives—
Followed the Piper for their lives.
From street to street he piped advancing,
And step by step they followed dancing,
Until they came to the river Weser
Wherein all plunged and perished
Save one, who, stout as Julius Caesar,
Swam across and lived to carry
(As he the manuscript he cherished)
To Rat-land home his commentary,

Which was, "At the first shrill notes of the pipe,
I heard a sound as of scraping tripe,
And putting apples, wondrous ripe,
Into a cider press's gripe;
And a moving away of pickle-tub boards,
And a drawing the corks of train-oil flasks,
And a breaking the hoops of butter casks;
And it seemed as if a voice
(Sweeter far than by harp or by psaltery
Is breathed) called out, Oh, rats! rejoice!
The world is grown to one vast drysaltery!
To munch on, crunch on, take your nuncheon,
Breakfast, supper, dinner, luncheon!
And just as a bulky sugar puncheon,
All ready staved, like a great sun shone
Glorious scarce an inch before me,
Just as methought it said, come, bore me!
—I found the Weser rolling o'er me."

You should have heard the Hamelin people
Ringing the bells till they rocked the steeple.
"Go," cried the Mayor, "and get long poles!
Poke out the nests and block up the holes!
Consult with carpenters and builders,
And leave in our town not even a trace
Of the rats!"—when suddenly up the face
Of the Piper perked in the market-place,
With a, "First, if you please, my thousand
    guilders!"

413

BRUEGEL, PIETER, THE ELDER (1525?–1569)

The painter Pieter Bruegel (or Brueghel) the Elder is best known for landscapes and peasant scenes. He was born in the Netherlands sometime between 1525 and 1530. Very little is known about his early life, but he became a master in the Antwerp Painters Guild in 1551.

Like many artists of his day, Bruegel looked to Italy for inspiration. He was in Rome in 1553 and returned home across the Alps by 1555. He had always been interested in landscape painting, but his travels in the Alps led him to portray nature in a grander and more unified way.

In Antwerp, Bruegel made drawings for engravings that were widely distributed. The drawings often portrayed serious ideas in humorous form. They showed his interest in popular subjects, his observations on the foolishness of people, and his concern for freedom of religion.

Bruegel's paintings were usually made for private patrons. They dealt with many themes.

He was interested in the human figure. In many of his paintings, crowds of people cover the canvas, creating a brightly colored pattern. But he was also concerned with nature and how it affects people's lives. This can be seen in the five paintings that remain of a series called the *Months. Hunters in the Snow* (1565) is a winter scene from the series, probably representing January.

Bruegel was well known in his time and knew many important people. In 1563 he married and moved to Brussels. He died there on September 9, 1569. Many of his works were then acquired by collectors. Two of his sons also became famous painters. Pieter the Younger (1564–1638) made many copies and variations of his father's works. He was nicknamed Hell for the scenes of Hell he painted. Jan (1568–1625) was a painter whose elegant style earned him the nickname Velvet Bruegel.

LOLA B. GELLMAN
City University of New York

In *Hunters in the Snow*, the hunters are part of a vast, wintry landscape. Bruegel arranged the elements in this scene to show how nature dominates people's lives.

BRUNEI

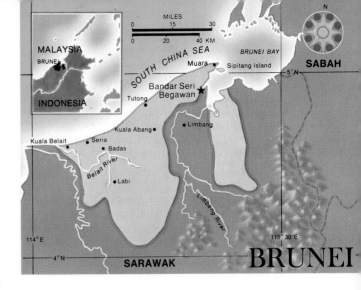

BRUNEI

The small Asian nation of Brunei is located on the northwestern coast of the island of Borneo. Except for its border on the South China Sea, Brunei is entirely surrounded by the territory of Sarawak, a state of the nation of Malaysia. Although small in area and population, Brunei has considerable deposits of petroleum and natural gas, which have given it one of the highest incomes per person in the world.

The People. The majority of Bruneians are Malays. Chinese make up about 25 percent of the population. The remainder include native ethnic groups and people who have come from elsewhere in Asia to work in Brunei. Most of the people live in the capital, Bandar Seri Begawan, and in towns along the coast.

Brunei's official language is Malay. English, Chinese, and native dialects also are spoken. Islam (the religion of the Muslims) is the official state religion, although other religions are permitted.

The Land. Brunei is divided into two unconnected parts, separated by the Limbang River valley off Sarawak. Dense forests cover about 70 percent of the country. The climate is tropical, with high temperatures and humidity and heavy rainfall.

Economy. Brunei's economy is dependent on its petroleum and natural gas. These account for nearly all its exports and more than 75 percent of its wealth. The traditional economic activities of agriculture and fishing have declined, and Brunei must import most of its food. About half of the work force is employed by the government, which also provides free education and medical care and many other social services. Brunei has no income tax. Because Brunei's petroleum reserves are expected to be exhausted by about the year 2010, the government has invested much of its income in economic projects at home and abroad.

History and Government. Brunei's first sultans, or rulers, date from the 14th or 15th century. By the 16th century Brunei had expanded to become the dominant state in the region. It soon declined in size and power, however. In 1888, with the agreement of the then-ruling sultan, Brunei became a British protectorate.

Petroleum was known to exist in Brunei by the early 20th century. But it was not until 1929 that the first large oil field was discovered and commercial production of oil began. Brunei's oil attracted the Japanese, who occupied the region during World War II. After the war ended in 1945, Britain resumed its protectorate over the territory. Brunei became self-governing under its own constitution in 1959. It regained complete independence in 1984.

Brunei is ruled by Sultan Sir Muda Hassanal Bolkiah, who succeeded his father in 1967. Although he governs with the aid of a cabinet, the Sultan holds complete power as both head of state and government.

ROBERT O. TILMAN
North Carolina State University

FACTS AND FIGURES

BRUNEI DARUSSALAM (Brunei, Abode of Peace) is the official name of the country.

THE PEOPLE are known as Bruneians.

LOCATION: Southeast Asia, on the northwestern coast of Borneo.

AREA: 2,226 sq mi (5,765 km²).

POPULATION: 216,000 (estimate).

CAPITAL AND LARGEST CITY: Bandar Seri Begawan.

MAJOR LANGUAGES: Malay (official), English, Chinese.

MAJOR RELIGIONS: Muslim, Buddhist, Christian.

GOVERNMENT: Sultanate (monarchy). **Head of state and government**—sultan.

CHIEF PRODUCTS: Petroleum, natural gas.

MONETARY UNIT: Brunei dollar (1 dollar = 100 cents).

NATIONAL ANTHEM: *Ya Allah Lanjutkan lah usia* ("Oh God, long live our majesty the sultan").

BRYAN, WILLIAM JENNINGS (1860–1925)

William Jennings Bryan was a leader of the Democratic Party for more than 20 years. He was also one of the most powerful speakers of all time. Known as the silver-tongued orator, he is best remembered for his moving Cross of Gold speech and for his work as a prosecutor in the famous Scopes "monkey" trial.

Bryan was born in Salem, Illinois, on March 19, 1860. In 1887 he moved to Nebraska, where he became interested in politics. In 1890 he was elected to the U.S. House of Representatives.

Toward the end of the 1900's, a great argument existed over what kind of money the nation should use. Silver-mine owners and farmers wanted the government to issue silver as well as gold. The farmers felt that free (unlimited) silver coinage would put more money into circulation and raise prices for crops. But people in business wanted money backed by a gold standard. At the Democratic convention of 1896, Bryan, a Free Silver Democrat, excited quarreling delegates to applause with these words from the Cross of Gold speech, "We will answer their demand for a gold standard by saying to them . . . you shall not crucify mankind upon a cross of gold." Bryan's speech won him the Democratic presidential nomination. But he lost the election to Republican William McKinley.

In 1900, Bryan again lost the presidential election to McKinley. In 1908 he ran against William Howard Taft and was defeated for a third time. Yet Bryan still had great influence, and he used it to help Woodrow Wilson win the presidential nomination in 1912. When Wilson became president, he appointed Bryan secretary of state.

In 1925, John Scopes, a high school biology teacher was brought to trial in Dayton, Tennessee, for teaching Darwin's theory of evolution in violation of state law. Many people felt that Darwin's theory denied the biblical story of creation. A deeply religious man, Bryan went to Dayton to help in the case against Scopes. Bryan won the case. Five days after the trial, he died in Dayton on July 26, 1925.

Reviewed by PAOLO E. COLETTA
Author, *William Jennings Bryan*

BRYANT, WILLIAM CULLEN (1794–1878)

The American poet and editor William Cullen Bryant was born on November 3, 1794, in Cummington, Massachusetts. His father was a doctor, who encouraged his son Cullen to write. When the boy was only 13, he published a long satirical poem, "The Embargo." He wrote his most famous poem, "Thanatopsis," a meditation on death, while he was a student at Williams College.

Bryant had to leave college because he lacked funds to support himself. He was apprenticed to a lawyer and passed his bar examination before he was 20. After moving to Great Barrington, Massachusetts, he pursued a successful law career. In 1821 he married Frances Fairchild. He celebrated their romance in "Oh Fairest of the Rural Maids."

Bryant wrote sensitive descriptions of nature and the American landscape in such poems as "To a Waterfowl," "The Yellow Violet," and "Green River." Collections of his poems issued in 1821 and 1832 established Bryant as the leading American poet of his time.

In 1825, Bryant moved to New York City to begin a new career in journalism. He rose to editor in chief on the *New York Evening Post* by 1829. He worked for the *Post* for over 50 years. On its editorial pages, Bryant supported such causes as abolition and the labor movement. He helped form the Republican Party and elect Abraham Lincoln.

Bryant also continued to compose poems. In "The Flood of Years," he pondered life after death, and in "The Prairies," he described the vast American West. After his wife's death in 1865, Bryant began his popular translation of the *Iliad* and of the *Odyssey,* published in 1870 and 1872. He lived an active life until his death on June 12, 1878.

JOHN B. PICKARD
University of Florida

BUBONIC PLAGUE. See DISEASES (Descriptions of Some Diseases).

JAMES BUCHANAN (1791–1868)
15th President of the United States

FACTS ABOUT BUCHANAN

Birthplace: Cove Gap, Pennsylvania
Religion: Presbyterian
College Attended: Dickinson College, Carlisle, Pennsylvania
Occupation: Lawyer
Marriage: None
Political Party: Democratic
Nickname: "Old Buck"
Post Held Before Becoming President: Minister to Great Britain
President Who Preceded Him: Franklin Pierce
Age on Becoming President: 65
Terms Served: One
Years in the Presidency: 1857–1861
Vice President: John C. Breckinridge
President Who Succeeded Him: Abraham Lincoln
Age at Death: 77
Burial Place: Woodward Hill Cemetery, Lancaster, Pennsylvania

DURING BUCHANAN'S PRESIDENCY

Minnesota (1858), Oregon (1859), and Kansas (1861) became states. *Below:* The first transatlantic telegraph cable was laid between Newfoundland and Ireland (1858). *Left:* John Brown, attempting to start a slave rebellion, attacked the U.S. arsenal (1860) at Harpers Ferry, Virginia (now West Virginia). Brown was hanged. *Above:* The Pony Express was established (1860) to carry mail from St. Joseph, Missouri, to Sacramento, California. The first Japanese delegation arrived in the United States (1860). South Carolina seceded from the Union (1860), followed by other Southern states that together formed the Confederate States of America.

BUCHANAN, JAMES. James Buchanan, the 15th president of the United States, also served his country as a congressman, senator, ambassador, and secretary of state. But many people remember mainly two things about him: that he was the only president who never married; and that the Civil War followed his administration.

▶ EARLY LIFE

Buchanan was born on April 23, 1791, in a log cabin near the frontier settlement of Cove Gap, Pennsylvania. His father, a Scotch-Irish immigrant, had come to America in 1783. When James was 6, the family moved to Mercersburg, Pennsylvania, where his father opened a general store. James's mother had little schooling, but she loved to read and she inspired her son with a love of learning.

James was able to go to school in Mercersburg. When he was not studying, he helped his father in the store. James's father was fond of his son, but he made him work hard and pay close attention to business. Mr. Buchanan

taught James that he must be ready to care for his nine younger brothers and sisters if their parents should die. In later years, after his father died, James Buchanan became responsible for the care of his mother and four of his brothers and sisters.

When James was 16, his father sent him to Dickinson College in Carlisle, Pennsylvania. Young Buchanan was a serious student, but he also wanted to have a good time. He began to drink and smoke with some of the other students. Even though his marks were excellent, he was expelled for bad conduct at the end of his first term. James pleaded to be taken back and promised to turn over a new leaf. He was allowed to return and went on to graduate with honors.

Buchanan then went to Lancaster, Pennsylvania, to study law. Hard work and intelligence made him a very good lawyer. Before long he was earning more than $11,000 a year, a huge sum in those days.

In 1814, Buchanan became a candidate for the Pennsylvania legislature. But the War of

Buchanan's birthplace as it now stands at Mercersburg Academy, Pennsylvania.

Ann Coleman (1796?–1819).

1812 was raging, and the British had just burned Washington. Buchanan felt that the United States should not have gone to war against Great Britain. However, he knew it was his duty to serve his country, and he joined a volunteer cavalry company.

Buchanan returned in time for the election and won his seat in the legislature. He served a second term and then returned to Lancaster to continue his law practice.

▶A TRAGIC LOVE STORY

As his practice grew, Buchanan became an important figure in town. He was invited to parties at some of the best homes in Lancaster. At one party he met and fell in love with beautiful Ann Coleman. In 1819 Ann and James were engaged to be married, but their happiness was destined to end quickly.

During the fall of 1819 Buchanan often had to be out of town on business. While he was away rumors spread that he wanted to marry Ann only for her money. There was gossip about another woman. All of this was untrue, but Ann was heartbroken. Because of a misunderstanding, she broke her engagement to James.

A short time later Ann died. Buchanan was so grief-stricken that he vowed he would never marry. Years later, after his death, a package of Ann's letters, yellow with age, was found among his papers. They were burned, according to his last wishes, without being opened.

▶HE RETURNS TO POLITICS

Buchanan turned to politics to forget his sorrow. The Federalist Party was looking for a candidate for Congress. Buchanan agreed to run, and in 1820 he was elected to the House of Representatives, where he served for 10 years. During his years in Congress, Buchanan changed his political party. He joined the Jacksonian Democrats (named for Andrew Jackson), and became a leader of the Jacksonians in Pennsylvania.

In 1831 President Jackson asked Buchanan to become minister to Russia. Buchanan went to Russia the following year. While there he negotiated the first trade agreement between Russia and the United States.

On his return to the United States, Buchanan was elected to the Senate. He served until 1845, and became chairman of the important committee on foreign affairs.

Buchanan applied all his training as a lawyer to his work in the Senate. The Constitution, he said, was the basis of all political power. But the Constitution also strictly limited the powers of the federal government. Buchanan believed that a constitutional republic could adjust serious differences between its people only by compromise and legal procedure.

▶SECRETARY OF STATE

By 1844 Buchanan had become an important political figure. Though he hoped for the presidential nomination, he gave his support to James K. Polk, who won the nomination and the election. President Polk appointed Buchanan secretary of state.

During Polk's term as president, war broke out between the United States and Mexico. Buchanan, as secretary of state, helped to arrange the treaty of peace in 1848. By this Treaty of Guadalupe Hidalgo the United States purchased from Mexico the region

Photograph of President Buchanan, taken about 1859.

President Pierce made Buchanan minister to Great Britain in 1853. Shortly thereafter Pierce instructed the American ministers in Europe to draw up proposals to "detach" Cuba from Spain. This led to the Ostend Manifesto, named after the Belgian city where the ministers met. The Manifesto defined a plan to purchase Cuba. But it also included a proposal many people condemned: that the United States would be justified in seizing Cuba if Spain refused to sell the island. Buchanan's political opponents severely denounced the Ostend Manifesto, and nothing ever came of the plan. Buchanan wrote of it: "Never did I obey any instructions so reluctantly."

While Buchanan was in England, Congress passed the Kansas-Nebraska Act, permitting slavery in regions of the Northwest from which the Missouri Compromise of 1820 had formerly excluded it. This new law marked the beginning of the Republican Party, which vowed to prevent any further expansion of slavery, and it split the Democratic Party into northern and southern groups. As Buchanan had been in England during the Congressional fight over the Kansas-Nebraska bill, he remained friendly with both sections of his party. When the Democrats met in 1856 to pick a new candidate for president, they needed someone who would be accepted by both the North and the South. Buchanan proved to be the man. This time he won the nomination and the election.

▶ PRESIDENT BUCHANAN

On March 4, 1857, Buchanan was inaugurated as president. Since Buchanan had no wife, his 27-year-old orphan niece, Harriet Lane, acted as his hostess. She was very popular, and Buchanan's administration was a great social success. White House guests included the first Japanese representatives to the United States and the Prince of Wales (who later became King Edward VII of England). The Prince arrived with such a large party that the President had to give up his own bed and sleep on a couch.

The Dred Scott Decision

But the political situation was getting worse. Two days after Buchanan's inauguration, the Supreme Court gave its historic

extending west from Texas to the Pacific Ocean.

Another problem concerned the vast Oregon territory, which both Great Britain and the United States claimed. The dispute became so bad that war threatened. But Buchanan arranged a compromise, and the Oregon Treaty of 1846 settled the Northwestern boundary between Canada and the United States.

When Polk left office, Buchanan also retired. For 4 years he lived the life of a country gentleman. He bought the famous mansion, Wheatland, near Lancaster, Pennsylvania, partly to have a suitable place to entertain political guests, but mainly to care for a growing family. Although Buchanan remained a bachelor, he had over the years become a kind of foster father to a score of nephews and nieces, seven of them orphans. They often visited him at Wheatland, and two made their home with him there, cared for in his absence by his faithful housekeeper, Miss Hetty Parker.

But Buchanan could not stay out of politics for long. In 1852 he was again a candidate for the presidential nomination. He was beaten by a little-known candidate, Franklin Pierce.

President Buchanan received the first Japanese delegation to the United States in 1860.

IMPORTANT DATES IN THE LIFE OF JAMES BUCHANAN

1791	Born at Cove Gap, Pennsylvania, April 23.
1809	Graduated from Dickinson College.
1814	Elected to the Pennsylvania legislature.
1819	Death of Ann Coleman.
1821–1831	Served in the United States House of Representatives.
1832–1833	Minister to Russia.
1835–1845	Served in the United States Senate.
1845–1849	Secretary of state.
1853–1856	Minister to Great Britain.
1857–1861	15th president of the United States.
1868	Died near Lancaster, Pennsylvania, June 1.

decision in the case of the slave Dred Scott, who sued for his freedom because he had been taken to a nonslave territory. However, the court decided that Congress could not outlaw slavery in United States territories. Buchanan thought slavery was wrong, but unfortunately the Constitution then recognized it. He hoped the Dred Scott decision would calm the country. Instead, people in the North refused to accept the court's decision. Thus the North and South became more divided than ever.

South Carolina Secedes from the Union

The crisis came in December, 1860. Abraham Lincoln had just been elected president, but he did not take office until March, 1861. Until that time Buchanan was still president.

When the news of Lincoln's victory reached the South, the state of South Carolina seceded from the Union, declaring that it was no longer a part of the United States. By February, 1861, six more southern states had broken away from the Union. The split in the nation that Buchanan feared had taken place.

In this crisis Buchanan wanted to keep the remaining slave states loyal to the Union. He said he would do nothing to provoke a war but he would try to protect federal property and enforce the laws in the South. He asked Congress to call a Constitutional Convention and to vote him the men and money needed to enforce the laws. But Congress refused.

▶THE COMING OF WAR

On March 5, 1861, Buchanan left Washington and returned to Wheatland. He was happy to leave the presidency and hopeful that the president who followed him could maintain peace and restore the Union. But 5 weeks after Lincoln's inauguration, the South fired on Fort Sumter and the Civil War began.

Buchanan spent his last years writing a book about his term as president. He died at Wheatland on June 1, 1868.

Could Buchanan have prevented the Civil War? Historians do not agree. Some say that a stronger president, one with more imagination, could have prevented the war. Others argue that the Civil War was inevitable: it would have happened no matter who was president, and if Buchanan had used force against the southern states, the war would only have started earlier.

Buchanan tried to solve the problems of the United States by acting within its laws. He failed. Whether any man could have succeeded will never be known.

Reviewed by PHILIP S. KLEIN
Author, *President James Buchanan*

See also DRED SCOTT DECISION; KANSAS-NEBRASKA ACT; MISSOURI COMPROMISE.

BUCK, PEARL (1892–1973)

Pearl Sydenstricker Buck, American author, was born on June 26, 1892, in Hillsboro, West Virginia. Her parents, Presbyterian missionaries in China, were home on leave. They returned to China five months later.

China was Pearl Buck's home for 42 years. She learned to speak Chinese before she learned English. All her schooling was in China until she attended Randolph-Macon College and, later, Cornell University.

Her marriage to Dr. John Buck, an agricultural missionary, took her to a small town in northern China. She described the region in her best-known novel, *The Good Earth* (1931). After five years she moved to Nanking and taught English literature to university students. When revolutionary soldiers invaded Nanking in March, 1927, she was rescued by an American gunboat and went to Japan. The next winter she returned to China, but by 1934 the situation was so dangerous for foreigners that she knew she must leave. She decided to make her home in Pennsylvania. She was divorced from Dr. Buck in 1935 and married Richard J. Walsh, her publisher.

Pearl Buck received many honors for her writing. *The Good Earth* won the Pulitzer prize in 1932, and in 1938 she became the first American woman to win the Nobel prize for literature. Her humanitarian activities were also numerous. In 1949 she founded Welcome House, an adoption agency for American children of Asian ancestry. In 1964 she established the Pearl S. Buck Foundation, which aids neglected American-Asian children living overseas. Pearl Buck died in Danby, Vermont, on March 6, 1973.

Reviewed by PAUL A. DOYLE
Author, *Pearl S. Buck*

▶ THE GOOD EARTH

Pearl Buck's most famous novel, *The Good Earth,* describes the daily life of a Chinese peasant family. In the following passage, Wang Lung and his wife O-Lan face unexpected disaster in the form of a plague of locusts.

And as if to cure him of the root of his ceaseless thought of his own troubles, there came out of the south one day a small slight cloud. At first it hung on the horizon small and smooth as a mist, except it did not come hither and thither as clouds blown by the wind do, but it stood steady until it spread fanwise up into the air.

The men of the village watched it and talked of it and fear hung over them, for what they feared was this, that locusts had come out of the south to devour what was planted in the fields. Wang Lung stood there also, and he watched, and they gazed and at last a wind blew something to their feet, and one stooped hastily and picked it up and it was a dead locust, dead and lighter than the living hosts behind.

Then Wang Lung forgot everything that troubled him. Women and sons and uncle, he forgot them all, and he rushed among the frightened villagers, and he shouted at them,

"Now for our good land we will fight these enemies from the skies!"

But there were some who shook their heads, hopeless from the start, and these said,

"No, and there is no use in anything. Heaven has ordained that this year we shall starve, and why should we waste ourselves in struggle against it, seeing that in the end we must starve?"

And women went weeping to the town to buy incense to thrust before the earth gods in the little temple, and some went to the big temple in the town, where the gods of heaven were, and thus earth and heaven were worshipped.

But still the locusts spread up into the air and on over the land.

Then Wang Lung called his own laborers and Ching stood silent and ready beside him and there were others of the younger farmers, and with their own hands these set fire to certain fields and they burned the good wheat that stood almost ripe for cutting and they dug wide moats and ran water into them from the wells, and they worked without sleeping. O-Lan brought them food and the women brought their men food, and the men ate standing and in the field, gulping it down as beasts do, as they worked night and day.

Then the sky grew black and the air was filled with the deep still roar of many wings beating against each other, and upon the land the locusts fell, flying over this field and leaving it whole, and falling upon that field, and eating it as bare as winter. And men sighed and said, "So Heaven wills," but Wang Lung was furious and he beat the locusts and trampled on them and his men flailed them with flails and the locusts fell into the fires that were kindled and they floated dead upon the waters of the moats that were dug. And many millions of them died, but to those that were left it was nothing.

Nevertheless, for all his fighting Wang Lung had this as his reward: the best of his fields were spared and when the cloud moved on and they could rest themselves, there was still wheat that he could reap and his young rice beds were spared and he was content.

BUDAPEST

Budapest, the capital and largest city of Hungary, is a double city, split in two by the Danube River. In fact, Buda and Pest were once separate, rival cities, with a stormy history going back thousands of years. Together with neighboring Óbuda (Old Buda), they were united legally in 1873.

Today Budapest is one of the most beautiful and dramatically situated cities in the world, with a population of about 2,000,000. It lies astride the Danube just below the point where the river turns south to cut through Hungary.

Ferries, steamers, and excursion boats continually ply this busy waterway. And eight bridges span the Danube, linking the two parts of the city. The older, fortresslike Buda lies on the steep hills of the river's western bank. The more modern Pest is spread out along the eastern shore of the river.

▶TOURING BUDAPEST

A cogwheel tram takes visitors to the many scenic hills of Buda. The high ground is studded with Gothic and Renaissance structures, most of them rebuilt one or more times. The Citadel, a fortress on Gellért Hill, has walls more than 3 meters (10 feet) thick. Nearby stands the towering Liberation Monument, built in memory of Soviet soldiers who were killed during World War II.

Ramparts from the Middle Ages enclose the Castle Hill district of Buda, where elegant homes of long ago line cobbled lanes. The most impressive buildings in this area are the 18th-century Royal Palace and the 13th-century Matthias Church (Coronation Church), where kings were crowned. Nearby is the Fishermen's Bastion—a fantasy of towers, turrets, para-

The Fishermen's Bastion lies high above the Danube River near the Castle Hill district of Buda. Across the river in Pest is the domed House of Parliament.

pets, and statues, built along the rim of the hill. From this point, visitors have a memorable view of the opposite bank, which is occupied by former palaces and the majestic House of Parliament.

Once in the heights, the cogwheel tram connects with the narrow-gauge Pioneer Railway. With the exception of the engineers, the owners and operators of this railway are all fifteen years old or younger. It is part of Pioneers' Town, a state-sponsored camp where hundreds of young people live and govern themselves with little adult supervision.

The Pest side of the Danube is crisscrossed with wide avenues, graced by leafy parks and gardens, and dotted with pretty squares. At the center is the Inner City. This is the oldest section of Pest.

Pest's many theaters, two opera houses, and numerous concert halls reflect the city's rich cultural life. Also located on the Pest side is Eötvös Loránd University. Students at the university take courses in music, drama, and the fine arts, as well as in economics, agriculture, and technical subjects.

Budapest has about two dozen museums. The National Museum, in the Inner City district, has both historical and natural history collections. The National Gallery, also in this district, contains collections of the Hungarian fine arts. The Museum of Fine Arts, in Heroes' Square, is rich in Flemish, Dutch, and Spanish old masters.

Perhaps no other city in Europe can compare with Budapest when darkness falls. Strings of soft lights, like strands of pearls, come on along the Chain Bridge, the oldest of the bridges across the Danube. Pink skies serve as a backdrop to the line of hilltop spires. The entire scene is mirrored in the waters of the river, producing a dazzling effect. For this reason many people consider Budapest to be the showcase of Eastern Europe.

▶ TWO FACES OF THE CITY

Budapest was once known as the most glittering capital on the continent of Europe. Today, the elegance and gaiety of the past have faded slightly. But much of the city's sparkle remains, and Budapest is still one of the loveliest cities in Europe. This is especially so on a sunny weekend. Couples stroll arm in arm along the riverside. Families sun themselves

Budapest, the capital of Hungary, is built on both sides of the Danube River. Bridges link the city's two parts.

and have picnics in city parks. On Margaret Island, a green oasis in the river, thousands of people make use of swimming pools, tennis courts, and soccer fields. They walk on garden paths and enjoy themselves in open-air terrace cafés. Margaret Island provides a resortlike atmosphere right in the heart of the bustling city.

Late in the afternoon, almost everyone stops for coffee and cake or an elaborate ice cream treat. The pastry shop and café on Vörösmarty Square, in business since 1858, has long been a favorite place to chat and sip coffee.

In the evening, Budapest's many restaurants have no difficulty in attracting customers. Orchestras play haunting folk melodies while people dine on the richly seasoned dishes that have long been among the glories of Hungary.

But on a working day, Budapest wears a different face. Well before dawn, people are off to their jobs in factories or in the industrial plants that ring the city. They ride the oldest subway system in continental Europe, built in 1896, or crowd into noisy streetcars. The streetcars operate on the honor system—no one checks to see whether passengers have paid for their tickets. Most working people travel on a low-cost monthly pass. The streets are clogged with traffic, mainly trucks. There are few private cars. Smog-filled skies dull the brilliance of the setting.

Most of the people are employed in industries that produce machine tools, precision instruments, locomotives, chemicals, and textiles. Many of these products are shipped to the Soviet Union, rather than being sold in the world market. For this reason, the industries of Budapest receive only a limited amount of money for their products. All businesses are owned and operated by the government. There is very little private enterprise.

Because Hungary's economy is controlled by the government, almost everyone in Budapest has a job. But few people have a chance to become wealthy. Prices for such goods as furniture and clothing are high compared to the level of the salaries. On the other hand, the cost of books is low, and almost everyone can afford to go to the theater, the opera, or the many concerts. For many people, enjoyment of music, literature, and the theater helps to soften the harsher side of life.

▶ HISTORY

Settlements have existed at Budapest's strategic river site since the earliest times. A Roman outpost, called Aquincum, was established at the site in the first century A.D. And more than a thousand years ago, the Magyars (a people from central Asia) moved in. Their descendants are the people of modern Hungary.

Budapest has been no stranger to repression and revolt. In the Middle Ages, it suffered invasions by Mongols and Tatars and by the Turks, who occupied Buda for almost 150 years. During two centuries of domination by the Austrian Habsburg rulers, revolts by Magyar inhabitants became almost commonplace.

Budapest was severely damaged toward the end of World War II. Its major monuments were destroyed, and all of its bridges were bombed. The Hungarian revolt of 1956, seven years after Hungary came under Soviet domination, centered in and around Budapest. Soviet troops put down the revolt by force.

The miracle of Budapest is the way in which the city has been able to rebuild itself again and again. Equally remarkable is the way in which the people have carried on in spite of hardship, strengthened by the belief that they live in the loveliest city in the world.

HELMUT KOENIG
Travel writer

BUDDHA AND BUDDHISM

More than 2,500 years ago, a man in India made a discovery. He discovered the cause of unhappiness and its cure. The man was named Siddhartha Gautama, but he is much better known as the **Buddha**, which means "the wise one" or "the enlightened one." The Buddha's teachings are the basis for one of the world's great religions, Buddhism.

▶ HOW SIDDHARTHA BECAME "THE WISE ONE"

Siddhartha Gautama was born about 563 B.C. His father ruled a small state in northern India near the Himalayas. Strangely enough, the man who discovered the cause of unhappiness knew little about it when he was young. His father tried to protect him from all knowledge of sickness, pain, suffering, and death. Siddhartha spent his early years within palaces and gardens where all was beautiful and pleasant. When he left the palace grounds, his father sent servants to clear the road of any painful sights. As a result, Siddhartha knew nothing about unhappiness.

In spite of all his father did, Siddhartha did eventually learn of unhappiness. Once as he was riding in his chariot he came upon a frail old man. Then he saw another man suffering from a dread disease. Later he met some men carrying the body of one who had died. When Siddhartha asked about those who suffered from old age, disease, and death, he was told: "This happens to all men." For the first time Siddhartha understood that unhappiness was a part of life.

Siddhartha thought about what he had learned. He realized that he could no longer live cut off from the sight of all suffering, as he had in the past. Now that he had begun to learn about life, he could never be content until he understood the whole truth. One night Siddhartha left his father and his wife and child and gave up his great personal fortune. He thought that wealth and comfort would only interfere with his search for understanding.

At first Siddhartha tried to learn wisdom from some holy men, but after 6 years he knew that this was not the way. He then decided to look for the truth within himself. He seated himself beneath a tree (which Buddhists now call the Bo Tree) and vowed that he would not leave until he understood the whole meaning of life. He sat there for 49 days, and then the truth came to him. Siddhartha, the seeker for wisdom, had become the Buddha—the wise one.

The Buddha spent the next 45 years teaching men what he had learned under the Bo Tree. He died about 483 B.C., when he was 80. Shortly before his death he reminded his followers that they should not grieve because "everything must die."

A golden statue of the Buddha in the city of Mandalay, Burma.

▶ WHAT THE WISE ONE TAUGHT

The Buddha wrote no books. He taught his followers, and they taught their followers, who in turn did the same. For hundreds of years the Buddha's teachings were passed on by word of mouth. When men did finally try to write down the teachings in books, they no longer agreed about them. Some had learned one thing; some had learned another. For this reason there is no single collection of writings that serves as a Buddhist bible.

However, most Buddhists do agree about certain teachings. They agree that the Buddha taught that pain, suffering, and unhappiness must be expected as a natural part of life. They tell of a woman who came to the Buddha hoping that he could bring her dead son back to life, for she had heard that he had remarkable powers. The Buddha told her to borrow a cup of mustard seed from a family that had not known of death. The woman went from door to door, but, of course, she could find no such family. She then understood what the Buddha was trying to teach her. No one could escape death and unhappiness. We must expect it and accept it. Men expect only happiness and they are disappointed when they do not receive it. To avoid disappointment, the Buddha taught that one should expect nothing.

If one knows the cause of unhappiness, the Buddha said, one also knows its cure. One can escape unhappiness by getting rid of all selfish desires. How can this be done? By thinking as much of others as we do of ourselves. The man who understands the whole truth and accepts it will understand that he should never steal or cheat or grow angry. He will

not stir up trouble by repeating hurtful things. The man who understands what the Buddha taught will "bear the burdens of those who are tired and weary," and he will "harm no living thing."

Once a man completely overcomes all selfishness, he will know a kind of freedom from care that the Buddhists call **nirvana**. The word "nirvana" means "the going out of fire," especially the fire of anger, greed, and desire. It is evidently hard to describe nirvana to those who do not know it. It is like trying to explain how salt tastes to someone who has never tasted it.

▶ DIFFERENT KINDS OF BUDDHISM

A hundred years after the Buddha's death, men already had different ideas about what he had taught. Each man believed what he had learned from his own teacher, and he taught this to his own students.

One group insisted that they remain true to the **Theravada**, which means "the way of the elders." The Buddha had taught, they said, that each man must find his own way to nirvana. No one can help him, not even the gods and spirits. The Buddha did all that one person can do for others; he showed them what they must do for themselves.

Young Burmese pupils study Buddhist scriptures in a monastery school.

The Great Buddha, at Kamakura, Japan. The huge statue is visited by thousands of pilgrims each year.

Another group said that the Theravada was only a part of the Buddha's teachings. He taught these "lesser ideas" first, but to those able to understand them he gave a greater teaching called the **Mahayana**, which means "the greater vehicle." Mahayana Buddhists refer to Theravada teachings as the **Hinayana**, "the little vehicle."

Mahayana Buddhists also teach that men should follow the Buddha's example of doing good to others. But they believe that the Buddha did more than provide an example. Mahayana Buddhists believe that the Buddha is a god who aids and protects those who pray to him and call upon him. They also believe that men can call upon a number of good spirits, called **Bodhisattvas**, who devote themselves to helping suffering mankind.

From these two divisions of Buddhism have come a number of others. It is said that there are more than 60 different Buddhist groups in Japan today. The differences among the various kinds of Buddhism are great. There are Buddhists, such as those of Tibet, who combine belief in the Buddha with a belief in a large number of spirits and demons. They believe that these spirits and demons can be controlled by magic. Other groups, such as Zen Buddhists of Japan, say very little about gods and spirits. Zen Buddhists, in fact, say

that it is impossible to explain Buddhist teachings in words at all. Either you understand what enlightenment is, or you do not. If you do not, there is nothing that can be said to make it clear to you.

Since Buddhism includes such a variety of branches, it has been described as a group of religions and of ways of thinking rather than a single religion.

▶ BUDDHIST MONKS

During the Buddha's lifetime some of his followers gave up all they had and shared their master's way of life. They spent their time learning the teacher's words and trying to do as he did. We call these men **monks** and the houses they live in **monasteries**.

Some men still choose to live as Buddhist monks. A Buddhist monk owns nothing except his yellow or orange robe, his bowl, his razor, and a few other personal items. Many monks depend entirely upon gifts of food for their living. They spend their time learning and reciting the Buddha's teachings. Monks also teach others, both by their words and by the example of their lives. Some monks care for the sick, for the Buddha once said, "He who would care for me should care for the sick."

Some monks spend their entire lives in the

monasteries. Others may live as monks for a short time. This has been true in Burma, where many boys have spent a few weeks or months living as monks.

BUDDHISM IN THE WORLD TODAY

It is impossible to say how many Buddhists there are in the world today. All that can be said for sure is that Buddhism is one of the world's major religions. A Buddhist is simply a person who believes that there is truth in some form of Buddhism.

Almost all Buddhists live in Asia, but only a small number live in India, where Buddhism began. Most Buddhists are found in Sri Lanka, Burma, Thailand, Cambodia, Tibet, China, and Japan. There are only a few people practicing Buddhism as a religion in Europe and America. But many Europeans and Americans have read and studied Buddhist teaching.

The Buddhists of the country of Sri Lanka follow the Theravada—the way of the elders. They take pride in the fact that Buddhism has been in their country for a long time. Buddhist missionaries went to Sri Lanka 2,200 years ago, bringing with them a cutting from Buddha's sacred Bo Tree. Sri Lankan Buddhists say that the cutting grew into a tree that still stands.

In Tibet the everyday life of the people revolves around a form of Buddhism known as Lamaism. The lamas, or monks, were once very powerful. The highest monk of one order, the Dalai Lama, was both the spiritual and political head of Tibet for several centuries. Although he was forced to leave Tibet for political reasons, the present Dalai Lama is still a spiritual leader.

Travelers carried Mahayana Buddhism to China before A.D. 100, where it became one of the three main religions. The Chinese adopted Buddhist teachings without giving up their old Confucianist beliefs. Some persons might consider themselves both Buddhists and Confucianists. This is why it is so hard to decide how many Buddhists there are.

In about A.D. 372 Buddhist monks carried their teachings to Korea, China's eastern neighbor. About 200 years later Buddhists from both Korea and China carried Buddhist books and images to the island kingdom of Japan. Today Buddhism is one of Japan's two major religions.

KENNETH S. COOPER
George Peabody College

BUDGETS, FAMILY

Most families have far more money than they realize. The ones who get the most from their money seem to have learned how to manage the money they have very well.

A plan for spending the money is called a budget. You, as a member of a family, share in the money spent for food, shelter, clothing, medical care, education, and recreation in your family. It is well to know how much thought and planning often has to be done to provide for the family's basic needs and the individual wants of each member.

Each family must decide for itself exactly how much planning it wants to do. However, there are useful steps that any family can follow for this purpose.

Step 1. Decide whether to divide the budget into periods of 1 week, 2 weeks, or 1 month. Most people find that the time between paydays is the best budgeting period.

WEEKLY BUDGET	
Fixed Expenses	Cost
Rent and Mortgage	
Insurance	
Transportation	
Taxes and Savings	
Time payments	
Living Expenses	
Food	
Clothing	
Utilities	
Recreation	
Contributions	
Medical	
Automobile	
Others	
Total	

Step 2. List all fixed expenses. Include every bill for which the exact amount is known in advance, such as payments for rent, mortgage, insurance, the car, and any other installment purchases.

Step 3. List all regular living expenses for which the amounts vary. Estimate how much each costs during a pay period. Accurate estimates will require time and experience since the amount spent on living expenses depends on such things as how much care is shown by the shopper and the time of year it is. For example, food costs can be kept down by the person who shops and cooks wisely; more water is used in summer, and more fuel and electricity in winter. The cost of clothing and its care can be spread out over the whole year instead of spending large amounts in the fall and spring. The home-maker who knows what to look for in selecting clothing, who has a wardrobe plan that will prevent unwise purchases, and who can sew, will need less money than another person.

Step 4. List any expected major expenses too large to be paid in a single pay period.

Decide how much should be set aside each payday to meet such expenses when they occur. Taxes can usually be estimated in advance, and enough money saved to pay them. Home appliances and furnishings can be bought with savings.

Step 5. Total all expenses. Compare this total with the family's income for the budgeting period. If the expenses are too high, look for ways to cut them. If there is money left, some of it should be set aside regularly in an emergency fund and some in a savings or investment program.

Step 6. Use a budget book or make a chart. Write down the family's plans for using its money. In the following weeks and months, compare this budget with what is actually spent and make any necessary changes.

Even a good budget will not help the family control its spending unless all family members co-operate. Young people who get experience in good money management as they grow up will have little difficulty in working out a family budget of their own.

KATHERINE R. CONAFAY
Author, *Family Budgets*

BUENOS AIRES

Buenos Aires is Argentina's largest city, its capital, and its gateway to the world. It is situated on the Río de la Plata (the River Plate), about 275 kilometers (170 miles) from the sea. Buenos Aires is one of the largest ports in the Americas. Greater Buenos Aires has about 9,000,000 people—over one third of Argentina's total population. The city itself has about 3,000,000 people. Most of the country's roads, railroads, manufacturing plants, ocean shipping, and commerce are centered in Buenos Aires.

The name of the city was given to it by the early Spanish explorers. Buenos Aires means "good airs." A first settlement in 1536 failed because of Indian attacks. A permanent settlement was finally achieved in 1580.

Buenos Aires was a modest city until the end of the 19th century. In time thousands of immigrants—Italians, Germans, Swedes, and people of other nationalities—made it the wonder city it is today. Buenos Aires is set

on a flat plain like a huge, sprawling giant. Its highways and streets stretch out in all directions as far as the eye can see. Seen from above at night, with its countless lights stabbing at the darkness, the city looks like a vast field of glittering diamonds.

On a sunny day the center of the city bustles with sound and movement. Automobile horns honk sharply, and river freighters whistle mournfully. Cheerful, busy people go about their errands, talking in Spanish

Buenos Aires is the bustling capital and commercial center of Argentina. Above: The Palace of the National Congress. Below left: Shoppers throng the city streets. Below right: Avenida 9 de Julio, one of the widest streets in the world.

and as many other languages as are likely to be heard in New York. There is also the dull rumble of the subway trains from deep beneath the sidewalk.

Buenos Aires is a great port whose ships go all over the world. Cement docks line the Río de la Plata. Warehouses, meat-packing plants, grain elevators, and the smokestacks of oceangoing ships loom against the sunny sky. Long freight trains pull into busy yards. Some of these trains have come hundreds of kilometers across the pampas, or plains, with wool to be shipped to distant countries. Most imports also come through the city.

Buenos Aires is a city of sunny plazas and wide boulevards. It is a city of pleasant living. People stroll to the many sidewalk cafés, sit at outdoor tables, and sip black coffee. Many of the streets and avenues are bordered with flowers.

Buenos Aires is the home of the tango. It is a city of music, of drama, of fine libraries and modern schools. World-famous opera stars come to the luxurious Teatro Colón to perform. Open-air performances of ballet are given at the Palermo Gardens. And here a symphony orchestra plays for crowds of appreciative listeners.

It is a city that loves to watch and play sports—golf, tennis, swimming, rowing, polo, and above all soccer, car racing, and horse racing. Champion sports figures become national heroes. One of the largest stadiums in the world, said to have a capacity of about 100,000 people, is in Buenos Aires.

These are some of the sights and sounds of the largest city in the Southern Hemisphere. This is Buenos Aires.

Reviewed by ERNESTO SÁBATO
Author, *On Heroes and Tombs*

BUFFALO AND BISON

Buffalo and bison are big, strong animals. They have horns on their heads. Their feet have cloven hooves. Buffalo and bison are members of the large group of animals called hoofed mammals. Cows and oxen are hoofed mammals, too. Cows, oxen, buffalo, and bison are all in the cattle family.

Like other cattle, buffalo and bison eat only plants. Those that live on plains eat mostly grass. Those that live in forests eat leaves.

Cows and oxen have been tamed for several thousand years. But only one kind of buffalo has ever been tamed. That is the Asian water

buffalo. Bison have almost never been tamed and put to work for people.

▶BUFFALO

Buffalo live in Asia and Africa. They look a lot like oxen except for their horns. For instance, two kinds—the Asian water buffalo and the African Cape buffalo—have big, sweeping horns. These are broad and flat at the base, where they grow out of the head.

The water buffalo is used in India and Southeast Asia to pull plows and do other heavy work. It likes to spend time in the water

The water buffalo (*left*) is very tame when it is in familiar surroundings. In parts of Asia, even very young children handle this huge beast with ease. In contrast, the bison (*right*) has little patience with human beings and will charge quickly if disturbed.

or to wallow in the mud, probably to keep flies away. These buffalo are also raised for milk, meat, and hides.

The Cape buffalo lives in Africa. Hunters have called it the world's most dangerous hoofed animal. Two kinds of forest buffalo also live in Africa.

Pygmy buffalo live in the Philippines and certain islands of Southeast Asia. They are just under 1 meter (about 3 feet) high at the shoulder.

▶BISON

A bison is a large, dark, shaggy animal. It has a thick growth of hair on its head, neck, shoulders, and front legs. It also has a beard and short, curved horns. There is a hump of fat on its shoulders. Bison may stand as high as 1.8 meters (6 feet) at the shoulder.

The American bison once ran in huge herds across the plains and prairies of North America. As the land was settled, people hunted these animals until the big herds were nearly wiped out. Then some people decided that the bison must be saved. There are now thousands of American bison. Most of them live in national parks and wildlife refuges. These animals are often called "buffalo," but "bison" is the correct name for them.

The European bison, or wisent, once ranged throughout Europe. Like its American cousin, it also faced extinction before efforts were made to save it. Today there are fewer than 2,000 of these animals. Most of them live in a protected forest in eastern Europe.

Reviewed by Robert M. McClung
Author, science books for children

See also Hoofed Mammals.

BUFFALO BILL (WILLIAM FREDERICK CODY) (1846–1917)

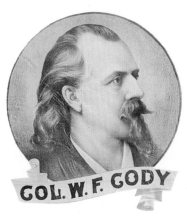

Buffalo Bill was the last of the famous American frontier scouts. He was a sharpshooter and an expert guide and hunter. His Wild West shows did much to establish the popular image of the Old West.

Buffalo Bill, whose real name was William Frederick Cody, was born in Le Claire, Iowa, on February 26, 1846. At the age of 14 he was carrying mail for the Pony Express. During the U.S. Civil War, he was a Union Army scout. Later he hunted Bison (often called buffalo) to supply meat for workers building a railroad across Kansas. It is said that Cody killed 69 bison in one day, and over 4,000 in 8 months. He became known everywhere as

Buffalo Bill. When war with the Sioux and Cheyenne Indians broke out in 1875, Cody again became a scout for the cavalry. He is said to have fought a hand-to-hand duel with Yellow Hand, the son of a Cheyenne chief, and killed him.

In 1883, Cody organized his famous traveling Wild West shows. These shows included a huge cast of cowboys, Indians, and sharpshooters, as well as herds of bison, elk, ponies, steers, and wild horses. Historic events such as Custer's Last Stand were re-enacted. Sitting Bull, the Sioux chief whose warriors had helped defeat General Custer's soldiers, traveled with the show in 1885. Annie Oakley, the famous sharpshooter, was another star. Thousands of people in the United States, Canada, and Europe saw the show before Cody lost it in 1913 because of debts.

Cody died on January 10, 1917. His grave and the Cody Memorial Museum are on top of Lookout Mountain in Colorado. Other Cody museums include the Buffalo Bill Historical Center in Cody, Wyoming, where scenes from the old Wild West shows are re-created every summer, and Buffalo Bill's Ranch State Historical Park in North Platte, Nebraska.

Reviewed by Thomas B. Morrison
Buffalo Bill's Ranch State Historical Park

The 110-story **World Trade Center** towers in New York City are among the most impressive buildings in the world. New skyscrapers are constantly being built.

BUILDING CONSTRUCTION

The construction of a building requires the talents and skills of many people who work with a variety of materials and processes. Architects and engineers design buildings. Workers in forests, quarries, mills, and factories produce the materials from which buildings are made. Contractors bring together the materials and the workers to assemble the buildings, and building inspectors make sure each building is constructed so it will be safe and healthy for the people who use it. Working together, these people create the fabric of our cities—buildings ranging from simple sheds to skyscrapers.

Materials of Construction

Two basic types of materials are used in buildings: structural and nonstructural. Structural materials hold up the building against such forces as gravity, wind, and earthquakes.

Such materials include stone, bricks, concrete blocks, concrete, wood, and steel. Nonstructural materials keep out the weather and finish the building in useful and attractive ways. There are many nonstructural materials used in buildings, but the most important are roofing materials, thermal insulation, glass, and gypsum.

Structural Materials. The major kinds of stone used in construction are granite, sandstone, limestone, and marble. Quarry workers cut large pieces of stone from the earth. At factories these pieces are sawed into blocks and slabs that will be used to make buildings. Stone is expensive because it is hard to cut and heavy to transport. But with its many colors and patterns, it is among the most beautiful of materials. It is also very durable.

Bricks are molded from moist clay. After drying, they are put into a kiln (a kind of oven), where they are heated to very high temperatures and converted into hard, stonelike blocks. Concrete blocks are molded from fresh concrete. Then they are hardened in a steam chamber.

People who work with stones, bricks, and concrete blocks are called masons. Any construction that uses these materials is called masonry. To make a masonry wall, masons set the blocks or stones in a thick layer of mortar, which is a mudlike mixture of sand, portland cement, and water. (Portland cement is a fine gray powder made from clay and limestone.) The mortar soon hardens into a rocklike material that holds the wall together and makes it weathertight.

Concrete is a mixture of sand, crushed stone, and portland cement. When blended with water, the cement powder hardens into a very strong adhesive that binds the sand and crushed stone into a rocklike material.

Masonry and concrete stand up well against pressing or squeezing forces known as **compression.** These materials are used in walls and columns that must withstand the compression created by the building's weight, or **load.** But masonry and concrete are brittle; they break when exposed to stretching forces, or **tension.** Nonbrittle materials that retain their strength when stretched are also necessary in building construction. Wood and steel, for example, are materials that can be used for beams and slabs that span horizontally between walls and columns.

Wood is used for structures of small or medium size. It is also used for the walls of small structures such as houses. Because wood can burn, however, it is not used in the construction of large buildings. Wood used in buildings must be kept dry and off the ground so it does not rot or become infested with insects.

Steel is a form of iron. Because of its great strength, steel is used for the frames of the tallest skyscrapers. Although it will not burn, steel will lose its strength at very high temperatures. In a large building, steel is covered with fire-resistant materials such as gypsum to protect it from becoming too hot should a fire occur in the building.

The brittleness of concrete can be overcome by embedding steel rods in it. This forms **reinforced concrete.** Beams and slabs of reinforced concrete can also span horizontal distances and are very resistant to fire.

Nonstructural Materials. Many nonstructural materials are just as important as structural materials. Roofing materials prevent rain and snow from leaking into the rooms below and causing structural damage. Buildings with sloping roofs, such as houses, typically are roofed with shingles. These are small, overlapping squares or rectangles of wood, slate, or asphalt. Flat roofs tend to hold rather than shed rainwater and snow. Because shingles have many seams, they are not watertight when used on flat roofs. Seamless sheets of asphalt or synthetic rubber must be used on flat roofs to keep water out.

Thermal insulating materials are also extremely important. They make buildings more comfortable and greatly reduce the amount of energy needed for heating and cooling. Insulating materials include loose mats of mineral fibers and lightweight boards of plastic foam.

Glass, another important nonstructural material, is made by melting sand, soda ash, and lime together. It is cast into large, smooth sheets that are cut into squares for use in windows. Gypsum is a common mineral that is made into plaster and plasterboard for walls and ceilings inside a building. Gypsum creates hard, smooth surfaces and is very resistant to fire. Gypsum plaster and plasterboard play a very important role in protecting structural materials from fire and preventing the spread of fire from one room of a building to another.

Constructing a House

Most houses are built by small crews of builders working with relatively simple tools and methods. The plans for a house may be specially drawn by an architect or team of architects to meet the needs or desires of a homeowner or builder. For an ordinary house, the builder may draw the plans or buy standard predrawn plans from a catalog. After the builder receives a building permit from the city or town building inspector, construction can begin. The first step is for an excavator to dig a hole for the foundation. Then workers construct the foundation, using concrete that has been poured into forms, concrete blocks, or wood treated with chemicals to prevent decay. The foundation must be strong enough to support the weight of the house.

Building a house: The first steps include digging for a foundation (*left*) and pouring concrete foundation walls and floors (*right*). Workers must spread and smooth the concrete for the floor before it hardens.

Sometimes the ground floor of the house is a concrete slab poured directly on the ground. More often it is made of wood. To make a wood floor, carpenters first bolt planks of wood, called **sills,** to the top of the foundation. Then horizontal pieces of lumber called **joists** are nailed to the sills. The joists are covered with sheets of plywood to create a level unfinished floor called the **subfloor.**

Walls of a house are framed with vertical pieces of lumber called **studs.** The subfloor is

Building a house: The foundation has been "capped" with a subfloor. *Above:* **Workers are putting up wall frames.** *Right:* **The wall frames are up and the slanting roof beams—rafters—are in place. A worker is nailing sheathing to the frame.** *Below:* **A diagram shows the main parts of a house.**

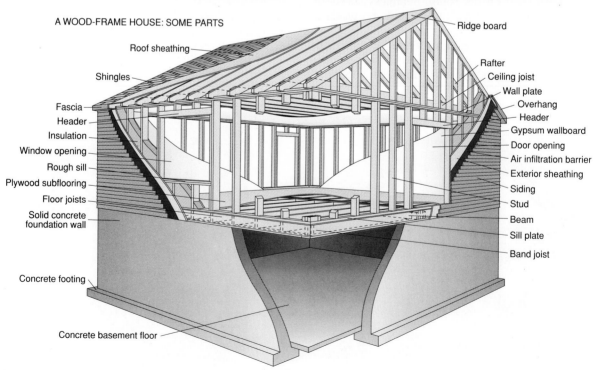

A WOOD-FRAME HOUSE: SOME PARTS

Ridge board
Roof sheathing
Rafter
Shingles
Ceiling joist
Wall plate
Fascia
Overhang
Header
Header
Insulation
Gypsum wallboard
Window opening
Door opening
Rough sill
Air infiltration barrier
Plywood subflooring
Exterior sheathing
Floor joists
Siding
Solid concrete foundation wall
Stud
Beam
Sill plate
Band joist
Concrete footing

Concrete basement floor

used as a kind of table on which sections of wall framing are assembled. Carpenters tilt finished sections of wall framing up into place and nail them to the floor frame. If the house is to be two stories high, the second floor joists rest on top of the first floor walls. Then the second story walls are assembled on the second floor, tilted up, and nailed down.

The attic floor and the sloping roof **rafters** are the last pieces of the house frame to be installed. The roof and all the outside walls are covered with a **sheathing** of wood boards, plywood, or sheets of wood composition board. Then carpenters can begin finishing the exterior of the house. First the roof is made watertight by nailing on the shingles. Then windows and doors that have been preassembled at a factory are installed in wall openings left for them. Finally, wood, vinyl, or aluminum siding is applied to the wall sheathing. Brick, stone, or stucco can also be used as siding.

Building a house: When the main frame is up, there is much left to do. *Below:* Pipes for water and wires for electricity must be run throughout the house. *Bottom:* A worker nails siding on the outside. *Below left:* Insulation is installed and large sheets of gypsum wallboard cover the framing inside. *Left:* Overlapping layers of shingles make the roof watertight.

Building a house: Finishing work (*above*) includes filling each wallboard joint with plaster and installing decorative trim. Painting or staining the house outside (*right*) makes the house look nice and protects it from the weather.

Why is a tree or an American flag sometimes placed on the highest part of a building under construction?

A tree or flag placed on, or nailed to, the highest part of a building under construction is a modern version of the ancient "topping out" ceremony. Topping out, still practiced in many parts of the world, is meant to indicate that the frame of the structure has been completed. During a topping out ceremony of long ago, a barrel of beer might be drunk while a tree or wreath was attached to the ridge of a building's newly completed roof. Today, finishing the frame of a building is still cause for celebration.

Even before the exterior of the house is finished, work inside begins. Masons may construct a fireplace and chimney. Electricians, plumbers, and sheet metal workers install the electrical wiring, the pipes and plumbing fixtures, and the heating and air conditioning systems. Workers stuff blankets of insulation into all the spaces between the exterior wall studs and ceiling joists. Insulation helps keep heat inside the house during cold weather. The interior walls are then covered with gypsum plaster or sheets of gypsum wallboard. Decorative wood trim is nailed around interior windows and doors. Finish flooring, cabinets, and lighting fixtures are the last items to be installed. Unfinished surfaces are painted, stained, varnished, and wallpapered. Driveway, sidewalk, and landscaping work can take place outside. After a final cleanup the house is ready to live in.

Constructing Larger Buildings

A larger building is much more complicated than a house. Each one is specially designed by a team of professionals that includes both **architects** and **engineers.** Architects design the exterior form, interior spaces, and surfaces of the building. Engineers, who work closely with the architects, design the foundations, the structural skeleton, the heating and cooling system, the electrical wiring, and the plumbing. The design work is complicated and takes many months. The architects and engineers work with the owner of the building to design a structure that is attractive and sturdy, and meets the owner's requirements. They also work with the city building inspector to be sure that the building is constructed according to the building code, which is a set of rules for making buildings safe and healthy. The building code may require that the building is made of fireproof materials; that enough toilets and lavatories are provided for everyone in the building; and that there are at least two safe ways for people to escape from the building in case of fire. Even in buildings that are made from materials that will not burn, the contents of the rooms may burn, causing dangerous fires. The designers must always take fire safety into account.

After the design work has been completed, the architects and engineers make blueprints of their final drawings and give them to the **building contractor.** He or she is responsible for seeing that the building is constructed exactly as it was designed. The contractor buys the materials for the building, hires many kinds of workers to put the materials together, and manages the entire construction process.

Larger buildings are much, much heavier than houses and need larger and stronger foundations. If the soil beneath a building is very firm and the building is not too tall, the foundations may be ordinary concrete **footings,** which are the flat strips and squares of concrete that lie in the ground and support the walls and columns of the building. If the soil is not so firm or the building is tall, more elaborate kinds of foundations have to be built. Sometimes the building is placed on one giant concrete footing that is as broad as the building; this is called a **mat** or **raft** foundation. Sometimes large drills may be used to bore holes several feet in diameter straight down through softer layers of soil until solid rock or a very firm soil is reached. This may lie a hundred feet (about 30 meters) or more beneath the surface of the ground. Then each hole is filled with concrete to make a type of foundation called either a **pier** or a **caisson.** It takes dozens of caissons to support a building; each one can support a single column or a part of a foundation wall. **Pile foundations** are used in some types of soft soil. Workers hammer **piles** into the ground using machines called pile drivers. Piles are long, slender pieces of wood, steel, or concrete. After the pile has been pounded firmly into the soil like a giant nail, it can support a considerable amount of weight. A cluster of piles can support each column of the building. Many clusters of piles in a line can hold up a wall.

Buildings larger than houses must be built of stronger, more fire-resistant materials than those used in houses. Large wood beams and columns can be used in structures less than five stories high. The frames of most large buildings, however, are built entirely of stronger materials such as steel or concrete.

In some large buildings, masonry or concrete walls support floors made of steel beams or concrete slabs. In smaller buildings, the floors might be made of wood joists or beams. This type of construction is called **bearing wall construction** because the walls bear, or support, the weight of the floors and roof. This weight is finally transferred to the foundation, on which the bearing walls are built.

Large buildings need sturdy foundations. Some rest on hundreds of piles, which are driven deep into the ground by powerful machines called pile drivers.

Most large buildings are held up by an open framework of vertical columns and horizontal beams. This type of construction is called **skeleton construction** because it resembles the bony structure that holds up a human body. A building's skeletal frame may be made of steel or concrete. Steel building frames are put up by people called **ironworkers.** Ironworkers use cranes to lift the heavy beams and columns into place. Then they bolt and weld the parts of the frame together. Diagonal braces are also installed to prevent the building from swaying due to wind or earthquakes.

Why don't tall buildings blow down in a strong wind?

Tall buildings must be braced throughout their height with cross-bracing, rigid connections, or stiff structural walls called shear walls. Most tall buildings are constructed of steel or reinforced concrete. These materials are flexible—that is, they can bend slightly without breaking. When strong winds blow, the steel and concrete buildings give way to the force of the wind by bending a little. For example, the World Trade Center towers in New York City were designed to sway as much as two feet (0.6 meters). If the buildings did not sway, they could be snapped in two by violent wind. The buildings are not pulled out of the ground because they are firmly anchored in strong foundations.

Reinforced concrete can be used to make bearing walls, columns, beams, and flat floor structures called slabs. The simplest kind of concrete structure is made up of columns and flat slabs, without any beams. For buildings with greater distances between columns, or where heavier weights must be supported, beams are used to hold up the slabs. In order to span longer distances, slabs are sometimes made with a ribbed or a waffle-like pattern underneath. These slabs are very strong and stiff without being too heavy or using too much concrete.

There are two ways of making a concrete building. One is called **sitecast construction.** In this method, workers construct wooden molds, or forms, into which steel rods are placed. Then wet concrete is poured, or "cast," into the forms, surrounding the steel reinforcing rods. After a few days the concrete has hardened and the forms are pulled off and re-used for another portion of the building.

The other way of making a concrete building is to cast the concrete in large pieces at a factory. The finished pieces of concrete are brought to the building site on trucks and are assembled in almost the same way as steel beams and columns. This is called **precast concrete construction.**

As soon as the steel or concrete frame of the building is finished, roofers apply a water-proof roof surface to keep out rain and snow. Crews of plumbers, electricians, and sheet metal workers install pipes, wires, air ducts, and elevators. Other workers install the exterior walls, which they bolt to the building frame. These walls are called **curtain walls** because they hang on the building (by means of the bolts), much like a curtain hangs on a wall. Curtain walls can be made of masonry, thin slabs of stone, panels of precast concrete, or light frames of aluminum holding sheets of glass and metal. Thermal insulation materials are put in the walls to make the building easier and more economical to heat and cool.

Once the outside walls are in place, interior partitions, ceilings, and floors can be installed. Interior partitions divide the inside of a building into separate spaces but do not bear any of the building's weight. Painters and a cleanup crew complete the construction.

Some kinds of structures, like basketball arenas, exhibition halls, and auditoriums, need roofs that span very long horizontal distances between the supporting walls or columns. Even steel beams may not be strong enough to safely span such distances. Instead, architects and engineers design other types of

The frame, or skeleton, of a skyscraper is made of sturdy steel columns and beams. The steel is lifted to the top by huge cranes or derricks. Thin "curtain walls" can be hung on the finished frame.

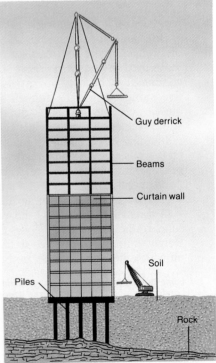

Guy derrick

Beams

Curtain wall

Soil

Piles

Rock

Cloth used in the construction of this airport at Riyadh, Saudi Arabia, makes it look like a huge tent. Air flowing through the waiting area cools people while hot air escapes through openings in the roof.

structural systems that are able to span longer distances. Domes or arches of reinforced concrete or heavy timbers can be designed to span hundreds of feet. Steel can make not only domes and arches, but also trusses and cable-supported roofs. A truss is used like a beam and is made up of slender pieces of steel that are connected together to make a series of open triangles. Cable-supported roofs are held up by strong wire ropes. A new type of long-span roof has been used in recent years on a number of covered stadiums. It is a thin, air-tight fabric reinforced with steel cables and held up by slight air pressure from within the stadium. The air pressure needed to hold the roof up—created by blowers in the heating and air conditioning system—is so slight that most people do not even notice it.

How We Learned to Build

Our earliest ancestors built from whatever materials were easily available. In forested areas tree trunks, branches, and saplings were fashioned into shelters of many kinds. Where stone was abundant, it was gathered and stacked into walls, with mud sometimes used between the stones. In regions with no stone, buildings were made of mud. Mud could be smeared over loosely woven mats of sticks, vines, or reeds to make thin walls. Or it could be mixed with straw and piled up to make very heavy, thick walls. Mud could also be molded into bricks that were dried by the sun. The bricks, joined by wet mud, could then be stacked into walls.

Although materials of construction (mud, stone, and wood) did not change for many thousands of years, people gradually learned how to build better buildings from them. These buildings were warmer, dryer, longer lasting, and more beautiful. People found that by raising the floors of their buildings off the ground, they could stay dry even during wet seasons. They learned to protect wooden building parts from water so they would not rot. They discovered ways to build sloping roofs from shingles or thatch (bundles of grass, reeds, or palm leaves) that would shed water without leaking. In cold climates, they discovered ways to build fires inside their buildings to keep warm in the winter, using holes in the roofs to let out the smoke. In hot, dry climates they learned that thick, heavy walls and roofs of stone or mud keep rooms cool even in the hottest weather. In humid tropical climates, where heavy walls would be damp, people developed light, airy houses on stilts so cooling breezes could pass through the rooms.

As time passed, builders became more skilled at cutting stone from quarries and carving it to the exact shapes they wanted for their buildings. They learned to make their mud bricks hard and durable by heating them to high temperatures in wood-fired kilns. Fireplaces and chimneys were developed to heat buildings better and remove smoke from the rooms. With metal saws and axes, tree trunks were squared into heavy posts and beams and sliced into thin boards for exterior and interior

Prefabricated buildings are those that were partly made in a factory. Large sections are transported to the site and assembled there to make a complete structure.

surfaces. Such metals as bronze, lead, and iron gradually came into use for fastening stones and timbers together and for covering roofs of public buildings.

More than 2,000 years ago the ancient Romans discovered how to make concrete, which they used to construct their enormous temples, baths, markets, and law courts. During the Middle Ages, the knowledge of how to make concrete was lost, but masons continued to develop their skills, building impressive churches, mosques, and public buildings that were covered with soaring domes and vaults (arched ceilings or roofs) made of brick or stone.

The Industrial Revolution began in the 18th century. During that time, people began using iron for columns and beams in buildings, especially factories. In the late 1800's, Gustave Eiffel built his famous iron tower in Paris. The making of concrete was revived, and glass-makers learned how to make larger and clearer sheets of glass for windows. Skyscrapers were built in Chicago and New York City using frames made of iron and steel. The first true skyscraper was the ten-story Home Insurance Building in Chicago, completed in 1885. Architects and engineers began using mathematics to make sure that their building frames were strong enough to stand up safely.

During the 20th century there have been many changes in building construction. Many kinds of machines are used on the construction site to cut, shape, lift, and install building materials. The use of mathematics in building design has increased so much that engineers now use computers to do most of their calculations. Much building construction is now done in factories rather than at the building site. Whole finished pieces of buildings are transported to the site and assembled rapidly in a process called **prefabrication.** Prefabrication saves money and time because it is faster and easier for the work to be done in a factory than out in the open.

Over the last century, ways have been developed to keep buildings well lighted and comfortable year-round. Electric lights, telephones, and computer networks are made possible by copper wiring run through buildings. Buildings are heated and cooled with many machines and devices designed to heat or chill air and control humidity. Sunlight is also better used to heat and light buildings. Modern plumbing systems enable people to wash, bathe, and cook in complete comfort and convenience. Computers are already used to control heating and cooling systems in some buildings. In years to come computers will be used more and more, not only to design buildings, but to manage every aspect of their operation as well.

EDWARD ALLEN
Author, *Fundamentals of Building Construction*

See also ARCHITECTURE; BRICKS AND MASONRY; CEMENT AND CONCRETE; IRON AND STEEL; STONE.

BULGARIA

BULGARIA

Bulgaria is situated on the Balkan Peninsula of southeastern Europe, a location that has played an important role in the nation's history. For although it is now a small country, Bulgaria was a great power in the region during much of the Middle Ages. In the late 1300's, however, Bulgaria was conquered by the Ottoman Turks, who ruled it as part of their empire for nearly 500 years. A self-governing Bulgarian state, greatly reduced in size, was re-established in1878. A fully independent kingdom of Bulgaria, with borders similar to the country's present-day borders, was proclaimed in 1908.

After World War II (1939–45), the Communist Party took over the Bulgarian government. It ruled Bulgaria as a dictatorship until 1989, when it yielded to demands for reform and accepted the idea of a multiparty political system.

A democratic constitution was adopted in 1991, and free elections held that same year were won by a coalition, or alliance, of non-Communist political parties. The first presidential election was held in 1992.

▶ THE PEOPLE

Migrating Slavic tribes settled in what is now Bulgaria during the A.D. 500's. In the 600's, the Bulgars, a nomadic people from Asia, conquered the Slavs and established a Bulgarian kingdom. The Bulgars eventually were absorbed into the much larger Slavic population. Little trace of them remains today, except for their name and a few words in the Bulgarian language.

Most of the people are Bulgarian Slavs. Turks form the largest minority group, making up about 9 percent of the population. Bulgaria also has smaller numbers of Gypsies, Armenians, Greeks, and Russians.

Bulgaria is a land of rugged mountains and fertile plains. The Rhodope Mountains, shown here, are the highest in the Balkans and form Bulgaria's boundary with Greece. The woman at right wears the traditional dress of Bulgaria's Plovdiv district.

Left: Blue denims are as popular with young Bulgarians as they are with teenagers the world over. *Below:* A bishop of the Bulgarian Orthodox Church blesses a parishioner. Religious observance was discouraged during the years of Communist rule, but today Bulgarians of all religions are free to practice their faiths.

Language and Religion. Bulgarian, the official language of the country, belongs to the South Slavic group of the Slavic languages. Bulgarian is closely related to Russian. Like Russian, it is written in the Cyrillic alphabet.

Historically, most Bulgarians have belonged to the Bulgarian Orthodox Church, an independent branch of the Eastern Orthodox Church. The head of the Bulgarian church is the Patriarch. Most of the Turks in Bulgaria, and also some Bulgarians, are Muslims. Bulgarian-speaking Muslims are called Pomaks. There are also small communities of Jews, Roman Catholics, and Protestants.

During the era of Communist rule, the government discouraged the practice of religion and regulated the conduct of the clergy. The policy of the new government includes respect for the independence of the country's religious institutions, and customary Christian holidays such as Christmas and Easter have been restored. The constitution proclaims Orthodox Christianity the traditional religion of the nation but gives it no special privileges. Bulgarians of other religions are free to practice their own faiths.

Way of Life. Before World War II, Bulgaria was mainly an agricultural country. Only about one quarter of the population lived in urban areas (cities and towns). After the Communists came to power, Bulgaria experienced vast changes in its way of life. The economy was nationalized, or brought under government control. Private farms were transformed into large, state-run collective farms, which

FACTS and figures

REPUBLIC OF BULGARIA is the official name of the country.

LOCATION: Balkan Peninsula in southeastern Europe.

AREA: 42,823 sq mi (110,912 km²).

POPULATION: 9,000,000 (estimate).

CAPITAL AND LARGEST CITY: Sofia.

MAJOR LANGUAGE: Bulgarian (official).

MAJOR RELIGION: Bulgarian Orthodox.

GOVERNMENT: Republic. **Head of state**—president. **Head of government**—prime minister. **Legislature**—National Assembly.

CHIEF PRODUCTS: Agricultural—wheat, corn, and other grains, sugar beets, grapes and other fruits, tobacco, sunflower seeds, roses. **Manufactured**—processed agricultural products, machinery, chemicals, metal products. **Mineral**—lignite (brown coal), iron ore (limited amounts), copper, zinc, lead, petroleum (limited amounts).

MONETARY UNIT: Lev (1 lev = 100 stotinki).

needed fewer workers. Industrialization led to the rapid growth of urban areas, where about two thirds of Bulgarians now live.

Major Cities. Sofia is Bulgaria's capital, commercial center, and largest city, with a population of more than 1 million. Although Sofia first became the national capital after it was freed from the Turks in 1878, the city has been a site of settlement since ancient times. Its oldest structure, the Church of St. George, was built on the remains of a public bath dating from Roman times.

Plovdiv is Bulgaria's second city, both in population and economic importance. Other major Bulgarian cities include Varna, Ruse, and Burgas.

▶ **THE LAND AND CLIMATE**

The Major Regions. Bulgaria has four major geographic regions: the Balkan Mountains, the Danube Plateau, the Thracian Plain, and the Rhodope Mountains.

The Balkan Mountains run east and west and split Bulgaria in two. They act as a divider between the two main climatic regions. North of the mountains the Danube Plateau slopes gradually to the Danube River, which separates Bulgaria from Romania. The Danube Plateau is an important agricultural area. It has a continental climate, marked by hot summers and cold winters. Between the Balkan Mountains and the Rhodope Mountains lies the Thracian Plain, drained by the Maritsa River, which has an especially fertile valley. The Rhodope Mountains, highest in the Balkan Peninsula, form the southern boundary between Bulgaria and Greece.

The Maritsa Valley is protected by the Balkan Mountains from the cold winds of the Russian plains. The valley has a Mediterranean climate, with mild but rainy winters and dry, hot summers.

The famous Valley of Roses, which lies in the heart of the country, is the center of Bulgaria's rose-growing industry. It produces attar of roses, an oil used in making perfumes. Bulgaria has nearly a world monopoly in the production of this attar.

Natural Resources. About one third of Bulgaria is covered with valuable forests. Some three quarters of the forests in the mountains are broadleaf; the rest are coniferous. Beech trees and evergreen scrub plants are found along the Maritsa Valley and the Turkish border. The country's wild animal life includes bears, wolves, foxes, elk, and wildcats, which roam the mountain forests.

Bulgaria has a variety of mineral resources, including coal, iron ore, copper, zinc, and lead. But most of its coal is a low-grade kind called lignite (brown coal), and its iron deposits are limited. Some petroleum is produced in the Black Sea region, but not enough to meet the country's energy needs.

Sunshine barely penetrates the winter mist covering Sofia, Bulgaria's capital and largest city. Although the site dates from ancient times, Sofia first became the national capital after it was freed from Turkish rule in 1878.

▶ THE ECONOMY

Until recently, Bulgaria, like other Communist nations, had a centrally planned economy, under which the government determined what the country's economic goals would be. After 1989, however, the country's leaders decided to abandon this system, which had led to severe economic problems, in favor of a market economy with large elements of private enterprise.

Agriculture. About half of Bulgaria's land is suitable for agriculture. The rest is too dry, too marshy, or too mountainous. Much of the farmland, however, is very fertile. The chief crops are wheat, corn, and other grains, grapes and other fruits, tobacco, sunflower seeds, and roses.

Under the Communist system, most of the country's agricultural production came from large agricultural complexes operated by the government. Individuals were permitted to cultivate only small plots of their own, which were usually devoted to raising livestock and animal feed. In 1991 the government adopted a law providing for the return of most of the land to private ownership.

Industry and Trade. Before the end of World War II, Bulgaria was one of the least industrialized countries in Europe. Emphasis by the government on this sector of the economy brought about the rapid development of industry, which is now the most important sector of the economy. The main categories of manufactured goods are processed agricultural products, machinery, chemicals, and metal products.

Most of Bulgaria's foreign trade traditionally had been with the former Soviet Union and other Communist nations. In the 1990's the country's leaders sought expanded trade relations with the countries of Western Europe and the United States. The country's main exports are machinery, foods, wine, rose oil, and metal products. Its chief imports include fuels, iron ore, and other raw materials.

▶ GOVERNMENT

Under the constitution of 1991, the Bulgarian state is headed by a president, who is elected by the people for a 5-year term. The government is led by a prime minister, who is chosen by the political party or coalition (alliance of parties) having the largest number of seats in the National Assembly, the country's parliament, or legislature.

In the 1991 elections for the National Assembly, the Union of Democratic Forces (UDF), a non-Communist alliance, won the largest number of seats and formed the government, in coalition with the Movement for Rights and Freedom (MRF), which represents primarily the Turkish minority. The Bulgarian Socialist Party (BSP), the new name adopted by the Bulgarian Communists, received the second largest number of seats and makes up the current opposition. The 1992 presidential election was won by Zheliu Zhelev, the original leader of the UDF.

Below: Bulgaria's Valley of Roses is the world's chief source of attar of roses, used in making perfume. *Right:* Industry, including steel production, is now the most important sector of the Bulgarian economy.

▶ HISTORY

The First Bulgarian Empire. The Bulgars arrived in the region from Central Asia in the A.D. 600's and conquered the part of the Balkan Peninsula inhabited by Slavs from the Byzantine Empire. In 681, Byzantium recognized the first Bulgarian empire, which lasted until 1018. Although they ruled the country, the Bulgars adopted the language and most of the customs of the conquered Slavs.

Bulgaria in the Middle Ages was a great military power. It fought many wars against the Byzantine Empire and against other neighbors and invaders. In 865 the Bulgarian ruler Czar Boris I accepted Christianity. He established the independent Bulgarian church and introduced the Cyrillic alphabet. This alphabet and the Orthodox religion were spread from Bulgaria to other parts of eastern Europe, including Russia. Boris' son Czar Simeon I (reigned 893–927) was one of Bulgaria's greatest rulers. During his reign, Bulgaria flourished as a center of Slavic culture and learning. Simeon I also conquered many new territories. At his death in 927, Bulgaria stretched from the Black Sea on the east to the Adriatic Sea on the west.

Byzantine Rule and the Second Empire. Bulgaria declined in importance after Simeon's death. In 1018 the Byzantine emperor Basil II conquered the country and ended the first Bulgarian empire. Bulgaria remained part of the Byzantine Empire until 1186.

In 1186, John Asen I and his brother Peter regained Bulgaria's independence. Their descendant Czar John Asen II (reigned 1218–41) established the second Bulgarian empire, which included most of the Balkan Peninsula. Art and literature flourished, and many new churches were founded. But in 1396, along with the rest of the Balkan states, Bulgaria was conquered by the Ottoman Turks.

Turkish Rule. Bulgaria remained a part of the Ottoman Empire for nearly 500 years. During that time the Bulgarian nobility disappeared, and Bulgarian farmers were made serfs to Turkish masters. The Bulgarian church, too, lost its independence and was placed under the control of the Greek Patriarch in Constantinople (now Istanbul).

The Bulgarians almost lost their national identity, for the ability to read and write had declined and few could remember the history of their people. However, a Bulgarian national

The Rila Monastery is one of the glories of Bulgaria's past. Originally built in the A.D. 900's, it was destroyed and rebuilt several times over the centuries.

revival began in the 1800's. An independent Bulgarian church was restored in 1870. Some Bulgarians took to the mountains and began a guerrilla campaign against Turkish rule.

Independence. Russia helped Bulgaria to win political independence from the Turks in the Russo-Turkish War of 1877–78. But the western European powers feared possible Russian expansion. Therefore, only the northern part of Bulgaria was made independent. In 1885, however, the southern part of the country, called Eastern Rumelia, broke away from Turkey and was reunited with Bulgaria.

The European powers did not believe that the Bulgarians were experienced enough to govern themselves in a fully democratic way, so they required the country to accept a foreign monarch. Its first prince was Alexander Battenberg, but he gave up the throne in 1886. That same year, Prince Ferdinand of Saxe-Coburg-Gotha was chosen as the new ruler.

Balkan Wars. In 1908, Ferdinand took the title of Czar and claimed the rest of the areas

Pro-democracy demonstrators in Sofia signaled "V" for victory after Bulgaria's Communist government yielded to demands for political and economic reforms. Elections held under a new constitution in 1991 brought to power a non-Communist government pledged to maintain democracy and to build a free-market economy.

of old Bulgaria, especially Macedonia. A Balkan alliance between Bulgaria, Serbia, Montenegro, and Greece was formed. This alliance fought against the Turks in the First Balkan War, in 1912. Victorious over the Turks, the Balkan allies quarreled among themselves. In the Second Balkan War, in 1913, Bulgaria was defeated by an alliance of Greece, Serbia, Romania, and Turkey, and was forced to give up its claims to Macedonia.

Two World Wars. In World War I (1914–18), Bulgaria, as an ally of Germany and Austria-Hungary, found itself on the losing side, and was compelled to give up more territory. Ferdinand was forced to abdicate, and the throne was inherited by his son Boris III. Heavy war reparations (compensation Bulgaria had to pay) and a flood of refugees from Macedonia caused economic and political instability during the 1920's and 1930's. In 1934, Czar Boris and the Army outlawed the country's political parties and made Bulgaria a dictatorship.

In 1941, during World War II, Bulgaria again allied itself with Germany. But although it declared war on the United States and Britain, Bulgaria did not declare war on the Soviet Union. Boris III died in 1943. The following year the Bulgarian government opened peace talks with the Allies.

Communism to Democracy. But the government had moved too slowly. While the talks were underway, the Soviet Union declared war against Bulgaria, and Bulgarian Communist leaders seized power. In 1946 the monarchy was abolished. The young czar, Simeon II, went into exile and Bulgaria adopted a Communist form of government.

During their years of rule, the Communists stressed the rapid growth of industry, but they allowed little political or cultural freedom. By the late 1980's, however, the far-reaching political changes that were sweeping the Soviet Union and other Communist nations of Eastern Europe had also affected Bulgaria. In 1989, Todor Zhivkov, who had led the Bulgarian Communist Party since 1954, was removed from power by his fellow Communist leaders. The new leadership allowed the formation of opposition political parties and the creation of a free press.

The first elections under the new 1991 Constitution were won by opponents of the Communists, who promised to maintain political democracy and to build a market economy, one based on private, rather than state-controlled, enterprise. Although the new government took office under difficult conditions, political and economic reforms proceeded without violence.

GEORGE W. HOFFMAN
University of Texas at Austin

Revised and updated by JOHN D. BELL
University of Maryland (Baltimore County)
Author, *The Bulgarian Communist Party from Blagoev to Zhivkov*

BULIMIA. See DISEASES (Descriptions of Some Diseases).

BULLETIN BOARDS

A bulletin board is a board for posting notices and other bits of information. A bulletin board of your own can serve many purposes. Perhaps it can make you smile by reminding you of the wonderful vacation you had last summer. It might make you feel proud by displaying your very best school papers. Maybe it can help keep you organized by providing a place to put important schedules and reminders. However you might use it, a bulletin board is a decorative showcase for your interests and accomplishments.

Ready-made bulletin boards are available at hardware and stationery stores. They come in a variety of sizes, ranging from the very large ones usually used in classrooms to the more usual 60- by 90-centimeter (2- by 3-foot) home size. Most bulletin boards are made out of cork. They can be purchased with a plain wood or metal frame or with no frame at all.

Bulletin boards are easy to make. Cork squares found in a hardware or decorating supply store can be used singly or in groups. A sheet of fiberboard (a material sometimes used to make walls), available at building supply stores, makes a good bulletin board. You can even use layers of cardboard glued together. Cover them with fabric or any of the other materials suggested below, and you have an attractive bulletin board at little or no cost.

Bulletin boards are usually hung like pictures on walls. But there are other places where bulletin boards can be just as effective. Try putting a large one behind your bed as a headboard. Or tack cork to the back of a bookcase or a dresser. In this way you can turn a piece of furniture that has an unfinished back into a free-standing piece that makes an excellent room divider.

Just as a bulletin board does not have to be on the wall, neither does it have to be a rectangle. You can easily cut cork or cardboard to any shape. Perhaps you can pick up a decorative shape, such as a flower or a star, from a fabric in your room. Or you can reflect an interesting hobby in the shape of your bulletin board. A car shape, baseball bat shape, or even the letters of your name or initials, cut out of cork and mounted, can provide a decorative touch to your room.

Background Material. There are many materials that can give a nice texture or design to the background of your bulletin board. Paper is a good choice because it can be changed easily when you change your board display. Try large sheets of poster board, construction paper, wallpaper, gift wrap, adhesive-backed paper, or shelf paper. Effective for certain themes are road maps, newsprint, or even aluminum foil. For a more permanent covering, fabrics are a good choice. Burlap, felt, leather, suede, or even fake fur lend good texture to the surface.

Borders. Borders give a finished look to your bulletin board. There are many ways to make effective borders. Pieces of braided or twisted yarn, crepe paper, ribbon, or paper chains can be used. Try stringing halves of paper plates or paper doilies together. See Diagram A on the following page for the technique of making cut-paper borders.

Lettering. If you want to label your bulletin board display, letters can be cut from magazines or made freehand. They can be made from paper or fabric. Diagram B on page 447 shows how to fold and cut paper to make letters.

Fasteners. Use straight pins, map pins, push pins, or double-faced tape to put materials on your bulletin board. Or try gluing magnets to the back of pictures. The magnets will stick to thumbtacks on the board.

On the following two pages, you will find some sample bulletin boards. They should give you some ideas for possible themes and techniques to make your bulletin board exciting and attractive.

ESTHER FINTON
Author, *Bulletin Boards Should Be More Than Something to Look At . . .*

BORDERS

1. Cut large sheets of colored construction paper into strips of 46 X 8 cm (18 X 3 in). Make as many as you need to surround your bulletin board.

2. Fold each strip in half, and in half again.

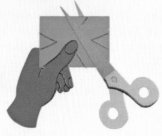

3. Select a pattern from the examples at right. You may want to make a cardboard sample of your pattern to trace onto each of your folded strips. Cut along the pencil lines indicated in your pattern.

4. Use straight pins to place the unfolded strips around your bulletin board.

Sample Borders

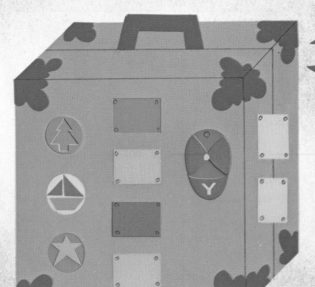

ABOUT THE BULLETIN BOARDS

Left: Reminders of summer camp include badges, a camp hat, and perhaps some photos of friends. The trunk-shaped board makes an appropriate background for any travel display. **Above right:** The food theme board decorated with heart borders is a handy place to keep school lunch menus or recipes. **Above far right:** A board cut into the shape of a fish is as decorative as an aquarium — and the cut paper fish do not have to be fed! **Right:** A semicircle bordered with paper umbrellas serves as a weather reporting station.

dieta

LETTERS

Cut pieces of paper or fabric to the letter size you want. Fold each piece as indicated by the dotted line on the letter you wish to make. Some letters require a vertical fold; others a horizontal; and letters G, J, N, Q, S, and Z require no fold at all. Using the entire paper, cut the shape for your letter, unfold — and enjoy the professional-looking results. You can change the style of your letters by rounding the edges or by changing the shape of the paper.

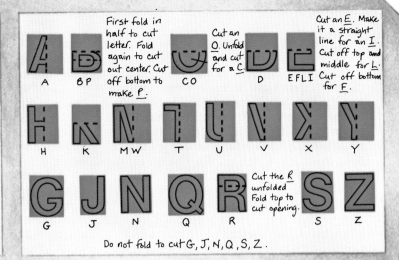

First fold in half to cut letter. Fold again to cut out center. Cut off bottom to make P.

A   B P   C O   D   E F L I

Cut an O. Unfold and cut for a C.

Cut an E. Make it a straight line for an I. Cut off top and middle for L. Cut off bottom for F.

H   K   M W   T   U   V   X   Y

G   J   N   Q   R   S   Z

Cut the R unfolded. Fold top to cut opening.

Do not fold to cut G, J, N, Q, S, Z.

447

BULLFIGHTING

Bullfighting has been called Spain's favorite sport. But to call it this is wrong for two reasons: first, soccer (called *fútbol* in Spain) is the most popular sport; and second, bullfighting cannot really be called a sport. It should be called, more properly, a spectacle, an exhibition, or a performance, like a ballet. However, this ballet is like dancing on a tightrope, because if the bullfighter makes a mistake, he is likely to be injured or killed.

A bullfight is not really a contest between a man and a bull. Actually it is a contest between a man and himself. The audience goes to the ring to see a man conquer his own fear of the horns and take as many chances with the bull as possible. The men who most gracefully execute the most daring maneuvers become the stars.

Bullfighting is one of the few ways a poor boy can become rich and famous in Spain and Latin America—and many *matadores* have become millionaires. But for every successful *matador,* there are hundreds who have fallen by the wayside and are forgotten. Many do not have the necessary grace and skill. Some are crippled by the bulls, and some are killed.

▶ HOW DID BULLFIGHTING BEGIN?

Bullfighting has existed in one form or another for more than 2,000 years. The ancient Cretans used to perform what they called bull dancing. Both men and women would leap over the bulls' horns in graceful, reckless exhibitions.

One of the reasons that Spain has been the leading place for bullfighting is that the fighting bull first lived there. Bullfighting cannot be done with ordinary animals. It requires the special *toro de lidia,* or *toro bravo,* which is as different from a domestic bull as a cobra is from a gopher snake, or a wolf is from a dog. For centuries, herds of these fierce bulls roamed wild over Spain. The Romans imported them for their savage battles against men and other animals in the Colosseum. The bulls usually won, even when pitted against lions and tigers. The Arabs in Spain helped make bullfighting popular around the early 12th century. In those days the spectacle consisted of a skillful horseman killing a wild bull with a lance while guiding his horse so as to avoid injury both to his mount and to himself. It is said that the famous cavalier El Cid was the first Spaniard to take part in organized bullfighting in an arena.

Bullfighting quickly became very popular, and for centuries rich Moors and Christians, nobles, and even kings practiced it. No feast day was complete without a *corrida de toros.*

The common people used to help the nobles fight the bulls, but they did so on foot. They used capes to distract the bull and keep it from charging at their bodies. Little by little this became the more exciting part of the act, and the ritual developed as we know it today.

Left: *Paseo,* or entrance parade, into the bullring in Madrid. Each *matador* leads his *cuadrilla,* or team of assistants. Right: The *matador* performs a classic *verónica.* The bull charges hard, passing before the *matador,* who swings the cape in front of its nose.

THE ARENA AND THE TOREROS

The first thing a person sees in the *plaza de toros,* or arena, is the gaily dressed and excited crowd. When the band strikes up, *toreros* stride into the arena and parade around it while the *aficionados,* or fans, cheer.

All people who fight bulls are called *toreros.* The *matadores* are the stars of the show, and there are usually three in an afternoon's program. Each one has two *picadores* and three *banderilleros* to help him. It is old-fashioned and incorrect to refer to bullfighters as *toreadores.* (The "toreador" of Bizet's opera *Carmen* is actually a *matador.*)

THE CONTEST

The men stride across the sand of the arena, and then the ring is cleared and the bull charges in. The bull has not been trained or tortured or starved; yet, because of its centuries of breeding, it knows it is supposed to fight. A *banderillero* will run out and swirl his cape a few times in front of the animal to demonstrate to his *matador* how this particular animal charges, since each bull has a different style of fighting.

Now the *matador* goes out. Where the *banderillero* was awkward and stayed safely away from the bull's horns, the *matador,* being the star, must stand very close to the animal. He swings the cape gracefully and lets the horns slice just by his legs. On each pass that the *matador* performs well, the crowd yells and cheers. If the *matador* bends over awkwardly and steps back out of the path of the bull as the *banderillero* did, the crowd boos loudly. The audience would like to see the bullfighters behave exactly opposite from the way they would behave if they had to stand in front of a huge bull with only a cape for protection. The bull goes at the cloth not because it is red, but because the *matador* knows just how to shake the cape to attract the animal and make it go at the lure instead of his body. The cape is yellow on one side and red on the other, but because bulls are color-blind, it makes no difference which side the *matador* presents to the animal.

After the *matador* does several passes, called *verónicas,* a trumpet blows and the *picadores* enter on horseback. They prick the bull with their lances in order to weaken his neck muscles. They do this so that at the end the *matador* will be able to reach over the horns and place the sword blade where it should go—between the bull's shoulder blades. The horses have been safely padded since 1930, so there is less chance that they will be injured by the charging bull.

Next, each of the three *banderilleros* places two *banderillas* ("barbed sticks") in the animal's shoulders. These further weaken the bull's neck muscles.

Finally the *matador* goes out with the sword and a little cape called the *muleta.* This is the most dangerous time of the fight, in spite of the fact that the bull is tired. There have been about 125 great *matadores* since 1700, and 42 of them have been killed, generally during this part of the bullfight. This is because the little cape is so small, the bull has learned so much during the course of the fight, and the man must make his most dangerous passes at this time.

THE KILL

Killing the bull, called "the moment of truth," is the most dangerous maneuver of all. The man must run at the bull at the same time that the bull runs at him, and plunge the sword between the shoulder blades. When this is done correctly, the bull will drop over dead almost instantly.

If the *matador* has done his job well, the crowd applauds, and he is awarded the ear of the bull as a trophy. If he has done a superior job, he is given both ears and the tail. The meat of the bulls is sometimes given to the poor, but usually the animals are butchered in back of the arena and sold for steaks.

Joselito and Manolete, two of the greatest bullfighters of the 20th century, were killed by bulls. Joselito died when he was only 25; Manolete at the age of 30. Many other *matadores,* like the great Antonio Ordóñez and El Cordobés of Spain, have been severely injured in the bullring. The ambition of most bullfighters, who usually come from poor families, is to make enough money to buy a bull ranch and retire at about the age of 30.

The best fights in Spain are held in Madrid, Seville, Valencia, and Málaga during the spring and summer. In Latin America the best fights can be seen in Mexico City or Lima, Peru. In Portugal the only ring of importance is in Lisbon.

BARNABY CONRAD
Author, *La Fiesta Brava, The Death of Manolete*

BUNCHE, RALPH (1904–1971)

Ralph Bunche was the first black to be awarded the Nobel peace prize. He received this honor in 1950 for his work as a United Nations mediator in the Middle East.

Bunche, the grandson of a slave, was born in Detroit, Michigan, on August 7, 1904. His parents died when he was 13, and he and his sister went to live with their grandmother in California. He received a scholarship to the University of California but still had to take odd jobs to pay for his books, meals, and carfare. Nevertheless he managed to play on three basketball championship teams and to graduate with highest honors. He continued his education at Harvard University, receiving an M.A. degree in 1928.

Bunche began his career teaching political science at Howard University and, soon after, married Ruth Harris, who had been one of his students. The couple had three children. Bunche left Howard for a time to continue his studies at Harvard and received a Ph.D. degree in 1934.

From 1938 to 1940, Bunche worked as the chief assistant to Swedish sociologist Gunnar Myrdal on a survey of race relations in America. The result was an important book titled *An American Dilemma* (1944). He later worked for the U.S. Government, eventually becoming the first black to head a division of the U.S. State Department. In 1946 he accepted a permanent post at the United Nations.

In 1948, war broke out between Israel and its Arab neighbors. Count Folke Bernadotte was appointed by the United Nations to help end the dispute. When Bernadotte was assassinated, Bunche took his place. He received the Nobel peace prize for his role in persuading the warring countries to stop fighting.

He continued to serve the United Nations in various troubled parts of the world, including the Congo (now Zaïre) and Cyprus as well as the Middle East. From 1967 until his retirement in 1971, he was the under secretary–general of the United Nations. Bunche died on December 9, 1971.

Reviewed by MARGUERITE CARTWRIGHT
Hunter College, City University of New York

BUNKER HILL, BATTLE OF. See REVOLUTIONARY WAR.
BUOYANCY. See FLOATING.

BURBANK, LUTHER (1849–1926)

Luther Burbank once remarked: "I shall be contented if because of me there shall be better fruits and fairer flowers." In 50 years of work, he more than achieved his goal. He developed 618 new varieties of plants.

Burbank was born on a farm near Lancaster, Massachusetts, on March 7, 1849. In his early years, Luther attended a one-room school. At 15 he entered Lancaster Academy, where he received some instruction in science. But it was in the Lancaster library that Burbank—at the age of 19—discovered the writings of Charles Darwin. From Darwin, Burbank learned how better varieties of plants could be developed. The secret was to select seeds from those plants with the most desirable traits and to breed for those traits.

A few years later, Burbank was able to purchase land near Lunenburg, Massachusetts. There he set about developing his first "new creation," a larger and firmer potato. He planted potato seeds and selected the best potatoes from the resulting crop for replanting.

The variety he developed in this way is still known as the Burbank potato.

In 1875, Burbank sold his farm and moved to Santa Rosa, California. There he set up a small nursery garden, greenhouse, and orchard, where he grew and sold plants to support his research. What he had done with the potato, he now began to do with other plants and fruits, such as plums and berries. He also developed new plants, such as his famous Shasta daisy, by crossbreeding.

Burbank bought more acres and established what became a world-famous experimental farm. The yearly catalog, *New Creations*, that he issued from 1893 to 1901 described his experiments. Although he used scientific principles and methods, Burbank's main interest was in practical results.

Burbank died on April 11, 1926. His work lives on in his plants. In California alone, his varieties form the basis of a industry.

JOHN S. BOWMAN
Author and science editor

BURKINA

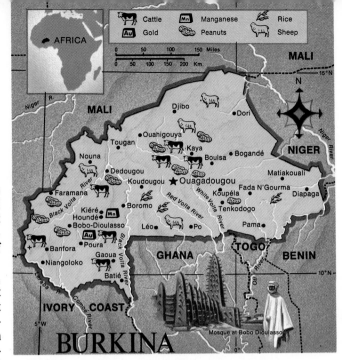

Mosque at Bobo Dioulasso

BURKINA

Burkina is an inland nation of West Africa. For centuries it was the site of a great empire ruled by the Mossi people. The Mossi are still the most numerous people of Burkina. But their empire has long ceased to exist, and Burkina today is one of the poorest nations of Africa.

Burkina was at one time a colony of France, before gaining its independence in 1960. It was called Upper Volta until 1984, when it adopted the African name Burkina. The country's official name is Burkina Faso, which is sometimes translated as "land of the honest [or upright] people." Politically, "Faso" has the approximate meaning of People's Republic.

▶THE PEOPLE

Most of Burkina's people live in the central and southwestern parts of the country. The Mossi, who inhabit the central region, make up about one third of the population. Other ethnic groups include the Bobo, Lobi-Dagari, Senufo, Gurunsi, and Mande. The sparsely settled northeast is the home of the Songhai, Fulani, and Tuareg.

Language and Religion. French is the official language, but each of Burkina's peoples has its own language or dialect. Moré, the language of the Mossi, is widely spoken in central Burkina.

The majority of the people practice traditional African religions. About 25 percent are Muslims and some 10 percent Christian.

Way of Life. The Mossi way of life still reflects the discipline enforced by early Mossi rulers. The actions of every individual must conform to a strict code of behavior. The family is the most important unit. Each family lives in a walled compound containing several small, round clay-and-mud huts. Most Mossi are farmers. The family fields surround the compound.

The Bobo, like the Mossi, are family-centered. Their dwellings, however, are larger than those of the Mossi and are built together in compact villages and towns.

The Fulani and Tuareg of the northeast are nomadic herders, who travel with their livestock seeking grazing land.

▶THE LAND

Most of Burkina is a vast plateau consisting of savanna, or grassland. The northeast is part of the Sahel, a region of sparse vegetation on the edge of the Sahara desert. The country's three principal rivers are the Red Volta, the Black Volta, and the White Volta.

The soil is generally poor, although crops can be grown where there is adequate rainfall. When the rains are long ·delayed, however, drought results.

Climate. Burkina has a hot, dry climate, with an average daytime temperature of 82°F (28°C). Rainfall is heaviest in the southwest and scantiest in the northeast. During the hottest season, from about March to May, the harmattan, a dry, searing wind, blows south from the Sahara.

Cities. Ouagadougou, which lies in central Burkina, was once a capital of the Mossi empire. It is now Burkina's capital and largest city, with a population of more than 240,000. Bobo-Dioulasso, the second largest city, is located in the southwest.

▶ECONOMY

Burkina's economy is based on agriculture and the raising of livestock, particularly cattle, sheep, and goats. The chief food crops include sorghum, millet, rice, corn, and beans. The country's major exports are livestock and livestock products, cotton, peanuts, sesame seeds, and shea nuts. (Shea nuts yield an oil that is used in cooking.) All land was nationalized, or brought under government control, in 1984.

Burkina has limited industry. Much of it involves the processing of agricultural and animal products.

The country has suffered frequent periods of severe drought, which have devastated the economy. Burkina's economic problems, in turn, have had a negative effect on the country's political life.

▶HISTORY AND GOVERNMENT

Early History. The ancestors of the Mossi probably arrived in what is now Burkina in the 11th century. Because of their superior organization, they were able to conquer the people already living in the region. They founded several kingdoms, the most important of which was centered at Ouagadougou.

Europeans first arrived in the region in the late 19th century. France became the dominant power, subduing the Mossi kings and establishing a protectorate over the area. The colony of Upper Volta was created by the French in 1919. It was divided among the other colonies of French West Africa in 1932 but was restored as a separate territory in 1948. Upper Volta gained self-government in 1958 and complete independence in 1960.

Since Independence. The country's history since independence has been stormy. The first president, Maurice Yaméogo, was deposed in

FACTS AND FIGURES

BURKINA FASO is the official name of the country.

THE PEOPLE are known as Burkinabe.

LOCATION: West Africa.

AREA: 105,869 sq mi (274,200 km²).

POPULATION: 8,000,000 (estimate).

CAPITAL AND LARGEST CITY: Ouagadougou.

MAJOR LANGUAGES: French (official), Moré, other African languages.

MAJOR RELIGIONS: Traditional African religions, Muslim, Christian.

GOVERNMENT: Republic (under military rule). **Head of state and government**—chairman of the Popular Front. **Legislature**—National Assembly (dissolved).

CHIEF PRODUCTS: Livestock (cattle, sheep, goats) and livestock products, cotton, peanuts, sesame seeds, shea nuts, sorghum, millet, rice, corn, beans.

MONETARY UNIT: African Financial Community (CFA) franc (1 franc = 100 centimes).

NATIONAL ANTHEM: *Ditaniya.*

1966 in a military coup led by Lieutenant Colonel Sangoulé Lamizana. Lamizana remained in power, either as president or as head of a military government, until 1980, when the worsening economic situation brought about his overthrow. Struggles for power within the military led to the formation of new governments following military coups in 1983 and 1987. The country's name was changed to Burkina Faso in 1984 to end a link to its colonial past.

H. R. JARRETT
University of Newcastle (Australia)
Author, *Physical Geography for West African Schools*

The distinctive architecture of the people of southwestern Burkina is shown in this mosque (Muslim house of worship), located near the city of Bobo-Dioulasso.

BURMA (MYANMAR)

Burma is a nation of Southeast Asia and the largest of the mainland Southeast Asian countries. It has sometimes been called the Land of Pagodas, because of the many pagodas, or Buddhist shrines, that dot the landscape.

Although it shares borders with a number of countries, Burma has been isolated for much of its long history. It was shut off first by the mountains that enclose it on three sides, but also by the choice of its ancient kings and some of its recent political leaders. In 1989, Burma's leaders changed its name to Myanmar, which is "Burma" spelled in Burmese, the national language.

▶THE PEOPLE

Ethnic Groups. The people of Burma come from many different ethnic groups, but the Burmans are the most numerous, making up about two thirds of the population. Their ancestors migrated to what is now Burma from the mountains of southern China more than a thousand years ago and mixed with the people already living in the region.

The main non-Burman peoples include the Chin, the Kachin, the Shan, the Karen, and the Mon. They mostly occupy the mountains and hills and border areas, and some live in neighboring countries as well. Many have never been under the complete control of the central Burmese government. There are many smaller groups, each of which has its own culture. There are also ethnic Indians, Bangladeshis, and Chinese.

Burma has been called the Land of Pagodas, because of the many pagodas, or Buddhist shrines, found throughout the country. Burmese pagodas are distinctive for their cone-shaped spires, which are often covered in gold leaf.

Language and Education. More than 120 different languages and dialects are spoken, but Burmese, the language of the Burmans, is the country's official language. Since it is taught in the schools, it is spoken or understood by most of the people. Burmese is related to Tibetan, which in turn is related to Chinese. English is used as a second language, particularly by educated Burmese. It is a reminder of the time, from the late 1800's to 1948, when Burma was ruled by Britain.

Basic education consists of one year of kindergarten, followed by four years of primary school, four years of middle school, and two years of high school. However, since government budgets are limited and the country is large, there are still shortages of schools and teachers in the smaller and remote areas. The

453

A young Burmese boy wears the saffron-colored robes of a Buddhist monk. Burmese boys traditionally spend a period of time serving as novice, or beginning, monks.

country's major universities are located in the cities of Rangoon (Yangon), the capital, and Mandalay.

All formal education is government sponsored. But because schools are crowded and standards have fallen, many families in the cities and towns send their children to private tutoring schools in addition to public schools.

Religion.   The first Burman kings adopted the Buddhist religion (which originated in India) from the Mon people, whom they conquered in the A.D. 1000's. Today almost all Burmans are Buddhists, as are the Shan and Mon. Some of the hill peoples still follow ancient tribal religions, while others were converted to Christianity by British and American missionaries. Burma also has substantial Hindu and Muslim minorities, chiefly the Indians and Bangladeshis.

▶ **WAY OF LIFE**

The Role of Buddhism.   Buddhism plays an important role in the life of the people. Burmese boys between the ages of 6 and 13 serve as novice (beginning) monks for a short time, and some remain in the monkhood. Almost every village has a monastery, headed by a monk who is a teacher as well as a spiritual leader. The monastery is the center of village life. In addition to providing for the religious needs of the people, it often serves as a school, a social center, a place for the traveler to rest, and even as a hospital or clinic.

At one time, before the advent of public education, most village children went to monastery schools, where they learned to read and write and studied Buddhist scriptures. Because of this, traditional Burma had one of the highest literacy rates (the percentage of people able to read and write) in Asia.

The Farm Village.   Most Burmese live in villages and are farmers. Farm houses are often built on poles with walls of matting and roofs made of palm-leaf thatch. Houses usually have a porch, which serves as both a living and dining area. The houses are grouped together, along dirt paths, with each having a small garden where vegetables and fruits are grown and where domestic animals may be kept. Most farmers plow their land with water buffalo.

Since generous giving and helping others is a part of Buddhist belief, visitors are always offered something to eat, and wayfarers can be assured of water to ease their thirst.

Food and Dress.   The Burmese eat their meals at low tables while seated on woven mats on the floor. Rice is the staple food and is eaten at every meal. Burmese use spoons as eating utensils, but do not usually use forks. Rice is rolled into small balls with the fingers and dipped into various dishes.

FACTS and figures

UNION OF MYANMAR is the official name of the country. Historically, it has been known as Burma.

LOCATION: Southeast Asia.

AREA: 261,218 sq mi (676,552 km²).

POPULATION: 41,500,000 (estimate).

CAPITAL AND LARGEST CITY: Rangoon (Yangon).

MAJOR LANGUAGES: Burmese (official), English, numerous other languages.

MAJOR RELIGION: Buddhist.

GOVERNMENT: Republic, under military rule: Since a military coup in 1988, the government has been led by the State Law and Order Restoration Council (SLORC).

CHIEF PRODUCTS: Agricultural—rice, sugarcane, sesame, peanuts, peas, beans, spices, fruits, coconuts. **Manufactured**—processed foods, lumber (particularly teak), cement, textiles, fertilizers. **Mineral**—lead, silver, zinc, tin, copper, tungsten, natural gas, jade, rubies, sapphires.

MONETARY UNIT: Kyat (1 kyat = 100 pyas).

Burmese food is tasty and spicy. Curries (dishes spiced with curry powder), vegetables, and fish are particularly favored. A sauce or paste made from fish or shrimp is commonly used as a seasoning. Since Buddhism discourages the killing of animals, meat is eaten only rarely. Coconut and coconut milk are also important ingredients in Burmese cooking, as are fruits such as mangoes, papaya, and bananas.

Most Burmese wear a sarong-like skirt called a *longyi* (or *lungyi*), with men's and women's garments differing in patterns and the way they are tied. On formal occasions men wear a colorful cloth headdress called a *gaungbaung*. Women go bareheaded but often wear flowers in their hair, especially young, unmarried women who frequently tie their lustrous black hair in a ponytail. Married women traditionally wear their hair in a bun.

Names and Social Attitudes. Burmese have given names, but no family names. The first syllable of the given name is usually determined by the day of the week on which one is born. Titles of respect are related to concepts of family, so that an older woman of good reputation is called *Daw,* or "aunt," rather than Mrs. (or Miss or Ms.). A man is addressed as *U* (pronounced 'oo'), meaning "uncle," rather than Mr. Male friends may refer to each other as "elder brother" or "younger brother."

In general, Burma has had a very open social system, without great landed wealth or restrictions based on birth or occupation. One may rise socially through education, the monkhood, the military, and politics. Women have always been treated with respect in Burmese society and traditionally have kept their own property when they married. They are active in business and in many professions, and include an opposition political leader.

Holidays. Some Burmese holidays commemorate national events, but the most important are religious in nature. The Burmese New Year, or Water Festival (*Thingyan*), occurs in April. This is a time when the heat is intense, and celebrants sprinkle water on images of the Buddha as well as on one another as a blessing. This often becomes an excuse for good natured water fights. The Festival of Lights, or *Thadingyut*, comes in October. It celebrates Buddha's return to earth from the realm of the gods and is marked by the lighting of thousands of candles in pagodas and homes.

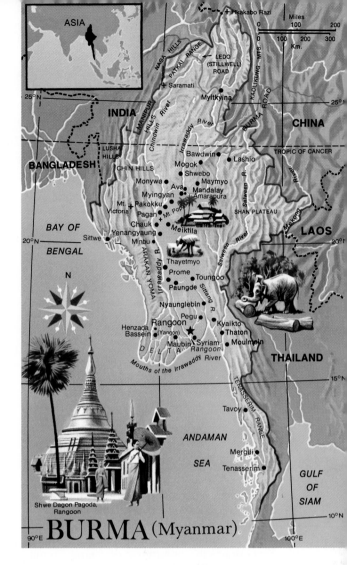

Shwe Dagon Pagoda, Rangoon

BURMA (Myanmar)

▶**THE LAND**

Mountains and Seas. Burma shares mountainous or ruggedly hilly boundaries with China on the north and northeast, Thailand and Laos on the east, and India and Bangladesh on the west. In the north the mountains form part of the high Himalayan range and some are permanently snowcapped. Even the less mountainous areas are difficult to cross, although the tribal hill peoples do so for purposes of trade. In the south, Burma has a long coastline on the Bay of Bengal and Andaman Sea, arms of the Indian Ocean.

The River System. Burma's major river is the Irrawaddy, which rises in the far north. The Irrawaddy is the chief communications link between central and southern Burma. It was the "road to Mandalay" in Rudyard Kip-

Right: Most of Burma's rice, its chief crop, is grown in the fertile area drained by the major rivers. Some of the mountains that enclose Burma on three sides can be seen in the distance. *Below:* Water buffalo haul logs of teak, a valuable hardwood that is the country's main export.

ling's famous poem *Mandalay* (see Cities section). The Salween River to the east is less important, because it is not navigable (usable by ships) for most of its length. The Sittang River drains the eastern part of central Burma.

Most Burmese live in the area drained by the Irrawaddy, its western tributary (branch), the Chindwin River, and the Sittang. Sediment deposited by the rivers in flood have enriched the soil, creating Burma's most fertile region.

A Monsoon Climate. Burma has three seasons, based on the monsoon winds. From October through February the winds bring dry weather with warm days and cool nights. In March the hot dry season begins. The rainy season begins in June, as humid winds sweep in from the Bay of Bengal, bringing up to 200 inches (5,080 millimeters) of rainfall along the coast. The rains are dissipated by the mountains, however, and central Burma remains relatively dry. It is after the first rains that the hard, dry, compacted earth is moistened and farmers can plow and plant their rice and other crops.

▶**THE ECONOMY**

Compared to other Asian countries, Burma has an abundance of fertile land and is not overpopulated. Although the people have fewer goods than in wealthier nations, there are also fewer differences between rich and poor than in most societies. Whatever its problems, Burma has rarely suffered from a shortage of food.

Economic Experiments. From independence in 1948 until 1988, Burmese governments were socialist in ideology, and much of the country's industry was state-controlled. This was a reaction against the domination of the economy by foreigners—British, Indians, and Chinese—during the colonial period. An extreme period of state control over the economy was begun in 1963 under military rule. This economic system failed, and the potentially rich country became even poorer. Since 1988 the government has encouraged private enterprise in many fields, as well as foreign investment, although certain industries remain a state monopoly.

Agriculture. The country's basic crop is rice, which is grown in wet, irrigated fields on the plains and in dry fields in the highlands. At one time, Burma was the world's leading exporter of rice, and rice remains a principal export. Sesame, peanuts, peas, beans, sugarcane, peppers, cotton, and various fruits are also grown in the lowlands.

In the highlands, *swidden* (slash and burn) agriculture is practiced among certain tribes. Trees and brush are felled and burned, and crops are planted. The soil is enriched this way for a few years. Then, as crop production diminishes, these fields are abandoned and new ones found. As populations increased, this system became wasteful and caused damage to the environment.

In remote regions, where government influence is limited, opium poppies are grown. The opium is made into heroin, which then enters the world drug market. The government has tried to control this illegal practice, but with little success.

Manufacturing, Forestry, Mining. Chief manufactured products include processed foods, lumber, cement and other construction materials, textiles, and fertilizers. Consumer goods were often smuggled, or brought into the country illegally. This was because Burmese industry could not produce them efficiently and they could not legally be imported. Many of these goods came overland through the mountainous regions of Thailand and China. The government has since legalized this trade.

Forests, which cover nearly half the land, are one of Burma's most valuable natural resources. Burma has about 75 percent of the world's reserves of teak and is the leading supplier of this valuable hardwood, which is used chiefly in making furniture. Teak is now the country's main export.

Burma has extensive mineral deposits, including lead, tin, tungsten, zinc, silver, copper, coal, and natural gas. It is also famed for such gemstones as jade, rubies, and sapphires. Although once an oil-exporting nation, Burma must now import some of this fuel.

▶ **CITIES**

Rangoon (or Yangon), in the south, is the country's capital, largest city, and chief seaport. It has a population of more than 2.5 million. One of the city's most impressive sites is the thousand-year-old Shwe Dagon Pagoda, the most revered Buddhist shrine in Southeast Asia. Most of Burma's industry is located in the city and nearby.

Mandalay, the second largest city, lies on the Irrawaddy River in central Burma. The capital of the kingdom of Burma from 1860 to 1885, it is the country's cultural center. Other important cities are Moulmein, a port on the Salween River in the southeast; Bassein in the delta region in the south; and Pegu, a city near Rangoon that was once a Mon capital.

▶ **HISTORY AND GOVERNMENT**

Early History. After migrating south from China in the A.D. 700's, the Burmans unified the country beginning with King Anawratha (1044–77). Their magnificent capital on the banks of the Irrawaddy River, Pagan, a city of some 5,000 pagodas, remains one of the most important historical sites of Southeast Asia. The classical age of Burma collapsed when Pagan fell to the troops of China's Mongol emperor Kublai Khan, in 1287.

Following a period of Shan rule, two powerful Burman kingdoms arose. The Toungoo dynasty (1484–1752) controlled Burma and northern Thailand. The Konbaung dynasty (1752–1885) pushed into eastern India, bringing Burma into conflict with Britain and its Indian colony.

British Rule to Independence. Beginning in 1824, three wars were fought by the British and Burmese. Known as the Anglo-Burmese wars, they gradually eliminated Burma as an independent kingdom. In 1886, Burma became a British colony, governed from India.

Although in ruins, Pagan, capital of the first Burman kings, reflects the splendor of Burma's past.

Anti-government demonstrations, begun by students and monks (*right*), forced Burma's military rulers to hold multiparty elections in 1990. But the results, a victory for the opposition, led by Aung San Suu Kyi (*above*), were ignored by the military, which held on to power. Aung San Suu Kyi, who was under house arrest, was awarded the 1991 Nobel peace prize.

Burmese resistance to colonial rule never really ceased. After demands for more control over its own affairs, Burma was separated from India in 1937 and given limited self-government within the British Empire. In 1941, during World War II, the Japanese invaded Burma, drove out the British, and established a Burmese state under Japanese rule.

Burma was reoccupied by the British in 1945, aided by Burmese nationalists. General Aung San, considered the father of independent Burma, negotiated his country's independence from Britain. Although Aung San was killed in 1947, an independent Burma came into existence the next year. U Nu was its first prime minister.

Recent History. From 1948 until 1958, the Union of Burma was a parliamentary democracy. The union was a weak one, however. Some ethnic groups, along with Communists and other dissidents, were in revolt against the central government.

In 1958 the military led by General Ne Win overthrew U Nu and took control of the country. They relinquished power to U Nu after elections in 1960, but seized control of the government again in 1962, ruling by decree. In 1974 a new constitution established a highly centralized government under a single political party, the Burma Socialist Program Party (BSPP), dominated by the military in civilian clothes.

Military rule created social and economic inequality as well as political repression. In 1988 student unrest triggered massive demonstrations that forced the abandonment of the single party system, the end of the BSPP, and the opening up of the economy. As continuing demonstrations were about to topple the regime, a new military group seized power in September 1988, during which thousands of Burmese were said to have been killed. The new military rulers governed as the State Law and Order Restoration Council (SLORC).

The SLORC promised multiparty elections for the National Assembly, which were held in May 1990. The opposition, led by Aung San's daughter, Aung San Suu Kyi, who had been placed under house arrest, won 80 percent of the seats. But the election results were ignored by the military, who jailed many opposition leaders. For her efforts to achieve democracy by nonviolent means, Aung San Suu Kyi was awarded the Nobel peace prize in 1991, while still under confinement.

THOMAS F. BARTON
Indiana University
Revised and updated by DAVID I. STEINBERG
Georgetown University
Author, *Burma's Road to Development*

BURNS. See FIRST AID.

BURNS, ROBERT (1759–1796)

Robert Burns, Scotland's greatest poet, becomes the world's favorite each New Year's Eve with the traditional singing of his "Auld Lang Syne." It is fitting tribute to a poet who loved good company, good song, and simple pleasures.

Robert was born on January 25, 1759, in Ayrshire, Scotland. His father was a poverty-stricken farmer, but a man of great character who valued education and strict morality. Although Robert's help was needed on the farm, his father encouraged him to read and gave him as much schooling as he could.

Robert read everything he could, from collections of songs to Shakespeare and Milton. He carried small volumes in his pocket and studied them while he was in the fields or at the table. He began writing his own verses and collected them in a scrapbook.

When his father died in 1784, Robert and his brother Gilbert tried to make a success of farming but failed. Robert fell in love with Jean Armour, but her father, a prosperous builder, refused to have him as a son-in-law. Robert then planned to seek his fortune in Jamaica. But first, he published *Poems, Chiefly in the Scottish Dialect* (1786). The poems were so successful that he was urged to try his luck in Edinburgh instead.

Burns became a favorite of prominent people there, and in 1787 a second edition of his poems appeared. He began to collect, adapt, and compose lyrics of folk songs for a publication called *The Scots Musical Museum*. For this and for George Thomson's *Select Collection of Original Scottish Airs* (1793), Burns composed over 300 lyrics. Some of his best-known poems are "Sweet Afton," "To a Mouse," "John Anderson, My Jo," and the patriotic "Scots, Wha Hae."

In 1788, Burns began a new life of farming, at Ellisland, near Dumfries, and finally married Jean Armour. But he failed again at farming. He took a government position as a tax officer and moved to Dumfries in 1791. His outspoken sympathy for the French Revolution damaged his popularity. Illness added to his troubles. He died on July 21, 1796, a broken and bitter man. But his poems found a permanent place in literature.

Reviewed by GEORGIA DUNBAR
Hofstra University

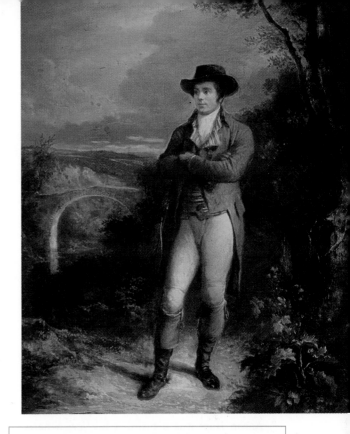

Robert Burns wrote in both standard English and the dialect of the Scottish farmers and villagers he had known all his life. Some of his poetry was written in a mixed language, using English grammar and Scottish vocabulary. Sometimes he simply spelled English words in the Scots fashion. In the following poem, the Scottish word "gang" means "go," and "weel" means "well."

A RED, RED ROSE

O, my luve is like a red, red rose,
That's newly sprung in June
O, my luve is like the melodie,
That's sweetly played in tune.

As fair art thou, my bonie lass,
So deep in luve am I,
And I will luve thee still, my dear,
Till a' the seas gang dry.

Till a' the seas gang dry, my dear,
And the rocks melt wi' the sun!
And I will luve thee still, my dear,
While the sands o' life shall run.

And fare thee weel, my only luve,
And fare thee weel a while!
And I will come again, my luve,
Tho' it were ten thousand mile!

Aaron Burr was a Revolutionary War hero and a leading lawyer and politician whose career was destroyed by poor judgment and uncontrolled ambition.

BURR, AARON (1756–1836)

Aaron Burr was a brilliant lawyer, a hero of the Revolutionary War, and a vice-president of the United States. But most Americans remember Burr only as the man who killed Alexander Hamilton in a duel.

Burr was born in Newark, New Jersey, on February 6, 1756. His father was president of the College of New Jersey (now Princeton University). Aaron was admitted to the college when he was 13 and graduated with honors at 16. Later he studied law.

At the outbreak of the Revolutionary War, Burr joined the Continental Army. He served in the American march on Quebec in 1775. Later he was a staff officer under George Washington. Once, by disobeying orders, he saved an entire brigade from capture by the British. But poor health cut short his military career, and Burr left the army in 1779.

In 1782, Burr married Theodosia Prevost, the widow of a British officer. They had one child, a girl named Theodosia after her mother. Burr carefully educated his daughter since he believed girls should be as well educated as boys. Burr's wife lived only 12 years after their marriage, but she was a steadying influence on her husband.

Burr was a leading figure in the legal, social, and political life of New York. He served in the U.S. Senate and in the New York State Assembly. In his early years in New York, Burr had become friendly with another prominent young lawyer, Alexander Hamilton. But political rivalry soon turned the two men into bitter enemies.

In the presidential election of 1800, Burr and Thomas Jefferson both received the same number of votes. So the election was decided by the House of Representatives. After 36 ballots, Jefferson was elected president, and Burr became vice-president.

Hamilton had led the fight to block Burr's election. The hatred between the two men finally led to a duel near Weehawken, New Jersey, on July 11, 1804. Hamilton fired into the air, but Burr's bullet hit home. Hamilton died the next day, and Burr fled to escape arrest.

After leaving the vice-presidency in 1805, Burr found private life dull. He could not live in New York again because of the duel. He began to plan an expedition against Spain's Mexican possessions. In 1805 and 1806 he traveled down the Mississippi River, but his real reasons for this journey are still a mystery. Some people said that he planned to set up his own empire in the Southwest, with himself as emperor.

In 1807, General James Wilkinson, who was secretly in the pay of the Spanish, denounced Burr to Jefferson. The President ordered Burr's arrest for treason. He was tried at Richmond, Virginia, with Supreme Court Justice John Marshall as judge. Burr was accused of trying to separate the western states from the Union. Marshall ruled that there was no clear proof of treason, and Burr was freed. But his reputation was ruined.

Burr went to Europe and did not return to the United States until 1812. He had hoped to devote his declining years to his daughter and grandson. But both Theodosia and her son died within a year of each other.

Burr spent his last years practicing law. He died, almost forgotten, on Staten Island, New York, on September 14, 1836, and was buried at Princeton, near his father.

Perhaps Thomas Jefferson best summed up the fatal flaw in Burr's character when he wrote: "No man's history proves better the value of honesty. With that, what might he not have been?"

Reviewed by RICHARD B. MORRIS
Columbia University

See also HAMILTON, ALEXANDER.

BURUNDI

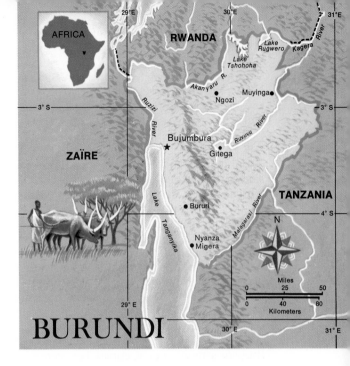

BURUNDI

Burundi is a small, densely populated nation located in the heart of east central Africa. Formerly known as Urundi, it was at one time a colony of Germany. Later, it was governed by Belgium. Burundi gained its independence as a kingdom in 1962. It became a republic in 1966.

▶ THE PEOPLE

The people of Burundi belong to three major ethnic groups—the Hutu, the Tutsi (also known as Watusi), and the Twa.

Most of Burundi's people are Hutu. The Hutu live mainly by farming. Tutsi, who make up about 15 percent of the population, are cattle raisers. Most of the Tutsi are extremely tall. In the past they were the warriors who controlled and defended the land, dominating their Hutu neighbors. The Twa are Pygmies who live by hunting and fishing. They were the earliest inhabitants of the region. Today they make up a small part of the population.

The most widely used language is Kirundi. French, which dates from the time when Belgium governed Burundi, is also spoken. Both are official languages of the country. Over three quarters of the people are Christians, mostly Roman Catholics. Some of the people of Burundi are Muslims. The rest of the people practice traditional African religions.

Some children do not receive an education because of a shortage of neighborhood schools or because they are needed at home. Even very young children herd cattle, sheep, and goats in the mountain pastures. But the educational system is expanding. There is a university in Bujumbura, the capital city.

While many of the people wear European-style clothing in Bujumbura, outside the capital traditional dress is more common. Women usually wear long, colorfully patterned garments. Tutsi men traditionally wear full-length white cotton robes. Almost all the people live in rural areas, often in large family groups. Houses have a distinctive beehive shape, with high, pointed thatched roofs. The houses are sometimes grouped to form villages, around which are fields for food crops.

▶ THE ECONOMY

Burundi is a poor country whose economy is based largely on agriculture. Coffee, cotton, and tea are the main commercial crops. Coffee is the leading export. Great numbers of cattle, sheep, and goats also are raised. Cattle are especially valued, not only for their meat, milk, and hides, but as signs of importance and wealth.

FACTS AND FIGURES

REPUBLIC OF BURUNDI is the official name of the country. (It is called République du Burundi in French and Republika yu Burundi in Kirundi.)

THE PEOPLE are known as Burundi.

LOCATION: East Central Africa.

AREA: 10,747 sq mi (27,834 km²).

POPULATION: 5,000,000 (estimate).

CAPITAL AND LARGEST CITY: Bujumbura.

MAJOR LANGUAGES: Kirundi, French (both official).

MAJOR RELIGIONS: Christian, Muslim, traditional African religions.

GOVERNMENT: Republic (under military rule). **Head of state and government**—chairman of the Military Committee for National Salvation.

CHIEF PRODUCTS: Coffee, cotton, tea, sweet potatoes, manioc (cassava), corn, beans, potatoes, sorghum, bananas, livestock, meat, milk, hides.

MONETARY UNIT: Burundi franc (1 franc = 100 centimes).

NATIONAL ANTHEM: *Bwacu Burundi* ("Beloved Burundi").

Burundi produces few minerals. But it is known to have large, untapped deposits of several minerals, especially vanadium and nickel.

▶THE LAND

Burundi lies in the mountains that form one side of the great Rift Valley in the heart of Africa. Lake Tanganyika borders the country on the southwest.

Most of Burundi is between 5,000 and 8,000 feet (1,500 and 2,400 meters) above sea level. Although the country is near the equator, the high elevation makes the climate quite pleasant. Temperatures average 50 to 80°F (10 to 27°C) all year long. Only in the lowlands near Lake Tanganyika is the weather warmer. Rainfall in the mountains averages about 40 to 60 inches (1,000 to 1,500 millimeters) a year. Burundi's rainy season comes between September and May. During the dry season there often is no rain at all.

Bujumbura, the capital, is Burundi's principal city. Located on Lake Tanganyika, it is the country's chief port, linking Burundi by ship with neighboring Zaïre and Tanzania. It has a population of about 200,000. The second largest town, Gitega, is situated in the central part of the country.

▶HISTORY AND GOVERNMENT

Burundi was one of the last African lands to become a European colony. It was annexed at the end of the 19th century by Germany, which made it part of the colony of German East Africa. After Germany's defeat in World War I, the League of Nations placed Burundi and what is now the country of Rwanda under the administration of Belgium. The territory was then known as Ruanda-Urundi. Belgium continued to govern the region, as a trust territory of the United Nations, until 1962, when Ruanda-Urundi became the independent nations of Rwanda and Burundi.

Since Independence. Following independence, Burundi was a constitutional monarchy ruled by a *mwami* (king). In 1966 the *mwami* was deposed by the prime minister, Michel Micombero, who proclaimed Burundi a republic with himself as president. Economic problems and hostilities between the Hutu and Tutsi people threatened the stability of the country. In 1976, Micombero was overthrown in a military coup led by Colonel Jean-Baptiste Bagaza, who became president.

Bagaza served as president until 1987, when his government was overthrown by the military while he was out of the country. His opponents charged Bagaza with violating fundamental human rights, corruption, and an inconsistent economic policy. A constitution that had been adopted in 1981 was suspended, the legislature was dissolved, and the country was placed under the rule of the Military Committee for National Salvation.

ANN E. LARIMORE
Michigan State University

See also RWANDA.

Burundi is a small, densely populated country. To utilize all the available land, farmers often cultivate crops on terraced hillsides (*left*). Burundi women in colorfully patterned traditional garments (*right*) sell food at a local market.

Local bus lines operate in about 1,000 U.S. cities. Schedules and routes are planned for the convenience of short-distance travelers, such as people traveling to and from work.

BUSES AND BUS TRAVEL

Every day, buses carry millions of people to work from their homes in the cities or the suburbs and back again in the evening. Thousands of other passengers take long bus trips for business or pleasure, and millions of children rely on buses to get to school.

Yet the bus is relatively new as a means of travel. Motor buses came into use only when automobile travel began to gain popularity in the early 1900's. But the bus has ancestors much older than the automobile.

▶ EARLY BUSES AND THEIR ANCESTORS

In colonial days, stagecoaches traveled over muddy, rutted roads between Boston, New York, and Philadelphia. Six or eight passengers were crowded inside the coach. Several more sat on top with the driver and the baggage. The trip from Boston to New York took anywhere from two days to a week, depending on the weather and the condition of the roads. The journey from New York City to Philadelphia, less than 100 miles (160 kilometers), took a day and a half.

In the 1820's, twelve-passenger horse-drawn carriages began carrying people along Broadway in New York City. This marked the start of public transportation in the United States. The idea was a huge success. Similar vehicles called omnibuses, began to be used in other cities as well. *Omnibus* is a Latin word meaning "for all," and the omnibus served everyone who had the fare. Eventually, these omnibuses were replaced by the horse-drawn streetcars that ran on rails laid in the street.

In the late 1800's, steam engines and electric motors began to replace horses as the power for vehicles. For long-distance travel, people used steamships and trains instead of coaches. In the cities, some motorized bus lines were operating as early as 1905. But in many cities, horsecars were replaced by trolley cars. These cars were driven by electric power that was supplied by overhead wires. Trolley cars were also used for short trips between cities and towns. By the 1920's, more than 1,000 U.S. cities and towns had trolley systems. But because the cars could go only where there were tracks for them, routes were limited.

With the growing popularity of the automobile, public transportation became less important to city dwellers. The freedom and convenience of movement made possible by the automobile, combined with a large supply of inexpensive fuel, soon made the automobile the favorite type of transportation in the United States.

Some people began to use their automobiles to carry passengers for a fare. They called attention to their services by painting signs saying "5¢" on their cars. These vehicles—forerunners of today's taxis—competed with regular motor-bus lines.

The early buses were built by truck manufacturers. These buses were designed to transport heavy loads rather than to provide for the

Above: In the United States more than 20,000,000 students are transported to and from school by school buses. *Right:* Buses specially equipped with ramps or lifts enable those who are physically disabled to use public transportation.

comfort of passengers. The heavy-duty truck springs gave a bumpy ride. Dust came in through cracks in the floorboards, and there was no heating system to keep passengers warm in winter.

The first buses that were designed specifically for passenger comfort appeared in the early 1920's. Unlike the truck-type buses, they were built close to the ground. This design gave a smoother ride with less swaying and decreased the danger of tipping over. The new buses were also easier for passengers to board.

▶TODAY'S BUSES

During the following years, buses were further improved to make the ride more comfortable. Today there are many kinds of buses, and they are used in many different ways.

School Buses. The school bus has changed the life of schoolchildren. Once there were thousands of small one-room schools with one teacher for all the grades. This was because every child who lived on a farm had to be near enough to a school to walk to it. These one-room schoolhouses have been replaced by large central schools that serve a wide territory. School buses pick up children each day at their homes and take them back when school is over. School buses are usually painted bright yellow or orange so that they can be seen easily. As a further safety measure, most states forbid automobile drivers to pass a school bus that has stopped to pick up children or let them off. In addition, many communities have passed local laws requiring seat belts on school buses because it has been proved that seat belts reduce the risk of injury in traffic accidents.

Public Transit. The bus is an important part of the public transportation systems. In 1985 the total number of trips made by transit buses in the United States came to almost 5,700,000,000. Hundreds of bus routes may crisscross a single city. Special routes may link city hotels with shopping areas, museums, and other points of interest.

Many cities are able to offer bus service within ¼ mile (0.4 kilometer) of nearly all their residents. Today's public-transit buses offer improved comfort and convenience. The newest buses have more comfortable seats, a lower floor for easier boarding, improved safety features such as shock-absorbing bumpers, and other features that make them easier to maintain. On some buses, a ramp or lift makes boarding easier for elderly and disabled persons. In some areas, door-to-door services called "Dial-a-Ride" use small buses or vans to carry older people or others who may have trouble using the regular system.

Vehicles called articulated buses have long been popular in Europe and are now seen in some U.S. cities. These buses are actually two bus units connected by a hinge mechanism that looks somewhat like a giant accordion.

They can carry nearly twice as many riders as standard transit buses. The hinge mechanism makes it easier for the bus to turn corners.

Transit systems have adopted the computer as a tool to improve scheduling, routing, and maintenance. In Japan, passengers waiting at bus stops can look at computerized sensors that display the movement of a bus along its route.

In many areas, public-transit buses are part of special systems that make getting from place to place easier. Express buses for commuters run on special lanes on some major highways so that they can bypass traffic and get into town very quickly. In some downtown areas, automobiles have been banned from certain streets to create transit malls. Buses and pedestrians move freely through these malls.

Long-Distance Travel. The long-distance bus that travels the highways today is designed to be comfortable and convenient. It is heated in winter and air-conditioned in summer. The passengers sit in upholstered chairs that can be tilted back for resting or sleeping. Each seat has its own reading light, so that a passenger can read while the person alongside, who may wish to sleep, is not disturbed. The large windows are tinted to keep out the sun's glare without cutting off the view. Most long-distance buses have washrooms with hot and cold running water. Under the floor is a huge baggage compartment.

Bus companies operate long-distance lines all over the United States and Canada. Their routes extend from coast to coast and from Alaska to Mexico. Some terminals resemble railroad stations, with checkrooms, restaurants, barbershops, and newsstands.

Tour Buses. A popular form of bus travel for vacationers is the chartered tour. All over the world, wherever there are tourists, there are buses that are specially designed for sightseeing. Tourists may take short sight-seeing trips to see local historic landmarks or other places of interest. They may also take long bus tours that can last several weeks and tour one or more countries. On long bus tours, bus companies usually make all the arrangements for the passengers' needs, such as meals and hotel room accommodations.

Modern tour buses are equipped with special sound systems and large tinted windows for easy viewing. A group will be assigned its own driver as well as a tour guide who stands at the front of the bus and speaks to the passengers through a microphone to point out interesting sites along the route and answer questions about the passing scenery and local history. A tour guide is also an important ally for tourists who are unable to communicate in the local language.

GAIL E. WILLIAMS
Public Affairs Specialist
Urban Mass Transportation Administration
U.S. Department of Transportation

Left: The increased passenger capacity of double-decker buses, such as those in London, helps reduce traffic. *Below:* Buses are often chartered by groups of people who wish to travel together, be it on a day's outing or a lengthy tour.

GEORGE BUSH (1924-   )
41st President of the United States

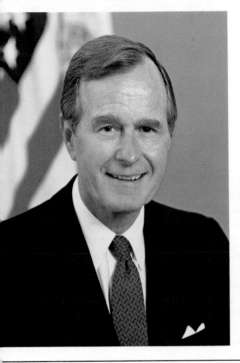

FACTS ABOUT BUSH

Birthplace: Milton, Massachusetts
Religion: Episcopalian
College Attended: Yale University
Occupation: Businessman, public official
Married: Barbara Pierce
Children: George W., John (Jeb), Neil,
   Marvin, Dorothy (Robin, died 1953)
Political Party: Republican
Office Held Before Becoming President:
   Vice President
President Who Preceded Him:
   Ronald W. Reagan

Age on Becoming President: 64
Years in Presidency: 1989–93
Vice President:
   James Danforth (Dan) Quayle
President Who Succeeded Him:
   William Clinton

Bush won the presidential nomination
in 1988 at the Republican convention in
New Orleans, Louisiana. He won renomination in Houston, Texas, in 1992.

BUSH, GEORGE. Few presidents in recent years have entered the White House with as much broad experience in government as George Bush. He served as a member of Congress and as U.S. representative to the United Nations. He was one of the first officials to represent the United States in the People's Republic of China. He is a former director of the Central Intelligence Agency (CIA). And he was vice president under President Ronald Reagan for eight years, before winning the presidency himself in 1988. Bush was the first sitting vice president to be elected president since Martin Van Buren won office in 1836.

▶EARLY YEARS

George Herbert Walker Bush was born in Milton, Massachusetts, on June 12, 1924. His parents were Prescott Sheldon Bush and Dorothy Walker Bush. His father was a Wall Street investment banker and later served as a U.S. senator from Connecticut. Four other children, three sons and a daughter, were born to the Bushes. George was named after his maternal grandfather, George Herbert Walker, who established the Walker Cup trophy for American and British amateur golfers.

When George was still an infant, the Bush family moved to Greenwich, Connecticut. There he was raised amid wealth. Three maids tended to the needs of the family. A chauffeur drove young George to the Greenwich Country Day School. The Bushes spent the summers at their vacation home in Kennebunkport, Maine, where George loved to go boating and fishing for mackerel in the waters of the Atlantic Ocean. Bush still maintains a summer home in Kennebunkport.

Bush attended an exclusive prep school, Phillips Academy, in Andover, Massachusetts. He was captain of the basketball and soccer teams, played on the baseball team, and was elected president of his senior class. During his senior year, on December 7, 1941, the Japanese attacked Pearl Harbor, Hawaii, drawing the United States into World War II. Bush was impatient to graduate in 1942 so that he could volunteer for the Navy air service.

▶WAR SERVICE, MARRIAGE, AND COLLEGE

On his 18th birthday, Bush enlisted in the Navy as a seaman second class. Following flight training, he was commissioned as an ensign in 1943 and became a torpedo bomber pilot. At age 19, he was the youngest pilot then serving in the U.S. Navy. During 1943 and 1944, he took part in 58 combat missions in the Pacific. His worst wartime experience occurred in 1944, when his plane was hit by Japanese anti-aircraft fire over Chichi Jima, one of the Bonin Islands. His two crewmen were killed. Bush parachuted to the water. He lay helpless in a rubber raft until he was rescued by a U.S. submarine.

In 1945, while still in uniform, Bush married Barbara Pierce, the daughter of a magazine publisher. The Bushes had five children who lived to maturity, George W., John (known as Jeb), Neil, Marvin, and Dorothy. Another daughter, Robin, died in 1953.

When the war ended in 1945, Bush was discharged from the Navy with the rank of lieutenant, junior grade. He had won the Distinguished Flying Cross and three Air Medals.

Bush resumed his education at Yale University, where he majored in economics. Still interested in sports, he played first base on the Yale baseball team. In 1948, during the home game against Princeton University, Bush got a chance to meet one of his baseball heroes, Babe Ruth. In one of his last public appearances before his death that year, Babe Ruth presented Bush, then the team captain, with the manuscript of his autobiography, which he was donating to Yale.

▶OIL AND POLITICS IN TEXAS

On his graduation from Yale in 1948, Bush was offered a job in his father's investment banking firm. But Bush preferred to make it on his own. With his wife and young son, he headed for Texas. His first job was painting oil rigs. But soon he was selling oil drilling equipment. In 1950 he and a partner formed a company that bought land in hopes of finding oil or natural gas. Three years later, Bush merged the company with the operations of other oil speculators, founding the Zapata Petroleum Corporation. From 1953 to 1966, Bush was the head of the Zapata Off Shore Company, which was a supplier of the drilling equipment used to explore for oil beneath the ocean floor.

A U.S. Navy pilot during World War II, Bush later graduated from Yale University, where he played on the baseball team.

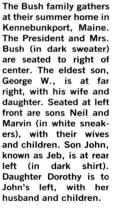

The Bush family gathers at their summer home in Kennebunkport, Maine. The President and Mrs. Bush (in dark sweater) are seated to right of center. The eldest son, George W., is at far right, with his wife and daughter. Seated at left front are sons Neil and Marvin (in white sneakers), with their wives and children. Son John, known as Jeb, is at rear left (in dark shirt). Daughter Dorothy is to John's left, with her husband and children.

Above: Bush served as vice president in Ronald Reagan's administration, from 1981 to 1989. *Right:* President and Mrs. Bush visited U.S. troops in Saudi Arabia on Thanksgiving 1990, two months before the successful allied ground offensive against Iraqi forces in Kuwait.

Meanwhile, Bush had settled his family in Houston, Texas, and had become active in Republican Party politics. In 1964 he ran for the U.S. Senate, but was defeated. Setting his sights a little lower, Bush won election to the U.S. House of Representatives in 1966. He was the first Republican to represent Houston in Congress. He was re-elected in 1968. In 1970, Bush again ran for the Senate and again was defeated.

▶**APPOINTIVE OFFICES**

United Nations Representative. In 1971, President Richard M. Nixon appointed Bush U.S. Permanent Representative to the United Nations. It was a crucial time for the world organization. The United States had agreed to allow the admission of the People's Republic of China to the United Nations for the first time since 1949, when the Communists took over the mainland of China. Bush argued forcefully for a so-called "two-China" policy. Under this compromise, a special seat would have been created for the Republic of China (Taiwan), which had held the China seat since the founding of the United Nations in 1945. But the United Nations rejected the two-China plan and expelled the Taiwan government in favor of the People's Republic.

Party Chairman. In 1973, Bush was named chairman of the Republican National Committee. At this time, President Nixon and the Republican Party were under the cloud of the Watergate scandal. For a long time, Bush defended Nixon, because he believed the president when he said that he had taken no part in attempts to cover up illegal activities by some members of his administration. But when the White House tape recordings were made public and exposed Nixon's involvement, Bush, acting for the Republican Party, asked Nixon to resign. Nixon did so on August 9, 1974.

Envoy to China and CIA Director. The new president, Gerald R. Ford, appointed Bush to what was then the top diplomatic post in the People's Republic of China, chief of the U.S. Liaison Office, in 1974. He remained in China until he was called home at Ford's request to become director of the Central Intelligence Agency (CIA). Bush served in that post from late January 1976 until the beginning of Jimmy Carter's administration in January 1977.

▶**VICE PRESIDENT**

Bush lost the Republican presidential nomination to Ronald Reagan in 1980 but was named as his vice-presidential running mate. The Reagan-Bush ticket won easily in 1980. They were re-elected overwhelmingly in 1984.

Two Presidential Emergencies. On March 30, 1981, President Reagan was shot in an assassination attempt. While Reagan was recovering, Vice President Bush met regularly with the cabinet, White House officials, and congressional leaders. On July 13, 1985, the powers of the presidency were transferred temporarily to Bush while Reagan underwent cancer surgery.

The Iran-Contra Affair. In 1986 it became known that presidential aides had secretly sold arms to Iran in exchange for the release of American hostages in the Middle East. Some of the arms profits were used, illegally, to help contra guerrillas in their war against the government of Nicaragua. Bush's role in the arms sale to Iran is unclear.

The Presidential Campaign. With Reagan forced to retire after two terms, Bush again sought the Republican presidential nomination in 1988. At the Republican convention in New Orleans, Louisiana, he won the nomination without opposition. Bush surprised many people by selecting 41-year-old Senator Dan Quayle of Indiana as his vice-presidential candidate. Bush and Quayle went on to defeat the Democratic candidates for president and vice president, Governor Michael Dukakis of Massachusetts and Senator Lloyd Bentsen, Jr., of Texas. The Bush and Quayle ticket won 54 percent of the popular vote and received 426 electoral votes to 111 for the Democrats.

▶**PRESIDENT**

Domestic Affairs. In February 1989, Bush proposed a major plan to bail out the nation's troubled savings and loan associations. Although Congress passed a $159 billion ten-year plan to rescue the industry, the scope of the problem grew. Also in 1989, Bush signed into law a bill that raised the federal minimum hourly wage to $4.25 in 1991, after first vetoing a higher raise. The large federal budget deficit, inherited from the Reagan administration, was a major concern of Bush's presidency. Like his predecessor, Bush took a strong anti-abortion stance.

Following the resignation of U.S. Supreme Court Justice William J. Brennan in 1990, Bush named Judge David H. Souter of New Hampshire to the post. In 1991 he appointed Clarence Thomas, a 43-year-old black federal judge, to the court to succeed the retiring Thurgood Marshall. Thomas was confirmed after much controversy. Bush agreed to a compromise civil rights bill in 1991, after he had vetoed an earlier measure in 1990.

Two other important domestic issues were a proposed balanced budget amendment to the constitution and a family leave bill.

Foreign Affairs. Bush presided over a period of great political change in many of the world's countries. Between 1989 and 1992, the Communist regimes of Eastern Europe fell and were replaced by representative governments. Germany was reunited as a nation in 1990. The Soviet Union, against which Bush and other U.S. presidents had long contended in the Cold War, broke apart in late 1991.

In late 1989, Bush authorized the use of U.S. troops to oust Panama's dictator, General Manuel Noriega. Taken to the United States in 1990 to face trial on drug trafficking charges, Noriega was found guilty in 1992 and sentenced to a long prison term.

In 1992, Bush, along with the leaders of Canada and Mexico, signed the North American Free Trade Agreement, which would establish the world's largest free trade zone. The treaty must be approved by the Senate.

After Iraq invaded Kuwait in 1990, Bush led an international effort to counter the aggression. An alliance headed by U.S. forces, and approved by the United Nations, forced the Iraqis' swift withdrawal in 1991.

Defeat in 1992. But Bush's successes in foreign affairs were offset by an economic recession at home, which showed no sign of easing as time approached for the 1992 presidential election. Bush easily won renomination. His Democratic opponent was William (Bill) Clinton, the 46-year-old governor of Arkansas. The entry of a strong independent candidate, H. Ross Perot, a Texas businessman, made it a three-way contest.

The campaign revolved around such issues as the faltering economy, family values, and affordable health care. Bush fell behind in the early polls and was never able to gain the lead, although he closed strongly. No candidate received a majority of the popular vote, but Clinton won the election overwhelmingly, with 370 electoral votes to Bush's 168.

WILLIAM A. DE GREGORIO
Author, *The Complete Book of U.S. Presidents*

Updated by JAMES E. CHURCHILL, JR.
Executive Editor, *The Americana Annual*

IMPORTANT DATES IN THE LIFE OF GEORGE BUSH

1924 Born in Milton, Massachusetts, June 12.
1942– Served in the U.S. Navy.
1945
1945 Married Barbara Pierce.
1948 Graduated from Yale University.
1953– Was president and then chairman of the board
1966 of the Zapata Off Shore Company, Texas.
1967– Served in the U.S. Congress.
1971
1971– U.S. Permanent Representative to the United
1972 Nations.
1973– Chairman of the Republican National
1974 Committee.
1974– Chief of the U.S. Liaison Office, China.
1975
1976– Director of the Central Intelligence Agency.
1977
1981– Vice president of the United States.
1989
1989– 41st president of the United States.
1993

The fortunate individual who owns and operates this business is able to work outdoors, surrounded by the beautiful flowers and colorful balloons he sells.

BUSINESS

How do your parents earn their living? How will you earn your living? Chances are that the answers to both questions will involve a business. Most people earn their livelihood either by working for a business owned by someone else, or by operating their own business.

There are many kinds of businesses, from small shops owned and operated by one person to large companies owned by many people and employing thousands of workers. A factory is a business. A store is a business. Other examples include beauty salons, professional sports, and all kinds of entertainment.

A business is any establishment that produces or distributes goods and services. Goods are tangible items like clothing and food. Services are intangible things like entertainment and the services of doctors and lawyers.

▶TYPES OF BUSINESS ORGANIZATION

There are three basic types of business organization: (1) the individual proprietorship; (2) the partnership; and (3) the corporation.

The Individual Proprietorship

An individual proprietorship is a business owned and managed by a single individual. This owner, or **proprietor**, makes all business decisions, receives all profits from the business, and is legally responsible for all of the losses and debts of the business. This legal responsibility for losses and debts, known as **unlimited liability**, is a major disadvantage of an individual proprietorship. It means that if debts cannot be paid, the owner can lose the business and also personal assets such as savings, home, and automobile. While an individual proprietorship can be started rather easily, often with little money, it is usually difficult to raise money for expansion or to improve efficiency. For this reason, it is often difficult for a proprietorship to compete successfully with larger businesses. An individual proprietorship also has a limited life. If the proprietor dies or retires, the business may cease to exist.

The Partnership

A partnership is a business owned by two or more individuals who are called partners. These partners make business decisions together and share all business profits and losses. They also share in unlimited liability for the business. As in a proprietorship, this means that all debts are the responsibility of all of the partners. If debts cannot be paid, they could lose the business as well as their own personal assets.

A partnership is relatively easy and inexpensive to establish. Since more than one person is involved, it is also generally easier to

The partners in an accounting firm meet often to discuss how to attract new clients and make decisions that will affect the firm's profitability.

raise money for expansion or other needs. A partnership also provides an opportunity for specialization, allowing one partner to specialize in production, another in finances, still another in sales, and so on. This usually enables a partnership to handle more work than an individual proprietorship. A partnership also has a limited life. If one partner dies, retires, or resigns, the business may be forced to close unless other partners are willing and able to buy out that partner's share of the business.

The Corporation

A corporation is a business that has the legal status of an individual but is owned collectively by many people. Most large businesses that employ hundreds or thousands of workers are corporations.

To establish a corporation, the potential owners must meet various legal requirements of federal, state, and local governments. One basic requirement is a corporate charter, which is a legal document that gives the corporation the authority to operate in a particular state. The charter establishes the corporation as a legal entity that can enter into contracts and make commitments under its own name. This means that the individual owners of the corporation have only a limited liability. No matter what happens to the corporation, the owners can lose no more than their initial investment, and they cannot be held personally liable for corporate debts or losses. This is one of the major advantages of a corporation.

Another advantage of a corporation is its unlimited life. When owners die or choose to leave the business, the corporation continues to operate unchanged because their shares in the company can be sold to other people. A corporation also has the ability to raise large sums of money through the sale of stocks. One disadvantage of a corporation is that because of its size and complexity decision-making may become slow. Sometimes it may not be able to respond as quickly as it should to changing economic conditions.

How a Corporation Works. A corporate charter authorizes the sale of shares of stock in order to raise money for starting a corporation, for expanding its business, or for other needs. The people who buy these shares of stock are called **stockholders**. In return for their investment, stockholders receive **dividends**, or shares of the corporation's profits.

Boards of directors of large corporations establish and review the basic policies their companies will follow and hire the executive officers who will actually manage their businesses.

The stockholders are the actual owners of a corporation and it is their responsibility to vote on major corporate issues. In most cases, stockholders have one vote for each share of stock owned. Stockholders also elect a board of directors, which is responsible for determining basic corporate policies and for hiring executive officers to carry out the decisions of directors and stockholders. These executive officers are responsible for the day-to-day operations of the corporation. To help them do this, they hire managers for specialized departments within the corporation. The number of managers and departments depends on the size of the corporation and the types of goods or services it provides. Most corporations have at least three specialized departments to provide the services of production, finance, and marketing. Corporations may also have personnel, research, and public relations departments.

WONDER QUESTION

What are gross income and net income?

Gross income is the total amount of money a business earns without considering expenses. Net income, also known as profit, is the total amount of money a business earns after expenses and other operating costs have been subtracted.

HOW TO BE AN ENTREPRENEUR

An **entrepreneur** is a person who sees the need for a particular product or service and then creates a business to supply that product or service. There are many opportunities for young people to become entrepreneurs. In some communities there may be a need for services such as babysitting, taking care of pets, or making deliveries. They might produce and sell goods — for example, growing and selling fresh fruits or vegetables or making and selling lemonade. Or they could become involved in woodworking, knitting, quilting, or pottery, and sell their finished products.

Before starting any business, a smart entrepreneur will find out if there is a need or market for a particular good or service, whether or not anyone is already providing it, and the possible costs of running the business. You will probably want to do some research at your local library. Additional information might be available from your town or city hall, chamber of commerce, church hall, or local newspaper. These might also be good places to **advertise** your product or service after your business has been established. Researching such issues is one of an entrepreneur's most important tasks. Now let us look at an example of how to become an entrepreneur.

Suppose your community has many homes with large lawns. You begin to wonder if some homeowners would pay you to mow their lawns. The potential may exist for a lawn-mowing business. You decide to become an entrepreneur.

You begin by asking neighbors if they would like to have their lawns mowed. You might also advertise by posting announcements on bulletin boards in schools, churches, supermarkets, and community centers. After lining up customers, you buy a lawn mower. The money you spend for it is consid-

ered an **investment** in your business. If the money comes from your savings, it is called **capital**. If it is borrowed, it is called a **capital loan**. Of course, if you borrow money you will have to pay it back, perhaps with **interest** — a fee that a lender charges for loaning money.

The income you receive from your business is called **revenue**. Out of this you must pay for fuel and any other costs, called **operating expenses**. If revenue is greater than expenses, your business has made a **profit**. If expenses are greater than revenue, your business has sustained a **loss**.

As your business grows, you decide to buy another lawn mower and hire a friend to help. Now you have become an **employer**, and your friend is your **employee**. The **wages** you pay your employee are part of your operating expenses.

After a few weeks, someone else starts a lawn-mowing service as **competition** to yours. With competition, the price of your service becomes very important. If one person charges less, or **undersells**, the other, the person charging more may begin to lose customers and eventually may be forced out of business. On the other hand, if one person charges too little, the income may not be enough to cover expenses and that business may go **bankrupt**. However, you and your competitor charge similar prices, and there are plenty of customers for both businesses.

As your business grows, you discover that some customers want the grass clippings removed from their lawns. You purchase grass catchers for your lawn mowers and consider paying someone to haul away the clippings. But then you have an idea — grass clippings make good mulch to place around shrubs, flowers, and vegetables. They could, therefore, be considered a product with a potential market. Soon you have found customers who want to buy mulch — you have created a new business and a new source of revenue.

You are a successful entrepreneur and manager of two businesses! The profit you earn is what motivated you to start your businesses, and it is what keeps them in operation. It is the potential for earning a profit that motivates most entrepreneurs.

▶BUSINESS IN A FREE ENTERPRISE SYSTEM

In a free enterprise system, such as the economies of the United States and Canada, businesses produce the goods and services people need and want. While doing this, they also try to make a profit—to have more income than expenses. Profit is essential for a business to remain in operation, and it is one of the most important principles of a free enterprise system.

One of the key factors affecting profit is competition. If a business has competitors—other companies producing and selling similar goods or services—it cannot charge prices that are much higher than those of its competitors without losing customers. However, it cannot charge prices that would result in less income than expenses without jeopardizing the survival of the business. Competition thus helps regulate profits businesses earn and prices consumers pay for goods and services.

Government Regulation of Businesses

Businesses often adjust their operations and their prices in an attempt to increase profits. But in the United States, Canada, and other countries with free enterprise systems, the government often establishes regulations concerning what a business can and cannot do.

The government often enacts laws to promote safe working conditions and to ensure safe products. For example, there are laws designed to limit the number of hours people can work and to provide certain safety standards in the workplace. Product safety is another concern. For example, if a company develops a new medicine, a government agency requires extensive testing to determine the safety and effectiveness of the medicine before allowing it to be sold to the public.

Government regulates business in other ways as well. Antitrust laws are enacted to help prevent companies from merging, or joining together, in order to control the supply

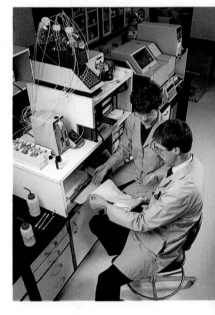

By opening restaurants so close together, these businesses face stiff competition from one another. Each business must offer good food and service at low prices to attract and keep customers. They must also be careful not to let costs exceed earnings or they will lose money and be forced to close.

New drugs and medicines must undergo extensive testing before the federal government allows doctors to prescribe them for their patients.

and price of a product or service. These laws help maintain competition among businesses. In certain industries, such as public utilities that supply gas, electricity, and water, the government often grants one company the exclusive right of operating in a specific market but then establishes regulations to ensure that the quality of its services is adequate and its prices are not too high.

Aside from regulations to ensure safety, to promote competition, and to protect consumers, businesses in a free enterprise system are generally left alone to operate according to the laws of supply and demand.

ALLEN SMITH
Author, *Understanding Economics*

See also BANKS AND BANKING; ECONOMICS; STOCKS AND BONDS.

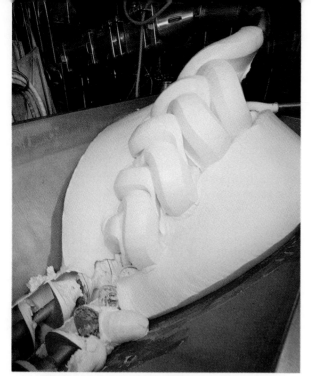

The spiral blades of a continuous churn push braids of freshly kneaded butter into stainless steel tanks. The butter is then pumped to machines for packaging.

BUTTER

Butter is a dairy product made from butterfat, a fat found in milk. It is used chiefly in cooking and baking and as a spread for bread. All of the butter produced in the United States is made from cow's milk, although in many other countries butter is made from the milk of reindeer, sheep, goats, water buffalo, or even horses. About 10 quarts (9.5 liters) of milk are needed to make 1 pound (0.45 kilograms) of butter.

Years ago buttermaking was a long and tiring job. After a batch of cream had been skimmed from milk, it would be left to cool and ripen in an earthernware crock. After several days, the slightly sour, or ripe, cream would be poured into a bell-shaped wooden churn. It would then be beaten with a long plunger until the butterfat separated from the rest of the cream into lumps about the size of peas. After draining off the leftover liquid, or buttermilk, the butter would be washed and kneaded until it was smooth.

In the 1930's automated churns were developed to make the production of butter more efficient, economical, and consistent. Today continuous churns can produce up to 15,000 pounds (6,800 kilograms) of butter an hour.

Most of the butter sold today is made by large creameries that buy milk from many different farmers. The manufacturing process begins by mechanically separating the cream (containing 35 to 40 percent butterfat) from the milk. The cream is then pasteurized (heated to destroy bacteria). Then the pasteurized cream moves into huge rotating cylinders, called churns, where it is beaten until the butterfat separates from the buttermilk. The buttermilk is drained off and dried into a powder to be used in foods, such as baked goods, ice cream, and pancake mixes. The remaining butterfat is washed and kneaded until it has a smooth, firm texture. Salt is usually added to improve the flavor and stop the growth of bacteria. Vegetable coloring, such as annatto, may be added to produce a desirable color.

In 1923 Congress delcared that butter could be made only from milk or cream and that the resulting product must consist of at least 80 percent fat. Today, butter is tested, evaluated, and graded by the U.S. Department of Agriculture according to its flavor, texture, and aroma. Grade AA is the best quality followed by Grades A, B, and C. Inferior butter, graded UG for undergrade, is usually reprocessed for industrial uses.

As a food, butter is a rich source of Vitamin A. It also contains limited amounts of vitamins D and E, calcium, phosphorus, sodium, and potassium. One tablespoon of butter contains approximately 100 calories.

Because butter is relatively high in cholesterol (a natural element found in all animal fats that has been linked to heart disease and hardening of the arteries), consumers who are health conscious have been using less and less butter each year. In the past 20 years, average yearly consumption of butter in the United States has fallen from nearly 8 pounds (3 kilograms) to just under 4 pounds (2 kilograms) per person. Margarine and other spreads made from vegetable oils that have little or no cholesterol in them have risen in popularity as butter substitutes.

The world's leading butter-consuming nations, per capita, are Germany, followed by New Zealand, Ireland, Denmark, and Finland. In the United States, the leading butter-producing states are Wisconsin, California, and Minnesota.

ROBERT L. BRADLEY, JR.
University of Wisconsin

BUTTERFLIES AND MOTHS

Anyone who touches the wings of a butterfly or a moth finds that something like dust comes off on the fingers. The dust is actually made up of tiny scales. The scales grow in rows and give the wings their patterns of colors. The scales also account for the scientific name for butterflies and moths. Together they are called Lepidoptera, which means "scaly winged."

There are about 112,000 different kinds of moths and butterflies in the world, and they live in almost every kind of environment. In the United States and Canada there are probably about 11,000 species, or kinds, of butterflies and moths.

As microscope shows, a butterfly's wing has rows of scales that give it color and pattern.

How Can You Tell a Butterfly from a Moth?

Many butterflies and moths look very much alike. Yet it is possible to tell them apart. In general, butterflies are brighter in color than moths. This is not always true—a few moths are as bright and beautiful as any butterfly. Butterflies are active during the day. Most moths are active only at night and are attracted by lights.

Butterflies and moths differ in other ways, too. Moths have thicker, more hairy bodies. Both have two pairs of wings. But a resting moth usually folds its front wings back upon its hind ones. A butterfly at rest leaves its wings full and erect.

A butterfly, like a moth, has two antennae (feelers) on its head. A butterfly's antennae have slightly enlarged tips, while a moth's antennae do not. In some moth species the antennae have featherlike plumes but the tips are never enlarged.

▶LIFE CYCLE

Butterflies and moths are among the insects that pass through four stages of development in their life cycles.

The first stage is the egg. Adult females lay eggs on the kind of plant their young will later need as food.

The eggs hatch into wormlike creatures known as **larvae**. The common name for the larvae of butterflies and moths is caterpillar. Caterpillars are busy and hungry. They may

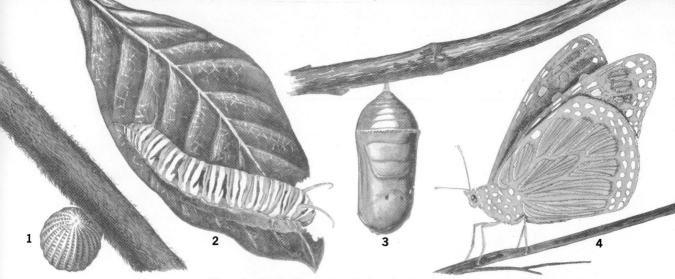

Life cycle of butterflies and moths includes four stages (not shown in scale here). First comes the egg (1), which hatches into a larva (2), familiar as a caterpillar. Larva then becomes pupa (3), a resting stage that lasts until body develops and adult emerges (4). Butterfly shown is a monarch. Third pair of legs is too small to show on thorax.

eat once or twice their own weight in leaves each day. After several days of such constant feeding, caterpillars outgrow their own skins. When this happens they molt, splitting the skin and crawling out of it. Caterpillars may shed their skins four or five times in this second stage of the life cycle.

In the third stage the caterpillar goes into a resting state and is called a **pupa**. Different caterpillars pupate in different ways. For example, many moth caterpillars burrow into the ground; others hide behind loose bark or in hollow logs. Some caterpillars rest in silken cocoons, which they make by spinning thread from their mouths. (Silk cloth is made from the threads in the cocoon of the silkworm moth.) The pupa does nothing except rest. This stage may last two weeks; it may last a whole winter. During this period the caterpillar changes into a full-grown butterfly or moth.

In its new and adult form, the butterfly or moth emerges wet and shaky from the cocoon. As blood flows into the veins of the wings the adult flutters and dries them. In a few hours, when the wings are strong and dry, the butterfly or moth flies off to live out its fourth, or adult, stage.

▶WHERE THE COLORS COME FROM

The colors that mark an adult may be of several types. Some scales hold pigment, or colored matter; it accounts for the blacks, browns, reds, oranges, yellows, and whites. Other scales catch the sunlight and separate it into different colors. This second effect may

be caused by a thin, oily film on the scales or by a scale's fine lines or ridges. (The green of many caterpillars is caused by their diet of plants.)

▶THE SENSES

Both moths and butterflies have keen senses of sight, smell, and taste. A few moths are able to hear, too. The organs of taste in most butterflies and moths are in the mouth. Most organs of smell are on the antennae. However, the mourning cloak, the red admiral, and some other butterflies smell things through "noses" on their feet.

Sight

The eyes of butterflies are very sensitive to colors. Butterflies are especially attracted to red flowers. Moths, most active at night, are attracted to light-colored flowers. Most night-blooming flowers are white.

Scents and Smell

Many butterflies and moths have odors, or scents, which they use for two purposes. One kind of scent is used to attract the opposite sex. The other kind of scent is used to drive away enemies.

The scents of male butterflies come from scales in pockets on their hind wings. During courtship a male monarch butterfly may scatter these scent scales over the female. The scents of many kinds of male butterflies resemble those of flowers or spices and are often pleasing to humans.

Female butterflies produce their scents in

Adult life of butterfly begins when it emerges from pupal case, as shown in these photos of monarch butterfly. Legs break out, grab case, and pull rest of body free.

Within about 2 minutes, butterfly is free and hangs on empty pupal case. Newly emerged butterfly, still crumpled and wet, has small, fleshy wings and a flat abdomen.

As butterfly hangs there, its abdomen pulsates vigorously. This causes body fluids to circulate. After 10 or 20 minutes, wings will have expanded to full size.

Even after wings are fully expanded, adult butterfly remains clinging to pupal case for several hours, depending on weather, before it tries its first flight.

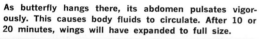

Monarch butterflies gather in dense, hanging clusters on the branches of trees and bushes.

Mexico and other southern areas. In spring the young female lays her eggs on the milkweed plants that have begun to grow. The caterpillars that hatch from the eggs feed on the milkweed leaves. When the adult butterflies develop, they fly some distance north. There they mate and lay eggs on the milkweed that has just begun to grow with the advance of spring. Thus, within a few months' time, several generations of monarch butterflies travel farther and farther north in search of milkweed. By late summer, descendants of the original monarchs reach Canada.

With the cooler weather of autumn, surviving monarchs fly back south in great swarms. There are reports of monarchs spread out in a swarm more than 20 miles (30 kilometers) wide. Year after year such masses of butterflies follow the same routes. Every night they settle on trees and bushes, which are often called butterfly trees.

special glands in their bodies. Most of these female odors are disagreeable to the human nose.

Taste

The taste organs of a butterfly are far more sensitive to sweet things than our tongues are. Their chief food, flower nectar, is a sugar solution, and they are easily able to find it. When a butterfly finds nectar in a flower, it uncoils its proboscis, a long, hollow tongue-like structure, and sucks in the liquid.

Not all butterflies live on nectar. Some are attracted to rotting fruits. A few prefer the flesh of dead animals.

▶MIGRATING BUTTERFLIES AND MOTHS

People have known for hundreds of years that birds travel over special routes during certain seasons. Such travel is called migration. Recently it has been learned that many butterflies, and some moths, also migrate. For example, the painted-lady butterfly travels from Mexico to California each spring. The same kind of butterfly flies across the Mediterranean Sea in spring, from North Africa to Europe. In butterfly migration thousands, even millions, of insects travel together.

The Monarch Butterfly

The best known of the migrating butterflies is the monarch that winters along the Gulf of

▶ENEMIES AND DEFENSES

Butterflies and moths have many enemies. There are tiny wasps that lay their eggs inside the eggs of the butterfly. The wasp larvae then feed on the butterfly eggs. Caterpillars also have enemies. Birds and bats eat them. Tiny flies and wasps invade caterpillars and live inside them. Farmers and gardeners also kill the ever-hungry caterpillars in order to protect their plants.

From all the eggs that hatch, only two caterpillars out of every hundred live to become butterflies. If this were not so, caterpillars would be much more serious pests than they are. Caterpillars eat the leaves and fruit of plants and bore into the trunks and roots. The larvae of the clothes moth chew holes in wool and silk and also eat fur.

A few kinds of butterflies and moths have developed defenses against their natural enemies. Some are nearly invisible because they look like twigs or dead leaves. Some caterpillars have stinging hairs or poison spines that drive off enemies. Others release bad odors. The monarch butterfly seems to taste bad to birds, and birds leave the handsome orange and black creature alone.

More kinds of butterflies and moths are shown in the pictures on pages 480–483.

ROSS E. HUTCHINS
Author, *Insects*

See also INSECTS; METAMORPHOSIS.

The kallima butterfly of southern Asia and the Pacific islands, the hawkmoth, and the geometrid moth and its caterpillar (also called looper, measuring worm, or inchworm) are nearly invisible to their enemies. They have a protective coloring or shape that camouflages them and makes them look like plant life. Can you find the butterfly, the moths, and the caterpillar in the pictures on this page?

Kallima butterfly or leaf?

Hawkmoth or tree bark?

Geometrid caterpillar or twig?

Geometrid moth or leaf?

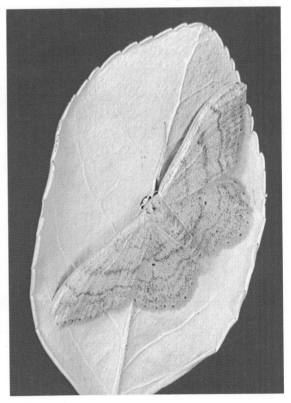

BUTTERFLIES OF THE WORLD

AGRIAS
SARDANAPALUS

EUROPEAN
SWALLOWTAIL
(PAPILIO
MACHAON)

BLUE MOUNTAIN
BUTTERFLY
(PAPILIO ULYSSES)

CHRISTMAS
BUTTERFLY
(PAPILIO
DEMODOCUS)

ORCHARD
SWALLOWTAIL
(PAPILIO AEGEUS)

SILVERSTRIPE
(PANDORIANA
PANDORA)

ANCYLURIS
FORMOSISSIMA

PEACOCK
(NYMPHALIS IO)

PAPILIO
SEMPERI

APOLLO
(PARNASSIUS
APOLLO)

MESENE
PHARAEUS

480

MORPHO
CYPRIS

BRIMSTONE
(GONEPTERYX
RHAMNI)

TAILED
BIRDWING
(PAPILIO
PARADISEA)

BUTTERFLIES OF THE UNITED STATES

QUESTION MARK
ANGLEWING
(POLYGONIA
INTERROGATIONIS)

MORNING CLOAK
(NYMPHALIS
ANTIOPA)

WOOD NYMPH
(MINOIS ALOPE)

PAINTED LADY
(VANESSA CARDUI)

MONARCH
(DANAUS
PLEXIPPUS)

DOG FACE
(COLIAS
CESONIA)

GREAT PURPLE
HAIRSTREAK
(ALTIDES HALESUS)

GIANT SWALLOWTAIL
(PAPILIO CRESPHONTES)

LEONARDUS SKIPPER
(HESPERIA LEONARDUS)

VARIEGATED FRITILLARY
(EUPTOIETA CLAUDIA)

WHITE ADMIRAL
(LIMENITIS
ARTHEMIS)

BLACK SWALLOWTAIL
(PAPILIO POLYXENES
ASTERIUS)

CABBAGE

CABBAGE LARVA
(PIERIS RAPAE)

ZEBRA SWALLOWTAIL
(PAPILIO MARCELLUS)

481

MOTHS OF THE WORLD

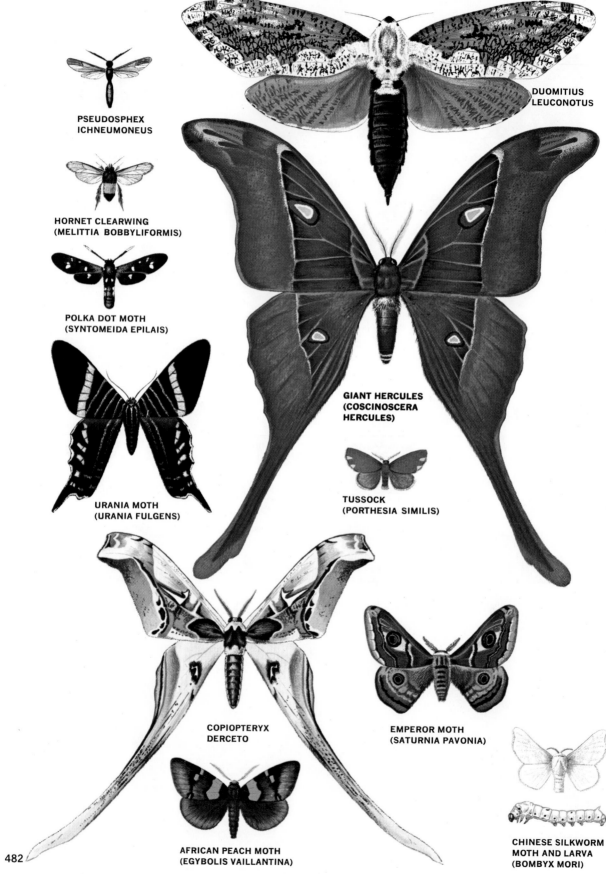

PSEUDOSPHEX
ICHNEUMONEUS

HORNET CLEARWING
(MELITTIA BOBBYLIFORMIS)

POLKA DOT MOTH
(SYNTOMEIDA EPILAIS)

URANIA MOTH
(URANIA FULGENS)

DUOMITIUS
LEUCONOTUS

GIANT HERCULES
(COSCINOSCERA
HERCULES)

TUSSOCK
(PORTHESIA SIMILIS)

COPIOPTERYX
DERCETO

AFRICAN PEACH MOTH
(EGYBOLIS VAILLANTINA)

EMPEROR MOTH
(SATURNIA PAVONIA)

CHINESE SILKWORM
MOTH AND LARVA
(BOMBYX MORI)

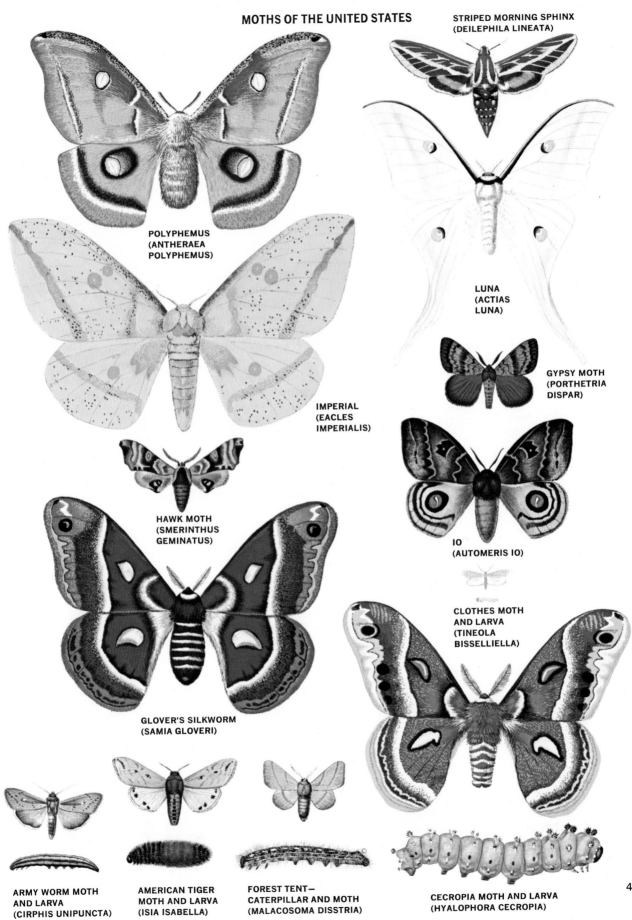

MOTHS OF THE UNITED STATES

STRIPED MORNING SPHINX
(DEILEPHILA LINEATA)

POLYPHEMUS
(ANTHERAEA
POLYPHEMUS)

LUNA
(ACTIAS
LUNA)

IMPERIAL
(EACLES
IMPERIALIS)

GYPSY MOTH
(PORTHETRIA
DISPAR)

HAWK MOTH
(SMERINTHUS
GEMINATUS)

IO
(AUTOMERIS IO)

CLOTHES MOTH
AND LARVA
(TINEOLA
BISSELLIELLA)

GLOVER'S SILKWORM
(SAMIA GLOVERI)

ARMY WORM MOTH
AND LARVA
(CIRPHIS UNIPUNCTA)

AMERICAN TIGER
MOTH AND LARVA
(ISIA ISABELLA)

FOREST TENT—
CATERPILLAR AND MOTH
(MALACOSOMA DISSTRIA)

CECROPIA MOTH AND LARVA
(HYALOPHORA CECROPIA)

483

A glass button (*left*) shows the English countryside, 1770–85. Above is a 19th-century French button of painted enamel.

BUTTONS

Buttons were probably first used to hold clothes together in the 13th century. At that time most people still fastened their clothes with clasps, but the nobility used beautiful buttons of silver and gold, hammered out by craftsmen.

In the next few centuries an almost endless variety of materials and designs were used by button makers. A popular button covering in the 1700's was made of metal threads wound into an intricate pattern. The button maker needed all his skill and patience to weave the threads of different colors into tiny stars or triangles. Miniature scenes were painted on buttons of ivory or glass. Some buttons were covered with beads and pearls. Button makers also cut designs in hard button bases and filled the cuts with silver.

The buttons that took almost the longest time and most painstaking care to make were surprisingly enough made of paper. The pieces of paper were cut with fine paring tools into shapes of tiny houses, people, or various other forms. These were made into scenes and fastened onto strong button bases.

Buttons were made by hand in these elaborate styles until the 19th century. Manufacturers then began to use powered machines to turn out large quantities of buttons cheaply. Brass buttons became very popular because designs could be stamped on them quickly. Many of the brass buttons were made for work clothes and had railroad signs or colorful slogans on them. Children's buttons were often stamped with a tiny Jack Horner or some other nursery hero.

New materials changed button manufacturing, too. Hard-rubber buttons were tried in the 1840's, but they did not wear well. Celluloid, a synthetic compound that looks like ivory, was developed toward the end of the 19th century. Delicate buttons that seemed to be hand painted could be mass-produced in the new material.

Buttons today are made of plastics or natural materials such as wood, leather, metal, pearl, and shell. Shanks, which are the fastening loops on the backs of buttons, can be put on in minutes by machines. Other buttons have holes punched out so that they can be sewn on clothes. Automatic machines cut and shape most buttons, but some buttons are still finished by hand. There are as many different ways of making buttons as there are kinds of buttons. Button making still demands the imagination and skill of the craftsman.

Collecting Buttons

Collecting pretty and unusual buttons is a popular hobby and an easy one to start. To have an interesting collection and not just a lot of buttons rattling around in an old shoe box, it is best to work according to some plan.

You may want to collect buttons made of certain materials such as pewter, brass, enamel, bone, glass, wood, porcelain, silver, or gold. Or you may prefer to collect according to subjects, choosing perhaps fairy tales, animals, flags, ships, or your favorite sport. Perhaps covered buttons will interest you most, or you might want variety.

Whatever you decide on, you will certainly want to display your collection. Buttons should be mounted if they are to be seen to the best advantage. A good way to mount them is on cards. Posterboard is a good weight. Plain cardboard that is faced with colored paper is often used.

The National Button Society has a junior division for boys and girls ages 8 to 18. It publishes the *News-Sheet* and provides adult leadership. For information write to NBS, 2733 Juno Place, Akron, Ohio 44313.

Reviewed by THEODORE ABRAMS
Associated Button Company, Inc.

From left are a shiny glass button with enamel from the late 1800's, a hand-painted Japanese button from about 1900, and a French button showing a hare and a hunting horn, 1850–75.

BYRD, RICHARD EVELYN (1888–1957)

Rear Admiral Richard E. Byrd was a daring aviator and America's greatest Antarctic explorer. He was the first man to fly over both the North and South Poles. His five expeditions to Antarctica helped to unlock the mysteries of that vast, frozen continent.

Byrd was born on October 25, 1888, in Winchester, Virginia. In 1912 he graduated from the United States Naval Academy. A leg injury forced him to retire from active sea duty in 1916, but he was soon back in the Navy as an aviator.

On May 9, 1926, Byrd and his copilot, Floyd Bennett, took off from Spitzbergen in the Arctic Ocean. They circled the North Pole and returned almost 16 hours later. For their achievement Byrd and Bennett each won the Congressional Medal of Honor. The following year, with a crew of three men, Byrd attempted a nonstop flight from New York to Paris, carrying the first transatlantic airmail. But bad weather forced him to crash land on the coast of France.

In 1928 Byrd led his first expedition to Antarctica. He established his base, Little America, on the Ross Ice Shelf near the Bay of Whales. The camp of more than a dozen huts was equipped with electricity and telephones. Airplanes were used to explore large areas of the continent. On November 28 and 29, 1929, Byrd and three crewmen, including his pilot Bernt Balchen, made the first flight over the South Pole.

During Byrd's second expedition, from 1933 to 1935, great emphasis was placed on scientific research. But research nearly cost Byrd his life. To gather weather information, he lived alone at a weather station for five months. His tiny cabin was built under the snow, 198 kilometers (123 miles) from Little America. Fumes from a leaky stove almost poisoned him before he was rescued. He wrote about this experience in his book *Alone*.

Byrd headed a third expedition, which began in 1939. In 1946–47 he was officer-in-charge of the largest Antarctic expedition in history—a project of the U.S. Navy called Operation High Jump. More than 4,000 persons and many ships and planes took part. The purpose was to continue the work of exploring and mapping the South Polar region.

On his last journey, in 1955–56, Byrd helped supervise another project, Operation Deep Freeze, in preparation for the International Geophysical Year, 1957–58. He died in Boston on March 11, 1957.

Reviewed by D. M. COONEY
Rear Admiral, U.S. Navy

See also ANTARCTICA; ARCTIC; EXPLORATION AND DISCOVERY.

BYRON, GEORGE GORDON, LORD (1788–1824)

George Gordon Byron, English poet, was born in London on January 22, 1788. His mother was Scottish. His father, an aristocrat and a gambler, died in 1791. Byron became the sixth Baron Byron in 1798, when his great-uncle died. He was born with a lame foot, and he tried all his life to disguise it by acts of physical daring.

Byron attended Harrow, a famous boys' school, and in 1805 he entered Trinity College, Cambridge. He had a volume of his poems printed privately in 1806. A year later, his first published work, *Hours of Idleness,* appeared. When it was harshly criticized in the *Edinburgh Review,* he wrote a satire, *English Bards and Scotch Reviewers* (1809), in reply.

In the summer of 1809, Byron and a Cambridge friend, John Cam Hobhouse, began two years of travel in Europe and the Middle East. The first two cantos of *Childe Harold's Pilgrimage* record some of his first year's experiences. The poem, published in 1812, made Byron famous, and he was sought after by London society. But scandalous love affairs damaged his reputation. He married Anne Isabella Milbanke in 1815. She left him a year later, shortly after the birth of a daughter. Byron was cast out by society, and in April, 1816, he left England forever.

In Geneva, Switzerland, he joined the poet Percy Bysshe Shelley. Byron finished the third canto of *Childe Harold,* wrote *The Prisoner of Chillon,* and began the poetic drama *Manfred.* In October, 1816, he and Hobhouse moved to Venice, Italy. The fourth canto of *Childe Harold* concerns a visit to Rome in the spring of 1817. *Beppo,* published anonymously in February, 1818, satirizes life in Venice. Byron's greatest work, *Don Juan,* was begun in September, 1818. It continues the satiric style of *Beppo.*

In 1819 he met Countess Teresa Guiccioli, whose love gave him a new steadiness. In their years together he completed *Don Juan* and wrote the satire *The Vision of Judgement,* seven poetic dramas, and many shorter poems.

In 1823 he was elected to a committee helping Greece gain freedom from Turkey. He went to Greece and was warmly welcomed by the Greek leaders. He was eager to lead an attack. But he died, instead, of a fever in the city of Missolonghi on April 19, 1824.

GEORGIA DUNBAR
Hofstra University

CHILDE HAROLD'S PILGRIMAGE
(excerpt from Canto III, describing the eve of the Battle of Waterloo)

There was a sound of revelry by night,
And Belgium's capital had gathered then
Her Beauty and her Chivalry, and bright
The lamps shone o'er fair women and brave men;
A thousand hearts beat happily; and when
Music arose with its voluptuous swell,
Soft eyes looked love to eyes which spake again,
And all went merry as a marriage bell;
But hush! hark! a deep sound strikes like a rising knell!

Did ye not hear it?—No; 'twas but the wind,
Or the car rattling o'er the stony street;
On with the dance! let joy be unconfined;
No sleep till morn, when Youth and Pleasure meet
To chase the glowing Hours with flying feet—

But hark!—that heavy sound breaks in once more,
As if the clouds its echo would repeat;
And nearer, clearer, deadlier than before!
Arm! Arm! it is—it is—the cannon's opening roar!

Within a windowed niche of that high hall
Sat Brunswick's fated chieftain; he did hear
That sound the first amidst the festival,
And caught its tone with Death's prophetic ear;
And when they smiled because he deemed it near,
His heart more truly knew that peal too well
Which stretched his father on a bloody bier,
And roused the vengeance blood alone could quell;
He rushed into the field, and, foremost fighting, fell.

THE PRISONER OF CHILLON
(excerpt; the story of a man imprisoned for trying to free Geneva from a tyrant)

There are seven pillars of Gothic mold,
In Chillon's dungeons deep and old,
There are seven columns, massy and gray,
Dim with a dull imprisoned ray,
A sunbeam which hath lost its way,
And through the crevice and the cleft
Of the thick wall is fallen and left;
Creeping o'er the floor so damp,
Like a marsh's meteor lamp:
And in each pillar there is a ring,
And in each ring there is a chain;
That iron is a cankering thing,
For in these limbs its teeth remain,
With marks that will not wear away,
Till I have done with this new day,
Which now is painful to these eyes,
Which have not seen the sun so rise
For years—I cannot count them o'er,
I lost their long and heavy score,
When my last brother drooped and died,
And I lay living by his side.

They chained us each to a column stone,
And we were three—yet, each alone;
We could not move a single pace,
We could not see each other's face,
But with that pale and livid light
That made us strangers in our sight:
And thus together—yet apart,
Fettered in hand, but joined in heart,
'Twas still some solace, in the dearth
Of the pure elements of earth,
To hearken to each other's speech,
And each turn comforter to each
With some new hope, or legend old,
Or song heroically bold;
But even these at length grew cold.
Our voices took a dreary tone,
An echo of the dungeon stone,
  A grating sound, not full and free,
  As they of yore were wont to be:
  It might be fancy, but to me
They never sounded like our own.

BYZANTINE ART AND ARCHITECTURE

Byzantine art is the art of the Eastern Roman Empire. Constantine, the first Christian emperor of the Roman Empire, moved his capital from Rome to the old Greek city of Byzantium. He renamed the city Constantinople after himself. But the art of the Eastern Roman Empire that he founded is known as Byzantine.

Byzantine art extends from the founding of Constantinople in A.D. 330 until the Turks captured the city in 1453. However, long after the fall of Constantinople, artists in the Greek islands, in the Balkans, and in Russia continued to create works in the Byzantine style.

In the days of its glory, Constantinople was the most magnificent city in the world. Above the gates and towers of the city walls rose the golden domes of the churches and the tall, shining columns set up by the emperors. Some of the most famous statues of ancient Greece had been brought to the city. The huge palace of the emperor blazed with gold and silver, marble and mosaics. There the emperor, covered with jewels, was surrounded by priests in shining robes and by men-at-arms of every barbarian race.

The Byzantine Empire was a religious state. The emperor was not only the ruler of his people but God's representative on earth. The ceremonies of the church and of the court were meant to show the emperor's sacred character. His magnificent jewels, robes, and crown were intended to give him a majestic and saintly appearance.

The purpose of Byzantine art was to glorify the Christian religion and to express its mystery. All of Byzantine art is filled with a kind of spiritual symbolism—things on earth are meant to stand for the order of heaven. Another characteristic of the art of this rich empire is a love of splendor.

Byzantine art is a combination of Eastern and classical Western art. The Byzantine Empire inherited the ideas and forms of art of the classical world of Greece and Rome. However, part of the empire was in Asia and Africa. The shores of Asia could be seen from Constantinople. It was natural that the art of this empire should be greatly influenced by the art of the Near East.

The art of Greece and Rome was naturalistic—artists wanted to show the world about them as it actually looked. Their greatest interest was in the human body. To create an ideal beauty, they showed the body as it would look if it were perfect.

The art of the ancient Near East was more an art of decoration. Artists filled large, flat areas with patterns that were repeated again and again. Instead of copying nature, they made natural forms into flat patterns. They did not have the great interest in the human body that classical artists had, and they did not hesitate to change the shape of the body to fit into their designs. Another characteristic of Eastern art was a use of glowing color.

▶ THE LATE ANTIQUE PERIOD: THE BEGINNING OF THE BYZANTINE STYLE (330–527)

For the first 200 years of the Byzantine Empire, artists worked in the same style as the artists of ancient Greece and Rome. Because the art was still based on that of the old classical world, these years are called the Late Antique period. During these years the new Byzantine style gradually grew out of the decaying art of the classical world.

In this period the Roman Empire lost its lands to the barbarian invaders from the north. Much of the art of this time of violence and disorder shows a loss of skill and craftsmanship. Artists were no longer able to make the human body look like that of a living person. They could no longer achieve the realism or ideal beauty that Greek and Roman artists had. Instead, for representing heads and bodies, they used certain rules that made human figures look unreal—stiff and wooden. This unreality was made-to-order for expressing the spiritual ideals of Christianity.

▶ THE FIRST GOLDEN AGE (527–726)

The earliest true Byzantine style appeared in the First Golden Age. By the 6th century Byzantine artists had broken away from the classical styles. They had created a new style to show the supernatural nature of Christ and the sacredness and grandeur of the emperor.

Justinian

The most important ruler of the First Golden Age was the Emperor Justinian. He is remembered for his code of laws and his

Above: *Theodora and her Court*, a 6th-century mosaic in the church of San Vitale, Ravenna. Below: A mosaic of the Emperor Justinian in the same church.

great building projects in Constantinople and Italy. After recapturing much of Italy from the Goths, Justinian chose the city of Ravenna as the center of Byzantine rule in Italy.

There is a famous mosaic picture of the great emperor in the church of San Vitale at Ravenna. He is shown surrounded by his attendants. His stiff pose and rich robes make him a symbol of majesty. On the opposite wall is a picture of his wife, the Empress Theodora, with her ladies-in-waiting. At the end of the church, in the half dome behind the altar, Christ is shown among the angels. Christ, the All-Ruler, is surrounded by the members of his court in heaven just as Justinian and Theodora are surrounded by a court on earth.

These pictures are done in mosaic. A mosaic picture or design is made of thousands of small glass or marble cubes, called **tesserae**, set in cement. The walls and domes of the great churches of Ravenna and Constantinople were decorated with glass tesserae, brilliantly colored or covered with gold.

A picture made out of many pieces of glass cannot be as freely done or copy nature as exactly as a painting. In the pictures of Justinian and Theodora in San Vitale, the figures are stiff. The bodies are flat, and the magnificent robes do not seem to cover any solid shapes. The feet point downward on the flat ground, giving the illusion that the bodies are floating in air. However, the stiff poses of the rulers, and their long, flat shapes, are not simply the result of the use of mosaic. These are characteristics of the new Byzantine style. The heads of the figures show us that the artist was capable of a much more realistic portrayal. The faces are almost like portraits in the old Roman tradition. However, Byzantine artists were not interested in realism, in showing solid forms in real space. Instead, they developed a formal style, a style in which the body is just another part of a flat design.

Hagia Sophia, the Church of Holy Wisdom

The greatest building of the whole Byzantine world is the church of Hagia Sophia, in Constantinople. Hagia Sophia, known as the Church of Holy Wisdom, was built on the site of an ancient temple to Pallas Athene, the Greek goddess of wisdom. It was dedicated to the Virgin Mary.

The church was designed by the architects Anthemius of Tralles and Isidorus of Miletus. Construction was begun in A.D. 532, and it is believed that the Emperor Justinian himself personally supervised the work. A legend tells that he followed the orders of an angel.

Hagia Sophia is so large that the human eye cannot take in the whole huge shape of the interior. If you stand inside the great church, you must look at it one part at a time. Your eyes are led from the pillars to the vaults, then to the smaller domes, finally to the central dome 180 feet (55 meters) high. This may be what the architects wanted. The eyes of the worshiper finally come to rest on the great mosaic figure of Christ in the dome, looking down as though from heaven itself. The feeling of endless space in Hagia Sophia makes it one of the most impressive buildings in the world. The many marble columns are enormous, but in the huge interior they seem small. At the same time the mounting of domes of increasing sizes up to the great central dome gives a feeling of order.

The splendor of Hagia Sophia also comes from color. The columns, brought from every corner of the empire, are of stone and marble of many different colors—blue, green, and blood-red. Even more brilliant in color is the mosaic decoration. The floor is covered with marble mosaic and the walls glitter with glass mosaics. The mosaics have designs of vines and pomegranates—the fruit of the pomegran-

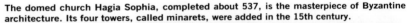

The domed church Hagia Sophia, completed about 537, is the masterpiece of Byzantine architecture. Its four towers, called minarets, were added in the 15th century.

ate was a symbol of life after death—and imaginary beasts. Below the central dome are mosaic pictures of star-eyed angels. On the golden background of the vast, topmost dome is the figure of Christ as judge and ruler of all.

The Dome on Pendentives

Byzantine architects did not invent the plans or building methods that they used; they adapted them from the architecture of the Near East and Rome. However, the architects of Hagia Sophia did solve the problem of placing a round dome on the square plan of the walls that support it. They did this by building up masonry from the corners of the walls in the shape of a triangle. This contruction is called a pendentive. Pendentives not only support the dome but join the dome to the walls in one continuous sweep.

The pendentives of Hagia Sophia rest on four massive piers. The stone blocks of these piers are set in lead rather than in mortar. The dome is also made stronger by half domes that carry its outward-pushing weight to huge buttresses, or supports, on the outside. To make it lighter the dome was built out of a special kind of light brick.

Some scholars believe that Byzantine architects learned how to build domes from earlier Roman buildings. Others think that they learned from Near Eastern architecture. However, the meaning of the dome in religious architecture came from Persia. In the ancient Near East, people thought that heaven was like a cup placed upside down over the earth. In Persia from the 3rd to 7th century A.D., architects used the shape of the dome to suggest the architecture of heaven. Since Byzantine architects also used this idea, it seems likely that both the knowledge of how to build a dome and the meaning of this shape came to Byzantium from her eastern neighbors.

Ivory Carving: A Bishop's Throne

The Byzantine Church did not approve of sculpture in the round—sculpture that can be seen from all sides. The Church feared that it would recall the idols of the Greek and Roman religions. However, small carvings in relief (raised from a flat surface), especially in ivory, were allowed as church decoration. One of the most beautiful examples of ivory carving of the First Golden Age is the throne of the Bishop Maximian at Ravenna. He is the priest to the right of Justinian in the mosaic at San Vitale.

The wooden chair is covered with many ivory panels of different sizes. In the center of the long rectangular panel on the front of the throne is the monogram of Christ. On either side are carved peacocks, symbols of paradise or everlasting life, and grapevines, symbols of the wine of Communion. Byzantine designs of birds and animals placed among the curling branches of vines are like the complicated patterns in Oriental rugs. Byzantine artists probably adapted these designs from textiles or carvings made in the Near East.

Four ivory carvings on the front of the throne show Saint John the Baptist and the four Gospel writers. The thinness of the saints

The throne of Bishop Maximian, Ravenna, is a fine example of Byzantine relief carving. It is made of wood and covered with elaborately carved ivory panels.

and their haggard appearance is typical of Byzantine art. In the early centuries of Christianity, many holy men fasted and tormented themselves. One famous hermit, Saint Simeon Stylites, even spent many years sitting on top of a column. The bodies of such holy men were very different from the healthy bodies of the Greek athletes. Extreme thinness came to be a sign of holiness, and this is one reason that the artist has carved such tall figures. By making the bodies of the saints very tall and fragile, they appear to be more spirit than flesh. The flat pattern of the saints' robes also makes their bodies look weightless, as if the cloth did not fall over any solid shapes.

The entire chair is carved with great precision and delicacy. The patterns of vines, birds, and beasts are wonderful examples of the Byzantine craftsman's creativeness in making a rich and exciting pattern.

▶ THE PERIOD OF ICONOCLASM (726–843)

In the 8th century the mosaics of the churches of Byzantium were covered with whitewash, and the sculpture was destroyed. This was done by the iconoclasts (image-breakers), who did not approve of representations of the saints or the Holy Family. They believed that many people really worshiped the picture or statue instead of the holy figure it represented. During the period when the iconoclasts were in power, no pictures of the Deity were allowed. The iconoclast movement not only interrupted the development of Byzantine art but caused the destruction of nearly all the great treasures of the First Golden Age.

▶ THE SECOND GOLDEN AGE (843–1204)

When the iconoclasts lost power, a new golden age began. Constantinople was still a city of great treasures, shimmering with gold. It was the richest city in the world. The art of this period shows an Eastern fondness for things that are richly ornamented and perfectly made. Everything is on a smaller scale. Artists made small, beautiful things that are delicate rather than impressive. Compared with the grand monuments of the time of Justinian, the churches of this period are tiny. Religious art was made to appeal to the worshiper in much more human terms. Instead of the solemn grandeur that made Christ unapproachable, there was a new emphasis on his sufferings as a man.

The Little Metropole, in Athens, was built during the Second Golden Age. Its small size and square, balanced plan are typical of the churches of this period.

Architecture

The churches of the Second Golden Age are like little jewel boxes in stone. They are most impressive from the outside, where the harmony and logic of the construction can be seen. The plan is square. Within the square is a cross with arms of equal length. A typical example is the Little Metropole in Athens. Three stories high, the church has a blocklike ground floor. The arms of the cross plan project into the second story. On the third level a small dome is placed over the center of the cross. Domes are also built between the arms of the cross plan on the second level, but these cannot be seen from the outside.

Another feature of the buildings of the Second Golden Age is the texture of the walls. In some places the surface is rough, in others smooth. This kind of surface causes an ever-changing activity of light and shade. The walls of the church at Athens are decorated with fragments of ancient Greek carving as well as reliefs of that time.

Saint Mark's. The famous church of Saint Mark's in Venice has nearly the same plan as the Little Metropolitan but is many times larger. Begun in 1063, it was probably copied from a church in Constantinople. The domes, like those in Hagia Sophia, have a ring of windows at their bases to let in light. The sunlight shining on the gold mosaics makes the domes look like golden shells hung in the air. The glow of gold mosaics and the sheen of colored marble make the visitor feel that he is really in a heaven brought to earth. On the outside the round domes are covered by domes of fantastic shape that make Saint Mark's look like an Eastern fairy palace. Marbles and mosaics of many different periods decorate the outside of the church.

The Mosaics at Daphni

The style of the mosaics of the Second Golden Age is like an echo of the great age of Greek art. In Greece, not far from Athens, is the church of Daphni. Inside the church are some of the finest mosaics in the whole history of Byzantine art.

In the dome there is a large picture of Christ. Only his head and shoulders are shown. His hand is raised in blessing, but his bearded face is solemn, even frightening. The large size of this picture, the beard, and the fearful solemnness of the face are like an ancient representation of the Greek god Zeus. The artist wanted to show Christ as the tremendous power that rules over the fate of man. It was natural that he should have turned to the noble beauty of Greek art for inspiration. He may even have been influenced by the bearded head of a statue of a Greek god.

On the pendentives are four scenes from the life of Christ. In the Crucifixion scene there are only three figures: Christ is on the cross, and Mary and Saint John are at the foot of the cross, one on each side. The figures are arranged in the shape of a triangle against the empty golden background. Each figure is separate and yet unified with the other figures.

Begun in the 11th century, Saint Mark's cathedral in Venice took centuries to build. The last details of this colorful church were added in the 1400's.

An 11th-century Italian cross made of enamels and gold.

A 14th-century mosaic in a Constantinople church shows the Holy Family paying taxes.

The balanced arrangement is like that used by Greek sculptors in placing their figures in the pediments of temples. Also, the position of Saint John—bending, with his weight on one leg—is a pose often used by Greek sculptors. The body of Christ is almost like that of a classic athlete. However, unlike Greek sculpture, the anatomy is not true to life. The Byzantine artist changed the body into a pattern of flat shapes. In doing this he tried to show Christ as perfect, unlike any ordinary human being.

The faces of Saint John and the Madonna have the flatness and heavy lines of the Byzantine style, but they express the calm of Greek statues. The emptiness of the background and the nobility of the figures show that this is an event that is not part of the everyday world. The artist has not tried to make a picture of the actual happening or to show what the real scene was actually like. Instead he has made a symbol of the Crucifixion.

Our Lady of Vladimir

Few examples of paintings on wooden panels have survived from the Second Golden Age. One of them is the famous Madonna of Vladimir, one of the first paintings to depict the Madonna and Child as mother and son, showing affection for each other. The picture reveals a new interest in human feeling. The softness of the features and the expression of

sadness in the eyes are like the technique and feeling of late Greek painting.

Our Lady of Vladimir was taken to Russia in the 11th or 12th century and became the model there for many later representations of the Madonna. This new, more human idea of divinity also influenced the religious painting of Italy in the 14th century.

Byzantine artists were not supposed to invent new compositions but to repeat as closely as possible the shapes of famous images. The Church wanted the representations of religious figures always to look the same. Artists followed rules written in manuals. In a beautiful ivory carving of the Madonna and Child, we can see that the artist has followed certain of these rules. The Madonna is carved in one of the standard poses—standing, she holds the Christ Child on her left arm. The carver has also used the Byzantine system of proportion for the body. The Madonna's body is extremely long and drawn out—9 or 10 times as long as the head. In ancient Greece artists usually made the bodies of athletes or gods seven times as long as the head.

The ivory carving has features that are typical of the Second Golden Age. The carved Madonna has the same sad, wistful look as the Madonna of Vladimir. Her oval head is delicate, with large, almond-shaped eyes and a tiny mouth. The strange, ghostly face under a heavy hood makes us feel that we are looking at a being from another world.

A delicately carved ivory panel of a Byzantine empress holding her scepter and orb.

A particularly beautiful feature of this ivory is the flattened pattern of the drapery arranged in a fanlike design.

The End of the Second Golden Age

The Second Golden Age came to an end with the capture of Constantinople by the Venetian crusaders in 1204. Like earlier crusades, it had been organized to fight the Turks in the Holy Land. Instead the crusaders attacked the most powerful city in the Christian world. When Constantinople fell into their hands, the invaders plundered the churches and palaces and burned the libraries. Many ancient works that had lasted from Greek and Roman times were lost in the flames. When the Venetians were finally driven out,

the last period of Byzantine civilization, the Third Golden Age, began.

▶ THE THIRD GOLDEN AGE (1261–1453)

The architecture typical of the Third Golden Age can be seen in many churches in the Balkans. These buildings differ from earlier churches like the Little Metropolitan because they give the impression of being tall, soaring buildings. Tiny domes are set on tall bases that sprout from the first story. The upward feeling is increased by the number of **pilasters** on the outside of the church. Pilasters are column-like strips built into the side of a wall. These churches do not look massive and solid like the churches of the Second Golden Age.

The Paintings of Kharieh Djami

In the paintings of this period, we seem to be looking at real dramatic happenings. The painters of the wall paintings of the church of Kharieh Djami in Constantinople were interested in storytelling. The figures in the Christian stories are placed in actual settings instead of on an empty golden background. Many of the old rules survive, but there is a new life and movement and a real beauty of color. Byzantine painters finally became interested in experimenting with realism, and in this respect they are the equals of their famous contemporaries in 14th-century Italy.

The End of Byzantium

Hagia Sophia was the spiritual center of the Byzantine Empire for 900 years. There the sacred emperors were crowned; there the priests celebrated the mass until that last dark night in Byzantine history, May 29, 1453. On that night the crowds prayed for the last time in the shadow of the great dome as the armies of the Turkish sultan attacked the city. Gathered inside the church, waiting for a miracle, they must have heard the crumbling of the city's walls. They must have heard the rattle of bridle chains in the streets, the clamor of the Turkish soldiers, the sound of axes hewing down the great doors as the sultan came to still forever the heart of the Byzantine world.

BENJAMIN ROWLAND, JR.
Harvard University

See also ARCHITECTURE; DECORATIVE ARTS; PAINTING; SCULPTURE.

BYZANTINE EMPIRE

A thousand years ago Constantinople was probably the largest and richest city on earth. It was the capital of the great Byzantine Empire. About a million people lived in Constantinople, and visitors marveled at its huge palaces, beautiful churches, and many shops. One visitor wrote that if he described a hundredth part of its wealth, it would seem like a lie and no one would believe it.

In A.D. 330 Constantine, the Roman emperor, had moved the seat of government from Rome to the old Greek city of Byzantium. Constantine named his capital New Rome, but most people called it Constantinople (Constantine's city), or still used the old name, Byzantium.

After Constantine died, the emperors who succeeded him found it difficult to rule the vast Roman Empire. In 395 the empire was officially divided; the lands in the east were ruled from Constantinople and those in the west from Rome. In the 100 years that followed the division, Rome lost most of the lands of the Western Empire (Italy, Spain, France, Britain, northwest Africa). In the east, however, the emperors still ruled. This part of the Roman Empire, ruled by emperors living in Byzantium, is known as the Byzantine Empire. But the rulers of the Byzantine Empire still called themselves Romans, and, for a time, the Byzantine Empire was still called the Eastern Roman Empire. The language of the Eastern Empire was Greek, rather than Latin, the Roman language.

▶ DEFENDING THE EMPIRE

The Byzantine Empire lasted for hundreds of years. It had a long life, but not an easy one. Its neighbors tried for centuries to overrun it. The Persians threatened the empire at one time. They had scarcely been defeated in 628 before the Arabs began a conquest of the East. The Byzantines at different times had to stand off attacks by a number of peoples from Asia, such as the Avars, Bulgars, and Turks. Because of the invasions the size of the empire varied from time to time. Generally the Byzantine emperors ruled most of the Balkan Peninsula and Asia Minor.

▶ THE ARMY

The Byzantine Empire lasted as long as it did because of its military strength. The armies were usually well organized and equipped. They had medical and ambulance services, signalmen who flashed messages with mirrors, and even marching bands to keep up their spirits. The navy possessed a secret weapon, "Greek fire." This was an inflammable mixture that was thrown on enemy ships in hand grenades or sprayed, flaming, from tubes in the prows of Byzan-

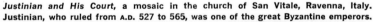

Justinian and His Court, a mosaic in the church of San Vitale, Ravenna, Italy. Justinian, who ruled from A.D. 527 to 565, was one of the great Byzantine emperors.

tine ships. Greek fire was a fearful weapon in the days of wooden ships. It was no wonder that the Byzantines kept the directions for its manufacture a carefully guarded secret.

▶THE WONDERS OF THE CAPITAL CITY

The Byzantines encouraged foreign rulers and ambassadors to visit their capital. They went to great lengths to impress the visitors with the wealth and power of the emperors. When an ambassador was presented to the emperor, he was ushered into a large, richly decorated hall. Before the throne stood a gilded bronze tree. On its branches were little mechanical golden birds that whistled beautiful songs. On either side of the throne stood lifelike bronze lions that roared and beat their tails. As the awe-struck foreigner bowed to the floor the throne on which the emperor sat rose slowly toward the ceiling. Ambassadors who had never seen such marvelous devices were always impressed by the clever Byzantines. Foreign visitors also gazed in wonder at the gold- and marble-covered walls of the palaces and churches. In particular they noticed the great church of Hagia Sophia, which still stands today. Although Constantinople had many poor people, visitors gave them little attention. They were more impressed with the large number of rich people, who rode fine horses and wore silk garments.

▶THE TRADE OF THE EMPIRE

Most people within the empire worked on the land, but the wealth of the capital came largely from trade. The city stood at a crossroads. All ships carrying goods between the Mediterranean Sea and the Black Sea had to pass Constantinople. The main road from Europe to the Middle East also passed through the city. The emperors taxed all goods carried in or out of their crossroads capital.

Goods from far-off places filled the markets of Constantinople. There were furs from Russia, spices from Ceylon, rugs from Asia, leather from Morocco, and ivory from East Africa. Skilled craftsmen made the fine cloth, jewelry, and other rich goods sold in the shops. The emperors owned the only workshops permitted to make silk cloth. The shops were grouped together according to their business. The perfume shops were all located near the palace so that their wares would sweeten the air.

▶SCHOOLS AND BOOKS

Constantinople had schools as well as shops. Since Greek was the language of the Byzantines, they studied the writings of such ancient Greeks as Plato and Aristotle. Many ancient books would have been lost had they not been kept and studied in the Byzantine schools, for scarcely anyone could read Greek in the West at this time. Byzantine authors also wrote new books, especially histories.

▶THE BYZANTINE CHURCH

The Byzantine Empire was a Christian empire. Its missionaries spread Christianity among the Slavic peoples of eastern Europe, including the Russians. Byzantine Christians disagreed with those of the West about a number of matters. The pope at Rome condemned the Eastern emperor's great powers over the church. Eastern Christians, however, did not recognize the pope's authority. Disagreements between the Eastern and Western churches grew so great that they divided in 1054. Churches that grew from the church of the Byzantines are known as the Orthodox churches—for example, the Greek Orthodox Church and the Russian Orthodox Church.

▶THE END OF THE EMPIRE

The struggle to rule was often a bitter one. Sometimes an emperor's son inherited his father's place, but often the throne was seized by a strong man. Some men would stop at nothing to be emperor—not even murder.

These struggles weakened the empire. It was during a struggle for the throne that an army of Crusaders from the West captured Constantinople in 1204. The rule of the Westerners lasted only until 1261, but the Byzantine emperors never became powerful again. A Muslim people, the Turks, conquered the Byzantine lands piece by piece until only Constantinople remained, a capital without an empire. Finally, in 1453, a Turkish army took the city. The last piece of the old Roman Empire had finally fallen.

KENNETH S. COOPER
George Peabody College

See also EASTERN ORTHODOX CHURCHES.

DICTIONARY ENTRIES

The following list contains brief biographies and short entries on many different subjects. It can be used for quick reference. To find references to all the information in the encyclopedia on a particular subject, consult the Index.

Baal Shem Tov (BOL SHEM tove) (Israel ben Eliezer) (1700?–60), Jewish teacher and founder of Hasidism, b. in what is now Ukraine. He appealed to common people as well as scholars in his belief that God exists in all things and is approachable through joyous and sincere prayer rather than merely through the intellect.

Babbitt, Natalie (1932–   ), American author and illustrator of children's books, b. Dayton, Ohio. Her *Kneeknock Rise* was an American Library Association Notable Book in 1970. Among other books she has written and illustrated for children are *The Something* (1970), *Herbert Rowbarge* (1982), and *The Devil's Other Storybook* (1987).

Babel (BAY-bel), **Tower of,** in the Old Testament (Genesis 11, 1–9), a tower in the plain of Shinar, or Babylonia, in ancient Mesopotamia. It was built by the descendants of Noah, who wished to build a tower reaching to heaven. This angered God, and He punished the builders by making them unable to understand each other's speech. They scattered over the earth in small groups, each speaking a language alien to the others. According to Scripture, this is the reason for the diversity of races and languages.

Baby's breath, a decorative plant native to Europe, Asia, and northern Africa, introduced into North America. It grows up to 3 feet (1 meter) tall and has numerous small white or pink flowers. It is often used by florists in trimming bouquets.

Bacall, Lauren (Betty Joan Perske) (1924–   ), American actress, b. New York, N.Y. She made a famous film debut at 19 in *To Have and Have Not,* starring with Humphrey Bogart, whom she married in 1945. Her other films include *Key Largo* (1948), *How to Marry a Millionaire* (1953), and *Murder on the Orient Express* (1974). She became a musical comedy star with *Applause* (1969) and *Woman of the Year* (1980), winning Tony awards for both performances.

Baer (BARE), **Karl Ernst von** (1792–1876), German biologist, b. Estonia. This pioneer in embryology (the study of animal development in the stages before birth or hatching) was the first person to see the female reproductive cell, or egg. Von Baer's law states that an embryo (unborn organism) develops the basic features of the group it belongs to before it develops the special features that separate the adult members of the group.

Baffin Bay, part of the North Atlantic Ocean between Greenland and the Canadian Northwest Territories. The bay is partially ice-free during summer months. It was discovered by the English explorer William Baffin during his search for a northwest passage (1616).

Bahá'í (BA-ha-i) **Faith** (the Faith of Baha'u'llah), was founded (1844) in Persia (now Iran) by Ali Mohammed of Shiraz, called the Báb ("the Gate"), who announced the coming of a new prophet. In 1863 Mirza Husayn Ali proclaimed himself the awaited Messiah. He took the name Baha'u'llah ("Splendor of God"), and it is on his teachings that the religion is based. World headquarters are in Haifa, Israel, and the Universal House of Justice is the international governing body. Members believe in one God and one evolving religion. They strive to eliminate all forms of prejudice. U.S. headquarters are located in Wilmette, Illinois. In recent years, members of the Bahá'í Faith have been subject to persecution in Iran.

Bailey, Pearl (1918–90), American entertainer, b. Newport News, Va. She was known for her distinctive singing style, which she combined with a steady stream of comical remarks. She performed in nightclubs, in concerts, and on Broadway, starring in an all-black production of *Hello, Dolly!* in 1967. She also appeared in films and on television. In 1976 she became a member of the U.S. Mission to the United Nations.

Baird, John Logie (1888–1946), Scottish inventor, b. Helensburgh. A pioneer in the development of television, he gave the first public demonstration of true television in London in 1926. He also pioneered in transatlantic and color television and invented the Noctovisor, a device for seeing in the dark.

Baird, Spencer Fullerton (1823–87), American zoologist and naturalist, b. Reading, Pa. As secretary of the Smithsonian Institution, he increased its collections, improved cataloging methods, and founded the National Museum. As first head of U.S. Commission of Fish and Fisheries, he founded Woods Hole Marine Biology Station. One of America's greatest naturalists, Baird wrote *Catalogue of North American Birds* and *Catalogue of North American Mammals.*

Baker, Josephine (1906–75), American singer and dancer, b. St. Louis, Mo. She spent most of her adult life in France, where she developed an international reputation. During World War II, Josephine Baker served in the Air Auxiliary of the Free French Forces and was awarded the French Legion of Honor medal. She adopted 12 orphans of different races and nationalities, and she sponsored a children's village at Les Milandes in France.

Baker, Russell Wayne (1925–   ), American writer, b. Morrisonville, Va. Baker won the Pulitzer prize twice—in 1979 for his humorous "Observer" columns in *The New York Times* and in 1982 for his autobiography, *Growing Up.* He began his newspaper career in 1947 as a reporter for the *Baltimore Sun.* In 1954 he joined *The New York Times,* reporting political news from Washington, D.C. He began the "Observer" in 1962 and soon established himself as a witty commentator on a wide range of subjects. His columns have been collected in book form, including *Poor Russell's Almanac* (1972) and *So This Is Depravity* (1980).

Balaklava (bahl-uh-KLAH-vuh), **Battle of** (1854), during the Crimean War, is best known for the charge of the British light cavalry brigade against overwhelming Russian artillery, as a result of a misunderstood command. Of more than 670 cavalrymen, less than 200 survived. It is the subject of Tennyson's poem *The Charge of the Light Brigade,* which glorifies the bravery and obedience of soldiers.

Balanchine, George (Georgi Militonovitch Balanchivadze) (1904–83), Russian-American ballet choreographer, b. St. Petersburg. Balanchine was trained as a dancer at the State Academic (Maryinsky) Theater. In 1924 he left a dance group touring Germany to go to Paris, where he joined the Ballets Russes de Monte Carlo. In 1933 he emigrated to the United States. There he created dances for several ballet companies and for Broadway shows, including *On Your Toes* (1936). In 1948 he helped found the New York City Ballet, a company he headed until shortly before his death. Typical of Balanchine's more than 200 ballets were *Apollo* (1928), *Agon* (1957), and *Don Quixote* (1965). They drew on classical traditions but were staged simply, so that the dancing would be the main element.

Balchen (BOL-ken), **Bernt** (1899–1973), American aviator, b. Topdal, Norway. As chief pilot of Byrd's Antarctic Expedition (1928–30), Balchen piloted the first flight over the South Pole. Active in the Norwegian underground during World War II, he entered the U.S. Army Air Corps in 1941, rising to the rank of colonel. Balchen wrote *Come North with Me.*

Baldwin I (1058–1118), French crusader and king of Jerusalem. With his brother Godfrey of Bouillon, he was one of the original leaders of the First Crusade. He succeeded Godfrey as ruler of Jerusalem (1100).

Baldwin I (1171–1205?), French crusader and emperor of Constantinople. As Baldwin IX of Flanders, he joined the Fourth Crusade and was elected first Latin emperor of Constantinople when the city was captured (1204). He was defeated at the Battle of Adrianople (1205).

Baldwin, Matthias William (1795–1866), American industrialist and philanthropist, b. Elizabethtown, N.J. Baldwin was the first U.S. manufacturer of bookbinders' tools and calico printers' rolls. He built "Old Ironsides," one of the first American locomotives; established a school for black children; and helped found the Franklin Institute.

Baldwin, Stanley, 1st Earl Baldwin of Bewdley (1867–1947), English statesman, b. Bewdley. Baldwin was first elected Conservative member of Parliament in 1908. He served as chancellor of the exchequer (1922–23) and three terms as prime minister (1923–24; 1924–29; 1935–37). Baldwin came to symbolize the qualities of moderation and trustworthiness.

Ball, Lucille (1911–89), American actress and TV producer, b. Jamestown, N.Y. She appeared in numerous films during the 1930's and 1940's, but is perhaps best-known as one of television's top comediennes. Her shows *I Love Lucy, The Lucy Show,* and *Here's Lucy* were consistently top-rated.

Banda (BON-da), **Hastings Kamuzu** (1906–), president of Malawi, b. Kasungu District, Nyasaland. He was prime minister of Nyasaland (1963–64) and remained prime minister when Nyasaland won independence as Malawi (1964). When

Malawi became a republic (1966), Banda was elected its first president. He was named president for life in 1971.

Bandaranaike (bon-da-ra-NY-kee), **Sirimavo Rawatte Dias** (1916–), Sri Lankan (Ceylonese) political leader, b. Bandaranaike, Sirimavo Rawatte Balangoda. She was the first woman prime minister of a modern nation, serving Sri Lanka in this office 1959–65 and 1970–77. She succeeded her husband, **Solomon West Ridgeway Bandaranaike** (1899–1959; b. Colombo), who was assassinated. He founded the Sri Lanka Freedom Party and was prime minister (1956–59).

Banda (BON-da) **Sea,** part of the Pacific Ocean encircled by the Indonesian islands. The sea contains the Banda Islands, noted for spices since their discovery by the Portuguese in the 16th century.

Bannister, Sir Roger Gilbert (1929–), English runner, b. Harrow. On May 6, 1954, he made track history by becoming the first person to run a mile in less than four minutes. His time of 3 min. 59.4 sec. was broken just 46 days later when John Landy ran the mile in 3 min. 58.0 sec. However, Bannister beat Landy about a month later. He retired from competition shortly thereafter and wrote his autobiography, *First Four Minutes* (1955). Bannister, who became a medical doctor, was knighted in 1975 by Queen Elizabeth II.

Banshee (or banshie), in Celtic folklore, supernatural being or spirit whose appearance or wailing foretells the death of some person. The word comes from the Gaelic *bean,* meaning "woman," and *sidth,* meaning "fairy." The banshee is portrayed in Irish folklore as either a lovely weeping maiden or an ugly old hag.

Baraka, Imamu Amiri (originally [Everett] LeRoi Jones) (1934–), American writer and political activist, b. Newark, N.J. His writings encourage the development of a strong cultural identity among blacks. They are rich in forceful language and images. His published works include the plays *Dutchman and The Slave* (1964), the poetry collection *Black Magic* (1969), and the collection of essays *Home* (1966). Baraka was also active in politics.

Barbary Wars, the name given to two conflicts between the United States and the former Barbary States of the North African coast. After independence, the United States, following the custom of most other maritime nations, paid yearly sums of money to the rulers of the Barbary States—Tripoli, Algiers, Tunis, and Morocco—to protect its merchant ships in the Mediterranean Sea from attack by the Barbary corsairs, or pirates. The Tripolitan War (1801–05) resulted when the pasha (ruler) of Tripoli (now in Libya) demanded additional tribute. Chiefly a naval war, it ended when a U.S. naval and land force captured the Tripolitan fortress of Derna. A war with Algiers (1815) was fought to suppress a new outbreak of piracy. A U.S. naval squadron under Commodore Stephen Decatur entered the harbor of Algiers (now the capital of Algeria) and forced its dey (ruler), under the threat of the destruction of his fleet and city, to sign a treaty ending the U.S. payment of tribute. Similar treaties were signed with the other Barbary States.

Barber, Samuel (1910–81), American composer, b. West Chester, Pa. He wrote the music for the opera *Vanessa,* which won a Pulitzer prize in 1958. In 1963 his *Concerto for Piano*

and Orchestra received the same honor. His *Essay No. 1* and an arrangement of another early work, performed as *Adagio,* were played on radio in 1938. They brought his music to international attention. Barber composed works for voice, ballet, string quartet, and full orchestra.

Bardeen, John (1908–), American physicist, b. Madison, Wis. He was the first person to receive two Nobel prizes in the same field. In 1948, Bardeen, W.H. Brattain, and W. Shockley invented the transistor. In 1956 they received the Nobel prize in physics for work on semiconductors, from which transistors are made. In 1972, Bardeen shared a second Nobel prize with Leon N. Cooper and John R. Schrieffer for work in superconductivity.

Barenboim, Daniel (1942–), Israeli pianist and conductor, b. Buenos Aires, Argentina. He gave his first public recital in Buenos Aires at the age of 7. His family settled in Israel in 1952, and he made his conducting debut there in 1962. Barenboim has played with leading orchestras of the world. He has served as music director of the Orchestre de Paris and the Bastille Opera of Paris. He was named (1989) as the future director of the Chicago Symphony, to succeed Georg Solti.

Barnard, Christiaan Neethling (1922–), South African surgeon, b. Beaufort West, S.A. He performed the first successful human heart transplant at Cape Town in December, 1967. The patient lived 18 days. Dr. Barnard had his most notable success with transplant patient Dr. Philip Blaiberg, who lived for 19 months with his new heart. Dr. Barnard is the creator of the Barnard valve, used in open-heart surgery. He is the author of several books, among them *Good Life/Good Death.*

Barnum, Phineas Taylor (1810–91), American showman, b. Bethel, Conn. As a boy, he worked in his father's grocery store. An ardent abolitionist, he published a Danbury newspaper, the *Herald of Freedom.* In 1834, he entered show business. An imaginative promoter, he won fame by sponsoring such attractions as Tom Thumb and Jenny Lind. In 1881 he and John Bailey produced the famous circus now run by Ringling Bros.

Barth, John (1930–), American novelist, b. Cambridge, Md. His book *Chimera* won the 1973 National Book Award for fiction. Serious philosophical questions come to light as his fantastic and humorous stories unfold. His other works include *The Sot-Weed Factor* (1960), *Giles Goat-Boy* (1966), and *Sabbatical: A Romance* (1982).

Barth (BART), **Karl** (1886–1968), Swiss Protestant theologian, b. Basel. Professor of theology at the University of Basel, Barth stressed that man could not know God through the power of reason, but only through the Bible and through Christ.

Barthelme (BAR-tuhl-mee), **Donald** (1931–89), American author, b. Philadelphia, Pa. He was a well-known writer of short stories, which have been collected in *60 Stories* (1981), *Overnight to Many Distant Cities* (1983), and other books. His book for young readers, *The Slightly Irregular Fire Engine, or the Hithering Thithering Djiin,* won a National Book Award in 1972.

Bartolommeo (bart-o-lo-MAY-o), **Fra** (Bartolommeo di Pagolo del Fattorini) (1475–1517), Italian painter, b. Savignano, Tuscany. He was also called Baccio della Porta. An important figure in the Florentine school in the High Renaissance, he excelled in coloring. Most of his works are found today in the Pitti Palace, Florence, including his masterpiece, *St. Mark.*

Bartram, John (1699–1777), American botanist, b. Chester County, Pa. The self-educated botanist is known as the father of American botany. In 1728 he founded the country's first botanical garden at Kingsessing, Pa. He was also responsible for the introduction of various European plants into America and American plants into Europe.

Baryshnikov, Mikhail Nikolayevich (1948–), Russian dancer, b. Riga, Latvia. He studied dance in Riga and in 1966 joined the famed Kirov Ballet of Leningrad. Although he received wide acclaim in the Soviet Union, he felt his artistic expression was limited. In 1974, while with the Bolshoi Ballet in Canada, he defected. He joined American Ballet Theatre that same year and the New York City Ballet in 1978. He returned to American Ballet Theatre two years later as artistic director, a post he held until 1989.

Barzun, Jacques (1907–), American educator and author, b. Crétail, France. He became a member of the Columbia University faculty in 1927, was dean of faculties and provost (1958–67), and university professor emeritus. His many books include *Berlioz and the Romantic Century* (1950), *The House of Intellect* (1959), *The American University* (1968), and *A Stroll With William James* (1983).

Basic English, system using 850 normal English words, designed by British scholar C. K. Ogden about 1925. It was devised for use in international communication and is used to teach English and to simplify writings in English.

Basie, Count (William Basie) (1904–84), American bandleader and jazz pianist, b. Red Bank, N.J. In his teens Basie went to Harlem, where he learned piano technique from the great jazz pianist Fats Waller. Basie formed his own band in 1935, and it soon became one of the most successful groups of the "Big Band" era of the 1930's and 1940's. Its strong rhythm section—including Count Basie's distinctive, spare piano playing—was especially influential. The band's most popular numbers include "One O'Clock Jump" and "April in Paris." In 1981, Basie received a Kennedy Center award for achievement in the performing arts.

Basilica (ba-SIL-ica) (from Greek word *basilikos,* meaning "royal"), a long rectangular building with interior colonnades and at least one apse (semicircular projection). Basilicas were originally Greek and Roman justice or assembly halls. Their architectural plan was widely used for churches.

Basil (BAZ-il) **the Great, Saint** (330?–379), doctor of the Christian Church, b. Caesarea, Cappadocia. He founded the first monastery in Asia Minor at Pontus (about 360) and became known as the Patriarch of Eastern Monasticism. He was ordained a priest (about 365), and later became bishop of Caesarea (370). Basil tried to stamp out heresies within the Church, especially Arianism, which denied the divinity of Christ. His feast is celebrated on January 1 in the Eastern Church and January 2 in the Western.

Basques (BASKS), a people who live in the foothills of the Pyrenees Mountains, on both sides of the border between Spain and France. They number nearly 3,000,000. Their language is

Basques (continued)

not related to any known language in the world. The largest city of the Basque region is Bilbao, Spain. Some Basques want to form an independent nation. A Spanish Basque organization known as ETA (initials standing for the Basque words for Basque Homeland and Freedom) has committed acts of violence against the Spanish government. In 1980, a limited form of home rule went into effect in the Spanish Basque provinces.

Batista y Zaldívar (ba-TI-sta e sal-DEE-var), **Fulgencio** (1901–73), Cuban dictator, b. Banes. He took part in the military overthrow of dictator Gerardo Machado (1931–33) and became chief of staff of the Cuban Army (1933–39). After a second coup (1952), he became dictator (1954). He was deposed (1959) by rebels under Fidel Castro and died in exile in Spain.

Batlle y Ordóñez (BAT-yay e or-DONE-yes), **José** (1856–1929), Uruguayan statesman and journalist, b. Montevideo. He established the newspaper *El Día* (1886), through which he publicized his political proposals later incorporated into the Constitution of 1918. He led the liberal Colorado Party and was president of Uruguay (1903–07, 1911–15), introducing an executive council based on the Swiss system. His leadership led to universal suffrage and increased governmental roles in business, welfare, and labor reform.

Battle, Kathleen (1948–), American soprano, b. Portsmouth, Ohio. The daughter of a steelworker, she taught music at the elementary school level while pursuing a career as a professional singer. She made her singing debut in 1972 at the Spoleto, Italy, Festival of Two Worlds. Her Metropolitan Opera debut (1977) was as the Shepherd in Wagner's *Tannhäuser*. She is admired for her sensitive interpretation of music as well as for her purity of voice.

Baudouin (BO-dwan) (1930–), king of the Belgians, b. Brussels. Baudouin became Prince Royal (1950) when his father, Leopold III, transferred royal constitutional powers to him because of political unrest. He became king when his father abdicated (1951). In 1960, he married a Spanish noblewoman, Fabiola de Mora y Aragón.

Baum (BOHM), **L. Frank** (Lyman Frank Baum) (1856–1919), American journalist and author of children's stories, b. Chittenango, N.Y. He is best known for a series of fantasies for children about the land of Oz, beginning with *The Wonderful Wizard of Oz.* Thirteen other Oz stories followed. The first Oz book was made into a movie in 1939.

Bayberry, shrub of eastern coastal North America. It has dark-green leaves, small flowers, and round, waxy, grayish-white berries. The sweet-smelling wax from the berries is used in making candles.

Baylor, Elgin (1934–), American basketball player, b. Washington, D.C. He was among the leading scorers in National Basketball Association history. He joined the Minneapolis Lakers in 1958 and was named NBA Rookie of the Year. The Lakers moved to Los Angeles in 1960, and Baylor remained with the team until his retirement in 1972. He was named to the NBA All-Star team ten times. In 1976, he was elected to the Basketball Hall of Fame.

Bay Psalm Book (correct title, *The Whole Booke of Psalmes Faithfully Translated into English Metre),* book of psalms adapted by several Puritan ministers in Massachusetts Bay Colony for use with familiar hymn tunes. It is famous as the first book in English printed in the New World (1640).

Beamon, Bob (Robert Beamon) (1946–), American track-and-field star, b. New York, N.Y. At the 1968 Olympics in Mexico City, he set a world record in the long jump, considered by many experts to be the greatest single performance in track history. His record jump, at 29 ft 2½ in (8.90 m), was 21½ in (55 cm) longer than the previous record.

Beard, Charles Austin (1874–1948), American historian, writer, and educator, b. near Knightstown, Ind. Beard was professor of politics, Columbia University (1915–17) and helped found the New School for Social Research. Books written with his wife, **Mary Ritter Beard** (1876–1958), include *A Basic History of the United States* and *The Rise of American Civilization.*

Beardsley, Aubrey Vincent (1872–98), English book illustrator, b. Brighton. Beardsley is known for his stylized, decorative line drawings in black and white. His works include illustrations for Ben Jonson's *Volpone,* Oscar Wilde's *Salomé,* and the English periodical *Yellow Book.*

Beatification (be-at-if-ic-A-tion), in Roman Catholic Church, papal act by which a holy person is declared blessed after death. Often this is the first step to canonization (being declared a saint). To become beatified, a person must have led a life of heroic virtue and have performed at least two miracles.

Beaton, Cecil Walter Hardy (1904–80), English photographer, writer, and designer, b. London. His work became known through magazines in England and other countries. He was noted especially for his photographs of beautiful women. He wrote *Air of Glory* and other books while working for the British Ministry of Information during World War II. His other books include *The Book of Beauty* and *Cecil Beaton's New York.* His designs include the costumes for the musical *My Fair Lady* (1956).

Beatrix (BAY-a-trix) (1938–), queen of the Netherlands, b. Soestdijk. She succeeded to the throne in 1980, when her mother, Queen Juliana, abdicated. Beatrix, the eldest child of Queen Juliana and Prince Bernhard, became crown princess in 1948, when her mother succeeded to the throne. In 1966 she married Claus-Georg von Amsberg, a German. They have three sons.

Beattie, Ann (1947–), American writer, b. Washington, D.C. In her novels and short stories, Beattie uses a simple, unemotional writing style, realistic dialogue, and unresolved endings to show the lives of her troubled characters. *Distortions,* her first collection of stories (most of which had first appeared in *The New Yorker* magazine), was published in 1976. Her first novel, *Chilly Scenes of Winter,* was published the same year. Beattie's other works include the short story collections *The Burning House* (1982) and *Where You'll Find Me* (1986) and the novels *Falling in Place* (1980) and *Love Always* (1985).

Beauregard (BO-re-gard), **Pierre Gustave Toutant de** (1818–93), American Confederate general, b. near New Orleans, La. Beauregard ordered firing on Fort Sumter, which began the Civil War (1861). He led the South to victory at Bull Run (1861), defended Charleston (1862–64), and together with General Bushrod Johnson surrendered to General Sherman (1865). His writings include *Principles and Maxims of the Art of War.*

Beauvoir (boh-VWAHR), **Simone de** (1908–86), French writer, b. Paris. After studying at the Sorbonne, she taught philosophy from 1931 until 1943, when she began to write full time. She maintained a lifelong association with the French writer Jean-Paul Sartre, whose existentialist philosophy she shared. Her own writings are shaped by this philosophy, particularly the belief that people create their own moral values. Her works include novels, essays, and four volumes of autobiography. Her best-known book is *The Second Sex* (1949), a feminist essay that made her an influential figure in the women's movement.

Becker, Boris (1967–   ), German tennis player, b. Leimen. He is a three-time winner of the All-England (Wimbledon) men's singles championship (1985, 1986, 1989). With his 1985 Wimbledon championship, Becker became the youngest and the first unseeded (unranked) player to win the title. He also won the U.S. Open men's singles championship in 1989.

Beckett, Samuel (1906–89), Irish playwright and novelist, b. Dublin. He settled permanently in France in 1937 and wrote in French after 1945. He translated several of his own works into English. Beckett's characters are defeated by their failure to communicate with one another and by an inability to understand their existence. His best-known plays are *Waiting for Godot* (1952), *Endgame* (1957), and *Krapp's Last Tape* (1959). His novel *Molloy* (1951) is the first of a trilogy that takes place mainly in the minds of its narrators. In 1969, he received the Nobel prize for literature.

Bedlam, hospital of Saint Mary of Bethlehem in London (name became slurred in popular usage: "Bethlem" and then "Bedlam"). It was built as a monastery (1247) and was later used as a lunatic asylum. Hence the term also refers to any place of noise and confusion.

Beecham, Sir Thomas (1879–1961), English symphony and opera conductor and impresario, b. St. Helens, Lancashire. He used his personal fortune to back several orchestras and opera companies, including Covent Garden Opera Company, London Philharmonic Orchestra, and Royal Philharmonic Orchestra. He introduced many operas to English audiences and toured extensively.

Beelzebub (be-EL-ze-bub) (from Hebrew *Baal-zebub,* meaning "Lord of Flies"), Philistine god worshiped at Ekron. Considered a false god by Jews in the Old Testament (II Kings 1: 3,6), he is mentioned in the New Testament (Matthew, Mark, and Luke) as the prince of devils. He appears in Milton's *Paradise Lost* as a fallen angel ranking second only to Satan.

Begin (BAY-ghin), **Menahem** (1913–92), Israeli political leader, b. Brest-Litovsk, Russian Poland (now Brest, Belarus). Begin served as prime minister of Israel from 1977 until his resignation in 1983. During his time in office, Israel signed a peace treaty with Egypt (1979), annexed the Golan Heights (1981), invaded Lebanon (1982), and encouraged the establishment of Israeli settlements in the West Bank. Begin grew up in Poland and led a Zionist youth group in the 1930's. After World War II, he led forces fighting for an independent Jewish state in the Middle East. He became a member of parliament after Israel was established. In 1978, Begin shared the Nobel peace prize with Egyptian president Anwar el-Sadat.

Behring (BEAR-ing), **Emil von** (1854–1917), German bacteriologist, b. Hansdorf. Known for his work on diphtheria and tetanus, he discovered that blood serum of an animal infected with one of these diseases, when injected into a healthy animal, provided immunity against that disease. He introduced the word "antitoxin" to describe these substances and was awarded the first Nobel prize in physiology or medicine in 1901.

Belafonte (bel-af-ON-tay), **Harry** (Harold George Belafonte, Jr.) (1927–   ), American folksinger and actor, b. New York, N.Y. He appeared on Broadway and in films but is best known for his recordings of Jamaican calypso music. He was active in civil rights work and in relief efforts for Ethiopia. In 1987 he was appointed Ambassador-at-large for UNICEF.

Belasco, David (1854–1931), American theatrical producer and playwright, b. San Francisco, Calif. He was stage manager of various New York theaters before he opened the first of his own theaters (1902). His success is attributed to careful attention to stage detail, and he was the first to conceal footlights from the audience. He was author and collaborator of many plays, including *The Girl of the Golden West.*

Bellini, Vincenzo (1801–35), Italian composer, b. Catania, Sicily. Known chiefly for his operas, he is noted for the elegance of his melodic style, which has been compared to Chopin's. His best-known operas are *I Puritani, La Sonnambula,* and *Norma.*

Belloc, Hilaire (Joseph Hilary Pierre Belloc) (1870–1953), English writer, b. St. Cloud, France. Today he is remembered mainly for his light comic verse, such as *The Bad Child's Book of Beasts* (1896) and *Cautionary Tales* (1907). During his lifetime he was also known as an essayist and as a leader of intellectual Catholicism in England. He was a Liberal member of Parliament from 1906 to 1910. Belloc's other works include a four-volume *History of England* (1925–31) and a travel journal, *The Path to Rome* (1902).

Bemelmans (BEM-el-mans), **Ludwig** (1898–1962), American author and illustrator, b. Merano, Austria (now in Italy). He went to the United States in 1914 and became a citizen in 1918. He wrote and illustrated books for children and adults. He is known for his humor and whimsical charm of his stories and paintings. His books for children include *Parsley, Quito Express,* and *Madeline's Rescue,* which won the Caldecott medal in 1954. Some of his adult books are *How to Travel Incognito* and *Best of Times.*

Ben Bella, Ahmed (1916–   ), former premier of Algeria, b. Marnia. One of the "nine fathers of Algerian independence," he took part in nationalist activities and was captured and jailed by the French (1956–61). He was named premier when Algeria won independence (1962). He was president of the Republic of Algeria (1963–65). Ousted by a military coup, he was held a prisoner until 1981.

Bench, Johnny (Johnny Lee Bench) (1947–   ), American baseball player, b. Oklahoma City, Okla. He was baseball's best catcher during the 1970's and one of the finest of all time. He spent his entire career (1967–83) with the Cincinnati Reds. During that time he was voted the National League (NL) Rookie of the Year (1968) and twice was named the NL Most Valuable Player (1970, 1972). As the NL's best defensive catcher, Bench also won ten Gold Gloves (1968–77). He had a career .267 batting average, 2,048 hits, 1,376 runs batted in, and 389 home runs. He was inducted into the Baseball Hall of Fame (1989).

Benchley, Robert Charles (1889–1945), American humorist, writer, and actor, b. Worcester, Mass. His whimsical sketches, mainly about everyday problems, were collected in *The Early Worm* (1927), *Inside Benchley* (1942), and other books. He was drama critic for *Life* and *The New Yorker* and also performed in films and on radio. Benchley's son **Nathaniel** and grandson **Peter** were also writers. Peter wrote *Jaws* (1974) and other popular adventure novels.

Benedict, Ruth Fulton (1887–1948), American anthropologist, b. New York, N.Y. She taught at Columbia University (1923–48). Her book about Japan, *The Chrysanthemum and the Sword,* was helpful in shaping U.S. policy there. She believed anthropologists should participate in solving social problems. In *Race: Science and Politics* she tried to disprove theories of racial superiority. She was the author of *Patterns of Culture*.

Benedict of Nursia, Saint (480?–543?), Italian monk, called Patriarch of Western Monasticism, b. Nursia, Umbria. He was educated in Rome, where he became disillusioned by the corrupt life around him. He retreated to a cave in Subiaco (500?) but was sought out by admiring disciples. He established a monastery (529?) on Monte Cassino that became the center of the Benedictine Order. He wrote *Regula Monachorum,* a set of strict rules that govern monks of this order.

Benelux, economic union of Belgium, the Netherlands, and Luxembourg. The original agreement, signed in 1944, was put into effect in 1948. Its primary goal of removing tariff barriers was achieved (1950), but other aims, such as uniform taxes, wages, and prices, have yet to be realized. An example of prosperity through cooperation, it was a precursor of the European Common Market.

Beneš (BEN-esh), **Edvard** (1884–1948), Czechoslovakian statesman, b. Kožlany, Bohemia. He worked with Tomáš Masaryk for a Czechoslovak national state (formed 1918). A delegate to Versailles peace conference (1919–20) and to League of Nations (1923–27), he was elected Czechoslovak president (1935). He resigned when Germans invaded (1938) and became head of Czech government-in-exile (1939–45). He was reelected president after war (1946) but resigned (1948) rather than co-operate with Communists in the government. His writings include *My War Memories* and *Democracy: Today and Tomorrow*.

Bennett, Floyd (1890–1928), American aviator, b. Warrensburg, N.Y. In 1926, with Rear Admiral Richard E. Byrd, Bennett piloted the first plane to fly over the North Pole. He and Byrd were awarded the Congressional Medal of Honor for their achievements. Bennett also flew with Byrd on an expedition to Greenland in 1925.

Bennett, Richard Bedford, Viscount Bennett (1870–1947), Canadian statesman, b. Hopewell Hill, New Brunswick. Conservative member of the Canadian House of Commons (1911–17, 1925–39), he was minister of justice and attorney general (1921), minister of finance (1926), leader of the Conservative Party (1927–38), and prime minister (1930–35). During his administration the Bank of Canada and the Canadian Broadcasting Commission were established.

Benny, Jack (Benjamin Kubelsky) (1894–1974), American comedian, b. Waukegan, Ill. He started his career as a violinist in 1912. "The Jack Benny Show," first heard on radio in 1932, was on TV from 1950 to 1964. Benny was given a special award (1957) by the National Academy of Television Arts and Sciences for the best continued performance by a male entertainer.

Bentham, Jeremy (1748–1832), English reformer and philosopher, b. London. He was a leading advocate of utilitarianism, a system of ethics defining the highest good as "the greatest good for the greatest number." He gave up his law practice in order to devote himself entirely to social criticism and reform. His works include *Introduction to the Principles of Morals and Legislation*.

Ben-Zvi (ben-tz-VE), **Isaac** (or Itzhak) (1884–1963), Israeli statesman, b. Poltava, Russia. He organized the Zionist movement in Russia. He fled to Palestine (1907) and helped organize the Jewish forces that later became the underground army Haganah. As head of the governing Council of Palestine, he was a spokesman for Israeli independence under the British mandate. He served as second president of Israel (1952–63). A noted Oriental scholar, he wrote on archaeology, ethnology, and the history of the Near East.

Berbers, people of the Hamitic language group who are the earliest known inhabitants of North Africa. The majority are farmers or raise livestock. Some, such as the Tuareg Berbers, are nomadic herders organized into clans, which are united into groups, each headed by a chief. They are Muslims.

Berg (BAIRG), **Alban** (1885–1935), Austrian composer, b. Vienna. He was one of the leading composers of the early 20th century. A pupil and disciple of Arnold Schoenberg, he wrote songs, chamber music, and orchestral works, but he is chiefly known for his operas *Wozzeck* and *Lulu* and his *Violin Concerto*.

Berg (BERG), **Patty** (Patricia Jane Berg) (1918–   ), American golfer, b. Minneapolis, Minn. She won 83 major golf tournaments, both amateur and professional, including U.S. Women's Amateur (1938) and U.S. Women's Titleholders (seven times between 1937 and 1957). She was chosen three times as outstanding woman athlete of the year by Associated Press. In 1951, Berg was elected to the Hall of Fame of the Ladies Professional Golfers' Association.

Bergman, Ingrid (1915–82), Swedish stage and screen actress, b. Stockholm. She gained international fame from her first American film, *Intermezzo,* with Leslie Howard (1939). She won the Antoinette Perry (Tony) award for her Broadway performance as *Joan of Lorraine* (1947) and Academy Awards for *Gaslight* (1944), *Anastasia* (1956), and *Murder on the Orient Express* (1975). Her other films include *For Whom the Bell Tolls* and *Casablanca*. In 1982 she won an Emmy for her last film performance in *A Woman Called Golda,* a movie made for television.

Berlin, Congress of (1878), assembly in Berlin of delegates from Germany, Austria-Hungary, France, Britain, Italy, Russia, and the Turkish Ottoman Empire. Its aim was to reverse territorial gains won by Russia in the Balkans following Russia's victory in the Russo-Turkish War of 1877–78. The delegates signed the Treaty of Berlin, which confirmed independence for Serbia and Montenegro (now parts of Yugoslavia), and Romania. The treaty divided Bulgaria into three parts and gave Britain, a leader of opposition to Russia, control of Cyprus.

Berliner, Emile (1851–1929), German-American inventor, b. Hanover, Germany. Among his many inventions were the microphone; the gramophone, forerunner of the modern flat-disk phonograph; and an improved telephone transmitter.

Bernadette of Lourdes (Marie Bernarde Soubirous), **Saint** (1844–79), a French peasant girl said to have had visions of the Virgin Mary at Lourdes in 1858, b. Lourdes, Hautes-Pyrénées. Through her, the waters at Lourdes, believed to have miraculous healing powers, became known. She joined the Sisters of Charity at Nevers in 1866. She was canonized in 1933.

Bernhardt, Sarah (Henriette Rosine Bernard) (1844–1923), French actress, b. Paris. Called Divine Sarah, she was known for her *voix d'or* (''golden voice''). She performed with the Comédie Française (1874–80), touring Europe and the United States with great success. She was noted for her performances in plays by Hugo, Sardou, and Racine. Despite a leg amputation (1915), she continued her acting career. She wrote a volume of memoirs and several plays and managed her own theater in Paris.

Bernstein, Leonard (1918–90), American conductor, pianist, and composer, b. Lawrence, Mass. Associated with the New York Philharmonic from 1943 and musical director 1958–69, he was the first person born and trained in the United States to hold that position. His compositions, ranging from classical to popular, include symphonies *The Age of Anxiety* and *Jeremiah;* a ballet, *Fancy Free;* the theatrical rock *Mass;* and scores of several musical shows, such as *Wonderful Town* and *West Side Story.*

Berra, Yogi (Lawrence Peter Berra) (1925–   ), American baseball player, b. St. Louis, Mo. He was a catcher for the New York Yankees (1946–63) and was chosen to play in the All-Star game 14 times. He was the American League's Most Valuable Player in 1951, 1954, and 1955. Berra managed the Yankees in 1964. He was a coach (1965–72) and manager (1972–75) of the New York Mets. He rejoined the Yankees as a coach (1976–83) and manager (1984 and part of 1985). He became a coach for the Houston Astros in 1986. Berra was inducted into the Baseball Hall of Fame in 1972.

Berton, Pierre (1920–   ), Canadian writer and television personality, b. Whitehorse, Yukon Terr. Berton worked as a journalist for newspapers in Vancouver and Toronto and for *Maclean's* magazine. He also appeared frequently on Canadian television as host of his own shows or as a panelist. Berton is especially well known for his books about Canadian history. These include *Klondike Fever* (1958), which tells the story of the Klondike gold rush of 1898; *The National Dream* (1970), about the building of the Canadian Pacific Railway; and *The Promised Land* (1984), a history of the settling of the Canadian West.

Betjeman (BET-je-man), **Sir John** (1906–84), English poet and writer, b. London. He was poet laureate of England from 1972 until his death and he was celebrated as a poet whose work was popular with ordinary readers. Many of his lyric poems captured the England of days gone by and the sadness he felt at its passing. Others were lighthearted views of the England of his day. *Collected Poems* (1958) and *Summoned by Bells* (1960), a verse autobiography, were among his books of poetry. He was also a literary critic and a writer on architecture. He was knighted in 1969.

Bettelheim (BET-tel-hime), **Bruno** (1903–90), American psychologist and educator, b. Vienna, Austria. He is well known for studies of emotionally disturbed children, including *Love Is Not Enough* (1950) and *A Home for the Heart* (1974). His imprisonment in a Nazi concentration camp in 1938 was the basis for several works in later years on group behavior. He emigrated to the United States in 1939. Later, he taught at the University of Chicago and directed its school for emotionally disturbed children (1944–73). Bettelheim also wrote many books and articles on general education and child development. In 1977 he received a National Book Award for *The Uses of Enchantment: The Meaning and Importance of Fairy Tales.*

Better Business bureaus, nonprofit agencies in United States and Canada that protect both public and business from misleading or fraudulent business practices.

Bhutto, Benazir (1953–   ), Pakistani political leader, b. Sind Province. She became prime minister of Pakistan in 1988, the first woman to head the government of a modern Islamic nation. The daughter of former Pakistani prime minister Zulfikar Ali Bhutto, she received her college education in the United States and Britain. She returned home just before her father's overthrow in a military coup (1977). After his execution (1979), she assumed the leadership of the Pakistan People's Party. She succeeded to office in elections that followed the death of Pakistan's longtime ruler, Mohammed Zia ul-Haq. She was dismissed from office (1990) on charges of corruption in her government.

Big Brothers/Big Sisters of America (BB/BSA), a social service organization of federated local agencies in the United States. The organization provides an adult volunteer to act as a Big Brother or Big Sister to a boy or girl from a single-parent home. The volunteer spends time each week with the same youngster, providing companionship and guidance. Big Brothers was founded in 1903 and Big Sisters in 1908. The groups merged in 1977. Big Brothers/Big Sisters of America has headquarters in Philadelphia, Pennsylvania. Big Brothers of Canada, an independent organization, has headquarters in Burlington, Ontario.

Bigfoot, a mysterious creature said to live in the mountains of the northwestern United States and British Columbia, Canada. Its name comes from huge footprints found in the region that were supposedly made by the creature. Except for their size—about 16 in (41 cm) long—they resemble human footprints. In

Bigfoot (continued)

reported sightings, Bigfoot is described as shy, apelike in appearance, and 7 to 10 ft (2 to 3 m) tall. It is also known by the Indian name Sasquatch.

Bikini, a coral atoll in the Marshall Islands, west central Pacific. The people who lived on the island were moved in 1946 so that the United States could use the region for nuclear testing. They returned (1968) but were relocated again (1978) because of dangerous radioactivity.

Billy the Kid (1859–81), American outlaw, believed to have been born in New York, N.Y. Billy the Kid was a notorious thief and killer who became a legendary figure in the American West. He lived in New Mexico under several aliases (William H. Bonney, Henry McCarty, Henry or Billy Antrim). In 1878, the Kid became involved in a feud called the Lincoln County cattle war, and he began a spree of killings and cattle thefts. He was shot and killed by Sheriff Pat Garrett in July, 1881. The Kid was said to have killed 21 people, but the true number was probably far smaller.

Biological warfare (also called germ, or bacteriological, warfare), warfare in which living organisms are used to transmit disease to an enemy. Bacteria of such diseases as diphtheria, typhus, and smallpox are introduced into the air or drinking water of an enemy. Infected animals also can be used to transmit disease. Although techniques are available for such warfare, it has rarely been used.

Bird, Larry (1956–   ), American basketball player, b. French Lick, Indiana. He is considered by many to be the best all-around player in professional basketball history, adept at scoring, rebounding, passing, and defense. A forward for the Boston Celtics, Bird was named NBA Rookie of the Year in 1980. He has been a member of the all-NBA team every year he has played, and he has won the NBA Most Valuable Player award three times (1984, 1985, 1986). Prior to his professional career, Bird was an All-American at Indiana State University. He is 6 ft 9 in (206 cm) tall.

Bishop, Billy (William Avery Bishop) (1894–1956), Canadian aviator, b. Owen Sound, Ontario. He is credited with shooting down 72 German aircraft during World War I and was awarded many medals, including the Victoria Cross (1917), Britain's highest award for bravery. As a member of British Air Ministry, he established a separate Canadian Air Force (1918). He was co-founder of one of the first commercial aviation companies in Canada. He was honorary air vice-marshal and director of air force recruiting.

Bittersweet, woody vine that grows in most of North America. Up to 25 ft (8 m) long, it bears clusters of small greenish-white flowers. Its yellow fruit shows red seeds. "Bitter sweet" is also a popular name for nightshade, a woody climbing shrub with purple flowers and poisonous red berries, found in North America, Europe, and Asia.

Bizet (bi-ZAY), **Georges** (Alexandre César Léopold Bizet) (1838–75), French composer, b. Paris. He is best known for the opera *Carmen.* Bizet greatly influenced French dramatic music. Besides *Carmen,* his operas include *The Pearl-Fishers* and *The Fair Maid of Perth.* He also wrote the suite *Children's Games,* and a symphony in C.

Black, Hugo La Fayette (1886–1971), American jurist, b. Harlan, Ala. Black received his law degree from the University of Alabama (1906). He practiced law in Birmingham and was active in local Democratic politics. In 1926, and again in 1932, he was elected U.S. senator. He was a strong supporter of President Franklin D. Roosevelt's New Deal policies, and in 1937 Roosevelt appointed him to fill a vacancy as Associate Justice of the U.S. Supreme Court. Black was a strong advocate of individual liberties and civil rights. He retired in 1971.

Blackbeard (Edward Teach, or Thatch) (?–1718), British pirate, b. Bristol. He is thought to have been a privateer for the British in the West Indies during the War of the Spanish Succession (1701–13). Later, he turned to piracy, plundering areas of the Caribbean and along the coasts of North Carolina and Virginia. Blackbeard was killed during an attack by ships sent against him by planters and the governor of Virginia.

Black box, a term usually referring to an electronic device whose internal workings are not known or understood by the person using the device. Someone using such a device can understand what it does without knowing how it operates. In aviation, however, the term "black box" refers specifically to an aircraft's flight recorder, an electronic instrument that records information about the performance of an aircraft in flight.

Black Hole of Calcutta, a dungeon within Fort William, a British East India company establishment in Calcutta, India. In 1756 the fort was occupied by the nawab (provincial governor) of Bengal after mediation failed to settle a dispute. The nawab's officers confined approximately 64 Englishmen in the Black Hole. During the night, about 43 of them died of suffocation. This incident served as justification for anti-Indian sentiment in England.

Blacklist, a list of people or companies that are boycotted or discriminated against. Governments in wartime have put together blacklists of companies in other countries suspected of dealing with the enemy. For example, Arab countries in the 1970's drew up a blacklist against U.S. firms that did business with Israel. In the 1950's, U.S. motion picture companies and radio and TV broadcasters placed workers accused of being pro-Communist on a blacklist that denied employment to many people for a number of years.

Black market, illegal market where goods are bought and sold in violation of government regulations. Black markets may develop where and when commodities are scarce and people are willing to pay high prices. The term may also apply to the unofficial trading of currency.

Blackout, covering or putting out of all lights to hide an area or object as protective measure against air attack. Blackouts were used especially as defense against Nazi air attacks during World War II. The term "blackout" is sometimes used to describe widespread electrical power failures.

Blake, Eubie (James Hubert Blake) (1883–1983), American composer and pianist, b. Baltimore, Md. Over a long career, Blake became known as a master of ragtime. Born of parents who had been slaves, he showed early musical talent and, in 1901, made his show business debut with a traveling medicine show. Blake and songwriter Noble Sissle together wrote such musicals as *Shuffle Along* (1921) and *The Chocolate*

Dandies (1924). One of Blake's biggest hits was the song, "I'm Just Wild About Harry," adopted by Harry S. Truman for the 1948 presidential campaign.

Blanchard, Doc (Felix Anthony Blanchard) (1924–   ), American football star and U.S. Army officer, b. McColl, S.C. He was an outstanding fullback for the U.S. Military Academy at West Point (1944–46), winning the Heisman Trophy as the best college football player (1945). He served in the Army (1946–71), rising to the rank of colonel. Blanchard was elected to the National Football Hall of Fame in 1956.

Blanchard (blon-SHAR), **Jean-Pierre François** (1753–1809), French balloonist, b. Les Andelys. He made his first balloon ascent in 1784. With American physician Dr. John Jeffries, he piloted the first air trip across the English Channel (1785). Blanchard made numerous first ascents in Europe and the United States (1785–96).

Bland, James Allen (1854–1911), American self-trained songwriter and minstrel performer, b. Flushing, N.Y. He wrote Virginia's official state song, "Carry Me Back to Old Virginny," in addition to "Oh Dem Golden Slippers," "In the Evening by the Moonlight," and "Climbing up the Goldden Stairs."

Blankers-Koen, Fanny (Francina Blankers-Koen) (1918–   ), Dutch track star, b. Amsterdam. At the age of 30 she won four gold medals in the 1948 Olympics, more than any other track-and-field competitor. She won the 100-m and 200-m sprints and the 80-m hurdles. She also led her team to a 400-m relay victory. Between 1938 and 1951 she set world records in seven individual events.

Blarney stone, an inscribed stone supposed to impart the gift of words, especially of flattery, persuasion, or deception, to anyone who kisses it. It is located in 15th-century Blarney Castle in County Cork, Ireland, where tourists or pilgrims lean over backward to reach it.

Blitzkrieg (BLITZ-kreeg) (German for "lightning war"), sudden military attack launched by combined air and ground forces with overwhelming speed and force, designed to cause an enemy's rapid surrender. It was first used by Germans during their invasion of Poland (1939).

Bloch, Ernest (1880–1959), Swiss-born American composer, b. Geneva. Bloch went to the United States in 1916, after first winning critical acclaim for his compositions in Europe. He was director of the Cleveland Institute of Music (1920–25) and director of the San Francisco Conservatory (1925–30). Much of his music, such as *Trois Poèmes Juifs, Schelomo,* and *Suite Hébraïque,* was inspired by his Jewish heritage. Bloch also wrote an opera, *Macbeth,* and the rhapsody *America.*

Bloch (BLOCK), **Konrad** (1912–   ), American biochemist, b. Neisse, Germany. Higgins professor of biochemistry at Harvard University (since 1954), he won the Nobel prize in physiology or medicine (1964) for studies that showed how cholesterol is made and used.

Blockade, the use of warships (and airplanes) to prevent arms, munitions, and other supplies of war from entering an enemy's ports. The right of blockade is recognized in international law, but it must first be declared to all parties concerned and then strictly enforced to be binding.

Bloomer, Amelia Jenks (1818–94), American reformer, b. Homer, N.Y. She wrote and lectured on temperance and women's rights and popularized a new style in women's dress designed by Elizabeth Smith Miller. Consisting of a short-skirted dress over trousers, it became known as a bloomer costume, and the pants as bloomers.

Bloomsbury Group, a circle of English intellectuals active from about 1905 to 1939. They often gathered informally in the Bloomsbury section of London, where several of them lived. Notable members were the novelist Virginia Woolf and her sister, the painter Vanessa Bell; their husbands, Leonard Woolf, an author and publisher, and Clive Bell, an art critic; the biographer Lytton Strachey; the novelist E. M. Forster; the painter Duncan Grant; and the economist John Maynard Keynes. Though not a formal movement, the group influenced the thinking of their time, especially in their rejection of the artistic and social values of the preceding Victorian period.

Blue laws, legislation that seeks to regulate matters of individual conscience or conduct, such as laws prohibiting drinking or working on Sunday. The term originated during colonial days in New Haven, Conn., where such laws were bound in blue paper.

Bluestocking, term for a literary or intellectual woman, sometimes implying only affected or superficial interest in intellectual matters. The term derived from a women's literary discussion group in 18th-century London, called The Bluestocking Club because of the informal blue stockings worn by a guest.

B'nai B'rith International ("B'nai B'rith" is from the Hebrew, meaning "sons of the covenant"), a Jewish organization founded in 1843 to unite Jews in cultural, social, and other activities that benefit themselves as well as all of humanity. There are over 3,500 local groups in many countries throughout the world. Major programs include the Hillel chapters on college campuses, the B'nai B'rith Youth Organization, and the Anti-Defamation League. B'nai B'rith International also sponsors a variety of educational programs and volunteer and counseling services. Its publications include the *International Jewish Monthly.* International headquarters are in Washington, D.C.

Body language, body signs, such as facial expressions, postures, and gestures, that reveal emotions and attitudes. For example, certain gestures and facial expressions signify pain among people everywhere. Body language can communicate a message that might not be conveyed through speech. Used together with speech, it can express attitudes that words alone cannot.

Bogart, Humphrey (1899–1957), American actor, b. New York, N.Y. His portrayals of hardened and cynical characters, starting with stage and screen versions of *The Petrified Forest* (1935–36), made him one of Hollywood's greatest box-office attractions. Appearing in over 50 motion pictures, he won the Academy Award for best actor for his performance in *The African Queen* (1951).

Bohemia, once a historical region in central Europe and now the geographical name for the western part of Czechoslo-

Bohemia (continued)

vakia. It is an agricultural and industrial region, famous for hops, glass, and ceramics. As a kingdom, Bohemia was at the height of its power during the 1300's. It was part of Austria from 1526 until 1918, when, at the end of World War I, it became part of the new nation of Czechoslovakia.

Bonaire (bo-NAIRE) (or Buen Aire; Buen Ayre), island of the Netherlands Antilles in the Caribbean Sea. Tourism is the main industry. The island is also a leading exporter of aloes (plants used in cosmetics and medicines). Kralendijk is the chief city.

Bonaparte family (Buonaparte in Italian), Corsican family of Italian descent, brought to prominence in Europe by French emperor **Napoleon I** (1769–1821). **Joseph** (1768–1844), brother of Napoleon I, was king of Naples (1806–08) and king of Spain (1808–13). **Louis** (1778–1846), brother of Napoleon I, was king of the Netherlands (1806–10). **Jérôme** (1784–1860), brother of Napoleon I, was king of Westphalia (1807–13). **François Charles Joseph,** or **Napoleon II** (1811–32), son of Napoleon I, was titular king of Rome. **Charles Louis Napoleon,** or **Napoleon III** (1808–73), son of Louis and nephew of Napoleon I, was emperor of France (1852–70).

Bond, Julian (1940–　), American politician and civil rights leader, b. Nashville, Tenn. Bond became a member of the Georgia House of Representatives in 1965. In 1966, he was barred from his seat for his stand against the Vietnam War, but the U.S. Supreme Court ruled that his constitutional rights had been violated. He served until 1975, when he became a state senator. Bond was a founder of the Student Non-violent (now National) Coordinating Committee (1960) and the first black to be nominated for vice-president (1968 Democratic convention).

Bonheur (bon-ER), **Rosa** (Marie Rosalie Bonheur) (1822–99), French painter, b. Bordeaux. She is known for spirited animal paintings, such as *Horse Fair*.

Bonhoeffer, Dietrich (1906–45), German Protestant theologian and pastor, b. Breslau. Barred from teaching because of his early opposition to Nazism, he was active in international activities of his church. He joined in underground German resistance to Hitler, was arrested in 1943, and hanged in 1945. In *Letters and Papers from Prison* published in 1951, he stressed the need for religion to involve itself in worldly activities.

Bonin (Ogasawara) **Islands,** volcanic islands in the Pacific Ocean south of Tokyo. Iwo Jima, one of the Bonin Islands, was the site of a major World War II battle. The islands came under U.S. control in 1946 and were returned to Japan in 1968.

Bontemps (BON-tomp), **Arna Wendell** (1902–73), American author, b. Alexandria, La. He was a distinguished member of a group of black writers and poets known as the Harlem Renaissance Group. His books include *The Story of the Negro* and *Black Thunder*.

Book of the Dead, collection of Egyptian hymns, prayers, and magic chants that made up funeral rites of ancient Egypt. It was based on the Osirian religion and remained in use from about 1500 B.C. to the early centuries of the Christian era. Only fragments written centuries apart exist today. Writings have been found on pyramid walls, on mummy cases, and on papyri in sarcophagi (coffins).

Boomerang, a flat, curved throwing stick. The returning boomerang, invented by Australian aborigines, is thrown mainly for sport. It circles in midair and returns near the thrower. Nonreturning boomerangs are used as hunting weapons. Boomerangs usually are made of a hard wood. They vary widely in size, with larger ones up to 30 in (76 cm) in length.

Boom town, a town that grows suddenly because of industrial activity or the discovery of a valuable natural resource. Boom towns, such as San Francisco, Calif., and Tombstone, Ariz., developed in the United States during the 1800's when the discovery of gold or silver brought an influx of people to the town. Rochester, N.Y., became a boom town with the opening of the Erie Canal.

Booth, Edwin Thomas (1833–93), American actor, b. Bel Air, Md. The greatest tragedian of his day, known especially for Shakespearean roles, he set a record when he appeared in 100 consecutive performances of *Hamlet*. He built the Booth Theater in New York, N.Y. (1869), and founded the Players Club there (1888). He was the brother of John Wilkes Booth, Lincoln's assassin.

Booth family, English family of evangelists associated with the Salvation Army. The Army was started by **General William** (1829–1912) as a Christian Mission in the Whitechapel district of London (1865). It later (1878) became the Salvation Army, with chapters around the world; **William Bramwell** (1856–1929) succeeded his father as general, and another son, **Ballington** (1859–1940), withdrew to found Volunteers of America; other descendants have continued in Salvation Army affairs.

Borg, Bjorn (1956–　), Swedish tennis player, b. Södertälje. Among his many victories were five consecutive singles titles at Wimbledon (1976–80)—a record in modern competition—and six French championships (1974–75, 1978–81), also a record. In 1975 Borg was a member of the first Swedish team to win the Davis Cup. He retired from tournament tennis in 1983.

Borges (BOR-hace), **Jorge Luis** (1899–1986), Argentine author and university professor, b. Buenos Aires. Raised and educated in Europe, Borges celebrated his native city in his first book of poetry, *Fervor de Buenos Aires* (1923). He is best known as a short-story writer. His stories are collected in *Ficciones* (1944) and other books. Borges became blind in the 1950's but continued to write by dictating his poems and stories.

Borgia (BOR-ja) **family,** noble Italian family of Spanish origin, powerful during the 15th and 16th centuries. **Alfonso** (1378–1458) became Pope Calixtus III (1455), and **Rodrigo** (1431?–1503) became Pope Alexander VI (1492). Rodrigo's son **Cesare** (1475?–1507) was a cardinal who left his office and tried to conquer a kingdom in central Italy. Cesare was known for his cruelty and treachery. His methods are praised in Machiavelli's *The Prince*. Rodrigo's daughter **Lucrezia** (1480–1519) was a great patron of the arts. She was reputed to have been cruel and villainous, but probably did not commit many of the crimes of which she has been accused.

Borja Cevallos, Rodrigo (1935–   ), Ecuadorean political leader, b. Quito. He was president of Ecuador from 1988 to 1992. A lawyer, Borja entered politics by winning election to the Ecuadorean Congress (1962) and was a founder (1970) of the Democratic Left Party. He twice previously (1979 and 1984) had been his party's unsuccessful candidate for the presidency.

Bormann (BOR-monn), **Martin Ludwig** (1900–45?), German Nazi leader, b. Halberstadt. Chief of staff of the Nazi Party (1933–41), he became Hitler's secretary and closest adviser in 1941. He was sentenced in absentia at the Nuremberg Trials (1946) to die as a war criminal. For many years Bormann's fate was unknown, until evidence appeared in 1972 that he had probably died in 1945 during the final battle for Berlin.

Bossy, Mike (Michael Bossy) (1957–   ), Canadian hockey player, b. Montreal, Que. A right wing for the New York Islanders of the National Hockey League (NHL), Bossy scored at least 50 goals in each of his first nine seasons, a feat no one else has ever accomplished. He was NHL Rookie of the Year in 1978. Bossy helped lead the Islanders to four consecutive Stanley Cups (1980–83).

Botha (BO-ta), **Pieter Willem** (1916–   ), South African political leader, b. Orange Free State. He served as prime minister of South Africa (1978–84) and as state president (1984–89). His government's adoption of a new constitution (1984) gave limited representation to South Africa's Coloureds and Asians. Some restrictions against blacks also were reduced. But blacks were still denied political rights in South Africa, and Botha's last years in office were marked by increasingly violent anti-government demonstrations in black townships.

Bourbon, House of, French royal family whose members ruled France from 1589 to 1792 and from 1814 to 1830. Louis XIV (reigned 1641–1715) was among the most powerful and influential rulers in European history. Louis XVI (reigned 1774–92) was removed from power and finally put to death in the French Revolution. The reign of the House of Bourbon was briefly restored in the 1800's. A grandson of Louis XIV became Philip V of Spain in 1700, and his descendants reigned there almost continuously into the 1900's. Other Bourbons ruled several principalities that are now part of Italy.

Bowditch (BOWD-itch), **Nathaniel** (1773–1838), American mathematician and astronomer, b. Salem, Mass. A self-educated man, he went to sea in 1795 as a clerk and became a ship's master in 1802. His revision of J. H. Moore's *The Practical Navigator,* which appeared as *The New American Practical Navigator* in 1802, was made the standard authority of the United States Navy Department. Bowditch worked on astronomical problems in his leisure time and wrote articles on the subject.

Bowdoin (BO-din), **James** (1726–90), American statesman, b. Boston, Mass. He was a member of Massachusetts General Court (1753–56) and Council (1757–69) and of the Constitutional Convention (1779). As governor of state (1785–87) he put down Shays' Rebellion. He was a delegate to national constitutional convention and first president of American Academy of Arts and Sciences (1780–90). Bowdoin College in Maine is named for him.

Bowell, Sir Mackenzie (1823–1917), Canadian prime minister, b. Rickinghall, England. Prime minister of Canada from 1894–96, he was one of only two Canadians to serve in that office at the same time they held Senate seats. He went to Canada at age 10 and became a printer's apprentice. He rose to owner and editor of the Belleville *Intelligencer* before being elected to the House of Commons in 1867. He became a senator in 1892 and served as minister of customs and of trade before becoming prime minister in December, 1894. Dissatisfaction with his leadership arose in Bowell's cabinet, and he resigned in April, 1896. He continued to serve in the Senate until 1906.

Boxer Rebellion (1900), an uprising against foreigners in China. Boxers was a name given to a Chinese secret society called the Righteous and Harmonious Fists (I-ho ch'üan), who opposed foreigners for their economic and political control over parts of China and their influence on Chinese society. Boxers believed that they could not be harmed by foreign bullets. Violence spread when the Chinese empress ordered all foreigners to be killed. About 500 foreigners were besieged in Peking for 55 days until an international rescue force captured the city.

Boycott, refusal to deal with an individual, organization, or country to show disapproval or to force acceptance of demands. Boycotts are used by organized labor against employers whom they consider to be unfair and sometimes by nations for political purposes. The term originated in Ireland when **Captain Charles Cunningham Boycott** (1832–97) treated tenants on his estate so unjustly that they refused to deal with him.

Boys' State, convention, sponsored by the American Legion, of high school boys, usually juniors, chosen for leadership, character, scholarship, and service. It has been held annually (since 1935), usually at a college or university. Its object is to show members how government operates. A similar program, Girls' State, is run for girls.

Bradbury, Ray (1920–   ), American writer, b. Waukegan, Ill. Bradbury is best known for collections of science fiction short stories, such as *The Martian Chronicles* (1950). Many of his stories warn that human values may be lost as technology expands and the use of machines grows. The novels *Fahrenheit 451* (1953) and *Dandelion Wine* (1957) and the short story collections *The Illustrated Man* (1951) and *The Toynbee Convector* (1988) are among his other popular works.

Bradley, Omar Nelson (1893–1981), American army officer, b. Clark, Mo. During World War II he led the U.S. First Army in the Normandy invasion on D-Day (June 6, 1944). As commander of the Twelfth Army Group (1945) he commanded the largest American force ever to serve under one field leader. He became a general of the Army (5-star general) in 1945. He served as head of the Veterans Administration (1945–48), chief of staff of the Army (1948–49), first chairman of Joint Chiefs of Staff (1949–53), and chairman of the military committee of NATO (1949–53). Bradley was chairman of the board of the Bulova Watch Company from 1958 to 1973.

Bradley, Thomas (1917–   ), American politician, b. Calvert, Texas. He was the first black to become mayor of Los Angeles, California (1973). He was re-elected in 1977, 1981, and 1985. In 1989 he was elected to an unprecedented fifth term. Bradley served on the Los Angeles police force from 1940 to 1961. He then established a private law practice. He was a

Bradley, Thomas (continued)
member of the Los Angeles city council from 1963 until his election as mayor. He ran unsuccessfully for governor of California in 1982 and 1986.

Brady, Diamond Jim (James Buchanan Brady) (1856–1917), American financier, b. New York, N.Y. A longtime employee of New York Central Railroad, he made his fortune as a promoter and executive for companies manufacturing railroad equipment. His nickname comes from his love of valuable jewels. He used part of his money for producing Broadway shows and for charity.

Brady, Mathew B. (1823?–96), American photographer, b. Warren County, N.Y. In 1845, Brady started a series of photographic portraits, which were published in *A Gallery of Illustrious Americans* (1850). However, he is chiefly remembered for his photographic documentation of the American Civil War (1861–65). He and his assistants traveled with the Union armies, and their photos provide a fascinating pictorial account of that conflict. In addition, about one third of the 100 known photographs of Abraham Lincoln were taken by Brady. His negatives are preserved in the National Archives and the Library of Congress.

Brain drain, migration of specialists and technicians from one country to another. The term was originally used with special reference to the immigration of British engineers, doctors, and scientists to the United States and to countries of the Commonwealth. However, similar brain drains have affected other countries. They are particularly serious when underdeveloped countries lose highly trained people.

Brainstorming, method used to solve problems through unstructured group discussion. The method is based on the idea that more effective solutions can be reached through the interplay of several minds than by one individual alone.

Brainwashing, the common term for systematically forcing people to accept ideas and information against their will or without their knowledge. The term became well known during the Korean War (1950–53), when brainwashing was used to change the thinking of prisoners of war. The prisoners were deprived of food, rest, and the company of others. Some gradually accepted the beliefs of their Communist captors rather than endure further harsh treatment. In recent years various cults have been accused of brainwashing members by subjecting them to lives of strict discipline, without freedom of thought.

Brandeis, Louis Dembitz (1856–1941), U.S. Supreme Court justice, b. Louisville, Ky. Brandeis studied law at Harvard and became a successful lawyer. He was named to the Supreme Court in 1916 by President Woodrow Wilson and served as an associate justice until 1939. On the court, Brandeis became known as a crusader for social justice. His ideas strongly influenced the development of the New Deal programs of the 1930's. He was also a leader of the Jewish community and strongly supported the creation of a Jewish homeland in Palestine. Brandeis University in Waltham, Mass., was named in his honor.

Brando, Marlon (1924–   ), American actor, b. Omaha, Neb. He appeared on Broadway in *I Remember Mama, Candida,* and *A Streetcar Named Desire.* Hollywood introduced him to the film public in 1950 in *The Men.* He then did the film

version of *A Streetcar Named Desire* and followed it with a memorable performance in *On the Waterfront,* for which he won an Academy Award in 1954. Other films include *The Young Lions, Mutiny on the Bounty, The Godfather,* and *Apocalypse Now.*

Brandt (BRONT), **Willy** (Herbert Frahm) (1913–92), German political leader, b. Lübeck. A member of the Social Democratic Party, he fled Germany when Nazis gained power. He was a journalist in Norway and Sweden (1933–45) and correspondent for Scandinavian newspapers in Berlin, Germany (1945–47). He returned to Germany and regained German citizenship in 1948. He was member of Bundestag (1949–57), president of Berlin House of Representatives (1955–57), and governing mayor of West Berlin (1957–66). He was vice-chancellor and foreign minister of West Germany (1966–69), and became chancellor in 1969. He resigned in 1974 but remained chairman of the Social Democratic Party until 1987. He was awarded the Nobel peace prize in 1971.

Branley, Franklyn M. (1915–   ), American science writer, b. New Rochelle, N.Y. A graduate of New York and Columbia Universities, he has taught high school science and has written about 50 books on all phases of science for young people from beginning readers up. Among his books are *Air Is All Around You, The Big Dipper,* and *Man in Space to the Moon.*

Braxton, Carter (1736–97), American statesman, b. Newington, Va. He was a member of the Virginia House of Burgesses between 1761 and 1775 and then served at the Continental Congress (1775–76, 1777–83, 1785), where he signed the Declaration of Independence.

Breakwater, a wall-like structure built out into the sea or a lake to break the force of the waves and so protect the harbor or beach. A breakwater differs from a jetty, which has the function of directing the course of water to make it carry sediment farther out.

Brennan, William Joseph (1906–   ), American jurist, b. Newark, N.J. After graduation from the University of Pennsylvania (1928), he earned his law degree from Harvard (1931). He practiced law in Newark until 1949. From 1949 to 1956 he served successively as judge of the New Jersey Supreme Court, Appelate Division; and the State Supreme Court. In 1956 Eisenhower appointed Brennan associate justice of the U.S. Supreme Court. He served until his retirement in 1990. Justice Brennan was identified with the more liberal element in his opinions dealing with civil rights.

Brewster, Sir David (1781–1868), Scottish physicist, b. Jedburgh. He made important studies of light and lenses, discovering the law, named for him, that deals with reflected light. His theories led him to invent such instruments as the kaleidoscope and a lens used in lighthouses.

Briggs, Raymond (1934–   ), English illustrator, b. London. He was awarded the Kate Greenaway Medal in 1966 for *The Mother Goose Treasury,* which contains almost 900 illustrations of nursery rhymes. His other works include *Father Christmas* (1973), *The Snowman* (1978), *When the Wind Blows* (1982), and *The Tin-Pot Foreign General and the Old Woman* (1985).

British Indian Ocean Territory (Chagos Archipelago), British dependency in the Indian Ocean. The territory was formed in 1965 to provide defense and communications bases for Britain and the United States, including a U.S. military base on the island of Diego Garcia.

Brooks, Gwendolyn (1917–), American poet, b. Topeka, Kans. She was the first black woman to win a Pulitzer prize (1950), which was awarded to her for her collection of poems *Annie Allen*. Her other collections include *A Street in Bronzeville* and *Bean Eaters*.

Brooks, Mel (Melvin Kaminsky) (1926?–), American comedy writer and filmmaker, b. Brooklyn, N.Y. His film *The Producers* won an Academy Award for best original screenplay of 1968. Brooks was a television comedy writer in the 1950's. He later became known for playing the comic 2,000-Year-Old Man character on television and record albums. His other films include *Blazing Saddles* (1974), *Silent Movie* (1976), *High Anxiety* (1977), *History of the World—Part I* (1981), and *Spaceballs* (1987).

Brotherhood/Sisterhood Week, observance dedicated to increasing understanding among people of different ethnic and religious backgrounds. Established in 1946 by the National Conference of Christians and Jews, it is celebrated during the week of Washington's birthday.

Brown, Claude (1937–), American author, b. New York, N.Y. His autobiography, *Manchild in the Promised Land* (1965), is a description of life in a black ghetto.

Brown, Jim (James Nathaniel Brown) (1936–), American football player, b. St. Simons Island, Ga. Brown is considered by many to be the greatest running back of all time. During his National Football Association career as a fullback for the Cleveland Browns (1957–65), he gained 12,312 yards. This was the career rushing record until it was broken by Walter Payton in 1984. Brown was an all-American at Syracuse University in lacrosse as well as football. As a professional, he was named NFL Player of the Year in 1958 and 1963. In 1971, Brown was inducted into the Professional Football Hall of Fame. After he retired from football, he became a movie actor.

Brown, Marcia (1918–), American author and artist, b. Rochester, N.Y. She illustrates books for children. Three of her books—*Cinderella* (1955), *Once a Mouse* (1962), and *Shadow* (1983)—won Caldecott Medals.

Brown, Margaret Wise (1910–52), author and editor of children's books, b. New York, N.Y. Under the pen name Golden MacDonald and under her own name she wrote more than 60 books, including *Goodnight Moon, Little Lost Lamb,* the "Noisy" books, and *Little Island*.

Brown, Sterling Allan (1901–89), American poet, author, and professor, b. Washington, D.C. He incorporated black folk themes and exact dialect into his poetry. He was editor of the Federal Writer's Project (1936–39) and staff member of the Carnegie-Myrdal Study (1939). He became the first black professor at Vassar (1945). He wrote *Southern Road* (1932) and co-edited *The Negro Caravan* (1941).

Brown, William Wells (1816?–84), American reformer, historian, and writer, b. Lexington, Ky. A slave, he escaped to Ohio and adopted the name Wells Brown from a Quaker who had helped him. He worked as steward on a Lake Erie steamboat and helped many blacks to freedom (1843–49). He lectured before abolitionist societies in New York and Massachusetts and was also interested in the temperance movement, women's suffrage, and prison reform. His works include *Narrative of William W. Brown: A Fugitive Slave,* and *The Black Man: His Antecedents, His Genius and His Achievements.*

Browning, John Moses (1855–1926), American inventor of firearms, b. Ogden, Utah. He received the first rifle patent (1879) and devised automatic pistols, repeating rifles, and machine guns. He manufactured arms with his brother, **Jonathan Edmund Browning** (1859–1939). Browning machine guns and automatic rifles (known as BAR's) were used extensively by the United States in World War II and in the Korean War.

Brubeck, Dave (David Warren Brubeck) (1920–), American jazz pianist and composer, b. Concord, Calif. He began his career with small dance bands in San Francisco. He organized and played piano with the Dave Brubeck Quartet in the 1950's. Later, with his three sons, he formed a group called Two Generations of Brubeck. His many recordings include *Jazz Impressions of Japan* and *Adventures in Time.*

Bruce, Blanche Kelso (1841–98), American politician, b. Farmville, Va. He held several local and state offices, then served (1875–81) as one of the two black senators from Mississippi during the Reconstruction period. He was recorder of deeds in Washington, D.C. (1889–95).

Brummell, Beau (George Bryan Brummell) (1778–1840), English dandy and wit, b. London. A close friend of the Prince of Wales (later George IV), he set standards of fashion, including trousers and black evening wear, that are still popular. He gambled away a large inheritance and fled to France in 1816 to avoid his creditors. He died in an insane asylum in Caen.

Brundtland (BRUNT-lahnd), **Gro Harlem** (1939–), Norwegian political leader, b. Oslo. She served briefly as Norway's first woman prime minister in 1981. A physician, she worked in government health services and as minister of environment before becoming vice-chairman of the Labor Party in 1975. She was named leader of the Party in 1981, and in 1986 she took office as prime minister a second time.

Brunhoff, Jean de (1899–1937), French author and illustrator, b. Paris. His *Babar* stories have become classics for children. His books include *The Story of Babar, The Little Elephant,* and *Travels of Babar.* Babar's adventures have been continued by Jean's son, **Laurent de Brunhoff** (1925–).

Brzezinski, Zbigniew (brezh-IN-skee, ZHBIG-nyef) (1928–), American government official and author, b. Warsaw, Poland. He served as assistant to the president for national security affairs from 1977 to 1981. Brzezinski is a noted authority on Soviet politics. He was a member of the policy planning staff of the U.S. Department of State from 1966 to 1968. He also served on the faculties of Harvard and Columbia

Brzezinski, Zbigniew (continued)
universities. His published works include *The Soviet Bloc: Unity and Conflict* (1960), *Between Two Ages* (1970), and *Power and Principle* (1983).

Buber (BU-ber), **Martin** (1878–1965), Jewish religious philosopher, b. Vienna, Austria. A professor of comparative religion at the University of Frankfurt (1923–33), he was forced by Nazis to leave Germany. He went to Israel and became professor of social philosophy at Hebrew University in Jerusalem (1938–51). He played an important role in the Zionist movement and in reviving literature and culture of the Hasidic sect. Buber's philosophy is set forth in *I and Thou* (1923). In this book he compares the ways people relate to objects, to each other, and to God.

Bubka, Sergei (1963–   ), Soviet pole vaulter, b. Voroshilovgrad. After setting his first world record in 1983, he established himself as one of the best pole vaulters of all time by breaking his own record eight times over the next five years. At the time of his ninth record-setting vault of 19 ft 10½ in (6.06 m), Bubka had to his credit the six highest pole vaults ever. He won the gold medal in this event in the 1988 Olympic Games.

Buckley, William F., Jr. (1925–   ), American writer and editor, b. New York, N.Y. He was a leading representative of conservative political thought in the United States. In 1955 he founded the conservative magazine *National Review*, and in 1962 he became a syndicated newspaper columnist. He also became known for his sharp wit and debating ability as host of the television program *Firing Line*, which began in 1966. His books include *God and Man at Yale* (1951), *Atlantic High* (1982), and *Overdrive* (1983). He also wrote spy novels, including *Saving the Queen* (1976) and *The Story of Henri Tod* (1984).

Budge, Don (John Donald Budge) (1915–), American tennis player, b. Oakland, Calif. He was first to achieve tennis "Grand Slam," winning U.S., British, Australian, and French singles championships in same year (1938). He became a professional player (1939) and thereafter won several professional championships.

Bugging, or electronic eavesdropping, is the practice of using supersensitive listening devices for the purpose of intercepting private conversations. The propriety of government use of these devices for law enforcement has been controversial. In the United States, it is regulated by law.

Bulganin (bull-GAN-yin), **Nikolai Aleksandrovich** (1895–1975), Russian political leader, b. Nizhni-Novgorod (now Gorki). He joined the Communist Party in 1917 and served with the secret police (1918–22). He held various Party offices, including membership on the Central Committee (1939–61), Politburo (1948–52), and Party Presidium (1952–59). He was minister of defense (1953–55), member of the Supreme Soviet (1937–58), and premier (chairman) of the Council of Ministers of the Soviet Union (1955–58) until removed from office on a charge of conspiring against the Party.

Bumbry, Grace (1937–), American soprano, b. St. Louis, Mo. She sang with the State Opera in Basel, Switzerland (1960–63), and was the first black to sing at the Bayreuth Festival in Germany. Her Metropolitan Opera debut (1965) was as Princess Eboli in *Don Carlos*. Her other roles include the title role in *Carmen,* Amneris in *Aida,* and Venus in *Tannhäuser.*

Bunyan, John (1628–88), English writer and preacher, b. Elstow, Bedfordshire. His masterpiece is *The Pilgrim's Progress* (1678), a symbolic account of a Christian's religious life. Bunyan, the son of a tinker (a mender of household utensils), served as a soldier before taking up his father's trade. In 1653 he joined a nonconformist church (one that was not in full agreement with the Church of England) and in 1657 began to preach. In 1660 he was arrested for preaching unlawfully and was imprisoned for more than eleven years. He wrote many religious books both in prison and after his release, but *The Pilgrim's Progress* is the best known. This powerful allegory (a work using fictional characters and events to express general truths) has been translated into more than 100 languages.

Bureaucracy, a term generally used to refer to the administrative machinery of a government. It is sometimes applied to any large organization divided into many departments or bureaus with a hierarchy of employees each responsible to a superior. It is often used as a term of disparagement.

Burleigh (BUR-li), **Henry Thacker** (1866–1949), American singer and composer, b. Erie, Pa. He introduced black spirituals on concert stages in the United States and abroad, and he preserved, in writing, folk songs of black people, which were previously handed down orally. His best-known works include songs "Little Mother of Mine," "Deep River," and "Just You."

Burne-Jones, Sir Edward Coley (1833–98), English painter, b. Birmingham. He was associated with pre-Raphaelite artists Dante Gabriel Rossetti and William Morris. His paintings are characterized by dreamlike, romantic idealism. They include *The Golden Stairs, The Depths of the Sea,* and *King Cophetua and the Beggar Maid.* He also designed tapestries and stained-glass windows for firm of William Morris.

Burnford, Sheila (1918–), Canadian author, b. Scotland. She wrote the popular animal stories *The Incredible Journey* and *Field of Noon,* as well as articles for *Punch,* the Glasgow *Herald,* and *Canadian Poetry.*

Burningham, John Mackintosh (1936–   ), English author and illustrator of children's books and graphic designer, b. Farnham, Surrey. He has received several awards for his illustrations, among them two Kate Greenaway Medals—in 1963 for *Borka: The Adventures of a Goose with No Feathers* and in 1970 for *Mr. Gumpy's Outing.* In addition to his own books, he has illustrated the work of others, including Ian Fleming's *Chitty Chitty Bang Bang: The Magical Car* (1964). Burningham's design work has been exhibited by the American Institute of Graphic Arts.

Burns, George (Nathan Birnbaum) (1896–   ), American comedian, b. New York, N.Y. Burns and **Gracie Allen** (1906–64), his wife, were a remarkably successful comedy team. She retired in 1958, and Burns continued to perform alone on television and in nightclubs and movies. A cigar and unfinished songs were his trademarks. He won an Academy Award as best supporting actor of 1976 for his role in *The Sunshine Boys.* His other films include *Oh, God!* (1977) and *Going in Style* (1979).

Burns, Tommy (Noah Bursso) (1881–1955), Canadian boxer, b. Hanover, Ontario. He won heavyweight title (1906) in 20-round decision over Marvin Hart but lost title (1908) to Jack Johnson in a fight so brutal police had to stop it in 14th round.

Burroughs (BURR-ose), **John** (1837–1921), American naturalist and writer, b. near Roxbury, N.Y. He was the author of many works based on his observations of nature, particularly birds. His writings showed a poetic appreciation for and deep knowledge of nature. He was a frequent contributor to *Atlantic Monthly* and wrote the first biography of his close friend Walt Whitman. Other books include *Wake-Robin* and *Birds and Poets*.

Burroughs, William Seward (1855–98), American inventor, b. Rochester, N.Y. He worked on machines for solving arithmetic problems and organized American Arithmometer Co. to manufacture them (1885). He was granted a patent for first practicable calculating machine (1888).

Burton, Richard (Richard Jenkins) (1925–84), British actor, b. Pontrhydfen, Wales. His first stage appearance (1943) was in *Druid's Rest* in Liverpool. He acted in various Shakespearean plays in England and the United States and in films such as *Look Back in Anger, Becket, The Spy Who Came in from the Cold*, and *Who's Afraid of Virginia Woolf?* One of his best-known roles was as King Arthur in the Broadway musical *Camelot*.

Burton, Virginia Lee (1909–68), American illustrator and author of children's books, b. Newton Center, Mass. She was awarded the Caldecott medal (1943) for *The Little house*. Her other books include *Katy and the Big Snow* and *Mike Mulligan and His Steam Shovel*.

Bushido (from Japanese, meaning "the way of the warrior"), Japanese system of ethical conduct developed from the code of samurai (warrior class). It includes loyalty to the overlord, honor in family and social relationships, and courage in all conflicts, extending to the duty of harakiri, or ritual suicide. It influences Japanese life, although the formal code no longer applies.

Bushmen, an African tribal people living in southern Africa, also known as the San. They are of slight build and are thought to be related to Pygmies. They live in small nomadic bands, each with its own leader.

Byars, Betsy (1928–   ), American author, b. Charlotte, N.C. She won the Newbery medal in 1971 for *The Summer of the Swans*. Her other books for young readers include *Clementine (1962), The Midnight Fox (1968), The Night Swimmers,* which won an American Book Award in 1981, *The Two-Thousand-Pound Goldfish (1982)*, and *The Burning Questions of Bingo Brown (1988)*.

Bylaws, laws or rules by which a city, corporation, or other organization governs its affairs and members. In the case of a municipality a bylaw has the force of law, whereas in other organizations it is merely an agreement among members. The term also refers to a secondary rule subordinate to a constitution.

Index

Bacon's Rebellion   U:175
  Indian wars   I:202
  Virginia, history of   V:359
Bacteria   B:10–12; M:208, 275; *picture(s)* A:264;
    M:274 *see also* Antiseptics; Bacterial diseases;
    Disinfectants; Microbiology
  aid digestion   D:163
  antibiotics   A:306; D:334
  bacteriostatic antiseptics   D:214
  cell structure of   L:200
  cheesemaking   D:12
  dental caries   T:44
  fermentation   F:91
  food spoilage   F:341, 351–52
  gene splicing   G:89–91
  genetic research in the 20th century   B:202
  insulin now produced from   V:369
  kingdoms of living things   K:251
  Koch, Robert, is called the father of bacteriology
      K:291
  nitrogen fixation   E:54
  pasteurization of milk   D:9–10
  penicillin kills bacteria, *picture(s)* A:307
  place in the food chain   L:205
  plant pests   P:286–87
  smallest cells   C:159
  soils, microorganisms in   S:232
  vitamin K produced by   V:371
  waste-water treatment   S:33
  white cells defend body against   B:257
  yogurt   D:11
Bacterial diseases   B:11; D:181–83, 208
  boils   D:195
  diphtheria   D:192
  gonorrhea   D:193
  impetigo   D:195
  pneumonia   D:199
  scarlet fever   D:201
  streptococcal sore throats   D:202
  syphilis   D:202–3
  tetanus   D:203
  tonsillitis   D:203–4
  tuberculosis   D:204–5
  typhoid fever   D:205
  typhus   D:205
  whooping cough   D:205
Bacterial viruses *see* Bacteriophages
Bacteriological warfare *see* Biological warfare
Bacteriology laboratories   M:209
Bacteriophages (bac-TER-i-o-phages) (bacterial viruses)
    V:364–65; *picture(s)* V:361
Bactrian camels   C:35; H:212; *picture(s)* H:213
Bad Axe, Battle of (1832)   I:75, 205
Baden-Powell (BADE-en PO-well), Agnes (English
    founder of Girl Guides)   G:218
Baden-Powell, Robert (English soldier, founder of
    scouting movement)   B:360; G:218
Badger baiting (sport)   O:257
Badgers   O:256–57; *picture(s)* A:269
Badger State (nickname for Wisconsin)   W:197
Badges (in heraldry)   H:112
Badges, merit *see* Merit badges
Badges of honor *see* Medals
Badlands (area in Great Plains region, North America)
  Alberta (Canada)   A:164; *picture(s)* A:166
  Montana   M:430, 438
  North Dakota   N:324; *picture(s)* N:323
  South Dakota   S:315; *picture(s)* E:17; S:314
Badlands National Park (South Dakota)   S:322;
    picture(s) S:314

Badminton (sport)   B:13–14
  Olympic sport   O:107
Badshahi Mosque (Lahore, Pakistan), *picture(s)* P:37
Baekeland (BAKE-land), Leo Hendrik (American chemist
    and inventor)   P:324
Baer (BARE), Karl Ernst von (German biologist)   B:497
Baer, Max (American boxer)   B:353
Baffin, William (English navigator)   N:338
Baffin Bay (part of the North Atlantic Ocean)   B:497
Baffin Island (Arctic Ocean)   C:55; I:362; N:340;
    picture(s) C:53
Baganda (a people of Africa)   U:4–5
Bagasse (ba-GASS) (fibrous part of sugarcane)   S:484
  sweet grasses   G:319
Bagatelle (musical form)   M:543
Bagaza, Jean-Baptiste (Burundi president)   B:462
Baggage (personal belongings of travelers)   A:126–27
Baggataway (bag-GAT-a-way) (Canadian Indian game)
  lacrosse is a national sport of Canada   L:20–21
Baghdad (capital of Iraq)   B:15; I:315; *picture(s)*
    M:298
  capital of Islamic empire   I:349
  Kadhimain Mosque, *picture(s)* I:349
Bag ladies *see* Homeless people
Bagnell Dam (Missouri), *picture(s)* M:369
Bagpipe   F:330; *picture(s)* D:29; F:329; U:55
Baguios (BOG-yos) (hurricanes in Philippines)   H:292
Bahá'í (BA-ha-i) Faith   B:497; R:152
  headquarters in Haifa (Israel)   I:370
Bahamas (ba-HA-mas)   B:16–17
  Columbus' discovery   C:446
  flag, *picture(s)* F:239
Bahasa Indonesia (national language of Indonesia)
    I:206; S:330
Bahasa Malaysia (national language of Malaysia)   M:54;
    S:330
Bahia (Brazil) *see* Salvador
Bahrain (bah-RAIN) (emirate in the Persian Gulf)
    B:18–19
  flag, *picture(s)* F:230
Bahutu *see* Hutu
Baikal (by-KALL), Lake (Russia)   L:31; R:361–62;
    U:39; *picture(s)* L:25
Baikal-Amur Mainline Railroad (Russia)   S:170
Bail (in law)   C:567
Bailey (of a castle)   C:131; F:375; *picture(s)* C:132
Bailey, James Anthony (American circus owner)   M:272
Bailey, Pearl (American entertainer)   B:497
Bainbridge, William (American naval officer)   N:179
Baird, John Logie (Scottish inventor)   B:497; T:66
Baird, Spencer Fullerton (American zoologist and
    naturalist)   B:497
Bait (for fishing)   F:205–6
Bait casting (fishing)   F:206–9
Baja (BA-ha) California (Mexico)   M:244
  off-road racing   A:538
Bajans (name for the people of Barbados)   B:60
Bakelite (BAKE-el-ite) (plastic)   P:324
Baker, Dorsey S. (American railroad builder)   W:25
Baker, Ellen (American astronaut), *picture(s)* S:344
Baker, Howard Henry, Jr. (American politician)   T:88
Baker, James A., III (United States secretary of state),
    picture(s) S:436
Baker, Josephine (American singer and dancer)   B:497
Baker, Russell Wayne (American writer)   B:497
Baker, Samuel White (British explorer)   U:6
Baker Island *see* Howland, Baker, and Jarvis islands
Baker v. Carr (1962)   S:509
Baking and bakery products   B:385–88b; C:533 *see
    also* Flour and flour milling

Baking and bakery products (continued)
metric conversions for the kitchen, *table(s)* W:113
recipes for cookies and cupcakes R:116
Baking powder B:386, 388b
Bakke decision *see* Affirmative action
Bakken Amusement Park (Copenhagen, Denmark)
P:79
Baklava (pastry) F:335–36
Bakongo (African people) A:260; C:498
Bakony Mountains (Hungary) H:285
Bakota (a people of Gabon) G:2
Bakst, Léon (Russian artist)
costume for *The Firebird*, *picture(s)* R:381
Baku (capital of Azerbaijan) A:571–72; U:43
Balafo (African musical instrument), *picture(s)* A:79
Balaguer, Joaquín (Dominican president) D:285
Balakirev, Mily Alekseevich (Russian composer) R:381
Balaklava (bahl-uh-KLAH-vuh), Battle of (1854)
B:498; C:577
Balance (in design) D:133–34
interior decorating I:258
Balance, sense of E:5–6
Balance beam (use in gymnastics) G:432; *picture(s)*
G:433
Balance of nature E:54–55, 296
cat family C:136
communities of living things affect each other
K:259
Balance of payments (of trade) I:275–76
Balance of power (among nations) I:274
disarmament D:180
Balance scales (for weighing) W:114
Balance sheet (in bookkeeping) B:312
Balance wheel (in watches and clocks) C:370–71;
W:44
Balanchine, George (Russian-American ballet
choreographer) B:30, 33, 498; D:26
Allegro Brillante (ballet), *picture(s)* B:33
Jewels (ballet), *picture(s)* B:32
Balante (African people) G:407
Balata (ba-LA-ta) (gum) R:185
Balaton (BALL-a-ton), Lake (Hungary) H:285; L:31
Balbas, Jeronimo (Mexican sculptor) L:64
Balboa (bol-BO-a) (Panama) P:47
Balboa, Vasco Núñez de (Spanish explorer) B:20;
E:412; P:48
Panama City statue, *picture(s)* P:45
Balchen (BOL-ken), Bernt (American aviator) B:498
Balcones (bal-CO-nes) Escarpment (Texas) T:126
Balcony (second floor of a theater) T:158
Balcony, The (painting by Manet), *picture(s)* I:104
Bald cypress (tree), *picture(s)* T:302 *see also* Cypress
state tree of Louisiana, *picture(s)* L:299
Bald eagles A:277; B:225; E:2; *picture(s)* B:207,
217, 230; C:520; U:89
endangered species E:211
Great Seal of the United States G:329
Balder (Norse god) N:279
Baldness (loss of hair) H:6
Baldwin, James (American writer) A:214a; B:21;
N:363
Baldwin, Matthias William (American industrialist and
philanthropist) B:498
Baldwin, Robert (Canadian statesman) C:74; O:135
Baldwin, Stanley (English statesman) B:498
Baldwin I (French crusader and emperor of
Constantinople) B:498
Baldwin I (French crusader and king of Jerusalem)
B:498; C:589

Balearic (bal-e-ARR-ic) Islands (off the east coast of
Spain) I:362; S:378
Baleen (ba-LEEN) (whalebone) W:147, 152
Baleen whales (mysticetes) M:70; W:149, 152
Balers (farm machines) F:58; *picture(s)* D:8; F:59
Balfour, Arthur James (British statesman) B:21
Balfour Declaration (1917) B:21; J:110; Z:379
Bali (BA-li) (Indonesia) I:206, 209–10
dancing is an ancient art D:32; *picture(s)* D:31;
I:210
funeral ceremony (cremation), *picture(s)* F:495
Balk (in baseball) B:83
Balkan Mountains B:22, 441
Balkans B:22–23
Albania A:159–62
architecture: late Byzantine churches B:494
Bulgaria B:439–44
Crimean War C:577
Macedonia M:4
Romania R:296–301
Serbia S:124–25
Slovenia S:199–200
World War I W:275
World War II W:290
Yugoslavia Y:354–59
Balkan Wars B:22–23, 444
Balkhash (bol-KASH), Lake (Kazakhstan) L:32
Ball (used in sports and games) B:23
antique baseball started museum B:88
baseball B:78
basketball B:95–95h
bowling ball B:348–49
golf G:253, 261
handball H:18
jai alai J:12
paddleball R:34a
paddle tennis P:11
platform tennis R:34c
racquetball R:34b
soccer S:217
softball S:229
squash racquets R:34
volleyball V:387
Ball, Lucille (American actress and TV producer)
B:498
I Love Lucy, *picture(s)* T:70
Balla (BA-la), Giacomo (Italian futurist painter) M:391
Dog on a Leash (painting), *picture(s)* M:390
Ballade (bal-LOD) (musical form) M:543
Ballade (poetic form) P:353
Ballads (BAL-lads) B:24; L:259; M:543
American folk ballads F:310–11
country music C:564
folklore F:303
folk music F:318, 328
narrative poems suitable for singing P:354
Scandinavian literature S:58f
Spanish romances S:389
Ball-and-socket joints (in the skeleton) S:184b
Ballast (for railroad roadbeds) R:78
Ballast (weights) F:251
Ballet (BAL-lay) B:25–33; D:25–26, 34
Canada C:67
dance music development D:35–36
musical comedy's first use as part of the plot
M:550
New York City Ballet at Lincoln Center L:248
Stravinsky's ballet music R:382; S:467
Ballet at the Paris Opera (drawing by Degas), *picture(s)*
D:306

Ballet Russe de Monte Carlo   B:32
Ballet skiing   S:184d
Ballets Russes (ballet company organized by Diaghilev)
    B:29–30; D:26
Ballets Russes (ballet company organized by Sergei
    Diaghilev)
    France, music of   F:447–48
Ballett (musical form)   E:292
Ballinger, Richard A. (American politician)   T:5
Ballistic missiles   M:343–44, 346–49
Ball lightning   T:187; U:32
Balloonfish, picture(s)   F:183
Ballooning (of spiders)   S:406
Balloons and ballooning   B:34–38; picture(s) C:428
    aerodynamics, principles of   A:41
    aviation history   A:558
    helium used to inflate   H:106; N:105
    International Hot Air Balloon Fiesta, picture(s)
        N:192
    Missouri's place in the history of air transportation
        M:375
    Piccard, Auguste   P:244
    transportation, history of   T:287
    weather balloon, picture(s)   W:86
    What makes a balloon rise?   B:36
    Why do balloons float?   F:250–51
Ballot (BAL-lot)   E:131
    origin of the word   B:23
Ballpoint pens   P:146–47
    ink   I:229
Ballroom dancing (social dancing)   D:26–28
Ball's Bluff (Virginia, site of Civil War battle)   C:340
Ball valves, diagram(s)   V:269
Balmaceda (bal-ma-SADE-a), José Manuel (president of
        Chile)   C:255
Balsa (BALL-sa) (tree)
    Ecuador is major producer   E:68
    lightest wood in commercial use   W:227
    wood used for airplane models   A:107
Balsam fir (tree)
    leaves, needlelike, picture(s)   L:117
Balsas (reed boats)   P:161; picture(s) B:308; P:160
Baltic (BALL-tic) languages   E:352
Baltic Sea   E:343; O:43
Baltic States
    Estonia   E:323–25
    Latvia   L:81–83
    Lithuania   L:261–63
    World War II   W:287–88
Baltimore (Maryland)   B:39; M:120, 123–24, 127,
        134; picture(s) M:121
    cargo ship in harbor, picture(s)   M:126
    Harborplace   M:128; picture(s) M:129
    National Aquarium, picture(s)   M:125
Baltimore, Lord see Calvert, George
Baltimore and Ohio Railroad   B:39; M:134; R:89
    first electric locomotive   L:281
    first in United States   T:285
    Maryland section   M:120
Baltimore Clippers (sailing ships)   M:120
Baltimore orioles (birds), picture(s)   B:242
    Maryland, state bird of, picture(s)   M:121
Baltimore Sun (newspaper)   M:127
Baltimore-Washington International Airport   M:127
Balto-Finnic languages   E:323
Baltoro Glacier (Kashmir), picture(s)   H:126
Balto-Slavic languages   L:39
Baluba (ba-LU-ba) (a people of Africa)   A:76
    sculpture, picture(s)   A:75
Baluchis (a people of Asia)   K:193

Balustrades (of escalators)   E:188
Balzac, Honoré de (French writer)   B:40; F:441
    great European novelists   N:360
    Rodin's Monument to Balzac, picture(s)   M:387
Bamako (ba-ma-KO) (capital of Mali)   M:62
Bambara (bom-BAR-a) (a people of central West Africa)
    African sculpture   A:72, 76; picture(s) A:70, 75
    Mali   M:61
Bambara (language)   M:61
Bambara, Toni Cade (American writer)   A:214a
Bambi (animated cartoon), picture(s)   D:216
Bamboo (giant grass)   G:318
    books made from   B:320
    jungle growth   J:153
    pandas' main food   P:50
Banaba (island in the Pacific Ocean)   K:265
Banabans (people of Ocean Island)   K:265
Banabhatta (Indian poet)   I:141
Banana   B:40–42; F:484; picture(s) C:173, 514;
        G:398
    flower, picture(s)   F:279
    Honduras is a leading producer   H:195–97
    important agricultural products   A:90–91
Banaras (India)   G:25
    Hindu pilgrims bathing, picture(s)   A:445; H:129
Banat (region of Romania)   R:297
Bancroft, George (American historian)   A:204; H:139
Banda (BON-da), Hastings Kamuzu (president of
        Malawi)   B:498; M:53
Bandai-san (volcano, Japan)   V:382
Bandana (kerchief worn by cowboys)   C:569
Bandaranaike (bon-da-ra-NY-kee), Sirimavo Rawatte Dias
        (Sri Lankan political leader)   B:498; S:416
Bandar Seri Begawan (capital of Brunei)   B:415
Banda (BON-da) Sea (part of the Pacific Ocean)
        B:498
Banderillos (bon-dai-RI-lyos) (in bullfighting)   B:449
Bandicoots (marsupials)   M:113
Banding (of birds) see Birdbanding
Bands and band music   B:42–45 see also Orchestra;
        Percussion instruments
    American pop music   R:262a, 262b
    circus music   C:310
    drums, use of   D:335–38
    fife and drum band, picture(s)   P:61
    how bands differ from orchestras   O:192–93
    jazz bands   J:59
    marching band, picture(s)   U:98
    Marine Corps Band   U:123
    military marches of Elgar   E:188
    percussion instruments   P:151–53
    wind instruments   W:182–83
Band saws (tools)   T:235
Bandung Conference (1955)   A:467
Banff National Park (Alberta, Canada)   B:46; picture(s)
        A:167; C:50
Banff School of Fine Arts   B:46
Bang, Molly (American author)   C:238
    illustration from The Paper Crane, picture(s)   C:236
Bangkok (Krung Thep) (capital of Thailand)   B:47;
        T:149, 152; picture(s) S:330, 334
Bangla see Bengali
Bangladesh (BANG-la-desh) (formerly East Pakistan)
        B:48–51
    flag, picture(s)   F:231
    India's role in formation of new nation   I:134
    jute preparation, picture(s)   A:462
    Pakistan, history of   P:40a
    Red Cross relief effort, picture(s)   F:354
Bangor (Maine)   M:43, 48

Bangui (capital of Central African Republic) C:171
Banjarmasin (bon-jer-MA-sin) (Indonesia) B:337; I:211
Banjo F:330; *picture(s)* F:329; S:469
Banjul (formerly Bathurst) (capital of The Gambia) G:8; *picture(s)* G:9
Bank cards (credit cards issued by banks) B:58; C:572
Bank holidays (in Great Britain) H:151, 157
Banking (lateral slant)
    airplane flight A:112
    road surfaces R:250
Banking Insurance Fund (BIF) B:58
Bank notes B:54
Bank of Canada B:59
Bank of England L:285; U:69
Bank of the United States B:53
    Andrew Jackson opposes J:7; U:182
    Philadelphia building, *picture(s)* B:52
    Tyler, John T:367
Bankruptcy (in economics) B:472
Banks (of the continental shelf) F:218
Banks and banking B:52–59 *see also* Inflation and deflation; Money
    automatic teller, *picture(s)* C:489; E:159
    automation employed in A:532
    Comptroller of the Currency T:294
    depressions and recessions D:122
    Federal Reserve System D:259; M:412
    inflation and deflation, control of I:228
    interest I:255
    Jackson's pet banks J:7
    Medici M:201
    Roosevelt institutes deposit insurance R:323
    Rothschild family R:339
    Switzerland is a center of international banking S:543
    trust fund T:328
    truth-in-lending laws C:528
Bannack (Montana) M:438, 442; *picture(s)* M:439
Banneker, Benjamin (American mathematician and astronomer) B:250e
    Washington, D.C., history of W:32, 35
Banners (flags) F:225
    heraldry H:110
Bannister, Sir Roger Gilbert (English runner) B:498; T:263; *picture(s)* T:262
Bannockburn, Battle of (1314) R:251; S:88
Bannock Indians (of North America) I:59; *picture(s)* I:163
Banshee (in Celtic folklore) B:498
Bantam chickens P:178, 414
Bantamweight (in boxing) B:352
Banting, Sir Frederick Grant (Canadian doctor and scientist) B:59
Bantu (people of Africa)
    Angola A:260
    Basotho L:156
    Botswana B:344
    Congo C:498
    languages A:55
    Malawi M:52–53
    Namibia N:8
    sculpture A:76
    South Africa S:268
    Tanzania T:16
    Uganda U:4–5
    Zaïre Z:367
    Zambia Z:371
    Zimbabwe Z:374, 376

Bantustans (homelands for Bantus of South Africa) S:269
Banyankole (a people of Africa) U:4
Banyan trees T:305
Banyoro (a people of Africa) U:4
Banzer Suárez, Hugo (Bolivian president) B:310
Bao Dai (emperor of South Vietnam) V:334d, 336
Baptism
    Easter symbols E:44
    Jesus Christ J:84
    sacrament of Roman Catholic Church R:294
Baptist Church P:492
    Russia R:358
Baptistery of Florence Cathedral (Baptistery of San Giovanni) F:256–57
    Ghiberti's doors I:395; R:164; *picture(s)* R:165
Baptistery of Pisa Cathedral
    Nicola Pisano's pulpit, *picture(s)* I:393
Bar (measure) (in musical notation) M:539–40
Bara, Theda (American actress) M:475
Barabbas (bar-AB-as) (in the New Testament) B:167
Barada River (Syria) S:548–49
Baraka, Imamu Amiri (American writer and political activist) B:498
Baranof (ba-RA-nof), Alexander (first Russian governor of Alaska) A:156–57
Baratieri Falls (Ethiopia) W:63
Barb (type of horse) H:238
Barbados (bar-BAY-doze) B:60; C:113–15
    flag, *picture(s)* F:239
    life in Latin America L:47–61
"Barbara Allen" (folk song) F:318
Barbarossa (Ottoman corsair) *see* Khayr-ad-Din
Barbarossa, Frederick *see* Frederick I (Frederick Barbarossa) (king of the Germans and Holy Roman emperor)
Barbary corsairs (pirates) P:263
Barbary States (North Africa) P:263
Barbary Wars (between the United States and the former Barbary States) B:498; U:179
Barbeau, Marius (Canadian folk music collector) C:67
Barbecueing O:263–64
Barbed wire W:274; *picture(s)* P:480
Barbells (weights used for exercise) W:107
Barbels (feelers of fish) F:193
Barber, Samuel (American composer) B:498–99
Barber of Seville, The (opera by Rossini) O:150
Barberry (plant) F:498
Barbie (fashion doll) D:270; *picture(s)* D:271
Barbieri, Francisco Asenjo (Spanish composer) S:392d
Barbiturates (bar-BIT-u-rates) (drugs) D:331
Barbizon School (of French painting) F:429; P:29
    modern art M:387
    romanticism R:303
Barbosa (bar-BO-sa), Ruy (Brazilian diplomat, jurist, and writer) B:384
Barbuda *see* Antigua·and Barbuda
Barca, Pedro Calderón de la *see* Calderón de la Barca, Pedro
Barcarolle (musical form) M:543
Barcelona (bar-cel-O-na) (Spain) S:377–78; *picture(s)* S:376
    Church of the Holy Family, *picture(s)* S:387
    city planning C:324
    Gaudí, Antonio S:387
    Olympic Games (1992) O:119–20
Bar codes (read by optical scanners) C:483; *picture(s)* E:158
Barco Vargas, Virgilio (Colombian political leader) C:408

Bardeen, John (American physicist) B:499
　history of electronics, *picture(s)* E:162
Bards (wandering poet-singers)
　Africa's bards or minstrels A:76b
　Celtic civilization C:164
Barefoot skiing W:73
Barenboim, Daniel (Israeli pianist and conductor)
　B:499; I:371
Barents (BAR-ents), Willem (Dutch navigator) E:416
Barents Sea O:43
Bar examinations (for lawyers) L:90–91
Barge canals C:86–88
Barge Haulers on the Volga (painting by Repin),
　picture(s) R:374
Bargello stitch *see* Florentine stitch
Barges (boats) T:289; *picture(s)* M:365
　dredging operations, use in D:319–20
Bar graphs G:309–11
Bar Harbor (Maine) M:44
Barite (mineral), *chart(s)* M:315; *picture(s)* M:314
　Nevada is a leading producer N:129
Baritone (male voice) C:283; M:540; V:375
Barium (BARR-ium) (element) E:171
　spectrum, *picture(s)* L:219
　used in taking X rays M:208h; X:341
Bark (kind of ship), *picture(s)* S:152
Bark (of trees) P:290; T:306
　cork oak tree C:549
　wood and wood products W:225
Barkentine (kind of ship), *picture(s)* S:152
Barking (of dogs) D:247
Barking owls O:285
Barkley, Alben W. (American statesman) T:326; V:330
Barley (grain) G:282, 284–86, 318; *picture(s)* G:283
　North Dakota is nation's leading producer N:322
Barlow, Joel (American poet and diplomat) A:201
Barm (liquid yeast) B:386
Bar Mitzvah (ceremony in Judaism) J:146; *picture(s)*
　J:139
Barnacles (kind of crustacean) A:281; C:592
　goose barnacles, *picture(s)* C:591
Barnard, Christiaan Neethling (South African surgeon)
　B:499
Barnard, Henry (American educator) C:509; E:83
Barnburners (faction of New York State Democratic
　Party) V:275
Barn dances *see* Square dances
Barnes, Edward Larrabee (American architect) U:136
Barn owls O:284–85; *picture(s)* A:269
Barns (for dairy cattle) D:7
Barnum, Phineas Taylor (American showman) B:499
　exhibited Jumbo the elephant E:184
　was mayor of Bridgeport (Connecticut) C:513
Barograph (instrument that measures air pressure)
　W:85
Baroja (ba-RO-ha), Pío (Spanish writer) S:392a
Barometer (ba-ROM-et-er) (used to measure air
　pressure) B:61; W:78, 85
　how to make W:93
　use of vacuum principle V:265
　weather forecasting W:95
Barometric pressure *see* Air pressure
Barons (members of the nobility, feudal lords)
　England, power struggle with king E:238–41
　Magna Carta and King John M:26
Baroque (ba-ROKE) architecture B:62–69
　architecture, history of A:380
　Brussels City Hall, *picture(s)* B:135
　German architecture G:170–71
　Latin America L:63–64

Russia, architecture of R:372
　Spain S:385
　Vienna V:333
Baroque art B:62–69
　decorative arts D:77
　drawing, history of D:315–16
　France, art of F:427
　furniture design F:508
　Italy I:400–401
　Latin America L:64
　painting P:23
　sculpture S:100–101
　Spanish art influenced by Caravaggio S:383–84
Baroque literature
　French Academy combats F:437
Baroque music B:69–73
　German composers G:184–85
　opera, development of the aria in O:140–41
　sonatas S:350; M:547
Baroque pearl B:62
Barotseland (region, Zambia) Z:371–72
Barracudas (barr-a-CU-das) (fish) F:188; *picture(s)*
　F:183
Barrage balloons (to block enemy aircraft) B:36
Barranquilla (ba-ron-KI-ya) (Colombia) C:406
Barre (railing used in ballet practice), *picture(s)* B:26
Barre (BAR-rie) (Vermont) V:314
Barred Plymouth Rock (chicken) P:416
Barred spiral galaxies U:214; *picture(s)* U:215
Barrel cacti C:5
Barrel racing (rodeo event) R:278; *picture(s)* H:227
Barrels (of guns) G:425
Barrels, wooden D:91
Barrel vault (in architecture) A:374
Barren Ground caribou H:214
Barrett, Stan (American automobile racer) A:538
Barrie, Sir James Matthew (Scottish writer) B:74
　dressed his realism in fantasy and humor D:301
　English literature, place in E:289
　Peter Pan, *excerpt(s)* P:165–66
Barrientos Ortuño, René (president of Bolivia) B:310
Barrier beaches
　Louisiana L:301
　New Jersey N:166–67
　Texas T:126
Barrier islands I:360
Barrier reefs C:548
　Great Barrier Reef (Australia) A:502
Barringer Crater *see* Meteor Crater
Barristers (lawyers) L:91
Barron, Robert (English inventor) L:276
Barry, Charles (English architect) E:262
Barrymore family (American actors) B:74
Bars, steel I:336
BART *see* Bay Area Rapid Transit System
Barter (system of economics) T:264
　use of money replaces barter M:409
Bartered Bride, The (opera by Smetana) O:150–51
Barter Theater (Abingdon, Virginia) V:353
Barth, Heinrich (German explorer) E:414
Barth, John (American novelist) A:214a; B:499
Barth (BART), Karl (Swiss theologian) B:499
Barthelme (BAR-tuhl-mee), Donald (American author)
　A:214a; B:499
Bartholdi (bart-OL-di), Frédéric Auguste (French
　sculptor) L:169
Bartholomew (bar-THOL-o-mew), Saint (one of the 12
　Apostles) A:329
Bartholomew Fair (England) F:10; *picture(s)* F:11
Bartlesville (Oklahoma) O:87

Bartlett, Josiah (American physician and Revolutionary War patriot)   N:161
Bartlett pear   P:112
Bartlett's Familiar Quotations   R:129
Bartók (BAR-toke), Béla (Hungarian composer)   B:75; C:184; H:284; M:398
Bartolommeo (bart-o-lo-MAY-o), Fra (Italian painter)   B:499
Barton, Clara (founder of American Red Cross)   B:75
   Red Cross   R:127
Barton, Otis (American inventor and explorer)   E:417–18; U:20
Barton, William (co-designer of Great Seal of the United States)   G:329
Bartram, John (American botanist)   B:499
Barú (mountain, Panama)   P:43
Baruch (BAY-rook) (apocryphal book of Bible)   B:163
Baruch (bar-OOK), Bernard Mannes (American economist and financier)   S:309
Baruch Plan (1946, to control nuclear weapons)   D:179
Barye (ba-RE), Antoine Louis (French sculptor)   S:102
   statue of a boa and a stag, *picture(s)*   S:102
Baryshnikov, Mikhail Nikolayevich (Russian dancer)   B:499; D:34
   in *The Sleeping Beauty*, *picture(s)*   B:33
Barzun, Jacques (American educator and author)   B:499
Basal readers   R:109
Basalt (ba-SALT) (lava rock)   R:264–65
   crust of the Earth   E:12, 23; G:111
   moon   M:454
   volcanic action   V:379
Basalt ware (kind of pottery)   P:413
Basant (Holi) (religious holiday in India)   R:154
Base (in algebra)   A:184
Base-4 system (of numeration)   N:407–9
Base-10 system *see* Decimal system
Base-12 system *see* Duodecimal system
Baseball   B:76–93 *see also* Little League Baseball; Softball
   Canada   C:69
   Japan   J:33
   Little League Baseball   L:264–67
   major league records   B:85
   National Hall of Fame and Museum   B:88
   Olympic sport   O:107
   physical fitness   P:225
   Robinson, Jackie   R:252
   Russian game *lapta* is similar   R:359; U:36
   Ruth, Babe   R:383
   softball   S:229
   Tee Ball, Little League   L:266
   World Series   B:86
Baseball Writers' Association of America   B:88
Baseburner (coal-burning stove)   H:95
Basedow (ba-zed-O), Johann (German educator)   P:223
Basel (BA-zel) (Switzerland)   S:542
Base line (of a graph)   G:309
Basenji (ba-SEN-jee) (dog), *picture(s)*   D:250
Bases (in chemistry)   C:204
BASIC (computer language)   C:486–88
Basic English   B:499
Basic oxygen process (in steelmaking)   I:332–33
Basic research   C:197; R:181
Basie, Count (American bandleader and jazz pianist)   B:499; J:60
Basil (BAZ-il) (herb)   H:114; *picture(s)* H:115
Basil II (Byzantine emperor)   B:443
Basilar membrane (of the inner ear)   E:4

Basilica (ba-SIL-ica) (building plan)   B:499
   church architecture   A:374, 376; I:392
   France, architecture of   F:422
Basil (BAZ-il) the Great, Saint (doctor of the Christian Church)   B:499; C:289
Basin and Range Province (United States)   U:82
Basins (of lakes)   L:24–25
Baskerville (typeface), *picture(s)*   B:327
Baskerville, John (English type designer)   T:369
Basketball (sport)   B:94–96; *picture(s)* G:137; I:149; M:141; N:311
   common terms   B:95j
   Lithuania   L:262
   Olympic Games   O:107
   women's basketball   B:95i, 96
Baskets, hanging, *picture(s)*   G:38
Basketweave bond (in masonry), *picture(s)*   B:391
Basketweave stitch (in needlepoint)   N:100
Basket weaving
   Hopi basket, *picture(s)*   I:183
   Indian art   I:186, 189
Basking sharks   S:140, 142; *picture(s)* S:141
Bas Mitzvah *see* Bat Mitzvah
Basotho (Basuto) (African people)   L:156–57; S:272
Basque (BASK) language   L:40
   Pyrenees section of Spain   S:374, 388
Basques (BASKS) (a people of Spain and France)   B:499–500; S:374
   folk dancers, *picture(s)*   F:298
   Idaho, immigrants to   I:50–51
   independence movement   T:117
   jai alai   J:12
Basra (BOS-ra) (Iraq)   I:315
   oil refinery, *picture(s)*   I:314
Bas-relief (BA-rel-IEF) (in sculpture)   S:90
Bass (BASE) (in music)   C:283; M:540
   voice training   V:375
Bass (fish), *picture(s)*   F:210
   baits   F:206
   sea bass   F:214
Bass, George (English explorer and doctor)   A:515
Bass clarinet, *picture(s)*   M:555
Bass clef (F clef) (in musical notation)   M:533–34
Bass drum   D:336–37
Bassein (Burma)   B:457
Bassetaille (enameling technique)   E:202
Basseterre (capital of Saint Kitts and Nevis)   S:15
Basset hound (dog)   D:244; *picture(s)* D:246
Basso continuo *see* Continuo
Bassoon (bas-SOON) (musical instrument)   M:555; *picture(s)* W:182
   orchestra seating plan   O:196
Basswood (tree)
   uses of the wood and its grain, *picture(s)*   W:223
Bast fibers   F:106
Bastille, fall of the (1789)   F:468; *picture(s)* E:365, 463; F:417, 467
   Place de la Bastille (Paris)   P:74
Bastille Day (July 14)   F:468; H:156; J:148
   importance to French history   F:406, 416
Basting stitches (in sewing)   S:128b
Bastions (of forts)   F:375, 377
Basuto *see* Basotho
Basutoland (ba-SU-to-land) *see* Lesotho
Bat, baseball   B:78
Bat, The (operetta) *see* Fledermaus, Die
Bata (Equatorial Guinea)   E:305
Bataan (ba-TAN) (Philippines)   W:294
Batavia (bat-A-via) (former name of Jakarta)   J:14
Batavian Republic (in Dutch history)   N:121

Batéké (a people of Africa) C:498
Batéké plateau (Congo) C:499
Bates, Katherine Lee (American professor and author)
    N:23
Ba'th Party (in Syria) S:550
Baths and bathing
    Ganges River (India) religious bathing G:25
    Indian ritual I:121
    Japan J:29
    knights of the bath K:277
Bathsheba (bath-SHE-ba) (in the Old Testament)
    B:167
Bathurst (Australia) A:516
Bathurst (New Brunswick, Canada) N:138f
Bathurst (The Gambia) see Banjul
Bathurst Island (Northwest Territories, Canada) G:437
Bathyl zone (of the ocean) O:23
Bathyscaphe (BATHI-scaph) (underwater ship) P:244
    oceanographic research O:42
    underwater exploration E:418; U:20–21
Bathysphere (used in underwater research) E:418;
    O:42; U:20
Batik (ba-TEEK) (method of printing textiles) M:57
    Indian decorative art D:72
    Indonesian industry I:207; picture(s) D:370;
    I:209
Batista y Zaldívar (ba-TI-sta e sal-DEE-var), Fulgencio
    (Cuban dictator) B:500
    Castro and Cuba C:133, 599
Batlle y Ordóñez (BAT-yay e or-DONE-yes), José
    (Uruguayan statesman and journalist) B:500;
    U:240
Bat Mitzvah (ceremony in Judaism) J:146
Baton Rouge (capital of Louisiana) L:209
Batoro (a people of Africa) U:4
Bats B:97–100; picture(s) A:269; M:73
    body changes in hibernation, table(s) H:119
    cave dwellers C:154–55
    echo E:49
    guano C:155, 158
    hand pattern changed for flying F:84
    hibernation H:120
    How do bats find their way in the dark? B:100
    mammals' food adaptations M:70
    nectar-feeding bat A:282; picture(s) F:281
    sensory system S:366; S:265
Battalion (army troop unit) U:109
Battambang (BAT-tam-bang) (Kampuchea) K:172
Battelle Memorial Institute (Columbus, Ohio) C:444
Battered children (victims of physical abuse) C:222
Batteries (devices that produce electricity) B:101–3;
    E:142–44
    automobiles A:541, 547–48
    bacterial fermentation produces electricity F:92;
        picture(s) F:91
    clocks, battery-operated C:370–71
    Davy's experiments E:138
    electric motors E:154
    electronic watches W:44–46
    Grove battery, picture(s) I:279
    ionization, principle of I:289
    lead used in storage batteries L:92
    solar batteries S:239
Battery (artillery troop unit) U:109
Batting average (in baseball) B:83
Battle, Kathleen (American soprano) B:500
Battle, trial by D:345; M:291
    jury replaces J:159
Battle Creek (Michigan) M:271
"Battle Cry of Freedom, The" (song) N:23

Battledore and Shuttlecock (game) see Badminton
Battlefields, national see National battlefields
"Battle Hymn of the Republic, The" (by Howe) N:23
Battlement (of a castle) C:131
Battle of Constantine, The (painting by Piero della
    Francesca)
    detail, picture(s) R:167
Battleship Potemkin (motion picture) M:486
Battleships see Warships
Batutsi see Tutsi
Batwa see Twa
Baucis see Philemon and Baucis
Baudelaire (bode-LAIRE), Charles (French poet) F:441
Baudot (bo-DO), Emile (French inventor) T:54
Baudouin (BO-dwan) (king of the Belgians) B:500
Baudry, Patrick (French astronaut), picture(s) S:351
Bauer, Georg see Agricola, Georgius
Bauer, Wolfgang (German dramatist) D:302
Bauhaus (BOW-hows) (design school in Germany)
    architecture, history of A:383
    furniture design F:510
    industrial design I:214
    influence on decorative arts D:79
    Kandinsky, Wassily K:173
    Mies van der Rohe, Ludwig M:306
    twentieth century German art and architecture
        G:173
Baule (Baoulé) (African tribe) I:417
    sculpture, picture(s) A:75
Baum (BOHM), L. Frank (American journalist and
    author of children's stories) B:500
Bauxite (BOK-site) (ore of aluminum) A:194c; O:217
    Arkansas leads U.S. production A:422, 424
    Australia is the world's largest producer A:509
    bauxite-producing regions of North America N:293
    Guyana is an important producer G:428a
    Hungary has large reserves H:285–86
    Jamaica is a leading producer J:17
    natural resource N:62–63
    world distribution W:261
Bavaria (ba-VAIR-ia) (Germany)
    food specialties G:151–52
    Neuschwanstein (castle), picture(s) G:149
    Thompson, Benjamin, service in government T:180
Bavarian Alps (Austria and Germany) G:153–54
BAWI (Balance Agriculture with Industry) program (in
    Mississippi) M:354
Bay (geographic term) O:43 see also the names of
    bays, as Fundy, Bay of
Bayaderka (ballet), picture(s) D:32
Bayamón (Puerto Rico) P:531
Bayar, Celal (president of Turkey) T:349
Bayard, James Asheton (American statesman) D:101
Bayard, Thomas F. (American statesman) D:101
Bay Area Rapid Transit System (BART) (California)
    S:31
Bayberry (shrub) B:500
    wax obtained from W:76
Bayeux (by-UH) tapestry (medieval embroidery) N:100;
    picture(s) E:238; W:173
Bayezid I (Ottoman sultan) O:261
Baying (of dogs) D:247
Bay leaves (spice) H:114; picture(s) H:115
Baylor, Elgin (American basketball player) B:500
Bay lynxes see Bobcats
Bay of Pigs Invasion see Pigs, Bay of
Bayous (BY-os) (marshy creeks in Louisiana) L:298;
    picture(s) L:307
Bayou State (nickname for Louisiana) L:299
Bay Psalm Book B:500; H:310

Bayreuth (by-ROIT) (Germany)
Festival of Wagner's operas **M:**558; **W:**2
Bay State (nickname for Massachusetts) **M:**136
Bazán, Emilia Pardo see Pardo Bazán, Emilia
Bazin, Marc (president of Haiti) **H:**12
Bazookas (small rocket launchers) **T:**14
BBC see British Broadcasting Company
BB gun (air rifle) **G:**424
B.C. (abbreviation used with dates) **C:**16
B.C.E. (abbreviation used with dates) **C:**16
B cells (in the immune system) **I:**96–97
BCG (vaccine against tuberculosis) **D:**205
B-complex vitamins **V:**370c–370d
B.E. 2a (early British airplane) **A:**560
Beaches
barrier beaches of Louisiana **L:**301
erosion **E:**313
Beach plum **P:**108
Beacon Hill (Boston, Massachusetts), *picture(s)* **H:**174
Beaconsfield, Earl of see Disraeli
Beaded lizard **L:**270
Bead lightning see Chain lightning
Beads (jewelry)
early glass articles **G:**229
Indian beadwork, *picture(s)* **I:**180
Beads (of a tire) **T:**209
Beagle (dog) **D:**250
Beagle, **H.M.S.** (British ship) **D:**40; **E:**376–77
Beagle Channel dispute (between Argentina and Chile)
A:396; **C:**252
Beaks (bills) (of birds) **A:**277; **B:**217
eagles **E:**2
waterfowl **D:**341, 343
Beam bridges **B:**395; *picture(s)* **B:**396
Beamon, Bob (American track-and-field star) **B:**500;
T:263
Beams, steel **I:**336
Beanies (hats) **H:**45
Beans **V:**289 see also Soybeans
food shopping **F:**350
nutrition **N:**425
seed, structure of, *picture(s)* **F:**286
Bear cats see Binturongs
Beard, Charles Austin (American historian, writer, and
educator) **B:**500
Bearded collie (dog), *picture(s)* **D:**250
Beardmore Glacier (Antarctica) **G:**224
Beardsley, Aubrey Vincent (English book illustrator)
B:500
Bear Festival (of the Ainu) **J:**41
Bear Flag Revolt (California) **T:**111
Bearings (of machinery)
made of diamonds **D:**145
watches **W:**44
Bearing wall construction (of buildings) **B:**435
Bear Mountain Bridge (New York), *picture(s)* **N:**214
Bears **B:**104–7
black bear, *picture(s)* **B:**206
brown bears, *picture(s)* **U:**89
cave bears of the Ice Age **I:**12
circus act, *picture(s)* **C:**309
foot bones **F:**81
pandas are related animals **P:**50
partial hibernation of **H:**118
polar bears, *picture(s)* **E:**210
Yellowstone National Park **Y:**345
Bears and bulls (in stock exchanges) **S:**459
Beast epics **F:**4
Beasts of burden **T:**281

Beat (in music) **M:**540; **S:**262
orchestra conducting **O:**199
Beatification (be-at-if-ic-A-tion) (in Roman Catholic
Church) **B:**500
Beatles, The (English rock group) **B:**108; **R:**262c,
262d
Beaton, Cecil Walter Hardy (English photographer,
writer, and designer) **B:**500
Beatrice (Dante's ideal and inspiration) **D:**37; **I:**405–6
Beatrix (BAY-a-trix) (queen of the Netherlands) **B:**500;
N:120d
Beats (sections of a city)
assignments of newspaper reporters **N:**201
covered by patrol officers **P:**363
Beats, The (group of poets) **A:**213
Beat the Story Drum, Pum-Pum (book by Bryan),
picture(s) **C:**243
Beattie, Ann (American writer) **B:**500
Beaubourg (art museum, Paris) see Pompidou Center
Beauchamp (bo-SHON), **Charles Pierre** (French ballet
dancer and choreographer) **B:**26; **D:**25
Beau de Rochas, Alphonse (French engineer) **I:**268
Beaufort (BO-fort) **Sea** (part of the Arctic Ocean) **O:**43
Beauharnois (bo-HARN-wa) (Quebec, Canada) **C:**57
Beaujoyeulx (bo-jwa-YER), **Balthazar de** (Italian-born
French choreographer) **B:**25
Beaumarchais, Pierre Augustin Caron de (French
playwright) **D:**300; **F:**440
Beaumont (BO-mont), **Francis** (English dramatist)
D:298
Beaumont, William (American frontier surgeon) **B:**109
contribution to medicine **M:**207
Beauregard (BO-re-gard), **Pierre Gustave Toutant de**
(American Confederate general) **B:**501; **C:**334,
339
Beauty culture see Cosmetics; Perfumes
Beauvoir (boh-VWAHR), **Simone de** (French writer)
B:501; **F:**443
Beaux-arts style (in architecture) **U:**131
Beaverbrook, Lord (English newspaper publisher and
politician) **N:**138g
statue, *picture(s)* **N:**138f
Beaver Island (in Lake Michigan) **M:**269
Beavers **B:**110–12
aplodontia (mountain beaver) **R:**274
fur **F:**517
hats **F:**511
homes of **M:**71
Beaver Scouts **B:**360
Beaver State (nickname for Oregon) **O:**203
Bebop (early name for modern jazz) **J:**60
Becharof Lake (Alaska) **A:**149
Bechet (besh-AY), **Sidney** (jazz musician) **J:**58
Bechuanaland see Botswana
Becker, Boris (German tennis player) **B:**501
Becket, Saint Thomas à (English churchman) **B:**113
kings versus clergy in English history **E:**240
Beckett, Samuel (Irish playwright and novelist) **B:**501;
I:328; **N:**363
absurdist drama **D:**303
France, literature of **F:**442
Waiting for Godot, picture(s) **D:**303
Becknell, William (American pioneer) **M:**374; **O:**273
Bécquer (BA-ker), **Gustavo Adolfo** (Spanish poet)
S:391
Becquerel (BECK-rel), **Antoine Henri** (French physicist)
B:113
chemistry, history of **C:**210–11
science, history of **S:**76
uranium studied by **U:**231

Bed (of a platen press) **P:**474
Bedbugs (insects) **H:**263
Bede, the Venerable (English historian-monk) **C:**290;
    E:269
"Bed in Summer" (poem by Stevenson) **S:**451
Bedivere (knight of King Arthur's court) **A:**440
Bedlam (hospital in London) **B:**501
Bedloe's Island (New York Harbor) see Liberty Island
Bedouins (BED-du-ins) (nomadic Arabic tribes) **A:**344;
    D:128; picture(s) **A:**344–45
  Egypt **E:**103
  homes **H:**176
  Kuwait **K:**305, 307
  Saudi Arabia **S:**57–58
  Syria **S:**548
Beds
  camp beds **C:**43
  crewelwork bed hangings **N:**97
Bed warmer, picture(s) **C:**410
Beebe (BEE-be), William (American naturalist, explorer,
    and author) **E:**417–18
  bathysphere **O:**42; **U:**20
Beech (tree)
  American beech, picture(s) **T:**304
  uses of the wood and its grain, picture(s) **W:**223
Beecham, Sir Thomas (English conductor) **B:**501
Beecher, Anson and Ebenezer (American inventors)
    M:152
Beecher, Henry Ward (American preacher) **B:**114
  "Beecher's Bibles" shipped to Kansas **C:**337
Beecher, Thaddeus (American educator) **E:**83
Beech Starship (airplane) **A:**117; picture(s) **A:**569
Bee-eaters (birds), picture(s) **B:**230
Beef (meat of cattle) **C:**148; **M:**196
  cuts of beef, picture(s) **M:**197
  inspection and grading of meat **M:**198
  what you eat depends on where you live **F:**332
Beef cattle **C:**147–48, 153–54
Beefeaters see Yeomen of the Guard
Beehive State (nickname for Utah) **U:**243
Bee hummingbird **A:**271
Beekeeping **H:**202; picture(s) **B:**116
Beelzebub (be-EL-ze-bub) (Philistine god) **B:**501
Beer, Jakob Liebmann see Meyerbeer, Giacomo
Beer and brewing **B:**114–15
  German festival, picture(s) **G:**150
  malt extract from barley **G:**284–85
Beerbohm (BEER-bome), Sir Max (English writer)
    E:288
Bees (insects) **B:**116–21 see also Honey
  animal communication **C:**462
  biological classification **L:**207
  clock-compass **H:**193
  color vision **C:**428
  eggs in the hive, picture(s) **E:**100
  flower pollination **F:**282
  fossil bee, picture(s) **F:**381
  homing, example of **H:**185
  honey **H:**200–202
  How do honeybees make honey? **H:**200
  mouthparts, picture(s) **I:**238
  strength of **I:**241
  vectors **V:**284
Bees (social gatherings to accomplish tasks) **C:**412
Beeswax **W:**76
  candles made of **C:**94
  storing of honey **H:**202
Beethoven (BATE-ho-ven), Ludwig van (German
    composer) **B:**122; **G:**186; picture(s) **G:**185
  chamber music **C:**184

choral music **C:**284
classical age, compositions of the **C:**349, 351–52
  Fidelio was his only opera **C:**351; **O:**144, 154
  symphonies **M:**549
Beetle Bailey (comic strip), picture(s) **C:**129
Beetles (insects) **B:**123–27; picture(s) **I:**248
  boll weevil **C:**561–62; picture(s) **C:**560
  bombardier beetle **I:**243
  carpet beetles **H:**263
  plant pests **P:**284–85, 287–88
  scavenger beetle, picture(s) **I:**234
  strength of **I:**241
  tiger beetles, picture(s) **I:**230
  used as biological control for weeds **W:**106
  vectors **V:**284–85
  wings, picture(s) **I:**240
Beets **V:**289; picture(s) **P:**306
  sugar beets **S:**485–86
Beet sugar **S:**485–86
B.E.F. see British Expeditionary Force
Befana (bay-FA-na), La (Italian Santa Claus) **C:**300
Beggar's Opera (play by Gay) **E:**277, 292–93; **O:**142–
  43
  scene painted by William Hogarth, picture(s)
    E:277
Begin (BAY-ghin), Menahem (Israeli political leader)
    B:501; **I:**376; picture(s) **U:**202
Begonia (be-GO-nia) (plant), picture(s) **B:**132
Behaim, Martin (German merchant and navigator)
    M:98
Behan, Brendan (Irish playwright) **I:**328
Béhanzin (bay-HON-zin) (king of Dahomey) **B:**143
Behavior, animal see Animal intelligence and behavior
Behavior, human
  brain function **B:**363, 369
  effect of drugs on **D:**326
  ethics **E:**328–29
  etiquette **E:**337–39
  hypnosis **H:**313–15
  identical twins raised apart **T:**364
  impulses to take drugs **N:**14
  learning **L:**98–106
  lie detection **L:**193
  lies **L:**194
  mental health **M:**223–25
  mental illness **M:**225–28
  sociology, study of **S:**226–27
  What is personality? **P:**497
Behavioral objectives (in education) **P:**483
Behaviorism (psychology) **P:**504–5
Behring (BEAR-ing), Emil von (German bacteriologist)
    B:501
Behring, Vitus see Bering, Vitus
Beiderbecke, Bix (American jazz musician) **J:**59
Beijerinck (BAY-jer-ink), M. W. (Dutch scientist) **V:**362
Beijing (China) see Peking
Beirut (bay-ROOT) (capital of Lebanon) **L:**121–23
Bekaa plain (Lebanon) **L:**120
Bel see Baal
Béla III (king of Hungary) **H:**287
Belafonte (bel-af-ON-tay), Harry (American folksinger
    and actor) **B:**501
Belarus **B:**128–29; **U:**34
  Commonwealth of Independent States **C:**460
  flag, picture(s) **F:**235
  Minsk **U:**43
Belasco, David (American theatrical producer and
    playwright) **B:**501; **D:**304
Belau, Republic of (Pacific island group) **P:**6; **U:**93,
    101

Belaúnde (bay-la-ON-day) **Terry, Fernando** (president of Peru) **P:**164
Bel canto (style of singing) **M:**540
Belém (bel-EM) (Brazil) **B:**383; *picture(s)* **B:**382
Belfast (capital of Northern Ireland) **U:**67; *picture(s)* **U:**66
Belgian Congo *see* Zaïre
Belgian horse, *picture(s)* **H:**240
Belgian sheepdog **D:**241
Belgium **B:**130–35
  Albert I **A:**163
  flag, *picture(s)* **F:**235
  Flemish and Dutch art **D:**351–64
  Industrial Revolution **I:**224
  invasion by Hitler (1940) **W:**288–89
  invasion in World War I **W:**271–72
  Where and what are the Low Countries? **E:**356
  Zaïre **Z:**370
Belgrade (capital of Yugoslavia) **S:**125; **Y:**356–58
Belinsky, Vissarion (Russian writer) **R:**377
Belize (Central America) **B:**136–37; **C:**172–75
  flag, *picture(s)* **F:**241
  Peace Corps activities, *picture(s)* **P:**104
Belize City (former capital of Belize) **B:**136
Bell, Alexander Graham (Scottish-born American inventor and scientist) **B:**138–39; **I:**285; *picture(s)* **I:**283; **T:**57
  airplane research **A:**560
  Alexander Graham Bell Museum (Nova Scotia) **N:**355–56
  Bell Homestead (Ontario) **O:**133
  invented the Graphophone **O:**57
  telephone **C:**468; **T:**47
Bell, Currer, Ellis, and Acton *see* Brontë, Anne; Brontë, Charlotte; Brontë, Emily
Bell, John (American statesman) **T:**87
Bell, Joseph (English doctor and model for Sherlock Holmes) **D:**289
Bell, Mabel Hubbard (wife of Alexander Graham Bell)
  parent-teacher associations **P:**67
Bella Bella (Indians of North America) **I:**188
Bella Coola (Indians of North America) **I:**188
Belladonna (deadly nightshade) (poisonous plant) **P:**322
  medicinal plants **P:**314; *picture(s)* **P:**315
Bellange, Jacques (French artist) **F:**426
Bellay (bel-LAY), **Joachim du** (French poet) **F:**435, 437
Belle Isle, Strait of (north of Newfoundland, Canada) **C:**126; **N:**140
Bellerophon (bell-ER-o-phon) (hero in Greek mythology) **G:**367
Belleville Breviary (illuminated manuscript), *picture(s)* **B:**321; **D:**68
Bellevue (Nebraska) **N:**92, 95
Bellingrath Gardens (Alabama) **A:**139
Bellingshausen (BELL-ings-how-zen), **Fabian von** (Russian admiral) **A:**295; **E:**416
Bellini (bel-LI-ni), **Giovanni** (Venetian painter) **B:**139; **I:**398; **P:**21; **R:**169
  Madonna of the Trees (painting), *picture(s)* **B:**139
  Titian was a pupil of Bellini **T:**210
Bellini, Vincenzo (Italian composer) **B:**501; **I:**412
  Italian styles in opera **O:**145
  Norma (opera) **O:**159
Bellini family (Italian painters) **B:**139
Bellman, Carl Michael (Swedish poet and singer) **S:**58g
Bello (BAY-o), **Andrés** (South American educator, statesman, and author) **L:**70

Bello, Joaquín Edwards (Chilean writer) **C:**250
Belloc, Hilaire (English writer) **B:**501
  The Yak (nonsense rhyme) **N:**274
Bellow, Saul (American novelist) **A:**214a; **B:**140; **N:**363
Bellows (devices for making hotter fires) **F:**144
Bellows, George Wesley (American artist) **C:**444; **O:**73; **P:**30
  Cliff Dwellers (painting), *picture(s)* **U:**132
  Dempsey Through the Ropes (painting), *picture(s)* **B:**351
Bells **B:**140–41
  Christmas customs **C:**299
  communication, use in **C:**467
  early mechanical clocks **T:**201
  Liberty Bell **L:**170
  orchestra, use in **P:**153
Bell's vireo (bird), *picture(s)* **B:**206
Bell system (telephone system) **P:**523
Bell towers *see* Campaniles
Bell X-1 (airplane) **A:**116
Bell XS-1 (research rocket plane) **A:**565
Bell XV-15 (airplane), *picture(s)* **A:**121
Bell XV-22 (tilt-rotor aircraft) **A:**569
Belmont Stakes (horse race) **H:**232
Belmopan (capital of Belize) **B:**136
Belo Horizonte (Brazil), *picture(s)* **L:**53
Belorussia *see* Belarus
Belpre Farmers' Library (Ohio) **O:**68
Belshazzar (bel-SHAZZ-ar) (in the Old Testament) **B:**167
Belt (to drive an alternator) **A:**547
Belted-bias tires **T:**209
Beltsville Small White (turkey), *picture(s)* **P:**416
Belugas (whales) **W:**147; *picture(s)* **W:**149
Bely, Andrei (Russian author) **R:**379
Belyayev, Pavel (Soviet cosmonaut) **S:**346
Bemba (a people of Africa) **Z:**371
Bemelmans (BEM-el-mans), **Ludwig** (American author and illustrator) **B:**501
  Madeline's Rescue, cover from, *picture(s)* **C:**229
Ben (meaning in names) **N:**5
Benalcázar, Sebastian de (Spanish conquistador) **E:**69
Ben Ali, Zine el-Abidine (Tunisian president) **T:**336
Benares (India) *see* Banaras
Benavente (bay-na-VEN-tay), **Jacinto** (Spanish writer) **S:**392a
Ben Bella, Ahmed (premier of Algeria) **A:**188; **B:**501
Bench, Johnny (American baseball player) **B:**502
Benchley, Robert Charles (American humorist, writer, and actor) **B:**502
Bendjedid, Chadli (Algerian political leader) **A:**188
Bends (knots) **K:**288
Bends, the (caisson disease) **B:**400; **O:**41; **U:**19
  helium mixture helps prevent **H:**106
Benedict, Ruth Fulton (American anthropologist) **B:**502
Benedict X (antipope) **R:**290
Benedict XIII (antipope) **R:**291
Benedict I (pope) **R:**290
Benedict II, Saint (pope) **R:**290
Benedict III, Saint (pope) **R:**290
Benedict IV (pope) **R:**290
Benedict V (pope) **R:**290
Benedict VI (pope) **R:**290
Benedict VII (pope) **R:**290
Benedict VIII (pope) **R:**290
Benedict IX (pope) **R:**290
Benedict XI (pope) **R:**291
Benedict XII (pope) **R:**291

Benedict XIII (pope) **R:**291
Benedict XIV (pope) **R:**291
Benedict XV (pope) **R:**291–92
Benedictine Cloister Church (Ottobeuren, Germany),
    picture(s) **G:**171
Benedictines (Rule of Saint Benedict) (religious order)
    C:289; **M:**294; **R:**285
Benedict of Nursia, Saint (Italian monk) **B:**502
Benefice (BEN-e-fis) **system** (in the Roman Catholic
    Church) **R:**287
Beneficiary (of a trust fund) **T:**328
Benefits (part of wage agreement) **L:**8
Benefit societies (industrial organizations formed to aid
    members who could not work) **S:**221
Ben Eliezer, Israel *see* Baal Shem Tov
Benelux (economic union of Belgium, the Netherlands,
    and Luxembourg) **B:**502; **N:**121
Beneš (BEN-esh), Edvard (Czechoslovakian statesman)
    B:502; **C:**610; **M:**135
Benevolent and Protective Order of Elks *see* Elks,
    Benevolent and Protective Order of (BPOE)
Bengal, Bay of (arm of the Indian Ocean) **O:**45
Bengali (Bangla) (language) **B:**48, 51
Bengalis (a people of Bangladesh and India) **B:**48,
    51; *picture(s)* **B:**49
Bengal tigers *see* Indian tigers
Benghazi (ben-GHA-zi) (Libya) **L:**189
Ben-Gurion (ben-GU-ri-on), David (first prime minister of
    Israel) **B:**141; *picture(s)* **P:**459
Ben-Haim, Paul (Israeli composer) **I:**371
Ben Hur (motion pictures) **M:**476
Benign tumors (of the body) **C:**90; **D:**190
Beni Hasan (Egypt) **E:**113
Benin (ben-ENE) (kingdom in Africa) **N:**257
    art achievements **A:**71–72; **N:**254
    ivory carvings, *picture(s)* **A:**73
Benin (modern African country) **B:**142–43
    flag, *picture(s)* **F:**226
    literature **A:**76b, 76c
Benin City (Nigeria) **N:**256
Benjamin (in the Old Testament) **B:**167; **J:**133
Benjamin, Judah Philip (British-born American lawyer
    and statesman) **L:**311
Bennett, Floyd (American aviator) **B:**502
    Byrd and Bennett **B:**485
Bennett, Richard Bedford (Canadian statesman)
    B:502; **N:**138g
Bennett, Robert Russell (American composer) **M:**380
Bennett, William Andrew (Canadian political leader)
    B:406d
Bennett's cassowaries (flightless birds) **O:**247
Ben Nevis (highest mountain in the United Kingdom)
    S:86; **U:**61
Bennington (Vermont)
    saltbox house, *picture(s)* **C:**415
Bennington, Battle of (1777) **R:**204
    monument **V:**316
Benny, Jack (American comedian) **B:**502; **T:**326
Benoit, Joan (American runner) **O:**117
Benson, Benny (designed Alaska's flag) **A:**144
Bentham, Jeremy (English reformer and philosopher)
    B:502
    ethics **E:**328
Benthic (bottom) environment (of the ocean) **O:**23, 26
Benthos (organisms living on the ocean bottom) **O:**26
Bentley, E. C. (English author) **M:**563
Benton, Thomas Hart (American artist) **M:**379–80;
    U:132

Independence and the Opening of the West (mural),
    picture(s) **M:**380
    teacher of Jackson Pollock **P:**378
Benton, Thomas Hart (American statesman) **M:**379
Bentonville, Battle of (1865) **N:**319
Bent's Fort (Colorado) **C:**440; **F:**376
Benue (BEN-oo-ay) River (west Africa) **N:**255
Benz (BENTS), Karl (German engineer and automobile
    manufacturer) **A:**540; **T:**286
Benzene (colorless, highly flammable liquid) **F:**47;
    P:174
    molecule arrangement, *picture(s)* **A:**485
Ben-Zvi (ben-tz-VE), Isaac (Israeli statesman) **B:**502
Beograd (Yugoslavia) *see* Belgrade
Beothuk Indians (of Newfoundland) **N:**141
Beowulf (BAY-o-wulf) (epic poem) **B:**144–45; **E:**265,
    268
Be Prepared (Scout motto) **B:**358
Bequia (island, Saint Vincent and the Grenadines)
    S:19
Berbera (Somalia) **S:**254
Berbers (people) **A:**185; **B:**502; **M:**461
Berceo, Gonzalo de *see* Gonzalo de Berceo
Berceuse (ber-SUHZ) (musical form) **M:**543
Berea (ber-E-a) College (Berea, Kentucky) **K:**219
Beregovoi, Georgi T. (Soviet cosmonaut) **S:**346
Bérégovoy, Pierre (French premier) **F:**420
Berezovoi, Anatoly (Soviet cosmonaut) **S:**348
Berg (BAIRG), Alban (Austrian composer) **B:**502;
    G:189
    chamber music **C:**184
    modern music **M:**398
    Wozzeck **O:**165
Berg (BERG), Patty (American golfer) **B:**502
Bergelson, David (Yiddish author) **Y:**351
Bergen (Norway) **N:**347
Bergen, Edgar (American ventriloquist) **V:**302
Bergerac, Cyrano de *see* Cyrano de Bergerac
Bergman, Ingmar (Swedish film director) **M:**490, 492
Bergman, Ingrid (Swedish actress) **B:**502–3
Bergy bits (melted-down icebergs) **I:**18
Beriberi (disease) **V:**370a, 370c–370d
Bering (BAR-ing), Vitus (Danish explorer) **A:**156;
    B:145; **D:**110; **E:**416
Beringia (Ice Age plain connecting Alaska and Siberia)
    I:164
Bering Sea **A:**387; **O:**43–44
Bering Strait (separating Asia and North America)
    B:145; **O:**43–44
    Alaska's distance from Asia **A:**144
Berisha, Sali (Albanian president) **A:**162
Berkeley, Sir William (English colonial governor) **I:**202
Berkelium (BER-kli-um) (element) **E:**171
Berkshire Hills (Massachusetts) **M:**138
Berkshire Music Festival (at Tanglewood in Lenox,
    Massachusetts) **M:**559
Berkshire Valley (Massachusetts) **M:**138
Berle, Milton (American comedian) **T:**70
Berlin (Germany) **B:**146–49; **G:**154, 156
    American sector border sign, *picture(s)* **G:**166
    children play in rubble, *picture(s)* **G:**164
    "Cold War" between East and West **G:**164
    made an enclave at end of World War II **W:**306
    Olympic Games (1936) **O:**109–10
    Soviet soldier and flag (1945), *picture(s)* **U:**50
    war memorial, *picture(s)* **B:**147
Berlin (New Hampshire) **N:**160, 193
Berlin, Congress of **B:**503; *picture(s)* **I:**273
    Russia **U:**47

Berlin, Irving (American songwriter) B:150; M:550;
    U:208–9
  Christmas songs C:118
  patriotic songs N:23
Berlin Airlift B:149; G:164; T:327; U:197; picture(s)
    B:148
Berliner, Emile (German-American inventor) B:503
  phonograph records P:195; R:123
Berliner Ensemble (theater, Berlin) T:160
Berlin Wall (separating East and West Berlin) B:146,
    149; G:166
Berlioz (BAIR-li-ose), Hector (French composer) B:150
  band music B:43
  choral music C:285
  France, music of F:446
  harp, use of H:36
  La Damnation de Faust F:73
  opera O:147
  romantic orchestral music R:304
  symphonies M:549
Bermuda (ber-MU-da) (British crown colony of islands in
    the Atlantic Ocean) B:151–52
  limestone quarry, picture(s) Q:5
  What is the Bermuda Triangle? B:152
Bermuda grass G:317
Bermuda onions O:123
Bermuda Triangle B:152
Bermúdez (ber-MU-deth), Juan de (Spanish navigator)
    B:152
Bern (capital of Switzerland) S:542
Bernadette of Lourdes, Saint B:503
Bernadotte, Count Folke (Swedish diplomat) S:529
Bernadotte, Jean Baptiste see Charles XIV John (king of
    Sweden and Norway)
Bernard (bair-NAR), Claude (French physiologist)
    B:201; M:207
Bern Convention (1886) C:547
Bernese Alps (Switzerland) A:194b
Bernhard, Thomas (German dramatist) D:302
Bernhardt, Sarah (French actress) B:503
Bernini (ber-NI-ni), Giovanni Lorenzo (Italian sculptor,
    painter, and architect) B:152
  Apollo and Daphne (sculpture), picture(s) I:400
  baroque architecture B:64, 66
  equestrian statue of Louis XIV, picture(s) B:152
  fountains F:394
  high altar in St. Peter's Basilica V:282; picture(s)
    V:281
  Italy, art and architecture of I:400
  place in the history of sculpture S:100–101
  statue of David, picture(s) J:103; S:100
  Throne of Saint Peter, picture(s) I:400
  Vision of Saint Theresa (sculpture), picture(s) B:63
Bernoulli (bair-NOOL-li), Daniel (Swiss scientist and
    mathematician) A:37
Bernoulli's principle (law in physics) A:37, 109
Bernstein, Leonard (American conductor, pianist, and
    composer) B:503; picture(s) U:210
  dance music D:36
  musical comedy, history of M:551
Berra, Yogi (American baseball player) B:503
Berries (fruit)
  food shopping F:350
  garden fruits G:51
  poisonous plants P:322–23
  uses in cooking C:534
Berruguete (bair-ru-GAY-tay), Alonso (Spanish artist)
    S:386
  Saint Sebastian (sculpture), picture(s) S:386
Berry, Chuck (American rock music performer) R:262c

Berryman, John (American poet) A:214
Berry's World (cartoon) C:129
Bertha (Berthrada) (mother of Charlemagne)
  believed to be original Mother Goose N:410
Berthold Missal (illuminated manuscript), picture(s)
    G:167
Berthrada see Bertha
Bertin, Rose (French seamstress) C:381
Berton, Pierre (Canadian writer and television
    personality) B:503
Beryl (gem mineral) G:71; chart(s) M:315; picture(s)
    M:314
Beryllium (ber-ILL-ium) (element) E:171
  particulate pollutant A:123
  used in space vehicles and nuclear equipment
    M:318
Berzelius (ber-ZE-lius), Jöns Jakob (Swedish chemist)
    C:209–10
Bessarabia (bess-a-RAY-bia) (Moldova and Ukraine)
    M:403; R:300
Bessel, Friedrich Wilhelm (German astronomer) A:474,
    476
Bessemer (BESS-em-er), Sir Henry (English inventor of
    Bessemer steel process) B:153; I:333
Bessemer process (for producing steel) B:153
  iron and steel I:333, 338
Bessette, Alfred see André, Brother
Best, Charles H. (Canadian physiologist) B:59
Best Friend of Charleston (locomotive) L:278
  early transportation in South Carolina S:302
  railroads, early history of R:89
Best in Show (dog show award) D:248
Best of Breed (dog show award) D:248
Beta brass (alloy) B:410
Betancourt (bate-an-COOR), Rómulo (Venezuelan
    statesman) V:299
Betancur Cuartas, Belisario (Colombian president)
    C:408
Beta (BAY-ta) particles (of radioactive atoms) R:45, 67
Beta rays (streams of beta particles of radioactive
    elements) R:67
Beta video cassette system V:332d
Betelgeuse (BET-el-geuse) (star) C:524; S:431–32
Bethesda (in the New Testament) J:82
Bethlehem (Jordan)
  birthplace of Jesus Christ J:84
  Christmas customs C:300
Bethlehem (Pennsylvania) P:142; picture(s) C:413
  Bach festival M:560
Bethune, Mary McLeod (American educator) B:153;
    F:271
Betjeman (BET-je-man), Sir John (English poet and
    writer) B:503
Betrothed, The (novel) see Promessi sposi, I
Betsy Ross House (Philadelphia, Pennsylvania) P:180
Bettelheim (BET-tel-hime), Bruno (American
    psychologist and educator) B:503
Better Business bureaus B:503
Bev (unit of energy in nuclear physics) see Electron volt
Bevel gears G:66
Beverages
  beer B:114–15
  coffee C:396–97
  grain products G:284–85
  tea T:34–36
  what you drink depends on where you live F:332
  whiskey and other distilled beverages W:159
  wine W:188–89
Bewick, Thomas (English engraver) C:234
Beyle, Marie Henri see Stendhal

Bile (secretion of the liver)   B:277; D:161–63; G:227
Bilingual education   E:90
    Hispanic Americans   H:135
Bilingual Education Act (United States, 1968)   H:135
Billboards (used for outdoor advertising)   A:29–30
    Ogden Nash poem against   H:280
Billets (steel ingots)   I:334
Bill Haley and the Comets (rock music group)   R:262c
Billiard balls   P:324
Billiards   B:179–81
Billings (Montana)   M:440
Billings, William (American hymn composer)   H:310
Billingsgate (London)   L:289
Bill of Rights, American   B:181–84 see also Civil
        rights; United States, Constitution of the
    civil rights, historical origins of   C:330
    The Federalist, position of   F:78
    freedom of religion, speech, and press   F:462
    jury, trial by   J:159
    Madison was the principal author   M:12
    ten original amendments to the Constitution
        U:147, 155–56
Bill of Rights, Canadian see Charter of Rights and
        Freedoms
Bill of Rights, English   B:184; E:246
    civil rights, historical origins of   C:330
    English Bill of Rights and taxation   T:24
    jury trial, right to   J:159
Bill of Rights, French see Declaration of the Rights of
        Man and of the Citizen
Bill of Rights, GI see GI Bill of Rights
Bill of Rights, Universal see Universal Declaration of
        Human Rights
Bill of Rights Day   B:181
Bills (of birds) see Beaks
Bills (suggested laws)   U:142–44, 166–68
Billy goats   G:244
Billy the Kid (American outlaw)   B:504
Biloxi (bil-OX-i) (Mississippi)   M:354, 361; picture(s)
        M:355
Biltmore House and Gardens (Asheville, North Carolina)
        N:314
Bimetallic strips (in thermometers)   T:164
Bimini Islands (Bahamas)   B:17
    Ponce de León's search for the Fountain of Youth
        P:382
Binary (BY-nary) form (basic design used in writing
        music)   M:543
Binary number system   C:485; N:409
    automation   A:530
    computers   C:481
    fiber optic telephone transmission   T:56
Binary stars   A:474; S:433
    mutual eclipses   E:50
Binchois, Gilles (Flemish composer)   D:365; F:444
    Renaissance music   R:172
Binder's board (for book covers)   B:333
Binding knots   K:288
Binding of books see Bookbinding
Bindweed   W:104
Binet (bi-NAY), Alfred (French psychologist)   I:253–54
Bingen, Hildegard von see Hildegard von Bingen
Bingham, Hiram (American missionary in Hawaii)
        H:62
Bingham Canyon copper mine (Utah)   U:249
Binnig, Gerd (German scientist)   E:164
Binoculars   O:181; picture(s) O:180
    prism binoculars   L:147
Binocular vision see Stereoscopic vision

Binomial (by-NO-mial) theorem (mathematical formula
        worked out by Newton)   N:206
Binominal (name of two terms to show genus and
        species)   K:252
Binturongs (bear cats) (mammals related to mongooses)
        G:92, 94; picture(s) G:93
Biochemistry (study of the composition of living things)
        B:185–88; C:205, 210 see also Body chemistry;
        Genetics; Photosynthesis
    biological studies in the 20th century   B:201
    body chemistry   B:291–99
    chemistry, history of   C:211
    life   L:198–200
    medical laboratory tests   M:209
    Pasteur, Louis   P:99
Biodegradable materials   W:64
    detergents and soap   D:141
Biofeedback (method to control body processes),
        picture(s)   D:239
Biogenesis (by-o-GEN-e-sis), Pasteur's theory of   B:200
Biogeography (by-o-ge-OG-raphy) (study of geography of
        plants and animals)   G:105–6
Biographical novel   B:190
Biography (by-OG-raphy) (author's account of a person's
        life)   B:189–90
    Boswell's Life of Samuel Johnson   E:279; J:125
    English literature   E:288
    library arrangement   L:183
    literature, types of   L:258
    Pulitzer prizes   P:536–37
Bioko (formerly Fernando Po) (province of Equatorial
        Guinea)   E:305–6
Biological clock   B:191–92; L:203–4 see also Rhythm
        (in plant and animal life)
    clock-compass in birds and bees   B:233, 235;
        H:193
    millipedes   C:169
Biological control (of pests)   F:57, 482; I:249–50;
        P:288
    vegetable growing   V:288
Biological rhythm see Rhythm (in plant and animal life)
Biological warfare (warfare in which living organisms are
        used to transmit disease to an enemy)   B:504
    disarmament   D:180
Biologic response modifiers (natural substances that
        help the body fight cancer)   C:93
Biology (by-OL-ogy)   B:193–202 see also Evolution
    biochemistry   B:185–88
    biological clock   L:203–4
    biological oceanography   O:37–39
    cells   C:159–62
    genetic engineering   G:88–91
    genetics   G:77–88
    medicine, history of   M:203–8c
    Mendel created a new experiment combining biology
        and statistics   M:220
    science, advances in   S:77
    science and society   S:79
    taxonomy   T:26–29
Bioluminescence (by-o-lu-min-ES-cence) (light emitted
        by living organisms)   B:203
    centipedes and millipedes   C:169
    comb jellies   J:75
    ocean life   O:24, 27
Biomedical engineers   E:225
Biomes (communities of plants and animals)   B:204–
        10
    specific regions of the biosphere   L:203
Biondi, Matt (American swimmer)   O:118
Biophysics   P:238

Biopsy (examination of living tissue) C:92; M:209
Biorhythm *see* Rhythm (in plant and animal life)
Biosatellite (satellite that carries living matter into space) S:340d
Biosphere L:201–6
   biomes B:204–10
Biotechnology
   control of plant pests P:289
Biotic patterns (in geography) G:103
Biotin (B-complex vitamin) V:370d
Bipolar transistors T:276
Birch (tree), *picture(s)* P:292
   paper birch, *picture(s)* T:304
   shapes of leaves, *picture(s)* L:114
   state tree of New Hampshire, *picture(s)* N:149
   uses of the wood and its grain, *picture(s)* W:223
   white birch, *picture(s)* M:328
Bird, Larry (American basketball player) B:504; I:156; *picture(s)* B:95g; I:157
Birdbanding, *picture(s)* H:187
   Audubon made first banding experiments A:491
"Bird Came Down the Walk, A" (poem by Dickinson) D:153
Bird Day *see* Arbor Day
Birdie (golf score) G:254
Bird in Space (sculpture by Brancusi) B:370; *picture(s)* S:105
Bird of paradise A:270
Birds A:266; B:211–44
   acid rain's effects A:8
   animal communication A:284
   Audubon's paintings A:491
   beaks (bills) A:277; B:217
   biological clocks and compasses B:191
   caring for their young B:232
   cassowaries O:247
   chemical poisoning of the environment by DDT E:210
   descended from dinosaurs D:168
   ducks, geese, and swans D:341–44
   eagles E:2
   Earth, history of E:29
   eggs and embryos E:100
   eggs and incubation B:226–27
   emus O:247
   extinct and endangered species B:243–44
   feeding their young B:229, 232
   feet A:276; F:84
   finches showing adaptations supporting Darwin's theory of natural selection, *picture(s)* E:377
   flightless birds O:244–47
   fossil birds B:243
   four-chambered heart M:76
   habitats B:244
   history and evolution of B:243
   imprinting B:228
   kiwis O:247
   largest A:271
   life cycle B:224–25
   life spans A:83
   mating B:224
   migration B:233–35; H:186–88, 191–92; M:139
   navigation H:192–93
   nest building B:224–26
   New Zealand birdlife N:239–40
   oil spills' effect on W:67–68
   orders of, *picture(s)* B:230–31
   ostriches O:245
   owls O:284–85
   pelicans P:120–20a
   penguins P:120b–126
   pets B:245–47; P:178–79
   pollination of flowers P:282
   pollution in the food chain B:244
   poultry P:414–17
   prehistoric animals P:434
   protective coloration B:214
   provincial *see* individual Canadian province articles
   reproduction R:178
   rheas O:245–47
   smallest A:271
   songs and other sounds B:223
   state U:86 *see also* individual state articles for pictures
   "talking" birds P:85–88
   turkeys T:350
Birds as pets B:245–47; P:178–79
Birdseye, Clarence (American inventor) I:286
   food preservation F:343
Bird snakes S:207
Bird's-nest fungi F:500
Birds of prey A:276
   eagles E:2
Birdsongs B:223
Birdwatching B:221
Bird Woman *see* Sacagawea
Birendra (king of Nepal) N:110
Birettas (hats) H:46
Birmingham (Alabama) A:130, 136, 140–41
Birmingham (England) U:64–65
Birney (BER-ni), Alice McLellan (American educator) P:67
Birney, James G. (American abolitionist) B:250f; P:376
Biro, Laszlo (Hungarian inventor) P:146–47
Birr Castle (Ireland)
   gardens, *picture(s)* G:32
Birth control B:247–49
   Supreme Court decisions W:213
Birth control pills *see* Pill
Birthday cards (how to make) G:376
Birthday parties P:89–93
   Why do we put lighted candles on a birthday cake and then blow them out? C:94
Birthdays (of famous people)
   arranged by the month *see* individual month articles
   holidays honoring H:151–53
Birthday stones *see* Birthstones
Birth defects *see* Congenital disabilities and diseases
Birthing rooms (in hospitals) H:247
"Birthmark, The" (story by Hawthorne) S:162
Birth of a Nation, The (motion picture) M:474
Birth of Venus, The (painting by Botticelli) U:3
Birth rate (number of births per 1,000 people) P:385
   countries with highest and lowest birth rates, *list(s)* P:386
Birthstones G:72 *see also* the names of stones and articles on individual months
Biscayne National Park (Florida) F:267
Biscuits (food) B:388b
Bishkek (capital of Kyrgyzstan) K:311
Bishop, Billy (Canadian aviator) B:504
Bishop, Charles Reed (American banker in Hawaii) H:62
Bishop, Elizabeth (American poet) A:213
Bishop, Maurice (prime minister of Grenada) G:379
Bishops (of a church)
   cathedral is a church containing the bishop's throne C:133

Bishops (continued)
  Christianity, history of **C:**287; **R:**283
  Roman Catholic Church, government of the **R:**294
Bishops' schools see Cathedral schools
Bishop's University (Lennoxville, Quebec) **Q:**11
Bislama (language) **V:**279
Bismarck (capital of North Dakota) **N:**330
Bismarck, Otto von (German statesman) **B:**250;
  G:161; picture(s) **I:**273; **P:**459
  Franco-Prussian War **F:**452
  William II dismissing Bismarck, cartoon of, picture(s)
  G:162
Bismarck Archipelago (Pacific island group) **P:**58d
Bismarck Sea **O:**44
Bismuth (element) **E:**171
Bisnaga (kind of cactus) **C:**5
Bison (BY-son) (hoofed mammals) **B:**428–29;
  picture(s) **H:**216; **I:**181; **U:**89
  Ice Age **I:**12
  National Bison Range (Montana) **M:**439
  prehistoric carving, picture(s) **A:**438
  slaughter in Kansas **K:**176
  Wood Buffalo National Park (Alberta, Canada) **C:**60
Bisque (BISK) **dolls** **D:**267–68
Bissau (capital of Guinea-Bissau) **G:**408
Bissell, Emily P. (American social welfare worker)
  D:101
Bissell, George (American lawyer) **P:**101
Bisymmetrical (by-sim-MET-ric-al) **balance** (in design)
  D:133
Bit (mouthpiece for a horse) **H:**228
Bit cells (of microchips) **C:**483
Bite (in dentistry) **O:**236
Bites (of animals)
  animal bites, first aid for **F:**162
  How do mosquitoes bite? **M:**470
  insect bites, first aid for **F:**162
Bitonality (in music) **M:**398
Bits (binary digits) (of information) **C:**481, 485; **T:**48
Bitter (sense of taste) **B:**286
Bitterroot (flower)
  state flower of Montana, picture(s) **M:**429
Bittersweet (woody vine) **B:**504
Bitumen (hydrocarbon) **P:**175
Bituminous (bit-TU-min-ous) **coal** (soft coal) **C:**388
  fuels **F:**487
Bivalves (mollusks with two shells) **O:**289–92; **S:**148
Biwa, Lake (Japan) **J:**35
Biya, Paul (Cameroon president) **C:**37
Bizerte (bi-ZERT) (Tunisia) **T:**336; picture(s) **T:**334
Bizet (bi-ZAY), **Georges** (French composer) **B:**504
  Carmen **O:**152
Bjørnson (BYERN-son), **Bjørnstjerne** (Norwegian writer)
  N:345; **S:**58f, 58g
Blab schools **L:**242
Black (color) **C:**425
  Christian funeral custom **F:**494
  symbolism of **C:**372, 429
Black, Hugo La Fayette (American jurist) **B:**504
Black, Joseph (Scottish scientist) **M:**27; **S:**70–72
Black, Shirley Temple see Temple, Shirley
Black Americans **B:**250a–250q; **U:**157 see also the
  names of black Americans
  Abolitionist movement **B:**250e–250f
  baseball **B:**88, 91–92
  Boston's Black Heritage Trail **B:**342
  children's literature **C:**238–39
  civil rights movements **C:**331
  Civil War, United States **C:**334–38, 346
  Confederate States **C:**496

Congress, first African-American members of,
  picture(s) **U:**143
Dred Scott decision **D:**321
education in the United States **E:**90
Emancipation Proclamation **B:**250f–250g; **E:**199–
  200
English language **E:**267
folklore **F:**313
folk music **F:**327
genealogical research **G:**76d
hymns and spirituals **F:**324; **H:**310–11
jazz **J:**57–62; **U:**208
jazz-style big bands **R:**262a
Liberia settled by freed American slaves **L:**165,
  168
literature **A:**199–200, 202, 208, 211, 213–14a
Maryland's population **M:**124
motion pictures **M:**491
New Negro Movement **B:**250j
newspapers **N:**198
newspapers: Baltimore's Afro-American **M:**127
novels **N:**363
physicians trained at Meharry Medical College
  N:17
Reconstruction Period **R:**117–20
rhythm and blues music **R:**262a, 262b
rock music **R:**262c
segregation **S:**113–15
slavery **S:**194–97
Spingarn Medal **S:**409–10
thirteen American colonies **T:**166, 178; picture(s)
  T:168
trickster stories carried from Africa **A:**76b
Uncle Tom's Cabin by Harriet Beecher Stowe
  S:465
Underground Railroad **U:**14–16
universities and colleges **U:**220
Washington, D.C., history of **W:**32, 34
Black-and-tan coonhound (dog) **D:**250
Black-and-white negative film (in photography) **P:**204–
  5, 210–11
Black Arts Movement **A:**214
Blackball (to vote against) **B:**23
Blackbeard (British pirate) **B:**504; **P:**264
Black bears **B:**105–6; picture(s) **B:**107
  Yellowstone National Park **Y:**345
Black Belt (area of Alabama) **A:**133
Black belt (in karate) **K:**195
Blackberries **G:**298, 301
Black box (electronic device not understood by the
  person using it) **B:**504
Blackbuck (antelope) **A:**297
Black Canyon of the Gunnison National Monument
  (Colorado) **C:**440
Black-capped chickadee (bird), picture(s) **B:**216
Black cats **S:**504
Black Codes (laws passed by Southern states just after
  Civil War) **R:**118; **U:**186
  Johnson, Andrew **J:**118
Black-crowned night heron (bird), picture(s) **B:**231
Black Death see Bubonic plague
Black-eyed Susans (flowers), picture(s) **W:**170
  Maryland, state flower of, picture(s) **M:**121
Black-figure pottery (of ancient Greece) **P:**408
Blackfish (Shawnee Indian leader) **B:**334
Blackfoot (Indians of North America) **I:**180
Black-footed ferret (weasel) **E:**54, 208, 211; picture(s)
  E:210
Black Forest (Germany) **G:**153
  acid rain effects, picture(s) **E:**300

Blackfriars (London theater) **S:**132
Black Hawk (Indian chief) **I:**74–75, 204–5, 303
  Black Hawk Historic Site (Rock Island, Illinois)
    I:70
  Iowa nicknamed Hawkeye State in his honor **I:**290
Black Hawk War **I:**74–75; **W:**207
Blackheads (clogged skin pores) **D:**187
Black Hills (South Dakota and Wyoming) **S:**312, 315;
    W:323; *picture(s)* **S:**319
  gold rush **G:**252
Black Hills National Forest (South Dakota and
    Wyoming), *picture(s)* **N:**29
Black hole (in astronomy) **A:**476; **S:**76, 435; **U:**212–
    13, 215
  galactic nucleus **M:**309
  quasars may contain **U:**217
Black Hole of Calcutta (dungeon in India) **B:**504
Black homelands (South Africa) *see* Bantustans
Black Iris (painting by O'Keeffe), *picture(s)* **U:**132
Blackjack oak (tree)
  shapes of leaves, *picture(s)* **L:**114
Black Kettle (Cheyenne Indian chief) **I:**180
Blackland Prairies (of Texas) **T:**130, 132
Black light *see* Ultraviolet radiation
Blacklist (people or companies boycotted or
    discriminated against) **B:**504
Black lung (disease that comes from breathing coal
    dust) **C:**391
Black Madonna (Polish religious symbol) **P:**358
Black market (market in violation of government
    regulations) **B:**504
Black Mesa State Park (Oklahoma) **O:**90; *picture(s)*
    O:82
Blackmun, Harry Andrew (American jurist) **S:**508;
    picture(s) **U:**171
Black Muslims *see* World Community of Islam in the
    West
Black olives **O:**101
Blackout (putting out of all lights) **B:**504
Black Panther Party **B:**250o
Black Peter *see* Swarte Piet
Black plague (disease) *see* Bubonic plague
Black powder (early gunpowder) **E:**422–23
  guns and ammunition **G:**414
Black power (slogan of the civil rights movement)
    B:250p
Black racer (snake), *picture(s)* **S:**205
Black Reflections (painting by Kline), *picture(s)*
    M:396a
Black Renaissance *see* Harlem Renaissance
Blacks **B:**250a–250q *see also* Black Americans; the
    names of African countries, black leaders, and
    organizations
  Africa **A:**55
  Africa, early kingdoms of **A:**67
  African literature **A:**76a–76d
  art **A:**70–76
  Brazil **B:**373–74
  folklore and folk songs **F:**313, 319, 324
  Haiti **H:**9, 11
  Jamaica **J:**15, 18
  Latin America **L:**49–50
  Latin American dance **D:**30; **L:**69
  music **A:**77–79; **L:**74
  sickle-cell anemia **D:**201
  slavery **S:**193–97
  Suriname **S:**516
  work songs **F:**319
Black Sea **O:**44; **U:**39
Blackshirts (fascist parties)
  British **F:**64
  Italian fascists and Mussolini **F:**63; **M:**560
Black snake, *picture(s)* **S:**205
Black Sox Scandal (in baseball) **B:**90
Black spirituals *see* Spirituals
Black Stone of Mecca *see* Kaaba
Blackstone River (Massachusetts and Rhode Island)
    R:214–15
Blackstrap molasses **H:**79; **S:**483
Black tea **T:**34–35
Blacktip sharks **S:**143; *picture(s)* **S:**141
Blackton, J. Stuart (American illustrator) **A:**290
Blacktop (asphalt for roads) **R:**250
Black walnuts **N:**431–32
Black Warrior River (Alabama) **A:**133
Blackwater River (Ireland) **I:**319
Blackwell, Elizabeth (English-American physician)
    B:250r
Blackwell, Rosa (American slave) **S:**195
Black widow spiders, *picture(s)* **F:**162
Bladder **B:**282
Blades (of broad leaves) **L:**112
Blade tools (of prehistoric people) **P:**440
Blaiberg, Philip *see* Barnard, Christiaan
Blaine, James Gillespie (American statesman) **G:**54;
    M:49
Blair, Bonnie (American speed skater) **O:**119–20;
    picture(s) **I:**42
Blair, Eric *see* Orwell, George
Blais, Marie-Claire (Canadian writer) **C:**85
Blaize, Herbert A. (prime minister of Grenada) **G:**379
Blake, Eubie (American composer and pianist) **B:**504–
    5
Blake, Lyman Reed (American shoe manufacturer)
    S:158
Blake, Nicholas *see* Day Lewis, C.
Blake, William (English poet and artist) **B:**250r
  book illustration **E:**261
  children's literature **C:**237
  English literature **E:**278
  engraving from *Songs of Experience*, *picture(s)*
    E:278
  illustration of books **I:**80
  Jacob's Ladder (painting), *picture(s)* **R:**302
  romanticism **R:**302; *picture(s)* **R:**303
Blanc (BLON), Mont (mountain between France and
    Italy) **A:**194b; **F:**407; *picture(s)* **F:**409; **G:**98
  first successful ascent **M:**495
Blanchard, Doc (American football star and Army
    officer) **B:**505
Blanchard (blon-SHAR), Jean-Pierre François (French
    balloonist) **B:**35, 505
Blanchard, Madeline-Sophie (French balloonist) **B:**35
Bland, James Allen (American songwriter and minstrel
    performer) **B:**505
Bland-Allison Bill (1877) **H:**71
Blanes, Juan Manuel (Uruguayan artist) **L:**65
Blankers-Koen, Fanny (Dutch track star) **B:**505;
    O:110; **T:**263
Blanket primary elections **E:**129
Blanket toss (Eskimo game), *picture(s)* **E:**320
Blank verse (unrhymed verse) **P:**353
  quotations from Shakespeare's plays **S:**133–37
Blantyre (Malawi) **M:**53
Blarney stone **B:**505
Blasco Ibáñez (BLAS-co-e-BON-yeth), Vicente (Spanish
    author) **S:**392
Blast (of a nuclear explosion) **N:**376
Blast furnaces **I:**330–32; *picture(s)* **P:**135
  fuel **F:**488

Bluebirds
    Idaho, mountain bluebird state bird of, *picture(s)*
      I:47
    Missouri, state bird of, *picture(s)* **M:**367
    Nevada, mountain bluebird state bird of, *picture(s)*
      N:123
    New York, state bird of, *picture(s)* **N:**211
Blue Birds (of Camp Fire, Inc.) **C:**40; *picture(s)* **C:**38
    awards, *picture(s)* **C:**39
Blue Boat, The (painting by Homer), *picture(s)* **U:**130
Bluebonnet (state flower of Texas), *picture(s)* **T:**125
Bluebottle flies, *picture(s)* **I:**244–45
Blue Boy, The (painting by Gainsborough), *picture(s)*
    G:4
Blue cheeses **D:**12
Blue chip stocks **S:**455
Blue crabs (crustaceans) **C:**571
Blue Dancers (drawing by Degas), *picture(s)* **F:**430
Bluefin (fish) **F:**215
Bluefish **F:**188
Blue-footed booby, *picture(s)* **B:**216
Bluegill (fish), *picture(s)* **F:**209
Blue goose (bird) **D:**344
Bluegrass Basin (of Kentucky) **K:**215
Bluegrass music **C:**563
Bluegrass State (nickname for Kentucky) **K:**212–13
Blue Grotto (Capri, Italy) **C:**157; **I:**363
Blueground (kimberlite) (diamond-bearing rock) **G:**70
Blue hen chicken
    state bird of Delaware, *picture(s)* **D:**89
Blue Hen State (nickname for Delaware) **D:**88–89
Blue jays (birds) **B:**242; **P:**88; *picture(s)* **B:**217, 230
Blue laws (to regulate individual conduct) **B:**505
Blue Men (nomads of Morocco) **M:**458
Blue Mosque (Istanbul, Turkey) *see* Sultan Ahmed
    Mosque
Blue Mountains (Jamaica) **J:**16
Blue Mountains (Oregon and Washington) **O:**205;
    W:14–15
Blue Nile River (Africa) **E:**331; **N:**260; **S:**477–78;
    picture(s) **A:**46
Blue ox (Babe, belonging to Paul Bunyan) **F:**312
Blue Plate, Legend of the **L:**133
Blue point Siamese cats **C:**144
Blueprint (photographic reproduction method) **B:**259
Blue Riband (award for the fastest Atlantic crossing)
    O:31
Blue Rider, The (modern art group in Germany) **E:**426;
    M:391–92
    German art **G:**172
    Kandinsky, Wassily **K:**173
    Klee, Paul **K:**271
Blue Ridge (mountain range, eastern United States),
    picture(s) **G:**133; **N:**104
    Maryland **M:**122; *picture(s)* **M:**121
    North Carolina **N:**308
    South Carolina **S:**298
    Tennessee **T:**76
    Virginia **V:**346; *picture(s)* **V:**347
Blue Ridge Parkway **N:**314; **V:**355; *picture(s)* **N:**51
Blues (in printing) **B:**330–31
Blues, the (music) **J:**57–58
    black American folklore **F:**313
    black American music **B:**250k
    contributions to jazz **U:**208
    folk musicians **F:**318
    folk songs **F:**304
    gospel songs **H:**311
Blue spruce (tree)

state tree of Colorado, *picture(s)* **C:**431
state tree of Utah, *picture(s)* **U:**243
Bluestocking (term for a literary woman) **B:**505
Blue whales **W:**149
    endangered species **E:**208; *chart(s)* **E:**209
    largest mammal **M:**65
Blue-winged teal (duck) **D:**341
Bluffing (animal defense) **L:**271
Blum (BLOOM), Léon (French statesman) **F:**419
Blume, Judy (American writer) **B:**259
Blumenschein, Ernest L. (American artist) **N:**193–94
Blunderbuss (smooth-bore gun) **G:**420
Blushing (body action) **B:**300
Bly, Nellie (American newspaper reporter) **B:**260
B lymphocytes *see* B cells
BMX (bicycle motocross) bicycles **B:**175, 177;
    picture(s) **B:**176
B'nai B'rith International (Jewish organization) **B:**505
Board games **G:**12–15
Boarding pass (permission to board an airplane)
    A:126–27
Boarding schools **P:**443
Board of directors (of a corporation) **B:**471
Boardsailing (sport) **B:**260–61
Boars (male pigs) **H:**211; **P:**248
    wild boar **C:**149; *picture(s)* **H:**210
"Boar's Head, The" (English carol) **C:**118
Boas (snakes) **S:**206–7; *picture(s)* **S:**212
Boas, Franz (German-American anthropologist) **B:**261
Boat racing **B:**265
    rowing competition **R:**340–41
Boats and boating **B:**262–65 *see also* Canoeing;
    Rowing; Sailing; Water sports
    ancient water craft **S:**151
    Bangladesh riverboats, *picture(s)* **B:**50
    canal boats **E:**311
    canoeing **C:**97–99
    Chinese dwellings **C:**264
    dhows of Bahrain **B:**18
    Dragon Boat Festival (China), *picture(s)* **H:**159
    early transportation **T:**281
    felucca on the Nile, *picture(s)* **R:**238
    gondolas on the canals (Venice), *picture(s)* **B:**62
    Grand Canyon National Park, *picture(s)* **G:**292
    houseboats **H:**176–77
    hydrofoils **H:**301
    iceboating **I:**19–20
    inventions in water transportation **I:**280
    johnboats for float fishing **M:**366
    junks, *picture(s)* **R:**247
    kayaks **C:**99; **E:**317; *picture(s)* **G:**374a
    Mississippi riverboats, *picture(s)* **M:**352
    reed boats on Lake Titicaca **P:**161; *picture(s)*
      B:308; **P:**160
    rowing **R:**340–41
    safety measures **S:**6–7
    sailboats, types of, *picture(s)* **S:**9
    sailing **S:**9–14
    toy boats, *picture(s)* **T:**249
    umiaks **E:**316
    Why do boats float? **F:**250
Boats and Sea, Deer Isle, Maine (painting by Marin),
    picture(s) **W:**61
Boats at Argenteuil (painting by Monet), *picture(s)*
    M:408
Bobber (for pole and line fishing) **F:**205
Bobbies (English policemen) **L:**288; **P:**368
Bobbin (spool for holding thread) **I:**218
Bobbin lace **L:**19
Bobcats **C:**141; *picture(s)* **C:**142

Bobko, Karol J. (American astronaut) *picture(s)* **S:**351
Bobo (a people of Africa) **B:**451
Bobo Dioulasso (BO-bo diu-LA-so) (Burkina) **B:**451;
picture(s) **B:**452
Bobsledding **B:**266–67
Olympic event **O:**107
Bobwhite (bird) **B:**239
Bocachee *see* Tomochichi
Boccaccio (bo-CA-chi-o), **Giovanni** (Italian writer)
I:383, 406; **S:**161
Boccherini (bo-car-E-ni), **Luigi** (Italian composer)
C:184
Boccioni (bo-CHO-ni), **Umberto** (Italian painter) **I:**403
futurism in sculpture **S:**104
modern art **M:**391
Unique Forms of Continuity in Space (painting),
picture(s) **I:**403
Bock beer **B:**115
Böcklin (BUK-lene), **Arnold** (Swiss artist) **G:**171
Bode (BO-da), **Johannes** (German astronomer) **S:**242–
43
Bodecker, N. M. (American author and illustrator)
illustration from *Hurry, Hurry, Mary Dear!*, *picture(s)*
C:248
Bode's law **S:**242–43
Bodhisattvas (bo-dis-AT-vas) (Buddhist deities) **B:**424
Bodleian (bod-LE-ian) **Library** (Oxford University)
L:174
Body (of an automobile) **A:**546, 551
Body, human **B:**268–88
adolescence, changes during **A:**22
aging **A:**81
air pollution's effects on **A:**122–24
antibodies and antigens **A:**313
biological clock **B:**191–92
blood **B:**255–58
bodybuilding **B:**289–90
body signals **B:**300–301
brain **B:**363–69
cancer **C:**90–93
cells **C:**159
chemistry *see* Body chemistry
child development **C:**224–25
circulatory system **C:**304–6
defenses against disease **D:**210
digestive system **D:**161–63
diseases **D:**181–213
drawing, history of **D:**314
dreaming **D:**317–18
drugs affect **D:**333
ear **E:**4–6
energy, source of **E:**214–15
eye **E:**429–32
feet and hands, basic pattern of **F:**79–80, 84
g-forces and weightlessness **S:**340L–341
glands **G:**226–28
hair **H:**5–7
health **H:**74–77
heart **H:**80–83
human body is seventy percent water **L:**202
immune system **I:**95–98
Leonardo's studies **L:**153
lie detection **L:**193
mental health **M:**225
nervous system **N:**115–18
osmosis **O:**242–43
physical anthropology **A:**301
physical examination by a doctor **M:**208e–208h
physical fitness **P:**224–29
reproductive organs **R:**178–79
skeletal system **S:**183–84b
smoking, effects of **S:**203
teeth **T:**42–44
voice apparatus **V:**375
water is most important substance in **W:**50
What is the largest organ of your body? **B:**272
X rays **X:**340–41
Bodybuilding (exercises for developing muscles)
B:289–90
weight lifting **W:**107
Body chemistry **B:**291–99
aging **A:**84–85
biochemistry **B:**187–88
biological studies in the 20th century **B:**201
body, human **B:**268–69
digestive system **D:**161–63
drugs supply hormones **D:**333
endocrine system **B:**287–88
enzymes **E:**303
glands **G:**226–28
immune system **I:**95–98
living matter, chemical makeup of **L:**198–200
nutrition **N:**423–26
Body drop (automobile assembling)
Model T, *picture(s)* **A:**543
Body language **B:**505
Body signals **B:**300–301
Body's senses
nervous system, biological studies of **B:**201
Body temperature
amphibians **A:**214b
anesthesia produced by lowering **A:**258–59
circulatory system regulates **C:**305–6
dinosaurs **D:**165, 173
hibernation **H:**117–20
how a nurse takes temperature **N:**422
medical examination, techniques of **M:**208e
sleep lowers **S:**198
Boehm, Gottfried German architect
Cologne building complex, *picture(s)* **G:**173
Boeing 247 (airplane) **A:**562
Boeing 314 (flying boat) **A:**563
Boeing 707 (jet airliner) **A:**565–66
Boeing 747 (jet airliner) **A:**566, 569; *picture(s)*
A:110, 119
Boeing Company **W:**19
Boerhaave (BOOR-ha-va), **Hermann** (Dutch doctor)
M:206
Boers (Dutch settlers in South Africa) **A:**69; **S:**272
Boer War **B:**302
Lesotho, history of **L:**157
Boer War (1899–1902) **B:**302
Africa, struggle for **A:**69
England, history of **E:**251
South Africa, history of **S:**273
use of spy kites **K:**267
Bogalusa (Louisiana) **L:**310
Bogart, Humphrey (American actor) **B:**505
Bogdan (Moldavian prince) **M:**403
Bogdanovich, Peter (American motion picture director)
M:493
Bogey (BOAG-y) (golf score) **G:**254
Bogie wheels (of tanks) **T:**14
Bog iron **N:**169
Bogotá (bo-go-TA) (capital of Colombia) **B:**303;
C:407; *picture(s)* **C:**402
University of the Andes, *picture(s)* **S:**285
Bogs **N:**63
cranberry bog, *picture(s)* **G:**300
Bog turtles **T:**355

Bogue Sound (North Carolina) N:308
Bohème (bo-EM), *La* (opera by Puccini) O:151
Bohemia (western part of Czechoslovakia) B:505–6;
　　C:608, 610; *picture(s)* C:606
　　Habsburgs H:2
　　Thirty Years' War T:179
Böhl de Faber (BURL day fa-BER), Cecilia *see*
　　Caballero, Fernán
Bohr, Niels (Danish atomic physicist) B:304; C:211;
　　D:110; *picture(s)* P:232
　　quantum theory L:226
　　science, history of S:76
Boiardo (bo-YAR-do), Matteo Maria (Italian poet) I:406
Boileau-Despréaux (bwa-LO-day-pray-O), Nicolas (French
　　poet) F:438
Boilers H:96–97; S:445
Boiling (method of cooking) C:533–34
Boiling point H:90–91
　　different boiling points make distillation possible
　　　　D:218–19
　　geysers G:193
　　liquids, properties of L:255
　　liquids boil at lower temperatures in a vacuum
　　　　V:262
　　water W:48
Boils (skin infections) D:195
Boise (BOI-se) (capital of Idaho) I:51, 55
Boitano, Brian (American figure skater) O:119;
　　picture(s) I:45
Bokassa, General Jean-Bedel (emperor of the Central
　　African Empire) C:171
Bokher, Eli (Yiddish author) Y:350
Bok Singing Tower (Florida) F:269
Bolas (hunting devices) I:108, 199
Bolden, Charles F. Jr. (American astronaut) S:350;
　　picture(s) S:341
Bolero (kind of jacket) C:377
Bolero (love song of Latin America) L:69
Boleyn (BULL-in), Anne (2nd queen of Henry VIII of
　　England) E:242; H:108
　　Reformation in England C:292
Bolívar, Pico (highest point in Venezuela) V:296
Bolívar (bo-LI-var), Simón (South American liberator and
　　patriot) B:305, 310
　　Colombia's independence C:408
　　present Organization of American States outgrowth of
　　　　his ideal O:220
　　San Martín, José, meeting with S:36
　　Simón Bolívar's birthday holiday H:152–53
　　Venezuela, history of V:298–99
Bolivia (bo-LIV-ia) B:306–10; *picture(s)* S:274, 278
　　Catavi tin mine, *picture(s)* S:278; T:207
　　corn harvest, *picture(s)* S:290
　　flag, *picture(s)* F:238
　　Indian folk dancing L:69
　　Indians, American I:196
　　life in Latin America L:47–61
　　Tiwanaku civilization I:170
Bolkiah, Sultan Sir Muda Hassanal *see* Hassanal
　　Bolkiah, Sultan Sir Muda
Böll, Heinrich (German writer) G:182
Bolling, Richard Walker (American politician) U:142
Boll weevil C:561–62; *picture(s)* B:126; C:560;
　　I:234; P:286
　　Alabama's monument to cotton pest A:137
　　beetles and their environment B:127
Bollworm, pink *see* Pink bollworm
Bologna, University of I:381; U:219
Bolshevik Party (in Russian history) C:473; L:140;
　　R:367; U:48–49

1917 coup, *picture(s)* R:368
Stalin's Great Purge U:50
Stalin was an organizer for S:419
Bolshoi Ballet, *picture(s)* B:30
Bolt-action (of guns and rifles) G:418–19
Bolter, The (painting by Russell), *picture(s)* C:569
Bolton, Guy (English-born American dramatist) M:550
Bolts (fasteners) N:3
Bolus (chewed food) S:460
Bolyai, Johann (Hungarian mathematician) M:162
Bombardier, Joseph-Armand (Canadian inventor of the
　　snowmobile) S:215
Bombardier beetle B:125; I:243; *picture(s)* B:124
Bombay (India) B:310a–310b
　　Catholic church, *picture(s)* R:149
　　commercial center of India I:122
　　Marine Drive, *picture(s)* I:123
Bombers (airplanes) U:112
Bombs *see* Atomic weapons; Hydrogen bomb; Neutron
　　bomb; Nuclear weapons
Bomb squads (in police departments) P:365
Bomoseen, Lake (Vermont) V:309
Bon (kind of nature worship) B:154
Bonaire (bo-NAIRE) (island in the Caribbean Sea)
　　B:506; C:114
Bonanza (television program), *picture(s)* T:70
Bonanza farms (in North Dakota) N:335
Bonaparte, Louis Napoleon *see* Napoleon III
Bonaparte, Napoleon *see* Napoleon I
Bonaparte family B:506
Bonar Law, Andrew *see* Law, Andrew Bonar
Bonavista (Newfoundland) N:145
Bond, Carrie Jacobs (American songwriter) W:206
Bond, Edward (English dramatist) D:303
Bond, George (American naval officer) U:23
Bond, James (literary and motion picture character)
　　M:491
Bond, Julian (American politician and civil rights leader)
　　B:506
Bonding (of adhesives) G:242
Bondone, Giotto di *see* Giotto di Bondone
Bonds (certificates of loans) S:454–55
　　Savings Bonds Division T:294
Bonds, chemical C:201, 204; M:153–54
Bone china (kind of porcelain) P:412
Bone marrow *see* Marrow
Bones (of animals and humans)
　　anthropological studies A:301
　　babies have more bones than adults S:184a
　　birds B:218
　　body, human B:274
　　feet F:80–82
　　first aid for broken bones F:161
　　hands F:83–84
　　periodontal disease causes deterioration of bones
　　　　that support the teeth D:198
　　skeletal system S:183–84b
　　What is a backbone? K:251
　　X rays, medical uses of X:340
Bongo (antelope) A:297; H:220; *picture(s)* H:218
Bongo, Omar (Gabonese president) G:4
Bongo drums D:338; *picture(s)* D:337
Bonheur (bon-ER), Rosa (French painter) B:506
Bonhoeffer, Dietrich (German Protestant theologian and
　　pastor) B:506
Bonhomme Richard (ship commanded by John Paul
　　Jones) J:127–28; R:205–6
Boniface, Saint (English missionary) C:290; R:284
Boniface (BON-i-face) VII (antipope) R:290
Boniface I, Saint (pope) R:290

Boniface II (pope) **R:**290
Boniface III (pope) **R:**290
Boniface IV, Saint (pope) **R:**290
Boniface V (pope) **R:**290
Boniface VI (pope) **R:**290
Boniface VIII (pope) **R:**287, 291
Boniface IX (pope) **R:**291
Bonin (Ogasawara) Islands (Pacific Ocean) **B:**506; **J:**35; **P:**6
Bonito (bon-E-to) (fish) **F:**188
Bon Marché (bon mar-SHAY) (early department store in Paris) **D:**119
Bonn (Germany) **B:**146; **G:**157
Bonnefoy, Yves (French poet) **F:**442
Bonnets, feathered (worn by American Indians) **H:**46
Bonneville (BON-nev-ille), Benjamin L. E. de (French-born American explorer) **O:**276
Bonneville, Lake (Utah) **L:**28; **U:**247
Bonneville Dam (Oregon and Washington) **D:**19; **O:**216; picture(s) **O:**207
Bonneville Salt Flats (Utah) **U:**244–45, 247
automobile racing **A:**538
Bonney, William H. see Billy the Kid
Bonspiel (curling tournament) **C:**69, 602
Bontemps (BON-tomp), Arna Wendell (American author) **B:**506
Booby (seabird)
blue-footed booby, picture(s) **B:**216
masked booby, picture(s) **B:**232
Book, Shrine of the (Jerusalem) see Shrine of the Book
Book awards see Awards, literary
Bookbinding **B:**332–33
printing **P:**471
Book clubs **P:**524
paperbacks for young people **P:**58a
Book design **B:**327, 329
encyclopedias **E:**204
medieval books **B:**321
typefaces **T:**369–70
Book fair (exhibition of books)
Frankfurt (Germany) **P:**525
Bookkeeping **B:**311–13
checking accounts in banks **B:**57
Bookkeeping machines **O:**54
Booklist (periodical) **L:**181
Book of Common Prayer see Prayer, Book of Common
Book of Hours (illustrated prayer book), picture(s) **E:**362
Book of Kells see Kells, Book of
Book of Mormon **M:**457; **S:**201
Book of the Dead (collection of Egyptian hymns, prayers, and magic chants) **B:**506
"Book of the Duchess, The" (poem by Chaucer) **C:**191
Book of the Year for Children Award **C:**232
Book reports **B:**314–17
Book reviews **B:**314
news of books **B:**333
Books **B:**318–33 see also Illuminated manuscripts; Libraries
from author to reader **B:**323–33
Aztec books had no words **A:**575
back matter **B:**329
bibliographic form **R:**183
binding see Bookbinding
blind, books for the **B:**253
bookmaking **B:**323–33
care of **L:**181–82
children's book awards **C:**228–31
children's literature **C:**232–48
collecting autographed books **A:**526–27

commercial art **C:**457–58
copyright protection **C:**547
design see Book design
education, history of **E:**77
encyclopedias **E:**203–7
etiquette books **E:**337
Frankfurt Book Fair **P:**525
front matter **B:**329
history of bookmaking **B:**318–22
illuminated see Illuminated manuscripts
illustration and illustrators **I:**79–84
indexes see Indexes and indexing
invention of **I:**284
Islamic illustrations **I:**357–58
layout **B:**329
Leipzig book and fur fair **F:**11–12
manuscript books **C:**463
mass communication tool **C:**471
Newbery, John **N:**137
novels **N:**358–63
paper **P:**51–57
paperback books **P:**58–58a, 524
prayer books **P:**430
printing **P:**468–79
programmed instruction **P:**483
publishing **P:**523–25
reference books **R:**129
reports and reviews **B:**314–17
on storytelling **S:**464
textbooks **T:**141–42
What is a talking book? **B:**254
word origins **W:**241
writing as a career **W:**321
Boom (of a sailboard) **B:**260
Boomerang (throwing stick) **A:**6a; **B:**506
Boomers (land seekers) **O:**95
Boomslangs (snakes) **S:**207
Boom town (town that grows suddenly) **B:**506
Boone, Daniel (American pioneer) **B:**334
birthplace (Daniel Boone Homestead) **P:**139
Horn in the West (outdoor drama, Boone, North Carolina) **N:**312
settlement of Kentucky **K:**225–26
westward movement **W:**145
Wilderness Road **O:**271
Boonesborough (frontier fort) **F:**376
Boone's Lick Trail (early road in Missouri) **M:**374
Boone's Trace (pioneer road) **P:**260
Booster shots (of vaccines) **M:**210; **V:**261
Booster stage (of multistage rockets) **R:**259–60
Boot camps (for recruits)
United States Marine Corps **U:**124
Boötes (bo-O-tese) (constellation) **C:**525
Booth, Edwin Thomas (American actor) **B:**506
Booth, John Wilkes (assassin of Lincoln) **B:**335; **C:**346; **L:**247
Boothe, Clare see Luce, Clare Boothe
Bootheel (area of Missouri) **M:**367
Booth family (English family of evangelists associated with the Salvation Army) **B:**506
Bootleggers (in the Roaring Twenties) **C:**539
Boots and shoes see Shoes
Bora (BO-ra) (wind of Adriatic region) **A:**161; **M:**213
Borah, William Edgar (American lawyer and political leader) **I:**58–59
Borah Peak (highest point in Idaho) **I:**48
Borax (mineral) **C:**24–25
Bordaberry, Juan M. (Uruguayan president) **U:**240
Bordeaux (France) **F:**412
Borden (Prince Edward Island, Canada) **P:**460, 462

Borden, Sir Robert Laird (Canadian statesman) B:335
  Canada, history of C:75–76
Border states (in the American Civil War) C:495
Borduas, Paul-Emile (Canadian artist) C:83
Boreal forests B:208
Borecole see Kale
Bores (of guns) G:414–15
Bores (tidal waves) T:196–97
  Bay of Fundy (Canada) N:138
Borg, Bjorn (Swedish tennis player) B:506; T:99;
  picture(s) T:93
Borges (BOR-hace), Jorge Luis (Argentine author and
  university professor) A:391; B:506; L:72
Borgia (BOR-ja) family (noble Italian family) B:506
Borglum, Gutzon (American sculptor) I:58
  Mount Rushmore National Memorial, picture(s)
  S:322
Boring see Drilling and boring
Boris I (BO-ris) (czar of Bulgaria) B:443
Boris III (king of Bulgaria) B:444
Boris Godunov (BOR-is goo-du-NOF) (play by Pushkin)
  D:300; R:377
Boris Godunov (opera by Mussorgsky) O:151
Borja Cevallos, Rodrigo (Ecuadorean political leader)
  B:507; E:69
Borlaug, Norman Ernest (American agricultural scientist)
  I:302; W:156
Borman, Frank (American astronaut) S:346; picture(s)
  S:347
Bormann (BOR-monn), Martin Ludwig (German Nazi
  leader) B:507
Borneo B:336–37; I:208–9 see also Malaysia
  Brunei, Sultanate of B:415
Bornholm (BORN-holm) (island, Denmark) D:110,
  112
Borodin (BO-ro-din), Alexander (Russian scientist and
  composer) O:146; R:381
Borodino, Battle of (1812), picture(s) U:46
Boron (element) E:171
  nuclear reactor safety N:372
  p-type semiconductors T:275
Bororo (American Indian language) I:197
Borstal Boy (book by Behan) I:328
Borzoi (dog) D:245–46
Borzov, Valery (Soviet runner) O:113
Börzsöny Mountains (Hungary) H:285
Bosch, Hieronymus (Flemish painter) D:354; P:23
  Temptation of Saint Anthony (painting), picture(s)
  D:357
Bosch (BOSH), Juan (Dominican president) D:285
Bosnia and Herzegovina (HER-tze-go-vi-na) B:23, 338;
  Y:357, 359
  flag, picture(s) F:235
Bosnian Muslims (a people of Europe), picture(s)
  Y:354
Bosons (subatomic particles) A:487–88
Bosporus (strait, Turkey) I:377; T:345, 347
Bossier City (Louisiana) L:310
Bossy, Mike (Canadian hockey player) B:507
Boston (capital of Massachusetts) B:339–42; M:136,
  142–43, 149–50; picture(s) M:137, 143
  Beacon Hill, picture(s) H:174
  Boston Metropolitan Area M:145
  colonial newspapers N:198
  colonial sites you can visit today C:422
  Faneuil Hall, picture(s) M:137
  first high school (1820) E:83–84
  Museum of Fine Art, picture(s) M:519
  museums and libraries M:141
  Old North Church, picture(s) C:423

outdoor market, picture(s) M:141
  police strike, Coolidge's stand C:538–39
  Quincy Grammar School was the first graded
  elementary school S:58i
  Quincy Markets A:386a
  State House, picture(s) M:145
  urban landscape of New England N:138h
Boston Brahmins (wealthy Boston families) M:150
Boston Celtics (basketball team) B:96; picture(s)
  M:141
Boston Latin Academy B:340; C:418
Boston Marathon B:341; M:141
Boston Massacre (1770) R:196; U:176
  Adams, John A:10
  Adams, Samuel A:18
  Attucks, Crispus, killed B:250c
  events leading to Declaration of Independence
  D:58
Boston Mountains (Arkansas) A:418
Boston Port Bill (1774) R:197–98
Boston Public Library L:175
Boston Symphony Orchestra M:559
Boston Tea Party (1773) R:197; U:176; picture(s)
  M:148
  Adams, Samuel, organizes A:18
  described in Johnny Tremain R:209
  events leading to Declaration of Independence
  D:58–59
  Revere, Paul, participates in R:192–93
Boston terrier (dog) D:244–45
Boswell, James (Scottish biographer) E:279
  early travel diary D:148
  Johnson, Samuel J:125
Botanical (bo-TAN-ic-al) gardens B:342–43
Botany (BOT-any) (study of plants) B:196, 343;
  P:290–304 see also Plants
  archaeological studies A:358–59, 361
  botanical gardens B:342–43
  Carver's agricultural research C:130
  cell structure C:159–62
  classification of plants (taxonomy) T:26–29
  food plants P:305–10
  fossils F:378–87
  fruit defined F:283
  genetic engineering G:88–91
  genetics G:77–88
  kingdoms of living things K:249–59
  leaves L:112–18
  Linnaeus invented classification system L:251
  medicinal plants P:310–15
  Mendel's experiments G:79–82; M:220
  odd and interesting plants P:316–20
  photosynthesis P:219–21
  poisonous plants P:321–23
  reproduction R:175–76
  taxonomy T:26–29
Botany Bay (Australia) A:515
Botero, Fernando (Colombian artist) L:67
  painting, picture(s) L:66
Botha (BO-ta), Pieter Willem (South African political
  leader) B:507; S:273
Bothnia, Gulf of (arm of the Baltic Sea) O:43
Bothwell, James Hepburn, 4th earl of (husband of Mary,
  Queen of Scots) M:118
Botocudo (American Indian language) I:197
Botrange (mountain, Belgium) B:133
Bo Tree (sacred to Buddhists) B:423
Botswana (bot-SWA-na) B:344
  children, picture(s) A:54
  flag, picture(s) F:226

Botticelli (bo-ti-CHEL-li), **Sandro** (Italian painter)
   B:345; **I:**396; **R:**162, 166
   The Adoration of the Magi (painting), *picture(s)*
      N:37
   Florentine painting **P:**20
   Primavera (painting) **B:**345
   Saint Augustine of Hippo (painting), *picture(s)*
      C:288
Bottled gas **F:**489
Bottlenose dolphins **D:**274–75, 277
Bottlenose whales **W:**147, 149
Bottles and bottling **B:**346–47
   modern baby bottle design, *picture(s)* **I:**213
   vacuum (thermos) bottles **V:**263–64
Bottomfish *see* Groundfish
Botulism (BOT-ul-ism) (type of food poisoning) **B:**11;
   F:352
   anaerobic bacteria **L:**203
   bacteria can grow in a vacuum **V:**264
Boucher (bu-SHAY), **François** (French painter) **F:**428
   drawing, history of **D:**316
   rococo style in painting **P:**24
Boucher, Gaétan (Canadian speed skater) **O:**118
Bouffant (bou-FONT) (shape in fashion design) **F:**65
Bougainville (BOU-gan-vil) (island in southwestern
      Pacific) **P:**59
"Bought Me a Cat" (folk song) **F:**322
Boulanger, Nadia (French composer) **F:**448; **M:**399;
   picture(s) **M:**397
Boulder (Colorado) **C:**441
   solar home, *picture(s)* **H:**184
Boulder caves **C:**157
Boulder clay (soil deposited by glaciers) **S:**234
Boulder Dam *see* Hoover Dam
Boulez, Pierre (French composer) **F:**448
Boulle (BOOL), **André** (French cabinetmaker) **D:**77;
   F:508
Boulton (BOLT-on), **Matthew** (English businessman)
   I:221
Boumedienne, Houari (Algerian political leader) **A:**188
Boundaries
   defined by rivers **R:**239
   territorial expansion of the United States **T:**105–15
Bounties (for military service) **D:**291–92
Bounty, Mutiny on the **B:**251
Bouquet garni (used to flavor soups and stews) **H:**115
Bourassa (BOO-ras-sa), **Henri** (Canadian journalist)
   Q:13
Bourbon, House of (French royal family) **B:**507
   France, history of **F:**415–16
Bourbon Street (New Orleans, Louisiana), *picture(s)*
   N:196
Bourgeoisie (social class) **F:**467
Bourguiba (boor-GHE-ba), **Habib** (president of Tunisia)
   T:336
Bourke-White, Margaret (American photographer)
   Louisville Flood Victims (photograph), *picture(s)*
      P:215
Bournonville, Auguste (father of Danish ballet) **B:**31–
   32
Bourse (money exchange) **S:**455
Boutet de Monvel, Bernard (French illustrator) **I:**82
Bouto dolphins, *picture(s)* **D:**275
Bouts, Dierik (Dutch painter) **D:**353
   The Last Supper (painting), *picture(s)* **D:**356
Bovidae (BO-vi-de) (family of mammals) **H:**217, 220
   antelopes **A:**297–98
   cattle **C:**147
Bovines (BO-vines) (cattlelike hoofed mammals)
   H:217, 220; *picture(s)* **H:**216

Bow, Clara (American actress) **M:**475
Bow and arrow *see* Bows and arrows
Bowditch (BOWD-itch), **Nathaniel** (American
      mathematician and astronomer) **B:**507
Bowdoin (BO-din), **James** (American statesman) **B:**507
Bowdoin College (Brunswick, Maine) **M:**44
Bow drill (tool) **T:**227–28
Bowed instruments **M:**553–54
Bowell, Sir Mackenzie (Canadian prime minister)
   B:507; **O:**135
Bowel movements *see* Feces
Bowen, Elizabeth (English writer) **E:**290
Bowersox, Kenneth D. (American astronaut), *picture(s)*
   S:343
Bowhunters (people who hunt with bows and arrows)
   A:364
Bowie (BOO-ie), **James** (American soldier and
      frontiersman) **B:**347
   Travis succeeds him as Alamo commander **T:**138
Bowie knife **B:**347
Bowker, R. R., Company *see* R. R. Bowker Company
Bow kite **K:**269–70
Bow knots **K:**287
Bowler hats **H:**45; *picture(s)* **L:**285
Bowl games (in football) **F:**364–65
Bowlines (knots), *picture(s)* **K:**286
Bowling (game) **B:**348–50b
Bowling (pitching in cricket) **C:**573
Bowl riding (skateboarding) **S:**182
Bowls (lawn bowling) **B:**350b
Bows and arrows **A:**364–66
Bow-steerers (iceboats) **I:**19–20
Bow Street Runners (early London police) **P:**368
Box (in geometry) **G:**127
Boxcars (of railroads) **R:**82
Boxer (dog) **D:**245
Boxer Rebellion (uprising against foreigners in China)
   B:507; **C:**270
   Open-Door policy **M:**194
   Peking's Legation Quarter **P:**118
Boxing **B:**351–54
   Olympic Games **O:**107
   related to fencing **F:**85
Boxing Day **H:**157
Box kites **K:**268–69
   used in scientific experiments and weather
      forecasting **K:**267
Box turtles **T:**356–57; *picture(s)* **T:**355
   pets **P:**179
Box wrenches (tools) **T:**232
"Boy Blue" (nursery rhyme) **N:**414
Boyce, William D. (American publisher, organized Boy
      Scouts of America) **B:**360
Boycott **B:**507
   Martin Luther King's bus boycott **K:**247
   Olympic Games **O:**107, 114–15, 117
   struggle for black civil rights **B:**250m–250n, 250p
Boyd, Belle (American Civil War spy) **S:**408
Boyden, Seth (American inventor and manufacturer)
   N:178
Boyer, Jean Pierre (Haitian president) **H:**11
Boy Jesus (Bible story) **B:**173–74
Boyle, Richard (English architect) **A:**380
Boyle, Robert (English scientist) **B:**354; **C:**207–8
   vacuum experiments **V:**265
Boyle's law **B:**354; **C:**207; **G:**56
Boyne, Battle of the (1690) **I:**323
Boyne River (Ireland) **I:**319
Boy Prisoners in the Tower (legend)
   What happened to the Princes in the Tower? **E:**241

Boys' camps *see* Camping, organized
Boys' Clubs of America B:355
Boy Scouts B:356–60
    Burmese, *picture(s)* A:457
Boy Scouts of Canada B:360; *picture(s)* F:205
Boysenberries G:301
Boy's Life (magazine) M:17
Boys' State (convention) B:507
Boys Town (Nebraska) N:92
Bozeman Trail (frontier trail) W:330, 337
BPOE *see* Elks, Benevolent and Protective Order of
Bracchae (trousers worn in the Middle Ages) C:375
Brace-and-bit (tool) T:231
Bracelets (jewelry) J:99–100
Braces (tools of the orthodontist) O:236–37
Brachiosaurus (dinosaur) D:171
Brackenridge, Hugh Henry (American novelist) A:202
Bracket fungi F:500
Bracts (of plants) P:295
Bradbury, Ray (American writer) B:507
Braddock, General Edward (British soldier) F:465;
    W:37
Braddock, James J. (American boxer) B:353
Bradford, Andrew (American printer and magazine
    publisher) M:19
Bradford, Roark (American novelist) T:88
Bradford, William (governor of Plymouth Colony)
    M:148; P:347; T:172; *picture(s)* T:171
    American literature A:197
Bradley, Omar Nelson (American army officer) B:507
Bradley, Thomas (American politician) B:507–8
Bradstreet, Anne (American poet) A:197
Brady, Diamond Jim (American financier) B:508
Brady, Mathew B. (American photographer) B:508
Braga (BRA-ga) (Portugal) P:393
Bragg, Braxton (American Civil War general) C:344
    Mexican War M:239b
Bragi (BROG-i) (Norse god) N:280
Brahe (BRA-uh), Tycho (Danish astronomer) A:472;
    B:361; D:110
Brahma (Hindu god) H:129
    bronze statue, *picture(s)* H:128
Brahman (Atman) (Hindu spiritual principle) H:129
Brahmans (caste in Hindu society) H:128; *picture(s)*
    H:130
    education of ancient times E:75
Brahmaputra (brah-ma-PU-tra) River (Asia) R:240
    joins the Ganges G:25
    rivers of India I:124
Brahms, Johannes (German composer) B:362; G:187
    choral music C:285
    First Symphony O:199–201
    symphonies M:549
Braided rug R:356
Braille (BRAIL) (alphabet of the blind) B:253–54
    children's book, *picture(s)* B:322
Braille, Louis (French teacher and musician) B:253
Brain B:363–69
    aging process A:83–85
    balance, sense of E:5–6
    body's senses B:201, 287
    central nervous system N:118
    cerebral palsy is caused by brain damage D:190
    child development C:225
    computerized image, *picture(s)* D:206
    damage caused by alcoholism A:173
    damage caused by a stroke D:202
    Did ancient Egyptians understand the importance of
        the brain? L:104

disabled people D:177
Does a larger brain mean greater intelligence?
    B:366
dreaming D:317–18
electroencephalograms M:208h–209
epilepsy D:192
in fishes, size of regions related to senses F:190
gray matter N:117
how we hear E:5
learning L:100–101
mammals M:65
medical and surgical techniques M:208h–210
nerve cell, *picture(s)* C:159
nervous system B:284–85; N:115–16
operations in hyperbaric chambers M:210
primates M:418
psychology P:496–511
Reye's syndrome affects D:200
ultrasonoscope detects abnormal conditions M:209
Brain coral, *picture(s)* J:74
Brain drain (migration of specialists and technicians
    from one country to another) B:508
Braine, John (English novelist) E:290
Brain stem N:116
Brainstorming B:508
Brainteasers (puzzles) T:313
Brainwashing B:508
Brakemen (on trains) R:86
Brakes
    air brakes H:300; R:88
    automobiles A:543–44, 546, 550–51
    hydraulic brakes H:299
    trucks T:319
    Westinghouse, George, and air brakes W:125
Bramante (brom-ON-tay), Donato (Italian architect)
    I:397
    Renaissance architecture R:167
    Tempietto of San Pietro Church (Rome), *picture(s)*
        I:397
Bran (of grain)
    flour and flour milling F:275
    rice R:229
    wheat G:281; W:154; *picture(s)* W:155
Branca (BRON-ca), Giovanni (Italian architect) E:229
    showed principle of steam turbine T:342
Branches (of department stores) D:119
Brancusi (bran-KOO-see), Constantin (Romanian-French
    sculptor) B:370; S:103
    Bird in Space (sculpture) *picture(s)* S:105
    French school of art F:432
    Mademoiselle Pogany (sculpture), *picture(s)* B:370
    Princesse X (sculpture), *picture(s)* A:437
Brand, Vance (American astronaut) S:348; *picture(s)*
    S:349–50
Brandeis, Louis Dembitz (Supreme Court justice)
    B:508; K:225–26
Brandenburg (former state, Germany)
    Frederick William (elector) F:461
Brandenburg Gate (Berlin, Germany) B:147
Brandenstein, Daniel C. (American astronaut) S:350;
    picture(s) S:351–52
Branding (of cattle) C:569–70; R:104–5
Brand names *see* Trademarks
Brando, Marlon (American actor) B:508
Brandon (Manitoba, Canada) M:85
Brandt (BRONT), Willy (German political leader)
    B:508; G:165
Brandy (distilled beverage) W:159
Branford Trolley Museum (East Haven, Connecticut)
    C:512

Branle (dance)   D:29
Branley, Franklyn M. (American science writer)   B:508;
    C:240
Bransfield, Edward (British naval officer)   A:295
Brant, Joseph (Thayendanegea) (Mohawk Indian)
    B:370–71; I:176, 204; R:205
Brants (geese)   D:343
Braque (BROC), Georges (French painter)   B:371;
    F:432; P:30
    Collage, picture(s)   C:400
    Guéridon, Le (painting), *picture(s)*   B:371
    modern art   M:390
    Picasso and Braque   P:243
Braque, Georges (French painter)
    The Portuguese (painting), *picture(s)*   F:431
Brasília (bra-ZI-lia) (capital of Brazil)   B:380, 383;
    picture(s) L:59; S:295; U:234
    architecture   A:386; L:67
    Niemeyer was its chief architect   A:386
    work of Brazil's leading designers   B:376–77
Brass   B:410
    alloys   A:190–91
    antiques   A:316b
    buttons   B:484
    major Connecticut industry   C:507
    zinc   Z:378
Brass band   B:42
Brass instruments   M:555–56
    orchestra   O:193; *picture(s)* O:197
    orchestra seating plan   O:196
    wind instruments   W:182–83
Brass rubbings   R:348b
Brasstown Bald Mountain (Georgia)   G:134
Bratislava (BRA-ti-sla-va) (Czechoslovakia)   C:609
Brattain, Walter H. (American physicist), *picture(s)*
    E:162
Braun, Wernher von see Von Braun, Wernher
Brave New World (novel by Huxley)   E:289
Braxton, Carter (American statesman)   B:508
Brazil   B:372–84
    Amazon Basin's endangered monkeys   E:208
    Amazon River   A:194e–194f; *picture(s)* R:241
    Belo Horizonte, *picture(s)*   L:53
    Carnival food, *picture(s)*   F:334
    coffee   C:397
    coffee beans drying, *picture(s)*   S:289
    feijoada is the most popular dish   F:339
    flag, *picture(s)*   F:238
    government, history of   L:59
    Lagoa dos Patos   L:30
    landforms of South America   S:276
    Latin-American art and architecture   L:64
    life in Latin America   L:47–61
    Marajoara civilization   I:170
    origin of name   D:371
    Portugal, history of   P:395
    Rio de Janeiro   R:234–35
    rubber trees   R:344
    São Paulo   S:38–39
Brazil Current (of Atlantic Ocean)   A:479; S:279
Brazilein (bra-ZIL-le-in) (dye)   D:371
Brazil nuts   N:428–29
Brazilwood (tree)   B:372
    dyes and dyeing   D:371
Brazing and soldering   S:249
Brazos River (Texas)   T:127
Brazza (BRA-tza), Count Pierre Paul François Camille
    Savorgnan de (French explorer)   C:500; G:4
Brazzaville (capital of the People's Republic of the
    Congo)   C:498–500

Bread   B:385–88b see also Flour and flour milling
    black or rye bread   R:386
    Egyptian statue of a baker, *picture(s)*   A:350
    Egyptians were the first to make leavened bread
        C:532
    experiments: growing bread molds   A:312
    flour from different kinds of wheat   F:274
    food regulations and laws   F:346
    mold   F:496–97
    nutrition   N:425
    unleavened and leavened compared   F:89
    wheat   W:154, 156
Bread-and-butter notes   L:160
Bread and Butter State (nickname for Minnesota)
    M:326
Breadfruit (tropical fruit)   M:78; *picture(s)* E:413
    introduced into Jamaica by Captain Bligh   J:18
Bread Loaf Writers' Conference (Middlebury College,
    Vermont)   V:315
Bread mold   F:496–97; *picture(s)* P:292
    experiments   A:312
Bread wheats   W:156
Breakers (giant waves)   S:511
Breakers (hard-coal preparation plants)   C:390
Breakfast cereals   G:284
Breakfast in Bed (painting by Cassatt), *picture(s)*
    C:130
Breaking a mirror (superstition)   S:504
Breaking a wishbone (superstition)   S:504
Breaking Home Ties (painting by Rockwell), *picture(s)*
    R:270
Breakwater   B:508
Breastbone see Sternum
Breast cancer   C:92
Breastfeeding (of babies)   B:3
    mammary glands   G:227
    mother with AIDS can infect baby   A:100b
Breaststroke (in swimming)   S:536; *picture(s)* S:533
Breastworks (field fortifications)   F:377
Breathing   B:278–79 see also Respiration
    crocodilian adaptations for staying underwater
        C:583–84
    dolphins   D:275
    emphysema affects   D:192
    first aid for stoppage of breathing   F:159
    hiccups   B:300
    narcotics, effects of   N:13
    oxygen and oxidation   O:287
    plants, respiration of   P:294
    problems of premature babies   B:2
    rescue breathing   F:159
    respiratory system of fishes   F:186–87
    turtles   T:356
    voice training and singing   V:375
Breathless (motion picture)   M:491
Brecht (BRECKT), Bertolt (German playwright)   D:302;
    G:181
Breckinridge, John (American senator and attorney
    general)   K:225
Breckinridge, John Cabell (vice president of the United
    States)   K:225; V:327
    Confederate general in Civil War   C:338
Breech-loaders (guns)   G:418
Breed associations (of dairy farmers)   D:4–5
Breeder reactor (type of nuclear reactor)   N:370
Breeding, animal
    advances in agriculture   A:99
    cats, pedigreed   C:143
    cattle   C:147
    dairy cattle   D:4–5

dogs **D**:247, 249–51
fur colors, by mutation **F**:514
genetic engineering **G**:88
goats **C**:150
horses **H**:237–38, 241, 244; *picture(s)* **H**:239–40
pigs **C**:149–50
poultry **P**:414–15, 417
sheep **C**:150
zoo animals **Z**:384, 386
Breeding, plant
advances in agriculture **A**:99–100
Burbank's contributions to **B**:450
cereal grains for the future **G**:286
food plants **P**:305
genetic engineering **G**:88–91
Mendel, work of **G**:79–81
wheat varieties **W**:155–56
Breedlove, Craig (American automobile racer) **A**:538
Breed's Hill (Boston, near Bunker Hill) **R**:200
Breezes, sea *see* Sea breezes
Breezing Up (painting by Homer), *picture(s)* **H**:167
Bregenz Festival (Austria) **A**:519
Breitenfeld, Battle of (1631) **T**:179
Bremen (BREM-en) (Germany) **G**:157
Brendan (Brenainn), Saint (Irish saint)
exploration and discovery **E**:403
Brennan, William Joseph (American jurist) **B**:508
Brenner Pass (through the Alps) **A**:194b
Brent, Margaret (American feminist) **M**:132
Brenton, Howard (English dramatist) **D**:303
Brer Rabbit (character in Joel Chandler Harris stories) **A**:76b
Brest-Litovsk, Treaty of (1918) **R**:368; **U**:49
Brétigny, Treaty of (1360) **E**:241
Breton, André (French poet and surrealist) **F**:442; **M**:394; **S**:518
Brett, Philip Milledoler (American dollhouse maker) **D**:262
Bretton Woods (New Hampshire) **N**:160
Breuer, Lee (American dramatist) **D**:305
Breuer (BROI-er), **Marcel** (Hungarian furniture designer and architect) **F**:510
Brewer, Margaret A. (American brigadier general) **U**:122
Brewer's yeast **B**:386; **H**:79
Brewis (colonial American dish) **C**:411
Brewster, Sir David (Scottish physicist) **B**:508; **K**:168
Brezhnev (BRAYGE-nef), **Leonid Ilyich** (Soviet political leader) **B**:389; **C**:211; **U**:51
Brian Boru (king of Ireland) **I**:323
Briand (bri-ON), **Aristide** (French statesman) **P**:106
Briand-Kellogg Pact (1928) *see* Kellogg-Briand Pact
Brices Cross Roads National Battlefield Site (Mississippi) **M**:359
Bricklaying **B**:392–93
Bricks **B**:390–94
adobe **H**:173–74
ancient cities built with clay bricks **A**:219
architecture, history of **A**:370–71, 373
building construction **B**:430, 437
houses **H**:174–75
Brico, Antonia (American conductor) **M**:493
Bridal rings *see* Wedding rings
Bridalveil (waterfall, California) **W**:63
Bridal Veil (waterfall, New York) **N**:243
Bridal veils **W**:100
Bridge (in music) **M**:540
Bridge, The (German art group) *see* Brücke, Die

Bridge at Sevres, The (painting by Sisley), *picture(s)* **I**:105
Bridge cranes (overhead traveling cranes) (machines) **H**:147; *picture(s)* **H**:146
Bridge layers (specialized tanks) **T**:15
Bridge of Sighs (Venice, Italy) **B**:401
Bridgeport (Connecticut) **C**:513
Bridger, Jim (American pioneer) **F**:523
overland trails **O**:276
Wyoming, settlement of **W**:335
Yellowstone National Park **Y**:345
Bridges **B**:395–401 *see also* Covered bridges
Brooklyn Bridge, *picture(s)* **I**:329
Chesapeake Bay Bridge-Tunnel **M**:122
Federal Highway Administration **T**:293
New York City **N**:229–30
reinforced concrete used in **C**:166
swinging bridge, *picture(s)* **J**:153
Why were some of the early bridges in America covered? **B**:401
Bridges (of ships) **O**:32
Bridges, Robert (English poet) **E**:287
Bridge to Terabithia (book by Paterson)
Donna Diamond illustration, *picture(s)* **C**:238
Bridgetown (capital of Barbados) **B**:60
Brig (kind of ship), *picture(s)* **S**:152
Brigade system (for fur trading) **F**:523
Brigantine (kind of ship), *picture(s)* **S**:152
Briggs, Raymond (English illustrator) **B**:508
Brigham Young University (Provo, Utah) **U**:250–51
Brighella (clown) **C**:386
Brightness (of stars) *see* Magnitude
Bright's disease *see* Nephritis
Brilliance (of pigment colors) **C**:425
Brimstone *see* Sulfur
Brindle coats (of dogs) **D**:245
Brine (salt and water solution) **S**:22–23
food preservation and processing **F**:343, 345
leather process for preserving hides **L**:108
processing of fish **F**:212, 221
refrigerated warehouses, use in **R**:136
water desalting **W**:56
Brine shrimps (crustaceans) **C**:591
Brinkley, David (American news commentator) **N**:320
Brisbane (capital of Queensland, Australia) **A**:511, 513, 515
Brisco-Hooks, Valerie (American athlete) **O**:117
Bristlecone pine (tree) **P**:317; **T**:300
Bristle worms (polychaetes) **W**:310
Bristol Clock Museum (Bristol, Connecticut) **C**:512
Bristow, George F. (American composer) **U**:206
Britain (ancient name of England, Scotland, Wales)
Celtic tribes **C**:163
discovered by Pytheas **E**:402
early history of England **E**:235–38
Britain, Battle of (1940) **W**:289–90
Britannia metal **K**:285
British Broadcasting Company (BBC) **R**:57; **U**:59
British Columbia (Canada) **B**:402–7
Canada's Cordillera **C**:54–55
Expo 86 (Vancouver) **F**:18
gold discoveries **G**:252
Indians, American **I**:188–90
Vancouver **V**:276; *picture(s)* **C**:67
British Columbia, University of **B**:406a
British Commonwealth of Nations *see* Commonwealth of Nations
British East India Company **E**:47; **I**:132–33
British Empire **E**:249, 251 *see also* Commonwealth of Nations

British Empire (continued)
extent of (1939) E:252
United Kingdom of Great Britain and Northern
Ireland U:54, 57
British Expeditionary Force (B.E.F.) W:273, 288
British Guiana see Guyana
British Honduras see Belize
British Indian Ocean Territory (Chagos Archipelago)
(British dependency in the Indian Ocean)
B:509
British Isles (group that includes Great Britain, Ireland,
and many smaller islands) U:57
British Library (national library of Britain) L:179
British Mountains (Yukon Territory, Canada) Y:360
British Museum (London) M:515–16, 519
library L:179
British Nationality Act (1983) I:94
British North America Act (now Constitution Act) (1867)
C:74, 77; M:2
British Open (golf tournament) G:260
British Patent Office P:101
British Society for the Promotion of Permanent and
Universal Peace P:105
British Somaliland (now Somalia) S:255
British South Africa Company Z:372, 376
British thermal units (Btu's) (measure of heat) H:89
British Togoland (United Nations trust territory, west
Africa) G:194, 198; T:215
British Virgin Islands see Virgin Islands, British
Britons (early people of England) E:235–37
settled Brittany F:403
Brittany (region of France), picture(s) F:410, 413;
W:68
Brittany spaniel (dog) D:249
Britten, Benjamin (English composer) E:293
opera O:148
Peter Grimes (opera) O:161
Briullov, Karl (Russian painter) R:373
The Rider (painting), picture(s) R:373
Brno (BER-no) (Czechoslovakia) C:609
Broad-Breasted Bronze (turkey) P:417
Broad-Breasted Large White (turkey) P:417
Broadcasting (of seed) A:98
Broadcasting (radio and television) R:50, 53–58; T:68
advertising A:29
communication, history of C:469
radio programs R:59–61
television programs T:70–71
Broadheads (arrows with sharp-bladed tips) A:366
Broad jump see Long jump
Broadsides (newssheets)
ballads B:24
political songs N:22
Broadtail (fur) F:518
Broadway Boogie-Woogie (painting by Mondrian),
picture(s) M:407
Broadway theater district (New York City) N:233–34;
T:161
Broadwood, John (English piano builder) P:242
Broccoli (vegetable) V:289
flowers we eat P:307–8; picture(s) P:309
food shopping F:350
Broch, Hermann (German writer) G:182
Brock, Sir Isaac (British soldier) O:135; W:10
Brockton (Massachusetts) M:145
Broilers (chickens) P:415
Broiling (method of cooking) C:533
Brokaw, Irving (American ice-skating promoter) I:45
Broken-color technique (in painting) I:104
Brokers (agents) (negotiators of sales and purchases)

real estate R:113
stocks and bonds, dealers in S:457–58
Brolga (Australian crane) A:506
Bromeliads (plants) B:210
Bromfield, Louis (American author) O:73
Bromine (BRO-mene) (element) E:171
minerals in the ocean O:28
Bronchial (BRONC-ial) tubes (of the respiratory system)
B:279
Bronchitis (bron-KY-tis) (inflammation of the bronchial
tubes) D:189–90
acid rain's effects A:8
emphysema D:192
Broncos (untamed horses) C:569; R:277 see also
Mustangs
Brong-Ahafo (a people of Africa) G:194
Brontë (BRON-te), Anne (English novelist) B:408;
E:286
Brontë, Branwell (English painter and writer) B:408
Brontë, Charlotte (English novelist) B:408; E:286
themes of her novels N:359
Brontë, Emily (English novelist) B:408; E:286
themes of her novels N:359
Brontosaurus (dinosaur) see Apatosaurus
Bronx (New York City) N:227–28
Bronx Community College, picture(s) N:232
Bronx Zoo (New York City) Z:383, 386
Bronze B:409–10
African sculpture, picture(s) A:71, 73; N:254
alloys A:190
armor A:433
Babylonian art A:236
bell casting B:140
chemistry, history of C:206
Chinese decorative arts C:276
decorative arts D:70, 72, 74–76; picture(s) D:71
door, picture(s) L:122
Islamic candlestick, picture(s) I:358
Japanese gilt bronze sculptures J:48
metallurgy, history of M:236
Bronze Age B:409
metallurgy M:236
prehistoric people P:442
time of the Trojan War T:316
Bronze Star (American award), picture(s) D:66
Brooches (BROACH-es) (jewelry) J:99
gold brooch designed by Leonor Fini, picture(s)
D:69
Brood parasites (birds that use others' nests) B:227–
28
Brood patch (in birds) B:227
Brood pouch (of a crustacean) C:592
Brooke, Edward William (United States senator) M:148
Brooke, Sir James (British ruler, White Rajah) of
Sarawak M:58
Brooke, Rupert (English poet) E:287
Brook Farm (utopian community, Massachusetts)
A:204
Brooklyn (New York City) N:228, 235
Brooklyn Bridge (New York City) B:398; N:230;
picture(s) I:329
Brooklyn Dodgers (baseball team) B:91–92
Brooks, Gwendolyn (American poet) A:214; B:509
Brooks, Mel (American comedy writer and filmmaker)
B:509; M:493
Brooks, Phillips (American Episcopal bishop) C:118
Brooks Range (Alaska) A:147, 150
Brook trout (fish), picture(s) F:210
Broomcorn (kind of sorghum) O:86
"Brooms" (poem by Aldis) F:120

Brossard, Nicole (Canadian writer)   C:85
Brosse, Salomon de (French architect)   F:425
Brotherhood/Sisterhood Week   B:509
Brothers Karamazov (novel by Dostoevski)   D:287
Brotulids (bro-TU-lids) (deep-sea fishes)   F:197
Broughton, Jack (English boxing champion)   B:353
Broughton, William R. (English explorer)   O:215
Brown, Charles Brockden (American novelist)   A:202
Brown, Claude (American author)   B:509
Brown, Edmund Gerald (Pat) (American politician)
     C:32
Brown, Edmund Gerald, Jr. (Jerry) (American politician)
     C:32
Brown, Father (fictional character created by Chesterton)
     M:563
Brown, Ford Madox (English artist)   E:263
Brown, George (Canadian statesman)   B:411; M:2
Brown, Jim (American football player)   B:509
Brown, Joe E. (American comedian)   O:73
Brown, John (American abolitionist)   B:250f, 411;
     S:196–97
   events leading to Civil War   C:337
   John Brown Memorial State Park (Osawatomie,
     Kansas)   K:184
   John Brown's Body (song)   N:23
Brown, Joseph Rogers (American inventor)   R:218
Brown, Karen (American ballerina), *picture(s)*   B:33
Brown, Marcia (American author and artist)   B:509
Brown, Margaret Wise (author and editor of children's
     books)   B:509
   illustration by Clement Hurd for *Goodnight Moon*,
     picture(s)   C:241
Brown, Robert (English botanist)   S:73
Brown, Sterling Allan (American poet, author, and
     professor)   B:509
Brown, William Hill (American novelist)   A:202
Brown, William Wells (American reformer, historian, and
     writer)   B:509
Brown bears   B:104, 107; *picture(s)* B:106; U:89
   foot, *picture(s)*   B:105
Brown coal *see* Lignite
Browne, Frances (Irish writer)   F:21
Browne, Sir Thomas (English author)   E:274
Brown family (American manufacturers and
     philanthropists)   R:224
Brown hyenas (animals)   H:305
Brownie Girl Scouts   G:215; *picture(s)* G:214
Browning, Elizabeth Barrett (English poet)   B:412;
     E:284–85
   "How do I love thee?"   B:412
Browning, John Moses (American inventor of firearms)
     B:509; U:254
Browning, Robert (English poet)   B:412–13; E:284
   "The Pied Piper of Hamelin," *excerpt(s)*   B:413
   quotation from *Pippa Passes*   Q:19
Brownlee, Don (American astronomer)   C:452
Brownlee particles (dust from asteroids and comets)
     C:452
Brown lung (respiratory disease)   O:12
Brown rat *see* Norway rat
Brown recluse spiders   S:406
Brown rice   G:282; H:79; R:229
Brownshirts (Nazi storm troopers)   F:64; N:80–81
Brown sugar   S:483
Brown Swiss (breed of cattle)   C:149; *picture(s)* D:5
Brown thrashers (birds)
   state bird of Georgia, *picture(s)*   G:133
Brown University (Providence, Rhode Island)   R:220;
     picture(s) R:221

Brown v. *Board of Education of Topeka, Kansas* (1954)
     B:250m; E:90; S:115, 509
Brownville (Nebraska)   N:92
Broz, Josip *see* Tito
Brubeck, Dave (American jazz pianist and composer)
     B:509
Bruce, Ailsa Mellon (American philanthropist)   N:37–
     38
Bruce, Blanche Kelso (American politician)   B:509
Bruce, James (Scottish explorer)   A:68; E:414
Bruce, Robert *see* Robert I (The Bruce) (king of
     Scotland)
Brucellosis (bru-cel-LO-sis) (undulant fever) (disease)
     D:212
Brücke, Die (German art group)   E:426; G:172; M:391
Bruckner (BROOK-ner), Anton (Austrian composer and
     organist)   G:188
   choral music   C:285
   symphonies   M:549
Bruegel (Brueghel) (BRUR-ghel), Jan (Flemish painter)
     B:414
Bruegel, Pieter, The Elder (Flemish painter)   B:414
   Children's Games (painting), *picture(s)*   D:356
   Dutch and Flemish art   D:354
   The Harvesters (painting), *picture(s)*   R:170
   Hunters in The Snow (painting), *picture(s)*   B:414
Bruegel, Pieter, The Younger (Flemish painter)   B:414
Bruges (BRUGE) (Belgium), *picture(s)*   B:131
Bruises (injuries)   F:161
Brulé (bru-LAY), Étienne (French explorer)   G:327–28;
     M:272
Brumel, Valery (Russian athlete)   O:111
Brumidi, Constantino (Italian-American painter)   C:104
Brummell, Beau (English dandy and wit)   B:509
Brundtland (BRUNT-lahnd), Gro Harlem (Norwegian
     political leader)   B:509
Brunei (BRUNE-i) (sultanate on the island of Borneo)
     B:336–37, 415; S:328
   flag, *picture(s)*   F:231
Brunel (bru-NEL), Isambard Kingdom (British engineer)
     O:33; T:339
Brunel, Marc (French-English inventor)   T:339
Brunelleschi (bru-nel-LESC-i), Filippo (Italian architect)
     A:378; I:395
   Foundling Hospital (Florence)   R:164; *picture(s)*
     R:165
   perspective, rules of   D:311
   Renaissance architecture   R:161, 164
Bruner, Jerome (American psychologist)   L:100
Brunhoff, Jean de (French author and illustrator)
     B:509
Brünnhilde *see* Brynhild
Brush, George de Forest (American painter)   T:88
Brushes (for painting)   P:34; W:58
Brushes (of electric generators and motors)   E:134,
     153
Brusilov (bru-SI-lof), Aleksei (Russian general)   W:278
Brussels (capital of Belgium)   B:133
   city hall, *picture(s)*   B:135
   German troops (1914), *picture(s)*   W:272
   rug-weaving   R:353
Brussels sprouts (vegetable related to cabbage)   V:287
   food shopping   F:350
   leaves we eat   P:307; *picture(s)* P:306
Brussels Universal and International Exhibition (1958)
     F:17
Brutus, Lucius Junius (Roman hero)   R:310
Brutus, Marcus Junius (Roman statesman)   A:317;
     C:6; R:316
Bryan, Ashley (American author and illustrator)

Bryan, Ashley (continued)
illustration from *Beat the Story Drum, Pum-Pum,* *picture(s)* **C:**243
Bryan, Charles Wayland (American governor) **N:**93
Bryan, John Neely (first settler in Dallas, Texas) **D:**14
Bryan, William Jennings (American politician and orator) **B:**416; **O:**191
Darrow and Bryan **D:**38
McKinley and Bryan **M:**192
Bryant, Paul ("Bear") (American football coach) **A:**142
Bryant, William Cullen (American poet and editor) **A:**203; **B:**416
Bryce Canyon National Park (Utah) **U:**252
Bryde's whales **W:**149–50
Brynhild (BRURN-hilt) (in Norse mythology) **N:**281
in Wagner's operas called Brünnhilde **O:**162–63
Bryophyllum (life plant), *picture(s)* **P:**300
leaves, special kinds of, *picture(s)* **L:**118
Brzezinski, Zbigniew (brezh-IN-skee, ZHBIG-nyef) (American government official and author) **B:**509–10
Btu's *see* British thermal units
Bubble chamber (in physics) **A:**194d
cosmic rays **C:**555
Buber (BU-ber), **Martin** (Jewish religious philosopher) **B:**510
Bubi (a people of Africa) **E:**305
Bubka, Sergei (Soviet pole vaulter) **B:**510
pole vault, *picture(s)* **T:**254
Bubonic plague (disease) **D:**190
disaster at the end of the Middle Ages **M:**295
Florence (Italy) **F:**257
medieval England **E:**240
Norway **N:**349
Roman Catholic Church damaged by **R:**287
Buccaneers (buc-ca-NEERS) (pirates of the Spanish Main) **P:**263
Buchanan, James (15th president of the United States) **B:**417–20; *picture(s)* **P:**450
Bucharest (bu-ca-REST) (capital of Romania) **R:**297–98; *picture(s)* **R:**299–300
Buchli, James F. (American astronaut) **S:**350
Büchner, Georg (German dramatist) **G:**179
Buck, Pearl (American author) **B:**421
The Good Earth, excerpt(s) **B:**421
Bucket brigades (for fire fighting) **F:**146
Bucket dredge *see* Ladder bucket dredge
Buckeye (state tree of Ohio), *picture(s)* **O:**61
Buckeye State (nickname for Ohio) **O:**61, 63–64
Bucking (in logging) **L:**323–24
Buckingham Palace (of Britain's royal family) **L:**286
Buckland-Wright, John (English artist)
Nymphe Surprise II (engraving), *picture(s)* **E:**294
Buckley, William F., Jr. (American writer and editor) **B:**510
Bucks (male deer) **D:**81–82
Buckskin (leather from deer) **L:**107
Buck teeth (orthodontic problem) **O:**236
Buckwheat (grain) **G:**284; *picture(s)* **G:**283
Bucrania (bu-CRAY-nia) (sculptured ornament) **D:**74
Buda (section of Budapest) **B:**422–22b
Budapest (BU-da-pest) (capital of Hungary) **B:**422–22b; **H:**286; *picture(s)* **E:**287, 359; **H:**284
Buddha (BU-dha), **Prince Siddhartha Gautama** (founder of Buddhism) **B:**422b–425
Buddha Amida (statue by Jocho), *picture(s)* **J:**48
Great Buddha of Kamakura (Japan), *picture(s)* **J:**27; **R:**147; **S:**90
sculpture, *picture(s)* **I:**135

Buddhism (religion founded by Buddha) **B:**423–25
Asia, chief religions of **A:**458
Buddhist scriptures, oldest existing set of **K:**298
Burma **B:**454–55
China **C:**260, 278
dance combines with religion **D:**31
fables and folk tales **F:**3
food taboos **F:**334
funeral customs **F:**492
India, art and architecture of **I:**135–36
India, literature of **I:**141
Japan **J:**27, 32, 41
Japanese art and architecture **J:**48–49
Lamaism in Tibet **T:**189–90
Laos **L:**42
marriage rites **W:**103
monks, *picture(s)* **A:**445, 458; **S:**331
oriental sculpture **O:**222–23, 229; *picture(s)* **O:**226
originated in India **I:**130
religions of the world **R:**147
religious holidays **R:**154
Russia **R:**358
sculpture **C:**277
Southeast Asia **S:**331
temple, *picture(s)* **I:**138
Thailand **T:**149; *picture(s)* **T:**152
Union of Soviet Socialist Republics **U:**35
Budding (plant propagation by grafting) **N:**428
apple trees **A:**331, 333
orange trees **O:**188
stone fruit trees **P:**108
Budding (type of reproduction) **R:**175
hydra **J:**73
sea anemones **J:**74
Budge, Don (American tennis player) **B:**510
Budgerigars (BUDGE-eri-gars) ("talking" birds) **B:**245; **P:**85; *picture(s)* **P:**86
Budget, national *see* National budget
Budgets, family **B:**425–26
Budgets, municipal, *diagram(s)* **M:**512
Budgies *see* Budgerigars
Buds (of trees) **T:**308–9
Bud scales (of plants) **P:**295
Buen Aire *see* Bonaire
Buenaventura (Colombia) **C:**407
Buena Vista (BUANE-a VE-sta), **Battle of** (1847) **M:**239b; **T:**32
Buenos Aires (BUANE-os I-res) (capital of Argentina) **A:**390, 394–95; **B:**426–28
Buero Vallejo, Antonio (Spanish dramatist) **S:**392b
Buffalo (hoofed mammals) **B:**428–29; *picture(s)* **H:**216
Asian work animal **A:**448–49
Australia **A:**506
Buffalo (New York) **N:**222–23
Buffalo, American *see* Bison
Buffalo Bill (William Frederick Cody) (American scout) **B:**429; **C:**570; **P:**383
Nebraska state historical park **N:**91
Buffalo National River (Arkansas) **A:**426; *picture(s)* **A:**426
Bugaku (Japanese dance) **D:**32; **T:**162
Buganda (bu-GAN-da) (former kingdom, now a region in Uganda) **U:**6–7
Bugging (electronic eavesdropping) **B:**510; **S:**409
Bugle (musical instrument) **M:**556 *see also* Trumpet
Bug River (Europe) **P:**359
Bugs *see* Insects

Bugs Bunny (cartoon character), *picture(s)* A:289
Builders (in detergents) D:141
Building code B:434
Building construction B:430–38; *picture(s)* I:336
  air conditioning A:101–3
  architecture A:368–86a
  bricks and masonry B:390–94
  bridges B:395–401
  castles C:131
  construction engineers E:225
  earth-moving machinery E:30–32
  elevators and escalators E:185–88
  explosives in construction E:425
  heating systems H:94–97
  hoisting and loading machinery H:146–47
  invention of tools for I:286
  kinds of industry I:225
  masonry B:392–94
  mechanical drawing M:200
  plumbing P:341–42
  stone masonry B:393–94
  trucks, use of T:321
  Why don't tall buildings blow down in a strong wind?
    B:435
  Why is a tree or an American flag sometimes placed
    on the highest part of a building under
    construction? B:434
Building materials B:430–31
  acid rain's effects A:8
  adobe houses H:173–74
  bricks and brick masonry B:390–94
  cement and concrete C:165–66
  ceramics C:177–78
  engineering E:224
  fireproofing B:434
  glass as a structural material G:237
  homes H:171–77
  influenced architecture A:373, 381–85
  iron and steel I:329–38
  lumber and lumbering L:322–29
  stone masonry B:393–94
  wood and wood products W:222–27
Bujumbura (capital of Burundi) B:461–62
Bukhara (early state in Central Asia) T:11; U:258
Bükk Mountains (Hungary) H:285
Bukovina (bu-ko-VI-na) (Romania) M:403; R:297, 300
Bulawayo (Zimbabwe) Z:375
Bulbs (underground stems) P:300
  gardens and gardening G:40; *picture(s)* G:41
  garden selection G:29
  houseplants H:269
  leaves, special kinds of L:118
Bulfinch, Charles (American architect) U:128
  completed the United States Capitol C:104–5
  Massachusetts State House, *picture(s)* M:145
  Old State House (Hartford, Connecticut) C:515
Bulgakov, Mikhail (Russian writer) R:380
Bulganin (bull-GAN-yin), Nikolai Aleksandrovich (Russian
    political leader) B:510
Bulgaria (bul-GAIR-ia) B:439–44
  Balkans B:22
  flag, *picture(s)* F:235
  World War I W:275, 281
Bulgarian Orthodox Church B:440, 443
Bulgars (people) B:439, 443
Bulge, Battle of the (1944–45) W:304
  Belgium B:135
  Eisenhower, Dwight D. E:124
Bulimia (eating disorder) D:190

Bulk food sales F:349; S:498
Bull (constellation) *see* Taurus
Bull, John (English composer) N:20
Bull, Ole (Norwegian violinist) G:380
  founded Norwegian Theater (Bergen) I:2
Bullboats (made of buffalo hide) M:383
Bull dancing (of ancient Crete) B:448
Bulldog D:244–45, 251
Bulldozers E:30
  roads and highways R:249
  tanks used for military support T:15
  used on farms F:53–54
Bulletin boards (for posting information) B:445–47
  computer bulletin boards C:489; L:160b
Bullets (ammunition for guns) G:414, 417
  made of lead L:92
Bullet trains *see* Turbo trains
Bullfighting B:448–49
  Costa Rica C:557
  How did bullfighting begin? B:448
  Mexico M:242
  Nicaragua N:245
  South America, *picture(s)* S:285
  Spain S:374; *picture(s)* S:372
Bullfrogs F:477; *picture(s)* A:214b
Bullheads (fish) F:216
  baits F:206
Bull-horn acacia (tree) A:324
Bullion (gold bars) G:247
Bull leaping (sport of ancient Crete) A:227
Bull Moose Party *see* Progressive Party
Bullocks *see* Steers
Bullpen (in baseball) B:83
Bull Run, Battles of (1861, 1862, Civil War) C:339,
    341; J:9
Bulls C:147
  Assyrian art A:240; *picture(s)* A:241
  dairy cattle D:5
  elephants E:180, 182
  rodeo riding R:277
Bulls and bears (in stock exchanges) S:459
Bull sharks, *picture(s)* S:141
Bull Shoals Dam (Arkansas), *picture(s)* A:420
Bull-tossing (sport in Venezuela) V:296
Bully (starting play in field hockey) F:115
Bulwer-Lytton, Edward *see* Lytton, Edward George Earle
    Bulwer-Lytton, 1st Baron
Bumblebees B:121
  flower pollination F:282
Bumbry, Grace (American soprano) B:510
Bumi (African people)
  traditional hairstyle, *picture(s)* H:6
Bumppo, Natty (hero of Cooper's *Leatherstocking Tales*)
    A:202; C:541
Bunche, Ralph (American educator and United Nations
    mediator) B:250k, 450; W:34
Bunching onions (without bulbs) O:123
Bund, The (street, Shanghai, China) S:138
Bundesrat (German parliament, upper house) G:157
Bundestag (German parliament, lower house) G:157
Bunin (BOON-yin), Ivan (Russian author) R:379
Bunker Hill, Battle of (1775) R:200
Bunraku (Japanese puppet play) J:32–33, 53; P:545;
    T:162
Bunt (in baseball) B:83
Buntline, Ned *see* Judson, Edward
Buntline Special (Colt revolver) G:422
Buñuel, Luis (Spanish motion picture director) M:491

Bunyan, John (English writer and preacher) B:510;
    E:276
    children's literature C:233
Bunyan, Paul (American folk hero) F:312; G:202
    children's literature C:237
    statue in Bangor (Maine) M:48
    statue in Bemidji (Minnesota) M:334
Bunyoro (bun-YO-ro) (former kingdom, Uganda) U:6
Buonaparte family see Bonaparte family
Buonarroti, Michelangelo see Michelangelo
Buoninsegna, Duccio di see Duccio di Buoninsegna
Buoyancy (BOY-an-cy) (upward push on a floating
    object) F:250
    Archimedes' principle A:367
    salinity affects O:17
Buoys (floats)
    navigational aids N:73
    oceanographic research O:40
Buran (Soviet space shuttle) S:369
Burbage, James (English actor) D:298
Burbage, Richard (English actor) S:131
Burbank, Luther (American horticulturalist) B:450
Burchell's zebra H:244
Burckhardt, Johann (Swiss explorer) E:415
Burdock (weed), picture(s) W:105
Bureaucracy B:510 see also Civil service
Bureaus (of the United States government) see
    individual names
Burgan oil field (Kuwait) K:307
Burger, Warren Earl (American jurist) M:338;
    picture(s) C:325
Burgess, Anthony (English novelist) E:290; N:363
Burgess, Gelett (American humorist)
    "I Wish That My Room Had a Floor" N:274
Burghers of Calais (statues by Rodin), picture(s) S:102
Burghley, Lord see Cecil, William
Burglary (crime) J:163
Burgoyne, John (English military commander) R:203–
    4; W:40
Burgundian (bur-GUN-dian) period (in Dutch and
    Flemish music) D:365
Burgundians (Germanic people) F:403
Burgundy (wine) W:189
Buri (Norse god) N:277
Burial customs see Funeral and burial customs
Burial mounds (of the Mound Builder Indians) O:60
Buried treasure P:264
Burins (tools used in engraving) D:76; E:294; G:303;
    W:229
Burke, Edmund (English statesman) O:191
Burke, Robert O'Hara (British explorer) E:413
Burkert, Nancy Ekholm (American illustrator)
    illustration for Lear's Scroobious Pip, picture(s)
    C:237
Burkina B:451–52
    flag, picture(s) F:226
    Mali, relations with M:62
    marketplace, picture(s) A:59
    Mossi dignitary, picture(s) A:54
Burleigh (BUR-li), Henry Thacker (American singer and
    composer) B:510
Burlesque (form of humor) H:280
Burlington (Vermont) V:311, 317; picture(s) V:319
Burma (Myanmar) B:453–58
    Boy Scout, picture(s) A:457
    bride and groom, picture(s) F:44
    dance D:31
    flag, picture(s) F:231
    gemstones found in G:70

Mandalay Buddha, picture(s) B:423
pupils in a monastery school, picture(s) B:424
Thant, U T:156
World War II W:294, 302, 306
Burmese cats C:144; picture(s) C:145
Burne-Jones, Sir Edward Coley (English painter)
    B:510; E:263
    Praising Angels (tapestry), picture(s) T:21
Burnett, Peter H. (American pioneer) O:277
Burney, Charles (English music scholar) M:532
Burnford, Sheila (Canadian author) B:510
Burnham, Forbes (political leader of Guyana) G:428a
Burning see Combustion
Burningham, John Mackintosh (English author and
    illustrator) B:510
Burns, George (American comedian) B:510
Burns, Lucy (American reformer) W:212b
Burns, Robert (Scottish poet) B:459; E:278
    miniature 1786 edition of his Poems D:262
    quotation from "To a Louse" Q:20
    "A Red, Red Rose" B:459
Burns, Tommy (Canadian boxer) B:353, 511
Burns and scalds F:162; S:3–4
Burnside, Ambrose (American soldier and statesman)
    C:342
Burping (body action) B:301
Burr, Aaron (American lawyer and politician) B:460;
    N:178
    Blennerhassett Island (West Virginia) W:136
    duels and dueling D:346; picture(s) D:345
    Hamilton and Burr H:16
    Jefferson and Burr J:68
    as vice president, picture(s) V:325
Burritt, Elihu (American advocate of peace) P:105
Burros (donkeys) H:235
    Colorado miners' work animal, monument to C:430
Burroughs, Edgar Rice (American author) S:84
Burroughs (BURR-ose), John (American naturalist and
    writer) B:511; N:212
Burroughs, William Seward (American inventor) B:511
Burrowing bees B:121
Burrowing owls B:239; O:285
Burrowing snakes S:207
Burrows (of animals)
    rodents R:274
Bursae (fluid sacs in the joints of the skeleton)
    S:184b
Bursters (office machines) O:58
Burstyn, Ellen (American actress) M:493
Burton, Richard (British explorer) E:414
Burton, Richard (Richard Jenkins) (British actor)
    B:511
Burton, Robert (English author) E:274
Burton, Virginia Lee (American illustrator and author of
    children's books) B:511
Burundi (bur-UN-di) B:135, 461–62
    flag, picture(s) F:226
Bus and truck tours (of theater groups) T:161
Buses and bus travel B:463–65; T:288
    airport shuttle buses A:126, 128
    bus segregation case S:115
    double deckers in London, picture(s) L:287
    New York City N:230
    United States U:102–3
Bush, Barbara Pierce (wife of George Bush) B:467;
    F:180b; picture(s) B:468
Bush, George (41st president of the United States)
    B:466–69; R:112b; picture(s) P:204, 456;
    U:170, 204

Bush babies see Galagos
Bush balladists (Australian poets) A:500
Bushido (Japanese system of conduct) B:511; R:149
Bushmen (African tribal people) B:344, 511; N:8
   hunting A:62; picture(s) A:302
   language A:55
   South Africa S:269
Bushnell, David (American inventor) S:473
Bushongo (a people of Africa) A:76
Bush people (of Suriname) S:516
Bushpigs (wild pigs) P:248
Bush pilots (of airplanes), picture(s) A:153
Bushwhackers (proslavery men of pre-Civil War days)
   C:337
Bushy Run, Battle of (1763) P:145
Business B:470-73
   advertising A:27-34
   agribusiness A:95
   bookkeeping and accounting B:311-13
   commercial art created for a business purpose
     C:456-58
   computers used in C:488-91, 493-94
   credit cards C:572
   depressions and recessions D:121
   fairs and expositions F:9-18
   farming as a business F:60-61
   how to be an entrepreneur B:472
   international trade I:275-76
   magazines M:16
   mail order M:34-35
   office machines O:53-58
   public relations P:517-18
   ranching R:103-4
   sales and marketing S:20-21
   special libraries L:179
   stocks and bonds S:454-59
   tariff influences buyers T:23
   trademarks T:266-67
   unemployment U:29-30
   What are gross income and net income? B:471
   white-collar crime C:575
Business cycles (recurring series of good times and bad)
   depressions and recessions D:121-22
   inflation and deflation I:227-28
   unemployment U:29
Business letters L:160b-161
Business machines see Office machines
Business managers (for plays) P:336
Busing (of students) B:250p; S:115
Busnois (bu-NWA), Antoine (French musician) D:365
Butadiene (bu-ta-DIE-ene) (gas) R:348
Butane (BU-tane) (gas) F:489
Butcher bird see Shrike
Butchering see Meat and meat packing
Butler, John (American Loyalist) R:205
Butler, Nicholas Murray (American educator) P:106
Butler, Samuel (English satirist) E:286
Butte (BUTE) (Montana) M:440
Butter B:474; D:10
   ghee (clarified butter) F:337
   measurements for cooking C:532
   oils and fats O:76
Buttercups (flowers), picture(s) W:168
   biological classification L:209
Butterflies B:475-81; picture(s) I:248
   How can you tell a butterfly from a moth? B:475
   how insects protect themselves I:243
   metamorphosis M:238
   migration H:188-89
   monarch butterflies, picture(s) I:245

   mouthparts, picture(s) I:238
   peacock butterfly, picture(s) I:230
   wings, picture(s) I:240
Butterfly fish, picture(s) F:183
Butterfly stroke (in swimming) S:536-37
Butterfly valves, diagram(s) V:269
Buttermere, Lake (England), picture(s) U:61
Buttermilk (liquid left over from making butter) B:474;
   C:534; D:10
Butterwort (plant), picture(s) P:316
Buttes (landforms) W:323
Button, Dick (American figure skater) I:44
Button, Sir Thomas (British explorer-trader in Canada)
   M:86
Buttons (fasteners) B:484
Buttonwood Tree Agreement (1792) S:456
Buttress (in architecture) A:376
   Gothic flying buttress G:266; picture(s) G:265
Buttress dams see Hollow concrete dams
Butyl (BU-til) (synthetic rubber) R:348
Butyl alcohol F:91
Buvelot, Louis (Swiss painter) A:501
Buxtehude (boox-teh-HU-de), Dietrich (German
   composer) B:71-72
Buyers (for stores) D:118-19; F:70
Buying C:527-28
Buying on margin (stock purchase in which only a part
   of price is paid) S:458
Buys Ballot's law (of winds and pressure) W:186
By, John (British engineer) O:250-51
Byars, Betsy (American author) B:511
Byblos (BIB-los) (ancient town, Lebanon) A:193
Byelorussia see Belarus
Bylaws B:511; P:81
Byrd (BIRD), Harry F. (United States senator) V:360
Byrd, Richard Evelyn (American explorer) B:485;
   E:416
   polar exploration A:295, 386d
Byrd, William (English composer) E:291
   chamber music C:184
   Renaissance music R:173
Byrd, William, II (Virginia diarist) A:197
Byrnes, James Francis (American statesman) S:309
Byron, George Gordon, Lord (English poet) B:485-86
   Childe Harold's Pilgrimage, excerpt(s) B:486
   place in English literature E:281-82
   The Prisoner of Chillon, excerpt(s) B:486
   romanticism R:303
Byssus (BISS-us) (filaments of mussels) O:290
Bytes (of computer-stored information) C:481-82,
   484-85
Bytown (former name of Ottawa, Canada) O:250, 252
Byzantine (BIZ-an-tene) architecture B:487-94
   cathedrals C:134
   church architecture A:375
   Russia, architecture of R:370
Byzantine art B:487-94
   art as a record A:438a
   decorative arts D:74
   early Christian art in Italy I:391-92
   enameling E:202
   illuminated manuscripts I:77
   imperialism I:100
   jewelry designs J:94
   mosaics P:17-18; picture(s) B:495; P:16
Byzantine Empire (Eastern Roman Empire) B:495-96
   art and architecture see Byzantine architecture;
     Byzantine art
   Constantine the Great C:522

PHOTO CREDITS

The following list credits the sources of photos used in THE NEW BOOK OF KNOWLEDGE. Credits are listed, by page, photo by photo—left to right, top to bottom. Wherever appropriate, the name of the photographer has been listed with the source, the two being separated by a dash. When two or more photos by different photographers appear on one page, their credits are separated by semicolons.

B

2 Silvester—Rapho/Photo Researchers
4 © Enrico Ferorelli—DOT
5 Giraudon—Art Resource
6 The Granger Collection
10 Dr. Tony Brain—Photo Researchers; Dr. Tony Brain—Photo Researchers; Dr. J. Burgess—Photo Researchers.
11 © M. Abbey—Photo Researchers
12 © Joe Munroe—Photo Researchers
15 © Nik Wheeler—Black Star
16 Bahamas Ministry of Tourism
20 The Granger Collection
21 © J. Donoso—Sygma
26 © Martha Swope; © H Koelbl—Leo de Wys.
27 © Martha Swope
28 Martha Swope
29 Bettmann Archive
30 Mira—Hurok Attractions
31 Jack Vartoogian
32 Martha Swope
33 Martha Swope; Jack Vartoogian.
34 Raven Industries Inc.
35 Bettmann Archive
37 National Scientific Balloon Facility, Palestine, Texas
38 UPI
39 Stuart L. Craig—Bruce Coleman Inc.
41 Carl Frank
45 U.S. Marine Corps; Canadian Government Travel Bureau.
46 G. Hunter; Malak.
47 Grolier International, Bangkok
49 Jason Laure; Bernard Pierre Wolf—Alpha.
50 Shostal; Jason Laure; Jason Laure.
52 © Charlie Borland—Tele-Photo; K.B. Kaplan Photography.
53 © K.B. Kaplan Photography
55 © K.B. Kaplan Photography
56 © H. Mark Weidman
57 © Kent Oppenheimer
58 © K.B. Kaplan Photography; © Kent Oppenheimer.
62 Ray Manley—Shostal
63 Scala—Art Resource
64 The Metropolitan Museum of Art, Purchase, 1871; Art Reference Bureau.
65 Art Reference Bureau
68 Scala—Art Resource; © The Frick Collection, New York.
70 Rapho Guillumette
71 Ivor Ashmore—Rapho Guillumette
72 Bettmann Archive
76 © Steven E. Sutton—Duomo
77 © Bobby Noel Kramer—Rising Stock; © Mitchell B. Reibel—Sportschrome, Inc.; © Brain Drake—Focus West; © Mitchell B. Reibel—Sportschrome, Inc.
79 © Rick Stewart—Focus West
80 © Stephen Green—Journalism Services; © Mitchell B. Reibel—Sportschrome, Inc.
81 Focus on Sports; © Ronald C. Modra—Sports Illustrated.
82 © V.J. Lovero—Focus West
87 © The Granger Collection; © Bob Daemmrich.
88 © National Baseball Hall of Fame and Museum, Inc.
89 © National Baseball Hall of Fame and Museum, Inc.; © National Baseball Hall of Fame and Museum, Inc.; © National Baseball Hall of Fame and Museum, Inc.
90 © National Baseball Hall of Fame and Museum, Inc.; © Focus on Sports; Brown Brothers.
91 © Focus on Sports; © Focus on Sports; © Focus on Sports; © Mickey Palmer—Focus

on Sports.
92 © Mitchell B. Reibel—Sportschrome, Inc.; © Focus on Sports; Mitchell B. Reibel—Sportschrome, Inc.
93 © Mark Gamba—Journalism Services
94 © Andrew D. Bernstein—NBA Photos
95a Focus on Sports
95b UPI—Bettmann Newsphotos; Focus on Sports.
95c Focus on Sports
95e Focus on Sports
95f Focus on Sports
95g Focus on Sports
95i Focus on Sports
97 © R. Mitchell—Tom Stack & Assoc.
98 © François Gohier—Photo Researchers
99 © Merlin Tuttle—Photo Researchers; © Peter Ward—Bruce Coleman Inc.
104 Courtesy of Horizon and The Museum of Modern Art, New York
105 Collection, The Museum of Modern Art, New York
106 T. Grant—National Film Board of Canada; C. J. Ott—Photo Researchers; Tom Hollyman—Photo Researchers; Mac's Foto Service.
107 Buckey Reeves—NAS—Photo Researchers; Wangi—Jacana.
108 Russe Kinne—Photo Researchers; Wangi—Jacana.
110 © Harry Engels—Animals Animals; © Stephen J. Krasemann—Photo Researchers
112 © Leonard Lee Rue III—Photo Researchers; © Johnny Johnson—Animals Animals.
115 © Peter Vanderwarker—Jackson & Company
116 © John Shaw—Tom Stack & Assoc.; © Charlton Photos.
118 © Scott Camazine; © Scott Camazine.
119 © D. Wilder—Tom Stack & Assoc.; © Scott Camazine.
120 © Walt Anderson—Tom Stack & Assoc.
122 Mary Evans Picture Library
123 © Gregory G. Dimijian—Photo Researchers; © Donald Specker—Animals Animals.
124 © Dr. Thomas Eisner; © Wendy Shattil/Bob Rozinski—Tom Stack & Assoc.
127 © Robert Noonan—Photo Researchers; © Don and Esther Phillips—Tom Stack & Assoc.
129 © Ria-Novosti—Sovfoto
131 Robert Davis—Photo Researchers; FPG.
132 Robert Davis—Photo Researchers; Farrell Grehan; Robert Davis—Photo Researchers.
135 © Fridmar Damn—Leo deWys; Lee Snider—Photo Image.
136 Tom Hollyman—Photo Researchers
137 © Charles R. Meyer—Photo Researchers
138 © The Bettmann Archive
139 Thomas Victor © 1979
140 © David Dobbs
141 Courtesy of Ben-Gurion University
143 © Lois Greenfield—Bruce Coleman Inc.
146 © Philip Temple—Tony Stone Worldwide
147 © The Granger Collection; © G. Anderson—The Stock Market; © Mark Romanelli—The Image Bank.
148 UPI—Bettmann Newsphotos
149 Alexandra Avakian—Woodfin Camp & Assoc.
150 © Bettmann Archive
151 © Jeanetta Baker—Leo deWys
152 Robert Emmet Bright—Rapho
154 © Larry Dale Gordon—The Image Bank
155 P. P. Karan
156 Leo Strashin—Rapho Guillumette
161 Courtesy of the British Museum; Jewish Theological Seminary; Lee Boltin.
162 Art Reference Bureau
165 The New York Public Library
175 © David Stoecklein—The Stock Solution
176 © Perrin—Tardy—Gamma Liaison; © Scott

Markewitz—The Stock Solution; © Julian Baum—Bruce Coleman Inc.
177 © John Kane
181 © Stephen R. Brown—National Archives
186 University of Göttingen
187 Brookhaven National Laboratory; Chas. Pfizer & Co., Inc.; Dr. Bruce R. Voeller—Rockefeller Institute.
191 © Dan Suzio—Photo Researchers; © Dan Suzio—Photo Researchers.
192 © Todd Powell—Profiles West; © Tim Davis—Photo Researchers.
194 Art Reference Bureau
195 Culver; Bettmann Archive.
196 "British Crown Copyright, Science Museum, London"
199 Claude Nuridsany
201 Corson—Fotogram
202 California Institute of Technology
203 © Kjell Sandved—Bruce Coleman Inc.; © Raymond Blythe—Animals Animals.
204 © Stephen J. Krasemann—Photo Researchers
205 © Lou Jacobs, Jr.—Grant Heilman Photography
208 © Thomas Kitchin—Tom Stack & Assoc.
210 © Morley Read—Photo Researchers
211 © Margot Conte—Animals Animals; © Z. Leszczynski—Animals Animals; © Stephen G. Maka—Photo-Nats.
212 © The Granger Collection; © Jeff Foott; © Roger and Donna Aitkenhead—Animals Animals.
213 © Ron Austing—Photo Researchers
215 © Ray Richardson—Animals Animals; © Don Enger—Animals Animals; © Peggy Daly—Profiles West.
216 © Steve Kaufman—Peter Arnold, Inc.; © Jim Nachel—Root Resources; © B.G. Murray, Jr.—Animals Animals.
217 © Jeff Foott; © Gregory Scott; © Jeff Foott.
219 © Jeff Foott; © Francois Gohier—Photo Researchers.
222 © Ben Goldstein—Root Resources; © Tom McHugh—Photo Researchers; © Jeff Foott; © L. J. Tinstman—Profiles West.
223 © Jeff Foott; © Jeff Foott.
224 © Jeff Foott; © Sidney Bahrt—Photo Researchers; © Grace DeWolf—Root Resources.
225 © Jeff Foott; © L.L.T. Rhodes—Animals Animals; © Gregory K. Scott; © Mary A. Root—Root Resources.
226 © Rick Wicker—Denver Museum of Natural History
227 © L.J. Tinstman—Profiles West; © Jeff Foott; © Jeff Foott.
228 © Jerome Wexler—Photo Researchers; © Jerome Wexler—Photo Researchers; © Jerome Wexler—Photo Researchers; © Jerome Wexler—Photo Researchers; © Stephen J. Krasemann—Photo Researchers.
229 © Pat & Tom Lesson—Photo Researchers; © Richard R. Hansen—Photo Researchers; © Gregory K. Scott.
232 © Jeff Foott; © Jeff Foott; © Clarence Postmus—Root Resources; © Doug Allan—Animals Animals.
233 © Jeff Foott
234 © Jeff Foott
243 © Alex—Sipa Press
245 © Erika Stone—Photo Researchers
246 © H. V. Lacey—Annan
247 © Tom McHugh—Photo Researchers
248 © Tonya A. Evatt; © John Kaprielian—Photo Researchers; © Tonya A. Evatt; © SIU—Photo Researchers.
249 © Tonya A. Evatt; © Tonya A. Evatt; © Tonya A. Evatt; © Hank Morgan—Photo Researchers.